FOR MEMBERS ONLY

A hard-to-get reservation is prized among serious restaurant-goers, but a table limited to members only is the Philadelphia diner's Holy Grail. Palizzi Social Club has been a gathering place for the Italian American community in South Philly for a century, but it was after chef Joey Baldino took over from his late uncle Ernie that business really started to boom.

The pocket-size dining room feels exclusive, warm, and authentic. Palizzi has mastered the balance of old-school Italian kitsch and super-high-quality food and cocktails. If the neon is on outside, they're open. Seventy adaptable, accessible recipes throughout include dishes like:

FENNEL AND ORANGE SALAD ||| ARANCINI WITH RAGU AND PEAS
SPAGHETTI WITH CRABS ||| STROMBOLI ||| HAZELNUT TORRONE

COME ON IN, AND JOIN THE CLUB.

PALIZZI

FILIPPO PALIZZI
CLUB

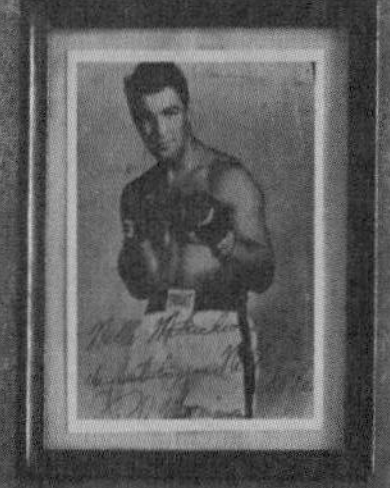

DINNER AT THE CLUB

100 YEARS OF STORIES AND RECIPES FROM SOUTH PHILLY'S PALIZZI SOCIAL CLUB

JOEY BALDINO
ADAM ERACE

RUNNING PRESS
PHILADELPHIA

Running Press
Hachette Book Group
1290 Avenue of the Americas
New York, NY 10104
www.runningpress.com
@Running_Press

Printed in China

First Edition: October 2019

Published by Running Press, an imprint of Perseus Books, LLC, a subsidiary of Hachette Book Group, Inc. The Running Press name and logo is a trademark of the Hachette Book Group.

Print book cover and interior design by Joshua McDonnell

Library of Congress Control Number: 2019936681

ISBNs: 978-0-7624-9386-9 (hardcover), 978-0-7624-9387-6 (ebook)

LREX

10 9 8 7 6 5 4 3 2 1

This book is dedicated to the founding fathers of the Filippo Palizzi Society and to all of its members, past and present.

—J. B.

CONTENTS

FLAVORS AND CARAMEL
TERLATO ARTISAN SPIRITS

FOREWORD

I was standing on the landing of Palizzi Social Club on a humid, early fall evening. After nearly two decades of living in Philadelphia, there is a fluency in the way in which we posture on stoops. I was leaning on the front of the building, my right elbow against the door, and my left hand in my pocket, gazing up and down 12th Street waiting for some friends.

I imagined the waves of immigrants arriving from the green mountains and open sea of Abruzzo to the stark, concrete setting of South Philadelphia. Their new life promised backbreaking work, a new language, and uneasy integration. Farmers, teachers, and musicians became bricklayers, factory workers, and tailors. Neighborhoods with their different dialects were established and the foundation of the American Dream was spread over the streets of South Philly. For these newcomers, bowls of pasta and gravy and platters of sausage became as iconic and important as church.

South Philadelphia got rough. Grandparents passed away. Parents moved to suburbs in South Jersey for better schools and a better quality of life. Some stayed, like the Baldino family, and held close to their hearts traditions of suppers, serenades, and sausage sandwiches while the neighborhood changed around them.

Joey Baldino and I first met in the kitchen at Vetri in 2003. What first impressed me about this young cook was his work ethic and his drive. He didn't stop. Not in a screaming, frantic way but a no-nonsense "I have a job to do and won't stop until it is done" way. I've learned, over time, that many of us grasp at success by stepping on those around us. From day one in the tiny but electric Vetri kitchen, I watched Joey accomplish goal after goal, elevate, grow, and inspire, while boosting everyone around him. He has always been the first to comfort, crack a joke, flash his famous grin, and tell you with words or action that he is your family and will have your back.

I clearly remember Joey saving my life one morning at Vetri, by throwing himself in front of my body as I came crashing down the basement steps while carrying cases of produce into the walk-in. I came to, flat on my back, covered with boxes and bags of heirloom lettuce, with Baldino's arms wrapped around me like he was cradling a baby. (I was at least 30 pounds heavier than him.) The image, I realize, is hilarious but sums up exactly who Joey is, where he comes from, and how he cares for his family.

Many years later, in the neighborhood in which Joey was born and raised, Palizzi Social Club is filled with aunts and uncles and punks like me and my obnoxious hipster friends who come for spaghetti and crabs, perfect stromboli, and hot espresso. Some come to experience the place that served their ancestors. I, however, come to give Joey bear hugs and try to get him to flash a smile. And, while my face is covered with gravy, I can't help but to think how fortunate I am to be part of Joey's family.

—**Michael Solomonov**, chef and co-owner of Zahav

PaLizzi Society Voting BaLLot.
Dec. 17.78 Nominee Candidate.
PLease Vote For OnLy One Nominee.
For President. Frank ALLizzo.
" " Charles DeMatteo.
For Vice Pres. SiLvio AndoLfi
" " Tony IppoLito
For Manager. Tony ALLizzo.
" " Albert Cerrone.

PALIZZI M. B. SOCIETY
Official Ballot
FOR PRESIDENT
(VOTE FOR ONE)

PART 1

THE CLUB

The official name of the row house at 1408 South 12th Street in South Philadelphia is Filippo Palizzi Societa di Mutuo Soccorso di Vasto, but we always just called it the Club.

Filippo Palizzi was a famous painter from Vasto, a seaside village in Abruzzo on Italy's Adriatic coast. When Dominico DiCicco and other immigrants from the town resettled in South Philly and founded the Club in 1918, they chose the artist as its namesake. These newcomers to America didn't have much money or speak the language, so this smoky, wood-paneled, row home hangout became a way for them to preserve their traditions and take care of one another. In the early years, membership dues would pay for health care, funerals, and benefits for member families in need. Over the decades, the assembly grew to two hundred members, relaxing the charter rules to first allow Italians from outside Abruzzo, then women. Italian American entertainers would drop by when they were in town—boxers, comedians, even Frank Sinatra, whose signed headshot hangs on the wall.

From the very beginning, I've had a familial connection to the Club. Dominico's daughter-in-law, Angela Rosa Catrambone DiCicco, and my maternal grandmother, Marianne Catrambone Mazza, were sisters, and part of the wave of immigration to South Philly from Calabria. My grandmother had five kids: Regina, my mom; my uncles Joseph and Al; my aunt Roma; and my Aunt Mary. Mary married Ernest Mezzaroba around the time the Club began granting membership to non-Abruzzese Italians. In 1975, Uncle Ernie became president.

Uncle Ernie and Aunt Mary were both great cooks. In the tiny kitchen in back, Ernie would make food for the guys when they were hanging out. I can remember, as a kid coming here in the '80s and early '90s, we'd have huge pans of stuffed shells and whole roasted suckling pigs at family events, such as my cousin's Holy Communion party. I remember the tables, Formica tops with ridged chrome edges.

FEDERAL TRUST COMPANY
OF PHILADELPHIA 4341

(6)

Deed.

391819

Saverio Del Borrello
and Concetta, his wife

To

"SOCIETA Di MUTUO SOCCORSO
"FILIPPO PALIZZI" Di VASTO"
a corporation chartered under the laws of the State of Pennsylvania.

PREMISES

1408 S. 12th Street

26th Ward, Philadelphia

Michael Francis Doyle
Attorney-at-Law
Philadelphia.

1.45

NOV 21 1922

The Club was a huge part of my childhood growing up in South Philly, but by the time I was old enough to really appreciate it, things were on the decline. Back in the day, there were dozens of Italian social clubs in the various neighborhoods, but as those original immigrants and the following generations became more educated, affluent, and mainstreamed into American society, their significance fell off. Social clubs became more of a nostalgia thing than the vital institution they once were, and Palizzi was no exception. Uncle Ernie would open three nights a week, then dropped it to two nights a week, then eventually would just open Sundays for the guys to hang out for a couple hours after Mass. By 2016, he was the last member left, and dying of cancer.

I had no plans to open another restaurant. I was happy with Zeppoli, my little Sicilian spot over the bridge in Jersey, seven years old and still busy. There was a lot of talk about the future of the Club, but me taking over...that wasn't even on my radar. Then one day, Uncle Ernie and my three older cousins approached me, "Well, what about you?"

At first I said no. I wasn't interested. Then my Cousin Al took me by the Club, and it was the first time I had been there in probably six years. It was like an older relative I had gotten too busy to visit more often, and I had forgotten what it was all about. Being there, looking through boxes of old war uniforms, mementos from Vasto, even the original gavel the members used at their meetings, I realized what a special place it was, and how important it was to these guys. There were all these old leather-bound ledgers with the most meticulous notes in flowing Catholic-school cursive. They kept minutes of all their meetings, whether they were planning a beef-and-beer for someone's sick kid or just shooting the shit about politics and sports. I didn't want to just let it die.

Uncle Ernie did, shortly after selling me the Club. If I hadn't taken it over, it would have just become a row home or apartment building, and I couldn't let that happen. I opened the "new" Palizzi Social Club in February 2017, and I wish Uncle Ernie were alive to see it. I think he'd be proud of the work we've done to the place: expanding the kitchen so I can serve a full dinner menu four nights a week, turning the huge old safe into a service station, bringing the rainbow of vinyl barstools back to a bowling-ball sparkle, hauling the old cigarette machine up from the basement, hanging a black-and-white picture of him and Aunt Mary on the wall across from the bar. I even fixed the hole in the floor in the kitchen, the one Uncle Ernie fell through one night (drunk) and broke his arm.

Our membership is booming under a new, inclusive charter. Now your last name doesn't need to end in a vowel to be a member. Anyone can apply—Italian, Jewish, Irish, black, Mexican, Asian, or any of the other colors and backgrounds that make up this crazy, idiosyncratic, vibrant part of Philadelphia I call home and care so much about. Thursday through Sunday, the neon is on, and Filippo Palizzi Societa di Mutuo Soccorso di Vasto is ready to be your home away from home. Officially, we've shortened the name to the Palizzi Social Club—but you're always welcome to just call it the Club.

FILIPPO PALIZZI SOCIETY PRESIDENTS

Caesar LaVerghetta 1918–1920
Giuseppe Molino 1920–1928
Luigi Smargiassi 1928–1930
Dominico DiCicco 1930–1935
Giustino DiCicco 1935–1942
Saverio DelBorrello 1942–1943
Michael Vergara 1943–1946
Michele Bozzelli 1946–1951
Joseph Florio 1951–1955
Angelo Allizzo 1955–1958
Anthony Ippolito 1958–1960
Nick D'Adamo 1960–1961
Vincent Milando 1961–1962
Pete DelBorrello 1962–1975
Ernest Mezzaroba 1975–2016
Joey Baldino 2016–present

DICICCO / MEZZAROBA / BALDINO FAMILY TREE

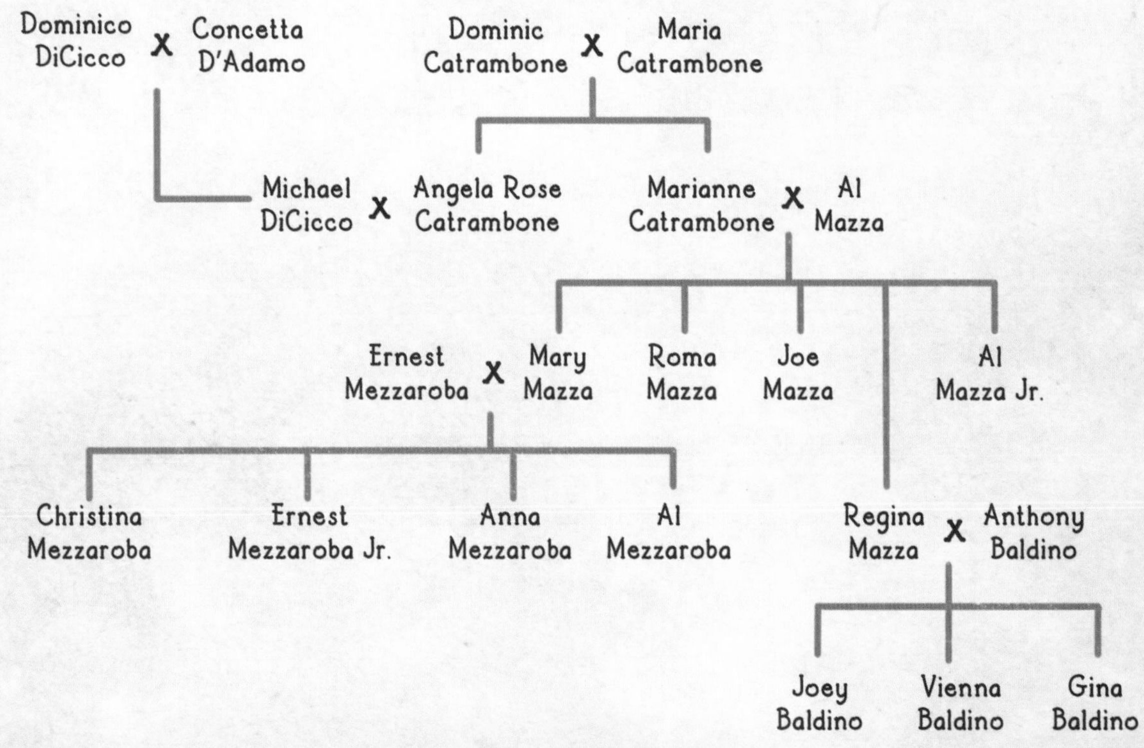

HOUSE RULES

MEMBERS ONLY & CASH ONLY

NO LOUD OBNOXIOUS BEHAVIOR.

PROPER ATTIRE REQUIRED.
Gentlemen must remove hats, and no flip-flops or sweatpants are allowed.

DO NOT LINGER OUTSIDE THE FRONT STOOP.
Smokers can use the backyard.

WHAT HAPPENS AT PALIZZI STAYS AT PALIZZI.
No pictures or excessive cell phone use.
No blogging, reviewing, or tagging on social media.

EACH MEMBER MAY BRING THREE (3) NON-MEMBERS.
If you wouldn't bring them to your mom's house, don't bring them here.

A MEMBERSHIP DOES NOT GUARANTEE ENTRY.
Please have patience when we are at capacity.

EXIT BRISKLY AND SILENTLY.
Our neighbors are sleeping next door.

EAT A LOT, DRINK MORE, AND MOSTLY: BE SOCIAL.

OUR RULES EXIST FOR THE BENEFIT OF ALL OUR MEMBERS; WE RESERVE THE RIGHT TO DENY OR REVOKE MEMBERSHIP FOR REFUSAL TO COMPLY WITH ANY OF THE ABOVE.

EGGPLANT

WE ACCEPT
ACCESS
Habanero
Okra
Escarole
Leeks
Carrots
Beets

PART 2

THE NEIGHBORHOOD

South Philly has always been a haven for immigrants. Although the countries of origin have changed over the last 150 years—the Eastern Europeans, Irish, Italians, and Lebanese of the late 1800s and early 1900s and African Americans of the Great Migration are the Mexicans, Syrians, and Southeast Asians of today—it remains a place where someone far from home can make a new one. Our narrow streets and sturdy brick buildings adapt well to newcomers, whether they're from Jakarta or New Jersey. The nineteenth-century synagogues around Mifflin Square have become Cambodian Buddhist temples. The old Edward W. Bok technical school, a concrete monster built in 1938 and decommissioned in 2013, is now a creative hive of photographers, jewelers, bakers, and calligraphers, with a restaurant on the roof.

Despite its outsize presence in the city's history and lore, South Philly takes up a relatively small part of Philadelphia, only about 10 percent by square miles. The Delaware River borders the area to the east, sweeping down along the old Navy Yard and sports complex to form the southern boundary as well, where it links up with the Schuylkill River on the west. Those borders are undisputed. The northern one, depends on whom you ask. Traditionally, everything below South Street is South Philly, but over the decades, the upper reaches have been absorbed into Center City. Even parts of Bella Vista, the historic heart of Italian American South Philly, feel more uptown than downtown these days.

The Club is in the neighborhood directly to the south of Bella Vista, in East Passyunk, which runs between Washington and Snyder Avenues, Broad and 8th Streets. Back in the day, Catholic parishes identified the areas within—you were from Saint Nick's or Annunciation—but as the neighborhood's DNA has changed, so has the church-centered cartography. Now real estate agents divide the district in two distinct adjacent areas, Passyunk Square and East Passyunk Crossing, but everyone here these days just says East Passyunk, which is also the name of the main commercial strip running diagonally through the neighborhood.

Coinciding with the decline of social clubs in the area, East Passyunk in the '80s and '90s had been dealing with depopulation of its core customers as white flight sent many middle-class Italian Americans over the bridge into New Jersey. (Washington Township, New Jersey, earned the nickname South Philly with Grass during this period.) Vacancies darkened Passyunk Avenue like missing teeth. Sure, people still went there for their Holy Communion outfits and Catholic school uniforms, or freshly made mozzarella balls swaddled in deli paper from Mr. Mancuso's—but things were way off from the strip's heyday as the vital spine of South Philly commerce.

Around the turn of the millennium Bella Vista began gaining traction as a cool and affordable neighborhood for those priced out of Center City, and as home prices there surged, buyers who never before crossed Washington Avenue started doing so and discovering East Passyunk. You know what happens next, same as it has in hundreds of other neighborhoods in hundreds of other cities across the country: galleries, cafés, a new generation of independent shops, and fantastic new restaurants to complement the been-there-forever ones like Mr. Martino's, where I bussed and waited tables as a teenager. In the span of a decade, East Passyunk became one of the hottest neighborhoods in Philly.

Many neighborhoods caught up in a real estate gold rush lose their identity. Thus far, that hasn't happened here. East Passyunk has been able to preserve its original spirit. There are tons of OGs still living here, sweeping their pavements and grumbling about parking and holding court on their stoops with bottles of bathtub limoncello, and the best of the old businesses are still in business, including Mancuso's, where my mom still buys cheese. Even though my version of the Club is "new," I feel that I'm the steward of something very old, something whose preservation is of essential importance. For my family and for the neighborhood.

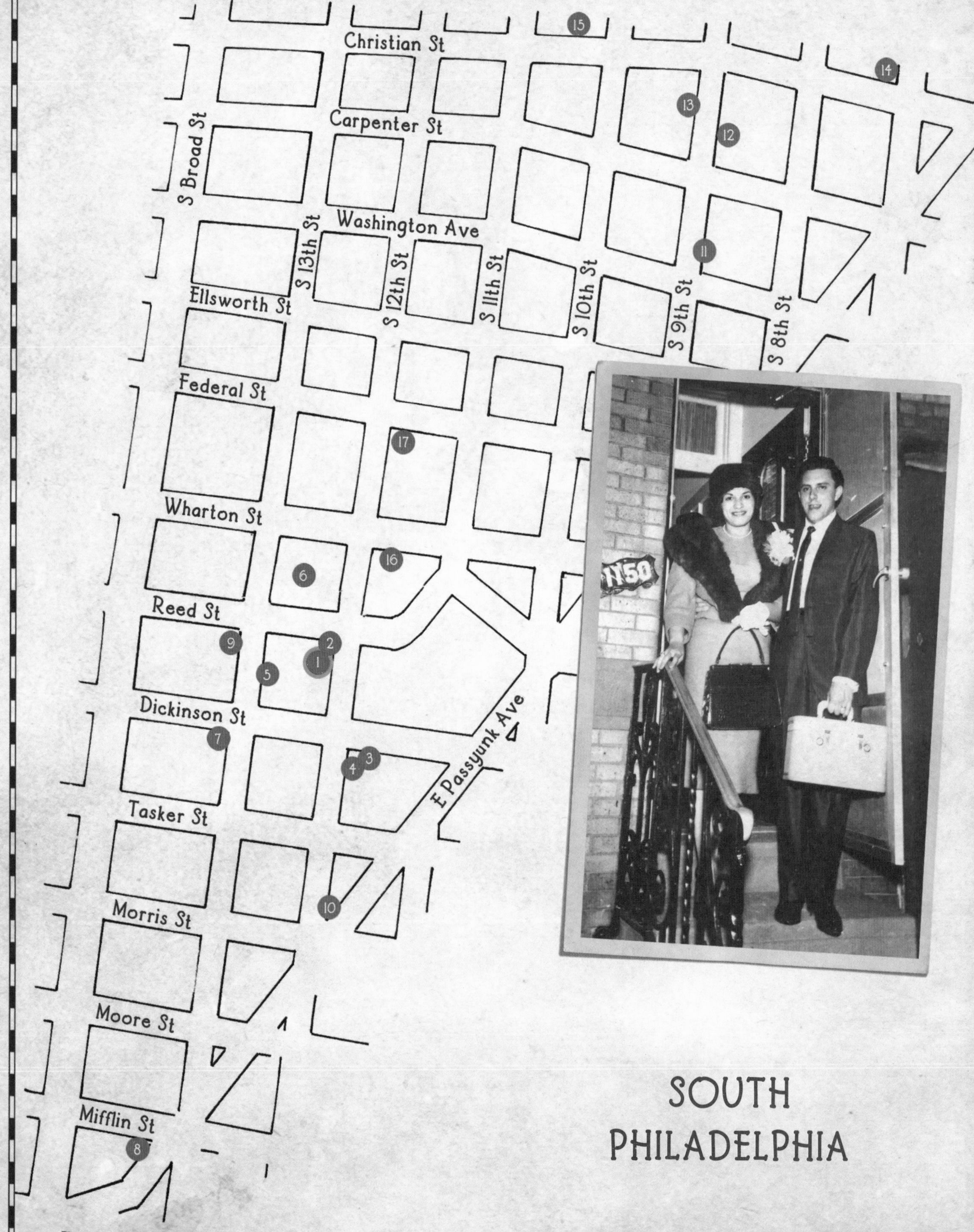
Christian St
Carpenter St
S Broad St
Washington Ave
S 13th St
S 12th St
S 11th St
S 10th St
S 9th St
S 8th St
Ellsworth St
Federal St
Wharton St
Reed St
Dickinson St
E Passyunk Ave
Tasker St
Morris St
Moore St
Mifflin St
1150
1
2
3
4
5
6
7
8
9
10
11
12
13
14
15
16
17

SOUTH PHILADELPHIA

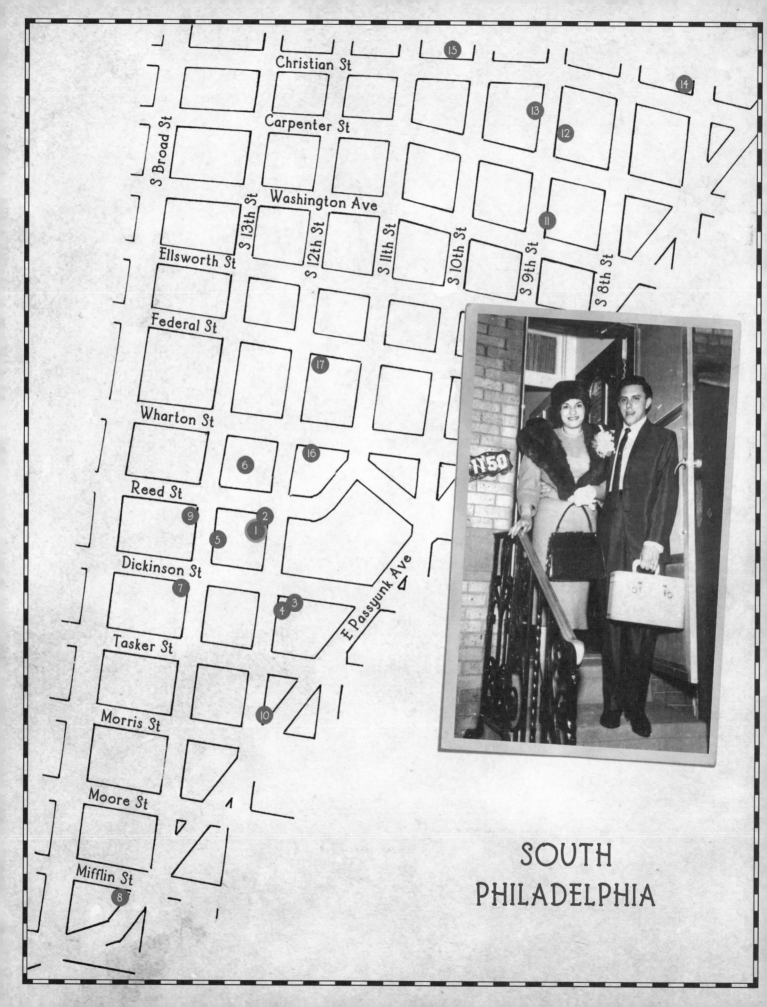

MAP KEY

1. The Club

2. Al Mazza's: This is the restaurant my mom's parents opened in 1964. Originally they all lived on Cross Street, but moved above the restaurant after my grandparents bought the building. For the guys in the neighborhood, a common night out was dinner at Al Mazza's, then drinks at the Club. My mom's brother, Uncle Al, took over in 1974 and ran it until 1998. It's now a commissary for a food manufacturer.

3. Baldino Family Home: My childhood home, also the home my mom grew up in before they moved above Al Mazza's

4. Mezzaroba Family Home: Aunt Mary and Uncle Ernie's place, site of many Christmas Eve dinners and almost back to back with my family's house

5. Aunt Roma's Home

6. Columbus Square: My neighborhood park, where I grew up hanging out and playing baseball

7. Ippolito's: Five generations of Sam D'Angelo's family have run this neighborhood fish market originally opened in 1929. As big seafood eaters, my family has always shopped here. Things get crazy here around Christmas Eve, when residents descend en masse to purchase octopus, baccala, shrimp, clams, mussels, and more for the Feast of the Seven Fishes (see page 112).

8. Lucio J. Mancuso & Son: Phil Mancuso is an East Passyunk legend. His father opened this eponymous cheese shop in 1940, and Phil took over in 1971. We buy all our mozzarella here—Phil makes it fresh throughout the day—as well as the basket cheese for our Pizzagaina (page 48) and pepperoni for our Stromboli (page 37).

9. Faragalli's: My family didn't bake much bread at home, and why would they with Faragalli's as our local bakery right around the corner? This is the only bakery in South Philly with a wood-fired oven, which has been turning out the crustiest, most delicious Italian loaves since 1948.

10. Mr. Martino's: Marc and Maria Farnese's Mr. Martino's BYOB on Passyunk Avenue was my first job in the restaurant industry. Even as Passyunk has boomed with new restaurants in the last decade, this one remains. It's still cash-only, still weekends-only, and still beloved in the neighborhood.

11. Giordano and Giordano Fruit & Produce: My family has always bought our fruits and vegetables at this stand on the corner of 9th and Washington in the Italian Market. I still shop from these guys for my restaurants.

12. Cannuli's Quality Meat & Poultry: Butchers in the Italian Market since 1927, Cannuli supplies us with most of our meats, including the star of our Whole Roasted Suckling Pig (page 157).

13. Claudio Specialty Foods: Like Mancuso's, Claudio makes its mozzarella fresh in house, but I go to this circa-1950s cheese and gourmet shop for ricotta and specialty pastas like La Fabbrica della Pasta del Gragnano "'o Vesuvio" twists we use in our Timballo (page 84).

14. John's Water Ice: Served in a waxed paper cup, often with a pretzel rod stuck into it like a flagpole, water ice is a summertime staple in South Philly, and John's has been making the best since 1945. I live around the corner from the stand now, and nothing is better on a hot day than a cup of its lemon.

15. Isgro Pasticceria: My favorite cannoli comes from Isgro's pastry shop, which has been in business on Christian Street, a block off the Italian Market in Bella Vista, since 1904.

16. Wharton Street Lofts: Before the building was converted into lofts, this was the site of Annunciation of the Blessed Virgin Mary grade school. I went to school here for kindergarten through fifth grade, right down the street from Al Mazza's and the Club.

17. Andrew Jackson Elementary School: After getting kicked out of Annunciation—I was a mischievous kid who maybe liked to throw things at the nuns—I finished up fifth through eighth grade at Andrew Jackson, our neighborhood public school.

EXTRA-LARGE EGGS
DETECTO
Tomatoes
125

FROM PAPERBOY TO BUSBOY

I never loved school, but I always loved work. I was a paperboy for the *Philadelphia Daily News*, and if a thirteen-year-old kid could be passionate about being a paperboy, well, I was that kid. It also led me to cooking and to my lifelong mentors.

My route was huge: Broad to 9th Streets, Mifflin up to Reed. I met a lot of really nice people on my route. They would invite me into their houses and give me gifts at Christmas. Kevin was one customer. He and his wife lived on East Passyunk. He was a photographer and at the time was working on a book, *America Then & Now*, which featured photos from the late 1800s juxtaposed against contemporary ones—the New York City skyline in 1876 next to the same skyline in 1992, for example. They wanted a picture of a paperboy, and Kevin asked whether I wanted to do it.

It was a hot summer day. I wore a Mickey Mouse tank top and a Phillies hat. My mom held the reflector. Kevin took some pictures in front of Ippolito's, my *Daily News* bag slung around my shoulder, one high-top propped up on my skateboard. And that photo, paired with a black-and-white one of a paperboy in 1918 became the front cover of the book.

This experience launched not my modeling career but inadvertently, my cooking career. Kevin told me about a restaurant that had just opened across the street from him, Mr. Martino's, a BYOB run by a couple named Marc and Maria Farnese. Marc was an antiques dealer by trade. Maria was an artist. And they decided to open up this little restaurant, her cooking, him doing everything else from shopping for ingredients to running the (very in demand) reservation book. Kevin said they might be looking for busboys.

Mr. Martino's was right next to an empty lot where my buddies and I played stickball. After a game one day, I sent my friends home and stopped into the restaurant, met Marc, and asked if he needed help. See, I grew up in the restaurant industry because of Al Mazza's, but I was too young to actually work there. My sisters and cousins all worked there, but I just kind of hung out. It was in my blood, but I hadn't been able to really access the experience of working in a restaurant. I wanted to.

Marc took my name and number and hired me around the time I turned fourteen. I started out bussing tables and worked my way up to server. I worked there all through high school and college. I left when I was twenty-five.

Working at Mr. Martino's opened my eyes to so many different things and people and inspired me to go into the restaurant industry professionally. I really think of Marc and Maria as my mentors, second set of parents, and best friends. When I opened Zeppoli, they gave me their old tables. When I opened the Club, Maria helped me paint the walls and made them glow red and gold.

Two years ago, they were short a dishwasher for New Year's Eve. I didn't have plans, so I went over to Mr. Martino's, put on an apron, and washed dishes for them. If I'm not working, I will do whatever they need. I owe them a lot and am so happy their restaurant is still going strong, twenty-five years after that stickball game. So much about the neighborhood and the Avenue has changed, it's very special when places like Mr. Martino's stay the same.

PART 3

THE FOOD

The recipes in the pages that follow are not fancy and, for the most part, not complicated. They come from or are inspired by our family dinners and holiday meals prepared by my mother and her sisters, a sorority of great cooks I've been learning from since I was old enough to hold a knife, long before I knew I wanted to cook professionally. They come from the Club and my Uncle Ernie, who I'd find in the backyard tending lamb chops on the grill (page 146), or hovered over the deep fryer tending a batch of Fritto Misto (page 105).

Some of these recipes are authentic as to how they're prepared exactly at my family home on Cross Street in South Philly. I don't mess around with my mom's Calamari and Peas (page 117), which calls for canned peas in all their grayish-green glory, or the Escarole and Beans (page 96). But I'm a chef, too, so I've sharpened, tightened, and upgraded many of the recipes through a professional filter. The fat content of boneless short rib makes the best Braciole (page 133), for example, and a trick from a chef from Lombardy makes my Marinara (page 54) different from my mom's. At its essence, though, this collection of recipes is about home cooking. And these *are* recipes you can cook at home, all of them. None requires major professional equipment or hard-to-source ingredients, but here are a few specifics to keep in mind while cooking from this book:

Cheese: We prefer ricotta and mozzarella made with whole milk. For mozzarella, recipes specify "dry," which is best for grating, or fresh. If you're in Philly, Mr. Mancuso on the 1900 block of East Passyunk has been making the beautiful fresh mozzarella since 1940, and for the best ricotta in town, we like Claudio's in the Italian Market.

Chiles: We use dried Arbol chiles as our default heat source. They're small, have a clean chile flavor, are widely available, and are pretty hot—I'd give them a 7 out of 10 on the heat scale. Recipes in this book also call for oil-packed Calabrian chiles, which you can find at Italian and specialty stores; and pizzeria-standard red pepper flakes.

Oils: For olive oil, extra-virgin only. We use Ursini brand from Abruzzo to cook and to finish. It's a medium-intensity oil that's not too spicy and won't overwhelm the other ingredients in a given dish. Throughout the book you'll also see us call for "blended oil," mostly in recipes for salad dressings (where straight olive oil would be too assertive) and for searing meat (which requires a higher smoke point). To make blended oil, combine one part extra-virgin olive oil with three parts canola oil. We keep it in a plastic squeeze bottle for easy use. Any dishes that call for deep-frying, we use canola oil.

Pasta: We have two fresh pasta recipes in this book, both of which use our 20-Yolk Pasta Dough (page 56). The remaining call for store-bought dried pastas. Our preferred brand is De Cecco for widely available shapes such as spaghetti and penne. For specialty shapes like the "'o Vesuvio" twists in the Timballo (page 84), we source Fabbrica della Pasta di Gragnano, a brand from a town outside Naples famous for dried pasta, from Claudio's in the Italian Market.

Salt: Sicilian sea salt is the standard for all recipes in this book. Kosher salt is used for curing and is specified where needed. Kosher is also used for salting pasta water at a ratio of 10 tablespoons (100 g) of salt for every gallon (4 L) of water. (These salt and water measurements will not appear in the ingredient lists for recipes calling for boiling pasta.) This ratio creates nice briny water that will season pasta as it cooks. Note: We use Diamond Crystal brand kosher salt, which is much lighter than the more common kosher salt, Morton's. One cup of Diamond Crystal, for example, is about 140 grams, while the same amount of Morton's is 260 grams, so purchase or adjust appropriately.

Tomatoes: We prefer imported, canned, whole peeled San Marzano tomatoes, which have a beautiful balance of sweetness and acidity. That said, every tomato is different, and there are variations batch to batch, can to can, fruit to fruit. Taste the tomatoes before using them. If they taste very sharp, balance that out with ¼ teaspoon sugar per 28-ounce (794 g) can. This also applies to fresh tomatoes, which vary even more depending on where they're from and when they're picked. Local and ripened on the vine is always best. For tomato paste, Fontanella is more condensed than other brands and has a thick, full flavor.

Flours: Making bread and pizza doughs, cakes, and pasta all require different types of flour. Finely milled Antimo Caputo 00 (double zero) flour creates the silkiest pastas, but we also use it as our all-purpose flour. Recipes in the book also call for semolina, durum, and bread flours, each one suited specifically to the desired structure and gluten content, so don't substitute one for another. Buy flours as fresh as possible and keep them stored in a cool, dry place for best results.

And some general notes:

Eggs are large unless otherwise specified.

Milk is whole unless otherwise specified.

Fruits and vegetables are medium in size unless otherwise specified.

Fruits and vegetables are peeled unless otherwise specified.

Citrus juice is freshly squeezed. Zest, freshly grated.

For onions, we'll specify red when required, but otherwise, I am almost always using yellow. I don't call for white onions because I find them to be too sharp. Keep them for hoagies.

Most importantly: This is food from the heart, and it's meant to be cooked as such. Use the recipes as a guide, not as a bible. Things can change based on humidity, oven temperature, and sweetness and acidity of different ingredients at different times of the year. If you feel a recipe needs a little more or less of something, don't overthink it. Dough seems too sticky? Add more flour. Tomato sauce not salty enough for your taste? Add more salt. For my family, my cooks, and me, cooking is more about feeling than science. (You think my nonna had a digital scale?) The good news is, the more you do it, the stronger that intuition becomes. I hope these recipes bring you lots of joy and happy memories.

Charter
of
Societa' di Mutuo Soccorso Filippo Palizzi di Vasto.
(Mutual Benefit Society Filippo Palizzi of Vasto...)
"Societa' di Mutuo Soccorso Filippo Palizzi di Vasto"
USE
QUARTER
AND
NICKEL
ONLY
35¢
KOOL
KENT

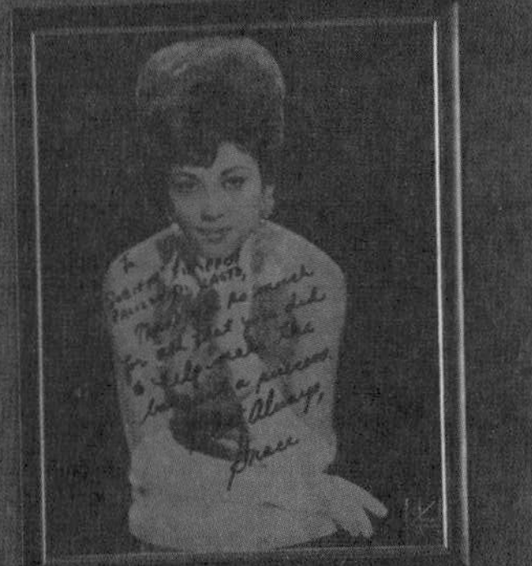

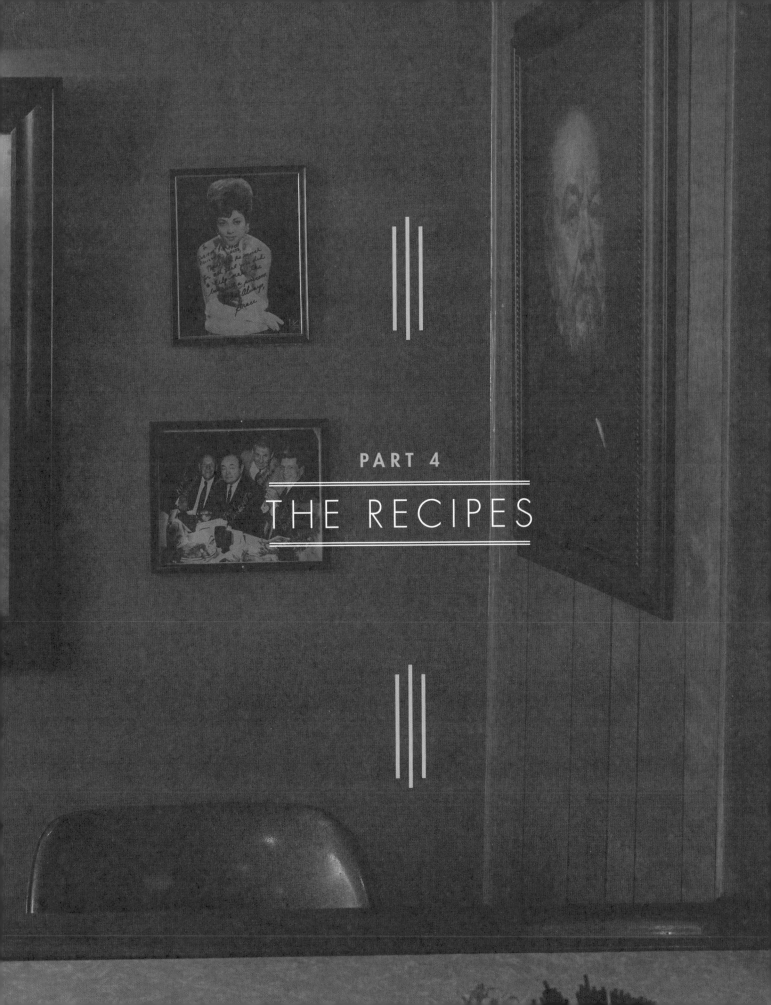

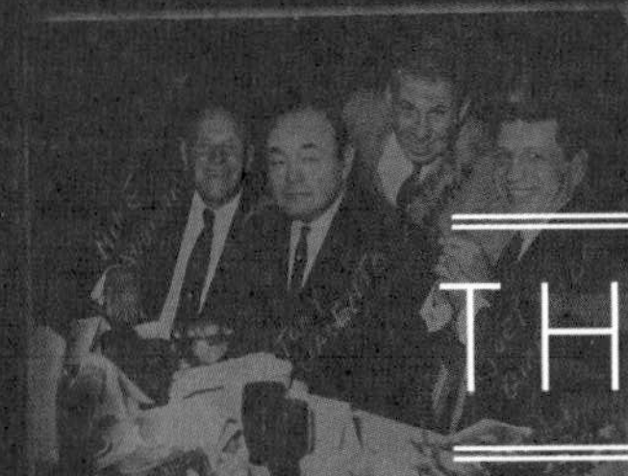

PART 4

THE RECIPES

National

STARTERS AND BREAD

SESAME SEMOLINA BREAD

SALSA PICANTE

MOZZARELLA AND ANCHOVY PANZAROTTI

MARINATED OLIVES AND LUPINI BEANS

FAVA BEAN PURÉE WITH MARINATED BLACK OLIVES

STROMBOLI

TOMATO PIE

FENNEL AND ORANGE SALAD

CAESAR SALAD

PIZZAGAINA

TOMATO PANZANELLA

SESAME SEMOLINA BREAD

Growing up, a nice loaf of crusty bread was always on the table. We use the word *scarpetta* in my family, which means "slipper" in Italian but represents the hunk of bread you use to mop up any leftover sauce in a bowl. This semolina bread is ideal for scooping up any last bits of Escarole and Beans (page 96) and Calamari and Peas (page 117), but it's also perfect on its own. At the Club, it's the foundation of our bread service; as soon as you sit down, we welcome you with a wooden bowl with semolina bread, our crunchy skinny breadsticks, Mozzarella and Anchovy Panzarotti (page 30), and Salsa Picante (page 27). Any leftovers get repurposed into croutons for our Tomato Panzanella (page 51) and Caesar Salad (page 46) and breadcrumbs. This recipe is modeled on the sesame-seeded loaves you'll find in bakeries from Abruzzo all the way down to Sicily—and in South Philly. (My family's spot, Faragalli's, is around the corner from the Club, and has been in business since 1948.) We add a little malt syrup to create complexity of flavor, but if you can't find it, it's fine to omit.

MAKES 3 LOAVES

3½ teaspoons (11 g) active dry yeast

2 cups (480 ml) warm water

1 teaspoon barley malt syrup

1¼ cups (173 g) bread flour, plus more for dusting

1½ cups (255 g) semolina flour, plus more for dusting

1½ cups (230 g) durum flour

2½ teaspoons salt

½ cup (75 g) white sesame seeds

Salsa Picante (page 27) for serving

Combine the yeast, water, and malt syrup in the bowl of a stand mixer and bloom for 8 minutes. Add the flours and mix on low speed with the dough hook attachment until the dough comes together into a ball, about 3 minutes. Increase the speed to medium and knead for 3 minutes. Add the salt and mix for 1 minute. At this point, the dough should be fairly smooth and should not stick to your hands. Remove the dough from the bowl, form it into a ball, and pinch the bottom closed. Lightly dust a medium bowl with bread flour and put the dough in the bowl, lightly dusting the top with more bread flour. Cover the bowl with plastic wrap and allow the dough to rise for 2 hours, or until almost doubled in size.

Portion the dough into 3 ball-shaped loaves, about 13 ounces (369 g) each. Pinch the bottom of each ball closed to form a tight round loaf. Put the sesame seeds into a small bowl. Fill a small spray bottle with water and spritz the tops of each ball of dough with water. Invert each dough ball and press lightly into the bowl of sesame seeds to cover the top. Flour a baking sheet with semolina flour. Place the dough balls on the prepared baking sheet, allowing at least 3 inches (7.5 cm) between each. Cover the baking sheet with plastic wrap and let the dough rise in a warm space for 1 hour, or until nearly doubled in size.

Preheat the oven to 450°F (230°C). Put a small pan of water in the bottom of the oven to create humidity. Uncover the pan and lightly score the top of each dough ball with a knife, cutting just through the surface, not too deep. Gently place the pan on the middle rack of the oven and bake for 15 minutes. Rotate the pan 180 degrees and bake for 10 to 15 additional minutes, or until the loaves are crusty and deep golden brown. Remove the loaves from the oven and let cool. Slice and serve warm with salsa picante.

SALSA PICANTE

This sauce first greets you as a dip for our Sesame Semolina Bread (page 26), but I tell people to hang on to it through the meal because it makes an amazing condiment for any meat or fish dish. It doesn't look like much—kind of chunky and reddish brown—but it packs so much flavor. I first had a version of it when I was in Sicily, studying with Anna Tasca Lanza, the queen of Sicilian cooking. I really didn't know what was in it except for eggplant, but through lots of trial and error I was able to recreate a picante sauce that works with roasted mushrooms, garlic, and a good hit of heat from chile picante concentrate. I use Alfonso Esposito brand, but if you can't find it online or in Italian specialty stores, harissa makes a great substitution. This recipe makes a quart. Half feeds four people, and the remaining half can be stored in the fridge for one week or in the freezer for three months. If you're cooking for a crowd, you can serve the whole quart at once, just add an extra chopped garlic clove to the final step.

MAKES 1 QUART (1 L) SAUCE

ROASTED GARLIC

- 1 head garlic
- 1 teaspoon extra-virgin olive oil

Preheat the oven to 425°F (220°C). Cut off the top of the head of garlic, place on a piece of aluminum foil, add the olive oil, and wrap tightly in the foil. Roast for 30 minutes, or until golden and soft. Remove from the oven and let cool to room temperature.

PICANTE SAUCE

- 1 eggplant, stemmed
- 4 teaspoons salt, divided
- 12 cracks black pepper
- 2¼ cups (531 ml) extra-virgin olive oil, divided
- 10 button mushrooms
- 2 tablespoons picante chile purée
- ¼ cup (55 g) Marinara (page 54)
- 1 cup (240 g) tomato paste
- 1 raw garlic clove, minced
- Sesame Semolina Bread (page 26) for serving

Preheat the oven to 425°F (220°C). Cut the eggplant lengthwise and score the flesh by crisscrossing with a knife. Salt the eggplant with 1 teaspoon of the salt and the pepper and let it sit for 10 minutes. Brush the eggplant with ¼ cup (59 ml) of the olive oil and roast in the oven until dark golden brown, about 20 minutes, or until a knife easily goes through the stem end. Remove from the oven and let cool to room temperature.

Toss the mushrooms with ½ cup (118 ml) of the olive oil and 1 teaspoon of the salt. Put the mushrooms in a roasting pan and cover with aluminum foil. Roast, covered, in the oven for 15 minutes. Remove the foil and continue to roast until dark golden brown, about 10 more minutes. Remove from the oven and let cool to room temperature.

When the mushrooms are cool enough to handle, finely chop them and transfer to a bowl. Remove the flesh of the eggplant and the skin of the roasted garlic, finely chop into a paste, and add it to the bowl. Add the remaining 2 teaspoons of salt, remaining 1½ cups (354 ml) of olive oil, and the chile purée, marinara, and tomato paste and mix all the ingredients well. The consistency should be like that of a pesto. Divide the salsa picante in half (store the extra in the refrigerator for 1 week or freeze for up to 3 months) and adjust the seasoning with salt and pepper to taste. Add the minced raw garlic to the remaining half of the salsa picante for serving. Serve with sliced semolina bread.

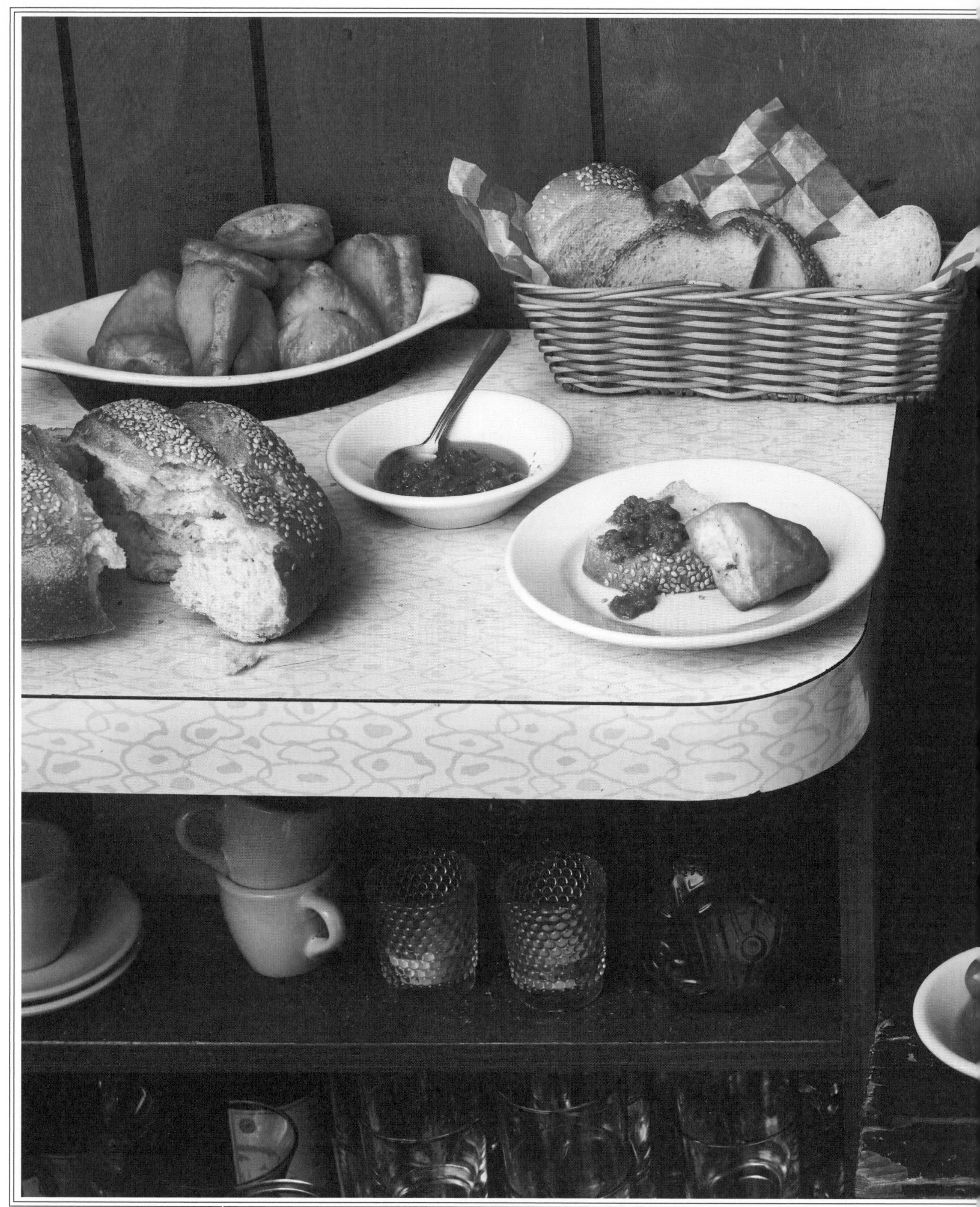

Sesame Semolina Bread / Mozzarella and Anchovy Panzarotti / Salsa Picante

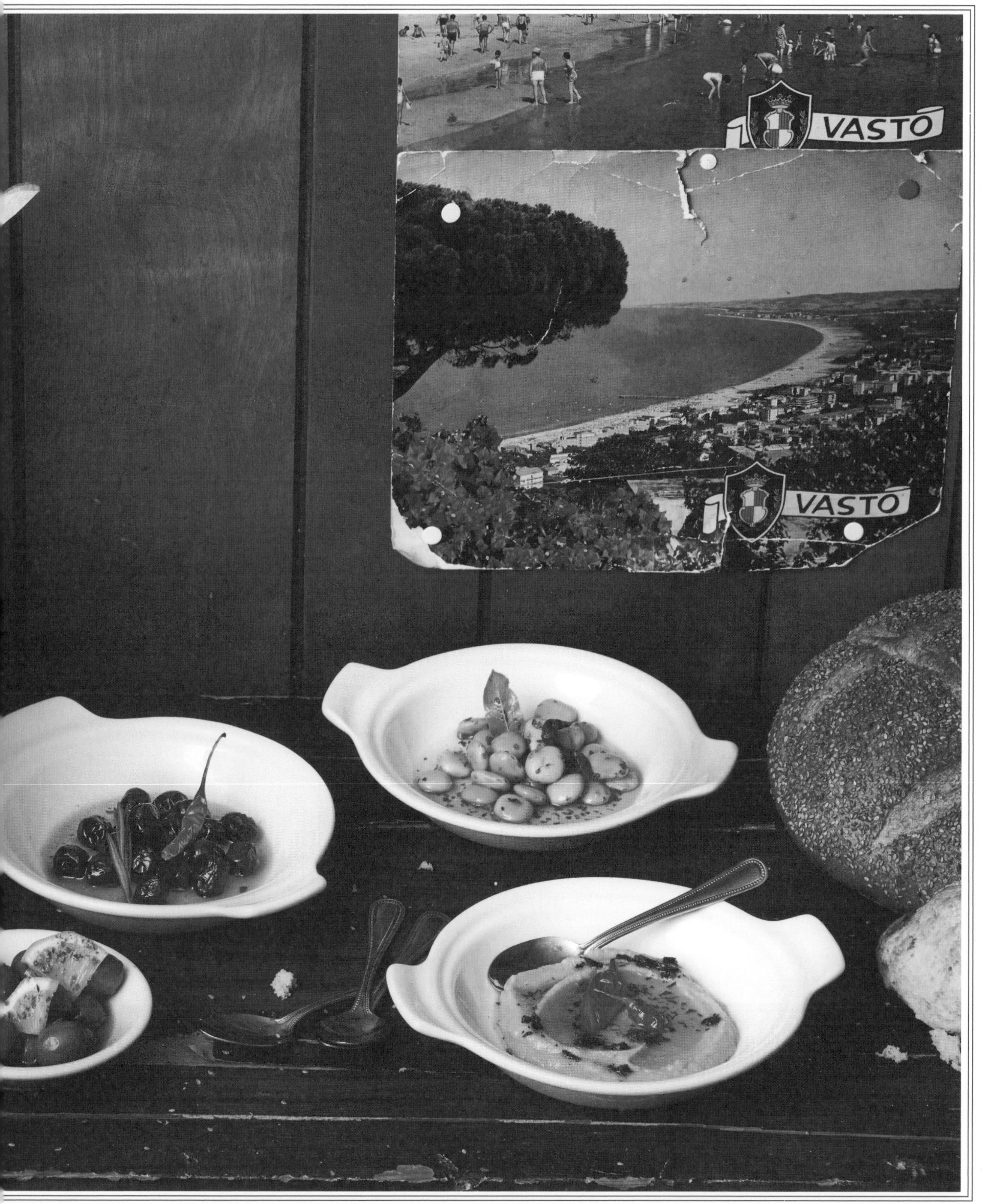

Marinated Olives and Lupini Beans / Fava Bean Purée with Marinated Black Olives

MOZZARELLA AND ANCHOVY PANZAROTTI

Think of these panzarotti as savory donuts. They're a staple of my family's Christmas Eve dinner at my cousin's house—crispy and golden on the outside, soft and gooey in the center, a little salty from the anchovy, which counts as one of the seven fish we eat that night. My mom keeps the dough in a big bowl by the stove and she'll just grab a hunk, flatten it out in her palm, stuff it with the cheese and anchovy, then pinch it closed and drop it in the hot oil. At the Club, we put a little more work into it, rolling out the dough and forming neat triangles as this recipe outlines, but my mom's version works just as well if you're pressed for time. This dough is also really customizable. Sometimes I'll omit the mozzarella and anchovy, fry them plain, then drape thin slices of prosciutto over the top, or make them sweet. This batch makes a lot of panzarotti, but you don't need to fry them all at once. Once they're stuffed and sealed, freeze any extras in a single layer on a baking sheet, then store them in a resealable plastic bag, where they'll keep for months. The panzarotti can go directly from freezer to fryer.

MAKES 49 PANZAROTTI

1¼ teaspoons (5 g) active dry yeast
¾ cup (177 ml) whole milk, at room temperature
½ teaspoon granulated sugar
1½ cups plus 3 tablespoons (233 g) bread flour, divided, plus more for dusting
17 oil-packed anchovy fillets, cut into 3 pieces each
1 garlic clove, minced
2 tablespoons plus ¼ teaspoon (30 g) unsalted butter, cubed, at room temperature
2 teaspoons salt, divided
20 cracks black pepper
2 quarts (2 L) canola oil
4 ounces (115 g) dry mozzarella, cut into 49 roughly equal (¼ inch [6 mm]) cubes
Salsa Picante (page 27) for serving

Make the starter by combining the yeast, milk, and sugar in a small mixing bowl and blooming for 8 minutes. Whisk in half of the flour and cover the bowl with plastic wrap. Set in a warm place for 2 to 2½ hours, or until the mixture is visibly bubbly looking and starting to rise. While the starter is proofing, mix together the anchovy and garlic in a small bowl and set aside.

Place the remaining flour in the bowl of a stand mixer fitted with the dough hook. Make a well in the flour and scrape all the starter into the center. Mix on low speed for 3 minutes, slowly adding the softened butter a cube at a time. Increase the speed to medium and mix until all the butter has been well incorporated, about 5 minutes. Add half of the salt and mix for 1 minute.

Turn out the dough onto a lightly floured surface. Knead the dough, folding it on top of itself like a book 10 to 15 times, until smooth. The dough should be soft but not stick to your hands or work surface. Transfer the dough to a lightly floured medium bowl and score the top with a cross. Lightly dust the surface of the dough with flour and cover the bowl with plastic wrap. Let it rest in a warm place for 2 to 2½ hours, or until almost doubled in size.

Turn out the dough onto a lightly floured surface and roll out to a roughly 15-inch (38 cm) square that's ⅛ inch (3 mm) thick. Square off the dough by removing ½ inch (1.3 cm) from each side and season it with the remaining salt and the black pepper. Using a pizza wheel, make 6 cuts across the dough at 2-inch (5 cm) intervals, followed by 6 vertical cuts at the same interval, leaving you with 49 (2-inch [5 cm]) squares.

Heat the canola oil in a deep pot on the stove until it registers 360°F (182°C). Place 1 cube of mozzarella and 1 slice of anchovy in the center of each square. Moisten the edges of each square with a pastry brush dipped in water. Fold over each square into a triangle shape and press the edges firmly to seal. Arrange the panzarotti in single layer on a lightly floured baking sheet, separated slightly so they don't stick together. Add the panzarotti to the hot oil a few at a time, being careful not to crowd the pot. Deep-fry them for about 3 minutes per batch, moving them around gently but constantly in the oil, until evenly golden brown, and transfer to a baking sheet lined with paper towels to absorb excess oil. Serve immediately with salsa picante for dipping.

MARINATED OLIVES AND LUPINI BEANS

You can get so many different flavors into olives depending how you marinate them. At the Club, we start dinner with two kinds, green Castelvetranos with oregano and lemon and oil-cured Moroccan black olives with orange and chile. You get a sharp contrast in flavor and texture: the Castelvetranos are young, mild, and fruity, whereas the Moroccans are strong, oily, and salty. These are perfect to put out for a cocktail party or happy hour, along with our garlicky marinated lupini beans. All can be made ahead of time.

BLACK OLIVES WITH ORANGE AND CHILE

MAKES 2 CUPS (440 G) OLIVES

- 2 cups (350 g) oil-cured black olives, drained
- 3 sprigs rosemary
- 20 Arbol chiles
- Grated zest of ½ orange
- 10 bay leaves
- 2 cups (480 ml) blended oil (see page 19)

Mix together all the ingredients, except the oil, in a bowl and allow them to sit together for 15 minutes. Add the oil, toss, and serve immediately, or transfer to an airtight container and store in the fridge for up to 2 weeks.

GREEN OLIVES WITH OREGANO AND LEMON

MAKES 2 CUPS (440 G) OLIVES

- 1 small lemon
- 2 cups (350 g) Castelvetrano olives, drained
- 1½ tablespoons dried oregano
- 15 bay leaves
- 3 garlic cloves, thinly sliced
- 2 cups (480 ml) blended oil (see page 19)

Trim the ends of the lemon and cut in half lengthwise. Slice each half of the lemon crosswise in thirds, creating 6 half-moons. Mix together all the ingredients, except the oil, in a bowl and allow them to sit together for 15 minutes. Add the oil, toss, and serve immediately, or transfer to an airtight container and store in the fridge for up to 1 week.

GARLIC LUPINI BEANS

MAKES 2 CUPS (440 G) BEANS

- 2 cups (350 g) brined lupini beans, drained
- 2 garlic cloves, peeled and smashed
- 1½ tablespoons dried oregano
- 12 bay leaves
- 20 Arbol chiles
- 2 tablespoons white wine vinegar
- 2 cups (480 ml) blended oil (see page 19)

Mix together all the ingredients, except the oil, in a bowl and allow them to sit together for 15 minutes. Add the oil, toss, and serve immediately, or transfer to an airtight container and store in the fridge for up to 2 weeks.

FAVA BEAN PURÉE WITH MARINATED BLACK OLIVES

In the Italian tradition of having something small to snack on while you drink, we put out little bowls of Abruzzese dried, salted, and toasted fava beans at the bar. I find them impossible to stop eating, and not just because I really love fava beans. Another one of my favorite ways to serve favas is this hummus-esque dip. We simmer dried fava beans for an hour, then buzz them up into a purée flavored with roasted garlic, then top it with marinated olives and herbaceous salsa verde. The contrast between the richness of the beans and the brininess of the olives makes this a strong player in a spread of snacks. Put out a bowl with some Mozzarella and Anchovy Panzarotti (page 30), a Fritto Misto (page 105), and a big Caesar Salad (page 46) and you're good to go. This recipe scales up easily and can be made one day before serving.

SERVES 4 TO 6

SALSA VERDE

MAKES 2 CUPS (448 G) SALSA VERDE

1 tablespoon capers
2 oil-packed anchovy fillets
1 cup (40 g) finely chopped parsley leaves
1 tablespoon finely chopped garlic
¼ teaspoon finely chopped red pepper flakes
1½ cups (355 ml) extra-virgin olive oil

Finely chop the capers and anchovies and place in a small bowl with the parsley, garlic, and red pepper flakes. Cover with the olive oil and stir to combine. Use immediately as a condiment for grilled meats and fish, or store, covered, in the refrigerator until serving. The salsa keeps for 1 day refrigerated.

FAVA BEAN PURÉE

1 head garlic, halved, plus 1 clove, divided
2 cups (330 g) dried fava beans
1 celery rib
½ carrot
½ yellow onion
4 sprigs parsley
2 sprigs rosemary
2 sprigs sage
2 teaspoons salt, divided
10 cracks black pepper, divided
½ Arbol chile
1 bay leaf
1½ quarts (1.5 L) water
1 head Roasted Garlic (page 27)
¼ teaspoon smoked paprika, plus more for serving
Juice of 2 lemons
½ cup (118 ml) extra-virgin olive oil
1 cup (220 g) Marinated Black Olives (page 34) for serving
¼ cup (56 g) Salsa Verde
Sesame Semolina Bread (page 26) for serving

Combine the halved garlic, favas, celery, carrot, onion, herbs, ½ teaspoon of the salt, half of the black pepper, and the chile, bay leaf, and water in a medium Dutch oven over low heat. Cook for 1 hour, or until the beans are soft. After an hour, the favas' skins will have split, the interiors will be very tender, and the liquid should be mostly reduced and slightly below the surface of the beans. Remove and discard the celery, carrot, onion, herbs, and chile.

Combine the roasted garlic and fresh garlic clove, paprika, and lemon juice in a blender and pulse for 30 seconds. Add the favas with their liquid and blend on medium speed until very smooth. Pour the purée into a medium bowl and whisk in the olive oil, remaining 1½ teaspoons of salt and the remaining black pepper. Transfer to a large platter and create a well in the center of the purée. Add the marinated olives to the well and drizzle with the salsa verde. Sprinkle with more paprika and serve with grilled slices of semolina bread.

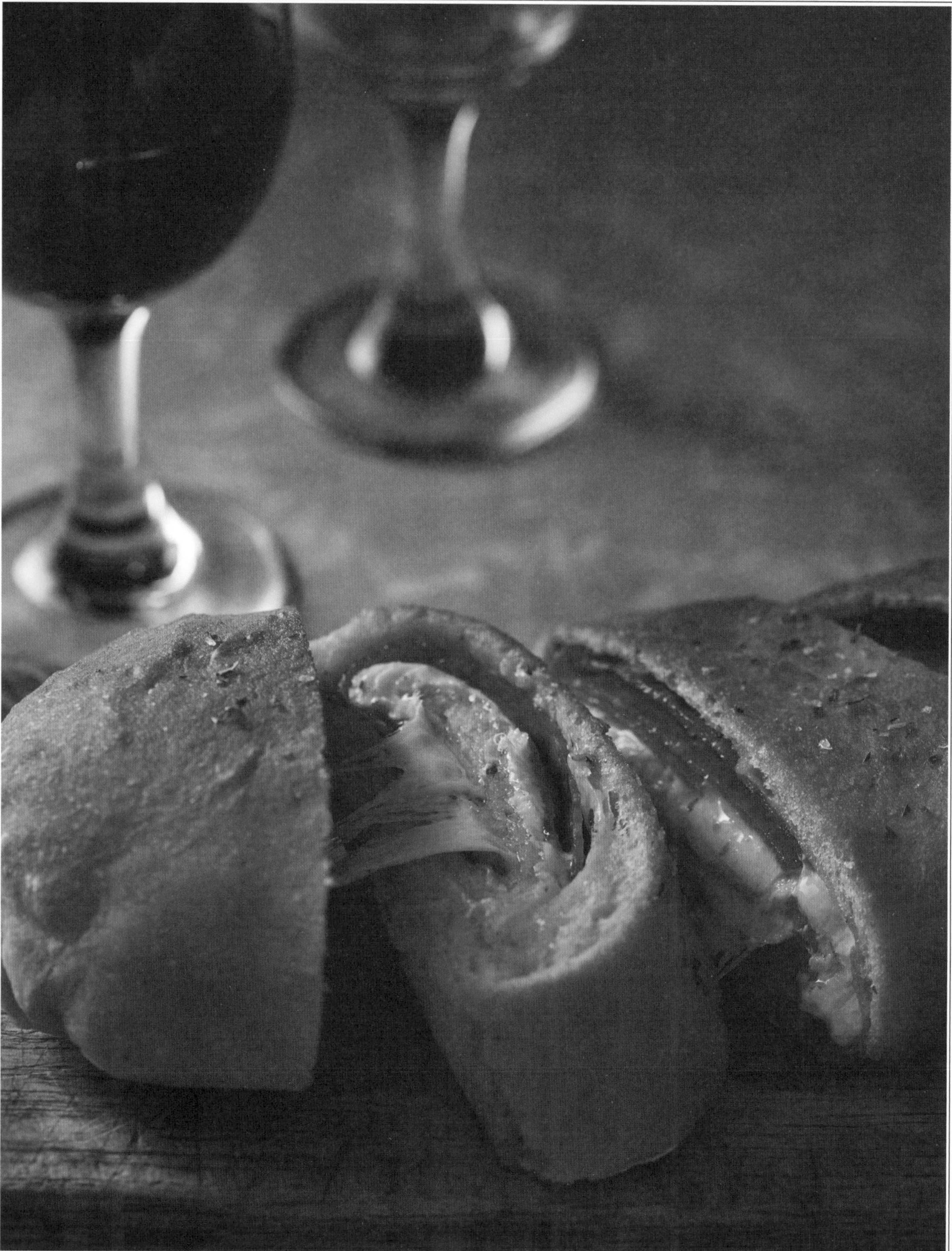

STROMBOLI

Stromboli, homemade pizza, or Pasta and Ceci (page 75). Every Friday night, my mom would make one of those three things for dinner. This recipe is a faithful recreation of the stromboli I've been watching her make since I was a kid: twice risen, stuffed with mozzarella and pepperoni, flavored with garlic and oregano. Unlike a lot of stromboli recipes, ours does not use tomato sauce. A lot of people ask why, but that's just how my mom does it. Feel free to serve the stromboli with a small bowl of warm Marinara (page 54) on the side for dipping. This recipe makes four stromboli; once they've completely cooled, you can wrap and freeze any leftovers. This way you'll always have stromboli to pop into the oven on a Friday night.

MAKES 4 STROMBOLI

(recipe continues)

STARTER

- ½ cup (118 ml) warm water
- 2 teaspoons (8 g) active dry yeast
- ½ teaspoon granulated sugar
- 1 cup (138 g) bread flour

Make the starter the day before you want to make the stromboli. Combine the water, yeast, and sugar in a medium bowl and bloom for 8 minutes. Add the bread flour and stir until well combined. Cover the bowl with plastic wrap and allow it to rest in a warm place until doubled in size, 3 to 4 hours. Transfer the starter to the refrigerator to rest overnight.

DOUGH

- 1¼ teaspoons (5 g) active dry yeast
- 1 cup (236 ml) warm water
- ½ teaspoon barley malt syrup
- 2¼ cups (344 g) durum flour
- 1½ teaspoons salt
- Bread flour for dusting

Remove the starter from the fridge, uncover, and allow it to come to room temperature. Place the yeast, water, and malt syrup in the bowl of a stand mixer fitted with the dough hook attachment and bloom for 8 minutes. Add the starter and durum flour to the bowl and mix on low speed to combine, about 4 minutes. Increase the speed to medium and knead the dough for 3 minutes. When the dough is smooth and starts to climb up the side of the bowl, add the salt and mix for 1 minute. Form the dough into a ball, pinching the bottom closed. Place the dough in a lightly floured medium bowl and dust the top lightly with bread flour. Cover the dough with plastic wrap and allow it to rise until almost doubled in size, about 2 hours.

Scrape out the dough onto a floured surface and divide into 4 equal portions, 7 to 8 ounces (198 to 225 g) each. Form each into a tight ball, pinching the bottom closed, and place them back on the floured surface. Lightly dust the tops of the balls with bread flour and drape the plastic wrap over the top to completely cover. Let them rise in a warm place for 1½ to 2 hours, or until doubled in size.

FILLING

- ¼ cup (59 ml) extra-virgin olive oil
- 3 garlic cloves, chopped
- 1 teaspoon dried oregano
- 1 tablespoon salt
- ½ teaspoon freshly ground black pepper
- 32 thin slices grande pepperoni
- 20 thin 3-inch (8 cm) slices dry mozzarella
- 1 large egg, beaten

Mix together the olive oil, chopped garlic, and oregano in a small bowl. Roll out the dough balls to a ¼-inch (6 mm)-thick round and season the side facing you with one fourth each of the salt and pepper. Brush the dough with one fourth of the oil mixture, leaving a ¾-inch (2 cm) border around the edges. Place 8 slices of pepperoni evenly on the dough, leaving ¾-inch (2 cm) border around the edges. Place 5 slices of mozzarella on top of the pepperoni, leaving ¾-inch (2 cm) border around the edges. Brush the border of the dough with the beaten egg. Gently pull out corners of the dough to make the round into more of a square shape. Fold each dough square into thirds, folding it toward you from back to front. After each fold, press gently on the sides to seal. After the third fold, with the seam of the dough on the bottom, close the ends and trim off ½ inch (1.3 cm) from both sides, and fold in the ends underneath. Repeat for the 3 remaining balls.

Place the stromboli on a baking sheet lined with parchment paper, leaving at least 3 inches (7.5 cm) between each. Brush the tops of the stromboli with the remaining oil mixture and drape with plastic wrap. Allow to rest for 15 minutes somewhere warm. Meanwhile, preheat the oven to 425°F (220°C). Unwrap the stromboli and bake on the middle rack for 15 minutes. Rotate the pan 180 degrees and bake for an additional 10 to 12 minutes, or until golden brown. Cut into slices and serve.

TOMATO PIE

Almost every Italian bakery in South Philly sells tomato pie, which isn't a pie in the dessert sense of the word, but a savory focaccia topped with marinara. It's a fixture of impromptu family get-togethers, one o'clock Eagles games, Holy Communion after-parties, and day trips down the Shore. When someone asks, "What can I bring?" to an afternoon gathering, a tomato pie is usually the answer. Each place makes tomato pie differently. Some bakeries add a dusting of Locatelli or Parmigiano after baking; to others, that's sacrilege. Some apply a layer of tomato sauce so thin the dimpled surface of the finished pie looks spray-painted; others ladle it on so heavily the pie is equal parts dough and tomatoes. On the tomato front, ours falls somewhere in between the thick and thin camps. We skip the cheese, but feel free to finish with some if you like. This recipe requires nearly three hours from mixing and rising to baking. If you don't have that much time, you can cut out an hour by starting with premade dough from your neighborhood bakery or pizzeria that's already completed a first rise. Just pick up the recipe from getting the dough into the oiled baking sheet and you'll be on your way to freshly baked tomato pie in about an hour and a half.

MAKES ONE 18 X 13-INCH (44.5 X 33 CM) TOMATO PIE

2 teaspoons (8 g) active dry yeast
2¼ teaspoons granulated sugar
1¾ cups (420 ml) lukewarm water
3½ cups (483 g) bread flour
¾ cup (177 ml) extra-virgin olive oil, divided into thirds, plus more for garnish
2 teaspoons salt, plus more for garnish
2 cups (473 ml) Marinara (page 54)

Combine the yeast, sugar, and water in the bowl of a stand mixer and bloom for 8 minutes. Add the bread flour and ¼ cup (59 ml) of the olive oil and mix on low speed for 1 minute with the paddle attachment. Increase the speed to medium. Mix until the dough comes off the sides of the bowl, 6 to 8 minutes. Add the salt and mix for 30 seconds. Remove the dough and place in a bowl that's been oiled with ¼ cup (59 ml) of the olive oil. Cover the bowl with a dish towel and let the dough rest at room temperature 1 hour, or until doubled in size.

When the dough is ready, oil an 18 x 13-inch (45.5 x 33 cm) baking sheet with the oil from the bowl plus the remaining ¼ cup (59 ml) of olive oil. Be sure to get the oil into the corners and up the sides of the pan. Place the dough on the pan, then flip the dough over and poke it down with your fingers to spread it out evenly on the pan. Cover the baking sheet with plastic wrap and allow the dough to rise for 1 hour, or until it fully fills out the pan.

After the second rise, uncover the dough, spread it gently to the edges to fit the pan, and poke lightly with your fingers again, creating a dimpled pattern. Let rest for 10 minutes, uncovered, on the counter.

Preheat the oven to 450°F (230°C). Bake the dough on the middle rack for 15 minutes. Rotate 180 degrees and bake for 10 additional minutes, or until golden brown, then remove from the oven. Spread the tomato sauce evenly across the pie and bake for 5 additional minutes. Remove the tomato pie from the oven and garnish with olive oil and salt. Cut into wedges and serve.

AMERICAN CHEESE ON A PIZZA? THE ONLY-IN-PHILLY PIZZAZZ PIE

If nothing else, this cookbook will probably be the only Italian one in the world to have a recipe featuring American cheese. Those mild, perfectly meltable, processed white squares are essential to pizzazz pizza, one of South Philly's strangest and greatest foods. It's a pie layered with American cheese, sliced fresh tomato, and the electric yellow, spicy-sour pickled pepper rings most often seen peeking out of hoagies. Sounds weird, tastes amazing.

Celebre's Pizza in Packer Park, the South Philly neighborhood built on reclaimed swampland in the 1950s, lays claim to creating the pizzazz. Celebre's has been around since 1961, but didn't invent the pizza until sometime in the 1980s, according to the current owner, Michael Spina. Two brothers owned the pizzeria at the time, Ronald and Robert Celebre, first-generation Italian Americans. Ronnie loved grilled cheese sandwiches from when he was a kid. They weren't made with mozzarella or provolone or any other cheese from his immigrant parents' pantry. They were made with American.

All the time, immigrants are navigating the food available to them in the context of their own culinary traditions, and that carries on through the generations. Like the Celebres, my parents were the first in their families to be born in America, and assimilating American foods into their Italian repertoire was common. When I was a kid, we used to have a soft pretzel guy in the neighborhood who would ride his cart up and down the streets on Sunday mornings, yelling, "Freeeesssssh pretzels!" My dad would go out and get a bunch, still warm in their brown paper bag. My mom would slice them in half like bagels and load them up with mortadella and sopressata—Italian sandwiches on Philly pretzels. (Years ago, she sent the recipe to a magazine recipe contest. She didn't win, but years later she got the magazine, and there was a recipe for a pretzel sandwich inside. She still kinda thinks she got ripped off.)

Ronald wanted to make a pizza that tasted like a grilled cheese and got to layering white American over dough one day. He added fresh tomatoes and onions, then nixed the onions in favor of pickled peppers. The Celebre's staff, the original pizzazz guinea pigs, loved the wacky pizza. Ronnie named the pie after his brother's boat, the *Pizzazz*. It went on the menu and became a South Philly phenomenon.

Most pizzerias in South Philly now make pizzazz, but if you don't live here, you can make the Palizzi version at home. Start by following the dough process for the Tomato Pie (page 40). After laying out the dough in a pan and letting it rest for 10 minutes, bake the pie on the middle rack in a 450°F (230°C) oven for 15 minutes and rotate 180 degrees. Bake for 10 additional minutes, or until golden brown, and remove from the oven. Mix together 3 chopped garlic cloves, ¼ cup (59 ml) of olive oil, and 1 teaspoon of dried oregano in a small bowl and evenly spread the mixture on the crust. Top the crust with 14 slices of white American cheese, then with 1¼ cups (130 g) drained pickled wax pepper rings, then 12 (¼-inch [6 mm]-thick) slices of vine-ripened tomatoes. Bake for 5 to 10 more minutes, until the cheese is melted and just starting to brown. Finish with coarse sea salt and a drizzle of olive oil.

FENNEL AND ORANGE SALAD

Fennel grows wild all over Sicily. I couldn't get away from it when I was cooking there, nor could I get away from it back home, where my Uncle Ernie would tear off the tender fronds and snack on them like pretzel sticks. Shaved fennel is the star of this crunchy, cool, and refreshing salad. We toss it with our Marinated Black Olives (page 34) for salinity and orange vinaigrette for sweetness and acidity. The dressing also has a little bit of ground aniseeds, which tie into the licorice notes in the fennel. We pile the whole thing over a big platter of fresh orange slices, and it's the best summertime salad you can have.

SERVES 4

2 navel oranges, divided

1 blood orange

1 large fennel bulb with fronds

3 tablespoons Champagne vinegar

2 tablespoons honey

¼ cup (59 ml) extra-virgin olive oil

1 cup (15 g) loosely packed fresh parsley leaves

Pinch of ground aniseeds

2 teaspoons salt

20 cracks black pepper

17 Marinated Black Olives (page 34)

Remove the peel and pith from 1 of the navel oranges and from the blood orange and cut the peeled fruits into ½-inch (1.3 cm)-thick slices. Arrange the orange slices on a large platter. Remove the tender fronds of the fennel and finely chop enough to make ¼ cup (25 g). Discard the remaining ribs. Core the fennel bulb and thinly shave with a knife or on a mandoline. Squeeze the juice from the remaining orange. Whisk together 3 tablespoons (45 ml) of the juice plus the vinegar, honey, olive oil, parsley, aniseeds, salt, and pepper in a medium bowl. Pit the olives and add them to the vinaigrette, along with the shaved fennel bulb and fronds. Toss the ingredients to coat in the vinaigrette, then drape over the orange slices.

CAESAR SALAD

Having a Caesar on the menu at the Club was nonnegotiable. While this salad was invented in Mexico, it was quickly adopted by and became a classic of Italian American restaurants. Everything about our version looks like a traditional Caesar, down to the wooden bowls we serve it in, but we put our little twist on it, balancing the intense heat of the garlic with milder shallot and adding a sprinkle of thyme to round out the flavor. We also use two different kinds of cheese, Locatelli (sheep's milk) in the dressing and Parmigiano-Reggiano (cow's milk) to finish. Locatelli is a brand of pecorino that's so prevalent in South Philly, people just refer to it by name, as if it's its own style of cheese. Our families didn't have the money to spend on expensive Parmigiano, so the sharp, salty, grated Locatelli was the macaroni cheese in the shaker on the table growing up. You get that kick in our Caesar dressing, but also the rich nuttiness of Parm shaved over top of the salad. This recipe makes about 3 cups of dressing, which you'll need about half of depending on how dressed you like your salad. Any extra will keep in the fridge up to a week.

SERVES 4

SEMOLINA CROUTONS

- ½ loaf Sesame Semolina Bread (page 26)
- ½ cup (125 ml) blended oil (see page 19)
- 2 garlic cloves, halved

Preheat the oven to 350°F (180°C). Cut the bread into 4 slices, each ¾ inch (2 cm) thick. Brush both sides of the slices with the blended oil and place on a baking sheet. Toast the bread until golden brown, about 8 minutes, then rub both sides of each piece with the cut sides of the garlic cloves. Cut the toasted bread into cubes. Place back in the oven and bake for 5 to 8 minutes, or until the croutons look golden and crunchy. Let cool to room temperature on the pan.

CAESAR DRESSING AND SALAD

- 2 large egg yolks
- ⅓ cup (80 ml) red wine vinegar
- Juice of 1 lemon
- 2 garlic cloves
- 6 oil-packed anchovy fillets plus 8 fillets for serving
- 1 small shallot
- 2 teaspoons salt
- 13 cracks black pepper
- 1 tablespoon Dijon mustard
- 1 tablespoon fresh thyme leaves
- 2 cups (480 ml) blended oil (see page 19)
- ⅓ cup (40 g) grated Locatelli pecorino
- 3 heads romaine hearts, halved lengthwise and cut into 1-inch (2.5 cm) strips
- Parmigiano-Reggiano for serving

In a food processor, pulse the egg yolks, vinegar, lemon juice, garlic, 6 anchovies, shallot, salt, pepper, mustard, and thyme until smooth. While the food processor is running, slowly drizzle in the blended oil to create a smooth emulsion. Add the grated pecorino and blend until smooth. Pour half of the dressing into a large bowl, reserving the remaining half for a future use. Add the romaine and the croutons and toss to coat. Adjust the salt and pepper to taste. Divide among 4 salad bowls and garnish each with 2 anchovy fillets and grated Parmigiano.

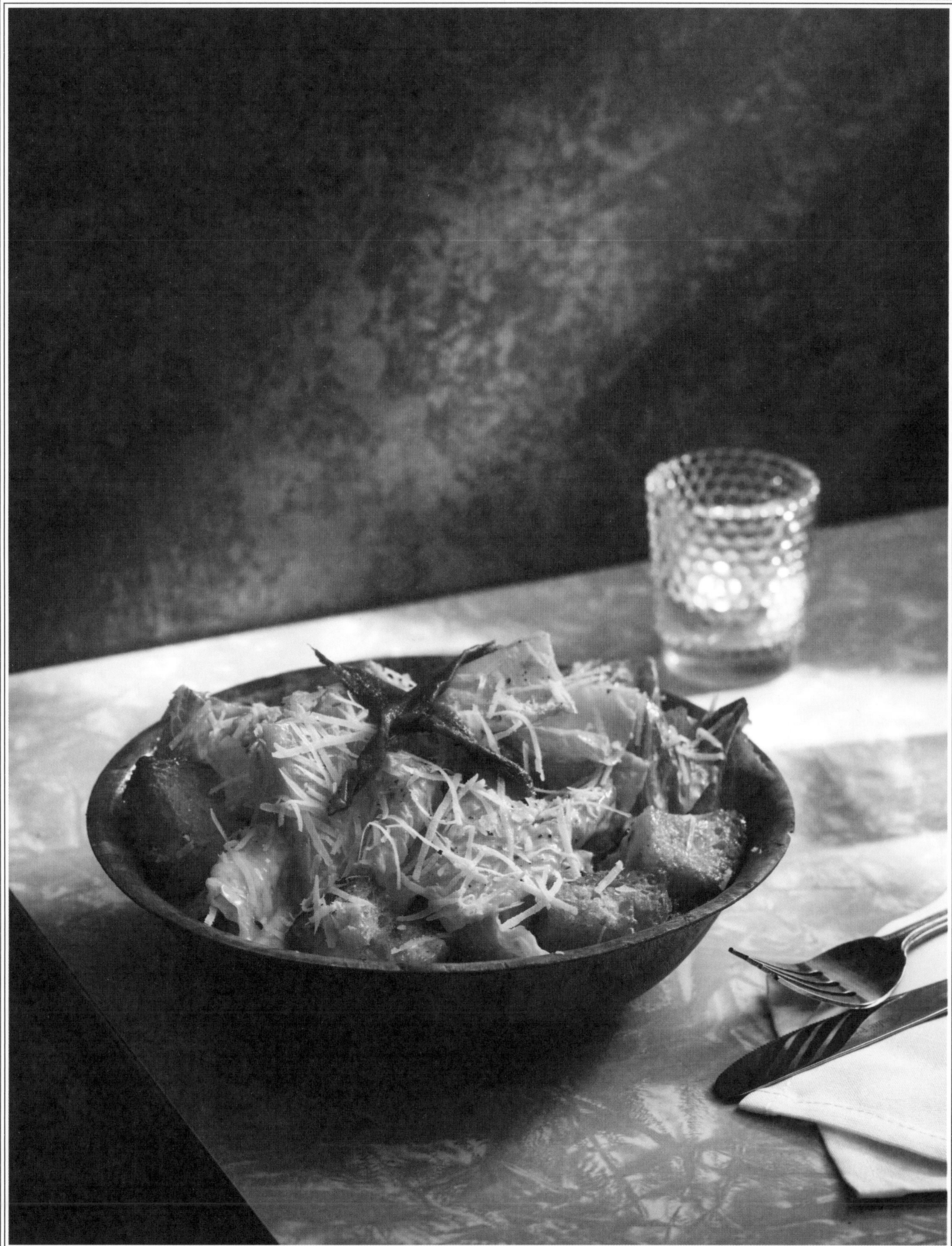

PIZZAGAINA

During Lent, the period of time leading up to Easter, many Catholics don't eat meat. The most common custom is to stick to seafood on Fridays only, but the superobservant like my grandparents and other Italian immigrants or first-generation Americans of their generation avoided it entirely from Ash Wednesday until midnight on Easter Sunday. Pizzagaina, also called ham pie, is part of this tradition, a celebratory dish that feels as if it's filled with five weeks' worth of meats. Imagine salty pieces of ham, salami, pepperoni, and capicola suspended in a cheesy egg frittata, all gift-wrapped in flaky pastry crust. That's ham pie. My mom would assemble and bake it off the day before Easter, and it would just sit there all day, filling the house with the most amazing, tempting, mouthwatering smell. We were not allowed to go near it until midnight, Easter Sunday, but as soon as the clock struck twelve, we'd all gather around the table for thick slices.

This year at the Club, I rolled out my own pizzagaina on midnight on the last night of Lent. Our members are such a mix of old South Philly, new South Philly, people that have nothing to do with South Philly at all. So, to see the dining room full of people eating something that's such a part of my heritage but may or may not have anything to do with theirs, was so cool and special. I love carrying on traditions like this.

The Italian meats we call for in this recipe are pretty widely available, but the basket cheese, a strained cow's milk cheese, might give you trouble if you don't have an Italian deli nearby. If you can't find basket cheese, use all ricotta.

SERVES 8

(recipe continues)

DOUGH

- 2⅓ cups plus 1 tablespoon (335 g) 00 flour, divided
- 3 large eggs
- 4 tablespoons (57 g) melted and cooled unsalted butter
- ¼ cup (60 ml) cold water

Place half of the flour in the bowl of a stand mixer fitted with the dough hook. Make a well in the flour and add the eggs, butter, and cold water to the center of the well. Mix on low speed until all the ingredients are combined. Turn out the dough onto a work surface and knead by hand, adding the remaining flour as you go, until the dough is smooth and not sticky, about 4 minutes. Wrap with plastic wrap and refrigerate for at least 1 hour and up to overnight.

HARD-BOILED EGGS

- 2 large eggs

Place the eggs in a pot, cover with cold water, and set over high heat. Start a timer for 6 minutes as soon as the water comes to a boil. At the 6-minute point, remove the eggs and shock them in ice water. Peel and chill until ready to use. Chop just before adding to the filling.

FILLING

- 1 cup (120 g) grated Parmigiano-Reggiano
- ½ cup (70 g) diced capicola (¼-inch [6 mm] dice)
- ½ cup (80 g) diced salami (¼-inch [6 mm] dice)
- ½ cup (75 g) diced ham (¼-inch [6 mm] dice)
- ½ cup (50 g) diced pepperoni (¼-inch [6 mm] dice)
- ½ cup (150 g) basket cheese
- ½ cup (63 g) grated dry mozzarella
- 10 cracks black pepper
- 1 teaspoon salt
- 8 ounces (227 g) ricotta
- ¼ cup (10 g) chopped fresh parsley leaves
- 2 large fresh eggs

Combine all the filling ingredients, except the eggs, in a large bowl and mix well. Gently fold in the fresh eggs, 1 at a time, then fold in the 2 chopped hard-boiled eggs. Set aside at room temperature.

TO BAKE

- Unsalted butter for pan
- 00 flour for dusting
- 1 large egg, beaten

Preheat the oven to 325°F (170°C), and lightly butter a 10-inch (25.5 cm) deep pie plate. Remove the chilled dough from the fridge and place on a lightly floured surface. Divide it in half. Roll out 1 portion to ⅛ inch (3 mm) thick and carefully drape it over the prepared pan. Gently push it down into the edges, leaving about ½ inch (1.3 cm) of overhang. (If you get holes, use some excess dough to patch.) Pour the filling into the pan. Roll out the remaining dough to the same thickness and place over the filled dish. Crimp the edges with a fork to seal. Trim off any excess dough around the sides. Brush the beaten egg over the surface and around the edges of the pie. Vent the top of the pie with a few slits. Bake the pie for 60 to 70 minutes, or until golden brown. A cake tester inserted into the center should come out clean. Remove the pie from the oven and allow it to rest for a minimum of 4 hours before serving at room temperature.

TOMATO PANZANELLA

You could toss all the ingredients in this recipe together in a bowl and make a pretty good panzanella salad. To make a great one, though, you need time. We build this summery salad in stages over twenty-five minutes. First, the tomatoes, basil, salt, and pepper hang out for ten, giving the seasonings time to really penetrate. Vinegar goes in next, and after two minutes, the olive oil, cucumber, and onion. If you add the oil too early, it will coat the vegetables and form a shield so no other flavors can get in. After ten more minutes, the oil, vinegar, and juices from the tomatoes will form a healthy amount of super-flavorful dressing in the bottom of the bowl. We toss that liquid with arugula and croutons, pile it on a platter, and top it with the tomato mixture. Try it as an opener for the Herb Butter–Roasted Orata (page 126) or alongside the Grilled Lamb Chops (page 146).

SERVES 4

4 tomatoes, cored and quartered
10 cracks black pepper
¼ teaspoon granulated sugar (optional)
10 fresh basil leaves, torn
½ teaspoon salt, divided
2 tablespoons red wine vinegar
¼ cup (59 ml) extra-virgin olive oil
½ cucumber, sliced ¼ inch (6 mm) thick
1 ounce (26 g) thinly sliced red onion
5 ounces (142 g) arugula
1 cup Semolina Croutons (page 46)
6 white anchovy fillets

Toss the tomatoes, pepper, sugar (if needed), basil, and ¼ teaspoon of the salt together in a medium bowl and let them sit for 10 minutes. Add the vinegar and let sit for 2 minutes. Add the olive oil, cucumber, and red onion and mix. Let sit for 10 minutes. Strain off 3 tablespoons (45 ml) of the liquid in the bottom of the bowl and place in a separate bowl along with the arugula, croutons, and remaining ¼ teaspoon of salt. Toss the arugula and croutons and arrange on a serving platter. Top with the tomato salad and garnish with the anchovies.

Societa' di Mutuo Soccorso
"Filippo Palizzi" di Vasto
1408 So. 12th STREET • PHILADELPHIA 47, PA.

PASTA AND RICE

MARINARA

"Tomato sauce" means different things to different people. Some take it as sauce slowly braised with cuts of pork or beef, what we call Sunday Gravy (page 133), others as a vegetarian situation, what we call marinara. In some South Philly households, the *r*'s become *d*'s and you drop the final *a* to arrive at the colloquial pronunciation, "madinad." Basically, our tomato sauce is both a self-contained dressing for pasta as well as an ingredient in other dishes, such as the Stuffed Peppers (page 93) and String Beans and Potatoes (page 94).

When my mom makes marinara, she chops and sautés the onion and garlic before adding the tomatoes, no big deal. I make mine a little bit different, based on a trick I learned from a chef from Lombardy for whom I once worked at a small BYOB. I knew I wanted my first restaurant, Zeppoli, to be a BYOB, so I wanted to get some experience in that kind of kitchen following my time at Vetri. The chef taught me to take the onion and garlic superslow, until they almost melt. When you run them through a sieve, they become almost a purée, and that robust flavor permeates the whole pot of marinara. Once I learned this method, I never went back.

MAKES 2 QUARTS (2 L) SAUCE

½ cup (118 ml) extra-virgin olive oil

3 small yellow onions, thinly shaved

3 garlic cloves, thinly shaved

1 bay leaf

1 Arbol chile

4 sprigs basil

2 (28-ounce [794 g]) cans whole peeled tomatoes

1 teaspoon salt

10 cracks black pepper

¼ teaspoon granulated sugar (optional)

Combine the olive oil, onions, garlic, bay leaf, chile, and basil in a medium Dutch oven over very low heat. Sweat the ingredients until the onions are melted and almost translucent, stirring frequently, about 45 minutes.

Meanwhile, combine the tomatoes, salt, black pepper, and sugar (if needed) in a medium bowl and crush the tomatoes as much as possible with your hands. Set a coarse sieve over a second medium bowl. Transfer the cooked onion mixture to the sieve and press through with a wooden spoon, until all that's left in the sieve is the bay leaf, chile, and basil stems. (This will take some elbow grease and about 5 minutes.) Be sure to scrape everything off the bottom of the sieve with a rubber spatula. Add the sieved onion mixture back to the pot, add the tomatoes, and simmer over very low heat for 2 to 3 hours, stirring frequently to prevent sticking. The marinara is done when it is reduced by a third and has a sweet, tomatoey flavor. Use immediately or let cool and store for up to 5 days in the refrigerator.

MEAT RAGU

Hearty with beef, pork, and veal, this ragu is less a pasta sauce than a dense, thick, Bolognese-like filling, which we use in our Arancini (page 82) and Timballo (page 84). The most common pitfall in making sauces with ground meat is overcrowding the pan. Add it all at once and the meat steams instead of browns. So, pull out the largest skillet in your cabinet and cook the beef, pork, and veal in two batches, taking the time to really sear them hard and develop a dark fond on the bottom of the pan. If you want to turn this ragu into a pasta sauce, triple the amount of marinara. It would be delicious with wide rigatoni, cheese tortellini, or layered into a lasagna.

MAKES 2 QUARTS (2 L) RAGU

½ cup (125 ml) extra-virgin olive oil, divided

1 pound (454 g) ground beef

4 ounces (113 g) ground pork

4 ounces (113 g) ground veal

2 teaspoons salt

8 cracks black pepper

1 cup (150 g) finely diced onion

½ cup (55 g) finely diced carrot

½ cup (55 g) finely diced celery

1 tablespoon finely chopped garlic

2 sprigs rosemary, tied together with kitchen twine

Pinch of red pepper flakes

1 Parmigiano-Reggiano rind, about 3 ounces (85 g)

1 whole prosciutto rind, about 5.3 ounces (150 g)

¼ cup (60 g) tomato paste

2 cups (473 ml) water

1 cup (236 g) Marinara (page 54)

Heat half of the olive oil in a large Dutch oven over medium-high heat until it shimmers. Working in 2 batches, add the ground meats and immediately begin to break them up with a wooden spoon. Cook until the meat is well browned and a fond begins to form on the bottom of the pot. Season with the salt and black pepper. Remove the meat from the pot and transfer it to a plate. Add the remaining oil and lower the heat to low. Add the onion, carrot, celery, and garlic and cook, stirring occasionally, until the vegetables are soft and the onion is translucent, about 5 minutes. Add the rosemary, red pepper flakes, Parmigiano rind, and prosciutto rind. Make a space in the pot and add the tomato paste. Cook the paste for about 6 minutes, until it turns from bright red to copper. Add the browned meat, water, and marinara. Cover and simmer for 1½ hours over low heat, checking and stirring every 10 minutes. Let the ragu cool overnight in the refrigerator, covered. Remove and discard the rosemary and rinds and transfer the ragu to airtight containers, where it will keep in the fridge for 1 week or in the freezer for 3 months.

20-YOLK PASTA DOUGH

The nearly two dozen yolks in this fresh dough is where our Tagliatelle (page 58) and Giant Raviolo (page 62) get their vibrant gold color and smooth, silky texture from. Be careful not to overmix it; stop kneading just as the dough begins to come together into a solid ball, and be sure to rest it for at least two hours so the gluten can chill out. Tightly wrapped with plastic wrap, the dough will hold in the fridge for two days. Longer than that, the yolks will begin to oxidize and the dough will turn green. You can also roll out the dough into pasta sheets and freeze them in a flour-dusted airtight container. And if you're wondering what to do with all those egg whites: make Hazelnut Torrone (page 190).

MAKES ABOUT 1½ POUNDS (680 G) DOUGH

2⅓ cups plus 2 tablespoons (335 g) 00 flour, plus more for dusting

¾ cup plus 1 tablespoon (125 g) durum flour

20 large egg yolks

1½ teaspoons extra-virgin olive oil

¾ cup (177 ml) water

Place the 00 and durum flours in the bowl of a stand mixer fitted with the dough hook. Make a well in the flour with your hands and add the egg yolks, olive oil, and water in the center. Mix on low speed until combined. Remove the dough from the mixer and knead by hand for 8 minutes, or until smooth. Wrap the dough with plastic wrap and refrigerate for at least 2 hours before using.

Professional 5 Plus

TAGLIATELLE WITH LEMON AND BOTTARGA

I was in Sorrento, the resort town on the Gulf of Naples, having lunch at one of those ridiculously scenic, only-in-Italy restaurants high up on a cliff overlooking the sea and surrounded by lemon trees. Sorrento is famous for its fat, perfumey lemons, and this restaurant had a lemon pasta on the menu. I was a young cook at the time, and I thought the dish would be weird. But I ordered it anyway. And it was a complete wow moment. I said to myself, *When I'm the chef of my own place someday, I want to have this on the menu.*

That's this pasta, long strands of tagliatelle glossed in a sauce that consists mostly of lemon juice and water. It might seem as if something that simple can't have much impact, but it does. The black pepper, chile, and oregano lend flavor, but the sauce at its core is a lightning bolt of citrus aimed at the eggy richness of the pasta. We top it with freshly grated bottarga, cured and pressed mullet roe, which I got to know well while studying in Sicily. It adds an aromatic, oceanic top note. If you don't get down with bottarga, we also do this pasta with slivers of prosciutto.

SERVES 4

- **1 pound (454 g) 20-Yolk Pasta Dough (page 56)**
- **00 flour for dusting**
- **Pinch of red pepper flakes**
- **Grated zest of 2 lemons**
- **7 ounces (207 g) freshly squeezed lemon juice**
- **8 cracks black pepper**
- **10 leaves fresh oregano, torn**
- **½ teaspoon salt**
- **1½ cups (355 ml) water**
- **2 tablespoons unsalted butter**
- **2 tablespoons extra-virgin olive oil, plus more for serving**
- **Grated bottarga for serving**

Cut the pasta dough in 8 pieces. Working with 1 piece at a time, roll the dough through a pasta sheeter, starting with the widest setting and working your way down to the thinnest setting, lightly flouring the dough each time you roll it through. Gently fold each sheet of dough into thirds and slice it crosswise with a pasta cutter or sharp knife to make tagliatelle. Lightly flour the pasta and set aside, covered, on a baking sheet at room temperature. This will give you four 4-ounce (112 g) portions.

Combine the red pepper flakes, lemon zest and juice, black pepper, oregano, salt, and water in a large sauté pan set over low heat. Meanwhile, bring a large pot of water to a boil and salt generously. Add the pasta to the boiling water and cook for 2 minutes, stirring occasionally. Drain the pasta and transfer it to the sauté pan. Increase the heat under the sauté pan to medium-low and toss the pasta with the lemon sauce for 1 minute. Add the butter and olive oil and toss for 1 additional minute. Transfer the pasta to a platter and top with the grated bottarga and more olive oil.

GIANT RAVIOLO DI VASTO WITH SAGE BROWN BUTTER

My cousin, Mike DiCicco, is the grandson of Dominico DiCicco, one of the Club's charter members. When the Club first came into existence, all the members had emigrated from the Abruzzese town of Vasto. Mike had spent some time there in his ancestral home during a vacation in Italy. As soon as he got back to Philly, I quizzed him on all the things he ate in Vasto, looking for heirloom recipes I might be able to add to the menu at the Club. Mike told me about a giant ravioli filled with eggplant, which was crazy to hear since I had been making my own giant raviolo for years. They are stuffed with a mix of spinach and ricotta, with a whole egg yolk nestled into the filling, and dressed with sage-scented brown butter. When you cut the pasta down the center, the barely cooked yolk oozes out, bleeding into the brown butter and creating an incredibly rich, flavorful sauce. This is one of those dishes, you can see our members in the dining room nodding their head *yes* as they eat it. When you see the head nod, you know it's a winner.

The flavor payoff is huge in this dish, but because of the temperamental yolks, it requires a lot of care to get there. You need to cook each ravioli separately in two steps: first at a slow boil, then finished in a pan with the brown butter. This process happens very quickly, but we've written the recipe so that each ravioli finishes cooking at the exact same time its butter has browned.

SERVES 5

½ cup (125 g) blanched, chopped, and patted-dry spinach

1 cup (210 g) ricotta

½ cup (32 g) grated dry mozzarella

¼ cup (30 g) grated Parmigiano-Reggiano, plus more for serving

Pinch of freshly grated nutmeg

1 teaspoon salt

10 cracks black pepper

1 pound (454 g) 20-Yolk Pasta Dough (page 56)

00 flour for dusting

5 large egg yolks, divided

7½ tablespoons (106 g) unsalted butter, divided

25 fresh sage leaves, divided

Make the filling by mixing the spinach, ricotta, mozzarella, Parmigiano-Reggiano, nutmeg, salt, and pepper in a medium bowl until all the ingredients are evenly combined.

Roll the dough through a pasta sheeter, starting with the widest setting and working your way down to the second-thinnest setting. (These raviolo require a slightly sturdier dough than the Tagliatelle, page 58.) Fold the dough into thirds and lightly flour it each time you roll it through. Cut the dough with a pizza wheel into 5 pieces measuring 12 x 7 inches (30 x 18 cm). Lay out a piece of pasta horizontally. Imagine an invisible line dividing it in half like the spine of a book. Center a 3-inch (7.6 cm) ring mold on one "page" of the pasta book. Fill the ring mold with 3 tablespoons (55 g) of the filling and create a small indentation in the center with the back of a spoon. Place 1 egg yolk in the indentation. With a pastry brush dipped in water, brush all the edges of the pasta and fold the empty side over the filling side so the edges meet and create a square. Press firmly on the edges to seal all sides, being careful to keep the yolk intact. Repeat the process for the 4 remaining pieces of pasta dough, arranging the raviolo as you go on a lightly floured baking sheet. Keep the pan covered with parchment paper and a very lightly dampened dish towel. If not using the raviolo immediately, wrap the pan with plastic wrap and refrigerate up to 6 hours.

Bring a large pot of water to a boil and salt generously. Once the water hits a boil, lower the water to a very low boil and add a ravioli. Note: As the ravioli boils, it will float and some parts may become exposed. If that happens, ladle boiling water over any parts that aren't submerged, so the pasta cooks evenly.

After the ravioli has been in the water for 1 minute, place 1½ tablespoons of the butter and 5 sage leaves in a small sauté pan and cook over high heat. After 2 minutes total cooking, the ravioli will be finishing cooking and the butter will be browned and smell nutty. Remove the brown butter from the heat. Using a large slotted spoon or spider, transfer the ravioli to a baking sheet lined with a towel and dab dry. Place the ravioli on a plate and spoon the brown butter over top. Garnish with lots of grated Parmigiano-Reggiano and serve immediately. Repeat the process for each remaining ravioli.

SEMOLINA GNOCCHETTI WITH SHORT RIB RAGU

On a chilly night, there's nothing better than this dish. Short ribs cook down with red wine into soft, hearty ragu that makes the whole house smell good. It takes three hours, perfect for a lazy Sunday when the Eagles are playing. Sorry, that's World Champion Philadelphia Eagles (at least at the time of this writing). As the ragu simmers, you make the gnocchetti. Smaller in size and made with semolina, they're a different animal than the traditional gnocchi we use in our Potato Gnocchi with Gorgonzola (page 68). You make the dough in a pot on the stovetop, similarly to French pâte à choux, then form it into little balls. The gnocchetti go in a baking dish, get smothered with ragu, and bake in the oven until golden and bubbling. This recipe calls for doing the whole batch at once in a single baking dish, but you can also assemble it in individual crocks, which makes a nice presentation if you're having people over.

SERVES 6

SHORT RIB RAGU

- 3 cups (720 ml) Burgundy
- 2½ pounds (1.1 kg) boneless short rib
- 3 tablespoons kosher salt
- 30 cracks black pepper, divided
- 1 (28-ounce [794 g]) can whole peeled tomatoes
- 1 teaspoon salt
- 1 teaspoon granulated sugar (optional)
- ½ cup (120 ml) blended oil (see page 19)
- ¼ cup (60 ml) extra-virgin olive oil
- ½ yellow onion
- ½ red onion
- 1 carrot, halved
- 2 celery ribs, halved
- 1 head garlic, halved
- 3 sprigs rosemary
- ½ bunch fresh parsley
- 2 bay leaves
- ½ Arbol chile
- 1 tablespoon tomato paste
- 3 cups (720 ml) water

Bring the red wine to a boil in a saucepan over medium-high heat. While the wine is boiling for 4 minutes, season the short rib with the kosher salt and 20 cracks of black pepper. Combine the tomatoes, remaining black pepper, salt, and sugar (if needed) in a medium bowl and crush the tomatoes as much as possible with your hands. Remove the wine from the heat.

Heat the blended oil in a large Dutch oven over medium-high heat until almost smoking. Add the seasoned short ribs carefully and brown evenly on all sides until dark caramel in color. Remove the short ribs and discard the oil. Set the same Dutch oven over very low heat and add the olive oil, onions, carrot, celery, garlic, rosemary, parsley, bay leaves, and chile and allow to slowly cook for 5 to 8 minutes, until the onions are soft and translucent. Make a space in the pot and add the tomato paste. Cook, stirring, for 6 minutes, or until the paste turns from bright red to copper. Add the reduced red wine and increase the heat to medium-low. Add the seasoned tomatoes. Pour the water into the tomato bowl, swishing around to collect all the bits left behind, and add it to the pot. Return the short ribs to the pot and cover tightly with a lid. Simmer over very low heat for 3 hours, or until the short ribs are tender and shred easily with a spoon. Let cool completely in the pot.

When cooled, remove the short ribs. Shred the meat over a plate, removing and discarding any big pieces of fat. Grind the tomato sauce through a food mill into a large bowl. Transfer 1 quart (1 L) of the tomato sauce to a quart-size container and refrigerate for up to 1 week (or freeze) for a future use. Combine all the shredded short rib with the remaining tomato sauce. Divide the ragu between 2 quart-size containers. Reserve 1 quart of ragu at room temperature for the pasta. Refrigerate the other quart for up to 1 week (or freeze) for a future use.

SEMOLINA GNOCCHETTI

- 1 whole clove
- 1 garlic clove
- 2 cups (480 ml) whole milk
- ¼ teaspoon freshly grated nutmeg
- 1 sprig rosemary
- 2 teaspoons unsalted butter
- 2 tablespoons salt
- 20 cracks black pepper
- 1 bay leaf
- 1 cup (170 g) semolina flour
- ¼ cup (67 g) ricotta
- 1 large egg yolk
- ¼ cup (85 g) small diced Toma cheese
- ¼ cup (30 g) grated Parmigiano-Reggiano, plus more for serving
- ¼ cup (13 g) chopped fresh parsley leaves
- Extra-virgin olive oil for serving

Stick the clove into the garlic clove. Heat the milk, garlic, nutmeg, rosemary, butter, salt, and pepper in a medium saucepan over medium-high heat until just shy of boiling, about 6 minutes. Add the bay leaf and continue to cook for 2 minutes. Remove and discard the bay leaf, garlic, and rosemary. Bring the milk to a boil. Whisk in the semolina flour, working quickly to avoid clumps. Switch to a wooden spoon and continue to cook over medium-high heat, stirring until the semolina is dry and comes easily off the sides of the pot, about 4 minutes. Transfer the semolina to a medium bowl and cover with plastic wrap, pressing it down onto the surface of the dough. Let cool to room temperature.

Preheat the oven to 425°F (220°C). Add the ricotta, egg yolk, Toma, Parmigiano, and parsley to the cooled semolina and mix thoroughly, first with a wooden spoon, then with your hands, to create the dough. Use a 2-ounce (56 g) cookie scoop to form the gnocchetti, adding the pasta to the baking dish as you go. (You should wind up with about 32 pieces.) Ladle 1 quart (800 g) of the short rib ragu over the gnocchetti and bake until lightly browned, about 8 minutes. Remove the pan from the oven and garnish with Parmigiano and extra-virgin olive oil.

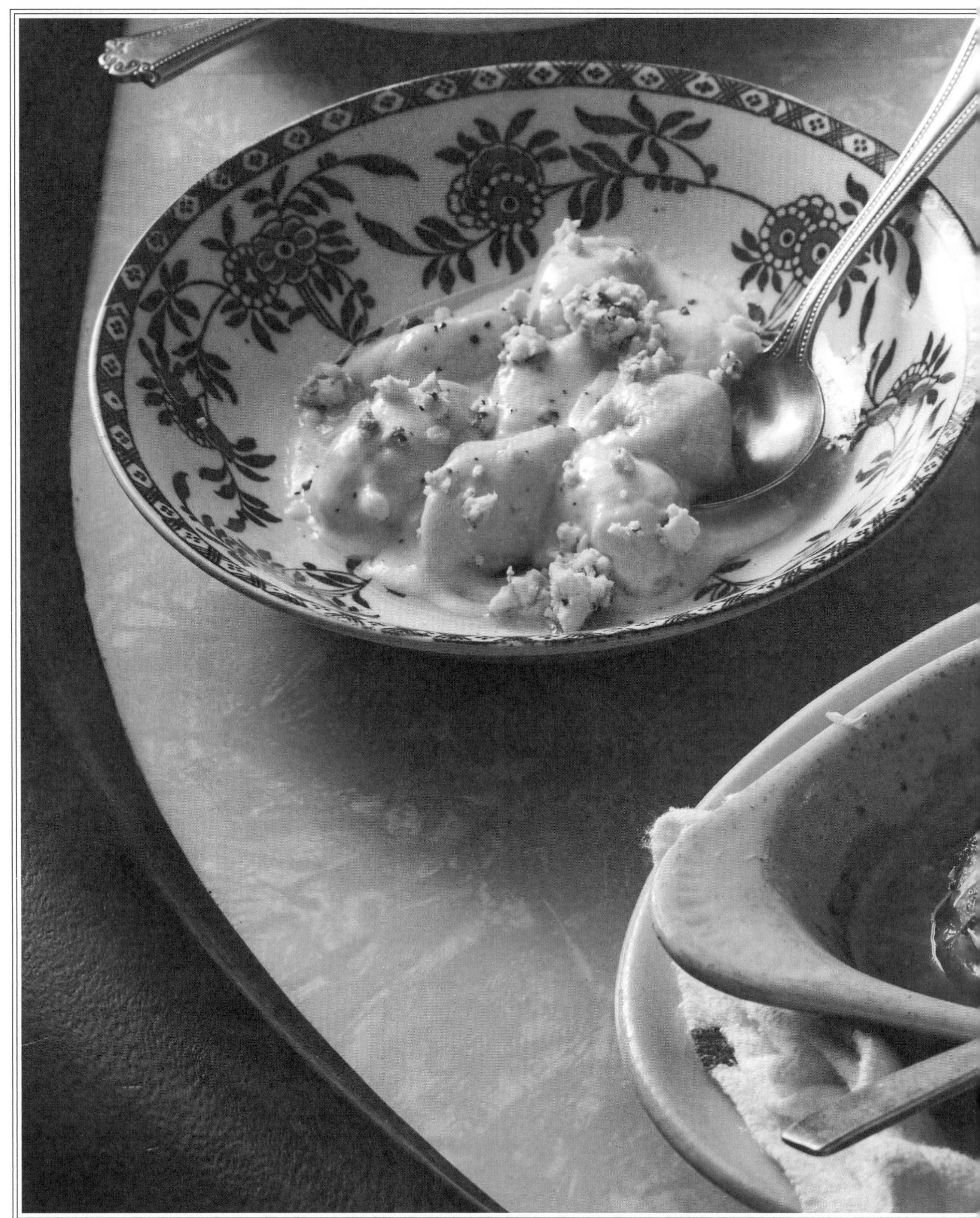

Potato Gnocchi with Gorgonzola on left, Semolina Gnocchi with Short Rib Ragu on right

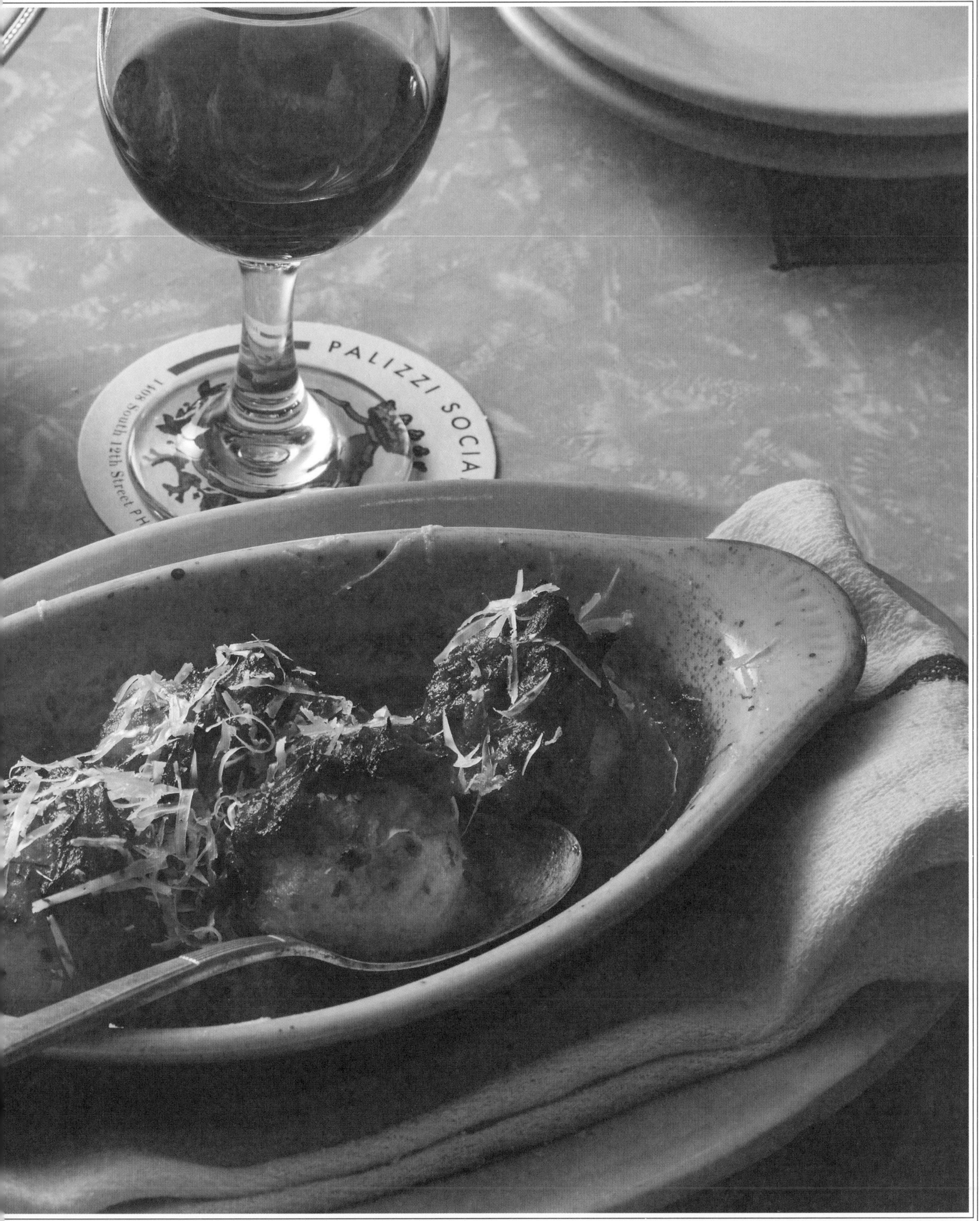
PALIZZI SOCIA
1408 South 12th Street PH

POTATO GNOCCHI WITH GORGONZOLA

This dish is for my dad, who's been rolling gnocchi on Sundays since I was a kid. The silky, tangy Gorgonzola sauce outlined here is his favorite, but these light potato dumplings are so versatile you can pair them with Marinara (page 54), sage brown butter from our Giant Raviolo (page 62), or just blistered cherry tomatoes. Instead of boiling the potatoes, which can make them waterlogged, I bake them in the oven, then run them through a food mill once they've slightly cooled. You wind up with dry, fluffy, riced potatoes that are easy to work into a dough without overkneading. This recipe makes 2 pounds of pasta, but you only need 1 pound for the finished dish. Fortunately the gnocchi freeze beautifully. To freeze, lay them flat on a baking sheet, being careful not to overlap. Let them freeze all the way through, then transfer to a resealable freezer bag. Then, they can go right from the freezer to the pot, but make sure the water is very aggressively boiling since the frozen pasta will instantly drop the temperature. It's also a good idea to use your largest pot. If you overcrowd, you'll wind up with one giant lump.

SERVES 6

POTATO GNOCCHI

MAKES 2 POUNDS (908 G) PASTA

- 6 medium-size white potatoes, about 8 ounces (240 g) each
- 3 cups (420 g) 00 flour
- 1½ teaspoons salt
- 15 cracks black pepper
- ½ teaspoon freshly grated nutmeg
- ⅓ cup (40 g) grated Parmigiano-Reggiano
- 2 large eggs
- ½ teaspoon extra-virgin olive oil

Preheat the oven to 350°F (180°C), wrap the potatoes separately with aluminum foil, and bake until fork-tender, about 1 hour. Remove from the oven, remove the foil, let cool slightly, and peel off the skins while still warm.

Using a food mill with a medium-size screen, mill the warm potatoes onto a clean work surface (you want them to be fluffy, not mashed). Dust the flour onto the potatoes. Create a well in the center. Season the walls of the well with the salt, pepper, nutmeg, and Parmigiano. Add the eggs and olive oil to the center of the well. Whisk the eggs and the oil with a fork, then slowly incorporate the surrounding potatoes into the well, continuing to whisk until a ball starts to form. Rest the dough for 5 minutes, covered with plastic wrap or a very lightly dampened towel.

Cut into 8 equal pieces. Using both hands, evenly roll out the pieces into ½-inch (1.3 cm)-diameter snakes. Cut across the snakes with a bench scraper or knife on a slight bias into roughly ¾-inch (2 cm) pieces. This will make about 75 gnocchi. Equally divide the pasta between 2 floured baking sheets. Chill 1 pan, covered, until ready to cook. Freeze the other for future use.

GORGONZOLA CREAM

MAKES 3 CUPS (710 ML) CREAM

- 1 whole clove
- 1 garlic clove
- 1½ cups (360 ml) heavy whipping cream
- 1 bay leaf
- 8 ounces (230 g) crumbled Gorgonzola
- 1 teaspoon salt
- 12 cracks black pepper

Stick the clove into the garlic clove and place in a medium pot along with the cream and bay leaf. Simmer over medium heat until reduced by half, about 10 minutes. Remove and discard the garlic and bay leaf and lower the heat to low. Whisk in the Gorgonzola in thirds and season with the salt and pepper. Set aside and keep warm.

TO SERVE

- 10 cracks black pepper
- ¼ cup (30 g) grated Parmigiano-Reggiano
- Crumbled Gorgonzola
- Extra-virgin olive oil

Bring a large pot of water to a boil and salt generously. Add the chilled gnocchi and cook until they float to the surface, 3 to 4 minutes. Drain the gnocchi and add them to the warm Gorgonzola cream along with the pepper and Parmigiano, gently stirring to coat. Transfer the gnocchi to a serving platter and garnish with crumbled Gorgonzola and olive oil.

FUSILLI WITH PISTACHIO PESTO

Pistachios and citrus fruits are two crops tightly associated with Sicily. The island produces some of the best of each in the world, and both appear in this riff on traditional pesto Genovese. Instead of pine nuts, we use pistachios and almonds at a two-to-one ratio (just to make the dish more cost-effective: pistachios are expensive!) and zests of lemon and orange, which help the sauce pop. Imported Sicilian pistachios are ideal, with Iranian ones coming in a close second, but at the Club we use high-quality California nuts, and the results are terrific. I love this recipe because it's so versatile. You can turn it into an excellent pasta salad, for example, just by switching to a short cut, such as penne or rotelle, and tossing in some extras like sun-dried tomatoes or crab meat. The pesto portion of this recipes makes about 4 cups, but you only need 2 cups per pound of pasta. The extra will keep for a week in the fridge and up to two months frozen.

SERVES 4

PISTACHIO PESTO

- 2 cups (250 g) shelled raw pistachios
- 1 cup (160 g) blanched almonds
- 1 garlic clove
- 3 sprigs (6 g) fresh oregano, picked leaves
- Grated zest of 1 lemon
- Grated zest of 1 orange
- 2 fistfuls fresh basil
- 10 cracks black pepper
- 2½ teaspoons salt
- ¼ cup (60 ml) extra-virgin olive oil
- 2¼ cups (532 ml) blended oil (see page 19)

Place the pistachios and almonds in a food processor and pulse until coarsely ground. Add the remaining ingredients and mix for 1 minute, or until smooth. Reserve 2 cups (420 g) for the dish. Refrigerate the remainder for up to 1 week or freeze for up to 2 months.

PASTA

- 1 pound (454 g) dried long fusilli
- 2 cups (420 g) Pistachio Pesto
- 1 cup (237 ml) water
- ¼ cup (30 g) grated Parmigiano-Reggiano
- 1 teaspoon salt
- 2 tablespoons extra-virgin olive oil

Bring a large pot of water to a boil and salt generously. Add the fusilli. Stirring every 2 minutes, cook the pasta for 1 minute less than the time specified on the package directions. While the pasta is cooking, heat the pesto and 1 cup (237 ml) of water in a large sauté pan over medium-low heat until warmed through. Drain the pasta and add it to the pan, tossing the pasta with the pesto for 1 minute. Remove the pan from the heat, stir in the Parmigiano, salt, and olive oil, and serve.

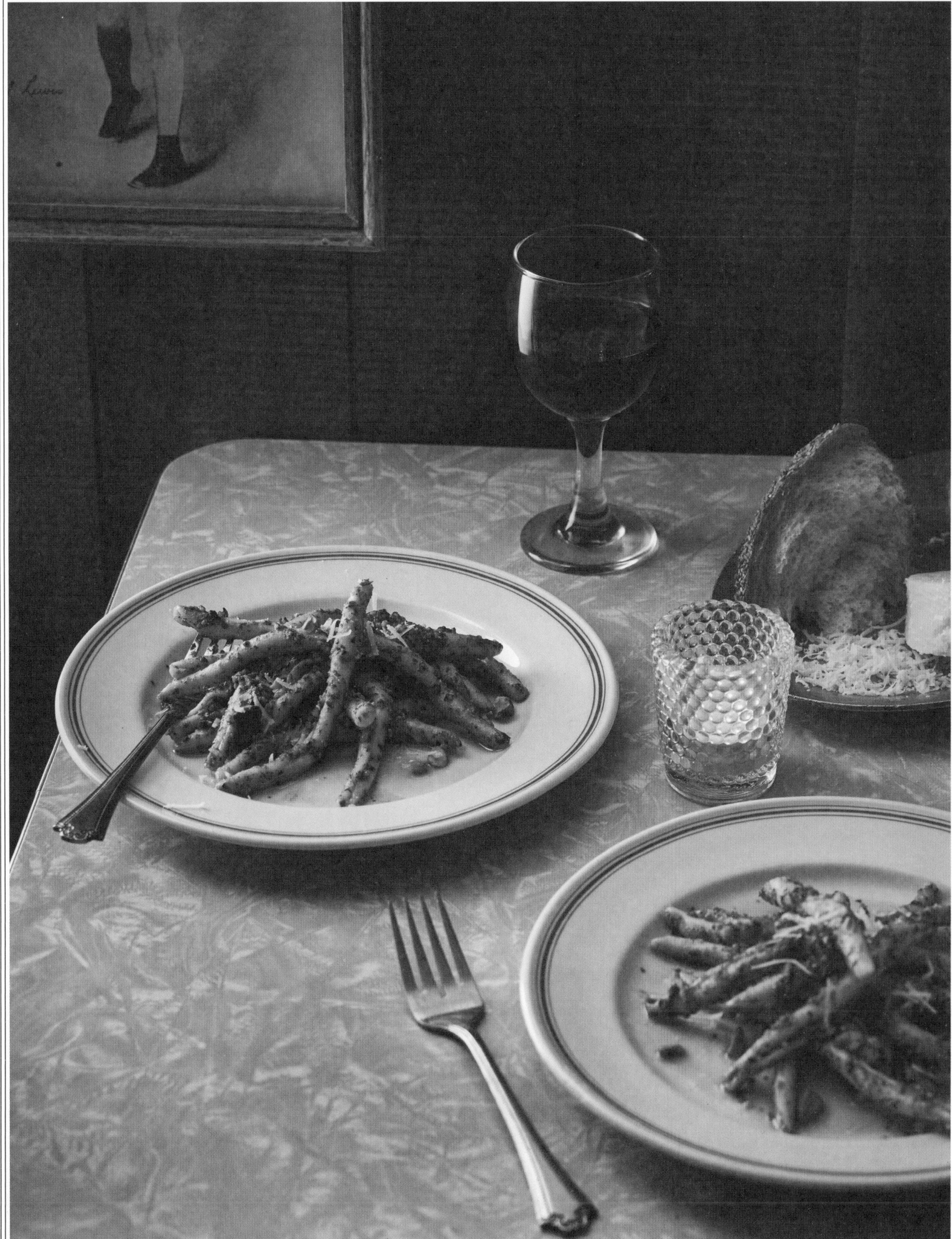

SPAGHETTI AND CRABS

The most popular dishes on the menu at the Club are the most quintessentially South Philly things: the Escarole and Beans (page 96), the Stuffed Artichokes (page 90), and definitely this pasta, paired with whole blue crustaceans slowly simmered in marinara until they meld into the sauce colloquially called crab gravy. Crab gravy is the name of the sauce, but it's also the name of the complete dish. Some families down here also refer to it as crabs and macaroni, but to keep it clear to our members who didn't grow up with it, we call it spaghetti and crabs.

Like in Maryland nearby, blue crabs are the dominant species down the shore in South Jersey, to which many South Philly families decamp to escape the brutal summers in the city. This is a dish strongly associated with that time of year, when our usual Sunday gravy hearty with meatballs, sausages, Braciole (page 133), or braising cuts of beef and pork takes a vacation in favor of this lighter seafood sauce. At the Club, we build the gravy with anchovies, brandy, and wine, additions you won't find in most households' recipes, but ones I think improve the overall flavor. Clam juice is another unusual ingredient in our crab gravy. You know when you open canned tomatoes, empty them out, and you add some water to swirl around to collect those bits left behind in the can? Instead of water, which adds no flavor, we add the clam juice, which punches up the gravy's oceanic profile for no extra work.

When buying crabs, live (and lively) is best. Frozen ones will work, too, but take longer to brown because of the moisture content. Blue crabs don't have the huge deposits of meat of their West Coast relatives, so look for larger ones to hedge your bets. Whomever you're cooking for, you want them to have something they can get into. White shirts should be left at home.

SERVES 6

(recipe continues)

CRAB GRAVY

MAKES 1 ½ QUARTS (1.4 L)

- ¼ cup (59 ml) blended oil (see page 19)
- 5 large blue crabs (500 g), cleaned
- 4 teaspoons salt, divided
- 20 cracks black pepper, divided
- ½ teaspoon dried oregano, divided
- 1 (28-ounce [794 g]) cans whole peeled tomatoes
- ¼ teaspoon granulated sugar (optional)
- 2 tablespoons extra-virgin olive oil
- ½ red onion, thinly sliced
- ½ yellow onion, thinly sliced
- 3 garlic cloves, thinly sliced
- 1 cup (60 g) fresh parsley
- 3 sprigs basil
- 1 sprig oregano
- 1 bay leaf
- 1 Arbol chile
- 1 tablespoon tomato paste
- 3 oil-packed anchovy fillets
- ½ cup (125 ml) Chablis
- ¼ cup (59 ml) brandy
- ½ cup (125 ml) clam juice
- 1 cup (240 ml) water

Heat the blended oil in a large Dutch oven set over medium-high heat. Evenly season the crabs on both sides with half each of the salt, black pepper, and oregano. Slowly sear the crabs, top shell-side down, until they turn dark red in color, about 5 minutes. Flip and continue to sear for 5 minutes. Remove the top shells and reserve. Flip the crabs again and sear the insides until dark brown, about 6 minutes. Remove the browned crabs and set aside in a shallow dish. Discard the oil and allow the pot to cool for 5 minutes.

While the pot is cooling, combine the tomatoes, sugar (if needed), and remaining salt, pepper, and oregano in a medium bowl and crush the tomatoes as much as possible with your hands. Set aside at room temperature.

Wipe out the pot, making sure to remove any burned crab parts that might be stuck to the bottom. Set the pot over low heat and add the olive oil, onion, garlic, herbs, and chile. Sweat until the onions are translucent, about 8 minutes. Make a space in the pot and add the tomato paste and anchovies. Cook for 5 minutes, or until the paste turns from bright red to copper. Return the crabs and reserved shells to the pot. Pour the Chablis into the dish that held the crabs, swishing around to collect any extra crab bits and juices, then add the wine to the pot. Reduce until almost dry, about 3 minutes. Add the brandy and simmer until the alcohol has cooked off, about 5 minutes. Add the seasoned crushed tomatoes. Pour the clam juice into the tomato bowl and swish around to collect any leftover tomato bits. Add the mixture to the pot along with the water and lower the heat to maintain a slow simmer. Cook for 2 hours, partially covered, gently stirring about every 10 minutes, then let cool completely to room temperature.

When the sauce has cooled, remove the crabs. If needed, scrape out and discard the lungs. Scrape out any roe and other innards and add them to the sauce. Cut the crabs in half and set aside at room temperature.

Set a chinois (conical strainer) over a clean pot. Working in batches, ladle the cooked sauce into the china cap, pressing as much into the clean pot as possible. Be sure to scrape everything off the outside of the chinois with a rubber spatula into the strained sauce. Discard the remaining solids. Stir the sauce well and keep over low heat.

SPAGHETTI

- 1 pound (454 g) dried spaghetti
- ¼ teaspoon finely chopped garlic
- 1 very small pinch red pepper flakes
- ¼ cup (59 ml) extra-virgin olive oil, divided, plus more for serving
- 2 tablespoons unsalted butter
- 10 fresh basil leaves, torn
- 10 ounces (283 g) fresh lump crabmeat

Bring a large pot of water to a boil and salt generously. Add the spaghetti and cook for 1 minute less than the time specified on the package directions.

Meanwhile, combine the garlic, red pepper flakes, and half of the olive oil in a large sauté pan set over medium-low heat. Sweat the ingredients for 1 minute, then add the crab gravy. Increase the heat to medium-high and simmer the sauce until reduced by half, about 5 minutes.

Strain the spaghetti, reserving the pasta water. Add the spaghetti to the gravy with the remaining olive oil and the butter, basil, and crabmeat. Lower the heat to medium and cook for 2 minutes, tossing to combine. While the pasta is finishing cooking, return half of the pasta water to the empty pot used to cook the pasta and bring to a simmer. Place the cooked crabs in the simmering water. When warm, remove the crabs from the pot, shaking off the excess water, and arrange them on top of the plated spaghetti. Drizzle with olive oil and serve.

PASTA AND CECI

Growing up, pasta and ceci was a classic dish we would have usually on Friday nights in the fall and winter, when my mom didn't want to cook a whole entire crazy meal. She'd get dough from Faragalli's and make pizza along with a pot of this cozy pasta-and-chickpea stew. She does red and white versions of the dish, which is why the tomatoes are optional in the recipe. Dried chickpeas are best if you have the time to soak them overnight—they won't get mushy—but if you want something quick and easy for a weeknight, my mom uses Cento canned chickpeas, and nobody ever complains.

SERVES 6

¾ cup (180 ml) extra-virgin olive oil, divided

½ yellow onion (70 g), minced

1 bay leaf

2 garlic cloves, 1 smashed, 1 minced, divided

1 Arbol chile

20 cracks black pepper

2 (19-ounce [539 g]) cans chickpeas with liquid

1 cup (15 g) loosely packed fresh sage

1 pound (454 g) tubetti pasta

2 tablespoons blended oil (see page 19)

3 tablespoons chopped fresh parsley leaves

Pinch of red pepper flakes

½ cup canned whole peeled tomatoes, crushed by hand (optional)

1 teaspoon salt

½ cup grated Parmigiano-Reggiano (60 g), plus more for serving

Heat ½ cup of the extra-virgin olive oil, onion, bay leaf, smashed garlic, chile, and black pepper in a large Dutch oven. Cook over low heat, stirring occasionally, until the onion is translucent, about 10 minutes. Add the chickpeas with their liquid and the sage and simmer for 5 minutes. Remove the pot from the heat and allow to cool to room temperature. Remove and discard the bay leaf, sage, chile, and garlic.

Bring a large pot of water to a boil and salt generously. Add the tubetti and cook for 1 minute less than the cook time on the package. Strain and toss the pasta with the blended oil. Set aside at room temperature.

Combine the remaining olive oil and the minced garlic, parsley, and red pepper flakes in a large Dutch oven over medium heat. Cook for 2 minutes, stirring occasionally, until the garlic is fragrant. (If using crushed tomatoes, add them now and cook until their liquid evaporates.) Add the cooled chickpeas and bring to a simmer. Add the pasta and salt and continue to simmer, stirring continually, for 1 to 2 minutes. Remove from the heat and stir in the Parmigiano-Reggiano. Garnish with more grated Parmigiano-Reggiano and serve.

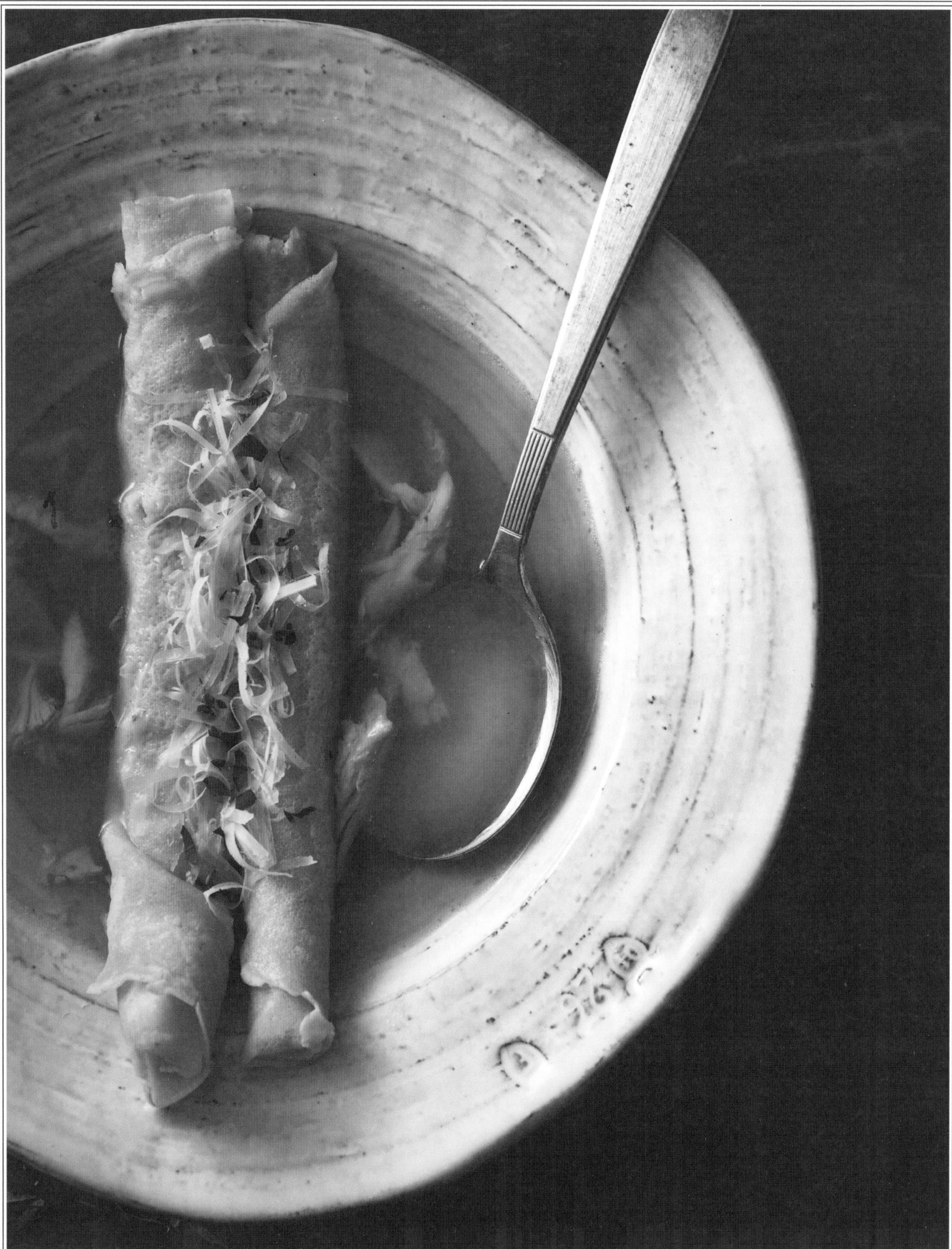

PARMIGIANO CRESPELLE EN BRODO

This is a classic soup from Abruzzo, tightly rolled Parmigiano crêpes (also sometimes called scrippelle) with chicken broth poured over the top, incredibly simple but incredibly satisfying when it's cool outside. My Uncle Ernie would always have this soup at the Club. He taught my Aunt Mary how to make it, and she turned it into a tradition in our family, the first course in every holiday meal. The delicate crespelle need to be made one at a time, but you can do them in advance and freeze them after rolling. My mom makes them in big batches and keeps them frozen in a resealable plastic bag so she and my dad can have this soup whenever they feel like it. Once you taste a bowl, you'll probably do the same.

SERVES 4

CHICKEN BRODO

- 1 whole chicken, about 2 pounds (907 g)
- 1 head garlic, halved
- 1 yellow onion, halved
- 1 carrot
- 2 sprigs rosemary
- 12 cracks black pepper
- 1 Arbol chile
- 2 bay leaves
- 1½ tablespoons salt
- 3 quarts (3 L) water

Combine the chicken, garlic, onion, carrot, rosemary, black pepper, chile, bay leaves, salt, and water in a large pot. Simmer for 2½ hours over medium heat, then let cool to room temperature. Remove the chicken, then strain the brodo and discard the solids. Return the brodo to the pot over medium heat. Shred the meat off the chicken thighs and legs, discarding the bones and skin, and return to the brodo. Refrigerate the breasts for another future use. Bring the brodo to a low simmer and keep warm.

PARMIGIANO CRESPELLE

- 1 cup (240 ml) whole milk
- 3 large eggs
- 3 tablespoons melted and cooled unsalted butter, plus 2 teaspoons not melted
- 1 cup (140 g) 00 flour, sifted
- Pinch of salt
- ½ cup (60 g) grated Parmigiano-Reggiano

Whisk the milk, eggs, and melted butter together in a medium bowl. Slowly whisk in the flour and salt. The batter should be smooth and runny. Melt ¼ teaspoon of the remaining butter in a 6-inch (15 cm) nonstick pan over low heat. Using a 1-ounce (28 ml) ladle, add the batter to the pan and increase the heat to medium-low. Tilt the pan to evenly spread the batter around. When the edges are just starting to color, about 2 minutes, gently loosen the perimeter of the crespelle with a rubber spatula and flip. Cook on the other side for 1 minute; don't let them get too dark. Transfer the crespelle to a plate and repeat the same process, greasing the pan with additional butter between each crespelle, until all the batter is gone. Equally divide the Parmigiano among the crespelle and tightly roll each one like a cigar. Set aside at room temperature.

TO SERVE

- Chopped fresh parsley leaves

Set out 4 soup bowls and put 2 rolled crespelle in each. Remove the chicken from the brodo with a slotted spoon and evenly distribute it among the bowls. Ladle ½ cup (120 ml) of warm brodo into each bowl. Garnish with the chopped parsley and serve.

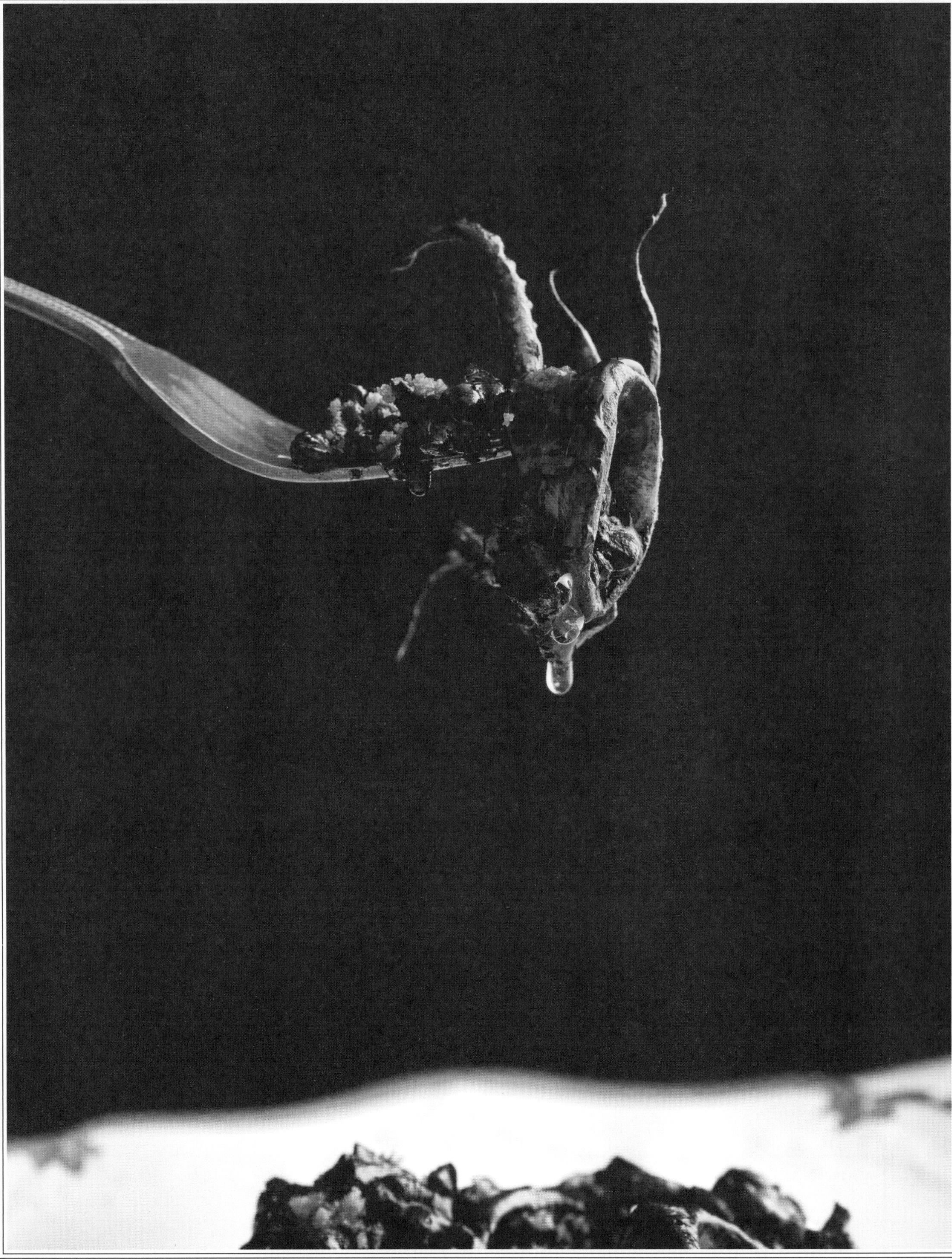

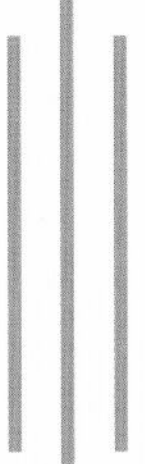

RISOTTO NERO WITH STEWED CALAMARI

When we run this calamari risotto on special at the Club, every order is spoken for within half an hour. The jet black color, from squid or sepia ink, catches the eye as it moves through the dining room. Some people assume that the ink, which you can pick up at better fish markets or online, and the calamari make this risotto fishy, but it actually has a very mild oceany flavor because we make the rice with water, not fish or seafood stock. In fact, I prefer to make most risottos with water, finishing with flavor at the end instead of putting it into the rice.

We use Northern Atlantic squid, usually from Rhode Island, for all our calamari recipes, and buy them as large as possible so the rings are meaty and thick. Always buy fresh whole squid, the dirty stuff, and either clean it yourself or have your fishmonger clean it for you. Frozen calamari is often precleaned with chemicals that can alter the texture. This recipe makes eight portions of risotto; turn any leftovers into arancini by following the rolling, breading, and frying process for our Arancini with Ragu and Peas (page 82).

SERVES 8

(recipe continues)

STEWED CALAMARI

- ½ cup (118 ml) olive oil
- 2 bay leaves
- 1 Arbol chile
- ½ lemon
- 1 head garlic, halved
- ½ yellow onion
- 1 pound (453 g) cleaned fresh calamari; tubes cut into ½-inch (1.3 cm) rings and tentacles cut in half
- 1½ tablespoons salt
- 25 cracks black pepper
- 1 teaspoon granulated sugar
- 1 cup (60 g) fresh parsley
- 1 sprig basil
- 1 sprig rosemary
- 1¼ cups (355 ml) Chablis

Combine the olive oil, bay leaves, chile, lemon, garlic, and onion in a large Dutch oven over low heat. Slowly cook to flavor the oil, about 8 minutes. Meanwhile, in a medium bowl, season the calamari with the salt, black pepper, and sugar. Move the vegetables to 1 side of the pot and increase the heat to medium-high. Wait 2 minutes, then add the calamari in a single layer as evenly as possible. Sear the calamari on 1 side for 3 minutes. While the calamari cooks, tie the parsley, basil, and rosemary into a bundle with kitchen twine. Add the herb bundle and Chablis to the pot and bring to a boil. Add enough water to just cover the calamari and lower the heat to a medium simmer. Cover and cook for 1 to 1½ hours, or until the calamari are very tender. Let cool to room temperature. Remove and discard the bay leaves, chile, lemon, garlic, onion, and herb bundle. Set aside at room temperature.

SEASONED BREADCRUMBS

- 4 cups (500 g) plain breadcrumbs
- 8 tablespoons (113 g) melted unsalted butter
- 2 garlic cloves, very finely chopped
- 20 cracks black pepper
- 1 cup (120 g) grated Parmigiano-Reggiano
- 3 tablespoons extra-virgin olive oil
- ½ cup (30 g) chopped fresh parsley leaves
- 1 teaspoon salt

Preheat the oven to 325°F (170°C). Toast the breadcrumbs on a dry baking sheet for 8 to 10 minutes, tossing halfway through, or until golden brown. Remove the pan from the oven and let the crumbs cool completely, then transfer to a medium bowl, add the remaining ingredients, and mix thoroughly. The texture will be like wet sand. Use immediately or store in freezer up to 2 weeks.

RISOTTO NERO

- 1 sprig oregano
- 1 sprig rosemary
- 1 whole clove
- 1 clove garlic
- 6 cups (1.4 L) water
- 1 shallot, finely diced
- 1 bay leaf
- ¼ cup (59 ml) extra-virgin olive oil, plus more for serving
- 1 oil-packed anchovy fillet
- Pinch of red pepper flakes
- 1½ teaspoons tomato paste
- 2 cups (380 g) uncooked arborio rice
- ½ cup (120 ml) Chablis
- ½ cup (120 ml) clam juice
- ¼ cup (60 g) cored and finely diced tomatoes
- ½ teaspoon squid or sepia ink
- 2 teaspoons salt
- 1 tablespoon unsalted butter
- 1 tablespoon chopped fresh parsley
- 4 fresh basil leaves, torn
- 2 cups (880 g) Stewed Calamari for serving
- 1 cup (104 g) Seasoned Breadcrumbs for serving

Tie the oregano and rosemary into a bundle with kitchen twine and set aside. Stick the clove into the garlic clove and set aside. Heat the water in a medium saucepan to just below boiling and keep over low heat.

Place the shallot, bay leaf, clove-studded garlic, herb bundle, and olive oil in a large Dutch oven. Set the pot over low heat and sweat until the shallots turn translucent, about 6 minutes. Add the anchovy, red pepper flakes, and tomato paste and cook until the anchovy melts and the paste turns from bright red to copper, about 5 minutes. Increase the heat to medium-high and add the rice, stirring continuously until fragrant and toasted, about 4 minutes. Stir in the wine and cook until dry. Add a third of the hot water, stirring continuously until almost completely absorbed, about 6 minutes. Repeat with another third of the hot water. Repeat for the final third of the hot water, then add the clam juice, tomatoes, and ink, and lower the heat to medium. Reduce until almost dry, at which point the rice should be tender to the bite and opaque. Stir in the salt, butter, parsley, and basil. Transfer the risotto to a serving dish and top with the calamari, then garnish with breadcrumbs and extra-virgin olive oil.

ARANCINI WITH RAGU AND PEAS

Al Mazza was my mom's dad. He and my grandmother Marianne ran Al Mazza's restaurant two doors down from the Club. He tended bar, my grandmother cooked, and my mom and her siblings lived upstairs. My mom tells stories how, at the dinner table growing up, she had to eat whatever the adults were eating: tongue, tripe; you weren't getting up from the table until you finished your plate. For my grandparents, who came to America from Calabria as small children and grew up with very little, not wasting food was so important. That mentality got passed on to my mom. Her leftover mashed potatoes become crispy potato croquettes. On chicken cutlet night, extra Cutlet Crumbs are blended with egg and become delicious fritters from almost nothing. Yesterday's risotto is today's arancini.

At the Club, we don't have risotto on the menu, so the starchy rice used to make these ragu-stuffed, pea-studded arancini is made fresh, then chilled overnight. Letting the risotto rest before rolling the arancini is essential, making this recipe a great way to use up any leftovers from the Risotto Nero (page 79). That's probably what my mom would do. The longer I cook, the more like her I become. The no-waste philosophy she learned from my grandfather is very much a part of my two restaurants. A lot of young chefs who come from fancy restaurants to work for me, if there are leftover ingredients from service, they're tempted to just throw them away. I try to break that habit. We can use that food for the staff meal, or transform it into something great, such as the seared squares of Maiale Fritti (page 161) my chef de cuisine Joe Gugliuzza makes with leftovers from our Whole Roasted Suckling Pig (page 157).

MAKES 12 ARANCINI

CUTLET CRUMBS

- 4 cups (500 g) plain breadcrumbs
- 1 tablespoon dried oregano
- 20 cracks black pepper
- 1 cup (120 g) grated Parmigiano-Reggiano
- 1 teaspoon salt

Combine all the ingredients in a medium bowl and mix thoroughly. Use immediately or store in the fridge or freezer up to 1 month.

ARANCINI

- 2 quarts (2 L) water
- 1 teaspoon saffron threads
- 4 tablespoons (57 g) unsalted butter
- ¼ cup (59 ml) extra-virgin olive oil, plus more for serving
- 1½ cups (225 g) very finely diced yellow onion
- 2 tablespoons very finely chopped garlic
- 1 bay leaf
- 2 cups (380 g) uncooked arborio rice
- ¾ cup (177 ml) Chablis
- 2 cups (240 g) grated Parmigiano-Reggiano, plus more for serving
- ½ cup (60 g) grated Caciocavallo cheese or mild provolone
- 2 tablespoons salt
- 1 gallon (4 L) vegetable oil
- 8 large eggs, divided
- 1 quart (1 L) Meat Ragu (page 55)
- 1½ pounds (680 g) grated scamorza cheese or smoked mozzarella
- 1 pound (454 g) peas, blanched and drained if fresh, or frozen
- 1 cup (140 g) 00 flour
- 4 cups (420 g) Cutlet Crumbs

Heat the water and saffron together in a pot until just under boiling. Keep hot on the stove.

Meanwhile, heat the butter and olive oil in a large Dutch oven over low heat. When the butter is melted, add the onion, garlic, and bay leaf and cook slowly until the onion is soft and translucent, about 6 minutes. Increase the heat to medium-high and add the rice, stirring continuously until fragrant and very lightly toasted. Stir in the Chablis and cook until dry. Add a third of the hot saffron water, stirring continuously until almost completely absorbed, about 6 minutes. Repeat with another third of the hot water. Repeat for the final third of the hot water, at which point the rice should be opaque and tender to the bite. You should be able to create a well in the risotto so it stands up for a few seconds and is not too loose. Turn off the heat and stir in the Parmigiano, Caciocavallo, and salt. Pour the risotto out onto a baking sheet in an even layer. Remove the bay leaf and let the rice cool to room temperature. Wrap the pan with plastic wrap and chill in the refrigerator, at least 4 hours or ideally overnight.

Preheat the oven to 425°F (220°C), and bring the vegetable oil to 350°F (180°C) in a 10-quart (9.5 L) Dutch oven. Mix together the cooled risotto and 2 of the eggs in a bowl. Mix together the ragu, scamorza, and peas in a separate bowl. On a large work surface lined with plastic wrap, divide the risotto-egg mixture into 12 equal piles. Flatten each pile down with your hand to about 1 inch (2.5 cm) thick. Add 2 tablespoons (75 g) of the ragu mixture to the center of each risotto pile. Gently pick up a risotto pile and hold it in the palm of one hand. Use your other hand to fold the sides over to completely conceal the ragu filling. Roll the arancino between your palms into a smooth round shape. Repeat for the remaining risotto piles.

Lightly beat the remaining 6 eggs in a medium bowl. Set up a breading station, with the flour, eggs, and cutlet crumbs in separate medium bowls. Using one hand for the flour and the other for the egg, gently roll an arancino in flour, then in the beaten egg, then in the crumbs. Make sure it's completely covered in crumbs and place on a large baking sheet. Repeat the breading process for the remaining arancini.

Set up 1 baking sheet lined with paper towels and another lined with parchment. Lower the arancini, 2 at a time, into the hot oil and deep-fry until golden brown, about 4 minutes per batch. As they finish, set the arancini on the paper towel–lined pan to absorb any excess oil. When all the arancini are fried, transfer them to the parchment-lined pan and bake in the center of the oven for 6 minutes, or until hot in the center (an instant-read thermometer should register 160°F [71°C]). Serve warm with drizzle of extra-virgin olive oil and grated Parmigiano.

TIMBALLO

If you've seen the 1996 movie *Big Night*, you know what a showstopper this family-style pasta bombe is. We make ours a little different from Tony Shaloub's character in the film. His timpano (the dish's other name) features layers of garganelli, ragu, meatballs, hard-boiled eggs, and mozzarella wrapped in a layer of thin pasta dough. For our version, we mix little pasta twists called Vesuvios with our ragu, plus scamorza for a smoky note and ricotta and peas for lightness; and instead of more pasta, the dome is surrounded by overlapping shingles of golden fried eggplant. It's ridiculous. We do the timballo at the Club as a first course for special events, and people go wild for it, but it also makes a great centerpiece for lunch or brunch. For a wow moment, present the timballo tableside after you've flipped the bowl into a platter or cutting board, and watch your guests' eyes pop out of their head when you slowly remove the bowl. The key to clean liftoff: butter the bowl well so the eggplant doesn't stick.

SERVES 6

- **1 eggplant, stemmed and sliced lengthwise in ¼-inch (6 mm)-thick slices**
- **2 teaspoons salt, divided**
- **12 cracks black pepper, divided**
- **4 ounces (113 g) dried "'o Vesuvio" pasta or short fusilli**
- **¼ cup (59 ml) plus 1 teaspoon extra-virgin olive oil, divided**
- **2 garlic cloves**
- **2 cups (400 g) Meat Ragu (page 55)**
- **1 cup (100 g) grated scamorza or smoked mozzarella**
- **¼ cup (80 g) ricotta**
- **¼ cup (30 g) grated Parmigiano-Reggiano**
- **½ cup (70 g) peas, frozen or (90 g) canned and drained**
- **½ teaspoon unsalted butter**
- **Marinara (page 54), warmed, for serving (optional)**

Season the sliced eggplant with half each of the salt and pepper. Drain on paper towels for 20 minutes and set aside at room temperature.

Meanwhile bring a large pot of water to a boil and salt generously. Add the pasta and cook for 3 minutes less than the time specified on the package instructions. Drain, then toss the pasta with 1 teaspoon of the olive oil. Transfer the oiled pasta to a baking sheet and allow it to cool to room temperature.

Heat 2 tablespoons of the remaining olive oil in a large skillet with 1 clove of garlic over medium-high heat. Add the eggplant and cook in 2 batches, 3 to 4 minutes per side, until the slices are golden, refreshing the olive oil and garlic between batches. Drain the eggplant on paper towels and set aside at room temperature.

Preheat the oven to 350°F (180°C). In a medium bowl, stir together the ragu, cheeses, and the remaining salt and pepper. Gently fold in the pasta and peas. Butter an ovenproof ceramic bowl measuring 6 inches (15 cm) wide and 3 inches (7.5 cm) deep. Layer in the fried eggplant, overlapping to eliminate gaps. The entire inside of the bowl, including up the sides, should be covered with a layer of eggplant. Add the ragu mixture and press in firmly. Put a small piece of parchment paper on top and tightly wrap the entire bowl with aluminum foil. Place on a baking sheet and bake for 30 to 40 minutes, or until a cake tester inserted into the center of the timballo comes out hot. Remove the timballo from the oven and let cool for 20 minutes. Remove the foil and parchment and place a round serving platter on top of the timballo. While holding the platter firmly, carefully but quickly flip the timballo over and slowly lift off the bowl. Slice into 6 portions and serve with warm marinara, if desired.

PALIZZI

VEGETABLES

GIAMBOTTA

Think of giambotta as Italian ratatouille: zucchini, eggplant, peppers, tomatoes, and potatoes all simmered together with roasted garlic and fresh herbs. During the summer, when backyard gardens are exploding with these vegetables, a big bowl of giambotta was a constant presence at family lunch spreads on Saturdays. Alongside the giambotta, there was a huge platter of lunch meats and cheeses and plenty of rolls for building sandwiches. My mom does hers with egg, which threads the melted vegetables together in a light, freeform scramble that's delicious tucked into our Sesame Semolina Bread (page 26). That's the recipe we've got here. (For a vegan version that's still full of flavor, just omit the eggs.) Giambotta can be served hot, warm, room temperature, or cool, making it a versatile side for picnics, barbecues, and beach days.

SERVES 8

½ cup (118 ml) extra-virgin olive oil

1 cup (150 g) finely diced red onion

3 garlic cloves, thinly sliced

1 bay leaf

1 Arbol chile

1 sprig rosemary

1 sprig basil

1 sprig parsley, plus chopped leaves for serving

1 green bell pepper, seeded and finely diced

1 yellow bell pepper, seeded and finely diced

1 red bell pepper, seeded and finely diced

4 teaspoons salt, divided

24 cracks black pepper

1 yellow squash, finely diced

1 zucchini, finely diced

2 tomatoes, cored and diced

1 large white potato, boiled and finely diced

10 large eggs

2 tablespoons whole milk

6 cloves Roasted Garlic (page 27)

Sesame Semolina Bread (page 26) for serving

Heat 5 tablespoons (74 ml) of the olive oil in a large Dutch oven over medium-low heat. Add the red onion, garlic, bay leaf, chile, and herbs and cook for 10 minutes, or until very soft. Add the bell peppers, 3 teaspoons of the salt, and 12 cracks of the black pepper and cook for 10 minutes, or until soft. Add the squash and zucchini and cook for 10 minutes, or until soft. Add the tomato and potato and cook for 20 minutes until soft and the tomato liquid has evaporated. Let cool to room temperature and remove the bay leaf, herbs, and chile.

Whisk the eggs and milk together in a medium bowl. Add the cooled vegetables and stir to combine. Season with the remaining salt and pepper and set aside at room temperature. Meanwhile, smash the roasted garlic cloves and heat them in the remaining 3 tablespoons of olive oil in a large Dutch oven over medium-low heat, about 2 minutes. Add the vegetable mixture to the pan, increase the heat to medium, and cook, stirring, for 4 minutes, or until the eggs are softly scrambled. Garnish with parsley leaves and serve with toasted semolina bread.

STUFFED ARTICHOKES

On holidays and special occasions, you can count on stuffed artichokes showing up as reliably as a bunch of extra cousins. My mom would use these huge artichokes, separate the leaves, stuff them with stale bread, and bake them standing up like a bouquet of greenish-gray flowers. My family would sit around with a giant artichoke in front of each person's plate, surgically picking it apart leaf by leaf, like a crab feast but with thistles. Should you find yourself at my mom's house for Easter, the way to eat these suckers is pretty specific: you pop a stuffing-lined leaf between your teeth, and scrape the edible bits off. After the meal, it's an artichoke graveyard, plates covered in stripped leaves and abandoned chokes way too woody to eat. On the original menu at the Club, we did the stuffed artichokes my mom's way, but nobody wanted to put in the work of eating them. So, we scrapped the colossal artichokes and went to smaller ones that, after a quick removal of the toughest outer leaves and a couple of hours in the oven, are edible from stem to crown. You get the same taste effect, with way less work.

SERVES 6

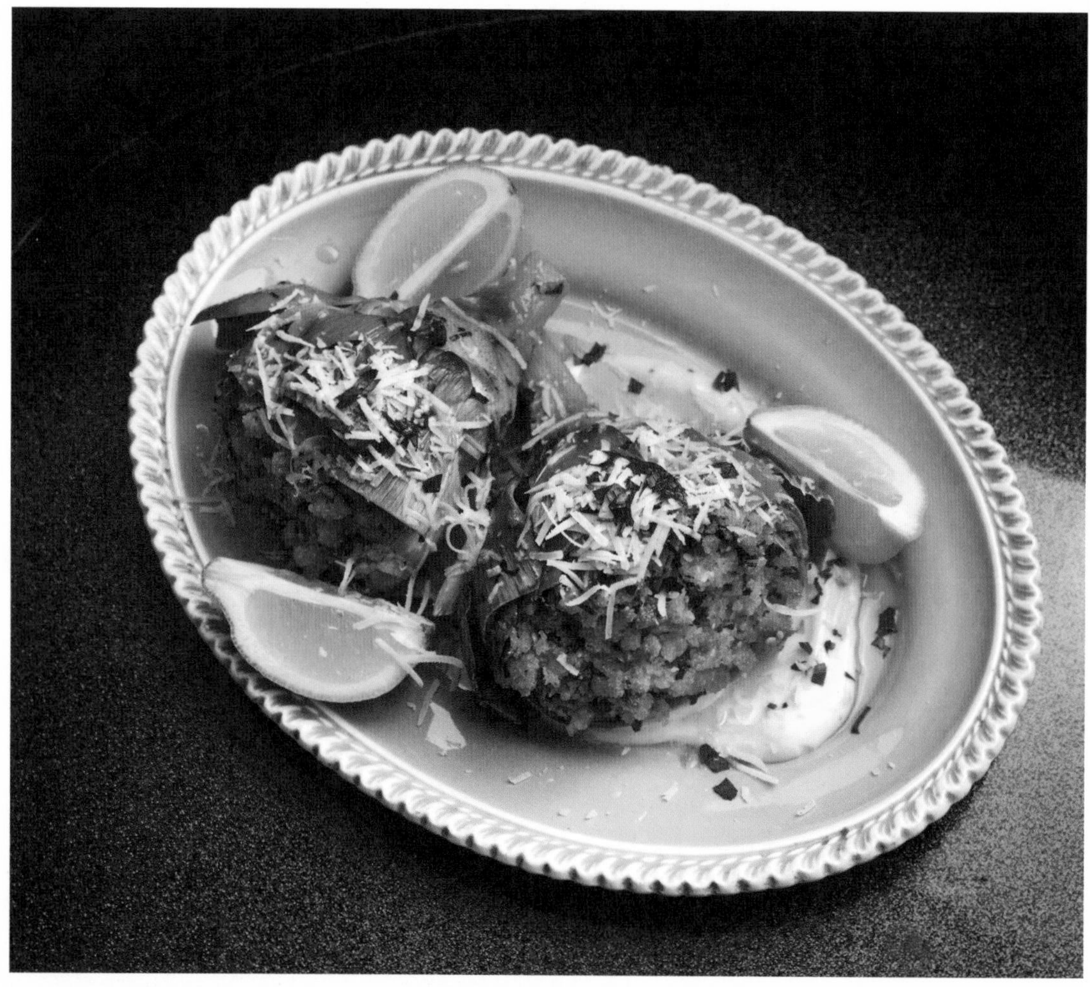

BRAISING LIQUID

- ¼ cup (59 ml) Chablis
- 2 cups (473 ml) water
- ½ yellow onion
- ½ lemon
- 2 bay leaves
- 1 dried Arbol chile
- 2 garlic cloves, smashed
- 5 whole black peppercorns
- 1 sprig rosemary
- 5 sprigs flat-leaf parsley
- 2 sprigs oregano
- 3 tablespoons salt
- 1 teaspoon granulated sugar

Combine the Chablis, water, onion, lemon, bay leaves, chile, garlic, peppercorns, herbs, salt, and sugar in a medium pot. Simmer over medium heat until the sugar and salt are dissolved, about 5 minutes. Remove from the heat and set aside.

STUFFED ARTICHOKES

- ½ loaf day-old Sesame Semolina Bread (page 26) or any rustic Italian bread, diced in very small cubes (about 2 cups [70 g])
- 8 tablespoons (113 g) unsalted butter, melted
- ½ cup plus 2 tablespoons (148 ml) extra-virgin olive oil, divided
- 3 garlic cloves, finely chopped
- ¼ cup (30 g) grated Parmigiano-Reggiano, plus more for serving
- 3 tablespoons chopped fresh flat-leaf parsley leaves
- 2 teaspoons salt
- ½ teaspoon freshly ground black pepper
- 6 cups (1.4 L) cold water
- 2 lemons, plus wedges for serving
- 6 artichokes, about 4 inches (10 cm) long
- Roasted Garlic Aioli (page 106) for serving

Combine the bread, butter, ½ cup (120 ml) of the olive oil, and the garlic, Parmigiano, parsley, salt, and pepper in a medium bowl. Mix together well with your hands to get the flavor of the garlic into the bread. The stuffing should be wet and clump together when you squeeze it.

Place the cold water in a bowl. Squeeze the juice of the 2 lemons into the water. Trim ¼ inch (6 mm) off the top and stem end of each artichoke. Working with 1 artichoke at a time, using your hands or a paring knife, remove the dark green outer leaves to expose lighter, yellow leaves. Using a peeler, remove the green exterior of the stem to reveal the lighter and less fibrous part of the stem. Using your thumbs, loosen the leaves, pushing them gently outward from the center to create room for the stuffing. Place each artichoke in the lemon water as you complete prepping it.

Preheat the oven to 350°F (180°C). Stuff each artichoke with the stuffing, using your thumbs to push it in hard between all the layers of leaves. Arrange the artichokes to stand up in a Dutch oven that's at least 4 inches (10 cm) deep. They should fit snugly. Carefully pour the prepared braising liquid into the pot, being careful not to get the tops of the artichokes wet. The liquid should be at least halfway up the artichokes. Put a lid on the pot. Place the pot in middle rack of the oven and bake for 2 to 2½ hours, or until a small knife easily penetrates the outer leaves. Remove the pot from the oven and let cool completely. Don't remove the artichokes from the braising liquid until you're ready to serve.

To serve, preheat the oven to 375°F (190°C). Arrange the artichokes on a baking sheet and drizzle the tops with the remaining 2 tablespoons of olive oil. Bake for 10 minutes, or until the stuffing begins to brown. Serve with grated Parmigiano-Reggiano, more olive oil, the aioli, and lemon wedges.

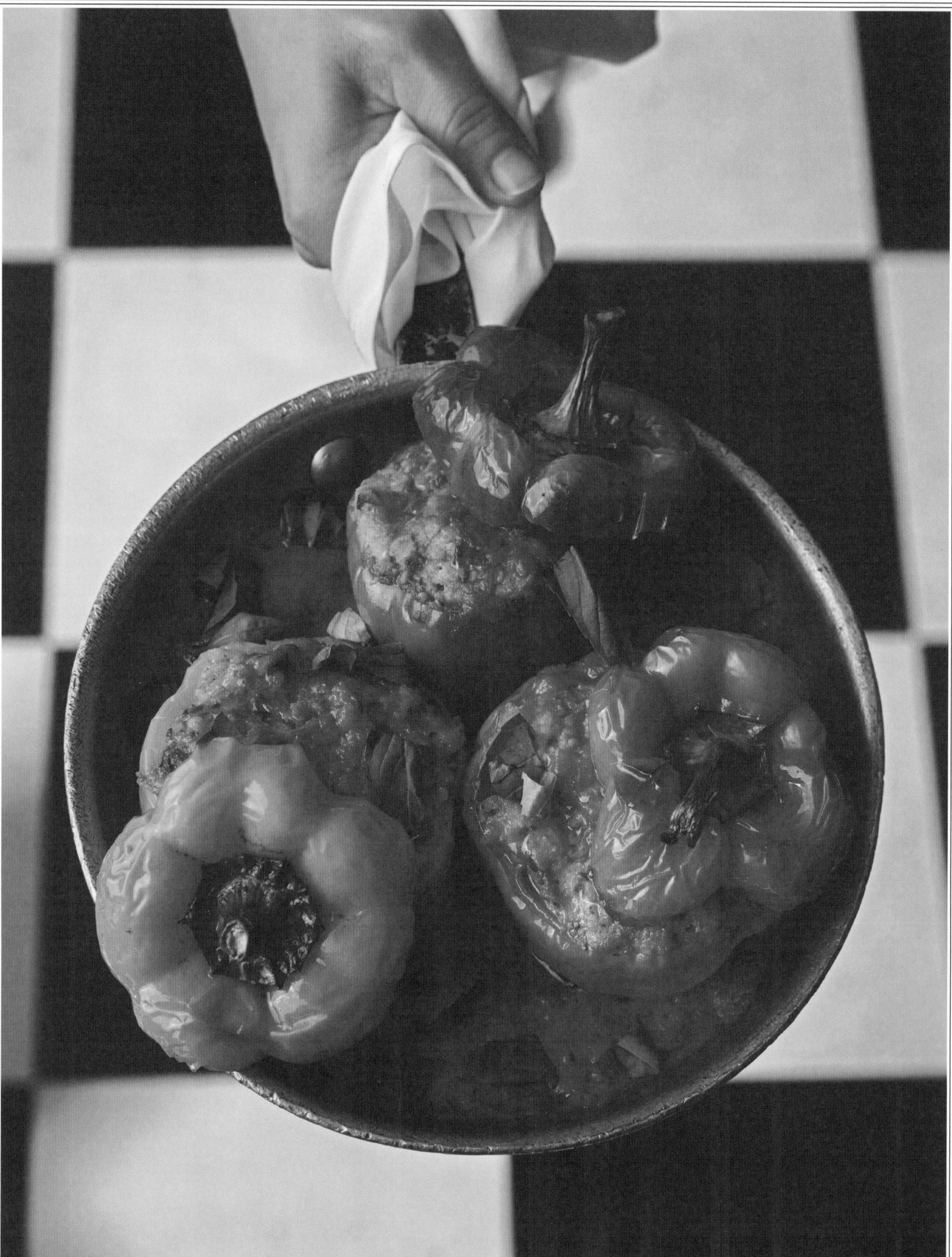

STUFFED PEPPERS

Stuffed peppers are a South Philly classic you can do a dozen different ways. At the Club, we pack red bells with tomatoey risotto beefed up with ragu and bake them in marinara until the stuffing is set and the peppers are soft and slightly slouching. They make a great side dish to Steak Pizzaiola (page 150) or Grilled Octopus (page 103), but are substantial enough to stand on their own as an entrée. Although we use bell peppers in this recipe, the same stuffing works well with banana, Cubanelle, or any other long green Italian frying peppers, which we always called "fryers." These are a little trickier to stuff (and you need to bake them lying down on their sides), but it's worth the extra effort if you like a pepper with some heat.

SERVES 6

5½ cups (1.3 L) water, divided

½ cup (118 ml) extra-virgin olive oil

1 tablespoon unsalted butter

1 bay leaf

¾ cup (80 g) finely diced yellow onion

1 garlic clove, chopped

2½ cups (475 g) uncooked arborio rice

1 cup (240 ml) Chablis

2 teaspoons salt, divided

2½ cups (500 g) Meat Ragu (page 55)

½ cup (30 g) fresh parsley leaves, chopped

1½ cups (180 g) grated Parmigiano-Reggiano, plus more for serving

1 large egg

1 cup (125 g) plain breadcrumbs

6 red bell peppers, tops and seeds removed

1 quart (946 ml) Marinara (page 54), divided

Heat 4½ cups (1.1 L) of the water until just under boiling. Keep hot on the stove.

Meanwhile, combine the olive oil, butter, bay leaf, onion, and garlic in a large Dutch oven over low heat and sweat until the onion is translucent, about 10 minutes. Increase the heat to medium and add the rice, stirring continuously until fragrant and very lightly toasted. Add the Chablis and cook until dry, about 2 minutes. Add a third of the hot water, stirring continuously until almost completely absorbed, about 8 minutes. Repeat with another third of the hot water. Repeat for the final third of the hot water, at which point the rice should be opaque and tender to the bite. Remove the rice from the heat, stir in half of the salt, and pour out onto a baking sheet lined with parchment. Remove the bay leaf and garlic and let the rice cool to room temperature.

Preheat the oven to 350°F (180°C). When the rice is cool, transfer it to a bowl and add the ragu, parsley, Parmigiano, egg, breadcrumbs, and remaining salt. Mix to combine all the ingredients. Arrange the peppers upright in a baking dish. Evenly divide the stuffing among the peppers and spoon a third of the marinara over the top. Pour the remaining marinara and the remaining 1 cup (240 ml) of water into the bottom of the baking dish. Cover the peppers with parchment and wrap the dish tightly with aluminum foil. Bake for 1 hour 15 minutes, uncovering for the last 15 minutes. The peppers should be soft and hot in the center, and a knife should easily pierce the sides. Serve with the marinara from the pan and grated Parmigiano on top.

STRING BEANS AND POTATOES

So much of southern Italian food is peasant food, and few dishes are as emblematic of that as string beans and potatoes. The namesake ingredients are abundant, cheap, and unsexy, but being able to take these humble things and turn them into something outrageously delicious and satisfying is the ingenuity of peasant cooking. You've gotta make the best of what you've got, and here that means a little cured pork (pepperoni in this case) and tomato sauce. The beans and potatoes soften and break as they simmer in the marinara, the starches thickening and transforming the sauce from a pasta condiment to a hearty vegetable stew. It's wonderful as a side dish to Veal Cutlets (page 141) and Roasted Chicken (page 145) or on its own as a light dinner. Omit the pepperoni for a vegetarian version, the pepperoni and the Parm for vegan.

SERVES 6

½ cup (118 ml) extra-virgin olive oil
6 garlic cloves, thinly sliced
2 ounces (57 g) stick pepperoni
1 sprig rosemary
1 sprig parsley
1 bay leaf
1 Arbol chile
1 teaspoon tomato paste
2 pounds (908 g) white potatoes, cut into large chunks
1 pound (454 g) fresh green beans (we have always called them string beans)
1¾ cups (414 ml) Marinara (page 54)
1½ teaspoons salt
8 cracks black pepper
1½ cups (355 ml) water
Grated Parmigiano-Reggiano for serving
Sesame Semolina Bread (page 26) for serving

Heat the olive oil in a large Dutch oven over medium-low heat. Add the garlic, pepperoni, herbs, and chile and sweat for 4 to 6 minutes. Add the tomato paste and cook for about 4 minutes, until it turns from bright red to copper. Add the potatoes and beans, lower the heat to low, and cook for 8 minutes. Add the marinara, salt, pepper, and water and increase the heat to medium-low. Cover the pot and simmer for 45 to 60 minutes, or until the potatoes are very soft and the beans are tender. Remove the herbs and discard. Garnish with grated Parmigiano and serve with sliced semolina bread.

ESCAROLE AND BEANS

Escarole is a bitter leafy green that takes well to long simmers in brothy soups and stews like this cold-weather staple. It's a classic: just escarole, cannellini beans, water, and some aromatics. You can add bacon or pancetta to the recipe, but I prefer it vegetarian, just the beans and the greens that you can scoop up with a spoon or dunk with a hunk of Sesame Semolina Bread (page 26). Leave out the grated cheese, and it's vegan. To achieve the best results, you want to cook the beans and the escarole separately, which ensures the former doesn't overcook and the latter can develop its own flavor, then marry them together in a fresh pan.

SERVES 6

CANNELLINI BEANS

- **$2\frac{1}{2}$ cups (500 g) dried cannellini beans, soaked overnight**
- **$1\frac{1}{2}$ quarts (1.4 L) water**
- **$\frac{1}{2}$ yellow onion**
- **2 garlic cloves**
- **1 carrot**
- **1 celery rib**
- **1 bay leaf**
- **4 sprigs sage**
- **2 sprigs rosemary**
- **4 sprigs parsley**
- **1 sprig oregano**
- **1 tablespoon salt**
- **30 cracks black pepper**
- **1 Arbol chile**

Drain the beans from the soaking water and place them in a large pot with the remaining ingredients, including the fresh water. Cover the pot and simmer the beans over medium-low heat, stirring occasionally, until tender, about 2 hours. Remove the onion, garlic, carrot, celery, bay leaf, herbs, and chile. Set the beans aside at room temperature.

ESCAROLE

- **2 heads escarole, cut into 1-inch (2.5 cm) pieces**
- **2 garlic cloves, thinly sliced**
- **1 Arbol chile**
- **1 bay leaf**
- **$\frac{1}{4}$ cup (59 ml) extra-virgin olive oil**
- **2 teaspoons salt**
- **15 cracks black pepper**
- **1 quart (1 L) water**

Wash the escarole well in cold water. If it's very dirty, fill a large container with the water and wash several times, lifting out the escarole and changing the water each time until absolutely no sand or dirt is left. Drain the escarole in a colander. Combine the sliced garlic, chile, bay leaf, and olive oil in a large Dutch oven. Cook over low heat until the garlic is translucent, about 2 minutes. Add the washed greens, salt, black pepper, and water. Cover the pot and increase the heat to medium. Cook for 45 minutes to 1 hour, or until the greens are very tender, keeping an eye on the level of water as the greens cook. By the end of the cooking time, there should still be enough liquid in the pot to just cover the greens. Remove the chile and bay leaf.

TO SERVE

- **$\frac{1}{4}$ cup (59 ml) extra-virgin olive oil**
- **1 teaspoon chopped garlic**
- **$\frac{1}{4}$ teaspoon red pepper flakes**
- **2 tablespoons chopped fresh parsley leaves**
- **Grated Parmigiano-Reggiano**
- **Sesame Semolina Bread (page 26), grilled**

Combine the olive oil, garlic, red pepper flakes, and parsley in a large Dutch oven over medium heat. When the garlic begins to sizzle, add the beans and escarole along with 1 cup each of their cooking liquid and bring to a simmer. Cook until creamy and soupy, about 5 minutes. Garnish with grated Parmigiano and serve with grilled bread.

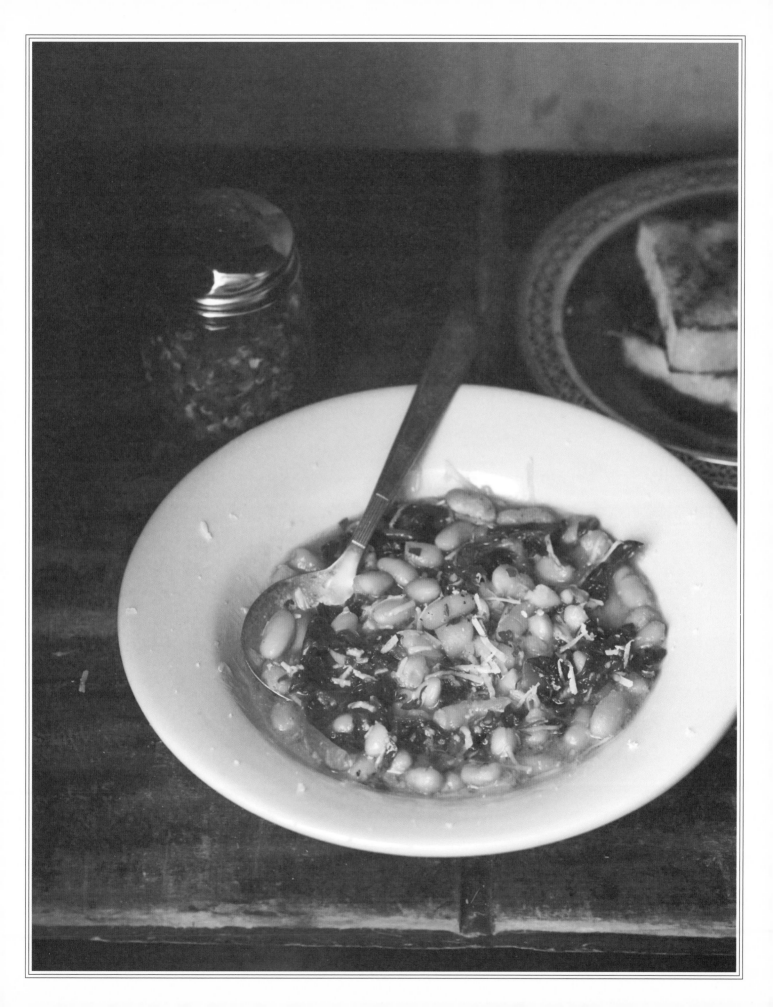

SPINACH SFORMATO

During those twelve years I bussed and waited tables at Mr. Martino's on Passyunk Avenue, Ellen Yin, a hospitality legend in Philly (she owns Fork and High Street on Market), was a regular. Over the years, we became friends, and when I told her I was planning to go to Sicily to study, Ellen connected me with Anna Tasca Lanza, who had hosted a recent dinner at Fork. I spent two months at Anna's farm in central Sicily, and this sformato was one of my favorite things I learned to make there. Imagine creamed spinach, but set into a soft, silky custard. We flavor the sformato with nutmeg and black pepper, two spices that pair beautifully with spinach, and bake it in a water bath like flan. The warm Gorgonzola cream sauce from our Potato Gnocchi (page 68) goes over the top.

SERVES 6

- 1 pound (454 g) fresh spinach
- 2 large eggs
- ¼ teaspoon salt
- ¼ teaspoon freshly grated nutmeg
- 2 tablespoons 00 flour
- ½ cup (125 ml) heavy whipping cream
- 8 cracks black pepper
- 1 tablespoon unsalted butter, melted
- Gorgonzola Cream (page 69) for serving

Bring a large pot of water to a boil and salt generously. Add the spinach and cook for 4 minutes. Remove the spinach and immediately shock in ice water. Strain out the water, squeeze the spinach dry with your hands, and then lay it out on paper towels to absorb any excess water. You should be left with about 10 ounces (283 g) of spinach after blanching. Transfer the spinach to a food processor and purée into a smooth paste. Add the eggs, salt, and nutmeg and pulse for 20 seconds. Set aside.

Place the flour in a bowl and slowly whisk in the cream. Add the pepper and the spinach mixture to the bowl, mixing well until it takes on the consistency of cake batter. Grease six 4-ounce (120 ml) aluminum molds or ramekins with the melted butter and divide the spinach batter equally among them. The batter should fill about three quarters of each mold. Set the molds in a baking pan and fill the pan with hot water until the water reaches halfway up the sides of the molds. Cover the pan with foil and set over medium heat on the stove. Steam for 8 to 10 minutes, or until the sformati are firm and have risen. Carefully remove the sformati from the pan and flip, upside-down, onto a plate. Serve immediately topped with Gorgonzola cream.

GARLIC-CHILE BROCCOLI RABE

When I was in grade school at Annunciation, my neighborhood Catholic school down the street from the Club (now loft apartments with a green roof), they would let us go home for lunch. I would walk the half-block to Al Mazza's, my grandparents' restaurant, and my grandmom would make me broccoli rabe on crusty bread. Five days a week, that was my lunch, and I couldn't have been happier. Even today, broccoli rabe is one of my electric-chair dinner foods. That, some Sesame Semolina Bread (page 26), and our Marinated Black Olives (page 34), and I'd die happy. When making broccoli rabe, a lot of people boil, then sauté, but I don't like how the boiling process strips away so much of the vitamins and minerals. This approach preserves all that good stuff by slowly cooking the rabe all the way through in a pot of garlicky oil with a little water. While it simmers, the juices of the rabe mingle with the oil and water and create their own self-contained sauce with no extra work, and the rabe comes out soft but not mushy. We serve this alongside our Sweet Fennel Sausage (page 138) and Whole Roasted Suckling Pig (page 157), but you should also try my grandmom's move, tangled up over a slab of bread.

SERVES 4

¼ cup (59 ml) extra-virgin olive oil
1 garlic clove, smashed
1 Arbol chile
1 bay leaf
1 bunch broccoli rabe, about 1 pound (454 g)
½ teaspoon salt
10 cracks black pepper
1 cup (235 ml) water

Combine the olive oil, garlic, chile, and bay leaf in a large Dutch oven. Cook over medium-low heat until the garlic just begins to color, about 5 minutes. Add the broccoli rabe, salt, black pepper, and water, cover, and lower the heat to low. Cook until the rabe is tender, about 20 minutes.

MEMBERS
MEMBER
VETERAN BOXERS ASSOC.
RING #1
PHILA., PENNA. TONY MORGANO PRES.

SEAFOOD

GRILLED SWORDFISH SPIEDINI

GRILLED OCTOPUS WITH SALSA VERDE AND MARINATED OLIVES

FRITTO MISTO

WHIPPED BACCALA

BACCALA SALAD

CALAMARI AND PEAS

SHRIMP AND BEANS

SCALLOP AND MUSHROOM CAPESANTE

CIOPPINO WITH SAFFRON COUSCOUS

HERB BUTTER–ROASTED ORATA

GRILLED SWORDFISH SPIEDINI

We use the Club Rub, a trio of parsley, garlic, and red pepper flakes, on many of our meat and seafood dishes, starting with these swordfish skewers. The rub goes on dry and we only add oil to it after the aromatics and meat have had some time to hang out together. If you add the oil immediately, it forms a barrier that prevents the seasonings from penetrating. You'll see this marinating method repeated throughout the rest of the book, and it's how we pack so much flavor into fairly neutral-tasting swordfish. These spiedini come off the grill juicy and slightly smoky, and when you slide the first cube off the skewer and into your mouth, it's a rush of citrus and garlic and herbs. This recipe scales up easily for a cookout, and you can assemble all the spiedini in advance for grilling later. Budget a few per person if you're using them as a picky (what we call a snack, in South Philly parlance), or pair them with the Grilled Octopus (page 103), Grilled Lamb Chops (page 146), and Sweet Fennel Sausage (page 138) for a family-style mixed grill.

SERVES 4

CLUB RUB

- 2 cups (30 g) loosely packed fresh parsley leaves
- 2 garlic cloves
- ¼ teaspoon red pepper flakes

Finely chop all the ingredients, mix, and store in an airtight container.

SWORDFISH

- 2 pounds (1 kg) swordfish loin, belly attached
- ½ cup (25 g) Club Rub
- ½ lemon, thinly sliced into half-moons, plus wedges for serving
- 10 bay leaves
- 2 tablespoons blended oil (see page 19)
- 1 tablespoon salt
- 20 cracks black pepper
- 1 teaspoon unsalted butter, at room temperature
- 1 cup (200 g) Salsa Verde (page 35) for serving
- ½ cup (110 g) Marinated Black Olives (page 34) for serving
- ½ cup (110 g) Marinated Green Olives (page 34) for serving
- ½ cup (110 g) Marinated Lupini Beans (page 34) for serving

Have ready 10-inch (25.5 cm) metal skewers. (Note that if using bamboo skewers, they should be soaked in hot water for at least 3 hours and preferably overnight to prevent burning on the grill.)

Get a grill very hot. Cut the swordfish into 1-inch (2.5 cm) cubes and toss in a bowl with the rub, lemon slices, and bay leaves. Allow the fish to sit at room temperature for 15 minutes. Add the oil, salt, and pepper and toss to coat. Divide the marinated swordfish between the skewers. Grill the skewers over direct heat for 2 minutes per side, then move to a cooler part of the grill. Distribute the butter in small pieces on top of the skewers, cover the grill, and cook for 4 additional minutes. Serve on a platter with the salsa verde, lemon wedges, marinated olives, and lupini beans.

GRILLED OCTOPUS WITH SALSA VERDE AND MARINATED OLIVES

My dad had a theory about cooking octopus with a wine cork. The myth probably started, he says, because a bunch of guys were drinking wine while a pot of octopus was cooking on the stove. As they finished each bottle, they tossed the cork in the pot, and by the time the octopus was done, they were so drunk they thought it was tender. In reality, the cork probably does nothing to help tenderize the octopus in this recipe, but I add it anyway for tradition's sake. What actually has way more impact on texture is where the octopus comes from. Spain, in my opinion, produces the best. It's tenderized before packaging and has a beautiful clean and oceanic flavor. Portuguese and Italian work well, too, and fresh or frozen is acceptable for this recipe.

SERVES 4

1½ lemons, plus wedges for serving
1 (5-pound [2 kg]) Spanish octopus
1 head garlic, halved lengthwise
1 yellow onion, halved
1 celery rib
2 tablespoons black peppercorns
12 bay leaves, divided
1 cup (40 g) fresh basil
4 sprigs rosemary
4 sprigs oregano
1 cup (60 g) fresh parsley
1¾ cups (245 g) kosher salt
2 tablespoons granulated sugar
1 wine cork
2 Arbol chiles
4 cups (946 ml) Chablis
1½ gallons (5 L) water
1 cup (50 g) Club Rub (page 102)
¼ cup (59 ml) blended oil (see page 19)
Salsa Verde (page 35) for serving
Marinated Black Olives (page 34) for serving
Marinated Green Olives (page 34) for serving

Thinly slice the half lemon into half-moons and set aside. Cut the whole lemon in half. Bring the octopus, garlic, onion, 2 lemon halves, celery, peppercorns, 4 of the bay leaves, and the basil, rosemary, oregano, parsley, kosher salt, sugar, wine cork, chiles, wine, and water to a simmer in a stockpot. Cook, covered, over medium heat for 45 minutes to 1 hour, or until you can easily poke a small knife through the thickest part of the tentacles. Let the octopus cool to room temperature in the liquid, then transfer it to a baking sheet. When it's cool enough to handle, remove the head and separate each tentacle with a knife. Using your fingers, scrape off the loose skin, working your way from the thickest part of the tentacle to the tip. Be sure to keep their suckers on.

Get a grill very hot. While the grill is heating, toss the cleaned octopus in a medium bowl with the thinly sliced lemon, rub, and remaining 8 bay leaves. Allow the octopus to sit at room temperature for 15 minutes, then add the blended oil and mix well to coat. Grill the octopus until evenly charred, about 3 minutes per side. Drizzle with salsa verde and serve with marinated olives and lemon wedges.

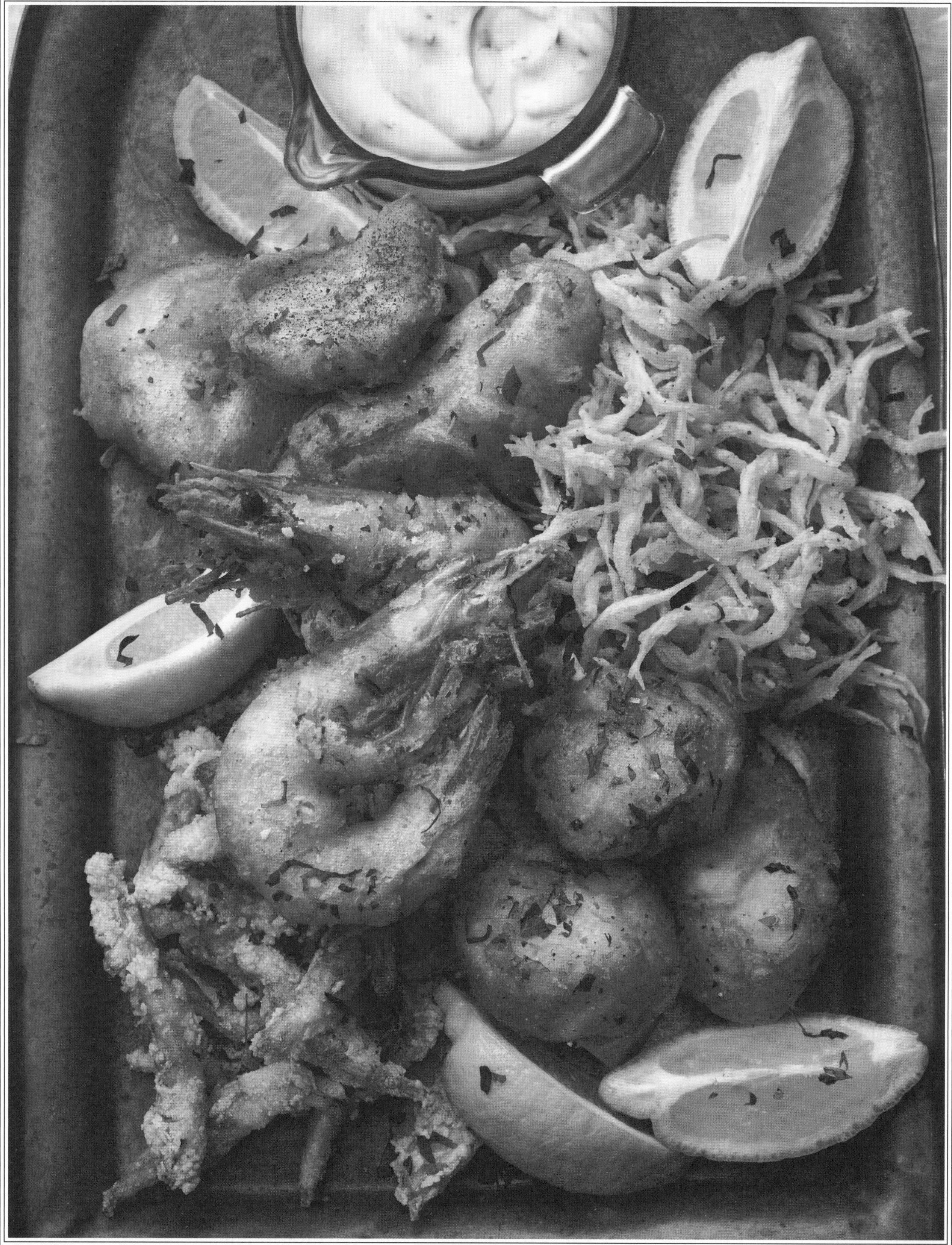

FRITTO MISTO

A few dishes have been served at the Club for decades. Fritto misto is one of them. When the guys would come in, my uncle would fry up whatever fish he had in the fridge: smelts, calamari, shrimp, and almost always baccala (salt cod). It can be an acquired taste, but it's essential in South Philly—especially on Christmas Eve, when Italian American families prepare the Seven Fishes, a seafood feast that leaves everyone stuffed and their clothes smelling like fryer oil. (You should see the lines at Ippolito's, the fish market in our neighborhood, in the days leading up to the holiday; it's insane.) Whether part of a huge holiday dinner or on its own with a couple of cold beers, this fritto misto gives you everything you want in an opening snack: salt, heat, crunch, plus a little balancing creaminess from the aioli. Along with the baccala, it features silverfish, juvenile white fish that are about the length of eyelashes. They fry up into this delicious crispy nest, but if you can't find them, shrimp, scallops, filleted sardines, and smelts work well, too. Note that the baccala will need to be soaked for two days prior to your cooking the fritto misto.

SERVES 4

(recipe continues)

ROASTED GARLIC AIOLI

- 1 head Roasted Garlic (page 27)
- 1 garlic clove
- 2 large egg yolks
- 1 tablespoon freshly squeezed lemon juice
- 1 teaspoon water
- 2 cups (480 ml) blended oil (see page 19)
- ¼ teaspoon salt
- 10 cracks black pepper
- 1 tablespoon chopped fresh parsley leaves

Combine the roasted garlic, garlic clove, egg yolks, lemon juice, and water in a food processor and turn it on. While the processor is running, slowly drizzle in the oil to emulsify. Turn off the processor, add the salt, pepper, and parsley, and pulse for 5 seconds to combine. Refrigerate until ready to use.

FISH FLOUR

- 2 cups (280 g) 00 flour
- ¾ cup (128 g) semolina flour
- Pinch of ground Arbol chile

Whisk together all the ingredients in a bowl until smooth. This mixture will be used for frying the silverfish and smelts. Store in a clean, airtight container until ready to use.

FISH BATTER

- ½ cup (70 g) 00 flour
- 3 tablespoons cornstarch
- 1½ teaspoons baking powder
- ¾ teaspoon kosher salt
- 6 ounces (178 ml) beer, such as Peroni

When ready to fry the baccala, scallops, and shrimp, whisk together all the batter ingredients in a bowl until smooth.

FRITTO MISTO

- 12 ounces (350 g) baccala, cut in 6 roughly equal pieces and soaked in cold water in the fridge for 2 days with the water changed daily
- 4 scallops, about 1 ounce (28 g) each
- 8 small shrimp, peeled and deveined
- ½ cup (25 g) Club Rub (page 102)
- 1 gallon (4 L) vegetable oil
- 1 cup (237 ml) white wine vinegar
- ¼ teaspoon ground Arbol chile
- 1 garlic clove, smashed
- 1 teaspoon salt, divided
- 3 ounces (85 g) silverfish
- 10 smelts
- 16 cracks black pepper, divided
- Chopped parsley leaves for serving
- Lemon wedges for serving

Toss the soaked baccala, scallops, and shrimp with the rub in a medium bowl. While the seafood is marinating, bring the vegetable oil to 350°F (180°C) in a large Dutch oven set over medium heat, and line a baking sheet with paper towels. Combine the vinegar, chile, garlic, and ¼ teaspoon of the salt in a small bowl. Once the baccala, scallops, and shrimp have been marinating for 20 minutes, add the silverfish and smelts to the vinegar mixture.

Add the baccala, scallops, and shrimp to the fish batter and mix well to evenly coat. Working with 1 piece at a time, gently remove the seafood from the batter, allowing some excess to drip off, and slowly lower into the hot oil, being careful not to allow to sink and stick to the bottom of the pot. Fry until golden brown, 3 to 4 minutes, and transfer to the paper towel–lined pan. Immediately season the seafood with half of the black pepper.

Place 1½ cups (250 g) of the fish flour in a bowl (store the leftover mixture in its container for a later use). Bring the oil back up to 350°F (180°C), if necessary. Strain out the silverfish and smelts from the vinegar. Add them to the fish flour and toss well to coat, making sure nothing is stuck together. Remove the smelts from the flour, shake off any excess, and gently lower into the oil. Fry for 2 minutes, then remove the silverfish from the flour, shake off any excess, and gently lower into the oil. Fry for 2 minutes, until all the seafood is golden brown. Transfer to the paper towel–lined pan and immediately season with the remaining salt and black pepper. Transfer the fritto misto to a platter and garnish with chopped parsley. Serve with the aioli and lemon wedges.

WHIPPED BACCALA

Baccala is huge in our culture. At Italian stores and fish markets, such as Ippolito's, which has been selling seafood in South Philly since 1929, petrified white planks of it dangle from the ceilings like wind chimes. If you're hesitant to cook baccala, know that it's really no big deal. All you have to do is rehydrate it, soaking and simmering for two days and two hours, respectively, and it comes back to life looking like a fresh piece of fish. Whipped baccala is similar to the French *brandade*, basically salt cod and potatoes cooked together with milk, cream, and aromatics, then buzzed in the food processor into a smooth, luscious spread.

SERVES 8

- 1 side dried baccala, about 37 ounces (1.1 kg)
- 4 sprigs thyme
- 4 sprigs rosemary
- 4 sprigs sage
- 2½ pounds (1.1 kg) white potatoes, diced
- 1 head garlic, halved
- 2 bay leaves
- 1 Arbol chile
- 1 small yellow onion, halved
- 5 cups (1.2 L) whole milk
- 2 cups (473 ml) heavy whipping cream
- 1 tablespoon salt
- Smoked paprika for serving
- Extra-virgin olive oil for serving
- Sesame Semolina Bread (page 26) for serving

Soak the baccala in cold water in the fridge for 2 days, changing the water daily. Weigh out 2 pounds (907 g) of the cod and cut into 2-inch (5 cm)-square pieces. Wrap and place the remaining rehydrated cod in the freezer for future use.

Tie the thyme, rosemary, and sage into a bundle with kitchen twine and place in a large Dutch oven along with the cod, potatoes, garlic, bay leaves, chile, onion, milk, cream, and salt. Cover and simmer very slowly over low heat for 2 hours, stirring occasionally to prevent sticking, until the potatoes begin to fall apart and the cod begins to flake. Remove the pot from the heat and let the mixture cool to room temperature. Squeeze the garlic cloves out of their papery skins into the cooked fish. Remove and discard the herbs, onion, bay leaves, and chile. Drain off the liquid through a strainer and reserve. Working in 3 batches, transfer the cod and potatoes to a food processor and slowly pulse to combine, being careful not to purée, which can make the whipped baccala gluey. Transfer the mixture to a large bowl and gently fold in 2 cups (473 ml) of the cooking liquid with a wooden spoon. Garnish with smoked paprika, olive oil, and grilled bread.

BACCALA SALAD

If the Whipped Baccala (page 108) is cold-weather comfort, this salt cod dish is pure summer: citrusy, refreshing, and light. You start with soaked baccala, simmer it until it flakes apart, then toss it with crunchy celery, briny black olives and capers, parsley, garlic, and lots of lemon and olive oil. Enjoy this salad as is, bulk it up with the saffron couscous from our Cioppino (page 122), or spoon it over toasted slices of Sesame Semolina Bread (page 26) for crostini.

SERVES 4

1 pound (454 g) dried baccala
4 sprigs parsley, plus 3 tablespoons chopped fresh leaves
4 sprigs basil
4 sprigs oregano
1 small yellow onion, halved
2 cups (473 ml) Chablis
1½ teaspoons granulated sugar
1 tablespoon salt
20 whole black peppercorns
1 Arbol chile
1 bay leaf
½ lemon, plus 2 tablespoons freshly squeezed lemon juice
3 cups (710 ml) water
2 tablespoons white wine vinegar
3 celery ribs, thinly sliced and leaves torn
20 pitted black olives, coarsely chopped
1 tablespoon capers
1 garlic clove, finely chopped
3 tablespoons extra-virgin olive oil, plus more for serving
Sesame Semolina Bread (page 26) for serving

Soak the baccala in cold water in the fridge for 2 days, changing the water daily. Weigh out 11 ounces (310 g) of the cod. Wrap and place the remaining cod in the freezer for future use.

Combine the baccala, parsley sprigs, basil, oregano, onion, wine, sugar, salt, peppercorns, chile, bay leaf, and half lemon, plus the water, in a medium Dutch oven. Simmer over low heat until the cod begins to flake apart, about 45 minutes. Remove the pot from the heat and let cool to room temperature. Remove the cod from the cooled liquid, flake completely, and transfer to a mixing bowl. Discard the cooking liquid along with its solids. Add the lemon juice, vinegar, celery, olives, capers, garlic, and olive oil and gently mix. Drizzle with more olive oil and serve with semolina bread.

THE MIRACLE ON
MERRY CH

SOUTH 13TH ST
RISTMAS
PESTO
NO PARKING
TIME
2 HR PARKING
8 AM - 7 PM

THE FEAST OF THE SEVEN FISHES

If such a thing as an Italian American calendar existed for South Philly, Christmas Eve would be the most important day of the year. It would be highlighted, underscored, and circled in red magic marker. Four days before the date would be a reminder: "Order the fish"—seven fish at least.

The Feast of the Seven Fishes, as the big Christmas Eve gathering is known, is not exclusively a South Philly thing, or even a Philly thing. All across the country, where there are descendants of Italian immigrants of the early 1900s, there are Christmas Eve spreads stacked with flounder francese, scungilli salad, mussels fra daviolo, stewed baccala, shrimp scampi, and dozens of other seafood dishes. Nobody knows whether the tradition has legit roots in Italy or was something immigrants invented after coming to America, and the significance of the number seven is similarly up for debate. The seven virtues, the seven sacraments, the seven days of creation all get credit.

Seven is a floor, not a ceiling, and many cooks take a more-is-more approach. While I was growing up, the spread at my Uncle Ernie and Aunt Mary's featured probably twenty different dishes served family style on their huge dining room table. Their son, my cousin Al, has carried on the tradition, and it's still a family effort. I order all the fish. My mom, sisters, and cousins clean and prep it. Al cooks it. The abundance of food has not changed, either. At least one dish is routinely forgotten—"Oh, no! We forgot the shrimp in the fridge!"—but it's always okay because we just head back over for leftovers on the day after Christmas.

There are no set species; each family has their own repertoire and favorites. For some, it's not Christmas Eve dinner without fried smelts and braised eel. For others, clams and macaroni in white sauce is sacred. Putting on this meal is a major undertaking, and eventually, hopefully, and sometimes not without a power struggle, the torch gets passed to the next generation, which has to navigate its own balance of traditional and "modern" dishes. In the '80s, that meant shrimp cocktail and bacon-wrapped scallops. Today, it's fish tacos and sushi trays. While some die-hard relatives might gripe, the tradition is less about the seafood than the gathering, having that day on the calendar every year that everyone in the family knows exactly where they're supposed to be and what they'll be doing, which is spending time together.

You don't need to be Italian to throw a Seven Fishes feast. Our neighborhood is more diverse than ever, and lots of newcomers have adopted the tradition and made it their own. Several recipes in this chapter appear on my family's Christmas Eve table every year. Try one or the entire menu. Just make sure to invite plenty of people over.

FEAST OF THE SEVEN FISHES MENU

From left to right: Calamari and Peas / Herb Butter–Roasted Orata / Fritto Misto / Crabs and Spaghetti

Shrimp and Beans / Grilled Octopus with Salsa Verde and Marinated Chives / Scallop and Mushroom Capesante

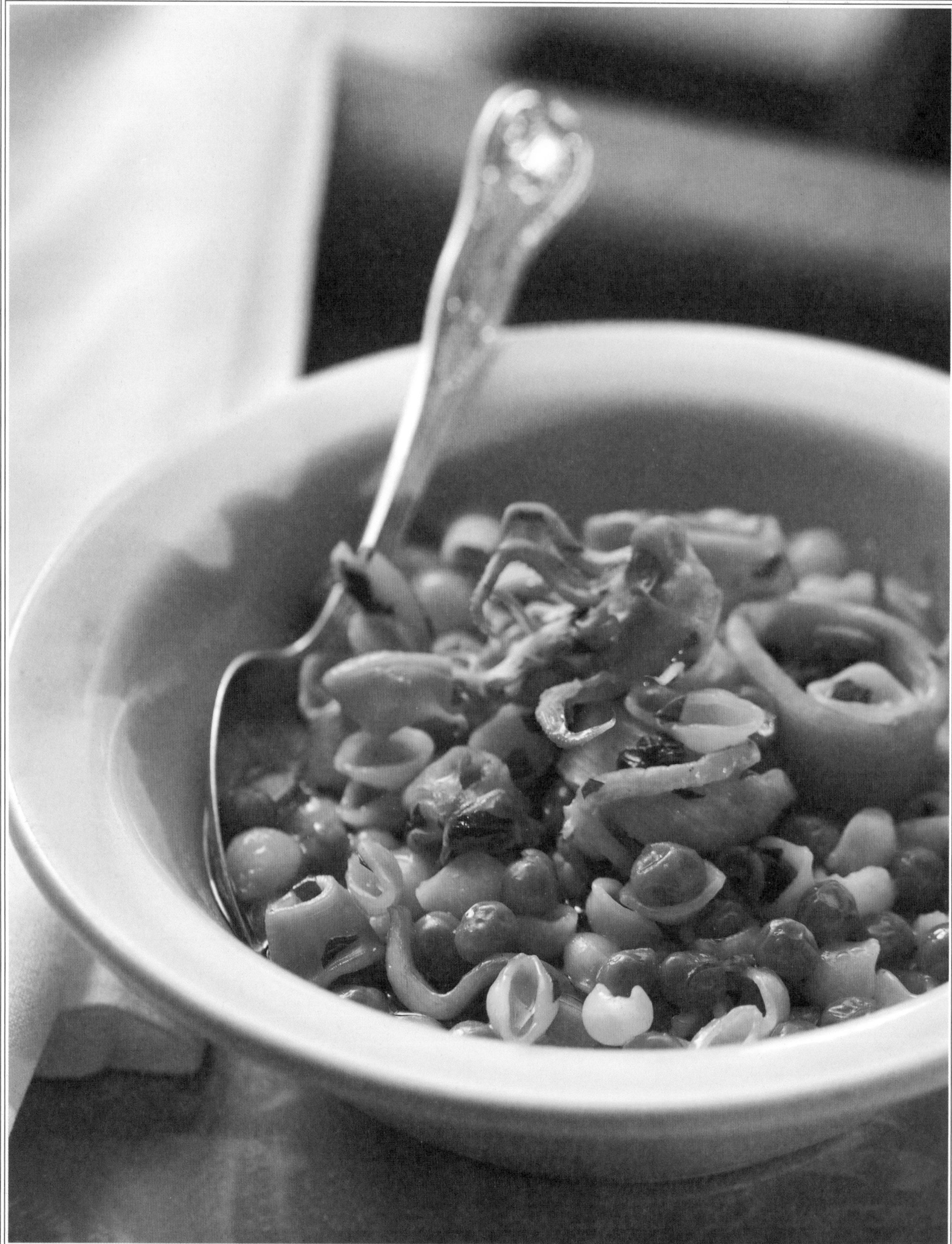

CALAMARI AND PEAS

Canned peas have a bad reputation, but give them a chance in this satisfying squid stew, which is less about the peas themselves than the liquid in which they're packed. This juice is a magic ingredient, subtly sweet and the foundation of the broth that lightly coats the calamari. You can serve this as a soup on its own or bulk it up with cooked pasta, which is how we do it at the Club. Small shells or tubetti work particularly well, as their holes catch the peas, but I also love this with our Potato Gnocchi (page 68).

SERVES 4

½ cup (80 g) very small diced yellow onion

1 garlic clove, smashed, plus 1 tablespoon chopped

2 bay leaves

20 cracks black pepper

¼ cup (59 ml) plus 2 tablespoons extra-virgin olive oil

3 (8½-ounce [241 g]) cans sweet peas

2 tablespoons chopped fresh parsley leaves

Pinch of red pepper flakes

2 cups (440 g) Stewed Calamari (page 80)

Grated Parmigiano-Reggiano for serving

Heat the onion, smashed garlic clove, bay leaves, black pepper, and ¼ cup (59 ml) of the olive oil over low heat in a medium pot. Cook until the onion is translucent, about 10 minutes. Add the peas and their liquid to the pot and increase the heat to medium. Bring to a simmer and remove from the heat. Remove and discard the bay leaf and smashed garlic.

Heat the remaining 2 tablespoons of olive oil and the chopped garlic, parsley, and red pepper flakes in a large Dutch oven over medium heat until fragrant, about 2 minutes. Add the pea mixture and the calamari and bring to a simmer, occasionally stirring until the calamari is warmed through, about 6 minutes (it should be brothy). Garnish with grated Parmigiano-Reggiano.

SHRIMP AND BEANS

The fewer ingredients in a dish, the less room to hide. Aside from olive oil and spices, this dish has two ingredients, and they're right there in the name: shrimp and beans. So much of the cooking we do at the Club is simple food. But simple food can be messed up really easily, and if you're not buying the best ingredients you can afford and/or are available near you, it shows. For this scampi-ish stew, high-quality shrimp are essential. Get them fresh from a reputable fishmonger or seafood market (I like prawns from Louisiana) with their heads, which are packed with flavor. The sweet, oceany, slightly firm shrimp against the soft, creamy, herby cannellini beans (the same ones from our Escarole and Beans, page 96) is a pairing you'll keep going back to.

SERVES 2

1½ cups (380 g) cooked Cannellini Beans, with their liquid (page 96)

¼ cup (59 ml) extra-virgin olive oil

6 head-on, peeled and deveined U-9 shrimp, about 11 ounces (310 g)

¼ teaspoon salt

12 cracks black pepper

2 garlic cloves, minced

Pinch of red pepper flakes

½ cup (20 g) chopped fresh parsley leaves

1 lemon, halved

Heat the beans in a medium pot over low heat.

Meanwhile, heat the olive oil to almost smoking over high heat in a large sauté pan. Season 1 side of the shrimp with the salt and black pepper. Carefully place the shrimp into the hot oil, unseasoned-side down. Cook until the sides of the shrimp in contact with the oil are golden and the other sides are just starting to become opaque, about 4 minutes. Take the pan off the heat and flip the shrimp. Add the garlic, red pepper flakes, and parsley. Return the pan to the heat for 30 seconds to cook the garlic. Transfer the warm beans to a serving platter. Remove the sauté pan from the heat and, using a small strainer to catch the seeds, squeeze the lemon juice into the pan. Pour the shrimp mixture over the beans and serve immediately.

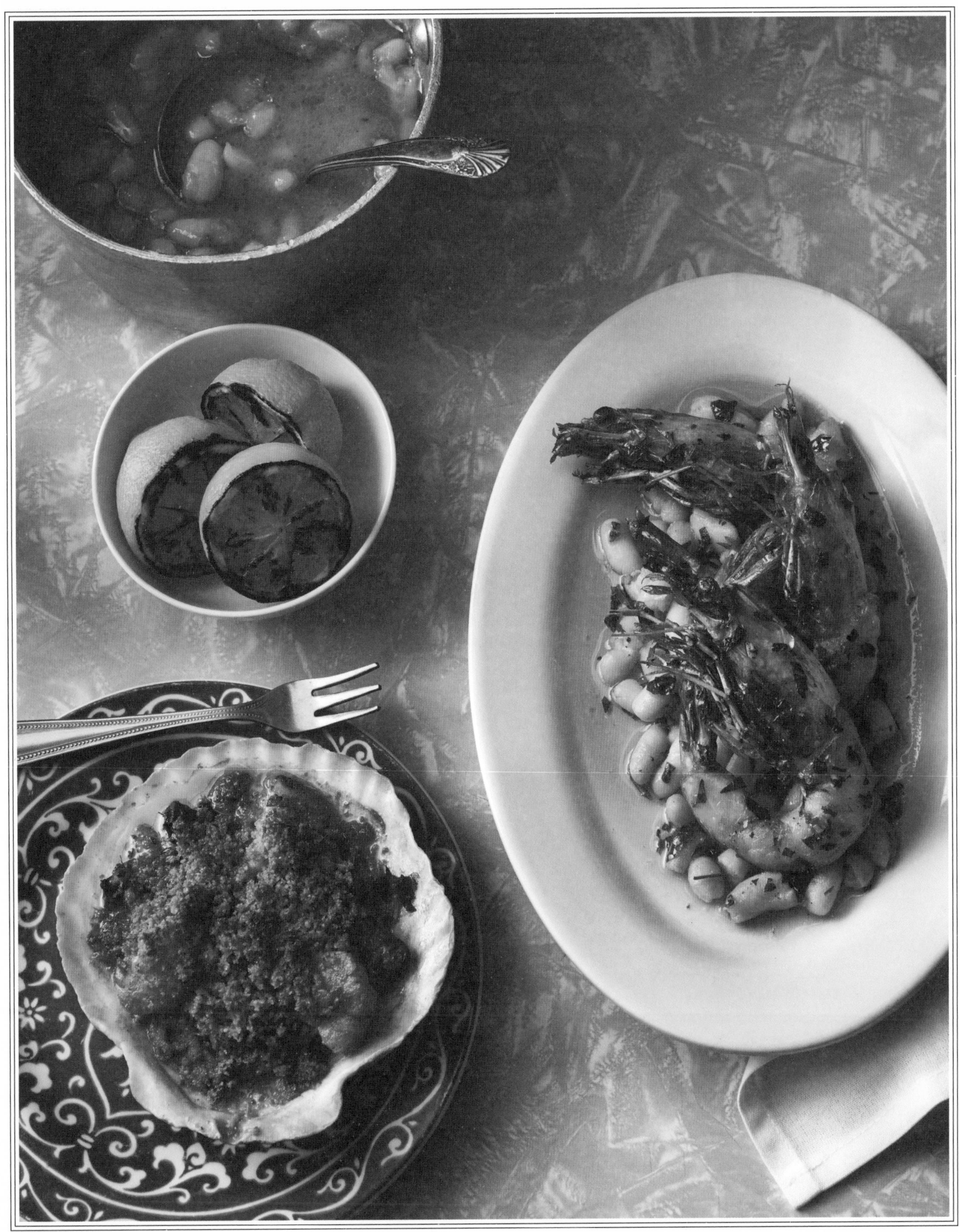

Scallop and Mushroom Capesante on left, Shrimp and Beans on right

SCALLOP AND MUSHROOM CAPESANTE

After I decided that I was going to take up my Uncle Ernie on his offer and reopen the Club, I spent several weeks here cleaning and organizing along with my dad and his brother, Frank. While we worked, I'd pass the time mentally menu planning. One day I was sweeping the floor, I just looked around, really taking in the atmosphere, and one thought came into my head: clams casino. They're so of the Club's era and were always on the menu at my grandparents' restaurant, Al Mazza's. This dish is not clams casino, but lives in the same category of warm, cheesy, definitely untrendy, gratinéed seafood appetizer. It's the anti-crudo.

To make the capesante, we blend scallops, crab, and clams with two kinds of Italian cheeses and chopped mushrooms that have been browned, truffled, brandied, and creamed. This rich mixture goes down into scallop shells (use crème brûlée dishes if you can't find them) and gets gratinéed in the oven with breadcrumbs until golden and bubbling. The combination is fantastic. Some people freak out when they see cheese and fish together, but I don't believe in that. There are some seafood dishes that don't pair well with cheese, sure, but our capesante is definitely not one of them.

SERVES 4

- ½ cup plus 1 tablespoon (135 ml) extra-virgin olive oil
- 1 pound (454 g) cremini or button mushrooms, sliced
- 2 teaspoons salt
- 20 cracks black pepper
- 1½ teaspoons unsalted butter
- ¼ teaspoon black truffle paste
- ½ teaspoon chopped fresh thyme leaves
- 1 sprig rosemary
- 1 garlic clove, chopped
- 1 tablespoon finely diced shallot
- 1 bay leaf
- ¼ cup (59 ml) brandy
- 1 cup (237 ml) water
- ½ cup (118 ml) heavy whipping cream
- 4 bay scallops (150 g), quartered
- 1 ounce (28 g) canned clams, drained
- 1.4 ounces (40 g) crab claw meat
- 3 tablespoons grated Parmigiano-Reggiano
- ¼ cup (28 g) grated Toma cheese
- 6 tablespoons (39 g) Seasoned Breadcrumbs (page 80)
- Fresh chopped parsley leaves for serving
- Lemon wedges for serving

Heat the olive oil over medium heat in a large Dutch oven until it just begins to shimmer. Add the mushrooms, spreading them out as flat and even as possible. Season with the salt and pepper and increase the heat to high, allowing their liquid to weep out and evaporate. When the liquid has cooked down to dry, add the butter. Cook the mushrooms until browned on the bottoms, then stir to get color on the remaining sides. Once the mushrooms are completely browned, lower the heat to low and add the truffle paste, thyme, rosemary, garlic, shallot, and bay leaf. Sweat the shallots and garlic until translucent, about 3 minutes. Off the heat, add the brandy very slowly. Continue to cook until the liquid has reduced to dry, then add the water. Bring to a simmer and cook for 10 minutes, or until the liquid takes on the color of the mushrooms. Add the cream and simmer for 10 minutes, or until slightly thickened. Remove the pot from the heat and let cool completely.

Preheat the oven to 450°F (230°C).

Remove the bay leaf and rosemary from the cooled mushrooms. Drain the mushrooms, reserving the liquid in a medium bowl. Coarsely chop the mushrooms and return to the bowl of liquid. Add the scallops, clams, crab, Parmigiano, and Toma and gently mix together.

Distribute the mixture among 4 scallop shells and arrange on a baking sheet. Bake for 10 minutes, or until the mixture is bubbling and the scallops are opaque. Remove the filled scallop shells from the oven and top each with 1½ tablespoons of seasoned breadcrumbs. Return the scallops to the oven and bake for an additional 3 to 5 minutes, or until golden brown. Garnish with chopped fresh parsley leaves and serve with lemon wedges.

Palizzi Society Membership Listing

Allizzo Angelo, of Galea. 1424 S. 13th St.
Allizzo Anthony Sr. 1424 S. 13th St.
Allizzo Anthony Jr. 1424 S. 13th St.
Allizzo Angelo, of Tony 1424 S. 13th St.
Allizzo Frank. 622 Sigel St.
Allizzo John. 34 Hampshire, Audubon N.J.
Andolfi Silvio. 1711 Watkins St.
Andolfi Michael. Miami Address
Bevilacqua Nick. 228 Glenside, Glenside, Pa.
Benedetto Albert. 1211 Tasker St.
Carrozza Anthony. 1009 Tasker St.
Carrozza Nicholas. 1009 Tasker St.
Celenza Michael. 2228 S. 19th St.
Celenza Michael. 3211 Rorer St.
Celenza Nicholas. 913 Dickinson St.
Celenza Domenic. 462 Center, Collingswood N.J.
Ciccotosto Joseph. 930 Fernon St.
Coppiolone Anthony. 2228 S. 19th St.
Coley William Jr. 206 Hazel Ave, Westmont N.J.
Cerrone M. Joseph. 1640 S. Clarion St.
Cerrone J. Americo. 1118 Cross St.
D'Adamo Nicholas. 1737 S. 12th St.
D'Adamo Michael. 1830 Hofman St.
D'Adamo Peter. 2216 Mifflin St.
De Felice Paul. 3119 S. Broad St.
Di Biase Nicholas. 825 Pierce St.
Di Biase Anthony 115 Grafton Ave, Bellmawr
Di Cicco Joseph, 1712 Summit, Union City N.J.
Di Foglio Domenic. 26 State Rd, Blackwood, N.J.
Del Fra Louis. 400 Folsom Ave, Folsom, Pa
Del Casale Charles. 6006 Springfield, Springfield, Pa
Del Casale Nicholas. 1719 Ritner St.
Del Bonifro Nicholas. 864 N. 66th St.
Del Borrello Angelo. S. 1405 Juniper St.
Del Borrello Peter. S. 1431 Juniper St.
Del Borrello Albert. S. 1401 Juniper St.
De Matteo Charles. 1214 Gerritt St.
Di Galbo Anthony. 1827 S. Etting St.
Del Conte Nicholas. 1634 S. Isemminger St.
Del Rossi Nicholas. 1521 S. Broad St.
Florio Joseph. 2010 S. Bouvier St.
Fabrizio Frank. 2023 S. Bancroft St.
Gullota Samuel Jr. 809 McClellan St.
Ippolito Anthony. 1409 S. Juniper St.
Iannuzzi Joseph. 1507 S. Isemminger St.
La Verghetta Caesar. 203 Arizona, Atlantic City N.J.
La Verghetta Dante. 2133 Vista St.
La Verghetta Nick. Cuthbert Rd. Apt. 37. Haddon Twp. N.J.
La Verghetta Nicholas 1812 Sigel St.
La Verghetta Nicholas 1423 S. Clarion St.
La Verghetta Carmen 1423 S. Clarion St.
Lavini Peter. 1021 Cantrell St.
Marinelli Anthony. 1216 N. 50th St.
Marchesani Nicholas. 1532 Tasker St.
Marchesani Michael. 1948 Dugfor St.
Marchesani Michael. 1228 Reed St.
Messina Joseph. 2122 Tyson Ave
Milando Joseph. 2028 S. 17th St.
Milando Vincent. 2028 S. 17th St.
Milando Domenic. 2028 S. 17th St.
Monteferrante Ralph. 447 Oaklyn, Maple Shade N.J.
Mezzacoba Ernest. 1507 S. 12th St.
Moccia Louis. 1039 Mercy St.
Pasqucci Nicholas. 1156 Passyunk Ave
Paolocca Dante. 1522 S. 13th St.
Reale Joseph. 1425 S. Broad St.
Reale Angelo. 628 N. 66th St.
Santini Nicholas. 330 Sussex Blvd, Broomall, Pa
Santore Saverio. 130 Henly Rd, Overbrook Heights
Silla Domenic. 800 Hillcrest Rd, Glenolden, Pa
Smargiassi Louis. 9M, Oakridge Rd, Hagerstone Md.
Smargiassi Daniel. 33 Sackavacker, Dover, De
Smargiassi Nicholas. Miami Address
Smargiassi Carmen. 1329 Porter St.
Spadaccini Domenic. 1918 S. Isemminger St.
Spadaccini Louis. 1232 McKean St.
Spadaccini Joseph 231 Fairmont, Blackwood, N.J.
Tenaglia Joseph. 814 Snyder Ave.
Tenaglia Ralph. Vasto. Italy.
Turchi Anthony. 1418 S. 13th St.
Ventura Frank. 310 Evergreen, Westmont, N.J.
Zaccaria James. 1829 Ritner St.
Zacco Michael. 1804 Wynnewood Rd

CIOPPINO WITH SAFFRON COUSCOUS

Some kids want pizza and ice cream on their birthdays; I always wanted cioppino. Even now that I'm forty-one years old, when we celebrate my birthday with a family dinner, my mom pulls out all the stops for a huge pot of this seafood stew loaded with shellfish, crabs, and fish. The name, you've probably heard, comes from Italian immigrants working San Francisco's wharves, "chipping in" various sea creatures to a communal broth tinted with tomato and fennel. Whether that origin story is legit or legend, where there are Italians by the sea (whether in Italy or in America), there are soups and stews made with whatever swims and skitters nearby. Orata (a.k.a. dorade), mussels, clams, cockles, shrimp, and crabs star in our version, with their shells and bones forming the foundation of an intensely flavored broth. In addition to the quality of the seafood, breaking this recipe into separate steps makes a huge difference. You have to carefully brown the scraps, building a fond in the pan whose flavor will carry through the entire soup, before adding your aromatics, liquids, and tomatoes, one at a time. This will create a bold, multidimensional sauce. We serve the cioppino over saffron couscous (the larger Israeli variety, also called pearl couscous), but you could also present it without pasta as more of a soup. Don't forget to include plenty of Sesame Semolina Bread (page 26) for soaking up the broth.

SERVES 4

(recipe continues)

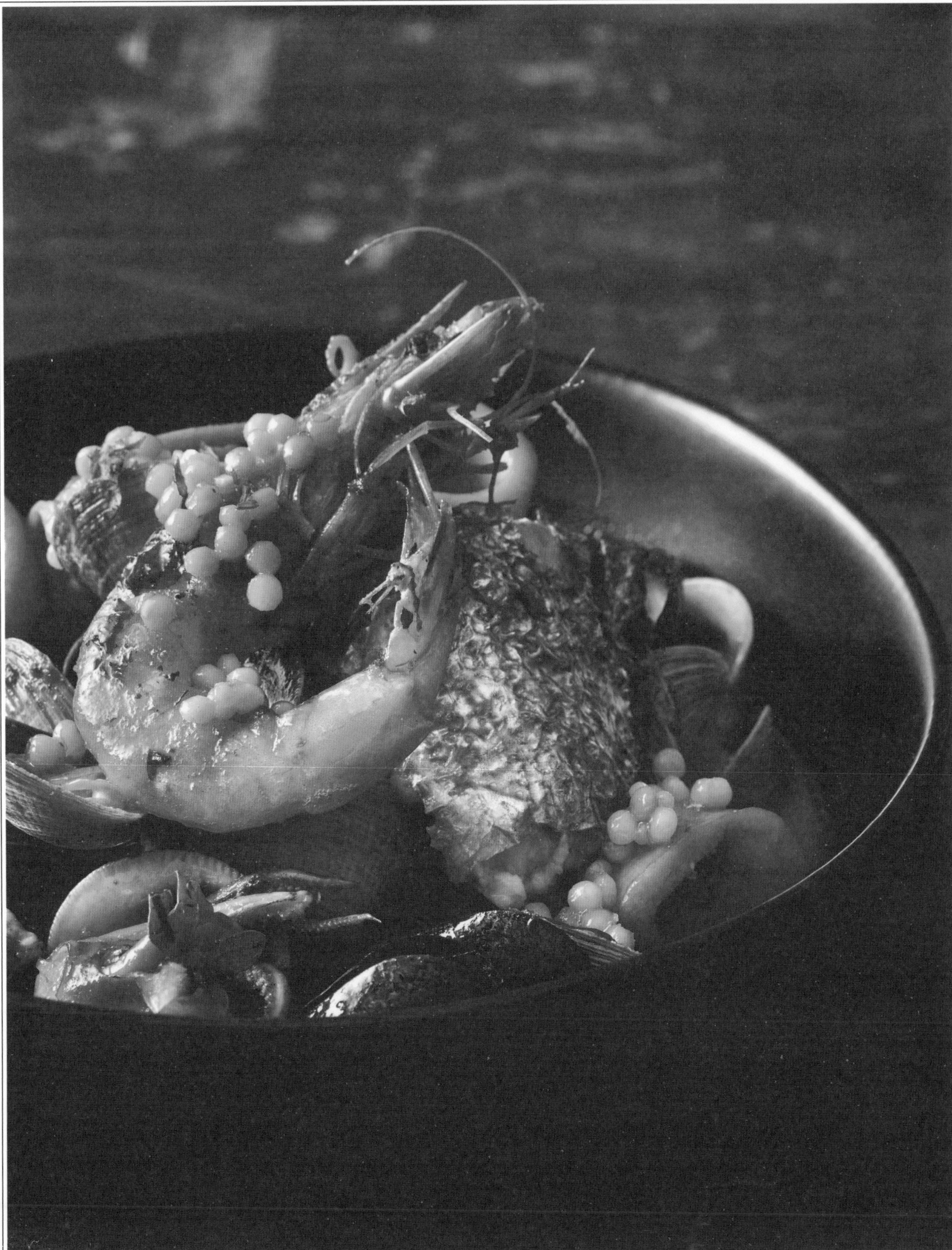

SEAFOOD BROTH

- **10 whole U-9 shrimp, about 1 pound (454 g)**
- **1 small fennel bulb, thinly sliced, fronds removed and reserved**
- **Fistful of fresh parsley**
- **3 sprigs basil**
- **¼ cup (59 ml) blended oil (see page 19)**
- **2 blue crabs (500 g), cleaned**
- **1 orata, about 1 pound (454 g), scaled and filleted with skeleton reserved**
- **1 tablespoon salt, divided**
- **14 cracks black pepper, divided, plus 10 black peppercorns**
- **3 tablespoons extra-virgin olive oil**
- **½ lemon**
- **½ orange**
- **1 head garlic, halved**
- **2 oil-packed anchovy fillets**
- **½ Arbol chile**
- **½ yellow onion, thinly sliced**
- **½ red onion, thinly sliced**
- **1 celery rib, thinly sliced**
- **1 carrot, thinly sliced**
- **2 (28-ounce [794 g]) cans whole peeled tomatoes**
- **¼ teaspoon granulated sugar (optional)**
- **1 teaspoon dried oregano**
- **1 cinnamon stick**
- **2 cloves**
- **1 bay leaf**
- **1 tablespoon tomato paste**
- **1 cup (250 ml) Chablis**
- **1 quart (1 L) water**
- **1 teaspoon fennel seeds**

Carefully peel and devein the shrimp, leaving the heads and tails on. Reserve the shells from 2 of the shrimp for the broth and discard the remaining shells. Chill all the peeled shrimp until using later in the recipe.

Tie the fennel fronds, parsley, and basil into a bundle with kitchen twine and set aside. Heat the blended oil in a large Dutch oven set over medium-high heat until shimmering. Season the crabs, shrimp shells, and fish bones (keep the fillets in the fridge) with 1 teaspoon of the salt and 14 cracks of the black pepper. Add the crabs to the oil first, immediately followed by the fish bones. Cook for 6 to 8 minutes, or until the crab shells become dark red. Flip the crabs and the fish bones, and add the reserved shrimp shells. Continue to sear for 6 minutes. Do not stir or sauté.

Remove the crabs, bones, and shells and set aside. Discard the oil. Add the olive oil to the pot and set over very low heat. Place the lemon, orange, and garlic, cut-side down, in the pot to infuse the oil. Add the peppercorns, anchovies, chile, onions, sliced fennel bulb, celery, and carrot and cook over low heat until soft, about 15 minutes. Season the tomatoes in a bowl with 2 teaspoons of the salt, the sugar (if needed), and the oregano and crush them by hand. Create a space in the pot and add the cinnamon, cloves, bay leaf, herb bundle, and tomato paste. Cook about 6 minutes, until the paste turns from bright red to copper. Add the wine, increase the heat to medium, and simmer until almost evaporated. Return the crabs, bones, and shells to the pot. Add the crushed seasoned tomatoes and water. Lower the heat to low and simmer, covered, for 3 hours, stirring every few minutes.

Remove the pot from the heat and add the fennel seeds. Let the broth cool to room temperature. Set a sieve over a clean pot. Ladle the broth into the sieve, using a wooden spoon to smash the seafood shells and push as much as possible of the vegetables and the seafood through the sieve. Discard the solids. Set aside the broth at room temperature.

SAFFRON COUSCOUS

- 1 bay leaf
- 1 garlic clove
- 1 whole clove
- 2 tablespoons extra-virgin olive oil
- 1 shallot, very finely diced
- 1 Arbol chile
- 1 sprig rosemary
- 2 cups (270 g) uncooked Israeli couscous
- 3 cups (710 ml) water
- ¼ teaspoon saffron threads
- 1 teaspoon salt

Press the bay leaf against the garlic clove and pierce with the whole clove to attach. Place the olive oil, garlic, shallot, chile, and rosemary in a large Dutch oven set over medium-low heat. Sauté until the shallot and garlic are soft, about 6 minutes. Add the couscous and increase the heat to medium-high. Lightly toast the couscous, stirring, until fragrant, about 4 minutes. Add the water and saffron and lower the heat to medium-low. Cook for 10 minutes, or until al dente. Pour the couscous onto a baking sheet, season with the salt, and let cool to room temperature. Set aside.

CIOPPINO

- Reserved skin-on orata fillets, cut into 4 roughly equal pieces
- 1 teaspoon salt, divided
- 10 cracks black pepper, divided
- 4 scallops, about 6 ounces (170 g)
- Peeled, head-on shrimp, reserved from the broth
- ¼ cup (59 ml) blended oil (see page 19)
- 3 tablespoons extra-virgin olive oil
- ¼ teaspoon chopped garlic
- 1 tablespoon chopped fresh parsley leaves
- Pinch of red pepper flakes
- ¼ cup (59 ml) Chablis
- 15 mussels, scrubbed and debearded
- 18 clams, scrubbed
- 2 cups (440 g) Stewed Calamari (page 80)

Season the flesh side of the orata with ½ teaspoon of the salt and 3 cracks of black pepper. Season the scallops and reserved shrimp on 1 side only with the remaining salt and black pepper.

Heat the blended oil in a large sauté pan set over high heat. Add the orata, skin-side down, and press each piece flat with a spatula. Cook the fish for 4 minutes, remove from the pan, and transfer to a plate. Add the scallops and shrimp to the pan, unseasoned-side down. Sear until golden brown, about 4 minutes, remove from pan, and transfer to the plate containing the cooked orata.

Discard the oil, wipe out the pot, and add the olive oil, garlic, parsley, and red pepper flakes. Sauté for 2 minutes. Add the wine, mussels, and clams and reduce until the wine has almost evaporated, about 3 minutes. Add the seafood broth and reduce by one third over high heat, about 4 minutes. Add the stewed calamari to the pot and add back the scallops, shrimp, and orata. Cover, lower the heat to medium-high, and cook for 3 minutes. Evenly divide the seafood and broth among 4 soup bowls. Top with the couscous and serve immediately.

HERB BUTTER–ROASTED ORATA

Minimizing food waste is very important to us (see Arancini with Ragu and Peas, page 82, for a leftovers manifesto), and roasting a whole fish is a great way to use an entire animal, not to mention make an impressive presentation. Cooking the fish whole gets you the moistest flesh and cracker-crisp skin with the bonus of a head-on skeleton that will make flavorful soup or stock. We rub our orata inside and out with a compound herb butter and stuff the cavity with rosemary, sear it on the stovetop, then finish it in the oven over a layer of potatoes. The sauce gets built right in the pan with lemon, caperberries (use a tablespoon of capers if you can't find the larger berries), black olives, and marinated zucchini. It all comes together in less than half an hour. If you can't find orata, any other medium-size, white-fleshed fish will work: branzino, red snapper, black bass, and so forth. Instead of getting hung up on species, go with whatever looks freshest, and you'll have solid results.

SERVES 4

MARINATED GRILLED ZUCCHINI

- 1 zucchini, cut on a bias in ½-inch (1.3 cm)-thick slices
- 1 tablespoon extra-virgin olive oil
- Pinch of salt
- 4 cracks black pepper
- 3 fresh basil leaves, torn
- 1 teaspoon red wine vinegar

Get a grill hot. Toss the zucchini, olive oil, salt, and pepper in a small bowl. Grill the zucchini over direct heat for 4 minutes per side. Put the basil leaves and vinegar on a plate and cover them with the zucchini to absorb. Set aside at room temperature.

HERB BUTTER

- 8 tablespoons (113 g) unsalted butter, at room temperature
- 3 tablespoons minced fresh chives
- 3 tablespoons minced fresh dill
- 3 tablespoons minced fresh parsley
- 1 teaspoon minced fresh oregano
- 1½ tablespoons minced red onion
- Grated zest of 1 lemon
- 1 garlic clove, minced
- ¼ teaspoon salt
- ¼ teaspoon granulated sugar
- ¼ teaspoon anchovy paste
- 5 cracks black pepper

Place the butter in a stand mixer fitted with the paddle attachment and whip on low speed, scraping down the sides with a rubber spatula as needed. Add the remaining ingredients and mix on low speed for 1 minute. Scrape down the sides and continue to mix until thoroughly combined. Set aside at room temperature.

ORATA

- 1 whole orata, about 2 pounds (907 g) scaled and gutted
- 3 sprigs rosemary
- 1 teaspoon salt
- 4 cracks black pepper
- ¼ cup (59 ml) blended oil (see page 19)
- ¼ cup (59 ml) extra-virgin olive oil
- 2 small white potatoes, cut in ¼-inch (6 mm) pieces
- 1 cup (237 ml) Chablis
- ½ cup (118 ml) water
- ¼ cup (28 g) Marinated Black Olives (page 34)
- 4 caperberries
- 1 oil-packed Calabrian chile
- 1 lemon, halved, plus wedges for serving

Preheat the oven to 450°F (230°C). Spread ¼ cup (57 g) of the herb butter all over the cavity of the fish. Add the rosemary to the cavity. Evenly season the outside of the fish with the salt and pepper. Set a large sauté pan over medium heat and add the blended oil. Heat until the oil begins to lightly smoke. Place the fish in the pan very carefully. Lightly shake the pan so the fish doesn't stick. Increase the heat to medium-high and cook the fish until golden brown, 3 to 4 minutes. Gently flip the fish and carefully drain off and discard the oil. Off the heat, add the olive oil to the pan. Add the potatoes. Place the fish on top of the potatoes and transfer the pan to the oven. Roast for 15 minutes. Check for doneness by inserting a cake tester into the thickest part of the fish for 5 seconds. If the tester is hot to the touch, the fish is done. If not done, roast for an additional 5 minutes. Remove the pan from the oven and gently transfer just the fish to a large serving platter.

Set the pan of potatoes over medium-low heat, add the wine and water, and reduce by half, then add the remaining herb butter. Stir for 1 minute to coat the potatoes. Stir in the marinated zucchini, olives, caperberries, and Calabrian chile and cook for 1 minute. Using a small strainer to catch the seeds, squeeze the juice from the lemon halves into the pan. Remove from the heat, stir, and pour the contents of the pan over the fish. Garnish with lemon wedges and serve immediately.

MEAT

BRACIOLE WITH SUNDAY GRAVY

LARDO

TOMATO AND CINNAMON–BRAISED TRIPE

SWEET FENNEL SAUSAGE

BRAISED RABBIT WITH TOMATO AND OREGANO

VEAL CUTLETS

ROASTED CHICKEN

GRILLED LAMB CHOPS

CHINOTTO RIBS

STEAK PIZZAIOLA

PANZETTA

WHOLE ROASTED SUCKLING PIG

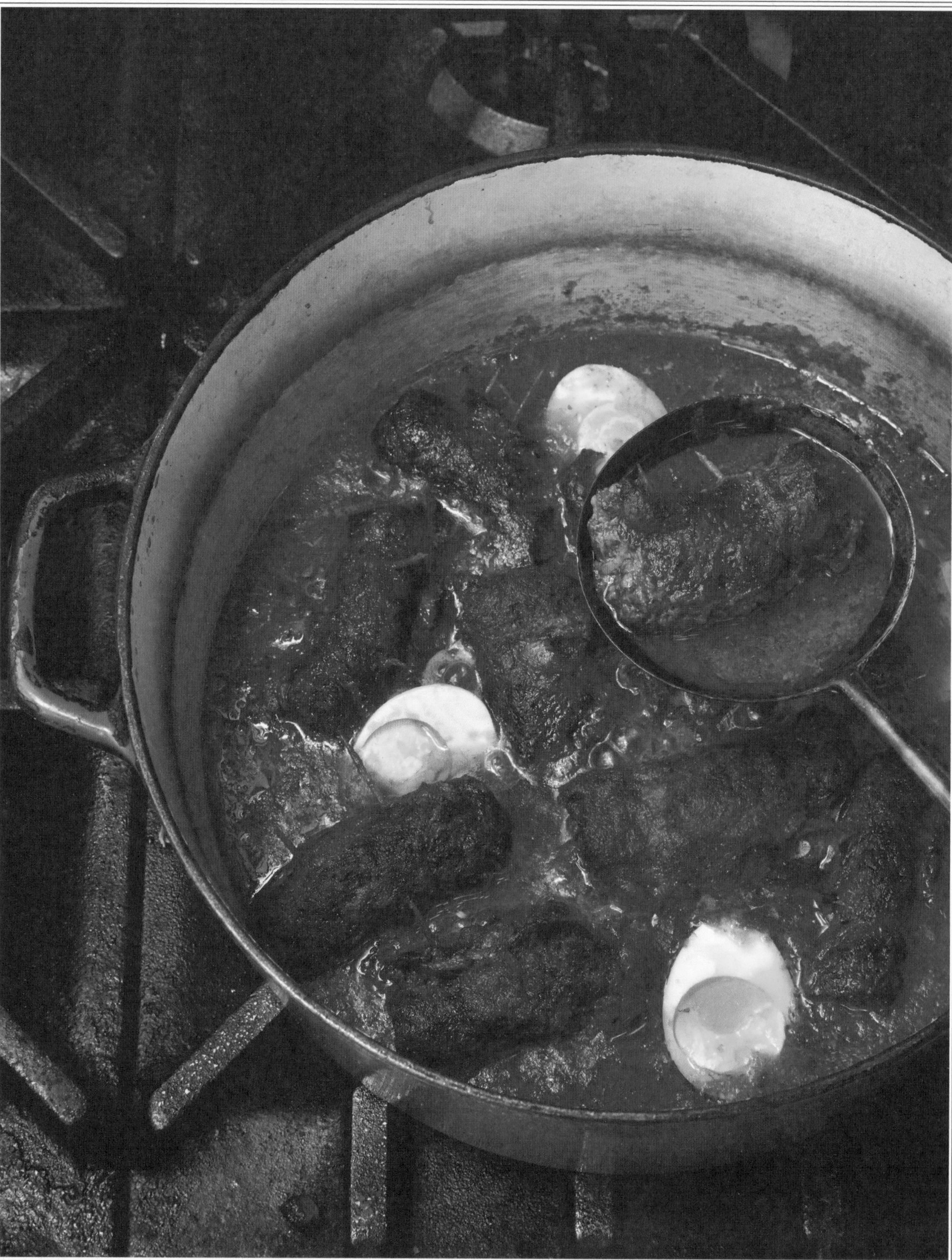

BRACIOLE WITH SUNDAY GRAVY

Making braciole with short rib is not traditional. These little stuffed bundles of beef, which my mom made every Sunday with her gravy, are usually done with top round and stuffed with hard-boiled egg. We tried the traditional cut when we were recipe testing for the Club, but it came out dry and chewy. We tested with rump, with shoulder, with flank—no dice. Eventually we hit on boneless short rib served with the egg on the side. It has a lot of fat, which slowly melts back into the meat, and to hedge our bets, we also spread each slice of beef with our house-made Lardo (page 135), which adds another layer of flavor and richness. But almost as important in making these braciole taste great is patience. It is so important to go slow, in this recipe and most others, a lesson I'm constantly trying to share with new cooks in my kitchens. Some new chefs get really enthusiastic and want to throw ingredients into the pan, cooking everything over a high flame. Yeah, you're getting it done quick, but you're creating one flavor as opposed to *building* flavor. This is why we call for cooking the aromatics, tomato paste, wine, and tomatoes all in separate steps. You wind up with a deeper, more developed flavor in the finished dish.

A note on serving: Toothpicks hold the braciole together, and obviously, you don't want to eat them, so let people know they're there. Do not remove all the picks before serving unless you're confident you won't have leftovers. If you try and reheat braciole after the toothpicks have been removed, they'll fall apart.

SERVES 7

(recipe continues)

- **2 pounds (907 g) trimmed boneless short rib**
- **6 cracks black pepper, divided**
- **3½ tablespoons salt, divided**
- **5 tablespoons (50 g) Lardo (page 135)**
- **4¼ cups (440 g) Seasoned Breadcrumbs (page 80), plus more for serving**
- **½ cup (118 ml) blended oil (see page 19)**
- **½ cup (118 ml) extra-virgin olive oil, plus more for serving**
- **1 red onion, thinly sliced**
- **1 yellow onion, thinly sliced**
- **4 garlic cloves, thinly sliced**
- **3 sprigs basil**
- **3 sprigs oregano**
- **Fistful of fresh parsley, plus 2 tablespoons chopped fresh leaves for serving**
- **2 bay leaves**
- **1 Arbol chile**
- **1 tablespoon tomato paste**
- **½ cup (118 ml) Chablis**
- **1 (28-ounce [794 g]) can whole peeled tomatoes, crushed by hand with 1 teaspoon salt**
- **2 cups (473 ml) water**
- **4 large hard-boiled eggs (see page 50)**
- **Grated Parmigiano-Reggiano for serving**

Cut the short rib in half and then lengthwise into ¼-inch (6 mm) slices. You should wind up with about 14 slices roughly 3 inches (7.5 cm) long and 2 inches (5 cm) wide. Lay the slices of short rib flat on plastic wrap and season with 3 cracks of black pepper and half of the salt. Cover with another piece of plastic wrap and pound lightly with a meat mallet to very thin. Flip the whole thing over and pound again. Remove the top sheet of plastic and season with remaining salt and pepper. Rub each piece with ½ teaspoon of the whipped lardo. Press ¼ cup (25 g) of the breadcrumbs onto each slice of short rib. Roll up each slice tightly and secure with 2 toothpicks per braciola.

Heat the blended oil in a large Dutch oven over medium heat. Working in 2 batches so as to not crowd the pan, lightly brown the braciole on all sides, about 3 minutes per batch. Remove the braciole and transfer to a plate. Discard the oil. To the same Dutch oven, add the olive oil, onions, garlic, herbs, bay leaves, and chile. Cook over very low heat until the onions are translucent, about 10 minutes. Clear a space in the pot and add the tomato paste. Cook the paste about 6 minutes, until it turns from bright red to copper. Add the wine and cook until evaporated. Add the salted crushed tomatoes and the water. Add all the braciole back to the pot, making sure they're completely covered by the tomato sauce. Cover and cook over low heat for 2 hours, stirring occasionally and checking the braciole every 15 minutes for tenderness. The braciole are done when a small knife goes through easily. Let them cool in sauce off the stove for 2 hours.

Transfer the cooled braciole to a clean pot and set a large sieve over it. Ladle the cooled tomato sauce through the sieve, pressing firmly to push as much of the sauce through as possible. Discard the solids. To serve, rewarm the braciole with the hard-boiled eggs in the pot of strained sauce over medium heat. Transfer them to a platter with sauce ladled over top. Cut the eggs in half. Garnish with olive oil, grated Parmigiano, chopped parsley, and breadcrumbs.

LARDO

This isn't the cured lardo that appears on charcuterie plates. Although both are made with pork fatback, ours acts like a meaty compound butter, a seasoning rather than something you eat on its own. It's the X-factor ingredient in the Braciole (page 133), the thing that makes people scratch their heads and wonder, *What is that flavor? Why is this so good?* You can also use it for sautéing vegetables and rubbing poultry or steak before roasting.

MAKES ABOUT 8 OUNCES (227 G) LARDO

8 ounces (227 g) pork fatback, finely diced

2 garlic cloves, minced

Leaves from 2 sprigs rosemary, minced

1 teaspoon salt

12 cracks black pepper

Pulse the pork in a food processor until smooth and transfer to a medium bowl. Mix the pork well with the remaining ingredients, form into a block, and wrap it tightly with plastic wrap. Store in the freezer up to 2 months.

TOMATO AND CINNAMON–BRAISED TRIPE

Brought to Sicily by Arab conquerors, cinnamon gives this soft wintery tripe stew its underlying warmth and spice. It also helps balance the honeycombed stomach lining, whose aroma and flavor can be a bit of an acquired taste. We don't sell much tripe at the Club, maybe five orders a night, but its permanent place on the menu is nonnegotiable, as one of those old-school dishes that represent the neighborhood and community's past. Recently a member poked his head in the kitchen and told me the tripe gave him the chills because it reminded him so much of his grandmother's. Our three-day process neutralizes a lot of tripe's innate funk. It soaks in milk for a day, brines for another, then gets boiled until tender and stewed with tomatoes, onions, herbs, Parmigiano rind, and the aforementioned cinnamon. The tripe almost melts into the sauce, perfect for scooping up with Sesame Semolina Bread (page 26).

SERVES 4

SOAKING AND BRINING THE TRIPE

- 4 pounds (2 kg) beef tripe, rinsed well
- 2 quarts (2 L) whole milk
- 3 sprigs fresh parsley
- 3 sprigs rosemary
- 3 sprigs oregano
- 3 sprigs basil
- 1 bay leaf
- 1 Arbol chile
- 1 lemon, halved
- 1 teaspoon black peppercorns
- 2 garlic cloves, smashed
- ½ yellow onion
- 5 tablespoons (75 g) granulated sugar
- 13 tablespoons (114 g) kosher salt
- 1 quart (1 L) ice water

Combine the tripe and milk in a large container. Weigh it down with a plate to keep it submerged, cover, and refrigerate for 8 hours, or overnight.

The following day, fill a pot with the 1 quart (1 L) of fresh water and add the herbs, chile, lemon, peppercorns, garlic, onion, sugar, and kosher salt. Set the pot over medium-low heat and simmer until the sugar and salt are dissolved. Place the ice water in a container large enough to fit the tripe. Pour the hot brine into the ice water and stir until chilled. Remove the tripe from the milk, rinse well under cool running water, and add it to the brine. Be sure the tripe is fully submerged, covering with a plate if necessary to keep it under the surface of the brine. Cover the container and refrigerate for 24 hours.

BRAISING THE TRIPE

- ½ yellow onion
- 2 garlic cloves, smashed
- 1 lemon, halved
- 1 Arbol chile
- 1 bay leaf
- 3 sprigs rosemary
- 3 sprigs oregano
- 3 sprigs parsley
- 3 sprigs basil
- 1 tablespoon white wine vinegar
- 1 tablespoon granulated sugar
- 1 teaspoon kosher salt
- 1 gallon (4 L) water

The following day, bring all the braising ingredients to a simmer in a large Dutch oven over medium-high heat. Add the brined tripe, weigh it down with a plate to keep it submerged, and simmer until tender. Begin testing for tenderness at 3 hours; it may take up to 4. Top up with water, if necessary. Let cool to room temperature.

STEWING THE TRIPE

- 1 (28 ounce [794 g]) can whole peeled tomatoes
- 1 teaspoon salt
- 10 cracks black pepper
- ¼ teaspoon sugar (optional)
- 3 sprigs rosemary
- 3 sprigs oregano
- 3 sprigs basil
- 3 sprigs parsley
- ¼ cup (59 ml) extra-virgin olive oil
- 1 yellow onion, thinly sliced
- 1 red onion, thinly sliced
- 4 garlic cloves, thinly sliced, plus 1 teaspoon chopped
- ½ cinnamon stick
- ½ Arbol chile
- 1 bay leaf
- 1 small beef bone, about 4 ounces (113 g)
- 3 ounces (85 g) Parmigiano-Reggiano rind
- 1 teaspoon dried oregano
- 1 tablespoon tomato paste
- ½ cup (118 ml) Chablis
- 2 cups (473 ml) water
- Grated Parmigiano-Reggiano for serving
- Sesame Semolina Bread (page 26) for serving

Combine the tomatoes, salt, pepper, and sugar (if needed) in a medium bowl and crush the tomatoes as much as possible with your hands. Set aside.

Tie all the fresh herbs into a bundle with kitchen twine and place in a large Dutch oven along with the olive oil, onions, sliced garlic, cinnamon stick, chile, bay leaf, beef bone, and Parmigiano rind. Sweat over low heat until the onions are soft and translucent, about 10 minutes. Meanwhile, cut the braised tripe into 1 x ½-inch (1.5 x 1.3 cm) pieces and toss in a bowl with the chopped garlic and dried oregano. Once the onions have finished cooking, make space in the pot and add the tomato paste. Cook until it turns from bright red to copper, about 3 minutes. Add the chopped seasoned tripe, stir to combine, and increase the heat to medium. Add the wine and reduce until completely evaporated. Add the crushed seasoned tomatoes and water. Lower the heat to low and simmer, covered, until the mixture takes on a stewlike consistency, about 2 hours. Remove the cinnamon stick, bay leaf, herb bundle, and beef bone. (If there's any meat on the bone, shred and add it back to the pot.) Garnish with grated Parmigiano and serve with grilled semolina bread.

SWEET FENNEL SAUSAGE

We tested so many sausage recipes before opening the Club, tweaking the seasonings and meat-to-fat ratio for weeks. Instead of adding spices to the sausage mix, we introduce flavor by marinating the pork shoulder in aromatics: garlic, fennel seeds, bay leaves, red pepper flakes, black pepper, and a glug of Sangiovese, which adds a winey kick to the finished product. Make sure all your equipment is very cold before grinding. The fatback should be frozen so it doesn't smear and clog the grinder or melt in the mixing bowl. Once ground, you can use the loose sausage immediately. Form it into patties or add it to the Meat Ragu (page 55). Brown it to bulk up the filling of the Stuffed Peppers (page 93) or toss it with orecchiette and Garlic-Chile Broccoli Rabe (page 99) for a classic pasta. That said, this recipe calls for casing, but know that if it doesn't go according to plan, you have options. It helps to have a sous chef to assist with the casing, especially if you haven't done this before.

Once cased, the best way to cook the sausage is to bake it in the oven 80 percent of the way before hitting the grill, which is how we do it at the Club. If we were cooking the sausage all the way through on the grill, it would take up valuable space on that station for over twenty minutes. This method cuts the grill time to four minutes, one of the rare restaurant shortcuts that translates well to home cooking. Prebaking also pulls out some of the fat, which minimizes split casings and flare-ups on the grill. Too cold to grill? You can cook this sausage completely in the oven. It's also wonderful simmered in a pot of bubbling Marinara (page 54).

SERVES 6 TO 8

- **1½ pounds (680 g) pork shoulder, trimmed of fat and diced into ½-inch (1.3 cm) pieces**
- **2 bay leaves**
- **¾ tablespoon salt**
- **1½ teaspoons red pepper flakes**
- **1 garlic clove, minced**
- **1 tablespoon fennel seeds**
- **20 cracks black pepper**
- **3 ounces (89 ml) Sangiovese**
- **8 ounces (227 g) fatback, diced in ½-inch (1.3 cm) pieces**
- **6 ounces (170 g) hog casing, defrosted**
- **Canola oil for grill**
- **Extra-virgin olive oil for serving**
- **Garlic-Chile Broccoli Rabe (page 99) for serving**
- **8 oil-packed Calabrian chiles for serving**

Mix the pork shoulder with the bay leaves, salt, red pepper flakes, garlic, fennel seeds, and black pepper and allow to sit at room temperature for 20 minutes. Add the wine, cover the bowl with plastic wrap, and marinate overnight in the refrigerator. Freeze the fatback overnight, along with all parts of a stand mixer's meat grinder attachment fitted with the coarse die.

Chill a bowl for 30 minutes. Remove the shoulder from the fridge and discard the bay leaves. Remove the fatback and the grinder attachment from the freezer. Grind the fatback and the marinated shoulder through the coarse die into the chilled bowl; the meat should not smear. Cover the bowl with plastic wrap and refrigerate while preparing the casing. Rinse the casing thoroughly in cold water. Assemble the sausage stuffer. Tie 1 end of the casing and fit it over the tube. Have a partner add the meat to the top of the stuffer and as it is pressed through, hold the casing firmly while allowing some slight slack. Fill the casing as tightly as possible, coiling the sausage as you go until all the meat is inside, then tie off the end.

Preheat the oven to 425°F (220°C) and a grill to medium-high. Oil the grill grates. Cook the sausage on a baking sheet in the oven for 6 to 8 minutes, until firm to the touch, then transfer to the grill. Grill over direct heat, watching for flare-ups, for 2 minutes per side. Remove from the grill and let rest for 5 minutes. Slice the sausage into big pieces and drizzle with olive oil. Serve with broccoli rabe and chiles.

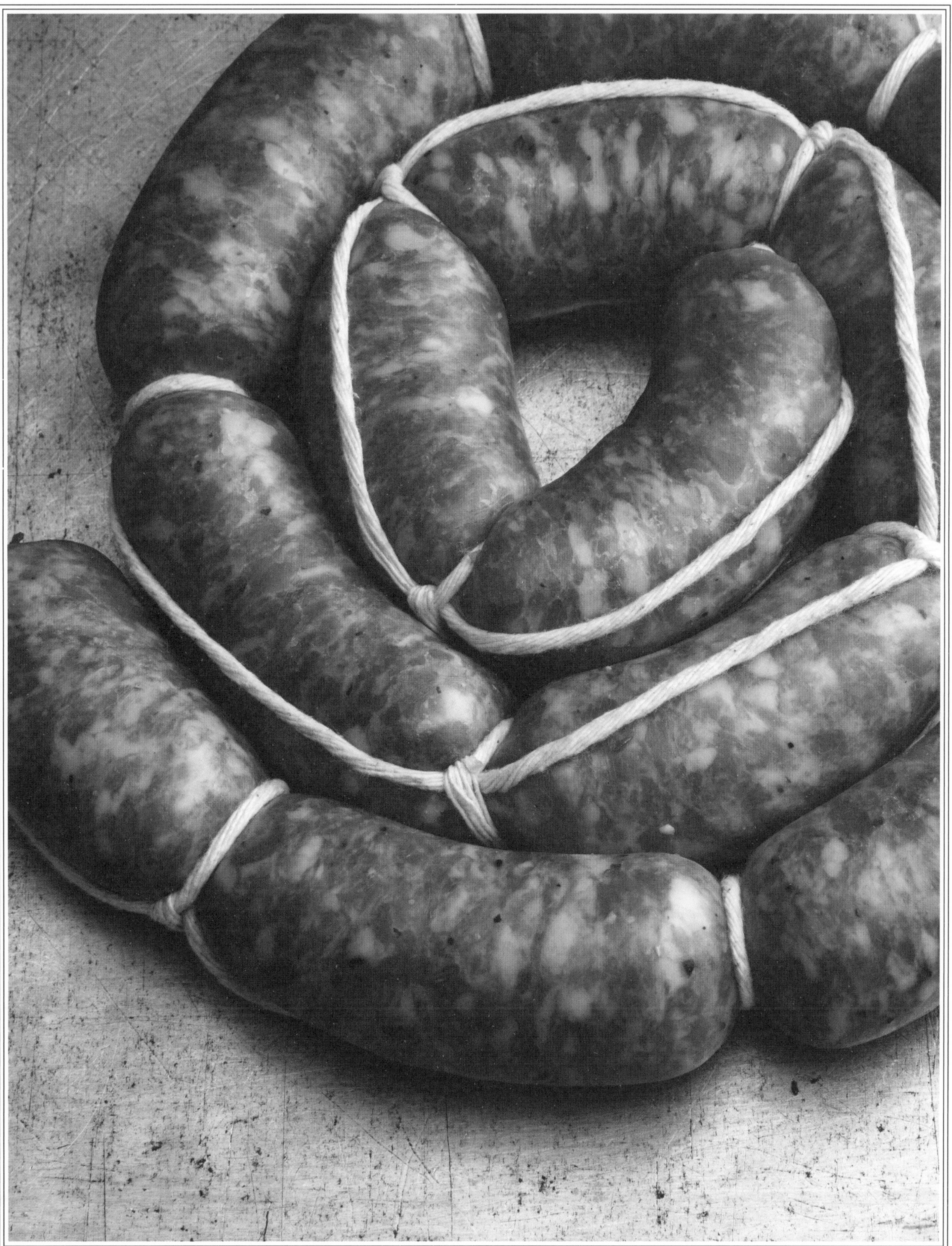

BRAISED RABBIT WITH TOMATO AND OREGANO

Rabbits rule Ischia. They're everywhere on the island, which sits right off the coast of Naples, and appear often in its traditional cuisine. I first had a version of this dish in Ischia and immediately began breaking it down and putting it back together as soon as I got back to Philly. First, we used whole rabbits, but because each part of the animal cooks differently (and there are so many tiny bones in the rib cage), we couldn't get it exactly right. Now we do it with legs only, and the results are much neater and more consistent. (We get them from D'Artagnan, which ships fresh rabbit all over the country.) An overnight salt cure puts seasoning *into* the mildly flavored meat while pulling moisture *out of* the surface of the meat, which makes for better browning before we braise the rabbit with tomatoes and oregano. That herb, overlooked in so many pizzeria shakers, forms the critical bookends to the entire dish. You have dried oregano in the cure that goes on the rabbit, zesty and familiar, in the beginning. And you have the velvety fresh leaves, wild and pungent and bright, finishing the dish. The aroma hits you as soon as you lift your first forkful and keeps pulling you back for more.

SERVES 4

6 garlic cloves, divided

4 skinned rabbit legs

¼ teaspoon dried oregano

1½ teaspoons kosher salt

22 cracks black pepper, divided

1 (28 ounce [794 g]) can whole peeled tomatoes

1 teaspoon salt

¼ teaspoon granulated sugar (optional)

2 sprigs parsley

2 sprigs oregano, plus fresh leaves for serving

2 sprigs rosemary

¼ cup (59 ml) extra-virgin olive oil

1 tablespoon unsalted butter

1 small yellow onion, thinly sliced

1 small red onion, thinly sliced

Pinch of red pepper flakes

¼ cup (59 ml) Chablis

½ cup (118 ml) water

Smash 2 of the garlic cloves with the side of a knife. Rub the rabbit with the garlic, oregano, kosher salt, and 12 cracks of the pepper, drape with a clean towel, and refrigerate overnight.

Remove the rabbit from the fridge, discard the garlic, and allow the rabbit to come to room temperature. Meanwhile, combine the tomatoes, salt, sugar (if needed), and remaining 10 cracks of black pepper in a medium bowl and crush the tomatoes as much as possible with your hands. Tie the herbs into a bundle with kitchen twine. Thinly slice the remaining 4 garlic cloves.

Preheat the oven to 350°F (180°C). When the rabbit is at room temperature, heat the olive oil in a large Dutch oven over medium heat until shimmering. Add the rabbit legs to the pan and sear for 5 minutes, or until golden brown. Flip and add the butter, then sear for 5 additional minutes, or until golden brown. Remove the legs and add the onions, sliced garlic, herb bundle, and red pepper flakes. Lower the heat to low and sweat the ingredients for 10 minutes. Add the wine and reduce until dry. Add the crushed seasoned tomatoes and the water, and add the rabbit back to the pot. Cook, covered, in the oven for 1½ hours, or until the legs are tender. Turn off the oven and let the pot sit in the oven for 15 minutes. Remove the pot from the oven and let the rabbit cool in the sauce. When cooled, remove the legs and set aside. Remove and discard the herb bundle. Using a food mill, grind the tomato sauce into a clean pot and set over medium-low heat. Add the rabbit legs and simmer until warmed through. Garnish with fresh oregano leaves and serve.

VEAL CUTLETS

Where the service station is at the Club now, Uncle Ernie had a long banquet table always set up. That table was always in the process of being depleted and replenished with food. Round and round that cycle went, any given Sunday. Piles of cutlets, chicken or veal, were regulars on the table, paved in breadcrumbs and fried in the back in a stovetop skillet of oil. The guys would drop a couple of bucks, grab a short stack of cutlets, and burn through them in minutes. Even today, when we run these veal cutlets on special, they're our biggest seller. Members will ask Guido Martelli, our manager, to call them when cutlets go on the menu. He does, and they come. We'll sell thirty orders a night (a lot for a restaurant that only seats thirty).

What makes them so good? The Parmigiano and oregano in our breadcrumbs, maybe, or the way we pound the veal enough to make it tender but not to dry it out. I think, more so, it's a nostalgia thing. Many of our members have personal connections to the foods we cook here. Any South Philly butcher shop with even a passing connection to Italy sells cutlets, both pounded for breading at home and already breaded for cooks in a hurry. Corner stores and delis stack golden fried cutlets by the register; they make outstanding on-the-go snacks. The luckiest kid in the lunchroom at Saint Monica's, the elementary school in one of the more ironclad Italian American neighborhoods downtown, is unwrapping an aluminum foil envelope of last night's chicken cutlets right now. Our approach at the Club is to take a culturally meaningful, beloved dish like this, and make the best version of it you've ever had.

We serve our veal cutlets topped with fresh tomato salad and grated sharp provolone, both of which bring acid and sharpness to balance the breading and fat. Garlic-Chile Broccoli Rabe (page 99) or Tomato Panzanella (page 51) make two other excellent pairings, or top them with Marinara (page 54) and fresh mozzarella and run them under the broiler for veal parm. If veal's not your thing, this recipe works exactly the same with boneless skinless chicken breasts. That's what most South Philly home cooks use anyway.

SERVES 2

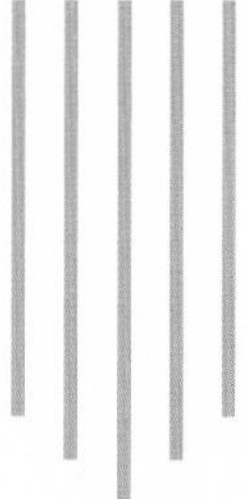

(recipe continues)

TOMATO SALAD

- 3 tomatoes, cored and quartered
- 6 cracks black pepper
- 5 fresh basil leaves, torn
- ¼ teaspoon salt
- 1 tablespoon finely diced red onion
- 1 tablespoon red wine vinegar
- 3 tablespoons extra-virgin olive oil

Combine the tomatoes, black pepper, basil, and salt in a medium bowl and let them sit for 5 minutes at room temperature. Add the red onion, vinegar, and olive oil, toss to stir to combine, and set aside at room temperature.

VEAL CUTLETS

- 2 veal cutlets, 6 ounces (170 g) each
- ½ cup (25 g) Club Rub (page 102)
- ½ lemon, thinly sliced
- 4 bay leaves
- ½ cup (118 ml) blended oil (see page 19)
- ¼ cup (35 g) 00 flour
- 2 large eggs, beaten
- 1 cup (108 g) Cutlet Crumbs (page 83)
- ¼ teaspoon salt
- 2 cracks black pepper
- Grated sharp provolone for serving
- Extra-virgin olive oil for serving

Lay out the cutlets on a cutting board between 2 pieces of plastic wrap. Pound each side of the cutlets with a meat mallet until very thin. Remove the plastic and sprinkle the cutlets on both sides with the rub. Lay the lemon slices and bay leaves on top of 1 cutlet, then lay the other cutlet on top, like a sandwich. Allow them to sit at room temperature for 5 minutes.

Set up a baking sheet lined with paper towels. Heat the blended oil in a large skillet over medium heat to 350°F (180°C). (The skillet should be large enough to fit both cutlets without touching. Alternatively, you can use a smaller skillet and fry them 1 at a time.) Set up a breading station, with the flour, eggs, and cutlet crumbs in separate medium bowls. Using 1 hand for the flour and the other for the egg, lightly dust 1 cutlet in the flour and shake off any excess. Submerge the floured cutlet in the eggs, then press it into the crumbs, making sure it's completely covered. Repeat the process for the other cutlet. Gently lower the cutlets into the hot oil. Fry until golden brown on the bottom, about 2 minutes. Flip and fry for another 2 minutes. Transfer the cutlets to the prepared pan and season with the salt on both sides and the pepper on 1 side. Serve on a platter topped with tomato salad, grated sharp provolone, and a drizzle of olive oil.

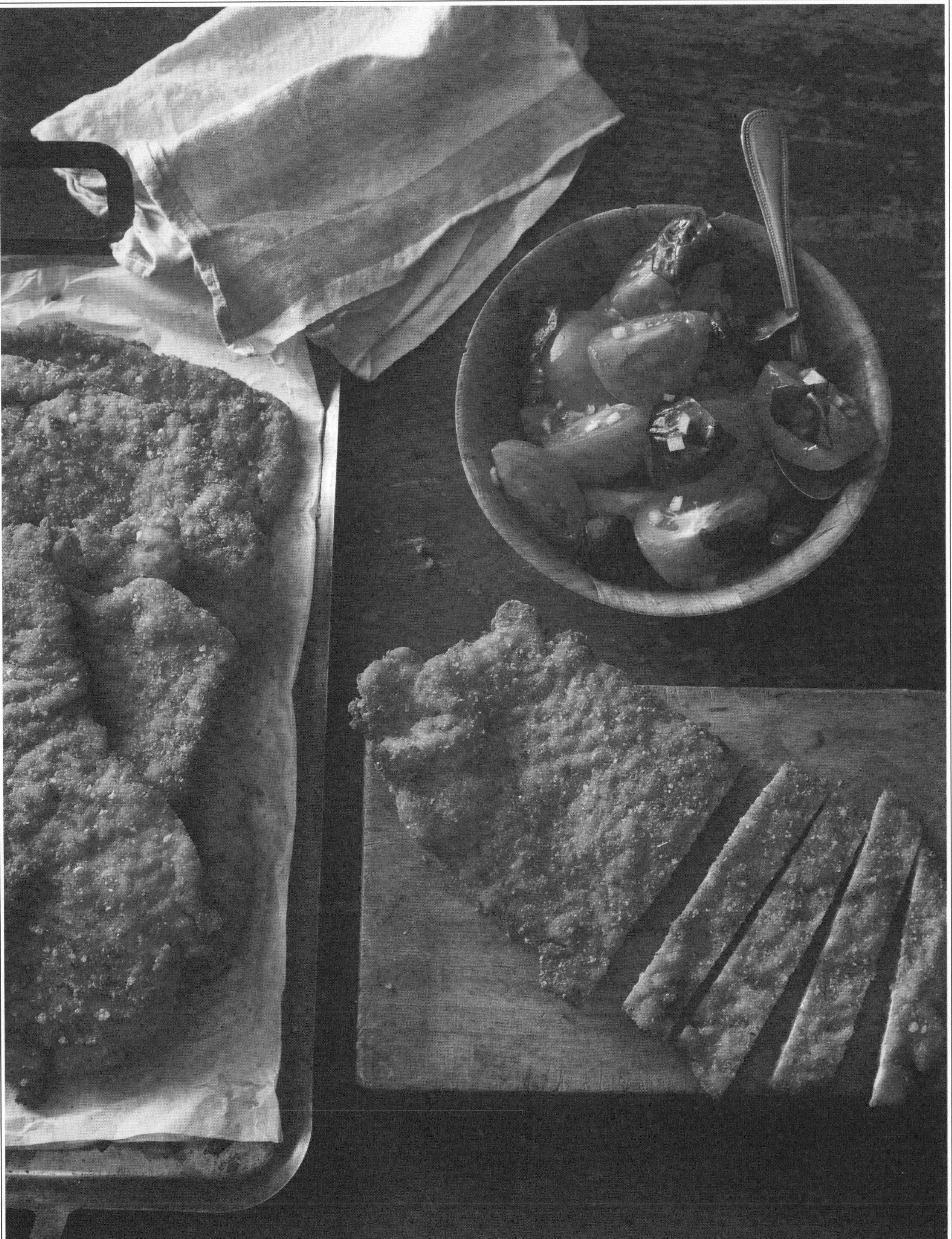

ROASTED CHICKEN

Moist meat. Skin that shines like gold foil. Tons of flavor. This superior roasted chicken has it all, with lemon, garlic, and fresh herbs like rosemary and sage reinforced through the recipe to create strokes of brightness, sweetness, woodsiness. We take a couple extra steps to ensure our bird comes out juicy inside and crisp outside. Size matters: as close to 4 pounds as you can get. We soak the chicken in a short brine, which typically I'm not a fan of, but it makes a difference here. Twelve to eighteen hours will get you there; anything longer will make the meat spongy. We also stuff the bird and inject a garlic-herb butter under the skin, which bastes the breasts from the inside out as the chicken roasts. Remember to rest the finished chicken for at least 25 minutes before carving. It will hold its heat with no problem, and the juices will have a chance to redistribute through the bird. Serve the chicken with Garlic-Chile Broccoli Rabe (page 99) for a heartier dinner plate, or pair with the Fennel and Orange Salad (page 44) for something fresher and lighter.

SERVES 4

- **1 quart (1 L) water**
- **2 heads garlic, halved, divided, plus 2 cloves, smashed**
- **1 yellow onion, thinly sliced**
- **26 sprigs sage, divided**
- **26 sprigs parsley, divided**
- **2 black peppercorns**
- **2 bay leaves**
- **½ cup (100 g) granulated sugar**
- **¾ cup (105 g) kosher salt**
- **3 lemons, halved, with one half cut in wedges for serving**
- **3 quarts (3 L) ice water**
- **1 (4-pound [1.8 kg]) fresh whole chicken**
- **8 tablespoons (113 g) unsalted butter**
- **6 sprigs rosemary, divided**
- **1 tablespoon salt**
- **30 cracks black pepper**

Combine the water with 1 halved head of the garlic, the onion, 20 sprigs each of the sage and parsley, and the peppercorns, bay leaves, sugar, and kosher salt in a medium pot. Squeeze the juice from and drop 2 of the lemons into the pot. Bring to a simmer over medium heat, stirring to completely dissolve the sugar and salt. Add the ice water to a stockpot and pour the hot brine over it. Stir until the liquid is cold. Submerge the chicken in the pot of brine, using a plate if necessary to keep it below the surface. Cover and transfer the pot to the fridge and brine for 12 to 18 hours.

After brining, remove the chicken from the liquid and let it come to room temperature, about 1 hour. After the chicken has rested for 50 minutes, preheat the oven to 500°F (260°C). Melt the butter in a skillet with the garlic cloves and 3 sprigs each of rosemary, sage, and parsley over low heat. Cook until the mixture starts to become fragrant, about 5 minutes, remove from the heat, and allow to cool. Remove and discard the herbs and garlic.

Using a flavor injector, pump 1 ounce (30 ml) of the melted garlic-herb butter into each breast and thigh. Place the chicken in a roasting pan, breast-side up, and stuff the cavity with the remaining 3 sprigs each of herbs, the remaining halved garlic head, and the remaining half lemon. Rub the chicken with the salt and pepper. Place the pan on the middle rack and roast for 15 minutes. Lower the temperature to 350°F (180°C) and continue to roast for 30 to 35 minutes, or until the skin becomes brown and crispy and the internal temperature reads 165°F (74°C) on an instant-read thermometer. Remove the chicken from the oven and let rest for 25 minutes. Carve, pour the pan jus over the pieces, and serve with lemon wedges.

GRILLED LAMB CHOPS

Very few houses in South Philly are blessed with a big backyard. You usually get an 8 x 10 patch of concrete framed by cinderblock or chain-link fences, about enough room for a patio set, some tomato plants or if you're lucky a fig tree, and a grill. Since the Club lives in a row home in the middle of a residential block, it's got the same backyard situation, small but big enough for my Uncle Ernie to tend a drum of glowing charcoal in the muggy summers.

Grilling was a huge thing here: sausage, pork chops, burgers, chicken breasts, and always lamb chops. When I reopened the Club, I knew I wanted to carry on that tradition. I installed a professional kitchen grill where we cook a handful of dishes, such as the Grilled Octopus (page 103), Grilled Swordfish Spiedini (page 102), and these lamb chops. I don't think the health department would be too happy if I was doing it in the yard. These are some of the simplest dishes we prepare, but also some of the most complicated. Live fire is temperamental. You need to know when to rotate, when to flip, where your hot spots are, when to pull the meat. It's very technical, but here's a tip: When you see the surface of these chops begin to glisten, then you know the juices are flowing and the lamb is just about done. Pull it then and let it rest.

This recipe calls for cooking the chops just to medium. Lamb has a lot of fat, and you need extra time for that fat to melt into the meat. But it's all up to your preference. Whenever I grill at home and my parents come over, I have to do the meat on two separate plates. You won't see even the tiniest drop of juice on my dad's plate of well-done meat. My mom's, meanwhile, is a pool of blood. When they come into the Club and my dad orders the lamb chops, my guys will be getting ready to plate, and I invariably have to tell them, no, no, put it back on the grill, otherwise it's coming back. This might not be a popular opinion among chefs, but I think we're here to learn those individual preferences and cook for people in whatever way will make them happy. Even if that means cooking the lamb a bit more.

SERVES 4

1 (2-pound [907 g]) rack of lamb, cut into 8 single chops

¼ lemon, thinly sliced in half-moons

3 sprigs rosemary

1 oil-packed anchovy fillet, smashed into a paste

8 bay leaves

½ cup (25 g) Club Rub (page 102)

2 tablespoons blended oil (see page 19)

1 tablespoon salt

32 cracks black pepper

Salsa Verde (page 35) for serving

Get a grill very hot. Meanwhile, combine the lamb, lemon slices, rosemary, anchovy, bay leaves, and rub in a medium bowl and mix well, being sure to massage the rub into the meat. Allow the marinated chops to sit at room temperature for 15 minutes. Add the oil and toss to coat. Transfer the chops to a baking sheet lined with parchment and season with the salt and pepper (2 cracks of pepper per side) on both sides. Grill the chops over direct heat for 3 minutes, rotating a quarter turn halfway through cooking to create crisscrossed grill marks. Flip and repeat on the other side, then move the chops to a cooler part of the grill and finish cooking until they are at medium doneness, about 5 minutes. Serve with salsa verde.

CHINOTTO RIBS

Pork has always been part of the Club, a tradition we carry on with these spareribs, which we run frequently as a special. They're a tribute to my uncle—he loved pork—but also my mom, who always slips a dose of Coca-Cola into her ribs at home. As they cook, the soda bastes the pork and creates a sweet glaze. To keep thematic with our heritage and our amari-focused bar, I thought, why not try it with Chinotto? Made by Pellegrino, this fizzy Italian soda tastes like a cross between Campari and Dr Pepper, and reduces down into a thick, bittersweet syrup so shiny you can see your reflection in it. In addition to these ribs, it's great as a glaze for ham or pork chops.

SERVES 4

BRINING THE RIBS

- 2 racks St. Louis–style ribs, about 5 pounds (2.3 kg) total
- 1 quart (1 L) water
- 1 cup (140 g) kosher salt
- ½ cup (100 g) granulated sugar
- 15 whole black peppercorns
- 2 Arbol chiles
- 2 bay leaves
- Fistful of fresh sage
- 3 sprigs rosemary
- Fistful of fresh parsley
- 2 tablespoons toasted fennel seeds
- 1 orange, halved
- 1 onion, halved
- 1 head garlic, halved
- 3 quarts (3 L) ice water

Combine all the brine ingredients, except the ice water, in a stockpot. Bring to a simmer while stirring to dissolve the salt and sugar. Meanwhile, put the ice water in a lidded container large enough to fit the ribs and all the liquid. Remove the ribs from the brine. Transfer the brine to the container of ice water and stir until everything is cold. Add the ribs to the container and cover with dinner plates to keep the meat submerged. Cover the container and brine for 48 hours in the refrigerator.

BRAISING THE RIBS

- 2 (6.75-ounce [200 ml]) bottles Chinotto soda
- 1 orange, halved
- 1 fistful fresh sage
- 1 fistful fresh parsley
- 3 sprigs fresh rosemary
- 1 head garlic, halved
- 1 yellow onion, halved
- 10 whole black peppercorns
- 2 bay leaves
- ¾ cup (355 ml) water

Preheat the oven to 325°F (170°C). Combine the Chinotto, the halved orange, herbs, garlic, onion, peppercorns, bay leaves, and water in the bottom of a roasting pan. Arrange the brined ribs on top. Place a layer of parchment paper directly over the ribs and wrap the pan tightly in 2 layers of aluminum foil. Bake for 2½ hours, or until a knife easily pierces the meat. Remove the pan from the oven and let cool for 1 hour, or until the contents reach room temperature. Rest the ribs in their cooking liquid overnight in the fridge.

GRILLING AND GLAZING THE RIBS

- 4 (6.75-ounce [200 ml]) bottles Chinotto soda
- ¼ cup (59 ml) white wine vinegar
- ¼ cup (78 g) honey
- Oil for grill
- Orange wedges for serving

Remove the ribs from their cooking liquid and brush off any aromatics sticking to them, as well as any congealed fat. Strain the liquid through a chinois, pushing through as much as possible with the back of a ladle. Reserve the liquid and discard the solids. Add the Chinotto to a large Dutch oven set over medium heat. Reduce the soda to a syrup, about 15 minutes. Add the reserved cooking liquid and bring to a simmer. Continue to cook until the liquid is reduced by half, 30 to 40 minutes. Stir in the vinegar and honey and keep the glaze warm.

Get a grill with well-oiled grates to medium heat. Place the ribs, meat-side down, over indirect heat and brush with the Chinotto glaze. Close the grill and let the ribs heat through for 8 minutes. Flip and brush the ribs with the glaze. Close the grill and cook for 8 more minutes. Increase the heat to medium-high. Carefully flip the ribs, placing over direct heat for 2 to 4 minutes. Brush the ribs with the glaze and flip again. Close the grill and cook for 2 more minutes, after which the ribs should be hot inside and appear crisp and caramelized on the outside. Remove the ribs and serve with orange slices and extra glaze.

STEAK PIZZAIOLA

Steak pizzaiola is always a big hit when we special it at the Club, but it's also a quick and easy dinner to cook at home. *Pizzaiola* means "in the style of the pizza maker." The story goes that at the end of his night, when he was done making his pies, the pizza maker would head home and his wife would cook him a steak with the leftover sauce from the pizza, extra fragrant with oregano and garlic. It's just a few ingredients, so make them the best you can afford. I like rib eye here, but the recipe also works well with sirloin and strip.

SERVES 2 TO 4

2 tablespoons extra-virgin olive oil, plus more for serving

2 rib-eye steaks, about 14 ounces (397 g) each, cut ½ inch (1.3 cm) thick

1½ teaspoons salt

20 cracks black pepper

2 garlic cloves, very thinly sliced

Pinch of red pepper flakes

1 sprig basil

1 cup (225 g) Marinara (page 54)

1 teaspoon dried oregano

Heat the olive oil in a large, heavy-bottomed sauté pan over medium-high heat. While the oil is heating, season the steaks on both sides with the salt and black pepper. When the oil is shimmering, add the steaks and increase the heat to high. Once the steaks are browned on 1 side, 4 to 6 minutes, gently flip them and drain off half the oil. Make some space in the pan, lower the heat to medium, and add the garlic. Continue to cook until the garlic is translucent and fragrant but not browned, about 1 minute. Add the red pepper flakes and basil and continue to cook for 30 seconds. Stir in the marinara and oregano and lower the heat to medium-low. Cook the sauce and steaks until the steaks reach 145°F (63°C) (medium-rare) on an instant-read thermometer, 2 to 4 minutes. Remove and discard the basil. Transfer the steaks to a serving platter and pour the sauce over the top. Drizzle with olive oil and serve.

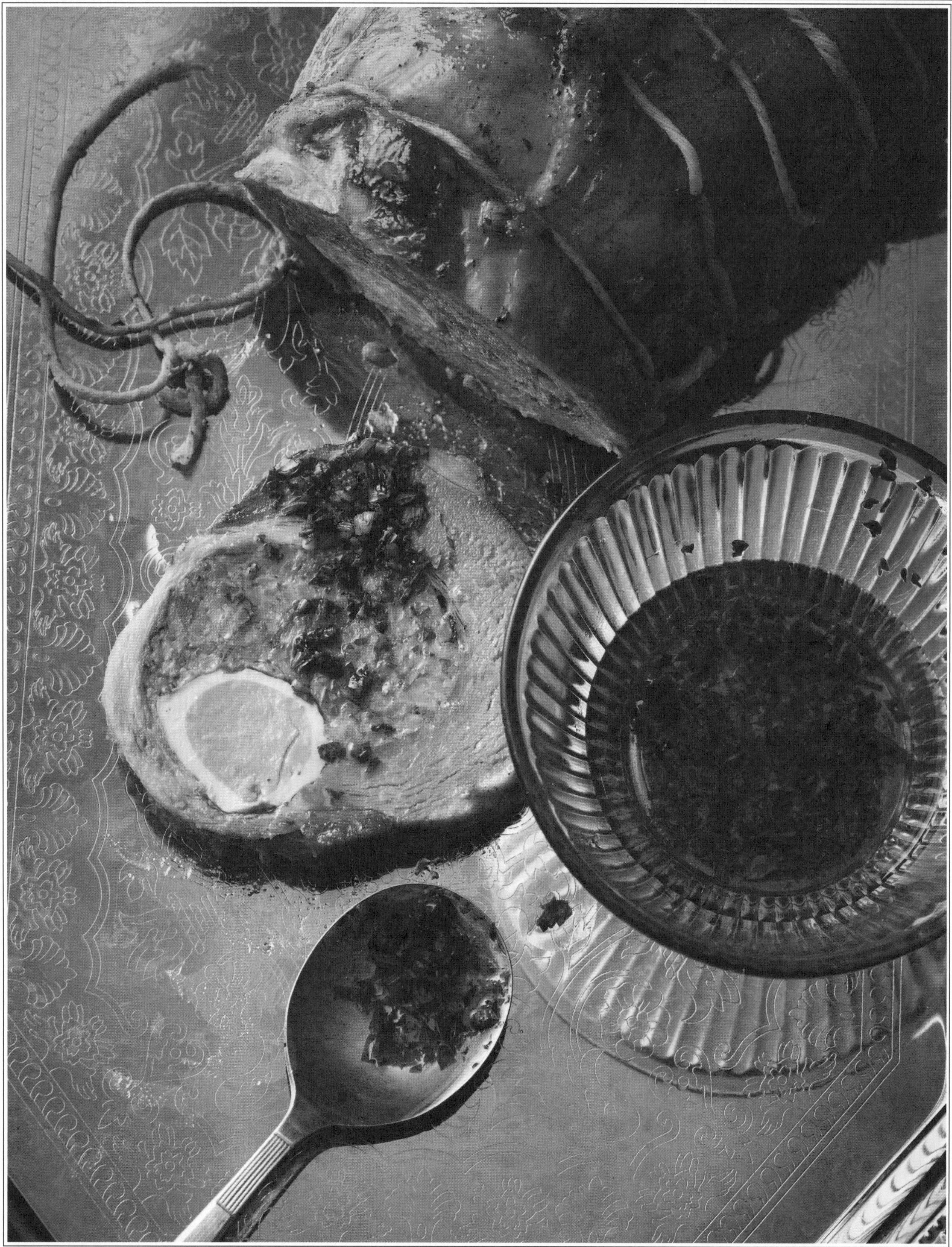

PANZETTA

When Braciole (page 133) won't cut it for a crowd, it's time to break out this slowly roasted, brawny, boned-out breast of veal stuffed with mortadella risotto and hard-boiled eggs. We know this dish by its Calabrese dialect name, *panzetta*, but it's basically a supersize braciola perfect for feeding a big group, whether you're hosting a holiday or dinner party or random get-together. You can stuff and roll it ahead time, then roast it off when people come over, or take the dish all the way to completion and reheat it in the oven before slicing and serving: the timeline is flexible. When buying the meat for this dish, ask your butcher to debone a 4-pound veal breast, and make sure he or she gives you the bone; it's key for flavoring the sauce as the veal roasts.

SERVES 10

(recipe continues)

PREPPING THE VEAL

- 4 pounds (1.8 kg) deboned veal breast, with bone reserved
- 1 tablespoon salt
- 40 cracks black pepper
- 1 cup (50 g) Club Rub (page 102)
- 5 bay leaves
- 1 sprig rosemary
- 1 sprig sage

Pound the breast between 2 pieces of plastic wrap to 1 inch (2.5 cm) thick. Season each side evenly with the salt and pepper. Massage the rub onto the veal, top with the bay leaves and herbs, and wrap with plastic wrap. Refrigerate overnight.

RISOTTO STUFFING

- ½ yellow onion, finely diced
- 3 garlic cloves, finely chopped, divided
- 1 bay leaf
- 2 tablespoons extra-virgin olive oil
- ¾ cup (143 g) uncooked arborio rice
- 3 tablespoons Chablis
- 1 quart (1 L) water
- 3½ teaspoons salt, divided
- 2 large eggs
- 2 cups (260 g) diced mortadella, finely ground in a food processor
- 8 ounces (227 g) ground veal
- ¾ cup (90 g) grated Parmigiano-Reggiano
- ½ cup (60 g) grated Caciocavallo cheese or mild provolone
- 1 cup (58 g) chopped fresh parsley leaves
- ¾ cup (94 g) plain breadcrumbs

Place the onion, 1 chopped garlic clove, and the bay leaf and olive oil in a large Dutch oven. Set the pot over low heat and sweat until the onion turns translucent, about 6 minutes. Increase the heat to medium-high and add the rice, stirring continuously until fragrant and toasted, about 4 minutes. Stir in the wine and cook until dry. Add the water, lower the heat to medium-low, and simmer for 20 minutes, or until the rice is tender. Stir in 1 tablespoon of the salt and pour the risotto onto a baking sheet to cool to room temperature. Transfer the cooled risotto to a large bowl. Add the remaining ½ teaspoon of salt, remaining 2 chopped garlic cloves, and the eggs, mortadella, ground veal, Parmigiano, Caciocavallo, parsley, and breadcrumbs and mix well. Set the stuffing aside at room temperature.

STUFFING AND ROASTING THE VEAL

- 10 large hard-boiled eggs (see page 50)
- Reserved veal bone
- 1 teaspoon salt
- 20 cracks black pepper
- 20 whole black peppercorns
- 2 bay leaves
- 2 Arbol chiles
- 1 yellow onion, halved
- 1 carrot
- 1 celery rib
- 1 head garlic, halved
- 3 sprigs rosemary
- 3 sprigs oregano
- 3 sprigs parsley
- 2 cups (473 ml) Chablis
- 2 cups (473 ml) water
- ½ cup (80 g) Lardo (page 135)
- Salsa Verde (page 35) for serving

Remove the marinated veal breast from the fridge, lay it out on a work surface, and remove the herbs and bay leaves. Add the risotto stuffing in an even layer across the breast, leaving a 2-inch (5 cm) border around all sides. Arrange the hard-boiled eggs, evenly spaced, on top of the stuffing. Tightly roll the breast, being careful not to squeeze the stuffing out of the ends. With the seam side down, tie 8 knots around the breast with kitchen twine to secure the roll. Close both of the ends of the rolled breast with 6 toothpicks each to prevent the rice from spilling out.

Preheat the oven to 325°F (170°C). Season the veal breast bone with the salt and pepper. Place the peppercorns, bay leaves, chiles, onion, carrot, celery, garlic, rosemary, oregano, parsley, wine, water, and the seasoned bone in the bottom of a large roasting pan. Place the stuffed veal breast on top, smear with the lardo, and cover with parchment, with the paper directly on top of the meat. Tightly wrap the pan in foil and roast for 4 hours, or until the fat has rendered and the meat is tender. Remove the pan from the oven, transfer the veal to a cutting board, and let rest for 20 minutes. Strain out the cooking liquid from the bottom of the pan and skim off the fat. If necessary, reduce in a small saucepot until thickened and shiny, while the veal rests. Keep the sauce warm. Cut the veal into thick slices and drizzle with the sauce. Serve with the remaining sauce and salsa verde.

WHOLE ROASTED SUCKLING PIG

Any big celebration at the Club automatically meant a pig. Young, roasted, and served whole. Sheathed in crispy skin. I used to sneak up and steal the ear; it's chewy, fatty, crackly, and still my favorite part. Continuing my uncle's tradition, this is our go-to for private events at the Club and while time-intensive, it's not very difficult to make at home. This recipe begins with a 10- to 15-pound suckling pig, which will fit in most home ovens without a problem. (For comparison, just picture your Thanksgiving turkey, which probably weighs about the same.) Any quality butcher shop should have no problem getting you one. The pig gets brined for three days and marinated for two, so plan accordingly. If you want to work way ahead, you can wrap the pig with plastic wrap and freeze after brining, then just pull it out three days before you want to cook it, thaw it completely, and proceed to marinating it.

After you roast and rest this beauty, put it on a long platter. Whoever you're cooking for is about to be very, very happy. We like to set this pig out with sandwich equipment: Sesame Semolina Bread (page 26), shaved sharp provolone, and Garlic-Chile Broccoli Rabe (page 99). Pick off all the leftover meat and pack it into quart-size containers. It'll keep for five days in the fridge, or you can freeze it. Even better, make Maiale Fritti (see sidebar, page 161).

SERVES 12

(recipe continues)

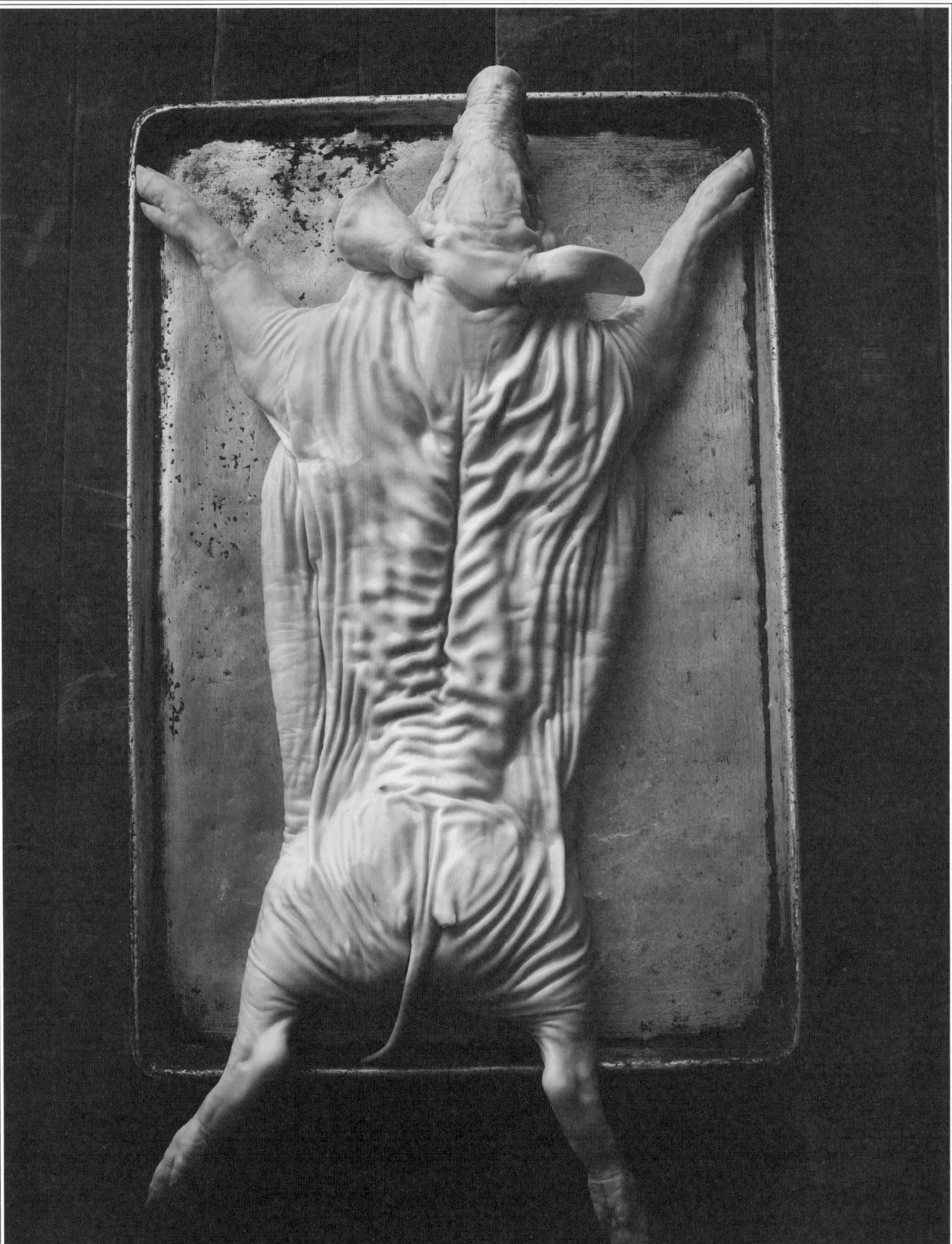

BRINING THE PIG

- 4 cups (560 g) kosher salt
- 2 cups (200 g) granulated sugar
- 2 oranges, halved
- ¼ cup (23 g) toasted fennel seeds
- 10 sprigs rosemary
- 10 sprigs parsley
- 2 tablespoons black peppercorns
- 2 Arbol chiles
- 2 heads garlic, halved
- 1 yellow onion, halved
- 3 tablespoons honey
- 2 cups (473 ml) Chablis
- 2 quarts (2 L) water
- 6 quarts (5.7 L) ice water
- 1 (10- to 15-pound [4.5 to 6.8 kg]) suckling pig

In a medium pot, combine the salt, sugar, oranges, fennel seeds, rosemary, parsley, peppercorns, chiles, garlic, onion, honey, wine, and water. Heat the ingredients over medium-low heat until the salt and sugar are completely dissolved, about 10 minutes. Be careful not to boil or reduce the brine. Place the ice water in a large pan measuring at least 21 x 13 x 6 inches (53 x 33 x 15 cm). Add the hot brine to the ice water and stir until cold. Rest the pig in the pan, making sure it's completely submerged. Cover the pan with cheesecloth and weigh down the surface with large dinner plates to keep the pig below the surface of the brine. Wrap the pan tightly with plastic wrap and refrigerate for 3 days.

MARINATING THE PIG

- 1 cup (58 g) chopped fresh parsley leaves
- 1 fennel frond, finely chopped
- 1 tablespoon ground toasted fennel seeds
- 2 tablespoons chopped garlic
- ¼ teaspoon red pepper flakes
- 40 cracks black pepper
- 1 cup (236 ml) extra-virgin olive oil

After 3 days, remove pig from the brine. Discard the brine and let the pig come to room temperature. Make the rub by whisking together all the marinating ingredients in a small bowl. Massage the marinade all over the outside and inside of the pig. Wrap tightly with plastic wrap and refrigerate for 2 days.

ROASTING THE PIG

- ½ bunch sage
- 1 fennel bulb, halved
- 1 yellow onion, halved
- 1 head garlic, halved
- 1 orange, halved
- 10 sprigs fresh parsley
- 10 sprigs fresh rosemary
- 1 Arbol chile
- 1 quart (1 L) water
- Garlic-Chile Broccoli Rabe (page 99) for serving
- Oil-packed Calabrian chiles for serving

Preheat the oven to 325°F (170°C). Place the sage, fennel, onion, garlic, orange, parsley, rosemary, Arbol chile, and water in a 21 x 13 x 6-inch (53 x 33 x 15 cm) pan. Unwrap the marinated pig and place on top. Place a piece of parchment paper over the top of the pig to cover completely, then wrap the pan tightly in 3 layers of aluminum foil. Roast in the oven for 3 to 4 hours. When the pig is ready, the skin will start to split and pull away from the bone and flesh should be fork-tender. Remove the foil and parchment and increase the heat to 350°F (180°C). Roast 15 to 20 minutes, or until the skin is golden brown. Remove the pan from the oven and let the pig rest in the liquid for 1 hour. Serve whole with broccoli rabe and Calabrian chiles.

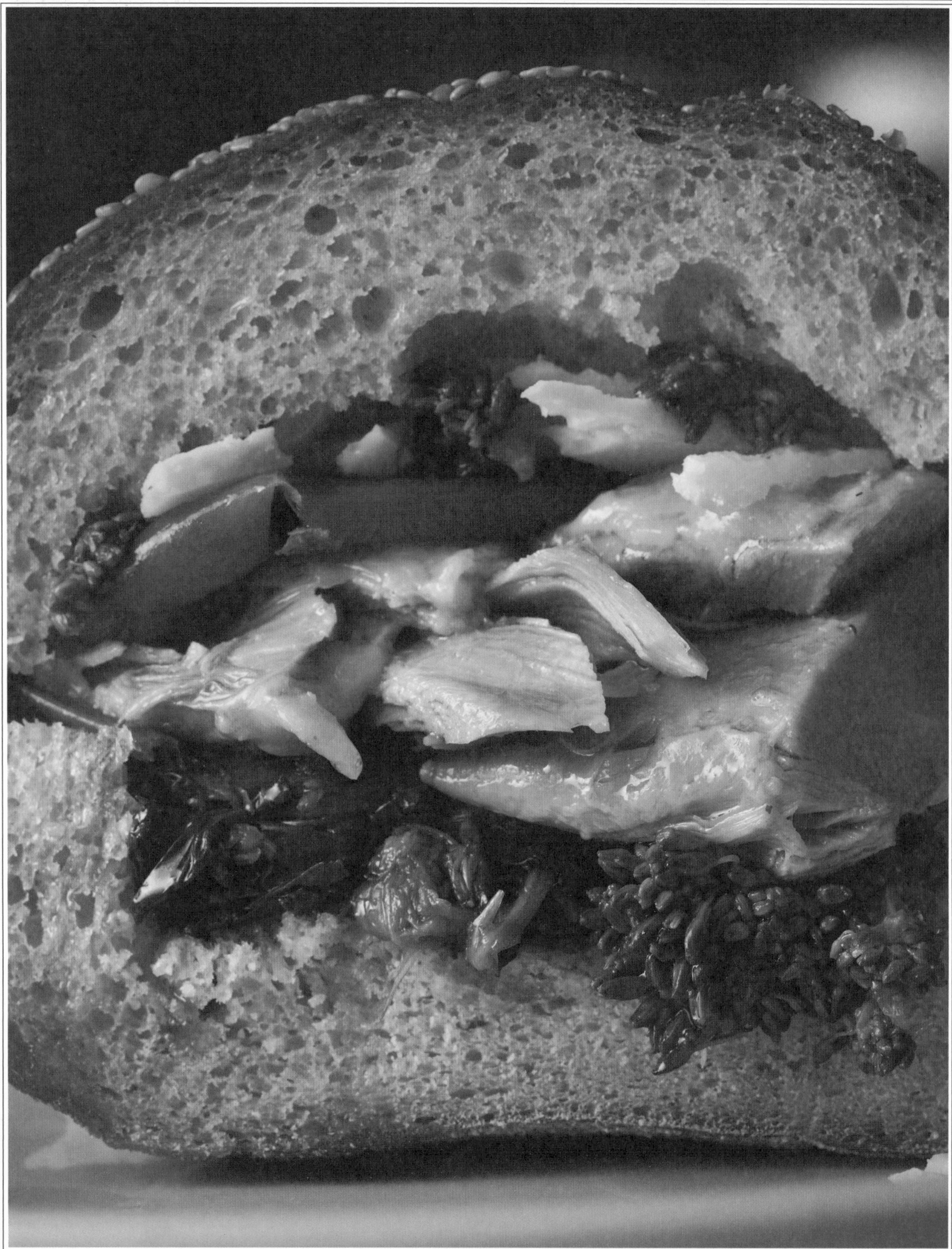

JOE G.'S MAIALE FRITTI

We have two Joes in the kitchen at the Club, me and my chef de cuisine, Joe Gugliuzza. Joe G. created these ingenious little snacks to use up leftovers from the whole pig. He makes these "fried pork" snacks by first separating the meat and the fat. He purées the fat in a food processor until smooth, then mixes it by hand with the picked meat and a spoonful of Club Rub (page 102). He presses that into a large roasting pan and weighs it down overnight in the fridge between pieces of plastic wrap. The following day, he cuts it into squares, prepares them with a standard flour-egg-breadcrumb breading (see Cutlet Crumbs, page 83), and deep-fries them until golden brown. Our staff devours the warm fritters with Salsa Verde (page 35) and Roasted Garlic Aioli (page 106) spiked with chopped capers.

COFFEE AND CAKE

EASTER BREAD

ESPRESSO GRANITA

CARAMEL GELATO

TROPICAL FRUIT SORBETTI

SPUMONI

LEMON CROSTATA

CHOCOLATE ALMOND CAKE

RICOTTA PIE

CINNAMON-SUGAR ZEPPOLI

CLASSIC CANNOLI

STRUFFOLI

HAZELNUT TORRONE

PIZZELLES

EASTER BREAD

Aunt Roma is the family baker. We wait all year long for Easter Sunday just to get this bread, a sweet yeasted and braided wreath glazed in white icing and decorated with rainbow sprinkles. The loaf winds around a hard-boiled egg, which signifies rebirth and the arrival of spring. Lots of the Italian bakeries in South Philly do a version of Easter bread; Faragalli's, for example, scents its bread with anise. Aunt Roma prefers a citrus profile, which we've re-created here with orange and lemon zests that balance the eggy, buttery richness of the plush, challah-like loaf. This recipe makes enough for two wreaths and can easily be divided in half, or make both and wrap and freeze the second loaf after baking; it'll keep for one month in the freezer. You want to eat this bread within a day of baking, as it can dry out quickly. I love it for breakfast with a swipe of soft, salty butter.

MAKES 2 LOAVES

1 cup (240 ml) plus 4½ teaspoons whole milk, divided

4 teaspoons (14 g) active dry yeast

7 tablespoons (82 g) granulated sugar, divided

1⅓ cups (184 g) bread flour

2½ cups (350 g) 00 flour

1 teaspoon salt

5 large eggs, divided

3 large egg yolks

½ cup plus 1 tablespoon (127 g) unsalted butter, at room temperature, plus more for pan

1½ tablespoons honey

¼ teaspoon grated lemon zest

¼ teaspoon grated orange zest

¼ cup (36 g) confectioners' sugar

Rainbow nonpareils for serving

Warm ¾ cup (180 ml) of the milk to just warm, not hot. Transfer it to a bowl and add the yeast and half of the granulated sugar. Allow the yeast to dissolve in the milk while preparing the remaining ingredients. Sift the flours, salt, and remaining granulated sugar and place them in the bowl of a stand mixer fitted with the dough hook. Beat 2 of the eggs and all the yolks in a small bowl and add to the dry ingredients, along with the butter, honey, and citrus zests. Mix on low speed until just combined, about 3 minutes. With the mixer still running, slowly add the milk mixture. When the dough comes together, increase the speed by 1 level and continue to mix for 8 minutes. The dough will be soft, elastic, and slightly sticky, but do not add more flour to it. Scrape the dough into a bowl, cover it with plastic wrap, and allow it to rest in a warm place until doubled in size, about 2 hours.

Place 2 of the eggs (in their shell) in a small pot and cover with cold water. Bring to a boil and start a timer for 8 minutes. Shock the eggs in ice water and place in the fridge.

After the dough has rested for 2 hours, divide it into 6 equal portions. Roll each portion into a snake roughly 24 inches (61 cm) long. Take 3 snakes of dough and arrange them so they meet at 1 end. Braid the 3 snakes and tuck the other ends underneath to create a round wreath. Place in a buttered baking pan and tuck a hard-boiled egg into part of the braid. Repeat the process for the other 3 snakes of dough. Wrap the pan with plastic wrap and allow it to rest in a warm area until doubled in size, about 2 hours.

Preheat the oven to 350°F (180°C). Place a small pan of water on the bottom rack of the oven for humidity. Beat the remaining egg and 1 tablespoon of the milk in a small bowl and brush the mixture onto the loaves. Bake the loaves on the middle rack for 15 minutes, rotate 180 degrees, and bake 15 minutes until golden brown. Remove from the oven and let cool completely.

Whisk the confectioners' sugar and remaining 1½ teaspoons of milk in a small bowl to create an icing. Brush the icing on the cooled loaves and dust with sprinkles. Slice and serve.

COFFEE AND CAKE

My mom has two older sisters, Mary and Roma, and they all lived within a block of one another. Our house and Aunt Mary's were roughly back to back. Our house was on Cross Street, a little street that runs crooked. Theirs was on 12th Street, where the homes are much wider and longer. So, our backyard basically faced their dining room window, and there was no fence or alley between us. Almost every night after dinner, we'd go over there for coffee and cake. I'd run out into the yard, Aunt Mary would open the window, and she or one of my cousins would bend down and lift me into the house.

Coffee and cake is the go-to casual gathering for Italian Americans of my parents' generation in South Philly. It's spur of the moment, relaxed, not a big to-do. If you have coffee and some type of baked good in the house, you can have people over. Your daughter is headed to the prom? Come over to see her and stay for coffee and cake. It's your cousin's birthday, but not a big-deal age that would warrant a full-on party? Coffee and cake, with a candle.

I can't overstate how pervasive this social tradition was for me growing up in South Philly. Being hospitable is a huge part of the culture. A lot of stereotypes about Italian Americans are false; that everyone is constantly trying to feed you is not one. As women (the primary cooks in many households) became more present in the workforce, their spending all day in the kitchen preparing elaborate meals—the way many of their mothers had, by necessity—became less of a thing. Coffee and cake was, and remains, a way to entertain without the fuss. And when there wasn't time to bake something, my family wasn't above opening up a boxed Entenmann's cake.

The "cake" in coffee and cake doesn't have to be actual cake. It can be a tin of Pizzelles (page 191), a ring of Easter Bread (page 166), or really any recipe from the following pages. It's less about the content of the dessert than the point of sharing something sweet with family and friends at the end of the day.

ESPRESSO GRANITA

Every Saturday and Sunday in the summer, my dad would take my cousins and me down to the Lakes. This is what we call FDR Park, 348 acres of fields and lagoons down by the stadiums. If you're living in South Philadelphia, it's where you get your nature. We would go fishing and catch sunnies and catfish (we'd throw them back) and head back to the neighborhood for John's Water Ice. If going to the Lakes was one thing we could count on in the summer in South Philly, water ice, a slushier descendant of Italian granita, was the second. Water ice stands like John's are all over the city, and every kid has a favorite flavor. This granita is my tribute to water ice, flavored with espresso and topped with cinnamon-dusted whipped cream. It's so easy to make and doesn't require an ice-cream maker. You mix the ingredients together, pour them into a shallow pan, and pop it into the freezer, scraping every forty minutes or so to create fluffy ice crystals. The texture of the granita against the cream is the perfect marriage of refreshing and rich.

SERVES 4

¾ cup (150 g) granulated sugar
2¼ cups (532 ml) brewed espresso, hot
1 cup (237 ml) heavy whipping cream
1 tablespoon confectioners' sugar
Ground cinnamon for serving

Place the granulated sugar in a heatproof bowl and pour the hot espresso over it. Stir to completely dissolve the sugar, then transfer the mixture to a medium baking dish. Place the dish in the freezer and scrape with a fork to create ice crystals every 40 minutes for 5 hours.

In a chilled mixing bowl or the chilled bowl of a stand mixer fitted with the whisk attachment, whip the cream with the confectioners' sugar to medium peaks, 3 to 4 minutes. Divide the granita among 4 bowls and top with whipped cream. Dust with cinnamon and serve immediately.

CARAMEL GELATO

Caramel is my favorite gelato flavor. To get that nutty, bittersweet complexity to carry through frozen dairy, you have to take the caramel very dark. Too light, and the resulting gelato will just taste sweet. When you're cooking the sugar, it should look like shiny liquid mahogany before you add milk and cream. This recipe makes 2 quarts, but you can spin half the base and freeze the rest. Then when you want to make another batch, just defrost in the fridge overnight.

SERVES 8

1 cup (237 ml) whole milk
1 cup (237 ml) heavy whipping cream
¼ teaspoon pure vanilla extract
Pinch of salt
1¾ cups (350 g) granulated sugar
3 tablespoons water
7 large egg yolks

Freeze the bowl of a 2-quart (2 L) ice-cream maker overnight.

Combine the milk, cream, vanilla, and salt in a pot set over medium-high heat. Bring the mixture to 180°F (82°C) and hold it at that temperature.

Meanwhile, place 1¼ cups (250 g) of the sugar and the water in a separate pan. Caramelize over medium-low heat until the sugar turns dark brown, about 6 minutes. Add the caramel in thirds to the scalded milk mixture, stirring constantly with rubber spatula, to create a caramel sauce.

While this is heating, combine the egg yolks and remaining sugar in the bowl of a stand mixer fitted with the whisk attachment. Whisk for 3 to 5 minutes, or until the mixture falls off the whisk in pale yellow ribbons. Add 1 ladleful of warm caramel sauce to temper the egg mixture, gently whisk to combine, then whisk in the remaining sauce to create the gelato base. Transfer the gelato base to a Dutch oven set over low heat. Cook the base, continuously stirring with a rubber spatula, until it coats the back of a spoon, about 6 minutes. Set a medium bowl over a large bowl filled with ice. Strain the gelato base through a fine sieve into the medium bowl. Stir the base to cool and prevent lumps from forming. Cover and refrigerate the base for at least 3 hours and up to overnight.

Set up the ice-cream maker. Add the cooled base to the frozen bowl and spin according to the manufacturer's instructions, until the mixture begins rising to the top of the bowl in creamy, semifrozen waves. Transfer the gelato to quart- (1 L)-size containers and allow to set in the freezer overnight before serving.

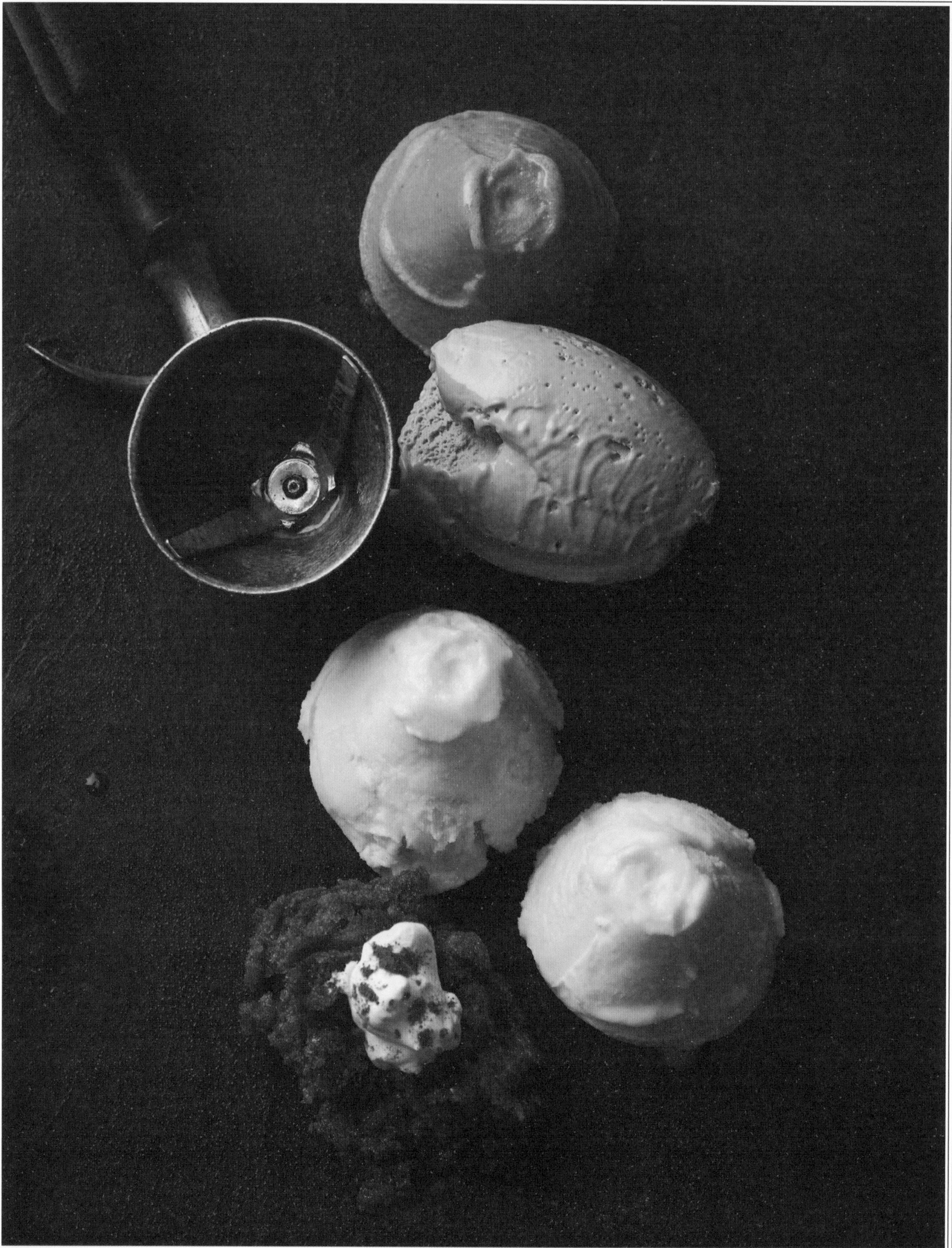

TROPICAL FRUIT SORBETTI

After a big meal, there's nothing as refreshing as cold, tropical fruit sorbet. We make three flavors: pineapple, cantaloupe, and prickly pear, the magenta cactus fruit that grows wild all over Sicily. Each flavor starts with our sorbetto syrup, the liquid sweetener to which we add different levels of water, fruit juice, and lemon. (Glucose and dextrose are available online.) The ratios are carefully calibrated for the right balance of sweetness and acidity, so get out your digital scale. You can enjoy each flavor on its own, but we recommend them as a trio, piled in a sundae glass and garnished with Pizzelles (page 191).

SERVES 8 PER FLAVOR

(recipe continues)

SORBETTO SYRUP

- 33.6 ounces (936 g) granulated sugar
- 11.1 ounces (315 g) glucose syrup
- 2.4 ounces (67.5 g) dextrose powder
- 16.6 ounces (471 g) warm water

Combine the sugar, glucose, dextrose, and warm water in a large Dutch oven set over low heat. Cook, stirring, for 8 minutes. When it begins to turn clear, increase the heat to medium and continue to cook until the sugar is completely dissolved and the syrup is crystal clear, about 8 minutes.

PRICKLY PEAR SORBETTO BASE

- 14.1 ounces (400 g) strained prickly pear purée
- 6.7 ounces (190 g) water
- 14.1 ounces (400 g) Sorbetto Syrup
- Juice of 1 lemon

Combine the prickly pear purée and water in a blender and purée until smooth. Transfer the purée to a medium bowl and whisk in the syrup, then the lemon juice.

PINEAPPLE SORBETTO BASE

- 14.1 ounces (400 g) strained pineapple purée
- 7.4 ounces (210 g) water
- 13.4 ounces (380 g) Sorbetto Syrup
- Juice of ½ lemon

Combine the pineapple purée and water in a blender and purée until smooth. Transfer the purée to a medium bowl and whisk in the syrup, then the lemon juice.

CANTALOUPE SORBETTO BASE

- 14.1 ounces (400 g) strained cantaloupe purée
- 5.6 ounces (160 g) water
- 11.3 ounces (320 g) Sorbetto Syrup
- Juice of ½ lemon

Combine the cantaloupe purée and water in a blender and purée until smooth. Transfer the purée to a medium bowl and whisk in the syrup, then the lemon juice.

TO SPIN

Freeze the bowl of a 2-quart (2 L) ice-cream maker for at least 12 hours.

Set up the ice-cream maker. Add your choice of the sorbetto base to the frozen bowl and spin according to the manufacturer's instructions until frozen. Transfer the sorbetto to quart- (1 L)-size containers and allow to set in the freezer for 1 hour. Remove from the freezer right before serving.

SPUMONI

All the old-time customers at the Club say our spumoni brings back memories. It's a lost Italian American dessert always on the sweet table at South Philly catering halls like Palumbo's, an institution that opened in 1940 and burned down in 1994. The flavors and corresponding colors—strawberry, vanilla, and pistachio—mimic the Italian flag, and I knew I had to have it on the menu here. We do our spumoni as a layered semifreddo, which means "partially frozen" in Italian. Instead of having an ice cream or gelato base made with cooked cream and cooked eggs, the semifreddo is made with whipped cream and whipped eggs, like a frozen mousse. Each flavor is made separately and frozen in a terrine mold to create the signature striped effect. If you don't have the time to dedicate to layering and freezing, you can freeze each flavor in separate pans, then just scoop them out and serve them together in a bowl as a green, white, and red sundae.

SERVES 10

26.5 ounces (750 g) heavy whipping cream, divided into thirds

9 large egg yolks, divided into 3 per color

3 large eggs, divided into 1 per color

1⅓ cups (260 g) plus 1 teaspoon granulated sugar, divided

¼ teaspoon pistachio extract

3 drops green food dye

1 vanilla bean

1 teaspoon pure vanilla extract

3 drops red food dye

1 (12-ounce [340 g]) jar strawberry jam

Miniature chocolate chips for serving

Toasted chopped pistachios for serving

Line a 14 x 5 x 4-inch (35.5 x 12.5 x 10 cm) terrine mold or loaf pan with plastic wrap inside and outside. Be sure the plastic is tucked down into the corners of the mold and there are no gaps.

Make the pistachio layer: On high speed, whip a third of the cream to stiff peaks in a stand mixer fitted with the whisk attachment, about 4 minutes. Gently scrape the whipped cream into a medium bowl and place in the freezer. Rinse the stand mixer bowl and attachment, then whip 3 of the egg yolks, 1 whole egg, ½ cup (100 g) of the sugar, the pistachio extract, and the green food dye in the mixer on high speed until ribbony, about 5 minutes. Remove the whipped cream from the freezer and gently fold in the pistachio mixture with a rubber spatula, careful not to deflate the cream. Pour the mixture into the prepared mold, using a rubber spatula to scrape the bowl. Place the mold in the freezer to set for 45 minutes.

Make the vanilla layer: Rinse the mixer bowl and attachment. Scrape the vanilla bean into the mixer bowl and add the second third of the cream. Whip the vanilla cream on high speed to stiff peaks, about 4 minutes. Gently scrape the whipped cream into a medium bowl and place in the freezer. Rinse the stand mixer bowl and attachment, then whip 3 of the yolks, 1 whole egg, ½ cup (100 g) of the sugar, and the vanilla extract on high speed until ribbony, about 5 minutes. Remove the whipped cream from the freezer and gently fold in the vanilla mixture with a rubber spatula, careful not to deflate the cream. Remove the spumoni mold from the freezer. Pour and scrape the vanilla mixture into the mold with a rubber spatula, starting at the corners and ends and working quickly toward the center. Place immediately back into the freezer to set for 2 hours.

Make the strawberry layer: Rinse the mixer bowl and attachment. Whip the final third of the cream on high speed to stiff peaks, about 4 minutes. Gently scrape the whipped cream into a medium bowl and place in the freezer. Rinse the mixer bowl and attachment, then whip the remaining 3 yolks, remaining egg, and remaining ⅓ cup plus 1 teaspoon (71 g) of sugar, and the red food dye on high speed until ribbony, about 5 minutes. Add the jam and mix for 20 seconds to combine. Remove the whipped cream from the freezer and gently fold in the egg-and-strawberry mixture with a rubber spatula, careful not to deflate the cream. Remove the spumoni mold from the freezer. Pour and scrape with a rubber spatula all of the strawberry layer into the mold, starting at the corners and ends and working quickly toward the center. Place immediately back into the freezer to set overnight.

When ready to serve, unmold the spumoni by turning it upside down onto a large sheet of parchment paper. Gently remove the plastic wrap and turn the spumoni over so the pistachio layer is on the bottom (the strawberry layer is the most volatile and melts quickest, due to the sugar content). Immediately place back into the freezer. Slice as needed and garnish each slice with chocolate chips and chopped pistachios. Store the leftover spumoni in the freezer, wrapped first in parchment, then tightly with plastic wrap.

LEMON CROSTATA

The worst kind of lemon desserts taste like a bucket of sugar with a splash of citrus. This tart is not that. Armored in a sturdy pasta frollo (Italian shortbread) crust, it stars an electric lemon curd filling that will probably send the citrus-shy running for our Chocolate Almond Cake (page 180). The curd is intentionally sharp, its sour edges lightly smoothed not with more sugar, but with the aromatic richness of vanilla, which gets folded into the dough, and a generous garnish of fresh whipped cream. After making this tart once, you can experiment with other citrus juices. Try replacing half of the lemon with lime, grapefruit, or blood orange juice to create different colors, flavors, and sweet-tart levels.

MAKES ONE 10-INCH (25.5 CM) CROSTATA

VANILLA BUTTER CRUST

- 1½ cups (210 g) 00 flour, plus more for dusting
- ⅔ cup (90 g) confectioners' sugar
- 1 teaspoon pure vanilla extract
- 2 large egg yolks
- 1½ tablespoons ice water
- 10½ tablespoons (150 g) cold unsalted butter

Mix together the flour and confectioners' sugar in a medium bowl and turn out onto a work surface. Create a well in the center and add the vanilla, egg yolks, ice water, and butter. Slowly work the dry ingredients into the wet until a dough begins to form. Knead for 6 minutes into a smooth ball. Wrap the dough with plastic wrap and refrigerate at least 1 hour, up to overnight.

Remove the dough from the fridge and allow it to rest at room temperature for 30 to 40 minutes. Meanwhile preheat the oven to 350°F (180°C). Lightly flour a work surface and roll out the dough to ¼ inch (6 mm) thick. Gently lay the dough over a 10-inch (25.5 cm) tart pan, pulling up the sides so it fits snugly. Press the dough down into the corners and press the edge of the pan to trim off the excess. Use the excess dough to fill in any tears or fortify any thin spots. Lay a piece of parchment paper over the crostata dough. Fill the crostata with dried beans or pie weights and blind bake for 30 minutes, or until the crust is golden brown all over. Remove from the oven, let cool completely, and remove the beans or pie weights. Set aside at room temperature.

LEMON CURD

- ¾ cup (175 ml) strained freshly squeezed lemon juice
- 10½ tablespoons (150 g) unsalted butter
- 1 cup (200 g) granulated sugar, divided
- 2 large eggs
- 3 large egg yolks
- ½ teaspoon salt
- Grated zest of 1 lemon
- Whipped cream for serving

Heat the lemon juice, butter, and half of the sugar in a small saucepot over low heat until the sugar dissolves. Whisk the eggs and yolks, the remaining sugar, and the salt and zest in a medium bowl until the mixture turns pale yellow and falls off the whisk in ribbons, 3 to 5 minutes. Slowly temper in ¼ cup (59 ml) of the hot lemon mixture, whisking continually to completely incorporate. Repeat the process ¼ cup (59 ml) at a time until all the lemon mixture is incorporated into the eggs. Transfer the curd to a large Dutch oven. Whisk over low heat until the curd is thick and begins to pull away from the sides of the pot, about 10 minutes. Allow the curd to cool to room temperature.

Preheat the oven to 350°F (180°C). Pour the cooled lemon curd into the shell and bake for 6 minutes. Remove from the oven and let cool to room temperature, 30 to 45 minutes. Invert a large dinner plate over the crostata to protect the curd and chill in the fridge for at least 2 hours and up to overnight before serving. Slice and serve with whipped cream.

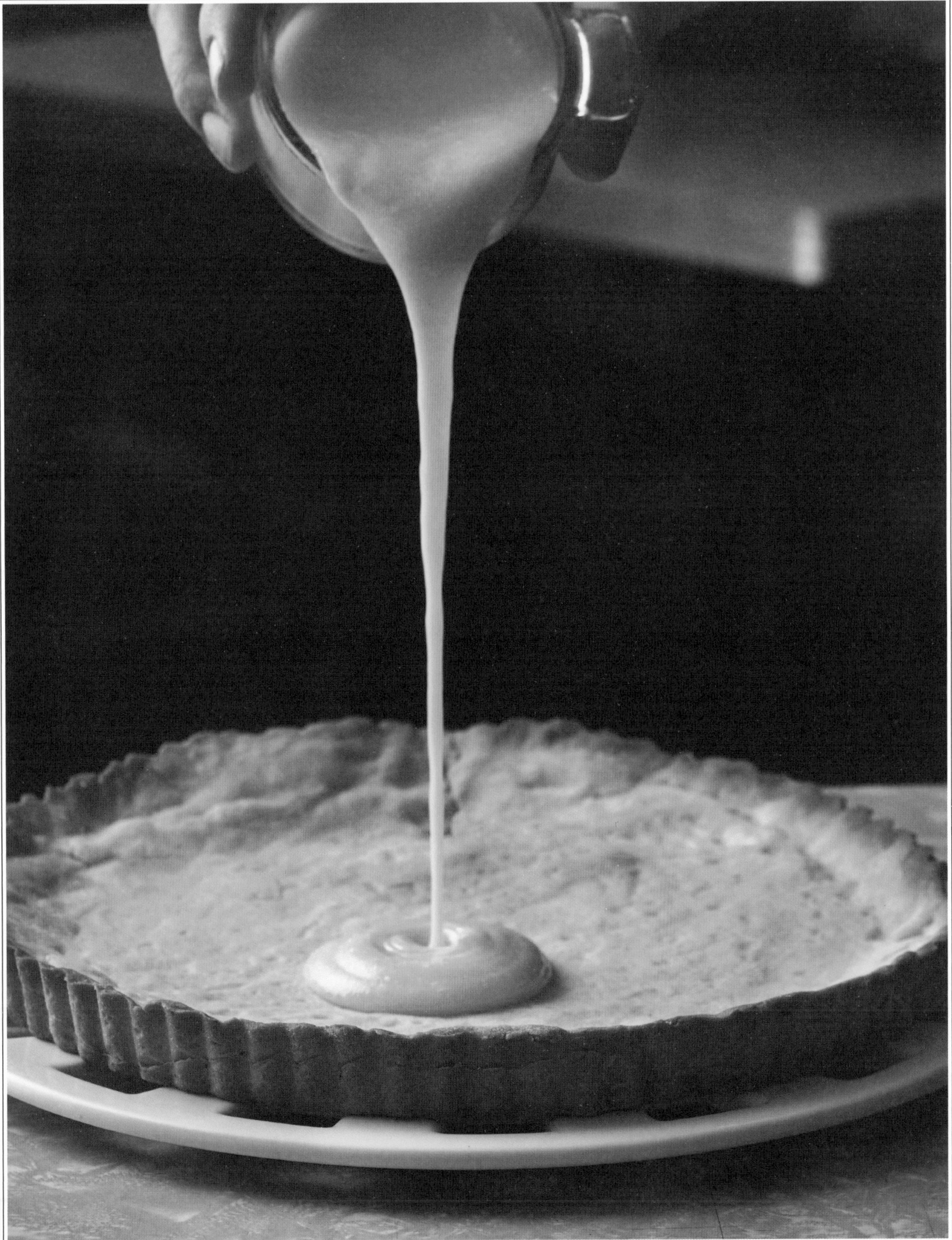

CHOCOLATE ALMOND CAKE

This fudgy, flourless cake is proof of how well chocolate and almonds work together. The cake gets its nuttiness from freshly ground almonds. Store-bought almond flour will work fine, but grinding your own takes two seconds and helps control the freshness. The almond flour gets folded into a mixture of chocolate and egg yolks, to which whipped egg whites are carefully added, similar to how you'd make the batter for a chocolate soufflé. This cake's dark, puffed dome is *supposed* to deflate. Budget for a two-hour rest after baking; room temperature is how you want to serve it. This also makes it a terrific make-ahead dessert. Bake it in the morning and let it hang out on the counter all day. Wrapped tightly with plastic wrap, it also freezes extremely well. Take it out two days before you want to serve it and let it defrost in the fridge, then let it come to room temperature two hours before serving. We recommend serving it with a dusting of confectioners' sugar and almond whipped cream, but it can take to fancier treatments, too. When members are celebrating birthdays at the Club and request a whole cake, we class it up with a coating of dark chocolate ganache.

This recipe makes two cakes. You can serve them together for a crowd or wrap the second cake with plastic wrap and freeze. Another option is to stack them into a layer cake, though the cakes are too heavy to use the almond whipped cream between. Use vanilla frosting doctored up with almond extract instead.

MAKES TWO 10-INCH (25.5 CM) CAKES

- **1 pound (454 g) raw almonds**
- **1 pound (440 g) unsalted butter, plus more for pans**
- **1 teaspoon pure vanilla extract**
- **¼ cup (59 ml) brewed espresso**
- **15½ ounces (440 g) chocolate (63% cacao)**
- **10 large eggs, whites and yolks separated**
- **15½ ounces (440 g) granulated sugar, divided**
- **00 flour, as needed, for dusting**
- **1 cup (240 ml) heavy whipping cream**
- **¼ teaspoon almond extract**
- **1 teaspoon confectioners' sugar, plus more for serving**
- **Toasted almonds for serving**

Grind the almonds in a food processor into a coarse flour. Measure out 15½ ounces (440 g) of almond flour and set aside.

Create a double boiler: Place a heatproof medium bowl over a saucepan partly filled with water (do not let the water touch the bowl's base) and bring the water to a boil over medium heat. Combine the butter, vanilla, espresso, and chocolate in the bowl and gently stir until the chocolate is completely melted, about 8 minutes. Whip the egg whites and two thirds of the granulated sugar in a stand mixer fitted with the whisk attachment to medium peaks, about 5 minutes. Whisk the yolks and the remaining granulated sugar in a separate medium bowl until the mixture turns pale yellow and falls off the whisk in ribbons, about 5 minutes. Off the heat, fold the yolk mixture in thirds into the chocolate mixture. Fold in the whipped egg whites in thirds, careful not to deflate. Carefully fold in the almond flour in thirds, combining just until there are no more streaks.

Preheat the oven to 350°F (180°C). Butter two 10-inch (25.5 cm) round springform pans and dust with 00 flour. Shake out the excess flour. Cut 2 rounds of parchment to fit the pans and place 1 in the bottom of each. Divide the batter evenly between the pans and bake for 20 minutes. Carefully rotate the pans 180 degrees and bake for 20 more minutes. Insert a cake tester into the center of a cake; the cakes are ready if it comes out clean. Remove from the oven and let the cakes cool to room temperature, about 2 hours.

After the cakes have cooled, make the whipped cream by combining the cream, almond extract, and confectioners' sugar in the bowl of a stand mixer fitted with the whisk attachment. Whip until medium peaks form and chill until cold.

Run a knife around the inside of each pan and remove the cake. Carefully invert the cake onto a serving platter. Dust with confectioners' sugar. Slice and serve with almond whipped cream and toasted almonds.

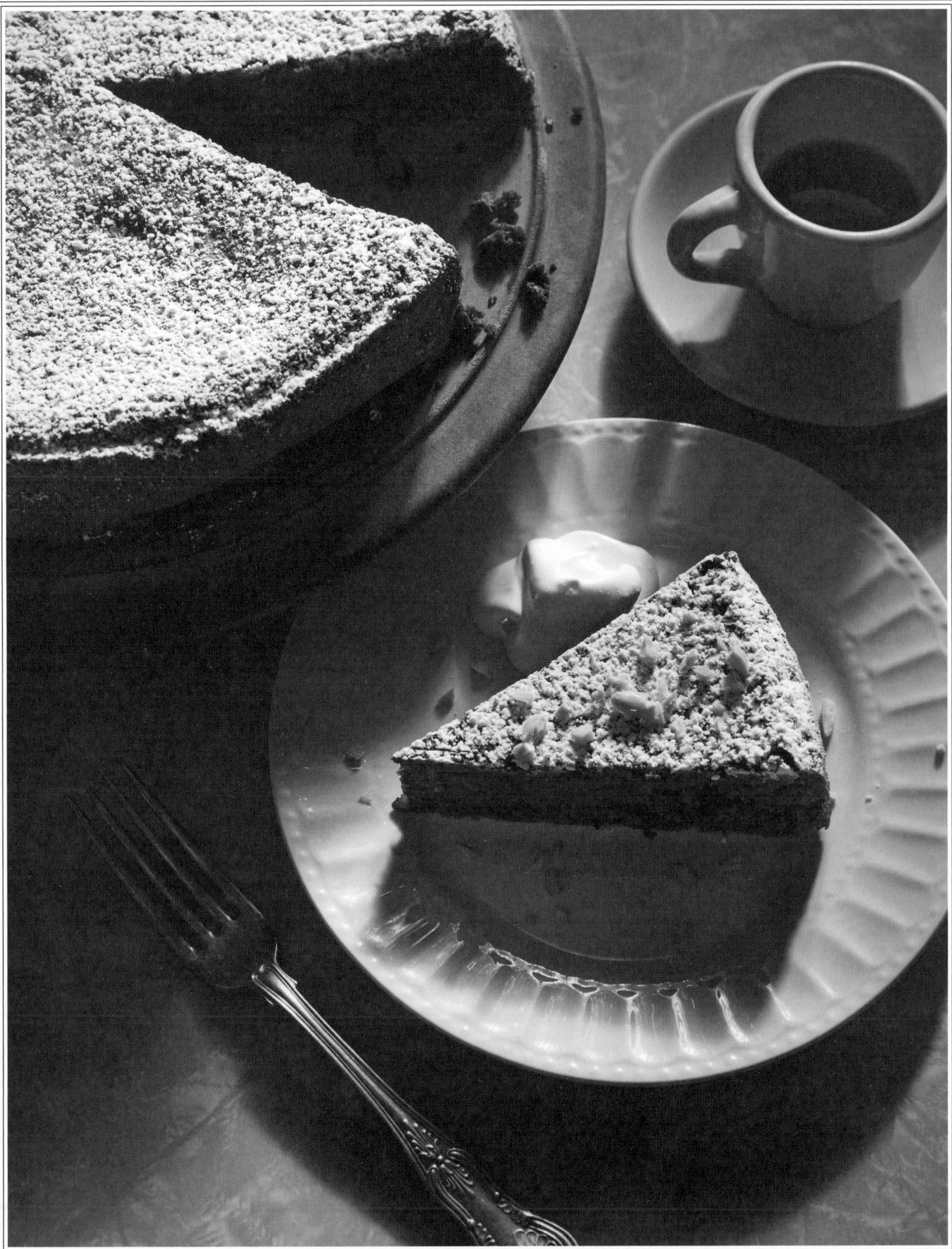

RICOTTA PIE

Ricotta pie isn't a pie in the usual American sense of the word. It's a cheesecake mainly composed of ricotta; in fact, the recipe my mom makes every year for Easter dinner is all ricotta, no crust or anything. For the pie we serve at the Club, I tweaked her formula with sour cream and extra egg yolks, which makes the pie a little richer and tangier, and added an almond crust. That sweet almond flavor in the crust carries through the filling, which has almond extract, vanilla, and lots of fresh citrus zest. Some South Philly bakers fold cooked rice or wheatberries into the filling. Everyone has their own version. This is mine.

MAKES ONE 10-INCH (25.5 CM) PIE

ALMOND CRUST

- 2 cups (220 g) slivered almonds
- ½ cup (100 g) granulated sugar
- ½ cup plus 2 tablespoons (88 g) 00 flour
- ¾ cup (177 ml) melted unsalted butter, plus more for pan
- 2 large egg yolks

Preheat the oven to 325°F (170°C). Grind the almonds in a food processor for 1 minute until coarsely ground. Add the remaining ingredients and pulse until evenly combined, to make the crust. Lightly butter a 10-inch (25 cm) round springform pan. Press the crust into the pan, packing it down with the end of a rolling pin to make it as flat and even as possible. Bake the crust for 6 to 10 minutes, or until golden brown. Remove from the oven and let cool completely.

PIE FILLING

- 24 ounces (680 g) cream cheese
- 1½ cups (340 g) sour cream
- 28 ounces (794 g) ricotta
- 1½ cups (300 g) granulated sugar
- ¼ teaspoon cornstarch
- 1 tablespoon white rum
- 1 teaspoon almond extract
- 1 teaspoon pure vanilla extract
- Grated zest of 1 lemon
- Grated zest of 1 orange
- 3 large eggs
- 2 large egg yolks
- Ground cinnamon for serving
- Amarena cherries in syrup for serving

Preheat the oven to 350°F (180°C). Whip the cream cheese, sour cream, ricotta, and sugar on medium speed for 2 minutes in a stand mixer fitted with the whisk attachment. Scrape down the sides of the bowl. Stir together the cornstarch and rum in a small bowl and add to the mixer, along with the extracts, zests, eggs, and egg yolks. Whip everything together on medium-high speed for 2 to 3 minutes. Scrape down the sides of the bowl and mix for 1 more minute, making sure everything is well combined. Pour the batter into the cooled crust; it should go three quarters of the way up the pan. Fill a large roasting pan with water and set the ricotta pie in the center; the water should go halfway up the sides of the pan. Place in the center rack of the oven and bake for 2 to 2½ hours, or until the filling is fully set (no jiggle). Turn off the oven and allow the pie to rest in the oven for 30 minutes. Crack open the oven door and let the pie continue to rest for another 20 minutes. Remove the pie and put plastic wrap directly on top of the pie. Let cool overnight in the refrigerator.

When ready to serve, run a small knife or spatula around the inside of the pan to loosen the pie. Remove the outer ring of the springform pan and transfer the pie to a platter. Dust cinnamon over the top and cut into 12 slices. Serve each slice topped with Amarena cherries and a drizzle of syrup. The pie will keep for 1 week wrapped in the fridge.

CINNAMON-SUGAR ZEPPOLI

March 19 is Saint Joseph's Day. In Catholic school, if you had a patron saint you were named after, it was like having a second birthday. Aunt Mary was my godmother and every March 19 until she died in 2000, she would come over to bring me Saint Joseph's cakes. Bakeries in South Philly make pretty versions from choux pastry piped into seashells, filled with ricotta or cream, and garnished with maraschino cherries, but Saint Joseph's cakes can also be as basic and rustic plain fried dough rolled in sugar, otherwise known as zeppoli. I love both types, but the latter are what I named my first restaurant after. Zeppoli go by other names—at the Club we call them sfingi—and every culture has its take, whether it's churros in Mexico, beignets in France, or funnel cake on the boardwalk down the shore. The key to this recipe is not to crowd the pot while frying the zeppoli; divide them into three batches and give them time to get golden all over.

SERVES 8

CINNAMON SUGAR

- ¼ cup (60 g) granulated sugar
- ½ teaspoon ground cinnamon

Whisk the sugar and cinnamon together in a medium bowl. Set aside at room temperature.

ZEPPOLI

- 4 teaspoons (14 g) active dry yeast
- ⅔ cup (155 ml) whole milk
- 6 tablespoons (72 g) granulated sugar, divided
- 2⅓ cups (340 g) 00 flour, plus more for dusting
- 1 large egg
- 1 large egg yolk
- 3½ tablespoons unsalted butter, at room temperature
- ¼ teaspoon pure vanilla extract
- ¼ teaspoon salt
- 1 gallon (4 L) canola oil
- Warmed Nutella for serving

Place the yeast, milk, and 1½ tablespoons (18 g) of the sugar in the bowl of a stand mixer and bloom for 8 minutes. Add the remaining sugar, flour, egg, and egg yolk. Mix on low speed with the dough hook attachment for 1 minute, or until the ingredients begin to combine. With the mixer running, slowly add the butter. Scrape down the sides and add the vanilla and salt. Mix on medium speed for 6 minutes, or until the dough is smooth and completely combined. Generously dust a medium bowl with 00 flour. Scrape the dough into the bowl and dust the surface with more flour. Cover with plastic wrap and allow the dough to rise for 1 hour, or until almost doubled in size.

Lightly flour a baking sheet and a work surface. Turn out the dough onto the work surface and gently roll it out to ½ inch (1.3 cm) thick. Using a 1-inch (2.5 cm) round cookie cutter, cut out the zeppoli and line them up on the floured pan. You can wrap and refrigerate them for up to 4 hours at this point.

Have ready the bowl of cinnamon sugar. Heat the oil in a large Dutch oven to 325°F (170°C). Fry the zeppoli in 3 batches, moving them around in the oil to attain an even golden brown color. Drain the zeppoli on a slotted spoon for a few seconds and transfer to the cinnamon sugar. Roll them around until lightly covered on all sides. Transfer to a serving platter, drizzle with Nutella or serve with the spread on the side for dipping. Serve immediately.

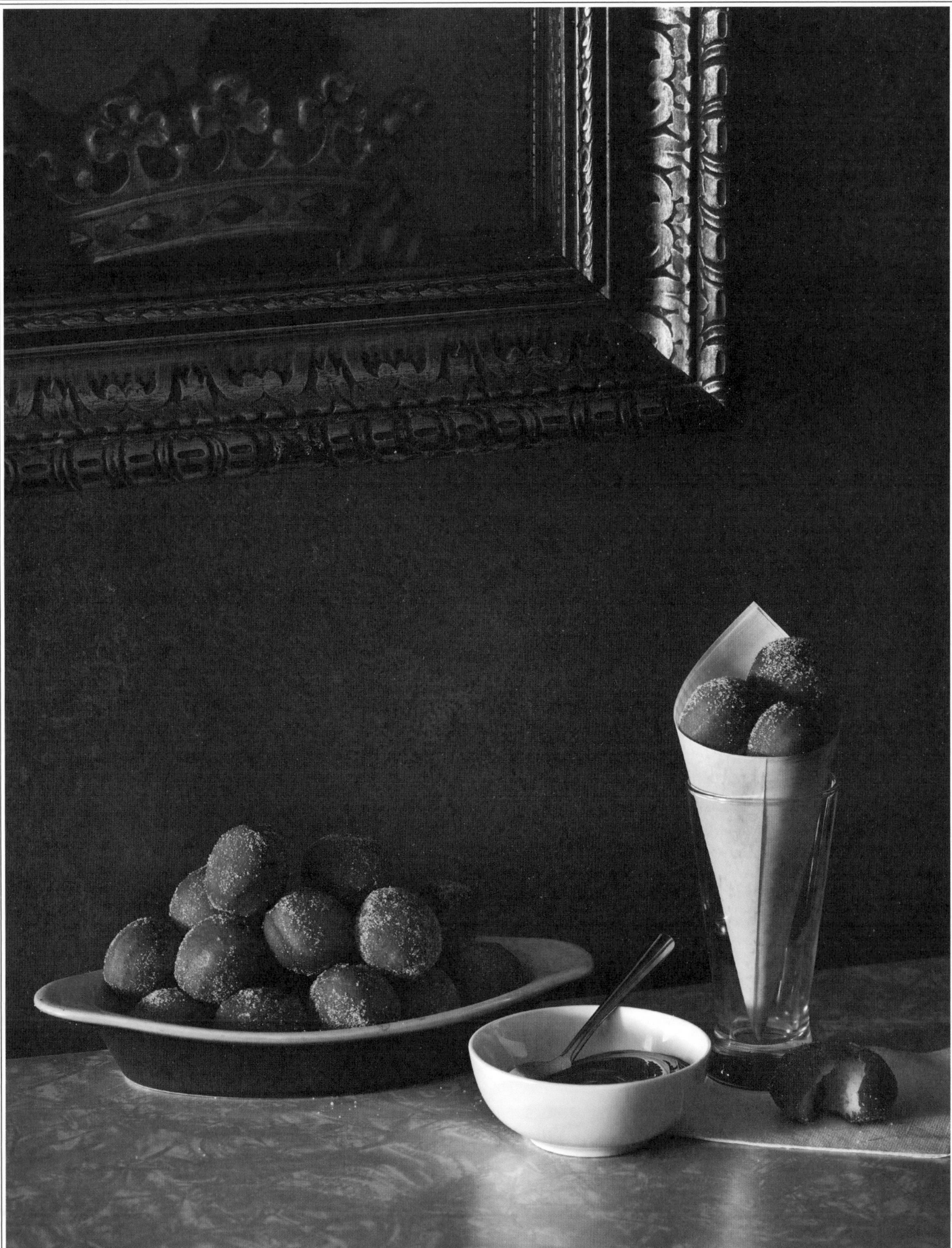

CLASSIC CANNOLI

You can get three types of cannoli at most South Philly bakeries: chocolate, vanilla, and ricotta. The first two varieties are filled with pastry cream and are almost always too sweet, which is why I go for the ricotta ones and only from Isgro's Pasticceria on Christian Street. When we make them at the Club, lemon and orange zests and orange blossom water give our ricotta filling more dimension, and our shells have coffee, cocoa, and Marsala in the dough. Note the technique when frying the shells: Plunging them in and out of the hot oil for the first ten seconds of cooking will create light, airy shells covered in little bubbles. They'll keep for a day packed in a cookie tin, and you can make the filling up to a week in advance. Whatever you do, fill the cannoli just before serving. As soon as the ricotta hits the shell, the clock is ticking toward sogginess, and a soggy cannolo isn't even worth eating.

MAKES 20 TO 24 CANNOLI

CANNOLI DOUGH

- 4 tablespoons (57 g) cold unsalted butter
- 1½ cups (227 g) 00 flour
- 2 tablespoons granulated sugar
- 1½ teaspoons unsweetened cocoa powder
- 1 tablespoon ground espresso powder
- ¼ teaspoon ground cinnamon
- ¼ teaspoon pure vanilla extract
- ¼ teaspoon Marsala
- 1 large egg yolk
- ¼ cup (57 ml) whole milk

Grate the butter on the large-holed side of a box grater and chill in the freezer for 20 minutes before starting the dough.

Combine the flour, sugar, cocoa powder, espresso powder, and cinnamon on a work surface. Create a well in the center of the dry ingredients and add the vanilla, Marsala, egg yolk, and milk. Slowly whisk the dry ingredients into the wet with a fork until a dough begins to form, about 3 minutes. Fold the chilled butter into the dough. Continue to fold the dough over onto itself until smooth, 8 to 10 minutes. It should feel moist but not sticky; if too dry, add ¼ teaspoon of water. Tightly wrap the dough with plastic wrap and refrigerate overnight.

RICOTTA FILLING

- 24 ounces (680 g) strained ricotta
- 6 ounces (170 g) cream cheese
- ¾ cup plus 4 teaspoons (170 g) granulated sugar
- ⅔ cup (90 g) confectioners' sugar
- ½ teaspoon pure vanilla extract
- ½ teaspoon orange blossom water

Place the ricotta, cream cheese, and sugars in the bowl of a stand mixer fitted with the paddle attachment. Cream the ingredients on medium speed for 3 minutes. Scrape down the sides of the bowl, add the vanilla and orange blossom water, and mix for 2 minutes. Line a strainer with 4 layers of cheesecloth and set the strainer over a mixing bowl. Transfer the filling to the strainer and refrigerate overnight.

FRYING AND FILLING

- 1 large egg white, beaten
- 1 gallon (4 L) canola oil
- 1 cup (100 g) chopped toasted pistachios for serving
- Confectioners' sugar for dusting

Remove the cannoli dough from the refrigerator and roll it out to 4 inches (10 cm) wide and ¼ inch (6 mm) thick. Cut it in half. Fit a stand mixer with the pasta-rolling attachment. Roll out one half of the dough, starting with the largest setting and working down to the #3 setting. Repeat for the other half of the dough. Cut 10 to 12 rounds from each half of dough with a 3-inch (7.5 cm) ring mold (20 to 24 total). Wrap the dough rounds around cannoli molds, overlapping the ends and sealing with beaten egg white.

Place the canola oil in a large Dutch oven and bring to 325°F (170°C). Divide the shells into 4 batches. Load the first batch into a fryer basket and carefully dunk it into the hot oil. Quickly pull the shells out of the oil and repeat this dunking process for the first 10 seconds of cooking, then continue to fry as usual until golden brown, about 2 minutes. Transfer to a paper towel–lined baking sheet and let cool.

While the shells are cooling, fill a piping bag with the chilled ricotta filling. Take a shell and evenly fill it from both sides. Repeat for the remaining shells. Garnish the ends of the cannoli with chopped pistachios. Dust all over with confectioners' sugar and serve immediately.

STRUFFOLI

In Italy, the name for these little marbles of fried dough soaked in spiced honey syrup, stacked into a tall sticky tower, and covered in rainbow sprinkles varies region to region: struffoli in Naples, *pignalote* in Sicily, *cicheriate* in Abruzzo. Growing up, we always called them honey balls, and they were always made by my Aunt Roma. This recipe is faithfully hers, starting with a dough flavored with vanilla, Marsala, and citrus and lightened with ricotta. Once rested, the dough gets portioned into balls, fried, drained, and transferred to a Jacuzzi of warm honey syrup, which the struffoli absorb like sponges. Add a slug of Chianti to the dough and the syrup to turn honey balls into wine balls, another Roma favorite.

SERVES 8

STRUFFOLI DOUGH

- 2⅓ cups (350 g) 00 flour
- 1 tablespoon confectioners' sugar
- ¼ teaspoon salt
- 1 teaspoon baking powder
- 2 tablespoons ricotta
- 3 large eggs
- Grated zest of 1 orange
- Grated zest of 1 lemon
- 1 teaspoon orange blossom water
- 1 teaspoon pure vanilla extract
- 1 teaspoon Marsala
- 3½ tablespoons unsalted butter, cubed and frozen

Combine the flour, confectioners' sugar, salt, and baking powder on a work surface and make a well in the center. Add the ricotta, eggs, zests, orange blossom water, vanilla, and Marsala to the center of the well and slowly mix the dry ingredients into the wet with your hands until a dough begins to form. Cut in the butter with a bench scraper and work the dough until smooth, about 10 minutes. Wrap the dough with plastic wrap and refrigerate for at least 1 hour, up to overnight.

HONEY SYRUP

- 2 cups (620 g) honey
- 4 whole cloves
- 2 cinnamon sticks
- 1 tablespoon orange blossom water
- 1 tablespoon Marsala
- ¼ teaspoon salt
- 3 tablespoons Demerara Syrup (page 200)

Combine all the syrup ingredients in a medium pot and bring to a low simmer. Turn off the heat and keep the pot warm on the stovetop.

FRYING THE STRUFFOLI

- 1 gallon (4 L) canola oil
- Rainbow nonpareils for serving

Heat the oil in a large Dutch oven to 325°F (170°C).

Remove the dough from the fridge and cut it into 8 strips. Roll out the strips to snakes about ¼ inch (6 mm) in diameter. Cut each snake into ¼-inch (6 mm) pieces and roll each piece into a ball between your palms. Working in 3 batches, fry the pieces of dough until golden brown all over. Transfer to a baking sheet lined with paper towels to absorb any excess oil, then add the struffoli to the warm pot of honey syrup. Bring the syrup and struffoli up to a simmer over medium heat to allow the fried dough to absorb the flavor, stirring occasionally to coat, 2 to 3 minutes. Lift the struffoli out of the syrup with a slotted spoon. Remove and discard the whole spices and discard the excess syrup. Pile the struffoli on top of one another in a tall tower on a serving platter. Garnish with nonpareils.

HAZELNUT TORRONE

Almonds are classic in torrone, but our version of Italian nougat features hazelnuts, along with subtle notes of orange, lemon, and vanilla. You start with Italian meringue, made by streaming a hot honey mixture into whipped egg whites; cooking and cooling the mixture to the temperatures specified below ensures the finished torrone is firm and chewy, not soft and gooey. After the nuts and flavorings are folded into the meringue, the mixture gets poured into a pan lined with edible wafer paper (what Holy Communion is made from) to set. If you can't find it or don't have time to order it online, use edible rice paper. This recipe also works really well with pistachios, almonds, or a mix. Just match the extract to the appropriate nut.

MAKES ABOUT 60 PIECES

Unsalted butter for pan

Edible wafer paper for wrapping

3 large egg whites

1 cup plus 2 tablespoons (170 g) confectioners' sugar

¼ teaspoon cream of tartar

Pinch of salt

2¾ cups plus 2 teaspoons (560 g) granulated sugar

1 cup (330 g) honey

3½ cups (440 g) toasted and skinned hazelnuts

¼ teaspoon hazelnut extract or Frangelico

¼ teaspoon pure vanilla extract

Grated zest of 1 lemon

Grated zest of 1 orange

Nonstick cooking spray for shears

Lightly butter the bottom and sides of a 13 x 9-inch (33 x 23 cm) rimmed baking sheet. Line the pan with edible wafer paper, overlapping sheets to fit the bottom of the pan and go up the sides by at least 1 inch (2.5 cm). The paper should stick to the pan so it doesn't move around when you spread the hot torrone over it.

Beat the egg whites in the bowl of a stand mixer fitted with the whisk attachment at medium-high speed until soft peaks form, 3 to 4 minutes. Add the confectioners' sugar, cream of tartar, and salt and beat at medium speed until stiff peaks form, 3 to 4 minutes. While the meringue is mixing, combine the granulated sugar and honey in a medium saucepan and cook over medium heat, stirring occasionally, until it reaches 325°F (170°C) on a candy thermometer. Remove the mixture from the heat and stir until the temperature drops to 300°F (150°C), 1 to 2 minutes. With the mixer running, slowly pour the honey mixture into the meringue. This will cause the meringue to double in volume. Turn off the mixer and let the meringue stand until it returns to its previous volume, about 2 minutes. Continue beating the mixture at medium speed until thick, shiny, and marshmallowy, about 2 minutes. Fold in the hazelnuts, extracts, and zests. Pour the torrone mixture into the prepared pan and cover with another layer of paper. Rest the torrone on a rack until slightly cooled. Spray a pair of kitchen shears with nonstick cooking spray. Remove the torrone from the pan and cut into squares. Let cool completely and store in a cookie tin.

PIZZELLES

No self-respecting, cellophane-wrapped, South Philly cookie tray is complete without a tall stack of pizzelles. These thin, crisp, snowflake-shaped wafers start with a runny batter, not a dough, and come in many different flavors, anise and vanilla being the most traditional. My Aunt Roma also does rolled pizzelles filled with chocolate. She and my mom set up an assembly line: my mom tosses a pizzelle hot from the iron to Roma, who lays a thin bar of chocolate in the middle and gently rolls it up into a skinny cigar. Try that method after you master the original. You'll need a pizzelle iron and plenty of time. Since most irons only have space for two cookies at a time, making a batch of pizzelles can be a marathon. Put on a pot of coffee or open up a bottle of Anisette (page 214) and make a night of it.

MAKES 50 TO 60 PIZZELLES

ANISE BATTER

- 3 large eggs
- ¾ cup (150 g) granulated sugar
- 1¾ cups (245 g) 00 flour, sifted
- 2 teaspoons baking powder
- ½ cup (118 ml) vegetable oil
- 1 tablespoon pure vanilla extract
- 1½ teaspoons whole aniseeds
- Pinch of salt

Cream the eggs and sugar in a medium bowl with a whisk until smooth, about 3 minutes. Add the remaining ingredients for the anise batter and mix until completely incorporated, about 2 minutes.

VANILLA BATTER

- 1 vanilla bean, scraped
- 3 large eggs
- ¾ cup (150 g) granulated sugar
- 1¾ cups (245 g) 00 flour, sifted
- 2 teaspoons baking powder
- ½ cup (118 ml) vegetable oil
- 1 tablespoon pure vanilla extract
- Pinch of salt

Scrape out the vanilla bean and place it in a medium bowl along with the eggs and sugar. Cream the ingredients with a whisk until smooth, about 3 minutes. Add the remaining ingredients for the vanilla batter and mix until completely incorporated, about 2 minutes.

TO COOK

- Nonstick cooking spray or vegetable oil for pizzelle iron
- Confectioners' sugar for serving

Preheat a pizzelle iron. Spray the inside of the iron with nonstick spray or lightly brush with vegetable oil. Add 1 teaspoon of either batter to the center of each mold and close. Cook according the manufacturer's instructions. Carefully remove pizzelles and transfer to wire racks. Continue until all the batter is used. Dust with confectioners' sugar and serve.

From left to right: Cinnamon-Sugar Zeppoli / Pizzelles / Classic Cannoli / Struffoli / Hazelnut Torrone / Ricotta Pie

CREME DE
CACAO

COCKTAILS AND CORDIALS

THE LAVERGHETTA

THE MOLINO

THE SMARGIASSI

THE DICICCO

THE DELBORRELLO

THE BOZZELLI

THE D'ADAMO

THE MEZZAROBA

CLASSIC NEGRONI

NEGRONI MILK PUNCH

ORANGE BLOSSOM LIMONATA

ANISETTE

LIMONCELLO

Since its founding, the Club has been a place to relax and have a drink, but our mahogany bar wasn't installed until the formal repeal of Prohibition. It's so solidly constructed that when I took over, it only needed a good dusting and wipe down with furniture polish. The mirrored bar back is original; so is the cash register. You can feel the history that's seeped down into the wood. I can't really explain the feeling of seeing the bar lined with members, the way it must have been during the Club's heyday. Our cocktail menu specializes in riffs on classics, from the martini to the Cosmopolitan (yes, really). As a tribute, each is named after a past Club president.

From left to right: The Smargiassi / The Bozzelli / The LaVerghetta / The Molino

CLEOPATR
GRAPPA
GRA
di NO
DISTILLERIA
PALIZZI SOCIAL CLUB

THE LAVERGHETTA

NAMESAKE: CAESAR LAVERGHETTA, PRESIDENT 1918–1920

This is our take on the Aperol Spritz. It's a classic build enhanced with Ruby Red grapefruit juice and fresh basil, which we tear and rim the glass with. When you lift the glass to take a sip, that sweet, herbal basil fragrance hits you immediately.

MAKES 1 COCKTAIL

- **2 ounces (59 ml) Aperol**
- **1 ounce (30 ml) freshly squeezed Ruby Red grapefruit juice**
- **3 ounces (89 ml) Prosecco**
- **1½ ounces (44 ml) club soda**
- **6 large basil leaves for serving**

Place all the ingredients, except the basil, in a metal shaker. Add ice and pour the contents into a 16-ounce (475 ml) wine goblet. Rub the basil leaves around the rim of the glass, tear them in half, and drop them on the surface of the cocktail. Serve with 2 stirrers.

THE MOLINO

NAMESAKE: GIUSEPPE MOLINO, PRESIDENT 1920–1928

Not quite an Amaretto Sour, not quite a Whiskey Sour, the Molino splits the difference with three parts overproof rye and one part Luxardo amaretto. We do sour cocktails the proper way, with shaken egg white that creates a really smooth texture and a tall cap of foam.

DEMERARA SYRUP

MAKES ABOUT 12 OUNCES (350 ML)

- **2 cups (420 g) raw or turbinado sugar**
- **1 cup (237 ml) water**

Combine the sugar with the water in a small saucepan over medium heat. Stir until the sugar dissolves. Remove the syrup from the heat, let cool to room temperature, and transfer to a clean airtight container.

MAKES 1 COCKTAIL

- **1½ ounces (44 ml) overproof rye, such as Wild Turkey 101**
- **¾ ounce (22 ml) freshly squeezed lemon juice**
- **½ ounce (15 ml) amaretto**
- **½ ounce (15 ml) Demerara Syrup**
- **1 large egg white**
- **Amarena cherry for serving**

Place all the ingredients, except the cherry, in a metal shaker and vigorously dry shake for 30 seconds. Add ice, quickly shake, and double strain into a 6-ounce (177 ml) beer glass. Garnish with a skewered cherry, making sure any excess syrup has been wiped off the cherry so as to not stain the foam of the cocktail.

THE SMARGIASSI

NAMESAKE: LUIGI SMARGIASSI, PRESIDENT 1928–1930

Corn syrupy lime "juice" and bottom-shelf Triple Sec have defiled so many Cosmopolitans, the cocktail has become easy to snub. But made properly, the Cosmo is actually a well-balanced drink, and we wanted one on the menu at the Club. Our version uses Pierre Ferrand Dry Curaçao for that aromatic expression of orange and Moscato grappa, which is softer than most grappas. It'll make you rethink your feelings about the Cosmo.

MAKES 1 COCKTAIL

- **1½ ounces (44 ml) Moscato grappa**
- **¾ ounce (22 ml) orange curaçao**
- **¾ ounce (22 ml) cranberry cocktail**
- **½ ounce (15 ml) freshly squeezed lime juice**

Place all the ingredients in a metal shaker with ice. Shake for 10 seconds and double strain into a 4-ounce (118 ml) martini glass.

THE DICICCO

NAMESAKE: DOMINICO DICICCO, PRESIDENT 1930–1935

Fat washing is in an interesting bartending technique. Basically it's a method for infusing a savory flavor into a spirit. You can fat wash with bacon drippings, sesame oil, duck fat, and in the case of the DiCicco, olive oil. This is our house martini, starring vodka washed in extra-virgin, an easy overnight process. We stir the washed vodka with dry and blanc (bianco) vermouths, blanc being the soft and flowery third-party vermouth halfway between sweet and dry.

EXTRA-VIRGIN OLIVE OIL–WASHED VODKA

MAKES ABOUT 25 OUNCES (750 ML)

- **1 bottle (750 ml) premium vodka, such as Ketel One**
- **6 ounces (177 ml) extra-virgin olive oil**

Decant the vodka into a quart- (1 L)-size container and top with the olive oil. Cover and freeze overnight. When the olive oil is fully frozen, scrape it off with a small knife and discard. Strain, if necessary, then transfer the vodka back to its bottle and store in a cool, dark place.

MAKES 1 COCKTAIL

- **2 ounces (59 ml) Extra-Virgin Olive Oil–Washed Vodka**
- **½ ounce (15 ml) dry vermouth, such as Dolin Dry**
- **½ ounce (15 ml) white vermouth, such as Dolin Blanc**
- **1 (2-inch [5 cm]) piece lemon peel for serving**

Place all the ingredients, except the lemon peel, in a mixing glass with ice and stir briskly for 30 seconds. Strain into a 4-ounce (118 ml) martini glass. Twist the lemon peel, skin-side down, to express the oils, run it around the rim of the glass, and drop it into the martini.

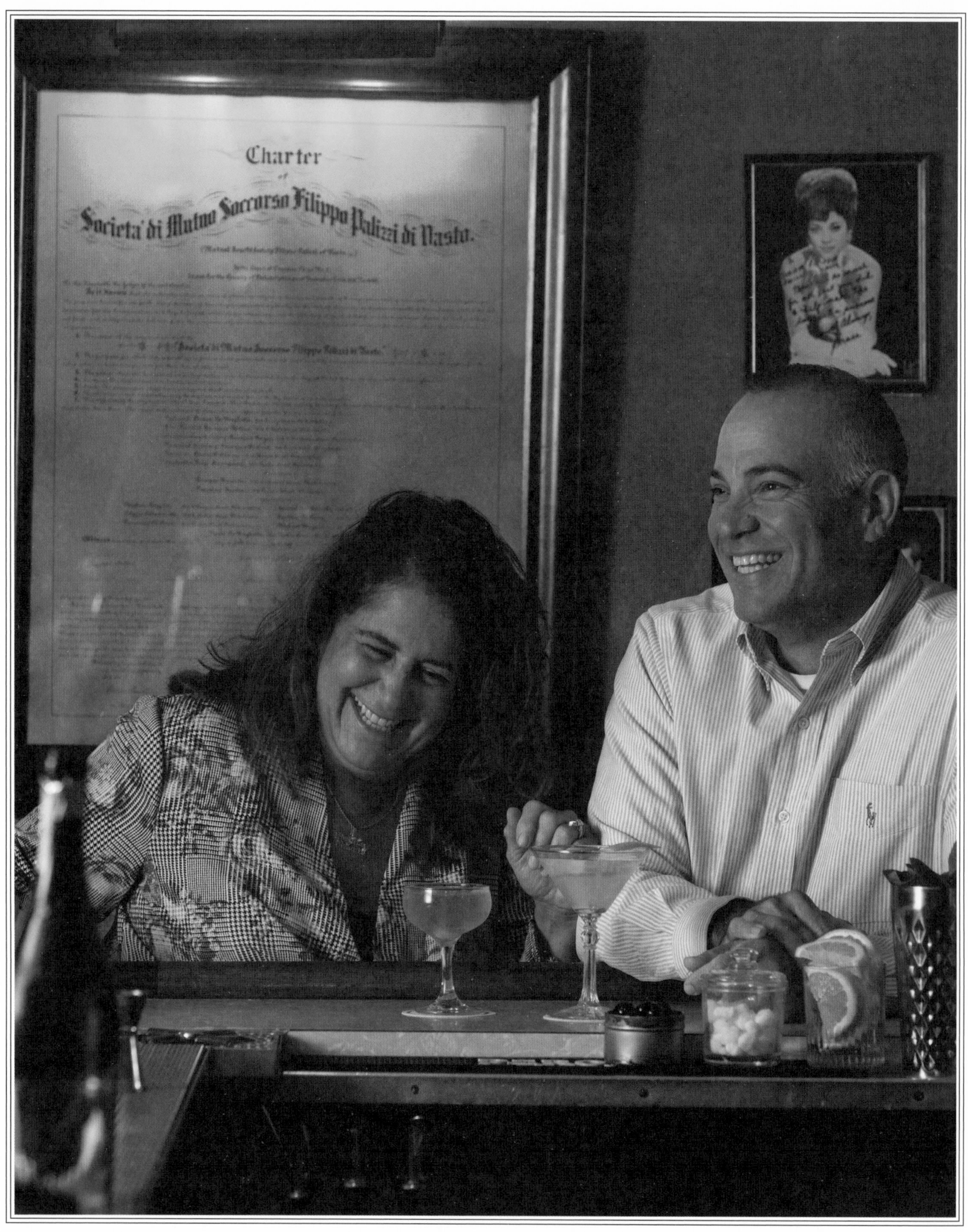

Karen DelBorrello Dougherty, daughter of 14th president Pete DelBorrello, and Jimmy DiCicco, great-grandson of 4th president Dominico DiCicco, drinking The Delborrello and The DiCicco.

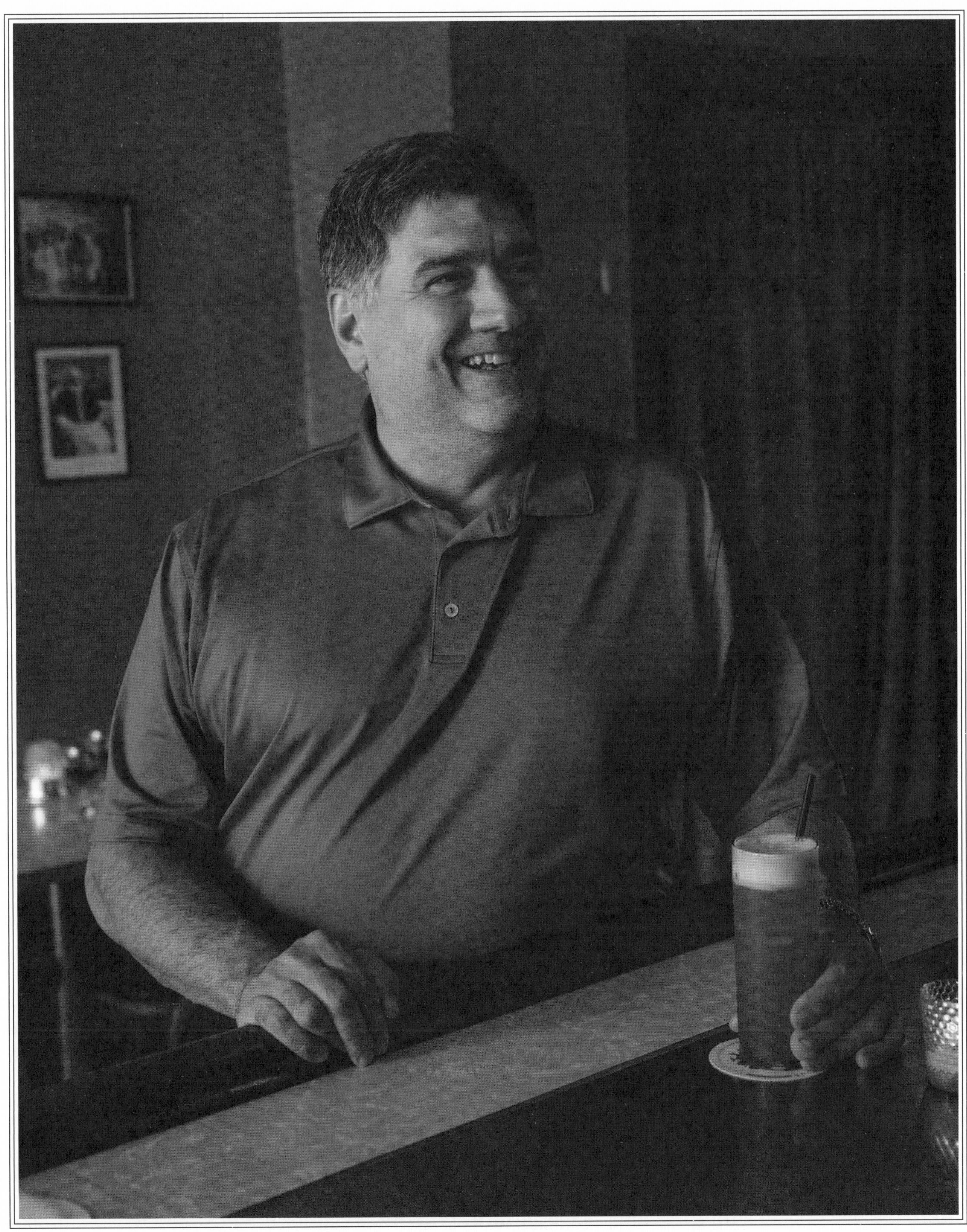

Al Mezzaroba, son of 15th president Ernest Mezzaroba, drinking The Mezzaroba.

THE DELBORRELLO

NAMESAKE: PETE DELBORRELLO, PRESIDENT 1962–1975

Our house bitters are a mix of Angostura, Regans', and Fee Brothers Indian Orange. We batch them together in an eyedropper bottle and use them in our Manhattan, Old-Fashioned, and pretty much any drink that calls for bitters. They have a featured role in the DelBorrello, our version of a Champagne Cocktail. We soak a sugar cube in the bitters, which slowly eats away at the cube. That mixture goes into a glass of Prosecco for a drink that's bittersweet, citrusy, and bubbly.

MAKES 1 COCKTAIL

1 sugar cube

2 dashes of Angostura Bitters

2 dashes of Regans' Orange Bitters No. 6

2 dashes of Fee Brothers West Indian Orange Bitters

3 ounces (89 ml) Prosecco

1 (2-inch [5 cm]) piece lemon peel for serving

Drop the sugar cube into a jigger. Shake the bitters over the sugar and let it rest for 45 seconds. Fill a 3-ounce (89 ml) Champagne coupe with Prosecco. Add the sugar and bitters to the Prosecco. Twist the lemon peel, run it around the rim of the glass, and discard.

Pete DelBorrello owned the Broadway Laundromats in South Philly, and much to his wife's chagrin, "the Vastaloo Club had a washing machine before we had one at home," says his daughter, Karen DelBorrello Dougherty, who grew up in the Club playing darts with her sister. "Vastaloo," derived from Vasto, was the family's nickname for the Club, and the washing machine was used to clean clams, not clothes.

THE BOZZELLI

NAMESAKE: MICHELE BOZZELLI, PRESIDENT 1946–1951

The Bozzelli is my favorite drink on the menu and how I test our bartenders. If they can correctly make this cocktail, a riff on a Last Word with Galliano and Cocchi Americano (an aromatized wine similar to Lillet Blanc), I know they're in good shape. The drink is cool and refreshing like a daiquiri, with notes of citrus and vanilla followed by a spicy finish from the Habanero Tincture. You have to calibrate the heat exactly right; it should be warm, but not sting your lips.

HABANERO TINCTURE

MAKES 6 3/4 OUNCES (200 ML)

10 fresh habanero chiles
6¾ ounces (200 ml) grain alcohol

Wearing gloves, roughly chop the habaneros and combine with the alcohol in a clean, airtight container. Steep for 24 hours. Strain the tincture through a fine-mesh strainer and bottle in a clean, airtight container. Store in a cool dark place; the tincture keeps indefinitely but loses its heat over time.

MAKES 1 COCKTAIL

¾ ounce (22 ml) London Dry gin, such as Beefeater
¾ ounce (22 ml) Galliano
¾ ounce (22 ml) Cocchi Americano
¾ ounce (22 ml) freshly squeezed lime juice
4 drops of Habanero Tincture

Place the ingredients in a metal shaker, add ice, and shake for 10 seconds. Double strain into a 3-ounce (89 ml) coupe.

THE D'ADAMO

NAMESAKE: NICK D'ADAMO, PRESIDENT 1960–1961

Sometimes you want coffee after dinner, sometimes you want dessert. When our members can't decide, we guide them to the D'Adamo, an espresso cocktail made with our Brown Butter–Washed Amaro. It's best to serve this drink at a party because you'll need to batch out the amaro first. You brown butter, add three different types of amari, and freeze overnight. Once the solid butter is strained off, you're left with a complex bitter elixir that has this fantastic nuttiness and velvety texture. Rittenhouse Rye and coffee liqueur are added to complete the batch, enough for about 16 cocktails. To make the drink, it's a simple two parts amaro and one part espresso shaken together, strained into a coupe, and garnished with sea salt. Sweet and savory, it's the perfect nightcap.

BROWN BUTTER–WASHED AMARO

MAKES 28 OUNCES (830 ML)
MAKES 16 COCKTAILS

- 8 tablespoons (112 g) unsalted butter
- 8 ounces (237 ml) Averna amaro
- 8 ounces (237 ml) Nardini amaro
- 4 ounces (118 ml) Cynar
- 4 ounces (118 ml) Patrón XO Café
- 4 ounces (118 ml) overproof rye
- 4 ounces (118 ml) Demerara Syrup (page 200)

Brown the butter in a saucepan over medium heat. Add the amari and stir for 10 seconds. Remove from the heat and steep for 30 minutes. Freeze overnight in the saucepan. Remove from the freezer and skim off the butter solids. Pour the amari through a fine-mesh strainer to clear any extra bits of butter. Add the Patrón, rye, and demerara syrup. Transfer to a clean, airtight container and store in a cool, dark place.

MAKES 1 COCKTAIL

- 2 ounces (59 ml) Brown Butter–Washed Amaro
- 1 ounce (30 ml) brewed espresso
- Salt for serving

Place all the ingredients, except the salt, in a metal shaker with ice. Shake for 10 seconds and double strain into a 3-ounce (89 ml) coupe glass. Garnish with a few grains of salt.

PALIZZI SOCIAL CLUB

THE MEZZAROBA

NAMESAKE: ERNEST MEZZAROBA, PRESIDENT 1975–2016

A Buck is any spirit plus citrus and ginger soda. You can have a Gin Buck, a Mezcal Buck, a Rye Buck, and at the Club, a Rum-and-Fernet Buck, also known as the Mezzaroba, after my Uncle Ernie. The spiciness of the Fernet and the smoothness of the aged rum (we like El Dorado 12 Year) work so well together with our house ginger beer. We make the soda from scratch with ginger and demerara syrups, fresh lime, and club. It's spicy and refreshing and complex and feels like a cocktail in its own right, making it a great alternative for anyone not drinking alcohol.

GINGER SYRUP

MAKES ABOUT 12 OUNCES (350 ML)

- 1 cup (96 g) finely chopped fresh ginger
- 1 cup (237 ml) freshly squeezed lime juice
- 1 cup (200 g) granulated sugar

Combine the ginger, lime juice, and sugar in a small saucepan over medium heat. Stir until the sugar dissolves. Remove the syrup from the heat and allow the ginger to steep for 30 minutes. Strain the syrup through a fine-mesh strainer, pressing the ginger to extract all the liquid. Let cool to room temperature and transfer to a clean, airtight container.

MAKES 1 COCKTAIL

- 1¼ ounces (37 ml) Fernet-Branca
- ¾ ounce (22 ml) aged rum
- ¾ ounce (22 ml) freshly squeezed lime juice
- ¾ ounce (22 ml) Ginger Syrup
- ½ ounce (15 ml) Demerara Syrup (page 200)
- 3 ounces (89 ml) club soda

Place all the ingredients, except the club soda, in a metal shaker. Quickly shake and strain into a highball glass. Top with the club soda and fill with ice.

CLASSIC NEGRONI

It's gotten trendy to make Negronis with a higher ratio of gin to Campari and sweet vermouth, but ours sticks to the original equal-parts formula. We prefer Beefeater in our Negroni, which, because it's distilled in the London Dry style, has more than enough kick to anchor the bitterness of the Campari and sweetness of the vermouth. Vermouth also really makes a difference in a Negroni, and while it might be a little off-brand for us to go with a French label here, Dolin Rouge brings a softness this drink needs.

MAKES 1 COCKTAIL

1 ounce (30 ml) London Dry gin, such as Beefeater

1 ounce (30 ml) Campari

1 ounce (30 ml) sweet vermouth, such as Dolin Rouge

1 half-moon orange slice for serving

Place all the ingredients, except the orange slice, in a mixing glass, add ice, and stir briskly for 30 seconds. Strain into a rocks glass filled with ice. Garnish with the half-moon of orange and a green straw.

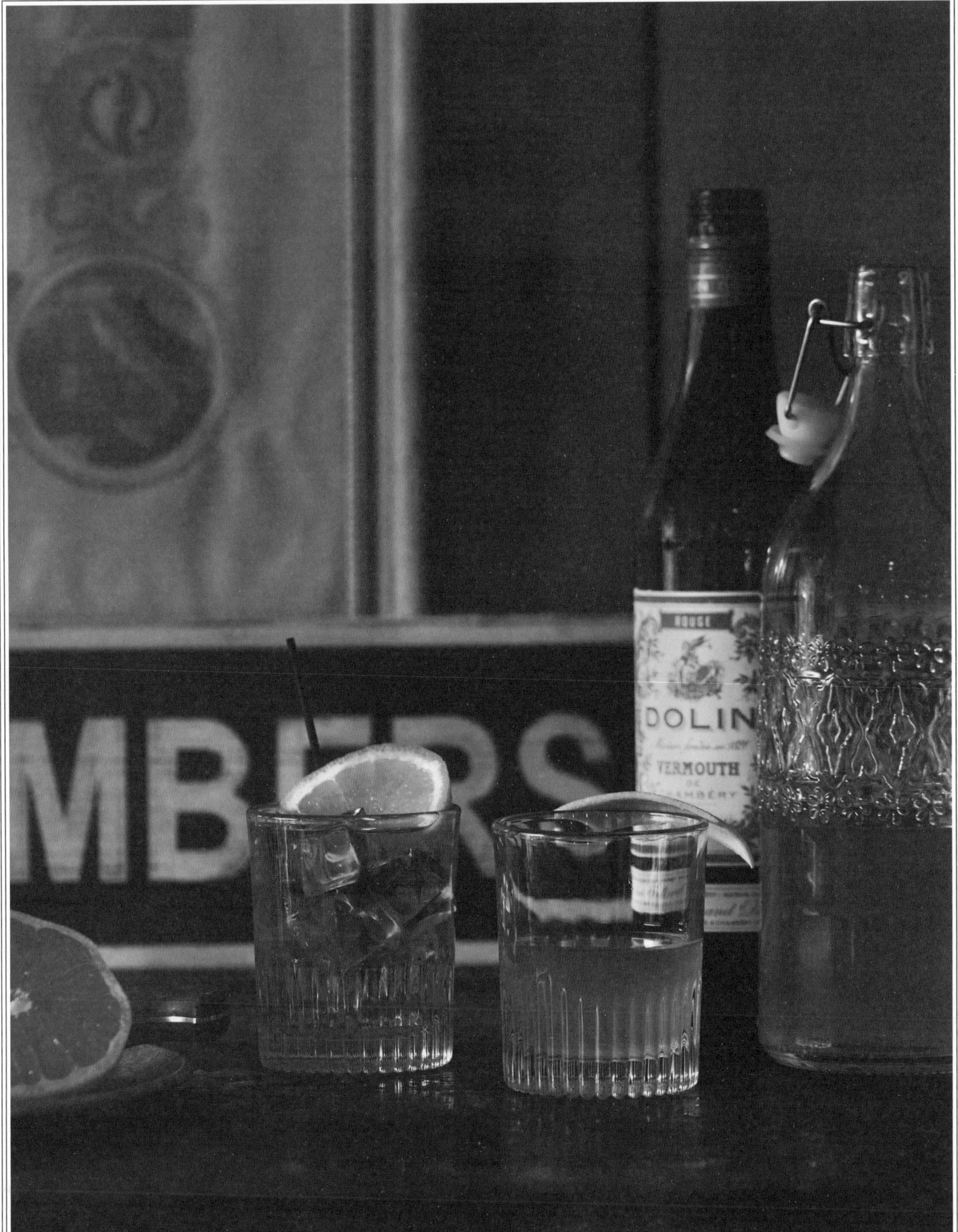

ROUGE
DOLIN
VERMOUTH

NEGRONI MILK PUNCH

Although we opt for delicate French vermouth in our straight Negroni, when we do that cocktail in the style of a clarified milk punch, we pull out the powerhouse that is Carpano Antica Formula, a regal sweet vermouth from Torino. To make the punch, we pour the vermouth and the grapefruit and lime juices over warm milk. The mix instantly curdles, not looking like anything you would want to drink, but after straining out the solids, you're left with a liquid that appears crystal clear but has the body and richness of dairy. We stir in gin and chill it down completely before serving. Like the D'Adamo, this recipe makes a sixteen-drink batch, so invite some people over.

NEGRONI MILK PUNCH

MAKES ABOUT 2 QUARTS (2 L);
MAKES 16 COCKTAILS

- 10 ounces (296 ml) Campari
- 10 ounces (296 ml) sweet vermouth
- 10 ounces (296 ml) freshly squeezed grapefruit juice
- 6 ounces (177 ml) freshly squeezed lime juice
- 30 ounces (890 ml) whole milk
- 20 ounces (590 ml) London Dry gin, such as Beefeater

Combine all the ingredients, except the milk and gin, in a clean, airtight container and refrigerate until cold. Warm the milk in a pot over medium heat until it reaches 180°F (82°C). Add the refrigerated cocktail mix to the warm milk and let it rest for 30 minutes. Strain through a chinois lined with cheesecloth. Repeat until the liquid is clear, which takes 2 or 3 strains. Add the gin, stir to combine, and bottle in a clean, airtight container. Refrigerate until completely chilled before serving. The milk punch keeps for about 4 weeks in the fridge.

MAKES 1 COCKTAIL

- 4 ounces (118 ml) Negroni Milk Punch, chilled
- 1 (3-inch [7.5 cm]) strip grapefruit peel for serving

Pour the milk punch into an 8-ounce (236 ml) rocks glass. Express the oils from the grapefruit peel over the punch and balance it on the rim of the glass.

ORANGE BLOSSOM LIMONATA

The fragrance of orange blossom water makes this summery Sicilian lemonade extra-special. It's a terrific mixer for vodka, but also perfectly delicious on its own as a non-alcoholic cooler. Switch out the water for seltzer to make it sparkle.

MAKES 4 DRINKS

- **5½ ounces (163 ml) freshly squeezed lemon juice**
- **5½ ounces (163 ml) Demerara Syrup (page 200)**
- **1½ teaspoons (7 ml) orange blossom water**
- **16 ounces (473 ml) water**
- **4 pinches of toasted ground aniseeds for serving**
- **8 star anise pods for serving**
- **4 thin orange slices for serving**
- **4 thin lemon slices for serving**

Stir together the lemon juice, syrup, orange blossom water, and water in a pitcher. Fill 4 highball glasses with ice. Pour the limonata over the ice and garnish each glass with a pinch of aniseeds, 2 star anise pods, and 1 slice each of lemon and orange.

ANISETTE

Bottles of homemade and store-bought liqueurs and digestifs just have a way of appearing on my family's dessert table. They're a great way to settle your stomach after a big meal (and keep the good times going). Anisette is one of my favorites. Most traditional recipes call for just aniseed, but I use star anise as well along with cinnamon, cloves, and vanilla bean to create a more complex drink. Serve the anisette solo, with chilled water as they do in Sicily, or poured into coffee or espresso for a café corretto.

MAKES ABOUT 2½ QUARTS (2.4 L)

1 quart (1 L) vodka
7 tablespoons (50 g) aniseeds
25 star anise pods
3 cinnamon sticks
8 whole cloves
½ vanilla bean, scraped
1 quart (1 L) Demerara Syrup (page 200)
¼ to ½ cup (59 to 118 ml) water

Place all the ingredients, except the syrup and water, in a nonreactive, airtight container. Steep for 1 month in a cool, dry place. Strain out the spices through a strainer lined with a large coffee filter, stir in the syrup, and adjust the strength of the anisette with the water to taste. Serve chilled.

LIMONCELLO

I make several different types of 'cello, including pistachio, almond, and coconut, but classic lemon is so refreshing. I actually add a little orange peel to mine, just to round out the flavor. Look for lemons with thick rinds, and if you're buying all that citrus anyway, you might as well bake our Lemon Crostata (page 178) with the leftover fruit.

MAKES ABOUT 2½ QUARTS (2.4 L) LIMONCELLO

2 quarts (2 L) grain alcohol
Grated zest of 15 lemons
Grated zest of 4 oranges
2 cups (473 ml) Demerara Syrup (page 200)

Place the alcohol and zests in a nonreactive, airtight container and steep for 3 weeks in a cool, dry place. Strain the mixture through a strainer lined with a large coffee filter. Stir in the syrup. Serve chilled.

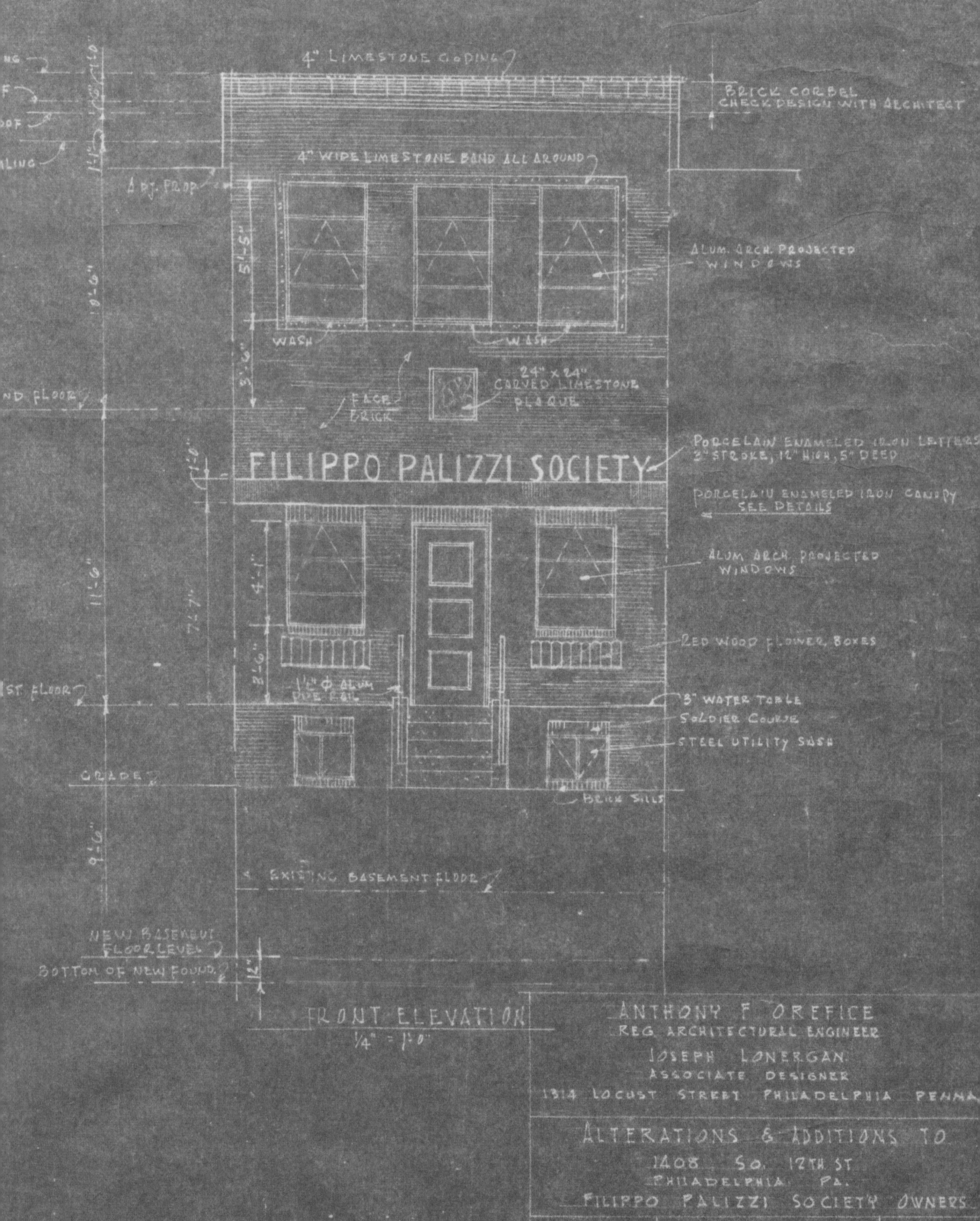

4" LIMESTONE COPING
BRICK CORBEL
CHECK DESIGN WITH ARCHITECT
4" WIDE LIMESTONE BAND ALL AROUND
ADJ. PROP.
ALUM. ARCH. PROJECTED WINDOWS
WASH
WASH
24" x 24" CARVED LIMESTONE PLAQUE
FACE BRICK
FILIPPO PALIZZI SOCIETY
PORCELAIN ENAMELED IRON LETTERS 3" STROKE, 12" HIGH, 5" DEEP
PORCELAIN ENAMELED IRON CANOPY SEE DETAILS
ALUM. ARCH. PROJECTED WINDOWS
RED WOOD FLOWER BOXES
1½" Φ ALUM. PIPE RAIL
3" WATER TABLE
SOLDIER COURSE
STEEL UTILITY SASH
BRICK SILLS
GRADE
EXISTING BASEMENT FLOOR
NEW BASEMENT FLOOR LEVEL
BOTTOM OF NEW FOUND.
FRONT ELEVATION
¼" = 1'0"
ANTHONY F. OREFICE
REG. ARCHITECTURAL ENGINEER
JOSEPH LONERGAN
ASSOCIATE DESIGNER
1314 LOCUST STREET PHILADELPHIA PENNA.
ALTERATIONS & ADDITIONS TO
1408 SO. 12TH ST.
PHILADELPHIA PA.
FILIPPO PALIZZI SOCIETY OWNERS
NOV. 10 1951
COMM. 51

INDEX

Note: Page references in *italics* indicate photographs.

R

S

T

V

Z

FOUNDED
1918

PALIZZI

Access certificates for WebTutor™ Advantage with Personal Trainer® can be bundled with the textbook or sold separately. For more information, including a demo, visit http://webtutor.swlearning.com. To adopt the course in either WebCT™ or Blackboard®, contact your sales representative or sign-up at http://webtutor.thomsonlearning.com.

Personal Trainer 3.0

Instructors consistently cite reading the text and completing graded homework assignments as a key to student success in financial accounting; however, most instructors do not have the time to grade homework. Personal Trainer solves this time problem by allowing professors to assign as many textbook exercises and problems as they like and Personal Trainer will grade all but the essay responses and post the grade in the gradebook, all real time! Personal Trainer is an Internet-based homework tutor where students can complete the textbook homework assignments, receive hints, submit their answers, and receive immediate feedback. For more information, including a demo, contact your sales representative.

Xtra! for Financial Accounting

Available as an optional, free bundle with every new textbook, Xtra! gives students FREE access to games and interactive quizzes so that students can test their understanding of the content of the fourth edition.

NEW! Thomson One

Keep your students current. Bundled free with each new text is an access card to get students into this rich, dynamic online resource. In addition to finding the latest financial information about the chapter focus and text flagship companies, students can address the questions posed in the new THOMSON ONE Business School Edition Cases at the end of each chapter. By using "live" data, students quickly see why accounting is the language of business!

To order call 1.800.423.0563

http://

For more information, visit:
http://porter.swlearning.com

The Porter/Norton Product Web site is designed specifically for ***Financial Accounting: The Impact on Decision Makers, The Alternative to Debits and Credits, 4e.*** The features include online and downloadable instructor and student resources, and an interactive study center, organized by chapter, with that contains learning objectives, Web links, online quizzes with automatic feedback, and more.

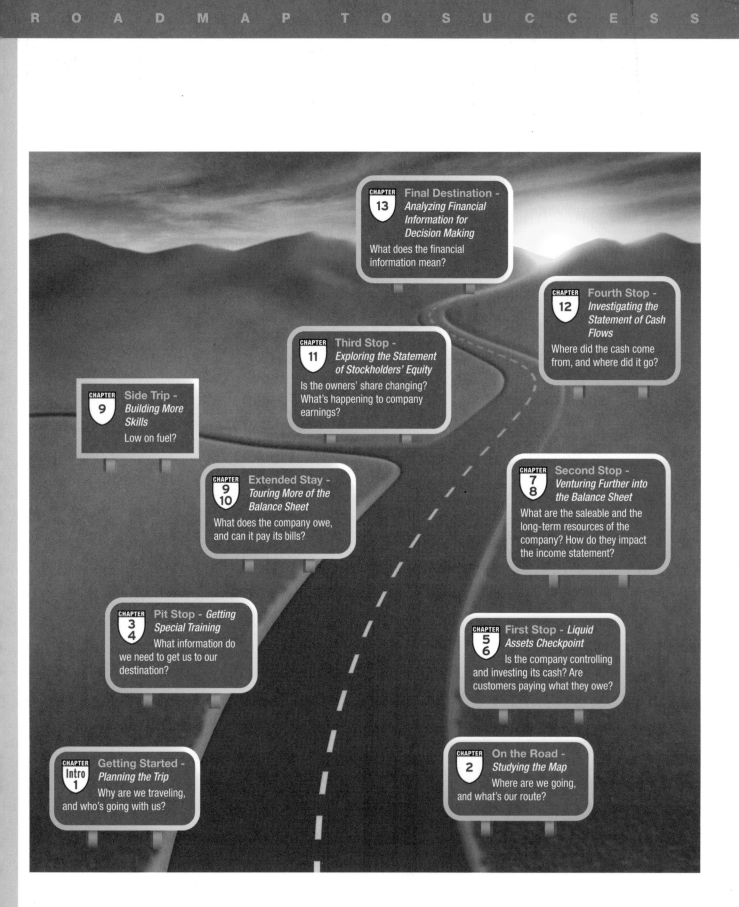

Final Destination - *Analyzing Financial Information for Decision Making*

What does the financial information mean?

Fourth Stop - *Investigating the Statement of Cash Flows*

Where did the cash come from, and where did it go?

Third Stop - *Exploring the Statement of Stockholders' Equity*

Is the owners' share changing? What's happening to company earnings?

Side Trip - *Building More Skills*

Low on fuel?

Extended Stay - *Touring More of the Balance Sheet*

What does the company owe, and can it pay its bills?

Second Stop - *Venturing Further into the Balance Sheet*

What are the saleable and the long-term resources of the company? How do they impact the income statement?

Pit Stop - *Getting Special Training*

What information do we need to get us to our destination?

First Stop - *Liquid Assets Checkpoint*

Is the company controlling and investing its cash? Are customers paying what they owe?

Getting Started - *Planning the Trip*

Why are we traveling, and who's going with us?

CHAPTER 2

On the Road - *Studying the Map*

Where are we going, and what's our route?

FINANCIAL ACCOUNTING

The Impact on Decision Makers

THE ALTERNATIVE TO DEBITS AND CREDITS

GARY A. PORTER

University of St. Thomas – Minnesota

CURTIS L. NORTON

Northern Illinois University

Australia · Canada · Mexico · Singapore · Spain · United Kingdom · United States

Financial Accounting: The Impact on Decision Makers
The Alternative to Debits and Credits, 4th Edition

Gary A. Porter and Curtis L. Norton

VP/Editorial Director:
Jack W. Calhoun

VP/Editor-in-Chief:
George Werthman

Acquisitions Editor:
Julie Lindsay Moulton

Developmental Editor:
Sara W. Wilson

Marketing Manager:
Heather MacMaster

Production Editor:
Robert Dreas

Media Developmental Editor:
Sally Nieman

Media Production Editor:
Robin K. Browning

Manufacturing Coordinator:
Doug Wilke

Production House:
Litten Editing and Production, Inc.

Compositor:
GGS Information Services, Inc.

Printer:
Quebecor World
Versailles, Kentucky

Sr. Design Project Manager:
Michelle Kunkler

Cover and Internal Designer:
Liz Harasymczuk Design

Cover Image:
© PictureQuest

Internal Illustrations:
Allan Moon Illustration & Design
Milton, Ontario

Photography Manager:
Deanna Ettinger

Printed in the United States of America
1 2 3 4 5 07 06 05 04

ISBN: 0-324-27266-9
ISBN: 0-324-23305-1 (Book)
Library of Congress Control Number: 2003114606

For more information, contact South-Western, 5191 Natorp Boulevard, Mason, Ohio 45040.
Or you can visit our Internet site at: http://www.swlearning.com

Winnebago Industries 2002 Annual Report reprinted with permission.

Monaco Coach Corporation 2002 Annual Report reprinted with permission.

Preface

WELCOME ABOARD THE FOURTH EDITION!

Follow our Roadmap to Success! As you and your students take the "trip" though our text, you will experience a "journey" that will reveal the primary information needed for understanding the business environment and the important role of financial accounting in that environment. You will venture through the process of transforming the information from transactions to financial reports, deciphering the important information contained in those reports, and then analyzing it to make financial decisions.

Follow Our Well-Developed Road to Success

Throughout the development of our first three editions, we have found an increasing number of instructors remove debits and credits substantially or entirely from the classroom. Many instructors are focusing their introductory financial accounting course on what decision makers want to know about accounting information, rather than how that information is prepared. They do so, in part, to broaden the scope of the course for their majors to include larger business issues and, in part, to help prepare non-majors to appreciate the financial information that will be important in their professional lives. Through this, our "Alternative to Debits and Credits" edition, we emphasize how to read and analyze financial information and make decisions. We continue our use of the transactions effects equation that shows graphically how each business transaction affects the accounting equation and financial statements.

Throughout this preface, we indicate the many new and continuing features and key supporting materials that focus student learning on financial understanding, analysis, and decision making. We provide *many choices* for coverage in order to meet the needs of your course and your students. As reflected in the table of contents, there are some end-of-chapter appendices that provide additional information and decision-focused coverage. Any one of these may be included or excluded as desired. In addition, there is a large selection of pedagogical elements and assignments to allow *flexibility* and *variety.*

TRAVEL ON A FIRM FOUNDATION

For the fourth edition, we remain committed to four principles that have been instrumental to the success of the earlier editions:

- An emphasis on *pedagogy* and *student appeal that accommodates most learning styles.*
- A focus on *financial statements.*
- A focus on *actual public companies.*
- A *decision-making* emphasis.

Our adherence to these principles has meant that thousands of business majors and accounting majors alike are prepared for future business success. We have continued and further enhanced and expanded those elements that have proven to be most effective.

Rely on the Text's Solid Infrastructure

Supporting the balance within the text is a basic internal structure, developed around the **balance sheet**. Assisting in tying that structure together are the flagship companies, to which students return many times as they develop their understanding of financial information. A roadmap provides a recurring visual to assist students in understanding where they are in their journey through the text.

NEW! Our **Roadmap to Success** guides students as they move through the text. The master roadmap appears at the beginning of the text, across from the title page, and provides an overview of the text. Each signpost displays one or more key questions for each chapter.

The roadmap reappears at the beginning of each chapter, where its sign expands to include a statement of the core focus of the chapter and serves as a continuing reminder of the text's direction and decision-making coverage.

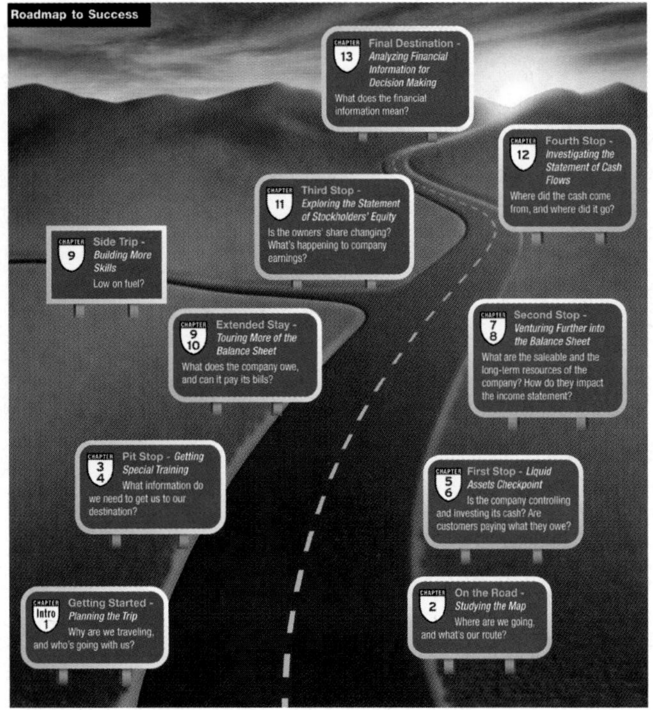

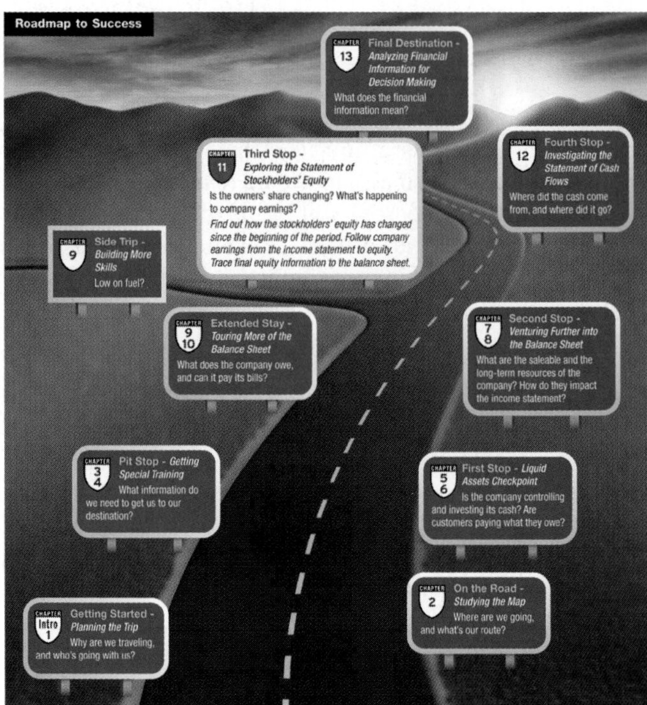

NEW! Information about **Winnebago Industries** and **Monaco Coach Corporation**, the new flagship companies, is interwoven throughout the text. Students are introduced to Winnebago Industries in the Introduction section and Chapter 1 and Monaco Coach Corporation in Chapter 2. In subsequent chapters, the flagship companies are revisited many times with the coverage identified by a feature icon. The entire Winnebago Industries and Monaco Coach Corporation 2002 Annual Reports are reproduced in Appendices A and B at the end of the text. Subsequent annual reports will be linked to the text's Web site (http://porter.swlearning.com) or may be accessed directly through the company sites (http://www.winnebagoind.com) and (http://www.monacocoach.com).

Part Openers. Each part is introduced by **A Word to Students**, which provides an overview of the coverage to come, the title of the chapters and appendices contained within the part, and a photo introducing the featured companies.

- **Part I—The Accounting Model**—begins with **Getting Started in Business**. This introduction is designed to help students orient themselves to the business world so that all members of the class will have basic information about the structure of businesses, the importance of financial accounting, and the decision makers in the business environment. The story of Winnebago Industries begins its path through the text in this introduction. From there, students move through Chapters 1–4. These chapters describe the four main financial statements and supporting information found in annual reports, GAAP, accrual accounting, and the basic processing of transactions through the accounting cycle.
- **Part II—Accounting for Assets**—and **Part III—Accounting for Liabilities and Owners' Equity**—"tour" the balance sheet, going from assets through liabilities to equity. We present the essential explanations of the statement's core content and clearly tie the balance sheet accounts to the other financial statements and disclosures.

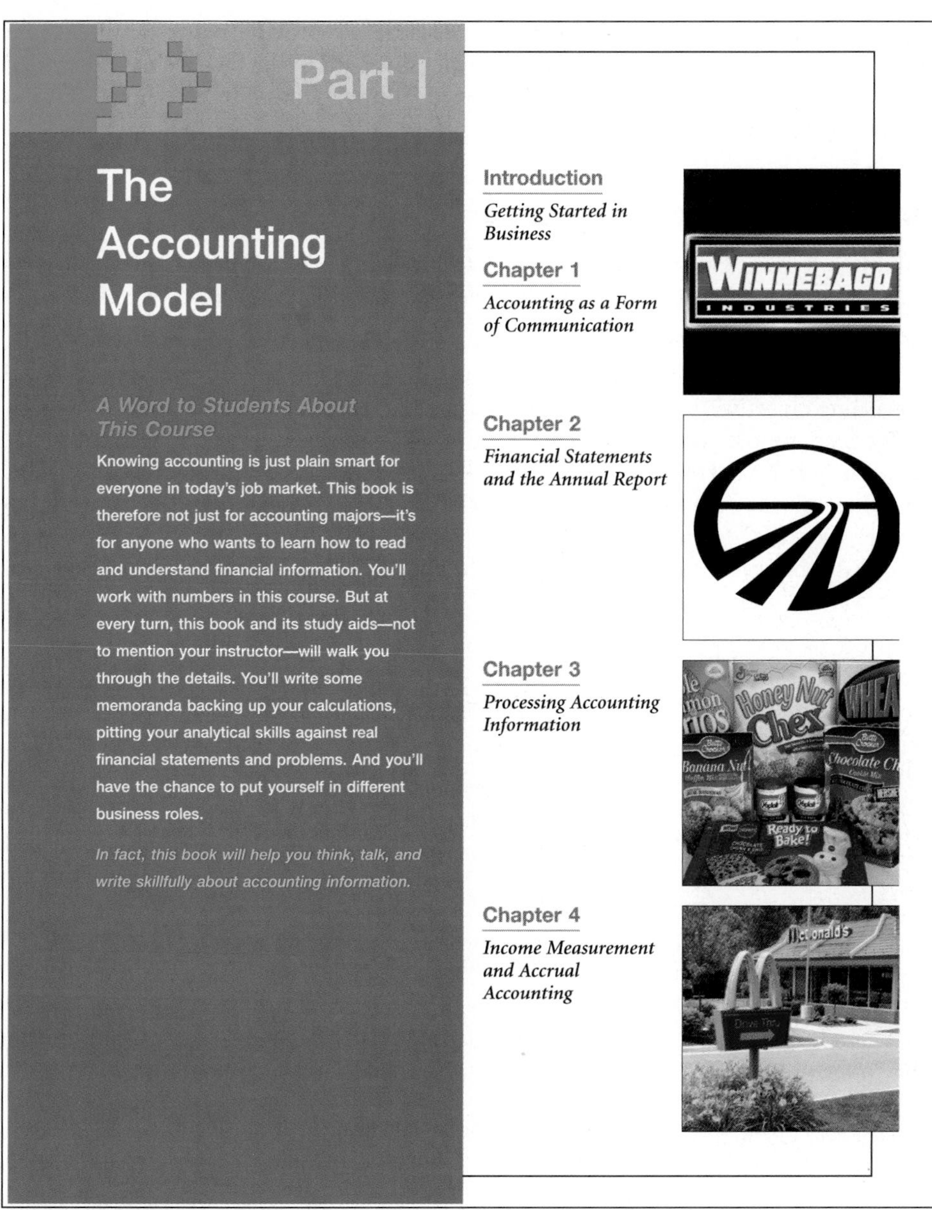

- **Part IV—Additional Topics in Financial Accounting**—provides an in-depth explanation of the statement of cash flows with descriptions of both the direct and indirect methods. This section also brings together and expands on all of the analysis coverage presented earlier in the text.

Tools. Supporting several chapters are appendices that contain special "tools" for students. These include coverage of *perpetual inventory costing method* (Ch. 7 appendix), *payroll accounting* (Ch. 9 appendix A), *using Excel for interest calculations* (Ch.9 appendix B), *accounting for unincorporated businesses* (Ch. 11), *statement of cash flows preparation using a work-sheet approach* (Ch. 12 appendix), and *reporting and analyzing non-ordinary items in the income statement* (Ch. 13 appendix).

Integrative Problem. We have strategically placed a comprehensive problem at the end of each part. Each assignment challenges the student to think through a multifaceted problem that requires knowledge learned throughout that section of the text.

Complete Glossary. For quick reference, a comprehensive glossary of key terms is located at the end of the text. Also included is the page number where each term was originally defined.

Company and Subject Indexes. Because we provide many examples and references to actual companies and other entities throughout the text, we have provided a separate company index for your convenience. This is followed by a complete subject index for quick referencing.

Navigate Our New Features

In addition to our new roadmap and new flagship companies, we have further enriched our text features to assist students with understanding financial accounting.

NEW! What External Decision Makers Want to Know. After students get their bearings from the chapter's roadmap, the introduction to the chapter's focus company, and the learning objectives reference list, they learn what it is about the content of the chapter that is so important. What do external decision makers want to know about topics like inventory and current liabilities? What kind of questions do these decision makers ask? Where do they find the basic information they need? What about accounting do they need to know to understand the information? How do they interpret that information? As the students study the chapter, they will gain a stronger understanding of the answers to these questions.

WHAT EXTERNAL DECISION MAKERS WANT TO KNOW ABOUT STOCKHOLDERS' EQUITY

DECISION MAKING

External decision makers want to know whether or not to buy stock in a company. They want to know what classes of stock the company currently has. They also want to know whether the company will issue dividends to the stockholders and whether the stock price will increase after the stock is purchased. Most importantly, they want to know whether the company will be profitable and how the company will use that profit. When profits are retained in the business, investors want to know how it will be used.

▸ *ASK ESSENTIAL QUESTIONS*

- Should potential investors buy stock in the company?
- Should existing stockholders continue or should they sell their stock?
- Can stockholders expect to receive a dividend from the company?
- Will the company need to issue more stock to finance its operations?

▸ *FIND BASIC INFORMATION*

The balance sheet and the statement of cash flows, along with the supporting notes, are the key sources of information about a company's stock and stockholders' equity. This information tells:

- the dollar amount of stock that has been issued,
- the different types or classes of stock,
- the amount of the profits that has been retained in the company,
- whether dividends have been declared by the company, and
- how much cash has been generated as a result of the stock

▸ *UNDERSTAND ACCOUNTING PRINCIPLES*

To understand the basic information that is found, decision makers must understand the underlying accounting principles (GAAP) that have been applied to create the reported information. For stockholders' equity, these principles determine:

- the amount of equity contributed to stockholders
- the equity earned by the company and retained within the company

▸ *INTERPRET ANALYTICAL INFORMATION*

The most important measure of the stock is the market value of the stock on the stock market or stock exchange. The amount of the dividends can be measured by computing the dividend payout ratio that indicates what portion of the company's profit has been paid out to stockholders. Another measure of the company's stock is the book value per share that indicates the rights of the stockholders if the company were liquidated.

NEW! Interpret: You Decide. As students learn about analyzing accounting information, they are presented with a challenge to think like a decision maker. They are asked to interpret financial information found in the text or other resources in the same way managers, investors, and others do everyday. Instructors are encouraged to use these challenges as a way to enrich student understanding.

> ***Interpret: You Decide.*** Take a close look at the stockholders' equity section of the balance sheet of Southwest Airlines provided in the chapter opener for this chapter. What is the number of shares authorized and number of shares issued at the balance sheet date? What does this indicate about the company's use of treasury stock? Also, use the Internet or *The Wall Street Journal* to find the company's stock price. What have been the high and low prices over the last year? What does this indicate about the company's stock as a potential investment?

NEW! Internal Decisions. Students will also see coverage of key Internal Decisions that involve accountants or others in management. These decisions are identified by an icon in the margin.

INTERNAL DECISION

NEW! Extensively Revised Chapters 5, 6, and 7. The coverage of Cash, Internal Controls, Receivables, Investments, and Inventories/Cost of Good Sold has been reorganized to better match the topics and enhance the flow of the material.

NEW! Comparing Two Companies in the Same Industry: Winnebago Industries and Monaco Coach Corporation. Each chapter contains a new **comparative case**. By completing these cases, students gain a greater understanding of two competitors in the same industry. They discover differences in approaches to reporting financial information and analyze the annual reports to get a better understanding of how financial information is used by decision makers.

Cases

Reading and Interpreting Financial Statements

http://www.winnebagoind.com
http://www.monacocoach.com

Case 4-1 ***Comparing Two Companies in the Same Industry: Winnebago Industries and Monaco Coach Corporation*** **LO 3, 4, 5**

Refer to the financial information for Winnebago Industries and Monaco Coach Corporation in Appendices A and B at the end of the book.

Required

1. Neither company reports on its balance sheet an account titled "Accounts Receivable." Identify the account or accounts on each company's balance sheet that is equivalent to Accounts Receivable.
2. What dollar amount does each company report in Prepaid Expenses on its balance sheet at the end of 2002? When the benefits from this asset expire in the future this account will be credited and an expense account will be debited. For each company, identify the account or accounts on its income statement that you would expect to be debited.
3. On its balance sheet, Winnebago Industries reports a "Property and Equipment" account and deducts from it "Accumulated Depreciation." How does this way of presenting the long-term tangible assets differ from the approach used by Monaco Coach on its balance sheet? Does Monaco Coach disclose the same type of information elsewhere in the annual report? If so, where? Why do you think these companies use different approaches to report this information?

In this Fourth Edition, the **From Concept to Practice** feature not only encourages students to think more about the focus companies but also about the two flagship companies, Winnebago Industries and Monaco Coach Corporation. By comparing these two competitors, students gain a better understanding of how different companies, in the same industry, communicate their financial information and how analysis can assist decision making. (Teaching notes are provided in the Instructor's Manual.)

From Concept to Practice 13.1

Reading the Annual Reports of Winnebago Industries and Monaco Coach Corporation

Where do Winnebago Industries' and Monaco Coach Corporation's annual reports provide financial summaries? How many years does each include? In terms of a trend over time, which item on each summary do you think is the most significant?

NEW! Updates for the Latest Pronouncements. Chapters 8 and 10 have been revised to reflect the impact of FASB Statements 141, 142, and 145. As new pronouncements arise that impact on text coverage, additional updates will be posted on our Web site (http://porter.swlearning.com).

- Chapter 8 includes discussion of the impact of the new rules for amortizing intangibles with finite lives and the impairment rules for intangible, such as goodwill. Care is taken throughout to focus attention on how these changes affect the financial statements rather than on the specifics of the authoritative standards, something better left to an intermediate accounting course.
- Chapter 10 reflects the recent change in the classification of any gain or loss on the early retirement of bonds. The new financial accounting standard reverses an earlier pronouncement, which required extraordinary treatment for these gains and losses.

NEW! Ratios for Decision Making. The purpose of this presentation, which appears in chapters where ratios and other key calculations are introduced, is to briefly review the core reason for use of the ratio(s) for decision making. The ratios are restated along with their formulas. In addition, the financial statement or note source of each ratio component is identified. This consolidated review of the chapters ratios provide students with a quick reference and reinforcement.

Ratios for Decision Making

Long-term assets are used to produce the products and services that allow a company to operate profitably. Therefore, it is important for investors and creditors to analyze whether the long-term assets are sufficient to support the company's activities. Investors and creditors should analyze the average life of the assets, the average age of the assets, and the asset turnover. The asset turnover is a measure of how many dollars of assets are necessary to generate a dollar of sales. The following ratios can be used to calculate the life, age, and turnover of the long-term assets (assuming the company is using the straight-line method of depreciation):

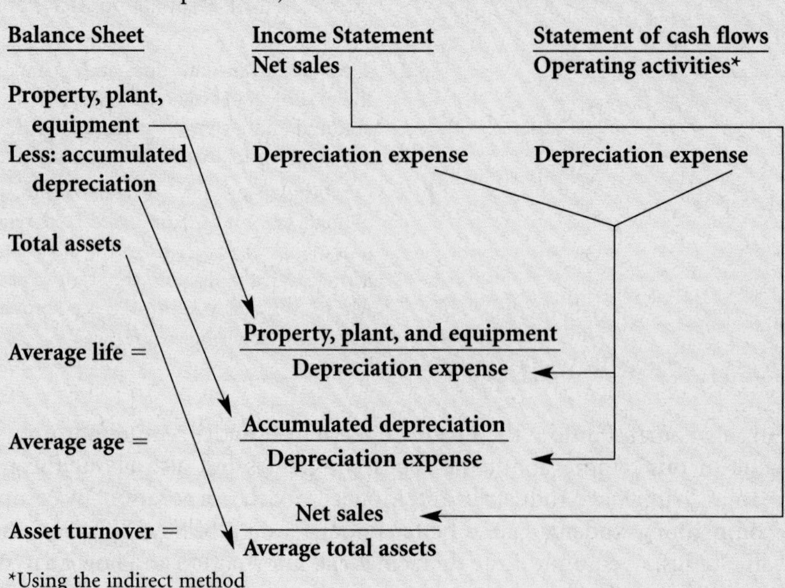

NEW! Impact on the Financial Reports. The purpose of this presentation is to show, in one place, the impact of the chapter's topical coverage on one or more of the four financial statements and the notes. This also reinforces how interconnected these reports are and where decision makers should expect to see impact and disclosure.

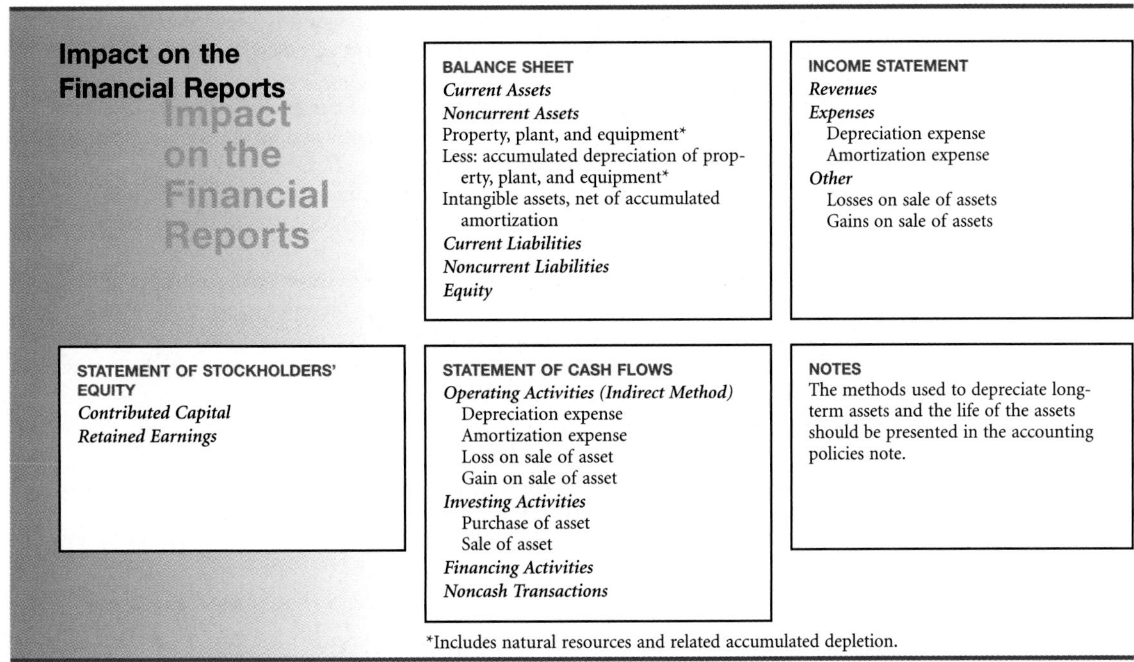

NEW! Introduction to Ethics in Accounting. Chapter 1 features expanded coverage of ethics, with an added framework that provides students with a structure for analyzing ethical issues. As students evaluate the issues raised in the **Ethics Cases** throughout the text, they can easily refer to this guide for assistance.

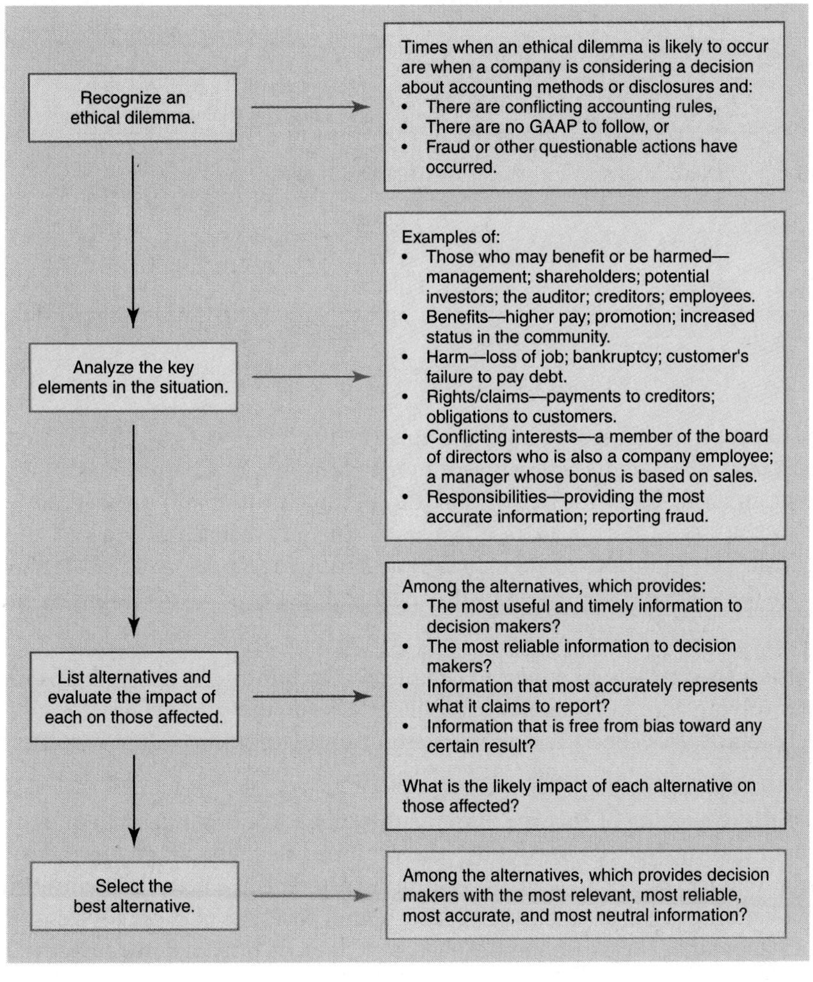

NEW! Ethics in Accounting. In select chapters, these new boxes contain easy-to-understand and timely information about ethical issues experienced by real companies. Questions are asked to encourage students to think about the situations and issues. (Teaching notes are provided in the Instructor's Manual.)

Ethics in Accounting

Enron Corporation

In late 2001, Enron, the nation's largest marketer of electricity and natural gas, reported massive losses and reductions in shareholder equity. At that time, the company issued a major restatement of their previously issued financial statements that covered a four-year period and then filed for bankruptcy.

Enron management, working closely with its chief consultant and auditor, Arthur Andersen, had set up several partnerships. These were owned by the Enron Corporation. Then, Enron accountants recorded a significant amount of Enron's long-term debt on the books of the partnerships rather than on the corporation's books. By doing this, Enron avoided reporting billions of dollars of debt on its own balance sheets.

During the period of these transactions, Enron executives were paid large bonuses that were based on Enron's earnings performance and increases in its stock price.

What did the company do that was of ethical concern? Why should Enron have disclosed the debt on its balance sheet instead of on that of the partnerships? How did not having the debt on Enron's books affect the company's earnings and its executives' bonuses?

Sources: Mitchell Pacelle, "Enron report gives details of deals that masked debt," *The Wall Street Journal*, September 23, 2002; "The Fall of Enron," *Business News Online*, December 17, 2001.

NEW! Spreadsheet Design. The introductory spreadsheet, presented in Ch. 3, has a new design to ease the transition for the student to the more comprehensive spreadsheet.

	Assets					= Liabilities		+ Owners' Equity + Revenues − Expenses	
TRANS. NO.	CASH	ACCT. REC.	EQUIP.	BLDG.	LAND	ACCT. PAY.	NOTES PAY.	CAPITAL STOCK	RET. EARN.
Bal.	$100,000							$100,000	
2				$150,000	$50,000		$200,000		
Bal.	$100,000			$150,000	$50,000		$200,000	$100,000	
Totals			$300,000					$300,000	

NEW! Assistance with Calculations. As instructors, we realize the varied approaches used to teach students time value of money concepts. In Chapter 9, as either an alternative or an addition to the use of tables to perform future and present value calculations, students are introduced to the use of financial calculators to aid the process. One of the most popular of these, a Texas Instrument model, is illustrated in the examples in the chapter. The use of a financial calculator is also reinforced in Chapter 10.

NEW! Excel as a Tool. A new appendix to Chapter 9, "Accounting Tools: Using Excel for Problems Involving Interest Calculations," illustrates for the student how one of the most widely used spreadsheets can serve as a tool in solving time value of money problems.

NEW! Expanded Coverage of Income Statement Items. It is not unusual to find an income statement that include the impact of a discontinued segment, an extraordinary item, or cumulative effect of a change in an accounting principle. To better prepare students for understanding these disclosures, we have added coverage of these topics in a new Chapter 13 appendix, "Reporting and Analyzing Other Income Statement Items."

Which Way To Go?

R&D Expense or Long-Term Asset?

For the past six months, Taz Industries has been struggling with a problem in its production line. The number of units produced each day has been steadily dropping. The company believes worn-out equipment is partly the cause. Three months ago, the plant manager put an engineer and the senior machinist to work, full time, to solve the problem. They created a new, electronic tool that, when used in the assembly process, significantly improves production. It is expected that this tool will be useful for at least the next five years.

The total cost of the salaries for the engineer and machinist for three months, plus the cost of materials used in the development process, is $35,000. This includes the cost of time and materials for creating early models that did not solve the problem.

Even though the company plans to use the new tool only for internal production and has no intention of selling it, management believes obtaining a patent is a good idea. The various fees involved in obtaining the patent are expected to total $10,000.

How should the company record the costs? Why should they be recorded in this manner?

NEW! Which Way to Go? In accounting, there are many decisions that must be made regarding how a transaction should be handled and what its effect will be on reported financial information. We have added this feature to allow you and your students to discuss some of those choices and their impact. Suggested solutions are provided in the Instructor's Resource Manual.

THOMSON ONE Business School Edition Case

Case 8-8 *Using THOMSON ONE for Walt Disney Company*

Use THOMSON ONE to obtain current information about the financial position and stock price of Walt Disney.

Begin by entering the company's ticker symbol, DIS, and then selecting "GO." On the opening screen you will see background information about the company, key financial ratios, and some recent data concerning stock price. To research their stock price further, you click the Prices tab. At the top of the Price Chart, click on the "Interactive Chart." To obtain a 1-year chart, go to "Time Frame," click on the down arrow, and select 1 year. Then click on "Draw," and a 1-year chart should appear.

http://disney.go.com

You can also find Walt Disney's recent financial statements. Near the top of the screen, click on "Financials" and select "Financial Statements." Refer to the stockholders equity portion of the company's balance sheet.

Based on your use of THOMSON ONE, answer the following questions:

1. Has the amount of intangible assets increased or decreased since the 2002 annual report? Which intangible assets have changed the most?
2. What is the current market price of the stock? How has the stock price responded since the relatively low stock prices of mid-2002?
3. What are the most important new television programs introduced by Walt Disney Company? What are the most important new movies developed by Walt Disney Company?

NEW! THOMSON ONE. Keep your students current. Bundled **free** with each new text is an access card to get students into this rich, dynamic online resource. In addition to finding the latest financial information about the chapter focus and text flagship companies, students can address the questions posed in the **new** THOMSON ONE Business School Edition Cases at the end of each chapter. By using "live" data, students quickly see why accounting is the language of business!

Explore the Real World

Coverage of well-known companies greatly enhances student interest. We have *fully updated* all of the financial and other relevant information related to the large number of publicly traded companies that we feature.

Focus on Financial Results. As each chapter opens, students are introduced to its focus company. This feature provides up-to-date background and key financial data that create an interest-generating, real-world setting for the reader. This company and its pertinent financial information thread throughout the chapter. All companies are well-known and publicly traded. In addition to Winnebago Industries and Monaco Coach Corporation, examples of chapter-focus companies are Walt Disney, PepsiCo, and Southwest Airlines.

You're in the Driver's Seat. This chapter-opening section contains questions relating to the focus company. Directives assist the reader in thinking about how the chapter's coverage provide answers to decision makers.

FOCUS ON FINANCIAL RESULTS

- Chapter-opening introduction illustrates a key financial issue related to the chapter.

Focus on Financial Results

What groups of people care about the financial performance of Winnebago Industries, one of the leading manufacturers of motor homes and recreational vehicles (RVs) in the United States? Since its founding over 40 years ago, the company's managers, investors, employees, dealers, and suppliers have all had a vested interest in the financial health of the company whose name is synonymous with RVs.

To communicate its financial performance, Winnebago Industries uses the language of accounting. The *selected financial data* shown here[1] summarize key measures including revenue, income, and assets. The information shows that while the company experienced a decline in both net revenues and net income in its 2001 fiscal year, both of these measures increased significantly in 2002. In fact, both revenues and net income reached record levels in 2002. As explained in management's discussion and analysis of its operations, the increase in revenues reflected a number of factors, including low interest rates, an increase in the company's market share, and continued acceptance of the company's new products.

What will be the future of Winnebago Industries? In its 2002 message to the stockholders, the company sounded quite optimistic about its future. In light of this optimism, the company elected to pay its shareholders a cash dividend of $0.20 per share for the sixth consecutive year. Another sign of the company's optimism for its future as well as that of the RV industry is its plans to unveil a new state-of-the-art manufacturing facility in early 2003. The expansion represents the company's most ambitious undertaking of this sort to date and is expected to increase its capacity by approximately 30 percent. Record revenues and earnings in 2002 and a significant rise in its ability to meet customer demand, along with the company's continued leadership position in the RV industry, do indeed give Winnebago Industries and its shareholders good reason to be optimistic about the future.

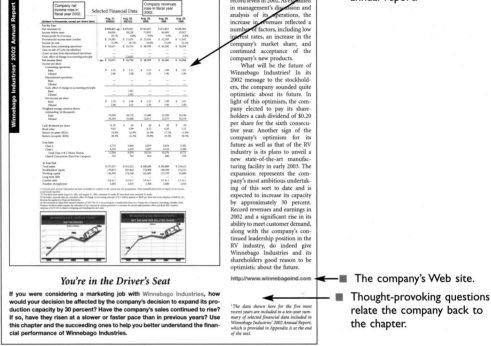

- A financial statement or excerpt from the company's annual report.

Winnebago Industries' 2002 Annual Report

Company net income rose in fiscal year 2002.

Selected Financial Data

Company revenues rose in fiscal year 2002.

(dollars in thousands, except per share data)	Aug. 31, 2002(2)	Aug. 25, 2001(3)	Aug. 26, 2000	Aug. 28, 1999	Aug. 29, 1998
For the Year					
Net revenues (4)	$ 828,403	$ 675,927	$ 747,637	$ 671,653	$ 529,363
Income before taxes	84,056	59,228	73,992	66,609	35,927
Pretax profit % of revenue	10.1%	8.8%	9.9%	9.9%	6.8%
Provision for income taxes (credits)	$ 29,385	$ 15,474	$ 25,593	$ 22,349	$ 11,543
Income tax rate	35.0%	26.1%	34.6%	33.6%	32.1%
Income from continuing operations	$ 54,671	$ 43,754	$ 48,399	$ 44,260	$ 24,384
Gain on sale of Cycle-Sat subsidiary	—	—	—	—	—
(Loss) income from discontinued operations	—	—	—	—	—
Cum. effect of change in accounting principle	—	(1,050)	—	—	—
Net income (loss)	$ 54,671	$ 42,704	$ 48,399	$ 44,260	$ 24,384
Income per share					
Continuing operations					
Basic	$ 2.74	$ 2.11	$ 2.23	$ 1.99	$ 1.01
Diluted	2.68	2.08	2.20	1.96	1.00
Discontinued operations					
Basic	—	—	—	—	—
Diluted	—	—	—	—	—
Cum. effect of change in accounting principle					
Basic	—	(.05)	—	—	—
Diluted	—	(.05)	—	—	—
Net income per share					
Basic	$ 2.74	$ 2.06	$ 2.23	$ 1.99	$ 1.01
Diluted	2.68	2.03	2.20	1.96	1.00
Weighted average common shares outstanding (in thousands)					
Basic	19,949	20,735	21,680	22,209	24,106
Diluted	20,384	21,040	22,011	22,537	24,314
Cash dividends per share	$ .20	$ .20	$ .20	$ .20	$ .20
Book value	9.63	9.99	8.22	6.69	5.11
Return on assets (ROA)	15.9%	12.9%	16.3%	17.1%	11.0%
Return on equity (ROE)	28.2%	22.3%	29.8%	33.3%	20.3%
Unit Sales					
Class A	6,725	5,666	6,819	6,054	5,381
Class C	4,329	3,410	3,697	4,222	3,390
Total Class A & C Motor Homes	11,054	9,076	10,516	10,276	8,771
Class B Conversions (EuroVan Campers)	763	703	854	600	978
At Year End					
Total assets	$ 337,077	$ 351,922	$ 308,686	$ 285,889	$ 230,612
Stockholders' equity	179,815	207,464	174,909	149,384	116,523
Working capital	144,995	174,248	141,683	123,720	92,800
Long-term debt	—	—	—	—	—
Current ratio	2.6 to 1	3.2 to 1	3.0 to 1	2.5 to 1	2.5 to 1
Number of employees	3,685	3,325	3,300	3,400	3,010

(1) Certain prior periods' information has been reclassified to conform to the current year-end presentation. These reclassifications have no impact on net income as previously reported.
(2) The fiscal years ended August 31, 2002, and August 31, 1996, contained 53 weeks; all other fiscal years contained 52 weeks.
(3) Includes a noncash after-tax cumulative effect of change in accounting principle of $1.1 million expense or $0.05 per share due to the adoption of SAB No. 101, Revenue Recognition in Financial Statements.
(4) Net revenues for fiscal 2002 required adoption of EITF No. 01-9 Accounting for Consideration Given by a Vendor for a Customer (Including a Reseller of the Vendor's Product) which requires the reduction of net revenues by certain payments to customers for certain sales incentive offers and fiscal 2001 required adoption of EITF 00-10 related to shipping and handling fees and costs.

NET REVENUES

NET INCOME PER DILUTED SHARE

http://www.winnebagoind.com

- The company's Web site.

You're in the Driver's Seat

If you were considering a marketing job with Winnebago Industries, how would your decision be affected by the company's decision to expand its production capacity by 30 percent? Have the company's sales continued to rise? If so, have they risen at a slower or faster pace than in previous years? Use this chapter and the succeeding ones to help you better understand the financial performance of Winnebago Industries.

[1] *The data shown here for the five most recent years are included in a ten-year summary of selected financial data included in Winnebago Industries' 2002 Annual Report, which is provided in Appendix A at the end of the text.*

- Thought-provoking questions relate the company back to the chapter.

Business Strategy. The current business environment can be very challenging to companies as many of them try to turn around declining positions and grow their businesses. What is the company doing to maintain a strong competitive edge in the marketplace? What are the management strategies? Where is the company placing most of its effort? Often including a global perspective, the information in these boxes answers these and other questions and brings to life the strategic viewpoint of each chapter's focus company. Students find this information to be very interesting and to add an in-depth understanding of the role of financial accounting in the business environment.

Instructors can use these strategy boxes as additional research topics by challenging their students to find out whether the goals of the company's strategy are being reached and what, if any, new strategies have been reported by management in the most recent annual report or other communications.

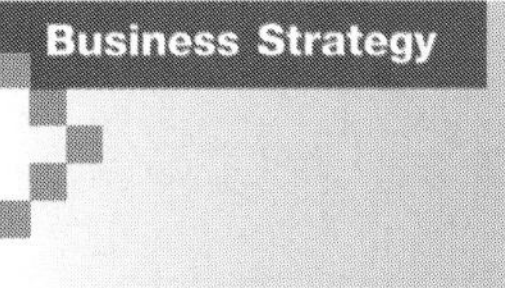

Putting Cash to Use

If a business has too little cash on hand, creditors can't be paid on a timely basis. If it has too much, it may miss opportunities to earn a better return than usually earned on cash in the bank. Cash management is certainly one of the most critical responsibilities of the treasurer's office in a company, and Gap Inc. is no exception. After an upswing in its performance, the specialty retailer found itself flush with cash at the end of 2002. The cash balance of roughly $3.4 billion accounted for nearly 35 percent of total assets!

In June 2003, Gap Inc. announced plans to put its cash to good use. First, the company entered into three-year secured $750 million revolving credit agreements with a group of commercial banks. In addition, Gap Inc. gained access to another $1.2 billion of funds through letter of credit agreements. Why would lenders stand ready to provide almost $2 billion in credit to Gap Inc.? The answer lies in those large cash balances the company built up and the security they provide lenders. For example, the letter of credit agreements were secured by about $1.2 billion in cash. While this portion of the company's cash will be reported as "restricted cash" on the balance sheet, Gap Inc. will continue to earn interest income on it.

Other Featured Companies. *Financial Accounting: The Impact on Decision Makers, The Alternative to Debits and Credits, 4e,* is rich with *recent financial information* about other public companies. Some of these are direct competitors of the chapter's focus company, such as Delta Air Lines, Inc., in Chapter 11 where Southwest Airlines is the featured company, and some are from other industries, such as Nike, Inc., in Chapter 7 where Circuit

Identifying the Components of the Stockholders' Equity Section of the Balance Sheet

LO 1 Identify the components of the Stockholders' Equity category of the balance sheet and the accounts found in each component.

http://www.delta.com

http://www.continental.com

The stockholders' equity portion of the balance sheet of **Delta Air Lines** is provided in Exhibit 11-3. We will focus on the Stockholders' (Shareholders') Equity category of the balance sheet. All corporations, including Delta Air Lines, begin the Stockholders' Equity category with a list of the firm's contributed capital. In some cases, there are two categories of stock: common stock and preferred stock (the latter is discussed later in this chapter). Common stock normally carries voting rights. The common stockholders elect the officers of the corporation and establish its bylaws and governing rules. It is not unusual for corporations to have more than one type of common stock, each with different rights or terms. For example, **Continental Airlines, Inc.**, one of Delta's competitors, has two classes of common stock listed on its 2002 balance sheet.

City Stores, Inc., is the chapter focus company. Information from many public companies is included in assignments, as well. Throughout the text, the *URL* of each company is provided for easy access to its Web site.

Reading and Interpreting Financial Statements. These cases require students to study the financial statement information of publicly traded companies, analyze that information, and prepare their responses. At least one of the cases in each chapter involves financial information for the text's flagship companies (Winnebago Industries and Monaco Coach Corporation).

Which Way to Go: Make Decisions

In addition to the many decision-making challenges involving real company information, the Fourth Edition provides students with the opportunity to place themselves in an important business role and apply reasoning to determine their responses.

Accounting for Your Decisions. Students assume the positions of user of financial information, decision maker, and business person, and are asked to respond to questions about realistic situations they may encounter in the future. Answers are offered to provide guidance to the students.

Accounting for Your Decisions

You Are the Sole Owner

Your accountant has presented you with three sets of financial statements—each with a different depreciation method—and asks you which depreciation method you prefer. You answer that other than for tax purposes, you don't really care. Should you?

ANS: For tax purposes you would prefer to use the accelerated depreciation method, which minimizes your net income so that you can pay the minimum allowable taxes. For financial statement purposes you may use a different method. As a sole owner, you may believe that the depreciation method chosen does not matter because you are more concerned with the cash flow of the firm and depreciation is a noncash item. However, the depreciation method is important if you are going to show your statements to external parties—for example, if you must present your statements to a banker in order to get a loan.

Making Financial Decisions. These cases feature financial information that students must analyze and use to make decisions. Students draw from the chapter content but must also think beyond it to determine their responses.

ETHICS

Accounting and Ethics Cases. As is very obvious in the current business environment, everyone engaged in the financial reporting and decision making must maintain a high level of ethical standards. Thus, is it essential for students throughout their academic studies to practice the process of reasoning through challenging ethical questions.

Learn from Dynamic Guides

On any new adventure, it is very helpful to have experienced guides. When the guide is one that provides dynamic ways to learn, the trip is more successful. Students will find many pedagogical elements in each chapter that create interest, challenge thinking, and strengthen understanding.

Learning Objectives. Students can concentrate on the important information by reviewing the learning objectives, which provide measurable goals. These objectives, which contain the page numbers where the relevant coverage begins, are repeated in the margins at the beginning of that coverage and are indicated by number next to reinforcing assignments.

LEARNING OBJECTIVES

After studying this chapter, you should be able to:

LO 1 Identify the primary users of accounting information and their needs. (p. 14)

LO 2 Explain the purpose of each of the financial statements and the relationships among them, and prepare a set of simple statements. (p. 16)

LO 3 Identify and explain the primary assumptions made in preparing financial statements. (p. 22)

LO 4 Describe the various roles of accountants in organizations. (p. 24)

Straight-line method A method by which the same dollar amount of depreciation is recorded in each year of asset use.

Study Tip

When interest rates increase, present values decrease. This is called an *inverse relationship.*

Marginal Glossaries. The definitions of key terms appear in the margin near their initial use in the text. (Student knowledge of these terms and their definitions is tested in the Key Terms Quiz at the end of the chapter.)

Study Tips. As students move through a chapter, these tips appear in the margin to help students focus on important concepts and provide a useful study tool when reviewing the chapter.

Two-Minute Review. How well do the students understand what they just read? This quick review helps them answer that question. Each chapter contains one or more reviews with the answers provided at the end of the chapter, just before the Warmup Exercises.

Two-Minute Review

1. *What items should be included when calculating the acquisition cost of an asset?*
2. *Which will be higher in the early years of an asset's life—straight-line depreciation or accelerated depreciation? Which will be higher in the later years? Which will be higher in total over the entire life of the asset?*

Answers on page 394.

Answers to the Two-Minute Reviews

Two-Minute Review on Page 377

1. *The general rule for calculating the acquisition cost of an asset is to include all of the costs that were necessary to acquire the asset and prepare it for use. Normally, that would include the purchase price but would also include costs such as freight costs, taxes, and installation costs if they were necessary to prepare the asset for use.*
2. *Accelerated depreciation will be higher in the early years of the asset, and straight-line will be higher in the later years. Over the life of the asset, the total amount of depreciation will be the same under all of the methods, assuming that the same amount of salvage value is estimated for each of the methods.*

Warmup Exercises with Suggested Solutions. These simple exercises preview the assignments to come and help students move from reading the text to doing the end-of-chapter assignments. Suggested solutions are provided as a self-check learning tool.

Warmup Exercises

Warmup Exercise 10-1 ***Bond Payable*** **LO 3, 5**

A bond due in 10 years, with face value of $1,000 and face rate of interest of 8%, is issued when the market rate of interest is 6%.

Required

1. What is the issue price of the bond?
2. What is the amount of premium or discount on the bond at the time of issuance?
3. What amount of interest expense will be shown on the income statement for the first year of the bond?
4. What amount of the premium or discount will be amortized during the first year of the bond?

Solutions to Warmup Exercises

Warmup Exercise 10-1

1. The issue price of the bond would be calculated at the present value:

$80 (7.360) =	$ 588.80	using Table 9-4, where i = 6% and n = 10
$1,000 (0.558) =	558.00	using Table 9-2, where i = 6% and n = 10
Issue price	$1,146.80	

You should perform the following steps when using a calculator to determine the present value:

ENTER	DISPLAY
10 N	N = 10
6 I/Y	I/Y = 8
80 PMT	PMT = 80
1000 FV	FV = 1000
CPT PV	PV = 1,147*
*(rounded)	

2. The amount of the premium is the difference between the issue price and the face value:

Premium = $1,146.80 − $1,000
= $146.80

Review Problem with Suggested Solution. Located at the end of every chapter, this problem and suggested solution tests student understanding of some of the major ideas in the chapter. These problems also serve as a walk-through demonstration with audio explanation in WebTutor Advantage.

A Large Number of EOC Choices. Assignments in the end-of-chapter section are numerous. These include:

- *Key Terms Quiz*—to test vocabulary knowledge (solutions are provided at the very end of the assignment material); an Alternate Terms list further enriches knowledge.
- *Questions*—to stimulate thinking and class discussion; these can be used for writing assignments to assist students in the practice of expressing and supporting their ideas.
- *Exercises*—to provide reinforcement of chapter content and prepare students for the challenge of the problem and case assignments; the first set of exercises is focused on a single learning objective, followed by a section of "multi-concept exercises;" exercises are primarily focused on application.
- *Problems*—to provide reinforcement of chapter content and focus on analysis and decision making; the first set of problems is tied to single learning objectives, followed by a section of "multi-concept problems;" a set of "alternate problems" provides additional assignment opportunities.
- *Cases*—to further reinforce analysis, decision making, professionalism, and research skills.

Icons for Quick Identification. Icons are like signposts that help you and your students identify key places along the way. For the Fourth Edition, we provide the following icons for the specific purposes indicated:

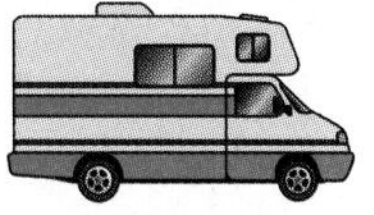

Winnebago Industries and Monaco Coach Corporation—After Chapter 2, this image will identify those places where key information relating to our flagship companies appears.

DECISION MAKING

Decision Making—The "What External Decision Makers Want to Know" coverage is identified by this icon. In addition, many assignments involving decision-making opportunities are indicated by this image.

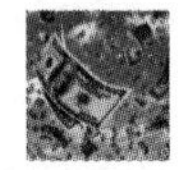

CASH FLOW

Impact on Cash Flows—To provide students with an easy way to quickly find how cash flows are affected, this new image identifies the key sections addressing this topic.

ANALYSIS

Analysis of Financial Information—This image identifies important sections coverage basic analytical information.

Global—Most corporations operate in an international environment and, therefore, have global accounting and strategic concerns. This icon serves as an indicator of where global coverage is provided.

SPREADSHEET

Spreadsheet—Assignments that are included in the Excel spreadsheet templates or that can easily be answered using spreadsheet software are identified by this image.

WebTutor Advantage—Problems demonstrated using PowerPoint® with audio as part of the online WebTutor Advantage product have this icon next to them.

ETHICS

Ethics in Accounting—Coverage addressing the very important and timely topic of ethics in the world of accounting is identified by this icon.

ADD POWER TO YOUR COURSE

With its many, quality options for you and your students, *Financial Accounting: The Impact on Decision Makers, The Alternative to Debits and Credits, 4e,* provides extra power to help pave the way to financial accounting excellence!

At the beginning of each chapter's assignment section, there is the following box that serves as a reminder to students to look at the technology information in this preface. In addition, students may want to refer to the inside front cover where resource information is also presented.

http://porter.swlearning.com

Technology and other resources for your success

If you need additional help, visit the text's Web site. Also, see this text's preface for a description of available technology and other resources. If your instructor is using PERSONAL Trainer in this course, you may complete, on line, the exercises and problems in the text.

Ahead of the Curve: Our Top-of-the-Line Technology

Personal Trainer® 3.0. Students can complete textbook end-of-chapter exercises and problems online and receive immediate feedback with Personal Trainer! Additionally, student results instantaneously flow into your gradebook! Each assignment begins with a warm-up, to get students started in the right direction; then hints provide additional assistance, if needed, once students receive the feedback on their work. This new, dynamic version of Personal Trainer offers many other helpful ways to assist both instructors and students.

WebTUTOR™ Advantage

WebTutor® Advantage with Personal Trainer. Available in either WebCT™ or Blackboard® platforms, this rich course management product is a specially designed extension of the classroom experience that enlivens the course by leveraging the power of the Internet with comprehensive educational content. WebTutor Advantage on WebCT™ or Blackboard® includes Personal Trainer to provide both students and instructors an unprecedented real-time, guided, self-correcting study outside the classroom. Instructors or students can use these resources along with those on the Product Web site to supplement the classroom experience. Use this effective resource as an integrated solution for your distance learning or web-enhanced course! This powerful, turnkey solution provides the following content (and more) customized for this edition:

- **E-Lectures**—PowerPoint® slides of the key topical coverage accompanied by audio explanations provide additional learning support.
- **Chapter Content Quizzes and Practice Problems**—Multiple choice, true/false, matching, and short problems, which test the knowledge of the chapter content, provide immediate feedback on the accuracy of the response. These quizzes help students pinpoint areas needing more study.
- **Problem Demonstrations**—The chapter review problem is presented, and an audio step-by-step explanation of the solution is provided to guide student understanding.
- **Video Clips**—Short, high-interest segments focus on chapter-related topics.
- **Chapter Summaries and Overviews**—Tied to each learning objective, these chapter reviews reinforce important concepts from each chapter.
- **Flashcards**—A terminology quiz helps students gain a complete understanding of the key terms from the chapter.
- **Spanish Dictionary of Accounting Terms**—To aid Spanish-speaking students, a Spanish dictionary of key financial accounting terms is provided.
- **Crossword Puzzles**—These interactive puzzles provide an alternative tool for students to test their understanding of terminology.
- **Quiz Bowl Game**—Students can review chapter content using this on-line game, which is similar to Jeopardy!®.
- **Personal Trainer**—This Internet-based homework tutor, described fully in the preceding section, is a rich tool for students and instructors.

Xtra! for Financial Accounting. This tool provides lecture enhancement resources and access to games and interactive quizzes so that students can test their understanding of the content of the Fourth Edition. *Free when bundled with a new text,* students receive an access code so that they can receive Xtra! reinforcement in financial accounting.

Text Web Site. (http://porter.swlearning.com) The Web site for the Fourth Edition has expanded to offer you and your student even more resources for teaching and learning than the Third Edition.

Among the many elements available to ***Students*** are:

- *Quizzes with feedback*
- *Hotlinks* to many resources on the Web, including all of the Web sites listed in the text; this provides a quick connection to key information
- *PowerPoint® presentation slides* for review of chapter coverage
- *Excel templates* for selected assignments in the text
- *Check figures* to selected assignments
- *Learning objectives* from the chapter provided as a study aid to keep clear focus on the core goals
- *Updates* for the latest information about changes in GAAP and any new, important information related to the text

*For **Instructors***, in addition to full access to the student resources listed above, a password-protected section of the Web site contains a number of resource files, including:

- *Solutions Manual, in MS Word*
- *Instructor's Manual, in MS Word*
- *Solutions to Excel templates*
- *Solution transparencies, in MS Word*
- Additional *updates* pertinent to instructors

Select from Other Helpful Support Materials

*For **Students:***

- *Study Guide*—Use the Study Guide to review the chapter's main focus, key concepts, and key terms and brush up your homework and test-taking skills. Solutions are provided.

*For **Instructors:***

- *Instructor's Resource Manual,* composed of the Instructor's Manual and the Solutions Manual, this ancillary's content is also available in electronic form on the Instructor's Resource CD-ROM and (restricted) on the product support Web site.
- *Test Bank* is a complete and plentiful set of newly revised test items that is also available in electronic form (using ExamView® software, provided) on the Instructor's Resource CD-ROM.
- *Solution Transparencies* consist of acetate transparencies of the numerical solutions to the exercises, problems, and cases.
- *Instructor's Resource CD-ROM with ExamView®* contains key instructor ancillaries (solutions manual, instructor's manual, test bank, and PowerPoint® presentation slides)—giving instructors the ultimate tool for customizing lectures and presentations. The testbank files on the CD-ROM are provided in ExamView® format. This program is an easy-to-use test-creation software compatible with Microsoft® Windows. Instructors can add or edit questions, instructions, and answers and select questions (randomly or numerically) by previewing them on the screen. Quizzes created can also be uploaded easily into the Blackboard or WebCT platforms.

- *PowerPoint® Presentation Slides* are located on the Instructor's Resource CD-ROM and on the text's Web site. These colorful slides reinforce chapter content and provide a rich tool for in-class lectures and out-of-class reviewing.

Additional Financial Accounting Resources

INSIDE LOOK: *Analysis From All Angles* Accounting is in the news *and* the classroom with access to this new Web site from Thomson/South-Western. The *Access Card* allows the instructor and the student to utilize information related to the Enron, Andersen, and other "names in the news" that involve accounting-related concerns. Well-known, popular news sources provide the background for the selected current events. Teaching tools are available to the instructor to implement class discussions, while analysis and questions are available to the student to utilize in many accounting discipline areas. This site is intended to help instructors teach and students to learn about critical current issues and understand them in the context of their accounting studies. **For a Demo, go to:** http://insidelook.swcollege.com.

Business & Professional Ethics for Accountants, 3e (by Leonard J. Brooks, Rotman School of Management, University of Toronto). Cases, readings, and textual material are blended to provide a concise, practical understanding of how to behave ethically in a post-Enron world for accounting and business students. This text provides a complete business and professional ethics guide to working in the age of accounting scandals. Issues and cases in this new edition cover: Enron and Enron-triggered changes in governance for corporations and the accounting profession; increased ethical sensitivity to ethical issues; calls for increased accountability to stakeholders, ethical decision making and behavior, and the development of ethical organization cultures domestically and internationally.

Accounting Ethics in the Post—Enron Age, 1e (by Iris Stuart and Bruce Stuart, of California State University—Fullerton). With the Enron/Andersen debacle, ethics is becoming an increasingly important (and interesting) part of accounting education. Ethics coverage is also required by the AACSB for accreditation purposes. Most texts include some limited ethics coverage, but many instructors would like to include more. This timely supplement contains ethics cases based on real situations in the business world. Examples include cases tied to Enron, Global Crossing, and Boston Chicken. Identifying ethical dilemmas and projecting their resolution will allow students to develop essential skills for success in their future careers. In each section of the textbook, the problems will be labeled according to subject matter (e.g., bad debt expense, revenue recognition). This allows the instructor to select problems consistent with the needs of the course.

The Financial Reporting Project and Readings, 3e (by Bruce A. Baldwin, of Arizona State University—West, and Clayton A. Hock, of Miami University). This project book requires students to obtain and analyze "live" financial statement from publicly traded firms. Also included in the book are several high-interest articles from popular publications, such as *The Wall Street Journal* and *Business Week*. The project has a flexible format and accommodates individual or team-based learning. Students are encouraged to compose short written responses to explain their analysis and to express their ideas based on the readings.

An Introduction to Accounting, Business Processes, and ERP (by Phil Reckers, Julie Smith David, and Harriet Maccracken, all of Arizona State University). Utilizing JD Edwards software demos, an industry leading ERP company, your students will learn an overview of the use of ERP software for accounting and business processes. Unlike any other product on the market, they will not only learn the advantages of technology in accessing business information but will also learn to apply it in three different business models. After each module, student learning is reinforced by quizzing. Equip your students with this class-tested and easy-to-use experience to help them meet the ever-changing challenges of business and technology!

InfoTrac® College Edition With this resource, your students can receive anytime, anywhere on-line access to a database of full-text articles from hundreds of popular and scholarly periodicals, such as *Newsweek, Fortune, Entrepreneur, Journal of Accountancy*, and *Nation's Business*, among others. Students can use its fast and easy search tools to find relevant news and analytical information among the tens of thousands of articles in the database—updated daily and going back as far as four years—all at a single Web site. InfoTrac is a great way to expose students to online research techniques, with the security that the content is academically based and reliable. An InfoTrac College Edition subscription card can be packaged free with new copies of our financial accounting texts. For more information, visit http://www.swcollege.com/infotrac/infotrac.html.

INTAACT Financial Accounting (by D.V. Rama and K. Raghunandan, both of Texas A&M International University). This Internet-based tutorial at http://rama.swcollege.com was designed for use in a financial accounting course or in any course where a review of the key financial concepts and terminology is needed. The program offers a visual, user-friendly way to reinforce accounting principles and includes tutorials, demonstration problems, exercises, and an interactive glossary. Users will receive an access certificate that will allow them to do the on-line tutorial over the full term of a course.

Accounting Career Consultant: Financial Accounting (by Charles Davis and Eric Sandburg). This resource is an online, interactive, tutored simulation. It is designed to complement both the classroom instruction and the text presentations. Each module includes links to review questions with customized feedback (approximately 20 questions), links to resources to further augment learning, and company profiles for the businesses discussed.

The Monopoly Game Practice Set (by Robert Knechel, of University of Florida). This fun practice set, based on the Monopoly game, helps students understand accounting information transaction as triggered by real business events. Each student's solution is unique but easily graded.

ACKNOWLEDGEMENTS

In preparing for this new edition of our text and the supporting materials, a number of individuals provided very helpful comments and suggestions. Among those are:

Walter Austin, Mercer University
Jane Baird, Minnesota State University—Mankato
Thomas J. Brady, University of Dayton
Sarah Brown, University of North Alabama
John M. Coulter, Western New England College
Marcia Agee Croteau, University of Maryland, Baltimore County
M. Taylor Ernst, Lehigh University
Susan Coomer Galbreath, Lipscomb University
Gloria Grayless, Sam Houston State University
John W. Hatcher, Purdue University
Herbert Hunt, California State University—Long Beach
Beth Kern, Indiana University—South Bend
Cindi Khanlarian, University of North Carolina—Greensboro
Greg Kordecki, Clayton College & State University
Cathy Larson, Middlesex Community College
Douglas Larson, Salem State College
Laurie Larson, Valencia Community College
Keith Leeseberg, Manatee Community College
Candace Leuck, University of North Carolina—Greensboro
Brian Leventhal, University of Illinois—Chicago
Elliott Levy, Bentley College
Larry Logan, University of Massachusetts—Dartmouth
Lois Mahoney, University of Central Florida
Susan D. Minke, Indiana University—Purdue University at Ft. Wayne
Linda Nichols, Texas Tech University
Betty S. Nolen, Floyd College

Margaret O'Reilly-Allen, Rider University
Elizabeth Plummer, Southern Methodist University
Linda Poulson, Elon University
Larry M. Prober, Rider University
Joseph M. Ragan, Saint Joseph's University
Angela Sandberg, Jacksonville State University
Karen Schoenebeck, Southwestern College
Cindy Seipel, New Mexico State University
Kathy Sevigny, Bridgewater State College
Diane Tanner, University of North Florida
Martin Taylor, University of Texas—Arlington
Uma Velury, University of Delaware
James Williamson, San Diego State University
Thomas L. Zeller, Loyola University—Chicago

We wish to thank those individuals for their contribution and Richard Friary, who provided valuable guidance to our ongoing effort to have the best teaching resources available for financial accounting.

Special acknowledgement and thanks goes to Iris and Bruce Stuart for their creative contribution to the expanded coverage of ethics in this edition.

Throughout the first three editions, many individuals have contributed helpful suggestions, which have resulted in several features that we have continued in the new fourth edition. We acknowledge these colleagues for their assistance.

Sheila Ammons, Austin Community College
David Angelovich, San Francisco State University
Mel Auerbach, California State Univ.—Dominguez Hills
Walter Austin, Mercer University
Alana Baier, Marquette University
Ray Bainbridge, Lehigh University
Amelia A. Baldwin-Morgan, Eastern Michigan University
Robert Ballenger, Babson College
Bobbe M. Barnes, University of Colorado at Denver
Maj. Curt Barry, U.S. Military Academy
Peter Battell, University of Vermont
Bob Bauman, Allan Hancock College
Paul Bayes, East Tennessee State University
Angela Bell, Jacksonville University
Dorcas Berg, Wingate University
Mark Bettner, Bucknell University
Frank Biegbeder, Rancho Santiago Community College
Francis Bird, University of Richmond
Karen Bird, University of Michigan
Eddy Birrer, Gonzaga University
Michelle Bissonnette, California State University—Fresno
John Blahnik, Lorain County Community College
Bruce Bolick, University of Mary Hardin Baylor
Frank Bouchlers, North Carolina State University
Thomas Brady, University of Dayton
Ed Bresnahan, American River College
Bob Brill, St. Bonaventure University
Doris Brown, Central Methodist University
Sarah Brown, University of North Alabama
David Brunn, Carthage College
Philip Buchanan, George Washington University
Rosie Bukics, Lafayette College
Gary Bulmash, American University
Bryan Burks, Harding University
Ronnie Burrows, University of Dayton
Judith Cadle, Tarleton State University
Carolyn Callahan, University of Notre Dame
Linda Campbell, University of Toledo
Jim Cashell, Miami University
Charles G. Carpenter, Miami University
Alice Cash, University of Southern Maine
Charles Caufield, Loyola University Chicago
David N. Champagne, Antelope Valley College
Gyan Chandra, Miami University
Mayer Chapman, California State University—Long Beach
Alan Cherry, Loyola Marymount University
Mike Claire, College of San Mateo
Teddy L. Coe, University of North Texas
David C. Coffee, Western Carolina University
John E. Coleman, University of Massachusetts at Boston
David Collins, Eastern Kentucky University
Gail Cook, University of Wisconsin—Parkside
Judith Cook, Grossmont Community College
John C. Corless, California State University—Sacramento
Rosalind Cranor, Virginia Polytechnic Institute
Dean Crawford, University of Toledo
Carrie Cristea, Augustana College, South Dakota
Fred Current, Furman University
Shirley J. Daniel, University of Hawaii at Manoa
Alan Davis, Community College of Philadelphia
Jim Davis, Clemson University

Henry H. Davis, Eastern Illinois University
Araya Debessay, University of Delaware
Lyle E. Dehning, Metropolitan State College—Denver
Sandra Devona, Northern Illinois University
Les Dlabay, Lake Forest College
Patricia Doherty, Boston University
Jaime Doran, Muhlenberg College
Margaret Douglas, University of Arkansas
Patricia Douglas, Loyola Marymount University
Alan Doyle, Pima Community College East
Alan Drebin, Northwestern University
Betty Driver, Murray State University
Kathy Dunne, Rider College
Dean Edmiston, Emporia State University
Kenneth Elvik, Iowa State University
Anette Estrada, Grand Valley State University
Ed Etter, Syracuse University
Alan Falcon, Loyola Marymount University
Charles Fazzi, Robert Morris College
Anita Feller, University of Illinois
Howard Felt, Temple University
David Fetyko, Kent State University
Richard File, University of Nebraska—Omaha
Ed Finkhauser, University of Utah
Jeannie M. Folk, College of DuPage
J. Patrick Forrest, Western Michigan University
Patrick Fort, University of Alaska—Fairbanks
Don Foster, Tacoma Community College
Diana Franz, University of Toledo
Tom Frecka, University of Notre Dame
Gary Freeman, University of Tulsa
Paquita Y. Friday, University of Notre Dame
Joan Friedman, Illinois Wesleyan University
Veronique Frucot, Rutgers University—Camden
Leo Gabriel, Bethel College
Susan Coomer Galbreath, Tennessee Tech University
Joe Gallo, Cuyahoga Community College
Michelle Gannon, Western Connecticut State University
Will Garland, Coastal Carolina University
John Gartska, Loyola Marymount University
Sharon Garvin, Wayne State College
Roger Gee, San Diego Mesa College
Cynthia Van Gelderen, Aquinas College
Linda Genduso, Nova University
Don E. Giacomino, Marquette University
Claudia Gilbertston, Anoka-Ramsey Community College
Hubert Gill, University of North Florida
Shirley Glass, Macomb Community College
Lorraine Glasscock, University of North Alabama
Larry Godwin, University of Montana
Art Goldman, University of Kentucky
Lynn Grace, Edison Community College
Bud Granger, Minnesota State University—Mankato
Marilyn Greenstein, Lehigh University
Paul Griffin, University of California—Davis
Jack Grinnell, University of Vermont
Bonnie Hairrell, Birmingham Southern
Jeanne Hamilton, Cypress College
Al Hannan, College of Notre Dame
Leon Hanouille, Syracuse University
Joseph Hargadon, Widener University
Suzanne Hartley, Franklin University
Coby Harmon, University of California, Santa Barbara
Robert Hartwig, Worcester State College
Jean Hatcher, University of South Carolina at Sumner
Donna Sue Hetzel, Western Michigan University
Thomas F. Hilgeman, St. Louis Community College—Meramec
Nathan Hindi, Shippensburgh University of Pennsylvania
Lee Hendrick, University of Tennessee
Robert E. Holtfreter, Ft. Hays State University
Betty Horn, Southern Connecticut State University
Kathy Horton, University of Illinois, Chicago
Fred Ihrke, Winona State University
Bruce Ikawa, Loyola Marymount University
Danny Ivancevich, University of Nevada—Las Vegas
Janet Jackson, Wichita State University
Sharon Jackson, Auburn University at Montgomery
Stanley Jenne, University of Montana
Patricia Johnson, Canisius College
Randy Johnston, Pennsylvania State University
Becky Jones, Baylor University
Christopher Jones, George Washington University
William Jones, Seton Hall University
Naida Kaen, University of New Hampshire
Manu Kai'ama, University of Hawaii at Manoa
Jane Kapral, Clark University
Mary Keim, California State University—Bakersfield
Anne Marie Keinath, Indiana University Northwest
Don Kellogg, Rock Valley College
Robert Kelly, Corning Community College
Marcia Kertz, San Jose State University
Jean Killey, Midlands Technical College
Ronald King, Washington University

Rita Kingery, University of Delaware
William Kinsella, Loyola Marymount University
Paul Kleichman, University of Richmond
George Klersey, Birmingham Southern College
Charles Konkol, University of Wisconsin—Milwaukee
Greg Krippel, Coastal Carolina University
Frank Korman, Mountain View College
Lynn Koshiyama, University of Alaska
Bobby Kuhlmann, Chaffey College
James Kurtenbach, Iowa State University
Jay LaGregs, Tyler Junior College
Michael Lagrone, Clemson University
Lucille E. Lammers, Illinois State University
Ellen Landgraf, Loyola University—Chicago
Horace Landry, Syracuse University
Laurie Larson, Valencia Community College
Kristine Lawyer, North Carolina State University
Terry Lease, Loyola Marymount University
Tom Lee, Winona State University
Susan Lightle, Wright State University
Tom Linsmeier, University of Iowa
Chao Liu, Tarleton State University
Chao-Shin Liu, University of Notre Dame
Alan Lord, Bowling Green State University
Gina Lord, Santa Rosa Junior College
Don Loster, University of California—Santa Barbara
Bruce Lubich, American University
Catherine Lumbattis, Southern Illinois University
Patsy Lund, Lakewood Community College
Raymond D. MacFee, Jr., University of Colorado
George Macklin, Susquehanna University
David Malone, University of Idaho
Janice Mardon, Green River Community College
Jim Martin, University of Montevallo
Spencer Martin, University of Rhode Island
Mary D. Maury, St. John's University
Al Maypers, University of North Texas
John C. McCabe, Ball State University
Nancy McClure, Lock Haven University
Margaret McCrory, Marist College
Christine McKeag, University of Evansville
Thomas D. McLaughlin, Monmouth College
Laura McNally, Black Hills State College
Mallory McWilliams, San Jose State University
Laurie McWhorter, University of Kentucky
E. James Meddaugh, Ohio University
Jim Meir, Cleveland State Community College
Barbara Merino, University of North Texas
Cynthia Miglietti, Bowling Green State University at Firelands
Paul Mihalek, University of Hartford
Cynthia Miller, GM Institute
Charles Milliner, Glendale Community College
William Mister, Colorado State University
Tami Mittelstaedt, University of Notre Dame
Perry Moore, Lipscomb University
Barbara Morris, Angelo State University
William Morris, Jr., University of North Texas
Mike Morris, University of Notre Dame
Theodore D. Morrison, Valparaiso University
Howard E. Mount, Seattle Pacific University
Rafael Munoz, University of Notre Dame
Muroki Mwaura, William Paterson University
Marcia Niles, University of Idaho
Mary J. Nisbet, University of California—Santa Barbara
Priscilla O'Clock, Xavier University
Mary Ellen O'Grady, Ramapo College
Nanne Olds, Doane College
Phil Olds, Virginia Commonwealth University
Bruce Oliver, Rochester Institute of Technology
Daniel O'Mara, Quinnipiac College
Michael O'Neill, Gannon University
Sylvia Ong (Paradise Valley Community College)
John Osborn, California State University—Fresno
Janet O'tousa, University of Notre Dame
Prakash Pai, Kent State University
Rimona Palas, William Paterson College of New Jersey
Beau Parent, Tulane University
Jane Park, California State University, Los Angeles
Paul Parkison, Ball State University
Victor Pastena, SUNY Buffalo
Sue Pattillo, University of Notre Dame
Charles A. Pauley, Gannon University
Ron Pawliczek, Boston College
Kathy Petroni, Michigan State University
Chris Pew, Galivan College
Donna Philbrick, Portland State University
Harry V. Poynter, Central Missouri State University
Les Price, Pierce College, University of Puget Sound
Joseph Ragan, St. Joseph's University
Mitchell Raiborn, Bradley University
Al Rainford, Greenfield Community College
Barbara Reider, University of Montana
John Rhode, University of San Francisco

Keith Richardson, Indiana State University
Ann Riley, American University
Mary Rolfes, Minnesota State University—Mankato
Robert Rouse, College of Charleston
Marc Rubin, Miami University
Donna Rudderow, Franklin University
Joseph Rue, Syracuse University
Leo A. Ruggle, Minnesota State University—Mankato
Victoria Rymer, University of Maryland
Judith Sage, University of Southern Colorado
Marilyn Sagrillo, University of Wisconsin—Green Bay
Rick Samuelson, San Diego State University
Gail Sanderson, Lebanon Valley College
George Sanderson, Moorhead State University
Richard Sathe, University of St. Thomas—Minnesota
Karen Saurlander, University of Toledo
Warren Schlesinger, Ithaca College
Edward S. Schwan, Susquehanna University
Don Schwartz, National University
Bradley Schwieger, St. Cloud State University
Richard Scott, University of Virginia
Karen Sedatole, Stephen F. Austin
John Sherman, University of Texas, Dallas
Richard Sherman, St. Joseph's University
Richard Silkoff, Quinnipiac College
Ron Singer, University of Wisconsin—Parkside
Ray Slager, Calvin College
David Smith, Metropolitan State University
David Smith, University of Dayton
Jill Smith, Idaho State University
William E. Smith, Xavier University
Kim Sorenson, Eastern Oregon State University
Amy Spielbauer, St. Norbert College
Charles Stanley, Baylor University
Catherine Staples, Virginia Commonwealth University
Anita Stellenwerf, Ramapo College
Jens Stephan, University of Cincinnati
Stephen Strange, Indiana University at Kokomo
Donna Street, James Madison University
David Strupeck, Indiana University NW
Linda Sugarman, University of Akron
Kathy Sullivan, George Washington University
Jeanie Sumner, Pacific Lutheran University
Judy Swingen, Rochester Institute of Technology
Tim Tancy, University of Notre Dame
Larry Tartaglino, Cabrillo College
H. Lee Tatum, University of Nebraska—Omaha
Martha Turner, Bowling Green State University
Bente Villadsen, Washington University
George Violette, University of Southern Maine
Alan K. Vogel, Cuyahoga Community College—Western
Vicki Vorell, Cuyahoga Community College—Western
Philip Walter, Bellevue Community College
Ann Watkins, Louisiana State University
Karen Walton, John Carroll University
Dewey Ward, Michigan State University
David P. Weiner, University of San Francisco
Michael Welker, Drexel University
Jane Wells, University of Kentucky
Jennifer Wells, University of San Francisco
Judy Wenzel, Gustavus Adolphus College
Charles Werner, Loyola University Chicago
Michael Werner, University of Miami
Paul Wertheim, Pepperdine University
Shari Wescott, Houston Baptist University
T. Sterling Wetzel, Oklahoma State University
Steven D. White, Western Kentucky University
Jill Whitley, Sioux Falls College
Jane Wiese, Valencia Community College
Samuel Wild, Loyola Marymount University
Jack Wilkerson, Wake Forest University
Michael Williams, Century College
David Willis, Illinois Wesleyan University
Lyle Wimmergren, Worcester Polytechnic Institute
Carol Wolk, University of Tennessee
Betty Wolterman, St. John's University, Minnesota
Steven Wong, San Jose City College
Gail Wright, Bryant College
Katherine Xenophon-Rybowiak
Robert Zahary, California State University at Los Angeles
Thomas L. Zeller, Loyola University Chicago
Linda Zucca, Kent State University

Finally, we are grateful to Kelli Harms and Winnebago Industries, as well as Mike Duncan and Monaco Coach Corporation, for their cooperation in our partnership between education and the real world of business.

Gary Porter
Curt Norton

Meet the Authors

Gary A. Porter is Professor of Accounting at the University of St. Thomas—Minnesota. He earned Ph.D. and M.B.A. degrees from the University of Colorado and his B.S.B.A. from Drake University. He has published in the *Journal of Accounting Education, Journal of Accounting, Auditing & Finance,* and *Journal of Accountancy*, among others and has conducted numerous workshops on the subjects of introductory accounting education and corporate financial reporting.

Dr. Porter's professional activities include experience as a staff accountant with Deloitte & Touche in Denver, a participant in KPMG Peat Marwick Foundation's Faculty Development program and as a leader in numerous bank training programs. He has won an Excellence in Teaching Award from the University of Colorado and Outstanding Professor Awards from both San Diego State University and the University of Montana.

He holds a CPA certificate in the state of Illinois and he served on the Illinois CPA Society's Innovations in Accounting Education Grants Committee, the steering committee of the Midwest region of the American Accounting Association, and the board of directors of the Chicago chapter of the Financial Executives International.

Curtis L. Norton is Deloitte & Touche Professor of Accountancy at Northern Illinois University. He earned his Ph.D. from Arizona State University, his M.B.A. from the University of South Dakota, and his B.S. from Jamestown College, North Dakota. His extensive list of publications include articles in *Accounting Horizons, The Journal of Accounting Education, Journal of Accountancy, Journal of Corporate Accounting, Journal of the American Taxation Association, Real Estate Review, The Accounting Review, CPA Journal*, and many others. In 1988-89, Dr. Norton received the University Excellence in Teaching Award, the highest university-wide teaching recognition at NIU. He is also a consultant and has conducted training programs for governmental authorities, bank, utilities, and other entities.

Dr. Norton is a member of the American Accounting Association and a member and officer of the Financial Executives International.

Brief Contents

Contents

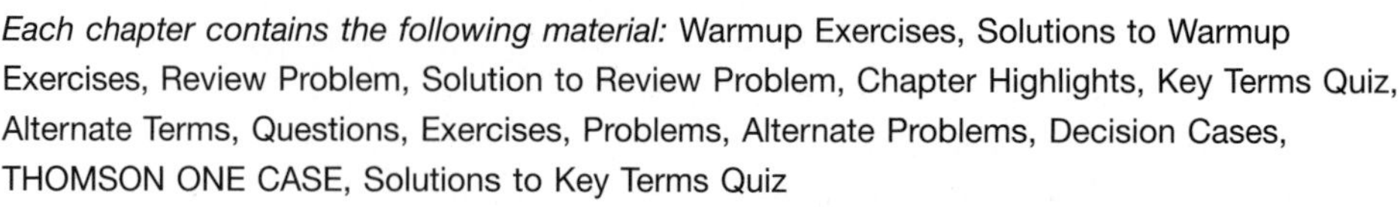
Each chapter contains the following material: Warmup Exercises, Solutions to Warmup Exercises, Review Problem, Solution to Review Problem, Chapter Highlights, Key Terms Quiz, Alternate Terms, Questions, Exercises, Problems, Alternate Problems, Decision Cases, THOMSON ONE CASE, Solutions to Key Terms Quiz

McDonald's
Drive-Thru

CIRCUIT
CITY

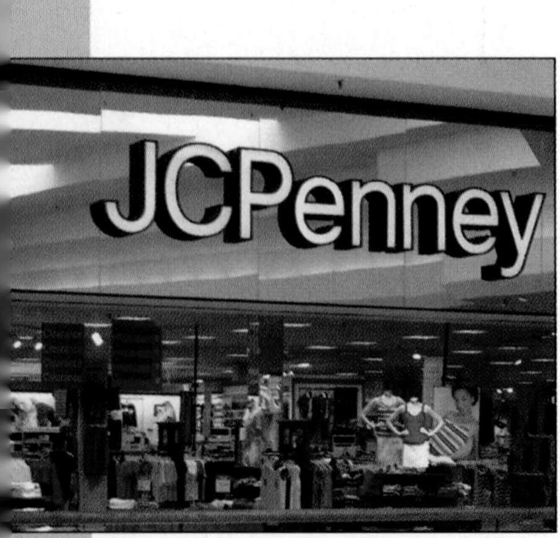
JCPenney

Coca-Cola
BOTTLING CO.

SOUTHWEST

WRIGLEY'S
SPEARMINT
DOUBLEMINT
JUICY FRUIT

To those who really "count":
Melissa
Kathy, Amy, Andrew

Part I

The Accounting Model

A Word to Students About This Course

Knowing accounting is just plain smart for everyone in today's job market. This book is therefore not just for accounting majors—it's for anyone who wants to learn how to read and understand financial information. You'll work with numbers in this course. But at every turn, this book and its study aids—not to mention your instructor—will walk you through the details. You'll write some memoranda backing up your calculations, pitting your analytical skills against real financial statements and problems. And you'll have the chance to put yourself in different business roles.

In fact, this book will help you think, talk, and write skillfully about accounting information.

Introduction

Getting Started in Business

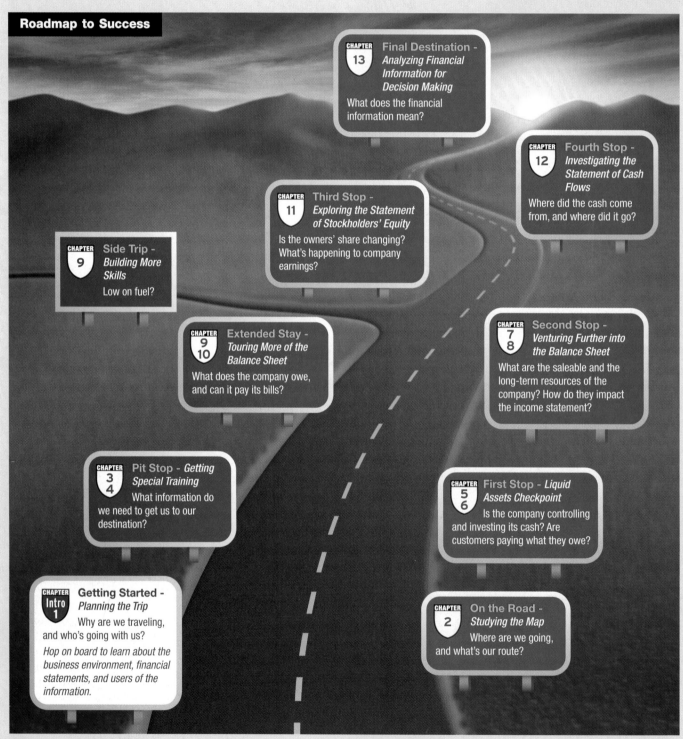

Roadmap to Success

CHAPTER Intro 1 **Getting Started -** *Planning the Trip*
Why are we traveling, and who's going with us?
Hop on board to learn about the business environment, financial statements, and users of the information.

CHAPTER 2 **On the Road -** *Studying the Map*
Where are we going, and what's our route?

CHAPTER 3 4 **Pit Stop -** *Getting Special Training*
What information do we need to get us to our destination?

CHAPTER 5 6 **First Stop -** *Liquid Assets Checkpoint*
Is the company controlling and investing its cash? Are customers paying what they owe?

CHAPTER 7 8 **Second Stop -** *Venturing Further into the Balance Sheet*
What are the saleable and the long-term resources of the company? How do they impact the income statement?

CHAPTER 9 10 **Extended Stay -** *Touring More of the Balance Sheet*
What does the company owe, and can it pay its bills?

CHAPTER 9 **Side Trip -** *Building More Skills*
Low on fuel?

CHAPTER 11 **Third Stop -** *Exploring the Statement of Stockholders' Equity*
Is the owners' share changing? What's happening to company earnings?

CHAPTER 12 **Fourth Stop -** *Investigating the Statement of Cash Flows*
Where did the cash come from, and where did it go?

CHAPTER 13 **Final Destination -** *Analyzing Financial Information for Decision Making*
What does the financial information mean?

*See the full road map at the front of the text.

LEARNING OBJECTIVES

After studying this module, you should be able to:

LO 1 Explain why financial information is important in making decisions. (p. 3)

LO 2 Understand what business is about. (p. 4)

LO 3 Distinguish among the forms of organization. (p. 5)

LO 4 Describe the various types of business activities. (p. 7)

Pick your favorite company. Maybe it is The Gap, because you buy all of your clothes there. Or maybe it is The Tribune Company because it owns your favorite team, the Chicago Cubs. Or is it Gateway because you like its commercials? At any rate, have you ever wondered how the company got started? Here is the abbreviated story of the birth of a well-known recreational vehicle manufacturer as told on its Web site:

In the mid-1950s, Forest City, Iowa, was looking at a bleak future. The farm economy was down and young people were leaving this rural area. Forward-looking members of the community set about bringing industry to town. In 1958, businessman John K. Hanson and others convinced a California company to open a travel trailer factory in Forest City. After a rough start, the operation was purchased by five Forest City residents, and John K. Hanson became president. In 1960 the name of the company was changed to Winnebago Industries.[1]

WINNEBAGO INDUSTRIES: THE NEED TO MAKE FINANCIAL DECISIONS

LO 1 Explain why financial information is important in making decisions.

From its humble beginnings, Winnebago Industries has made tremendous strides in its first 40 years. Revenues in 2002 exceeded $828 million. Numerous reasons account for the company's success, not the least of which is the strong desire people in the United States have for travel and leisure activities. However, any company owes a major part of its success to its ability to make *financial decisions.* Initially, John Hanson and his fellow investors made a crucial decision to invest their own money and buy the company. Would *you* have been willing to risk your savings to enter a new business? This was a financial decision these five Forest City residents had to make.

During the 1960s, the investors made significant strides to get the young company off the ground and on solid financial footing. For example, they introduced an assembly line to the motor home industry in an effort to reduce costs. That allowed Winnebago Industries to cut its costs to better compete against other companies. One of the most pivotal financial decisions in the life of Winnebago Industries was made in 1966. Many successful companies reach a point in their existence when it becomes necessary to consider "going public." January 25, 1966, marked the first time Winnebago Industries sold its stock to the public. The initial price was $12.50 per share. As is the case for many companies, a public offering of its stock provided the additional resources it needed to continue to grow and become a leader in its industry.

In 1970, the company was faced with another crucial financial decision. Should it move its operation to a larger manufacturing facility? Although this would certainly be a costly decision, the investors decided the move was in the best interests of their company. Did it prove to be a good decision? Apparently so, since a series of positive

In the mid-1950s, this early Winnebago was the primary product for the company. As reflected in both its annual report, at the end of this text, and its Web site, Winnebago Industries has greatly changed and expanded it product line. By providing investors and creditors with reliable financial information, the company has been able to get the resources it has needed to help it grow.

[1]This information, and that in the following section, is provided in more detail on Winnebago Industries' Web site in the section titled "Corporate Information—Our Story."

milestones in the following decades certainly support the decision made. In the same year as the expansion, Winnebago Industries' stock was first listed on the New York Stock Exchange, and in the following year, the stock had appreciated in price more than any other company's stock on the exchange. This significant increase reflected the confidence investors had in the future growth of the company. In 1977, Winnebago Industries became the first recreational vehicle (RV) manufacturer to build 100,000 units. Another milestone occurred in 1984 when sales topped $400 million for the first time in the company's history. Two years later, Winnebago Industries first appeared on *Fortune Magazine's* list of the top 500 U.S. corporations. Not bad for a company that less than 30 years earlier got its start when five residents in a small Iowa town made a decision to take a chance on not only a new business but on a whole new industry!

All the major events to date in the history of Winnebago Industries involved a need to take risks and make decisions. And in each of these decisions, the decision makers needed to rely on financial information. We all use financial information in making decisions. For example, when you were deciding whether to enroll at your present school, you needed information on the tuition and, in some cases, the room-and-board costs at the different schools you were considering. When a stockbroker decides whether to recommend to a client the purchase of stock in a company, the broker needs information on the company's profits and whether it pays dividends. When trying to decide whether to lend money to a company, a banker must consider the company's current debts.

In this book, we explore how accounting can help all of us in making informed financial decisions. Before we turn to the role played by accounting in decision making, we need to explore business in more detail. What *is* business? What forms of organization carry on business activities? In what types of business activities do those organizations engage?

WHAT IS BUSINESS?

LO 2 Understand what business is about.

Business All the activities necessary to provide the members of an economic system with goods and services.

Just as Winnebago Industries got its start in Forest City, Iowa, your study of accounting has to start somewhere. All disciplines have a foundation on which they rest. For accounting, that foundation is business.

Broadly defined, **business** consists of all the activities necessary to provide the members of an economic system with goods and services. Certain business activities focus on the providing of goods or products, such as ice cream, automobiles, and computers. Some of these companies produce or manufacture the products. Others are involved in the distribution of the goods, either as wholesalers (who sell to retail outlets) or retailers (who sell to consumers). Other business activities by their nature are service oriented. Corporate giants such as **Citicorp, Walt Disney, Time Warner,** and **United Airlines** remind us of the prominence of service activities in the world today. The relatively recent phenomenon of various "service providers," such as health-care organizations and Internet companies, are a testimony to the growing importance of the service sector in the U.S. economy.

To appreciate the kinds of business enterprises in our economy, consider the various types of companies that have a stake in the delivery of a pint of ice cream to the grocery store. We will use as an example the case of **Daisy's Dairy,** a producer of super-premium ice cream. First, Daisy's Dairy must contract with a local milk *supplier,* **Cramden Creamery.** As a *manufacturer* or *producer,* Daisy's Dairy takes the milk and other various raw materials, such as sugar and chocolate, and transforms them into a finished product. At this stage, a *distributor* or *wholesaler* gets involved. For example, Daisy's Dairy sells a considerable amount of its ice cream to **Duffy's Distributors.** Duffy's Distributors, in turn, sells the products to many different *retailers,* such as **Albertsons'** and **Safeway.** Although maybe less obvious, any number of *service* companies are also involved in the process. For example, ABC Transport hauls the milk to Daisy's Dairy for production, and others move the ice cream along to Duffy's Distributors. Still others get it to supermarkets and other retail outlets. Exhibit I-1 summarizes the process.

Exhibit I-1 Types of Businesses

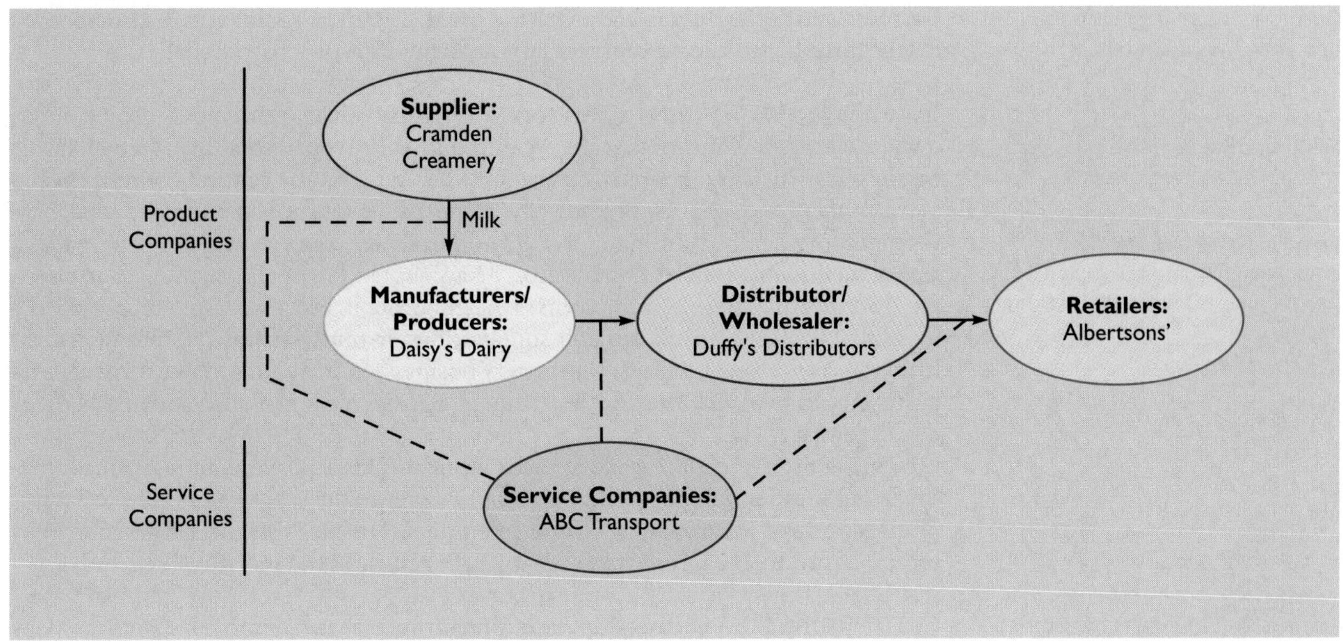

FORMS OF ORGANIZATION

LO 3 Distinguish among the forms of organization.

There are many different types of organizations in our society. One convenient way to categorize the myriad types is to distinguish between those that are organized to earn money and those that exist for some other purpose. Although the lines can become blurred, *business entities* generally are organized to earn a profit, whereas *nonbusiness entities* generally exist to serve various segments of society. Both types are summarized in Exhibit I-2.

Exhibit I-2 Forms of Organization

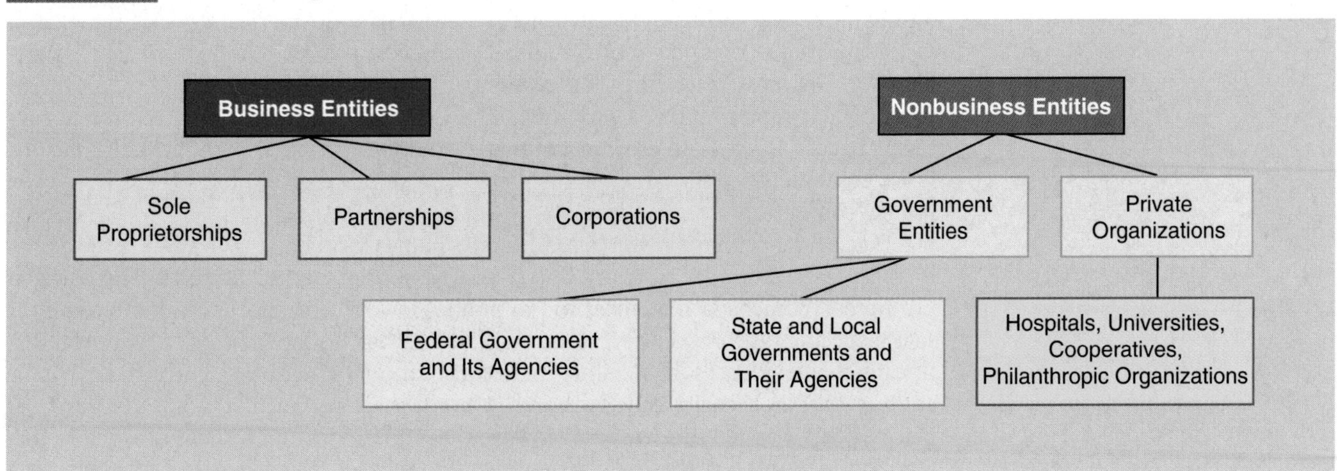

Business Entities

Business entity Organization operated to earn a profit.

Business entities are organized to earn a profit. Legally, a profit-oriented company is one of three types: a sole proprietorship, a partnership, or a corporation.

Sole proprietorship Form of organization with a single owner.

Economic entity concept The assumption that a single, identifiable unit must be accounted for in all situations.

Sole Proprietorships This form of organizaion is characterized by a single owner. Many small businesses are organized as **sole proprietorships.** Very often the business is owned and operated by the same person. Because of the close relationship between the owner and the business, the affairs of the two must be kept separate. This is one example in accounting of the **economic entity concept,** which requires that a single, identifiable unit of organization be accounted for in all situations. For example, assume that Bernie Berg owns a neighborhood grocery store. In paying the monthly bills, such as utilities and supplies, Bernie must separate his personal costs from the costs associated with the grocery business. In turn, financial statements prepared for the business must not intermingle Bernie's personal affairs with the affairs of the company.

Unlike the distinction made for accounting purposes between an individual's personal and business affairs, the IRS does not recognize the separate existence of a proprietorship from its owner. That is, a sole proprietorship is not a taxable entity; any profits earned by the business are taxed on the return of the individual.

Partnership A business owned by two or more individuals; organization form often used by accounting firms and law firms.

Partnerships A **partnership** is a business owned by two or more individuals. Many small businesses begin as partnerships. When two or more partners start out, they need some sort of agreement as to how much each will contribute to the business and how they will divide any profits. In many small partnerships, the agreement is often just an oral understanding between the partners. In large businesses, the partnership agreement is formalized in a written document.

Although a partnership may involve just two owners, some have thousands of partners. Public accounting firms, law firms, and other types of service companies are often organized as partnerships. Like a sole proprietorship, a partnership is not a taxable entity. The individual partners pay taxes on their proportionate shares of the profits of the business.

Corporation A form of entity organized under the laws of a particular state; ownership evidenced by shares of stock.

Share of stock A certificate that acts as evidence of ownership in a corporation.

Corporations Although sole proprietorships and partnerships dominate in sheer number, corporations control an overwhelming majority of the private resources in this country. A **corporation** is an entity organized under the laws of a particular state. Each of the 50 states is empowered to regulate the creation and operation of businesses organized as corporations in it.

To start a corporation, one must file articles of incorporation with the state. If the articles are approved by the state, a corporate charter is issued, and the corporation can begin to issue stock. A **share of stock** is a certificate that acts as evidence of ownership in a corporation. Although not always the case, stocks of many corporations are traded on organized stock exchanges, such as the New York and American Stock Exchanges.

What are the advantages of running a business as a corporation rather than a partnership? This was the question the owners of Winnebago Industries had to ask themselves. The company enjoyed early success in the market, and to capitalize on that success, it needed to grow. To grow meant that it would need a larger manufacturing facility, more equipment, and a larger staff. All of these things cost money. Where would the money come from?

Bond A certificate that represents a corporation's promise to repay a certain amount of money and interest in the future.

One of the primary advantages of the corporate form of organization is the ability to raise large amounts of money in a relatively brief period of time. This is what prompted Winnebago Industries to "go public" in 1966. To raise money, the company sold a specific type of security: stock. As stated earlier, a share of stock is simply a certificate that evidences ownership in a corporation. Sometimes, corporations issue another type of security called a bond. A **bond** is similar in that it is a certificate or piece of paper issued to someone. However, it is different from a share of stock in that a bond represents a promise by the company to repay a certain amount of money at a future date. In other words, if you were to buy a bond from a company, you would be lending it money. Interest on the bond is usually paid semiannually. We will have more to say about stocks and bonds when we discuss financing activities later.

The ease of transfer of ownership in a corporation is another advantage of this form of organization. If you hold shares of stock in a corporation whose stock is actively traded and you decide that you want out, you simply call your broker and put in an order to sell. Another distinct advantage is the limited liability of the stockholder. Generally speaking, a stockholder is liable only for the amount contributed to the business. That is, if a company goes out of business, the most the stockholder stands to lose is the amount invested. On the other hand, both proprietors and general partners usually can be held personally liable for the debts of the business.

Nonbusiness Entities

Most **nonbusiness entities** are organized for a purpose other than to earn a profit. They exist to serve the needs of various segments of society. For example, a hospital is organized to provide health care to its patients. A municipal government is operated for the benefit of its citizens. A local school district exists to meet the educational needs of the youth in the community.

Nonbusiness entity Organization operated for some purpose other than to earn a profit.

All these entities are distinguished by the lack of an identifiable owner. The lack of an identifiable owner and of the profit motive changes to some extent the type of accounting used by nonbusiness entities. This type, called *fund accounting,* is discussed in advanced accounting courses. Regardless of the lack of a profit motive in nonbusiness entities, there is still a demand for the information provided by an accounting system. For example, a local government needs detailed cost breakdowns in order to levy taxes. A hospital may want to borrow money and will need financial statements to present to the prospective lender.

Organizations and Social Responsibility

Although nonbusiness entities are organized specifically to serve members of society, U.S. business entities also have become more sensitive to their broader social responsibilities. Because they touch the lives of so many members of society, most large corporations recognize the societal aspects of their overall mission and have established programs to meet their social responsibilities. Some companies focus their efforts on local charities, while others donate to national or international causes. Certainly all of the companies showcased in the chapter openers of this book have programs in place to meet their objectives in the area of corporate giving.

THE NATURE OF BUSINESS ACTIVITY

LO 4 Describe the various types of business activities.

Because corporations dominate business activity in the United States, in this book we will focus on this form of organization. Corporations engage in a multitude of different types of activities. It is possible to categorize all of them into one of three types, however: financing, investing, and operating.

Financing Activities

All businesses must start with financing. Simply put, money is needed to start a business. John Hanson and his fellow investors needed money in the late 1950s to buy the travel trailer factory and get their business off the ground. As described earlier, Winnebago Industries found itself in need of additional financing in 1966 and thus made the decision to sell stock to the public. Some companies not only sell stock to raise money but also borrow from various sources to finance their operations.

As you will see throughout this book, accounting has its own unique terminology. In fact, accounting is often referred to as *the language of business.* The discussion of

Liability An obligation of a business.

Capital stock Indicates the owners' contributions to a corporation.

Stockholder One of the owners of a corporation.

Creditor Someone to whom a company or person has a debt.

financing activities brings up two important accounting terms: liabilities and capital stock. A **liability** is an obligation of a business; it can take many different forms. When a company borrows money at a bank, the liability is called a *note payable.* When a company sells bonds, the obligation is termed *bonds payable.* Amounts owed to the government for taxes are called *taxes payable.* Assume Winnebago Industries buys from Clear Glass Company the glass for the windows in its RVs. Assume that Clear Glass gives Winnebago Industries 30 days to pay for purchases. During this 30-day period, Winnebago Industries has an obligation called *accounts payable.*

Capital stock is the term used by accountants to indicate the dollar amount of stock sold to the public. Capital stock differs from liabilities in one very important respect. Those who buy stock in a corporation are not lending money to the business, as are those who buy bonds in the company or make a loan in some other form to the company. Someone who buys stock in a company is called a **stockholder,** and that person is providing a permanent form of financing to the business. In other words, there is not a due date at which time the stockholder will be repaid. Normally, the only way for a stockholder to get back his or her original investment from buying stock is to sell it to someone else. Someone who buys bonds in a company or in some other way makes a loan to it is called a **creditor.** A creditor does *not* provide a permanent form of financing to the business. That is, the creditor expects repayment of the amount loaned and, in many instances, payment of interest for the use of the money as well.

Investing Activities

There is a natural progression in a business from financing activities to investing activities. That is, once funds are generated from creditors and stockholders, money is available to invest. Winnebago Industries used the money it received from selling stock to grow and eventually open a new manufacturing facility.

Asset A future economic benefit.

An **asset** is a future economic benefit to a business. For example, cash is an asset to a company. To Winnebago Industries, its land, buildings, and machinery are assets. At any point in time, Winnebago Industries has a supply of materials to be used in building RVs. It also has RVs that are in the process of being manufactured and others that are ready to be sold to dealers. The finished RVs and the materials are called *inventory* and are another valuable asset of a company.

An asset represents the right to receive some sort of benefit in the future. The point is that not all assets are tangible in nature, as are inventories and plant and equipment. For example, assume that Winnebago Industries sells RVs to one of its dealers and allows this dealer to pay for its purchase at the end of 30 days. At the time of the sale, Winnebago Industries doesn't have cash yet, but it has another valuable asset. The right to collect the amount due from the customer in 30 days is an asset called an *account receivable.* As a second example, assume that a company acquires from an inventor a patent that will allow the company the exclusive right to manufacture a certain product. The right to the future economic benefits from the patent is an asset. In summary, an asset is a valuable resource to the company that controls it.

At this point, you should notice the inherent tie between assets and liabilities. How does a company satisfy its liabilities, that is, its obligations? Although there are some exceptions, most liabilities are settled by transferring assets. The asset most often used to settle a liability is cash.

Operating Activities

Once funds are obtained from financing activities and investments are made in productive assets, a business is ready to begin operations. Every business is organized with a purpose in mind. The purpose of some businesses is to sell a *product.* Winnebago Industries was organized to manufacture and sell RVs. Other companies provide *services.* Service-oriented businesses are becoming an increasingly important sector of the U.S. economy. Some of the largest corporations in this country, such as banks and airlines, sell services rather than products. Some companies sell both products and services.

Accountants have a name for the sale of products and services. **Revenue** is the inflow of assets resulting from the sale of products and services. When a company makes a cash sale, the asset it receives is cash. When a sale is made on credit, the asset received is an account receivable. For now, you should understand that revenue represents the dollar amount of sales of products and services for a specific period of time.

Revenue An inflow of assets resulting from the sale of goods and services.

We have thus far identified one important operating activity: the sale of products and services. However, costs must be incurred to operate a business. Employees must be paid salaries and wages. Suppliers must be paid for purchases of inventory, and the utility company has to be paid for heat and electricity. The government must be paid the taxes owed it. All of these are examples of important operating activities of a business. As you might expect by now, accountants use a specific name for the costs incurred in operating a business. An **expense** is the outflow of assets resulting from the sale of goods and services.

Expense An outflow of assets resulting from the sale of goods and services.

Exhibit I-3 summarizes the three types of activities conducted by a business. Our discussion and the exhibit present a simplification of business activity, but actual businesses are in a constant state of motion with many different financing, investing, and operating activities going on at any one time. The model as portrayed in Exhibit I-3 should be helpful as you begin the study of accounting, however. To summarize, a company obtains money from various types of financing activities, uses the money raised to invest in productive assets, and then provides goods and services to its customers.

Exhibit I-3 A Model of Business Activities

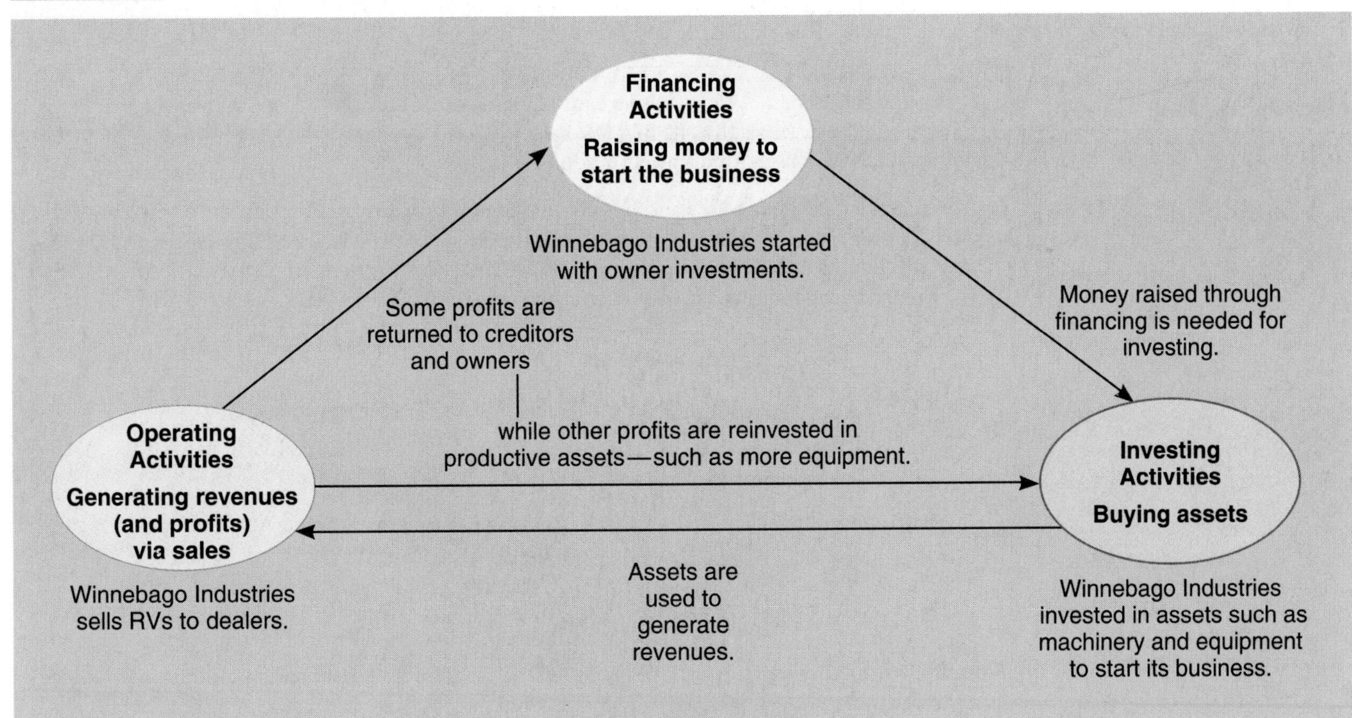

STARTING THE STUDY OF ACCOUNTING

The purpose of this module was to introduce you to business and help you to understand why it is the foundation on which accounting is based. Now that you have a basic understanding of what business is, the types of organizations that engage in business, and the various activities they conduct, you are ready to begin the study of accounting itself.

This module introduced you to business and decision making by telling a brief story of how Winnebago Industries got started. You will learn more about the company and its financial statements in Chapter 1. Beginning in Chapter 2, another new feature company will start off each chapter as a way of introducing the material in that chapter.

If you do not own stock in one of these companies, how can you get access to its financial statements and other information about it? One way is by calling or writing to the company's investor relations department. A much more efficient and timely approach to gathering this information, however, is to use the Internet. Nearly all major corporations, as well as many smaller ones, now post financial statements and other information on their Web sites. To help in your search, each chapter contains the URLs of the companies discussed there.

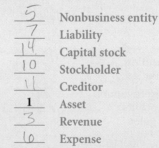

http://

http://porter.swlearning.com

Technology and other resources for your success

If you need additional help, visit the text's Web site. Also, see this text's preface for a description of available technology and other resources. If your instructor is using PERSONAL Trainer in this course, you may complete, on line, the exercises and problems in the text.

Key Terms Quiz

Note to the student: We conclude each chapter with a quiz on the key terms, which are in bold where they appear in the chapter. We have included a quiz for the numerous important terms introduced in this getting started module.

Read each definition below and then write the number of that definition in the blank beside the appropriate term it defines. The first one has been done for you. The solution appears at the end of this module. When reviewing terminology, come back to your completed key terms quiz. Study tip: Also check the glossary in the margin or at the end of the book.

15	Business	5	Nonbusiness entity
16	Business entity	7	Liability
13	Sole proprietorship	14	Capital stock
12	Economic entity concept	10	Stockholder
2	Partnership	11	Creditor
4	Corporation	1	Asset
8	Share of stock	3	Revenue
9	Bond	6	Expense

1. A future economic benefit.
2. A business owned by two or more individuals; organization form often used by accounting firms and law firms.
3. An inflow of assets resulting from the sale of goods and services.
4. A form of entity organized under the laws of a particular state; ownership evidenced by shares of stock.
5. Organization operated for some purpose other than to earn a profit.
6. An outflow of assets resulting from the sale of goods and services.
7. An obligation of a business.
8. A certificate that acts as evidence of ownership in a corporation.
9. A certificate that represents a corporation's promise to repay a certain amount of money and interest in the future.
10. One of the owners of a corporation.
11. Someone to whom a company or person has a debt.
12. The assumption that a single, identifiable unit must be accounted for in all situations.
13. Form of organization with a single owner.
14. Indicates the owners' contributions to a corporation.
15. All the activities necessary to provide the members of an economic system with goods and services.
16. Organization operated to earn a profit.

Alternate Terms

Creditor Lender

Stockholder Shareholder

Questions

1. What is business about? What do all businesses have in common?
2. What is an asset? Give three examples.
3. What is a liability? How does the definition of *liability* relate to the definition of *asset*?
4. Business entities are organized as one of three distinct forms. What are these three forms?
5. What are the three distinct types of business activity in which companies engage? Assume you start your own company to rent bicycles in the summer and skis in the winter. Give an example of at least one of each of the three types of business activities in which you would engage.

Solutions to Key Terms Quiz

15 Business (p. 4)
16 Business entity (p. 6)
13 Sole proprietorship (p. 6)
12 Economic entity concept (p. 6)
2 Partnership (p. 6)
4 Corporation (p. 6)
8 Share of stock (p. 6)
9 Bond (p. 6)
5 Nonbusiness entity (p. 7)
7 Liability (p. 8)
14 Capital stock (p. 8)
10 Stockholder (p. 8)
11 Creditor (p. 8)
1 Asset (p. 8)
3 Revenue (p. 9)
6 Expense (p. 9)

Chapter 1

Accounting as a Form of Communication

WINNEBAGO
INDUSTRIES

Roadmap to Success

CHAPTER 13 Final Destination - *Analyzing Financial Information for Decision Making*
What does the financial information mean?
CHAPTER 12 Fourth Stop - *Investigating the Statement of Cash Flows*
Where did the cash come from, and where did it go?
CHAPTER 11 Third Stop - *Exploring the Statement of Stockholders' Equity*
Is the owners' share changing? What's happening to company earnings?
CHAPTER 9 Side Trip - *Building More Skills*
Low on fuel?
CHAPTER 9 10 Extended Stay - *Touring More of the Balance Sheet*
What does the company owe, and can it pay its bills?
CHAPTER 7 8 Second Stop - *Venturing Further into the Balance Sheet*
What are the saleable and the long-term resources of the company? How do they impact the income statement?
CHAPTER 3 4 Pit Stop - *Getting Special Training*
What information do we need to get us to our destination?
CHAPTER 5 6 First Stop - *Liquid Assets Checkpoint*
Is the company controlling and investing its cash? Are customers paying what they owe?
CHAPTER Intro 1 Getting Started - *Planning the Trip*
Why are we traveling, and who's going with us?
Hop on board to learn about the business environment, financial statements, and users of the information.
CHAPTER 2 On the Road - *Studying the Map*
Where are we going, and what's our route?

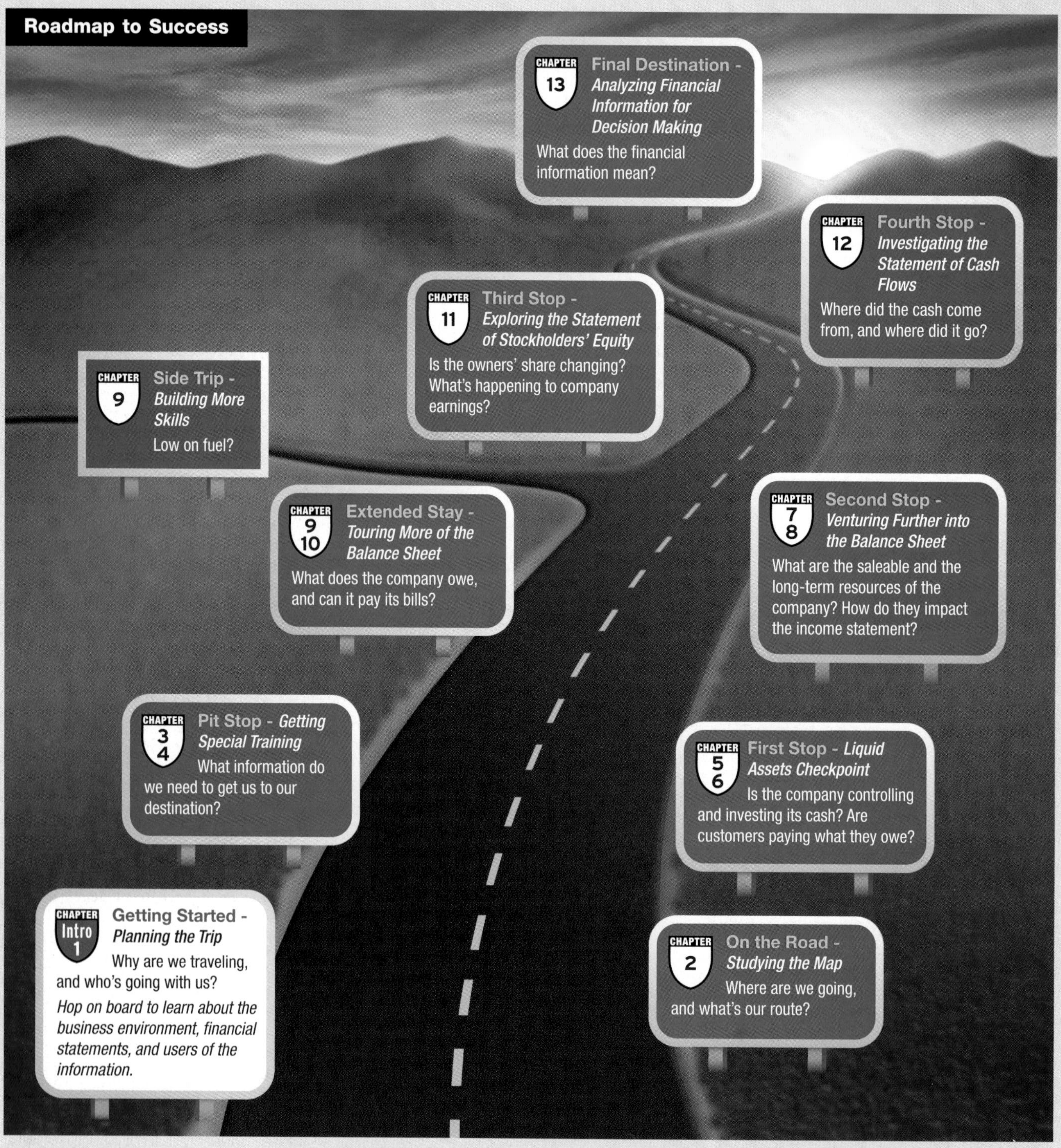

Focus on Financial Results

What groups of people care about the financial performance of Winnebago Industries, one of the leading manufacturers of motor homes and recreational vehicles (RVs) in the United States? Since its founding over 40 years ago, the company's managers, investors, employees, dealers, and suppliers have all had a vested interest in the financial health of the company whose name is synonymous with RVs.

To communicate its financial performance, Winnebago Industries uses the language of accounting. The *selected financial data* shown here[1] summarize key measures including revenue, income, and assets. The information shows that while the company experienced a decline in both net revenues and net income in its 2001 fiscal year, both of these measures increased significantly in 2002. In fact, both revenues and net income reached record levels in 2002. As explained in management's discussion and analysis of its operations, the increase in revenues reflected a number of factors, including low interest rates, an increase in the company's market share, and continued acceptance of the company's new products.

What will be the future of Winnebago Industries? In its 2002 message to the stockholders, the company sounded quite optimistic about its future. In light of this optimism, the company elected to pay its shareholders a cash dividend of $0.20 per share for the sixth consecutive year. Another sign of the company's optimism for its future as well as that of the RV industry is its plans to unveil a new state-of-the-art manufacturing facility in early 2003. The expansion represents the company's most ambitious undertaking of this sort to date and is expected to increase its capacity by approximately 30 percent. Record revenues and earnings in 2002 and a significant rise in its ability to meet customer demand, along with the company's continued leadership position in the RV industry, do indeed give Winnebago Industries and its shareholders good reason to be optimistic about the future.

http://www.winnebagoind.com

Winnebago Industries' 2002 Annual Report

Company net income rose in fiscal year 2002.

Company revenues rose in fiscal year 2002.

Selected Financial Data

(dollars in thousands, except per share data)	Aug. 31, 2002(2)	Aug. 25, 2001(3)	Aug. 26, 2000	Aug. 28, 1999	Aug. 29, 1998
For the Year					
Net revenues (4)	$ 828,403	$ 675,927	$ 747,637	$ 671,653	$ 529,363
Income before taxes	84,056	59,228	73,992	66,609	35,927
Pretax profit % of revenue	10.1%	8.8%	9.9%	9.9%	6.8%
Provision for income taxes (credits)	$ 29,385	$ 15,474	$ 25,593	$ 22,349	$ 11,543
Income tax rate	35.0%	26.1%	34.6%	33.6%	32.1%
Income from continuing operations	$ 54,671	$ 43,754	$ 48,399	$ 44,260	$ 24,384
Gain on sale of Cycle-Sat subsidiary	—	—	—	—	—
(Loss) income from discontinued operations	—	—	—	—	—
Cum. effect of change in accounting principle	—	(1,050)	—	—	—
Net income (loss)	$ 54,671	$ 42,704	$ 48,399	$ 44,260	$ 24,384
Income per share					
Continuing operations					
Basic	$ 2.74	$ 2.11	$ 2.23	$ 1.99	$ 1.01
Diluted	2.68	2.08	2.20	1.96	1.00
Discontinued operations					
Basic	—	—	—	—	—
Diluted	—	—	—	—	—
Cum. effect of change in accounting principle					
Basic	—	(.05)	—	—	—
Diluted	—	(.05)	—	—	—
Net income per share					
Basic	$ 2.74	$ 2.06	$ 2.23	$ 1.99	$ 1.01
Diluted	2.68	2.03	2.20	1.96	1.00
Weighted average common shares outstanding (in thousands)					
Basic	19,949	20,735	21,680	22,209	24,106
Diluted	20,384	21,040	22,011	22,537	24,314
Cash dividends per share	$ .20	$ .20	$ .20	$ .20	$ .20
Book value	9.63	9.99	8.22	6.69	5.11
Return on assets (ROA)	15.9%	12.9%	16.3%	17.1%	11.0%
Return on equity (ROE)	28.2%	22.3%	29.8%	33.3%	20.3%
Unit Sales					
Class A	6,725	5,666	6,819	6,054	5,381
Class C	4,329	3,410	3,697	4,222	3,390
Total Class A & C Motor Homes	11,054	9,076	10,516	10,276	8,771
Class B Conversions (EuroVan Campers)	763	703	854	600	978
At Year End					
Total assets	$ 337,077	$ 351,922	$ 308,686	$ 285,889	$ 230,612
Stockholders' equity	179,815	207,464	174,909	149,384	116,523
Working capital	144,995	174,248	141,683	123,720	92,800
Long-term debt	—	—	—	—	—
Current ratio	2.6 to 1	3.2 to 1	3.0 to 1	2.5 to 1	2.5 to 1
Number of employees	3,685	3,325	3,300	3,400	3,010

(1) Certain prior periods' information has been reclassified to conform to the current year-end presentation. These reclassifications have no impact on net income as previously reported.
(2) The fiscal years ended August 31, 2002, and August 31, 1996, contained 53 weeks; all other fiscal years contained 52 weeks.
(3) Includes a noncash after-tax cumulative effect of change in accounting principle of $1.1 million expense or $0.05 per share due to the adoption of SAB No.101, Revenue Recognition in Financial Statements.
(4) Net revenues for fiscal 2002 required adoption of EITF No. 01-9 Accounting for Consideration Given by a Vendor for a Customer (Including a Reseller of the Vendor's Product) which requires the reduction of net revenues by certain payments to customers for certain sales incentive offers and fiscal 2001 required adoption of EITF 00-10 related to shipping and handling fees and costs.

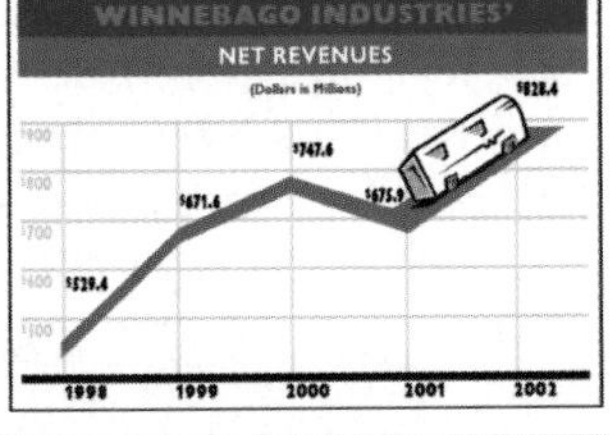

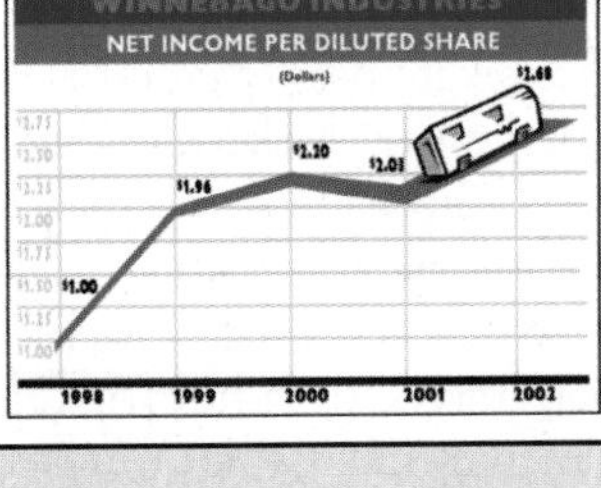

WINNEBAGO INDUSTRIES'
NET REVENUES
(Dollars in Millions)
1998 1999 2000 2001 2002

WINNEBAGO INDUSTRIES'
NET INCOME PER DILUTED SHARE
(Dollars)
1998 1999 2000 2001 2002

You're in the Driver's Seat

If you were considering a marketing job with Winnebago Industries, how would your decision be affected by the company's decision to expand its production capacity by 30 percent? Have the company's sales continued to rise? If so, have they risen at a slower or faster pace than in previous years? Use this chapter and the succeeding ones to help you better understand the financial performance of Winnebago Industries.

[1] *The data shown here for the five most recent years are included in a ten-year summary of selected financial data included in Winnebago Industries' 2002 Annual Report, which is provided in Appendix A at the end of the text.*

LEARNING OBJECTIVES

After studying this chapter, you should be able to:

LO 1 Identify the primary users of accounting information and their needs. (p. 14)

LO 2 Explain the purpose of each of the financial statements and the relationships among them, and prepare a set of simple statements. (p. 16)

LO 3 Identify and explain the primary assumptions made in preparing financial statements. (p. 22)

LO 4 Describe the various roles of accountants in organizations. (p. 24)

WHAT IS ACCOUNTING?

Accounting The process of identifying, measuring, and communicating economic information to various users.

Many people have preconceived notions about what accounting is. They think of it as a highly procedural activity practiced by people who are "good in math." This notion of accounting is very narrow and focuses only on the record-keeping or bookkeeping aspects of the discipline. Accounting is in fact much broader than this in its scope. Specifically, **accounting** is "the process of identifying, measuring, and communicating economic information to permit informed judgments and decisions by users of the information.[2]

Each of the three activities in this definition—*identifying, measuring,* and *communicating*—requires the judgment of a trained professional. We will return later in this chapter to acccounting as a profession and the various roles of accountants in our society. Note that the definition refers to the users of economic information and the decisions they make. Who *are* the users of accounting information? We turn now to this important question.

USERS OF ACCOUNTING INFORMATION AND THEIR NEEDS

LO 1 Identify the primary users of accounting information and their needs.

It is helpful to categorize users of accounting information on the basis of their relationship to the organization. Internal users, primarily the managers of a company, are involved in the daily affairs of the business. All other groups are external users.

Internal Users

Management accounting The branch of accounting concerned with providing management with information to facilitate planning and control.

The management of a company is in a position to obtain financial information in a way that best suits its needs. For example, if a plant manager at Winnebago Industries needs to know how much it costs to build a Winnebago Adventurer, the best selling motor home of its type on the market, this information exists in the accounting system and can be reported. If the same manager wants to find out if the monthly payroll is more or less than the budgeted amount, a report can be generated to provide the answer. **Management accounting** is the branch of accounting concerned with providing internal users (management) with information to facilitate planning and control. The ability to produce management accounting reports is limited only by the extent of the data available and the cost involved in generating the relevant information.

External Users

External users, those not involved directly in the operations of a business, need information that differs from that needed by internal users. In addition, the ability of exter-

[2]American Accounting Association, *A Statement of Basic Accounting Theory* (Evanston, Ill.: American Accounting Association, 1966), p. 1.

nal users to obtain the information is more limited. Without the day-to-day contact with the affairs of the business, outsiders must rely on the information presented to them by the management of the company.

Certain external users, such as the Internal Revenue Service, require that information be presented in a very specific manner, and they have the authority of the law to ensure that they get the required information. Stockholders, bondholders, and other creditors must rely on *financial statements* for their information.[3] **Financial accounting** is the branch of accounting concerned with communication with outsiders through financial statements.

Financial accounting The branch of accounting concerned with the preparation of financial statements for outsider use.

Stockholders and Potential Stockholders Both existing and potential stockholders need financial information about a business. If you currently own stock in a company, you need information that will aid in your decision either to continue to hold the stock or to sell it. If you are considering buying stock in a company, you need financial information that will help in choosing among competing alternative investments. What has been the recent performance of the company in the stock market? What were its profits for the most recent year? How do these profits compare with those of the prior year? How much did the company pay in dividends? One source for much of this information is the company's financial statements.

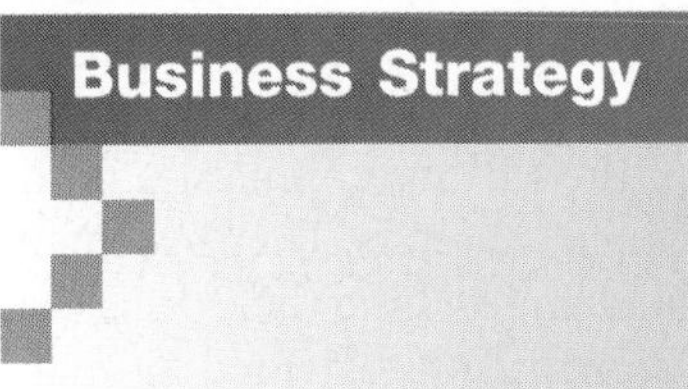

To Build or Not to Build?

What should be a company's strategy when it reports a decline in net revenues of nearly 10 percent from the prior year and over 10 percent in net income? Winnebago Industries explained in its 2001 annual report that the decrease in revenues was a reflection of the decline in consumer confidence levels and a slowdown in the economy. However, at the same time, the RV manufacturer felt that, in the long term, demographics would be in its favor. Supporting this positive outlook was the anticipated increase over the next 30 years of the number of people 50 years and older, which is a key target market for Winnebago Industries.

So what was Winnebago Industries' reaction to what could be construed as conflicting signals: a decline in revenues but some favorable demographics regarding its market? On April 1, 2002, the company left little doubt in the minds of its stockholders about its optimism for the future. On this day, it announced plans to build a new manufacturing facility, an expansion that would be the company's largest to date. Once the new plant in Charles City, Iowa, is operating at full capacity, it will increase Winnebago Industries' motor home production by about 30 percent. The new plant was set to open in early 2003.

Winnebago Industries' investors did not have to wait long to have their confidence boosted in the company's management. Less than three months later, on June 19, 2002, the company released its results for the third quarter of its 2002 fiscal year. Revenues had already begun to rebound from the declines in the earlier year, with a 26 percent increase compared to the revenues in the same quarter of the prior year. Net income for the quarter was up even more, showing a 45 percent increase from the comparable quarter in 2001. And then came the results for the full 2002 fiscal year: both revenues and earnings reached all-time highs. The stock market appeared to buy in to the quick recovery as evidenced by a market price that had dipped to $10.75 per share in 2001 and then reached as high as $51.43 in 2002. Only time will tell if the decision to build a new plant will contribute to a continuation of record sales and earnings for the leader in RVs, but early results should certainly help reassure its investors that it is on the right road. ■

Source: Winnebago Industries' 2002 and 2001 Annual Reports and Web site.

[3]Technically, stockholders are insiders because they own stock in the business. In most large corporations, however, it is not practical for stockholders to be involved in the daily affairs of the business. Thus, they are better categorized here as external users because they normally rely on general-purpose financial statements, as do creditors.

Bondholders, Bankers, and Other Creditors Before buying a bond in a company (remember you are lending money to the company), you need to feel comfortable that the company will be able to pay you the amount owed at maturity and the periodic interest payments. Financial statements can help you to decide whether to purchase a bond. Similarly, before lending money, a bank needs information that will help it to determine the company's ability to repay both the amount of the loan and interest. Therefore, a set of financial statements is a key ingredient in a loan proposal.

Government Agencies Numerous government agencies have information needs specified by law. For example, the Internal Revenue Service (IRS) is empowered to collect a tax on income from both individuals and corporations. Every year a company prepares a tax return to report to the IRS the amount of income it earned. Another government agency, the Securities and Exchange Commission (SEC), was created in the aftermath of the Great Depression. This regulatory agency sets the rules under which financial statements must be prepared for corporations that sell their stock to the public on organized stock exchanges. Similar to the IRS, the SEC prescribes the manner in which financial information is presented to it. Companies operating in specialized industries submit financial reports to other regulatory agencies, such as the Interstate Commerce Commission and the Federal Trade Commission.

http://www.irs.gov

http://www.sec.gov

Other External Users Many other individuals and groups rely on financial information given to them by businesses. A supplier of raw material needs to know the creditworthiness of a company before selling it a product on credit. To promote its industry, a trade association must gather financial information on the various companies in the industry. Other important users are stockbrokers and financial analysts. They use financial reports in advising their clients on investment decisions. In reaching their decisions, all of these users rely to a large extent on accounting information provided by management. Exhibit 1-1 summarizes the various users of financial information and the types of decisions they must make.

Exhibit 1-1 Users of Accounting Information

CATEGORIES OF USERS	EXAMPLES OF USERS	COMMON DECISION	RELEVANT QUESTION
Internal	Management	Should we build another new manufacturing facility?	What will be the cost to construct the new plant?
External	Stockholder	Should I buy shares of Winnebago Industries stock?	How much did the company earn last year?
	Banker	Should I lend money to Winnebago Industries?	What existing debts or liabilities does the company have?
	Employee	Should I ask for a raise?	How much are the company's sales, and how much is it paying out in salaries and wages? Is it paying out too much in compensation compared to its sales?
	Supplier	Should I allow Winnebago Industries to buy glass from me and pay me later?	What is the current amount of the company's accounts payable?

FINANCIAL STATEMENTS: HOW ACCOUNTANTS COMMUNICATE

LO 2 Explain the purpose of each of the financial statements and the relationships among them, and prepare a set of simple statements.

The primary focus of this book is financial accounting. This branch of accounting is concerned with informing management and outsiders about a company through financial statements. We turn our attention now to the composition of three of the major statements: the balance sheet, the income statement, and the statement of retained earnings.[4]

The Accounting Equation and the Balance Sheet

The accounting equation is the foundation for the entire accounting system:

Assets = Liabilities + Owners' Equity

The left side of the accounting equation refers to the *assets* of the company. Those items that are valuable economic resources and will provide future benefit to the company should appear on the left side of the equation. The right side of the equation indicates who provided, or has a claim to, those assets. Some of the assets were provided by creditors, and they have a claim to them. For example, if a company has a delivery truck, the dealer that provided the truck to the company has a claim to the assets until the dealer is paid. The delivery truck would appear on the left side of the equation as an asset to the company; the company's *liability* to the dealer would appear on the right side of the equation. Other assets are provided by the owners of the business. Their claims to these assets are represented by the portion of the right side of the equation called **owners' equity.**

The term *stockholders' equity* is used to refer to the owners' equity of a corporation. **Stockholders' equity** is the mathematical difference between a corporation's assets and its obligations or liabilities. That is, after the amounts owed to bondholders, banks, suppliers, and other creditors are subtracted from the assets, the amount remaining is the stockholders' equity, the amount of interest or claim that the owners have on the assets of the business.

Stockholders' equity arises in two distinct ways. First, it is created when a company issues stock to an investor. As we noted earlier, capital stock reflects ownership in a corporation in the form of a certificate. It represents the amounts contributed by the owners to the company. Second, as owners of shares in a corporation, stockholders have a claim on the assets of a business when it is profitable. **Retained earnings** represents the owners' claims to the company's assets that result from its earnings that have not been paid out in dividends. It is the earnings accumulated or retained by the company.

The **balance sheet** (sometimes called the *statement of financial position*) is the financial statement that summarizes the assets, liabilities, and owners' equity of a company. It is a "snapshot" of the business at a certain date. A balance sheet can be prepared on any day of the year, although it is most commonly prepared on the last day of a month, quarter, or year. At any point in time, the balance sheet must be "in balance." That is, assets must equal liabilities and owners' equity.

Balance sheets for Winnebago Industries at the end of two recent years are shown in Exhibit 1-2. Note the headings on the two columns of the balance sheet: August 31, 2002, and August 25, 2001. Winnebago Industries chooses to end its fiscal or accounting year on the last Saturday in August, which was August 31 in 2002 and August 25 in 2001. Although December 31 is the most common year-end, some companies such as Winnebago Industries use a date other than December 31 to end their year. Often this choice is based on when a company's peak selling season ends. For Winnebago Industries, most of its sales occur in spring and early summer. Thus, a year-end date near the end of August makes sense.

As the exhibit makes clear, there are the three main sections of the balance sheet corresponding to the three elements of the accounting equation: Assets, Liabilities, and Stockholders' Equity.

In the following table, note some of the main types of items that appear on the balance sheet. (NOTE: Here and throughout the book, the numbers that follow correspond to the highlighted numbers in the exhibit; numbers in this exhibit are stated in thousands of dollars.)

Study Tip

The accounting equation and the financial statements are at the heart of this course. Memorize the accounting equation, and make sure you study this introduction to how the financial statements should look, how to read them, and what they say about a company.

Owners' equity The owners' claims on the assets of an entity.

Stockholders' equity The owners' equity in a corporation.

Retained earnings The part of owners' equity that represents the income earned less dividends paid over the life of an entity.

Balance sheet The financial statement that summarizes the assets, liabilities, and owners' equity at a specific point in time.

[4]The fourth major financial statement is the statement of cash flows. This important statement will be introduced in Chapter 2.

Exhibit 1-2 Winnebago Industries Balance Sheets

Consolidated Balance Sheets

(dollars in thousands)

A = L + SE

	Assets	August 31, 2002	August 25, 2001
	Current assets (A)		
1	Cash and cash equivalents	$ 42,225	$102,280
2	Receivables, less allowance for doubtful accounts ($120 and $244, respectively)	28,616	21,571
	Dealer financing receivables, less allowance for doubtful accounts ($96 and $117, respectively)	37,880	40,263
3	Inventories	113,654	79,815
	Prepaid expenses	4,314	3,604
	Deferred income taxes	6,907	6,723
	Total current assets	233,596	254,256
4	Property and equipment, at cost		
	Land	972	1,029
	Buildings	47,953	45,992
	Machinery and equipment	86,744	82,182
	Transportation equipment	5,641	5,482
		141,310	134,685
	Less accumulated depreciation	92,383	88,149
	Total property and equipment, net	48,927	46,536
	Investment in life insurance	23,602	22,223
	Deferred income taxes	22,438	21,495
	Other assets	8,514	7,412
	Total assets	$337,077	$351,922

=

	Liabilities and Stockholders' Equity (L)	August 31, 2002	August 25, 2001
	Current liabilities		
5	Accounts payable, trade	$ 44,230	$ 40,678
	Income taxes payable	2,610	4,938
	Accrued expenses:		
	Accrued compensation	18,673	13,730
	Product warranties	8,151	8,072
	Insurance	5,967	4,567
	Promotional	4,499	3,181
	Other	4,471	4,842
	Total current liabilities	88,601	80,008
	Postretirement health care and deferred compensation benefits	68,661	64,450
	Contingent liabilities and commitments		

+

	Stockholders' equity (SE)	August 31, 2002	August 25, 2001
	Capital stock common, par value $0.50; authorized 60,000,000 shares, issued 25,888,000 and 25,886,000 shares, respectively	12,944	12,943
6	Additional paid-in capital	25,740	22,261
	Reinvested earnings	284,856	234,139
		323,540	269,343
	Less treasury stock, at cost	143,725	61,879
	Total stockholders' equity	179,815	207,464
	Total liabilities and stockholders' equity	$337,077	$351,922

See notes to consolidated financial statements.

1 Cash and Cash Equivalents: Includes cash on hand as well as cash in various checking and savings accounts

2 Receivables: Arises from selling RVs to dealers and allowing them to pay later

3 Inventories: Refers to the RVs and related products that the company sells

4 Property and Equipment: Includes land, buildings, machinery, and transportation equipment that are all needed to build and transport RVs

5 Accounts Payable, Trade: Arises from buying supplies and other materials and being allowed to pay later

6 Reinvested (or Retained) Earnings: Amount of income earned less dividends distributed over life of the company

Exhibit 1-3 summarizes the relationship between the accounting equation and the items that appear on a balance sheet.

Exhibit 1-3

The Relationship between the Accounting Equation and the Balance Sheet

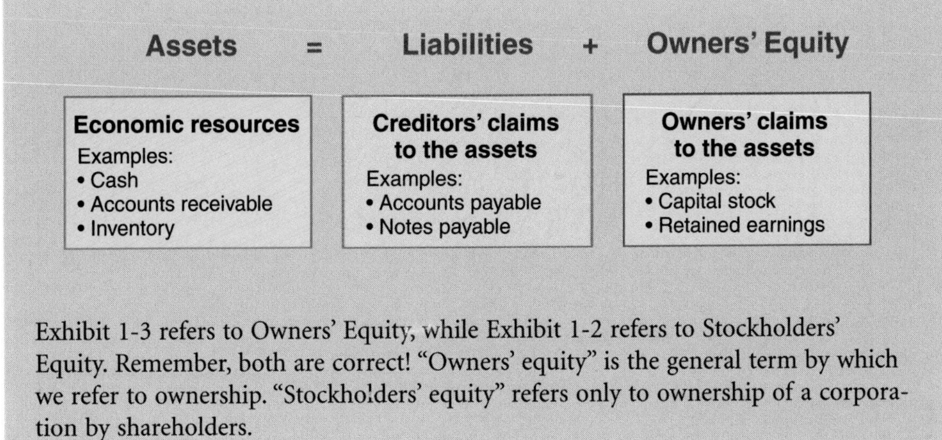

Exhibit 1-3 refers to Owners' Equity, while Exhibit 1-2 refers to Stockholders' Equity. Remember, both are correct! "Owners' equity" is the general term by which we refer to ownership. "Stockholders' equity" refers only to ownership of a corporation by shareholders.

The Income Statement

An **income statement,** or statement of income, as it is sometimes called, summarizes the revenues and expenses of a company for a period of time. Comparative income statements for Winnebago Industries for three recent years are shown in Exhibit 1-4. Unlike the balance sheet, an income statement is a *flow* statement. That is, it summarizes the flow of revenues and expenses for the year. As was the case for the balance sheet, you are not expected at this point to understand fully all of the complexities involved in preparing an income statement. However, note the two largest items on the income statement—Revenues: Manufactured products and Cost of manufactured products. For now, it is sufficient to understand that the former is Winnebago Industries' primary source of revenue and the latter is its most significant expense. Note that the excess of revenues over expenses, or **net income** as it is called, appears as the bottom line on the income statement. A company's net income is sometimes referred to as its profits or earnings.

Income statement A statement that summarizes revenues and expenses.

Net income The excess of revenues over expenses.

From Concept to Practice 1.1

Reading Winnebago Industries' Income Statement

Winnebago Industries' income statement reports that its "Revenues from manufactured products" increased in 2002 from the prior year. Does it seem logical that the "Cost of manufactured products" shown under "Costs and expenses" would also increase? Explain your answer and give some examples of the types of costs that would be included in "Cost of manufactured products" for Winnebago Industries.

Exhibit 1-4 Winnebago Industries Income Statements

Consolidated Statements of Income

Winnebago Industries' primary source of revenue

Winnebago Industries' most significant expense

(in thousands, except per share data)	Year Ended August 31, 2002(1)	August 25, 2001	August 26, 2000
Revenues:			
Manufactured products	$825,269	$671,686	$743,729
Dealer financing	3,134	4,241	3,908
Total net revenues	828,403	675,927	747,637
Costs and expenses:			
Cost of manufactured products	708,865	588,561	641,138
Selling	19,606	18,285	18,723
General and administrative	18,735	13,607	17,122
Total costs and expenses	747,206	620,453	676,983
Operating income	81,197	55,474	70,654
Financial income	2,859	3,754	3,338
Income before income taxes	84,056	59,228	73,992
Provision for taxes	29,385	15,474	25,593
Income before cumulative effect of change in accounting principle	54,671	43,754	48,399
Cumulative effect of change in accounting principle, net of taxes	—	(1,050)	—
Net income	$ 54,671	$ 42,704	$ 48,399

See notes to consolidated financial statements.

(1) Year ended August 31, 2002, contained 53 weeks; all other fiscal years contained 52 weeks.

The Statement of Retained Earnings

Dividends A distribution of the net income of a business to its owners.

Statement of retained earnings The statement that summarizes the income earned and dividends paid over the life of a business.

As discussed earlier, Retained Earnings represents the accumulated earnings of a corporation less the amount paid in dividends to stockholders. **Dividends** are distributions of the net income or profits of a business to its stockholders. Not all businesses pay cash dividends. Among those companies that do pay dividends, the frequency with which they pay differs. For example, Winnebago Industries currently pays a cash dividend of $0.10 per share twice each year.

A **statement of retained earnings** explains the change in retained earnings during the period. The basic format for the statement is as follows:

Beginning balance	$xxx,xxx
Add: Net income for the period	xxx,xxx
Deduct: Dividends for the period	xxx,xxx
Ending balance	$xxx,xxx

Revenues minus expenses, or net income, is an increase in retained earnings, and dividends are a decrease in the balance. Why are dividends shown on a statement of retained earnings instead of on an income statement? Dividends are not an expense and thus are not a component of net income, as are expenses. Instead, they are a *distribution* of the income of the business to its stockholders.

Recall that stockholders' equity consists of two parts: capital stock and retained earnings. In lieu of a separate statement of retained earnings, many corporations pre-

Accounting for Your Decisions

You Are a Potential Stockholder

You are deciding whether to invest in a company's stock. Which financial statement would you want to see, and which areas would you be most interested in?

ANS: All of them. The balance sheet will show the relative size of the assets and liabilities, and the stockholders' equity section should state how many shares of stock have been sold (outstanding shares) and how many more are available (authorized but not yet issued). The income statement's net sales, gross profit, operating income, and net income are important, not only for the most current year but also for previous years to determine trends. The statement of retained earnings will report whether dividends were paid and, if so, the amount.

pare a comprehensive statement to explain the changes both in the various capital stock accounts and in retained earnings during the period. Winnebago Industries, for example, presents the more comprehensive statement of changes in stockholders' equity. (It is not shown here, but you will find it in the printed annual report or online with Winnebago Industries' other financial statements.)

Relationships Among Winnebago Industries' Financial Statements

Because the statements of a company such as Winnebago Industries are complex, it may not be easy at this point to see the important links among them. The relationships among the statements are summarized for you in Exhibit 1-5. Recall that in its annual report, Winnebago Industries does not present a separate statement of retained earnings.

Exhibit 1-5

Relationships among Financial Statements: Winnebago Industries Example

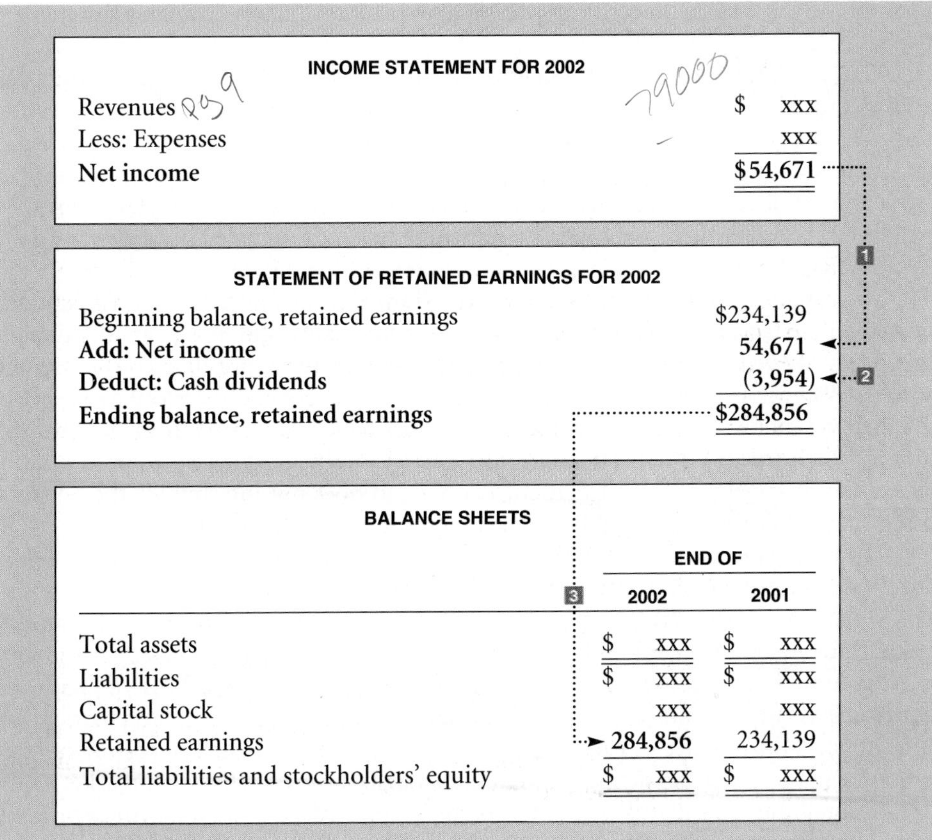

INCOME STATEMENT FOR 2002

Revenues	$ xxx
Less: Expenses	xxx
Net income	**$54,671**

1

STATEMENT OF RETAINED EARNINGS FOR 2002

Beginning balance, retained earnings	$234,139
Add: Net income	**54,671**
Deduct: Cash dividends	**(3,954)** 2
Ending balance, retained earnings	**$284,856**

BALANCE SHEETS

	END OF 2002 (3)	2001
Total assets	$ xxx	$ xxx
Liabilities	$ xxx	$ xxx
Capital stock	xxx	xxx
Retained earnings	**284,856**	234,139
Total liabilities and stockholders' equity	$ xxx	$ xxx

The information for the statement of retained earnings in Exhibit 1-5 appears as one of the columns in Winnebago Industries' statement of changes in stockholders' equity. Three important relationships are seen by examining the exhibit:

1. The 2002 income statement reports net income of $54,671. Net income increases retained earnings, as reported on the statement of retained earnings.
2. Cash dividends in the amount of $3,954 decrease retained earnings and, therefore, are shown as a deduction on the statement of retained earnings.
3. The ending balance of $284,856 in retained earnings, as reported on the statement of retained earnings for 2002, is transferred to the balance sheet at the end of 2002.

Two-Minute Review

1. *State the accounting equation, and indicate what each term means.*
2. *What are the three financial statements presented in this chapter?*
3. *How do amounts in the three statements interrelate?*

Answers on p. 33

THE CONCEPTUAL FRAMEWORK: FOUNDATION FOR FINANCIAL STATEMENTS

LO 3 Identify and explain the primary assumptions made in preparing financial statements.

Study Tip

The concepts in this section underlie everything you will learn throughout the course. You'll encounter them later in the context of specific topics.

Many people perceive the work of an accountant as being routine. In reality, accounting is anything but routine and requires a great deal of judgment on the part of the accountant. The record-keeping aspect of accounting—what we normally think of as bookkeeping—is the routine part of the accountant's work and only a small part of it. Most of the job deals with communicating relevant information to financial statement users.

The accounting profession has developed a *conceptual framework for accounting* that aids accountants in their role as interpreters and communicators of relevant information. The purpose of the framework is to act as a foundation for the specific principles and standards needed by the profession. An important part of the conceptual framework is a set of assumptions accountants make in preparing financial statements. We will briefly consider these assumptions, returning to a more detailed discussion of them in later chapters.

The *economic entity concept* was introduced in "Getting Started" when we first discussed different types of business entities. This assumption requires that an identifiable, specific entity be the subject of a set of financial statements. For example, even though some of Winnebago Industries' employees are stockholders and therefore own part of Winnebago Industries, their personal affairs must be kept separate from the business affairs. When we look at a balance sheet for the RV business, we need assurance that it shows the financial position of that entity only and does not intermingle the personal assets and liabilities of the employees or any of the other stockholders.

Cost principle Assets are recorded at the cost to acquire them.

The **cost principle** requires that accountants record assets at the cost paid to acquire them and continue to show this amount on all balance sheets until the company disposes of them. With a few exceptions, companies do not carry assets at their market value (how much they could sell the asset for today) but at original cost. Accountants use the term *historical cost* to refer to the original cost of an asset. Why not show an asset such as land at market value? The *subjectivity* inherent in determining market values supports the practice of carrying assets at their historical cost. The cost of an asset is verifiable by an independent observer and is much more *objective* than market value.

Going concern The assumption that an entity is not in the process of liquidation and that it will continue indefinitely.

Accountants assume that the entity being accounted for is a **going concern.** That is, they assume that Winnebago Industries is not in the process of liquidation and that it will continue indefinitely into the future. Another important reason for using historical cost rather than market value to report assets is the going concern assumption. If we assume that a business is *not* a going concern, then we assume that it is in the process of liquidation. If this is the case, market value might be more relevant than cost as a basis for recognizing the assets. But if we are able to assume that a business will continue indefinitely, cost can be more easily justified as a basis for valuation. The **monetary unit** used in preparing the statements of Winnebago Industries is the dollar. The reason for using the dollar as the monetary unit is that it is the recognized medium of exchange in the United States. It provides a convenient yardstick to measure the position and earnings of the business. As a yardstick, however, the dollar, like the currencies of all other countries, is subject to instability. We are all well aware that a dollar will not buy as much today as it did 10 years ago.

Monetary unit The yardstick used to measure amounts in financial statements; the dollar in the United States.

Inflation is evidenced by a general rise in the level of prices in an economy. Its effect on the measuring unit used in preparing financial statements is an important concern to the accounting profession. Although accountants have experimented with financial statements adjusted for the changing value of the measuring unit, the financial statements now prepared by corporations are prepared under the assumption that the monetary unit is relatively stable. At various times in the past, this has been a reasonable assumption and at other times not so reasonable.

Under the **time period** assumption, accountants assume that it is possible to prepare an income statement that accurately reflects net income or earnings for a specific time period. In the case of Winnebago Industries, this time period is one year. It is somewhat artificial to measure the earnings of a business for a period of time indicated on a calendar, whether it be a month, a quarter, or a year. Of course, the most accurate point in time to measure the earnings of a business would be at the end of its life. Accountants prepare periodic statements, however, because the users of the statements demand information about the entity on a regular basis.

Time period Artificial segment on the calendar, used as the basis for preparing financial statements.

Financial statements prepared by accountants must conform to **generally accepted accounting principles (GAAP).** This term refers to the various methods, rules, practices, and other procedures that have evolved over time in response to the need for some form of regulation over the preparation of financial statements. As changes have taken place in the business environment over time, GAAP have developed in response to these changes.

Generally accepted accounting principles (GAAP) The various methods, rules, practices, and other procedures that have evolved over time in response to the need to regulate the preparation of financial statements.

Accounting as a Social Science

Accounting is a service activity. As we have seen, its purpose is to provide financial information to decision makers. Thus, accounting is a *social* science. Accounting principles are much different from the rules that govern the *physical* sciences. For example, it is a rule of nature that an object dropped from your hand will eventually hit the ground rather than be suspended in air. There are no rules comparable to this in accounting. The principles that govern financial reporting are not governed by nature but instead develop in response to changing business conditions. For example, consider the lease of an office building. Leasing has developed in response to the need to have access to valuable assets, such as office space, without spending the large sum necessary to buy the asset. As leasing has increased in popularity, it has been left to the accounting profession to develop guidelines, some of which are quite complex, to be followed in accounting for leases. Those guidelines are now part of GAAP.

© AFP/CORBIS.

Enron's demise is a prime example of the downward spiral a company can take when investors question whether the company adhered to the rules of GAAP.

Two-Minute Review

1. *Name the four concepts (other than the economic entity concept) in the conceptual framework presented in this section.*
2. *Give a brief example of each concept.*
3. *What is "GAAP"?*

Answers on p. 33

Securities and Exchange Commission (SEC) The federal agency with ultimate authority to determine the rules for preparing statements for companies whose stock is sold to the public.

http://www.sec.gov

Financial Accounting Standards Board (FASB) The group in the private sector with authority to set accounting standards.

http://www.fasb.org

American Institute of Certified Public Accountants (AICPA) The professional organization for certified public accountants.

http://www.aicpa.org

Certified Public Accountant (CPA) The designation for an individual who has passed a uniform exam administered by the AICPA and met other requirements as determined by individual states.

International Accounting Standards Board (IASB) The organization formed to develop worldwide accounting standards.

http://www.iasc.org.uk

Who Determines the Rules of the Game?

Who determines the rules to be followed in preparing an income statement or a balance sheet? No one group is totally responsible for setting the standards or principles to be followed in preparing financial statements. The process is a joint effort among the following groups.

The federal government, through the **Securities and Exchange Commission (SEC),** has the ultimate authority to determine the rules for preparing financial statements by companies whose securities are sold to the general public. However, for the most part, the SEC has allowed the accounting profession to establish its own rules.

The **Financial Accounting Standards Board (FASB)** sets these accounting standards in the United States. A small independent group with a large staff, the board has issued more than 150 financial accounting standards, and seven statements of financial accounting concepts, since its creation in the early 1970s. These standards deal with a variety of financial reporting issues, such as the proper accounting for lease arrangements and pension plans, and the concepts are used to guide the board in setting accounting standards.

The **American Institute of Certified Public Accountants (AICPA)** is the professional organization of **certified public accountants** (CPAs). The CPA is the designation for an individual who has passed a uniform exam administered by the AICPA and met other requirements as determined by individual states. AICPA advises the FASB but is more involved in setting the auditing standards to be followed by public accounting firms.

Finally, if you are considering buying stock in Porsche, the German-based car manufacturer, you'll want to be sure that the rules Porsche follows in preparing the statements are similar to those the FASB requires for U.S. companies. Unfortunately, accounting standards can differ considerably from one country to another. The **International Accounting Standards Board (IASB)** was created in 2001. Prior to that time, the organization was known as the International Accounting Standards Committee (IASC), which was formed in 1973 to develop worldwide accounting standards. Organizations from many different countries, including the FASB in this country, participate in the IASB's efforts to develop international reporting standards. Although the group has made considerable progress, compliance with the standards of the IASB is strictly voluntary, and much work remains to be done in developing international accounting standards.

THE ACCOUNTING PROFESSION

LO 4 Describe the various roles of accountants in organizations.

Accountants play many different roles in society. Understanding the various roles will help you to appreciate more fully the importance of accounting in organizations.

Employment by Private Business

Many accountants work for business entities. Regardless of the types of activities companies engage in, accountants perform a number of important functions for them. A partial organization chart for a corporation is shown in Exhibit 1-6. The chart indicates that three individuals report directly to the chief financial officer: the controller, the treasurer, and the director of internal auditing.

Controller The chief accounting officer for a company.

The **controller** is the chief accounting officer for a company and typically has responsibility for the overall operation of the accounting system. Accountants working for the controller record the company's activities and prepare periodic financial statements. In this organization, the payroll function is assigned to the controller's office, as well as responsibility for the preparation of budgets.

Treasurer The officer responsible in an organization for the safeguarding and efficient use of a company's liquid assets.

The **treasurer** of an organization is typically responsible for the safeguarding, as well as the efficient use, of the company's liquid resources, such as cash. Note that the director of the tax department in this corporation reports to the treasurer. Accountants in the tax department are responsible for both preparing the company's tax returns and planning transactions in such a way that the company pays the least amount of taxes possible within the laws of the Internal Revenue Code.

Exhibit 1-6 Partial Organization Chart

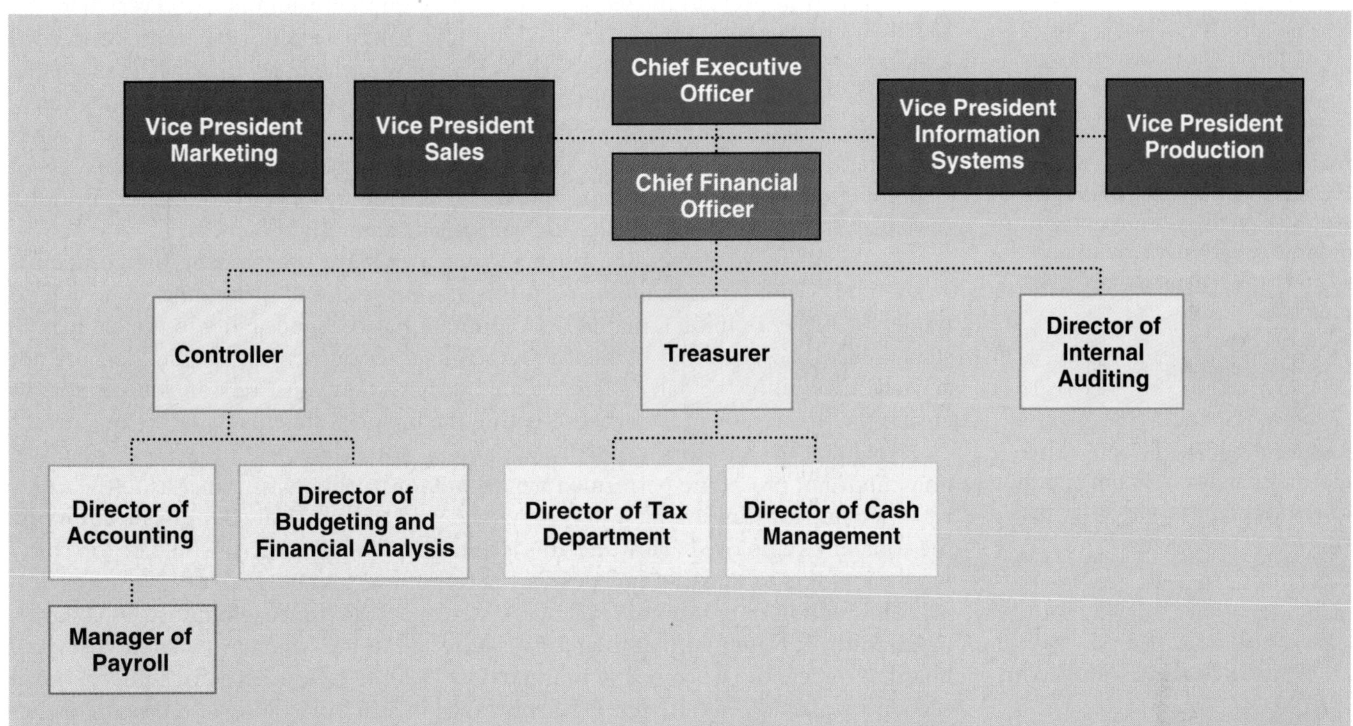

This partial organization chart does not show details of the other departments in the company—such as marketing, sales, production, and so on. That does not mean they are unimportant to the flow of accounting information. In fact, accounting information for internal decision making forms a complex system of reporting, responsibility, and control collectively known as management accounting.

Internal auditing is the department responsible in a company for the review and appraisal of accounting and administrative controls. The department must determine whether the company's assets are properly accounted for and protected from losses. Recommendations are made periodically to management for improvements in the various controls.

Internal auditing The department responsible in a company for the review and appraisal of its accounting and administrative controls.

Employment by Nonbusiness Entities

Nonbusiness organizations, such as hospitals, universities, and various branches of the government, have as much need for accountants as do companies organized to earn a profit. Although the profit motive is not paramount to nonbusiness entities, all organizations must have financial information to operate efficiently. A county government needs detailed cost information in determining the taxes to levy on its constituents. A university must pay close attention to its various operating costs in setting the annual tuition rates. Accountants working for nonbusiness entities perform most of the same tasks as their counterparts in the business sector. In fact, many of the job titles in business entities, such as controller and treasurer, are also used by nonbusiness entities.

Employment in Public Accounting

Public accounting firms provide valuable services in much the same way as do law firms or architectural firms. They provide a professional service for their clients in return for a fee. The usual services provided by public accounting firms include auditing and tax and management consulting services.

Auditing Services The auditing services rendered by public accountants are similar in certain respects to the work performed by internal auditors. However, there are key differences between the two types of auditing. Internal auditors are more concerned with the efficient operation of the various segments of the business, and therefore, the work they do is often called *operational auditing.* On the other hand, the primary objective of the external auditor, or public accountant, is to assure stockholders and other users that the statements are fairly presented. In this respect, **auditing** is the process of examining the financial statements and the underlying records of a company in order to render an opinion as to whether the statements are fairly presented.

Auditing The process of examining the financial statements and the underlying records of a company in order to render an opinion as to whether the statements are fairly presented.

As we discussed earlier, the financial statements are prepared by the company's accountants. The external auditor performs various tests and procedures to be able to render his or her opinion. The public accountant has a responsibility to the company's stockholders and any other users of the statements. Because most stockholders are not actively involved in the daily affairs of the business, they must rely on the auditors to ensure that management is fairly presenting the financial statements of the business.

Auditors' report The opinion rendered by a public accounting firm concerning the fairness of the presentation of the financial statements.

Note that the **auditors' report** is an *opinion,* not a statement of fact. For example, one important procedure performed by the auditor to obtain assurance as to the validity of a company's inventory is to observe the year-end physical count of inventory by the company's employees. However, this is done on a sample basis. It would be too costly for the auditors to make an independent count of every single item of inventory.

http://www.deloitte.com

The auditors' report on the financial statements for Winnebago Industries is shown in Exhibit 1-7. Note first that the report is directed to the company's shareholders and board of directors. The company is audited by Deloitte & Touche, a large international accounting firm. Public accounting firms range in size from those with a single owner to others, such as Deloitte & Touche, that have thousands of partners. The opinion given by Deloitte & Touche on the company's financial statements is the *standard auditors' report.* The first paragraph indicates that the firm has examined the company's balance sheet and the related statements of income, changes in stockholders' equity, and cash flows. Note that the second paragraph of the report indicates that evidence supporting the amounts and disclosures in the statements was examined on a *test* basis. The third paragraph states the firm's *opinion* that the financial statements are fairly presented in conformity with GAAP. (We have highlighted these paragraphs for clarity.)

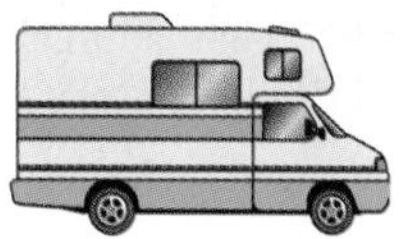

From Concept to Practice 1.2

Reading Winnebago Industries' Auditors' Report

Note the date at the bottom of the report. Why do you think it takes more than one month after the end of the fiscal year to issue this report?

Tax Services In addition to auditing, public accounting firms provide a variety of tax services. Firms often prepare the tax returns for the companies they audit. They also usually work throughout the year with management to plan acquisitions and other transactions to take full advantage of the tax laws. For example, if tax rates are scheduled to decline next year, a public accounting firm would advise its client to accelerate certain expenditures this year as much as possible to receive a higher tax deduction than would be possible by waiting until next year.

Management Consulting Services By working closely with management to provide auditing and tax services, a public accounting firm becomes very familiar with various aspects of a company's business. This vantage point allows the firm to provide expert advice to the company to improve its operations. In the past, management consulting services rendered by public accounting firms to their clients took a variety of forms. For example, the firm might advise the company on the design and installation of a computer system to fill its needs. However, as we will see later in this section, serious doubts have been raised about an auditor's ability to remain independent while providing these other services. These doubts have caused the federal government to place restrictions on the non-audit services the auditor can provide.

Exhibit 1-7 Winnebago Industries' Auditors' Report

REPORT OF INDEPENDENT AUDITORS
To the Board of Directors and Shareholders
Winnebago Industries, Inc.
Forest City, Iowa

We have audited the consolidated balance sheets of Winnebago Industries, Inc. and subsidiaries (the Company) as of August 31, 2002 and August 25, 2001, and the related consolidated statements of income, cash flows, and changes in stockholders' equity for each of the three years in the period ended August 31, 2002. These consolidated financial statements are the responsibility of the Company's management. Our responsibility is to express an opinion on these consolidated financial statements based on our audits.

We conducted our audits in accordance with auditing standards generally accepted in the United States of America. Those standards require that we plan and perform the audit to obtain reasonable assurance about whether the consolidated financial statements are free of material misstatement. An audit includes examining, on a test basis, evidence supporting the amounts and disclosures in the consolidated financial statements. An audit also includes assessing the accounting principles used and significant estimates made by management, as well as evaluating the overall financial statement presentation. We believe that our audits provide a reasonable basis for our opinion.

In our opinion, the consolidated financial statements present fairly, in all material respects, the financial position of the Company as of August 31, 2002 and August 25, 2001; and the results of its operations and its cash flows for each of the three years in the period ended August 31, 2002 in conformity with accounting principles generally accepted in the United States of America.

Deloitte & Touche LLP

Deloitte & Touche LLP
Minneapolis, Minnesota
October 4, 2002

Standard Auditors' Report

First Paragraph says that the auditor has examined the statements.

Second Paragraph indicates that evidence was gathered on a test basis.

Third Paragraph states the auditor's opinion.

Accountants in Education

Some accountants choose a career in education. As the demand for accountants in business entities, nonbusiness organizations, and public accounting has increased, so has the need for qualified professors to teach this discipline. Accounting programs range from two years of study at community colleges to doctoral programs at some universities. All these programs require the services of knowledgeable instructors. In addition to their teaching duties, many accounting educators are actively involved in research. The **American Accounting Association** is a professional organization of accounting educators and others interested in the future of the profession. The group advances its ideas through its many committees and the publication of a number of journals.

American Accounting Association The professional organization for accounting educators.

http://www.aaa-edu.org

Accounting as a Career

As you can see, a number of different career paths in accounting are possible. The stereotypical view of the accountant as a "numbers person and not a people person" is a seriously outdated notion. Various specialties are now emerging, including tax accounting, environmental accounting, forensic accounting, software development, and accounting in the entertainment and telecommunications industries. Some of these opportunities exist in both the business and the nonbusiness sectors. For example, forensic accounting has become an exciting career field as both corporations and various agencies of the federal government, such as the FBI, concern themselves with fraud and white-collar crime.

As in any profession, salaries in accounting vary considerably depending on numerous factors, including educational background and other credentials, number of years of experience, and size of the employer. For example, most employers pay a premium for candidates with a master's degree and professional certification, such as the CPA. Exhibit 1-8 indicates salaries for various positions within the accounting field.[5]

Exhibit 1-8

Salaries in the Accounting Profession

Position	Salary Range	
Public Accounting		
→ Staff Auditors (1–3 years' experience)	\$30,000–\$50,500	\$
Managers/Directors	\$64,000–\$116,500	\$\$
Partners	\$150,000+	\$\$\$
Industry		
→ Staff Accountants (1–3 years' experience)	\$34,000–\$49,500	\$
Corporate Controllers	\$56,750–\$147,000	\$\$–\$\$\$
Chief Financial Officers	\$85,250–\$353,750	\$\$–\$\$\$\$
→ Government (entry-level)		
Federal	\$32,788 average	\$
State/Local	\$33,595 average	\$

Accounting graduates start here.

Introduction to Ethics in Accounting

In the modern business world, rapidly changing markets, technological improvements, and business innovation all affect financial decisions. Decision makers consider information received from many sources such as others investors in the marketplace, analysts' forecasts, and companies whose corporate officers and executives may be encouraging "aggressive" accounting and reporting practices.

[5]The information in this section regarding career opportunities and salaries was drawn primarily from the AICPA's Web site (http://www.aicpa.org).

Accounting for Your Decisions

You Are a Student

As a student, you decide to go into the accounting profession. However, you are not sure which area to focus on: private, nonbusiness, public, or education. What information would you seek to help you make this decision?

ANS: You may want to consider the following (not necessarily in this order): (1) both starting and potential increases in salaries; (2) education requirements; (3) advancement opportunities; (4) fringe benefits; and (5) challenging work.

Recently, the news has been filled with reports of questionable accounting practices by some companies. As a decision maker outside of a company, you should be aware of the potential for ethical conflicts that arise within organizations and ask questions, do research, and not just accept everything as fact. If you are a decision maker within a company, you should stay alert for potential pressures on you or others to make choices that are not in the best interest of the company, its owners, and its employees as a whole. Companies may use aggressive accounting practices to misrepresent their earnings; executives may misuse their companies' funds. You may encounter a corporate board of directors that undermines the goals of its own company or a public accounting firm that fails its auditing duty to watch for and to disclose wrongdoing.

As a decision maker, you may analyze business information to project capital expansion, to open markets for new products, or to anticipate tax liabilities. You may be responsible for making financial reporting decisions that will affect others inside or outside of the organization. Knowledge of the professional standards of accounting procedures will be critical for your decision making process. It will also help you recognize when information is not consistent with the standards and needs to be questioned.

It is important to note that you may encounter circumstances when it appears as if generally accepted accounting principles (GAAP) may not have been used to resolve particular accounting issues. This may occur because there are several conflicting rules, because no specific GAAP rules seem applicable, or as a result of fraud. In such situations, an ethical dilemma is likely to exist. Resolving the dilemma may involve one or more decision makers. In most instances, an accountant plays a significant role in the process.

As accountants analyze and attempt to solve the ethical dilemmas posed by certain financial transactions and complex business reporting decisions, they can turn to their profession's conceptual framework. (You will learn more about this framework in Chapter 2.) According to the profession, "Financial reporting should provide information that is useful to present and potential investors and creditors and other users in making rational investment, credit, and similar decisions."[6]

When the accountant asks: "Is the quality of the information that is disclosed good or does it need to be improved?" the answer (which shapes all accounting decisions that follow) is: "If the information is *both* relevant and reliable, its quality is good."

Relevant information is information that is useful to the decision-making process. Relevant information may provide clear information about past financial events that is helpful for predicting the future. To be relevant, the information must also be timely; that is, it must be available at the time the decision is being made.

Accounting information should also be reliable; it should accurately represent what it claims to represent. Reliability includes *verifiability;* thus, there is documentation, from one or more independent parties, that supports the accuracy of the information. Reliability also includes *neutrality*, which means the presentation of

[6] *Original Pronouncements: Accounting Standards* (New York: John Wiley and Sons, Inc. 2001–2002 edition), III, Concept One, paragraph 34, p. 1014.

information is free from bias toward a particular result. Neutral information can be used by anyone, and it does not try to influence the decision in one direction. Basically, accounting information that is reliable will report economic activity that accurately represents the situation, without trying to influence behavior in any particular direction.[7]

This text presents ethics problems as brief case studies in "boxed" features of selected chapters and as end-of-chapter assignments. The cases and assignments will introduce dilemmas that you are expected to resolve by making the appropriate ethical decisions. Normally, the uncertainties of the business transactions and reporting decisions must be resolved in accordance with generally accepted accounting principles (GAAP) following the Financial Accounting Standards Board (FASB) statements. However, the appropriate application of accounting principles may not be easy to determine. You must be alert to pressures on the decision-making process that may be due to the self-interests of one or more of the decision makers. Bias, deception, and even fraud may distort the disclosed information. Whatever the circumstances, the dilemmas should be resolved by questioning and analyzing the situation.

All decision makers should consider the moral and social implications of their decisions. How will the decisions affect others, such as shareholders, creditors, employees, suppliers, customers, and the local community? The process of determining the most ethical choice involves identifying the most significant facts of the situation. For financial reporting, this includes identifying who may be affected and how, the relevant GAAP principles, and a realistic appraisal of the possible consequences of the decision. To assist your decision making for the cases and assignments, we offer an ethics model, shown in Exhibit 1-9 and explained here.

Identification

1. Recognize the ethical dilemma. A dilemma occurs when this awareness is combined with the inability to clearly apply accounting principles to represent the situation accurately.

Analysis

2. Analyze the key elements in the situation by answering these questions in sequence:
   a. Who may benefit or be harmed?
   b. How are they likely to benefit or be harmed?
   c. What rights or claims may be violated?
   d. What specific interests are in conflict?
   e. What are my responsibilities and obligations?
3. Determine what alternative methods are available to report the transaction, situation, or event. Answer the following questions:
   a. How relevant and reliable are the alternatives? Timeliness should be considered; potential bias must be identified.
   b. Does the report accurately represent the situation it claims to describe?
   c. Is the information free from bias?

Resolution

4. Select the best or most ethical alternative, considering all the circumstances and the consequences.

[7] *Original Pronouncements: Accounting Standards* (New York: John Wiley and Sons, Inc. 2001–2002 edition), III, p. 1022; FASB, paragraphs 46, 47, 48, 56, 63, 77, 81; pp. 48–49, 51–53, 56–59.

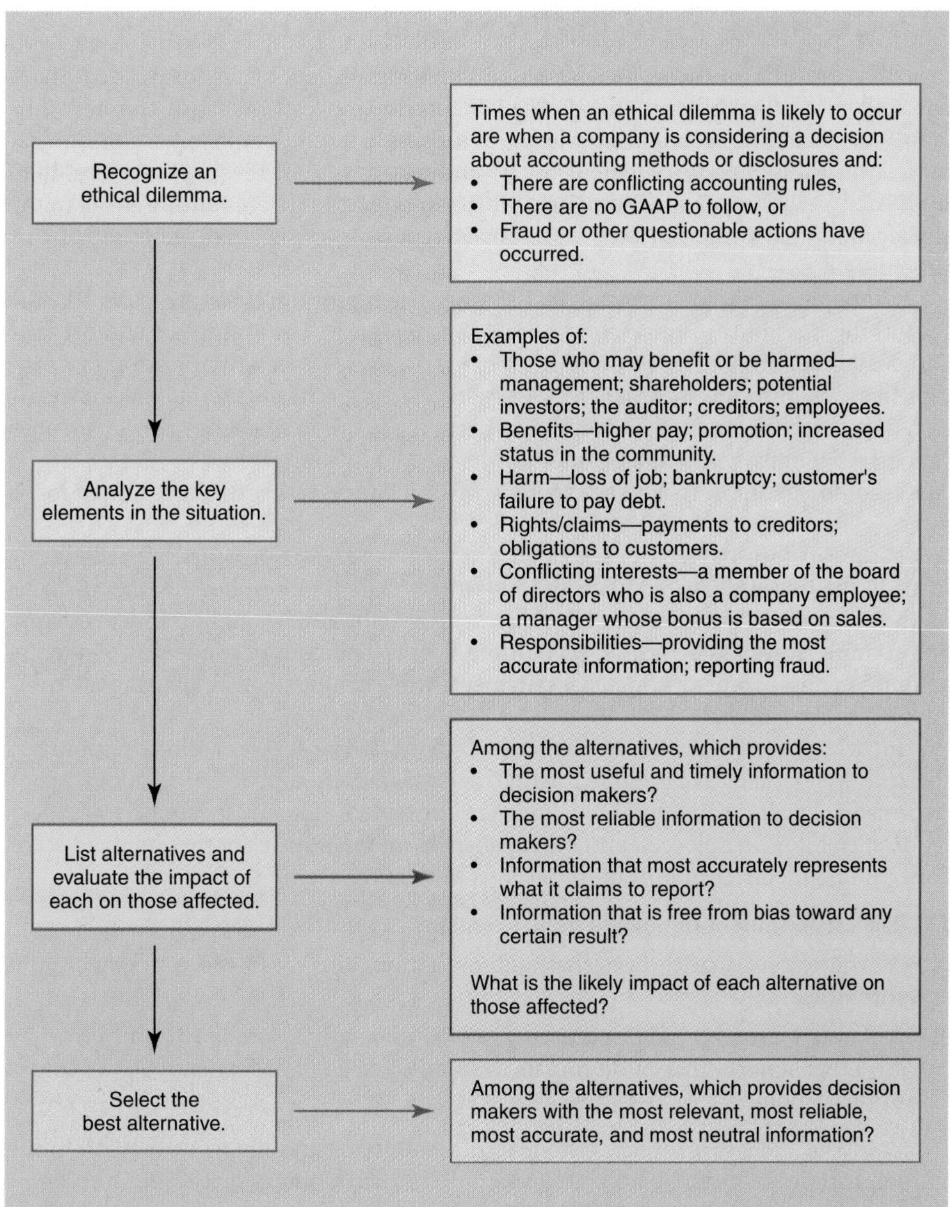

Exhibit 1-9

Ethics and Accounting: A Decision-Making Model

Accountants and Ethical Judgments

Remember the primary goal of accounting: to provide useful information to aid in the decision-making process. As we discussed, the work of the accountant in providing useful information is anything but routine and requires the accountant to make subjective judgments about what information to present and how to present it. The latitude given accountants in this respect is one of the major reasons accounting is a profession and its members are considered professionals. Along with this designation as a professional, however, comes a serious responsibility. As we noted, financial statements are prepared for external parties who must rely on these statements to provide information on which to base important decisions.

At the end of each chapter are cases titled "Accounting and Ethics: What Would You Do?" The cases require you to evaluate difficult issues and make a decision. Judgment is needed in deciding which accounting method to select or how to report a certain item in the statements. As you are faced with these decisions, keep in mind the trust placed in the accountant by various financial statement users. This is central to reaching an ethical decision.

The Changing Face of the Accounting Profession

Probably no time in the history of the accounting profession in the United States has seen more turmoil and change than the period since the start of the new millennium. Corporate scandals have led to some of the largest bankruptcies in the history of business. The involvement of the auditors in one of these scandals resulted in the demise of one of the oldest and most respected public accounting firms in the world. Many have referred to the "financial reporting crisis" that grew out of this time period.

Although the issues involved in the financial reporting crisis are complex, the accounting questions in these cases were often very basic. For example, the most fundamental accounting issue involved in the Enron case revolved around the entity concept that was introduced earlier in "Getting Started." Specifically, should various entities under the control of Enron have been included in the company's financial statements? Similarly, the major question in the WorldCom case was whether certain costs should have been treated as expenses when incurred rather than accounted for as assets.

Earlier in the chapter we described the various services provided by accounting firms to their clients. The scandals of the last few years have resulted in a major focus on the nonaudit services provided by these firms and the issue of auditor independence. For example, is it possible for an accounting firm to remain independent in rendering an opinion on a company's financial statements while simultaneously advising the company on other matters?

Sarbanes-Oxley Act An act of Congress in 2002 intended to bring reform to corporate accountability and stewardship in the wake of a number of major corporate scandals.

In 2002 Congress passed the **Sarbanes-Oxley Act**. The act was a direct response to the corporate scandals mentioned earlier and was an attempt to bring about major reforms in corporate accountability and stewardship, given the vast numbers of stockholders, creditors, employees, and others affected in one way or another by these scandals. Among the most important provisions in the new act are the following:

1. The establishment of a new Public Company Accounting Oversight Board.
2. A requirement that the external auditors report directly to the company's audit committee.
3. A clause to prohibit public accounting firms who audit a company from providing any other services that could impair their ability to act independently in the course of their audit.

Events of the last few years have placed accountants and the work they do in the spotlight more than ever before. More than ever, accountants realize the burden of responsibility they have to communicate openly and honestly with the public concerning the financial well being of businesses. Whether you will someday be an accountant or simply a user of the information an accountant provides, it is important to appreciate the critical role accounting plays in the smooth functioning of the free enterprise system.

A FINAL NOTE ABOUT WINNEBAGO INDUSTRIES

As you have seen in this chapter, accounting is a practical discipline. Financial statements of real companies, including Winnebago Industries, are used throughout the remainder of the book to help you learn more about this practical discipline. For example, some of the From Concept to Practice sidebars in future chapters will require you to return to the financial statements of Winnebago Industries, as will some of the cases at the end of the chapters. Because no two sets of financial statements look the same, however, you will be introduced to the financial statements of many other real companies as well. Use this opportunity to learn more not only about accounting but also about each of these companies.

Answers to the Two-Minute Reviews

Two-Minute Review on Page 22

1. *Assets = Liabilities + Owners' Equity*
   Assets are economic resources. Liabilities are creditors' claims against assets. Owners' Equity is owners' claims against assets. See Exhibit 1-3.
2. *The three financial statements are the balance sheet, the income statement, and the statement of retained earnings.*
3. *Net income on the income statement increases retained earnings on the statement of retained earnings. The ending balance in retained earnings is transferred to the balance sheet. See Exhibit 1-5.*

Two-Minute Review on Page 23

1. *Cost principle, going concern, monetary unit, and time period assumption.*
2. *Under the cost principle, we record assets at their cost rather than at market value. Example: Winnebago Industries would record a new machine at its purchase price. Under going concern, we assume that the company will continue existing indefinitely. Example: Winnebago Industries will continue to operate rather than begin liquidating its assets. The monetary unit, such as the dollar, is the company's recognized medium of exchange. Example: Winnebago Industries uses the dollar as the monetary unit. The time period assumption imposes, for reporting purposes, an arbitrary time period (such as a year) that is shorter than the company's life span. Example: Winnebago Industries' income statement is for the fiscal year ended August 31, 2002.*
3. *GAAP is the methods, rules, practices, and other procedures that have evolved to govern the preparation of financial statements.*

Warmup Exercises

Warmup Exercise 1-1 ***Your Assets and Liabilities*** **LO 2**
Consider your own situation in terms of assets and liabilities.

Required

1. Name three of your financial assets.
2. Name three of your financial liabilities.

Study Tip

Use these exercises to get accustomed to the assignments that follow.

Key to the Solution

Refer to Exhibit 1-3 for definitions of assets and liabilities.

Warmup Exercise 1-2 ***Winnebago Industries' Assets and Liabilities*** **LO 2**
Think about Winnebago Industries' business in balance sheet terms.

http://www.winnebagoind.com

Required

1. Name three of Winnebago Industries' assets.
2. Name three of Winnebago Industries' liabilities.

Key to the Solution

Refer to Exhibit 1-2 if you need to see Winnebago Industries' balance sheet. Also consult the list on page 19.

Warmup Exercise 1-3 ***Winnebago Industries and the Accounting Equation*** **LO 2**
Place Winnebago Industries' total assets, total liabilities, and total stockholders' equity in the form of the accounting equation.

http://www.winnebagoind.com

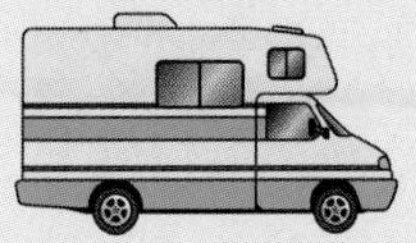

Key to the Solution

Refer to Exhibit 1-2. You will have to add up the liabilities since they are not totaled for you.

Solutions to Warmup Exercises

Warmup Exercise 1-1

1. Possible personal financial assets might include checking accounts, savings accounts, certificates of deposit, money market accounts, stocks, bonds, and mutual funds.
2. Possible personal financial liabilities might include student loans, car loans, home mortgages, and amounts borrowed from relatives.

Warmup Exercise 1-2

1. Winnebago Industries' assets are Cash and cash equivalents, Receivables, Inventories, Prepaid expenses, Deferred income taxes, Property and equipment, Investment in life insurance, and Other assets.
2. Winnebago Industries' liabilities are Accounts payable—Trade, Income taxes payable, Accrued expenses, and Postretirement health care and deferred compensation benefits.

Warmup Exercise 1-3

Assets	=	Liabilities	+	Stockholders' Equity
$337,077	=	$157,262	+	$179,815

Review Problem

WebTUTOR™ Advantage

Study Tip

Note to the student: At the end of each chapter is a problem to test your understanding of some of the major ideas presented in the chapter. Try to solve the problem before turning to the solution that follows it.

Greenway Corporation is organized on June 1, 2004. The company will provide lawn-care and tree-trimming services on a contract basis. Following is an alphabetical list of the items that should appear on its income statement for the first month and on its balance sheet at the end of the first month (you will need to determine on which statement each should appear).

Accounts payable	$ 800
Accounts receivable	500
Building	2,000
Capital stock	5,000
Cash	3,300
Gas, utilities, and other expenses	300
Land	4,000
Lawn-care revenue	1,500
Notes payable	6,000
Retained earnings (beginning balance)	–0–
Salaries and wages expense	900
Tools	800
Tree-trimming revenue	500
Truck	2,000

DECISION MAKING

Required

1. Prepare an income statement for the month of June.
2. Prepare a balance sheet at June 30, 2004. *Note:* You will need to determine the balance in Retained Earnings at the end of the month.
3. The financial statements you have just prepared are helpful, but in many ways they are a starting point. Assuming this is your business, what additional questions do they raise that you need to consider?

Solution to Review Problem

1.

GREENWAY CORPORATION
INCOME STATEMENT
FOR THE MONTH ENDED JUNE 30, 2004

Revenues:		
Lawn care	$1,500	
Tree trimming	500	$2,000

Expenses:		
Salaries and wages	$ 900	
Gas, utilities, and other expenses	300	1,200
Net income		$ 800

2.

GREENWAY CORPORATION
BALANCE SHEET
JUNE 30, 2004

Assets		Liabilities and Stockholders' Equity	
Cash	$ 3,300	Accounts payable	$ 800
Accounts receivable	500	Notes payable	6,000
Truck	2,000	Capital stock	5,000
Tools	800	Retained earnings	800
Building	2,000		
Land	4,000		
Total assets	$12,600	Total liabilities and stockholders' equity	$12,600

3. Following are examples of questions that the financial statements raise:
   - During June, 75% of the revenue was from lawn care and the other 25% from trimming trees. Will this relationship hold in future months?
   - Are the expenses representative of those that will be incurred in the future? Will any other expenses arise, such as advertising and income taxes?
   - When can we expect to collect the accounts receivable? Is there a chance that not all will be collected?
   - How soon will the accounts payable need to be paid?
   - What is the interest rate on the note payable? When is interest paid? When is the note itself due?

Chapter Highlights

1. **LO 1** Both individuals external to a business and those involved in the internal management of the company use accounting information. External users include present and potential stockholders, bankers and other creditors, government agencies, suppliers, trade associations, labor unions, and other interested groups.
2. **LO 2** The accounting equation is the basis for the entire accounting system: **Assets = Liabilities + Owners' Equity.** Assets are valuable economic resources. Liabilities are the claims of outsiders to the assets of a business. Owners' equity is the residual interest that remains after deducting liabilities from assets.
3. **LO 2** A balance sheet summarizes the financial position of a company at a *specific point in time.* An income statement reports on its revenues and expenses for a *period of time.* A statement of retained earnings explains the changes in retained earnings *during a particular period.*
4. **LO 3** A number of assumptions are made in preparing financial statements. Accounting is not an exact science, and judgment must be used in deciding what to report on financial statements and how to report the information. Generally accepted accounting principles (GAAP) have evolved over time and are based on a conceptual framework. The *Securities and Exchange Commission* in the public sector and the *Financial Accounting Standards Board* in the private sector have the most responsibility for developing GAAP at the present time.
5. **LO 4** Accountants are employed by business entities, nonbusiness entities, public accounting firms, and educational institutions. Public accounting firms provide audit services for their clients, as well as tax and management consulting services.

http://porter.swlearning.com

Technology and other resources for your success

If you need additional help, visit the text's Web site. Also, see this text's preface for a description of available technology and other resources. If your instructor is using PERSONAL Trainer in this course, you may complete, on line, the exercises and problems in the text.

Key Terms Quiz

Read each definition below and then write the number of that definition in the blank beside the appropriate term it defines. The quiz solutions appear at the end of the chapter.

_____ Accounting
_____ Management accounting
_____ Financial accounting
_____ Owners' equity
_____ Stockholders' equity
_____ Retained earnings
_____ Balance sheet
_____ Income statement
_____ Net income
_____ Dividends
_____ Statement of retained earnings
_____ Cost principle
_____ Going concern
_____ Monetary unit
_____ Time period
_____ Generally accepted accounting principles (GAAP)
_____ Securities and Exchange Commission (SEC)
_____ Financial Accounting Standards Board (FASB)
_____ American Institute of Certified Public Accountants (AICPA)
_____ Certified Public Accountant (CPA)
_____ International Accounting Standards Board (IASB)
_____ Controller
_____ Treasurer
_____ Internal auditing
_____ Auditing
_____ Auditors' report
_____ American Accounting Association
_____ Sarbanes-Oxley Act

1. A statement that summarizes revenues and expenses for a period of time.
2. The statement that summarizes the income earned and dividends paid over the life of a business.
3. The owners' equity of a corporation.
4. The process of identifying, measuring, and communicating economic information to various users.
5. The branch of accounting concerned with communication with outsiders through financial statements.
6. The owners' claims to the assets of an entity.
7. The financial statement that summarizes the assets, liabilities, and owners' equity at a specific point in time.
8. The part of owners' equity that represents the income earned less dividends paid over the life of an entity.
9. The branch of accounting concerned with providing management with information to facilitate the planning and control functions.
10. A distribution of the net income of a business to its stockholders.
11. The various methods, rules, practices, and other procedures that have evolved over time in response to the need to regulate the preparation of financial statements.
12. Assets are recorded and reported at the cost paid to acquire them.
13. The federal agency with ultimate authority to determine the rules for preparing statements for companies whose stock is sold to the public.
14. The professional organization for accounting educators.
15. The officer of an organization who is responsible for the safeguarding and efficient use of the company's liquid assets.
16. The assumption that an entity is not in the process of liquidation and that it will continue indefinitely.
17. The group in the private sector with authority to set accounting standards.
18. The yardstick used to measure amounts in financial statements; the dollar in the United States.
19. The professional organization for certified public accountants.
20. The department in a company responsible for the review and appraisal of a company's accounting and administrative controls.
21. A length of time on the calendar used as the basis for preparing financial statements.
22. The chief accounting officer for a company.
23. The process of examining the financial statements and the underlying records of a company in order to render an opinion as to whether the statements are fairly presented.
24. The organization formed to develop worldwide accounting standards.
25. The opinion rendered by a public accounting firm concerning the fairness of the presentation of the financial statements.
26. An act of Congress in 2002 intended to bring reform to corporate accountability and stewardship in the wake of a number of major corporate scandals.
27. The excess of revenues over expenses.
28. The designation for an individual who has passed a uniform exam administered by the AICPA and met other requirements as determined by individual states.

Answers on p. 54.

Alternate Terms

Auditors' report Report of independent accountants

Balance sheet Statement of financial position

Cost principle Original cost; historical cost

Income statement Statement of income

Net income Profits or earnings

Questions

1. What is accounting? Define it in terms understandable to someone without a business background.
2. How do financial accounting and management accounting differ?
3. What are five different groups of users of accounting information? Briefly describe the types of decisions each group must make.
4. How does owners' equity fit into the accounting equation?
5. What are the two distinct elements of owners' equity in a corporation? Define each element.
6. What is the purpose of a balance sheet?
7. How should a balance sheet be dated: as of a particular day or for a particular period of time? Explain your answer.
8. What does the term *cost principle* mean?
9. What is the purpose of an income statement?
10. How should an income statement be dated: as of a particular day or for a particular period of time? Explain your answer.
11. Rogers Corporation starts the year with a Retained Earnings balance of $55,000. Net income for the year is $27,000. The ending balance in Retained Earnings is $70,000. What was the amount of dividends for the year?
12. How do the duties of the controller of a corporation typically differ from those of the treasurer?
13. What are the three basic types of services performed by public accounting firms?
14. How would you evaluate the following statement: "The auditors are in the best position to evaluate a company because they have prepared the financial statements"?
15. What is the relationship between the cost principle and the going concern assumption?
16. Why does inflation present a challenge to the accountant? Relate your answer to the monetary unit assumption.
17. What is meant by the phrase *generally accepted accounting principles*?
18. What role has the Securities and Exchange Commission played in setting accounting standards? Contrast its role with that played by the Financial Accounting Standards Board.

Exercises

Exercise 1-1 ***Users of Accounting Information and Their Needs*** **LO 1**

Listed below are a number of the important users of accounting information. Below the list are descriptions of a major need of each of these various users. Fill in the blank with the one user group that is most likely to have the need described to the right of the blank.

Company management	**Banker**
Stockholder	**Supplier**
Securities and Exchange Commission	**Labor union**
Internal Revenue Service	

User Group	Needs Information About
____________________	1. The profitability of each division in the company
____________________	2. The prospects for future dividend payments
____________________	3. The profitability of the company since the last contract with the work force was signed
____________________	4. The financial status of a company issuing securities to the public for the first time
____________________	5. The prospects that a company will be able to meet its interest payments on time
____________________	6. The prospects that a company will be able to pay for its purchases on time
____________________	7. The profitability of the company based on the tax code

Exercise 1-2 ***The Accounting Equation*** **LO 2**

For each of the following independent cases, fill in the blank with the appropriate dollar amount.

	Assets	=	Liabilities	+	Owners' Equity
Case 1	$125,000		$ 75,000		$ _____
Case 2	400,000		_____		100,000
Case 3	_____		320,000		95,000

Exercise 1-3 ***The Accounting Equation*** **LO 2**

Ginger Enterprises began the year with total assets of $500,000 and total liabilities of $250,000. Using this information and the accounting equation, answer each of the following independent questions.

1. What was the amount of Ginger's owners' equity at the beginning of the year?
2. If Ginger's total assets increased by $100,000 and its total liabilities increased by $77,000 during the year, what was the amount of Ginger's owners' equity at the end of the year?
3. If Ginger's total liabilities increased by $33,000 and its owners' equity decreased by $58,000 during the year, what was the amount of its total assets at the end of the year?
4. If Ginger's total assets doubled to $1,000,000 and its owners' equity remained the same during the year, what was the amount of its total liabilities at the end of the year?

Exercise 1-4 ***The Accounting Equation*** **LO 2**

Using the accounting equation, answer each of the following independent questions.

1. Burlin Company starts the year with $100,000 in assets and $80,000 in liabilities. Net income for the year is $25,000, and no dividends are paid. How much is owners' equity at the end of the year?
2. Chapman Inc. doubles the amount of its assets from the beginning to the end of the year. Liabilities at the end of the year amount to $40,000, and owners' equity is $20,000. What is the amount of Chapman's assets at the beginning of the year?
3. During the year, the liabilities of Dixon Enterprises triple in amount. Assets at the beginning of the year amount to $30,000, and owners' equity is $10,000. What is the amount of liabilities at the end of the year?

Exercise 1-5 ***Changes in Owners' Equity*** **LO 2**

The following amounts are available from the records of Coaches and Carriages Inc. at the end of the years indicated:

December 31	Total Assets	Total Liabilities
2002	$ 25,000	$ 12,000
2003	79,000	67,000
2004	184,000	137,000

Required

1. Compute the changes in Coaches and Carriages' owners' equity during 2003 and 2004.
2. Compute the amount of Coaches and Carriages' net income (or loss) for 2003 assuming that no dividends were paid during the year.
3. Compute the amount of Coaches and Carriages' net income (or loss) for 2004 assuming that dividends paid during the year amounted to $10,000.

SPREADSHEET

Exercise 1-6 ***The Accounting Equation*** **LO 2**

For each of the following independent cases, fill in the blank with the appropriate dollar amount.

	Case 1	Case 2	Case 3	Case 4
Total assets, end of period	$40,000	$_____	$75,000	$50,000
Total liabilities, end of period	_____	15,000	25,000	10,000
Capital stock, end of period	10,000	5,000	20,000	15,000
Retained earnings, beginning of period	15,000	8,000	10,000	20,000
Net income for the period	8,000	7,000	_____	9,000
Dividends for the period	2,000	1,000	3,000	_____

Exercise 1-7 *Classification of Financial Statement Items* **LO 2**

Classify each of the following items according to (1) whether it belongs on the income statement (IS) or balance sheet (BS) and (2) whether it is a revenue (R), expense (E), asset (A), liability (L), or owners' equity (OE) item.

Item	Appears on the	Classified as
Example: Cash	BS	A
1. Salaries expense	________	________
2. Equipment	________	________
3. Accounts payable	________	________
4. Membership fees earned	________	________
5. Capital stock	________	________
6. Accounts receivable	________	________
7. Buildings	________	________
8. Advertising expense	________	________
9. Retained earnings	________	________

Exercise 1-8 *Net Income (or Loss) and Retained Earnings* **LO 2**

The following information is available from the records of Prestige Landscape Design Inc. at the end of the 2004 calendar year:

Accounts payable	$ 5,000	Office equipment	$ 7,500
Accounts receivable	4,000	Rent expense	6,500
Capital stock	8,000	Retained earnings, beginning of year	8,500
Cash	13,000	Salary and wage expense	12,000
Dividends paid during the year	3,000	Supplies	500
Landscaping revenues	25,000		

Required

Use the information above to answer the following questions:

1. What is Prestige's net income for the year ended December 31, 2004?
2. What is Prestige's retained earnings balance at the end of the year?
3. What is the total amount of Prestige's assets at the end of the year?
4. What is the total amount of Prestige's liabilities at the end of the year?
5. How much owners' equity does Prestige have at the end of the year?
6. What is Prestige's accounting equation at December 31, 2004?

Exercise 1-9 *Statement of Retained Earnings* **LO 2**

Ace Corporation has been in business for many years. Retained earnings on January 1, 2004, is $235,800. The following information is available for the first two months of 2004:

	January	February
Revenues	$83,000	$96,000
Expenses	89,000	82,000
Dividends paid	–0–	5,000

Required

Prepare a statement of retained earnings for the month ended February 28, 2004.

Exercise 1-10 *Accounting Principles and Assumptions* **LO 3**

The following basic accounting principles and assumptions were discussed in the chapter:

Economic entity
Monetary unit
Cost principle
Going concern
Time period

Fill in each of the blanks with the accounting principle or assumption that is relevant to the situation described.

______________________ 1. Genesis Corporation is now in its 30th year of business. The founder of the company is planning to retire at the end of the year and turn the business over to his daughter.

______________________ 2. Nordic Company purchased a 20-acre parcel of property on which to build a new factory. The company recorded the property on the records at the amount of cash given to acquire it.

______________________ 3. Jim Bailey enters into an agreement to operate a new law firm in partnership with a friend. Each partner will make an initial cash investment of $10,000. Jim opens a checking account in the name of the partnership and transfers $10,000 from his personal account into the new account.

______________________ 4. Multinational Corp. has a division in Japan. Prior to preparing the financial statements for the company and all its foreign divisions, Multinational translates the financial statements of its Japanese division from yen to U.S. dollars.

______________________ 5. Camden Company has always prepared financial statements annually, with a year-end of June 30. Because the company is going to sell its stock to the public for the first time, quarterly financial reports will also be required by the Securities and Exchange Commission.

Exercise 1-11 ***Organizations and Accounting*** **LO 4**

Match each of the organizations listed below with the statement that most adequately describes the role of the group.

Securities and Exchange Commission

International Accounting Standards Board

Financial Accounting Standards Board

American Institute of Certified Public Accountants

American Accounting Association

______________________ 1. Federal agency with ultimate authority to determine rules used for preparing financial statements for companies whose stock is sold to the public

______________________ 2. Professional organization for accounting educators

______________________ 3. Group in the private sector with authority to set accounting standards

______________________ 4. Professional organization for certified public accountants

______________________ 5. Organization formed to develop worldwide accounting standards

Multi-Concept Exercises

Exercise 1-12 ***Users of Accounting Information and the Financial Statements*** **LO 1, 2**

Listed below are a number of users of accounting information and examples of questions they need answered before making decisions. Fill in each blank to indicate whether the user is most likely to find the answer by looking at the income statement (IS), the balance sheet (BS), or the statement of retained earnings (RE).

User	Question	Financial Statement
Stockholder	How did this year's sales compare to last year's?	____________
Banker	How much debt does the company already have on its books?	____________
Supplier	How much does the company currently owe to its suppliers?	____________
Stockholder	How much did the company pay in dividends this past year?	____________
Advertising account manager	How much did the company spend this past year to generate sales?	____________
Banker	What collateral or security can the company provide to ensure that any loan I make will be repaid?	____________

Exercise 1-13 *Winnebago Industries' Inventories* LO 2, 3

Refer to Winnebago Industries' balance sheet reproduced in the chapter.

Required

What was the amount of Inventories at August 31, 2002? What does this amount represent (i.e., cost, market value)? Why does Winnebago Industries carry its inventories at one or the other?

Exercise 1-14 *Roles of Accountants* LO 1, 4

One day on campus, you overhear two nonbusiness majors discussing the reasons each did not major in accounting. "Accountants are bean counters. They just sit in a room and play with the books all day. They do not have people skills, but I suppose it really doesn't matter because no one ever looks at the statements they prepare," said the first student. The second student replied, "Oh, they are very intelligent, though, because they must know all about the tax laws, and that's too complicated for me."

Required

Comment on the students' perceptions of the roles of accountants in society. Do you agree that no one ever looks at the statements they prepare? If not, identify who the primary users are.

Problems

Problem 1-1 *You Won the Lottery* LO 1

You have won a lottery! You will receive $200,000, after taxes, each year for the next five years.

Required

Describe the process you will go through in determining how to invest your winnings. Consider at least two options and make a choice. You may consider the stock of a certain company, bonds, real estate investments, bank deposits, and so on. Be specific. What information did you need to make a final decision? How was your decision affected by the fact that you will receive the winnings over a five-year period rather than in one lump sum? Would you prefer one payment? Explain.

Problem 1-2 *Users of Accounting Information and Their Needs* LO 1

Havre Company would like to buy a building and equipment to produce a new product line. Some information about Havre is more useful to some people involved in the project than to others.

Required

Complete the chart in the margin on the next page by identifying the information listed on the right with the user's need to know the information. Identify the information as

a. *need* to know;

b. *helpful* to know; or

c. *not necessary* to know.

User of the Information			
Management	Stockholders	Banker	Information
_____	_____	_____	1. Amount of current debt, repayment schedule, and interest rate
_____	_____	_____	2. Fair market value of the building
_____	_____	_____	3. Condition of the roof and heating and cooling, electrical, and plumbing systems
_____	_____	_____	4. Total cost of the building, improvements, and equipment to set up production
_____	_____	_____	5. Expected sales from the new product, variable production costs, related selling costs

Problem 1-3 *Balance Sheet* LO 2

The following items are available from records of Freescia Corporation at the end of the 2004 calendar year:

Accounts payable	$12,550
Accounts receivable	23,920
Advertising expense	2,100
Buildings	85,000
Capital stock	25,000
Cash	4,220
Notes payable	50,000
Office equipment	12,000
Retained earnings, end of year	37,590
Salary and wage expense	8,230
Sales revenue	14,220

Required

Prepare a balance sheet. *Hint:* Not all the items listed should appear on a balance sheet. For each of these items, indicate where it should appear.

Problem 1-4 *Corrected Balance Sheet* LO 2

Dave is the president of Avon Consulting Inc. Avon began business on January 1, 2004. The company's controller is out of the country on business. Dave needs a copy of the company's balance sheet for a meeting tomorrow and asked his assistant to obtain the required information from the company's records. She presented Dave with the following balance sheet. He asks you to review it for accuracy.

AVON CONSULTING INC.
BALANCE SHEET
FOR THE YEAR ENDED DECEMBER 31, 2004

Assets		Liabilities and Stockholders' Equity	
Accounts payable	$13,000	Accounts receivable	$16,000
Cash	21,000	Capital stock	20,000
Cash dividends paid	16,000	Net income for 2004	72,000
Furniture and equipment	43,000	Supplies	9,000

Required

1. Prepare a corrected balance sheet.
2. Draft a memo explaining the major differences between the balance sheet Dave's assistant prepared and the one you prepared.

Problem 1-5 *Income Statement, Statement of Retained Earnings, and Balance Sheet* LO 2

SPREADSHEET

Shown below, in alphabetical order, is a list of the various items that regularly appear on the financial statements of Maple Park Theatres Corp. The amounts shown for balance sheet items are balances as of September 30, 2004 (with the exception of Retained Earnings, which is the balance on September 1, 2004), and the amounts shown for income statement items are balances for the month ended September 30, 2004:

Accounts payable	$17,600
Accounts receivable	6,410
Advertising expense	14,500
Buildings	60,000
Capital stock	50,000
Cash	15,230
Concessions revenue	60,300
Cost of concessions sold	23,450

Dividends paid during the month	$ 8,400
Furniture and fixtures	34,000
Land	26,000
Notes payable	20,000
Projection equipment	25,000
Rent expense-movies	50,600
Retained earnings	73,780
Salaries and wages expense	46,490
Ticket sales	95,100
Water, gas, and electricity	6,700

Required

1. Prepare an income statement for the month ended September 30, 2004.
2. Prepare a statement of retained earnings for the month ended September 30, 2004.
3. Prepare a balance sheet at September 30, 2004.
4. You have $1,000 to invest. On the basis of the statements you prepared, would you use it to buy stock in Maple Park? What other information would you want before making a final decision?

Problem 1-6 *Income Statement and Balance Sheet* LO 2

DECISION MAKING

Green Bay Corporation began business in July 2004 as a commercial fishing operation and passenger service between islands. Shares of stock were issued to the owners in exchange for cash. Boats were purchased by making a down payment in cash and signing a note payable for the balance. Fish are sold to local restaurants on open account, and customers are given 15 days to pay their account. Cash fares are collected for all passenger traffic. Rent for the dock facilities is paid at the beginning of each month. Salaries and wages are paid at the end of the month. The following amounts are from the records of Green Bay Corporation at the end of its first month of operations:

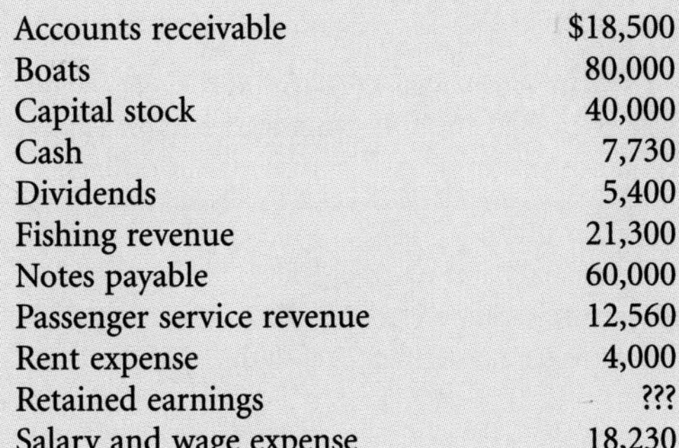

Accounts receivable	$18,500
Boats	80,000
Capital stock	40,000
Cash	7,730
Dividends	5,400
Fishing revenue	21,300
Notes payable	60,000
Passenger service revenue	12,560
Rent expense	4,000
Retained earnings	???
Salary and wage expense	18,230

Required

1. Prepare an income statement for the month ended July 31, 2004.
2. Prepare a balance sheet at July 31, 2004.
3. What information would you need about Notes Payable to assess fully Green Bay's long-term viability? Explain your answer.

Problem 1-7 *Corrected Financial Statements* LO 2

Hometown Cleaners Inc. operates a small dry-cleaning business. The company has always maintained a complete and accurate set of records. Unfortunately, the company's accountant left in a dispute with the president and took the 2004 financial statements with him. The following income statement and balance sheet were prepared by the company's president.

HOMETOWN CLEANERS INC.
INCOME STATEMENT
FOR THE YEAR ENDED DECEMBER 31, 2004

Revenues:		
Accounts receivable	$15,200	
Cleaning revenue—cash sales	32,500	$47,700
Expenses:		
Dividends	$ 4,000	
Accounts payable	4,500	
Utilities	12,200	
Salaries and wages	17,100	37,800
Net income		$ 9,900

HOMETOWN CLEANERS INC.
BALANCE SHEET
DECEMBER 31, 2004

Assets		Liabilities and Stockholders' Equity	
Cash	$ 7,400	Cleaning revenue—	
Building and equipment	80,000	credit sales	$26,200
Less: Notes payable	(50,000)	Capital stock	20,000
Land	40,000	Net income	9,900
		Retained earnings	21,300
		Total liabilities and	
Total assets	$77,400	stockholders' equity	$77,400

The president is very disappointed with the net income for the year because it has averaged $25,000 over the last 10 years. She has asked for your help in determining whether the reported net income accurately reflects the profitability of the company and whether the balance sheet is prepared correctly.

Required

1. Prepare a corrected income statement for the year ended December 31, 2004.
2. Prepare a statement of retained earnings for the year ended December 31, 2004. (The actual balance of retained earnings on January 1, 2004, was $42,700. Note that the December 31, 2004, retained earnings balance shown above is incorrect. The president simply "plugged" this amount in to make the balance sheet balance.)
3. Prepare a corrected balance sheet at December 31, 2004.
4. Draft a memo to the president explaining the major differences between the income statement she prepared and the one you prepared.

Problem 1-8 *Statement of Retained Earnings for the Walt Disney Company* LO 2

http://disney.go.com

The **Walt Disney Company** reported the following amounts in various statements included in its 2002 annual report (all amounts are stated in millions of dollars):

Net income for 2002	$ 1,236
Dividends declared and paid in 2002	428
Retained earnings, September 30, 2001	12,171
Retained earnings, September 30, 2002	12,979

Required

1. Prepare a statement of retained earnings for the Walt Disney Company for the year ended September 30, 2002.
2. The Walt Disney Company does not actually present a statement of retained earnings in its annual report. Instead, it presents a broader statement of stockholders' equity. Describe the information that would be included on this statement and that is not included on a statement of retained earnings.

Problem 1-9 *Role of the Accountant in Various Organizations* LO 4

The following positions in various entities require a knowledge of accounting practices:

1. Chief financial officer for the subsidiary of a large company
2. Tax adviser to a consolidated group of entities
3. Independent computer consultant
4. Financial planner in a bank
5. Real estate broker in an independent office
6. Production planner in a manufacturing facility
7. Quality control adviser
8. Superintendent of a school district
9. Manager of one store in a retail clothing chain
10. Salesperson for a company that offers subcontract services, such as food service and maintenance to hospitals

Required

For each position listed above, identify the entity in which it occurs as business or nonbusiness and describe the kind of accounting knowledge (such as financial, managerial, taxes, not-for-profit) required by each position.

Problem 1-10 ***Information Needs and Setting Accounting Standards*** **LO 1**

The Financial Accounting Standards Board requires companies to supplement their consolidated financial statements with disclosures about segments of their businesses. To comply with this standard, Time Warner's 2002 annual report provides various disclosures for the six segments in which it operates: AOL, Cable, Filmed Entertainment, Networks, Music, and Publishing.

http://www.timewarner.com

Required

Which users of accounting information do you think the Financial Accounting Standards Board had in mind when it set this standard? What types of disclosures do you think these users would find helpful?

Multi-Concept Problem

Problem 1-11 ***Primary Assumptions Made in Preparing Financial Statements*** **LO 2, 3**

Joe Hale opened a machine repair business in leased retail space, paying the first month's rent of $300 and a $1,000 security deposit with a check on his personal account. He took the tools worth about $7,500, from his garage to the shop. He also bought some equipment to get started. The new equipment had a list price of $5,000, but Joe was able to purchase it on sale at Sears for only $4,200. He charged the new equipment on his personal Sears charge card. Joe's first customer paid $400 for services rendered, so Joe opened a checking account for the company. He completed a second job, but the customer has not paid Joe the $2,500 for his work. At the end of the first month, Joe prepared the following balance sheet and income statement.

JOE'S MACHINE REPAIR SHOP
BALANCE SHEET
JULY 31, 2004

Cash	$ 400		
Equipment	5,000	Equity	$5,400
Total	$5,400	Total	$5,400

JOE'S MACHINE REPAIR SHOP
INCOME STATEMENT
FOR MONTH ENDED JULY 31, 2004

Sales		$ 2,900
Rent	$ 300	
Tools	4,200	4,500
Net loss		$(1,600)

Joe believes that he should show a greater profit next month because he won't have large expenses for items such as tools.

Required

Identify the assumptions that Joe has violated and explain how each event should have been handled. Prepare a corrected balance sheet and income statement.

Alternate Problems

Problem 1-1A ***What to Do with a Million Dollars*** **LO 1**

You have inherited $1 million!

Required

Describe the process you will go through in determining how to invest your inheritance. Consider at least two options and choose one. You may consider the stock of a certain company, bonds,

(continued)

real estate investments, bank deposits, and so on. Be specific. What information did you need to make a final decision? Where did you find the information you needed? What additional information will you need to consider if you want to make a change in your investment?

Problem 1-2A ***Users of Accounting Information and Their Needs*** **LO 1**

Billings Inc. would like to buy a franchise to provide a specialized service. Some information about Billings is more useful to some people involved in the project than to others.

Required

Complete the chart in the margin by identifying the information listed on the right with the user's need to know the information. Identify the information as

a. *need* to know;

b. *helpful* to know; or

c. *not necessary* to know.

User of the Information			
Manager	Stockholders	Franchisor	Information
____	____	____	1. Expected revenue from the new service.
____	____	____	2. Cost of the franchise fee and recurring fees to be paid to the franchisor.
____	____	____	3. Cash available to Billings, the franchisee, to operate the business after the franchise is purchased.
____	____	____	4. Expected overhead costs of the service outlet.
____	____	____	5. Billings' required return on its investment.

Problem 1-3A ***Balance Sheet*** **LO 2**

The following items are available from the records of Victor Corporation at the end of its fiscal year, July 31, 2004:

Accounts payable	$16,900
Accounts receivable	5,700
Buildings	35,000
Butter and cheese inventory	12,100
Capital stock	25,000
Cash	21,800
Computerized mixers	25,800
Delivery expense	4,600
Notes payable	50,000
Office equipment	12,000
Retained earnings, end of year	26,300
Salary and wage expense	8,230
Sales revenue	14,220
Tools	5,800

Required

Prepare a balance sheet. *Hint:* Not all the items listed should appear on a balance sheet. For each of these items, indicate where it should appear.

Problem 1-4A ***Corrected Balance Sheet*** **LO 2**

Pete is the president of Island Enterprises. Island Enterprises began business on January 1, 2004. The company's controller is out of the country on business. Pete needs a copy of the company's balance sheet for a meeting tomorrow and asked his assistant to obtain the required information from the company's records. She presented Pete with the following balance sheet. He asks you to review it for accuracy.

ISLAND ENTERPRISES
BALANCE SHEET
FOR THE YEAR ENDED DECEMBER 31, 2004

Assets		**Liabilities and Stockholders' Equity**	
Accounts payable	$ 29,600	Accounts receivable	$ 23,200
Building and equipment	177,300	Supplies	12,200
Cash	14,750	Capital stock	100,000
Cash dividends paid	16,000	Net income for 2004	113,850

Required

1. Prepare a corrected balance sheet.
2. Draft a memo explaining the major differences between the balance sheet Pete's assistant prepared and the one you prepared.

Problem 1-5A ***Income Statement, Statement of Retained Earnings, and Balance Sheet*** **LO 2**

SPREADSHEET

Shown below, in alphabetical order, is a list of the various items that regularly appear on the financial statements of Sterns Audio Book Rental Corp. The amounts shown for balance sheet items are balances as of December 31, 2004 (with the exception of retained earnings, which is the balance on January 1, 2004), and the amounts shown for income statement items are balances for the year ended December 31, 2004:

Accounts payable	$ 4,500
Accounts receivable	300
Advertising expense	14,500
Audio tape inventory	70,000
Capital stock	50,000
Cash	2,490
Display fixtures	45,000
Dividends paid during the year	12,000
Notes payable	10,000
Rental revenue	125,900
Rent paid on building	60,000
Retained earnings	35,390
Salaries and wages expense	17,900
Water, gas, and electricity	3,600

Required

1. Prepare an income statement for the year ended December 31, 2004.
2. Prepare a statement of retained earnings for the year ended December 31, 2004.
3. Prepare a balance sheet at December 31, 2004.
4. You have $1,000 to invest. On the basis of the statements you prepared, would you use it to buy stock in this company? What other information would you want before deciding?

Problem 1-6A ***Income Statement and Balance Sheet*** **LO 2**

DECISION MAKING

Fort Worth Corporation began business in January 2004 as a commercial carpet cleaning and drying service. Shares of stock were issued to the owners in exchange for cash. Equipment was purchased by making a down payment in cash and signing a note payable for the balance. Services are performed for local restaurants and office buildings on open account, and customers are given 15 days to pay their account. Rent for office and storage facilities is paid at the beginning of each month. Salaries and wages are paid at the end of the month. The following amounts are from the records of Fort Worth Corporation at the end of its first month of operations:

Accounts receivable	$24,750
Capital stock	80,000
Cash	51,650
Cleaning revenue	45,900
Dividends	5,500
Equipment	62,000
Notes payable	30,000
Rent expense	3,600
Retained earnings	???
Salary and wage expense	8,400

Required

1. Prepare an income statement for the month ended January 31, 2004.
2. Prepare a balance sheet at January 31, 2004.
3. What information would you need about Notes Payable to fully assess Fort Worth's long-term viability? Explain your answer.

Problem 1-7A *Corrected Financial Statements* LO 2

Heidi's Bakery Inc. operates a small pastry business. The company has always maintained a complete and accurate set of records. Unfortunately, the company's accountant left in a dispute with the president and took the 2004 financial statements with her. The balance sheet and the income statement shown below were prepared by the company's president.

HEIDI'S BAKERY INC.
INCOME STATEMENT
FOR THE YEAR ENDED DECEMBER 31, 2004

Revenues:		
Accounts receivable	$15,500	
Pastry revenue—cash sales	23,700	$39,200
Expenses:		
Dividends	$ 5,600	
Accounts payable	6,800	
Utilities	9,500	
Salaries and wages	18,200	40,100
Net loss		$ (900)

HEIDI'S BAKERY INC.
BALANCE SHEET
DECEMBER 31, 2004

Assets		Liabilities and Stockholders' Equity	
Cash	$ 3,700	Pastry revenue—	
Building and equipment	60,000	credit sales	$22,100
Less: Notes payable	(40,000)	Capital stock	30,000
Land	50,000	Net loss	(900)
		Retained earnings	22,500
		Total liabilities and	
Total assets	$73,700	stockholders' equity	$73,700

The president is very disappointed with the net loss for the year because net income has averaged $21,000 over the last 10 years. He has asked for your help in determining whether the reported net loss accurately reflects the profitability of the company and whether the balance sheet is prepared correctly.

Required

1. Prepare a corrected income statement for the year ended December 31, 2004.
2. Prepare a statement of retained earnings for the year ended December 31, 2004. (The actual amount of Retained Earnings on January 1, 2004, was $39,900. The December 31, 2004, retained earnings balance shown above is incorrect. The president simply "plugged" this amount in to make the balance sheet balance.)
3. Prepare a corrected balance sheet at December 31, 2004.
4. Draft a memo to the president explaining the major differences between the income statement he prepared and the one you prepared.

Problem 1-8A *Statement of Retained Earnings for Brunswick Corporation* LO 2

http://www.brunswick.com

Brunswick Corporation reported the following amounts in various statements included in its 2002 annual report (all amounts are stated in millions of dollars):

Net earnings for 2002	$ 78.4
Cash dividends declared and paid in 2002	45.1
Retained earnings, December 31, 2001	1,079.4
Retained earnings, December 31, 2002	1,112.7

Required

1. Prepare a statement of retained earnings for Brunswick Corporation for the year ended December 31, 2002.
2. Brunswick does not actually present a statement of retained earnings in its annual report. Instead, it presents a broader statement of shareholders' (stockholders') equity. Describe the information that would be included on this statement and that is not included on a statement of retained earnings.

Problem 1-9A *Role of the Accountant in Various Organizations* **LO 4**

The following positions in various entities require a knowledge of accounting practices:

__________ 1. Chief financial officer for the subsidiary of a large company

__________ 2. Tax adviser to a consolidated group of entities

__________ 3. Accounts receivable computer analyst

__________ 4. Financial planner in a bank

__________ 5. Budget analyst in a real estate office

__________ 6. Production planner in a manufacturing facility

__________ 7. Quality control adviser

__________ 8. Manager of the team conducting an audit on a state lottery

__________ 9. Assistant superintendent of a school district

__________ 10. Manager of one store in a retail clothing chain

__________ 11. Controller in a company that offers subcontract services, such as food service and maintenance to hospitals

__________ 12. Staff accountant in a large audit firm

Required

For each position listed above, fill in the blank to classify the position as one of the general categories of accountants listed below.

Financial accountant	**Accountant for not-for-profit organization**
Managerial accountant	**Auditor**
Tax accountant	**Not an accounting position**

Problem 1-10A *Information Needs and Setting Accounting Standards* **LO 1**

The Financial Accounting Standards Board requires companies to supplement their consolidated financial statements with disclosures about segments of their businesses. To comply with this standard, **Marriott International's** 2002 annual report provides various disclosures for the six segments in which it operates: Full-Service Lodging, Select-Service Lodging, Extended-Stay Lodging, Timeshare, Senior Living Services, and Distribution Services (includes a wholesale food-distribution business).

http://www.marriott.com

Required

Which users of accounting information do you think the Financial Accounting Standards Board had in mind when it set this standard? What types of disclosures do you think these users would find helpful?

Alternate Multi-Concept Problem

Problem 1-11A *Primary Assumptions Made in Preparing Financial Statements* **LO 2, 3**

Millie Abrams opened a ceramic studio in leased retail space, paying the first month's rent of $300 and a $1,000 security deposit with a check on her personal account. She took molds and paint, worth about $7,500, from her home to the studio. She also bought a new firing kiln to start the business. The new kiln had a list price of $5,000, but Millie was able to trade in her old kiln, worth $500 at the time of trade, on the new kiln, and therefore she paid only $4,500 cash. She wrote a check on her personal checking account. Millie's first customers paid a total of $1,400 to attend classes for the next two months. She opened a checking account in the company's name with the $1,400. She has conducted classes for one month and has sold for $3,000 unfinished ceramic pieces called *greenware.* Greenware sales are all cash. Millie incurred $1,000 of personal cost in making the greenware. At the end of the first month, Millie prepared the following balance sheet and income statement.

MILLIE'S CERAMIC STUDIO
BALANCE SHEET
JULY 31, 2004

Cash	$1,400		
Kiln	5,000	Equity	$6,400
Total	$6,400	Total	$6,400

MILLIE'S CERAMIC STUDIO
INCOME STATEMENT
FOR THE MONTH ENDED JULY 31, 2004

Sales		$4,400
Rent	$300	
Supplies	600	900
Net income		$3,500

Millie needs to earn at least $3,000 each month for the business to be worth her time. She is pleased with the results.

Required

Identify the assumptions that Millie has violated and explain how each event should have been handled. Prepare a corrected balance sheet and income statement.

Decision Cases

Reading and Interpreting Financial Statements

http://www.winnebagoind.com

Decision Case 1-1 ***An Annual Report as Ready Reference*** **LO 1, 2**

Refer to the **Winnebago Industries** annual report, reproduced in Appendix A, and identify where each of the following users of accounting information would first look to answer their respective questions about Winnebago Industries:

1. Investors: How much did the company earn for each share of stock I own? How much of those earnings did I receive, and how much was reinvested in the company?
2. Potential investors: What amount of earnings can I expect to see from Winnebago Industries in the near future?
3. Bankers and creditors: Should I extend the short-term borrowing limit to Winnebago Industries? Does it have sufficient cash or cash-like assets to repay short-term loans?
4. IRS: How much does Winnebago Industries owe for taxes?
5. Employees: How much money did the president and vice presidents earn? Should I ask for a raise?

http://www.winnebagoind.com

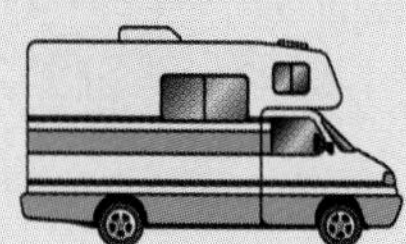

Decision Case 1-2 ***Reading and Interpreting Winnebago Industries' Financial Statements*** **LO 2**

Refer to the financial statements for **Winnebago Industries** reproduced in the chapter and answer the following questions:

1. What was the company's net income for 2002?
2. State Winnebago Industries' financial position on August 31, 2002, in terms of the accounting equation.
3. Explain the reasons for the change in retained (or reinvested) earnings from a balance of $234,139,000 on August 25, 2001, to a balance of $284,856,000 on August 31, 2002. Also, what amount of dividends did the company pay in 2002?

http://www.winnebagoind.com
http://www.monacocoach.com

Decision Case 1-3 ***Comparing Two Companies in the Same Industry: Winnebago Industries and Monaco Coach Corporation*** **LO 2, 4**

Refer to the financial information for **Winnebago Industries** and **Monaco Coach Corporation** reproduced in Appendices A and B at the end of the book and answer the following questions:

1. What was the total revenue amount for each company for 2002? (Note that Monaco Coach uses the term "net sales" rather than revenues.) Did each company's revenues increase or decrease from its total amount in 2001?

2. What was each company's net income for 2002? Did each company's net income increase or decrease from its net income for 2001?
3. What was the total asset balance for each company at the end of its 2002 fiscal year? Among its assets, what was the largest asset each reported on its 2002 fiscal year-end balance sheet?
4. Did either company pay its stockholders any dividends during 2002? Explain how you can tell whether they did or did not pay any dividends.
5. Compare the auditors' report for the two companies. Is the format of the reports the same? If not, how do they differ? Do they contain the same basic information?

Making Financial Decisions

Decision Case 1-4 ***An Investment Opportunity*** **LO 1**

DECISION MAKING

You have saved enough money to pay for your college tuition for the next three years when a high school friend comes to you with a deal. He is an artist who has spent most of the past two years drawing on the walls of old buildings. The buildings are about to be demolished and your friend thinks you should buy the walls before the buildings are demolished and open a gallery featuring his work. Of course, you are levelheaded and would normally say "No!" Recently, however, your friend has been featured on several local radio and television shows and is talking to some national networks about doing a feature on a well-known news show. To set up the gallery would take all your savings, but your friend feels that you will be able to sell his artwork for 10 times the cost of your investment. What kinds of information about the business do you need before deciding to invest all your savings? What kind of profit split would you suggest to your friend if you decide to open the gallery?

Decision Case 1-5 ***Preparation of Projected Statements for a New Business*** **LO 2**

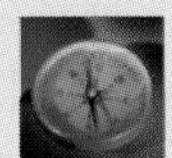

DECISION MAKING

Upon graduation from MegaState University, you and your roommate decide to start your respective careers in accounting and salmon fishing in Remote, Alaska. Your career as a CPA in Remote is going well, as is your roommate's job as a commercial fisherman. After one year in Remote, he approaches you with a business opportunity.

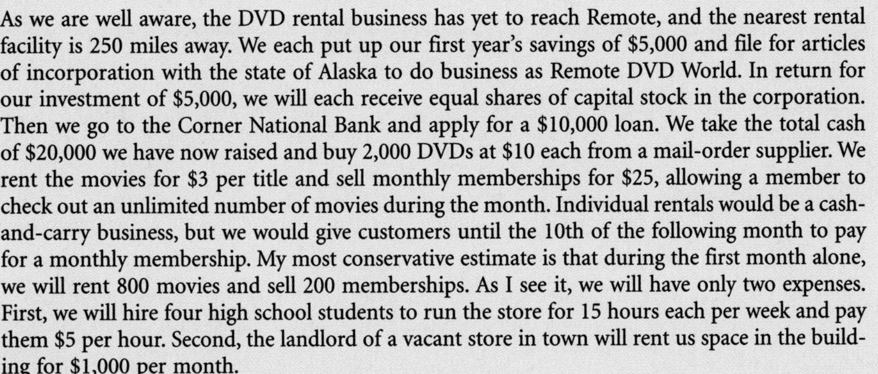

> As we are well aware, the DVD rental business has yet to reach Remote, and the nearest rental facility is 250 miles away. We each put up our first year's savings of $5,000 and file for articles of incorporation with the state of Alaska to do business as Remote DVD World. In return for our investment of $5,000, we will each receive equal shares of capital stock in the corporation. Then we go to the Corner National Bank and apply for a $10,000 loan. We take the total cash of $20,000 we have now raised and buy 2,000 DVDs at $10 each from a mail-order supplier. We rent the movies for $3 per title and sell monthly memberships for $25, allowing a member to check out an unlimited number of movies during the month. Individual rentals would be a cash-and-carry business, but we would give customers until the 10th of the following month to pay for a monthly membership. My most conservative estimate is that during the first month alone, we will rent 800 movies and sell 200 memberships. As I see it, we will have only two expenses. First, we will hire four high school students to run the store for 15 hours each per week and pay them $5 per hour. Second, the landlord of a vacant store in town will rent us space in the building for $1,000 per month.

Required

1. Prepare a projected income statement for the first month of operations.
2. Prepare a balance sheet as it would appear at the end of the first month of operations.
3. Assume that the bank is willing to make the $10,000 loan. Would you be willing to join your roommate in this business? Explain your response. Also, indicate any information other than what he has provided that you would like to have before making a final decision.

Accounting and Ethics: What Would You Do?

Decision Case 1-6 ***Identification of Errors in Financial Statements and Preparation of Revised Statements*** **LO 1, 2**

ETHICS

Lakeside Slammers Inc. is a minor-league baseball organization that has just completed its first season. You and three other investors organized the corporation; each put up $10,000 in cash for shares of capital stock. Because you live out of state, you have not been actively involved in the daily affairs of the club. However, you are thrilled to receive a dividend check for $10,000 at the end of the season—an amount equal to your original investment! Included with the check are the following financial statements, along with supporting explanations.

LAKESIDE SLAMMERS INC.
INCOME STATEMENT
FOR THE YEAR ENDED DECEMBER 31, 2004

Revenues:		
Single-game ticket revenue	$420,000	
Season-ticket revenue	140,000	
Concessions revenue	280,000	
Advertising revenue	100,000	$940,000
Expenses:		
Cost of concessions sold	$110,000	
Salary expense—players	225,000	
Salary and wage expense—staff	150,000	
Rent expense	210,000	695,000
Net income		$245,000

LAKESIDE SLAMMERS INC.
STATEMENT OF RETAINED EARNINGS
FOR THE YEAR ENDED DECEMBER 31, 2004

Beginning balance, January 1, 2004	$ 0
Add: Net income for 2004	245,000
Deduct: Cash dividends paid in 2004	(40,000)
Ending balance, December 31, 2004	$205,000

LAKESIDE SLAMMERS INC.
BALANCE SHEET
DECEMBER 31, 2004

Assets		**Liabilities and Stockholders' Equity**	
Cash	$ 5,000	Notes payable	$ 50,000
Accounts receivable:		Capital stock	40,000
Season tickets	140,000	Additional owners' capital	80,000
Advertisers	100,000	Parent club's equity	125,000
Auxiliary assets	80,000	Retained earnings	205,000
Equipment	50,000		
Player contracts	125,000	Total liabilities and	
Total assets	$500,000	stockholders' equity	$500,000

Additional information:

a. Single-game tickets sold for $4 per game. The team averaged 1,500 fans per game. With 70 home games × $4 per game × 1,500 fans, single-game ticket revenue amounted to $420,000.

b. No season tickets were sold during the first season. During the last three months of 2004, however, an aggressive sales campaign resulted in the sale of 500 season tickets for the 2005 season. Therefore, the controller (who is also one of the owners) chose to record an Account Receivable—Season Tickets and corresponding revenue for 500 tickets × $4 per game × 70 games, or $140,000.

c. Advertising revenue of $100,000 resulted from the sale of the 40 signs on the outfield wall at $2,500 each for the season. However, none of the advertisers have paid their bills yet (thus, an account receivable of $100,000 on the balance sheet) because the contract with Lakeside required them to pay only if the team averaged 2,000 fans per game during the 2004 season. The controller believes that the advertisers will be sympathetic to the difficulties of starting a new franchise and be willing to overlook the slight deficiency in the attendance requirement.

d. Lakeside has a working agreement with one of the major-league franchises. The minor-league team is required to pay $5,000 *every* year to the major-league team for each of the 25 players on its roster. The controller believes that each of the players is certainly an asset to the organization and has therefore recorded $5,000 × 25, or $125,000, as an asset called Player Contracts. The item on the right side of the balance sheet entitled Parent Club's Equity is the amount owed to the major league team by February 1, 2005, as payment for the players for the 2004 season.

e. In addition to the cost described in **d**, Lakeside directly pays each of its 25 players a $9,000 salary for the season. This amount—$225,000—has already been paid for the 2004 season and is reported on the income statement.

f. The items on the balance sheet entitled Auxiliary Assets on the left side and Additional Owners' Capital on the right side represent the value of the controller's personal residence. She has a mortgage with the bank for the full value of the house.

g. The $50,000 note payable resulted from a loan that was taken out at the beginning of the year to finance the purchase of bats, balls, uniforms, lawn mowers, and other miscellaneous supplies needed to operate the team (equipment is reported as an asset for the same amount). The loan, with interest, is due on April 15, 2005. Even though the team had a very successful first year, Lakeside is a little short of cash at the end of 2004 and has therefore asked the bank for a three-month extension of the loan. The controller reasons, "By the due date of April 15, 2005, the cash due from the new season ticket holders will be available, things will be cleared up with the advertisers, and the loan can be easily repaid."

Required

1. Identify any errors that you think the controller has made in preparing the financial statements.
2. On the basis of your answer in **1**, prepare a revised income statement, statement of retained earnings, and balance sheet.
3. On the basis of your revised financial statements, identify any ethical dilemma you now face. Does the information regarding the season ticket revenue provide reliable information to an outsider? Does the $100,000 advertising revenue on the income statement represent the underlying economic reality of the transaction? Do you have a responsibility to share these revisions with the other three owners? What is your responsibility to the bank?

Using Exhibit 1-9 and the related text as your guide, analyze the key elements in the situation and answer the following questions. Support your answers by explaining your reasoning.

a. Who may benefit or be harmed?
b. How are they likely to benefit or be harmed?
c. What rights or claims may be violated?
d. What specific interests are in conflict?
e. What are your responsibilities and obligations?
f. Do you believe the information provided by the organization is relevant, is reliable, accurately represents what it claims to report, and is unbiased?

THOMSON ONE Business School Edition Case

Case 1-7 ***Using THOMSON ONE for Winnebago Industries***

In the chapter we introduced the critical role that financial statements play in helping users of those statements make decisions. Exhibit 1-1 gave examples of various users of financial statements and common decisions they need to make. Success as measured on the various statements should translate to success in the market for a company's stock in the form of appreciation in its stock price and, if the company chooses, in the form of dividends to the stockholders. We can use THOMSON ONE to obtain information about both **Winnebago Industries**' performance as measured in its financial statements and in its stock price.

http://www.winnebagoind.com

Begin by entering the company's ticker symbol, WGO, and then selecting "GO." On the opening screen you will see background information about the company, key financial ratios, and some recent data concerning stock price. To research the company's stock price further, click the "Prices" tab. At the top of the Price Chart, click on the "Interactive Chart." To obtain a 1-year chart, go to "Time Frame," click on the down arrow and select "1 year." Then click on "Draw" and a 1-year chart should appear.

We can also find Winnebago Industries most recent financial statements. Near the top of the screen, click on "Financials" and select "Financial Statements." Refer to the comparative statements of earnings, statements of cash flows, and balance sheets.

Based on your use of THOMSON ONE, answer the following questions:

1. What was the amount of Winnebago Industries' revenues, cost of manufactured products, and net income for the most recent fiscal year as reported on its income statement? Was there an increase or decrease in these amounts from the prior year? What was the percentage increase or decrease in each amount from the prior year?

(continued)

2. What was the amount of cash dividends paid, both in total and per share, for the most recent fiscal year as reported on Winnebago Industries' statement of changes in stockholders' equity? Was there any change in the dividends paid per share from the prior year?
3. What has been Winnebago Industries' high and low stock price for the most recent year?
4. How does the company's stock performance compare to the other line on the stock price chart for the S & P 500?
5. Given your answers to each of the above questions, would you consider buying shares of stock in Winnebago Industries? Explain your reasoning.

Solutions to Key Terms Quiz

Answer	Term
4	Accounting (p. 14)
9	Management accounting (p. 14)
5	Financial accounting (p. 15)
6	Owners' equity (p. 17)
3	Stockholders' equity (p. 17)
8	Retained earnings (p. 17)
7	Balance sheet (p. 17)
1	Income statement (p. 19)
27	Net income (p. 19)
10	Dividends (p. 20)
2	Statement of retained earnings (p. 20)
12	Cost principle (p. 22)
16	Going concern (p. 22)
18	Monetary unit (p. 23)
21	Time period (p. 23)
11	Generally accepted accounting principles (GAAP) (p. 23)
13	Securities and Exchange Commission (SEC) (p. 24)
17	Financial Accounting Standards Board (FASB) (p. 24)
19	American Institute of Certified Public Accountants (AICPA) (p. 24)
28	Certified Public Accountant (CPA) (p. 24)
24	International Accounting Standards Board (IASB) (p. 24)
22	Controller (p. 24)
15	Treasurer (p. 24)
20	Internal auditing (p. 25)
23	Auditing (p. 26)
25	Auditors' report (p. 26)
14	American Accounting Association (p. 28)
26	Sarbanes-Oxley Act (p. 32)

Chapter 2

Financial Statements and the Annual Report

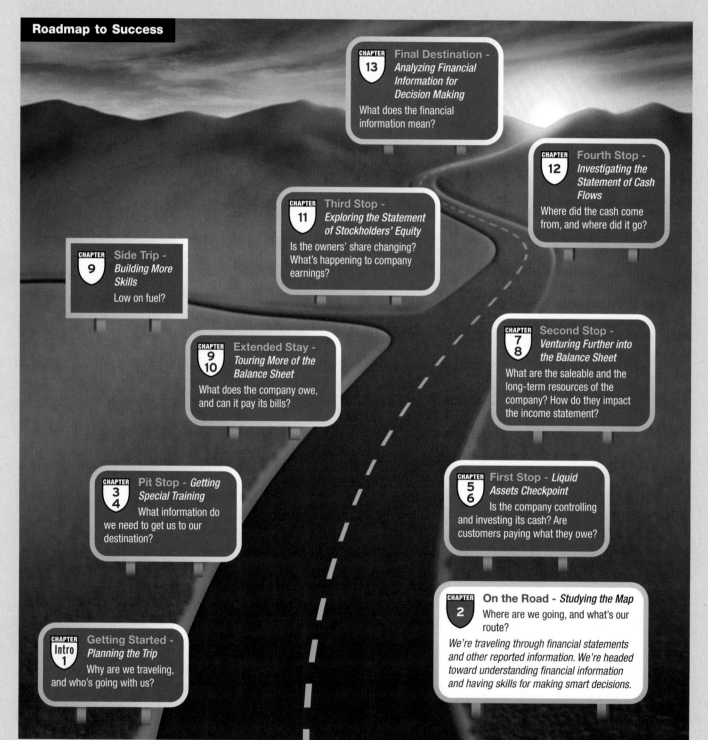

Roadmap to Success

CHAPTER 13 **Final Destination -** ***Analyzing Financial Information for Decision Making***
What does the financial information mean?

CHAPTER 12 **Fourth Stop -** ***Investigating the Statement of Cash Flows***
Where did the cash come from, and where did it go?

CHAPTER 11 **Third Stop -** ***Exploring the Statement of Stockholders' Equity***
Is the owners' share changing? What's happening to company earnings?

CHAPTER 9 **Side Trip -** ***Building More Skills***
Low on fuel?

CHAPTER 9 10 **Extended Stay -** ***Touring More of the Balance Sheet***
What does the company owe, and can it pay its bills?

CHAPTER 7 8 **Second Stop -** ***Venturing Further into the Balance Sheet***
What are the saleable and the long-term resources of the company? How do they impact the income statement?

CHAPTER 5 6 **First Stop -** ***Liquid Assets Checkpoint***
Is the company controlling and investing its cash? Are customers paying what they owe?

CHAPTER 3 4 **Pit Stop -** ***Getting Special Training***
What information do we need to get us to our destination?

CHAPTER 2 **On the Road -** ***Studying the Map***
Where are we going, and what's our route?
We're traveling through financial statements and other reported information. We're headed toward understanding financial information and having skills for making smart decisions.

CHAPTER Intro 1 **Getting Started -** ***Planning the Trip***
Why are we traveling, and who's going with us?

Focus on Financial Results

The year 2002 marked a significant milestone for Monaco Coach Corporation. It was the first time in its relatively short history that the Oregon-based maker of luxury motorcoaches and other recreational vehicles surpassed the billion dollar mark in sales. As seen in the accompanying financial highlights, Monaco Coach's record sales of over $1.2 billion reflected a 30 percent increase from those of the prior year.

The record sales also translated to a very positive "bottom line" for the company. In fact, Monaco Coach's 2002 net income of over $44 million represented a nearly 80 percent increase from 2001.

All companies use a variety of both financial and nonfinancial measures to monitor their progress. Monaco Coach is no different, and one of the key indicators for it is the number of units it sells to its dealers in a given year. One need look no further than the company's unit sales in 2002 to understand why it topped the billion dollar mark in sales: during the year Monaco Coach sold a total of 11,211 RVs, also a record for the company. In its annual report, the company cites a number of factors for this success. First, the industry did well in 2002, recording a 20 percent increase in wholesale units shipped. And much like the housing market, the demand for recreational vehicles has benefited from the extremely low interest rates.

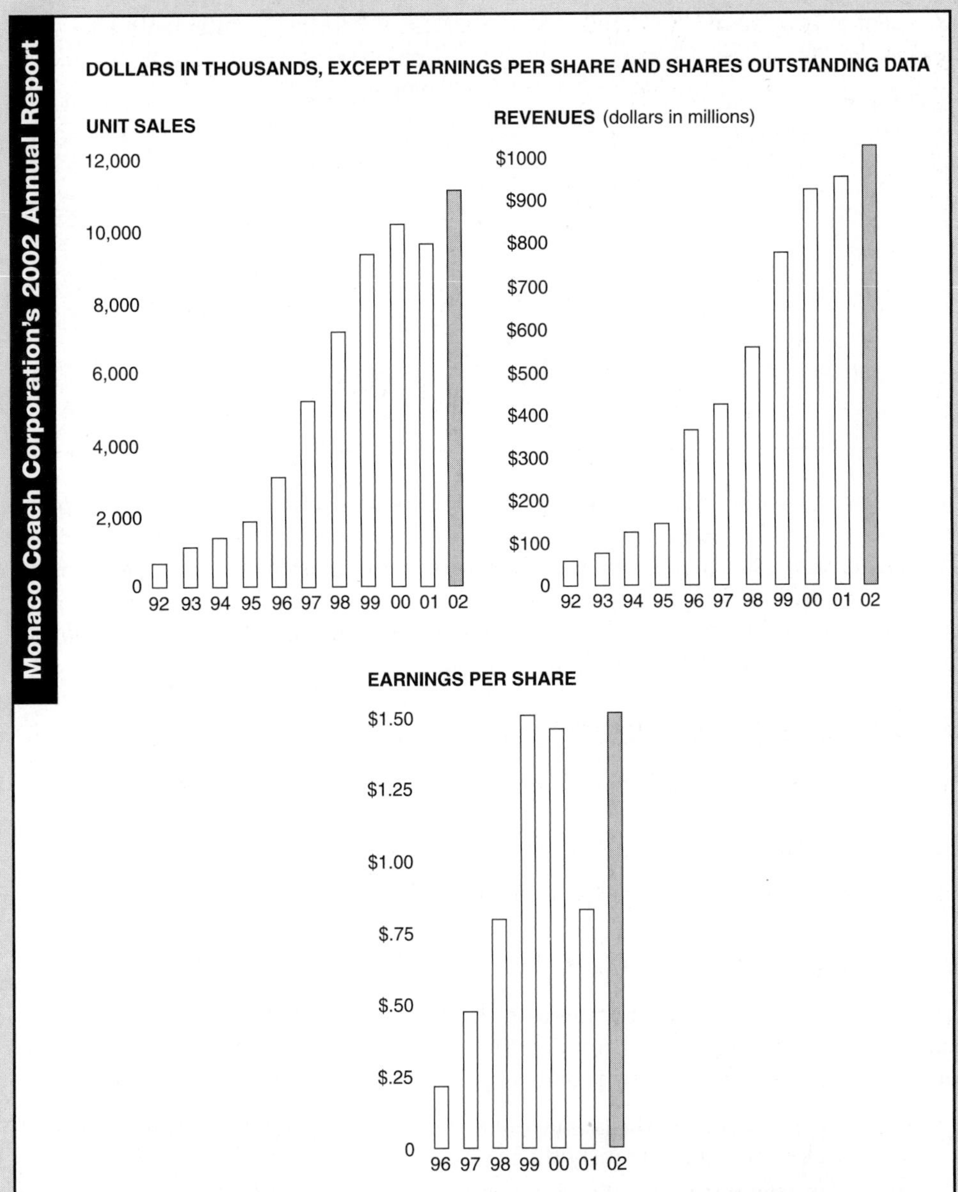

What does the future hold for Monaco Coach and the rest of the RV industry? According to Kay Toolson, Chairman and CEO, the company remains optimistic but also aware of the challenges and uncertainties in the market for its products. Certainly demographics favor the industry, as does an increasing interest in leisure travel. However, the company clearly understands the highly competitive nature of its industry. Only by continuing to focus attention on innovation and meeting the needs of its customers will Monaco Coach be able to surpass the high sales mark it set in 2002.

Source: Monaco Coach Corporation 2002 Annual Report.

You're in the Driver's Seat

If you were thinking of buying shares of Monaco Coach stock, what questions about Monaco Coach's future plans would you want answered? Use this chapter, Monaco Coach's annual report, and its Web site to help you identify and evaluate information about the company's financial performance and management's plans for use of the firm's resources.

http://www.monacocoach.com

LEARNING OBJECTIVES

After studying this chapter, you should be able to:

LO 1 Describe the objectives of financial reporting. (p. 59)

LO 2 Describe the qualitative characteristics of accounting information. (p. 61)

LO 3 Explain the concept and purpose of a classified balance sheet and prepare the statement. (p. 65)

LO 4 Use a classified balance sheet to analyze a company's financial position. (p. 70)

LO 5 Explain the difference between a single-step and a multiple-step income statement and prepare each type of income statement. (p. 72)

LO 6 Use a multiple-step income statement to analyze a company's operations. (p. 74)

LO 7 Identify the components of the statement of retained earnings and prepare the statement. (p. 75)

LO 8 Identify the components of the statement of cash flows and prepare the statement. (p. 76)

LO 9 Read and use the financial statements and other elements in the annual report of a publicly held company. (p. 77)

WHAT EXTERNAL DECISION MAKERS WANT TO KNOW ABOUT FINANCIAL STATEMENTS

DECISION MAKING

As we saw in Chapter 1, a variety of external users need information to make sound business decisions. These users include stockholders, bondholders, bankers, and other types of creditors, such as suppliers. All of these users must make an initial decision about investing in a company, regardless of whether it is in the form of a stock, a bond or a note. Beginning in this chapter, we will consider four basic steps that all decision makers must consider if they are to be successful:

▶ *ASK ESSENTIAL QUESTIONS*

Wise business decisions start with asking the right questions. All external users need answers to these questions:

- Will the company be able to pay its debts as they come due?
- Will the company be profitable in the future?

▶ *FIND BASIC INFORMATION*

The balance sheet, the income statement, the statement of cash flows, along with the supporting notes and other information found in an annual report, are the key sources of information about a company's ability to pay its debts and its profitability. Specifically,

- the balance sheet tells what obligations will be due in the near future and what assets will be available to satisfy them,
- the income statement tells the revenues and expenses for a period of time,
- the statement of cash flows tells where cash came from and how it was used during the period, and
- the notes provide essential details about the company's accounting policies and other key factors that affect its financial condition and performance.

▶ *UNDERSTAND ACCOUNTING PRINCIPLES*

To use the basic information that is found, decision makers must understand the underlying accounting principles (GAAP) that have been applied to create the reported information in the statements. In preparing financial statements, accountants consider:

- the objectives of financial reporting
- the characteristics that make accounting information useful
- the most useful way to display the information found in the balance sheet, the income statement, and the statement of cash flows

▶ *INTERPRET ANALYTICAL INFORMATION*

To make sound business decisions, external users must interpret the information they are given in the statements and in the notes. In other words, what does the information tell you about the company and its future? Throughout this book we will consider various tools that allow users to analyze financial statements. Among the most important of these tools are a number of ratios that can be developed from the statements. In this chapter we begin by looking at three of these ratios. The current ratio provides insight into a company's ability to pay its debts as the come due. The gross profit ratio and the profit margin are key indicators of profitability.

WHY DOES ACCOUNTING INFORMATION NEED TO BE USEFUL? OBJECTIVES OF FINANCIAL REPORTING

LO 1 Describe the objectives of financial reporting.

The users of financial information are the main reason financial statements are prepared. After all, it is the investors, creditors, and other groups and individuals outside and inside the company who must make economic decisions based on these statements. Therefore, as we learned in Chapter 1, financial statements must be based on agreed-upon assumptions like time-period, going concern, and other generally accepted accounting principles.

Moreover, when the accountants for companies like Winnebago Industries and Monaco Coach prepare their financial statements, they must keep in mind financial reporting objectives, which are focused on providing the most understandable and useful information possible. Financial reporting has one overall objective and a set of related objectives, all of them concerned with how the information may be most useful to the readers.

The Primary Objective: Provide Information for Decision Making

The primary objective of financial reporting is to provide economic information to permit users of the information to make informed decisions. Users include both the management of a company (internal users) and others not involved in the daily operations of the business (external users). Without access to the detailed records of the business and without the benefit of daily involvement in the affairs of the company, external users make their decisions based on *financial statements* prepared by management. According to the Financial Accounting Standards Board (FASB), "Financial reporting should provide information that is useful to present and potential investors and creditors and other users in making rational investment, credit, and similar decisions".[1]

We see from this statement how closely the objective of financial reporting is tied to decision making. The purpose of financial reporting is to help the users reach their decisions in an informed manner.

[1] *Statement of Financial Accounting Concepts [SFAC] No. 1,* "Objectives of Financial Reporting by Business Enterprises" (Stamford, Conn.: Financial Accounting Standards Board, November 1978), par. 34.

Secondary Objective: Reflect Prospective Cash Receipts to Investors and Creditors

Present stockholders must decide whether to hold their stock in a company or sell it. For potential stockholders, the decision is whether to buy the stock in the first place. Bankers, suppliers, and other types of creditors must decide whether to lend money to a company. In making their decisions, all these groups rely partially on the information provided in financial statements. (Other sources of information are sometimes as important, or more important, in reaching a decision. For example, the most recent income statement may report the highest profits in the history of a company. However, a potential investor may choose not to buy stock in a company if *The Wall Street Journal* or *Business Week* reports that a strike is likely to shut down operations for an indeterminable period of time.)

http://www.wsj.com
http://www.businessweek.com

If you buy stock in a company, your primary concern is the *future cash to be received from the investment.* First, how much, if anything, will you periodically receive in *cash dividends?* Second, how much cash will you receive from the *sale of the stock?* The interests of a creditor, such as a banker, are similar. The banker is concerned with receiving the original amount of money lent and the interest on the loan. In summary, another objective of financial reporting is to "provide information to help present and potential investors and creditors and other users in assessing the amounts, timing, and uncertainty of prospective cash receipts from dividends or interest and the proceeds from the sale, redemption, or maturity of securities or loans."[2]

Secondary Objective: Reflect Prospective Cash Flows to the Enterprise

As an investor your ultimate concern is not the company's cash flows—how much comes in and goes out in the course of doing business—but the cash you receive from your investment. But since your investment depends to some extent on the company's business skills in managing its cash flows, another objective of accounting is to provide information that will allow users to make decisions about the cash flows of a company. (We will discuss cash flows briefly later in the chapter and will return to them in Chapter 12.)

Secondary Objective: Reflect the Enterprise's Resources and Claims to Its Resources

The FASB emphasizes the roles of the balance sheet and the income statement in providing useful information. These financial statements should reflect what *resources* (or assets) the company or enterprise has, what *claims to these resources* (liabilities and stockholders' equity) there are, and the effects of transactions and events that change these resources and claims.[3] Thus, another objective of financial reporting is to show the effect of transactions on the entity's "accounting equation."

Exhibit 2-1 summarizes the objectives of financial reporting as they pertain to someone considering whether to buy stock in Monaco Coach. The exhibit should help you to understand how something as abstract as a set of financial reporting objectives can be applied to a decision-making situation.

[2]*SFAC No. 1*, par. 37.
[3]*SFAC No. 1*, par. 40.

Exhibit 2-1 The Application of Financial Reporting Objectives

FINANCIAL REPORTING OBJECTIVE	POTENTIAL INVESTOR'S QUESTIONS
1. The primary objective: Provide information for decision making.	"Based on the financial information, should I buy shares of stock in Monaco Coach?"
2. Secondary objective: Reflect prospective cash receipts to investors and creditors.	"How much cash will I receive in dividends each year and from the sale of the stock of Monaco Coach in the future?"
3. Secondary objective: Reflect prospective cash flows to an enterprise.	"After paying its suppliers and employees, and meeting all of its obligations, how much cash will Monaco Coach take in during the time I own the stock?"
4. Secondary objective: Reflect resources and claims to resources.	"How much has Monaco Coach invested in new plant and equipment?"

WHAT MAKES ACCOUNTING INFORMATION USEFUL? QUALITATIVE CHARACTERISTICS

LO 2 Describe the qualitative characteristics of accounting information.

Since accounting information must be useful for decision making, what makes this information useful? This section focuses on the qualities that accountants strive for in their financial reporting and on some of the challenges they face in making reporting judgments. It also reveals what users of financial information expect from financial statements.

Quantitative considerations, such as tuition costs, certainly were a concern when you chose your current school. In addition, your decision required you to make subjective judgments about the *qualitative* characteristics you were looking for in a college. Similarly, there are certain qualities that make accounting information useful.

Understandability

For anything to be useful, it must be understandable. Usefulness and understandability go hand in hand. However, **understandability** of financial information varies considerably, depending on the background of the user. For example, should financial statements be prepared so that they are understandable by anyone with a college education? Or should it be assumed that all readers of financial statements have completed at least one accounting course? Is a background in business necessary for a good understanding of financial reports, regardless of one's formal training? As you might expect, there are no simple answers to these questions. However, the FASB believes that financial information should be comprehensible to *those who are willing to spend the time to understand it:* "Financial information is a tool and, like most tools, cannot be of much direct help to those who are unable or unwilling to use it or who misuse it. Its use can be learned, however, and financial reporting should provide information that can be used by all—nonprofessionals as well as professionals—who are willing to learn to use it properly."[4]

Understandability The quality of accounting information that makes it comprehensible to those willing to spend the necessary time.

Relevance

Understandability alone is certainly not enough to render information useful. To be useful, information must be relevant. **Relevance** is the capacity of information to make a difference in a decision.[5] For example, assume that you are a banker evaluating the financial statements of a company that has come to you for a loan. All of the financial

Relevance The capacity of information to make a difference in a decision.

[4]*SFAC No. 1,* par. 36.

[5]*Statement of Financial Accounting Concepts [SFAC] No. 2,* "Qualitative Characteristics of Accounting Information" (Stamford, Conn.: Financial Accounting Standards Board, May 1980), par. 47.

statements point to a strong and profitable company. However, today's newspaper revealed that the company has been named in a multimillion-dollar lawsuit. Undoubtedly, this information would be relevant to your talks with the company, and disclosure of the lawsuit in the financial statements would make them even more relevant to your lending decision.

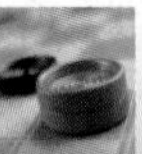

Accounting for Your Decisions

You Are the Stockholder

ABC Technology produces a highly technical product used in the computer industry. You are a stockholder and are currently in the process of reading this year's annual report. You find that you can't understand the report because it contains so much accounting jargon. But the annual report contains a 1-800 number for shareholder inquiries. You call the number and complain about the annual report, but the corporate spokesman politely tells you that "that's the way people talk in accounting." Is your complaint valid?

ANS: One of the purposes of an annual report is to interest potential stockholders in the company. A small percentage of those potential investors are professional money managers who are familiar with the accounting terminology. However, most readers are individual investors who probably don't have a sophisticated accounting background. It is true that the report must assume a minimum level of formal education; accountants expect those who read the report to take the time to understand it. Technicalities aside, however, it is important to write an annual report for as broad an audience as possible.

Reliability

What makes accounting information reliable? According to the FASB, "Accounting information is reliable to the extent that users can depend on it to represent the economic conditions or events that it purports to represent."[6]

Reliability The quality that makes accounting information dependable in representing the events that it purports to represent.

Reliability has three basic characteristics:

- *Verifiability* Information is verifiable when we can make sure that it is free from error—for example, by looking up the cost paid for an asset in a contract or an invoice.
- *Representational faithfulness* Information is representationally faithful when it corresponds to an actual event—such as when the purchase of land corresponds to a transaction in the company's records.
- *Neutrality* Information is neutral when it is not slanted to portray a company's position in a better or worse light than the actual circumstances would dictate—such as when the probable losses from a major lawsuit are disclosed accurately in the notes to the financial statements, with all its potential effects on the company, rather than minimized as a very remote possible loss.

Comparability For accounting information, the quality that allows a user to analyze two or more companies and look for similarities and differences.

Depreciation The process of allocating the cost of a long-term tangible asset over its useful life.

Comparability and Consistency

Comparability allows comparisons to be made *between or among companies.* Generally accepted accounting principles (GAAP) allow a certain amount of freedom in choosing among competing alternative treatments for certain transactions.

For example, under GAAP, companies may choose from a number of methods of accounting for the depreciation of certain long-term assets. **Depreciation** is the *process of allocating* the cost of a long-term tangible asset, such as a building or equipment, over

[6] *SFAC No. 2,* par. 62.

its useful life. Each method may affect the value of the assets differently. (We discuss depreciation in Chapter 8.) How does this freedom of choice affect the ability of investors to make comparisons between companies?

Assume you were considering buying stock in one of three companies. As their annual reports indicate, two of the companies use what is called the "accelerated" depreciation method, and the other company uses what is called the "straight-line" depreciation method. (We'll learn about these methods in a later chapter.) Does this lack of a common depreciation method make it impossible for you to compare the performance of the three companies?

Obviously, comparisons among the companies would be easier and more meaningful if all three used the same depreciation method. However, comparisons are not impossible just because companies use different methods. Certainly, the more alike—that is, uniform—statements are in terms of the principles used to prepare them, the more comparable they will be. However, the profession allows a certain freedom of choice in selecting from among alternative generally accepted accounting principles.

To render statements of companies using different methods more meaningful, *disclosure* assumes a very important role. For example, as we will see later in this chapter, the first note in the annual report of a publicly traded company is the disclosure of its accounting policies. The reader of this note for each of the three companies is made aware that the companies do not use the same depreciation method. Disclosure of accounting policies allows the reader to make some sort of subjective adjustment to the statements of one or more of the companies and thus to compensate for the different depreciation method being used.

Consistency is closely related to the concept of comparability. Both involve the relationship between two numbers. *However, whereas financial statements are comparable when they can be compared between one company and another, statements are* consistent *when they can be compared within a single company from one accounting period to the next.*

Consistency For accounting information, the quality that allows a user to compare two or more accounting periods for a single company.

Occasionally, companies decide to change from one accounting method to another. Will it be possible to compare a company's earnings in a period in which it switches methods with its earnings in prior years if the methods differ? Like the different methods used by different companies, changes in accounting methods from one period to the next do not make comparisons impossible, only more difficult. When a company makes an accounting change, accounting standards require various disclosures to help the reader evaluate the impact of the change.

INTERNAL DECISION

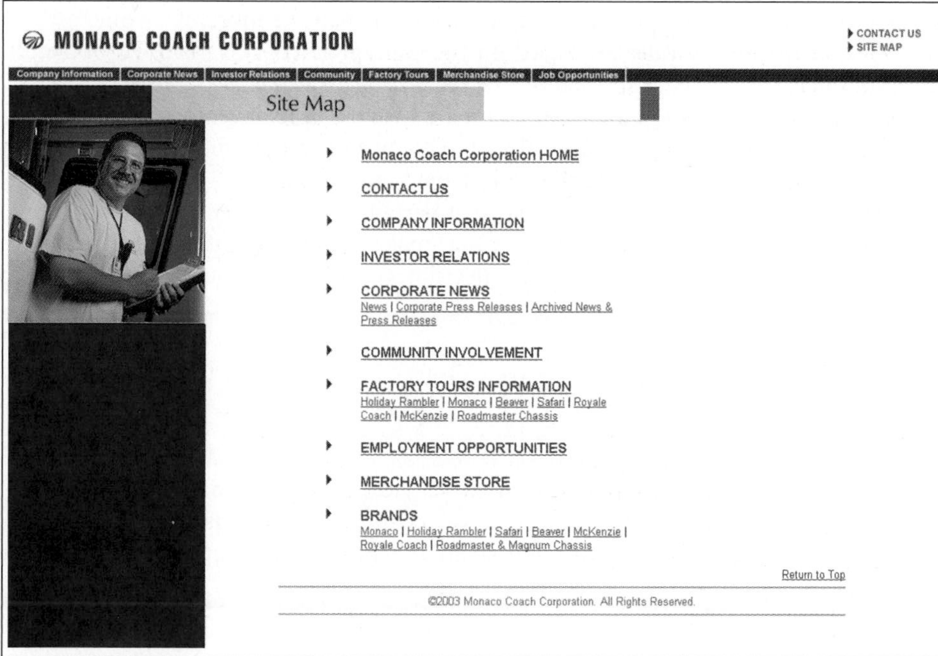

Companies still produce printed annual reports as a way to summarize the past year's business activities, discuss the firm's performance, preview upcoming products and business trends, and give investors and other users of financial information a format for analyzing the financial information. But most companies also provide annual report information—along with news reports and current information—at the Investor Relations *page on their Web site. You can search for Monaco Coach's at http://www.monacocoach.com.*

Materiality

Materiality The magnitude of an accounting information omission or misstatement that will affect the judgment of someone relying on the information.

INTERNAL DECISION

For accounting information to be useful, it must be relevant to a decision. The concept of **materiality** is closely related to relevance and deals with the size of an error in accounting information. The issue is whether the error is large enough to affect the judgment of someone relying on the information. Consider the following example. A company pays cash for two separate purchases: one for a $5 pencil sharpener and the other for a $50,000 computer. Theoretically, each expenditure results in the acquisition of an asset that should be depreciated over its useful life. However, what if the company decides to account for the $5 as an expense of the period rather than treat it in the theoretically correct manner by depreciating it over the life of the pencil sharpener? *Will this error in any way affect the judgment of someone relying on the financial statements?* Because such a slight error will *not* affect any decisions, minor expenditures of this nature are considered *immaterial* and are accounted for as an expense of the period.

The *threshold* for determining materiality will vary from one company to the next, depending to a large extent on the size of the company. Many companies establish policies that *any* expenditure under a certain dollar amount should be accounted for as an expense of the period. The threshold might be $50 for the corner grocery store but $1,000 for a large corporation. Finally, in some instances the amount of a transaction may be immaterial by company standards but may still be considered significant by financial statement users. For example, a transaction involving either illegal or unethical behavior by a company officer would be of concern, regardless of the dollar amounts involved.

Conservatism

Conservatism The practice of using the least optimistic estimate when two estimates of amounts are about equally likely.

The concept of **conservatism** is a holdover from earlier days when the primary financial statement was the balance sheet and the primary user of this statement was the banker. It was customary to deliberately understate assets on the balance sheet because this resulted in an even larger margin of safety that the assets being provided as collateral for a loan were sufficient.

Today the balance sheet is not the only financial statement, and deliberate understatement of assets is no longer considered desirable. The practice of conservatism is reserved for those situations in which there is *uncertainty* about how to account for a particular item or transaction: "Thus, if two estimates of amounts to be received or paid in the future are about equally likely, conservatism dictates using the less optimistic estimate; however, if two amounts are not equally likely, conservatism does not necessarily dictate using the more pessimistic amount rather than the more likely one."[7]

Various accounting rules are based on the concept of conservatism. For example, inventory held for resale is reported on the balance sheet at *the lower-of-cost-or-market value.* This rule requires a company to compare the cost of its inventory with the market price, or current cost to replace that inventory, and report the lower of the two amounts on the balance sheet at the end of the year. In Chapter 7 we will more fully explore the lower-of-cost-or-market rule as it pertains to inventory.

Exhibit 2-2 summarizes the qualities that make accounting information useful as these characteristics pertain to a banker's decision regarding whether to lend money to a company.

FINANCIAL REPORTING: AN INTERNATIONAL PERSPECTIVE

In Chapter 1 we introduced the International Accounting Standards Board (IASB) and its efforts to improve the development of accounting standards around the world. Interestingly, four of the most influential members of this group, representing the

[7] *SFAC No. 2,* par. 95.

Exhibit 2-2 Qualitative Characteristics of Accounting Information

SITUATION A bank is trying to decide whether to extend a $1 million loan to Russell Corporation. Russell presents the bank with its most recent balance sheet, showing its financial position on a historical cost basis. Each quality of the information is summarized in the form of a question.

QUALITY	QUESTION
Understandability	Can the information be used by those willing to learn to use it properly?
Relevance	Would the information be useful in deciding whether or not to loan money to Russell?
Reliability	
Verifiability	Can the information be verified? Is the information free from error?
Representational faithfulness	Is there agreement between the information and the events represented?
Neutrality	Is the information slanted in any way to present the company more favorably than is warranted?
Comparability	Are the methods used in assigning amounts to assets the same as those used by other companies?
Consistency	Are the methods used in assigning amounts to assets the same as those used in prior years?
Materiality	Will a specific error in any way affect the judgment of someone relying on the financial statements?
Conservatism	If there is any uncertainty about any of the amounts assigned to items on the balance sheet, are they recognized using the least optimistic estimate?

standard-setting bodies in the United States, the United Kingdom, Canada, and Australia, agree on the primary objective of financial reporting. All recognize that the primary objective is to provide information useful in making economic decisions.

The standard-setting body in the United Kingdom distinguishes between qualitative characteristics that relate to *content* of the information presented and those that relate to *presentation.* Similar to the FASB, this group recognizes relevance and reliability as the primary characteristics related to content. Comparability and understandability are the primary qualities related to the presentation of the information.

The concept of conservatism is also recognized in other countries. For example, both the IASB and the standard-setting body in the United Kingdom list "prudence" among their qualitative characteristics. Prudence requires the use of caution in making the various estimates required in accounting. Like the U.S. standard-setting body, these groups recognize that prudence does not justify the deliberate understatement of assets or revenues or the deliberate overstatement of liabilities or expenses.

THE CLASSIFIED BALANCE SHEET

LO 3 Explain the concept and purpose of a classified balance sheet and prepare the statement.

Now that we have learned about the conceptual framework of accounting, we turn to the outputs of the system: the financial statements. First, we will consider the significance of a *classified balance sheet.* We will then examine the *income statement,* the *statement of retained earnings,* and the *statement of cash flows.* The chapter concludes with a brief look at the financial statements of a real company, Monaco Coach, and at the other elements in an annual report.

What Are the Parts of the Balance Sheet? Understanding the Operating Cycle

Operating cycle The period of time between the purchase of inventory and the collection of any receivable from the sale of the inventory.

In the first part of this chapter, we stressed the importance of *cash flow.* For a company that sells a product, the **operating cycle** begins when cash is invested in inventory and ends when cash is collected by the enterprise from its customers.

Assume that on August 1 a retailer, Laptop Computer Sales, buys a computer for $5,000 from the manufacturer, BIM Corp. At this point, Laptop has merely substituted one asset, cash, for another, inventory. On August 20, twenty days after buying the computer, Laptop sells it to an accounting firm, Price & Company, for $6,000. Under the purchase agreement, Price will pay for the computer within the next 30 days. At this point, both the form of the asset and the amount have changed. The form of the asset held by Laptop has changed from inventory to accounts receivable. Also, because the inventory has been sold for $1,000 more than its cost of $5,000, the size of the asset held, the account receivable, is now $6,000. Finally, on September 20, Price pays $6,000 to Laptop, and the operating cycle is complete. As we will explore more fully in later chapters, Laptop has earned $1,000, the difference between what it sold the computer for and what it initially paid for the computer. The cycle starts again when Laptop buys another computer for resale.

Study Tip

The operating cycle of a business is the basis for deciding which assets are current and which are noncurrent. When you look at a company's balance sheet, be sure you understand the length of its operating cycle so you are clear about how it classifies its assets.

Laptop's operating cycle is summarized in Exhibit 2-3. The length of the company's operating cycle was 50 days. The operating cycle consisted of two distinct parts. From the time Laptop purchased the inventory, 20 days elapsed before it sold the computer. Another 30 days passed before the account receivable was collected. The length of the operating cycle depends to a large extent on the nature of a company's business. For example, in our illustration, the manufacturer of the computer, BIM Corp., received cash immediately from Laptop and did not have to wait to collect a receivable. However, additional time is added to the operating cycle of BIM Corp. to *manufacture* the computer.

The operating cycle of the accounting firm in our example, Price & Company, differs from that of either the manufacturer or the retailer. Price sells a service rather than a product. Its operating cycle is determined by two factors: the length of time involved

Exhibit 2-3 The Operating Cycle for a Retailer

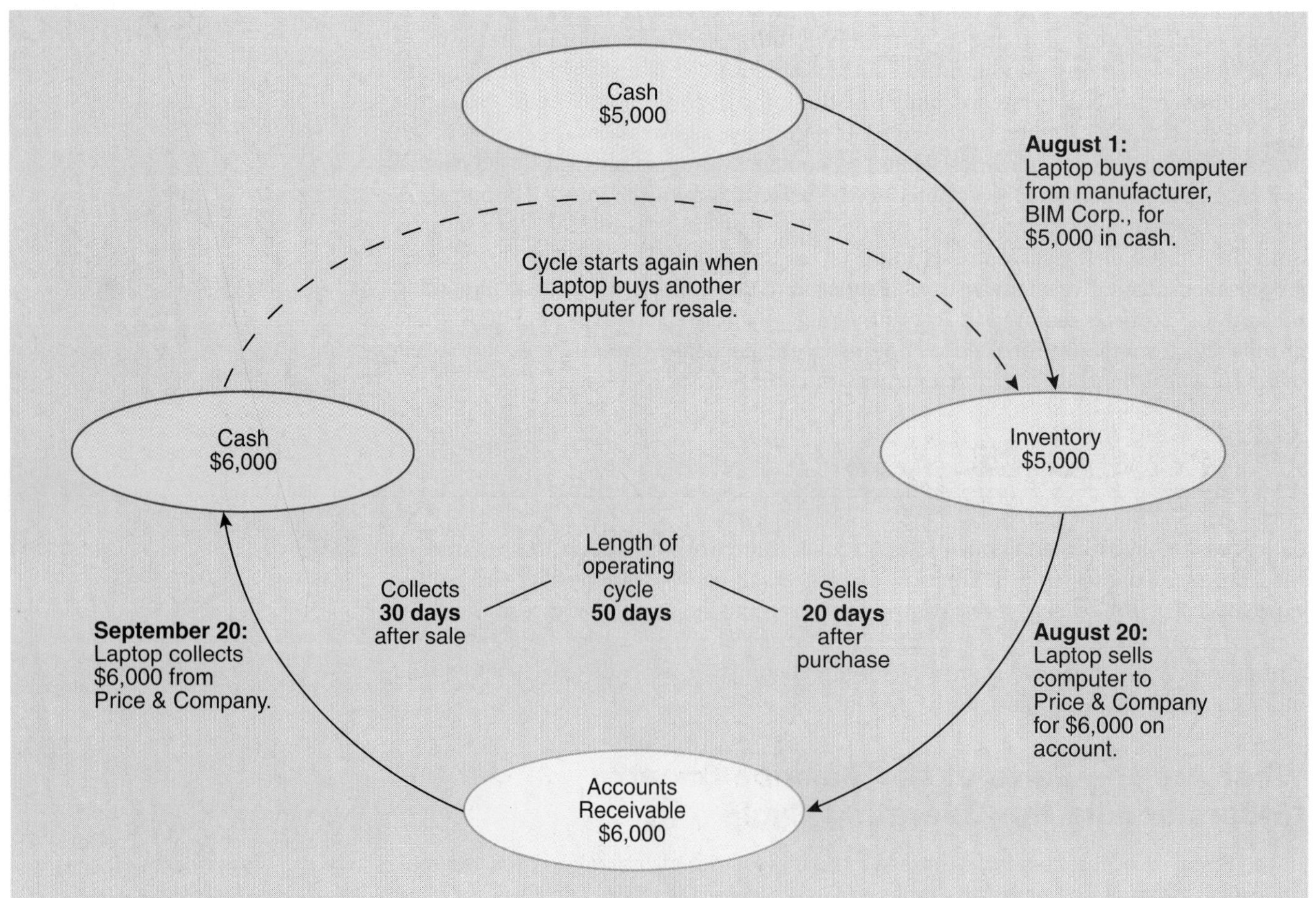

in providing a service to the client and the amount of time required to collect any account receivable.

A classified balance sheet for a hypothetical company, Dixon Sporting Goods Inc., is shown in Exhibit 2-4. You will want to refer to it as you learn about the different categories on a classified balance sheet. (The bulleted numbers below refer to Exhibit 2-4.)

Current Assets 1

The basic distinction on a classified balance sheet is between current and noncurrent items. **Current assets** are "cash and other assets that are reasonably expected to be

Current asset An asset that is expected to be realized in cash or sold or consumed during the operating cycle or within one year if the cycle is shorter than one year.

Exhibit 2-4 Balance Sheet for Dixon Sporting Goods

DIXON SPORTING GOODS INC.
BALANCE SHEET
AT DECEMBER 31, 2004

	ASSETS			
1	**Current assets**			
These assets are realizable, sold, or consumed in one year or operating cycle.	Cash		$ 5,000	
	Marketable securities		11,000	
	Accounts receivable		23,000	
	Merchandise inventory		73,500	
	Prepaid insurance		4,800	
	Store supplies		700	
	Total current assets			$118,000
2 These assets will not be realizable, sold, or consumed within one year or operating cycle.	**Investments**			
	Land held for future office site			150,000
	Property, plant, and equipment			
	Land		$100,000	
	Buildings	$150,000		
	Less: Accumulated depreciation	60,000	90,000	
	Store furniture and fixtures	$ 42,000		
	Less: Accumulated depreciation	12,600	29,400	
	Total property, plant, and equipment			219,400
	Intangible assets			
	Franchise agreement			55,000
	Total assets			$542,400
	LIABILITIES			
3 These are liabilities that will be satisfied within one year or operating cycle.	**Current liabilities**			
	Accounts payable		$ 15,700	
	Salaries and wages payable		9,500	
	Income taxes payable		7,200	
	Interest payable		2,500	
	Bank loan payable		25,000	
	Total current liabilities			$ 59,900
4 These are liabilities that will not be satisfied within one year or operating cycle.	**Long-term debt**			
	Notes payable, due December 31, 2014			120,000
	Total liabilities			$179,900
	STOCKHOLDERS' EQUITY			
5	**Contributed capital**			
	Capital stock, $10 par, 5,000 shares issued and outstanding		$ 50,000	
These are owners' claims on assets.	Paid-in capital in excess of par value		25,000	
	Total contributed capital		$ 75,000	
	Retained earnings		287,500	
	Total stockholders' equity			362,500
	Total liabilities and stockholders' equity			$542,400

realized in cash or sold or consumed during the normal operating cycle of a business or within one year if the operating cycle is shorter than one year."[8]

Most businesses have an operating cycle shorter than one year. The operating cycle for Laptop Computer Sales in our illustration was 50 days. Therefore cash, accounts receivable, and inventory are classified as current assets because they *are* cash, will be *realized* in (converted to) cash (accounts receivable), or will be *sold* (inventory) within one year.

Can you think of a situation in which a company's operating cycle is longer than one year? A construction company is a good example. A construction company essentially builds an item of inventory, such as an office building, to a customer's specifications. The entire process, including constructing the building and collecting the sales amount from the customer, may take three years to complete. According to our earlier definition, because the inventory will be sold and the account receivable will be collected within the operating cycle, they will still qualify as current assets.

© SKIP NALL/GETTYIMAGES/PHOTODISC

Compare the length of the operating cycle of a builder of an office building (or of communications equipment for the Internet) to that of a computer retailer. From the time a construction project "launches" to cash collection may be years, not weeks or months.

In addition to cash, accounts receivable, and inventory, the two other most common types of current assets are marketable securities and prepaid expenses. Excess cash is often invested in the stocks and bonds of other companies, as well as in various government instruments. If the investments are made for the short term, they are classified as current and are typically called either *short-term investments* or *marketable securities.* (Alternatively, some investments are made for the purpose of exercising influence over another company and thus are made for the long term. These investments are classified as noncurrent assets.) Various prepayments, such as office supplies, rent, and insurance, are classified as *prepaid expenses* and thus are current assets. These assets qualify as current because they will usually be *consumed* within one year.

Noncurrent Assets 2

Any assets that do not meet the definition of a current asset are classified as *long-term* or *noncurrent assets.* Three common categories of long-term assets are: investments; property, plant, and equipment; and intangibles.

Investments Recall, from the discussion of current assets, that stocks and bonds expected to be sold within the next year are classified as current assets. Securities that are not expected to be sold within the next year are classified as *investments.* In many cases, the investment is in the common stock of another company. Sometimes companies invest in another company either to exercise some influence or actually to control the operation of the other company. Other types of assets classified as investments are land held for future use and buildings and equipment not currently used in operations. Finally, a special fund held for the retirement of debt or for the construction of new facilities is also classified as an investment.

Property, Plant, and Equipment This category consists of the various *tangible, productive assets* used in the operation of a business. Land, buildings, equipment, machinery, furniture and fixtures, trucks, and tools are all examples of assets held for use in the *operation* of a business rather than for *resale.* The distinction between inventory and equipment, for example, depends on the company's *intent* in acquiring the asset. For example, IBM classifies a computer system as inventory because its intent in manufacturing the asset is to offer it for resale. However, this same computer in the hands of a law firm would be classified as equipment because its intent in buying the asset from IBM is to use it in the long-term operation of the business.

http://www.ibm.com

The relative size of property, plant, and equipment depends largely on a company's business. Consider Xcel Energy, a utility company with over $27 billion in total assets at the end of 2002. Almost 70 percent of the total assets was invested in property, plant,

http://www.xcelenergy.com

[8]Accounting Principles Board, *Statement of the Accounting Principles Board, No. 4,* "Basic Concepts and Accounting Principles Underlying Financial Statements of Business Enterprises" (New York: American Institute of Certified Public Accountants, 1970), par. 198.

and equipment. On the other hand, property and equipment represented less than 4 percent of the total assets of Microsoft, the highly successful software company. Regardless of the relative size of property, plant, and equipment, all assets in this category are subject to depreciation, with the exception of land. A separate accumulated depreciation account is used to account for the depreciation recorded on each of these assets over its life.

http://www.microsoft.com

Intangibles Intangible assets are similar to property, plant, and equipment in that they provide benefits to the firm over the long term. The distinction, however, is in the *form* of the asset. *Intangible assets lack physical substance.* Trademarks, copyrights, franchise rights, patents, and goodwill are examples of intangible assets. The cost principle governs the accounting for intangibles, just as it does for tangible assets. For example, the amount paid to an inventor for the patent rights to a new project is recorded as an intangible asset. Similarly, the amount paid to purchase a franchise for a fast-food restaurant for the exclusive right to operate in a certain geographic area is recorded as an intangible asset. With a few exceptions, intangibles are written off to expense over their useful lives. *Depreciation* is the name given to the process of writing off tangible assets; the same process for intangible assets is called *amortization.* Depreciation and amortization are both explained more fully in Chapter 8.

Two-Minute Review

1. *Give at least three examples of current assets.*
2. *Give the three common categories of noncurrent assets.*

Answers on page 84.

Accounting for Your Decisions

You Are a Student

Identify any assets you currently have, and then categorize them as either current or noncurrent.

ANS: Among your current assets would be cash and any investments you expect to sell in the near future. Your car would be a noncurrent asset.

Current Liabilities 3

The definition of a current liability is closely tied to that of a current asset. A **current liability** is an obligation that will be satisfied within the next operating cycle or within one year, if the cycle is shorter than one year. For example, the classification of a note payable on the balance sheet depends on its maturity date. If the note will be paid within the next year, it is classified as current; otherwise, it is classified as a long-term liability. On the other hand, accounts payable, wages payable, and income taxes payable are all short-term or current liabilities.

Current liability An obligation that will be satisfied within the next operating cycle or within one year if the cycle is shorter than one year.

Most liabilities, such as those for purchases of merchandise on credit, are satisfied by the payment of cash. However, certain liabilities are eliminated from the balance sheet when the company performs services. For example, the liability Subscriptions Received in Advance, which would appear on the balance sheet of a magazine publisher, is satisfied not by the payment of any cash but by the delivery of the magazine to the customers. Finally, it is possible to satisfy one liability by substituting another in its place. For example, a supplier might ask a customer to sign a written promissory note to replace an existing account payable if the customer is unable to pay at the present time.

Long-Term Liabilities 4

Any obligation that will not be paid or otherwise satisfied within the next year or the operating cycle, whichever is longer, is classified as a long-term liability, or long-term debt. Notes payable and bonds payable, both promises to pay money in the future, are two common forms of long-term debt. Some bonds have a life as long as 25 or 30 years.

Stockholders' Equity 5

Recall that stockholders' equity represents the owners' claims on the assets of the business. These claims arise from two sources: *contributed capital* and *earned capital.* Contributed capital appears on the balance sheet in the form of capital stock, and earned capital takes the form of retained earnings. *Capital stock* indicates the owners' investment in the business. *Retained earnings* represents the accumulated earnings, or net income, of the business since its inception less all dividends paid during that time.

Most companies have a single class of capital stock called *common stock.* This is the most basic form of ownership in a business. All other claims against the company, such as those of *creditors* and *preferred stockholders,* take priority. *Preferred stock* is a form of capital stock that, as the name implies, carries with it certain preferences. For example, the company must pay dividends on preferred stock before it makes any distribution of dividends on common stock. In the event of liquidation, preferred stockholders have priority over common stockholders in the distribution of the entity's assets.

Capital stock may appear as two separate items on the balance sheet: *Par Value* and *Paid-in Capital in Excess of Par Value.* The total of these two items tells us the amount that has been paid by the owners for the stock. We will take a closer look at these items in Chapter 11.

USING A CLASSIFIED BALANCE SHEET

LO 4 Use a classified balance sheet to analyze a company's financial position.

As we have now seen, a classified balance sheet separates both assets and liabilities into those that are current and those that are noncurrent. This distinction is very useful in any analysis of a company's financial position.

Working Capital

Liquidity The ability of a company to pay its debts as they come due.

Working capital Current assets minus current liabilities.

Investors, bankers, and other interested readers use the balance sheet to evaluate the liquidity of a business. Liquidity is a relative term and deals with the ability of a company to pay its debts as they come due. As you might expect, bankers and other creditors are particularly interested in the liquidity of businesses to which they have lent money. A comparison of current assets and current liabilities is a starting point in evaluating the ability of a company to meet its obligations. **Working capital** is the difference between current assets and current liabilities at a point in time. Referring back to Exhibit 2-4, we see that the working capital for Dixon Sporting Goods on December 31, 2004, is as follows:

WORKING CAPITAL

FORMULA	FOR DIXON SPORTING GOODS
Current Assets − Current Liabilities	$118,000 − $59,900 = $58,100

The management of working capital is an important task for any business. A company must continually strive for a *balance* in managing its working capital. For example, too little working capital—or in the extreme, negative working capital—may signal the inability to pay creditors on a timely basis. However, an overabundance of working capital could indicate that the company is not investing enough of its available funds in productive resources, such as new machinery and equipment.

Current Ratio

Because it is an absolute dollar amount, working capital is limited in its informational value. For example, $1 million may be an inadequate amount of working capital for a large corporation but far too much for a smaller company. In addition, a certain dollar amount of working capital may have been adequate for a company earlier in its life but is inadequate now. However, a related measure of liquidity, the **current ratio,** allows us to *compare* the liquidity of companies of different sizes and of a single company over time. The ratio is computed by dividing current assets by current liabilities. Dixon Sporting Goods has a current ratio of just under 2 to 1:

Current ratio Current assets divided by current liabilities.

CURRENT RATIO

FORMULA	FOR DIXON SPORTING GOODS
$\frac{\text{Current Assets}}{\text{Current Liabilities}}$	$\frac{\$118,000}{\$59,900} = \underline{\underline{1.97 \text{ to } 1}}$

Some analysts use a rule of thumb of 2 to 1 for the current ratio as a sign of short-term financial health. However, as is always the case, rules of thumb can be dangerous. Historically, companies in certain industries have operated quite efficiently with a current ratio of less than 2 to 1, whereas a ratio much higher than this is necessary to survive in other industries. Consider Gap Inc., the popular clothing company. At the end of the fiscal year 2002, it had a current ratio of 2.11 to 1. On the other hand, companies in the telephone communication business routinely have current ratios from well under 1 to 1. Sprint's current ratio at the end of 2002 was only 0.78 to 1.

http://www.gap.com

http://www.sprint.com

Unfortunately, neither the amount of working capital nor the current ratio tells us anything about the *composition* of current assets and current liabilities. For example, assume two companies both have total current assets equal to $100,000. Company A has cash of $10,000, accounts receivable of $50,000, and inventory of $40,000. Company B also has cash of $10,000 but accounts receivable of $20,000 and inventory of $70,000. All other things being equal, Company A is more liquid than Company B because more of its total current assets are in receivables than inventory. Receivables are only one step away from being cash, whereas inventory must be sold and then the receivable collected. Note that Dixon's inventory of $73,500 makes up a large portion of its total current assets of $118,000. An examination of the *relative* size of the various current assets for a company may reveal certain strengths and weaknesses not evident in the current ratio.

In addition to the composition of the current assets, the *frequency* with which they are "turned over" is important. For instance, how long does it take to sell an item of inventory? How long is required to collect an account receivable? Many companies could not exist with the current ratio of 0.71 reported by the McDonald's Corporation at the end of 2002. However, think about the nature of the fast-food business. The frequency of its sales and thus the numerous operating cycles within a single year mean that it can operate with a much lower current ratio than a manufacturing company, for example.

http://www.mcdonalds.com

THE INCOME STATEMENT

The income statement is used to summarize the results of operations of an entity for a *period of time.* At a minimum, all companies prepare income statements at least once a year. Companies that must report to the Securities and Exchange Commission prepare financial statements, including an income statement, every three months. Monthly income statements are usually prepared for internal use by management.

http://www.sec.gov

What Appears on the Income Statement?

From an accounting perspective, it is important to understand what transactions of an entity should appear on the income statement. In general, the income statement reports the excess of *revenue over expense,* that is, the *net income,* or in the event of an excess of *expense over revenue,* the *net loss* of the period. As a reference to the "bottom line" on an income statement, it is common to use the terms *profits* or *earnings* as synonyms for *net income.*

As discussed in Chapter 1, *revenue* is the inflow of assets resulting from the sale of products and services. It represents the dollar amount of sales of products and services for a period of time. An *expense* is the outflow of assets resulting from the sale of goods and services for a period of time. The cost of products sold, wages and salaries, and taxes are all examples of expenses.

Certain special types of revenues, called *gains,* are sometimes reported on the income statement, as are certain special types of expenses, called *losses.* For example, assume that Sanders Company holds a parcel of land for a future building site. The company paid $50,000 for the land 10 years ago. The state pays Sanders $60,000 for the property to use in a new highway project. Sanders has a special type of revenue from the condemnation of its property. It will recognize a *gain* of $10,000: the excess of the cash received from the state, $60,000, over the cost of the land, $50,000.

Format of the Income Statement

LO 5 Explain the difference between a single-step and a multiple-step income statement and prepare each type of income statement.

INTERNAL DECISION

Different formats are used by corporations to present their results. The major choice a company makes is whether to prepare the income statement in a single-step or a multiple-step form. Both forms are generally accepted. According to the AICPA's annual survey of 600 companies, over three times as many use the multiple-step form than the single-step form. Next, we'll explain the differences between the two forms and their variations.

Single-step income statement An income statement in which all expenses are added together and subtracted from all revenues.

Single-Step Format for the Income Statement In a **single-step income statement,** all expenses and losses are added together and then are deducted *in a single step* from all revenues and gains to arrive at net income. A single-step format for the income statement of Dixon Sporting Goods is presented in Exhibit 2-5. The primary advantage of the single-step form is its simplicity. No attempt is made to classify either revenues or expenses or to associate any of the expenses with any of the revenues.

Exhibit 2-5 Income Statement (Single-Step Format) for Dixon Sporting Goods Inc.

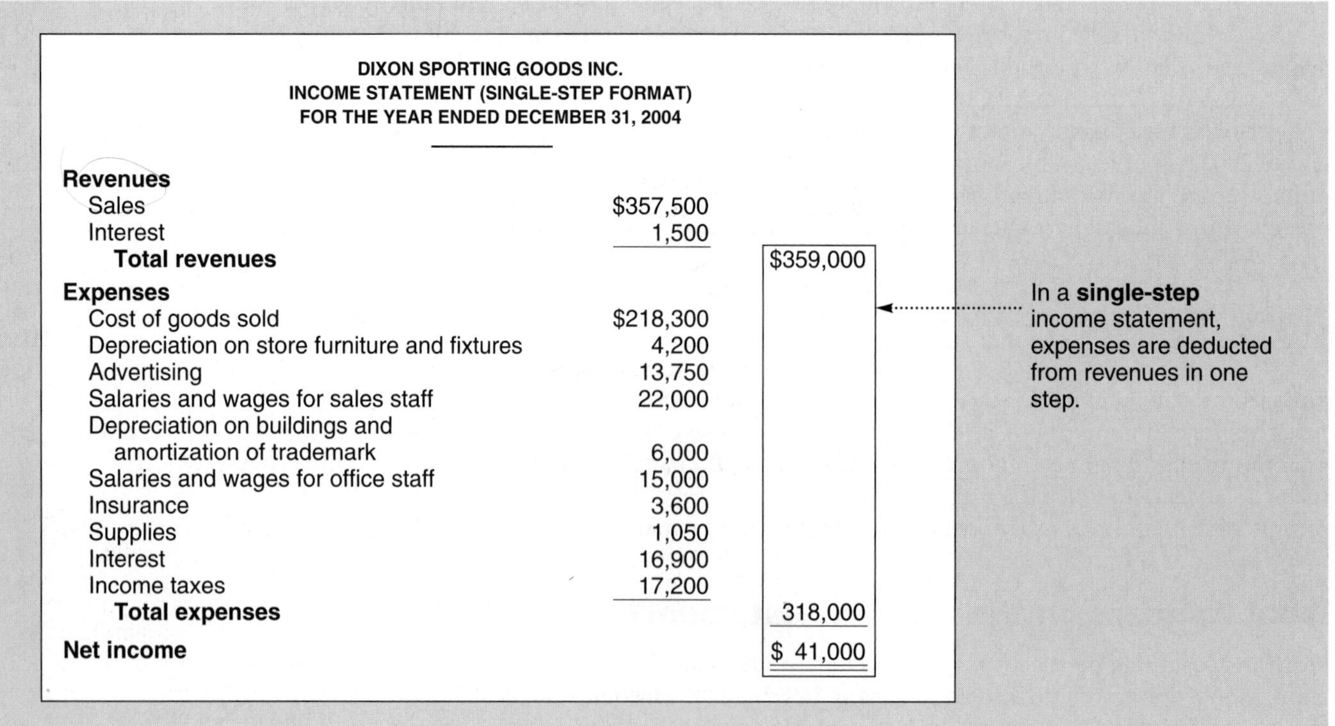

DIXON SPORTING GOODS INC.
INCOME STATEMENT (SINGLE-STEP FORMAT)
FOR THE YEAR ENDED DECEMBER 31, 2004

Revenues		
Sales	$357,500	
Interest	1,500	
Total revenues		$359,000
Expenses		
Cost of goods sold	$218,300	
Depreciation on store furniture and fixtures	4,200	
Advertising	13,750	
Salaries and wages for sales staff	22,000	
Depreciation on buildings and amortization of trademark	6,000	
Salaries and wages for office staff	15,000	
Insurance	3,600	
Supplies	1,050	
Interest	16,900	
Income taxes	17,200	
Total expenses		318,000
Net income		$ 41,000

In a **single-step** income statement, expenses are deducted from revenues in one step.

Multiple-Step Format for the Income Statement The purpose of the **multiple-step income statement** is to subdivide the income statement into specific sections and provide the reader with important subtotals. This format is illustrated for Dixon Sporting Goods in Exhibit 2-6.

Multiple-step income statement An income statement that shows classifications of revenues and expenses as well as important subtotals.

The multiple-step income statement for Dixon indicates three important subtotals. First, **1** cost of goods sold is deducted from sales to arrive at **gross profit:**

Gross profit Sales less cost of goods sold.

Gross Profit = Sales − Cost of Goods Sold

Sales	$357,500
Cost of goods sold	218,300
Gross profit	$139,200

Cost of goods sold, as the name implies, is the cost of the units of inventory sold during the year. It is logical to associate cost of goods sold with the sales revenue for the year because the latter represents the *selling price* of the inventory sold during the period.

The second important subtotal on Dixon's income statement is **2** *income from operations* of $73,600. This is found by subtracting *total operating expenses* of $65,600 from the gross profit of $139,200. Operating expenses are further subdivided between *selling expenses* and *general and administrative expenses.* For example, note that two depreciation amounts are included in operating expenses. Depreciation on store furniture and fixtures is classified as a selling expense because the store is where sales take place. On the other hand, we will assume that the buildings are offices for the administrative staff

Exhibit 2-6 Income Statement (Multiple-Step Format) for Dixon Sporting Goods

In a **multiple-step** income statement:

- Sales and the **costs** of sales are compared. **1**
- Expenses of the business are detailed.
- Isolating expenses and revenues by type is useful in analyzing a business.
- Operating income is highlighted. **2**
- "Nonoperating" revenues and expenses are included here. **3** **4**

DIXON SPORTING GOODS INC.
INCOME STATEMENT (MULTIPLE-STEP FORMAT)
FOR THE YEAR ENDED DECEMBER 31, 2004

Sales		$357,500	
Cost of goods sold		218,300	
Gross profit			$139,200
Operating expenses			
Selling expenses			
Depreciation on store furniture and fixtures	$ 4,200		
Advertising	13,750		
Salaries and wages	22,000		
Total selling expenses		$ 39,950	
General and administrative expenses			
Depreciation on buildings and amortization of trademark	$ 6,000		
Salaries and wages	15,000		
Insurance	3,600		
Supplies	1,050		
Total general and administrative expenses		25,650	
Total operating expenses			65,600
Income from operations			$ 73,600
Other revenues and expenses			
Interest revenue		$ 1,500	
Interest expense		16,900	
Excess of other expenses over other revenue			15,400
Income before income taxes			$ 58,200
Income tax expense			17,200
Net income			$ 41,000

and thus depreciation on the buildings is classified as a general and administrative expense.

The third important subtotal on the income statement is **3** *income before income taxes* of $58,200. Interest revenue and interest expense, neither of which is an operating item, are included in *other revenues and expenses.* The excess of interest expense of $16,900 over interest revenue of $1,500, which equals $15,400, is subtracted from income from operations to arrive at income before income taxes. Finally, **4** *income tax expense* of $17,200 is deducted to arrive at *net income* of $41,000.

Two-Minute Review

1. *Give at least two examples of items that would appear on a multiple-step income statement but not a single-step statement.*
2. *Classify each of the following expenses as either selling or general and administrative: advertising, depreciation on office building, salespersons' commissions and office salaries.*

Answers on page 84.

Using a Multiple-Step Income Statement

LO 6 Use a multiple-step income statement to analyze a company's operations.

An important advantage of the multiple-step income statement is that it provides additional information to the reader. Although all the amounts needed to calculate certain ratios are available on a single-step statement, such calculations are easier to figure with a multiple-step statement. For example, the deduction of cost of goods sold from sales to arrive at gross profit, or *gross margin* as it is sometimes called, allows us to quickly calculate the **gross profit ratio.** The ratio of Dixon's gross profit to its sales, rounded to the nearest percent, is as follows:

Gross profit ratio Gross profit divided by sales.

GROSS PROFIT RATIO

FORMULA	FOR DIXON SPORTING GOODS
Gross Profit / **Sales**	$\frac{\$139{,}200}{\$357{,}500} = 39\%$

The gross profit ratio tells us that after paying for the product, for every dollar of sales, 39¢ is available to cover other expenses and earn a profit. The complement of the gross profit ratio is the ratio of cost of goods sold to sales. For Dixon, this ratio is 1 − 0.39 = 0.61, or 61%. For every dollar of sales, Dixon spends $0.61 on the cost of the product.

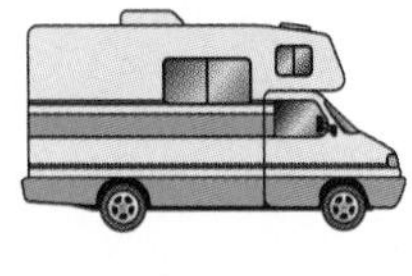

From Concept to Practice 2.1

Read Winnebago Industries' *and* Monaco Coach Corporation's *Income Statements. Note that Winnebago Industries' income statement does not report gross profit while Monaco Coach Corporation's statement does. However, what two items on Winnebago Industries' statement can be used to determine its gross profit? Calculate each companys' gross profit ratio for 2002 and 2001. By what percentage did it go up or down between the two years?*

An important use of the income statement is to evaluate the *profitability* of a business. For example, a company's **profit margin** is the ratio of its net income to its sales. Some analysts refer to a company's profit margin as its *return on sales.* Dixon's profit margin is as follows:

Profit margin Net income divided by sales.

PROFIT MARGIN

FORMULA	FOR DIXON SPORTING GOODS
Net Income / **Sales**	$\frac{\$41{,}000}{\$357{,}500} = 11\%$

For every dollar of sales, Dixon has $0.11 in net income.

Two important factors should be kept in mind in evaluating any financial statement ratio. First, how does this year's ratio differ from ratios of prior years? For example, a decrease in the profit margin may indicate that the company is having trouble this year controlling certain costs. Second, how does the ratio compare with industry norms? For example, in some industries the profit margin is considerably lower than in many others, such as in mass merchandising (Wal-Mart's profit margin was only 3.3% for the year ended January 31, 2003). It is always helpful to compare key ratios, such as the profit margin, with an industry average or with the same ratio for a close competitor of the company.

http://www.walmart.com

THE STATEMENT OF RETAINED EARNINGS

The purpose of a statement of stockholders' equity is to explain the changes in the components of owners' equity during the period. Retained earnings and capital stock are the two primary components of stockholders' equity. If there are no changes during the period in a company's capital stock, it may choose to present a statement of retained earnings instead of a statement of stockholders' equity. A statement of retained earnings for Dixon Sporting Goods is shown in Exhibit 2-7.

LO 7 Identify the components of the statement of retained earnings and prepare the statement.

Exhibit 2-7

Statement of Retained Earnings for Dixon Sporting Goods Inc.

DIXON SPORTING GOODS INC. STATEMENT OF RETAINED EARNINGS FOR THE YEAR ENDED DECEMBER 31, 2004	
Retained earnings, January 1, 2004	$271,500
Add: Net income for 2004	41,000
	$312,500
Less: Dividends declared and paid in 2004	(25,000)
Retained earnings, December 31, 2004	$287,500

The statement of retained earnings provides an important link between the income statement and the balance sheet. Dixon's net income of $41,000, as detailed on the income statement, is an *addition* to retained earnings. Note that the dividends declared and paid of $25,000 do not appear on the income statement because they are a payout, or *distribution,* of net income to stockholders rather than one of the expenses deducted to arrive at net income. Accordingly, they appear as a direct deduction on the statement of retained earnings. The beginning balance in retained earnings is carried forward from last year's statement of retained earnings.

THE STATEMENT OF CASH FLOWS

All publicly held corporations are required to present a statement of cash flows in their annual reports. The purpose of the statement is to summarize the cash flow effects of a company's operating, investing, and financing activities for the period.

CASH FLOW

The Cash Flow Statement for Dixon Sporting Goods

The statement for Dixon Sporting Goods is shown in Exhibit 2-8. The statement consists of three categories: operating activities, investing activities, and financing activities. Each of these three categories can result in a net inflow of cash or a net outflow of cash.

LO 8 Identify the components of the statement of cash flows and prepare the statement.

Exhibit 2-8 Statement of Cash Flows for Dixon Sporting Goods Inc.

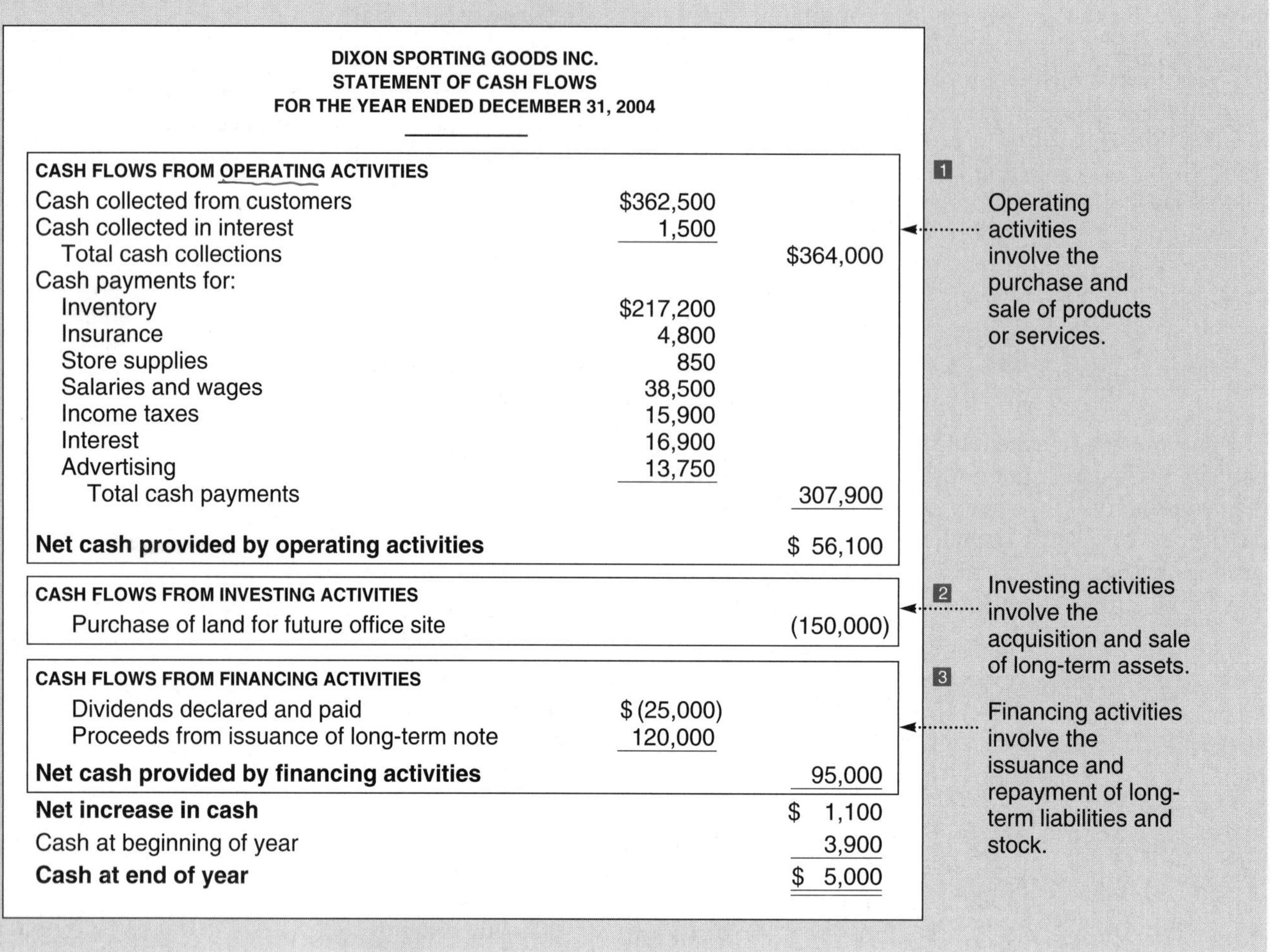

DIXON SPORTING GOODS INC.
STATEMENT OF CASH FLOWS
FOR THE YEAR ENDED DECEMBER 31, 2004

CASH FLOWS FROM OPERATING ACTIVITIES		
Cash collected from customers	$362,500	
Cash collected in interest	1,500	
Total cash collections		$364,000
Cash payments for:		
Inventory	$217,200	
Insurance	4,800	
Store supplies	850	
Salaries and wages	38,500	
Income taxes	15,900	
Interest	16,900	
Advertising	13,750	
Total cash payments		307,900
Net cash provided by operating activities		$ 56,100
CASH FLOWS FROM INVESTING ACTIVITIES		
Purchase of land for future office site		(150,000)
CASH FLOWS FROM FINANCING ACTIVITIES		
Dividends declared and paid	$ (25,000)	
Proceeds from issuance of long-term note	120,000	
Net cash provided by financing activities		95,000
Net increase in cash		$ 1,100
Cash at beginning of year		3,900
Cash at end of year		$ 5,000

Dixon's *operating activities* generated $56,100 of cash during the period. Operating activities 1 concern the purchase and sale of a product, in this case the acquisition of sporting goods from distributors and the subsequent sale of those goods. As we can readily see, Dixon had one major source of cash, the collection from its customers of $362,500. Similarly, Dixon's largest use of cash was the $217,200 it paid for inventory. In Chapter 12, we will discuss the statement of cash flows in detail and the preparation of this section of the statement.

Financing and investing activities were described in the book's introduction. *Investing activities* 2 involve the acquisition and sale of long-term or noncurrent assets, such as long-term investments, property, plant, and equipment, and intangible assets. *Financing activities* 3 result from the issuance and repayment, or retirement, of long-term liabilities and capital stock. The one investing activity on Dixon's statement of cash flows, the purchase of land for a future office site, required the use of cash and thus is shown as a net outflow of $150,000. Dixon had two financing activities: dividends of $25,000 required the use of cash, and the issuance of a long-term note generated cash of $120,000. The balance in cash on the bottom of the statement of $5,000 must agree with the balance for this item as shown on the balance sheet in Exhibit 2-4.

1
Operating activities involve the purchase and sale of products or services.
2
Investing activities involve the acquisition and sale of long-term assets.
3
Financing activities involve the issuance and repayment of long-term liabilities and stock.

THE FINANCIAL STATEMENTS FOR MONACO COACH CORPORATION

LO 9 Read and use the financial statements and other elements in the annual report of a publicly held company.

The financial statements for our hypothetical company, Dixon Sporting Goods Inc., introduced the major categories on each of the statements. We now turn to the financial statements of an actual company, **Monaco Coach Corporation.** These statements are more complex and require additional analysis and a better understanding of accounting to fully appreciate them. However, we will concentrate on certain elements of the statements. At this stage in your study, look for the similarities rather than the differences between these statements and those of Dixon.

As we will see later, the notes to a set of financial statements give the reader a variety of information about a company. Like the statements of many other companies, Monaco Coach's financials include a note that describes its business:

> Monaco Coach Corporation and its subsidiaries (the "Company") manufacture premium motor coaches, bus conversions, and towable recreational vehicles at manufacturing facilities in Oregon and Indiana. These products are sold to independent dealers primarily throughout the United States and Canada. In addition, the Company also owns three motor coach resort properties, the developed lots of which, are sold to retail customers.[9]

Monaco Coach's Balance Sheet

INTERNAL DECISION

The balance sheets for Monaco Coach at the end of each of two years are shown in Exhibit 2-9. Note that the date on Monaco Coach's most recent balance sheet is December 28, 2002. Unlike many companies that choose to end their accounting or fiscal year on December 31, Monaco ends its year on the Saturday closest to December 31. Some companies choose a fiscal year that ends at a point when sales are at their lowest in the annual cycle. For example, Wal-Mart ends its fiscal year on January 31, after the busy holiday season.

Monaco Coach releases what are called *consolidated financial statements,* which reflect the position and results of all operations that are controlled by a single entity. Like most other large corporations, Monaco Coach owns other companies. Often these companies are legally separate and are called *subsidiaries.* How a company accounts for its investment in a subsidiary is covered in advanced accounting courses.

Monaco Coach presents comparative balance sheets to indicate its financial position at the end of each of the last two years. As a minimum standard, the Securities and Exchange Commission requires that the annual report include balance sheets as of the two most recent years and income statements for each of the three most recent years. Note that all amounts on the balance sheet are stated in thousands of dollars. This type of rounding is a common practice in the financial statements of large corporations and is justified under the materiality concept. Knowing the exact dollar amount of each asset would not change a decision made by an investor.

The presentation of comparative balance sheets allows the reader to make comparisons between years. For example, Monaco Coach's *working capital* increased significantly during 2002:

WORKING CAPITAL

	DECEMBER 29, 2001	DECEMBER 28, 2002
Current Assets − Current Liabilities	$239,350 − $175,656 = $63,694	$356,130 − $241,889 = $114,241

Monaco Coach's *current ratio* at each of the two dates follows:

CURRENT RATIO

	DECEMBER 29, 2001	DECEMBER 28, 2002
$\frac{\text{Current Assets}}{\text{Current Liabilities}}$	$\frac{\$239,350}{\$175,656} = 1.36 \text{ to } 1$	$\frac{\$356,130}{\$241,889} = 1.47 \text{ to } 1$

[9] *Monaco Coach Corporation 2002 Annual Report, p. 22.*

Exhibit 2-9 Comparative Balance Sheets for Monaco Coach Corporation

CONSOLIDATED BALANCE SHEETS
(in thousands of dollars, except share and per share data)

ASSETS	December 29, 2001	December 28, 2002
Current assets:		
Trade receivables, net of $541 and $799, respectively	$82,885	$116,647
Inventories	127,075	175,609
Resort lot inventory	0	26,883
Prepaid expenses	2,063	3,612
Deferred income taxes	27,327	33,379
Total current assets	239,350	356,130
Notes receivable	8,157	0
Property, plant, and equipment, net	122,795	135,350
Debt issuance costs, net of accumulated amortization of $75 and $389, respectively	940	683
Goodwill, net of accumulated amortization or $5,320 and $5,320, respectively	55,856	55,254
Total assets	$427,098	$547,417
LIABILITIES		
Current liabilities:		
Book overdraft	$5,889	$3,518
Line of credit	26,004	51,413
Current portion of long-term note payable	10,000	21,667
Accounts payable	66,859	78,055
Product liability reserve	19,856	21,322
Product warranty reserve	27,799	31,745
Income taxes payable	0	4,536
Accrued expenses and other liabilities	19,249	29,633
Total current liabilities	175,656	241,889
Long-term note payable	30,000	30,333
Deferred income taxes	8,312	14,568
	213,968	286,790
Commitments and contigencies (Note 16)		
STOCKHOLDER'S EQUITY		
Common stock, $.01 par value; 50,000,000 shares authorized 28,632,774 and 28,871,144 issued and outstanding, respectively	286	289
Additional paid-in captial	48,522	51,501
Retained earnings	164,322	208,837
Total stockholders' equity	213,130	260,627
Total liabilities and stockholders' equity	$427,098	$547,417

Use these to find:
- Working capital
- Current ratio

The accompanying notes are an integral part of the consolidated financial statements.

Note that both the amount of working capital and the current ratio increased between 2001 and 2002. Both trade receivables and inventories increased significantly, while on the liability side of the balance sheet there was a significant increase in the company's line of credit.

Monoco Coach's Income Statement

We have examined two basic formats for the income statement: the single-step format and the multiple-step format. In practice, numerous variations on these two basic formats exist, depending to a large extent on the nature of a company's business. For example, the multiple-step form, with its presentation of gross profit, is not used by service businesses because they do not sell a product. (Remember that gross profit is sales less cost of goods sold.) As we will see for Monaco Coach, the form of the income statement is a reflection of a company's operations.

Multiple-step income statements for Monaco Coach for a three-year period are presented in Exhibit 2-10. Monaco Coach's *gross profit ratio* increased slightly from 2001 to 2002:

GROSS PROFIT RATIO

	2001	2002
$\frac{\text{Gross Profit}}{\text{Net Sales}}$	$\frac{\$113{,}990}{\$937{,}073} = 12\%$	$\frac{\$163{,}129}{\$1{,}222{,}689} = 13\%$

Also, note the inclusion of net income per share information at the bottom of the statement. The per share information helps users of the statement in various ways and is discussed in more detail in Chapter 12.

From Concept to Practice 2.2

Reading Winnebago Industries' and Monaco Coach Corporation's Income Statements

Compute each company's profit margin for the past two years. Did it go up or down from the prior year to the current year?

Other Elements of an Annual Report

No two annual reports look the same. The appearance of an annual report depends not only on the size of a company but also on the budget devoted to the preparation of the report. Some companies publish "bare-bones" annual reports, whereas others issue a glossy report complete with pictures of company products and employees. In recent years, many companies, as a cost-cutting measure, have scaled back the amount spent on the annual report.

Privately held companies tend to distribute only financial statements, without the additional information normally included in the annual reports of public companies. For the annual reports of public companies, however, certain basic elements are considered standard. A letter to the stockholders from either the president or the chairman of the board of directors appears in the first few pages of most annual reports. A section describing the company's products and markets is usually included. At the heart of any annual report is the financial report or review, which consists of the financial statements accompanied by notes to explain various items on the statements. We will now consider these other elements as presented in the 2002 annual report of Monaco Coach Corporation.

Report of Independent Accountants As you see in Exhibit 2-11, Monaco Coach is audited by PricewaterhouseCoopers LLP, one of the largest international

http://www.pwcglobal.com

Exhibit 2-10 Consolidated Income Statements for Monaco Coach Corporation

CONSOLIDATED STATEMENTS OF INCOME
for the years ended December 30, 2000, December 29, 2001, and December 28, 2002
(in thousands of dollars, except per share amounts)

	2000	2001	2002
Net sales	$901,890	$937,073	$1,222,689
Cost of sales	772,240	823,083	1,059,560
Gross profit	129,650	113,990	163,129
Selling, general and administrative expenses	59,175	70,687	87,202
Amortization of goodwill	645	645	0
Operating income	69,830	42,658	75,927
Other income, net	182	334	105
Interest expense	(632)	(2,357)	(2,752)
Income before income taxes	69,380	40,635	73,280
Provision for income taxes	26,859	15,716	28,765
Net Income	$ 42,521	$ 24,919	$ 44,515
Earnings per common share:			
Basic	$ 1.50	$ .87	$ 1.55
Diluted	$ 1.47	$ .85	$ 1.51
Weighted average common shares outstanding:			
Basic	28,377,123	28,531,593	28,812,473
Diluted	28,978,265	29,288,688	29,573,420

Use these to find:
• Gross profit ratio

The accompanying notes are an integral part of the consolidated financial statements.

accounting firms. Two key phrases should be noted in the first sentence of the independent accountants' report: *in our opinion* and *present fairly.* The report indicates that responsibility for the statements rests with Monaco Coach and that the auditors' job is to *express an opinion* on the statements, based on certain tests. It would be impossible for an auditing firm to spend the time or money to retrace and verify every single transaction entered into during the year by Monaco Coach. Instead, the auditing firm performs various tests of the accounting records to be able to assure itself that the statements are free of *material misstatement.* Auditors do not "certify" the total accuracy of a set of financial statements but render an opinion as to the reasonableness of those statements. Finally, note that this format for the auditors' report differs from the one for Winnebago Industries presented in Chapter 1. However, both formats contain the same basic information.

ETHICS

The Ethical Responsibility of Management and the Auditors The management of a company and its auditors share a common purpose: to protect the interests of stockholders. In large corporations, the stockholders are normally removed from the daily affairs of the business. The need for a professional management team to run the business is a practical necessity, as is the need for a periodic audit of the company's records. Because stockholders cannot run the business themselves, they need assurances that the business is being operated effectively and efficiently and that the financial statements presented by management are a fair representation of the company's operations and financial position. The management and the auditors have a very important ethical responsibility to their constituents, the stockholders of the company.

Exhibit 2-11 Report of Independent Accountants for Monaco Coach Corporation

Report of Independent Accountants
To the Stockholders and Board of Directors of Monaco Coach Coporation

In our opinion, the accompanying consolidated balance sheets and the related consolidated statements of income, of stockholders' equity, and of cash flows present fairly, in all material respects, the financial position of Monaco Coach Corporation and its Subsidiaries (the Company) at December 29, 2001 and December 28, 2002, and the results of their operations and their cash flows for each of the three years in the period ended December 28, 2002 in conformity with accounting principles generally accepted in the United States of America. These financial statements are the responsibility of the Company's management; our responsibility is to express an opinion on these financial statements based on our audits. We conducted our audits of these statements in accordance with auditing standards generally accepted in the United States of America, which require that we plan and perform the audit to obtain reasonable assurance about whether the financial statements are free of material misstatement. An audit includes examining, on a test basis, evidence supporting the amounts and disclosures in the financial statements, assessing the accounting principles used and significant estimates made by management, and evaluating the overall financial statement presentation. We believe that our audits provide a reasonable basis for our opinion.

As discussed in Note 1 to the consolidated financial statements, the Company adopted the provisions of Statement of Financial Accounting Standards No. 142, Goodwill and Other Intangible Assets.

PricewaterhouseCoopers LLP

PricewaterhouseCoopers LLP
Portland, Oregon
January 28, 2003

Management Discussion and Analysis Preceding the financial statements is a section of Monaco Coach's annual report titled "Management's Discussion and Analysis of Financial Condition and Results of Operations." This report gives management the opportunity to discuss the financial statements and provide the stockholders with explanations for certain amounts reported in the statements. For example, management explains the change in its selling, general, and administrative expenses as follows:

> Selling, general, and administrative expenses increased by $16.5 million from $70.7 million in 2001 to $87.2 million in 2002 and decreased as a percentage of sales from 7.5% in 2001 to 7.1% in 2002. Increases in spending over the prior year were due to those items that fluctuate with the increase in sales such as sales commissions, product liability expenses, advertising, promotions, general insurance, and printed brochure costs. The reduction as a percentage of sales was mostly due to the large increase in sales compared to overall spending.[10]

Notes to Consolidated Financial Statements The sentence "The accompanying notes are an integral part of these consolidated financial statements" appears at the bottom of each of Monaco Coach's four financial statements. These comments, or *notes*, as they are commonly called, are necessary to satisfy the need for *full disclo-*

[10]Monaco Coach Corporation 2002 Annual Report, p. 11.

Business Strategy

Focused on Growth

How does a company increase its sales from $46 million in 1991 to $1.2 billion a mere eleven years later? Innovation in its product line has been one key element in the success of Monaco Coach Corporation. In addition, low interest rates and favorable demographics have benefited the entire RV industry. But one need look no further than Monaco Coach's history of acquisitions to understand much of the reason for its growth.

Monaco Coach's merger activity began in earnest in 1996 when it acquired the Holiday Rambler division and certain related dealerships from Harley Davidson. Up to this time Monaco Coach was known primarily as a specialty builder of luxury motorcoaches. This acquisition moved Monaco Coach into the industry's mainstream for the first time. And with this acquisition sales began to take off, more than doubling in 1996 alone. Next came the 2001 buyout of Monaco Coach's highly competitive Oregon-based neighbor, SMC Corporation, and with it came the popular Beaver and Safari brands. It didn't take long for the purchase of SMC to pay off for Monaco Coach and its stockholders. In the first full year after the acquisition, sales increased by 30 percent and topped the $1 billion mark (on October 25, 2002) long before year end.

All companies are well aware that growing sales doesn't always translate to a growth in the bottom line. Monaco Coach's success in operating profitably after the SMC purchase can be traced to the close attention it paid to the two plants where the Beaver and Safari brands were built. Monaco Coach chose to retain the Beaver plant because it was relatively efficient and a move of its operations to Monaco Coach's main facilities 120 miles away would have meant the loss of loyal Beaver employees. In contrast, the Safari plant did not have the necessary capacity to grow its brand. The decision to close this plant and integrate its operations into Monaco Coach's main base of operations was made even easier by the mere eight miles between the two facilities. The company's bottom line in 2002 suggests that Monaco Coach's decisions to buy SMC, keep one of its plants intact, and move the operations of the other were wise ones: net income increased by almost 80 percent from the year before to $44.5 million. ■

Sources: Monaco Coach Corporation's 2001 and 2002 Annual Reports.

sure of all the facts relevant to a company's results and financial position. The first note in all annual reports is a summary of *significant accounting policies.* A company's policies for valuing inventories, depreciating assets, and recognizing revenue are among the important items contained in this note. For example, Monaco Coach describes its policy for depreciating its plant and equipment as follows:

> The cost of plant and equipment is depreciated using the straight-line method over the estimated useful lives of the related assets. Buildings are generally depreciated over 39 years and equipment is depreciated over 3 to 10 years.[11]

In addition to the summary of significant accounting policies, other notes discuss such topics as income taxes and stock option plans.

This completes our discussion of the makeup of the annual report. By now you should appreciate the flexibility that companies have in assembling the report, aside from the need to follow generally accepted accounting principles in preparing the statements. The accounting standards followed in preparing the statements, as well as the appearance of the annual report itself, differ in other countries. As has been noted elsewhere, although many corporations operate internationally, accounting principles are far from being standardized.

[11]*Monaco Coach Corporation 2002 Annual Report, p. 23.*

Interpret: You Decide. Review the current ratio, gross profit ratio, and profit margin as they were computed for Monaco Coach Corporation for both 2001 and 2002. As someone considering making a loan to the company, do you think the company will be able to pays its debts as they fall due? And as a potential stockholder, do you feel assured that the company will remain profitable in the future? Explain your reasoning for each of your answers.

Ratios for Decision Making

The purpose of this presentation, which will appear in chapters where ratios and other key calculations are introduced, is to briefly review the core reason for use of the ratio(s) for decision making.

Reporting and Analyzing Financial Statement Information Related to a Company's Liquidity and Profitability In order to continue operating, a company must be able to pay its bills when they come due. Checking the working capital information on the balance sheet to make sure there are enough current assets to cover the current liabilities is a simple way to get an idea about the company's liquidity. Then, calculating the current ratio provides decision makers with information about how adequate that coverage is.

The income statement provides important profitability information. The proportion of each sales dollar available after covering the cost of the products sold gives decision makers a better idea of how well the company is operating. The greater the gross profit percentage, the greater the amount of sales dollars available to cover costs and to provide a profit. Also, knowing how the profit margin (or return on sales) has changed from year to year helps decision makers assess the direction the company is going and use that information to help predict future profitability.

In this chapter, you have learned about three new ratios and another calculation that are used for decision making. These four items and the sources of information needed for their analysis are as follows:

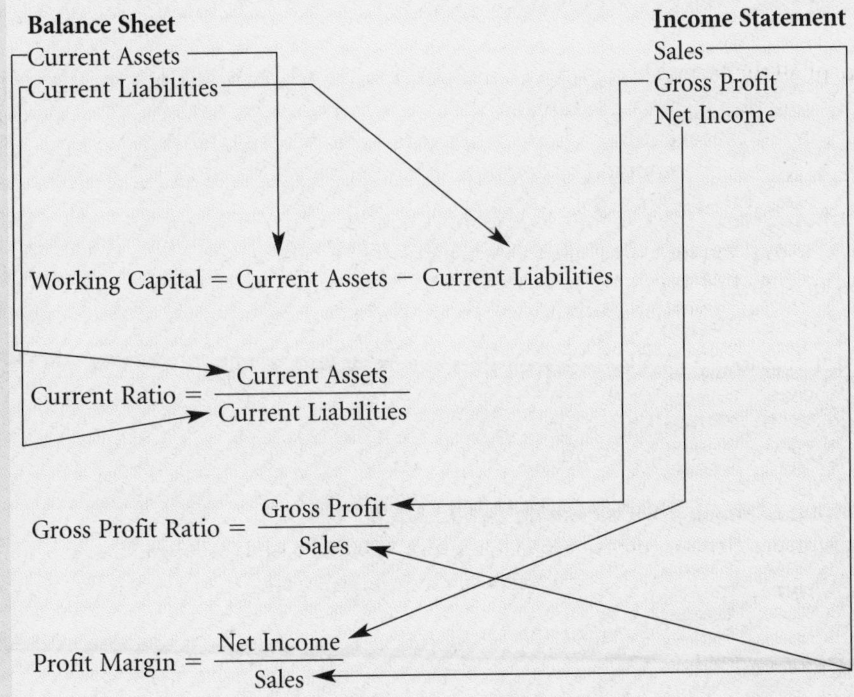

Impact on the Financial Reports

Impact on the Financial Reports

BALANCE SHEET
Current Assets
Noncurrent Assets
Current Liabilities
Noncurrent Liabilities
Stockholders' Equity

INCOME STATEMENT
Revenues
Expenses
Other

STATEMENT OF STOCKHOLDERS' EQUITY
Contributed Capital
Retained Earnings

STATEMENT OF CASH FLOWS
Operating Activities
Investing Activities
Financing Activities
Noncash Transactions

NOTES
Summary of Significant Accounting Policies

The purpose of this presentation is to show, in one place, the impact of the chapter's topical coverage on one or more of the four financial statements and the notes. This also reinforces how interconnected these reports are and shows where decision makers should expect to see impact and disclosure. The primary sections of each statement are as illustrated.

Answers to the Two-Minute Reviews

Two-Minute Review on Page 69

1. *Cash, accounts receivable, inventory, short-term investments, and prepaid expenses.*
2. *Investments; property, plant, and equipment; and intangibles.*

Two-Minute Review on Page 74

1. *Gross profit, income from operations and income before income taxes.*
2. *Advertising: selling; Depreciation on office building: general and administrative; Salespersons' commissions: selling; Office salaries: general and administrative*

Warmup Exercises

Warmup Exercise 2-1 ***Identifying Ratios*** **LO 4, 6**

State the equation for each of the following ratios:

1. Current ratio
2. Gross profit ratio
3. Profit margin

Key to the Solution

Review the various ratios as discussed in the chapter.

Warmup Exercise 2-2 ***Calculating Ratios*** **LO 6**

Bridger reported net income of $150,000, sales of $1,000,000, and cost of goods sold of $800,000.

Required

Compute each of the following ratios for Bridger:

1. Gross profit ratio
2. Profit margin

Key to the Solution

Recall the equation for each of these ratios as presented in the chapter.

Warmup Exercise 2-3 *Determining Liquidity* LO 4

Big has current assets of $500,000 and current liabilities of $400,000. Small reports current assets of $80,000 and current liabilities of $20,000.

Required

Which company is more liquid? Why?

Key to the Solution

Calculate the current ratio for each company and compare them.

Solutions to Warmup Exercises

Warmup Exercise 2-1

1. Current ratio $= \dfrac{\text{Current Assets}}{\text{Current Liabilities}}$

2. Gross profit ratio $= \dfrac{\text{Gross Profit}}{\text{Sales}}$

3. Profit margin $= \dfrac{\text{Net income}}{\text{Sales}}$

Warmup Exercise 2-2

1. $\dfrac{\$1{,}000{,}000 - \$800{,}000}{\$1{,}000{,}000} = \dfrac{\$200{,}000}{\$1{,}000{,}000} = \underline{\underline{20\%}}$

2. $\dfrac{\$150{,}000}{\$1{,}000{,}000} = \underline{\underline{15\%}}$

Warmup Exercise 2-3

Small Company appears on the surface to be more liquid. Its current ratio of $80,000/$20,000, or 4 to 1, is significantly higher than Big's current ratio of $500,000/$400,000, or 1.25 to 1.

The following review problem will give you the opportunity to apply what you have learned by preparing both an income statement and a balance sheet.

Review Problem

WebTUTOR™ Advantage

Shown below, in alphabetical order, are items taken from the records of Grizzly Inc., a chain of outdoor recreational stores in the Northwest. Use the items to prepare two statements. First, prepare an income statement for the year ended December 31, 2004. The income statement should be in multiple-step form. Second, prepare a classified balance sheet at December 31, 2004. All amounts are in thousands of dollars.

Accounts payable	$ 6,500
Accounts receivable	8,200
Accumulated depreciation—buildings	25,000
Accumulated depreciation—furniture and fixtures	15,000
Advertising expense	3,100
Buildings	80,000
Capital stock, $1 par, 10,000 shares issued and outstanding	10,000
Cash	2,400
Commissions expense	8,600
Cost of goods sold	110,000
Depreciation on buildings	2,500
Depreciation on furniture and fixtures	1,200
Furniture and fixtures	68,000
Income taxes payable	2,200

(continued)

Income tax expense	$ 13,000
Insurance expense	2,000
Interest expense	12,000
Interest payable	1,000
Interest revenue	2,000
Land	100,000
Long-term notes payable, due December 31, 2012	120,000
Merchandise inventories	6,000
Office supplies	900
Paid-in capital in excess of par value	40,000
Prepaid rent	3,000
Rent expense for salespersons' autos	9,000
Retained earnings	48,800
Salaries and wages for office staff	11,000
Sales revenue	190,000

Solution to Review Problem

1. Multiple-step income statement:

GRIZZLY INC.
INCOME STATEMENT
FOR THE YEAR ENDED DECEMBER 31, 2004
(IN THOUSANDS OF DOLLARS)

Sales revenue		$190,000	
Cost of goods sold		110,000	
Gross profit			$ 80,000
Operating expenses:			
Selling expenses:			
Advertising expense	$ 3,100		
Depreciation on furniture and fixtures	1,200		
Rent expense for salespersons' autos	9,000		
Commissions expense	8,600		
Total selling expenses		$ 21,900	
General and administrative expenses:			
Depreciation on buildings	$ 2,500		
Insurance expense	2,000		
Salaries and wages for office staff	11,000		
Total general and administrative expenses		15,500	
Total operating expenses			37,400
Income from operations			$ 42,600
Other revenues and expenses:			
Interest revenue		$ 2,000	
Interest expense		12,000	
Excess of other expenses over other revenue			10,000
Income before income taxes			$ 32,600
Income tax expense			13,000
Net income			$ 19,600

2. Classified balance sheet:

GRIZZLY INC.
BALANCE SHEET
AT DECEMBER 31, 2004
(IN THOUSANDS OF DOLLARS)

Assets

Current assets:		
Cash	$ 2,400	
Accounts receivable	8,200	
Merchandise inventories	6,000	
Office supplies	900	
Prepaid rent	3,000	
Total current assets		$ 20,500

Property, plant, and equipment:			
Land		$100,000	
Buildings	$ 80,000		
Less: Accumulated depreciation	25,000	55,000	
Furniture and fixtures	$ 68,000		
Less: Accumulated depreciation	15,000	53,000	
Total property, plant, and equipment			208,000
Total assets			$228,500
Liabilities			
Current liabilities:			
Accounts payable		$ 6,500	
Income taxes payable		2,200	
Interest payable		1,000	
Total current liabilities			$ 9,700
Long-term notes payable, due December 31, 2012			120,000
Total liabilities			$129,700
Stockholders' Equity			
Contributed capital:			
Capital stock, $1 par, 10,000 shares issued and outstanding		$ 10,000	
Paid-in capital in excess of par value		40,000	
Total contributed capital		$ 50,000	
Retained earnings		48,800	
Total stockholders' equity			98,800
Total liabilities and stockholders' equity			$228,500

Chapter Highlights

1. **LO 1** The primary objective of financial reporting is to provide information that is useful in making investment, credit, and similar decisions.
2. **LO 1** Investors and creditors are ultimately interested in their own prospective cash receipts from dividends or interest and the proceeds from the sale, redemption, or maturity of securities or loans. Because these expected cash flows are related to the expected cash flows to the company, its cash flows are of interest to investors and creditors. The entity's economic resources, claims to them, and the effects of transactions that change resources and claims to those resources are also of interest.
3. **LO 2** Financial information should be understandable to those who are willing to spend the time to understand it. To be useful, the information should be relevant and reliable. Relevant information has the capacity to make a difference in a decision. Reliable information can be depended on to represent the economic events that it purports to represent.
4. **LO 2** *Comparability* is the quality that allows for comparisons to be made between two or more companies, whereas *consistency* is the quality that allows for comparisons to be made within a single company from one period to the next. These two qualities of useful accounting information are aided by full disclosure—in the notes to the financial statements—of all relevant information.
5. **LO 3** The operating cycle depends to a large extent on the nature of a company's business. For a retailer, it encompasses the period of time from the investment of cash in inventory to the collection of any account receivable from sale of the product. The operating cycle for a manufacturer is expanded to include the period of time required to convert raw materials into finished products.
6. **LO 3** Current assets will be realized in cash or sold or consumed during the operating cycle or within one year if the cycle is shorter than one year. Because most businesses have numerous operating cycles within a year, the cutoff for classification as a current asset is usually one year. Cash, accounts receivable, inventory, and prepaid expenses are all examples of current assets.
7. **LO 3** The definition of *current liability* is related to that of *current asset.* A current liability is an obligation that will be satisfied within the operating cycle or within one year if the cycle is shorter than one year. Many liabilities are satisfied by making a cash payment. However, some obligations are settled by rendering a service.
8. **LO 4** A classified balance sheet is helpful in evaluating the liquidity of a business. Working capital, the difference between current assets and current liabilities, indicates the buffer of protection for creditors. The current ratio, current assets divided by current liabilities, provides the reader with a relative measure of liquidity.
9. **LO 5, 6** All expenses are added together and subtracted from all revenues in a single-step income statement. The multiple-step income statement provides the reader with classifications of revenues and expenses as well as with important subtotals. Cost of goods sold is subtracted from sales revenue on a multiple-step statement, with the result reported as gross profit. Profitability analysis includes such measures as the gross profit ratio (the ratio of gross profit to sales) and the profit margin (the ratio of net income to sales).

10. LO 7, 8 If there are no changes in the capital stock accounts, some companies present a statement of retained earnings or a combined statement of income and retained earnings in lieu of a statement of stockholders' equity. The statement of cash flows summarizes the operating, investing, and financing activities of an entity for the period.

11. LO 9 No two annual reports are the same. However, certain basic elements are included in most of them. In addition to the financial statements, annual reports include, among other items, the independent accountants' report, management's discussion of the amounts appearing in the statements, and notes to the statements.

http://

http://porter.swlearning.com

Technology and other resources for your success

If you need additional help, visit the text's Web site. Also, see this text's preface for a description of available technology and other resources. If your instructor is using PERSONAL*Trainer* in this course, you may complete, on line, the exercises and problems in the text.

Key Terms Quiz

Read each definition below and then write the number of that definition in the blank beside the appropriate term it defines. The quiz solutions appear at the end of the chapter.

_____ Understandability
_____ Relevance
_____ Reliability
_____ Comparability
_____ Depreciation
_____ Consistency
_____ Materiality
_____ Conservatism
_____ Operating cycle
_____ Current asset
_____ Current liability
_____ Liquidity
_____ Working capital
_____ Current ratio
_____ Single-step income statement
_____ Multiple-step income statement
_____ Gross profit
_____ Gross profit ratio
_____ Profit margin

1. An income statement in which all expenses are added together and subtracted from all revenues.
2. The magnitude of an omission or misstatement in accounting information that will affect the judgment of someone relying on the information.
3. The capacity of information to make a difference in a decision.
4. An income statement that provides the reader with classifications of revenues and expenses as well as with important subtotals.
5. The practice of using the least optimistic estimate when two estimates of amounts are about equally likely.
6. The quality of accounting information that makes it comprehensible to those willing to spend the necessary time.
7. Gross profit divided by sales.
8. Current assets divided by current liabilities.
9. The quality of accounting information that makes it dependable in representing the events that it purports to represent.
10. An obligation that will be satisfied within the next operating cycle or within one year if the cycle is shorter than one year.
11. The period of time between the purchase of inventory and the collection of any receivable from the sale of the inventory.
12. Current assets minus current liabilities.
13. Net income divided by sales.
14. The quality of accounting information that allows a user to analyze two or more companies and look for similarities and differences.
15. An asset that is expected to be realized in cash or sold or consumed during the operating cycle or within one year if the cycle is shorter than one year.
16. The ability of a company to pay its debts as they come due.
17. The quality of accounting information that allows a user to compare two or more accounting periods for a single company.
18. Sales less cost of goods sold.
19. The allocation of the cost of a tangible, long-term asset over its useful life.

Answers on p. 105.

Alternate Terms

Balance sheet Statement of financial position or condition

Capital stock Contributed capital

Cost of goods sold Cost of sales

Gross profit Gross margin

Income statement Statement of income

Income tax expense Provision for income taxes

Long-term assets Noncurrent assets

Long-term liability Long-term debt

Net income Profits or earnings

Report of independent accountants Auditors' report

Retained earnings Earned capital

Stockholders' equity Shareholders' equity

Questions

1. How would you evaluate the following statement: "The cash flows to a company are irrelevant to an investor; all the investor cares about is the potential for receiving dividends on the investment"?
2. A key characteristic of useful financial information is understandability. How does this qualitative characteristic relate to the background of the user of the information?
3. What does *relevance* mean with regard to the use of accounting information?
4. What is the qualitative characteristic of comparability, and why is it important in preparing financial statements?
5. What is the difference between comparability and consistency as they relate to the use of accounting information?
6. How does the concept of materiality relate to the size of a company?
7. How does the operating cycle of a retailer differ from that of a service company?
8. How does the concept of the operating cycle relate to the definition of a current asset?
9. What are two examples of the way a company's intent in using an asset affects classification of the asset on the balance sheet?
10. How would you evaluate the following statement: "A note payable with an original maturity of five years will be classified on the balance sheet as a long-term liability until it matures"?
11. How do the two basic forms of owners' equity items for a corporation—capital stock and retained earnings—differ?
12. What are the limitations of working capital as a measure of the liquidity of a business as opposed to the current ratio?
13. What is meant by a company's capital structure?
14. What is the major weakness of the single-step form for the income statement?
15. Why might a company's gross profit ratio increase from one year to the next but its profit margin ratio decrease?
16. How does a statement of retained earnings act as a link between an income statement and a balance sheet?
17. In auditing the financial statements of a company, does the auditor *certify* that the statements are totally accurate and without errors of any size or variety?
18. What is the first note in the annual report of all publicly held companies, and what is its purpose?

Exercises

Exercise 2-1 *Characteristics of Useful Accounting Information* **LO 2**

Fill in the blank with the qualitative characteristic for each of the following descriptions:

______________ 1. Information that users can depend on to represent the events that it purports to represent

______________ 2. Information that has the capacity to make a difference in a decision

______________ 3. Information that is valid, that indicates an agreement between the underlying data and the events represented

______________ 4. Information that allows for comparisons to be made from one accounting period to the next

______________ 5. Information that is free from error

______________ 6. Information that is meaningful to those who are willing to learn to use it properly

______________ 7. Information that is not slanted to portray a company's position any better or worse than the circumstances warrant

______________ 8. Information that allows for comparisons to be made between or among companies

Exercise 2-2 *Classification of Assets and Liabilities* **LO 3**

Indicate the appropriate classification of each of the following as a current asset (CA), noncurrent asset (NCA), current liability (CL), or long-term liability (LTL):

_____ 1. Inventory
_____ 2. Accounts payable
_____ 3. Cash
_____ 4. Patents
_____ 5. Notes payable, due in six months
_____ 6. Taxes payable
_____ 7. Prepaid rent (for the next nine months)
_____ 8. Bonds payable, due in 10 years
_____ 9. Machinery

Exercise 2-3 *Selling Expenses and General and Administrative Expenses* **LO 5**

Operating expenses are subdivided between selling expenses and general and administrative expenses when a multiple-step income statement is prepared. From the following list, identify each item as a selling expense (S) or general and administrative expense (G&A):

_____ 1. Advertising expense
_____ 2. Depreciation expense—store furniture and fixtures
_____ 3. Office rent expense
_____ 4. Office salaries expense
_____ 5. Store rent expense
_____ 6. Store salaries expense
_____ 7. Insurance expense
_____ 8. Supplies expense
_____ 9. Utilities expense

Exercise 2-4 *Missing Income Statement Amounts* **LO 5**

For each of the following independent cases, fill in the blank with the appropriate dollar amount:

	Sara's Coffee Shop	Amy's Deli	Jane's Bagels
Net sales	$35,000	$ _____	$78,000
Cost of goods sold	_____	45,000	_____
Gross profit	7,000	18,000	_____
Selling expenses	3,000	_____	9,000
General and administrative expenses	1,500	2,800	_____
Total operating expenses	_____	8,800	13,600
Net income	$ 2,500	$ 9,200	$25,400

Exercise 2-5 *Income Statement Ratios* **LO 6**

The 2004 income statement of Holly Enterprises shows net income of $45,000, comprising net sales of $134,800, cost of goods sold of $53,920, selling expenses of $18,310, general and administrative expenses of $16,990, and interest expense of $580. Holly's stockholders' equity was $280,000 at the beginning of the year and $320,000 at the end of the year. The company has 20,000 shares of stock outstanding at December 31, 2004.

Required

Compute Holly's (1) gross profit ratio and (2) profit margin. What other information would you need to be able to comment on whether these ratios are favorable?

Exercise 2-6 *Statement of Retained Earnings* **LO 7**

Landon Corporation was organized on January 2, 2002, with the investment of $100,000 by each of its two stockholders. Net income for its first year of business was $85,200. Net income increased during 2003 to $125,320 and to $145,480 during 2004. Landon paid $20,000 in dividends to each of the two stockholders in each of the three years.

Required

Prepare a statement of retained earnings for the year ended December 31, 2004.

Exercise 2-7 ***Components of the Statement of Cash Flows*** **LO 8**

From the following list, identify each item as operating (O), investing (I), financing (F), or not on the statement of cash flows (N):

______ 1. Paid for supplies
______ 2. Collected cash from customers
______ 3. Purchased land (held for resale)
______ 4. Purchased land (for construction of new building)
______ 5. Paid dividend
______ 6. Issued stock
______ 7. Purchased computers (for use in the business)
______ 8. Sold old equipment

Exercise 2-8 ***Basic Elements of Financial Statements*** **LO 9**

Most financial reports contain the list of basic elements on the following page. For each element, identify the person(s) who prepared the element and describe the information a user would expect to find in each element. Some information is verifiable; other information is subjectively chosen by management. Comment on the verifiability of information in each element.

1. Management's report
2. Product/markets of company
3. Financial statements
4. Notes to financial statements
5. Independent accountants' report

Multi-Concept Exercises

Exercise 2-9 ***Financial Statement Classification*** **LO 3, 5, 7**

Potential stockholders and lenders are interested in a company's financial statements. For the list below, identify the statement—balance sheet (BS), income statement (IS), retained earnings statement (RE)—on which each item would appear.

______ 1. Accounts payable
______ 2. Accounts receivable
______ 3. Advertising expense
______ 4. Bad debt expense
______ 5. Bonds payable
______ 6. Buildings
______ 7. Cash
______ 8. Common stock
______ 9. Deferred income taxes
______ 10. Depreciation expense
______ 11. Dividends
______ 12. Land held for future expansion
______ 13. Loss on the sale of equipment
______ 14. Office supplies
______ 15. Organizational costs
______ 16. Patent amortization expense
______ 17. Retained earnings
______ 18. Sales
______ 19. Unearned revenue
______ 20. Utilities expense

Exercise 2-10 ***Single- and Multiple-Step Income Statement*** **LO 5, 6**

Some headings and/or items are used on either the single-step or the multiple-step income statement. Some are used on both. For the list below, indicate the following: single-step (S), multiple-step (M), both formats (B), or not used on either income statement (N).

______ 1. Sales
______ 2. Cost of goods sold
______ 3. Selling expenses
______ 4. Total revenues
______ 5. Utilities expense
______ 6. Administrative expense
______ 7. Net loss
______ 8. Supplies on hand
______ 9. Accumulated depreciation
______ 10. Gross profit

Exercise 2-11 ***Multiple-Step Income Statement*** **LO 5, 6**

Gaynor Corporation's partial income statement follows:

Sales	$1,200,000
Cost of sales	450,000
Selling expenses	60,800
General and administrative expenses	75,000

Required

Determine the gross profit ratio and profit margin. Would you consider investing in Gaynor Corporation? Explain your answer.

Problems

Problem 2-1 ***Materiality*** **LO 2**

Joseph Knapp, a newly hired accountant, wanted to impress his boss, so he stayed late one night to analyze the office supplies expense. He determined the cost by month, for the past 12 months, of each of the following: computer paper, copy paper, fax paper, pencils and pens, note pads, postage, stationery, and miscellaneous items.

1. What did Joseph think his boss would learn from this information? What action might be taken as a result of knowing it?
2. Would this information be more relevant if Joseph worked for a hardware store or for a real estate company? Discuss.

Problem 2-2 ***Costs and Expenses*** **LO 2**

The following costs are incurred by a retailer:

1. Display fixtures in a retail store
2. Advertising
3. Merchandise for sale
4. Incorporation (i.e., legal costs, stock issue costs)
5. Cost of a franchise
6. Office supplies
7. Wages in a restaurant
8. Computer software
9. Computer hardware

Required

For each of these costs, explain whether all of the cost or only a portion of the cost would appear as an expense on the income statement for the period in which the cost was incurred. If not all of the cost would appear on the income statement for that period, explain why not.

Problem 2-3 ***Classified Balance Sheet*** **LO 3**

The following balance sheet items, listed in alphabetical order, are available from the records of Ruth Corporation at December 31, 2004:

Accounts payable	$ 18,255
Accounts receivable	23,450
Accumulated depreciation—automobiles	22,500
Accumulated depreciation—buildings	40,000
Automobiles	112,500
Bonds payable, due December 31, 2008	160,000
Buildings	200,000
Capital stock, $10 par value	150,000
Cash	13,230
Income taxes payable	6,200
Interest payable	1,500
Inventory	45,730

Land	$250,000
Long-term investments	85,000
Notes payable, due June 30, 2005	10,000
Office supplies	2,340
Paid-in capital in excess of par value	50,000
Patents	40,000
Prepaid rent	1,500
Retained earnings	311,095
Salaries and wages payable	4,200

Required

1. Prepare in good form a classified balance sheet as of December 31, 2004.
2. Compute Ruth's current ratio.
3. On the basis of your answer to requirement 2, does Ruth appear to be *liquid?* What other information do you need to fully answer this question?

Problem 2-4 ***Financial Statement Ratios*** **LO 4**

The items below, in alphabetical order, are available from the records of Walker Corporation as of December 31, 2004 and 2003:

	December 31, 2004	December 31, 2003
Accounts payable	$ 8,400	$ 5,200
Accounts receivable	13,230	19,570
Cash	10,200	9,450
Cleaning supplies	450	700
Interest payable	–0–	1,200
Inventory	24,600	26,200
Marketable securities	6,250	5,020
Note payable, due in six months	–0–	12,000
Prepaid rent	3,600	4,800
Taxes payable	1,450	1,230
Wages payable	1,200	1,600

Required

1. Calculate the following, as of December 31, 2004, and December 31, 2003:
   a. Working capital
   b. Current ratio
2. On the basis of your answers to **1**, comment on the relative liquidity of the company at the beginning and the end of the year. As part of your answer, explain the change in the company's liquidity from the beginning to the end of 2004.

Problem 2-5 ***Working Capital and Current Ratio*** **LO 4**

The balance sheet of Stevenson Inc. includes the following items:

Cash	$ 23,000
Accounts receivable	13,000
Inventory	45,000
Prepaid insurance	800
Land	80,000
Accounts payable	54,900
Salaries payable	1,200
Capital stock	100,000
Retained earnings	5,700

Required

1. Determine the current ratio and working capital.
2. Beyond the information provided in your answers to **1**, what does the composition of the current assets tell you about Stevenson's liquidity?
3. What other information do you need to fully assess Stevenson's liquidity?

Problem 2-6 ***Single-Step Income Statement*** **LO 5**

The following income statement items, arranged in alphabetical order, are taken from the records of Shaw Corporation for the year ended December 31, 2004:

Advertising expense	$ 1,500
Commissions expense	2,415
Cost of goods sold	29,200
Depreciation expense—office building	2,900
Income tax expense	1,540
Insurance expense—salesperson's auto	2,250
Interest expense	1,400
Interest revenue	1,340
Rent revenue	6,700
Salaries and wages expense—office	12,560
Sales revenue	48,300
Supplies expense—office	890

Required

1. Prepare a single-step income statement for the year ended December 31, 2004.
2. What weaknesses do you see in this form for the income statement?

Problem 2-7 ***Multiple-Step Income Statement*** **LO 5**

Refer to the list of income statement items in Problem 2-6. Assume that Shaw Corporation classifies all operating expenses into two categories: (1) selling and (2) general and administrative.

1. Prepare a multiple-step income statement for the year ended December 31, 2004.
2. Compute Shaw's gross profit ratio.
3. What does this ratio tell you about Shaw's markup on its products?

Problem 2-8 ***Albertsons' Gross Profit Ratio*** **LO 6**

http://www.albertsons.com

Albertsons Inc. is a large, retail food and drug chain, with nearly 2,300 stores throughout the western, midwestern, and southern states. The following items appeared in the company's 2002 annual report (all amounts are in millions of dollars):

	52 Weeks January 30, 2003	52 Weeks January 31, 2002	52 Weeks February 1, 2001
Sales	$35,626	$36,605	$35,501
Cost of goods sold	25,242	26,179	25,409

Required

1. Note that Albertsons' fiscal year ends toward the end of January (actually, on the Thursday nearest to January 31 each year). Why do you think this particular company would choose this time, rather than December 31, to end its accounting year?
2. Compute Albertsons' gross profit and its gross profit ratio for each of the three years.
3. Comment on the *change* in the gross profit ratio over the three-year period. What possible explanations are there for the change?

Problem 2-9 ***Statement of Cash Flows*** **LO 8**

Colorado Corporation was organized on January 1, 2004, with the investment of $250,000 in cash by its stockholders. The company immediately purchased an office building for $300,000, paying $210,000 in cash and signing a three-year promissory note for the balance. Colorado signed a five-year, $60,000 promissory note at a local bank during 2004 and received cash in the same amount. During its first year, Colorado collected $93,970 from its customers. It paid $65,600 for inventory, $20,400 in salaries and wages, and another $3,100 in taxes. Colorado paid $5,600 in cash dividends.

1. Prepare a statement of cash flows for the year ended December 31, 2004.
2. What does this statement tell you that an income statement does not?

Problem 2-10 ***Basic Elements of Financial Reports*** **LO 9**

Comparative income statements for Grammar Inc. are presented on the following page.

	2004	2003
Sales	$1,000,000	$500,000
Cost of sales	500,000	300,000
Gross margin	$ 500,000	$200,000
Operating expenses	120,000	100,000
Operating income	$ 380,000	$100,000
Loss on sale of subsidiary	(400,000)	—
Net income	$ (20,000)	$100,000

Required

The president and management believe that the company performed better in 2004 than it did in 2003. Write the president's letter to be included in the 2004 annual report. Explain why the company is financially sound and why shareholders should not be alarmed by the $20,000 loss in a year when sales have doubled.

Multi-Concept Problems

Problem 2-11 ***Comparing Coca-Cola and PepsiCo*** **LO 2, 4**

The current items, listed in alphabetical order, are taken from the consolidated balance sheets of Coca-Cola and PepsiCo as of December 31, 2002, and December 28, 2002, respectively (all amounts are in millions of dollars):

http://www.cocacola.com
http://www.pepsico.com

SPREADSHEET

Coca-Cola	
Accounts payable and accrued expenses	$3,692
Accrued income taxes	994
Cash and cash equivalents	2,126
Current maturities of long-term debt	180
Inventories	1,294
Loans and notes payable	2,475
Marketable securities	219
Prepaid expenses and other assets	1,616
Trade accounts receivable, less allowance of $55	2,097
PepsiCo	
Accounts and notes receivable, net	$2,531
Accounts payable and other current liabilities	4,998
Cash and cash equivalents	1,638
Income taxes payable	492
Inventories	1,342
Prepaid expenses and other current assets	695
Short-term investments, at cost	207
Short-term obligations	562

Required

1. Compute working capital and the current ratio for both companies.
2. On the basis of your answers to **1** above, which company appears to be more liquid?
3. As you know, other factors affect a company's liquidity in addition to its working capital and current ratio. Comment on the *composition* of each company's current assets and how this composition affects its liquidity.

Problem 2-12 ***Comparability and Consistency in Income Statements*** **LO 2, 5**

The following income statements were provided by Gleeson Company, a retailer:

2004 Income Statement		**2003 Income Statement**	
Sales	$1,700,000	Sales	$1,500,000
Cost of sales	520,000	Cost of sales	$ 450,000
Gross profit	$1,180,000	Sales salaries	398,000
Selling expense	$ 702,000	Advertising	175,000
Administrative expense	95,000	Office supplies	54,000
Total selling and		Depreciation—building	40,000
administrative expense	$ 797,000	Delivery expense	20,000
		Total expenses	$1,137,000
Net income	$ 383,000	Net income	$ 363,000

Required

1. Identify each income statement as either single-step or multiple-step format.
2. Convert the 2003 income statement to the same format as the 2004 income statement.

Problem 2-13 ***Classified Balance Sheet, Multiple-Step Income Statement, and Statement of Retained Earnings for Kellogg's*** **LO 3, 5, 7**

http://www.kelloggs.com

SPREADSHEET

In alphabetical order, the following items are taken from Kellogg's 2002 consolidated financial statements:

(millions, except per share data)	2002
Accounts payable	$ 619.0
Accounts receivable, net	741.0
Accumulated other comprehensive income (reduction of owners' equity listed after treasury stock)	(853.4)
Capital in excess of par value	49.9
Cash and cash equivalents	100.6
Cash dividends	(412.6)
Common stock	103.8
Cost of goods sold	4,569.0
Current maturities of long-term debt	776.4
Income taxes (expense)	423.4
Interest expense	391.2
Inventories	603.2
Long-term debt	4,519.4
Net sales	8,304.1
Notes payable (current liability)	420.9
Other assets (long-term assets)	5,615.7
Other current assets	318.6
Other current liabilities	1,198.6
Other income (expense), net	27.4
Other liabilities (long-term liabilities)	1,789.9
Property, net	2,840.2
Retained earnings, beginning of year	1,564.7
Selling, general, and administrative expense	2,227.0
Treasury stock at cost (reduction of owners' equity listed after retained earnings)	(278.2)

(NOTE: The descriptions in parentheses are not part of the items but have been added to provide you with hints as you complete this problem.)

Required

1. Prepare a multiple-step income statement for Kellogg's for the year ended December 31, 2002.
2. Prepare a statement of retained earnings for Kellogg's for the year ended December 31, 2002.
3. Prepare a classified balance sheet for Kellogg's at December 31, 2002.

SPREADSHEET

Problem 2-14 ***Using Kellogg's Classified Balance Sheet and Multiple-Step Income Statement*** **LO 4, 6**

(Note: Consider completing this problem after Problem 2-13 to ensure that you have the various items on the financial statements properly classified.)

Refer to the information set forth in Problem 2-13.

Required

1. Compute Kellogg's working capital and its current ratio at December 31, 2002.
2. Does Kellogg's appear to be liquid? What other factors need to be considered in answering this question?
3. Compute Kellogg's gross profit ratio and its profit margin for 2002.
4. As a Kellogg's stockholder, would you be satisfied with the company's gross profit ratio and its profit margin? What other factors need to be considered in answering this question?

Problem 2-15 *Cash Flow* LO 1, 4, 8

DECISION MAKING

Franklin Co., a specialty retailer, has a history of paying quarterly dividends of $0.50 per share. Management is trying to determine whether the company will have adequate cash on December 31, 2004, to pay a dividend if one is declared by the board of directors. The following additional information is available:

- All sales are on account, and accounts receivable are collected one month after the sale. Sales volume has been increasing 5% each month.
- All purchases of merchandise are on account, and accounts payable are paid one month after the purchase. Cost of sales is 40% of the sales price. Inventory levels are maintained at $75,000.
- Operating expenses in addition to the mortgage are paid in cash. They amount to $3,000 per month and are paid as they are incurred.

FRANKLIN CO.
BALANCE SHEET
SEPTEMBER 30, 2004

Cash	$ 5,000	Accounts payable	$ 5,000
Accounts receivable	12,500	Mortgage note**	150,000
Inventory	75,000	Common stock—$1 par	50,000
Note receivable*	10,000	Retained earnings	66,500
Building/Land	169,000	Total liabilities	
Total assets	$271,500	and stockholders' equity	$271,500

**Note receivable represents a one-year, 5% interest-bearing note, due November 1, 2004.*
***Mortgage note is a 30-year, 7% note due in monthly installments of $1,200.*

Required

Determine the cash that Franklin will have available to pay a dividend on December 31, 2004. Round all amounts to the nearest dollar. What can Franklin's management do to increase the cash available? Should management recommend that the board of directors declare a dividend?

Alternate Problems

Problem 2-1A *Materiality* LO 2

Jane Erving, a newly hired accountant, wanted to impress her boss, so she stayed late one night to analyze the long-distance calls by area code and time of day placed. She determined the monthly cost, for the past 12 months, by hour and area code called.

Required

1. What did Jane think her boss would learn from this information? What action might be taken as a result of knowing it?
2. Would this information be more relevant if Jane worked for a hardware store or for a real estate company? Discuss.

Problem 2-2A *Costs and Expenses* LO 2

The following costs are incurred by a retailer:

1. Point-of-sale systems in a retail store
2. An ad in the yellow pages
3. An inventory-control computer software system
4. Shipping merchandise for resale to chain outlets

For each of these costs, explain whether all of the cost or only a portion of the cost would appear as an expense on the income statement for the period in which the cost is incurred. If not all of the cost would appear on the income statement for that period, explain why not.

Problem 2-3A *Classified Balance Sheet* LO 3

The following balance sheet items, listed in alphabetical order, are available from the records of Singer Company at December 31, 2004:

(continued)

Accounts payable	$ 34,280
Accounts receivable	26,700
Accumulated depreciation—buildings	40,000
Accumulated depreciation—equipment	12,500
Bonds payable, due December 31, 2010	250,000
Buildings	150,000
Capital stock, $1 par value	200,000
Cash	60,790
Equipment	84,500
Income taxes payable	7,500
Interest payable	2,200
Land	250,000
Marketable securities	15,000
Merchandise inventory	112,900
Notes payable, due April 15, 2005	6,500
Office supplies	400
Paid-in capital in excess of par value	75,000
Patents	45,000
Prepaid rent	3,600
Retained earnings	113,510
Salaries payable	7,400

Required

1. Prepare a classified balance sheet as of December 31, 2004.
2. Compute Singer's current ratio.
3. On the basis of your answer to **2**, does Singer appear to be *liquid?* What other information do you need to fully answer this question?

Problem 2-4A *Financial Statement Ratios* LO 4

The following items, in alphabetical order, are available from the records of Quinn Corporation as of December 31, 2004 and 2003:

	December 31, 2004	December 31, 2003
Accounts payable	$10,500	$ 6,500
Accounts receivable	16,500	26,000
Cash	12,750	11,800
Interest receivable	200	–0–
Note receivable, due 12/31/2006	12,000	12,000
Office supplies	900	1,100
Prepaid insurance	400	250
Salaries payable	1,800	800
Taxes payable	10,000	5,800

Required

1. Calculate the following, as of December 31, 2004, and December 31, 2003:
   a. Working capital
   b. Current ratio
2. On the basis of your answers to **1**, comment on the relative liquidity of the company at the beginning and the end of the year. As part of your answer, explain the change in the company's liquidity from the beginning to the end of 2004.

Problem 2-5A *Working Capital and Current Ratio* LO 4

The balance sheet of Kapinski Inc. includes the following items:

Cash	$ 23,000
Accounts receivable	43,000
Inventory	75,000
Prepaid insurance	2,800
Land	80,000
Accounts payable	84,900
Salaries payable	3,200
Capital stock	100,000
Retained earnings	35,700

Required

1. Determine the current ratio and working capital.
2. Kapinski appears to have a positive current ratio and a large net working capital. Why would it have trouble paying bills as they come due?
3. Suggest three things that Kapinski can do to help pay its bills on time.

Problem 2-6A ***Single-Step Income Statement*** **LO 5**

The following income statement items, arranged in alphabetical order, are taken from the records of Corbin Enterprises, a software sales firm, for the year ended December 31, 2004:

Advertising expense	$ 9,000
Cost of goods sold	150,000
Depreciation expense—computer	4,500
Dividend revenue	2,700
Income tax expense	30,700
Interest expense	1,900
Rent expense—office	26,400
Rent expense—salesperson's car	18,000
Sales revenue	350,000
Supplies expense—office	1,300
Utilities expense	6,750
Wages expense—office	45,600

Required

1. Prepare a single-step income statement for the year ended December 31, 2004.
2. What weaknesses do you see in this form for the income statement?

Problem 2-7A ***Multiple-Step Income Statement*** **LO 5**

Refer to the list of income statement items in Problem 2-6A. Assume that Corbin Enterprises classifies all operating expenses into two categories: (1) selling and (2) general and administrative.

Required

1. Prepare a multiple-step income statement for the year ended December 31, 2004.
2. Compute Corbin's gross profit ratio.
3. What does this ratio tell you about Corbin's markup on its products?

Problem 2-8A ***Saks' Gross Profit Ratio*** **LO 6**

Saks Incorporated is a national retailer operating department stores under various names, with the most recognizable being Saks Fifth Avenue. The following items appeared in the company's 2002 annual report (all amounts are in thousands of dollars): **http://www.saksincorporated.com**

	February 1, 2003	February 2, 2002	February 3, 2001
Net sales	$5,911,122	$6,070,568	$6,581,236
Cost of goods sold	3,739,247	3,960,129	4,211,707

Required

1. Note that Saks' fiscal year ends toward the end of January (actually, on the Saturday closest to January 31 each year). Why do you think this particular company would choose this time to end its accounting year rather than December 31?
2. Compute Saks' gross profit and its gross profit ratio for each of the three years.
3. Comment on any *change* in the gross profit ratio over the three-year period. What possible explanations are there for the change?

Problem 2-9A ***Statement of Cash Flows*** **LO 8**

Wisconsin Corporation was organized on January 1, 2004, with the investment of $400,000 in cash by its stockholders. The company immediately purchased a manufacturing facility for $300,000, paying $150,000 in cash and signing a five-year promissory note for the balance. Wisconsin signed another five-year note at the bank for $50,000 during 2004 and received cash for the same amount. During its first year, Wisconsin collected $310,000 from its customers. It paid $185,000 for inventory, $30,100 in salaries and wages, and another $40,000 in taxes. Wisconsin paid $4,000 in cash dividends.

Required

1. Prepare a statement of cash flows for the year ended December 31, 2004.
2. What does this statement tell you that an income statement does not?

Problem 2-10A ***Basic Elements of Financial Reports*** **LO 9**

Comparative income statements for Thesaurus Inc. are presented below:

	2004	2003
Sales	$1,000,000	$500,000
Cost of sales	500,000	300,000
Gross margin	$ 500,000	$200,000
Operating expenses	120,000	100,000
Operating income	$ 380,000	$100,000
Gain on the sale of subsidiary	—	400,000
Net income	$ 380,000	$500,000

Required

The president and management believe that the company performed better in 2004 than it did in 2003. Write the president's letter to be included in the 2004 annual report. Explain why the company is financially sound and why shareholders should not be alarmed by the reduction in income in a year when sales have doubled.

Alternate Multi-Concept Problems

Problem 2-11A ***Comparing Gateway and Dell*** **LO 2, 4**

http://www.gateway.com
http://www.dell.com

The following current items, listed in alphabetical order, are taken from the consolidated balance sheets of Gateway, Inc., and Dell Computer Corporation as of December 31, 2002, and January 31, 2003, respectively (all amounts for Gateway are in thousands of dollars and amounts for Dell are in millions of dollars):

Gateway

Accounts payable	$278,609
Accounts receivable, net	197,817
Accrued liabilities	364,741
Accrued royalties (current liability)	56,684
Cash and cash equivalents	465,603
Inventory	88,761
Other current liabilities	240,315
Other, net (current asset)	602,073
Marketable securities	601,118

Dell

Accounts payable	$5,989
Accounts receivable, net	2,586
Accrued and other (current liabilities)	2,944
Cash and cash equivalents	4,232
Inventories	306
Other (current assets)	1,394
Short-term investments	406

(NOTE: The descriptions in parentheses are not part of the items but have been added to provide you with assistance as you complete this problem.)

Required

1. Compute working capital and the current ratio for both companies.
2. On the basis of your answers to 1 above, which company appears to be more liquid?
3. As you know, other factors affect a company's liquidity in addition to its working capital and current ratio. Comment on the *composition* of each company's current assets and how this composition affects its liquidity.

Problem 2-12A ***Comparability and Consistency in Income Statements*** **LO 2, 5**

The following income statements were provided by Chisholm Company, a wholesale food distributor:

	2004	2003
Sales	$1,700,000	$1,500,000
Cost of sales	$ 612,000	$ 450,000
Sales salaries	427,000	398,000
Delivery expense	180,000	175,000
Office supplies	55,000	54,000
Depreciation—truck	40,000	40,000
Computer line expense	23,000	20,000
Total expenses	$1,337,000	$1,137,000
Net income	$ 363,000	$ 363,000

Required

1. Identify each income statement as either single-step or multiple-step format.
2. Restate each item in the income statements as a percentage of sales. Why did net income remain unchanged when sales increased in 2004?

Problem 2-13A ***Classified Balance Sheet, Multiple-Step Income Statement, and Statement of Retained Earnings for Walgreens*** **LO 3, 5, 7**

Shown below, in alphabetical order, are items taken from Walgreens' 2002 consolidated financial statements. Walgreen Co. has a fiscal year ending August 31.

http://www.walgreens.com

	(dollars in millions)
Accounts receivable, net	$ 954.8
Accrued expenses and other liabilities	1,017.9
Cash and cash equivalents	449.9
Cash dividends declared	148.4
Common stock	80.1
Cost of sales	21,076.1
Deferred income taxes (noncurrent liability)	176.5
Income taxes (current liability)	100.9
Income tax provision (expense)	618.1
Interest income	6.9
Inventories	3,645.2
Net sales	28,681.1
Other current assets	116.6
Other income	6.2
Other noncurrent assets	120.9
Other noncurrent liabilities	516.9
Paid-in capital	748.4
Property and equipment, at cost, less accumulated depreciation and amortization	4,591.4
Retained earnings, beginning of year	4,530.9
Selling, occupancy, and administration (expense)	5,980.8
Trade accounts payable	1,836.4

(NOTE: The descriptions in parentheses are not part of the items but have been added to provide you with hints as you complete this problem.)

Required

1. Prepare a multiple-step income statement for Walgreens for the year ended August 31, 2002.
2. Prepare a statement of retained earnings for Walgreens for the year ended August 31, 2002.
3. Prepare a classified balance sheet for Walgreens at August 31, 2002.

Problem 2-14A ***Using Walgreens' Classified Balance Sheet and Multiple-Step Income Statement*** **LO 4, 6**

(Note: Consider completing this problem after Problem 2-13A to ensure that you have the various items on the financial statements properly classified.)

Refer to the information set forth in Problem 2-13A.

Required

1. Compute Walgreens' working capital and its current ratio at August 31, 2002.
2. Does Walgreens appear to be liquid? What other factors need to be considered in answering this question?
3. Compute Walgreens' gross profit ratio and its profit margin for the year ended August 31, 2002.
4. As a Walgreens stockholder, would you be satisfied with the company's gross profit ratio and its profit margin? What other factors need to be considered in answering this question?

Problem 2-15A *Cash Flow* LO 1, 4, 8

Roosevelt Inc., a consulting service, has a history of paying annual dividends of $1 per share. Management is trying to determine whether the company will have adequate cash on December 31, 2004, to pay a dividend if one is declared by the board of directors. The following additional information is available:

- All sales are on account, and accounts receivable are collected one month after the sale. Sales volume has been decreasing 5% each month.
- Operating expenses are paid in cash in the month incurred. Average monthly expenses are $10,000 (excluding the biweekly payroll).
- Biweekly payroll is $4,500, and it will be paid December 15 and December 31.
- Unearned revenue is expected to be earned in December. This amount was taken into consideration in the expected sales volume.

ROOSEVELT INC.
BALANCE SHEET
DECEMBER 1, 2004

Cash	$ 15,000	Unearned revenue	$ 2,000
Accounts receivable	40,000	Note payable*	30,000
Computer equipment	120,000	Common stock—$2 par	50,000
		Retained earnings	93,000
		Total liabilities and	
Total assets	$175,000	stockholder's equity	$175,000

**The note payable plus 3% interest for six months is due January 15, 2005.*

Required

Determine the cash that Roosevelt will have available to pay a dividend on December 31, 2004. Round all amounts to the nearest dollar. Should management recommend that the board of directors declare a dividend?

Decision Cases

Reading and Interpreting Financial Statements

Decision Case 2-1 *Boeing's Operating Cycle* LO 3

http://www.boeing.com

In Boeing's annual report, note 1, "Summary of Significant Accounting Policies," includes the following explanation of Boeing's inventories:

> *Inventories*
> Inventoried costs on commercial aircraft programs and long-term contracts include direct engineering, production and tooling costs, and applicable overhead, not in excess of estimated net realizable value. In accordance with industry practice, inventoried costs include amounts relating to programs and contracts with long production cycles, a portion of which is not expected to be realized within one year.[12]

[12] *Boeing Company 2002 Annual Report.*

Required

1. Based on the note above, describe Boeing's inventory. That is, what types of items would you expect to find in the inventory of this type of company?
2. Why would Boeing expect that a portion of its inventoried costs would *not* be realized within one year?
3. Based on your answer to **2** above, should Boeing classify its inventories as current or as non-current assets? Explain your answer.

Decision Case 2-2 ***Comparing Two Companies in the Same Industry: Winnebago Industries and Monaco Coach Corporation*** **LO 4**

Refer to the financial information for Winnebago Industries and Monaco Coach Corporation reproduced in Appendices A and B at the end of the book for the information needed to answer the following questions.

http://www.winnebagoind.com
http://www.monacocoach.com

Required

DECISION MAKING

1. Compute each company's working capital at the end of 2002 and 2001. Also, for each company, compute the change in working capital from the end of 2001 to the end of 2002.
2. Compute each company's current ratio at the end of 2002 and 2001. Compute the percentage change in the ratio from the end of 2001 to the end of 2002.
3. How do Winnebago Industries and Monaco Coach differ in terms of the accounts that made up their current assets at the end of 2002? What is the largest current asset each reports on the balance sheet at the end of 2002?
4. On the basis of your answers to questions **2** and **3**, which company appears to be the most liquid at the end of 2002? Explain your answer.

Decision Case 2-3 ***Interpreting Monaco Coach's Inventory*** **LO 3, 4**

Refer to Note 3 titled "Inventories" in Monaco Coach's 2002 annual report.

Required

1. What is the amount of Monaco Coach's inventory at December 28, 2002? Has this amount increased or decreased during 2002?
2. What are the three components of Monaco Coach's inventory?
3. Assume you are considering making a loan to Monaco Coach. Should you be concerned that inventory has increased in 2002? What possible explanations could there be for the increase?

Making Financial Decisions

Decision Case 2-4 ***Analysis of Cash Flow for a Small Business*** **LO 8**

DECISION MAKING

Charles, a financial consultant, has been self-employed for two years. His list of clients has grown, and he is earning a reputation as a shrewd investor. Charles rents a small office, uses the pool secretarial services, and has purchased a car that he is depreciating over three years. The following income statements cover Charles's first two years of business:

	Year 1	Year 2
Commissions revenue	$ 25,000	$65,000
Rent	$ 12,000	$12,000
Secretarial services	3,000	9,000
Car expenses, gas, insurance	6,000	6,500
Depreciation	15,000	15,000
Net income	$(11,000)	$22,500

Charles believes that he should earn more than $11,500 for working very hard for two years. He is thinking about going to work for an investment firm where he can earn $40,000 per year. What would you advise Charles to do?

Decision Case 2-5 ***Factors Involved in an Investment Decision*** **LO 9**

DECISION MAKING

As an investor, you are considering purchasing stock in a fast-food restaurant chain. The annual reports of several companies are available for comparison.

Required

Prepare an outline of the steps you would follow to make your comparison. Start by listing the first section that you would read in the financial reports. What would you expect to find there, and why did you choose that section to read first? Continue with the other sections of the financial report.

Many fast-food chains are owned by large conglomerates. What limitation does this create in your comparison? How would you solve it?

Accounting and Ethics: What Would You Do?

ETHICS

Decision Case 2-6 ***The Expenditure Approval Process*** **LO 2**

Roberto is the plant superintendent of a small manufacturing company that is owned by a large corporation. The corporation has a policy that any expenditure over $1,000 must be approved by the chief financial officer in the corporate headquarters. The approval process takes a minimum of three weeks. Roberto would like to order a new labeling machine that is expected to reduce costs and pay for itself in six months. The machine costs $2,200, but Roberto can buy the sales rep's demo for $1,800. Roberto has asked the sales rep to send two separate bills for $900 each.

What would you do if you were the sales rep? Do you agree or disagree with Roberto's actions? What do you think about the corporate policy?

ETHICS

Decision Case 2-7 ***Barbara Applies for a Loan*** **LO 4, 6**

Barbara Bites, owner of Bites of Bagels, a drive-through bagel shop, would like to expand her business from its current one location to a chain of bagel shops. Sales in the bagel shop have been increasing an average of 8 percent each quarter. Profits have been increasing accordingly. Barbara is conservative in spending and a very hard worker. She has an appointment with a banker to apply for a loan to expand the business. To prepare for the appointment, she instructs you, as the chief financial officer and payroll clerk, to copy the quarterly income statements for the past two years but not to include a balance sheet. Barbara already has a substantial loan from another bank. In fact, she has very little of her own money invested in the business.

Required

Before answering the following questions, you may want to refer to Exhibit 1-9 and the related text on pages 28–31. Support each answer with your reasoning.

1. What is the ethical dilemma in this case? Who would be affected and how would they be affected if you follow Barbara's instructions? (Would they benefit? Would they be harmed?) What responsibility do you have in this situation?
2. If the banker does not receive the balance sheet, will he have all of the relevant and reliable information needed for his decision-making process? Why or why not? Will the information provided by Barbara be free from bias?
3. What should you do? If the banker does not receive the balance sheet, has he examined all the information that is useful for his decision regarding the loan? Is the information provided by Barbara *free from bias*? Might anyone be harmed by her accounting decision?

THOMSON ONE Business School Edition Case

Case 2-8 ***Using THOMSON ONE for Monaco Coach Corporation***

In the chapter we saw how both a multiple-step income statement and a classified balance sheet can be useful in measuring company performance. The success of a company as indicated in its financial statements should translate to success in the market for a company's stock in the form of appreciation in its stock price and, if the company chooses, in the form of dividends to the stockholders. We can use THOMSON ONE to obtain information about both Monaco Coach's performance as measured in its financial statements and in its stock price.

Begin by entering the company's ticker symbol, MNC, and then selecting "GO." On the opening screen you will see background information about the company, key financial ratios, and some recent data concerning stock price. To research the company's stock price further, click the "Prices" tab. At the top of the Price Chart, click on the Interactive Chart." To obtain a 1-year chart, go to "Time Frame," click on the down arrow and select "1 year." Then click on "Draw" and a 1-year chart should appear.

We can also find Monaco Coach's most recent financial statements. Near the top of the screen, click on "Financials" and select "Financial Statements." Refer to the comparative statements of earnings, statements of cash flows, and balance sheets.

Based on your use of THOMSON ONE, answer the following questions:

1. What is Monaco Coach's current ratio for the most recent year available? By how much did this measure of liquidity increase or decrease from the prior year?
2. What is Monaco Coach's gross profit ratio and profit margin ratio for the most recent year available? By how much did each of these measures of profitability increase or decrease from the prior year?
3. What has been Monaco Coach's high and low stock price for the most recent year?
4. Does it appear to you that Monaco Coach's stock price during the current period is a reflection of its financial performance as measured by the ratios you computed in **1** and **2** above? Explain your answer.

Fill in your source for industry information:
http://www.__________.com

Monaco Coach and its main competitors:
http://www.monaco-online.com
http://www.__________.com
http://www.__________.com

Solutions to Key Terms Quiz

6	Understandability (p. 61)	10	Current liability (p. 69)
3	Relevance (p. 61)	16	Liquidity (p. 70)
9	Reliability (p. 62)	12	Working capital (p. 70)
14	Comparability (p. 62)	8	Current ratio (p. 71)
19	Depreciation (p. 62)	1	Single-step income statement (p. 72)
17	Consistency (p. 63)	4	Multiple-step income statement (p. 73)
2	Materiality (p. 64)	18	Gross profit (p. 73)
5	Conservatism (p. 64)	7	Gross profit ratio (p. 74)
11	Operating cycle (p. 65)	13	Profit margin (p. 74)
15	Current asset (p. 67)		

Chapter 3

Processing Accounting Information

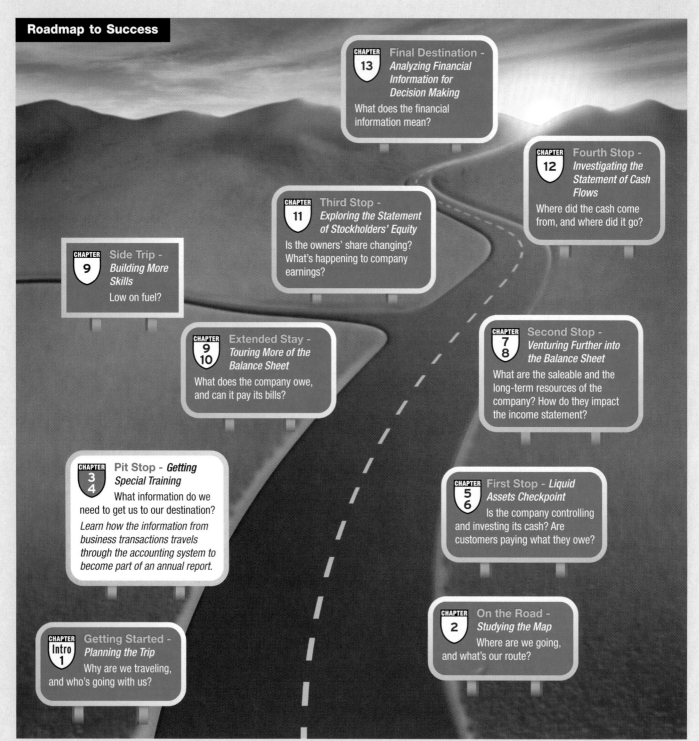

Roadmap to Success

CHAPTER Intro 1 — **Getting Started -** *Planning the Trip*
Why are we traveling, and who's going with us?

CHAPTER 2 — **On the Road -** *Studying the Map*
Where are we going, and what's our route?

CHAPTER 3 4 — **Pit Stop -** ***Getting Special Training***
What information do we need to get us to our destination?
Learn how the information from business transactions travels through the accounting system to become part of an annual report.

CHAPTER 5 6 — **First Stop -** ***Liquid Assets Checkpoint***
Is the company controlling and investing its cash? Are customers paying what they owe?

CHAPTER 7 8 — **Second Stop -** *Venturing Further into the Balance Sheet*
What are the saleable and the long-term resources of the company? How do they impact the income statement?

CHAPTER 9 10 — **Extended Stay -** *Touring More of the Balance Sheet*
What does the company owe, and can it pay its bills?

CHAPTER 9 — **Side Trip -** *Building More Skills*
Low on fuel?

CHAPTER 11 — **Third Stop -** *Exploring the Statement of Stockholders' Equity*
Is the owners' share changing? What's happening to company earnings?

CHAPTER 12 — **Fourth Stop -** *Investigating the Statement of Cash Flows*
Where did the cash come from, and where did it go?

CHAPTER 13 — **Final Destination -** *Analyzing Financial Information for Decision Making*
What does the financial information mean?

Focus on Financial Results

Brand names are the lifeblood of any consumer product company, and General Mills boasts some of the most recognizable names in the world. Who cannot identify with Cheerios® and Wheaties® in General Mills' Big G division? Or is there anyone who is not familiar with the name Betty Crocker®? Finally, the company leads the U.S. yogurt market with products such as Yoplait® and Colombo®.

Being a successful company requires growth, and General Mills is no exception to this rule. Sales, as shown on the accompanying income statement (or statement of earnings), increased 32 percent to $10.5 billion in the 2003 fiscal year. Companies use different strategies to grow, with one of the most popular being the acquisition of other businesses. The latter approach certainly contributed to General Mills' impressive sales in 2003. This represented the first full year of operations after the company's acquisition of Pillsbury® from Diageo plc. To its already impressive list of brands, the company added names like Green Giant®, Old El Paso®, and Haagen-Dazs®.

Adding new products to a consumer foods company may help to grow sales but is not a guarantee that a company's bottom line will improve. With the acquisition of another company comes additional recurring costs of running those businesses as well as the costs associated with integrating operations. The 2003 income statement shows that General Mills has managed to improve both its top and bottom lines since the acquisition. Net earnings more than doubled to a very impressive $917 million in 2003. What remains to be seen is whether the consumer foods powerhouse can continue to control costs and translate sales growth to its bottom line.

General Mills' 2003 Annual Report

General Mills, Inc.
Consolidated Statements of Earnings

In Millions, Except per Share Data; Fiscal Year Ended	May 25, 2003	May 26, 2002	May 27, 2001
Net Sales	**$10,506**	$7,949	$5,450
Costs and Expenses:			
Cost of sales	**6,109**	4,662	2,841
Selling, general and administrative	**2,472**	2,070	1,393
Interest, net	**547**	416	206
Restructuring and other exit costs	**62**	134	12
Total Costs and Expenses	**9,190**	7,282	4,452
Earnings before Taxes and Earnings from Joint Ventures	**1,316**	667	998
Income Taxes	**460**	239	350
Earnings from Joint Ventures	**61**	33	17
Earnings before Cumulative Effect of Change in Accounting Principle	**917**	461	665
Cumulative Effect of Change in Accounting Principle	**—**	(3)	—
Net Earnings	**$ 917**	$ 438	$ 665
Earnings per Share—Basic:			
Earnings before cumulative effect of change in Accounting Principle	**$2.49**	$1.39	$2.34
Cumulative effect of change in Accounting Principle	**—**	(0.01)	—
Earnings per Share—Basic	**$2.49**	$1.38	$2.34
Average Number of Common Shares	**369**	331	284
Earnings per Share—Diluted:			
Earnings before Cumulative Effect of Change in Accounting Principle	**$2.43**	$1.35	$2.28
Cumulative Effect of Change in Accounting Principle	**—**	(0.01)	—
Earnings per Share—Diluted	**$2.43**	$1.34	$2.28
Averge Number of Common Shares—Assuming Dilution	**378**	342	292

See accompanying notes to consolidated financial statements.

http://www.generalmills.com

You're in the Driver's Seat

General Mills' income statement, pictured here, tells a story of the need for generating growth while at the same time keeping a watchful eye over costs. How can the accounting system help you process the information needed to measure sales and various costs and expenses? As you study the accounting process introduced in this chapter, think about how the tools you are learning would be used to record the usual transactions of most companies.

LEARNING OBJECTIVES

After studying this chapter, you should be able to:

LO 1 Explain the difference between an external and an internal event. (p. 109)

LO 2 Explain the role of source documents in an accounting system. (p. 110)

LO 3 Analyze the effects of transactions on the accounting equation. (p. 111)

LO 4 Describe the use of the account and the general ledger to accumulate amounts of financial statement items. (p. 117)

LO 5 Explain the rules of debits and credits (Appendix). (p. 123)

LO 6 Explain the purposes of a journal and the posting process (Appendix). (p. 128)

LO 7 Explain the purpose of a trial balance (Appendix). (p. 130)

WHAT EXTERNAL DECISION MAKERS WANT TO KNOW ABOUT HOW ACCOUNTING INFORMATION IS PROCESSED

DECISION MAKING

In Chapter 2 we examined financial statements in detail, including a classified balance and a multiple-step income statement. We saw how financial statements and other elements in an annual report provide useful information in making decisions. In addition to understanding how to interpret and analyze the statements, decision makers must understand how the information that is reported in the statements is processed. To be successful, decision makers must:

▶ *ASK ESSENTIAL QUESTIONS*

- What types of events are recognized in the statements? Are all activities that affect a company reported somewhere in the financial statements?
- What is the evidence used in an accounting system to record the various transactions? What source documents support the amounts that appear in the statements?
- How are transactions recorded in an accounting system? And, how do the amounts recorded find their way into the financial statements?

▶ *FIND BASIC INFORMATION*

The balance sheet, the income statement, and the statement of cash flows, along with the supporting notes, are the key sources of information about a company's resources and the changes in those resources. In this chapter we explore how an accounting system is used to develop the information found in these statements and that is needed to make business decisions.

▶ *UNDERSTAND ACCOUNTING PRINCIPLES*

To use the information produced by an accounting system, decision makers must understand the underlying accounting principles (GAAP) that have been applied to create the reported information. In preparing financial statements, accountants consider:

- Which events are measurable and should be recognized, and
- The cost principle.

▶ *INTERPRET ANALYTICAL INFORMATION*

We began in Chapter 2 to consider how decision makers such as bankers and stockholders can interpret the financial statements with the help of various analytical tools such as ratios. Once we have seen how the accounting information is processed in this chapter, we will return to a consideration of the ways in which these parties can analyze the statements in making their decisions.

ECONOMIC EVENTS: THE BASIS FOR RECORDING TRANSACTIONS

LO 1 Explain the difference between an external and an internal event.

Many different types of economic events affect an entity during the year. A sale is made to a customer. Inventory is purchased from a supplier. A loan is taken out at the bank. A fire destroys a warehouse. A new contract is signed with the union. In short, "An **event** is a happening of consequence to an entity."[1]

Event A happening of consequence to an entity.

External and Internal Events

External event An event involving interaction between an entity and its environment.

Internal event An event occurring entirely within an entity.

Transaction Any event that is recognized in a set of financial statements.

Two types of events affect an entity: internal and external. An **external event** "involves interaction between the entity and its environment."[2] For example, the *purchase* of raw material from a supplier is an external event, as is the *sale* of inventory to a customer. An **internal event** occurs entirely within the entity. The *transfer* of raw material into production is an internal event, as is the use of a piece of equipment. We will use the term **transaction** to refer to any event, external or internal, that is recognized in a set of financial statements.[3]

INTERNAL DECISION

What is necessary to recognize an event in the records? Are all economic events recognized as transactions by the accountant? The answers to these questions involve the concept of *measurement*. An event must be measured to be recognized. Certain events are relatively easy to measure: the payroll for the week, the amount of inventory destroyed by an earthquake, or the sales for the day. Not all events that affect an entity can be measured *reliably*, however. For example, how does a manufacturer of breakfast cereal measure the effect of a drought on the price of wheat? A company hires a new chief executive. How can it reliably measure the value of the new officer to the company? There is no definitive answer to the measurement problem in accounting. It is a continuing challenge to the accounting profession and something we will return to throughout the text.

From Concept to Practice 3.1

Reading General Mills' Financial Statements

General Mills uses a variety of ingredients in making its products. Is the purchase of oats an internal or external event? The company subsequently uses oats to make Cheerios®. Is this an internal or external event?

[1] *Statement of Financial Accounting Concepts (SFAC) No. 3,* "Elements of Financial Statements of Business Enterprises" (Stamford, Conn.: Financial Accounting Standards Board, 1982), par. 65.

[2] *SFAC No. 3.*

[3] Technically, a *transaction* is defined by the Financial Accounting Standards Board as a special kind of external event in which the entity exchanges something of value with an outsider. Because the term *transaction* is used in practice to refer to any event that is recognized in the statements, we will use this broader definition.

Source documents like these receipts are records that document transactions that the business engages in. Shown here are an employee's travel expense receipts, which will be turned in to the company for reimbursement. Other source documents may be contracts, lease agreements, invoices, delivery vouchers, check stubs, and deposit slips.

The Role of Source Documents in Recording Transactions

LO 2 Explain the role of source documents in an accounting system.

Source document A piece of paper that is used as evidence to record a transaction.

The first step in the recording process is *identification.* A business needs a systematic method for recognizing events as transactions. A **source document** provides the evidence needed in an accounting system to record a transaction. Source documents take many different forms. An invoice received from a supplier is the source document for a purchase of inventory on credit. A cash register tape is the source document used by a retailer to recognize a cash sale. The payroll department sends the accountant the time cards for the week as the necessary documentation to record wages.

Not all recognizable events are supported by a standard source document. For certain events, some form of documentation must be generated. For example, no standard source document exists to recognize the financial consequences from a fire or the settlement of a lawsuit. Documentation is just as important for these types of events as it is for standard, recurring transactions.

Analyzing the Effects of Transactions on the Accounting Equation

LO 3 Analyze the effects of transactions on the accounting equation.

Economic events are the basis for recording transactions in an accounting system. For every transaction, it is essential to analyze its effect on the accounting equation:

Assets = Liabilities + Owners' Equity

We will now consider a series of events and their recognition as transactions for a hypothetical corporation, Glengarry Health Club. The transactions are for the month of January 2004, the first month of operations for the new business.

(1) *Issuance of capital stock.* The company is started when Mary Jo Kovach and Irene McGuinness file articles of incorporation with the state to obtain a charter. Each invests $50,000 in the business. In return, each receives 5,000 shares of capital stock. Thus, at this point, each of them owns 50% of the outstanding stock of the company and has a claim to 50% of its assets. The effect of this transaction on the accounting equation is to increase both assets and owners' equity:

	Assets					= Liabilities		+ Owners' Equity + Revenues − Expenses	
TRANS. NO.	**CASH**	**ACCT. REC.**	**EQUIP.**	**BLDG.**	**LAND**	**ACCT. PAY.**	**NOTES PAY.**	**CAPITAL STOCK**	**RET. EARN.**
1	$100,000							$100,000	
Totals			$100,000					$100,000	

As you see, each side of the accounting equation increases by $100,000. Cash is increased, and because the owners contributed this amount, their claim to the assets is increased in the form of Capital Stock.

(2) *Acquisition of property in exchange for a note.* The company buys a piece of property for $200,000. The seller agrees to accept a five-year promissory note. The note is given by the health club to the seller and is a written promise to repay the principal amount of the loan at the end of five years. To the company, the promissory note is a liability. The property consists of land valued at $50,000 and a newly constructed building valued at $150,000. The effect of this transaction on the accounting equation is to increase both assets and liabilities by $200,000:

	Assets					= Liabilities		+ Owners' Equity + Revenues − Expenses	
TRANS. NO.	**CASH**	**ACCT. REC.**	**EQUIP.**	**BLDG.**	**LAND**	**ACCT. PAY.**	**NOTES PAY.**	**CAPITAL STOCK**	**RET. EARN.**
Bal.	$100,000							$100,000	
2				$150,000	$50,000		$200,000		
Bal.	$100,000			$150,000	$50,000		$200,000	$100,000	
Totals			$300,000					$300,000	

(3) *Acquisition of equipment on an open account.* Mary Jo and Irene contact an equipment supplier and buy $20,000 of exercise equipment: treadmills, barbells, and stationary bicycles. The supplier agrees to accept payment in full in 30 days. The health club has acquired an asset and at the same time incurred a liability:

	Assets					= Liabilities		+ Owners' Equity + Revenues − Expenses	
TRANS. NO.	**CASH**	**ACCT. REC.**	**EQUIP.**	**BLDG.**	**LAND**	**ACCT. PAY.**	**NOTES PAY.**	**CAPITAL STOCK**	**RET. EARN.**
Bal.	$100,000			$150,000	$50,000		$200,000	$100,000	
3			$20,000			$20,000			
Bal.	$100,000		$20,000	$150,000	$50,000	$20,000	$200,000	$100,000	
Totals			$320,000					$320,000	

(**4**) *Sale of monthly memberships on account.* The owners open their doors for business. During January, they sell 300 monthly club memberships for $50 each, or a total of $15,000. The members have until the 10th of the following month to pay. Glengarry does not have cash from the new members but instead has a promise from each member to pay cash in the future. The promise from a customer to pay an amount owed is an asset called an *account receivable.* The other side of this transaction is an increase in the owners' equity in the business. In other words, assets have increased by $15,000 without any increase in a liability or decrease in another asset. The increase in owners' equity indicates that the owners' residual interest in the assets of the business has increased by this amount. More specifically, an inflow of assets resulting from the sale of goods and services by a business is called *revenue,* and in this case, membership revenue. Note in the accounting equation below that $15,000 is added to the column head "Revenues − Expenses:"

	Assets					= Liabilities		+ Owners' Equity + Revenues − Expenses		
TRANS. NO.	**CASH**	**ACCT. REC.**	**EQUIP.**	**BLDG.**	**LAND**	**ACCT. PAY.**	**NOTES PAY.**	**CAPITAL STOCK**	**RET. EARN.**	
Bal.	$100,000		$20,000	$150,000	$50,000	$20,000	$200,000	$100,000		
4		$15,000								$15,000
Bal.	$100,000	$15,000	$20,000	$150,000	$50,000	$20,000	$200,000	$100,000		$15,000
Totals			$335,000						$335,000	

The last column in the equation is treated as an extension of, or addition to, owners' equity on the right side of the accounting equation. This is because the inflow of cash is due to the sale of memberships, and therefore, the owners' claims to the assets of the business have increased by $15,000. More specifically, the retained earnings portion of owners' equity has increased by this amount. However, rather than treat the revenue as a direct increase in retained earnings, we account for it separately. Later we will see how the excess of revenue over expense makes its way into retained earnings.

(**5**) *Sale of court time for cash.* In addition to memberships, Glengarry sells court time. Court fees are paid at the time of use and amount to $5,000 for the first month:

	Assets					= Liabilities		+ Owners' Equity + Revenues − Expenses		
TRANS. NO.	**CASH**	**ACCT. REC.**	**EQUIP.**	**BLDG.**	**LAND**	**ACCT. PAY.**	**NOTES PAY.**	**CAPITAL STOCK**	**RET. EARN.**	
Bal.	$100,000	$15,000	$20,000	$150,000	$50,000	$20,000	$200,000	$100,000		$15,000
5	5,000									5,000
Bal.	$105,000	$15,000	$20,000	$150,000	$50,000	$20,000	$200,000	$100,000		$20,000
Totals			$340,000						$340,000	

The only difference between this transaction and (**4**) is that cash is received rather than a promise to pay at a later date. Both transactions result in an increase in an asset and an increase in the owners' claim to the assets in the form of revenue. In both cases, there is an inflow of assets, in the form of either Accounts Receivable or Cash. Thus, in both cases, the company has earned revenue.

(**6**) *Payment of wages and salaries.* The wages and salaries for the first month amount to $10,000. The payment of this amount results in a decrease in Cash and a decrease in the owners' claim on the assets. More specifically, an outflow of assets resulting from the sale of goods or services is called an *expense.* In this case, the club recognizes 10,000 of *wages and salaries* expense. The effect of this transaction is to decrease both sides of the accounting equation:

	Assets					= Liabilities		+ Owners' Equity + Revenues − Expenses	
TRANS. NO.	**CASH**	**ACCT. REC.**	**EQUIP.**	**BLDG.**	**LAND**	**ACCT. PAY.**	**NOTES PAY.**	**CAPITAL STOCK**	**RET. EARN.**
Bal.	$105,000	$15,000	$20,000	$150,000	$50,000	$20,000	$200,000	$100,000	$20,000
6	−10,000								−10,000
Bal.	$ 95,000	$15,000	$20,000	$150,000	$50,000	$20,000	$200,000	$100,000	$10,000
Totals			$330,000					$330,000	

(7) *Payment of utilities.* The cost of utilities for the first month is $3,000. Glengarry pays this amount in cash. Both the utilities and the salaries and wages are expenses, and they have the same effect on the accounting equation. Cash is decreased, accompanied by a corresponding decrease in the right side of the equation due to the expense recognized:

	Assets					= Liabilities		+ Owners' Equity + Revenues − Expenses	
TRANS. NO.	**CASH**	**ACCT. REC.**	**EQUIP.**	**BLDG.**	**LAND**	**ACCT. PAY.**	**NOTES PAY.**	**CAPITAL STOCK**	**RET. EARN.**
Bal.	$95,000	$15,000	$20,000	$150,000	$50,000	$20,000	$200,000	$100,000	$10,000
7	−3,000								−3,000
Bal.	$92,000	$15,000	$20,000	$150,000	$50,000	$20,000	$200,000	$100,000	$ 7,000
Totals			$327,000					$327,000	

(8) *Collection of accounts receivable.* Even though the January monthly memberships are not due until the 10th of the following month, some of the members pay their bills by the end of January. The amount received from members in payment of their accounts is $4,000. The effect of the collection of an open account is to increase Cash and decrease Accounts Receivable:

	Assets					= Liabilities		+ Owners' Equity + Revenues − Expenses	
TRANS. NO.	**CASH**	**ACCT. REC.**	**EQUIP.**	**BLDG.**	**LAND**	**ACCT. PAY.**	**NOTES PAY.**	**CAPITAL STOCK**	**RET. EARN.**
Bal.	$92,000	$15,000	$20,000	$150,000	$50,000	$20,000	$200,000	$100,000	$7,000
8	4,000	−4,000							
Bal.	$96,000	$11,000	$20,000	$150,000	$50,000	$20,000	$200,000	$100,000	$7,000
Totals			$327,000					$327,000	

This is the first transaction we have seen that affects only one side of the accounting equation. In fact, the company simply traded assets: Accounts Receivable for Cash. Thus, note that the totals for the accounting equation remain at $327,000. Also note that Retained Earnings is not affected by this transaction because revenue was recognized earlier, in **(4)**, when Accounts Receivable was increased.

(9) *Payment of dividends.* At the end of the month, Mary Jo and Irene, acting on behalf of Glengarry Health Club, decide to pay a dividend of $1,000 on the shares of stock owned by each of them, or $2,000 in total. The effect of this dividend is to decrease both Cash and Retained Earnings. That is, the company is returning cash to the owners, based on the profitable operations of the business for the first month. The transaction not only reduces Cash but also decreases the owners' claims on the assets of the company. Dividends are not an expense but rather a direct reduction of Retained Earnings. The effect on the accounting equation follows:

		Assets				= Liabilities		+ Owners' Equity + Revenues − Expenses		
TRANS. NO.	CASH	ACCT. REC.	EQUIP.	BLDG.	LAND	ACCT. PAY.	NOTES PAY.	CAPITAL STOCK	RET. EARN.	
Bal.	$96,000	$11,000	$20,000	$150,000	$50,000	$20,000	$200,000	$100,000		$7,000
9	−2,000								−2,000	
Bal.	$94,000	$11,000	$20,000	$150,000	$50,000	$20,000	$200,000	$100,000	−2,000	$7,000
Totals			$325,000						$325,000	

The Cost Principle An important principle governs the accounting for both the exercise equipment in **(3)** and the building and land in **(2)**. The *cost principle* requires that we record an asset at the cost to acquire it and continue to show this amount on all balance sheets until we dispose of the asset. With a few exceptions, an asset is not carried at its market value but at its original cost. Why not show the land on future balance sheets at its market value? Although this might seem more appropriate in certain instances, the subjectivity inherent in determining market values is a major reason behind the practice of carrying assets at their historical cost. The cost of an asset can be verified by an independent observer and is much more *objective* than market value.

Two-Minute Review

Assume that on February 1 Glengarry buys additional exercise equipment for $10,000 in cash.

1. *Indicate which two accounts are affected and the increase or decrease in each.*
2. *What will be the total dollar amount of each of the two sides of the accounting equation after this transaction is recorded?*

Answers on page 132.

Companies engage in transactions in many ways. The company from whom this woman is ordering supports sales transactions over the phone using a credit card number. A sales representative may be inputting the card number and the order information into an order database. The company links its order-processing system and other business systems to this customer input.

© PETER BECK/CORBIS

Balance Sheet and Income Statement for the Health Club

To summarize, Exhibit 3-1 indicates the effect of each transaction on the accounting equation, specifically the individual items increased or decreased by each transaction. Note the *dual* effect of each transaction. At least two items were involved in each transaction. For example, the initial investment by the owners resulted in an increase in an asset and an increase in Capital Stock. The payment of the dividends caused a decrease in an asset and a decrease in Retained Earnings.

You can now see the central idea behind the accounting equation: Even though individual transactions may change the amount and composition of the assets and liabilities, the *equation* must always balance *for* each transaction, and the *balance sheet* must balance *after* each transaction.

An income statement for Glengarry is shown in Exhibit 3-2. An income statement summarizes the revenues and expenses of a company for a period of time. In our example, the statement is for the month of January, as indicated on the third line of the heading of the statement. Glengarry earned revenues from two sources: (1) memberships and (2) court fees. Two types of expenses were incurred: (1) salaries and wages and (2) utilities. The difference between the total revenues of $20,000 and the total expenses of $13,000 is the net income for the month of $7,000.

Glengarry's statement of retained earnings is shown in Exhibit 3-3 on page 116. Recall from Chapter 1 that a statement of retained earnings provides a bridge between

Exhibit 3-1 Glengarry Health Club Transactions for the Month of January

	Assets					=	Liabilities	+	Owners' Equity	+ Revenues − Expenses	
TRANS. NO.	CASH	ACCOUNTS RECEIVABLE	EQUIPMENT	BUILDING	LAND		ACCOUNTS PAYABLE	NOTES PAYABLE	CAPITAL STOCK	RETAINED EARNINGS	
1	$100,000								$100,000		
2				$150,000	$50,000			$200,000			
Bal.	$100,000			$150,000	$50,000			$200,000	$100,000		
3			$20,000				$20,000				
Bal.	$100,000		$20,000	$150,000	$50,000		$20,000	$200,000	$100,000		
4		$15,000									$ 15,000
Bal.	$100,000	$15,000	$20,000	$150,000	$50,000		$20,000	$200,000	$100,000		$ 15,000
5	5,000										5,000
Bal.	$105,000	$15,000	$20,000	$150,000	$50,000		$20,000	$200,000	$100,000		$ 20,000
6	− 10,000										−10,000
Bal.	$ 95,000	$15,000	$20,000	$150,000	$50,000		$20,000	$200,000	$100,000		$ 10,000
7	− 3,000										− 3,000
Bal.	$ 92,000	$15,000	$20,000	$150,000	$50,000		$20,000	$200,000	$100,000		$ 7,000
8	4,000	− 4,000									
Bal.	$ 96,000	$11,000	$20,000	$150,000	$50,000		$20,000	$200,000	$100,000		$ 7,000
9	− 2,000									−2,000	
Bal.	$ 94,000	$11,000	$20,000	$150,000	$50,000		$20,000	$200,000	$100,000	$−2,000	$ 7,000

Total assets: $325,000 — Total liabilities and owners' equity: $325,000

a company's income statement and its balance sheet. Because the health club only began operating in January of 2004, the beginning balance in retained earnings is zero. January's net income of $7,000, as reported on the income statement in Exhibit 3-2, is added to the beginning balance, and the dividends of $2,000 are deducted. The reason that the dividends appear directly on the statement of retained earnings in Exhibit 3-3, rather than on the income statement, is because they are a *distribution* of net income for the period, not a *determinant* of net income as are expenses.

A balance sheet for the business appears in Exhibit 3-4. Note that the ending retained earnings from the statement of retained earnings appears on the right side of the balance sheet. All of the other information needed to prepare this statement is available in Exhibit 3-1. The balances at the bottom of this exhibit are entered on the balance sheet, with assets on the left side and liabilities and owners' equity on the right side.

We have seen how transactions are analyzed and how they affect the accounting equation and ultimately the financial statements. While the approach we took in analyzing the nine transactions of the Glengarry Health Club was manageable, can you

Exhibit 3-2

Income Statement for Glengarry Health Club

GLENGARRY HEALTH CLUB
INCOME STATEMENT
FOR THE MONTH ENDED JANUARY 31, 2004

Revenues:		
Memberships	$15,000	
Court fees	5,000	$20,000
Expenses:		
Salaries and wages	$10,000	
Utilities	3,000	13,000
Net income		$ 7,000

Exhibit 3-3

Statement of Retained Earnings for Glengarry Health Club

GLENGARRY HEALTH CLUB STATEMENT OF RETAINED EARNINGS FOR THE MONTH ENDED JANUARY 31, 2004	
Beginning balance, January 1, 2004	$ 0
Add: Net income for January	7,000
Deduct: Dividends for January	2,000
Ending balance, January 31, 2004	$5,000

Exhibit 3-4

Balance Sheet for Glengarry Health Club

GLENGARRY HEALTH CLUB
BALANCE SHEET
JANUARY 31, 2004

Assets		Liabilities and Owners' Equity	
Cash	$ 94,000	Accounts payable	$ 20,000
Accounts receivable	11,000	Notes payable	200,000
Equipment	20,000	Capital stock	100,000
Building	150,000	Retained earnings	5,000
Land	50,000	Total liabilities	
Total assets	$325,000	and owners' equity	$325,000

imagine using this type of analysis for a company with *thousands* of transactions in any one month? We now turn our attention to various *tools* used by the accountant to process a large volume of transactions effectively and efficiently.

Business Strategy

As mentioned in the chapter opener, General Mills completed the most significant transaction in its history with the acquisition of Pillsbury, another leading consumer foods company. The transaction was celebrated at the New York Stock Exchange on November 1, 2001, when the CEO of the new global General Mills was invited to ring the opening bell. The Pillsbury Doughboy™, the Trix Rabbit™, and other company mascots handed out "blue chip" cookies to traders on the floor.

When companies decide to grow by acquiring other businesses, they follow a variety of paths. Some choose to branch out into industries much different than their core business. At times this approach has been successful, and at other times the results have been disastrous. General Mills followed the more conventional route by acquiring another company that made similar products. The existing knowledge of the business, along with the ability to consolidate production facilities, are leading factors in the choice to go this route.

The strategic acquisition of Pillsbury has already begun to pay off for General Mills. According to Chairman and Chief Executive Officer Steve Sanger, the company's results in 2003, the first full year after the acquisition, met or exceeded performance objectives for the year. Probably the most impressive statistic in these 2003 results was the 6 percent total return to stockholders, compared to a negative 12 percent return for the S&P 500 index during the same time period. The next few annual reports will tell the story as to whether General Mills can continue to offer superior returns to stockholders who choose to invest in its stable of leading brand names in the consumer foods business. ■

Source: General Mills' 2001 and 2003 annual reports and Web site.

THE ACCOUNT: THE BASIC UNIT FOR RECORDING TRANSACTIONS

LO 4 Describe the use of the account and the general ledger to accumulate amounts of financial statement items.

An **account** is the record used to accumulate monetary amounts for each asset, liability, and component of owners' equity, such as Capital Stock, Retained Earnings, and Dividends. It is the basic recording unit for each element in the financial statements. Each revenue and expense has its own account. In the Glengarry Health Club example, ten accounts were used: Cash, Accounts Receivable, Equipment, Building, Land, Accounts Payable, Notes Payable, Capital Stock, Retained Earnings, and Revenues minus Expenses. In the real world, a company might have hundreds, or even thousands, of individual accounts.

Account Record used to accumulate amounts for each individual asset, liability, revenue, expense, and component of owners' equity.

No two entities have exactly the same set of accounts. To a certain extent, the accounts used by a company depend on its business. For example, a manufacturer normally has three inventory accounts: Raw Materials, Work in Process, and Finished Goods. A retailer uses just one account for inventory, a Merchandise Inventory account. A service business has no need for an inventory account.

INTERNAL DECISION

From Concept to Practice 3.2

Reading the Balance Sheets of Winnebago Industries and Monaco Coach Corporation

How many current asset accounts does each company report on its balance sheet? What is the dollar amount of the largest of these?

Chart of Accounts

Companies need a way to organize the large number of accounts they use to record transactions. A **chart of accounts** is a numerical list of all of the accounts an entity uses. The numbering system is a convenient way to identify accounts. For example, all asset accounts might be numbered from 100 to 199, liability accounts from 200 to 299, equity accounts from 300 to 399, revenues from 400 to 499, and expenses from 500 to 599. A chart of accounts for a hypothetical company, Widescreen Theaters Corporation, is shown in Exhibit 3-5. Note the division of account numbers within each of the financial statement categories. Within the asset category, the various cash accounts are numbered from 100 to 109, receivables from 110 to 119, etc. Not all of the numbers are currently assigned. For example, only three of the available nine numbers are currently utilized for cash accounts. This allows the company to add accounts as needed.

Chart of accounts A numerical list of all the accounts used by a company.

The General Ledger

Companies store their accounts in different ways, depending on their accounting system. In a manual system, a separate card or sheet is used to record the activity in each account. A **general ledger** is simply the file or book that contains the accounts.[4] For example, the general ledger for Widescreen Theaters Corporation might consist of a file of cards in a cabinet, with a card for each of the accounts listed in the chart of accounts.

General ledger A book, file, hard drive, or other device containing all the accounts.

In today's business world, most companies have an automated accounting system. The computer is ideally suited for the job of processing vast amounts of data rapidly. *All of the tools discussed in this chapter are as applicable to computerized systems as they are to manual systems. It is merely the appearance of the tools that differs between manual and computerized systems.* For example, the ledger in an automated system might be contained on a computer file server rather than stored in a file cabinet. Throughout the book, we will use a manual system to explain the various tools. The reason is that it is easier to illustrate and visualize the tools in a manual system. However, all of the ideas apply just as well to a computerized system of accounting.

INTERNAL DECISION

[4]In addition to a general ledger, many companies maintain subsidiary ledgers. For example, an accounts receivable subsidiary ledger contains a separate account for each customer. The use of a subsidiary ledger for Accounts Receivable is discussed further in Chapter 6.

Exhibit 3-5

Chart of Accounts for a Theater

100–199: ASSETS
  100–109: Cash
    101: Cash, Checking, Second National Bank
    102: Cash, Savings, Third State Bank
    103: Cash, Change, or Petty Cash Fund (coin and currency)
  110–119: Receivables
    111: Accounts Receivable
    112: Due from Employees
    113: Notes Receivable
  120–129: Prepaid Assets
    121: Cleaning Supplies
    122: Prepaid Insurance
  130–139: Property, Plant, and Equipment
    131: Land
    132: Theater Buildings
    133: Projection Equipment
    134: Furniture and Fixtures
200–299: LIABILITIES
  200–209: Short-Term Liabilities
    201: Accounts Payable
    202: Wages and Salaries Payable
    203: Taxes Payable
      203.1: Income Taxes Payable
      203.2: Sales Taxes Payable
      203.3: Unemployment Taxes Payable
    204: Short-Term Notes Payable
      204.1: Six-Month Note Payable to First State Bank
  210–219: Long-Term Liabilities
    211: Bonds Payable, due in 2013
300–399: STOCKHOLDERS' EQUITY
    301: Preferred Stock
    302: Common Stock
    303: Retained Earnings
400–499: REVENUES
    401: Tickets
    402: Video Rentals
    403: Concessions
    404: Interest
500–599: EXPENSES
  500–509: Rentals
    501: Films
    502: Videos
  510–519: Concessions
    511: Candy
    512: Soda
    513: Popcorn
  520–529: Wages and Salaries
    521: Hourly Employees
    522: Salaries
  530–539: Utilities
    531: Heat
    532: Electric
    533: Water
  540–549: Advertising
    541: Newspaper
    542: Radio
  550–559: Taxes
    551: Income Taxes
    552: Unemployment Taxes

PROCESSING ACCOUNTING INFORMATION

In this chapter, we analyzed the effects of the transactions of Glengarry Health Club on the accounting equation. Because the accounting equation is the basis for financial statements, the ability to analyze transactions in terms of their effect on the equation is an essential skill to master. In the appendix to this chapter, tools used by the accountant to effectively and efficiently process large volumes of transactions during the period are examined. One of the key tools used by the accountant is a system of debits and credits.

The emphasis throughout this book is on the *use* of financial statements to make decisions, as opposed to the tools used by accountants to process information. Therefore, in future chapters, our emphasis will not be on the accountant's various tools, such as debits and credits, but on the effects of transactions on the accounting equation and financial statements. Recall transaction 4 for the Glengarry Health Club, as it was originally summarized in Exhibit 3-1:

	Assets					= Liabilities		+ Owners' Equity + Revenues − Expenses	
NO.	CASH	ACCT. REC.	EQUIP.	BLDG.	LAND	ACCT. PAY.	NOTES PAY.	CAPITAL STOCK	RET. EARN.
4		$15,000							$15,000

Recall also that the sale of memberships increased both accounts receivable and revenue. In future chapters, we will use a variation of the format in Exhibit 3-1 to demonstrate the effects of various transactions on the accounting equation. For example,the sale of memberships would appear as follows in this version of the equation:

BALANCE SHEET						INCOME STATEMENT
ASSETS	=	LIABILITIES	+	OWNERS' EQUITY	+	REVENUES − EXPENSES
Accounts Receivable 15,000						Membership Revenue 15,000

Note two important changes in this version of the equation. First,rather than having a separate column for each individual financial statement item, the items are simply listed under the appropriate categories.For example, this transaction results in an increase in Accounts Receivable,which is shown in the assets category. Second, in this expanded version of the accounting equation, the income statement is viewed as an extension of the balance sheet. As you are aware, revenues do result in an increase in retained earnings and thus owners' equity, but they must first be recorded on the income statement.

To illustrate one additional transaction with this new format,recall transaction 6 for Glengarry in which $10,000 was paid in wages and salaries. The effect of this transaction on the accounting equation is:

BALANCE SHEET						INCOME STATEMENT
ASSETS	=	LIABILITIES	+	OWNERS' EQUITY	+	REVENUES − EXPENSES
Cash (10,000)						Wage and Salary Expense (10,000)

Exhibit 3-6 summarizes how the new transaction effects equation will be used in Chapters 4–13.

Exhibit 3-6 Using the Transaction Effects Equation

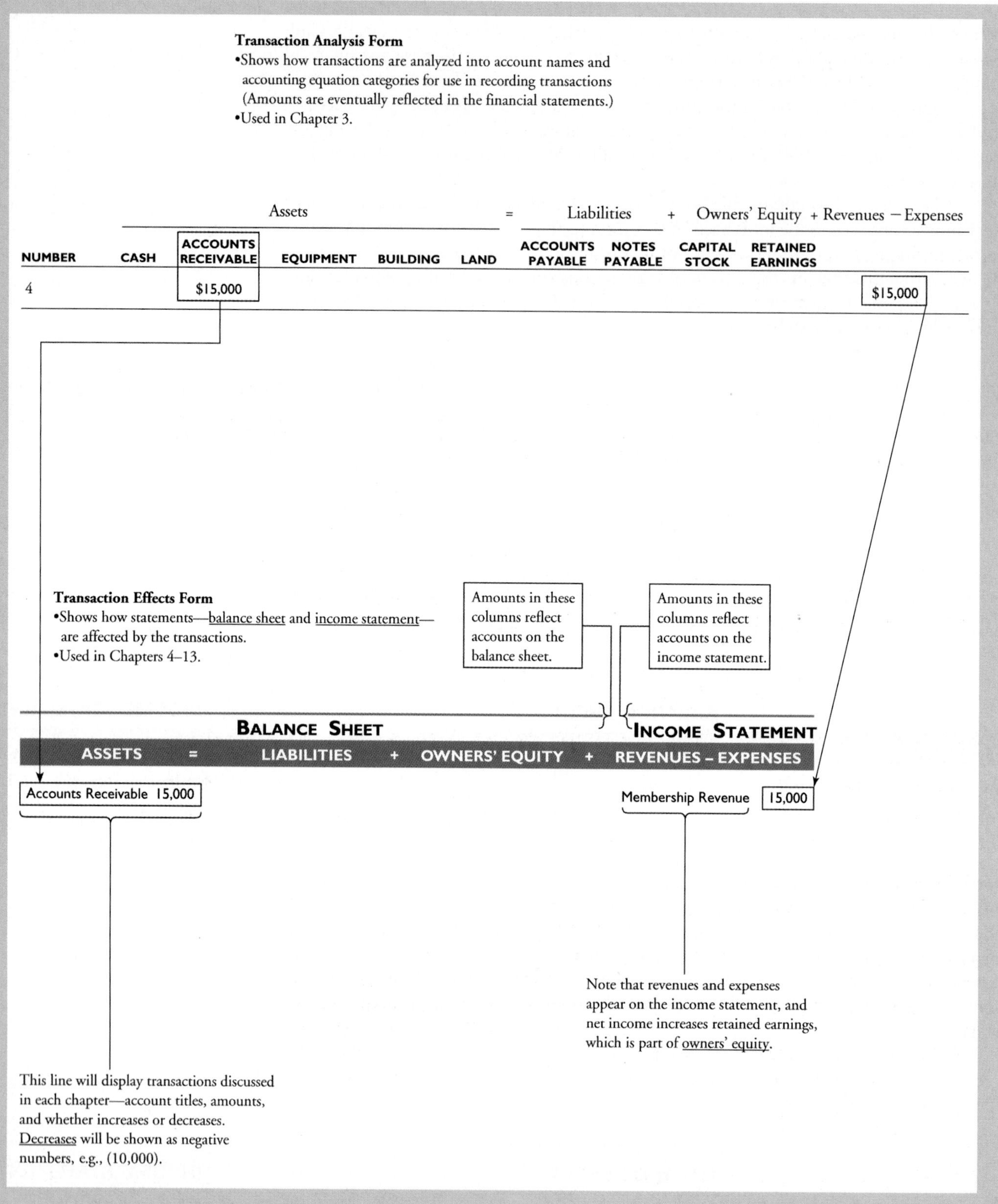

Transaction Analysis Form
•Shows how transactions are analyzed into account names and accounting equation categories for use in recording transactions (Amounts are eventually reflected in the financial statements.)
•Used in Chapter 3.
Assets = Liabilities + Owners' Equity + Revenues − Expenses
NUMBER
CASH
ACCOUNTS RECEIVABLE
EQUIPMENT
BUILDING
LAND
ACCOUNTS PAYABLE
NOTES PAYABLE
CAPITAL STOCK
RETAINED EARNINGS
4
$15,000
$15,000
Transaction Effects Form
•Shows how statements—balance sheet and income statement—are affected by the transactions.
•Used in Chapters 4–13.
Amounts in these columns reflect accounts on the balance sheet.
Amounts in these columns reflect accounts on the income statement.
BALANCE SHEET
INCOME STATEMENT
ASSETS = LIABILITIES + OWNERS' EQUITY + REVENUES – EXPENSES
Accounts Receivable 15,000
Membership Revenue 15,000
Note that revenues and expenses appear on the income statement, and net income increases retained earnings, which is part of owners' equity.
This line will display transactions discussed in each chapter—account titles, amounts, and whether increases or decreases. Decreases will be shown as negative numbers, e.g., (10,000).

Warmup Exercises

Warmup Exercise 3-1 ***Your Accounting Equation*** **LO 3**

Assume that you borrow $1,000 from your roommate by signing an agreement to repay the amount borrowed in six months.

Required

What is the effect of this transaction on your own accounting equation?

Key to the Solution

Recall Exhibit 3-1 for the effects of transactions on the accounting equation.

Warmup Exercise 3-2 ***A Bank's Accounting Equation*** **LO 3**

The Third State Bank loans a customer $5,000 in exchange for a promissory note.

Required

What is the effect of this transaction on the bank's accounting equation?

Key to the Solution

Recall Exhibit 3-1 for the effects of the transaction on the accounting equation.

Warmup Exercise 3-3 ***Accounting Equation for Winnebago Industries*** **LO 3**

Assume Winnebago Industries goes to its bank and borrows $50,000 by signing a promissory note. The next day the company uses the money to buy a piece of machinery for use in its manufacturing facility.

Required

What is the effect of each of these two transactions on Winnebago Industries' accounting equation?

Key to the Solution

Recall Exhibit 3-1 for the effects of transactions on the accounting equation.

Solutions to Warmup Exercises

Warmup Exercise 3-1

If you borrow $1,000 from your roommate, assets in the form of cash, increase $1,000, and liabilities in the form of a note payable, increase $1,000.

Warmup Exercise 3-2

If a bank loans a customer $5,000, the bank's assets, in the form of a note receivable, increase $5,000, and its assets, in the form of cash, decrease $5,000.

Warmup Exercise 3-3

If Winnebago Industries borrows $50,000 from its bank, assets, in the form of cash, increase $50,000, and liabilities, in the form of a note payable, increase $50,000. If the company uses the money to buy a machine, assets, in the form of machinery, increase $50,000, and assets, in the form of cash, decrease $50,000.

Review Problem

WebTUTOR™ Advantage

The following transactions are entered into by Sparkle Car Wash during its first month of operations:

a. Articles of incorporation are filed with the state, and 20,000 shares of capital stock are issued. Cash of $40,000 is received from the new owners for the shares.

b. A five-year promissory note is signed at the local bank. The cash received from the loan is $120,000.

c. An existing car wash is purchased for $150,000 in cash. The values assigned to the land, building, and equipment are $25,000, $75,000, and $50,000, respectively.

d. Cleaning supplies are purchased on account for $2,500 from a distributor. All of the supplies are used in the first month.

e. During the first month, $1,500 is paid to the distributor for the cleaning supplies. The remaining $1,000 will be paid next month.

f. Gross receipts from car washes during the first month of operations amount to $7,000.

g. Wages and salaries paid in the first month amount to $2,000.

h. The utility bill of $800 for the month is paid.

i. A total of $1,000 in dividends is paid to the owners.

Required

1. Prepare a table to summarize the preceding transactions as they affect the accounting equation. Use the format in Exhibit 3-1. Identify each transaction by letter.
2. Prepare an income statement for the month.
3. Prepare a balance sheet at the end of the month.

Solution to Review Problem

1.

SPARKLE CAR WASH
TRANSACTIONS FOR THE MONTH

	Assets				= Liabilities		+ Owners' Equity		+ Revenues − Expenses
TRANS.	**CASH**	**LAND**	**BUILDING**	**EQUIPMENT**	**ACCOUNTS PAYABLE**	**NOTES PAYABLE**	**CAPITAL STOCK**	**RETAINED EARNINGS**	
a.	$ 40,000						$40,000		
b.	120,000					$120,000			
Bal.	$160,000					$120,000	$40,000		
c.	−150,000	$25,000	$75,000	$50,000					
Bal.	$ 10,000	$25,000	$75,000	$50,000		$120,000	$40,000		
d.					$2,500				$−2,500
Bal.	$ 10,000	$25,000	$75,000	$50,000	$2,500	$120,000	$40,000		$−2,500
e.	−1,500				−1,500				
Bal.	$ 8,500	$25,000	$75,000	$50,000	$1,000	$120,000	$40,000		$−2,500
f.	7,000								7,000
Bal.	$ 15,500	$25,000	$75,000	$50,000	$1,000	$120,000	$40,000		$ 4,500
g.	−2,000								−2,000
Bal.	$ 13,500	$25,000	$75,000	$50,000	$1,000	$120,000	$40,000		$ 2,500
h.	−800								− 800
Bal.	$ 12,700	$25,000	$75,000	$50,000	$1,000	$120,000	$40,000		$ 1,700
i.	−1,000							−1,000	
Bal.	$ 11,700	$25,000	$75,000	$50,000	$1,000	$120,000	$40,000	$−1,000	$1,700

Total assets: $161,700

Total liabilities and owners' equity: $161,700

2.

SPARKLE CAR WASH
INCOME STATEMENT
FOR THE MONTH ENDED XX/XX/XX

Car wash revenue		$7,000
Expenses:		
Supplies	$2,500	
Wages and salaries	2,000	
Utilities	800	5,300
Net income		$1,700

3.

SPARKLE CAR WASH
BALANCE SHEET
XX/XX/XX

Assets		**Liabilities and Owners' Equity**	
Cash	$ 11,700	Accounts payable	$ 1,000
Land	25,000	Notes payable	120,000
Building	75,000	Capital stock	40,000
Equipment	50,000	Retained earnings	700
		Total liabilities	
Total assets	$161,700	and owners' equity	$161,700

Appendix: Accounting Tools: The Double-Entry System

The origin of the double-entry system of accounting can be traced to Venice, Italy, in 1494. In that year, Fra Luca Pacioli, a Franciscan monk, wrote a mathematical treatise. Included in his book was the concept of debits and credits that is still used almost universally today.

The T Account

The form for a general ledger account will be illustrated later in the chapter. However, the form of account often used to analyze transactions is called the *T account,* so named because it resembles the capital letter T. The name of the account appears across the horizontal line. One side is used to record increases and the other side decreases, but as you will see, the same side is not used for increases for every account. As a matter of convention, the *left* side of an *asset* account is used to record *increases* and the *right* side to record *decreases.* To illustrate a T account, we will look at the Cash account for Glengarry Health Club. The transactions recorded in the account can be traced to Exhibit 3-1.

INCREASES	CASH	DECREASES	
Investment by owners	100,000	Wages and salaries	10,000
Court fees collected	5,000	Utilities	3,000
Accounts collected	4,000	Dividends	2,000
	109,000		15,000
Bal.	94,000		

The amounts $109,000 and $15,000 are called *footings.* They represent the totals of the amounts on each side of the account. Neither these amounts nor the balance of $94,000 represents transactions. They are simply shown to indicate the totals and the balance in the account.

Debits and Credits

LO 5 Explain the rules of debits and credits.

Debit An entry on the left side of an account.

Credit An entry on the right side of an account.

Rather than refer to the left or right side of an account, accountants use specific labels for each side. The *left* side of any account is the **debit** side, and the *right* side of any account is the **credit** side. We will also use the terms *debit* and *credit* as verbs. If we *debit* the Cash account, we enter an amount on the left side. Similarly, if we want to enter an amount on the right side of an account, we *credit* the account. To *charge* an account has the same meaning as to *debit* it. No such synonym exists for the act of crediting an account.

Note that *debit* and *credit* are *locational* terms. They simply refer to the left or right side of a T account. They do *not* represent increases or decreases. As we will see, when one type of account is increased (for example, the Cash account), the increase is on the left or *debit* side. When certain other types of accounts are increased, however, the entry will be on the right or *credit* side.

As you would expect from your understanding of the accounting equation, the conventions for using T accounts for assets and liabilities are opposite. Assets are future economic benefits, and liabilities are obligations to transfer economic benefits in the future. If an asset is *increased* with a *debit,* how do you think a liability would be increased? *Because assets and liabilities are opposites, if an asset is increased with a debit, a liability is increased with a credit.* Thus, the right side, or credit side, of a liability account is used to record an increase. Like liabilities, owners' equity accounts are on the opposite side of the accounting equation from assets. *Thus, like a liability, an owners' equity account is increased with a credit.* We can summarize the logic of debits and credits, increases and decreases, and the accounting equation in the following way:

Study Tip

Once you know the rule to increase an asset with a debit, the rules for the other increases and decreases follow logically. For example, because a liability is the opposite of an asset, it is increased with a credit. And it follows logically that it would be decreased with a debit.

ASSETS		=	LIABILITIES		+	OWNERS' EQUITY	
Debits Increases +	Credits Decreases −		Debits Decreases −	Credits Increases +		Debits Decreases −	Credits Increases +

Note again that debits and credits are location-oriented. Debits are always on the left side of an account and credits on the right side.

Accounting for Your Decisions

You Are a Student

A classmate comes to you with a question about the bank statement she has received. Why does the bank credit her account when she makes a deposit to her account, but accounting rules state that cash is increased with a debit?

ANS: The bank is looking at customer deposits from its perspective and not the customers'. Checking account deposits represent liabilities to the bank, such as "Deposits Payable." Thus, when customers make deposits, the bank has increased its liability to those customers, with a credit to its "Deposits Payable."

Debits and Credits for Revenues, Expenses, and Dividends

In our Glengarry Health Club example, revenues increased the right side of the accounting equation. The sale of memberships was not only an increase in the asset Accounts Receivable but also an increase in the owners' claim on the assets of the business. Rather than being recorded directly in Retained Earnings, however, each revenue item is maintained in a separate account. The following logic is used to arrive at the rules for increasing and decreasing revenues:[5]

1. Retained Earnings is increased with a credit.
2. Revenue is an increase in Retained Earnings.
3. Revenue is increased with a credit.
4. Because revenue is increased with a credit, it is decreased with a debit.

The same logic is applied to the rules for increasing and decreasing expense accounts:

1. Retained Earnings is decreased with a debit.
2. Expense is a decrease in Retained Earnings.
3. Expense is increased with a debit.
4. Because expense is increased with a debit, it is decreased with a credit.

Recall that dividends reduce cash. But they also reduce the owners' claim on the assets of the business. Earlier we recognized this decrease in the owners' claim as a reduction of Retained Earnings. As we do for revenue and expense accounts, we will use a separate Dividends account:

1. Retained Earnings is decreased with a debit.
2. Dividends are a decrease in Retained Earnings.
3. Dividends are increased with a debit.
4. Because dividends are increased with a debit, they are decreased with a credit.

[5] We normally think of both revenues and expenses as being only increased, not decreased. Because we will need to decrease them as part of the closing procedure, it is important to know how to reduce these accounts as well as increase them.

Summary of the Rules for Increasing and Decreasing Accounts

The rules for increasing and decreasing the various types of accounts are summarized as follows:

Type of Account	Debit	Credit
Asset	Increase	Decrease
Liability	Decrease	Increase
Owners' Equity	Decrease	Increase
Revenue	Decrease	Increase
Expense	Increase	Decrease
Dividends	Increase	Decrease

Normal Account Balances

Each account has a "normal" balance. For example, assets normally have debit balances. Would it be possible for an asset such as Cash to have a credit balance? Assume that a company has a checking account with a bank. A credit balance in the account would indicate that the decreases in the account, from checks written and other bank charges, were more than the deposits into the account. If this were the case, however, the company would no longer have an asset, Cash, but instead would have a liability to the bank. The normal balances for the accounts we have looked at are as follows:

Type of Account	Normal Balance
Asset	Debit
Liability	Credit
Owners' Equity	Credit
Revenue	Credit
Expense	Debit
Dividends	Debit

Debits Aren't Bad, and Credits Aren't Good

Students often approach their first encounter with debits and credits with preconceived notions. The use of the terms *debit* and *credit* in everyday language leads to many of these notions. "Joe is a real credit to his team." "Nancy should be credited with saving Mary's career." These both appear to be very positive statements. You must resist the temptation to associate the term *credit* with something good or positive and the term *debit* with something bad or negative. *In accounting, debit means one thing: an entry made on the left side of an account. A credit means an entry made on the right side of an account.*

Debits and Credits Applied to Transactions

Recall the first transaction recorded by Glengarry Health Club earlier in the chapter: the owners invested $100,000 cash in the business. The transaction resulted in an increase in the Cash account and an increase in the Capital Stock account. Applying the rules of debits and credits, we would *debit* the Cash account for $100,000 and *credit* the Capital Stock account for the same amount:[6]

CASH	
(1) 100,000	

CAPITAL STOCK	
	100,000 (1)

[6]We will use the numbers of each transaction, as they were labeled earlier in the chapter, to identify the transactions. In practice, a formal ledger account is used, and transactions are entered according to their date.

Double-entry system A system of accounting in which every transaction is recorded with equal debits and credits and the accounting equation is kept in balance.

You now can see why we refer to the **double-entry system** of accounting. Every transaction is recorded so that the equality of debits and credits is maintained, and in the process, the accounting equation is kept in balance. *Every transaction is entered in at least two accounts on opposite sides of T accounts. Our first transaction resulted in an increase in an asset account and an increase in an owners' equity account. For every transaction, the debit side must equal the credit side. The debit of $100,000 to the Cash account equals the credit of $100,000 to the Capital Stock account.* It naturally follows that if the debit side must equal the credit side for every transaction, at any point in time the total of all debits recorded must equal the total of all credits recorded. Thus, the fundamental accounting equation remains in balance.

Transactions for Glengarry Health Club

Three distinct steps are involved in recording a transaction in the accounts.

1. First, we *analyze* the transaction. That is, we decide what accounts are increased or decreased and by how much.
2. Second, we *recall* the rules of debits and credits as they apply to the transaction we are analyzing.
3. Finally, we *record* the transaction using the rules of debits and credits.

We return to the transactions of the health club. We have already explained the logic for the debit to the Cash account and the credit to the Capital Stock account for the initial investment by the owners. We will now analyze the remaining eight transactions for the month. Refer to Exhibit 3-1 for a summary of the transactions.

(2) A building and land are exchanged for a promissory note.

(a) *Analyze:* Two asset accounts are increased: Building and Land. The liability account Notes Payable is also increased.

(b) *Recall the rules of debits and credits:* An asset is increased with a debit, and a liability is increased with a credit.

(c) *Record the transaction:*

BUILDING	
(2) 150,000	

NOTES PAYABLE	
	200,000 (2)

LAND	
(2) 50,000	

(3) Exercise equipment is purchased from a supplier on open account. The purchase price is $20,000.

(a) *Analyze:* An asset account, Equipment, is increased. A liability account, Accounts Payable, is also increased. Thus, the transaction is identical to the last transaction in that an asset or assets are increased and a liability is increased.

(b) *Recall the rules of debits and credits:* An asset is increased with a debit, and a liability is increased with a credit.

(c) *Record the transaction:*

EQUIPMENT	
(3) 20,000	

ACCOUNTS PAYABLE	
	20,000 (3)

(4) Three hundred club memberships are sold for $50 each. The members have until the 10th of the following month to pay.

(a) *Analyze:* The asset account Accounts Receivable is increased by $15,000. This amount is an asset because the company has the right to collect it in the future. The owners' claim to the assets is increased by the same amount. Recall, however, that we do not record these claims—revenues—directly in an owners' equity account but instead use a separate revenue account. We will call the account Membership Revenue.

(b) *Recall the rules of debits and credits:* An asset is increased with a debit. Owners' equity is increased with a credit. Because revenue is an increase in owners' equity, it is increased with a credit.

(c) *Record the transaction:*

ACCOUNTS RECEIVABLE	
(4) 15,000	

MEMBERSHIP REVENUE	
	15,000 (4)

(5) Court fees are paid at the time of use and amount to $5,000 for the first month.

(a) *Analyze:* The asset account Cash is increased by $5,000. The owners' claim to the assets is increased by the same amount. The account used to record the increase in the owners' claim is Court Fee Revenue.

(b) *Recall the rules of debits and credits:* An asset is increased with a debit. Owners' equity is increased with a credit. Because revenue is an increase in owners' equity, it is increased with a credit.

(c) *Record the transaction:*

CASH	
(1) 100,000	
(5) **5,000**	

COURT FEE REVENUE	
	5,000 (5)

(6) Wages and salaries amount to $10,000, and they are paid in cash.

(a) *Analyze:* The asset account, Cash, is decreased by $10,000. At the same time, the owners' claim to the assets is decreased by this amount. However, rather than record a decrease directly to Retained Earnings, we set up an expense account, Wage and Salary Expense.

(b) *Recall the rules of debits and credits:* An asset is decreased with a credit. Owners' equity is decreased with a debit. Because expense is a decrease in owners' equity, it is increased with a debit.

(c) *Record the transaction:*

CASH	
(1) 100,000	**10,000 (6)**
(5) 5,000	

WAGE AND SALARY EXPENSE	
(6) 10,000	

(7) The utility bill of $3,000 for the first month is paid in cash.

(a) *Analyze:* The asset account Cash is decreased by $3,000. At the same time, the owners' claim to the assets is decreased by this amount. However, rather than record a decrease directly to Retained Earnings, we set up an expense account, Utility Expense.

(b) *Recall the rules of debits and credits:* An asset is decreased with a credit. Owners' equity is decreased with a debit. Because expense is a decrease in owners' equity, it is increased with a debit.

(c) *Record the transaction:*

CASH	
(1) 100,000	10,000 (6)
(5) 5,000	**3,000 (7)**

UTILITIES EXPENSE	
(7) 3,000	

(8) Cash of $4,000 is collected from members for their January dues.

(a) *Analyze:* Cash is increased by the amount collected from the members. Another asset, Accounts Receivable, is decreased by the same amount. Glengarry has simply traded one asset for another.

(b) *Recall the rules of debits and credits:* An asset is increased with a debit and decreased with a credit. Thus, one asset is debited, and another is credited.

(c) *Record the transaction:*

CASH	
(1) 100,000	10,000 (6)
(5) 5,000	3,000 (7)
(8) 4,000	

ACCOUNTS RECEIVABLE	
(4) 15,000	**4,000 (8)**

(9) Dividends of $2,000 are distributed to the owners.

(a) *Analyze:* The asset account Cash is decreased by $2,000. At the same time, the owners' claim to the assets is decreased by this amount. Earlier in the chapter, we decreased Retained Earnings for dividends paid to the owners. Now we will use a separate account, Dividends, to record these distributions.

(b) *Recall the rules of debits and credits:* An asset is decreased with a credit. Retained earnings is decreased with a debit. Because dividends are a decrease in retained earnings, they are increased with a debit.

(c) *Record the transaction:*

CASH	
(1) 100,000	10,000 (6)
(5) 5,000	3,000 (7)
(8) 4,000	**2,000 (9)**

DIVIDENDS	
(9) 2,000	

Two-Minute Review

1. *Assume Glengarry pays the supplier the amount owed on open account. Record this transaction in the appropriate T accounts.*
2. *Assume Glengarry collects the remaining amount owed by members for dues. Record this transaction in the appropriate T accounts.*

Answers on page 132.

THE JOURNAL: THE FIRM'S CHRONOLOGICAL RECORD OF TRANSACTIONS

LO 6 Explain the purposes of a journal and the posting process.

Journal A chronological record of transactions, also known as the book of original entry.

Posting The process of transferring amounts from a journal to the ledger accounts.

Each of the nine transactions was entered directly in the ledger accounts. By looking at the Cash account, we see that it increased by $5,000 in transaction **(5)**. But what was the other side of this transaction? That is, what account was credited? To have a record of *each entry,* transactions are recorded first in a journal. A **journal** is a chronological record of transactions entered into by a business. Because a journal lists transactions in the order in which they took place, it is called the *book of original entry.* Transactions are recorded first in a journal and then are posted to the ledger accounts. **Posting** is the process of transferring a journal entry to the ledger accounts:

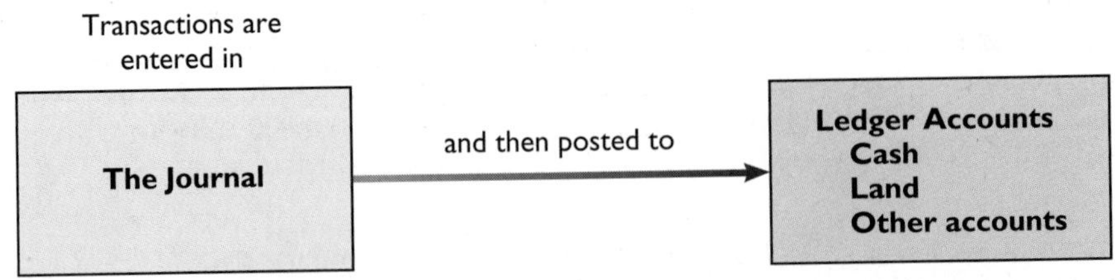

Note that posting does not result in any change in the amounts recorded. It is simply a process of re-sorting the transactions from a chronological order to a topical arrangement.

Journalizing The act of recording journal entries.

A journal entry is recorded for each transaction. **Journalizing** is the process of recording entries in a journal. A standard format is normally used for recording journal entries. Consider the original investment by the owners of Glengarry Health Club. The format of the journal entry is as follows:

		DEBIT	CREDIT
Jan. XX	Cash	100,000	
	Capital Stock		100,000
	To record the issuance of 10,000 shares of stock for cash.		

Each journal entry contains a date with columns for the amounts debited and credited. Accounts credited are indented to distinguish them from accounts debited. A brief explanation normally appears on the line below the entry.

Transactions are normally recorded in a **general journal.** Specialized journals may be used to record repetitive transactions. For example, a cash receipts journal may be used to record all transactions in which cash is received. Special journals accomplish the same purpose as a general journal, but they save time in recording similar transactions. In this chapter, we will use a general journal to record all transactions.

General journal The journal used in place of a specialized journal.

An excerpt from Glengarry Health Club's general journal appears in the top portion of Exhibit 3-7. One column needs further explanation. *Post. Ref.* is an abbreviation for *Posting Reference.* As part of the posting process explained below, the debit and credit amounts are posted to the appropriate accounts, and this column is filled in with the number assigned to the account.

From Concept to Practice 3.3

Reading Winnebago Industries' Financial Statements

Refer to Winnebago Industries' *income statement and its balance sheet. Using the appropriate accounts from these statements, prepare the journal entry Winnebago Industries would record if it sold an RV to a dealer for $100,000 and gave the dealer 30 days to pay.*

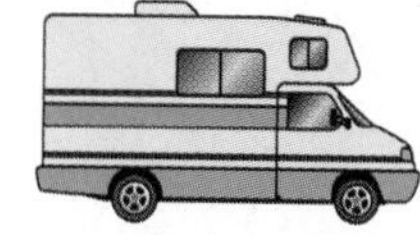

Journal entries and ledger accounts are both *tools* used by the accountant. The end result, a set of financial statements, is the most important part of the process. Journalizing provides us with a chronological record of each transaction. So why not just prepare financial statements directly from the journal entries? Isn't it just extra work to *post* the entries to the ledger accounts? In our simple example of Glengarry Health Club, it would be possible to prepare the statements directly from the journal entries. In real-world situations, however, the number of transactions in any given period is so large that it would be virtually impossible, if not terribly inefficient, to bypass the accounts. Accounts provide us with a convenient summary of the activity, as well as the balance, for a specific financial statement item.

The posting process for Glengarry Health Club is illustrated in Exhibit 3-7 for the health club's fifth transaction, in which cash is collected for court fees. Rather than a T-account format for the general ledger accounts, the *running balance form* is illustrated. A separate column indicates the balance in the ledger account after each transaction. The use of the explanation column in a ledger account is optional. Because an explanation of the entry in the account can be found by referring to the journal, this column is often left blank.

Note the cross-referencing between the journal and the ledger. As amounts are entered in the ledger accounts, the Posting Reference column is filled in with the page number of the journal. (For example, GJ1 to indicate page 1 from the general journal). At the same time, the Posting Reference column of the journal is filled in with the appropriate account number.

The frequency of posting differs among companies, partly based on the degree to which their accounting system is automated. For example, in some computerized systems,

Exhibit 3-7 Posting from the Journal to the Ledger

General Journal — Page No. 1

Date		Account Titles and Explanation	Post. Ref.	Debit	Credit
2004 Jan.	XX	Accounts Receivable	5	15000	
		Membership Revenue	40		15000
		Sold 300 memberships at $50 each.			
	XX	Cash	1	5000	
		Court Fee Revenue	44		5000
		Collected court fees.			

General Ledger
Cash — Account No. 1

Date		Explanation	Post. Ref.	Debit	Credit	Balance
2004 Jan.	XX		GJ1	100000		100000
	XX		GJ1	5000		105000

Court Fee Revenue — Account No. 44

Date		Explanation	Post. Ref.	Debit	Credit	Balance
2004 Jan.	XX		GJ1		5000	5000

amounts are posted to the ledger accounts at the time an entry is recorded in the journal. In a manual system, posting is normally done periodically, for example, daily, weekly, or monthly. Regardless of when performed, the posting process changes nothing. It simply reorganizes the transactions by account.

THE TRIAL BALANCE

LO 7 Explain the purpose of a trial balance.

Trial balance A list of each account and its balance; used to prove equality of debits and credits.

Accountants use one other tool to facilitate the preparation of a set of financial statements. A **trial balance** is a list of each account and its balance at a specific point in time. The trial balance is *not* a financial statement but merely a convenient device to prove the equality of the debit and credit balances in the accounts. It can be as informal as an adding-machine tape with the account titles penciled in next to the debit and credit amounts. A trial balance for Glengarry Health Club as of January 31, 2004, is shown in Exhibit 3-8. The balance in each account was determined by adding the increases and subtracting the decreases for the account for the transactions detailed earlier.

Certain types of errors are detectable from a trial balance. For example, if the balance of an account is incorrectly computed, the total of the debits and credits in the

GLENGARRY HEALTH CLUB TRIAL BALANCE JANUARY 31, 2004		
Account Titles	**Debits**	**Credits**
Cash	$ 94,000	
Accounts Receivable	11,000	
Equipment	20,000	
Building	150,000	
Land	50,000	
Accounts Payable		$ 20,000
Notes Payable		200,000
Capital Stock		100,000
Membership Revenue		15,000
Court Fee Revenue		5,000
Wage and Salary Expense	10,000	
Utility Expense	3,000	
Dividends	2,000	
Totals	$340,000	$340,000

Exhibit 3-8

Trial Balance for Glengarry Health Club

Study Tip

Remember from p. 125 that every account has a normal balance, either debit or credit. Note the normal balances for each account on this trial balance.

trial balance will not equal. If a debit is posted to an account as a credit, or vice versa, the trial balance will be out of balance. The omission of part of a journal entry in the posting process will also be detected by the preparation of a trial balance.

Do not attribute more significance to a trial balance, however, than is warranted. It does provide a convenient summary of account balances for preparing financial statements. It also assures us that the balances of all the debit accounts equal the balances of all the credit accounts. But an equality of debits and credits does not necessarily mean that the *correct* accounts were debited and credited in an entry. For example, the entry to record the purchase of land by signing a promissory note *should* result in a debit to Land and a credit to Notes Payable. If the accountant incorrectly debited Cash instead of Land, the trial balance would still show an equality of debits and credits. A trial balance can be prepared at any time; it is usually prepared before the release of a set of financial statements.

Accounting for Your Decisions

You Are the Manager

You are the community relations manager for a company. You need to determine whether the company is spending its money wisely in promoting its image in the local community.

1. What types of accounts would you examine? Give examples of the possible names for some of these accounts.
2. Would a general journal or a general ledger be more useful to you in making your determination? Explain your answer.

ANS: 1. Among the possible accounts that you want to examine are Entertainment, Travel, Promotions, Advertising, and Miscellaneous, in addition to any accounts that might contain expenditures related to community relations.

2. You may want to examine the general ledger for each of the accounts listed in part 1. The ledger contains a record for each of the accounts and the activity in them during the period.

Accounting for Your Decisions

You Are the Stockholder

You own 100 shares of stock in General Motors. Every year you receive GM's annual report, which includes a chairman's letter, a description of new models, a financial section, and notes to financial statements. Nowhere in the report do you see a general ledger or a trial balance. Is General Motors hiding something?

ANS: GM's balance sheet, income statement, and statement of cash flows are derived from the company's journal entries, general ledgers, trial balances, and so on. These documents are the building blocks of the final statements. There could literally be millions of transactions during the year—which even the most diehard accounting fan would tire of reading.

Answers to the Two-Minute Reviews

Two-Minute Review on Page 114

1. *Equipment will increase by $10,000, and Cash will decrease by $10,000.*
2. *$325,000 (the effect of the transaction is to increase and decrease assets by the same amount).*

Two-Minute Review on Page 128

1.

CASH	
	20,000

ACCOUNTS PAYABLE	
20,000	

2.

CASH	
11,000	

ACCOUNTS RECEIVABLE	
	11,000

Chapter Highlights

1. **LO 1** Both internal and external events affect an entity. External events, such as the purchase of materials, involve the entity and its environment. Internal events, such as the placement of the materials into production, do not involve an outside entity. For any event to be recorded, it must be measurable.
2. **LO 2** Source documents are used as the basis for recording events as transactions. For certain repetitive transactions, a standard source document is used, such as a time card to document the payroll for the week. For other nonrepetitive transactions, a source document has to be generated for the specific event.
3. **LO 3** Economic events are the basis for recording transactions. These transactions result in changes in the company's financial position. Transactions change the amount of individual items on the balance sheet, but the statement must balance after each transaction is recorded.
4. **LO 4** A separate account is used for each identifiable asset, liability, revenue, expense, and component of owners' equity. No standard set of accounts exists, and the types of accounts used depend to a certain extent on the nature of a company's business. A chart of accounts is a numerical list of all the accounts used by an entity. The general ledger in a manual system might consist of a set of cards, one for each account, in a file cabinet. In a computerized system, a magnetic tape or diskette might be used to store the accounts.
5. **LO 4** Accountants use T accounts as the basic form of analysis of transactions. The left side of an account is used for debits, and the right side is for credits. Transactions are recorded in the ledger in more formal accounts than the typical T account (Appendix).
6. **LO 5** By convention, the left side of an asset account is used to record increases. Thus, an asset account is increased with a debit. Because liabilities are on the opposite side of the accounting equation, they are increased with a credit. Similarly, owners' equity accounts are increased with a credit. Because revenue is an increase in owners' equity, it is increased with a credit. Thus, an expense, as well as a dividend, is increased with a debit. According to the double-entry system, there are two sides to every transaction. For each transaction, the debit or debits must equal the credit or credits (Appendix).

7. **LO 6** Transactions are not recorded directly in the accounts but are recorded initially in a journal. A separate entry is recorded in the journal for each transaction. The account(s) debited appears first in the entry, with the account(s) credited listed next and indented. Separate columns for debits and credits are used to indicate the amounts for each. A general journal is used in lieu of any specialized journals (Appendix).
8. **LO 6** Amounts appearing in journal entries are posted to the ledger accounts. Posting can be done either at the time the entry is recorded or periodically. The Post. Ref. column in a journal indicates the account number to which the amount is posted, and a similar column in the account acts as a convenient reference back to the particular page number in the journal (Appendix).
9. **LO 7** A trial balance proves the equality of the debits and credits in the accounts. If only one side of a transaction is posted to the accounts, the trial balance will not balance. Other types of errors are detectable from the process of preparing a trial balance. It cannot, however, detect all errors. A trial balance could be in balance even though the wrong asset account is debited in an entry (Appendix).

http://

http://porter.swlearning.com

Technology and other resources for your success

If you need additional help, visit the text's Web site. Also, see this text's preface for a description of available technology and other resources. If your instructor is using PERSONAL Trainer in this course, you may complete, on line, the exercises and problems in the text.

Key Terms Quiz

Note: A separate quiz is available for the terms in the Appendix to this chapter.

Read each definition below, and then write the number of the definition in the blank beside the appropriate term it defines. The quiz solutions appear at the end of the chapter.

Quiz 1: Processing Accounting Information

_____ Event
_____ External event
_____ Internal event
_____ Transaction
_____ Source document
_____ Account
_____ Chart of accounts
_____ General ledger

1. A numerical list of all the accounts used by a company.
2. A happening of consequence to an entity.
3. An event occurring entirely within an entity.
4. A piece of paper, such as a sales invoice, that is used as the evidence to record a transaction.
5. An event involving interaction between an entity and its environment.
6. The record used to accumulate monetary amounts for each individual asset, liability, revenue, expense, and component of owners' equity.
7. A book, file, hard drive, or other device containing all of a company's accounts.
8. Any event, external or internal, that is recognized in a set of financial statements.

Answers on p. 155.

Quiz 2: Appendix

_____ Debit
_____ Credit
_____ Double-entry system
_____ Journal
_____ Posting
_____ Journalizing
_____ General journal
_____ Trial balance

1. A list of each account and its balance at a specific point in time; used to prove the equality of debits and credits.
2. An entry on the right side of an account.
3. The act of recording journal entries.
4. An entry on the left side of an account.
5. The process of transferring amounts from a journal to the appropriate ledger accounts.
6. A chronological record of transactions, also known as the *book of original entry*.
7. The journal used in place of a specialized journal.
8. A system of accounting in which every transaction in recorded with equal debits and credits and the accounting equation is kept in balance.

Answers on p. 155.

Alternate Terms

Credit side of an account Right side of an account

Debit an account Charge an account

Debit side of an account Left side of an account

General ledger Set of accounts

Journal Book of original entry

Journalize an entry Record an entry

Posting an account Transferring an amount from the journal to the ledger

Questions

1. What are the two types of events that affect an entity? Describe each.
2. What is the significance of source documents to the recording process? Give two examples of source documents.
3. What are four different forms of cash?
4. How does an account receivable differ from a note receivable?
5. What is meant by the statement "One company's account receivable is another company's account payable"?
6. Owners' equity represents the claim of the owners on the assets of the business. What is the distinction relative to the owners' claim between the Capital Stock account and the Retained Earnings account?
7. What do accountants mean when they refer to the "double-entry system" of accounting? (Appendix)
8. If an asset account is increased with a debit, what is the logic for increasing a liability account with a credit? (Appendix)
9. A friend comes to you with the following plight: "I'm confused. An asset is something positive, and it is increased with a debit. However, an expense is something negative, and it is also increased with a debit. I don't get it." How can you straighten your friend out? (Appendix)
10. The payment of dividends reduces cash. If the Cash account is reduced with a credit, why is the Dividends account debited when dividends are paid? (Appendix)
11. If Cash is increased with a debit, why does the bank credit your account when you make a deposit? (Appendix)
12. Your friend presents the following criticism of the accounting system: "Accounting involves so much duplication of effort. First, entries are recorded in a journal, and then the same information is recorded in a ledger. No wonder accountants work such long hours!" Do you agree with this criticism? (Appendix)
13. How does the T account differ from the running balance form for an account? How are they similar? (Appendix)
14. What is the benefit of using a cross-referencing system between a ledger and a journal? (Appendix)
15. How often should a company post entries from the journal to the ledger? (Appendix)
16. What is the purpose of a trial balance? (Appendix)

Exercises

Exercise 3-1 *Types of Events* **LO 1**

For each of the following events, identify whether it is an external event that would be recorded as a transaction (E), an internal event that would be recorded as a transaction (I), or not recorded (NR):

_______________ 1. A supplier of a company's raw material is paid an amount owed on account.

_______________ 2. A customer pays its open account.

_______________ 3. A new chief executive officer is hired.

_______________ 4. The biweekly payroll is paid.

_______________ 5. Raw materials are entered into production.

_______________ 6. A new advertising agency is hired to develop a series of newspaper ads for the company.

_______________ 7. The advertising bill for the first month is paid.

_______________ 8. The accountant determines the federal income taxes owed based on the income earned during the period.

Exercise 3-2 *Source Documents Matched with Transactions* **LO 2**

Following are a list of source documents and a list of transactions. Indicate by letter next to each transaction the source document that would serve as evidence for the recording of the transaction.

Source Documents

a. Purchase invoice
b. Sales invoice
c. Cash register tape
d. Time cards
e. Promissory note
f. Stock certificates
g. Monthly statement from utility company
h. No standard source document would normally be available

Transactions

_______ **1.** Utilities expense for the month is recorded.
_______ **2.** A cash settlement is received from a pending lawsuit.
_______ **3.** Owners contribute cash to start a new corporation.
_______ **4.** The biweekly payroll is paid.
_______ **5.** Cash sales for the day are recorded.
_______ **6.** Equipment is acquired on a 30-day open account.
_______ **7.** A sale is made on open account.
_______ **8.** A building is acquired by signing an agreement to repay a stated amount plus interest in six months.

Exercise 3-3 *The Effect of Transactions on the Accounting Equation* LO 3

For each of the following transactions, indicate whether it increases (I), decreases (D), or has no effect (NE) on the total dollar amount of each of the elements of the accounting equation.

Transactions	Assets	= Liabilities	+ Owners' Equity
Example: Common stock is issued in exchange for cash.	I	NE	I
1. Equipment is purchased for cash.			
2. Sales are made on account.			
3. Cash sales are made.			
4. An account payable is paid off.			
5. Cash is collected on an account receivable.			
6. Buildings are purchased in exchange for a three-year note payable.			
7. Advertising bill for the month is paid.			
8. Dividends are paid to stockholders.			
9. Land is acquired by issuing shares of stock to the owner of the land.			

Exercise 3-4 *Types of Transactions* LO 3

As you found out in reading the chapter, there are three elements to the accounting equation: assets, liabilities, and owners' equity. You also learned that every transaction affects at least two of these elements. Although other possibilities exist, five types of transactions are described below. For *each* of these five types, write out descriptions of at least *two* transactions that illustrate these types of transactions.

Type of Transaction	Assets	= Liabilities	+ Owners' Equity
1.	Increase	Increase	
2.	Increase		Increase
3.	Decrease	Decrease	
4.	Decrease		Decrease
5.	Increase Decrease		

Exercise 3-5 *Analyzing Transactions* **LO 3**

Prepare a table to summarize the following transactions as they affect the accounting equation. Use the format in Exhibit 3-1.

1. Sales on account of $1,530.
2. Purchases of supplies on account for $1,365.
3. Cash sales of $750.
4. Purchase of equipment for cash of $4,240.
5. Issuance of a promissory note for $2,500.
6. Collections on account for $890.
7. Sale of capital stock in exchange for a parcel of land. The land is appraised at $50,000.
8. Payment of $4,000 in salaries and wages.
9. Payment of open account in the amount of $500.

Exercise 3-6 *Balance Sheet Accounts and Their Use* **LO 4**

Choose from the following list of account titles the one that most accurately fits the description of that account or is an example of that account. An account title may be used more than once or not at all.

Cash	**Accounts Receivable**	**Notes Receivable**
Prepaid Asset	**Land**	**Buildings**
Investments	**Accounts Payable**	**Notes Payable**
Taxes Payable	**Retained Earnings**	**Common Stock**
Preferred Stock		

______ 1. A written obligation to repay a fixed amount, with interest, at some time in the future

______ 2. Twenty acres of land held for speculation

______ 3. An amount owed by a customer

______ 4. Corporate income taxes owed to the federal government

______ 5. Ownership in a company that allows the owner to receive dividends before common shareholders receive any distributions

______ 6. Five acres of land used as the site for a factory

______ 7. Amounts owed on an open account to a supplier of raw materials, due in 90 days

______ 8. A checking account at the bank

______ 9. A warehouse used to store merchandise

______ 10. Claims by the owners on the undistributed net income of a business

______ 11. Rent paid on an office building in advance of use of the facility

Exercise 3-7 *Normal Account Balances (Appendix)* **LO 5**

Each account has a normal balance. For the following list of accounts, indicate whether the normal balance of each is a debit or a credit.

Account	Normal Balance
1. Cash	______
2. Prepaid Insurance	______
3. Retained Earnings	______
4. Bonds Payable	______
5. Investments	______
6. Capital Stock	______
7. Advertising Fees Earned	______
8. Wages and Salaries Expense	______
9. Wages and Salaries Payable	______
10. Office Supplies	______
11. Dividends	______

Exercise 3-8 *Debits and Credits (Appendix)* LO 5

The new bookkeeper for Darby Corporation is getting ready to mail the daily cash receipts to the bank for deposit. Because his previous job was at a bank, he is aware that the bank "credits" your account for all deposits and "debits" your account for all checks written. Therefore, he makes the following entry before sending the daily receipts to the bank:

June 5	Accounts Receivable	10,000	
	Sales Revenue	2,450	
	Cash		12,450
	To record cash received on June 5: $10,000 collections on account and $2,450 in cash sales.		

Required

Explain why this entry is wrong, and prepare the correct journal entry. Why does the bank refer to cash received from a customer as a *credit* to that customer's account?

Exercise 3-9 *Trial Balance (Appendix)* LO 7

The following list of accounts was taken from the general ledger of Spencer Corporation on December 31, 2004. The bookkeeper thought it would be helpful if the accounts were arranged in alphabetical order. Each account contains the balance normal for that type of account (for example, Cash normally has a debit balance). Prepare a trial balance as of this date, with the accounts arranged in the following order: (1) assets, (2) liabilities, (3) owners' equity, (4) revenues, (5) expenses, and (6) dividends.

Account	Balance
Accounts Payable	$ 7,650
Accounts Receivable	5,325
Automobiles	9,200
Buildings	150,000
Capital Stock	100,000
Cash	10,500
Commissions Expense	2,600
Commissions Revenue	12,750
Dividends	2,000
Equipment	85,000
Heat, Light, and Water Expense	1,400
Income Tax Expense	1,700
Income Taxes Payable	2,500
Interest Revenue	1,300
Land	50,000
Notes Payable	90,000
Office Salaries Expense	6,000
Office Supplies	500
Retained Earnings	110,025

Multi-Concept Exercises

Exercise 3-10 *Determining an Ending Account Balance* LO 3, 4

Jessie's Bead Shop was organized on June 1, 2004. The company received a contribution of $1,000 from each of the two principal owners. During the month, Jessie's Bead Shop had cash sales of $1,400, had sales on account of $450, received $250 from customers in payment of their accounts, purchased supplies on account for $600 and equipment on account for $1,350, received a utility bill for $250 which will not be paid until July, and paid the full amount due on the equipment. Determine the company's Cash balance on June 30, 2004.

Exercise 3-11 *Reconstructing a Beginning Account Balance* LO 3, 4

During the month, services performed for customers on account amounted to $7,500, and collections from customers in payment of their accounts totaled $6,000. At the end of the month, the Accounts Receivable account had a balance of $2,500. What was the Accounts Receivable balance at the beginning of the month?

Exercise 3-12 *Journal Entries Recorded Directly in T Accounts (Appendix)* **LO 3, 4, 5**

Record each transaction shown below directly in T accounts, using the numbers preceding the transactions to identify them in the accounts. Each account involved needs a separate T account.

1. Received contribution of $6,500 from each of the three principal owners of the We-Go Delivery Service in exchange for shares of stock.
2. Purchased office supplies for cash of $130.
3. Purchased a van for $15,000 on an open account. The company has 25 days to pay for the van.
4. Provided delivery services to residential customers for cash of $125.
5. Billed a local business $200 for delivery services. The customer is to pay the bill within 15 days.
6. Paid the amount due on the van.
7. Received the amount due from the local business billed in transaction (5) above.

Exercise 3-13 *Trial Balance (Appendix)* **LO 4, 7**

Refer to the transactions recorded directly in T accounts for the We-Go Delivery Service in Exercise 3-12. Assume that the transactions all took place during December 2004. Prepare a trial balance at December 31, 2004.

Exercise 3-14 *Journal Entries (Appendix)* **LO 3, 5, 6**

Prepare the journal entry to record each of the following independent transactions (use the number of the transaction in lieu of a date for identification purposes):

1. Sales on account of $1,530
2. Purchases of supplies on account for $1,365
3. Cash sales of $750
4. Purchase of equipment for cash of $4,240
5. Issuance of a promissory note for $2,500
6. Collections on account for $890
7. Sale of capital stock in exchange for a parcel of land; the land is appraised at $50,000
8. Payment of $4,000 in salaries and wages
9. Payment of open account in the amount of $500

Exercise 3-15 *Journal Entries (Appendix)* **LO 3, 5, 6**

Following is a list of transactions entered into during the first month of operations of Gardener Corporation, a new landscape service. Prepare in journal form the entry to record each transaction.

April 1: Articles of incorporation are filed with the state, and 100,000 shares of common stock are issued for $100,000 in cash.

April 4: A six-month promissory note is signed at the bank. Interest at 9% per annum will be repaid in six months along with the principal amount of the loan of $50,000.

April 8: Land and a storage shed are acquired for a lump sum of $80,000. On the basis of an appraisal, 25% of the value is assigned to the land and the remainder to the building.

April 10: Mowing equipment is purchased from a supplier at a total cost of $25,000. A down payment of $10,000 is made, with the remainder due by the end of the month.

April 18: Customers are billed for services provided during the first half of the month. The total amount billed of $5,500 is due within 10 days.

April 27: The remaining balance due on the mowing equipment is paid to the supplier.

April 28: The total amount of $5,500 due from customers is received.

April 30: Customers are billed for services provided during the second half of the month. The total amount billed is $9,850.

April 30: Salaries and wages of $4,650 for the month of April are paid.

Exercise 3-16 *The Process of Posting Journal Entries to General Ledger Accounts (Appendix)* **LO 5, 6**

On June 1, Campbell Corporation purchased 10 acres of land in exchange for a promissory note in the amount of $50,000. Using the formats shown in Exhibit 3-7, prepare the journal entry to record this transaction in a general journal, and post it to the appropriate general ledger accounts. The entry will be recorded on page 7 of the general journal. Use whatever account numbers you would like in the general ledger. Assume that none of the accounts to be debited or credited currently contain a balance.

If at a later date you wanted to review this transaction, would you examine the general ledger or the general journal? Explain your answer.

Problems

Problem 3-1 ***Events to Be Recorded in Accounts*** **LO 1**

The following events take place at Dillon's Drive-In:

1. Food is ordered from vendors, who will deliver the food within the week.
2. Vendors deliver food on account, payment due in 30 days.
3. Employees take frozen food from the freezers and prepare it for customers.
4. Food is served to customers, and sales are rung up on the cash register; sales will be totaled at the end of the day.
5. Trash is taken to dumpsters, and the floors are cleaned.
6. Cash registers are cleared at the end of the day.
7. Cash is deposited in the bank night depository.
8. Employees are paid weekly paychecks.
9. Vendors noted in item **2** are paid for the food delivered.

Required

Identify each event as internal (I) or external (E), and indicate whether each event would be recorded in the *accounts* of the company. For each event that is to be recorded, identify the names of at least two accounts that would be affected.

Problem 3-2 ***Transaction Analysis and Financial Statements*** **LO 3**

Just Rolling Along Inc. was organized on May 1, 2004, by two college students who recognized an opportunity to make money while spending their days at a beach along Lake Michigan. The two entrepreneurs plan to rent bicycles and in-line skates to weekend visitors to the lakefront. The following transactions occurred during the first month of operations:

May 1: Received contribution of $9,000 from each of the two principal owners of the new business in exchange for shares of stock.

May 1: Purchased 10 bicycles for $300 each on an open account. The company has 30 days to pay for the bicycles.

May 5: Registered as a vendor with the city and paid the $15 monthly fee.

May 9: Purchased 20 pairs of in-line skates at $125 per pair, 20 helmets at $50 each, and 20 sets of protective gear (knee and elbow pads and wrist guards) at $45 per set for cash.

May 10: Purchased $100 in miscellaneous supplies on account. The company has 30 days to pay for the supplies.

May 15: Paid $125 bill from local radio station for advertising for the last two weeks of May.

May 17: Customers rented in-line skates and bicycles for cash of $1,800.

May 24: Billed the local park district $1,200 for in-line skating lessons provided to neighborhood kids. The park district is to pay one-half of the bill within five working days and the rest within 30 days.

May 29: Received 50% of the amount billed to the park district.

May 30: Customers rented in-line skates and bicycles for cash of $3,000.

May 30: Paid wages of $160 to a friend who helped out over the weekend.

May 31: Paid the balance due on the bicycles.

Required

1. Prepare a table to summarize the preceding transactions as they affect the accounting equation. Use the format in Exhibit 3-1. Identify each transaction with the date.
2. Prepare an income statement for the month ended May 31, 2004.

(continued)

3. Prepare a classified balance sheet at May 31, 2004.
4. Why do you think the two college students decided to incorporate their business rather than operate it as a partnership?

Problem 3-3 *Transaction Analysis and Financial Statements* **LO 3**

SPREADSHEET

Expert Consulting Services Inc. was organized on March 1, 2004, by two former college roommates. The corporation will provide computer consulting services to small businesses. The following transactions occurred during the first month of operations:

March 2: Received contributions of $20,000 from each of the two principal owners of the new business in exchange for shares of stock.

March 7: Signed a two-year promissory note at the bank and received cash of $15,000. Interest, along with the $15,000, will be repaid at the end of the two years.

March 12: Purchased $700 in miscellaneous supplies on account. The company has 30 days to pay for the supplies.

March 19: Billed a client $4,000 for services rendered by Expert in helping to install a new computer system. The client is to pay 25% of the bill upon its receipt and the remaining balance within 30 days.

March 20: Paid $1,300 bill from the local newspaper for advertising for the month of March.

March 22: Received 25% of the amount billed the client on March 19.

March 26: Received cash of $2,800 for services provided in assisting a client in selecting software for its computer.

March 29: Purchased a computer system for $8,000 in cash.

March 30: Paid $3,300 of salaries and wages for March.

March 31: Received and paid $1,400 in gas, electric, and water bills.

Required

1. Prepare a table to summarize the preceding transactions as they affect the accounting equation. Use the format in Exhibit 3-1. Identify each transaction with the date.
2. Prepare an income statement for the month ended March 31, 2004.
3. Prepare a classified balance sheet at March 31, 2004.
4. From reading the balance sheet you prepared in part 3, what events would you expect to take place in April? Explain your answer.

Problem 3-4 *Transactions Reconstructed from Financial Statements* **LO 3**

The following financial statements are available for Elm Corporation for its first month of operations:

ELM CORPORATION
INCOME STATEMENT
FOR THE MONTH ENDED JUNE 30, 2004

Service revenue		$93,600
Expenses:		
Rent	$ 9,000	
Salaries and wages	27,900	
Utilities	13,800	50,700
Net income		$42,900

ELM CORPORATION
BALANCE SHEET
JUNE 30, 2004

Assets		**Liabilities and Owners' Equity**	
Cash	$ 22,800	Accounts payable	$ 18,000
Accounts receivable	21,600	Notes payable	90,000
Equipment	18,000	Capital stock	30,000
Building	90,000	Retained earnings	38,400
Land	24,000	Total liabilities and	
Total assets	$176,400	owners' equity	$176,400

Required

Using the format illustrated in Exhibit 3-1, prepare a table to summarize the transactions entered into by Elm Corporation during its first month of business. State any assumptions you believe are necessary in reconstructing the transactions.

Multi-Concept Problems

Problem 3-5 *Identification of Events with Source Documents* LO 1, 2

Many events are linked to a source document. The following is a list of events that occurred in an entity:

a. Paid a one-year insurance policy.
b. Paid employee payroll.
c. Sold merchandise to a customer on account.
d. Identified supplies in the storeroom destroyed by fire.
e. Received payment of bills from customers.
f. Purchased land for future expansion.
g. Calculated taxes due.
h. Entered into a car lease agreement and paid the tax, title, and license.

Required

For each item **a** through **h,** indicate whether the event should or should not be recorded in the entity's accounts. For each item that should be recorded in the entity's books:

1. Identify one or more source documents that are generated from the event.
2. Identify which source document would be used to record an event when it produces more than one source document.
3. For each document, identify the information that is most useful in recording the event in the accounts.

Problem 3-6 *Transaction Analaysis and Financial Statements* LO 1, 3

SPREADSHEET

Blue Jay Delivery Service is incorporated on January 2, 2004, and enters into the following transactions during its first month of operations:

January 2: Filed articles of incorporation with the state, and issued 100,000 shares of capital stock. Cash of $100,000 is received from the new owners for the shares.

January 3: Purchased a warehouse and land for $80,000 in cash. An appraiser values the land at $20,000 and the warehouse at $60,000.

January 4: Signed a three-year promissory note at the Third State Bank in the amount of $50,000.

January 6: Purchased five new delivery trucks for a total of $45,000 in cash.

January 31: Performed services on account that amounted to $15,900 during the month. Cash amounting to $7,490 was received from customers on account during the month.

January 31: Established an open account at a local service station at the beginning of the month. Purchases of gas and oil during January amounted to $3,230. Blue Jay has until the 10th of the following month to pay its bill.

Required

1. Prepare a table to summarize the preceding transactions as they affect the accounting equation. Ignore depreciation expense and interest expense. Use the format in Exhibit 3-1.
2. Prepare an income statement for the month ended January 31, 2004.
3. Prepare a classified balance sheet at January 31, 2004.
4. Assume that you are considering buying stock in this company. Beginning with the transaction to record the purchase of the property on January 3, list any additional information you would like to have about each of the transactions during the remainder of the month.

Problem 3-7 *Transaction Analysis and Financial Statements* LO 1, 3

Neveranerror Inc. was organized on June 2, 2004, by a group of accountants to provide accounting and tax services to small businesses. The following transactions occurred during the first month of business:

(continued)

June 2: Received contributions of $10,000 from each of the three owners of the business in exchange for shares of stock.

June 5: Purchased a computer system for $12,000. The agreement with the vendor requires a down payment of $2,500 with the balance due in 60 days.

June 8: Signed a two-year promissory note at the bank and received cash of $20,000.

June 15: Billed $12,350 to clients for the first half of June. Clients are billed twice a month for services performed during the month, and the bills are payable within 10 days.

June 17: Paid a $900 bill from the local newspaper for advertising for the month of June.

June 23: Received the amounts billed to clients for services performed during the first half of the month.

June 28: Received and paid gas, electric, and water bills. The total amount is $2,700.

June 29: Received the landlord's bill for $2,200 for rent on the office space that Neveranerror leases. The bill is payable by the 10th of the following month.

June 30: Paid salaries and wages for June. The total amount is $5,670.

June 30: Billed $18,400 to clients for the second half of June.

June 30: Declared and paid dividends in the amount of $6,000.

Required

1. Prepare a table to summarize the preceding transactions as they affect the accounting equation. Ignore depreciation expense and interest expense. Use the format in Exhibit 3-1.
2. Prepare the following financial statements:
   a. Income statement for the month ended June 30, 2004.
   b. Statement of retained earnings for the month ended June 30, 2004.
   c. Classified balance sheet at June 30, 2004.

DECISION MAKING

3. Assume that you have just graduated from college and have been approached to join this company as an accountant. From your reading of the financial statements for the first month, would you consider joining the company? Explain your answer. Limit your answer to financial considerations only.

Problem 3-8 ***Accounts Used to Record Transactions (Appendix)*** **LO 3, 5**

A list of accounts, with an identifying number for each, is shown below. Following the list of accounts is a series of transactions entered into by a company during its first year of operations.

Required

For each transaction, indicate the account or accounts that should be debited and credited.

1. Cash
2. Accounts Receivable
3. Office Supplies
4. Buildings
5. Automobiles
6. Land
7. Accounts Payable
8. Income Tax Payable
9. Notes Payable
10. Capital Stock
11. Retained Earnings
12. Service Revenue
13. Wage and Salary Expense
14. Selling Expense
15. Utilities Expense
16. Income Tax Expense

Transactions	Accounts Debited	Accounts Credited
Example: Purchased land and building in exchange for a three-year promissory note.	4, 6	9
a. Issued capital stock for cash.		
b. Purchased 10 automobiles; paid part in cash and signed a 60-day note for the balance.		
c. Purchased land in exchange for a note due in six months.		
d. Purchased office supplies; agreed to pay total bill by the 10th of the following month.		

e. Billed clients for services performed during the month, and gave them until the 15th of the following month to pay. ______ ______

f. Received cash on account from clients for services rendered to them in past months. ______ ______

g. Paid employees salaries and wages earned during the month. ______ ______

h. Paid newspaper for company ads appearing during the month. ______ ______

i. Received monthly gas and electric bill from the utility company; payment is due anytime within the first 10 days of the following month. ______ ______

j. Computed amount of taxes due based on the income of the period; amount will be paid in the following month. ______ ______

Problem 3-9 *Transaction Analysis and Journal Entries Recorded Directly in T Accounts (Appendix)* **LO 3, 4, 5**

Four brothers organized Beverly Entertainment Enterprises on October 1, 2004. The following transactions occurred during the first month of operations:

October 1: Received contribution of $10,000 from each of the four principal owners of the new business in exchange for shares of stock.

October 2: Purchased the Arcada Theater for $125,000. The seller agreed to accept a down payment of $12,500 and a seven-year promissory note for the balance. The Arcada property consists of land valued at $35,000 and a building valued at $90,000.

October 3: Purchased new seats for the theater at a cost of $5,000, paying $2,500 down and agreeing to pay the remainder in 60 days.

October 12: Purchased candy, popcorn, cups, and napkins for $3,700 on an open account. The company has 30 days to pay for the concession supplies.

October 13: Sold tickets for the opening-night movie for cash of $1,800, and took in $2,400 at the concession stand.

October 17: Rented out the theater to a local community group for $1,500. The community group is to pay one-half of the bill within five working days and has 30 days to pay the remainder.

October 23: Received 50% of the amount billed to the community group.

October 24: Sold movie tickets for cash of $2,000, and took in $2,800 at the concession stand.

October 26: The four brothers, acting on behalf of Beverly Entertainment, paid a dividend of $750 on the shares of stock owned by each of them, or $3,000 in total.

October 27: Paid $500 for utilities.

October 30: Paid wages and salaries of $2,400 total to the ushers, the projectionist, concession stand workers, and the maintenance crew.

October 31: Sold movie tickets for cash of $1,800, and took in $2,500 at the concession stand.

Required

1. Prepare a table to summarize the preceding transactions as they affect the accounting equation. Use the format in Exhibit 3-1. Identify each transaction with a date.
2. Record each transaction directly in T accounts, using the dates preceding the transactions to identify them in the accounts. Each account involved in the problem needs a separate T account.

Problem 3-10 *Trial Balance and Financial Statements (Appendix)* **LO 4, 7**

Refer to the table for Beverly Entertainment Enterprises in part **1** of Problem 3-9.

Required

1. Prepare a trial balance at October 31, 2004.
2. Prepare an income statement for the month ended October 31, 2004.
3. Prepare a statement of retained earnings for the month ended October 31, 2004.
4. Prepare a classified balance sheet at October 31, 2004.

Problem 3-11 *Journal Entries (Appendix)* **LO 3, 5, 6**

Atkins Advertising Agency began business on January 2, 2004. Listed on the following page are the transactions entered into by Atkins during its first month of operations.

a. Acquired its articles of incorporation from the state, and issued 100,000 shares of capital stock in exchange for $200,000 in cash.

b. Purchased an office building for $150,000 in cash. The building is valued at $110,000, and the remainder of the value is assigned to the land.

c. Signed a three-year promissory note at the bank for $125,000.

d. Purchased office equipment at a cost of $50,000, paying $10,000 down and agreeing to pay the remainder in 10 days.

e. Paid wages and salaries of $13,000 for the first half of the month. Office employees are paid twice a month.

f. Paid the balance due on the office equipment.

g. Sold $24,000 of advertising during the first month. Customers have until the 15th of the following month to pay their bills.

h. Paid wages and salaries of $15,000 for the second half of the month.

i. Recorded $3,500 in commissions earned by the salespeople during the month. They will be paid on the fifth of the following month.

Required

Prepare in journal form the entry to record each transaction.

Problem 3-12 ***Journal Entries Recorded Directly in T Accounts (Appendix)*** **LO 3, 4, 5**

Refer to the transactions for Atkins Advertising Agency in Problem 3-11.

Required

1. Record each transaction directly in T accounts, using the letters preceding the transactions to identify them in the accounts. Each account involved in the problem needs a separate T account.
2. Prepare a trial balance at January 31, 2004.

Problem 3-13 ***The Detection of Errors in a Trial Balance and Preparation of a Corrected Trial Balance (Appendix)*** **LO 3, 5, 7**

Malcolm Inc. was incorporated on January 1, 2004, with the issuance of capital stock in return for $90,000 of cash contributed by the owners. The only other transaction entered into prior to beginning operations was the issuance of a $75,300 note payable in exchange for building and equipment. The following trial balance was prepared at the end of the first month by the bookkeeper for Malcolm Inc.

MALCOLM INC.
TRIAL BALANCE
JANUARY 31, 2004

Account Titles	Debits	Credits
Cash	$ 9,980	
Accounts Receivable	8,640	
Land	80,000	
Building	50,000	
Equipment	23,500	
Notes Payable		75,300
Capital Stock		90,000
Service Revenue		50,340
Wage and Salary Expense	23,700	
Advertising Expense	4,600	
Utilities Expense	8,420	
Dividends		5,000
Totals	$208,840	$220,640

Required

1. Identify the *two* errors in the trial balance. Ignore depreciation expense and interest expense.
2. Prepare a corrected trial balance.

Problem 3-14 ***Journal Entries, Trial Balance, and Financial Statements (Appendix)***
LO 3, 5, 6, 7
Refer to the transactions for Blue Jay Delivery Service in Problem 3-6.

Required:

1. Prepare journal entries on the books of Blue Jay to record the transactions entered into during the month. Ignore depreciation expense and interest expense.
2. Prepare a trial balance at January 31, 2004.
3. Prepare an income statement for the month ended January 31, 2004.
4. Prepare a classified balance sheet at January 31, 2004.
5. Assume that you are considering buying stock in this company. Beginning with the transaction to record the purchase of the property on January 3, list any additional information you would like to have about each of the transactions during the remainder of the month.

Problem 3-15 ***Journal Entries, Trial Balance, and Financial Statements (Appendix)***
LO 3, 5, 6, 7
Refer to the transactions for Neveranerror Inc. in Problem 3-7.

Required:

1. Prepare journal entries on the books of Neveranerror to record the transactions entered into during the month. Ignore depreciation expense and interest expense.
2. Prepare a trial balance at June 30, 2004.
3. Prepare the following financial statements:
   a. Income statement for the month ended June 30, 2004.
   b. Statement of retained earnings for the month ended June 30, 2004.
   c. Classified balance sheet at June 30, 2004.
4. Assume that you have just graduated from college and have been approached to join this company as an accountant. From your reading of the financial statements for the first month, would you consider joining the company? Explain your answer. Limit your answer to financial considerations only.

Alternate Problems

Problem 3-1A ***Events to Be Recorded in Accounts*** **LO 1**

The following events take place at Anaconda Accountants Inc.:

1. Supplies are ordered from vendors, who will deliver the supplies within the week.
2. Vendors deliver supplies on account, payment due in 30 days.
3. New computer system is ordered.
4. Old computer system is sold for cash.
5. Services are rendered to customers on account. The invoices are mailed and due in 30 days.
6. Cash received from customer payments is deposited in the bank night depository.
7. Employees are paid weekly paychecks.
8. Vendors noted in item **2** are paid for the supplies delivered.

Required

Identify each event as internal (I) or external (E), and indicate whether each event would be recorded in the *accounts* of the company. For each event that is to be recorded, identify the names of at least two accounts that would be affected.

Problem 3-2A ***Transaction Analysis and Financial Statements*** **LO 3**
Beachway Enterprises was organized on June 1, 2004, by two college students who recognized an opportunity to make money while spending their days at a beach in Florida. The two entrepreneurs plan to rent beach umbrellas. The following transactions occurred during the first month of operations:

(continued)

June 1: Received contribution of $2,000 from each of the two principal owners of the new business in exchange for shares of stock.

June 1: Purchased 25 beach umbrellas for $250 each on account. The company has 30 days to pay for the beach umbrellas.

June 5: Registered as a vendor with the city and paid the $35 monthly fee.

June 10: Purchased $50 in miscellaneous supplies on an open account. The company has 30 days to pay for the supplies.

June 15: Paid $70 bill from a local radio station for advertising for the last two weeks of June.

June 17: Customers rented beach umbrellas for cash of $1,000.

June 24: Billed a local hotel $2,000 for beach umbrellas provided for use during a convention being held at the hotel. The hotel is to pay one-half of the bill in five days and the rest within 30 days.

June 29: Received 50% of the amount billed to the hotel.

June 30: Customers rented beach umbrellas for cash of $1,500.

June 30: Paid wages of $90 to a friend who helped out over the weekend.

June 30: Paid the balance due on the beach umbrellas.

Required

1. Prepare a table to summarize the preceding transactions as they affect the accounting equation. Use the format in Exhibit 3-1. Identify each transaction with a date.
2. Prepare an income statement for the month ended June 30, 2004.
3. Prepare a classified balance sheet at June 30, 2004.

Problem 3-3A *Transaction Analysis and Financial Statements* LO 3

SPREADSHEET

Dynamic Services Inc. was organized on March 1, 2004, by two former college roommates. The corporation will provide computer tax services to small businesses. The following transactions occurred during the first month of operations:

March 2: Received contributions of $10,000 from each of the two principal owners in exchange for shares of stock.

March 7: Signed a two-year promissory note at the bank and received cash of $7,500. Interest, along with the $7,500, will be repaid at the end of the two years.

March 12: Purchased miscellaneous supplies on account for $350, payment due in 30 days.

March 19: Billed a client $2,000 for tax-preparation services. According to an agreement between the two companies, the client is to pay 25% of the bill upon its receipt and the remaining balance within 30 days.

March 20: Paid a $650 bill from the local newspaper for advertising for the month of March.

March 22: Received 25% of the amount billed the client on March 19.

March 26: Received cash of $1,400 for services provided in assisting a client in preparing its tax return.

March 29: Purchased a computer system for $4,000 in cash.

March 30: Paid $1,650 in salaries and wages for March.

March 31: Received and paid $700 of gas, electric, and water bills.

Required

1. Prepare a table to summarize the preceding transactions as they affect the accounting equation. Use the format in Exhibit 3-1. Identify each transaction with the date.
2. Prepare an income statement for the month ended March 31, 2004.
3. Prepare a classified balance sheet at March 31, 2004.
4. From reading the balance sheet you prepared in part **3**, what events would you expect to take place in April? Explain your answer.

Problem 3-4A *Transactions Reconstructed from Financial Statements* LO 3

The following financial statements are available for Oak Corporation for its first month of operations:

OAK CORPORATION
INCOME STATEMENT
FOR THE MONTH ENDED JULY 31, 2004

Service revenue		$75,400
Expenses:		
Rent	$ 6,000	
Salaries and wages	24,600	
Utilities	12,700	43,300
Net income		$32,100

OAK CORPORATION
BALANCE SHEET
JULY 31, 2004

Assets		Liabilities and Owners' Equity	
Cash	$ 13,700	Wages payable	$ 6,000
Accounts receivable	25,700	Notes payable	50,000
Equipment	32,000	Unearned service revenue	4,500
Furniture	14,700	Capital stock	30,000
Land	24,000	Retained earnings	19,600
Total assets	$110,100	Total liabilities and owners' equity	$110,100

Required

Describe as many transactions as you can that were entered into by Oak Corporation during the first month of business.

Alternate Multi-Concept Problems

Problem 3-5A ***Identification of Events with Source Documents*** LO 1, 2

Many events are linked to a source document. The following is a list of events that occurred in an entity:

a. Paid a security deposit and six months' rent on a building.
b. Hired three employees and agreed to pay them $400 per week.
c. Sold merchandise to a customer for cash.
d. Reported a fire that destroyed a billboard that is on the entity's property and is owned and maintained by another entity.
e. Received payment of bills from customers.
f. Purchased stock in another entity to gain some control over it.
g. Signed a note at the bank and received cash.
h. Contracted with a cleaning service to maintain the interior of the building in good repair. No money is paid at this time.

Required

For each item **a** through **h,** indicate whether the event should or should not be recorded in the entity's accounts. For each item that should be recorded in the entity's books:

1. Identify one or more source documents that are generated from the event.
2. Identify which source document would be used to record an event when it produces more than one source document.
3. For each document, identify the information that is most useful in recording the event in the accounts.

Problem 3-6A ***Journal Entries*** LO 1, 3

Overnight Delivery Inc. is incorporated on January 2, 2004, and enters into the following transactions during its second month of operations:

February 2: Paid $400 for wages earned by employees for the week ending January 31.
February 3: Paid $3,230 for gas and oil billed on an open account in January.
February 4: Declared and paid $2,000 cash dividends to stockholders.

February 15: Received $8,000 cash from customer accounts.

February 26: Provided $16,800 of services on account during the month.

February 27: Received a $3,400 bill from the local service station for gas and oil used during February.

Required

1. Prepare a table to summarize the preceding transactions as they affect the accounting equation. Use the format in Exhibit 3-1.
2. For the transactions on February 2, 3, 4, and 27, indicate whether the amount is an expense of operating in the month of January or February or is not an expense in either month.

Problem 3-7A ***Journal Entries and a Balance Sheet*** **LO 1, 3**

Krittersbegone Inc. was organized on July 1, 2004, by a group of technicians to provide termite inspections and treatment to homeowners and small businesses. The following transactions occurred during the first month of business:

July 2: Received contributions of $3,000 from each of the six owners in exchange for shares of stock.

July 3: Paid $1,000 rent for the month of July.

July 5: Purchased flashlights, tools, spray equipment, and ladders for $18,000, with a down payment of $5,000 and the balance due in 30 days.

July 17: Paid a $200 bill for the distribution of door-to-door advertising.

July 28: Paid August rent and July utilities to the landlord in the amounts of $1,000 and $450, respectively.

July 30: Received $8,000 in cash from homeowners for services performed during the month. In addition, billed $7,500 to other customers for services performed during the month. Billings are due in 30 days.

July 30: Paid commissions of $9,500 to the technicians for July.

July 31: Received $600 from a business client to perform services over the next two months.

Required

1. Prepare a table to summarize the preceding transactions as they affect the accounting equation. Ignore depreciation expense. Use the format in Exhibit 3-1.
2. Prepare a classified balance sheet dated July 31, 2004. From the balance sheet, what cash inflow and what cash outflow can you predict in the month of August? Who would be interested in the cash flow information and why?

Problem 3-8A ***Accounts Used to Record Transactions (Appendix)*** **LO 3, 5**

A list of accounts, with an identifying number for each, is shown below. Following the list of accounts is a series of transactions entered into by a company during its first year of operations.

Required

For each transaction, indicate the account or accounts that should be debited and credited.

1. Cash
2. Accounts Receivable
3. Prepaid Insurance
4. Office Supplies
5. Automobiles
6. Land
7. Accounts Payable
8. Income Tax Payable
9. Notes Payable
10. Capital Stock
11. Retained Earnings
12. Service Revenue
13. Wage and Salary Expense
14. Utilities Expense
15. Income Tax Expense

Transactions	Accounts Debited	Accounts Credited
Example: Purchased office supplies for cash.	4	1
a. Issued capital stock for cash.		
b. Purchased an automobile and signed a 60-day note for the total amount.		

c. Acquired land in exchange for capital stock.	_____	_____
d. Received cash from clients for services performed during the month.	_____	_____
e. Paid employees salaries and wages earned during the month.	_____	_____
f. Purchased flyers and signs from a printer, payment due in 10 days.	_____	_____
g. Paid for the flyers and signs purchased in part **f.**	_____	_____
h. Received monthly telephone bill; payment is due within 10 days of receipt.	_____	_____
i. Paid for a six-month liability insurance policy.	_____	_____
j. Paid monthly telephone bill.	_____	_____
k. Computed amount of taxes due based on the income of the period and paid the amount.	_____	_____

Problem 3-9A *Transaction Analysis and Journal Entries Recorded Directly in T Accounts (Appendix)* LO 3, 4, 5

Three friends organized Rapid City Roller Rink on October 1, 2004. The following transactions occurred during the first month of operations:

October 1: Received contribution of $22,000 from each of the three principal owners of the new business in exchange for shares of stock.

October 2: Purchased land valued at $15,000 and a building valued at $75,000. The seller agreed to accept a down payment of $9,000 and a five-year promissory note for the balance.

October 3: Purchased new tables and chairs for the lounge at the roller rink at a cost of $25,000, paying $5,000 down and agreeing to pay for the remainder in 60 days.

October 9: Purchased 100 pairs of roller skates for cash at $35 per pair.

October 12: Purchased food and drinks for $2,500 on an open account. The company has 30 days to pay for the concession supplies.

October 13: Sold tickets for cash of $400 and took in $750 at the concession stand.

October 17: Rented out the roller rink to a local community group for $750. The community group is to pay one-half of the bill within five working days and has 30 days to pay the remainder.

October 23: Received 50% of the amount billed to the community group.

October 24: Sold tickets for cash of $500, and took in $1,200 at the concession stand.

October 26: The three friends, acting on behalf of Rapid City Roller Rink, paid a dividend of $250 on the shares of stock owned by each of them, or $750 in total.

October 27: Paid $1,275 for utilities.

October 30: Paid wages and salaries of $2,250.

October 31: Sold tickets for cash of $700, and took in $1,300 at the concession stand.

Required

1. Prepare a table to summarize the preceding transactions as they affect the accounting equation. Use the format in Exhibit 3-1. Identify each transaction with a date.
2. Record each transaction directly in T accounts, using the dates preceding the transactions to identify them in the accounts. Each account involved in the problem needs a separate T account.

Problem 3-10A *Trial Balance and Financial Statements (Appendix)* LO 4, 7

Refer to the table for Rapid City Roller Rink in part **1** of Problem 3-9A.

Required

1. Prepare a trial balance at October 31, 2004.
2. Prepare an income statement for the month ended October 31, 2004.
3. Prepare a statement of retained earnings for the month ended October 31, 2004.
4. Prepare a classified balance sheet at October 31, 2004.

Problem 3-11A *Journal Entries (Appendix)* LO 3, 5, 6

Castle Consulting Agency began business in February 2004. Listed below are the transactions entered into by Castle during its first month of operations.

a. Acquired articles of incorporation from the state, and issued 10,000 shares of capital stock in exchange for $150,000 in cash.

b. Paid monthly rent of $400.

c. Signed a five-year promissory note for $100,000 at the bank.

d. Received $5,000 cash from a customer for services to be performed over the next two months.

e. Purchased software to be used on future jobs. The software costs $950 and is expected to be used on five to eight jobs over the next two years.

f. Billed customers $12,500 for work performed during the month.

g. Paid office personnel $3,000 for the month of February.

h. Received a utility bill of $100. The total amount is due in 30 days.

Required

Prepare in journal form the entry to record each transaction.

Problem 3-12A *Journal Entries Recorded Directly in T Accounts (Appendix)* LO 3, 4, 5, 7

Refer to the transactions for Castle Consulting Agency in Problem 3-11A.

Required

1. Record each transaction directly in T accounts, using the letters preceding the transactions to identify them in the accounts. Each account involved in the problem needs a separate T account.
2. Prepare a trial balance at February 28, 2004.

Problem 3-13A *Entries Prepared from a Trial Balance and Proof of the Cash Balance (Appendix)* LO 3, 4, 5, 7

Russell Company was incorporated on January 1, 2004, with the issuance of capital stock in return for $120,000 of cash contributed by the owners. The only other transaction entered into prior to beginning operations was the issuance of a $50,000 note payable in exchange for equipment and fixtures. The following trial balance was prepared at the end of the first month by the bookkeeper for Russell Company:

RUSSELL COMPANY
TRIAL BALANCE
JANUARY 31, 2004

Account Titles	Debits	Credits
Cash	$???	
Accounts Receivable	30,500	
Equipment and Fixtures	50,000	
Wages Payable		$ 10,000
Notes Payable		50,000
Capital Stock		120,000
Service Revenue		60,500
Wage and Salary Expense	24,600	
Advertising Expense	12,500	
Rent Expense	5,200	

Required

1. Determine the balance in the Cash account.
2. Identify all of the transactions that affected the Cash account during the month. Use a T account to prove what the balance in Cash would be after all transactions are recorded.

Problem 3-14A *Journal Entries (Appendix)* LO 3, 5, 6

Refer to the transactions for Overnight Delivery Inc. in Problem 3-6A.

Required:

1. Prepare journal entries on the books of Overnight to record the transactions entered into during February.
2. For the transactions on February 2, 3, 4, and 27, indicate whether the amount is an expense of operating in the month of January or February or is not an expense in either month.

Problem 3-15A *Journal Entries and a Balance Sheet (Appendix)* **LO 3, 5, 6**

Refer to the transactions for Krittersbegone Inc. in Problem 3-7A.

Required:

1. Prepare journal entries on the books of Krittersbegone to record the transactions entered into during the month. Ignore depreciation expense.
2. Prepare a classified balance sheet dated July 31, 2004. From the balance sheet, what cash inflow and what cash outflow can you predict in the month of August? Who would be interested in the cash flow information and why?

Decision Cases

Reading and Interpreting Financial Statements

Decision Case 3-1 *Comparing Two Companies in the Same Industry: Winnebago Industries and Monaco Coach Corporation* **LO 4**

http://www.winnebagoind.com
http://www.monacocoach.com

Refer to the income statements for Winnebago Industries and Monaco Coach Corporation in Appendices A and B at the end of the book.

Required

1. How many accounts does each company report on its income statement? (Do not include in your answer any of the subtotals reported, such as operating income.)
2. Winnebago Industries reports an account on its income statement titled "Revenues: Manufactured products." What account is equivalent to this account on Monaco Coach Corporation's income statement?
3. One of the accounts on Monaco Coach Corporation's income statement is "Selling, general and administrative expenses." How are these expenses reported on Winnebago Industries' income statement?
4. Winnebago Industries reports taxes on its income statement on the line titled "Provision for taxes." Monaco Coach Corporation uses the account "Provision for income taxes." What is the dollar amount of taxes each reports on its income statement? Compute the ratio of taxes to income before income taxes for 2001 and for 2002 for each company. Is Winnebago Industries' ratio the same for both years? Is Monaco Coach Corporation's ratio the same for both years? Which company has the higher ratio for 2001? Which company has the higher ratio for 2002? What does this ratio information tell you?

Decision Case 3-2 *Reading and Interpreting Winnebago Industries' Statement of Cash Flows* **LO 3**

Refer to Winnebago Industries' statement of cash flows for the year ended August 31, 2002.

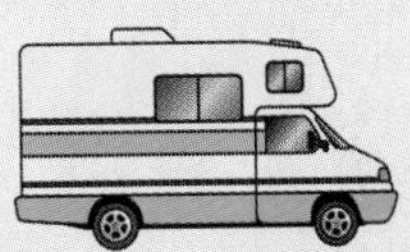

Required

1. What amount did the company spend on purchases of property and equipment during 2002? Determine the effect on the accounting equation from these purchases.
2. What amount did the company pay to stockholders in cash dividends during 2002? Determine the effect on the accounting equation from these dividends.

Decision Case 3-3 *Reading and Interpreting General Mills' Income Statement* **LO 4**

http://www.generalmills.com

Refer to the chapter opener and General Mills' income statement as shown there.

Required

1. General Mills' income statement does not provide a subtotal for gross profit. Compute gross profit and the gross profit percentage for the years 2002 and 2003. Did each of these increase or decrease in 2003?

(continued)

2. What is General Mills' largest expense? Compute the ratio of this expense to sales for 2002 and 2003. Did the ratio increase, decrease, or stay the same?
3. Compute General Mills' profit margin for 2002 and 2003. Did the ratio increase, decrease, or stay the same?

http://www.delta.com

Decision Case 3-4 ***Reading and Interpreting Delta's Balance Sheet*** **LO 1, 3**

The following item appears in the current liabilities section of Delta Air Lines' balance sheet at December 31, 2002:

Air traffic liability $1,270 million

In addition, one of Delta's notes states: "We record sales of passenger tickets as air traffic liability on our Consolidated Balance Sheets. Passenger revenues are recognized when we provide the transportation, reducing the related air traffic liability. We periodically evaluate the estimated air traffic liability and record any resulting adjustments in the Consolidated Statements of Operations in the period that the evaluations are completed."

Required

1. What economic event caused Delta to incur this liability? Was it an external or an internal event?
2. Describe the effect on the accounting equation from the transaction to record the air traffic liability.
3. Assume that one customer purchases a $500 ticket in advance. Determine the effect on the accounting equation from this transaction.
4. What economic event will cause Delta to reduce its air traffic liability? Is this an external or an internal event?

Making Financial Decisions

DECISION MAKING

Decision Case 3-5 ***Cash Flow versus Net Income*** **LO 2, 3**

Shelia Young started a real estate business at the beginning of January. After approval by the state for a charter to incorporate, she issued 1,000 shares of stock to herself and deposited $20,000 in a bank account under the name Young Properties. Because business was "booming," she spent all of her time during the first month selling properties rather than keeping financial records.

At the end of January, Shelia comes to you with the following plight:

> I put $20,000 in to start this business at the beginning of the month. My January 31 bank statement shows a balance of $17,000. After all of my efforts, it appears as if I'm "in the hole" already! On the other hand, that seems impossible—we sold five properties for clients during the month. The total sales value of these properties was $600,000, and I receive a commission of 5% on each sale. Granted, one of the five sellers still owes me an $8,000 commission on the sale, but the other four have been collected in full. Three of the sales, totaling $400,000, were actually made by my assistants. I pay them 4% of the sales value of a property. Sure, I have a few office expenses for my car, utilities, and a secretary, but that's about it. How can I have possibly lost $3,000 this month?

You agree to help Shelia figure out how she really did this month. The bank statement is helpful. The total deposits during the month amount to $22,000. Shelia explains that this amount represents the commissions on the four sales collected so far. The canceled checks reveal the following expenditures:

Check No.	Payee—Memo at Bottom of Check	Amount
101	Stevens Office Supply	$ 2,000
102	Why Walk, Let's Talk Motor Co.—new car	3,000
103	City of Westbrook—heat and lights	500
104	Alice Hill—secretary	2,200
105	Ace Property Management—office rent for month	1,200
106	Jerry Hayes (sales assistant)	10,000
107	Joan Harper (sales assistant)	6,000
108	Don's Fillitup—gas and oil for car	100

According to Shelia, the $2,000 check to Stevens Office Supply represents the down payment on a word processor and a copier for the office. The remaining balance is $3,000 and it must be paid to Stevens by February 15. Similarly, the $3,000 check is the down payment on a car for the business. A $12,000 note was given to the car dealer and is due along with interest in one year.

1. Prepare an income statement for the month of January for Young Properties.
2. Prepare a statement of cash flows for the month of January for Young Properties.
3. Draft a memorandum to Shelia Young explaining as simply and as clearly as possible why she *did* in fact have a profitable first month in business but experienced a decrease in her cash account. Support your explanation with any necessary figures.
4. The down payments on the car and the office equipment are reflected on the statement of cash flows. They are assets that will benefit the business for a number of years. Do you think that *any* of the cost associated with the acquisition of these assets should be recognized in some way on the income statement? Explain your answer.

Decision Case 3-6 *Loan Request* LO 1, 3, 4

DECISION MAKING

Simon Fraser started a landscaping and lawn-care business in April 2004 by investing $20,000 cash in the business in exchange for capital stock. Because his business is in the Midwest, the season begins in April and concludes in September. He prepared the following list of accounts and their balances (with accounts in alphabetical order) at the end of the first season in business.

	Balance
Accounts Payable	$13,000
Accounts Receivable	23,000
Capital Stock	20,000
Cash	1,200
Gas and Oil Expense	15,700
Insurance Expense	2,500
Landscaping Revenue	33,400
Lawn Care Revenue	24,000
Mowing Equipment	5,000
Rent Expense	6,000
Salaries Expense	22,000
Truck	15,000

Simon is pleased with his first year in business. "I paid myself a salary of $22,000 during the year and still have $1,200 in the bank. Sure, I have a few bills outstanding, but my accounts receivable will more than cover those." In fact, Simon is so happy with the first year, that he has come to you in your role as a lending officer at the local bank to ask for a $20,000 loan to allow him to add another truck and mowing equipment for the second season.

Required

1. From your reading of the trial balance, what does it appear to you that Simon did with the $20,000 in cash he originally contributed to the business? Determine the effect on the accounting equation from the transaction you think took place.
2. Prepare an income statement for the six months ended September 30, 2004.
3. The mowing equipment and truck are assets that will benefit the business for a number of years. Do you think that any of the costs associated with the purchase of these assets should have been recognized as expenses in the first year? How would this have affected the income statement?
4. Prepare a classified balance sheet as of September 30, 2004. As a banker, what two items on the balance sheet concern you the most? Explain your answer.
5. As a banker, would you loan Simon $20,000 to expand his business during the second year? Draft a memo to respond to Simon's request for the loan, indicating whether you will make the loan.

Accounting and Ethics: What Would You Do?

Decision Case 3-7 *Revenue Recognition* LO 1, 3

ETHICS

You are controller for an architectural firm whose accounting year ends on December 31. As part of the management team, you receive a year-end bonus directly related to the firm's earnings for the year. One of your duties is to review the transactions recorded by the bookkeepers. A new bookkeeper recorded the receipt of $10,000 in cash as an increase in cash and an increase in service revenue.

The $10,000 is a deposit and the bookkeeper explains to you that the firm plans to provide the services to the client in March of the following year.

1. Did the bookkeeper correctly record the client's deposit? Explain your answer.
2. What would you do as controller for the firm? Do you have a responsibility to do anything to correct the books?

Decision Case 3-8 ***Delay in the Posting of a Journal Entry (Appendix)*** **LO 3, 5, 6**

ETHICS

As assistant controller for a small consulting firm, you are responsible for recording and posting the daily cash receipts and disbursements to the ledger accounts. After you have posted the entries, your boss, the controller, prepares a trial balance and the financial statements. You make the following entries on June 30, 2004:

2004			
June 30	Cash	1,430	
	Accounts Receivable	1,950	
	Service Revenue		3,380
	To record daily cash receipts.		
June 30	Advertising Expense	12,500	
	Utilities Expense	22,600	
	Rent Expense	24,000	
	Salary and Wage Expense	17,400	
	Cash		76,500
	To record daily cash disbursements.		

The daily cash disbursements are much larger on June 30 than any other day because many of the company's major bills are paid on the last day of the month. After you have recorded these two transactions and *before* you have posted them to the ledger accounts, your boss comes to you with the following request:

> As you are aware, the first half of the year has been a tough one for the consulting industry and for our business in particular. With first-half bonuses based on net income, I am concerned whether you or I will get any bonus this time around. However, I have a suggestion that should allow us to receive something for our hard work and at the same time will not hurt anyone. Go ahead and post the June 30 cash receipts to the ledger but don't bother to post that day's cash disbursements. Even though the treasurer writes the checks on the last day of the month and you normally journalize the transaction on the same day, it is pretty silly to bother posting the entry to the ledger, since it takes at least a week for the checks to clear the bank.

Required

1. Explain why the controller's request will result in an increase in net income.
2. Do you agree with the controller's comment that the June 30th entry "will not hurt anyone"? Who might be hurt? Does omitting the entry provide information that is free from bias? Explain your answer.
3. What would you do if the controller had told you to do this? To whom should you talk about this matter? Is this situation an ethical dilemma? Why?

THOMSON ONE Business School Edition Case

Case 3-9 ***Using THOMSON ONE for General Mills***

http://www.generalmills.com

The acquisition of Pillsbury by General Mills immediately transformed the company into a global consumer foods giant. Like General Mills before the merger, Pillsbury maintained a leadership market position in no less than four food categories. We can use THOMSON ONE to obtain information about General Mills' performance since this key acquisition and the effect of its performance on its stock price.

Begin by entering the company's ticker symbol, GIS, and then selecting "GO." On the opening screen you will see background information about the company, key financial ratios, and some recent data concerning stock price. To research the company's stock price further, click the "Prices" tab. At the top of the Price Chart, click on the "Interactive Chart." To obtain a 1-year chart, go to "Time Frame," click on the down arrow, and select "1 year." Then click on "Draw," and a 1-year chart should appear.

We can also find General Mills' most recent financial statements. Near the top of the screen, click on "Financials" and select "Financial Statements." Refer to the comparative statements of earnings, statements of cash flows, and balance sheets.

Based on your use of THOMSON ONE, answer the following questions:

1. Based on the most recent year available, what are General Mills' sales and its net earnings?
2. Compare the number reported in part **1** to the corresponding amounts of sales and net earnings reported by General Mills in the 2003 fiscal year, the first full year after the acquisition of Pillsbury (refer to the chapter opener for the 2003 income statement).
3. What have been General Mills' high and low stock prices for the most recent year?
4. How does the company's stock performance compare to the other line on the stock price chart for the S&P 500?
5. Based on your answers to the above questions, do you think it was a wise decision for General Mills to acquire Pillsbury? Explain your reasoning.

Source: General Mills' 2003 Annual Report.

Solutions to Key Terms Quiz

Quiz 1: Processing Accounting Information

2	Event (p. 109)
5	External event (p. 109)
3	Internal event (p. 109)
8	Transaction (p. 109)
4	Source document (p. 110)
6	Account (p. 117)
1	Chart of accounts (p. 117)
7	General ledger (p. 117)

Quiz 2: Appendix

4	Debit (p. 123)
2	Credit (p. 123)
8	Double-entry system (p. 126)
6	Journal (p. 128)
5	Posting (p. 128)
3	Journalizing (p. 128)
7	General journal (p. 129)
1	Trial balance (p. 130)

Chapter 4

Income Measurement and Accrual Accounting

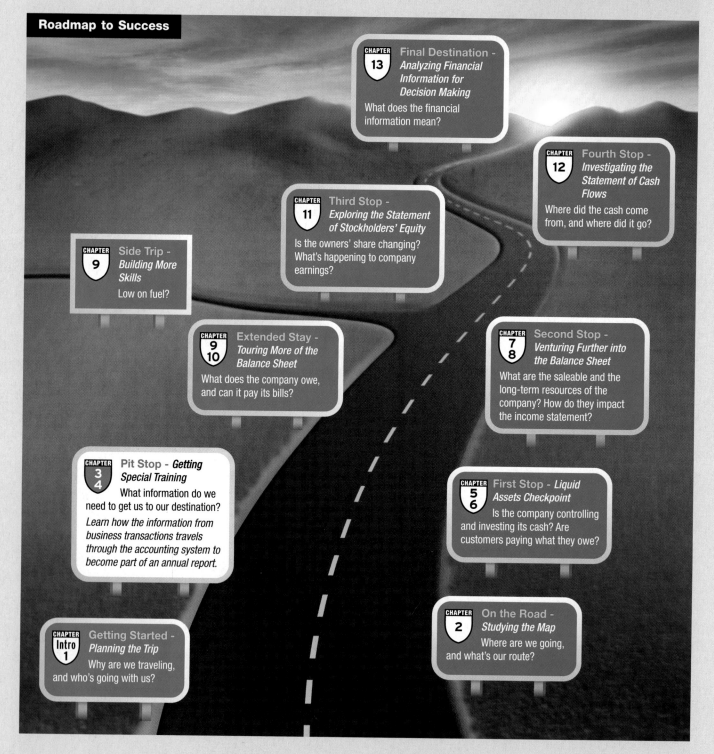

Roadmap to Success

CHAPTER 13 **Final Destination -** *Analyzing Financial Information for Decision Making*
What does the financial information mean?

CHAPTER 12 **Fourth Stop -** *Investigating the Statement of Cash Flows*
Where did the cash come from, and where did it go?

CHAPTER 11 **Third Stop -** *Exploring the Statement of Stockholders' Equity*
Is the owners' share changing? What's happening to company earnings?

CHAPTER 9 **Side Trip -** *Building More Skills*
Low on fuel?

CHAPTER 9 10 **Extended Stay -** *Touring More of the Balance Sheet*
What does the company owe, and can it pay its bills?

CHAPTER 7 8 **Second Stop -** *Venturing Further into the Balance Sheet*
What are the saleable and the long-term resources of the company? How do they impact the income statement?

CHAPTER 3 4 **Pit Stop -** ***Getting Special Training***
What information do we need to get us to our destination?
Learn how the information from business transactions travels through the accounting system to become part of an annual report.

CHAPTER 5 6 **First Stop -** ***Liquid Assets Checkpoint***
Is the company controlling and investing its cash? Are customers paying what they owe?

CHAPTER Intro 1 **Getting Started -** *Planning the Trip*
Why are we traveling, and who's going with us?

CHAPTER 2 **On the Road -** *Studying the Map*
Where are we going, and what's our route?

Focus on Financial Results

It would be difficult to find anyone in the world today who is not familiar with what McDonald's does. However, what may be less obvious are the two distinct ways in which the company generates revenue. As can be seen in the accompanying income statements, McDonald's relies on two different forms of revenues: sales by company-owned restaurants and revenues from franchised and affiliated restaurants. The first is easy to understand: every sale of a hamburger or fries at a restaurant owned by McDonald's adds to its top line. The second form of revenue, however, requires more explanation. Operators of the franchised and affiliated restaurants pay McDonald's a fee plus a share of their income for the right to operate as part of the chain. Thus, only a portion of the franchisee's revenue appears in the second line of the income statement pictured here. That portion of their revenue that they must pay, along with other fees, is what adds to the revenues of McDonald's.

The income statements show modest growth in both forms of revenue during 2002. Sales by company-operated restaurants of nearly $11.5 billion was an increase of just over 4% from 2001, while revenues from the franchised and affiliated restaurants grew about 2%. Together, the two forms of revenue resulted in a top line that exceeded $15 billion for the first time in the company's history.

As you will understand even better after reading this chapter, companies must focus not only on growing revenues, but on controlling costs as well. Only by doing so can they improve the all-important bottom line of net income. While McDonald's reported just under $900 million in net income in 2002, this was significantly less than the $1.6 billion in 2001 and the nearly $2 billion in 2000. Whether or not the growth in revenue will translate into an improved bottom line will be the challenge faced by management of the golden arches in the years ahead.

McDonald's 2002 Annual Report

Consolidated Statement of Income

(IN MILLIONS, EXCEPT PER SHARE DATA) *Years ended December 31,*	2002	2001	2000
REVENUES			
Sales by company-operated restaurants	$11,499.6	$11,040.7	$10,467.0
Revenues from franchised and affiliated restaurants	3,906.1	3,829.3	3,776.0
Total revenues	15,405.7	14,870.0	14,243.0
OPERATING COSTS AND EXPENSES			
Company-operated restaurant expenses			
Food & paper	3,917.4	3,802.1	3,557.1
Payroll & employee benefits	3,078.2	2,901.2	2,690.2
Occupancy & other operating expenses	2,911.0	2,750.4	2,502.8
Franchised restaurants–occupancy expenses	840.1	800.2	772.3
Selling, general & administrative expenses	1,712.8	1,661.7	1,587.3
Other operating (income) expense, net	833.3	257.4	(196.4)
Total operating costs and expenses	13,292.8	12,173.0	10,913.3
Operating income	2,112.9	2,697.0	3,329.7
Interest expense—net of capitalized interest of $14.3, $15.2 and $16.3	374.1	452.4	429.9
McDonald's Japan IPO gain		(137.1)	
Nonoperating expense, net	76.7	52.0	17.5
Income before provision for income taxes and cumulative effect of accounting change	1,662.1	2,329.7	2,882.3
Provision for income taxes	670.0	693.1	905.0
Income before cumulative effect of accounting change	992.1	1,636.6	1,977.3
Cumulative effect of accounting change, net of tax benefit of $17.6	(98.6)		
Net income	$ 893.5	$ 1,636.6	$ 1,977.3
Per common share–basic:			
Income before cumulative effect of accounting change	$ .78	$ 1.27	$ 1.49
Cumulative effect of accounting change	(.08)		
Net income	$ .70	$ 1.27	$ 1.49
Per common share–diluted:			
Income before cumulative effect of accounting change	$ .77	$ 1.25	$ 1.46
Cumulative effect of accounting change	(.07)		
Net income	$ .70	$ 1.25	$ 1.46
Dividends per common share	$ .24	$ .23	$ .22
Weighted-average shares–basic	1,273.1	1,289.7	1,323.2
Weighted-average shares–diluted	1,281.5	1,309.3	1,356.5

See notes to consolidated financial statements.

Maintaining growth in revenues will require global strategies.

You're in the Driver's Seat

What can McDonald's do to improve its bottom line? Should it focus more attention on the restaurants it owns or on those operated by its franchisees? As you study this chapter, you will begin to understand the effect of the timing of revenues and expenses and their impact on reported profits.

http://www.mcdonalds.com

LEARNING OBJECTIVES

After studying this chapter, you should be able to:

LO 1 Explain the significance of recognition and measurement in the preparation and use of financial statements. (p. 159)

LO 2 Explain the differences between the cash and accrual bases of accounting. (p. 161)

LO 3 Describe the revenue recognition principle and explain its application in various situations. (p. 164)

LO 4 Describe the matching principle and the various methods for recognizing expenses. (p. 168)

LO 5 Identify the four major types of adjustments and determine their effect on the accounting equation. (p. 170)

LO 6 Explain the steps in the accounting cycle and the significance of each step. (p. 182)

WHAT EXTERNAL DECISION MAKERS WANT TO KNOW ABOUT ACCRUAL ACCOUNTING

DECISION MAKING

As you know by now, financial statements provide the information needed to evaluate a company's profitability, liquidity, and overall financial health. When stockholders, bankers, and other external users pick up these financials, they must understand the foundation on which they rest. That foundation is the accrual basis of accounting. They also need to be clear on what events have been recognized in the statements and, most importantly, how these events have been measured. All decision makers must look for answers to the following questions:

▶ *ASK ESSENTIAL QUESTIONS*

- How are economic events communicated, or *recognized*, in the financial statements?
- How have the effects of these events been *measured* in the statements?
- How are events recognized differently under the accrual basis versus the the cash basis of accounting?

▶ *FIND BASIC INFORMATION*

Each of the financial statements plays a critical role in communicating information to external decision makers. In an accrual-based system of accounting:

- the balance sheet tells what stake the owners have in a business after taking into account the entity's obligations
- the income statement reveals how profitable the business has been over a distinct period of time, such as a month or a year
- the statement of cash flows indicates how successful the company has been in managing the cash resources at its disposal

▶ *UNDERSTAND ACCOUNTING PRINCIPLES*

To evaluate a business, decision makers must understand the generally accepted accounting principles (GAAP) that underlie the accrual system. These principles determine:

- which events are recognized
- when the events are recognized, i.e., the timing of both revenues and expenses
- the measurement basis, i.e., the amounts at which revenues and expenses are recognized in the statements

▸ *INTERPRET ANALYTICAL INFORMATION*

Financial statements only have value to stockholders, bankers, analysts, and others if they can use them to make decisions. That is, they must be able to interpret the statements and use them as a basis for predicting the future. For example, a banker reading a company's balance sheet needs some assurance that the assets recognized on the accrual basis will be available in time to satisfy outstanding obligations. An analyst reading an income statement needs to decide whether the current year's revenues and expenses bode well for the future profitability of the company. Finally, a stockholder needs to know what information is available on the statement of cash flows in order to decide whether the company is likely to pay a dividend in the near future.

RECOGNITION AND MEASUREMENT IN FINANCIAL STATEMENTS

LO 1 Explain the significance of recognition and measurement in the preparation and use of financial statements.

Accounting is a communication process. The dual concepts of recognition and measurement are crucial to the success of accounting as a form of communication.

Recognition

Recognition The process of recording an item in the financial statements as an asset, liability, revenue, expense, or the like.

"**Recognition** is the process of formally recording or incorporating an item into the financial statements of an entity as an asset, liability, revenue, expense, or the like. Recognition includes depiction of an item in both words and numbers, with the amount included in the totals of the financial statements."[1] We see in this definition the central idea behind general-purpose financial statements. They are a form of communication between the entity and external users. **Stockholders, bankers, and other creditors have limited access to relevant information about a company. They depend on the periodic financial statements issued by management to provide the necessary information to make their decisions.** Acting on behalf of management, accountants have a moral and ethical responsibility to provide users with financial information that will be useful in making their decisions. The process by which the accountant depicts, or describes, the effects of economic events on the entity is called *recognition.*

ETHICS

The items, such as assets, liabilities, revenues, and expenses, depicted in financial statements are *representations.* Simply stated, the accountant cannot show a stockholder or other user the company's assets, such as cash and buildings. What the user sees in a set of financial statements is a depiction of the real thing. That is, the accountant describes, with words and numbers, the various items in a set of financial statements. The system is imperfect at best and, for that reason, is always in the process of change. As society and the business environment have become more complex, the accounting profession has striven for ways to improve financial statements as a means of communicating with statement users.

Measurement

Accountants depict a financial statement item in both words and *numbers.* The accountant must *quantify* the effects of economic events on the entity. It is not enough to decide that an event is important and thus warrants recognition in the financial statements. To be able to recognize it, the statement preparer must measure the financial effects of the event on the company.

Measurement of an item in financial statements requires that two choices be made. First, the accountant must decide on the *attribute* to be measured. Second, a scale of measurement, or *unit of measure,* must be chosen.

[1] *Statement of Financial Accounting Concepts No. 5,* "Recognition and Measurement in Financial Statements of Business Enterprises" (Stamford, Conn.: Financial Accounting Standards Board, December 1984), par. 6.

INTERNAL DECISION

The Attribute to Be Measured Assume that a company holds a parcel of real estate as an investment. What attribute—that is, *characteristic*—of the property should be used to measure and thus recognize it as an asset on the balance sheet? The cost of the asset at the time it is acquired is the most logical choice. *Cost* is the amount of cash, or its equivalent, paid to acquire the asset. But how do we report the property on a balance sheet a year from now?

Historical cost The amount paid for an asset and used as a basis for recognizing it on the balance sheet and carrying it on later balance sheets.

Current value The amount of cash, or its equivalent, that could be received by selling an asset currently.

- The simplest approach is to show the property on the balance sheet at its original cost, thus the designation **historical cost.** The use of historical cost is not only simple but also *verifiable.* Assume that two accountants are asked to independently measure the cost of the asset. After examining the sales contract for the land, they should arrive at the same amount.
- An alternative to historical cost as the attribute to be measured is **current value.** Current value is the amount of cash, or its equivalent, that could be received currently from the sale of the asset. For the company's piece of property, current value is the *estimated* selling price of the land, reduced by any commissions or other fees involved in making the sale. But the amount is only an estimate, not an actual amount. If the company has not yet sold the property, how can we know for certain its selling price? We have to compare it to similar properties that *have* sold recently.

The choice between current value and historical cost as the attribute to be measured is a good example of the trade-off between *relevance* and *reliability.* As indicated earlier, historical cost is verifiable and is thus to a large extent a reliable measure. But is it as relevant to the needs of the decision makers as current value? **Put yourself in the position of a banker trying to decide whether to lend money to the company. In evaluating the company's assets as collateral for the loan, is it more relevant to your decision to know what the firm paid for a piece of land 20 years ago or what it could be sold for today?** But what *could* the property be sold for today? Two accountants might not necessarily arrive at the same current value for the land. Whereas value or selling price may be more relevant to your decision on the loan, the reliability of this amount is often questionable.

Because of its objective nature, historical cost is the attribute used to measure many of the assets recognized on the balance sheet. However, certain other attributes, such as current value, have increased in popularity in recent years. In other chapters of the book, we will discuss some of the alternatives to historical cost.

What events have economic consequences to a business? The destructive effects of a warehouse fire, for example, will result in losses to buildings and other business assets. These losses will surely be reflected in the next year's financial statements of the affected companies—possibly in the income statement, as a downturn in revenues due to lost sales. What other financial statements would be affected by a big fire?

The Unit of Measure Regardless of the attribute of an item to be measured, it is still necessary to choose a yardstick or unit of measure. The yardstick we currently use is units of money. *Money* is something accepted as a medium of exchange or as a means of payment. The unit of money in the United States is the dollar. In Japan the medium of exchange is the yen, and in Great Britain it is the pound.

The use of the dollar as a unit of measure for financial transactions is widely accepted. The *stability* of the dollar as a yardstick is subject to considerable debate, however. Consider an example. You are thinking about buying a certain parcel of land. As part of your decision process, you measure the dimensions of the property and determine that the lot is 80 feet wide and 120 feet deep. Thus, the unit of measure used to determine the lot's size is the square foot. The company that owns the land offers to sell it for $10,000. Although the offer sounds attractive, you decide against the purchase today.

You return in one year to take a second look at the lot. You measure the lot again and, not surprisingly, find the width to still be 80 feet and the depth 120 feet. The owner is still willing to sell the lot for $10,000. This may appear to be the same price as last year. But the *purchasing power* of the unit of measure, the dollar, may very possibly have changed since last year. Even though the foot is a stable measuring unit, the dollar often is not. A *decline* in the purchasing power of the dollar is evidenced by a continuing *rise* in the general level of prices in an economy. For example, rather than paying $10,000 last year to buy the lot, you could have spent the $10,000 on other goods or services.

However, a year later, the same $10,000 may very well not buy the same amount of goods and services.

Inflation, or a rise in the general level of prices in the economy, results in a decrease in purchasing power. In the past, the accounting profession has experimented with financial statements adjusted for the changing value of the dollar. As inflation has declined in recent years in the United States, the debate over the use of the dollar as a stable measuring unit has somewhat subsided.[2] It is still important to recognize the inherent weakness in the use of a measuring unit that is subject to change, however.

Summary of Recognition and Measurement in Financial Statements

The purpose of financial statements is to communicate various types of economic information about a company. The job of the accountant is to decide which information should be recognized in the financial statements and how the effects of that information on the entity should be measured. Exhibit 4-1 summarizes the role of recognition and measurement in the preparation of financial statements.

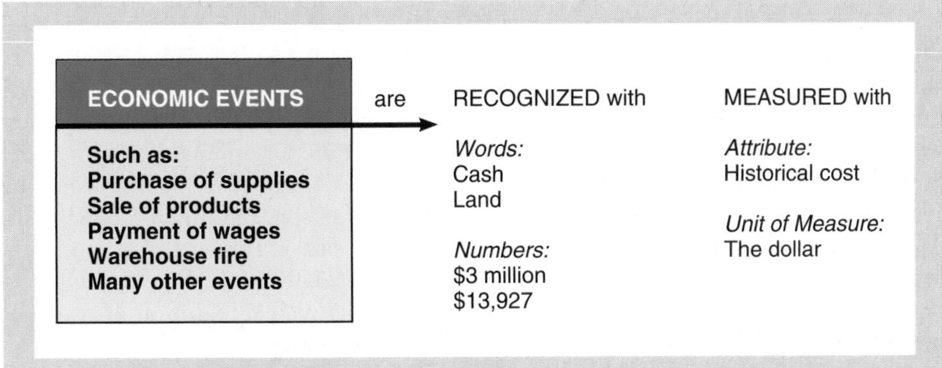

Exhibit 4-1
Recognition and Measurement in Financial Statements

THE ACCRUAL BASIS OF ACCOUNTING

LO 2 Explain the differences between the cash and accrual bases of accounting.

The accrual basis of accounting is the foundation for the measurement of income in our modern system of accounting. The best way to understand the accrual basis is to compare it with the simpler cash approach.

Comparing the Cash and Accrual Bases of Accounting

The cash and accrual bases of accounting differ with respect to the *timing* of the recognition of revenues and expenses. For example, assume that on July 24, Barbara White, a salesperson for Spiffy House Painters, contracts with a homeowner to repaint a house for $1,000. A large crew comes in and paints the house the next day, July 25. The customer has 30 days from the day of completion of the job to pay and does, in fact, pay Spiffy on August 25. *When* should Spiffy recognize the $1,000 as revenue? As soon as the contract is signed on July 24? Or on July 25, when the work is done? Or on August 25, when the customer pays the bill?

Cash basis A system of accounting in which revenues are recognized when cash is received and expenses when cash is paid.

Accrual basis A system of accounting in which revenues are recognized when earned and expenses when incurred.

In an income statement prepared on the **cash basis,** revenues are recognized when cash is *received.* Thus, on a cash basis, the $1,000 would not be recognized as revenue until the cash is collected, on August 25. On an **accrual basis,** revenue is recognized when it is *earned.* On this basis, the $1,000 would be recognized as revenue on July 25, when the house is painted. This is the point at which the revenue is earned.

[2]The rate of inflation in some countries, most noticeably those in South America, has far exceeded the rate in the United States. Companies operating in some of these countries with hyperinflationary economies are required to make adjustments to their statements.

Although cash has not yet been received, another asset, Accounts Receivable, is recognized. This asset represents the right to receive cash in the future. The effect on Spiffy's accounting equation when revenue is recognized before cash is received is as follows:

BALANCE SHEET							INCOME STATEMENT	
ASSETS		=	LIABILITIES	+	OWNERS' EQUITY	+	REVENUES – EXPENSES	
Accounts Receivable	1,000						Service Revenue	1,000

At the time cash is collected, accounts receivable is reduced and cash is increased. The effect on the accounting equation from this event is this:

BALANCE SHEET							INCOME STATEMENT
ASSETS		=	LIABILITIES	+	OWNERS' EQUITY	+	REVENUES – EXPENSES
Cash	1,000						
Accounts Receivable	(1,000)						

Assume that Barbara White is paid a 10% commission for all contracts and is paid on the 15th of the month following the month a house is painted. Thus, for this job, she will receive a $100 commission check on August 15. When should Spiffy recognize her commission of $100 as an expense? On July 24, when White gets the homeowner to sign a contract? When the work is completed, on July 25? Or on August 15, when she receives the commission check? Again, on a cash basis, commission expense would be recognized on August 15, when cash is *paid* to the salesperson. But on an accrual basis, expenses are recognized when they are *incurred*. In our example, the commission expense is incurred when the house is painted, on July 25.

Exhibit 4-2 summarizes the essential differences between recognition of revenues and expenses on a cash basis and recognition on an accrual basis.

Exhibit 4-2

Comparing the Cash and Accrual Bases of Accounting

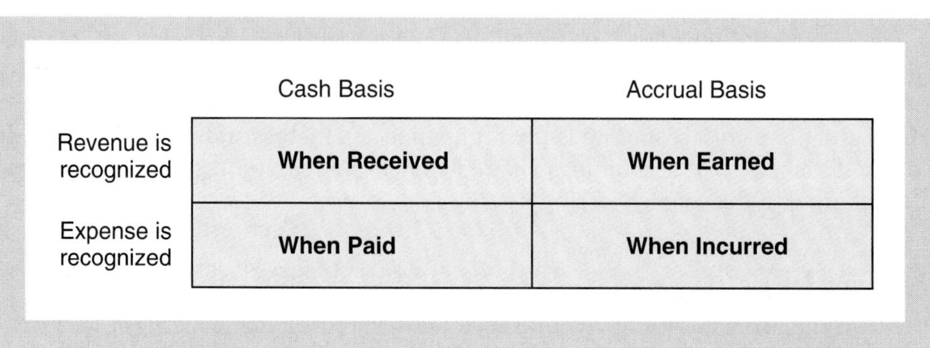

	Cash Basis	Accrual Basis
Revenue is recognized	**When Received**	**When Earned**
Expense is recognized	**When Paid**	**When Incurred**

What the Income Statement and the Statement of Cash Flows Reveal

Most business entities, other than the very smallest, use the accrual basis of accounting. Thus, the income statement reflects the accrual basis. Revenues are recognized when they are earned and expenses when they are incurred. At the same time, however, **stockholders and creditors are also interested in information concerning the cash flows of an entity.** The purpose of a statement of cash flows is to provide this information. Keep in mind that even though we present a statement of cash flows in a complete set of financial statements, the accrual basis is used for recording transactions and for preparing a balance sheet and an income statement.

Recall the example of Glengarry Health Club in Chapter 3. The club earned revenue from two sources, memberships and court fees. Both of these forms of revenue

Business Strategy

http://www.mcdonalds.com

Adding Customers to Restaurants

McDonald's has experienced a long run of rapid and continuous growth, both at home and abroad. Revenues over an 11-year period more than doubled, reaching a record level of $15.4 billion in 2002. However, as reported on the income statement at the beginning of this chapter, net income for 2002 declined sharply from the levels achieved in both 2000 and 2001. In his letter to the shareholders in the 2002 annual report, Jim Cantalupo, Chairman and CEO, talks about the company's disappointing financial performance and the fact that it has lost momentum.

Certainly economic conditions both in the United States and worldwide have contributed to this disappointing financial performance. As a reaction to the struggling economy, McDonald's started by adjusting downward its expectations for earnings growth. No longer does the company think that earnings per share growth in the 10 to 15 percent range is realistic. But the company realizes that its future depends also on the specific strategies it develops to grow and improve the bottom line. One of the most important of these is a conscious decision to lower its capital expenditures. While the 2001 report touted plans to open between 1,300 and 1,400 restaurants in the coming year, the 2002 report focuses attention on the 30,000 existing McDonald's restaurants.

The best way to characterize the new strategy is to hear what Cantalupo has to say: "In short, McDonald's is in transition from a company that emphasizes '*adding restaurants to customers*' to one that emphasizes '*adding customers to restaurants*.'" This strategy focuses attention directly on improving the dining experience in its existing restaurants rather than simply on adding more golden arches. ■

Sources: McDonald's 2002 and 2001 annual reports.

were recognized on the income statement presented in that chapter and are reproduced in the top portion of Exhibit 4-3. Recall, however, that members have 30 days to pay and that, at the end of the first month of operation, only $4,000 of the membership fees of $15,000 had been collected.

Now consider the statement of cash flows for the first month of operation, partially reproduced in the bottom portion of Exhibit 4-3. Because we want to compare the income statement to the statement of cash flows, only the Operating Activities section

Exhibit 4-3 Comparing the Income Statement and the Statement of Cash Flows

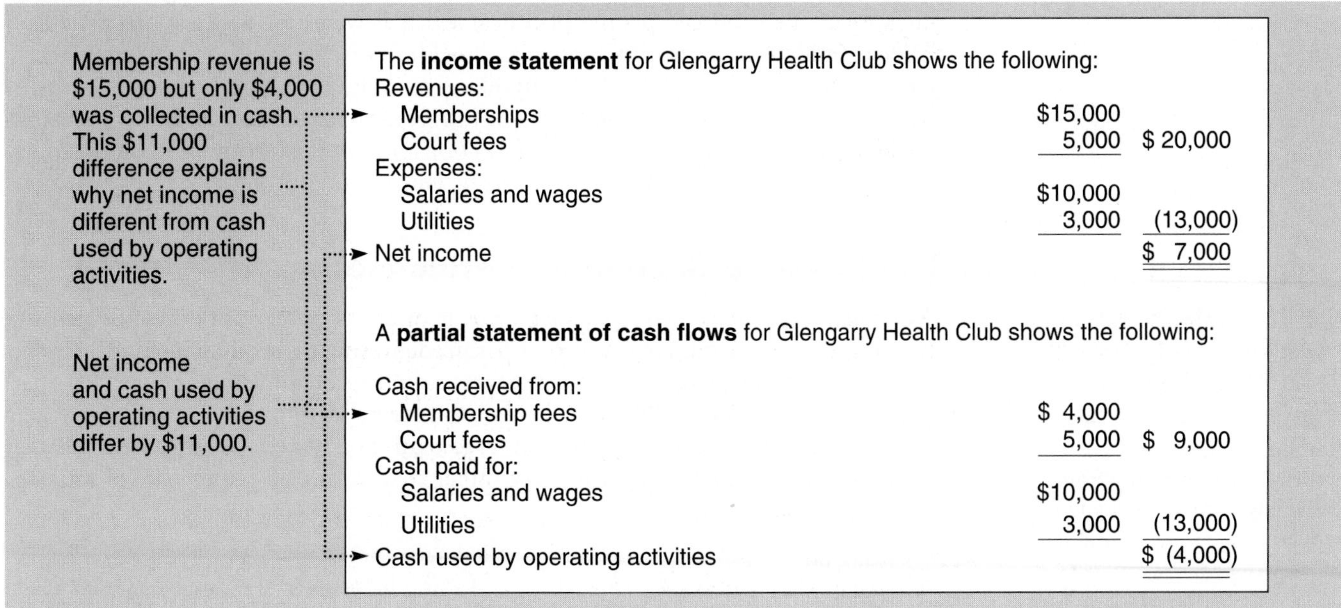

Membership revenue is $15,000 but only $4,000 was collected in cash. This $11,000 difference explains why net income is different from cash used by operating activities.
Net income and cash used by operating activities differ by $11,000.

The **income statement** for Glengarry Health Club shows the following:

Revenues:		
Memberships	$15,000	
Court fees	5,000	$ 20,000
Expenses:		
Salaries and wages	$10,000	
Utilities	3,000	(13,000)
Net income		$ 7,000

A **partial statement of cash flows** for Glengarry Health Club shows the following:

Cash received from:		
Membership fees	$ 4,000	
Court fees	5,000	$ 9,000
Cash paid for:		
Salaries and wages	$10,000	
Utilities	3,000	(13,000)
Cash used by operating activities		$ (4,000)

of the statement is shown. (The Investing and Financing Activities sections have been omitted from the statement.) Why is net income for the month a *positive* $7,000 but cash from operating activities a *negative* $4,000? Of the membership revenue of $15,000 reflected on the income statement, only $4,000 was collected in cash. Glengarry has accounts receivable for the other $11,000. Thus, cash from operating activities, as reflected on a statement of cash flows, is $11,000 *less* than net income of $7,000, or a negative $4,000.

Each of these two financial statements serves a useful purpose. The income statement reflects the revenues actually earned by the business, regardless of whether cash has been collected. The statement of cash flows tells the reader about the actual cash inflows during a period of time. The need for the information provided by both statements is summarized by the Financial Accounting Standards Board as follows:

> Statements of cash flows commonly show a great deal about an entity's current cash receipts and payments, but a cash flow statement provides an incomplete basis for assessing prospects for future cash flows because it cannot show interperiod relationships. Many current cash receipts, especially from operations, stem from activities of earlier periods, and many current cash payments are intended or expected to result in future, not current, cash receipts. Statements of earnings and comprehensive income, especially if used in conjunction with statements of financial position, usually provide a better basis for assessing future cash flow prospects of an entity than do cash flow statements alone.[3]

Accrual Accounting and Time Periods

The *time period* assumption was introduced in Chapter 1. We assume that it is possible to prepare an income statement that fairly reflects the earnings of a business for a specific period of time, such as a month or a year. It is somewhat artificial to divide the operations of a business into periods of time as indicated on a calendar. The conflict arises because earning income is a *process* that takes place *over a period of time* rather than *at any one point in time.*

Consider an alternative to our present system of reporting on the operations of a business on a periodic basis. A new business begins operations with an investment of $50,000. The business operates for 10 years, during which time no records are kept other than a checkbook for the cash on deposit at the bank. At the end of the 10 years, the owners decide to go their separate ways and convert all of their assets to cash. They split among them the balance of $80,000 in the bank account. What is the profit of the business for the 10-year period? The answer is $30,000, the difference between the original cash of $50,000 contributed and the cash of $80,000 available at liquidation.

The point of this simple example is that we could be very precise and accurate in our measurement of the income of a business if it were not necessary to artificially divide operations according to a calendar. **Stockholders, bankers, and other interested parties cannot wait until a business liquidates to make decisions, however. They need information on a periodic basis.** Thus, the justification for the accrual basis of accounting lies in the needs of financial statement users for periodic information on the financial position as well as the profitability of the entity.

The Revenue Recognition Principle

LO 3 Describe the revenue recognition principle and explain its application in various situations.

Revenues Inflows of assets or settlements of liabilities from delivering or producing goods, rendering services, or conducting other activities.

"**Revenues** are inflows or other enhancements of assets of an entity or settlements of its liabilities (or a combination of both) from delivering or producing goods, rendering services, or other activities that constitute the entity's ongoing major or central operations."[4] Two points should be noted about this formal definition of revenues. First, an asset is not always involved when revenue is recognized. The recognition of revenue may result from the settlement of a liability rather than from the acquisition of an asset.

[3] *SFAC No. 5,* par. 24c.
[4] *Statement of Financial Accounting Concepts No. 6,* "Elements of Financial Statements" (Stamford, Conn.: Financial Accounting Standards Board, December 1985), par. 78.

Second, entities generate revenue in different ways: some companies produce goods, others distribute or deliver the goods to users, and still others provide some type of service.

Accounting for Your Decisions

You Are the Marketing Manager

The end of the year is fast approaching, and your department has not sold its quota of computers. As you understand the company's accounting policies, revenues are recorded when computers are ordered and shipped to customers. You know that if your department does not make its quota, then your job could be in jeopardy. So you get an idea. You call up some friends and tell them to order computers that they don't really need yet. In return, you'll get them a great price on the machines. Besides, if they don't want the computers, they can send them back in January and get a full refund. Meanwhile, you'll make your quota. Do you think there is anything wrong with this idea?

ANS: Yes, there is something wrong with the idea. For one thing, it is very poor business judgment to push products on customers if you believe they will be returned. Although many customers will say no to your idea, others will go along to get a lower price, only to later regret buying something they don't need. And if the computers are indeed returned in January, then the company's auditors will be obliged to indicate that the company has not followed generally accepted accounting principles, because the intent of the transaction was merely to boost sales in the current year. This shortcut is not only unethical but in violation of the revenue recognition principle.

On the accrual basis, revenues are recognized when earned. However, the **revenue recognition principle** involves two factors. Revenues are recognized in the income statement when they are both *realized* and *earned*.[5] Revenues are *realized* when goods or services are exchanged for cash or claims to cash.

Revenue recognition principle Revenues are recognized in the income statement when they are realized, or realizable, and earned.

Accounting For Your Decisions

You Are the Stockholder

Assume that a construction company starts two projects during the year. One is a \$5 million contract for a bridge. The other is a \$4 million contract for a dam. Based on actual costs incurred to date and estimates of costs yet to be incurred, the contractor estimates that at the end of the year the bridge is 20% complete and the dam is 50% complete. Which would be more informative to you as a stockholder of the construction company: (1) an end-of-the-year report that indicates no revenue because no contracts are finished yet or (2) an end-of-the-year report that indicates revenue of \$1 million on the bridge (20% of \$5 million) and \$2 million on the dam (50% of \$4 million), both based on the extent of completion?

ANS: As a stockholder, you need information on a timely basis to evaluate your various investments. The percentage-of-completion method will allow you to assess the profitability of your investment in the construction company on a regular basis rather than only at the point when projects are completed.

[5]An alternative is to recognize revenues when they are *realizable* and earned. *Realizable* has a slightly different meaning, which will be explained later when we look at commodities.

Other Applications of the Revenue Recognition Principle

At what point are revenues realized and earned by an entity? As a practical rule, revenue is usually recognized at the time of sale. This is normally interpreted to mean at the time of delivery of the product or service to the customer. However, consider the following examples in which it is necessary either to modify or to interpret the meaning of the revenue recognition principle.

Percentage-of-completion method The method used by contractors to recognize revenue before the completion of a long-term contract.

http://www.wgint.com

Long-Term Contracts The **percentage-of-completion method** allows a contractor to recognize revenue over the life of a project rather than at its completion. For long-term contracts in which the sales price is fixed by contract and in which the realization of revenue depends only on production, such as constructing the bridge or the dam (see the box above), the method is a reasonable alternative to deferring the recognition of revenue until the project is completed. The following excerpt from the 2002 annual report of Washington Group International is an example of how revenue is recognized by most companies in the construction industry:

> Revenue is generally recognized on the "percentage-of-completion" method for construction-type contracts, and as work is performed and award and other fees are earned for cost-type and operation and maintenance-type contracts. There are various means of determining revenue under the percentage-of-completion method. Most of our fixed-price and target-price contracts use a cost-to-cost approach, where revenue is earned in proportion to costs incurred divided by total expected costs to be incurred. However, if a project includes significant materials or equipment costs, we require that the percentage-of-completion method be based on labor hours, labor dollars or some other appropriate approximation of physical completion rather than on a strict percentage of costs incurred. For certain long-term contracts involving mining and environmental and hazardous substance remediation, completion is measured on estimated physical completion or units of production.

Franchises Over the last 30 years, franchising has achieved enormous popularity as a way to conduct business. It has been especially prevalent in retail sales, including the fast-food (McDonald's), hotel (Holiday Inn), and car rental (Hertz) businesses. Typically, the franchisor grants the exclusive right to sell a product or service in a specific geographic area to the franchisee. As discussed in the chapter opener, a franchisor such as McDonald's generates revenues from one or both of two sources: (1) from the sale of the franchise and related services, such as help in selecting a site and hiring employees and (2) from continuing fees based on performance, for example, a fixed percentage of sales by the franchisee.

At what point should the revenue from the sale of a franchise be recognized? An FASB standard allows a franchisor such as McDonald's to recognize initial franchise fees as revenue only when it has made "substantial performance" of its obligations and when collection of the fee is reasonably assured.[6] An excerpt from McDonald's 2002 annual report indicates how it recognizes both the initial and continuing fees:

http://www.mcdonalds.com

> *Revenue Recognition*
> Sales by Company-operated restaurants are recognized on a cash basis. Revenues from franchised and affiliated restaurants include continuing rent and service fees, initial fees, and royalties received from foreign affiliates and developmental licensees. Continuing fees and royalties are recognized in the period earned. Initial fees are recognized upon opening of a restaurant, which is when the Company has performed substantially all initial services required by the franchise arrangement.

[6] *Statement of Financial Accounting Standards No. 45,* "Accounting for Franchise Fee Revenue" (Stamford, Conn.: Financial Accounting Standards Board, December 1981), par. 5.

From Concept to Practice 4.1

Reading McDonald's Income Statement

Refer to McDonald's comparative income statements for 2002, 2001, and 2000 in the chapter opener. What percentage of total revenues was derived from franchised restaurants? Has this percentage changed over the three-year period?

Commodities Corn, wheat, gold, silver, and other agricultural and mining products trade on the open market at established prices. Readily convertible assets such as these are interchangeable and can be sold at a quoted price in an active market that can absorb the quantity being sold without significantly affecting the price.[7] Earlier, we mentioned that to be recognized, revenues must be realized. An acceptable alternative is to recognize revenues when they are realizable. Revenues are *realizable* when assets received or held are readily convertible to known amounts of cash or claims to cash.

Assume that a company mines gold. Revenues are realizable by the company at the time the product is mined because each ounce of gold is interchangeable with another ounce of gold and the commodities market can absorb all of the gold the company sells without having an effect on the price. This is one of the few instances in which it is considered acceptable to recognize revenue *prior* to the point of sale. The exception is justified because the important event in the revenue-generation process is the *production* of the gold, not the sale of it. The **production method** of recognizing revenue is used for precious metals, as well as certain agricultural products and marketable securities.

Production method The method in which revenue is recognized when a commodity is produced rather than when it is sold.

Installment Sales Various consumer items, such as automobiles, appliances, and even vacation properties, are sold on an installment basis. A down payment is followed by a series of monthly payments over a period of years. Default on the payments and repossession of the item by the seller are more common in these types of sales than with most other arrangements. For this reason, it is considered acceptable, in limited circumstances, to defer the recognition of revenue on an installment sale until cash is actually collected. The **installment method,** which is essentially a cash basis of accounting,

Installment method The method in which revenue is recognized at the time cash is collected.

Ethics in Accounting

BRISTOL-MYERS SQUIBB

Bristol-Myers Squibb, a company that manufactures and sells medicines and healthcare products, had a very difficult year financially in 2002 and the company's stock price dropped more than 50%.

The company's customers are large wholesale companies that buy medicines and other products and then sell the goods to smaller companies, such as local drugstores. Usually, Bristol-Myers sells to its customers the amount of goods the customers can resell quickly. However, in 2001, the manufacturer pushed its customers to order much more than they needed.

As a result, the drug manufacturer recognized much higher sales than usual. In 2002, the SEC investigated this change in selling practice and pressured Bristol-Myers to significantly restate its reported revenue. Overall, the company estimated its aggressive selling tactics had resulted in its reporting excessive sales of $1.5 billion. Bristol-Myers' management claimed its accounting decisions were appropriate.

Why do you think the SEC required the restatements? Did an ethical dilemma exist for anyone involved? If you were an investor in 2001, how might you have benefited or been harmed? Were any investors harmed by the 2002 restatements? If so, how? What responsibility, if any, did Bristol-Myers' accountants owe to its customers? Were any GAAP rules violated?

Source: Gardiner Harris, "SEC is probing Bristol-Myers over sales-incentive accounting," *The Wall Street Journal*, July 12, 2002.

[7] *SFAC No. 5*, par. 83a.

is acceptable only when the seller has no reasonable basis for estimating the degree of collectibility. Note that the production and installment methods are at opposite ends of the spectrum. Under the production method, revenue is recognized *before* a sale takes place; with the installment method, revenue is recognized *after* the sale.

Rent and Interest In some cases, revenue is earned *continuously* over time. In these cases, a product or service is not delivered at a specific point in time; instead, the earnings process takes place with the passage of time. Rent and interest are two examples. Interest is the cost associated with the use of someone else's money. When should a bank recognize the interest earned from granting a 90-day loan? Even though the interest may not be received until the loan itself is repaid, interest is earned every day the loan is outstanding. Later in the chapter, we will look at the process for recognizing interest earned but not yet received. The same procedure is used to recognize revenue from rent that is earned but uncollected.

Long-term contracts, franchises, commodities, installment sales, rent, and interest are not the only situations in which the revenue recognition principle must be interpreted. The intent in examining these particular examples was to help you think about the variety of ways in which businesses generate revenue and about the need to apply judgment in deciding when to recognize revenue. These examples should help you to realize the subjective nature of the work of an accountant and to understand that the discipline is not as precise as it may sometimes seem.

Expense Recognition and the Matching Principle

LO 4 Describe the matching principle and the various methods for recognizing expenses.

Companies incur a variety of costs. A new office building is constructed. Inventory is purchased. Employees perform services. The electric meter is read. In each of these situations, the company incurs a cost, regardless of when it pays cash. Conceptually, *any time a cost is incurred, an asset is acquired.* However, according to the definition in Chapter 1, an asset represents a future economic benefit. An asset ceases being an asset and becomes an expense when the economic benefits from having incurred the cost have expired. Assets are unexpired costs, and expenses are expired costs.

At what point do costs expire and become expenses? The expense recognition principle requires that we recognize expenses in different ways, depending on the nature of the cost. The ideal approach to recognizing expenses is to match them with revenues. Under the **matching principle,** the accountant attempts to associate revenues of a period with the costs necessary to generate those revenues. For certain types of expenses, a direct form of matching is possible; for others, it is necessary to associate costs with a particular period. The classic example of direct matching is cost of goods sold expense with sales revenue. Cost of goods sold is the cost of the inventory associated with a particular sale. A cost is incurred and an asset is recorded when the inventory is purchased. The asset, inventory, becomes an expense when it is sold. Another example of a cost that can be matched directly with revenue is commissions. The commission paid to a salesperson can be matched directly with the sale.

Matching principle The association of revenue of a period with all of the costs necessary to generate that revenue.

An indirect form of matching is used to recognize the benefits associated with certain types of costs, most noticeably long-term assets, such as buildings and equipment. These costs benefit many periods, but usually it is not possible to match them directly with a specific sale of a product. Instead, they are matched with the periods during which they will provide benefits. For example, an office building may be useful to a company for 30 years. *Depreciation* is the process of allocating the cost of a tangible long-term asset to its useful life. Depreciation Expense is the account used to recognize this type of expense.

The benefits associated with the incurrence of certain other costs are treated in accounting as expiring simultaneously with their acquisition. The justification for this treatment is that no future benefits from the incurrence of the cost are discernible. This is true of most selling and administrative costs. For example, the costs of heat and light in a building benefit only the current period and therefore are recognized as expenses as soon as the costs are incurred. Likewise, income taxes incurred during the period do not benefit any period other than the current period and are thus written off as an expense in the period incurred.

The relationships among costs, assets, and expenses are depicted in Exhibit 4-4 using three examples. First, costs incurred for purchases of merchandise result in an asset, Merchandise Inventory, and are eventually matched with revenue at the time the product is sold. Second, costs incurred for office space result in an asset, Office Building, which is recognized as Depreciation Expense over the useful life of the building. Third, the cost of heating and lighting benefits only the current period and is thus recognized immediately as Utilities Expense.

Exhibit 4-4

Relationships among Costs, Assets, and Expenses

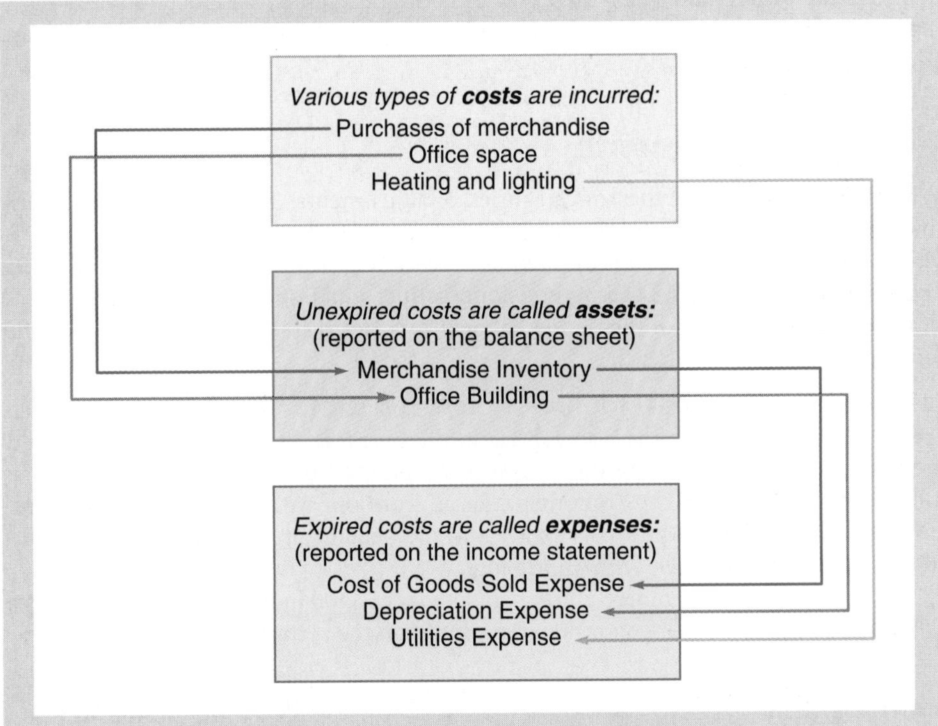

According to the FASB, **expenses** are "outflows or other using up of assets or incurrences of liabilities (or a combination of both) from delivering or producing goods, rendering services, or carrying out other activities that constitute the entity's ongoing major or central operations."[8] The key point to note about expenses is that they come about in two different ways: from the use of an asset or from the recognition of a liability. For example, when a retailer sells a product, the asset sacrificed is Inventory. Cost of Goods Sold is the expense account that is increased, and the Inventory account is decreased. As we will see in the next section, the incurrence of an expense may also result in a liability.

Expenses Outflows of assets or incurrences of liabilities resulting from delivering goods, rendering services, or carrying out other activities.

Two-Minute Review

1. *Explain the difference between the attribute to be measured and the unit of measure.*
2. *Give at least three examples of situations in which revenues are recognized other than at the time of sale.*
3. *Explain the different ways in which expenses are matched with revenues.*

Answers on pages 184 and 185.

[8]SFAC No. 6, par. 80.

ACCRUAL ACCOUNTING AND ADJUSTMENTS

LO 5 Identify the four major types of adjustments and determine their effect on the accounting equation.

Adjusting entries Journal entries made at the end of a period by a company using the accrual basis of accounting.

The accrual basis of accounting necessitates a number of adjustments at the end of a period. **Adjusting entries** are the journal entries the accountant makes at the end of a period for a company on the accrual basis of accounting. *Adjusting entries are not needed if a cash basis is used. It is the very nature of the accrual basis that results in the need for adjusting entries.* The frequency of the adjustment process depends on how often financial statements are prepared. Most businesses make adjustments at the end of each month. Recall from Chapter 3 that the emphasis throughout this book is on the *use* of financial statements rather than their preparation. Thus, rather than focus on the adjusting *entries* that the accountant makes, we will concern ourselves with the effect of these adjustments on the accounting equation.

Types of Adjustments

Why are there four basic types, or categories, of adjustments? The answer lies in the distinction between the cash and the accrual bases of accounting. On an accrual basis, *revenue* can be earned either *before* or *after* cash is received. *Expenses* can be incurred either *before* or *after* cash is paid. Each of these four distinct situations requires a different type of adjustment at the end of the period. We will consider each of the four categories and look at some examples of each.

(1) Cash Paid Before Expense Is Incurred (Deferred Expense) Assets are often acquired before their actual use in the business. Insurance policies typically are prepaid, as often is rent. Office supplies are purchased in advance of their use, as are all types of property and equipment. Recall from our earlier discussion that unexpired costs are assets. As the costs expire and the benefits are used up, the asset must be written off and replaced with an expense.

Assume that on September 1 a company prepays $2,400 in rent on its office space for the next 12 months. The effect of the prepayment on the accounting equation follows:

BALANCE SHEET							INCOME STATEMENT	
ASSETS		=	LIABILITIES	+	OWNERS' EQUITY	+	REVENUES − EXPENSES	
Prepaid Rent	2,400							
Cash	(2,400)							

The asset Prepaid Rent represents the benefits that the company will receive over the next 12 months. Because the rent is for a 12-month period, $200 of benefits from the asset expire at the end of each month. The adjustment at the end of September to record this expiration accomplishes two purposes: (1) it recognizes the reduction in the asset Prepaid Rent, and (2) it recognizes the expense associated with using up the benefits for one month. On September 30, the accountant makes an adjustment to recognize the expense and reduce the asset:

BALANCE SHEET							INCOME STATEMENT	
ASSETS		=	LIABILITIES	+	OWNERS' EQUITY	+	REVENUES − EXPENSES	
Prepaid Rent	(200)						Rent Expense	(200)

The balance in Prepaid Rent represents the unexpired benefits from the prepayment of rent for the remaining 11 months: $\$200 \times 11 = \$2{,}200$. Rent Expense reflects the expiration of benefits during the month of September.

As discussed earlier in the chapter, depreciation is the process of allocating the cost of a long-term tangible asset over its estimated useful life. The accountant does not attempt to measure the decline in *value* of the asset but simply tries to allocate its cost over its useful life. Thus, the adjustment for depreciation is similar to the one we made for rent expense. Assume that on January 1, a company buys a delivery truck, for which it pays $21,000. At this point, one asset is simply traded for another. The effect of the purchase of the truck on the accounting equation is as follows:

BALANCE SHEET							INCOME STATEMENT
ASSETS		=	LIABILITIES	+	OWNERS' EQUITY	+	REVENUES − EXPENSES
Delivery Truck	21,000						
Cash	(21,000)						

From Concept to Practice 4.2

Reading the Balance Sheets of Winnebago Industries and Monaco Coach Corporation

Refer to the balance sheets in Winnebago Industries' and Monaco Coach Corporation's annual reports. How does each company classify prepaid expenses? What types of prepaid expenses would you expect these companies to have?

Accounting for Your Decisions

You Are the Store Manager

You are responsible for managing a new running shoe store. The landlord requires a security deposit as well as prepayment of the first year's rent. The security deposit is refundable at the end of the first year. After the first year, rent is payable on a monthly basis. After three months in business, the owner asks you for an income statement. How should the security deposit and the prepayment of the first year's rent be recognized on this income statement?

ANS: The security deposit will not affect the income statement. It is an asset that will be converted to cash at the end of the first year, assuming that you are entitled to a full refund. One-fourth of the prepayment of the first year's rent should be recognized as an expense on the income statement for the first three months.

INTERNAL DECISION

Two estimates must be made in depreciating the delivery truck: (1) the useful life of the asset and (2) the salvage value of the truck at the end of its useful life. Estimated salvage value is the amount a company expects to be able to receive when it sells an asset at the end of its estimated useful life. Assume a five-year estimated life for the truck and an estimated salvage value of $3,000 at the end of that time. Thus, the *depreciable cost* of the truck is $21,000 − $3,000, or $18,000. In a later chapter, we will consider alternative methods for allocating the depreciable cost over the useful life of an asset. For now, we will use the simplest approach, called the **straight-line method,** which assigns an equal amount of depreciation to each period. The monthly depreciation is found by dividing the depreciable cost of $18,000 over the estimated useful life of 60 months, which equals $300 per month.

Straight-line method The assignment of an equal amount of depreciation to each period.

The adjustment to recognize depreciation is conceptually the same as the adjustment to write off Prepaid Rent. That is, the asset account is reduced, and an expense is recognized. However, accountants normally use a contra account to reduce the total amount of long-term tangible assets by the amount of depreciation. A **contra account** is any account that is used to offset another account. For example, Accumulated Depreciation is used to record the decrease in a long-term asset such as the delivery truck:

Contra account Any account that is used to offset another account.

BALANCE SHEET							INCOME STATEMENT	
ASSETS		=	LIABILITIES	+	OWNERS' EQUITY	+	REVENUES − EXPENSES	
Accumulated Depreciation	(300)						Depreciation Expense	(300)

Study Tip

Think of the Accumulated Depreciation account as simply an extension of the related asset account, in this case the truck. Therefore, although the truck account is not directly reduced for depreciation, an increase in its companion account, Accumulated Depreciation, has the effect of reducing the asset.

Why do companies use a contra account for depreciation rather than simply reducing the long-term asset directly? If the asset account were reduced each time depreciation is recorded, its original cost would not be readily determinable from the accounting records. Businesses need to know the original cost of each asset, for various reasons. One of the most important of these reasons is the need to know historical cost for computation of depreciation for tax purposes.

On a balance sheet prepared on January 31, the contra account is shown as a reduction in the carrying value of the truck:

Delivery Truck	$21,000	
Less: Accumulated Depreciation	300	$20,700

(2) Cash Received Before Revenue Is Earned (Deferred Revenue)

You can benefit greatly in your study of accounting by recognizing its *symmetry.* By this we mean that one company's asset is another company's liability. In the earlier example involving the rental of office space, a second company, the landlord, received the cash paid by the first company, the tenant. At the time cash is received, the landlord has a liability because it has taken cash from the tenant but has not yet performed the service to earn the revenue. The revenue will be earned with the passage of time. The effect on the accounting equation from the collection of cash on September 1 is as follows:

BALANCE SHEET							INCOME STATEMENT	
ASSETS		=	LIABILITIES		+	OWNERS' EQUITY	+	REVENUES – EXPENSES
Cash	2,400		Rent Collected in Advance	2,400				

The account Rent Collected in Advance is a liability. The landlord is obligated to provide the tenant uninterrupted use of the office facilities for the next 12 months. With the passage of time, the liability is satisified as the tenant is provided the use of the space. The adjustment at the end of each month accomplishes two purposes: It recognizes (1) the reduction in the liability and (2) the revenue earned each month as the tenant occupies the space:

BALANCE SHEET							INCOME STATEMENT	
ASSETS		=	LIABILITIES		+	OWNERS' EQUITY	+	REVENUES – EXPENSES
			Rent Collected in Advance	(200)				Rent Revenue 200

COURTESY OF AMAZON.COM, INC.

A gift certificate like this is a good example of a deferred revenue. **Amazon.com** *has received the $25 in payment for the certificate, but because it must wait for the recipient of the gift to pick out a book, it considers the obligation to deliver the book in the future a liability.*

After the adjustment is made, the landlord's remaining liability is \$2,400 − \$200, or \$2,200, which represents 11 months of unearned rent at \$200 per month.

In another example, many magazine subscriptions require the customer to pay in advance. For example, you pay \$12 for a one-year subscription to your favorite magazine, and the publisher in turn sends you 12 monthly issues. At the time you send money to the publisher, it incurs a liability. It has taken your money but has not yet done anything to earn it. The publisher has an obligation either to provide you with the magazine over the next 12 months or to refund your \$12.

At what point should the publisher recognize revenue from magazine sales? The publisher receives cash at the time the subscription is sold. The revenue has not been *earned* until the company publishes the magazine and mails it to you, however. Thus, a publisher usually recognizes revenue at the time of delivery. An excerpt from the 2002 annual report of Time Warner Inc. (which publishes such popular magazines as *Time, People,* and *Sports Illustrated*) reflects this policy:

http://www.timewarner.com

> The unearned portion of paid magazine subscriptions is deferred until magazines are delivered to subscribers. Upon each delivery, a proportionate share of the gross subscription price is included in revenues. Magazine advertising revenues are recognized when the advertisements are published.

Assume that on March 1 Time Warner sells 500 one-year subscriptions to a monthly magazine at a price of \$12 each. At this point, Time Warner has an obligation to deliver magazines over the next 12 months:

BALANCE SHEET							INCOME STATEMENT	
ASSETS		=	LIABILITIES		+	OWNERS' EQUITY	+ REVENUES − EXPENSES	
Cash	6,000		Subscriptions Collected in Advance	6,000				

Assuming that each of the subscriptions starts with the March issue of the magazine, at the end of March, Time Warner accountants would adjust the records to reflect the revenue earned for the first month:

BALANCE SHEET							INCOME STATEMENT	
ASSETS		=	LIABILITIES		+	OWNERS' EQUITY	+ REVENUES − EXPENSES	
			Subscriptions Collected in Advance	(500)			Subscription Revenue	500

After the adjustment is made, Time Warner's remaining liability is \$6,000 − \$500, or \$5,500, which represents 11 months of unearned revenue at \$500 per month.

As you know by now, accounting terminology differs among companies. The account title Subscriptions Collected in Advance is only one of any number of possible titles for the liability related to subscriptions. For example, Time Warner's balance sheet does not have this account title, but does report deferred revenue.

(3) Expense Incurred Before Cash Is Paid (Accrued Liability) This situation is just the opposite of (1). That is, cash is paid *after* an expense is actually incurred rather than *before* its incurrence, as was the case in (1). Many normal operating costs, such as payroll and utilities, fit this situation. The utility bill is received at the end of the month, but the company has 10 days to pay it. Or consider the biweekly payroll for Jones Corporation. The company pays a total of \$28,000 in wages on every other Friday. Assume that the last payday was Friday, May 31. The next two paydays will be Friday, June 14,

Accounting for Your Decisions

You Are the Banker

A new midwestern publisher comes to you for a loan. Through an aggressive ad campaign, the company sold a phenomenal number of subscriptions to a new sports magazine in its first six months and needs additional money to go national. The first issue of the magazine is due out next month. The publisher presents you an income statement for its first six months and you notice that it includes all of the revenue from the initial subscriptions sold in the Midwest. What concerns do you have?

ANS: First, the accounting treatment for the magazine revenue is improper. Because the magazine has not yet been delivered to the customer, the subscriptions have not yet been earned, and therefore no revenue should be recognized. As a banker, you should be sufficiently concerned that a potential customer would present improper financial statements, and you should deny the loan on that basis alone. That does not even take into account the fact that the company has yet to establish a sufficient track record to warrant the credit risk.

and Friday, June 28. The effect on the accounting equation on each of these paydays is the same:

BALANCE SHEET							INCOME STATEMENT	
ASSETS		=	LIABILITIES		+	OWNERS' EQUITY	+ REVENUES – EXPENSES	
Cash	(28,000)						Wages Expense	(28,000)

On a balance sheet prepared as of June 30, a liability must be recognized. Even though the next payment is not until July 12, Jones *owes* employees wages for the last two days of June and must recognize an expense for the wages earned by employees for these two days. We will assume that the company operates seven days a week and that the daily cost is 1/14th of the biweekly amount of $28,000, or $2,000. In addition to recognizing a liability on June 30, Jones must adjust the records to reflect an expense associated with the cost of wages for the last two days of the month:

BALANCE SHEET							INCOME STATEMENT	
ASSETS		=	LIABILITIES		+	OWNERS' EQUITY	+ REVENUES – EXPENSES	
			Wages Payable	4,000			Wages Expense	(4,000)

What adjustment will be made on the next payday, July 12? Jones will need to eliminate the liability of $4,000 for the last two days of wages recorded on June 30 because the amount has now been paid. An additional $24,000 of expense has been incurred for the $2,000 cost per day associated with the first 12 days in July. Finally, cash is reduced by $28,000, which represents the biweekly payroll:

BALANCE SHEET							INCOME STATEMENT	
ASSETS		=	LIABILITIES		+	OWNERS' EQUITY	+ REVENUES – EXPENSES	
Cash	(28,000)		Wages Payable	(4,000)			Wages Expense	(24,000)

The following time line illustrates the amount of expense incurred in each of the two months, June and July, for the biweekly payroll:

2 days' expense in June: $4,000	12 days' expense in July: $24,000	
Friday, June 28: Last payday	Friday, June 30: End of accounting period	Friday, July 12: Next payday

Another typical expense incurred before the payment of cash is interest. In many cases, the interest on a short-term loan is repaid with the amount of the loan, called the *principal*, on the maturity date. For example, Granger Company takes out a 9%, 90-day, $20,000 loan with its bank on March 1. The principal and interest will be repaid on May 30. On March 1, both an asset, Cash, and a liability, Notes Payable, are increased:

BALANCE SHEET							INCOME STATEMENT	
ASSETS		=	LIABILITIES		+	OWNERS' EQUITY	+ REVENUES – EXPENSES	
Cash	20,000		Notes Payable	20,000				

The basic formula for computing interest follows:

$$I = P \times R \times T,$$

where I = The dollar amount of interest
P = The principal amount of the loan
R = The annual rate of interest as a percentage
T = Time in years (often stated as a fraction of a year).

The total interest on Granger's loan is as follows:

$$\$20,000 \times .09 \times 3/12 = \underline{\underline{\$450}}$$

Therefore,the amount of interest that must be recognized as expense at the end of March is one-third of $450 because one month of a total of three has passed. Alternatively, the formula for finding the total interest on the loan can be modified to compute the interest for one month:[9]

$$\$20,000 \times .09 \times 1/12 = \underline{\underline{\$150}}$$

On March 31 and April 30, the accountant records adjustments to recognize interest both as an expense and as an obligation. The effect on the accounting equation from the adjustments for the two months combined is as follows:

BALANCE SHEET							INCOME STATEMENT	
ASSETS		=	LIABILITIES		+	OWNERS' EQUITY	+ REVENUES – EXPENSES	
			Interest Payable	300			Interest Expense	(300)

The effect on Granger's accounting equation on May 30 when it repays the principal and interest is

BALANCE SHEET							INCOME STATEMENT	
ASSETS		=	LIABILITIES		+	OWNERS' EQUITY	+ REVENUES – EXPENSES	
Cash	(20,450)		Interest Payable	(300)			Interest Expense	(150)
			Notes Payable	(20,000)				

[9]In practice, interest is calculated on the basis of days rather than months. For example, the interest for March would be $20,000 × .09 × 30/365, or $147.95, to reflect 30 days in the month out of a total of 365 days in the year. The number of days in March is 30 rather than 31 because in computing interest, businesses normally count the day a note matures but not the day it is signed. To simplify the calculations, we will use months, even though the result is slightly inaccurate.

Recognition of this transaction accomplishes three purposes. First, the $20,000 of principal and the total interest of $450 for three months is recognized as a decrease in Cash. Second, Interest Expense of $150 for the month of May is recognized. Finally, the two liabilities remaining on the books, Interest Payable and Notes Payable, are removed.[10]

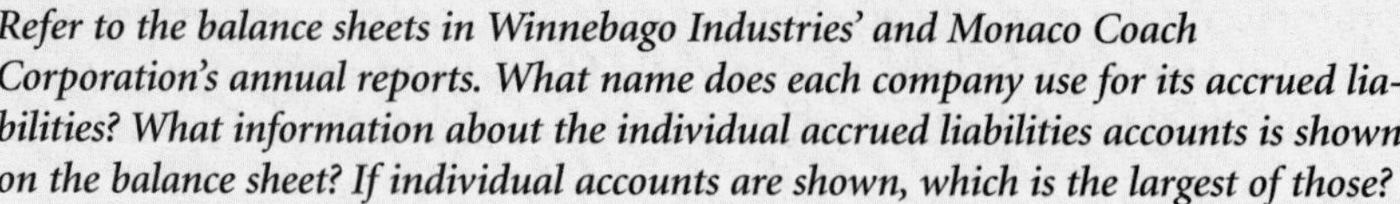

From Concept to Practice 4.3

Reading the Balance Sheets of Winnebago Industries and Monaco Coach Corporation

Refer to the balance sheets in Winnebago Industries' and Monaco Coach Corporation's annual reports. What name does each company use for its accrued liabilities? What information about the individual accrued liabilities accounts is shown on the balance sheet? If individual accounts are shown, which is the largest of those?

(4) Revenue Earned Before Cash Is Received (Accrued Asset)

Revenue is sometimes earned before the receipt of cash. Rent and interest are both earned with the passage of time and require an adjustment if cash has not yet been received. For example, assume that Grand Management Company rents warehouse space to a number of tenants. Most of its contracts call for prepayment of rent for six months at a time. Its agreement with one tenant, however, allows the tenant to pay Grand $2,500 in monthly rent anytime within the first 10 days of the following month. The adjustment on April 30, the end of the first month of the agreement, is as follows:

BALANCE SHEET						INCOME STATEMENT	
ASSETS		=	LIABILITIES	+	OWNERS' EQUITY	+	REVENUES – EXPENSES	
Rent Receivable	2,500					Rent Revenue	2,500

When the tenant pays its rent on May 7, the effect on Grand's accounting equation is as follows:

BALANCE SHEET						INCOME STATEMENT	
ASSETS		=	LIABILITIES	+	OWNERS' EQUITY	+	REVENUES – EXPENSES
Cash	2,500						
Rent Receivable	(2,500)						

Although we used the example of rent to illustrate this category, the membership revenue of Glengarry Health Club in Chapter 3 also could be used as an example. Whenever a company records revenue before cash is received, some type of receivable is increased and revenue is also increased. In that chapter, the health club earned membership revenue even though members had until the following month to pay their dues.

Study Tip

Now that we have seen examples of all four types of adjustments, think about a key difference between deferrals (the first two categories) and accruals (the last two categories). When we make adjustments involving deferrals, we must consider any existing balance in a deferred account. Conversely, there is no existing account when making an accrual.

Accruals and Deferrals

One of the challenges in learning accounting concepts is to gain an understanding of the terminology. Part of the difficulty stems from the alternative terms used by different accountants to mean the same thing. For example, the asset created when insurance is paid for in advance is termed a *prepaid asset* by some and a *prepaid expense* by others. Someone else might refer to it as a *deferred expense.*

We will use the term **deferral** to refer to a situation in which cash has been either paid or received but the expense or revenue has been deferred to a later time. A **deferred**

[10]This assumes that Granger did not make an adjustment prior to this to recognize interest expense for the month of May. If a separate adjustment had been made, Interest Payable would be reduced by $450.

expense indicates that cash has been paid but the recognition of expense has been deferred. Because a deferred expense represents a *future benefit* to a company, it is an *asset.* An alternative name for deferred expense is *prepaid expense.* Prepaid insurance and office supplies are deferred expenses. An adjustment is made periodically to record the portion of the deferred expense that has expired. A **deferred revenue** means that cash has been received but the recognition of any revenue has been deferred until a later time. Because a deferred revenue represents an *obligation* to a company, it is a *liability.* An alternative name for deferred revenue is *unearned revenue.* Rent collected in advance is deferred revenue. The periodic adjustment recognizes the portion of the deferred revenue that is earned in that period.

In this chapter, we have discussed in detail the accrual basis of accounting, which involves recognizing changes in resources and obligations as they occur, not simply when cash changes hands. More specifically, we will use the term **accrual** to refer to a situation in which no cash has been paid or received yet but it is necessary to recognize, or accrue, an expense or a revenue. An **accrued liability** is recognized at the end of the period in cases in which an expense has been incurred but cash has not yet been paid. Wages payable and interest payable are examples of accrued liabilities. An **accrued asset** is recorded when revenue has been earned but cash has not yet been collected. Rent receivable is an accrued asset.

Deferral Cash has either been paid or received, but expense or revenue has not yet been recognized.

Deferred expense An asset resulting from the payment of cash before the incurrence of expense.

Deferred revenue A liability resulting from the receipt of cash before the recognition of revenue.

Accrual Cash has not yet been paid or received, but expense has been incurred or revenue earned.

Accrued liability A liability resulting from the recognition of an expense before the payment of cash.

Accrued asset An asset resulting from the recognition of a revenue before the receipt of cash.

Summary of Adjustments

The four types of adjustments are summarized in Exhibit 4-5. Common examples of each are shown, along with the accounts affected by each. Finally, the following generalizations should help you in gaining a better understanding of adjustments and how they are used:

1. An adjustment is an internal transaction. It does not involve another entity.
2. Because it is an internal transaction, an adjustment *never* involves an increase or decrease in Cash.
3. At least one balance sheet account and one income statement account are involved in an adjustment. It is the nature of the adjustment process that an asset or liability account is adjusted with a corresponding change in either a revenue or an expense account.

Exhibit 4-5 Accruals and Deferrals

TYPE	SITUATION	EXAMPLES	ENTRY DURING PERIOD	ENTRY AT END OF PERIOD
Deferred expense	Cash paid before expense is incurred	Insurance policy Supplies Rent Buildings, equipment	Asset Cash	Expense Asset
Deferred revenue	Cash received before revenue is earned	Deposits, rent Subscriptions Gift certificates	Cash Liability	Liability Revenue
Accrued liability	Expense incurred before cash is paid	Salaries, wages Interest Taxes Rent	No Entry	Expense Liability
Accrued asset	Revenue earned before cash is received	Interest Rent	No Entry	Asset Revenue

Two-Minute Review

Assume a company wants to prepare financial statements at the end of its first month of operations. Each of the following transactions were recorded on the company's books on the first day of the month.

1. *Purchased a 24-month insurance policy for $3,600.*
2. *Collected $4,800 from a tenant for office space that the tenant has rented for the next 12 months.*
3. *Took out a 6%, 180-day, $10,000 loan at the bank.*

For each of these transactions, determine the effect on the accounting equation of the adjustment required at the end of the month.

Answers on page 185.

Comprehensive Example of Adjustments

We will now consider a comprehensive example involving the transactions for the first month of operations and the end-of-period adjustments for a hypothetical business, Duffy Transit Company. A list of accounts and their balances is shown for Duffy Transit at January 31, the end of the first month of operations (prior to making any adjustments):

Assets:	
Cash	$ 50,000
Prepaid Insurance	48,000
Land	20,000
Buildings—Garage	160,000
Equipment—Buses	300,000
Liabilities:	
Discount Tickets Sold in Advance	25,000
Notes Payable	150,000
Owners' Equity:	
Capital Stock	400,000
Revenues:	
Daily Ticket Revenue	30,000
Expenses:	
Gas, Oil, and Maintenance	12,000
Wages and Salaries	10,000
Dividends	5,000

Duffy wants to prepare a balance sheet at the end of January and an income statement for its first month of operations. Use of the accrual basis necessitates a number of adjustments to update certain asset and liability accounts and to recognize the correct amounts for the various revenues and expenses.

Adjustments at the End of January

(1) At the beginning of January, Duffy issued an 18-month, 12%, $150,000 promissory note for cash. Although interest will not be repaid until the loan's maturity date, Duffy must accrue interest for the first month. The calculation of interest for one month is $150,000 × .12 × 1/12. The adjustment is

BALANCE SHEET							INCOME STATEMENT	
ASSETS	=	LIABILITIES		+	OWNERS' EQUITY	+	REVENUES − EXPENSES	
		Interest Payable	1,500				Interest Expense	(1,500)

(**2**) Wages and salary expense of $10,000 reflects the amount paid to employees during January. Duffy owes employees an additional $2,800 in salaries and wages at January 31. The effect of the adjustment is as follows:

BALANCE SHEET						INCOME STATEMENT
ASSETS	=	LIABILITIES	+	OWNERS' EQUITY	+	REVENUES − EXPENSES
		Wages and Salaries Payable 2,800				Wage and Salary Expense (2,800)

(**3**) At the beginning of January, Duffy acquired a garage to house the buses at a cost of $160,000. Land is not subject to depreciation. The cost of the land acquired in connection with the purchase of the building will remain on the books until the property is sold. The garage has an estimated useful life of 20 years and an estimated salvage value of $16,000 at the end of its life. The monthly depreciation is found by dividing the depreciable cost of $144,000 by the useful life of 240 months:

$$\frac{\$160{,}000 - \$16{,}000}{20 \text{ years} \times 12 \text{ months}} = \frac{\$144{,}000}{240 \text{ months}} = \underline{\underline{\$600}} \text{ per month}$$

The adjustment to recognize the depreciation on the garage for January for a full month is

BALANCE SHEET						INCOME STATEMENT
ASSETS	=	LIABILITIES	+	OWNERS' EQUITY	+	REVENUES − EXPENSES
Accumulated Depreciation—Garage (600)						Depreciation Expense—Garage (600)

(**4**) Duffy purchased 10 buses for $30,000 each at the beginning of January. The buses have an estimated useful life of five years at which time the company plans to sell them for $6,000 each. The monthly depreciation on the 10 buses is

$$10 \times \frac{\$30{,}000 - \$6{,}000}{5 \text{ years} \times 12 \text{ months}} = 10 \times \frac{\$24{,}000}{60 \text{ months}} = \underline{\underline{\$4{,}000}} \text{ per month}$$

The adjustment to recognize the depreciation on the buses for the first month is

BALANCE SHEET						INCOME STATEMENT
ASSETS	=	LIABILITIES	+	OWNERS' EQUITY	+	REVENUES − EXPENSES
Accumulated Depreciation—Buses (4,000)						Depreciation Expense—Buses (4,000)

(**5**) An insurance policy was purchased for $48,000 on January 1. It provides property and liability protection for a 24-month period. The adjustment to allocate the cost to expense for the first month is

BALANCE SHEET						INCOME STATEMENT
ASSETS	=	LIABILITIES	+	OWNERS' EQUITY	+	REVENUES − EXPENSES
Prepaid Insurance (2,000)						Interest Expense (2,000)

(**6**) In addition to selling tickets on the bus, Duffy sells discount tickets at the terminal. The tickets are good for a ride anytime within 12 months of purchase. Thus, as these tickets are sold, Duffy increases Cash, as well as a liability account, Discount Tickets Sold in Advance.The sale of $25,000 worth of these tickets was recorded during January. At the end of the first month, Duffy counts the number of tickets that have been redeemed. Because $20,400 worth of tickets has been turned in, this is the amount by which the company reduces its liability and recognizes revenue for the month:

BALANCE SHEET					INCOME STATEMENT	
ASSETS	=	LIABILITIES		+ OWNERS' EQUITY	+ REVENUES – EXPENSES	
		Discount Tickets Sold in Advance	(20,400)		Discount Ticket Revenue	20,400

(7) Duffy does not need all the space in its garage and rents a section of it to another company for $2,500 per month. The tenant has until the 10th day of the following month to pay its rent. The adjustment on Duffy 's books on the last day of the month is

BALANCE SHEET					INCOME STATEMENT	
ASSETS		= LIABILITIES		+ OWNERS' EQUITY	+ REVENUES – EXPENSES	
Rent Receivable	2,500				Rent Revenue	2,500

(8) Corporations pay estimated taxes on a quarterly basis. Because Duffy is preparing an income statement for the month of January, it must estimate its taxes incurred for the month, which will be paid at the end of the quarter. We will assume a corporate tax rate of 34% on income before tax. The computation of Income Tax Expense is as follows (the amounts shown for the revenues and expenses reflect the effect of the adjustments):

Revenues:		
Daily Ticket Revenue	$30,000	
Discount Ticket Revenue	20,400	
Rent Revenue	2,500	$52,900
Expenses:		
Gas, Oil, and Maintenance Expense	$12,000	
Wage and Salary Expense	12,800	
Depreciation Expense	4,600	
Insurance Expense	2,000	
Interest Expense	1,500	32,900
Net Income before Tax		$20,000
Times the Corporate Tax Rate		× .34
Income Tax Expense		$ 6,800

Based on this estimate of taxes, the final adjustment Duffy makes is

BALANCE SHEET					INCOME STATEMENT	
ASSETS	=	LIABILITIES		+ OWNERS' EQUITY	+ REVENUES – EXPENSES	
		Income Tax Payable	6,800		Income Tax Expense	(6,800)

Income Statement and Balance Sheet for Duffy Transit

Now that the adjustments have been made, financial statements can be prepared. An income statement for January and a balance sheet as of January 31 are shown in Exhibit 4-6. Each of the account balances on the statements was determined by taking the balances in the list of accounts on page 178 and adding or subtracting as appropriate the necessary adjustments. Note the balance in Retained Earnings of $8,200. This amount was found by taking the net income of $13,200 and deducting the dividends of $5,000.

Exhibit 4-6

Financial Statements for Duffy Transit Company

DUFFY TRANSIT COMPANY
INCOME STATEMENT
FOR THE MONTH OF JANUARY

Revenues:		
Daily ticket revenue	$30,000	
Discount ticket revenue	20,400	
Rent revenue	2,500	$52,900
Expenses:		
Gas, oil, and maintenance	$12,000	
Wages and salaries	12,800	
Depreciation—garage	600	
Depreciation—buses	4,000	
Insurance	2,000	
Interest	1,500	
Income taxes	6,800	39,700
Net income		$13,200

DUFFY TRANSIT COMPANY
BALANCE SHEET
JANUARY 31

Assets			Liabilities and Owners' Equity	
Cash		$ 50,000	Discount tickets sold in advance	$ 4,600
Rent receivable		2,500	Notes payable	150,000
Prepaid insurance		46,000	Interest payable	1,500
Land		20,000	Wages and salaries payable	2,800
Buildings—garage	$160,000		Income tax payable	6,800
Accumulated depreciation	600	159,400	Capital stock	400,000
Equipment—buses	$300,000		Retained earnings	8,200
Accumulated depreciation	4,000	296,000		
Total assets		$573,900	Total liabilities and owners' equity	$573,900

Ethical Considerations for a Company on the Accrual Basis

ETHICS

As you have seen, the accrual basis requires the recognition of revenues when earned and expenses when incurred, regardless of when cash is received or paid. It was also noted earlier that adjusting entries are *internal* transactions in that they do not involve an exchange with an outside entity. Because adjustments do not involve another company, accountants may at times feel pressure from others within the organization to either speed or delay the recognition of certain adjustments.

Consider the following two examples for a construction company that is concerned about its "bottom line," that is, its net income. A number of jobs are in progress, but because of inclement weather, none of them is very far along. Management asks the accountant to recognize 50% of the revenue from a job in progress even though by the most liberal estimates it is only 25% complete. Further, the accountant has been asked to delay the recognition of various short-term accrued liabilities (and, of course, the accompanying expenses) until the beginning of the new year.

The "correct" response of the accountant to each of these requests may seem obvious: only 25% of the revenue on the one job should be recognized, and all accrued liabilities should be expensed at year-end. The pressures of the daily work environment make these decisions difficult for the accountant, however. **The accountant must always remember that his or her primary responsibility in preparing financial statements is to accurately portray the affairs of the company to the various outside users. Bankers, stockholders, and others rely on the accountant to serve their best interests.**

THE ACCOUNTING CYCLE

LO 6 Explain the steps in the accounting cycle and the significance of each step.

Accounting cycle A series of steps performed each period and culminating with the preparation of a set of financial statements.

We have focused our attention in this chapter on accrual accounting and the adjustments it necessitates. The adjustments the accountant makes are one key component in the **accounting cycle**. The accountant for a business follows a series of steps each period. The objective is always the same: *collect the necessary information to prepare a set of financial statements.* Together, these steps make up the accounting cycle. The name comes from the fact that the steps are repeated each period. It is possible that a company performs all of the steps in the accounting cycle once a *month*, although in practice, certain steps in the cycle may be carried out only once a *year.*

The steps in the accounting cycle are shown in Exhibit 4-7. Note that step 1 involves not only *collecting* information but also *analyzing* it. Transaction analysis is probably the most challenging of all the steps in the accounting cycle. It requires the ability to think logically about an event and its effect on the financial position of the entity. Once the transaction is analyzed, it is recorded in the journal, as indicated by the second step in the exhibit. The first two steps in the cycle take place continuously.

Transactions are posted to the accounts on a periodic basis. The frequency of posting to the accounts depends on two factors: the type of accounting system used by a company and the volume of transactions. In a manual system, entries might be posted daily, weekly, or even monthly, depending on the amount of activity. The larger the number of transactions a company records, the more often it posts. In an automated accounting system, posting is likely done automatically by the computer each time a transaction is recorded.

The Use of a Work Sheet

Work sheet A device used at the end of the period to gather the information needed to prepare financial statements without actually recording and posting adjustments.

Step 4 in Exhibit 4-7 calls for the preparation of a work sheet. The end of an accounting period is a busy time. In addition to recording daily recurring transactions, adjustments must be recorded as the basis for preparing financial statements. The time available to prepare the statements is usually very limited. The use of a **work sheet** allows the accountant to gather and organize the information required to adjust the accounts without actually recording and posting the adjustments to the accounts. Actually recording adjustments and posting them to the accounts can be done after the financial statements are prepared. *A work sheet itself is not a financial statement.* Instead, it is a useful device to *organize* the information needed to prepare the financial statements at the end of the period.

It is not essential that a work sheet be used before preparing financial statements. If it is not used, step 6, recording and posting adjustments, comes before step 5, preparing the financial statements.

The Closing Process

Real accounts The name given to balance sheet accounts because they are permanent and are not closed at the end of the period.

Nominal accounts The name given to revenue, expense, and dividend accounts because they are temporary and are closed at the end of the period.

Closing entries Journal entries made at the end of the period to return the balance in all nominal accounts to zero and transfer the net income or loss and the dividends to Retained Earnings.

Step 7 in Exhibit 4-7 is the closing process. For purposes of closing the books, accountants categorize accounts into two types. Balance sheet accounts are called **real accounts** because they are permanent in nature. For this reason, they are never closed.The balance in each of these accounts is carried over from one period to the next. In contrast, revenue, expense, and dividend accounts are temporary or **nominal accounts.**The balances in the income statement accounts and the Dividends account are *not* carried forward from one accounting period to the next. For this reason, these accounts are closed at the end of the period.

Closing entries serve two important purposes: (1) to return the balances in all temporary or nominal accounts to zero to start the next accounting period and (2) to transfer the net income (or net loss) and the dividends of the period to the Retained Earnings account.

Exhibit 4-7 Steps in the Accounting Cycle

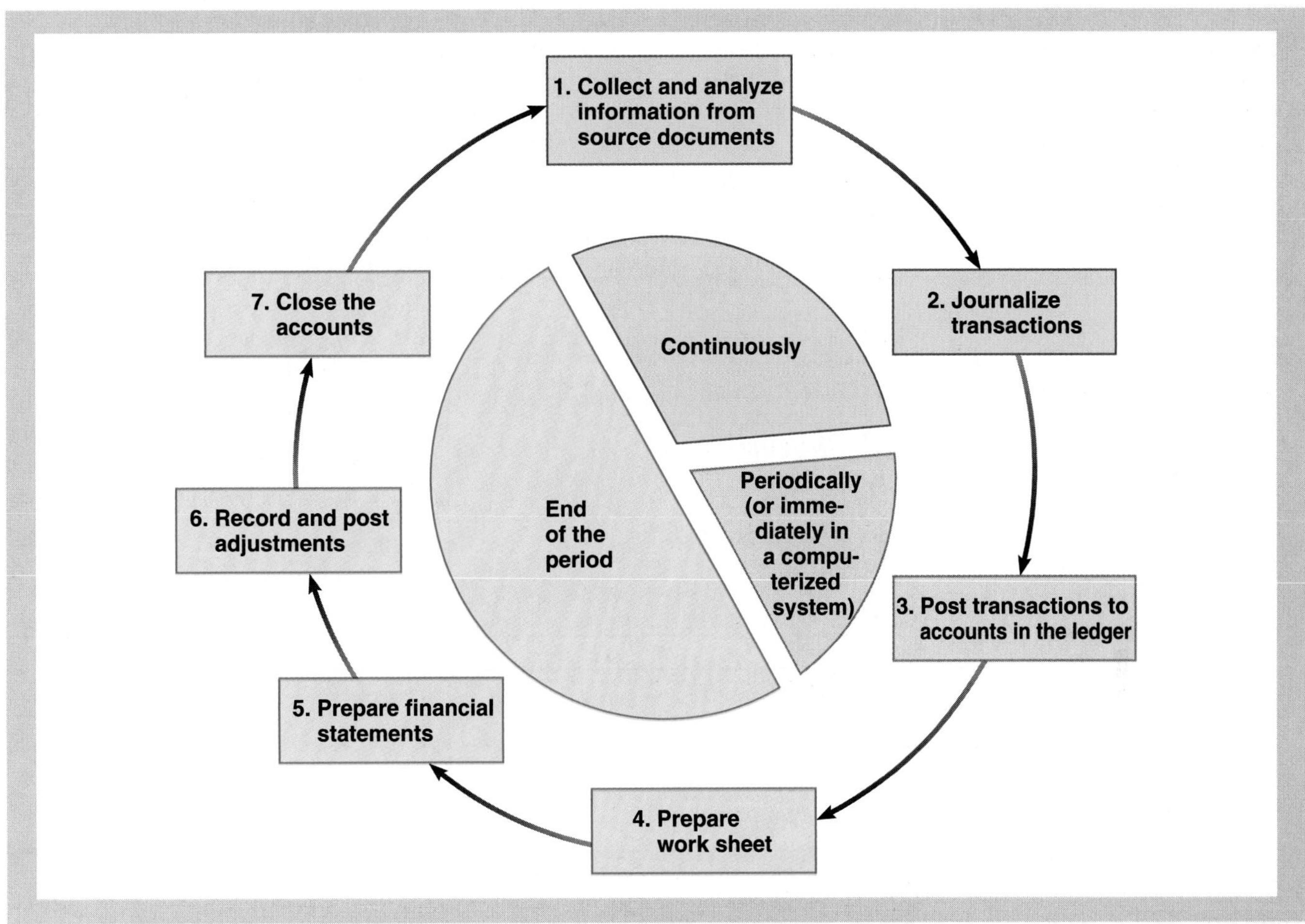

Interim Financial Statements

We mentioned earlier in this chapter that certain steps in the accounting cycle are sometimes carried out only once a year rather than each month as in our example. For ease of illustration, we assumed a monthly accounting cycle. Many companies adjust and close the accounts only once a year, however. They use a work sheet more frequently than this as the basis for preparing interim statements. Statements prepared monthly, quarterly, or at other intervals less than a year in duration are called **interim statements.** Many companies prepare monthly financial statements for their own internal use. Similarly, corporations whose shares are publicly traded on one of the stock exchanges are required to file quarterly financial statements with the Securities and Exchange Commission.

Interim statements Financial statements prepared monthly, quarterly, or at other intervals less than a year in duration.

Suppose that a company prepares monthly financial statements for internal use and completes the accounting cycle in its entirety only once a year. In this case, a work sheet is prepared each month as the basis for interim financial statements. Formally adjusting and closing the books is done only at the end of each year. The adjustments that appear on the monthly work sheet are not posted to the accounts. They are entered on the work sheet simply as a basis for preparing the monthly financial statements.

Interpret: You Decide. Refer back to McDonald's comparative income statements as presented at the beginning of this chapter. Consider the two forms of revenue presented on the statement and how the differences between them were explained in the chapter. Which of the two forms is McDonald's more reliant on for its revenues? Which form of revenue has grown more rapidly over the three-year period? Do you think McDonald's should focus its attention more on its own restaurants or on those of its franchisees? Explain your reasoning for each of your responses.

Impact on the Financial Reports

Impact on the Financial Reports

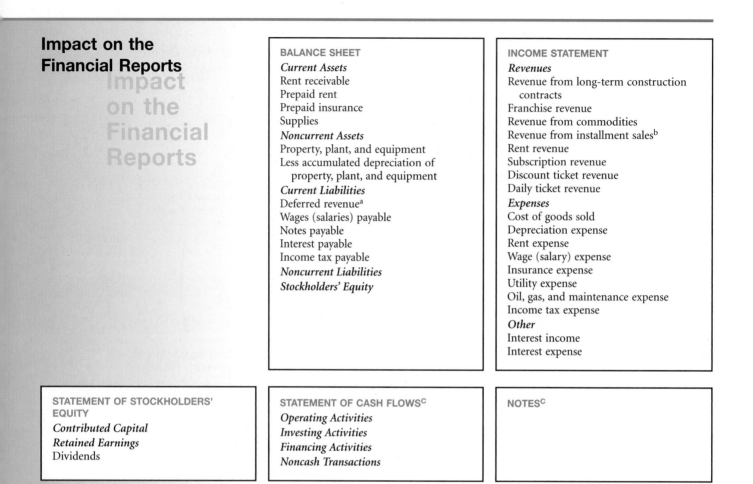

BALANCE SHEET

Current Assets
Rent receivable
Prepaid rent
Prepaid insurance
Supplies
Noncurrent Assets
Property, plant, and equipment
Less accumulated depreciation of property, plant, and equipment
Current Liabilities
Deferred revenue[a]
Wages (salaries) payable
Notes payable
Interest payable
Income tax payable
Noncurrent Liabilities
Stockholders' Equity

INCOME STATEMENT

Revenues
Revenue from long-term construction contracts
Franchise revenue
Revenue from commodities
Revenue from installment sales[b]
Rent revenue
Subscription revenue
Discount ticket revenue
Daily ticket revenue
Expenses
Cost of goods sold
Depreciation expense
Rent expense
Wage (salary) expense
Insurance expense
Utility expense
Oil, gas, and maintenance expense
Income tax expense
Other
Interest income
Interest expense

STATEMENT OF STOCKHOLDERS' EQUITY

Contributed Capital
Retained Earnings
Dividends

STATEMENT OF CASH FLOWS[c]

Operating Activities
Investing Activities
Financing Activities
Noncash Transactions

NOTES[c]

[a]For example, rent or subscriptions collected in advance, gift certificates, deposits, and discount tickets sold in advance.
[b]Rarely used.
[c]Future chapters will provide information about the impact on the statement of cash flows and the notes to the financial statements.

Answers to the Two-Minute Reviews

Two-Minute Review on Page 169

1. *Accountants must decide whether to use historical cost or another attribute or characteristic of an asset, such as its current value, to measure it. Regardless of the attribute measured, it is necessary to choose a yardstick, or unit of measure. In this country, accountants use the dollar to measure assets and other financial statement items.*
2. *The percentage-of-completion method, the production method, and the installment method are all alternatives to recognizing revenue at the point of sale. Also, franchisors normally recognize revenue when they have made substantial performance of their obligations.*
3. *For certain costs, such as cost of goods sold, it is possible to directly match the expense with revenue generated. For other costs, such as depreciation, an indirect form of matching is necessary in which expenses are allocated to the periods benefited, rather than matched with specific revenues. Finally, the*

(continued)

Answers to the Two-Minute Reviews (continued)

benefits associated with the incurrence of certain costs, such as utilities, expire immediately and therefore expense is recognized as soon as the cost is incurred.

Two-Minute Review on Page 178

BALANCE SHEET							INCOME STATEMENT	
ASSETS		=	LIABILITIES		+	OWNERS' EQUITY	+ REVENUES − EXPENSES	
1. Prepaid Insurance	(150)						Insurance Expense	(150)
2.			Rent Collected in Advance	(400)			Rent Revenue	400
3.			Interest Payable	50			Interest Expense	(50)

Warmup Exercises

Warmup Exercise 4-1 ***Prepaid Insurance*** **LO 5**

ABC Corp. purchases a 24-month fire insurance policy on January 1, 2004, for $5,400.

Required

Determine the effect on the accounting equation on January 31, 2004.

Key to the Solution

Determine what proportion and therefore what dollar amount of the policy has expired after one month.

Warmup Exercise 4-2 ***Depreciation*** **LO 5**

DEF Corp. purchased a new car for one of its salespeople on March 1, 2004, for $25,000. The estimated useful life of the car is four years with an estimated salvage value of $1,000.

Required

Determine the effect on the accounting equation on March 31, 2004.

Key to the Solution

Determine what dollar amount of the cost of the car should be depreciated and then how much should be depreciated each month.

Warmup Exercise 4-3 ***Interest on a Note*** **LO 5**

On April 1, 2004, GHI Corp. took out a 12%, 120-day, $10,000 loan at its bank.

Required

Determine the effect on the accounting equation on April 30, 2004.

Key to the Solution

Determine the monthly interest cost on a loan that accrues interest at the rate of 12% per year.

Solutions to Warmup Exercises

BALANCE SHEET						INCOME STATEMENT	
ASSETS		= LIABILITIES		+ OWNERS' EQUITY		+ REVENUES − EXPENSES	
1. Prepaid Insurance	(225)					Insurance Expense	(225)
2. Accumulated Depreciation	(500)					Rent Revenue	(500)
3.		Interest Payable	100			Interest Expense	(100)

Review Problem

WebTUTOR™ Advantage

A list of accounts for Northern Airlines at January 31 is shown below. It reflects the recurring transactions for the month of January, but it does not reflect any month-end adjustments.

Cash	$ 75,000
Parts Inventory	45,000
Land	80,000
Buildings—Hangars	250,000
Accumulated Depreciation—Hangars	24,000
Equipment—Aircraft	650,000
Accumulated Depreciation—Aircraft	120,000
Tickets Sold in Advance	85,000
Capital Stock	500,000
Retained Earnings	368,000
Ticket Revenue	52,000
Maintenance Expense	19,000
Wage and Salary Expense	30,000

The following additional information is available:

a. Airplane parts needed for repairs and maintenance are purchased regularly, and the amounts paid are added to the asset account Parts Inventory. At the end of each month, the inventory is counted. At the end of January, the amount of parts on hand is $36,100. *Hint:* What adjustment is needed to reduce the asset account to its proper carrying value? Any expense involved should be included in Maintenance Expense.

b. The estimated useful life of the hangar is 20 years with an estimated salvage value of $10,000 at the end of its life. The original cost of the hangar was $250,000.

c. The estimated useful life of the aircraft is 10 years with an estimated salvage value of $50,000. The original cost of the aircraft was $650,000.

d. As tickets are sold in advance, the amounts are added to Cash and to the liability account Tickets Sold in Advance. A count of the redeemed tickets reveals that $47,000 worth of tickets were used during January.

e. Wages and salaries owed to employees, but unpaid, at the end of January total $7,600.

f. Northern rents excess hangar space to other companies. The amount owed to Northern but unpaid at the end of January is $2,500.

g. Assume a corporate income tax rate of 34%.

Required

1. For each of the preceding items of additional information, determine the effect on the accounting equation.
2. Prepare an income statement for January and a balance sheet as of January 31.

Solution to Review Problem

1.

a.

BALANCE SHEET				INCOME STATEMENT
ASSETS	= LIABILITIES	+	OWNERS' EQUITY	+ REVENUES – EXPENSES
Parts Inventory (8,900)				Maintenance Expense (8,900)

b.

BALANCE SHEET				INCOME STATEMENT
ASSETS	= LIABILITIES	+	OWNERS' EQUITY	+ REVENUES – EXPENSES
Accumulated Depreciation—Hangars (1,000)				Depreciation Expense—Hangars (1,000)

c.

BALANCE SHEET				INCOME STATEMENT
ASSETS	= LIABILITIES	+	OWNERS' EQUITY	+ REVENUES – EXPENSES
Accumulated Depreciation—Aircraft (5,000)				Depreciation Expense—Aircraft (5,000)

d.

BALANCE SHEET				INCOME STATEMENT
ASSETS	= LIABILITIES	+	OWNERS' EQUITY	+ REVENUES – EXPENSES
	Tickets Sold in Advance (47,000)			Ticket Revenue 47,000

e.

BALANCE SHEET				INCOME STATEMENT
ASSETS	= LIABILITIES	+	OWNERS' EQUITY	+ REVENUES – EXPENSES
	Salaries and Wages Payable 7,600			Wage and Salary Expense (7,600)

f.

BALANCE SHEET				INCOME STATEMENT
ASSETS	= LIABILITIES	+	OWNERS' EQUITY	+ REVENUES – EXPENSES
Rent Receivable 2,500				Rent Revenue 2,500

g.

BALANCE SHEET				INCOME STATEMENT
ASSETS	= LIABILITIES	+	OWNERS' EQUITY	+ REVENUES – EXPENSES
	Income Tax Payable 10,200			Income Tax Expense (10,200)

3. Financial statements:

NORTHERN AIRLINES
INCOME STATEMENT
FOR THE MONTH OF JANUARY

Revenues:		
Ticket revenue	$99,000	
Rent revenue	2,500	$101,500
Expenses:		
Maintenance	$27,900	
Wages and salaries	37,600	
Depreciation—hangars	1,000	
Depreciation—aircraft	5,000	
Income taxes	10,200	81,700
Net income		$ 19,800

NORTHERN AIRLINES
BALANCE SHEET
JANUARY 31

Assets			Liabilities and Owners' Equity	
Cash		$ 75,000	Tickets sold in advance	$ 38,000
Rent receivable		2,500	Salaries and wages payable	7,600
Parts inventory		36,100	Income tax payable	10,200
Land		80,000	Capital stock	500,000
Buildings—Hangars	$250,000		Retained earnings	387,800
Accumulated depreciation	25,000	225,000		
Aircraft	$650,000			
Accumulated depreciation	125,000	525,000		
Total assets		$943,600	Total liabilities and owners' equity	$943,600

Chapter Highlights

1. **LO 1** The success of accounting as a form of communication depends on two concepts: recognition and measurement. The items depicted in financial statements are representations. The accountant cannot show the reader an asset but instead depicts it with words and numbers.

2. **LO 1** Measurement in accounting requires choosing an attribute and a unit of measure. Historical cost is the attribute used for many of the assets included in financial statements. One alternative to historical cost is current value. The dollar as a unit of measure is subject to instability, depending on the level of inflation.

3. **LO 2** Under the accrual basis of accounting, revenues are recognized when earned and expenses when incurred. The income statement is prepared on an accrual basis, and the statement of cash flows complements it by providing valuable information about the operating, financing, and investing cash flows of a business.

4. **LO 3** According to the revenue recognition principle, revenues are recognized when they are realized or realizable and earned. On a practical basis, revenue is normally recognized at the time a product or service is delivered to the customer. Certain types of sales arrangements, such as long-term contracts and franchises, present special problems in applying the principle.

5. **LO 4** The matching principle attempts to associate with the revenue of the period all costs necessary to generate that revenue. A direct form of matching is possible for certain types of costs, such as cost of goods sold and commissions. Costs, such as depreciation, are recognized as expenses on an indirect basis. Depreciation is the allocation of the cost of a tangible, long-term asset over its useful life. The benefits from most selling and administrative expenses expire immediately and are recognized as expenses in the period the costs are incurred.

6. **LO 5** The accrual basis necessitates adjustments at the end of a period. The four types of adjustments result from differences between the recognition of revenues and expenses on an accrual basis and the receipt or payment of cash.

7. **LO 5** Cash paid before expense is incurred results in a deferred expense, which is recognized as an asset on the balance sheet. The adjustment reduces the asset and recognizes a corresponding amount of expense. Cash received before revenue is earned requires the recognition of a liability, a deferred revenue. The adjustment reduces the liability and recognizes a corresponding amount of revenue.

8. **LO 5** If cash is paid after an expense is incurred, an adjustment is needed to recognize the accrued liability and the related expense. Similarly, if cash is received after the revenue is earned, the adjustment recognizes the accrued asset and the corre-

sponding revenue. The liability or asset is eliminated in a later period when cash is either paid or received.

9. **LO 6** Steps in the accounting cycle are carried out each period as a basis for the preparation of financial statements. Some of the steps, such as journalizing transactions, are performed continuously, while others, such as recording adjustments, are performed only at the end of the period.

10. **LO 6** After adjustments are recorded and posted to the accounts, certain accounts are closed. Closing serves two important purposes: (1) to return the balances in all revenue, expense, and dividend accounts to zero to start the following accounting period and (2) to transfer the net income (or net loss) and the dividends of the period to the Retained Earnings account.

http://

http://porter.swlearning.com

Technology and other resources for your success

If you need additional help, visit the text's Web site. Also, see this text's preface for a description of available technology and other resources. If your instructor is using PERSONAL *Trainer* in this course, you may complete, on line, the exercises and problems in the text.

Key Terms Quiz

Read each definition below and then write the number of that definition in the blank beside the appropriate term it defines. The quiz solutions appear at the end of the chapter.

_____ Recognition
_____ Historical cost
_____ Current value
_____ Cash basis
_____ Accrual basis
_____ Revenues
_____ Revenue recognition principle
_____ Percentage-of-completion method
_____ Production method
_____ Installment method
_____ Matching principle
_____ Expenses
_____ Adjusting entries
_____ Straight-line method
_____ Contra account
_____ Deferral
_____ Deferred expense
_____ Deferred revenue
_____ Accrual
_____ Accrued liability
_____ Accrued asset
_____ Accounting cycle
_____ Work sheet
_____ Real accounts
_____ Nominal accounts
_____ Closing entries
_____ Interim statements

1. A device used at the end of the period to gather the information needed to prepare financial statements without actually recording and posting adjustments.
2. Inflows or other enhancements of assets or settlements of liabilities from delivering or producing goods, rendering services, or other activities.
3. The method in which revenue is recognized when a commodity is produced rather than when it is sold.
4. Journal entries made at the end of a period by a company using the accrual basis of accounting.
5. Journal entries made at the end of the period to return the balance in all nominal accounts to zero and transfer the net income or loss and the dividends of the period to Retained Earnings.
6. The method used by contractors to recognize revenue before the completion of a long-term contract.
7. A liability resulting from the receipt of cash before the recognition of revenue.
8. The method in which revenue is recognized at the time cash is collected; used for various types of consumer items, such as automobiles and appliances.
9. The name given to balance sheet accounts because they are permanent and are not closed at the end of the period.
10. An asset resulting from the recognition of a revenue before the receipt of cash.
11. The amount of cash, or its equivalent, that could be received by selling an asset currently.
12. The assignment of an equal amount of depreciation to each period.
13. Cash has either been paid or received, but expense or revenue has not yet been recognized.
14. A system of accounting in which revenues are recognized when earned and expenses when incurred.
15. Cash has not yet been paid or received, but expense has been incurred or revenue earned.

16. Financial statements prepared monthly, quarterly, or at other intervals less than a year in duration.
17. Revenues are recognized in the income statement when they are realized, or realizable, and earned.
18. The process of recording an item in the financial statements as an asset, liability, revenue, expense, or the like.
19. An asset resulting from the payment of cash before the incurrence of expense.
20. The name given to revenue, expense, and dividend accounts because they are temporary and are closed at the end of the period.
21. A system of accounting in which revenues are recognized when cash is received and expenses when cash is paid.
22. A liability resulting from the recognition of an expense before the payment of cash.
23. The association of revenue of a period with all of the costs necessary to generate that revenue.
24. Any account that is used to offset another account.
25. The amount that is paid for an asset and that is used as a basis for recognizing it on the balance sheet and carrying it on later balance sheets.
26. Outflows or other using up of assets or incurrences of liabilities resulting from delivering goods, rendering services, or carrying out other activities.
27. A series of steps performed each period and culminating with the preparation of a set of financial statements.

Answers on p. 213.

Alternate Terms

Historical cost Original cost

Asset Unexpired cost

Deferred expense Prepaid expense, prepaid asset

Deferred revenue Unearned revenue

Expense Expired cost

Nominal account Temporary account

Real account Permanent account

Questions

1. What is meant by the following statement? "The items depicted in financial statements are merely *representations* of the real thing."
2. What is the meaning of the following statement? "The choice between historical cost and current value is a good example of the trade-off in accounting between relevance and reliability."
3. A realtor earns a 10% commission on the sale of a $150,000 home. The realtor lists the home on June 5, the sale occurs on June 12, and the seller pays the realtor the $15,000 commission on July 8. When should the realtor recognize revenue from the sale, assuming (a) the cash basis of accounting and (b) the accrual basis of accounting?
4. What does the following statement mean? "If I want to assess the cash flow prospects for a company down the road, I look at the company's most recent statement of cash flows. An income statement prepared under the accrual basis of accounting is useless for this purpose."
5. What is the relationship between the time period assumption and accrual accounting?
6. Is it necessary for an asset to be acquired when revenue is recognized? Explain your answer.
7. What is the justification for recognizing revenue on a long-term contract by the percentage-of-completion method?
8. Illinois Fried Chicken sells franchises granting the franchisee in a specific geographic area the exclusive right to use the company name and sell chicken using its secret recipe. An initial franchise fee of $50,000 is charged by Illinois, along with a continuing fee of 3% of sales. The initial fee is for Illinois' assistance in selecting a site and training personnel. When should Illinois recognize the $50,000 as revenue?
9. When should a publisher of magazines recognize revenue?
10. What is the justification for recognizing revenue in certain industries at the time the product is *produced* rather than when it is *sold?*
11. A friend says to you: "I just don't get it. Assets cost money. Expenses reduce income. There must be some relationship among *assets, costs,* and *expenses*—I'm just not sure what it is!" What is the relationship? Can you give an example of it?
12. What is the meaning of *depreciation* to the accountant?
13. What are the four basic types of adjustments? Give an example of each.
14. What is the difference between a real account and a nominal account?
15. What two purposes are served in making closing entries?

Exercises

Exercise 4-1 *Revenue Recognition* LO 3

The highway department contracted with a private company to collect tolls and maintain facilities on a turnpike. Users of the turnpike can pay cash as they approach the toll booth, or they can purchase a pass. The pass is equipped with an electronic sensor that subtracts the toll fee from the pass balance as the motorist slowly approaches a special toll booth. The passes are issued in $10 increments. Refunds are available to motorists who do not use the pass balance, but these are issued very infrequently. Last year $3,000,000 was collected at the traditional toll booths, $2,000,000 of passes were issued, and $1,700,000 of passes were used at the special toll booth. How much should the company recognize as revenue for the year? Explain how the revenue recognition rule should be applied in this case.

Exercise 4-2 ***The Matching Principle*** **LO 4**

Three methods of matching costs with revenue were described in the chapter: (a) directly match a specific form of revenue with a cost incurred in generating that revenue, (b) indirectly match a cost with the periods during which it will provide benefits or revenue, and (c) immediately recognize a cost incurred as an expense because no future benefits are expected. For each of the following costs, indicate how it is normally recognized as expense by indicating either *a*, *b*, or *c*. If you think there is more than one possible answer for any of the situations, explain why.

1. New office copier
2. Monthly bill from the utility company for electricity
3. Office supplies
4. Biweekly payroll for office employees
5. Commissions earned by salespeople
6. Interest incurred on a six-month loan from the bank
7. Cost of inventory sold during the current period
8. Taxes owed on income earned during current period
9. Cost of three-year insurance policy

Exercise 4-3 ***Accruals and Deferrals*** **LO 5**

For the following situations, indicate whether each involves a deferred expense (DE), a deferred revenue (DR), an accrued liability (AL), or an accrued asset (AA).

Example: ___DE___ Office supplies purchased in advance of their use.

_______ 1. Wages earned by employees but not yet paid

_______ 2. Cash collected from subscriptions in advance of publishing a magazine

_______ 3. Interest earned on a customer loan for which principal and interest have not yet been collected

_______ 4. One year's premium on life insurance policy paid in advance

_______ 5. Office building purchased for cash

_______ 6. Rent collected in advance from a tenant

_______ 7. State income taxes owed at the end of the year

_______ 8. Rent owed by a tenant but not yet collected

Exercise 4-4 ***Office Supplies*** **LO 5**

Somerville Corp. purchases office supplies once a month and prepares monthly financial statements. The asset account Office Supplies on Hand has a balance of $1,450 on May 1. Purchases of supplies during May amount to $1,100. Supplies on hand at May 31 amount to $920. Determine the effect on the accounting equation of the adjustment necessary on May 31. What would be the effect on net income for May if this entry is *not* recorded?

Exercise 4-5 ***Prepaid Rent—Quarterly Adjustments*** **LO 5**

On September 1, Northhampton Industries signed a six-month lease, effective September 1, for office space. Northhampton agreed to prepay the rent and mailed a check for $12,000 to the landlord on September 1. Assume that Northhampton prepares adjustments only four times a year, on March 31, June 30, September 30, and December 31.

Required

1. Compute the rental cost for each full month.
2. Determine the effect on the accounting equation of the entry necessary on September 1.

(continued)

3. Determine the effect on the accounting equation of the adjustment necessary on September 30.
4. Assume that the accountant prepares the adjustment on September 30 but forgets to record an adjustment on December 31. Will net income for the year be understated or overstated? By what amount?

Exercise 4-6 *Depreciation* LO 5

On July 1, 2004, Red Gate Farm buys a combine for $100,000 in cash. Assume that the combine is expected to have a seven-year life and an estimated salvage value of $16,000 at the end of that time.

Required

1. Determine the effect on the accounting equation of the purchase of the combine on July 1, 2004.
2. Compute the depreciable cost of the combine.
3. Using the straight-line method, compute the monthly depreciation.
4. Determine the effect on the accounting equation of the adjustment necessary to record depreciation at the end of July 2004.
5. Compute the combine's carrying value that will be shown on Red Gate's balance sheet prepared on December 31, 2004.

Exercise 4-7 *Prepaid Insurance—Annual Adjustments* LO 5

On April 1, 2004, Briggs Corp. purchases a 24-month property insurance policy for $72,000. The policy is effective immediately. Assume that Briggs prepares adjusting entries only once a year, on December 31.

Required

1. Compute the monthly cost of the insurance policy.
2. Determine the effect on the accounting equation of the purchase of the policy on April 1, 2004.
3. Determine the effect on the accounting equation of the adjustment necessary on December 31, 2004.
4. Assume that the accountant forgets to record an adjustment on December 31, 2004. Will net income for the year ended December 31, 2004, be understated or overstated? Explain your answer.

Exercise 4-8 *Subscriptions* LO 5

Horse Country Living publishes a monthly magazine for which a 12-month subscription costs $30. All subscriptions require payment of the full $30 in advance. On August 1, 2004, the balance in the Subscriptions Received in Advance account was $40,500. During the month of August, the company sold 900 yearly subscriptions. After the adjustment at the end of August, the balance in the Subscriptions Received in Advance account is $60,000.

Required

1. Determine the effect on the accounting equation of the sale of the 900 yearly subscriptions during the month of August.
2. Determine the effect on the accounting equation of the adjustment necessary on August 31.
3. Assume that the accountant made the correct entry during August to record the sale of the 900 subscriptions but forgot to make the adjustment on August 31. Would net income for August be overstated or understated? Explain your answer.

Exercise 4-9 *Customer Deposits* LO 5

Wolfe & Wolfe collected $9,000 from a customer on April 1 and agreed to provide legal services during the next three months. Wolfe & Wolfe expects to provide an equal amount of services each month.

Required

1. Determine the effect on the accounting equation of the receipt of the customer deposit on April 1.
2. Determine the effect on the accounting equation of the adjustment necessary on April 30.
3. What would be the effect on net income for April if the adjustment in (2) is not recorded?

Exercise 4-10 *Wages Payable* LO 5

Denton Corporation employs 50 workers in its plant. Each employee is paid $10 per hour and works seven hours per day, Monday through Friday. Employees are paid every Friday. The last payday was Friday, October 20.

Required

1. Compute the dollar amount of the weekly payroll.
2. Determine the effect on the accounting equation of the payment of the weekly payroll on Friday, October 27.
3. Denton prepares monthly financial statements. Determine the effect on the accounting equation of the adjustment necessary on Tuesday, October 31, the last day of the month.
4. Determine the effect on the accounting equation of the payment of the weekly payroll on Friday, November 3.
5. Would net income for the month of October be understated or overstated if Denton doesn't bother with an adjustment on October 31? Explain your answer.

Exercise 4-11 *Interest Payable* LO 5

Billings Company takes out a 12%, 90-day, $100,000 loan with First National Bank on March 1, 2004.

Required

1. Determine the effect on the accounting equation on March 1, 2004, when Billings takes out the loan.
2. Determine the effect on the accounting equation of the adjustments necessary for the months of March and April 2004.
3. Determine the effect on the accounting equation on May 30, 2004, when Billings repays the principal and interest to First National.

Exercise 4-12 *Property Taxes Payable—Annual Adjustments* LO 5

Lexington Builders owns property in Kaneland County. Lexington's 2003 property taxes amounted to $50,000. Kaneland County will send out the 2004 property tax bills to property owners during April 2005. Taxes must be paid by June 1, 2005. Assume that Lexington prepares adjusting entries only once a year, on December 31, and that property taxes for 2004 are expected to increase by 5% over those for 2003.

Required

1. Determine the effect on the accounting equation of the adjustment necessary to record the property taxes payable on December 31, 2004.
2. Determine the effect on the accounting equation of the payment of the 2004 property taxes on June 1, 2005.

Exercise 4-13 *Interest Receivable* LO 5

On June 1, 2004, MicroTel Enterprises lends $60,000 to MaxiDriver Inc. The loan will be repaid in 60 days with interest at 10%.

Required

1. Determine the effect on the accounting equation of the loan on MicroTel's books on June 1, 2004.
2. Determine the effect on the accounting equation of the adjustment necessary on MicroTel's books on June 30, 2004.
3. Determine the effect on the accounting equation for MicroTel's books on July 31, 2004, when MaxiDriver repays the principal and interest.

Exercise 4-14 *Unbilled Accounts Receivable* LO 5

Mike and Cary repair computers for small local businesses. Heavy thunderstorms during the last week of June resulted in a record number of service calls. Eager to review the results of operations for the month of June, Mike prepared an income statement and was puzzled by the lower-than-expected amount of revenues. Cary explained that he had not yet billed the company's customers for $40,000 of work performed during the last week of the month.

Required

1. Should revenue be recorded when services are performed or when customers are billed? Explain your answer.
2. Determine the effect on the accounting equation of the adjustment necessary on June 30.

Exercise 4-15 *The Effect of Ignoring Adjustments on Net Income* LO 5

For each of the following independent situations, determine whether the effect of ignoring the required adjustment will result in an understatement (U), an overstatement (O), or no effect (NE) on net income for the period.

Situation	Effect on Net Income
Example: Taxes owed but not yet paid are ignored.	O
1. A company fails to record depreciation on equipment.	
2. Sales made during the last week of the period are not recorded.	
3. A company neglects to record the expired portion of a prepaid insurance policy (its cost was originally recorded in an asset account).	
4. Interest due but not yet paid on a long-term note payable is ignored.	
5. Commissions earned by salespeople but not payable until the 10th of the following month are ignored.	
6. A landlord receives cash on the date a lease is signed for the rent for the first six months and records Unearned Rent Revenue. The landlord fails to make any adjustment at the end of the first month.	

Exercise 4-16 *The Effect of Adjustments on the Accounting Equation* LO 5

Determine whether recording each of the following adjustments will increase (I), decrease (D), or have no effect (NE) on each of the three elements of the accounting equation.

	Assets	= Liabilities	+ Owners' Equity
Example: Wages earned during the period but not yet paid are accrued.	NE	I	D
1. Prepaid insurance is reduced for the portion of the policy that has expired during the period.			
2. Interest incurred during the period but not yet paid is accrued.			
3. Depreciation for the period is recorded.			
4. Revenue is recorded for the earned portion of a liability for amounts collected in advance from customers.			
5. Rent revenue is recorded for amounts owed by a tenant but not yet received.			
6. Income taxes owed but not yet paid are accrued.			

Exercise 4-17 *The Accounting Cycle* LO 6

The steps in the accounting cycle are listed below in random order. Fill in the blank next to each step to indicate its *order* in the cycle. The first step in the cycle is filled in as an example.

Order	Procedure
	Prepare a work sheet.
	Close the accounts.
1	Collect and analyze information from source documents.
	Prepare financial statements.
	Post transactions to accounts in the ledger.
	Record and post adjustments.
	Journalize daily transactions.

Multi-Concept Exercises

Exercise 4-18 ***Revenue Recognition, Cash and Accrual Basis*** **LO 1, 2, 3**

Hathaway Health Club sold three-year memberships at a reduced rate during its opening promotion. It sold 1,000 three-year, nonrefundable memberships for $366 each. The club expects to sell 100 additional three-year memberships for $900 each over each of the next two years. Membership fees are paid when clients sign up. The club's bookkeeper has prepared the following income statement for the first year of business and projected income statements for Years 2 and 3.

Cash-basis income statements:

	Year 1	Year 2	Year 3
Sales	$366,000	$ 90,000	$ 90,000
Equipment*	$100,000	$ 0	$ 0
Salaries and wages	50,000	50,000	50,000
Advertising	5,000	5,000	5,000
Rent and utilities	36,000	36,000	36,000
Net income (loss)	$175,000	$ (1,000)	$ (1,000)

*Equipment was purchased at the beginning of Year 1 for $100,000 and is expected to last for three years and then to be worth $1,000.

Required

1. Convert the income statements for each of the three years to the accrual basis.
2. Describe how the revenue recognition principle applies. Do you believe that the cash-basis or the accrual-basis income statements are more useful to management? to investors? Why?

Exercise 4-19 ***The Effect of the Percentage-of-Completion Method on Financial Statements*** **LO 1, 2, 3**

Fox Valley Inc. is building a bridge. During the first year of the three-year project, Fox Valley incurred construction costs of $1.2 million. The company expects to spend an additional $600,000 in each of the next two years of the project. The state has agreed to pay Fox Valley $4 million for the bridge, $2 million in the first year and $2 million on completion. The company would like to use the percentage-of-completion method to report revenue and income.

Required

1. Complete the following table, comparing the percentage-of-completion method with the cash basis. Use the percentage of costs incurred to date to estimated total costs to determine the percentage of completion.

	Income Recognized under	
Year	Percentage-of-Completion	Cash Basis
1		
2		
3		
Total		

2. Explain how the revenue recognition principle applies to the percentage-of-completion method.

Exercise 4-20 ***Depreciation Expense*** **LO 4, 5**

During 2004, Carter Company acquired three assets with the following costs, estimated useful lives, and estimated salvage values:

Date	Asset	Cost	Estimated Useful Life	Estimated Salvage Value
March 28	Truck	$ 18,000	5 years	$ 3,000
June 22	Computer	55,000	10 years	5,000
October 3	Building	250,000	30 years	10,000

The company uses the straight-line method to depreciate all assets and computes depreciation to the nearest month. For example, the computer system will be depreciated for six months in 2004.

Required

1. Compute the depreciation expense that Carter will record on each of the three assets for 2004.
2. Comment on the following statement: "Accountants could save time and money by simply expensing the cost of long-term assets when they are purchased. In addition, this would be more accurate because depreciation requires estimates of useful life and salvage value."

Exercise 4-21 ***Accrual of Interest on a Loan*** **LO 4, 5**

On July 1, 2004, Paxson Corporation takes out a 12%, two-month, $50,000 loan at Friendly National Bank. Principal and interest are to be repaid on August 31.

Required

1. Determine the effects on the accounting equation of each of the following: (a) the borrowings on July 1 (b) the necessary adjustment for the accrual of interest on July 31 (c) repayment of the principal and interest.
2. Evaluate the following statement: "It would be much easier not to bother with an adjustment on July 31 and simply record interest expense on August 31 when the loan is repaid."

Problems

Problem 4-1 ***The Revenue Recognition Principle*** **LO 3**

Each of the following paragraphs describes a situation involving revenue recognition.

a. ABC Realty receives a 6% commission for every house it sells. It lists a house for a client on April 3 at a selling price of $150,000. ABC receives an offer from a buyer on April 28 to purchase the house at the asking price. The realtor's client accepts the offer on May 1. ABC will receive its 6% commission at a closing scheduled for May 16.

b. Chicken King is a fast-food franchisor on the West Coast. It charges all franchisees $10,000 to open an outlet in a designated city. In return for this fee, the franchisee receives the exclusive right to operate in the area, as well as assistance from Chicken King in selecting a site. On January 5, Chicken King signs an agreement with a franchisee and receives a down payment of $4,000, with the balance of $6,000 due in three months. On March 13, Chicken King meets with the new franchisee, and the two parties agree on a suitable site for the business. On April 5, the franchisee pays Chicken King the remaining $6,000.

c. Refer to part **b.** In addition to the initial fee, Chicken King charges a continuing fee equal to 2% of the franchisee's sales each month. Each month's fee is payable by the 10th of the following month. The franchisee opens for business on June 1. On July 3, Chicken King receives a report from the franchisee indicating its sales for the month of June amount to $60,000. On July 8, Chicken King receives its 2% fee for June sales.

d. Goldstar Mining Corporation mines and sells gold and other precious commodities on the open market. During August, the company mines 50 ounces of gold. The market price throughout August is $300 per ounce. The 50 ounces are eventually sold on the open market on September 5 for $310 per ounce.

e. Whatadeal Inc. sells used cars. Because of the uncertainties involved in collecting from customers, Whatadeal uses the installment basis of accounting. On December 2, Whatadeal sells a car for $10,000 with a 25% down payment and the balance due in 60 days. The company's accounting year ends on December 31. Whatadeal receives the balance of $7,500 on February 1.

Required

For each situation, indicate when revenue should be recognized, as well as the dollar amount. Give a brief explanation for each answer.

Problem 4-2 ***Adjustments*** **LO 5**

Water Corporation prepares monthly financial statements and therefore adjusts its accounts at the end of every month. The following information is available for March 2004:

a. Water Corporation takes out a 90-day, 8%, $15,000 note on March 1, 2004, with interest and principal to be paid at maturity.

b. The asset account Office Supplies on Hand has a balance of $1,280 on March 1, 2004. During March, Water adds $750 to the account for the purchases of the period. A count of the supplies on hand at the end of March indicates a balance of $1,370.

c. The company purchased office equipment last year for $62,600. The equipment has an estimated useful life of six years and an estimated salvage value of $5,000.

d. The company's plant operates seven days per week with a daily payroll of $950. Wage earners are paid every Sunday. The last day of the month is Saturday, March 31.

e. The company rented an idle warehouse to a neighboring business on February 1, 2004, at a rate of $2,500 per month. On this date, Water Corporation recorded Rent Collected in Advance for six months' rent received in advance.

f. On March 1, 2004, Water Corporation created a liability account, Customer Deposits, for $4,800. This sum represents an amount that a customer paid in advance and that will be earned evenly by Water over a four-month period.

g. Based on its income for the month, Water Corporation estimates that federal income taxes for March amount to $3,900.

Required

1. For each of the preceding situations, determine the effect on the accounting, equation of the adjustment necessary on March 31, 2004.
2. Assume that Water reports income of $23,000 before any of the adjustments. What net income will Water report for March?

Problem 4-3 *Annual Adjustments* LO 5

Palmer Industries prepares annual financial statements and adjusts its accounts only at the end of the year. The following information is available for the year ended December 31, 2004:

a. Palmer purchased computer equipment two years ago for $15,000. The equipment has an estimated useful life of five years and an estimated salvage value of $250.

b. The Office Supplies account had a balance of $3,600 on January 1, 2004. During 2004, Palmer added $17,600 to the account for purchases of office supplies during the year. A count of the supplies on hand at the end of December 2004 indicates a balance of $1,850.

c. On August 1, 2004, Palmer created a liability account, Customer Deposits, for $24,000. This sum represents an amount that a customer paid in advance and that will be earned evenly by Palmer over a six-month period.

d. Palmer rented some office space on November 1, 2004, at a rate of $2,700 per month. On that date, Palmer recorded Prepaid Rent for three months' rent paid in advance.

e. Palmer took out a 120-day, 9%, $200,000 note on November 1, 2004, with interest and principal to be paid at maturity.

f. Palmer operates five days per week with an average daily payroll of $500. Palmer pays its employees every Thursday. December 31, 2004, is a Friday.

Required

1. For each of the preceding situations, determine the effect on the accounting equation of the adjustment necessary on December 31, 2004.
2. Assume that Palmer's accountant forgets to record the adjustments on December 31, 2004. Will net income for the year be understated or overstated? By what amount? (Ignore the effect of income taxes.)

Problem 4-4 *Recurring Transactions and Adjustments* LO 5

The following are Butler Realty Corporation's accounts, identified by number. The company has been in the real estate business for 10 years and prepares financial statements monthly. Following the list of accounts is a series of transactions entered into by Butler. For each transaction, enter the number(s) of the account(s) affected.

Accounts

1. Cash	6. Accumulated Depreciation
2. Accounts Receivable	7. Land
3. Prepaid Rent	8. Accounts Payable
4. Office Supplies	9. Salaries and Wages Payable
5. Automobiles	10. Income Tax Payable

(continued)

11. Notes Payable
12. Capital Stock, $10 par
13. Paid-In Capital in Excess of Par
14. Commissions Revenue
15. Office Supply Expense
16. Rent Expense
17. Salaries and Wages Expense
18. Depreciation Expense
19. Interest Expense
20. Income Tax Expense

Transaction	
a. **Example:** Issued additional shares of stock to owners at amount in excess of par.	1, 12, 13
b. Purchased automobiles for cash.	______
c. Purchased land; made cash down payment and signed a promissory note for the balance.	______
d. Paid cash to landlord for rent for next 12 months.	______
e. Purchased office supplies on account.	______
f. Collected cash for commissions from clients for the properties sold during the month.	______
g. Collected cash for commissions from clients for the properties sold in the prior month.	______
h. During the month, sold properties for which cash for commissions will be collected from clients next month.	______
i. Paid for office supplies purchased on account in an earlier month.	______
j. Recorded an adjustment to recognize wages and salaries incurred but not yet paid.	______
k. Recorded an adjustment for office supplies used during the month.	______
l. Recorded an adjustment for the portion of prepaid rent that expired during the month.	______
m. Made required month-end payment on note taken out in **(c)**; payment is part principal and part interest.	______
n. Recorded adjustment for monthly depreciation on the autos.	______
o. Recorded adjustment for income taxes.	______

Problem 4-5 *Use of Account Balances as a Basis for Annual Adjustments* LO 5

The following account balances are taken from the records of Chauncey Company at December 31, 2004. The Prepaid Insurance account represents the cost of a three-year policy purchased on August 1, 2004. The Rent Collected in Advance account represents the cash received from a tenant on June 1, 2004, for 12 months' rent, beginning on that date. The Note Receivable represents a nine-month promissory note received from a customer on September 1, 2004. Principal and interest at an annual rate of 9% will be received on June 1, 2005.

Prepaid Insurance	$ 7,200
Rent Collected in Advance	6,000
Note Receivable	50,000

Required

1. For each of the three situations described above, determine the effect on the accounting equation of the adjustments necessary on December 31, 2004. Assume that Chauncey records adjustments only once a year, on December 31.
2. Assume that adjustments are made at the end of each month rather than only at the end of the year. What would be the balance in Prepaid Insurance *before* the December adjustment is recorded? Explain your answer.

Problem 4-6 *Use of Account Balances as a Basis for Adjustments* LO 5

Bob Reynolds operates a real estate business. A list of accounts on April 30, 2004, *before* recording any adjustments, appears as follows:

Cash	$15,700
Prepaid Insurance	450
Office Supplies	250
Office Equipment	50,000
Accumulated Depreciation—Office Equipment	5,000
Automobile	12,000
Accumulated Depreciation—Automobile	1,400
Accounts Payable	6,500
Unearned Commissions	9,500
Notes Payable	2,000
Capital Stock	10,000
Retained Earnings	40,000
Dividends	2,500
Commissions Earned	17,650
Utilities Expense	2,300
Salaries Expense	7,400
Advertising Expense	1,450

Other Data

a. The monthly insurance cost is $50.

b. Office supplies on hand on April 30, 2004, amount to $180.

c. The office equipment was purchased on April 1, 2003. On that date, it had an estimated useful life of 10 years.

d. On September 1, 2003, the automobile was purchased; it had an estimated useful life of five years.

e. A deposit is received in advance of providing any services for first-time customers. Amounts received in advance are recorded initially in the account Unearned Commissions. Based on services provided to these first-time customers, the balance in this account at the end of April should be $5,000.

f. Repeat customers are allowed to pay for services one month after the date of the sale of their property. Services rendered during the month but not yet collected or billed to these customers amount to $1,500.

g. Interest owed on the note payable but not yet paid amounts to $20.

h. Salaries owed to employees but unpaid at the end of the month amount to $2,500.

Required

1. For each of the items of other data, **a** through **h**, determine the effect on the accounting equation.
2. Compute the net increase or decrease in net income for the month from the recognition of the adjustments in part **1**. (Ignore income taxes).
3. Note the balance in Accumulated Depreciation—Office Equipment of $5,000. Explain *why* the account contains a balance of $5,000 on April 30, 2004.

Problem 4-7 ***Reconstruction of Adjustments from Account Balances*** LO 5

Taggart Corp. records adjustments each month before preparing monthly financial statements. The following selected account balances on May 31, 2004, and June 30, 2004, reflect month-end adjustments:

Account Title	May 31, 2004	June 30, 2004
Prepaid Insurance	$3,600	$3,450
Equipment	9,600	9,600
Accumulated Depreciation	1,280	1,360
Notes Payable	9,600	9,600
Interest Payable	2,304	2,448

Required

1. The company purchased a 36-month insurance policy on June 1, 2003. Determine the effect on the accounting equation of the adjustment that was made for insurance on June 30, 2004.

(continued)

2. What was the original cost of the insurance policy? Explain your answer.
3. The equipment was purchased on February 1, 2003, for $9,600. Taggart uses straight-line depreciation and estimates that the equipment will have no salvage value. Determine the effect on the accounting equation of the adjustment that was made for depreciation on June 30, 2004.
4. What is the equipment's estimated useful life in months? Explain your answer.
5. Taggart signed a two-year note payable on February 1, 2003, for the purchase of the equipment. Interest on the note accrues on a monthly basis and will be paid at maturity along with the principal amount of $9,600. Determine the effect on the accounting equation of the adjustment that was made for interest on June 30, 2004.
6. What is the *monthly* interest rate on the loan? Explain your answer.

Problem 4-8 ***Use of Account Balances as a Basis for Adjustments*** **LO 5**

The following is a list of accounts for Four Star Video at May 31, 2004. It reflects the recurring transactions for the month of May but does not reflect any month-end adjustments.

Cash	$ 4,000
Prepaid Rent	6,600
Video Inventory	25,600
Display Stands	8,900
Accumulated Depreciation	5,180
Accounts Payable	3,260
Customer Subscriptions	4,450
Capital Stock	5,000
Retained Earnings	22,170
Rental Revenue	9,200
Wage and Salary Expense	2,320
Utilities Expense	1,240
Advertising Expense	600

The following additional information is available:

a. Four Star rents a store in a shopping mall and prepays the annual rent of $7,200 on April 1 of each year.

b. The asset account Video Inventory represents the cost of videos purchased from suppliers. When a new title is purchased from a supplier, its cost is added to this account. When a title has served its useful life and can no longer be rented (even at a reduced price), it is removed from the inventory in the store. Based on the monthly count, the cost of titles on hand at the end of May is $23,140.

c. The display stands have an estimated useful life of five years and an estimated salvage value of $500.

d. Wages and salaries owed to employees but unpaid at the end of May amount to $1,450.

e. In addition to individual rentals, Four Star operates a popular discount subscription program. Customers pay an annual fee of $120 for an unlimited number of rentals. Based on the $10 per month earned on each of these subscriptions, the amount earned for the month of May is $2,440.

f. Four Star accrues income taxes using an estimated tax rate equal to 30% of the income for the month.

Required

1. For each of the items of additional information, **a** through **f**, determine the effect on the accounting equation.
2. On the basis of the information you have, does Four Star appear to be a profitable business? Explain your answer.

Multi-Concept Problems

Problem 4-9 ***Cash and Accrual Income Statements for a Manufacturer*** **LO 2, 3**

Drysdale Company was established to manufacture components for the auto industry. The components are shipped the same day they are produced. The following events took place during the first year of operations.

a. Issued common stock for a $50,000 cash investment.

b. Purchased delivery truck at the beginning of the year at a cost of $10,000 cash. The truck is expected to last five years and will be worthless at the end of that time.

c. Manufactured and sold 500,000 components the first year. The costs incurred to manufacture the components are (1) $1,000 monthly rent on a facility that included utilities and insurance, (2) $400,000 of raw materials purchased on account ($100,000 is still unpaid as of year-end, but all materials were used in manufacturing), and (3) $190,000 paid in salaries and wages to employees and supervisors.

d. Paid $100,000 to sales and office staff for salaries and wages.

e. Sold all components on account for $2 each. As of year-end, $150,000 is due from customers.

Required

1. How much revenue will Drysdale recognize under the cash basis and under the accrual basis?
2. Describe how Drysdale should apply the matching principle to recognize expenses.
3. Prepare an income statement under the accrual basis. Ignore income taxes.

Problem 4-10 ***Revenue Recognition on Installment Sales*** **LO 3, 4**

John Deare, an Illinois corn farmer, retired in South Carolina. While retired, he volunteered his time at the Small Business Administration office. One day, Frances Hirise, a condominium builder, came in with a question about the amount of sales she should recognize on her income statement. She had constructed a complex of 200 units. Half of the units sell for $50,000 each, and the other half sell for $60,000. The developer agreed to finance the sale of all units, and by the end of the year, 40 units at $50,000 and 30 units at $60,000 had been sold. Each buyer made a down payment of 10% cash and agreed to pay the remainder in equal annual payments plus interest on the unpaid balance over the next nine years. No payments have been received other than the down payments. John advised Frances that she should recognize sales of $11 million [(100 × $50,000) + (100 × $60,000)].

Required

Do you agree with John? Why did he suggest this amount? What amount of revenue would you suggest that Frances recognize in the current and subsequent years as a result of these sales? When should the costs to build the condos (lumber, labor, etc.) be recognized as expenses?

Problem 4-11 ***Revenue and Expense Recognition*** **LO 3, 4**

Two years ago, Darlene Darby opened a delivery service. Darby reports the following accounts on her income statement:

Sales	$69,000
Advertising expense	3,500
Salaries expense	39,000
Rent expense	10,000

These amounts represent two years of revenue and expenses. Darby has asked you how she can tell how much of the income is from the first year of business and how much is from the second year. She provides the following additional data:

a. Sales in the second year were double those of the first year.

b. Advertising expense is for a $500 opening promotion and weekly ads in the newspaper.

c. Salaries represent one employee for the first nine months and then two employees for the remainder of the time. Each is paid the same salary. No raises have been granted.

d. Rent has not changed since the business opened.

Required

1. Prepare income statements for Years 1 and 2.

Problem 4-12 ***Monthly Transactions, Adjustments, and Financial Statements*** **LO 5, 6**

Moonlight Bay Inn is incorporated on January 2, 2004, by its three owners, each of whom contributes $20,000 in cash in exchange for shares of stock in the business. In addition to the sale of stock, the transactions on the following page are entered into during the month of January.

January 2: A Victorian inn is purchased for $50,000 in cash. An appraisal performed on this date indicates that the land is worth $15,000 and the remaining balance of the purchase price is attributable to the house. The owners estimate that the house will have an estimated useful life of 25 years and an estimated salvage value of $5,000.

January 3: A two-year, 12%, $30,000 promissory note was signed at the Second State Bank. Interest and principal will be repaid on the maturity date of January 3, 2006.

January 4: New furniture for the inn is purchased at a cost of $15,000 in cash. The furniture has an estimated useful life of 10 years and no salvage value.

January 5: A 24-month property insurance policy is purchased for $6,000 in cash.

January 6: An advertisement for the inn is placed in the local newspaper. Moonlight Bay pays $450 cash for the ad, which will run in the paper throughout January.

January 7: Cleaning supplies are purchased on account for $950. The bill is payable within 30 days.

January 15: Wages of $4,230 for the first half of the month are paid in cash.

January 16: A guest mails the business $980 in cash as a deposit for a room to be rented for two weeks. The guest plans to stay at the inn during the last week of January and the first week of February.

January 31: Cash receipts from rentals of rooms for the month amount to $8,300.

January 31: Cash receipts from operation of the restaurant for the month amount to $6,600.

January 31: Each stockholder is paid $200 in cash dividends.

Required

1. Determine the effect on the accounting equation of each of the preceding transactions.
2. Prepare a list of accounts and their balances for Moonlight Bay Inn at January 31, 2004. Reflect the recurring transactions for the month of January but not the necessary month-end adjustments.
3. Determine the effect on the accounting equation of the necessary adjustments at January 31, 2004, for each of the following:
   a. Depreciation of the house
   b. Depreciation of the furniture
   c. Interest on the promissory note
   d. Recognition of the expired portion of the insurance
   e. Recognition of the earned portion of the guest's deposit
   f. Wages earned during the second half of January amount to $5,120 and will be paid on February 3.
   g. Cleaning supplies on hand on January 31 amount to $230.
   h. A gas and electric bill that is received from the city amounts to $740 and is payable by February 5.
   i. Income taxes are to be accrued at a rate of 30% of income before taxes.
4. Prepare in good form the following financial statements:
   a. Income statement for the month ended January 31, 2004
   b. Statement of retained earnings for the month ended January 31, 2004
   c. Balance sheet at January 31, 2004
5. Assume that you are the loan officer at Second State Bank (refer to the transaction on January 3). What are your reactions to Moonlight's first month of operations? Are you comfortable with the loan you made?

Alternate Problems

Problem 4-1A *The Revenue Recognition Principle* LO 3

Each of the following paragraphs describes a situation involving revenue recognition.

a. Zee Zitter Inc. paints and decorates office buildings. On September 30, 2004, it received $5,750 for work to be completed over the next six months.

b. Tan Us is a tanning salon franchisor in the Midwest. It charges all franchisees a fee of $2,500 to open a salon and an ongoing fee equal to 5% of all revenue during the first five years. The $2,500 is for training and accounting systems to be used in each salon. During January 2004, Tan Us signed an agreement with five individuals to open salons over the next three months.

c. On June 1, 2004, Dan Diver Bridge Building Inc. entered into a contract with the county to renovate an old covered bridge. The county gives Dan an advance of $500,000 and agrees to pay Dan $75,000 each month for 20 months, at which time the project should be completed.

d. Joe Cropper, a wheat grower, harvested the current year's crop and delivered it to the elevator for storage on October 1, 2004, until it is sold to one of several foreign countries. The expected sales value of the wheat is $450,000.

e. Shop-n-Here, a convenience store chain, constructed a strip shopping center next to one of its stores. The spaces are being sold to individuals who will open auto parts and repair facilities. One person is planning to open a brake-repair shop, another will set up a transmission-repair shop, a third will do 10-minute oil changes, and so on. The store spaces sell for $25,000 each. There are six spaces, four of which are sold in May of 2004.

Required

For each of the preceding situations, indicate when in 2004 revenue should be recognized, as well as the dollar amount. Give a brief explanation for each answer.

Problem 4-2A *Adjustments* LO 5

Flood Relief Inc. prepares monthly financial statements and therefore adjusts its accounts at the end of every month. The following information is available for June 2004:

a. Flood received a $10,000, 4%, two-year note receivable from a customer for services rendered. The principal and interest are due on June 1, 2006. Flood expects to be able to collect the note and interest in full at that time.

b. Office supplies totaling $5,600 were purchased during the month. The asset account Supplies is increased whenever a purchase is made. A count in the storeroom on June 30, 2004, indicated that supplies on hand amount to $507. The supplies on hand at the beginning of the month total $475.

c. The company purchased machines last year for $170,000. The machines are expected to be used for four years and have an estimated salvage value of $2,000.

d. On June 1, the company paid $4,650 for rent for June, July, and August, and increased the asset Prepaid Rent. It did not have a balance on June 1.

e. The company operates seven days per week with a weekly payroll of $7,000. Wage earners are paid every Sunday. The last day of the month is Saturday, June 30.

f. Based on its income for the month, Flood estimates that federal income taxes for June amount to $2,900.

Required

1. For each of the preceding situations, determine the effect on the accounting equation of the adjustment necessary on June 30, 2004.
2. Assume that Flood Relief reports income of $35,000 before any of the adjustments. What net income will Flood Relief report for June?

Problem 4-3A *Annual Adjustments* LO 5

Ogonquit Enterprises prepares annual financial statements and adjusts its accounts only at the end of the year. The following information is available for the year ended December 31, 2004:

a. Ogonquit purchased office furniture last year for $25,000. The furniture has an estimated useful life of seven years and an estimated salvage value of $4,000.

b. The Supplies account had a balance of $1,200 on January 1, 2004. During 2004, Ogonquit added $12,900 to the account for purchases of supplies during the year. A count of the supplies on hand at the end of December 2004 indicates a balance of $900.

c. On July 1, 2004, Ogonquit created a liability account, Customer Deposits, for $8,800. This sum represents an amount that a customer paid in advance and that will be earned evenly by Ogonquit over an eight-month period.

d. Ogonquit rented some warehouse space on September 1, 2004, at a rate of $4,000 per month. On that date, Ogonquit recorded Prepaid Rent for six months' rent paid in advance.

e. Ogonquit took out a 90-day, 6%, $30,000 note on November 1, 2004, with interest and principal to be paid at maturity.

f. Ogonquit operates five days per week with an average weekly payroll of $4,150. Ogonquit pays its employees every Thursday. December 31, 2004, is a Friday.

Required

1. For each of the preceding situations, determine the effect on the accounting equation of the adjustment necessary on December 31, 2004.
2. Assume that Ogonquit's accountant forgets to record the adjustments on December 31, 2004. Will net income for the year be understated or overstated? By what amount? (Ignore the effect of income taxes.)

Problem 4-4A *Recurring Transactions and Adjustments* LO 5

The following are the accounts of Dominique Inc., an interior decorator. The company has been in the decorating business for 10 years and prepares quarterly financial statements. Following the list of accounts is a series of transactions entered into by Dominique. For each transaction, enter the number(s) of the account(s) affected.

Accounts

1. Cash	11. Capital Stock, $1 par
2. Accounts Receivable	12. Paid-In Capital in Excess of Par
3. Prepaid Rent	13. Consulting Revenue
4. Office Supplies	14. Office Supply Expense
5. Office Equipment	15. Rent Expense
6. Accumulated Depreciation	16. Salaries and Wages Expense
7. Accounts Payable	17. Depreciation Expense
8. Salaries and Wages Payable	18. Interest Expense
9. Income Tax Payable	19. Income Tax Expense
10. Interim Financing Notes Payable	

Transaction

a. **Example:** Issued additional shares of stock to owners; shares issued at greater than par.	1, 11, 12
b. Purchased office equipment for cash.	______
c. Collected open accounts receivable from customer.	______
d. Purchased office supplies on account.	______
e. Paid office rent for the next six months.	______
f. Paid interest on an interim financing note.	______
g. Paid salaries and wages.	______
h. Purchased office equipment; made a down payment in cash and signed an interim financing note.	______
i. Provided services on account.	______
j. Recorded depreciation on equipment.	______
k. Recorded income taxes due next month.	______
l. Recorded the used office supplies.	______
m. Recorded the used portion of prepaid rent.	______

Problem 4-5A *Use of Account Balances as a Basis for Annual Adjustments* LO 5

The following account balances are taken from the records of Laugherty Inc. at December 31, 2004. The Supplies account represents the cost of supplies on hand at the beginning of the year plus all purchases. A physical count on December 31, 2004, shows only $1,520 of supplies on hand. The Unearned Revenue account represents the cash received from a customer on May 1,

2004, for 12 months of service, beginning on that date. The Note Payable represents a six-month promissory note signed with a supplier on September 1, 2004. Principal and interest at an annual rate of 10% will be paid on March 1, 2005.

Supplies	$ 5,790
Unearned Revenue	1,800
Note Payable	60,000

Required

1. For each of the three situations described above, determine the effect on the accounting equation of the adjustments necessary on December 31, 2004. Assume that Laugherty records adjustments only once a year, on December 31.
2. Assume that adjustments are made at the end of each month rather than only at the end of the year. What would be the balance in Unearned Revenue *before* the December adjustment is made? Explain your answer.

Problem 4-6A *Use of Account Balances as a Basis for Adjustments* **LO 5**

Lori Matlock operates a graphic arts business. A list of accounts on June 30, 2004, *before* recording any adjustments, appears as follows:

Cash	$ 7,000
Prepaid Rent	18,000
Supplies	15,210
Office Equipment	46,120
Accumulated Depreciation—Equipment	4,000
Accounts Payable	1,800
Notes Payable	2,000
Capital Stock	50,000
Retained Earnings	24,350
Dividends	8,400
Revenue	46,850
Utilities Expense	2,850
Salaries Expense	19,420
Advertising Expense	12,000

Other Data

a. The monthly rent cost is $600.

b. Supplies on hand on June 30, 2004, amount to $1,290.

c. The office equipment was purchased on June 1, 2003. On that date, it had an estimated useful life of 10 years and a salvage value of $6,120.

d. Interest owed on the note payable but not yet paid amounts to $50.

e. Salaries of $620 are owed to employees but unpaid at the end of the month.

Required

1. For each of the items of other data, **a** through **e**, determine the effect on the accounting equation.
2. Compute the net increase or decrease in net income for the month from the recognition of the adjustments in part **1** (ignore income taxes).
3. Note the balance in Accumulated Depreciation—Equipment is $4,000. Explain *why* the account contains a balance is $4,000 on June 30, 2004.

Problem 4-7A *Reconstruction of Adjustments from Account Balances* **LO 5**

Zola Corporation records adjustments each month before preparing monthly financial statements. The following selected account balances on May 31, 2004, and June 30, 2004, reflect month-end adjustments:

Account Title	May 31, 2004	June 30, 2004
Prepaid Rent	$4,000	$3,000
Equipment	9,600	9,600
Accumulated Depreciation	800	900
Notes Payable	9,600	9,600
Interest Payable	768	864

Required

1. The company paid for a six-month lease on April 1, 2004. Determine the effect on the accounting equation of the adjustment that was made for rent on June 30, 2004.
2. What amount was prepaid on April 1, 2004? Explain your answer.
3. The equipment was purchased on September 30, 2003, for $9,600. Zola uses straight-line depreciation and estimates that the equipment will have no salvage value. Determine the effect on the accounting equation of the adjustment that was made for depreciation on June 30, 2004.
4. What is the equipment's estimated useful life in months? Explain your answer.
5. Zola signed a two-year note on September 30, 2003, for the purchase of the equipment. Interest on the note accrues on a monthly basis and will be paid at maturity along with the principal amount of $9,600. Determine the effect on the accounting equation of the adjustment that was made for interest expense on June 30, 2004.
6. What is the *monthly* interest rate on the loan? Explain your answer.

Problem 4-8A ***Use of Account Balances as a Basis for Adjustments*** **LO 5**

Lewis and Associates has been in the termite inspection and treatment business for five years. The following is a list of accounts for Lewis on June 30, 2004. It reflects the recurring transactions for the month of June, but does not reflect any month-end adjustments.

Cash	$ 6,200
Accounts Receivable	10,400
Prepaid Rent	4,400
Chemical Inventory	9,400
Equipment	18,200
Accumulated Depreciation	1,050
Accounts Payable	1,180
Capital Stock	5,000
Retained Earnings	25,370
Treatment Revenue	40,600
Wages and Salary Expense	22,500
Utilities Expense	1,240
Advertising Expense	860

The following additional information is available:

a. Lewis rents a warehouse with office space and prepays the annual rent of $4,800 on May 1 of each year.

b. The asset account Equipment represents the cost of treatment equipment, which has an estimated useful life of 10 years and an estimated salvage value of $200.

c. Chemical inventory on hand equals $1,300.

d. Wages and salaries owed to employees but unpaid at the end of the month amount to $1,080.

e. Lewis accrues income taxes using an estimated tax rate equal to 30% of the income for the month.

Required

1. For each of the items of additional information, **a** through **e**, determine the effect on the accounting equation.
2. On the basis of the information you have, does Lewis appear to be a profitable business? Explain your answer.

Alternate Multi-Concept Problems

Problem 4-9A ***Cash and Accrual Income Statements for a Manufacturer*** **LO 2, 3, 4**

Marie's Catering makes sandwiches for vending machines. The sandwiches are delivered to the vendor on the same day that they are made. The following events took place during the first year of operations.

a. On the first day of the year, issued common stock for a $20,000 cash investment and a $10,000 investment of equipment. The equipment is expected to last 10 years and will be worthless at the end of that time.

b. Purchased a delivery truck at the beginning of the year at a cost of $14,000 cash. The truck is expected to last five years and will be worthless at the end of that time.

c. Made and sold 50,000 sandwiches during the first year of operations. The costs incurred to make the sandwiches are (1) $800 monthly rent on a facility that included utilities and insurance, (2) $25,000 of meat, cheese, bread, and condiments (all food was purchased on account, and $4,000 is still unpaid at year-end even though all of the food has been used), and (3) $35,000 paid in salaries and wages to employees and supervisors.

d. Paid $12,000 for part-time office staff salaries.

e. Sold all sandwiches on account for $2 each. As of year-end, $25,000 is still due from the vendors.

Required

1. How much revenue will Marie's Catering recognize under the cash basis and under the accrual basis?
2. Explain how accountants apply the revenue recognition principle to Marie's small business. What conditions would allow Marie's to use the cash method to recognize revenue?
3. Prepare an income statement according to the accrual method. Ignore income taxes.

Problem 4-10A *Revenue Recognition on the Percentage-of-Completion and Production Methods* LO 3, 4

Judy Darling owns a diamond mine in South Africa. While vacationing on an island in the Caribbean, she discussed with Marty Jones a recent dig that yielded $1.5 million of raw diamonds. The product is stored with an agent until a buyer is located. The agent expects it to take about two and a half years to sell all of the diamonds. Judy's company spent $1 million to extract the diamonds in 2004.

Marty's company constructs airplane runways and hangars. He is in the process of building a runway for the island and expects to incur the following costs over the next two and one-half years:

2004	$400,000
2005	500,000
2006	100,000

Local residents and the government have already paid Marty $1 million in 2004 and will pay another $500,000 when the project is completed in 2006.

Required

Explain the difference between revenue and cash flow for Judy and Marty. How much revenue will each recognize in 2004, 2005, and 2006?

Problem 4-11A *Revenue and Expense Recognition* LO 3, 4

Two years ago, Sue Stern opened an audio book rental shop. Sue reports the following accounts on her income statement:

Sales	$84,000
Advertising expense	10,500
Salaries expense	12,000
Depreciation on tapes	5,000
Rent expense	18,000

These amounts represent two years of revenue and expenses. Sue has asked you how she can tell how much of the income is from the first year and how much is from the second year of business. She provides the following additional data:

a. Sales in the second year are triple those of the first year.

b. Advertising expense is for a $1,500 opening promotion and weekly ads in the newspaper.

c. Salaries represent one employee who was hired eight months ago. No raises have been granted.

d. Rent has not changed since the shop opened.

Required

Prepare income statements for Years 1 and 2.

Problem 4-12A *Adjustments and Financial Statements* LO 5, 6

The account balances on the following page are available for Tenfour Trucking Company on January 31, 2004.

Cash	$ 27,340
Accounts Receivable	41,500
Prepaid Insurance	18,000
Warehouse	40,000
Accumulated Depreciation—Warehouse	21,600
Truck Fleet	240,000
Accumulated Depreciation—Truck Fleet	112,500
Land	20,000
Accounts Payable	32,880
Notes Payable	50,000
Interest Payable	4,500
Customer Deposits	6,000
Capital Stock	100,000
Retained Earnings	40,470
Freight Revenue	165,670
Gas and Oil Expense	57,330
Maintenance Expense	26,400
Wage and Salary Expense	43,050
Dividends	20,000

Required

1. Determine the effect on the accounting equation of the necessary adjustments at January 31, 2004, for each of the following:
   a. Prepaid insurance represents the cost of a 24-month policy purchased on January 1, 2004.
   b. The warehouse has an estimated useful life of 20 years and an estimated salvage value of $4,000.
   c. The truck fleet has an estimated useful life of six years and an estimated salvage value of $15,000.
   d. The promissory note was signed on January 1, 2003. Interest at an annual rate of 9% and the principal of $50,000 are due on December 31, 2004.
   e. The customer deposits represent amounts paid in advance by new customers. A total of $4,500 of the balance in Customer Deposits was earned during January 2004.
   f. Wages and salaries earned by employees at the end of January but not yet paid amount to $8,200.
   g. Income taxes are accrued at a rate of 30% at the end of each month.
2. Prepare in good form the following financial statements:
   a. Income statement for the month ended January 31, 2004
   b. Statement of retained earnings for the month ended January 31, 2004
   c. Balance sheet at January 31, 2004
3. Compute Tenfour's current ratio. What does this ratio tell you about the company's liquidity?
4. Explain why it is not possible to compute a gross profit ratio for Tenfour. Describe a ratio that you believe would be a meaningful measure of profitability for a trucking company. Feel free to "invent" a ratio if you think it would be a meaningful measure of profitability.

Decision Cases

Reading and Interpreting Financial Statements

http://www.winnebagoind.com
http://www.monacocoach.com

Decision Case 4-1 ***Comparing Two Companies in the Same Industry: Winnebago Industries and Monaco Coach Corporation*** **LO 3, 4, 5**

Refer to the financial information for Winnebago Industries and Monaco Coach Corporation in Appendices A and B at the end of the book.

Required

1. Neither company reports on its balance sheet an account titled "Accounts Receivable." Identify the account or accounts on each company's balance sheet that is equivalent to Accounts Receivable.

2. What dollar amount does each company report in Prepaid Expenses on its balance sheet at the end of 2002? When the benefits from this asset expire in the future this account will be reduced and an expense account will be increased. For each company, identify the account or accounts on its income statement that you would expect to be increased.
3. On its balance sheet, Winnebago Industries reports four accounts under "Property and Equipment" and from the total of the four deducts "Accumulated Depreciation." How does this way of presenting the long-term tangible assets differ from the approach used by Monaco Coach Corporation on its balance sheet? Does Monaco Coach Corporation disclose the same type of information elsewhere in the annual report? If so, where? Why do you think these companies use different approaches to report this information?

Decision Case 4-2 ***Reading and Interpreting McDonald's Notes—Revenue Recognition*** **LO 3**

Refer to the excerpt on page 166 where McDonald's explains how it recognizes franchise fees as revenue.

http://www.mcdonalds.com

Required

1. At what points in time does McDonald's recognize revenue from its company-owned restaurants?
2. When are continuing fees recognized as revenue by McDonald's? Does the way in which McDonald's recognizes these fees as revenue seem to be in agreement with the revenue recognition principle?
3. When are initial fees recognized as revenue by McDonald's? Does the way in which McDonald's recognizes these fees as revenue seem to be in agreement with the revenue recognition principle?
4. Refer to McDonald's income statement on page 157. How important are franchise fees as a form of revenue for the company? Support your answer with any necessary computations.

Decision Case 4-3 ***Reading and Interpreting Winnebago Industries' Notes—Revenue Recognition*** **LO 3**

Refer to Winnebago Industries' first note, "Nature of Business and Significant Accounting Policies," and specifically the section that discusses revenue recognition.

http://www.winnebagoind.com

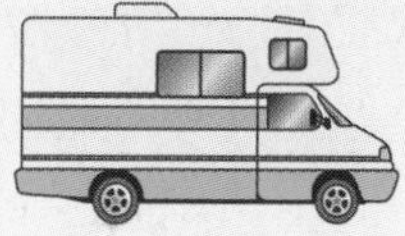

Required

1. At what point in time does Winnebago Industries recognize revenue?
2. Explain what "dealer floor plan receivables" are to Winnebago Industries.
3. How and when does Winnebago Industries recognize revenue from dealer floor plan receivables?

Decision Case 4-4 ***Reading and Interpreting Sears, Roebuck's Notes—Revenue Recognition*** **LO 3**

The following excerpt is taken from the Sears, Roebuck and Co. 2002 annual report: "Additionally, the Company sells extended service contracts with terms of coverage between 12 and 60 months. Revenues from the sale of these contracts are deferred and amortized over the lives of the contracts while the service costs are expensed as incurred."

http://www.sears.com

Required

1. Why do retailers recognize the revenue over the life of the service contract even though cash is received at the time of the sale?
2. If a product is sold in Year 1 for $2,500, including a $180 service contract that will cover three years, how much revenue is recognized in Years 1, 2, and 3? (Assume a straight-line approach.) What corresponding account can you look for in the financial statements to determine the amount of service contract revenue that will be recognized in the future?

Making Financial Decisions

Decision Case 4-5 ***The Use of Net Income and Cash Flow to Evaluate a Company*** **LO 2, 3, 4**

After you have gained five years of experience with a large CPA firm, one of your clients, Duke Inc., asks you to take over as chief financial officer for the business. Duke advises its clients on the purchase of software products and assists them in installing the programs on their computer

DECISION MAKING

systems. Because the business is relatively new (it began servicing clients in January 2004), its accounting records are somewhat limited. In fact, the only statement available is an income statement for the first year:

DUKE INC.
STATEMENT OF INCOME
FOR THE YEAR ENDED DECEMBER 31, 2004

Revenues		$1,250,000
Expenses:		
Salaries and wages	$480,000	
Supplies	65,000	
Utilities	30,000	
Rent	120,000	
Depreciation	345,000	
Interest	138,000	
Total expenses		1,178,000
Net income		$ 72,000

Based on its relatively modest profit margin of 5.76% (net income of $72,000 divided by revenues of $1,250,000), you are concerned about joining the new business. To alleviate your concerns, the president of the company is able to give you the following additional information:

a. Clients are given 90 days to pay their bills for consulting services provided by Duke. On December 31, 2004, $230,000 of the revenues is yet to be collected in cash.

b. Employees are paid on a monthly basis. Salaries and wages of $480,000 include the December payroll of $40,000, which will be paid on January 5, 2005.

c. The company purchased $100,000 of operating supplies when it began operations in January. The balance of supplies on hand at December 31 amounts to $35,000.

d. Office space is rented in a downtown high-rise building at a monthly rental of $10,000. When the company moved into the office in January, it prepaid its rent for the next 18 months, beginning January 1, 2004.

e. On January 1, 2004, Duke purchased its own computer system and related accessories at a cost of $1,725,000. The estimated useful life of the system is five years.

f. The computer system was purchased by signing a three-year, 8% note payable for $1,725,000 on the date of purchase. The principal amount of the note and interest for the three years are due on January 1, 2007.

Required

1. Based on the income statement and the additional information given, prepare a statement of cash flows for Duke for 2004. (*Hint:* Simply list all of the cash inflows and outflows that relate to operations.)
2. On the basis of the income statement given and the statement of cash flows prepared in part 1, do you think it would be a wise decision on your part to join the company as its chief financial officer? Include in your response any additional questions that you believe are appropriate to ask before joining the company.

DECISION MAKING

Decision Case 4-6 *Depreciation* LO 4

Jenner Inc., a graphic arts studio, is considering the purchase of computer equipment and software for a total cost of $18,000. Jenner can pay for the equipment and software over three years at the rate of $6,000 per year. The equipment is expected to last 10 to 20 years, but because of changing technology, Jenner believes it may need to replace the system as soon as three to five years. A three-year lease of similar equipment and software is available for $6,000 per year. Jenner's accountant has asked you to recommend whether the company should purchase or lease the equipment and software and to suggest the length of the period over which to depreciate the software and equipment if the company makes the purchase.

Required

Ignoring the effect of taxes, would you recommend the purchase or the lease? Why? Referring to the definition of *depreciation,* what is the appropriate useful life to use for the equipment and software?

Accounting and Ethics: What Would You Do?

ETHICS

Decision Case 4-7 ***Revenue Recognition and the Matching Principle*** **LO 2, 3, 4, 5**

Listum & Sellum Inc. is a medium-size midwestern real estate company. It was founded five years ago by its two principal stockholders, Willie Listum and Dewey Sellum. Willie is president of the company, and Dewey is vice-president of sales. Listum & Sellum has enjoyed tremendous growth since its inception by aggressively seeking out listings for residential real estate and paying a very generous commission to the selling agent.

The company receives a 6% commission for selling a client's property and gives two-thirds of this, or 4% of the selling price, to the selling agent. For example, if a house sells for $100,000, Listum & Sellum receives $6,000 and pays $4,000 of this to the selling agent. At the time of the sale, the company records $6,000 of Accounts Receivable and $6,000 of Sales Revenue. The accounts receivable is normally collected within 30 days. Also at the time of sale, the company records $4,000 of Commissions Expense and $4,000 of Commissions Payable. Sales agents are paid by the 15th of the month following the month of the sale. In addition to the commissions expense, Listum & Sellum's other two major expenses are advertising of listings in local newspapers and depreciation of the company fleet of Cadillacs (Dewey has always believed that all of the sales agents should drive Cadillacs). The newspaper ads are taken for one month, and the company has until the 10th of the following month to pay that month's bill. The automobiles are depreciated over four years (Dewey doesn't believe that any salesperson should drive a car that is more than four years old).

Due to a downturn in the economy in the Midwest, sales have been sluggish for the first 11 months of the current year, which ends on June 30. Willie is very disturbed by the slow sales this particular year because a large note payable to the local bank is due in July and the company plans to ask the bank to renew the note for another three years. Dewey seems less concerned by the unfortunate timing of the recession and has some suggestions as to how they can "paint the rosiest possible picture for the banker" when they go for the loan extension in July. In fact, he has some very specific recommendations for you as to how to account for transactions during June, the last month in the fiscal year.

You are the controller for Listum & Sellum and have been treated very well by Willie and Dewey since joining the company two years ago. In fact, Dewey insists that you personally drive the top-of-the-line Cadillac. Following are his suggestions:

> First, for any sales made in June, we can record the 6% commission revenue immediately but delay recording the 4% commission expense until July, when the sales agent is paid. We record the sales at the same time we always have, the sales agents get paid when they always have, the bank sees how profitable we have been, we get our loan, and everybody is happy!
>
> Second, since we won't be paying our advertising bills for the month of June until July 10, we can just wait until then to record the expense. The timing seems perfect, given that we are to meet with the bank for the loan extension on July 8.
>
> Third, since we will be depreciating the fleet of Caddys for the year ending June 30, how about just changing the estimated useful life on them to eight years instead of four years? We won't say anything to the sales agents; no need to rile them up about having to drive their cars for eight years. Anyhow, the change to eight years would just be for accounting purposes. In fact, we could even switch back to four years for accounting purposes next year. Likewise, the changes in recognizing commission expense and advertising expense don't need to be permanent either; these are just slight bookkeeping changes to help us get over the hump!

Required

1. Explain why each of the three proposed changes in accounting will result in an increase in net income for the year ending June 30.
2. Identify any concerns you have with each of the three proposed changes in accounting from the perspective of generally accepted accounting principles. If these changes are made, do the financial statements faithfully represent what they claim to represent? Are these changes merely minor bookkeeping changes?
3. Identify any concerns you have with each of the three proposed changes in accounting from an ethical perspective. Do the proposed changes provide information that is free from bias? Explain.
4. Does the controller benefit by making the proposed changes? Are outsiders harmed? Explain your answer.

Decision Case 4-8 *Advice to a Potential Investor* **LO 4**

ETHICS

Century Company was organized 15 months ago as a management consulting firm. At that time, the owners invested a total of $50,000 cash in exchange for stock. Century purchased equipment for $35,000 cash and supplies to be used in the business. The equipment is expected to last seven years with no salvage value. Supplies are purchased on account and paid for in the month after the purchase. Century normally has about $1,000 of supplies on hand. Its client base has increased so dramatically that the president and chief financial officer have approached an investor to provide additional cash for expansion. The balance sheet and income statement for the first year of business are presented below:

CENTURY COMPANY
BALANCE SHEET
DECEMBER 31, 2004

Assets		**Liabilities and Owners' Equity**	
Cash	$10,100	Accounts payable	$ 2,300
Accounts receivable	1,200	Common stock	50,000
Supplies	16,500	Retained earnings	10,500
Equipment	35,000		
Total	$62,800	Total	$62,800

CENTURY COMPANY
INCOME STATEMENT
FOR THE YEAR ENDED DECEMBER 31, 2004

Revenues		$82,500
Wages and salaries	$60,000	
Utilities	12,000	72,000
Net income		$10,500

Required

The investor has asked you to look at these financial statements and give an opinion about Century's future profitability. Are the statements prepared in accordance with generally accepted accounting principles? If not, explain why. Based on only these two statements, what would you advise? What additional information would you need in order to give an educated opinion?

THOMSON ONE Business School Edition Case

Case 4-9 *Using THOMSON ONE for McDonald's*

http://www.mcdonalds.com

In the chapter we saw how accrual accounting is used to measure a company's financial performance. The success of a company as indicated in its financial statements should translate to success in the market for a company's stock in the form of appreciation in its stock price and, if the company chooses, in the form of dividends to the stockholders. We can use THOMSON ONE to obtain information about McDonald's performance as measured in its financial statements and in its stock price.

Begin by entering the company's ticker symbol, MCD, and then selecting "GO." On the opening screen you will see background information about the company, key financial ratios, and some recent data concerning stock price. To research the company's stock price further, click the "Prices" tab. At the top of the Price Chart, click on the "Interactive Chart." To obtain a 1-year chart, go to "Time Frame," click on the down arrow, and select "1 year." Then click on "Draw," and a 1-year chart should appear.

We can also find McDonald's most recent financial statements. Near the top of the screen, click on "Financials" and select "Financial Statements." Refer to the comparative statements of earnings, statements of cash flows, and balance sheets.

Based on your use of THOMSON ONE, answer the following questions:

1. McDonald's total revenues include all the revenues from company-operated restaurants and a portion of the revenues of franchisees' restaurants.
   a. Looking at the most recent income statement, what are McDonald's total revenues? By how much did it increase or decrease from the prior year?
   b. McDonald's also refers to total "systemwide" sales in the management section of its annual report. Why is total revenue reported in the income statement and systemwide revenue not reported there? That is, why can't McDonald's place systemwide sales on its income statement?

2. Looking at the most recent income statement, what is McDonald's net income? By how much did it increase or decrease from the prior year?
3. What have been McDonald's high and low stock prices for the most recent year?
4. How does the company's stock performance compare to the other line on the stock price chart for the S&P 500?

Solutions to Key Terms Quiz

18	Recognition (p. 159)	24	Contra account (p. 171)
25	Historical cost (p. 160)	13	Deferral (p. 176)
11	Current value (p. 160)	19	Deferred expense (p. 176)
21	Cash basis (p. 161)	7	Deferred revenue (p. 177)
14	Accrual basis (p. 161)	15	Accrual (p. 177)
2	Revenues (p. 164)	22	Accrued liability (p. 177)
17	Revenue recognition principle (p. 165)	10	Accrued asset (p. 177)
6	Percentage-of-completion method (p. 166)	27	Accounting cycle (p. 182)
3	Production method (p. 167)	1	Work sheet (p. 182)
8	Installment method (p. 167)	9	Real accounts (p. 182)
23	Matching principle (p. 168)	20	Nominal accounts (p. 182)
26	Expenses (p. 169)	5	Closing entries (p. 182)
4	Adjusting entries (p. 170)	16	Interim statements (p. 183)
12	Straight-line method (p. 171)		

Part I

Integrative Problem

Completing Financial Statements, Computing Ratios, Comparing Accrual vs. Cash Income, and Evaluating the Company's Cash Needs

SPREADSHEET

Mountain Home Health Inc. provides home nursing services in the Great Smoky Mountains of Tennessee. When contacted by a client or referred by a physician, nurses visit with the patient and discuss needed services with the physician.

Mountain Home Health earns revenue from patient services. Most of the revenue comes from billing either insurance companies, the state of Tennessee, or the Medicare program. Amounts billed are recorded in the Billings Receivable account. Insurance companies, states, and the federal government do not fully fund all procedures. For example, the state of Tennessee pays an average 78% of billed amounts. Mountain Home Health has already removed the uncollectible amounts from the Billings Receivable account and reports it and Medical Services Revenue at the net amount. Services provided but not yet recorded totaled $16,000, net of allowances for uncollectible amounts. The firm earns a minor portion of its total revenue directly from patients in the form of cash.

Employee salaries, medical supplies, depreciation, and gasoline are the major expenses. Employees are paid every Friday for work performed during the Saturday-to-Friday pay period. Salaries amount to $800 per day. In 2003, December 31 falls on a Wednesday. Medical supplies (average use of $1,500 per week) are purchased periodically to support health care coverage. The inventory of supplies on hand on December 31 amounted to $8,653.

The firm owns five automobiles (all purchased at the same time) that average 50,000 miles per year and are replaced every three years. They typically have no residual value. The building has an expected life of 20 years with no residual value. Straight-line depreciation is used on all firm assets. Gasoline costs, which are a cash expenditure, average $375 per day. The firm purchases a three-year, extended warranty contract to cover maintenance costs. The contract costs $9,000 (assume equal use each year).

On December 29, 2003, Mountain Home Health declared a dividend of $10,000, payable on January 15, 2004. The firm makes annual payments of principal and interest each June 30 on the mortgage. The interest rate on the mortgage is 6%.

The following account balances are available for Mountain Home Health on December 31, 2003:

Cash	$ 77,400
Billings Receivable (net)	151,000
Medical Supplies	73,000
Extended Warranty	3,000
Automobiles	90,000
Accumulated Depreciation—Automobiles	60,000
Building	200,000
Accumulated Depreciation—Building	50,000
Accounts Payable	22,000
Dividend Payable	10,000
Mortgage Payable	100,000
Capital Stock	100,000
Additional Paid-In Capital	50,000
Retained Earnings	99,900
Medical Services Revenue	550,000
Salary and Wages Expense	288,000
Gasoline Expense	137,500
Utilities Expense	12,000
Dividends	10,000

Required

1. Determine the effect on the accounting equation of the necessary adjustments on December 31, 2003.
2. Prepare a statement of income and a statement of retained earnings for Mountain Home Health for the year ended December 31, 2003.
3. Prepare a balance sheet for Mountain Home Health as of December 31, 2003.
4. Compute the following as of December 31, 2003: **a.** Working capital **b.** Current ratio
5. Which of the adjustments might cause a difference between cash and accrual based income?
6. Mary Francis, controller of Mountain Home, became concerned about the company's cash flow after talking to a local bank loan officer. The firm tries to maintain a 7-week supply of cash to meet the demands of payroll, medical supply purchases, and gasoline. Determine the amount of cash Mountain Home needs to meet the 7-week supply.

Part II

Accounting for Assets

A Word to Students about Part II

In Part I you learned how companies communicate their activities and financial results to users of financial information. You also discovered new ways of thinking about events as transactions, and how these business transactions culminate in a company's financial statements. You learned specialized terminology, used the accounting equation, and began to understand the basis for making financial decisions.

Part II tells what happens when assets flow into the business. Chapter 5 introduces cash and the internal controls over it and the other assets that are necessary for keeping a business running smoothly. Chapter 6 discusses the inflow of receivables into a business from its sales efforts as well as considering how to account for investments it makes. Chapter 7 covers the various issues related to a company's inventory and how inventory transactions affect the statement of cash flows. Chapter 8 recognizes that a business must invest its cash and receivables in operating assets.

Finally, you'll focus on how investors and other financial statement users evaluate companies with ratios and make decisions based on that information.

Chapter 5

Cash and Internal Control

© TERRI MILLER/E-VISUAL COMMUNICATIONS, INC.

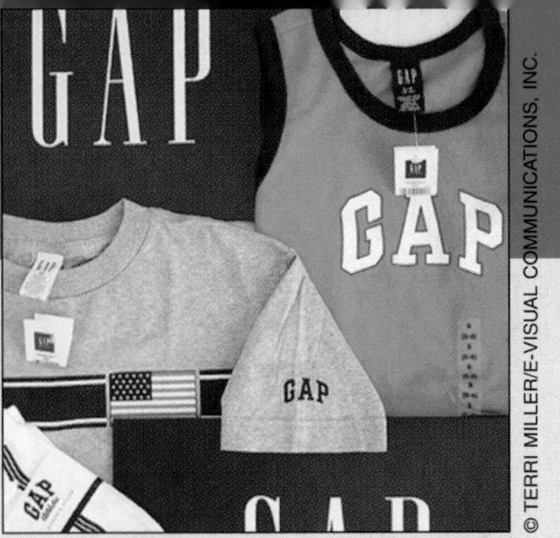

Roadmap to Success
CHAPTER 13 Final Destination - *Analyzing Financial Information for Decision Making*
What does the financial information mean?
CHAPTER 12 Fourth Stop - *Investigating the Statement of Cash Flows*
Where did the cash come from, and where did it go?
CHAPTER 11 Third Stop - *Exploring the Statement of Stockholders' Equity*
Is the owners' share changing? What's happening to company earnings?
CHAPTER 9 Side Trip - *Building More Skills*
Low on fuel?
CHAPTER 9 10 Extended Stay - *Touring More of the Balance Sheet*
What does the company owe, and can it pay its bills?
CHAPTER 7 8 Second Stop - *Venturing Further into the Balance Sheet*
What are the saleable and the long-term resources of the company? How do they impact the income statement?
CHAPTER 5 6 First Stop - *Liquid Assets Checkpoint*
Is the company controlling and investing its cash? Are customers paying what they owe?
Gain an understanding of accounting for and controlling cash and other near-cash assets.
CHAPTER 3 4 Pit Stop - *Getting Special Training*
What information do we need to get us to our destination?
CHAPTER 2 On the Road - *Studying the Map*
Where are we going, and what's our route?
CHAPTER Intro 1 Getting Started - *Planning the Trip*
Why are we traveling, and who's going with us?

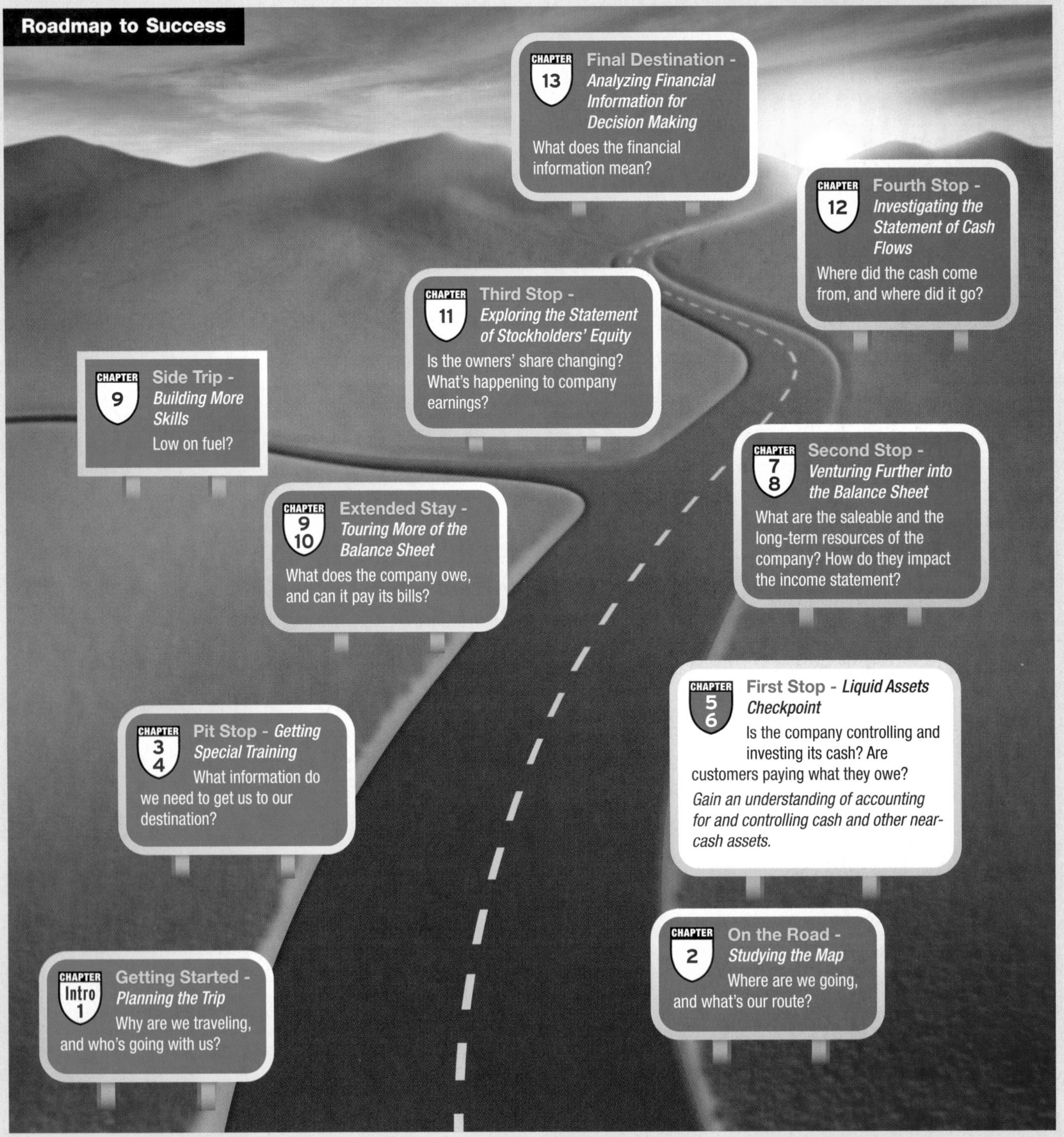

Focus on Financial Results

With over 4,200 stores in the United States, Canada, France, Germany, Japan, and the United Kingdom, Gap Inc. has become a global success story. This youth-oriented retailer of casual fashions, accessories, and personal care products encompasses three distinct brands—Gap®, Banana Republic®, and Old Navy®, in addition to its popular GapKids® and babyGap® lines. The company, like various other retailers, has found the Internet to be a highly efficient and economical alternative to selling its products in stores.

Also, like many of its competitors, Gap Inc. has found the last few years challenging, to say the least. Sales were nearly flat in 2001 and a net loss was reported for the year. However, the 2002 fiscal year would appear to be one in which the specialty retailer turned the corner. Sales reached record levels, topping $14 billion for the first time in company history. And earnings rebounded to an enviable $477 million.

Another indication of Gap Inc.'s turnaround is its vastly improved cash position, as reported on the comparative balance sheets shown here. Cash on hand at the end of 2002 (the year ended on February 1, 2003) was roughly $3.4 billion, up considerably from the balance at the end of the prior year. However, with an emphasis on improving its balance sheet, company management was especially pleased with its "net debt position," as measured by total long-term liabilities minus cash. As can be seen on the two balance sheets, this measure improved considerably between the two years. The company's net debt position was about $1 billion at the beginning of 2002; by the end of the year, cash was nearly equal to total long-term debt.

Gap Inc.'s 2002 Annual Report

Consolidated Balance Sheets

(In thousands except share and per value)	Feb. 1, 2003	Feb. 2, 2002
Assets		
Current Assets		
Cash and equivalents	$3,388,514	$1,035,749
Merchandise inventory	2,047,879	1,768,613
Other current assets	303,332	331,685
Total current assets	5,739,725	3,136,047
Property and Equipment		
Leasehold improvements	2,241,831	2,127,966
Furniture and equipment	3,438,805	3,327,819
Land and buildings	942,845	917,055
Construction-in-progress	202,839	246,691
	6,826,320	6,619,531
Accumulated depreciation and amortization	(3,049,477)	(2,458,241)
Property and equipment, net	3,776,843	4,161,290
Lease rights and other assets	385,436	385,486
Total assets	$9,902,004	$7,682,823
Liabilities and Shareholders' Equity		
Current Liabilities		
Notes payable	$ —	$41,889
Current maturities of long-term debt	499,979	—
Accounts payable	1,159,301	1,196,614
Accrued expenses and other current liabilities	1,067,294	874,977
Total current liabilities	2,726,574	2,113,480
Long-Term Liabilities		
Long-term debt	1,515,794	1,961,397
Senior convertible notes (a)	1,380,000	-
Deferred lease credits and other liabilities	621,424	598,365
Total long-term liabilities	3,517,218	2,559,762
Shareholders' Equity		
Common stock $.05 par value		
Authorized 2,300,000,000 shares; issued 968,010,453 and 948,597,949 shares; outstanding 887,322,707 and 865,726,890 shares	48,401	47,430
Additional paid-in capital	638,306	461,408
Retained earnings	5,289,480	4,890,375
Accumulated other comprehensive losses	(16,766)	(61,824)
Deferred compensation	(13,574)	(7,245)
Treasury stock, at cost	(2,287,635)	(2,320,563)
Total shareholders' equity	3,658,212	3,009,581
Total liabilities and shareholders' equity	$9,902,004	$7,682,823

See Notes to Consolidated Financial Statements.
(a) See Note B.

You're in the Driver's Seat

http://www.gap.com

Assume that you are considering whether to buy stock in Gap Inc. Have the improvements in the company's performance and its cash position affected how much you will have to pay for a share of stock? How much has the company paid in cash dividends to its stockholders recently?

LEARNING OBJECTIVES

After studying this chapter, you should be able to:

LO 1 Identify and describe the various forms of cash reported on a balance sheet. (p. 219)

LO 2 Demonstrate an understanding of various techniques that companies use to control cash. (p. 220)

LO 3 Explain the importance of internal control to a business. (p. 225)

LO 4 Describe the basic internal control procedures. (p. 228)

LO 5 Describe the various documents used in recording purchases and their role in controlling cash disbursements. (p. 231)

WHAT EXTERNAL DECISION MAKERS WANT TO KNOW ABOUT CASH AND INTERNAL CONTROL

DECISION MAKING

Stockholders, bankers, and other external decision makers all have an interest in a company's cash position. Cash is critical for all businesses and enough must be on hand to pay debts as they fall due. The effective management of cash is an important signal to outsiders that the company is maximizing the use of the cash at its disposal. Additionally, these decision makers need assurances that internal controls exist to safeguard cash in the business.

▶ *ASK ESSENTIAL QUESTIONS*

- Does the company maintain sufficient cash on hand to pay its debts?
- Does the company make good use of any excess cash that is not needed to pay its debts?
- Are sufficient controls in place to safeguard cash?

▶ *FIND BASIC INFORMATION*

The balance sheet and the statement of cash flows provide information about a company's cash. Specifically,

- the balance sheet reports the amount of cash on hand as of a particular date.
- the statement of cash flows summarizes the various sources and uses of cash during the period and reports the net increase or decrease for that period of time.

▶ *UNDERSTAND ACCOUNTING PRINCIPLES*

Decision makers must understand the forms of cash and cash equivalents as reported on a company's balance sheet. Accounting principles determine what is included in cash and cash equivalents as opposed to what is included in various forms of investments.

Gap Inc., like all businesses, relies on a steady flow of cash to function smoothly. For retailers such as Gap Inc., cash is needed to buy the merchandise it carries and eventually sells to customers. For manufacturers such as Winnebago Industries, cash is needed to buy the raw materials that it eventually turns into finished RVs. Regardless of their business, all companies must pay their employees salaries and wages. All companies must also regularly invest in new plant and equipment. In short, cash is needed for a variety of purposes and is the lifeblood of a business.

Cash is considered the most liquid of all assets in that it is the most acceptable medium of exchange for goods and services. Given its high degree of liquidity, businesses must have in place policies to safeguard cash. We consider in this chapter both the appropriate accounting for cash as an asset on the balance sheet and also the essential components of an effective system of internal control in a business.

WHAT CONSTITUTES CASH?

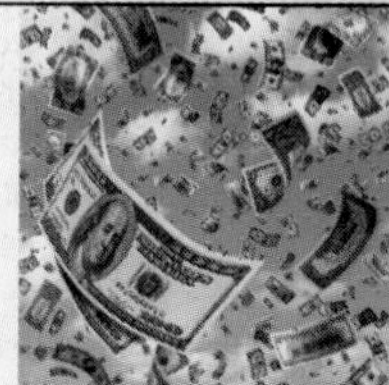

CASH FLOW

LO 1 Identify and describe the various forms of cash reported on a balance sheet.

Cash takes many different forms. Coin and currency on hand and cash on deposit in the form of checking, savings, and money market accounts are the most obvious forms of cash. Also included in cash are various forms of checks, including undeposited checks from customers, cashier's checks, and certified checks. The proliferation of different types of financial instruments on the market today makes it very difficult to decide on the appropriate classification of these various items. The key to the classification of an amount as cash is that it be *readily available to pay debts.* Technically, a bank has the legal right to demand that a customer notify it before making withdrawals from savings accounts, or time deposits, as they are often called. Because this right is rarely exercised, however, savings accounts are normally classified as cash. In contrast, a certificate of deposit has a specific maturity date and carries a penalty for early withdrawal and is therefore not included in cash.

Cash Equivalents and the Statement of Cash Flows

Note that the first item on Gap Inc.'s balance sheet is titled Cash and equivalents. Examples of items normally classified as cash equivalents are commercial paper issued by corporations, Treasury bills issued by the federal government, and money market funds offered by financial institutions. According to current accounting standards, classification as a **cash equivalent** is limited to those investments that are readily convertible to known amounts of cash and that have an original maturity to the investor of three months or less. Note that according to this definition, a six-month bank certificate of deposit would *not* be classified as a cash equivalent.

Cash equivalent An investment that is readily convertible to a known amount of cash and has an original maturity to the investor of three months or less.

From Concept to Practice 5.1

Reading Winnebago Industries' Notes

Locate in Note 1 of Winnebago Industries' notes a section titled "Statements of Cash Flows." In what types of securities are its cash equivalents invested?

The statement of cash flows that accompanies Gap Inc.'s balance sheet is shown in Exhibit 5-1. Note the direct tie between this statement and the balance sheet (refer to the Current Assets section of Gap Inc.'s balance sheet as shown in the chapter opener). The cash and equivalents of $3,388,514,000 at the end of 2002 (February 1, 2003), as shown at the bottom of the statement of cash flows, is the same amount that appears as the first line on the balance sheet. The reason for this is that the statement of cash flows traces the flow of cash from the beginning balance of cash for the year—$1,035,749,000—to the year's ending balance, $3,388,514,000. Cash provided by operating activities, $1,238,356,000, minus cash used for investing activities, $291,355,000, plus cash provided by financing activities, $1,378,478,000, plus the effect of exchange rate changes, $27,286,000, equals a net increase in cash of $2,352,765,000. Add $2,352,765,000 to the beginning cash balance to arrive at $3,388,514,000.

Exhibit 5-1 Gap Inc.'s Statement of Cash Flows

Consolidated Statement of Cash Flows

(in thousands)	52 Weeks Ended Feb. 1, 2003	52 Weeks Ended Feb. 2, 2002	52 Weeks Ended Feb. 3, 2001
Cash Flows from Operating Activities			
Net earnings (loss)	$ 477,457	$ (7,764)	$ 877,497
Adjustments to reconcile net earnings (loss) to net cash provided by operating activities:			
Depreciation and amortization	780,876	810,486	590,365
Tax benefit from exercise of stock options and vesting of restricted stock	44,219	58,444	130,882
Deferred income taxes	6,090	(28,512)	(38,872)
Loss on disposal	117,256	64,250	23,463
Change in operating assets and liabilites:			
Merchandise inventory	(258,222)	121,570	(454,595)
Prepaid expenses and other	32,802	(13,303)	(61,096)
Accounts payable	(46,669)	133,702	249,545
Accrued expenses	135,733	175,500	(56,541)
Deferred lease credits and other long-term liabilities	(51,186)	20,442	54,020
Net cash provided by operating activities	1,238,356	1,334,815	1,314,668
Cash Flows from Investing Activities			
Purchase of property and equipment	(303,284)	(957,054)	(1,882,125)
Proceeds from sale of property and equipment	8,513	—	—
Acquisition of lease rights, net increase (decrease) of other assets	3,416	(10,549)	(16,252)
Net cash used for investing activities	(291,355)	(967,603)	(1,898,377)
Cash Flows from Financing Activities			
Net increase (decrease) in notes payable	(41,942)	(734,927)	621,420
Net issuance of long-term debt	—	1,194,265	250,000
Net issuance of senior convertible notes	1,345,500	—	—
Payments of long-term debt	—	(250,000)	—
Issuance of common stock	153,272	139,105	152,105
Net purchase of treasury stock	—	(785)	(392,558)
Cash dividends paid	(78,352)	76,373	(75,488)
Net cash provided by financing activites	1,378,478	271,285	555,479
Effect of exchange rate fluctuations on cash	27,286	(11,542)	(13,328)
Net increase (decrease) in cash and equivalents	2,352,765	626,955	(41,558)
Cash and equivalents at beginning of year	1,035,749	408,794	450,352
Cash and equivalents at end of year	$3,388,514	$1,035,749	$ 408,794

See Notes to Consolidated Financial Statements.

CONTROL OVER CASH

LO 2 Demonstrate an understanding of various techniques that companies use to control cash.

Because cash is universally accepted as a medium of exchange, control over it is critical to the smooth functioning of any business, no matter how large or small.

Cash Management

In addition to the need to guard against theft and other abuses related to the physical custody of cash, management of this asset is also important. Cash management is necessary to ensure that at any point in time, a company has neither too little nor too much cash on hand. The need to have enough cash on hand is obvious: suppliers, employees, taxing agencies, banks, and all other creditors must be paid on time if an entity is to remain in business. It is equally important that a company not maintain cash on hand and on deposit in checking accounts beyond a minimal amount that is necessary to

Business Strategy

Putting Cash to Use

If a business has too little cash on hand, creditors can't be paid on a timely basis. If it has too much, it may miss opportunities to earn a better return than usually earned on cash in the bank. Cash management is certainly one of the most critical responsibilities of the treasurer's office in a company, and Gap Inc. is no exception. After an upswing in its performance, the specialty retailer found itself flush with cash at the end of 2002. The cash balance of roughly $3.4 billion accounted for nearly 35 percent of total assets!

In June 2003, Gap Inc. announced plans to put its cash to good use. First, the company entered into three-year secured $750 million revolving credit agreements with a group of commercial banks. In addition, Gap Inc. gained access to another $1.2 billion of funds through letter of credit agreements. Why would lenders stand ready to provide almost $2 billion in credit to Gap Inc.? The answer lies in those large cash balances the company built up and the security they provide lenders. For example, the letter of credit agreements were secured by about $1.2 billion in cash. While this portion of the company's cash will be reported as "restricted cash" on the balance sheet, Gap Inc. will continue to earn interest income on it.

In addition to providing the company with instant access to credit, the company expects the new agreements to lower its interest expense considerably. Gap Inc. projects that it will save about $10 million in interest for the remaining seven months in its 2003 fiscal year. This savings would amount to almost 5 percent of the total interest expense the company expects to incur for the year. The new credit structures have given the company increased financial flexibility and at the same time lowered the interest cost it does incur on borrowed funds, proving just how valuable good cash management is to a business. ■

Source: Gap Inc. press release—June 24, 2003.

support ongoing operations, since cash is essentially a nonearning asset. Granted, some checking accounts pay a very meager rate of interest. However, the superior return that could be earned by investing idle cash in various forms of marketable securities dictates that companies carefully monitor the amount of cash on hand at all times.

An important tool in the management of cash, the cash flows statement, is discussed in detail in Chapter 12. Cash budgets, which are also critical to the management of cash, are discussed in management accounting and business finance texts. Cash management is just one important aspect of control over cash. Beyond cash management, companies often use two other cash control features: bank reconciliations and petty cash funds. Before we turn to these control devices, we need to review the basic features of a bank statement.

Reading a Bank Statement

Two fundamental principles of internal control are applicable to cash. First, all cash receipts should be deposited daily intact, and second, all cash payments should be made by check. Checking accounts at banks are critical in this regard. These accounts allow a company to carefully monitor and control cash receipts and cash payments. Control is aided further by the monthly **bank statement.** Most banks mail their customers a monthly bank statement for each account. The statement provides a detailed list of all activity for a particular account during the month. An example of a typical bank statement is shown in Exhibit 5-2. Note that the bank statement indicates the activity in one of the cash accounts maintained by Weber Products Inc. at the Mt. Etna State Bank.

Bank statement A detailed list, provided by the bank, of all the activity for a particular account during the month.

Before we look at the various items that appear on a bank statement, it is important to understand the route a check takes after it is written. Assume that Weber writes a check on its account at the Mt. Etna State Bank. Weber mails the check to one of its suppliers, Keese Corp., which deposits the check in its account at the Second City Bank. At this point, Second City presents the check to Mt. Etna for payment, and Mt. Etna

Exhibit 5-2 Bank Statement

MT. ETNA STATE BANK
CHICAGO, ILLINOIS
STATEMENT OF ACCOUNT

Weber Products Inc.
502 Dodge St.
Chicago, IL 66606

FOR THE MONTH ENDING **June 30, 2004**
ACCOUNT **0371-22-514**

Date	Description	Subtractions	Additions	Balance
6-01	Previous balance			3,236.41
6-01	Check 497	723.40		2,513.01
6-02	Check 495	125.60		2,387.41
6-06	Check 491	500.00		1,887.41
6-07	Deposit		1,423.16	3,310.57
6-10	Check 494	185.16		3,125.41
6-13	NSF check	245.72		2,879.69
6-15	Deposit		755.50	3,635.19
6-18	Check 499	623.17		3,012.02
6-20	Check 492	125.00		2,887.02
6-22	Deposit		1,875.62	4,762.64
6-23	Service charge	20.00		4,742.64
6-24	Check 493	875.75		3,866.89
6-24	Check 503	402.10		3,464.79
6-26	Customer note, interest		550.00	4,014.79
6-26	Service fee on note	16.50		3,998.29
6-27	Check 500	1,235.40		2,762.89
6-28	Deposit		947.50	3,710.39
6-30	Check 498	417.25		3,293.14
6-30	Interest earned		15.45	3,308.59
6-30	Statement Totals	5,495.05	5,567.23	

reduces the balance in Weber's account accordingly. The canceled check has now "cleared" the banking system. Either the canceled check itself or a copy of it is returned with Weber's next bank statement.

The following types of items appear on Weber's bank statement:

Canceled checks—Weber's checks that cleared the bank during the month of June are listed with the corresponding check number and the date paid. Keep in mind that some of these checks may have been written by Weber in a previous month but were not presented for payment to the bank until June. You also should realize that during June, Weber may have written some checks that do not yet appear on the bank statement because they have not been presented for payment. A check written by a company but not yet presented to the bank for payment is called an **outstanding check.**

Outstanding check A check written by a company but not yet presented to the bank for payment.

Deposits—In keeping with the internal control principle calling for the deposit of all cash receipts intact, most companies deposit all checks, coin, and currency on a daily basis. For the sake of brevity, we have limited to four the number of deposits that Weber made during the month. Keep in mind that Weber also may have made a deposit on the last day or two of the month and that this deposit may not yet be reflected on the bank statement. This type of deposit is called a **deposit in transit.**

Deposit in transit A deposit recorded on the books but not yet reflected on the bank statement.

NSF check—NSF is an abbreviation for *not sufficient funds.* The NSF check listed on the bank statement on June 13 is a customer's check that Weber recorded on its books, deposited, and thus included in its cash account. When Mt. Etna State Bank learned that the check was not good because the customer did not have sufficient funds on hand in its bank account to cover the check, the bank deducted the amount from

Weber's account. Weber needs to contact its customer to collect the amount due; ideally, the customer will issue a new check once it has sufficient funds in its account.

Service charge—Banks charge for various services they provide to customers. Among the most common bank service charges are monthly activity fees, fees charged for new checks, for the rental of a lockbox at the bank in which to store valuable company documents, and for the collection of customer notes by the bank.

Customer note and interest—It is often convenient to have customers pay amounts owed to a company directly to that company's bank. The bank simply acts as a collection agency for the company.

Interest earned—Most checking accounts pay interest on the average daily balance in the account. Rates paid on checking accounts are usually significantly less than could be earned on most other forms of investment.

The Bank Reconciliation

A **bank reconciliation** should be prepared for each individual bank account as soon as the bank statement is received. Ideally, the reconciliation should be performed or, at a minimum, thoroughly reviewed by someone independent of custody, record-keeping, and authorization responsibilities relating to cash. As the name implies, the purpose of a bank reconciliation is to *reconcile* or resolve any differences between the balance that the bank shows for an account with the balance that appears on the company's books. Differences between the two amounts are investigated, and if necessary, adjustments are made. The following are the steps in preparing a bank reconciliation:

Bank reconciliation A form used by the accountant to reconcile or resolve any differences between the balance shown on the bank statement for a particular account with the balance shown in the accounting records.

1. Trace deposits listed on the bank statement to the books. Any deposits recorded on the books but not yet shown on the bank statement are deposits in transit. Prepare a list of the deposits in transit.
2. Arrange the canceled checks in numerical order, and trace each of them to the books. Any checks recorded on the books but not yet listed on the bank statement are outstanding. List the outstanding checks.
3. List all items, other than deposits, shown as additions on the bank statement, such as interest paid by the bank for the month and amounts collected by the bank from one of the company's customers. When the bank pays interest or collects an amount owed to a company by one of the company's customers, the bank increases or *credits* its liability to the company on its own books. For this reason, these items are called **credit memoranda.**
4. List all amounts, other than canceled checks, shown as subtractions on the bank statement, such as any NSF checks and the various service charges mentioned earlier. When a company deposits money in a bank, a liability is created on the books of the bank. Therefore, when the bank reduces the amount of its liability for these various items, it *debits* the liability on its own books. For this reason, these items are called **debit memoranda.**
5. Identify any errors made by the bank or by the company in recording the various cash transactions.
6. Use the information collected in steps **1** through **5** to prepare a bank reconciliation.

Credit memoranda Additions on a bank statement for such items as interest paid on the account and notes collected by the bank for the customer.

Debit memoranda Deductions on a bank statement for such items as NSF checks and various service charges.

Companies use a number of different *formats* in preparing bank reconciliations. For example, some companies take the balance shown on the bank statement and reconcile this amount to the balance shown on the books. Another approach, which we will illustrate for Weber Products, involves reconciling the bank balance and the book balance to an adjusted balance, rather than one to the other. As we will see, the advantage of this approach is that it yields the correct balance and makes it easy for the company to make any necessary adjustments to its books. A bank reconciliation for Weber Products is shown in Exhibit 5-3.

The following are explanations for the various items on the reconciliation:

1. The balance per bank statement of $3,308.59 is taken from the June statement as shown in Exhibit 5-2.

Exhibit 5-3

Bank Reconciliation

WEBER PRODUCTS BANK RECONCILIATION JUNE 30, 2004			
Balance per bank statement, June 30			$3,308.59
Add:	Deposit in transit		642.30
Deduct:	Outstanding checks:		
	No. 496	$ 79.89	
	No. 501	213.20	
	No. 502	424.75	(717.84)
Adjusted balance, June 30			$3,233.05
Balance per books, June 30			$2,895.82
Add:	Customer note collected	$500.00	
	Interest on customer note	50.00	
	Interest earned during June	15.45	
	Error in recording check 498	54.00	619.45
Deduct:	NSF check	$245.72	
	Collection fee on note	16.50	
	Service charge for lockbox	20.00	(282.22)
Adjusted balance, June 30			$3,233.05

Study Tip

Review your own bank statement to see the similarities and differences between it and the one illustrated here. Also, look on the reverse of your statement for the form of a reconciliation the bank provides. It may or may not be the same format as illustrated in Exhibit 5-3.

2. Weber's records showed a deposit for $642.30 made on June 30 that is not reflected on the bank statement. The deposit in transit is listed as an addition to the bank statement balance.
3. The accounting records indicate three checks written but not yet reflected on the bank statement. The three outstanding checks are as follows:

   496 $ 79.89
   501 $213.20
   502 $424.75

   Outstanding checks are the opposite of deposits in transit and therefore are deducted from the bank statement balance.
4. The adjusted balance of $3,233.05 is found by adding the deposit in transit and deducting the outstanding checks from the bank statement balance.
5. The $2,895.82 book balance on June 30 is taken from the company's records as of that date.
6. According to the bank statement, $550 was added to the account on June 26 for the collection of a note with interest. We assume that the repayment of the note itself accounted for $500 of this amount and that the other $50 was for interest. The bank statement notifies Weber that the note with interest has been collected. Therefore, Weber must add $550 to the book balance.
7. An entry on June 30 on the bank statement shows an increase of $15.45 for interest earned on the bank account during June. This amount is added to the book balance.
8. A review of the canceled checks returned with the bank statement detected an error made by Weber. The company records indicated that check 498 was recorded incorrectly as $471.25; the check was actually written for $417.25 and reflected as such on the bank statement. This error, referred to as a *transposition error,* resulted from transposing the 7 and the 1 in recording the check in the books. The error is the difference between the amount of $471.25 recorded and the amount of $417.25 that should have been recorded, or $54.00. Because Weber recorded the cash payment at too large an amount, $54.00 must be added back to the book balance.
9. In addition to canceled checks, three other deductions appear on the bank statement. Each of these must be deducted from the book balance:
   a. A customer's NSF check for $245.72 (see June 13 entry on bank statement)

b. A $16.50 fee charged by the bank to collect the customer's note discussed in item **6** (see June 26 entry on bank statement)

c. A service fee of $20.00 charged by the bank for rental of a lockbox (see June 23 entry on bank statement)

10. The additions of $619.45 and deductions of $282.22 resulted in an adjusted cash balance of $3,233.05. Note that this adjusted balance agrees with the adjusted bank statement balance on the bank reconciliation (see item **4**). Thus, all differences between the two balances have been explained.

The Bank Reconciliation and the Need for Adjustments to the Records

After it completes the bank reconciliation, Weber must prepare a number of adjustments to its records. In fact, all of the information for these adjustments will be from one section of the bank reconciliation. Do you think that the additions and deductions made to the bank balance or the ones made to the book balance are the basis for the adjustments? It is logical that the additions and deductions to the Cash account *on the books* should be the basis for the adjustments because these are items that Weber was unaware of before receiving the bank statement. Conversely, the additions and deductions to the bank's balance, that is, the deposits in transit and the outstanding checks, are items that Weber has already recorded on its books.

Establishing a Petty Cash Fund

Recall one of the fundamental rules in controlling cash: all disbursements should be made by check. Most businesses make an exception to this rule in the case of minor expenditures, for which they use a **petty cash fund.** This fund consists of coin and currency kept on hand to make minor disbursements. The necessary steps in setting up and maintaining a petty cash fund follow:

Petty cash fund Money kept on hand for making minor disbursements in coin and currency rather than by writing checks.

1. A check is written for a lump-sum amount, such as $100 or $500. The check is cashed, and the coin and currency are entrusted to a petty cash custodian.
2. A journal entry is made to record the establishment of the fund.
3. Upon presentation of the necessary documentation, employees receive minor disbursements from the fund. In essence, cash is traded from the fund in exchange for a receipt.
4. Periodically, the fund is replenished by writing and cashing a check in the amount necessary to bring the fund back to its original balance.
5. At the time the fund is replenished, an adjustment is made both to record its replenishment and to recognize the various expenses incurred.

The use of this fund is normally warranted on the basis of cost versus benefits. That is, the benefits in time saved in making minor disbursements from cash are thought to outweigh the cost associated with the risk of loss from decreased control over cash disbursements. The fund also serves a practical purpose for certain expenditures such as taxi fares and messengers which often must be paid in cash.

Now that we have considered the importance of control over cash, we turn our attention to the broader topic of internal control systems.

AN INTRODUCTION TO INTERNAL CONTROL

LO 3 Explain the importance of internal control to a business.

An employee of a large auto parts warehouse routinely takes spare parts home for personal use. A payroll clerk writes and signs two checks for an employee and then splits the amount of the second check with the worker. Through human error, an invoice is paid for merchandise never received from the supplier. These cases sound quite different from one another, but they share one important characteristic. They all point to a

Internal control system Policies and procedures necessary to ensure the safeguarding of an entity's assets, the reliability of its accounting records, and the accomplishment of overall company objectives.

deficiency in a company's internal control system. An **internal control system** consists of the policies and procedures necessary to ensure the safeguarding of an entity's assets, the reliability of its accounting records, and the accomplishment of its overall objectives.

Three assets are especially critical to the operation of a merchandising company such as Gap Inc.: cash, accounts receivable, and inventory. Activities related to these three assets compose the operating cycle of a business. Cash is used to buy inventory, the inventory is eventually sold, and assuming a sale on credit, the account receivable from the customer is collected. We turn now to the ways in which a company attempts to *control* the assets at its disposal. This section serves as an introduction to the important topic of internal control, which is explored further at appropriate points in the book.

The Report of Management: Showing Responsibility for Control

Modern business is characterized by absentee ownership. In most large corporations, it is impossible for the owners—the stockholders—to be actively involved in the daily affairs of the business. Professional managers have the primary responsibility for the business's smooth operation. They are also responsible for the content of the financial statements.

Report of management Written statement in the annual report indicating the responsibility of management for the financial statements.

Internal audit staff Department responsible for monitoring and evaluating the internal control system.

Most annual reports now include a **report of management** to the stockholders. A typical management report, in this case for **Gap Inc.,** is shown in Exhibit 5-4. The first paragraph of the report clearly spells out management's responsibility for the financial information presented in the annual report. The second paragraph refers to the system of internal controls within the company. One of the features of Gap Inc.'s internal control system is the use of an **internal audit staff.** Most large corporations today have a full-time staff of internal auditors who have the responsibility for evaluating the entity's internal control system.

The primary concern of the independent public accountants, or external auditors, is whether the financial statements have been presented fairly. Internal auditors focus more on the efficiency with which the organization is run. They are responsible for periodically reviewing both accounting and administrative controls, which we discuss later in this chapter. The internal audit staff also helps to ensure that the company's policies and procedures are followed.

The second paragraph of the report states that the company's independent public accountants have audited the company's financial statements. The management of most corporations would consider it cost-prohibitive for the auditors to verify the millions of transactions recorded in a single year. Instead, the auditors rely to a certain degree on the system of internal control as assurance that transactions are properly recorded and reported. The degree of reliance that they are able to place on the company's internal controls is a significant factor in determining the extent of their testing. The stronger the system of internal control, the less testing is necessary. A weak system of internal control requires that the auditors extend their tests of the records.

Board of directors Group composed of key officers of a corporation and outside members responsible for general oversight of the affairs of the entity.

Audit committee Board of directors subset that acts as a direct contact between stockholders and the independent accounting firm.

Foreign Corrupt Practices Act Legislation intended to increase the accountability of management for accurate records and reliable financial statements.

The **board of directors** of a corporation usually consists of key officers of the corporation as well as a number of directors whom it does not directly employ. For example, Gap Inc.'s board of 11 directors consists of 4 insiders and 7 outsiders. The outsiders often include presidents and key executive officers of other corporations and sometimes business school faculty. The board of directors is elected by the stockholders.

As referred to in the third paragraph of Exhibit 5-4, the **audit committee** (or the Audit and Finance Committee for Gap Inc.) of the board of directors provides direct contact between the stockholders and the independent accounting firm. Audit committees have assumed a much more active role since the passage of the **Foreign Corrupt Practices Act** in 1977. This legislation was passed in response to a growing concern over various types of improprieties by top management, such as kickbacks to politicians and bribes of foreign officials. The act includes a number of provisions intended to increase the accountability of management and the board of directors to stockholders. According to the act, management is responsible for keeping accurate records, and various provisions deal with the system of internal controls necessary to ensure the safeguarding of

Exhibit 5-4 Report of Management—Gap Inc.

Management's Report on Financial Information

Management is responsible for the integrity and consistency of all financial information presented in the Annual Report. The consolidated financial statements have been prepared in accordance with accounting principles generally accepted in the United States of America and necessarily include certain amounts based on Management's best estimates and judgments.

In fulfilling its responsibility for the reliability of financial information, Management has established and maintains accounting systems and procedures appropriately supported by internal accounting controls. Such controls include the selection and training of qualified personnel, an organizational structure providing for division of responsibility, communication of requirement for compliance with approved accounting control and business practices and a program of internal audit. The extent of our system of internal accounting control recognizes that the cost should not exceed the benefits derived and that the evaluation of those factors requires estimates and judgments by Management. Although no system can ensure that all errors or irregularities have been eliminated, Management believes that the internal accounting controls in use provide reasonable assurance that assets are safeguarded against loss from unauthorized use or disposition, that transactions are executed in accordance with Management's authorization and that the financial records are reliable for preparing financial statements and maintaining accountability for assets. The consolidated financial statements of the Company and subsidaries have been audited by Deloitte & Touche LLP, independent auditors, whose report appears below.

The Audit and Finance Committee (the "Committee") of the Board of Directors is comprised solely of directors who are not officers or employees of the Company. The Committee is responsible for recommending to the Board of Directors the retention and compensation of the independent auditors. It meets periodically with Management, the independent auditors and the internal auditors to ensure that they are carrying out their responsibilities. The Committee also reviews and monitors the financial, accounting and auditing procedures of the Company in addition to reviewing the Company's financial reports. Deloitte & Touche LLP and the internal auditors have full and free access to the Committee, with and without Management's presence.

First Paragraph
Management's responsibility for the financial information

Second Paragraph
System of internal controls

Third Paragraph
Role of the Audit and Finance Committee

assets and the reliability of the financial statements. Audit committees have become much more involved in the oversight of the financial reporting system since the enactment of the act.

From Concept to Practice 5.2

Reading Gap Inc.'s Management Report

Refer to management's report for Gap Inc. in Exhibit 5-4. What is the composition of its Audit and Finance Committee? Why do you think it is composed in this way?

The Control Environment

The success of an internal control system begins with the competence of the people in charge of it. Management's operating style will have a determinable impact on the effectiveness of various policies. An autocratic style in which a few key officers tightly control operations will result in an environment different from that of a decentralized organization in which departments have more freedom to make decisions. Personnel policies and practices form another factor in the internal control of a business. An appropriate system for hiring competent employees and firing incompetent ones is crucial to an efficient operation. After all, no internal control system will work very well if employees who are dishonest or poorly trained are on the payroll. On the other hand, too few people doing too many tasks defeats the purpose of an internal control system. Finally, the effectiveness of internal control in a business is influenced by the board of directors, particularly its audit committee.

© KEN REID/GETTY IMAGES/TAXIS

This woman is using the paper source document in her hand as a reference for entering data into the accounting system. From the standpoint of internal control, should she be the one who is ordering inventory, receiving it, and entering the information into the system? Is she authorized to make journal entries? If so, does her laptop have safeguards that prevent access by unauthorized personnel? These and other internal control procedures are part of the control environment within every company.

The Accounting System

An **accounting system** consists of all the methods and records used to accurately report an entity's transactions and to maintain accountability for its assets and liabilities. Regardless of the degree of computer automation, the use of a journal to record transactions is an integral part of all accounting systems. Refinements are sometimes made to the basic components of the system, depending on the company's needs. For example, most companies use specialized journals to record recurring transactions, such as sales of merchandise on credit.

An accounting system can be completely manual, fully computerized, or as is often the case, a mixture of the two. Internal controls are important to all businesses, regardless of the degree of automation of the accounting system. The system must be capable of handling both the volume and the complexity of transactions entered into by a business. Most businesses use computers because of the sheer volume of transactions. The computer is ideally suited to the task of processing large numbers of repetitive transactions efficiently and quickly.

The cost of computing has dropped so substantially that virtually every business can now afford a system. Today some computer software programs that are designed for home-based businesses cost under $100 and are meant to run on machines that cost less than $1,000. Inexpensive software programs that categorize expenses and print checks, produce financial statements, and analyze financial ratios are available.

LO 4 Describe the basic internal control procedures.

Accounting system Methods and records used to accurately report an entity's transactions and to maintain accountability for its assets and liabilities.

Administrative controls Procedures concerned with efficient operation of the business and adherence to managerial policies.

Accounting controls Procedures concerned with safeguarding the assets or the reliability of the financial statements.

Internal Control Procedures

Management establishes policies and procedures on a number of different levels to ensure that corporate objectives will be met. Some procedures are formalized in writing. Others may not be written but are just as important. Certain **administrative controls** within a company are more concerned with the efficient operation of the business and adherence to managerial policies than with the accurate reporting of financial information. For example, a company policy that requires all prospective employees to be interviewed by the personnel department is an administrative control. Other **accounting controls** primarily concern safeguarding assets and ensuring the reliability of the financial statements. We now turn to a discussion of some of the most important internal control procedures:

- Proper authorizations
- Segregation of duties
- Independent verification
- Safeguarding assets and records
- Independent review and appraisal
- The design and use of business documents

Proper Authorizations Management grants specific departments the authority to perform various activities. Along with the *authority* goes *responsibility.* Most large organizations give the authority to hire new employees to the personnel department. Management authorizes the purchasing department to order goods and services for the company and the credit department to establish specific policies for granting credit to customers. By specifically authorizing certain individuals to carry out specific tasks for the business, management is able to hold these same people responsible for the outcome of their actions.

The authorizations for some transactions are general in nature; others are specific. For example, a cashier authorizes the sale of a book in a bookstore by ringing up the transaction (a general authorization). It is likely, however, that the bookstore manager's approval is required before a book can be returned (a specific authorization).

Segregation of Duties What might happen if one employee is given the authority both to prepare checks and to sign them? What could happen if a single employee is allowed to order inventory and receive it from the shipper? Or what if the cashier at a checkout stand also records the daily receipts in the journal? If the employee in each of these situations is honest and never makes mistakes, nothing bad will happen. However, if the employee is dishonest or makes human errors, the company can experience losses. These situations all point to the need for the segregation of duties, which is one of the most fundamental of all internal control procedures. Without segregation of duties, an employee is able not only to perpetrate a fraud but also to conceal it. A good system of internal control requires that the *physical custody* of assets be separated from the *accounting* for those same assets.

Like most internal control principles, the concept of segregation of duties is an ideal that is not always completely attainable. For example, many smaller businesses simply do not have adequate personnel to achieve complete segregation of key functions. In certain instances, these businesses need to rely on the direct involvement of the owners in the business and on independent verification.

Accounting for Your Decisions

You Are the Chief Financial Officer

You have been hired by the owner of Mt. Rainier Broom Company to come in and replace the out-of-date accounting systems with a system that uses modern technology. The first thing you notice is that the company's bookkeeper, Mavis, is in charge of collecting receivables, recording payments, ordering and receiving inventory, and preparing and signing checks. When you suggest to her that she has too many duties, she gets angry and appeals to the owner. The owner backs up Mavis and tells you to focus entirely on new accounting technology. What should you do?

ANS: Ever so politely, you should inform the owner and Mavis in a three-way meeting that your suggestion that Mavis not do all the accounting functions is not meant as an insult but is simply good internal control. Even if Mavis is as honest as they come, there is a good chance that she will make errors, which could result in losses to the company. By having at least two people involved in a transaction, the chances are excellent that an error will be caught by one or the other.

Independent Verification Related to the principle of segregation of duties is the idea of independent verification. The work of one department should act as a check on the work of another. For example, the physical count of the inventory in a perpetual inventory system provides such a check. The accounting department maintains the general ledger card for inventory and updates it as sales and purchases are made. The physical count of the inventory by an independent department acts as the check on the work of the accounting department. As another example, consider the bank reconciliation that we saw earlier in the chapter (Exhibit 5-3) as a control device. The reconciliation of a company's bank account with the bank statement by someone not responsible for either the physical custody of cash or the cash records acts as an independent check on the work of these parties.

Safeguarding Assets and Records Adequate safeguards must be in place to protect assets and the accounting records from losses of various kinds. Cash registers, safes, and lockboxes are important safeguards for cash. Secured storage areas with limited access are essential for the safekeeping of inventory. Protection of the accounting records against misuse is equally important. For example, access to a computerized accounting record should be limited to those employees authorized to prepare journal entries. This can be done with the use of a personal identification number and a password to access the system.

Independent Review and Appraisal A well-designed system of internal control provides for periodic review and appraisal of the accounting system as well as the people operating it. The group primarily responsible for review and appraisal of the system is the internal audit staff. Internal auditors provide management with periodic reports on the effectiveness of the control system and the efficiency of operations.

The Design and Use of Business Documents *Business documents* are the crucial link between economic transactions entered into by an entity and the accounting record of these events. They are often called *source documents.* Many of these are generated by the computer, but a few may be completed manually. The source document for the recognition of the expense of an employee's wages is the time card. The source documents for a sale include the sales order, the sales invoice, and the related shipping document. Business documents must be designed so that they capture all relevant information about an economic event. They are also designed to ensure that related transactions are properly classified.

Business documents themselves must be properly controlled. For example, a key feature for documents is a *sequential numbering system* just like you have for your personal checks. This system results in a complete accounting for all documents in the series and negates the opportunity for an employee to misdirect one. Another key feature of well-designed business documents is the use of *multiple copies.* The various departments involved in a particular activity, such as sales or purchasing, are kept informed of the status of outstanding orders through the use of copies of documents. The next section provides an example of the use of business documents for a merchandiser.

Limitations on Internal Control

Internal control is a relative term. No system of internal control is totally foolproof. An entity's size affects the degree of control that it can obtain. In general, large organizations are able to devote a substantial amount of resources to safeguarding assets and records because these companies have the assets to justify the cost. Because the installation and maintenance of controls can be costly, an internal audit staff is a luxury that many small businesses cannot afford. The mere segregation of duties can result in added costs if two employees must be involved in a task previously performed by only one.

Segregation of duties can be effective in preventing collusion, but no system of internal control can ensure that it will not happen. It does no good to have one employee count the cash at the end of the day and another to record it if the two act in concert to steal from the company. Rotation of duties can help to lessen the likelihood for problems of this sort. An employee is less likely to collude with someone to steal if the assignment is a temporary one. Another control feature, a system of authorizations, is meaningless if management continually overrides it. Management must believe in a system of internal control enough to support it.

Intentional acts to misappropriate company assets are not the only problem. All sorts of human errors can weaken a system of internal control. Misunderstood instructions, carelessness, fatigue, and distraction can all lead to errors. A well-designed system of internal control should result in the best-possible people being hired to perform the various tasks, but no one is perfect.

Two-Minute Review

1. *Explain why an internal control system is important to the operation of a company that sells a product.*

2. *Explain the difference between administrative controls and accounting controls.*
3. *Explain how the concept of segregation of duties involves an evaluation of costs versus benefits.*

Answers on page 238.

COMPUTERIZED BUSINESS DOCUMENTS AND INTERNAL CONTROL

LO 5 Describe the various documents used in recording purchases of merchandise and their role in controlling cash disbursements.

Specific internal controls are necessary to control cash receipts and cash disbursements in a merchandising company such as Gap Inc. In addition to the separation of the custodianship of cash from the recording of it in the accounts, two other fundamental principles apply to its control. First, all cash receipts should be deposited *intact* in the bank on a *daily* basis. *Intact* means that no disbursements should be made from the cash received from customers. The second basic principle is related to the first: all cash disbursements should be made by check. The use of sequentially numbered checks results in a clear record of all disbursements. The only exception to this rule is the use of a petty cash fund to make cash disbursements for minor expenditures such as postage stamps and repairs.

Control over Cash Receipts

Most merchandisers receive checks and currency from customers in two distinct ways: (1) cash received over the counter, that is, from cash sales and (2) cash received in the mail, that is, cash collections from credit sales. Each of these types of cash receipts poses its own particular control problems.

Cash Received over the Counter Several control mechanisms are used to handle these cash payments. First, cash registers allow the customer to see the display, which deters the salesclerk from ringing up a sale for less than the amount received from the customer and pocketing the difference. A locked-in cash register tape is another control feature. At various times during the day, an employee other than the clerk unlocks the register, removes the tape, and forwards it to the accounting department. At the end of the shift, the salesclerk remits the coin and currency from the register to a central cashier. Any difference between the amount of cash remitted to the cashier and the amount on the tape submitted to the accounting department is investigated.

Finally, prenumbered customer receipts, prepared in duplicate, are a useful control mechanism. The customer is given a copy, and the salesclerk retains another. The salesclerk is accountable for all numbers in a specific series of receipts and must be able to explain any differences between the amount of cash remitted to the cashier and the amount collected per the receipts.

Cash Received in the Mail Most customers send checks rather than currency through the mail. Any form of cash received in the mail from customers should be applied to their account balances. The customer wants assurance that the account is appropriately reduced for the amount of the payment. The company must be assured that all cash received is deposited in the bank and that the account receivable is reduced accordingly.

To achieve a reasonable degree of control, two employees should be present when the mail is opened.[1] The first employee opens the mail in the presence of the second

[1] In some companies, this control procedure may be omitted because of the cost of having two employees present when the mail is opened.

employee, counts the money received, and prepares a control list of the amount received on that particular day. The list is often called a *prelist* and is prepared in triplicate. The second employee takes the original to the cashier along with the total cash received on that day. The cashier is the person who makes the bank deposit. One copy of the prelist is forwarded to the accounting department to be used as the basis for recording the increase in Cash and the decrease in Accounts Receivable. The other copy is retained by one of the two persons opening the mail. A comparison of the prelist to the bank deposit slip is a timely way to detect receipts that do not make it to the bank. Because the two employees acting in concert could circumvent the control process, rotation of duties is important.

Monthly customer statements act as an additional control device for customer payments received in the mail. Assume that the two employees responsible for opening the mail and remitting checks to the cashier decide to pocket a check received from a customer. Checks made payable to a company *can* be stolen and cashed. The customer provides the control element. Because the check is not remitted to the cashier, the accounting department will not be notified to reduce the customer's account for the payment. The monthly statement, however, should alert the customer to the problem. The amount the customer thought was owed will be smaller than the balance due on the statement. At this point, the customer should ask the company to investigate the discrepancy. As evidence of its payment on account, the customer will be able to point to a canceled check—which was cashed by the unscrupulous employees.

Finally, keep in mind that the use of customer statements as a control device will be effective only if the employees responsible for the custody of cash received through the mail, for record keeping, and for authorization of adjustments to customers' accounts are not allowed to prepare and mail statements to customers. Employees allowed to do so are in a position to alter customers' statements.

Cash Discrepancies Discrepancies occur occasionally due to theft by dishonest employees and to human error. For example, if a salesclerk either intentionally or unintentionally gives the wrong amount of change, the amount remitted to the cashier will not agree with the cash register tape. Any material differences should be investigated. Of particular significance are *recurring* differences between the amount remitted by any one cashier and the amount on the cash register tape.

The Role of Computerized Business Documents in Controlling Cash Disbursements

A company makes cash payments for a variety of purposes: to purchase merchandise, supplies, plant, and equipment; to pay operating expenditures; and to cover payroll expenses, to name a few. We will concentrate on the disbursement of cash to purchase goods for resale, focusing particularly on the role of business documents in the process. Merchandising companies rely on a smooth and orderly inflow of quality goods for resale to customers. It is imperative that suppliers be paid on time so that they will continue to make goods available.

Business documents play a vital role in the purchasing function. The example that follows begins with a requisition for merchandise by the tool department of Grizzly Hardware Stores. The example continues through the receipt of the goods and the eventual payment to the supplier. The entire process is summarized in Exhibit 5-5. You will want to refer to this exhibit throughout the remainder of this section.

Purchase Requisition The tool department at Grizzly Hardware Stores weekly reviews its stock to determine whether any items need replenishing. On the basis of its needs, the supervisor of the tool department fills out the **purchase requisition form** shown in Exhibit 5-6 on page 234. The form indicates the preferred supplier or vendor, A-1 Tool.

Purchase requisition form Form a department uses to initiate a request to order merchandise.

The purchasing department has the responsibility for making the final decision on a vendor. Giving the purchasing department this responsibility means that it is held

Exhibit 5-5 Document Flow for the Purchasing Function

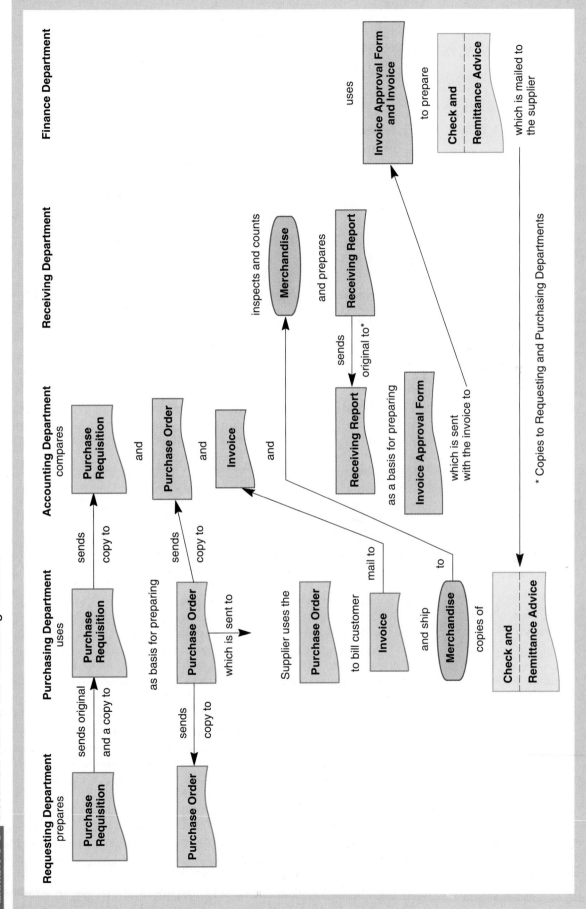

Requesting Department
prepares
Purchase Requisition
sends original and a copy to

Purchasing Department
uses
Purchase Requisition
sends copy to

Accounting Department
compares
Purchase Requisition
and
Purchase Order
and
Invoice
and

Receiving Department

Finance Department

(Purchasing Department) as basis for preparing
Purchase Order
sends copy to **Purchase Order** (Requesting Department)
sends copy to **Purchase Order** (Accounting Department)
which is sent to

Supplier uses the
Purchase Order
to bill customer
Invoice
mail to (Accounting Department)
and ship
Merchandise
to (Receiving Department)
copies of
Check and
Remittance Advice

(Receiving Department) inspects and counts
Merchandise
and prepares
Receiving Report
sends original to*
Receiving Report (Accounting Department)
as a basis for preparing
Invoice Approval Form
which is sent with the invoice to

(Finance Department) uses
Invoice Approval Form and Invoice
to prepare
Check and
Remittance Advice
which is mailed to the supplier

* Copies to Requesting and Purchasing Departments

Exhibit 5-6

Purchase Requisition

Grizzly Hardware Stores
676 Sentinel St.
Missoula, MT

PURCHASE REQUISITION

Date 5/28/04 **PR 75638**

Preferred vendor A-1 Tool Co.

Date needed by 6/5/04

The following items are requested for weekly dept. order

Item No.	**Quantity**	**Description/Vendor No.**
314627	24 ST	Hobby tool set/5265
323515	12 CD	Hobby blades 5 pk/7512
323682	6 ST	Screwdriver set 5/PC/1589

Requested by Joe Smith **Department** Tool department

accountable for acquiring the goods at the lowest price, given certain standards for merchandise quality. Grizzly assigns a separate item number to each of the thousands of individual items of merchandise it stocks. Note that the requisition also indicates the vendor's number for each item. The unit of measure for each item is indicated in the quantity column. For example, "24 ST" means 24 sets, and "12 CD" means 12 cards. The original and a copy of the purchase requisition are sent to the purchasing department. The tool department keeps one copy for its records.

Purchase Order Like many other businesses, Grizzly uses a computerized purchasing system. Most companies either have purchased software or have developed software internally to perform such functions as purchasing, sales, and payroll. The software is capable not only of increasing the speed and accuracy of the process but also of generating the necessary documents.

Purchase order Form sent by the purchasing department to the supplier.

A computer-generated **purchase order** is shown in Exhibit 5-7. Purchase orders are usually prenumbered; a company should periodically investigate any missing numbers. The purchasing department uses its copy of the purchase requisition as a basis for preparing the purchase order. An employee in the purchasing department keys in the relevant information from the purchase requisition and adds the unit cost for each item gathered from the vendor's price guide. The software program generates the purchase order as shown in Exhibit 5-7. You should trace all of the information for at least one of the three items ordered from the purchase requisition to the purchase order.

The system generates the original purchase order and three copies. As indicated in Exhibit 5-5, the original is sent to the supplier after a supervisor in the purchasing department approves it. One copy is sent to the accounting department, where it will be matched with the original requisition. A second copy is sent to the tool department as confirmation that its request for the items has been attended to by the purchasing department. The purchasing department keeps the third copy for its records.

A purchase order is not the basis for recording a purchase and a liability. Legally, the order is merely an offer by the company to purchase goods from the supplier. Technically, the receipt of goods from the supplier is the basis for the purchaser's recognition of a

Exhibit 5-7

Computer-Generated Purchase Order

Grizzly Hardware Stores
676 Sentinel St.
Missoula, MT

PURCHASE ORDER

TO: **PO 54296**

A-1 Tool Co.
590 West St.
Milwaukee, WI

Date 5/30/04 **Ship by** Best Express

Terms 2/10, net 30 **Date required** 6/5/04

Item No.	Quantity	Description/Vendor No.	Unit price	Amount
314627	24 ST	Hobby tool set/5265	$28.59	$686.16
323515	12 CD	Hobby blades 5 pk/7512	0.69	8.28
323682	6 ST	Screwdriver set 5/PC/1589	4.49	26.94
				$721.38

Approved by Mary Jones

liability. As a matter of practice, however, most companies record the payable upon receipt of the invoice.

Invoice When A-1 Tool ships the merchandise, it also mails an invoice to Grizzly, requesting payment according to the agreed-upon terms, in this case 2/10, net 30.[2] The **invoice** may be mailed separately or included with the shipment of merchandise. A-1 Tool, the seller, calls this document a *sales invoice;* it is the basis for recording a sale and an account receivable. Grizzly, the buyer, calls the same document a *purchase invoice,* which is the basis for recording a purchase and an account payable. The invoice that A-1 sent to Grizzly's accounting department is shown in Exhibit 5-8.

Invoice Form sent by the seller to the buyer as evidence of a sale.

Receiving Report The accounting department receives the invoice for the three items ordered. Within a few days before or after the receipt of the invoice, the merchandise arrives at Grizzly's warehouse. As soon as the items are unpacked, the receiving department inspects and counts them. The same software program that generated the purchase order also generates a receiving report, as shown in Exhibit 5-9.

Grizzly uses a **blind receiving report.** The column for the quantity received is left blank and is filled in by the receiving department. Rather than being able simply to indicate that the number ordered was received, an employee must count the items to determine that the number ordered is actually received. You should trace all of the relevant information for one of the three items ordered from the purchase order to the receiving report. The accounting system generates an original receiving report and three copies. The receiving department keeps one copy for its records and sends the original to the accounting department. One copy is sent to the purchasing department to be matched with the purchase order, and the other copy is sent to the tool department as verification that the items it originally requested have been received.

Blind receiving report Form used by the receiving department to account for the quantity and condition of merchandise received from a supplier.

[2]Terms for the purchase of inventory will be discussed more fully in Chapter 7. For now, understand that terms of 2/10, net 30 mean that the customer receives a 2 percent discount by paying within ten days of purchase; if not, the full amount is due within thirty days of purchase.

Exhibit 5-8
Invoice

NO. 427953

A-1 Tool Co.
590 West St.
Milwaukee, WI

INVOICE

Sold to Grizzly Hardware Stores
676 Sentinel St.
Missoula, MT
Ship to Same
Terms 2/10, net 30

Date 6/2/04
Order No. 54296
Shipped via Best Express
Date shipped 6/2/04

Quantity	Description/No.	Price	Amount
24 ST	Hobby tool set/5265	$28.59	$686.16
12 CD	Hobby blades 5 pk/7512	0.69	8.28
6 ST	Screwdriver set 5 PC/1589	4.49	26.94
			$721.38

Invoice approval form Form the accounting department uses before making payment to document the accuracy of all the information about a purchase.

Invoice Approval Form At this point, Grizzly's accounting department has copies of the purchase requisition from the tool department, the purchase order from the purchasing department, the invoice from the supplier, and the receiving report from the warehouse. The accounting department uses an **invoice approval form** to document the accuracy of the information on each of these other forms. The invoice approval form for Grizzly Hardware is shown in Exhibit 5-10.

The invoice is compared to the purchase requisition to ensure that the company is billed for goods that it requested. A comparison of the invoice with the purchase order ensures that the goods were in fact ordered. Finally, the receiving report is

Exhibit 5-9
Computer-Generated Receiving Report

Grizzly Hardware Stores
676 Sentinel St.
Missoula, MT

Receiving Report

RR 23637

Purchase Order No. 54296
Vendor A-1 Tool Co.
Ship via Best Express
Terms 2/10, net 30

Date ordered 5/30/04
Date required 6/5/04

Quantity received	Our Item No.	Description/Item No.	Remarks
24 ST	314627	Hobby tool set/5265	Box damaged but merchandise ok
12 CD	323515	Hobby blades 5 pk/7512	
6 ST	323682	Screwdriver set 5/PC/1589	

Received by Bob Reed

Date 6/4/04

Grizzly Hardware Stores
676 Sentinel St.
Missoula, MT

Invoice Approval Form

	No.	Check
Purchase Requisition	PR 75638	✓
Purchase Order	PO 54296	✓
Receiving Report	RR 23637	✓

Invoice:

No. 427953
Date 6/2/04
Price ✓
Extensions ✓
Footings ✓

Last Day to Pay for Discount 6/12/04

Approved for Payment by Alice Johnson

Exhibit 5-10
Invoice Approval Form

compared with the invoice to verify that all goods it is being billed for were received. An accounting department employee must also verify the mathematical accuracy of the amounts that appear on the invoice. The date the invoice must be paid to take advantage of the discount is noted so that the finance department will be sure to send the check by this date. At this point, the accounting department prepares the journal entry to increase the inventory and accounts payable accounts. The invoice approval form and the invoice are then sent to the finance department. Some businesses call the invoice approval form a *voucher;* it is used for all expenditures, not just for purchases of merchandise. Finally, it is worth noting that some businesses do not use a separate invoice approval form but simply note approval directly on the invoice itself.

Check with Remittance Advice Grizzly's finance department is responsible for issuing checks. This results from the need to segregate custody of cash (the signed check) from record keeping (the updating of the ledger). On receipt of the invoice approval form from the accounting department, a clerk in the finance department types a check with a remittance advice attached, as shown in Exhibit 5-11.[3]

Before the check is signed, the documents referred to on the invoice approval form are reviewed and canceled to prevent reuse. The clerk then forwards the check to one of the company officers authorized to sign checks. According to one of Grizzly's internal control policies, only the treasurer and the assistant treasurer are authorized to sign checks. Both officers must sign check amounts above a specified dollar limit. To maintain separation of duties, the finance department should mail the check. The remittance advice informs the supplier as to the nature of the payment and is torn off by the supplier before cashing the check.

[3]In some companies, an employee in the accounting department prepares checks and sends them to the finance department for review and signature. Also, many companies use computer-generated checks, rather than manually typed ones.

Exhibit 5-11

Check with Remittance Advice

3690

Grizzly Hardware Stores
676 Sentinel St.
Missoula, MT

June 12 20 04

PAY TO THE
ORDER OF A-1 Tool Co. $706.95

Seven hundred six and 95/100 DOLLARS

Second National Bank
Missoula, MT

3690 035932 9321

John B. Martin

Purchase Order No.	Invoice No.	Invoice Date	Description	Amount
PO 54296	427953	6/2/04	24 ST Hobby tool set	$686.16
			12 CD Hobby blades 5pk	8.28
			6 ST Screwdriver set 5PC	26.94
			Total	$721.38
			Less: 2% discount	14.43
			Net remitted	$706.95

Answers to the Two-Minute Reviews

Two-Minute Review on Pages 230–231

1. *An effective system of internal control is critical to protecting a company's investment in three of its major assets: cash, accounts receivable, and inventory. Without an effective system, these assets are subject to misuse.*
2. *Administrative controls are concerned with the efficient operation of a business and adherence to managerial policies. Alternatively, accounting controls deal with safeguarding assets and ensuring the reliability of the financial statements.*
3. *Involving more than one employee in a specific function reduces the likelihood of theft or other misuse of company assets. However, all businesses must decide whether the benefit of segregation of duties outweighs the additional cost of involving more than one employee in a specific function such as the preparation and distribution of the payroll.*

Warmup Exercises

Warmup Exercise 5-1 ***Composition of Cash*** **LO 1**

For the following items, indicate whether each should be included (I) or excluded (E) from the line item titled Cash and Cash Equivalents on the balance sheet.

_______ **1.** Certificate of deposit maturing in 60 days
_______ **2.** Checking account
_______ **3.** Certificate of deposit maturing in six months
_______ **4.** Savings account
_______ **5.** Shares of GM stock
_______ **6.** Petty cash
_______ **7.** Corporate bonds maturing in 30 days
_______ **8.** Certified check

Key to the Solution

Recall the key to classification as part of cash: the amount must be readily available to pay debts and cash equivalents must have an original maturity to the investor of three months or less.

Warmup Exercise 5-2 ***Internal Control*** **LO 4**

List the internal control procedures discussed in the text.

Key to the Solution

Refer to the section in the chapter that discusses internal control procedures.

Solutions to Warmup Exercises

Warmup Exercise 5-1

1. I **2.** I **3.** E **4.** I **5.** E **6.** I **7.** E **8.** I

Warmup Exercise 5-2

1. Proper authorizations
2. Segregation of duties
3. Independent verification
4. Safeguarding assets and records
5. Independent review and appraisal
6. Design and use of business documents

Review Problem

WebTUTOR™ Advantage

The following information is available for Woodbury Corp. on June 30, 2004:

a. The balance in cash as reported on the June 30, 2004, bank statement is $5,654.98.

b. Woodbury made a deposit of $865.00 on June 30 that is not included on the bank statement.

c. A comparison between the canceled checks returned with the bank statement and Woodbury's records indicated that two checks had not yet been returned to the bank for payment. The amounts of the two checks were $236.77 and $116.80.

d. The Cash account on the company's books reported a balance on June 30 of $4,165.66.

e. Woodbury rents some excess storage space in one of its warehouses and the tenant pays its monthly rent directly to the bank for deposit in Woodbury's account. The bank statement indicates that a deposit of $1,500.00 was made during the month of June.

f. Interest earned on the checking account and added to Woodbury's account during June was $11.75.

g. Bank services charges were $15.00 for the month of June as reported on the bank statement.

h. A comparison between the checks returned with the bank statement and the company's records revealed that a check written by the company in the amount of $56.00 was recorded by the company erroneously as a check for $560.00.

Required

Prepare a bank reconciliation for the month of June in good form.

Solution to Review Problem

WOODBURY CORP.
BANK RECONCILIATION
JUNE 30, 2004

Balance per bank statement, June 30		$5,654.98
Add: Deposit in transit		865.00
Deduct: Outstanding checks:		
	$ 236.77	
	116.80	(353.57)
Adjusted balance, June 30		$6,166.41
Balance per books, June 30		$4,165.66
Add: Tenant's rent collected by bank	$1,500.00	
Interest earned on checking account	11.75	
Error in recording check	504.00	2,015.75
Deduct: Bank service charges		(15.00)
Adjusted balance, June 30		$6,166.41

Chapter Highlights

1. **LO 1** The amount of cash reported on the balance sheet includes all items that are readily available to satisfy obligations. Items normally included in cash are coin and currency, petty cash funds, customers' undeposited checks, cashier's checks, certified checks, savings accounts, and checking accounts.
2. **LO 1** Cash equivalents include such items as commercial paper, money market funds, certificates of deposit, and Treasury bills. They are included with cash on the balance sheet and are limited to those investments that are readily convertible to known amounts of cash and have original maturities of three months or less.
3. **LO 2** A bank reconciliation is normally prepared monthly for all checking accounts to reconcile the amount of cash recorded on the books with the amount recorded on the bank statement. One popular form for the reconciliation, and the one illustrated in the chapter, reconciles the balance on the bank statement and the balance on the books to the correct balance. Adjustments must be made for all items in the balance per books section of the reconciliation.
4. **LO 2** Many companies use a petty cash fund to disburse small amounts of cash that would otherwise require the use of a check and a more lengthy approval process. The fund is established by writing and cashing a check and placing the coin and currency in a secure place controlled by a custodian. At this point, an adjustment is made to record the establishment of the fund. On presentation of a supporting receipt to the custodian, employees receive disbursements from the fund. The fund is replenished periodically, and an adjustment is made to record the replenishment and to recognize the various expenses incurred.
5. **LO 3** The purpose of an internal control system is to provide assurance that overall company objectives are met. Specifically, accounting controls are designed to safeguard the entity's assets and provide the company with reliable accounting records. Management has the primary responsibility for the reliability of the financial statements. Many companies employ a full-time internal audit staff to monitor and evaluate the internal control system.
6. **LO 4** Segregation of duties is the most fundamental of all internal control procedures. Possession of assets must be kept separate from the record-keeping function. Other important control procedures include a system of independent verifications, proper authorizations, adequate safeguards for assets and their records, independent review and appraisal of the accounting system, and the design and use of business documents.
7. **LO 5** Control over cash requires that all receipts be deposited intact on a daily basis and that all disbursements be made by check. Control procedures are important for cash received over the counter as well as for cash received in the mail. Any material discrepancies between the cash actually on hand and the amount that should be on hand need to be investigated.
8. **LO 5** Business documents play a vital role in various business activities such as the purchase of merchandise. The requesting department fills out a purchase requisition form and sends it to

the purchasing department. The purchasing department uses the requisition to complete a purchase order, which it sends to the supplier. The supplier mails an invoice to the buyer's accounting department. The accounting department also gets a receiving report from the warehouse to indicate the quantity and condition of the goods delivered. The accounting department fills out an invoice approval form, which it sends with the invoice to the finance department, which uses them as the basis for preparing and sending a check to the supplier.

http://

http://porter.swlearning.com

Technology and other resources for your success

If you need additional help, visit the text's Web site. Also, see this text's preface for a description of available technology and other resources. If your instructor is using PERSONAL Trainer in this course, you may complete, on line, the exercises and problems in the text.

Key Terms Quiz

Read each definition below and then write the number of the definition in the blank beside the appropriate term it defines. The quiz solutions appear at the end of the chapter.

_____	Cash equivalent	_____	Board of directors
_____	Bank statement	_____	Audit committee
_____	Outstanding check	_____	Foreign Corrupt Practices Act
_____	Deposit in transit	_____	Accounting system
_____	Bank reconciliation	_____	Administrative controls
_____	Credit memoranda	_____	Accounting controls
_____	Debit memoranda	_____	Purchase requisition form
_____	Petty cash fund	_____	Purchase order
_____	Internal control system	_____	Invoice
_____	Report of management	_____	Blind receiving report
_____	Internal audit staff	_____	Invoice approval form

1. The form sent by the seller to the buyer as evidence of a sale.
2. The group composed of key officers of a corporation and outside members responsible for the general oversight of the affairs of the entity.
3. Policies and procedures necessary to ensure the safeguarding of an entity's assets, the reliability of its accounting records, and the accomplishment of overall company objectives.
4. Procedures concerned with safeguarding the assets or the reliability of the financial statements.
5. The form a department uses to initiate a request to order merchandise.
6. A form the accounting department uses before making payment to document the accuracy of all the information about a purchase.
7. A form used by the accountant to reconcile the balance shown on the bank statement for a particular account with the balance shown in the accounting records.
8. An investment that is readily convertible to a known amount of cash and has an original maturity to the investor of three months or less.
9. Deductions on a bank statement for such items as NSF checks and various service charges.
10. A check written by a company but not yet presented to the bank for payment.
11. A detailed list, prepared by the bank, of all the activity for a particular account during the month.
12. Legislation intended to increase the accountability of management for accurate records and reliable financial statements.
13. A deposit recorded on the books but not yet reflected on the bank statement.
14. The methods and records used to accurately report an entity's transactions and to maintain accountability for its assets and liabilities.
15. Additions on a bank statement for such items as interest paid on the account and notes collected by the bank.
16. The board of directors subset that acts as a direct contact between the stockholders and the independent accounting firm.
17. Money kept on hand for making minor disbursements in coin and currency rather than by writing checks.

18. A written statement in the annual report indicating the responsibility of management for the financial statements.
19. A form used by the receiving department to account for the quantity and condition of merchandise received from a supplier.
20. Procedures concerned with efficient operation of the business and adherence to managerial policies.
21. The form sent by the purchasing department to the supplier.
22. The department responsible for monitoring and evaluating the internal control system.

Alternate Terms

Invoice Purchase invoice, sales invoice

Invoice approval form Voucher

Report of management Management's report

Questions

1. What is a cash equivalent? Why is it included with cash on the balance sheet?
2. Why does the purchase of an item classified as a cash equivalent *not* appear on the statement of cash flows as an investing activity?
3. A friend says to you: "I understand why it is important to deposit all receipts intact and not keep coin and currency sitting around the business. Beyond this control feature, however, I believe that a company should strive to keep the maximum amount possible in checking accounts to always be able to pay bills on time." How would you evaluate your friend's statement?
4. A friends says to you: "I'm confused. I have a memo included with my bank statement indicating a $20 service charge for printing new checks. If the bank is deducting this amount from my account, why do they call it a 'debit memorandum'? I thought a decrease in a cash account would be a credit, not a debit." How can you explain this?
5. Different formats for bank reconciliations are possible. What is the format for a bank reconciliation in which a service charge for a lockbox is *added* to the balance per the bank statement? Explain your answer.
6. How do the duties of an internal audit staff differ from those of the external auditors?
7. What is the typical composition of a board of directors of a publicly held corporation?
8. An order clerk fills out a purchase requisition for an expensive item of inventory and the receiving report when the merchandise arrives. The clerk takes the inventory home and then sends the invoice to the accounting department so that the supplier will be paid. What basic internal control procedure could have prevented this misuse of company assets?
9. What are some of the limitations on a company's effective system of internal control?
10. What two basic procedures are essential to an effective system of internal control over cash?
11. How would you evaluate the following statement? "The only reason a company positions its cash register so that customers can see the display is so customers feel comfortable they are being charged the correct amount for the purchase."
12. Which document, a purchase order or an invoice, is the basis for recording a purchase and a corresponding liability? Explain your answer.
13. What is a blind receiving report and how does it act as a control device?
14. What is the purpose of comparing a purchase invoice with a purchase order? Of comparing a receiving report with a purchase invoice?

Exercises

Exercise 5-1 ***Items on a Bank Reconciliation*** **LO 2**

Assume that a company is preparing a bank reconciliation for the month of June. It reconciles the bank balance and the book balance to the correct balance. For each of the following items, indicate whether the item is an addition to the bank balance (A-Bank), an addition to the book balance (A-Book), a deduction from the bank balance (D-Bank), a deduction from the book balance (D-Book), or would not appear on the June reconciliation (NA).

_______ 1. Check written in June but not yet returned to the bank for payment

_______ 2. Customer's NSF check

_______ 3. Customer's check written in the amount of $54 but recorded on the books in the amount of $45*

_______ 4. Service charge for new checks

______ 5. Principal and interest on a customer's note collected for the company by the bank

______ 6. Customer's check deposited on June 30 but not reflected on the bank statement

______ 7. Check written on the company's account, paid by the bank, and returned with the bank statement

______ 8. Check written on the company's account for $123 but recorded on the books as $132*

______ 9. Interest on the checking account for the month of June

*Answer in terms of the adjustment needed to correct for the error.

Exercise 5-2 *Internal Control* LO 4

The university drama club is planning a raffle. The president overheard you talking about internal control to another accounting student, so she has asked you to set up some guidelines to "be sure" that all money collected for the raffle is accounted for by the club.

Required

1. Describe guidelines that the club should follow to achieve an acceptable level of internal control.
2. Comment on the president 's request that she "be sure" all money is collected and recorded.

Exercise 5-3 *Segregation of Duties* LO 4

The following tasks are performed by three employees, each of whom is capable of performing all of them. Do not concern yourself with the time required to perform the tasks but with the need to provide for segregation of duties. Assign the duties by using a check mark to indicate which employee should perform each task. Remember that you may assign any one of the tasks to any of the employees.

	Employee		
Task	**Mary**	**Sue**	**John**
Prepare invoices			
Mail invoices			
Pick up mail from post office			
Open mail, separate checks			
List checks on deposit slip in triplicate			
Post payment to customer's account			
Deposit checks			
Prepare monthly schedule of accounts receivable			
Reconcile bank statements			

Multi-Concept Exercises

Exercise 5-4 *Composition of Cash* LO 1, 2

Using a Y for yes or an N for no, indicate whether each of the following items should be included in cash and cash equivalents on the balance sheet. If an item should not be included in cash and cash equivalents, indicate where it should appear on the balance sheet.

______ 1. Checking account at Third County Bank

______ 2. Petty cash fund

______ 3. Coin and currency

______ 4. Postage stamps

______ 5. An IOU from an employee

______ 6. Savings account at the Ft. Worth Savings & Loan

______ 7. A six-month CD

______ 8. Undeposited customer checks

______ 9. A customer's check returned by the bank and marked NSF

______ 10. Sixty-day U.S. Treasury bills

______ 11. A cashier's check

Exercise 5-5 *Cash Equivalents* **LO 1, 2**

Systematic Enterprises invested its excess cash in the following instruments during December 2004:

Certificate of deposit, due January 31, 2007	$ 75,000
Certificate of deposit, due March 30, 2005	150,000
Commercial paper, original maturity date February 28, 2005	125,000
Deposit into a money market fund	25,000
Investment in stock	65,000
90-day Treasury bills	100,000
Treasury note, due December 1, 2034	500,000

Required

Determine the amount of cash equivalents which should be combined with cash on the company's balance sheet at December 31, 2004, and for purposes of preparing a statement of cash flows for the year ended December 31, 2004.

Problems

Problem 5-1 *Bank Reconciliation* **LO 2**

The following information is available to assist you in preparing a bank reconciliation for Calico Corners on May 31, 2004:

a. The balance on the May 31, 2004, bank statement is $8,432.11.

b. Not included on the bank statement is a $1,250.00 deposit made by Calico Corners late on May 31.

c. A comparison between the canceled checks returned with the bank statement and the company records indicated that the following checks are outstanding at May 31:

No. 123	$ 23.40
No. 127	145.00
No. 128	210.80
No. 130	67.32

d. The Cash account on the company's books shows a balance of $9,965.34.

e. The bank acts as a collection agency for interest earned on some municipal bonds held by Calico Corners. The May bank statement indicates interest of $465.00 earned during the month.

f. Interest earned on the checking account and added to Calico Corners' account during May was $54.60. Miscellaneous bank service charges amounted to $50.00.

g. A customer's NSF check in the amount of $166.00 was returned with the May bank statement.

h. A comparison between the deposits listed on the bank statement and the company's books revealed that a customer's check in the amount of $123.45 was recorded on the books during May but was never added to the company's account. The bank erroneously added the check to the account of Calico Closet, which has an account at the same bank.

i. The comparison of deposits per the bank statement with those per the books revealed that another customer's check in the amount of $101.10 was correctly added to the company's account. In recording the check on the company's books, however, the accountant erroneously increased the Cash account $1,011.00.

Required

1. Prepare a bank reconciliation in good form.
2. A friend says to you: "I don't know why companies bother to prepare bank reconciliations—it seems a waste of time. Why don't they just do like I do and adjust the cash account for any difference between what the bank shows as a balance and what shows up in the books?" Explain to your friend *why* a bank reconciliation should be prepared as soon as a bank statement is received.

DECISION MAKING

Problem 5-2 *Internal Control Procedures* **LO 4**

You are opening a summer business, a chain of three drive-thru snow-cone stands. You have hired other college students to work and have purchased a cash register with locked-in tapes. You retain one key, and the other is available to the lead person on each shift.

Required

1. Write a list of the procedures for all employees to follow when ringing up sales and giving change.
2. Write a list of the procedures for the lead person to follow in closing out at the end of the day. Be as specific as you can so that employees will have few if any questions.
3. What is your main concern in the design of internal control for the snow-cone stands? How did you address that concern? Be specific.

Problem 5-3 ***The Design of Internal Control Documents*** **LO 5**

Motel $49.99 has purchased a large warehouse to store all supplies used by housekeeping departments in the company's expanding chain of motels. In the past, each motel bought supplies from local distributors and paid for the supplies from cash receipts.

Required

1. Name some potential problems with the old system.
2. Design a purchase requisition form and a receiving report to be used by the housekeeping departments and the warehouse. Indicate how many copies of each form should be used and who should receive each copy.

Multi-Concept Problems

Problem 5-4 ***Cash and Liquid Assets on the Balance Sheet*** **LO 1, 2**

The following accounts are listed in a company's general ledger. The accountant wants to place the items in order of liquidity on the balance sheet.

Accounts receivable
Certificates of deposit (six months)
Investment in stock
Prepaid rent
Money market fund
Petty cash fund

Required

Rank the accounts in terms of liquidity. Identify items to be included in the total of cash, and explain why the items not included in cash on the balance sheet are not as liquid as cash. Explain how these items should be classified.

Problem 5-5 ***Internal Control*** **LO 3, 4**

At Morris Mart Inc. all sales are on account. Mary Morris-Manning is responsible for mailing invoices to customers, recording the amount billed, opening mail, and recording the payment. Mary is very devoted to the family business and never takes off more than one or two days for a long weekend. The customers know Mary and sometimes send personal notes with their payments. Another clerk handles all aspects of accounts payable. Mary's brother, who is president of Morris Mart, has hired an accountant to help with expansion.

Required

1. List some problems with the current accounts receivable system.
2. What suggestions would you make to improve internal control?
3. How would you explain to Mary that she personally is not the problem?

Alternate Problems

Problem 5-1A ***Bank Reconciliation*** **LO 2**

The following information is available to assist you in preparing a bank reconciliation for Karen's Catering on March 31, 2004:

a. The balance on the March 31, 2004, bank statement is $6,506.10.
b. Not included on the bank statement is a deposit made by Karen's late on March 31 in the amount of $423.00.

(continued)

c. A comparison between the canceled checks listed on the bank statement and the company records indicated that the following checks are outstanding at March 31:

No. 112	$ 42.92
No. 117	307.00
No. 120	10.58
No. 122	75.67

d. The bank acts as a collection agency for checks returned for insufficient funds. The March bank statement indicates that one such check in the amount of $45.00 was collected and deposited and a collection fee of $4.50 was charged.

e. Interest earned on the checking account and credited to Karen's account during March was $4.30. Miscellaneous bank service charges amounted to $22.00.

f. A comparison between the deposits listed on the bank statement and the company's books revealed that a customer's check in the amount of $1,250.00 appears on the bank statement in March but was never credited to the customer's account on the company's books.

g. The comparison of checks cleared per the bank statement with those per the books revealed that the wrong amount was charged to the company's account for a check. The amount of the check was $990.00. The proof machine encoded the check in the amount of $909.00, the amount charged against the company's account.

Required

1. Determine the balance on the books before any adjustments as well as the corrected balance to be reported on the balance sheet.
2. What would you recommend Karen do as a result of the bank error in item **g** above? Why?

Problem 5-2A ***Internal Control Procedures*** **LO 4**

The loan department in a bank is subject to regulation. Internal auditors work for the bank to ensure that the loan department complies with requirements. The internal auditors must verify that each car loan file has a note signed by the maker, verification of insurance, and a title issued by the state that names the bank as co-owner.

Required

1. Explain why the bank and the regulatory agency are concerned with these documents.
2. Describe the internal control procedures that should be in place to ensure that these documents are obtained and safeguarded.

Problem 5-3A ***The Design of Internal Control Documents*** **LO 5**

Tiger's Group is a newly formed company that produces and sells children's movies about an imaginary character. The movies are in such great demand that they are shipped to retail outlets as soon as they are produced. The company must pay a royalty to several actors for each movie that it sold to retail outlets.

Required

1. Describe some internal control features that should be in place to ensure that all royalties are paid to the actors.
2. Design the shipping form that Tiger's Group should use for the movies. Be sure to include authorizations and indicate the number of copies and the routing of the copies.

Alternate Multi-Concept Problems

Problem 5-4A ***Cash and Liquid Assets on the Balance Sheet*** **LO 1, 2**

The following accounts are listed in a company's general ledger:

	December 31, 2004	December 31, 2003
Accounts receivable	$12,300	$10,000
Certificates of deposit (three months)	10,000	10,000
Marketable securities	4,500	4,000
Prepaid rent	1,200	1,500
Money market fund	25,800	28,000
Cash in checking account	6,000	6,000

Required

1. Which items are cash equivalents?
2. Explain where items that are not cash equivalents should be classified on the balance sheet.
3. What are the amount and the direction of change in cash and cash equivalents for 2004? Is the company as liquid at the end of 2004 as it was at the end of 2003? Explain your answer.

Problem 5-5A *Internal Control* LO 3, 4

Abbott Inc. is expanding and needs to hire more personnel in the accounting office. Barbara Barker, the chief accounting clerk, knew that her cousin Cheryl was looking for a job. Barbara and Cheryl are also roommates. Barbara offered Cheryl a job as her assistant. Barbara will be responsible for Cheryl's performance reviews and training.

Required

1. List some problems with the proposed personnel situations in the accounting department.
2. Explain why accountants are concerned with the hiring of personnel. What suggestions would you make to improve internal control at Abbott?
3. How would you explain to Barbara and Cheryl that they personally are not the problem?

Decision Cases

Reading and Interpreting Financial Statements

Decision Case 5-1 *Comparing Two Companies in the Same Industry: Winnebago Industries and Monaco Coach Corporation* LO 1

Refer to the financial information for Winnebago Industries and Monaco Coach Corporation reproduced in Appendices A and B of the book.

http://www.winnebagoind.com
http://www.monacocoach.com

Required:

1. What is the balance in "Cash and cash equivalents" on the balance sheet of Winnebago Industries on August 31, 2002? What is the amount of increase or decrease in this balance from August 25, 2001?
2. On what other statement in Winnebago Industries' annual report does the increase or decrease in cash and cash equivalents appear? Explain why it appears on this statement.
3. Note the *absence* of a cash account on the balance sheet of Monaco Coach Corporation. Also note that the first liability listed on its balance sheet is titled "Book overdraft." Explain the connection between the lack of a cash account and the book overdraft account. Even though Monaco Coach Corporation does not report a cash account on its balance sheet, what other statement in the annual report has lines for the net change in cash, the balance at the beginning of the period, and the balance at the end of the period? What amounts appear for each of these lines?

Decision Case 5-2 *Reading and Interpreting Gap Inc.'s Management Report* LO 3

Gap Inc.'s 2002 annual report includes a management's report. Included in the report is the following:

http://www.gap.com

> In fulfilling its responsibility for the reliability of financial information, Management has established and maintains accounting systems and procedures appropriately supported by internal accounting controls. Such controls include the selection and training of qualified personnel, an organizational structure providing for division of responsibility, communication of requirement for compliance with approved accounting control and business practices and a program of internal audit. The extent of our system of internal accounting control recognizes that the cost should not exceed the benefits derived and that the evaluation of those factors requires estimates and judgments by Management.

Required:

1. Why did management include this statement in the annual report?
2. What types of costs does Gap Inc. have in mind when it states that "the cost should not exceed the benefits derived"?

(continued)

3. Based on what you know about retail stores, and Gap Inc. stores in particular, list the kinds of accounting and system controls the company may have in place to safeguard assets.

Making Financial Decisions

Decision Case 5-3 ***Liquidity*** **LO 1, 2**

R Montague and J Capulet both distribute films to movie theaters. The following are the current assets for each at the end of the year (all amounts are in millions of dollars):

	R Montague	J Capulet
Cash	$10	$ 5
Six-month certificates of deposit	9	0
Short-term investments in stock	0	6
Accounts receivable	15	23
Allowance for doubtful accounts	(1)	(1)
Total current assets	$33	$33

Required

As a loan officer for the First National Bank of Verona Heights, assume that both companies have come to you asking for a $10 million, six-month loan. If you could lend money to only one of the two, which one would it be? Justify your answer by writing a brief memo to the president of the bank.

Accounting and Ethics: What Would You Do?

Decision Case 5-4 ***Cash Receipts in a Bookstore*** **LO 3, 4**

ETHICS

You were recently hired by a large retail bookstore chain. Your training involved spending a week at the largest and most profitable store in the district. The store manager assigned the head cashier to train you on the cash register and closing procedures required by the company's home office. In the process, the head cashier instructed you to keep an envelope for cash over and short that would include cash or IOUs equal to the net amount of overages or shortages in the cash drawer. "It is impossible to balance exactly, so just put extra cash in this envelope and use the cash when you are short." You studied accounting for one semester in college and remembered your professor saying that "all deposits should be made intact, daily."

Required

Draft a memorandum to the store manager detailing any problems you see with the current system. This memo should address the issue of the reliability of the cash receipts number. It should also answer the following question, "Does this method provide information to the company that would enable someone to detect whether or not theft has occurred during the particular day in question?" Your memo should suggest an alternative method of internal control for cash receipts.

THOMSON ONE Business School Edition Case

Case 5-5 ***Using THOMSON ONE for Gap, Inc.***

http://www.gap.com

In the chapter we saw the critical role that cash and the appropriate control of it play in the success of a company. The ability to manage and control cash should translate to success in the market for a company's stock in the form of appreciation in its stock price and, if the company chooses, in the form of dividends to the stockholders. We can use THOMSON ONE to obtain information about Gap Inc.'s performance as measured in its financial statements and in its stock price.

Begin by entering the company's ticker symbol, GPS, and then selecting "GO." On the opening screen you will see background information about the company, key financial ratios, and some recent data concerning stock price. To research the company's stock price further, click the "Prices" tab. At the top of the Price Chart, click on the "Interactive Chart." To obtain a 1-year chart, go to "Time Frame," click on the down arrow, and select "1 year." Then click on "Draw," and a 1-year chart should appear.

We can also find Gap Inc.'s most recent financial statements. Near the top of the screen, click on "Financials" and select "Financial Statements." Refer to the comparative statements of earnings, statements of cash flows, and balance sheets.

Based on your use of THOMSON ONE, answer the following questions:

1. For the most recent year available, what are Gap Inc.'s net sales and net earnings? How do they compare with the 2002 fiscal year, as mentioned in the Focus on Financial Results chapter opening vignette? What are some of the explanations for the changes in both net sales and net earnings since 2002?
2. For the most recent year available, what is Gap Inc.'s cash and equivalents balance on its balance sheet? Does this amount represent an increase or decrease from the amount of cash on hand at the end of 2002? What are some of the possible explanations for the change in cash and equivalents?
3. Gap Inc. measures it net debt position as the excess of total long-term liabilities over cash and equivalents. For the most recent year available, what is the company's net debt position? How does this compare with its position at the end of 2002? What are some of the possible explanations for the change in net debt position?
4. What have been Gap Inc.'s high and low stock prices for the most recent year?
5. How does the company's stock performance compare to the other line on the stock price chart for the S&P 500?

Solutions to Key Terms Quiz

8	Cash equivalent (p. 219)	2	Board of directors (p. 226)
11	Bank statement (p. 221)	16	Audit committee (p. 226)
10	Outstanding check (p. 222)	12	Foreign Corrupt Practices Act (p. 226)
13	Deposit in transit (p. 222)	14	Accounting system (p. 228)
7	Bank reconciliation (p. 223)	20	Administrative controls (p. 228)
15	Credit memoranda (p. 223)	4	Accounting controls (p. 228)
9	Debit memoranda (p. 223)	5	Purchase requisition form (p. 232)
17	Petty cash fund (p. 225)	21	Purchase order (p. 234)
3	Internal control system (p. 226)	1	Invoice (p. 235)
18	Report of management (p. 226)	19	Blind receiving report (p. 235)
22	Internal audit staff (p. 226)	6	Invoice approval form (p. 236)

Chapter 6

Investments and Receivables

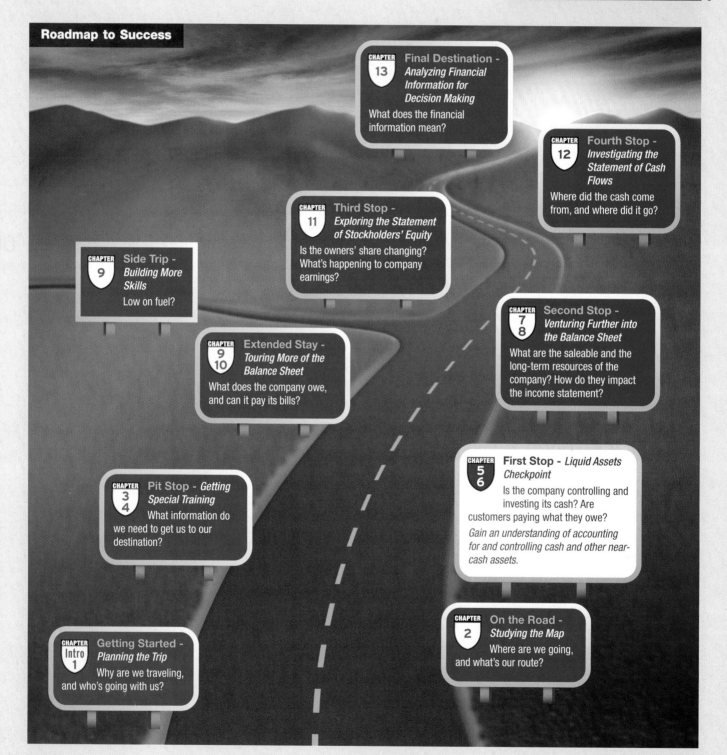

Roadmap to Success

CHAPTER 13 **Final Destination** - *Analyzing Financial Information for Decision Making*
What does the financial information mean?

CHAPTER 12 **Fourth Stop** - *Investigating the Statement of Cash Flows*
Where did the cash come from, and where did it go?

CHAPTER 11 **Third Stop** - *Exploring the Statement of Stockholders' Equity*
Is the owners' share changing? What's happening to company earnings?

CHAPTER 9 **Side Trip** - *Building More Skills*
Low on fuel?

CHAPTER 7 8 **Second Stop** - *Venturing Further into the Balance Sheet*
What are the saleable and the long-term resources of the company? How do they impact the income statement?

CHAPTER 9 10 **Extended Stay** - *Touring More of the Balance Sheet*
What does the company owe, and can it pay its bills?

CHAPTER 5 6 **First Stop** - *Liquid Assets Checkpoint*
Is the company controlling and investing its cash? Are customers paying what they owe?
Gain an understanding of accounting for and controlling cash and other near-cash assets.

CHAPTER 3 4 **Pit Stop** - *Getting Special Training*
What information do we need to get us to our destination?

CHAPTER 2 **On the Road** - *Studying the Map*
Where are we going, and what's our route?

CHAPTER Intro 1 **Getting Started** - *Planning the Trip*
Why are we traveling, and who's going with us?

Focus on Financial Results

For the last few years PepsiCo, one of the world's fastest growing consumer products companies, has been in the business of revamping itself. In the late 1990s, the company sold off some highly recognizable franchising businesses, such as KFC, Pizza Hut, and Taco Bell, to focus attention on its core brands, Frito-Lay snacks, Pepsi-Cola beverages, and Tropicana juices. The new millennium saw the company make the biggest strategic decision of its corporate life when, in 2001, it completed a merger with The Quaker Oats Company. This added not only all of the various Quaker food brands to PepsiCo's portfolio but also Gatorade, the pioneer in sports supplement drinks.

The assets section of PepsiCo's consolidated balance sheet pictured here reflects the combined muscle of the company and its new partner, Quaker Oats. Crucial to the future success of the consumer foods giant will be its ability to react quickly to new opportunities to invest valuable resources. Among the most liquid of these resources are PepsiCo's short-term investments, as shown on the second line of its balance sheet. Consumer food companies like PepsiCo also have sizeable amounts tied up in *accounts and notes receivable,* assets resulting from the commonly accepted business practice of extending credit to customers. The ability to collect from those customers on a timely basis and turn those receivables into cash will be a key factor in determining the success of the new and improved PepsiCo.

PepsiCo's 2002 Annual Report

Consolidated Balance Sheet

PepsiCo, Inc. and Subsidiaries
December 28, 2002 and December 29, 2001

(in millions except per share amounts)	2002	2001
ASSETS		
Current Assets		
Cash and cash equivalents	$ 1,638	$ 683
Short-term investments, at cost (Highly liquid resource)	207	966
	1,845	1,649
Accounts and notes receivable, net (Result of selling to customers on credit)	2,531	2,142
Inventories	1,342	1,310
Prepaid expenses and other current assets	695	752
Total Current Assets	6,413	5,853
Property, Plant and Equipment, net	7,390	6,876
Amortizable Intangible Assets, net	801	875
Nonamortizable Intangible Assets	4,418	3,966
Investments in Noncontrolled Affiliates	2,611	2,871
Other Assets	1,841	1,254
Total Assets	$ 23,474	$ 21,695

You're in the Driver's Seat

http://www.pepsico.com

PepsiCo, Inc., prides itself on its ability to earn profits for its shareholders. If you owned shares in the company, what questions would you ask about its liquid resources such as short-term investments and accounts and notes receivable? Study the chapter to find out how information about these assets is used to make decisions.

LEARNING OBJECTIVES

After studying this chapter, you should be able to:

LO 1 Demonstrate an understanding of the accounting for various types of investments companies make. (p. 253)

LO 2 Demonstrate an understanding of how to account for accounts receivable, including bad debts. (p. 263)

LO 3 Demonstrate an understanding of how to account for interest-bearing notes receivable. (p. 271)

LO 4 Demonstrate an understanding of how to account for non-interest-bearing notes receivable. (p. 272)

LO 5 Explain various techniques that companies use to accelerate the inflow of cash from sales. (p. 273)

LO 6 Explain the effects of transactions involving liquid assets on the statement of cash flows. (p. 275)

WHAT EXTERNAL DECISION MAKERS WANT TO KNOW ABOUT SHORT-TERM INVESTMENTS AND RECEIVABLES

DECISION MAKING

Both short-term investments and receivables are highly liquid assets. At some point in time, companies need to convert investments and receivables into cash in order to pay debts as they fall due. The liquidity of a business is of concern to stockholders, creditors, and others with a vested interest in that company's future. Creditors in particular need some assurance that short-term investments can be converted into cash in the near future. And they need to know whether all or some lesser percentage of the receivables are likely to be collected.

To be successful, decision makers must:

▶ *ASK ESSENTIAL QUESTIONS*

- What are the various investments the company has made?
- What is the annual amount of interest or dividends that the investments pay?
- What is the current market value of the investments?
- What is the net realizable value of the company's accounts receivables?
- Does the company have any other receivables outstanding, such as interest-bearing or non-interest-bearing notes receivable, and if so, what are their values?

▶ *FIND BASIC INFORMATION*

The balance sheet and income statement, along with the supporting notes, provide the information decision makers need about a company's investments and receivables. Specifically, this information tells

- the cost and market value of the company's investments,
- the dividends or interest that were received from the investments
- any gains or losses from sale of the investments
- the gross amount of accounts receivables and any allowance for doubtful accounts
- the carrying value of any other receivables

▶ *UNDERSTAND ACCOUNTING PRINCIPLES*

To understand the basic information that is found, decision makers must understand the underlying accounting principles (GAAP) that have been applied to create the reported information. These principles determine:

- how investments are reported on a company's balance sheet

- how periodic income is recognized from these investments, as well as any gains and losses from sale of the investments
- how accounts and notes receivable are reported on the balance sheet and how bad debts affect a company's earnings

▶ *INTERPRET ANALYTICAL INFORMATION*

Various ratios and other analytical tools are available to help decision makers assess a company's liquidity. As we saw in an earlier chapter, two of the most important of these are the current and quick ratios. The first is an indication of the relative amount of a company's current assets to its current liabilities. The quick ratio is similar to the current ratio, but it excludes inventory and prepayments from the numerator. Both short-term investments and accounts receivable are not only current assets but also quick assets and are thus included in both ratios. Both investors and creditors are interested in a company's ability to collect its receivables in a timely fashion. An important measure in this regard is the accounts receivable turnover ratio that is computed by dividing net credit sales by average accounts receivable.

PepsiCo Inc., like all other businesses, relies on *liquid assets* to function smoothly. *Liquidity* is a relative term. It deals with a company's ability to pay its debts as they fall due. Most obligations must be paid in cash, and therefore cash is considered the most liquid of all assets. Accounts and notes receivable are not as liquid as cash. Their collection does result in an inflow of cash, however. Because cash in its purest form does not earn a return, most businesses invest in various types of securities as a way to use idle cash over the short term. The Current Assets section of PepsiCo's balance sheet, as shown in the chapter opener, indicates three highly liquid assets: cash and cash equivalents, short-term investments, and accounts and notes receivable. Inventories are not considered as liquid as these three assets because they depend on a sale to be realized.

In the prior chapter, we considered the various forms cash can take and the importance of cash control to a business. Some companies invest cash in various types of financial instruments, as well as in the stocks and bonds of other companies. This chapter illustrates the accounting for these investments. In many instances the cash available to make these investments comes from the collection of receivables. The chapter concludes with a discussion of the accounting both for accounts receivable and for notes receivable.

ACCOUNTING FOR INVESTMENTS

LO 1 Demonstrate an understanding of the accounting for various types of investments companies make.

The investments that companies make take a variety of forms and are made for various reasons. Some corporations find themselves with excess cash during certain times of the year and invest this idle cash in various highly liquid financial instruments, such as certificates of deposit and money market funds. In Chapter 5 it was pointed out that these investments are included with cash and are called cash equivalents if they have an original maturity to the investor of three months or less. Otherwise they are accounted for as short-term investments.

In addition to investments in highly liquid financial instruments, some companies invest in the stocks and bonds of other corporations, as well as bonds issued by various government agencies. Securities issued by corporations as a form of ownership in the business, such as common stock and preferred stock, are called **equity securities.** Because these securities are a form of ownership, they do not have a maturity date. As we will see later, investments in equity securities can be classified as either current or long term, depending on the company's intent. Alternatively, bonds issued by corporations and governmental bodies as a form of borrowing are called **debt securities.** The term of a bond can be relatively short, such as 5 years, or much longer, such as 20 or 30 years. Regardless of the term, classification as a current or noncurrent asset by the investor depends on whether it plans to sell the debt securities within the next year.

Equity securities Securities issued by corporations as a form of ownership in the business.

Debt securities Bonds issued by corporations and governmental bodies as a form of borrowing.

INVESTMENTS IN HIGHLY LIQUID FINANCIAL INSTRUMENTS

We now turn our attention to the appropriate accounting for these various types of investments. We begin by considering the accounting for highly liquid financial instruments such as certificates of deposit and then turn to the accounting for investments in the stocks and bonds of other companies.

Investing Idle Cash

The seasonal nature of most businesses leads to the potential for a shortage of cash during certain times of the year and an excess of cash during other times. Companies typically deal with *cash shortages* by borrowing on a short-term basis, either from a bank in the form of notes or from other entities in the form of commercial paper. The maturities of the bank notes or the commercial paper generally range anywhere from 30 days to six months. These same companies use various financial instruments as a way to invest excess cash during other times of the year. We will present the accounting for the most common type of highly liquid financial instrument, a certificate of deposit (CD).

Accounting for an Investment in a Certificate of Deposit (CD)

Assume that on October 2, 2004, Creston Corp. invests $100,000 of excess cash in a 120-day certificate of deposit. The CD matures on January 30, 2005, at which time Creston receives the $100,000 invested and interest at an annual rate of 6%. On October 2, 2004, the company has simply traded one asset for another:

BALANCE SHEET					INCOME STATEMENT
ASSETS	=	LIABILITIES	+	OWNERS' EQUITY	+ REVENUES − EXPENSES
Short-Term Investments—CD 100,000					
Cash (100,000)					

Assuming December 31 is the end of Creston's fiscal year, an adjustment is needed on this date to record interest earned during 2004, even though no cash will be received until the CD matures in 2005. The adjustment recognizes a new asset as well as an addition on the income statement:

BALANCE SHEET					INCOME STATEMENT
ASSETS	=	LIABILITIES	+	OWNERS' EQUITY	+ REVENUES − EXPENSES
Interest Receivable 1,500					Interest Income 1,500

The basic formula to compute interest is as follows:

$$\text{Interest } (I) = \text{Principal } (P) \times \text{Interest Rate } (R) \times \text{Time } (T)$$

Because interest rates are normally stated on an annual basis, time is interpreted to mean the fraction of a year that the investment is outstanding. The amount of interest is based on the principal or amount invested ($100,000), times the rate of interest (6%), times the fraction of a year the CD was outstanding in 2004 (29 days in October + 30 days in November + 31 days in December = 90 days). To simplify calculations, it is easiest to assume 360 days in a year in computing interest. With the availability of computers to do the work, however, most businesses now use 365 days in a year to calculate interest. Throughout this book, we assume 360 days in a year to allow us to focus on concepts rather than detailed calculations. Thus, in our example, the fraction of a year that the CD is outstanding during 2004 is 90/360.

The effect of the receipt of the principal amount of the CD of $100,000 and interest for 120 days is:

BALANCE SHEET					INCOME STATEMENT	
ASSETS		= LIABILITIES	+	OWNERS' EQUITY	+ REVENUES – EXPENSES	
Cash	102,000				Interest Income	500
Short-Term Investments—CD	(100,000)					
Interest Receivalbe	(1,500)					

This transaction results in the removal of both the CD and the interest receivable from the records and the recognition of $500 in interest earned during the first 30 days of 2005: $100,000 × 0.06 × 30/360 = $500.

We now turn to situations in which companies invest in the stocks and bonds of other companies.

INVESTMENTS IN STOCKS AND BONDS

Corporations frequently invest in the securities of other businesses. These investments take two forms: debt securities and equity securities.

Corporations have varying motivations for investing in the stocks and bonds of other companies. We will refer to the company that invests as the *investor* and the company whose stocks or bonds are purchased as the *investee.* In addition to buying certificates of deposit and other financial instruments, companies invest excess funds in stocks and bonds over the short run. The seasonality of certain businesses may result in otherwise idle cash being available during certain times of the year. In other cases, stocks and bonds are purchased as a way to invest cash over the long run. Often these types of investments are made in anticipation of a need for cash at some distant point in the future. For example, a company may invest today in a combination of stocks and bonds because it will need cash 10 years from today to build a new plant. The investor may be primarily interested in periodic income in the form of interest and dividends, in appreciation in the value of the securities, or in some combination of the two.

Sometimes shares of stock in another company are bought with a different purpose in mind. If a company buys a relatively large percentage of the common stock of the investee, it may be able to secure significant influence over the policies of this company. For example, a company may buy 30% of the common stock of a supplier of its raw materials to ensure a steady source of inventory. When an investor is able to secure influence over the investee, the *equity method* of accounting is used. According to current accounting standards, this method is appropriate when an investor owns at least 20% of the common stock of the investee.

Finally, a corporation may buy stock in another company with the purpose of obtaining control over that other entity. Normally, this requires an investment in excess of 50% of the common stock of the investee. When an investor owns more than half the stock of another company, accountants normally prepare a set of *consolidated financial statements.* This involves combining the financial statements of the individual entities into a single set of statements. An investor with an interest of more than 50% in another company is called the *parent,* and the investee in these situations is called the *subsidiary.*

We will limit our discussion to how companies account for investments that do *not* give them any significant influence over the other company. (Accounting for investments in which there is either significant influence or control is covered in advanced accounting textbooks.) The following chart summarizes the accounting by an investor for investments in the common stock of another company:

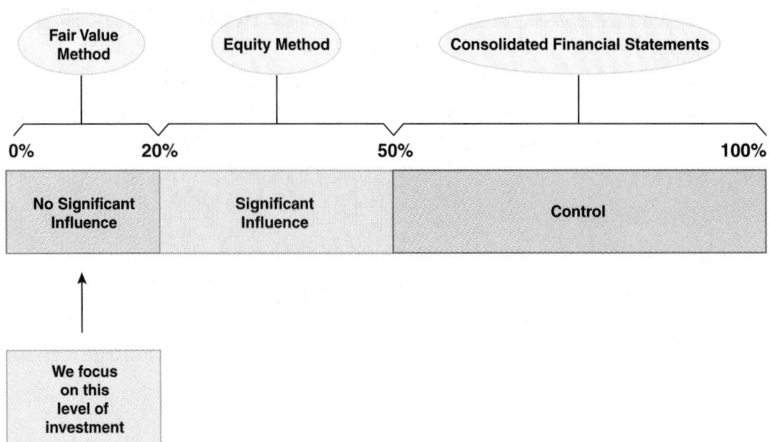

INVESTMENTS WITHOUT SIGNIFICANT INFLUENCE

Companies face a number of major issues in deciding how to account for and report on investments in the stocks and bonds of other companies:

1. What should be the basis for the recognition of periodic income from an investment? That is, what event causes income to be recognized?
2. How should an investment be valued and thus reported at the end of an accounting period? At original cost? At fair value?
3. How should an investment be classified on a balance sheet? As a current asset? As a noncurrent asset?

The answer to each of these questions depends on the type of investment. Accountants classify investments in the securities of other companies into one of three categories.[1]

Held-to-maturity securities Investments in bonds of other companies in which the investor has the positive intent and the ability to hold the securities to maturity.

Trading securities Stock and bonds of other companies bought and held for the purpose of selling them in the near term to generate profits on appreciation in their price.

Available-for-sale securities Stocks and bonds that are not classified as either held-to-maturity or trading securities.

Held-to-maturity securities are investments in the bonds of other companies when the investor has the positive intent and the ability to hold the securities to maturity. *Note that only bonds can qualify as held-to-maturity securities because shares of stock do not have a maturity date.*

Trading securities are stocks and bonds that are bought and held for the purpose of selling them in the near term. These securities are usually held for only a short period of time with the objective of generating profits on short-term appreciation in the market price of the stocks and bonds.

Available-for-sale securities are stocks and bonds that are not classified as either held-to-maturity or trading securities.

Investments in Held-to-Maturity Securities

By their nature, only bonds, not stock, can qualify as held-to-maturity securities. A bond is categorized as a held-to-maturity security if the investor plans to hold it until it matures. An investor may buy the bonds either on the original issuance date or later. If the investor buys them on the date they are originally issued, the purchase is from the issuer. It is also possible, however, for an investor to buy bonds on the *open market* after they have been outstanding for a period of time.

[1] *Statement of Financial Accounting Standards No. 115,* "Accounting for Certain Investments in Debt and Equity Securities" (Stamford, Conn.: Financial Accounting Standards Board, May 1993), pars. 7–12.

Consider the following example. On January 1, 2004, Simpson issues $10,000,000 of bonds that will mature in ten years. Homer buys $100,000 in face value of these bonds at face value, which is the amount that will be repaid to the investor when the bonds mature. In many instances, bonds are purchased at an amount more or less than face value. We will limit our discussion, however, to the simpler case in which bonds are purchased for face value. The bonds pay 10% interest semiannually on June 30 and December 31. This means Homer will receive 5% of $100,000 or $5,000 on each of these dates. The effect of the purchase on the accounting equation is as follows:

BALANCE SHEET					INCOME STATEMENT
ASSETS	=	LIABILITIES	+	OWNERS' EQUITY	+ REVENUES − EXPENSES
Investment in Bonds 100,000 Cash (100,000)					

On June 30, Homer must record the receipt of semiannual interest. The effect of the receipt of interest on this date would be:

BALANCE SHEET					INCOME STATEMENT
ASSETS	=	LIABILITIES	+	OWNERS' EQUITY	+ REVENUES − EXPENSES
Cash 5,000					Interest Income 5,000

Note that income was recognized when interest was received. If interest is not received at the end of an accounting period, a company should accrue interest earned but not yet received. Also note that an investment in held-to-maturity bonds is normally classified as a noncurrent asset. Any held-to-maturity bonds that are one year or less from maturity, however, are classified in the current assets section of a balance sheet.

Assume that before the maturity date, Homer needs cash and decides to sell the bonds. Keep in mind that this is a definite change in Homer's plans, since the bonds were initially categorized as held-to-maturity securities. Any difference between the proceeds received from the sale of the bonds and the amount paid for the bonds is recognized as either a gain or a loss.

Assume that on January 1, 2005, Homer sells all its Simpson bonds at 99. This means that the amount of cash received is .99 × $100,000, or $99,000. The effect on the accounting equation from the sale of the bonds is

BALANCE SHEET					INCOME STATEMENT
ASSETS	=	LIABILITIES	+	OWNERS' EQUITY	+ REVENUES − EXPENSES
Cash 99,000 Investment in Bonds (100,000)					Loss on Sale of Bonds (1,000)

The $1,000 loss on the sale of the bonds is the excess of the amount paid for the purchase of the bonds of $100,000 over the cash proceeds from the sale of $99,000. The loss is reported in the Other Income and Expenses section on the 2005 income statement.

Investments in Trading Securities

A company invests in trading securities as a way to profit from increases in the market prices of these securities over the short term. Because the intent is to hold them for the short term, trading securities are classified as current assets. All trading securities are recorded initially at cost, including any brokerage fees, commissions, or other fees paid to acquire the shares. Assume that Dexter Corp. invests in the following securities on November 30, 2004:

SECURITY	COST
Stuart common stock	$50,000
Menlo preferred stock	25,000
Total cost	$75,000

When Dexter buys the stocks, investments are increased and cash is reduced:

BALANCE SHEET					INCOME STATEMENT	
ASSETS		= LIABILITIES	+ OWNERS' EQUITY		+ REVENUES – EXPENSES	
Investment in Stuart Common Stock	50,000					
Investment in Menlo Preferred Stock	25,000					
Cash	(75,000)					

Many companies attempt to pay dividends every year as a signal of overall financial strength and profitability.[2] Assume that on December 10, 2004, Dexter received dividends of $1,000 from Stuart and $600 from Menlo. The dividends received from trading securities are recognized as income, as shown in the accounting equation:

BALANCE SHEET					INCOME STATEMENT	
ASSETS		= LIABILITIES	+ OWNERS' EQUITY		+ REVENUES – EXPENSES	
Cash	1,600				Dividend Income	1,600

Unlike interest on a bond or a note, dividends do not accrue over time. In fact, a company does not have a legal obligation to pay dividends until its board of directors declares them. Up to that point, the investor has no guarantee that dividends will ever be paid.

As noted earlier, trading securities are purchased with the intention of holding them for a short period of time. Assume that Dexter sells the Stuart stock on December 15, 2004, for $53,000. In this case, Dexter recognizes a gain for the excess of the cash proceeds, $53,000, over the amount recorded on the books, $50,000:

BALANCE SHEET					INCOME STATEMENT	
ASSETS		= LIABILITIES	+ OWNERS' EQUITY		+ REVENUES – EXPENSES	
Cash	53,000				Gain on Sale of Stock	3,000
Investment in Stuart Common Stock	(50,000)					

For accounting purposes, the gain is considered realized and is classified on the income statement as other income.

Assume that on December 22, 2004, Dexter replaces the Stuart stock in its portfolio by purchasing Canby common stock for $40,000:

BALANCE SHEET					INCOME STATEMENT	
ASSETS		= LIABILITIES	+ OWNERS' EQUITY		+ REVENUES – EXPENSES	
Investment in Canby Common Stock	40,000					
Cash	(40,000)					

[2]IBM's June 2003 dividend was the computer company's 353rd consecutive quarterly dividend, an uninterrupted string of more than 88 years in which it paid dividends.

Now, assume that Dexter ends its accounting period on December 31. Should it adjust the carrying value of its investments to reflect their fair values on this date? According to the accounting profession, fair values should be used to report investments in trading securities on a balance sheet. The fair values are thought to be relevant information to the various users of financial statements. Assume the following information for Dexter on December 31, 2004:

SECURITY	TOTAL COST	TOTAL FAIR VALUE ON DECEMBER 31, 2004	GAIN (LOSS)
Menlo preferred stock	$25,000	$27,500	$2,500
Canby common stock	40,000	39,000	(1,000)
Totals	$65,000	$66,500	$1,500

On December 31, Dexter will make an adjustment in its records that has the following effect on the accounting equation:

BALANCE SHEET						INCOME STATEMENT
ASSETS	=	LIABILITIES	+	OWNERS' EQUITY	+	REVENUES – EXPENSES
Investment in Menlo Preferred Stock 2,500						Unrealized Gain—Trading Securities 1,500
Investement in Canby Common Stock (1,000)						

Note that this adjustment results in each security being written up or down so that it will appear on the December 31 balance sheet at its market or fair value. This type of fair value accounting for trading securities is often referred to as a *mark to market* approach because at the end of each period, the value of each security is adjusted to its current market value. Also, it is important to realize that for trading securities, the changes in value are recognized on the income statement. The difference of $1,500 between the original cost of the two securities, $65,000, and their fair value, $66,500, is recorded in the account Unrealized Gain—Trading Securities to call attention to the fact that the securities have not been sold. Even though the gain or loss is *unrealized*, it is recognized on the income statement as a form of other income or loss.

Assume one final transaction in our Dexter example. On January 20, 2005, Dexter sells the Menlo stock for $27,000. The effect on the accounting equation of the sale is as follows:

BALANCE SHEET						INCOME STATEMENT
ASSETS	=	LIABILITIES	+	OWNERS' EQUITY	+	REVENUES – EXPENSES
Cash 27,000						Loss on Sale of Stock (500)
Investment in Menlo Preferred Stock (27,500)						

The important point to note about this entry is that the $500 loss represents the difference between the cash proceeds of $27,000 and the *fair value of the stock at the most recent reporting date,* $27,500. Because the Menlo stock was adjusted to a fair value of $27,500 on December 31, the excess of this amount over the cash proceeds of $27,000 results in a loss of $500. Keep in mind that a gain of $2,500 was recognized last year when the stock was adjusted to its fair value at the end of the year. Thus the *net* gain from the Menlo stock is the excess of the sales price of $27,000 over the cost of $25,000, or $2,000. The result is that this net amount is recognized in two periods: as a $2,500 holding gain in 2004 and a $500 loss on sale in 2005.

Investments in Available-for-Sale Securities

Stocks and bonds that do not qualify as trading securities and bonds that are not intended to be held to maturity are categorized as available-for-sale securities. The accounting for these securities is similar to the accounting for trading securities, with one major exception: *even though fair value accounting is used to report available-for-sale securities at the end of an accounting period, any gains or losses resulting from marking to market are not reported on the income statement but instead are accumulated in a stockholders' equity account.* This inconsistency is justified by the accounting profession on the grounds that the inclusion in income of fluctuations in the value of securities that are available for sale but that are not necessarily being actively traded could lead to volatility in reported earnings. Regardless, reporting gains and losses on the income statement for one class of securities but not for others is a subject of considerable debate. Investments in available-for-sale securities may be classified as either current or noncurrent assets.

INTERNAL DECISION

To understand the use of fair value accounting for available-for-sale securities, assume that Lenox Corp. purchases two different stocks late in 2004. The costs and fair values at the end of 2004 are as follows:

SECURITY	TOTAL COST	FAIR VALUE ON DECEMBER 31, 2004	GAIN (LOSS)
Adair preferred stock	$15,000	$16,000	$ 1,000
Casey common stock	35,000	32,500	(2,500)
Totals	$50,000	$48,500	$(1,500)

On December 31, Lenox adjusts its records to reflect the changes in value of the two securities:

BALANCE SHEET						INCOME STATEMENT	
ASSETS		= LIABILITIES	+	OWNERS' EQUITY		+ REVENUES – EXPENSES	
Investement in Adair Preferred Stock	1,000			Unrealized Gain/Loss—Available-for-Sale Securities	(1,500)		
Investment in Casey Common Stock	(2,500)						

Note the similarity between this adjustment and the one we made at the end of the period in the example for trading securities. In both instances, the individual investments are adjusted to their fair values for purposes of presenting them on the year-end balance sheet. The unrealized loss of $1,500 does not, however, affect income in this case. Instead, the loss is shown as a reduction of stockholders' equity on the balance sheet.

Now assume that Lenox sells its Casey stock for $34,500 on June 30, 2005. The effect of the sale on the accounting equation is as follows:

BALANCE SHEET						INCOME STATEMENT	
ASSETS		= LIABILITIES	+	OWNERS' EQUITY		+ REVENUES – EXPENSES	
Cash	34,500			Unrealized Gain/Loss—Available-for-Sale Securities	2,500	Loss on Sale of Stock	(500)
Investment in Casey Common Stock	(32,500)						

Lenox recognizes a *realized* loss on the income statement of $500, which represents the excess of the cost of the stock of $35,000 over the cash proceeds of $34,500. Note, however, that the Investment in Casey Common Stock is removed from the books at $32,500, the fair value at the end of the prior period. Thus, it is also necessary to adjust the Unrealized Gain/Loss account for $2,500, the difference between the original cost of $35,000 and the fair value at the end of 2004 of $32,500.

Finally, assume that Lenox does not buy any additional securities during the remainder of 2005 and that the fair value of the one investment it holds, the Adair preferred stock, is $19,000 on December 31, 2005. The adjustment on this date is as follows:

BALANCE SHEET							INCOME STATEMENT
ASSETS		=	LIABILITIES	+	OWNERS' EQUITY		+ REVENUES – EXPENSES
Investement in Adair Preferred Stock	3,000				Unrealized Gain/Loss— Available-for-Sale Securities	3,000	

The increase in the Investment in Adair Preferred Stock account results in a balance of $19,000 in this account, the fair value of the stock. The stockholders' equity account now has a *positive* balance of $4,000, as follows:

Adjustment on December 31, 2004	$(1,500)
Adjustment on June 30, 2005	2,500
Adjustment on December 31, 2005	3,000
Balance on December 31, 2005	$ 4,000

The balance of $4,000 in this account represents the excess of the $19,000 fair value of the one security now held over its original cost of $15,000.

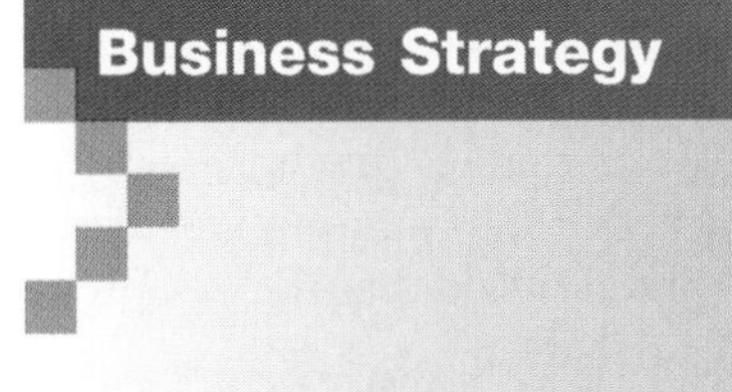

Adding Brands, Growing Sales, and Cutting Costs

The cover of PepsiCo's 2002 annual report proclaims a "Future to Cheer About" and backs up this prediction with statistics on "Performance to Cheer About." The results include growth in comparable earnings per share and net revenues of 14% and 4%, respectively. Keeping with the sports-oriented theme, the company touts a lineup that includes more than 500 products and international divisions that operate in over 175 countries.

Brands are naturally the lifeblood of consumer companies, and PepsiCo is no exception, with a portfolio of 15 brands that each generated more than $1 billion in annual retail sales. Contributing to this lineup of strong brands were those that came on board in August of 2001 when the company completed its merger with The Quaker Oats Company. With this transaction, the new PepsiCo added to its already impressive portfolio such household names as Quaker Oats® and Gatorade®.

Corporate mergers happen for a variety of reasons. Some reap rewards for the various stakeholders and others simply don't work out. With the acquisition of The Quaker Oats Company, PepsiCo undoubtedly hoped to grow sales just as does every other company that goes through a merger. However, part of the strategy also was aimed at achieving significant cost savings. For example, the 2001 annual report explains how PepsiCo was able to use Quaker's warehouse distribution system to deliver its Tropicana products to stores at a lower cost. And by the time the 2002 report came off the presses, the company could report that annual cost savings from the Quaker merger had reached approximately $250 million, exceeding the company's target. With a seemingly unlimited potential for growth and the ability to achieve significant cost savings, it does seem that PepsiCo has a future worth cheering about. ■

Sources: PepsiCo's 2002 and 2001 Annual Reports.

Summary of Accounting and Reporting Requirements

A summary of the accounting and reporting requirements for each of the three categories of investments is shown in Exhibit 6-1. Periodic income from each of these types of investments is recognized in the form of interest and dividends. Held-to-maturity bonds are reported on the balance sheet at *amortized cost* (see second footnote in Exhibit 6-1 below). Both trading securities and available-for-sale securities are reported on the balance sheet at fair value. Unrealized gains and losses from holding trading securities are recognized on the income statement, whereas these same gains and losses for available-for-sale securities are accumulated in a stockholders' equity account.

Exhibit 6-1 Accounting for Investments without Significant Influence

CATEGORIES	TYPES	ASSET CLASSIFIED ON BALANCE SHEET AS	RECOGNIZE AS INCOME	REPORT ON BALANCE SHEET AT	REPORT CHANGES IN FAIR VALUE ON
Held-to-maturity	Bonds	Noncurrent*	Interest	Cost**	Not applicable
Trading	Bonds, stock	Current	Interest, dividends	Fair value	Income statement
Available-for-sale	Bonds, stock	Current or noncurrent	Interest, dividends	Fair value	Balance sheet (in stockholders' equity)

*Reclassified as current if they mature within one year of the balance sheet date.
**As mentioned earlier, bonds are often purchased at an amount more or less than face value. When this is the case, the bond account must be adjusted periodically and the asset is reported on the balance sheet at amortized cost.

The Controversy over Fair Value Accounting

Only recently have accounting standards changed to require that certain investments be reported at fair value. Before the change, the lower-of-cost-or-market rule was followed when accounting for these investments. The use of market or fair values is clearly an exception to the cost principle as first introduced in Chapter 1. Whether the exception is justified has been, and will continue to be, a matter of debate.

One concern of financial statement users is the hybrid system now used to report assets on a balance sheet. Consider the following types of assets and how we report them on the balance sheet:

ASSET	REPORTED ON THE BALANCE SHEET AT
Inventories	Lower of cost or market
Investments	Either cost or fair value
Property, plant, and equipment	Original cost, less accumulated depreciation

It is difficult to justify so many different valuation methods to report the assets of a single company. The lower-of-cost-or-market approach to valuing inventory is based on conservatism. Why should it be used for inventories while fair value is used for investments? Proponents of fair values believe that the information provided to the reader of the statements is more relevant, and they argue that the subjectivity inherent in valuing other types of assets is not an issue when dealing with securities that have a ready market. The controversy surrounding the valuation of assets on a balance sheet is likely to continue.

Which Way to Go? Fair Value, Significant Influence, or Consolidation?

Taz Industries owns $10 million (40%) of the outstanding bonds and 10% of the voting common stock of the MMartian Corporation. In addition, Theron Ross, the president of Taz, is a member of the board of directors of MMartian. The management of MMartian is very interested in responding positively to the

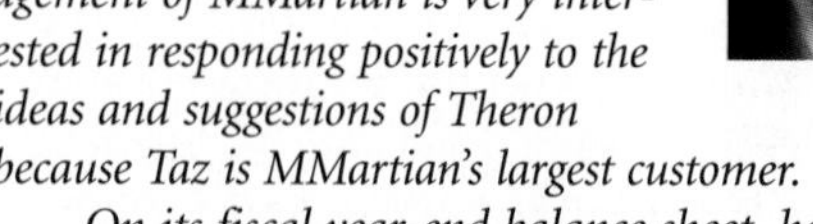

ideas and suggestions of Theron because Taz is MMartian's largest customer.

On its fiscal year-end balance sheet, how should Taz Industries value its investments in the MMartian bonds and common stock? Does Taz have significant influence in the MMartian Corporation? Should Taz use the fair value method, the equity method, or should it prepare consolidated financial statements that include MMartian Corporation's financial information? Why?

Two-Minute Review

1. *What are the three categories of investments?*
2. *Two of the three categories of investments can contain either stocks or bonds. Which one of the three can only contain bonds? Explain your answer.*
3. *What is the one major distinction between the reporting requirements for trading securities and those for available-for-sale securities?*

Answers on page 277.

ACCOUNTS RECEIVABLE

LO 2 Demonstrate an understanding of how to account for accounts receivable, including bad debts.

http://www.sears.com

To appreciate the significance of credit sales for many businesses, consider the case of Sears, Roebuck & Co. Sears operates retail outlets throughout the United States and around the world. The balance sheet of Sears reported total assets of approximately $50 billion at the end of 2002. Of this total amount, credit card receivables accounted for almost $31 billion, or 62%, of total assets. Sears or any other company would rather not sell on credit but would prefer to make all sales for cash. Selling on credit causes two problems: it slows down the inflow of cash to the company, and it raises the possibility that the customer may not pay its bill on time or possibly ever. To remain competitive, however, Sears and most other businesses must sell their products and services on credit. Large retailers such as Sears often extend credit through the use of their own credit cards.

From Concept to Practice 6.1

Reading PepsiCo's Financial Statements

Refer to PepsiCo's partial balance sheet as presented in the chapter opener. By what amount did accounts and notes receivable increase or decrease during 2002? How significant are accounts and notes receivable to the amount of total current assets at the end of 2002? What distinguishes the company's accounts receivable from its notes receivable?

http://www.pepsico.com

The types of receivables reported on a corporate balance sheet depend to some extent on a company's business. The "credit card receivables" on the balance sheet of Sears represent the interest-bearing accounts it carries with its retail customers. Alternatively, consider the case of PepsiCo. The beverage and snack-food businesses usually sell their products to distributors. The asset resulting from a sale by Pepsi on credit, with an oral promise that the customer will pay within a specified period of time, is called an account receivable. This type of account does not bear interest and often gives the customer a discount for early payment. For example, the terms of sale might be 2/10, net 30, which means the customer can deduct 2% from the amount due if the bill is paid within 10 days of the date of sale; otherwise, payment in full is required within 30 days. In some instances, PepsiCo requires from a customer at the time of sale a written promise in the form of a promissory note. The asset resulting from a sale on credit, with a written promise that the customer will pay within a specified period of time, is called a note receivable. This type of account usually bears interest.

The Use of a Subsidiary Ledger

As mentioned earlier, PepsiCo sells its beverages and snack foods through distributors. Assume that it sells $25,000 of Fritos to ABC Distributors on an open account. The sale results in the recognition of an asset and additional revenue:

BALANCE SHEET						INCOME STATEMENT
ASSETS	=	LIABILITIES	+	OWNERS' EQUITY	+	REVENUES − EXPENSES
Accounts Receivable 25,000						Sales Revenue 25,000

It is important for control purposes that PepsiCo keeps a record of *whom* the sale was to and includes this amount on a periodic statement or *bill* sent to the customer. What if a company has a hundred or a thousand different customers? Some mechanism is needed to track the balance owed by each of these customers. The mechanism companies use is called a **subsidiary ledger.**

Subsidiary ledger The detail for a number of individual items that collectively make up a single general ledger account.

Control account The general ledger account that is supported by a subsidiary ledger.

A subsidiary ledger contains the necessary detail on each of a number of items that collectively make up a single general ledger account, called the **control account.** In theory, any one of the accounts in the general ledger could be supported by a subsidiary ledger. In addition to Accounts Receivable, two other common accounts supported by subsidiary ledgers are Plant and Equipment and Accounts Payable. An accounts payable subsidiary ledger contains a separate account for each of the suppliers or vendors from which a company purchases inventory. A plant and equipment subsidiary ledger consists of individual accounts, along with their balances, for each of the various long-term tangible assets the company owns.

It is important to understand that a subsidiary ledger does *not* take the place of the control account in the general ledger. Instead, at any point in time, the balances of the accounts that make up the subsidiary ledger should total to the single balance in the related control account. In the remainder of this chapter we will illustrate the use of only the control account. Whenever a specific customer's account is increased or decreased we will, however, note the name of the customer next to the control account in the journal entry.

The Valuation of Accounts Receivable

The following presentation of receivables is taken from Winnebago Industries' 2002 annual report:

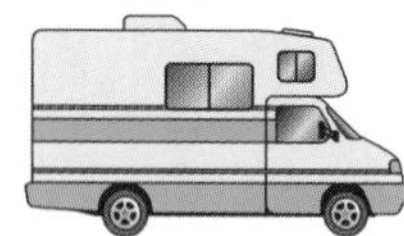

	2002	2001
Receivables, less allowance for doubtful accounts ($120 and $244, respectively)	$28,616	$21,571

As you read this excerpt from the balance sheets, keep two points in mind. First, all amounts are stated in thousands of dollars. Second, these are the balances at the *end* of each of the two years.

Winnebago Industries does not sell its products to distributors under the assumption that any particular customer will *not* pay its bill. In fact, the credit department of a business is responsible for performing a credit check on all potential customers before they are granted credit. Management of Winnebago Industries is not naive enough, however, to believe that all customers will be able to pay their accounts when due. This would be the case only if (1) all customers are completely trustworthy and (2) customers never experience unforeseen financial difficulties that make it impossible to pay on time.

Delivering such products as Pepsi's Frappuccino drink to retail stores on account creates large receivables for PepsiCo. Indeed, receivables are a large and important part of the asset side of balance sheets of many companies.

The reduction in Winnebago Industries' receivables for an allowance is the way in which most companies deal with bad debts in their accounting records. Bad debts are unpaid customer accounts that a company gives up trying to collect. Some companies such as Winnebago Industries describe the allowance more fully as the allowance for doubtful accounts, and others call it the allowance for uncollectible accounts. Using the end of 2002 as an example, Winnebago Industries believes that the *net recoverable amount* of its receivables is $28,616 thousand, even though the *gross* amount of receivables is $120 thousand higher than this amount. The company has reduced the gross receivables for an amount that it believes is necessary to reflect the asset on the books at the *net recoverable amount* or *net realizable value.* We now take a closer look at how a company accounts for bad debts.

Two Methods to Account for Bad Debts

Assume that Roberts Corp. makes a $500 sale to Dexter Inc. on November 10, 2004, with credit terms of 2/10, net 60. The effect on the accounting equation of the sale is as follows:

BALANCE SHEET					INCOME STATEMENT	
ASSETS		= LIABILITIES	+	OWNERS' EQUITY	+ REVENUES − EXPENSES	
Accounts Receivable—Dexter	500				Sales Revenue	500

Accounting for Your Decisions

You Are the Credit Manager

You are the credit manager of USA Department Store, which offers its customers USA Department Store credit cards. An existing customer, Jane Doe, has requested a credit line increase. In processing her request, you must determine the current balance of her account. How would you use the accounting system to find her current balance? What other factors might you consider in granting Jane's request?

ANS: You would find Jane's current balance by looking for her account in the accounts receivable subsidiary ledger. The subsidiary ledger should have a current balance because daily postings are made to each customer's account. Other factors to consider in processing Jane's request can include researching her payment history to see if she paid on time not only for this credit card but for all debts, checking to see if her income is sufficient to cover her existing debt and the new credit line increase, and verifying employment to ensure income stability.

Assume further that Dexter not only misses taking advantage of the discount for early payment but also is unable to pay within 60 days. After pursuing the account for four months into 2005, the credit department of Roberts informs the accounting department that it has given up on collecting the $500 from Dexter and advises that the account should be written off. To do so, the accounting department makes an adjustment:

BALANCE SHEET					INCOME STATEMENT	
ASSETS		= LIABILITIES	+	OWNERS' EQUITY	+ REVENUES − EXPENSES	
Accounts Receivable—Dexter	(500)				Bad Debts Expense	(500)

This approach to accounting for bad debts is called the **direct write-off method.** Do you see any problems with its use? What about Roberts's balance sheet at the end of 2004? By ignoring the possibility that not all of its outstanding accounts receivable will be collected, Roberts is overstating the value of this asset at December 31, 2004. Also, what about the income statement for 2004? By ignoring the possibility of bad debts on sales made during 2004, Roberts has violated the *matching principle.* This principle requires that all costs associated with making sales in a period should be matched with the sales of that period. Roberts has overstated net income for 2004 by ignoring bad debts as an expense. The problem is one of *timing:* even though any one particular account may not prove to be uncollectible until a later period (e.g., the Dexter account), the cost associated with making sales on credit (bad debts) should be recognized in the period of sale.

Direct write-off method The recognition of bad debts expense at the point an account is written off as uncollectible.

Accountants use the **allowance method** to overcome the deficiencies of the direct write-off method. They *estimate* the amount of bad debts before these debts actually occur. For example, assume that Roberts's total sales during 2004 amount to $600,000 and that at the end of the year the outstanding accounts receivable total $250,000. Also assume that Roberts estimates that on the basis of past experience, 1% of the sales of the period, or $6,000, eventually will prove to be uncollectible. Under the allowance method, Roberts makes the following adjustment at the end of 2004:

Allowance method A method of estimating bad debts on the basis of either the net credit sales of the period or the accounts receivable at the end of the period.

BALANCE SHEET						INCOME STATEMENT
ASSETS	=	LIABILITIES	+	OWNERS' EQUITY	+	REVENUES – EXPENSES
Allowance for Doubtful Accounts (6,000)						Bad Debts Expense (6,000)

Bad Debts Expense recognizes the cost associated with the reduction in value of the asset Accounts Receivable. A contra-asset account is used to reduce the asset to its net realizable value. This is accomplished by using an allowance account, Allowance for Doubtful Accounts. Roberts presents accounts receivable as follows on its December 31, 2004, balance sheet:

Accounts receivable	$250,000
Less: Allowance for doubtful accounts	(6,000)
Net accounts receivable	$244,000

Study Tip

Note the similarities between the Allowance for Doubtful Accounts contra account and another contra account, Accumulated Depreciation. Both are used to reduce an asset account to a lower carrying or book value.

Write-Offs of Uncollectible Accounts with the Allowance Method

Like the direct write-off method, the allowance method reduces Accounts Receivable to write off a specific customer's account. If the account receivable no longer exists, there is no need for the related allowance account and thus this account is reduced as well. For example, assume, as we did earlier, that Dexter's $500 account is written off on May 1, 2005. Under the allowance method, the effect of the write-off is as follows:

BALANCE SHEET						INCOME STATEMENT
ASSETS	=	LIABILITIES	+	OWNERS' EQUITY	+	REVENUES – EXPENSES
Allowance for Doubtful Accounts 500						
Accounts Receivable—Dexter (500)						

To summarize, whether the direct write-off method or the allowance method is used, the entry to write off a specific customer's account reduces the *gross* amount of Accounts Receivable. However, under the direct write-off method, an *expense* is recognized and under the allowance method, the *allowance* account is reduced.

Two Approaches to the Allowance Method of Accounting for Bad Debts

INTERNAL DECISION

Because the allowance method results in a better *matching*, accounting standards require the use of this method rather than the direct write-off method unless bad debts are immaterial in amount. Accountants use one of two different variations of the allowance method to estimate bad debts. One approach emphasizes matching bad debts expense with revenue on the income statement and bases bad debts on a percentage of the sales of the period. This was the method we illustrated earlier for Roberts Corp. The other approach emphasizes the net realizable amount (value) of accounts receivable on the balance sheet and bases bad debts on a percentage of the accounts receivable balance at the end of the period.

Percentage of Net Credit Sales Approach If a company has been in business for enough years, it may be able to use the past relationship between bad debts and *net* credit sales to predict bad debt amounts. *Net* means that credit sales have been adjusted for sales discounts and returns and allowances. Assume that the accounting records for Bosco Corp. reveal the following:

YEAR	NET CREDIT SALES	BAD DEBTS
1999	$1,250,000	$ 26,400
2000	1,340,000	29,350
2001	1,200,000	23,100
2002	1,650,000	32,150
2003	2,120,000	42,700
	$7,560,000	$153,700

INTERNAL DECISION

Although the exact percentage varied slightly over the five-year period, the average percentage of bad debts to net credit sales is very close to 2% ($153,700/$7,560,000 = 0.02033). Bosco needs to determine whether this estimate is realistic for the current period. For example, are current economic conditions considerably different from those in the prior years? Has the company made sales to any new customers with significantly different credit terms? If the answers to these types of questions are yes, Bosco should consider adjusting the 2% experience rate to estimate future bad debts. Otherwise, it should proceed with this estimate. Assuming that it uses the 2% rate and that its net credit sales during 2004 are $2,340,000, Bosco makes the following adjustment:

BALANCE SHEET					INCOME STATEMENT
ASSETS	=	LIABILITIES	+	OWNERS' EQUITY	+ REVENUES – EXPENSES
Allowance for Doubtful Accounts (46,800)					Bad Debts Expense (46,800)

Thus, Bosco matches bad debt expense of $46,800 with sales revenue of $2,340,000.

Percentage of Accounts Receivable Approach Some companies believe they can more accurately estimate bad debts by relating them to the balance in the Accounts Receivable account at the end of the period rather than to the sales of the period. The objective with both approaches is the same, however: to use past experience with bad debts to predict future amounts. Assume that the records for Cougar Corp. reveal the following:

YEAR	BALANCE IN ACCOUNTS RECEIVABLE DECEMBER 31	BAD DEBTS
1999	$ 650,000	$ 5,250
2000	785,000	6,230
2001	854,000	6,950
2002	824,000	6,450
2003	925,000	7,450
	$4,038,000	$32,330

Accounting for Your Decisions

You Are the Owner

Assume you own a retail business that offers credit sales. To estimate bad debts, your business uses the percentage of net credit sales approach. For the new fiscal year, how would you decide what percentage to use to estimate your bad debts?

ANS: To determine the bad debt percentage for the new fiscal year, you can (1) review historical records to see what the actual percentages of bad debts were, (2) check to see if credit policies have substantially changed, (3) consider current and future economic conditions, and (4) consult with your managers and salespeople to see if they are aware of any changes in customers' paying habits.

The ratio of bad debts to the ending balance in Accounts Receivable over the past five years is $32,330/$4,038,000, or approximately 0.008 (0.8%). Assuming balances in Accounts Receivable and the Allowance for Doubtful Accounts on December 31, 2004, of $865,000 and $2,100, respectively, Cougar adjusts its records as follows:

BALANCE SHEET						INCOME STATEMENT
ASSETS	=	LIABILITIES	+	OWNERS' EQUITY	+	REVENUES − EXPENSES
Allowance for Doubtful Accounts (4,820)						Bad Debts Expense (4,820)

The logic for the amount recognized as bad debts is as follows:

Balance required in allowance account after adjustment	$6,920
Less: Balance in allowance account before adjustment	2,100
Amount of adjustment	$4,820

Note the one major difference between this approach and the percentage of sales approach: *under the percentage of net credit sales approach, the balance in the allowance account is ignored, and the bad debts expense is simply a percentage of the sales of the period; under the percentage of accounts receivable approach, however, the balance in the allowance account must be considered.*

The net realizable value of Accounts Receivable is determined as follows:

Accounts receivable	$865,000
Less: Allowance for doubtful accounts	(6,920)
Net realizable value	$858,080

Aging of Accounts Receivable Some companies use a variation of the percentage of accounts receivable approach to estimate bad debts. This variation is actually a refinement of the approach because it considers the length of time that the receivables have been outstanding. It stands to reason that the older an account receivable is, the less likely it is to be collected. An **aging schedule** categorizes the various accounts by length of time outstanding. An example of an aging schedule is shown in Exhibit 6-2. We assume that the company's policy is to allow 30 days for payment of an outstanding account. After that time, the account is past due. An alphabetical list of customers appears in the first column, with the balance in each account shown in the appropriate column to the right. The dotted lines after A. Matt's account indicate that many more accounts appear in the

Aging schedule A form used to categorize the various individual accounts receivable according to the length of time each has been outstanding.

Exhibit 6-2

Aging Schedule

		Number of Days Past Due			
CUSTOMER	CURRENT	1–30	31–60	61–90	OVER 90
L. Ash	$ 4,400				
B. Budd	3,200				
C. Cox		$ 6,500			
E. Fudd					$6,300
G. Hoff			$ 900		
A. Matt	5,500				
......					
......					
......					
T. West				$ 3,100	
M. Young				4,200	
Totals*	$85,600	$31,200	$24,500	$18,000	$9,200

*Only a few of the customer accounts are illustrated; thus the column totals are higher than the amounts for the accounts illustrated.

records; we have included just a few to show the format of the schedule. The totals on the aging schedule are used as the basis for estimating bad debts, as shown in Exhibit 6-3.

Exhibit 6-3

Use of an Aging Schedule to Estimate Bad Debts

CATEGORY	AMOUNT	ESTIMATED PERCENT UNCOLLECTIBLE	ESTIMATED AMOUNT UNCOLLECTIBLE
Current	$ 85,600	1%	$ 856
Past due:			
1–30 days	31,200	4%	1,248
31–60 days	24,500	10%	2,450
61–90 days	18,000	30%	5,400
Over 90 days	9,200	50%	4,600
Totals	$168,500		$14,554

Note that the estimated percentage of uncollectibles increases as the period of time the accounts have been outstanding lengthens. If we assume that the Allowance for Doubtful Accounts has a balance of $1,230 before adjustment, the accountant makes the following adjustments:

BALANCE SHEET					INCOME STATEMENT
ASSETS	=	LIABILITIES	+	OWNERS' EQUITY	+ REVENUES – EXPENSES
Allowance for Doubtful Accounts (13,324)					Bad Debts Expense (13,324)

The logic for the amount recognized as bad debts is as follows:

Balance required in allowance account after adjustment	$14,554
Less: Balance in allowance account before adjustment	1,230
Amount of adjustment	$13,324

The net realizable value of accounts receivable would be determined as follows:

Accounts receivable	$168,500
Less: Allowance for doubtful accounts	14,554
Net realizable value	$153,946

From Concept to Practice 6.2

Reading Winnebago Industries' Notes

In the Winnebago Industries' annual report, locate the section in Note 1 that is titled "Allowance for Doubtful Accounts." From your reading of this, which method does it appear that Winnebago Industries uses to estimate bad debts? In what line item on the income statement would you expect bad debts expense to be included?

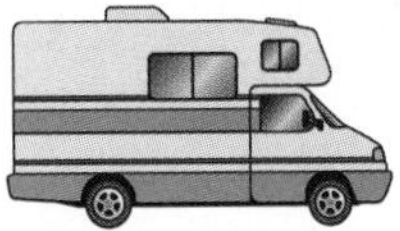

Two-Minute Review

1. *What is the theoretical justification for recognizing bad debts under the allowance method?*
2. *What accounts are used at the end of the period to recognize bad debts?*
3. *Two approaches are available to recognize bad debts. What are they? Which one of the two takes into account any existing balance in the Allowance for Doubtful Accounts account when the entry is made to recognize bad debts for the period?*

Answers on page 277.

ANALYZING THE ACCOUNTS RECEIVABLE RATE OF COLLECTION

ANALYSIS

Managers, investors, and creditors are keenly interested in how well a company manages its accounts receivable. One simple measure is to compare a company's sales to its accounts receivable. The result is the accounts receivable turnover ratio:

$$\text{Accounts Receivable Turnover} = \frac{\text{Net Credit Sales}}{\text{Average Accounts Receivable}}$$

Typically, the faster the turnover is, the better. For example, if a company has sales of $10 million and an average accounts receivable of $1 million, it turns over its accounts receivable 10 times per year. If we assume 360 days in a year, that is once every 36 days. An observer would compare that figure with historical figures to see if the company is experiencing slower or faster collections. A comparison could also be made to other companies in the same industry. If receivables are turning over too slowly, that could mean that the company's credit department is not operating effectively and the company therefore is missing opportunities with the cash that isn't available. On the other hand, a turnover rate that is too fast might mean that the company's credit policies are too stringent and that sales are being lost as a result.

Interpret: You Decide. Refer back to PepsiCo's partial balance sheet in the chapter opener. Also consider that during 2002 the company reported net sales of $25,112 million. Calculate the accounts and notes receivable turnover ratio for 2002. What is the average length of time that it takes to collect a receivable? Do you think the average time would be different for the company's accounts receivable compared to its notes receivable? Explain your answer. Does the average time to collect receivables seem reasonable for PepsiCo's type of business?

NOTES RECEIVABLE

Promissory note A written promise to repay a definite sum of money on demand or at a fixed or determinable date in the future.

Maker The party that agrees to repay the money for a promissory note at some future date.

Payee The party that will receive the money from a promissory note at some future date.

Note receivable An asset resulting from the acceptance of a promissory note from another company.

Note payable A liability resulting from the signing of a promissory note.

A **promissory note** is a written promise to repay a definite sum of money on demand or at a fixed or determinable date in the future. Promissory notes normally require the payment of interest for the use of someone else's money. The party that agrees to repay money is the **maker** of the note, and the party that receives money in the future is the **payee.** A company that holds a promissory note received from another company has an asset, called a **note receivable;** the company that makes or gives a promissory note to another company has a liability, a **note payable.** Over the life of the note, the maker incurs interest expense on its note payable, and the payee earns interest revenue on its note receivable. The following summarizes this relationship:

PARTY	RECOGNIZES ON BALANCE SHEET	RECOGNIZES ON INCOME STATEMENT
Maker	Note payable	Interest expense
Payee	Note receivable	Interest revenue

Promissory notes are used for a variety of purposes. Banks normally require a company to sign a promissory note to borrow money. They are often used in the sale of consumer durables with relatively high purchase prices, such as appliances and automobiles. At times a promissory note is issued to replace an existing overdue account receivable.

Important Terms Connected with Promissory Notes

It is important to understand the following terms when dealing with promissory notes:

Principal—the amount of cash received, or the fair value of the products or services received, by the maker when a promissory note is issued.

Maturity date—the date that the promissory note is due.

Term—the length of time a note is outstanding; that is, the period of time between the date it is issued and the date it matures.

Maturity value—the amount of cash the maker is to pay the payee on the maturity date of the note.

Interest—the difference between the principal amount of the note and its maturity value.

Key terms for promissory notes These terms, with their definitions in the text, are important for your understanding.

In some cases, the interest rate on a promissory note is stated explicitly on the face of the note. Even though the note's term may be less than a year, the interest rate is stated on an annual basis. In other cases, an interest rate does not appear on the face of the note. As we will see, however, there is *implicit* interest, because more is to be repaid at maturity than is owed at the time the note is signed. Notes in which an interest rate is explicitly stated are called **interest-bearing notes.** Notes in which interest is implicit in the agreement are called **non-interest-bearing notes.** We now look at the accounting for each of these types of notes.

Interest-bearing note A promissory note in which the interest rate is explicitly stated.

Non-interest-bearing note A promissory note in which interest is not explicitly stated but is implicit in the agreement.

Interest-Bearing Notes

LO 3 Demonstrate an understanding of how to account for interest-bearing notes receivable.

Assume that on December 13, 2004, HighTec sells a computer to Baker Corp. at an invoice price of $15,000. Because Baker is short of cash, it gives HighTec a 90-day, 12% promissory note. The total amount of interest due on the maturity date is determined as follows:

$$\$15{,}000 \times .12 \times 90/360 = \underline{\underline{\$450}}$$

The effect of the receipt of the note by HighTec is as follows:

BALANCE SHEET							INCOME STATEMENT	
ASSETS		=	LIABILITIES	+	OWNERS' EQUITY	+	REVENUES – EXPENSES	
Notes Receivable	15,000						Sales Revenue	15,000

If we assume that December 31 is the end of HighTec's accounting year, an adjustment is needed to recognize interest earned but not yet received. It is required when a company uses the accrual basis of accounting. The question is: how many days of interest have been earned during December? *It is normal practice to count the day a note matures, but not the day it is signed, in computing interest.* Thus, in our example, interest would be earned for 18 days (December 14 to December 31) during 2004 and for 72 days in 2005:

MONTH	NUMBER OF DAYS OUTSTANDING
December 2004	18 days
January 2005	31 days
February 2005	28 days
March 2005	13 days (matures on March 13, 2005)
Total days	90 days

Thus, the amount of interest earned during 2004 is $15,000 × .12 × 18/360, or $90. An adjustment is made on December 31 to record interest earned during 2004:

BALANCE SHEET							INCOME STATEMENT	
ASSETS		=	LIABILITIES	+	OWNERS' EQUITY	+	REVENUES – EXPENSES	
Interest Receivable	90						Interest Revenue	90

On March 13, 2005, HighTec collects the principal amount of the note and interest from Baker:

BALANCE SHEET					INCOME STATEMENT	
ASSETS		= LIABILITIES	+ OWNERS' EQUITY	+	REVENUES – EXPENSES	
Cash	15,450				Interest Revenue	360
Notes Receivable	(15,000)					
Interest Receivable	(90)					

This adjustment accomplishes a number of purposes. First, it removes the amount of $15,000 originally recorded in the Notes Receivable account. Second, it recognizes interest earned during the 72 days in 2005 that the note was outstanding. The calculation of interest earned during 2005 is as follows:

$$\$15{,}000 \times .12 \times 72/360 = \underline{\underline{\$360}}$$

Third, Interest Receivable for $90 is removed from the records now that the note has been collected. Finally, cash of $15,450 is collected, which represents the principal amount of the note, $15,000, plus interest of $450 for 90 days.

Non-Interest-Bearing Notes

LO 4 Demonstrate an understanding of how to account for non-interest-bearing notes receivable.

Assume that you walk in to an automobile dealership on November 1, 2004, and find the car of your dreams. After extensive negotiation, the dealer agrees to sell you the car outright for $10,000. Because you are short of cash, you give the dealer $1,000 as a down payment and sign a promissory note to pay $9,900 in six months. Even though interest is never mentioned, it is *implicitly* built into the transaction. You owe the car dealer $10,000 – $1,000, or $9,000, today, and you have agreed to pay $9,900 in six months. The $900 excess of the amount to be paid in six months over the amount owed today is *interest.* The note is called a non-interest-bearing note because no interest is *explicitly* stated. Anytime it is necessary to pay more in the future than is owed today, interest is involved. The *effective interest rate* can be found as follows:

1. The amount of interest implicit in the note: $9,900 – $9,000, or $900
2. The length of the note: 6 months
3. The number of 6-month periods in a year: 12/6 = 2
4. The amount of interest that would apply to a full year: $900 × 2, or $1,800
5. The effective annual interest rate: $1,800/$9,000, or 20%

In essence, the car dealer had you sign a promissory note in the amount of $9,900 but gave you credit equivalent to only $9,000 in cash, that is, the difference between the value of the car today, $10,000, and the amount of your down payment, $1,000. The dealer deducted interest of $900 in advance and gave you the equivalent of a $9,000 loan. Another name for this non-interest-bearing note is a **discounted note.** On the date the note is signed, the car dealer makes an adjustment as follows:

Discounted note An alternative name for a non-interest-bearing promissory note.

BALANCE SHEET					INCOME STATEMENT	
ASSETS		= LIABILITIES	+ OWNERS' EQUITY	+	REVENUES – EXPENSES	
Cash	1,000				Sales Revenue	10,000
Notes Receivable	9,900					
Discount on Notes Receivable	(900)					

The cash received represents the down payment. The increase in Notes Receivable of $9,900 is the maturity amount of the promissory note. Sales Revenue represents the amount the car could be sold for today. Discount on Notes Receivable is a contra account to the Notes Receivable account and represents the interest that the dealer will earn over the next six months. As interest is earned, this account will be reduced and Interest Revenue will be increased. For example, at the end of the year, the dealer will make an adjustment to recognize that two months' interest of the total of six months' interest has been earned:

BALANCE SHEET							INCOME STATEMENT	
ASSETS		=	LIABILITIES	+	OWNERS' EQUITY	+	REVENUES – EXPENSES	
Discount on Notes Receivable	300						Interest Revenue	300

The current assets section of the dealer's balance sheet at December 31, 2004, includes the following:

Notes receivable	$9,900	
Less: Discount on notes receivable	(600)	$9,300

On April 30, the dealer records the collection of the maturity amount of the note and the remaining interest earned:

BALANCE SHEET							INCOME STATEMENT	
ASSETS		=	LIABILITIES	+	OWNERS' EQUITY	+	REVENUES – EXPENSES	
Cash	9,900						Interest Revenue	600
Notes Receivable	(9,900)							
Discount on Notes Receivable	600							

ACCELERATING THE INFLOW OF CASH FROM SALES

LO 5 Explain various techniques that companies use to accelerate the inflow of cash from sales.

Earlier in the chapter we pointed out why cash sales are preferable to credit sales: credit sales slow down the inflow of cash to the company and create the potential for bad debts. To remain competitive, most businesses find it necessary to grant credit to customers. That is, if one company won't grant credit to a customer, the customer may find another company willing to do so. Companies have found it possible, however, to circumvent the problems inherent in credit sales. We now consider some approaches that companies use to speed up the flow of cash from sales.

Credit Card Sales

Most retail establishments, as well as many service businesses, accept one or more major credit cards. Among the most common cards are MasterCard®, VISA®, American Express®, Carte Blanche®, Discover Card®, and Diners Club®. Most merchants believe that they must honor at least one or more of these credit cards to remain competitive. In return for a fee, the merchant passes the responsibility for collection on to the credit card company. Thus, the credit card issuer assumes the risk of nonpayment. The basic relationships among the three parties—the customer, the merchant, and the credit card company—are illustrated in Exhibit 6-4. Assume that Joe Smith entertains clients at Club Cafe and charges $100 in meals to his Diners Club credit card. When Joe is presented with his bill at the end of the evening, he is asked to sign a multiple-copy **credit card draft** or invoice. Joe keeps one copy of the draft and leaves the other two copies at Club Cafe. The restaurant keeps one copy as the basis for recording its sales for the day and sends the other copy to Diners Club for payment. Diners Club uses the copy of the draft it gets for two purposes: to reimburse Club Cafe $95 (keeping $5 or 5% of the original sale as a collection fee) and to include Joe Smith's $100 purchase on the monthly bill it mails him.

Credit card draft A multiple-copy document used by a company that accepts a credit card for a sale.

Exhibit 6-4

Basic Relationships among Parties with Credit Card Sales

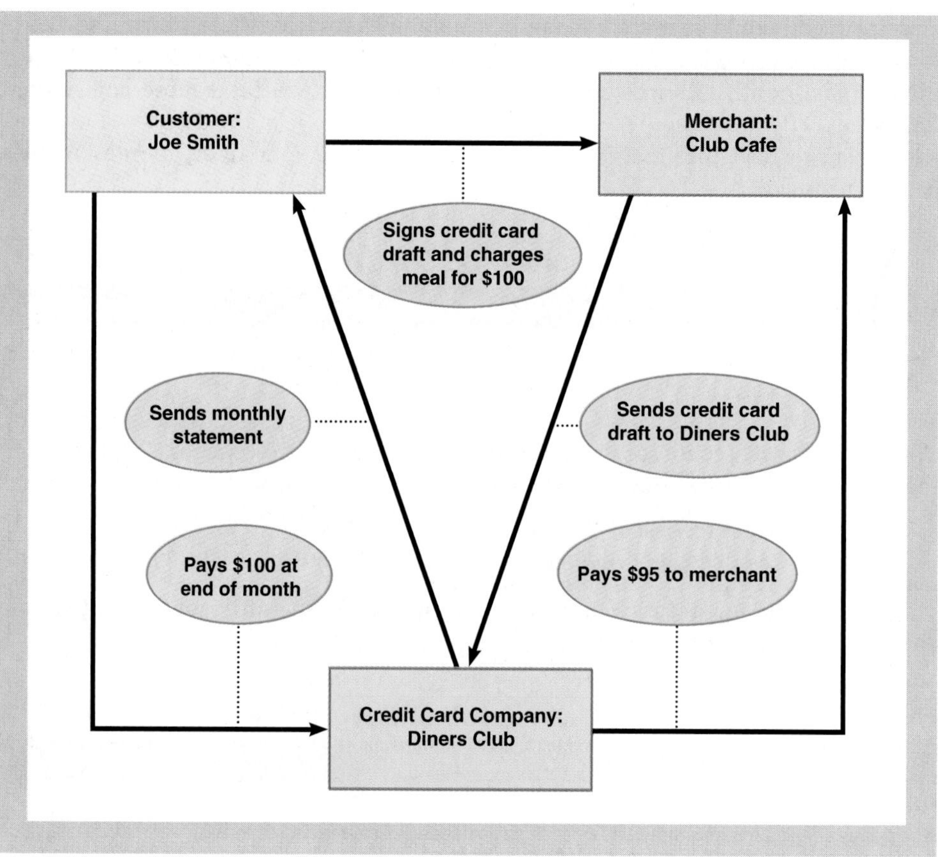

Assume that total credit card sales on June 5 amount to $800. The effect on the accounting equation is as follows:

BALANCE SHEET					INCOME STATEMENT	
ASSETS		= LIABILITIES	+ OWNERS' EQUITY	+	REVENUES − EXPENSES	
Accounts Receivable— Diners Club	800				Sales Revenue	800

Assume that Club Cafe remits the credit card drafts to Diners Club once a week and that the total sales for the week ending June 11 amount to $5,000. Further assume that on June 13 Diners Club pays the amount due to Club Cafe, after deducting a 5% collection fee. The adjustment is as follows:

BALANCE SHEET					INCOME STATEMENT	
ASSETS		= LIABILITIES	+ OWNERS' EQUITY	+	REVENUES − EXPENSES	
Cash	4,750				Collection Fee Expense	(250)
Accounts Receivable— Diners Club	(5,000)					

Some credit cards, such as MasterCard and VISA, allow a merchant to present a credit card draft directly for deposit in a bank account, in much the same way the merchant deposits checks, coins, and currency. Obviously, this type of arrangement is even more advantageous for the merchant because the funds are available as soon as the drafts are credited to the bank account. Assume that on July 9, Club Cafe presents VISA credit card drafts to its bank for payment in the amount of $2,000 and that the collection charge is 4%. The effect of the collection is as follows:

BALANCE SHEET					INCOME STATEMENT	
ASSETS	=	LIABILITIES	+	OWNERS' EQUITY	+ REVENUES − EXPENSES	
Cash	1,920				Collection Fee Expense	(80)
					Sales Revenue	2,000

Discounting Notes Receivable

Promissory notes are negotiable, which means that they can be endorsed and given to someone else for collection. In other words, a company can sign the back of a note, just as it would a check, sell it to a bank, and receive cash before the note's maturity date. This process is called **discounting** and is another way for companies to speed the collection of cash from receivables. A note can be sold immediately to a bank on the date it is issued, or it can be sold after it has been outstanding but before the due date.

Discounting The process of selling a promissory note.

When a note is discounted at a bank, it is normally done *with recourse.* This means that if the original customer fails to pay the bank the total amount due on the maturity date of the note, the company that transferred the note to the bank is liable for the full amount. Because there is *uncertainty* as to whether the company will have to make good on any particular note that it discounts at the bank, a *contingent liability* exists from the time the note is discounted until its maturity date. The accounting profession has adopted guidelines to decide whether a particular uncertainty requires that the company record a contingent liability on its balance sheet. Under these guidelines, the contingency created by the discounting of a note with recourse is not recorded as a liability. However, a *note* in the financial statements is used to inform the reader of the existing uncertainty.

HOW LIQUID ASSETS AFFECT THE STATEMENT OF CASH FLOWS

CASH FLOW

LO 6 Explain the effects of transactions involving liquid assets on the statement of cash flows.

As we discussed in Chapter 5, cash equivalents are combined with cash on the balance sheet. These items are very near maturity and do not present any significant risk of collectibility. Because of this, any purchases or redemptions of cash equivalents are not considered significant activities to be reported on a statement of cash flows.

The purchase and the sale of investments are considered significant activities and are therefore reported on the statement of cash flows. The classification of these activities on the statement depends on the type of investment. Cash flows from purchases, sales, and maturities of held-to-maturity securities and available-for-sale securities are classified as *investing* activities. On the other hand, these same types of cash flows for trading securities are classified as *operating* activities. We present a complete discussion of the statement of cash flows, including the reporting of investments, in Chapter 12.

The collection of either accounts receivable or notes receivable generates cash for a business and affects the Operating Activities section of the statement of cash flows. Most companies use the indirect method of reporting cash flows and begin the statement of cash flows with the net income of the period. Net income includes the sales revenue of the period. Therefore, a decrease in accounts or notes receivable during the period indicates that the company collected more cash than it recorded in sales revenue. Thus, *a decrease in accounts or notes receivable must be added back to net income because more cash was collected than is reflected in the sales revenue number.* Alternatively, an increase in accounts or notes receivable indicates that the company recorded more sales revenue than cash collected during the period. Therefore, *an increase in accounts or notes receivable requires a deduction from the net income of the period to arrive at cash flow from operating activities.* These adjustments, as well as the cash flows from buying and selling investments, are summarized in Exhibit 6-5. Note that any investments are assumed to be in either held-to-maturity or available-for-sale securities.

Exhibit 6-5

How Investments and Receivables Affect the Statement of Cash Flows

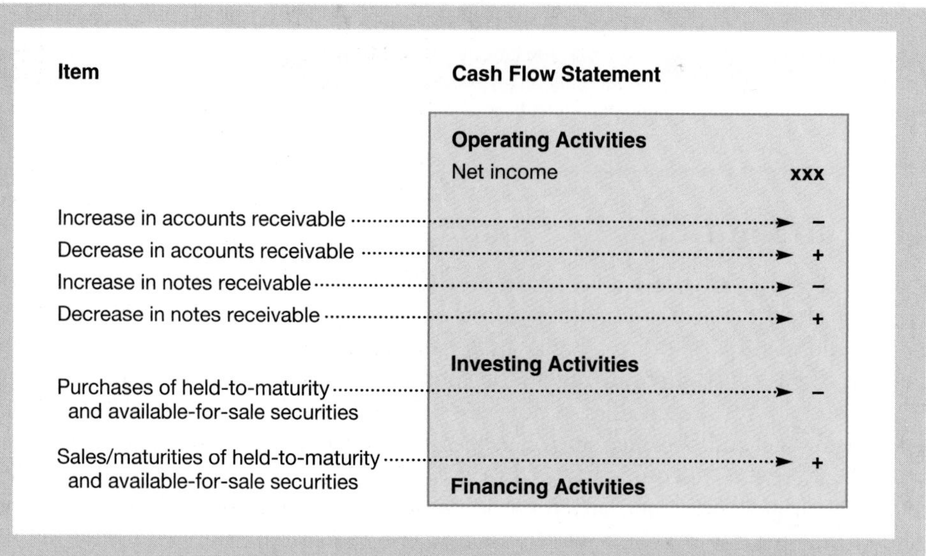

Ratios for Decision Making

Reporting and analyzing financial statement information related to a company's accounts receivable:
The accounts receivable turnover calculation provides information about how well the company is handling its collection of receivables from credit sales. The higher the number, the more frequently cash from credit sales is collected. Comparing the company's turnover rate with its rate in prior years or with the rate of other companies in the same industry can provide an estimate of how well the company is doing with managing its receivables.

Balance Sheet	Income Statement	Statement of Cash Flows	Notes
Accounts Receivable	**Net Sales**	**Cash received from accounts receivable** **Cash received from cash sales**	

$$\textbf{Accounts Receivable Turnover} = \frac{\textbf{Net Credit Sales*}}{\textbf{Average Accounts Receivable**}}$$

*Net credit sales are credit sales minus any sales discounts, returns, and allowances (these are discussed more fully in Chapter 7). Net credit sales can be estimated as follows:

Net Sales − cash received from cash sales as reported on the statement of cash flows

**Average accounts receivable can be estimated using the following calculation:

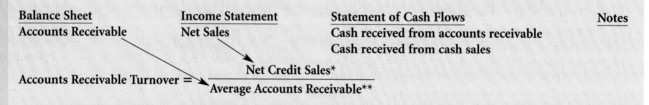

$$\frac{\text{Beginning Accounts Receivable} + \text{Ending Accounts Receivable}}{2}$$

Impact on the Financial Reports

Impact on the Financial Reports

BALANCE SHEET

Current Assets
Cash and cash equivalents
Short-term investments[1]
Accounts receivable[2]
Allowance for doubtful accounts
Notes receivable[3]
Discount on notes receivable
Interest receivable
Supplies
Noncurrent Assets
Current Liabilities
Noncurrent Liabilities
Stockholders' Equity
Unrealized gain (loss)—available-for-sale securities

INCOME STATEMENT

Revenues
Sales revenue
Expenses
Cost of goods sold
Bad debt expense
Rent expense—lockbox
Collection fee expense
Postage expense
Delivery expense
Office expense
Other
Interest revenue
Dividend income
Gain (loss) on sale of investments[4]
Unrealized gain (loss)—trading securities

STATEMENT OF STOCKHOLDERS' EQUITY

Contributed Capital
Retained Earnings

STATEMENT OF CASH FLOWS

Operating Activities[5]
Cash from sales
Cash received for accounts receivable
Cash received for interest from notes receivable and bond investments
Investing Activities
Cash received from (paid for) debt and equity security investments
Cash dividends received
Financing Activities
Noncash Transactions

NOTES

[1]May include certificates of deposit, investments in stocks, investments in bonds that mature or are expected to be sold within one year of the balance sheet date.
[2]Accounts receivable less allowance for doubtful accounts = net accounts receivable = net realizable value; accounts receivable includes credit card sales
[3]Notes receivable less discount on notes receivable = net notes receivable = net realizable value
[4]Includes gain (loss) from sale of stocks and bonds
[5]Under the indirect method (explained in detail in Chapter 12), any increase (or decrease) in accounts receivable and in notes receivable and any gain (or loss) from the sale of investments would be shown as a subtraction from (addition to) net income in this section and would replace the items listed above under "Operating Activities."

Answers to the Two-Minute Reviews

Two-Minute Review on Page 263

1. *Held-to-maturity, trading, and available-for-sale.*
2. *Bonds are the only securities that can be held to maturity. Stocks do not have a maturity date.*
3. *Any changes in fair value of trading securities are reported on the income statement. Changes in fair value of available-for-sale securities are reported in stockholders' equity on the balance sheet.*

Two-Minute Review on Page 269

1. *Use of the allowance method is an attempt by accountants to match bad debts as an expense with the revenue of the period in which a sale on credit took place.*
2. *Bad Debts expense is debited, and Allowance for Doubtful Accounts is credited.*
3. *The two approaches are the percentage of net credit sales approach and the percentage of accounts receivable approach. Only the latter takes into account the balance in the Allowance for Doubtful Accounts account.*

Warmup Exercises

Warmup Exercise 6-1 ***Investments*** **LO 1**

Indicate whether each of the following events will result in an increase (I), decrease (D), or no effect (NE) on net income for the period.

_______ **1.** Trading securities are sold for more than their carrying value.
_______ **2.** An interest check is received for held-to-maturity securities.
_______ **3.** Available-for-sale securities increase in value during the period.
_______ **4.** Available-for-sale securities are sold for less than their carrying value.
_______ **5.** Trading securities decrease in value during the period.
_______ **6.** Held-to-maturity securities are redeemed on their maturity date at face value.

Key to the Solution

Recall from earlier in the chapter the differences in accounting for the various types of investments.

Warmup Exercise 6-2 ***Accounting for Bad Debts*** **LO 4**

Brown Corp. ended the year with balances in Accounts Receivable of $60,000 and in Allowance for Doubtful Accounts of $800 (before adjustment). Net sales for the year amounted to $200,000. Determine the effect on the accounting equation, assuming the following:

1. Estimated percentage of net sales uncollectible is 1%.
2. Estimated percentage of year-end accounts receivable uncollectible is 4%.

Key to the Solution

Recall that the percentage of net sales approach does not take into account any existing balance in the allowance account but the percentage of receivables approach does.

Solutions to Warmup Exercises

Warmup Exercise 6-1

1. I **2.** I **3.** NE **4.** D **5.** D **6.** NE

Warmup Exercise 6-2

BALANCE SHEET						INCOME STATEMENT
ASSETS	**=**	**LIABILITIES**	**+**	**OWNERS' EQUITY**	**+**	**REVENUES − EXPENSES**
1. Allowance for Doubtful Accounts (2,000)						Bad Debts Expense (2,000)
2. Allowance for Doubtful Accounts (1,600)						Bad Debts Expense (1,600)

Review Problem

WebTUTOR™ Advantage

The following items pertain to the Current Assets section of the balance sheet for Jackson Corp. at the end of its accounting year, December 31, 2004. Each item must be considered, and any necessary adjustment recognized. Additionally, the accountant for Jackson wants to develop the Current Assets section of the balance sheet as of the end of 2004.

a. Cash and cash equivalents amount to $19,375.

b. A 9%, 120-day certificate of deposit was purchased on December 1, 2004, for $10,000.

c. Gross accounts receivable at December 31, 2004, amount to $44,000. Before adjustment, the balance in the Allowance for Doubtful Accounts is $340. Based on past experience, the accountant estimates that 3% of the gross accounts receivable outstanding at December 31, 2004, will prove to be uncollectible.

d. A customer's 12%, 90-day promissory note in the amount of $6,000 is held at the end of the year. The note has been held for 45 days during 2004.

Required

1. Determine the effect on the accounting equation from the adjustments required in parts **b,** **c,** and **d.**
2. Prepare the Current Assets section of Jackson's balance sheet as of December 31, 2004. In addition to items **a–d,** the balances in Inventory and Prepaid Insurance on this date are $65,000 and $4,800, respectively.

Solution to Review Problem

1. The effect on the accounting equation from each item is as follows:

b. Jackson needs an adjustment to record interest earned on the certificate of deposit. The CD has been outstanding for 30 days during 2004; therefore, the amount of interest earned is calculated as follows:

$$\$10{,}000 \times 0.09 \times 30/360 = \underline{\underline{\$75}}$$

The effect of the adjustment is as follows:

BALANCE SHEET							INCOME STATEMENT	
ASSETS		=	LIABILITIES	+	OWNERS' EQUITY	+	REVENUES – EXPENSES	
Interest Receivable	75						Interest Revenue	75

c. Based on gross accounts receivable of $44,000 at year-end and an estimate that 3% of this amount will be uncollectible, the balance in the Allowance for Doubtful Accounts should be $1,320 ($44,000 × 3%). Given a current balance of $340, an adjustment for $980 ($1,320 − $340) is needed to bring the balance to the desired amount of $1,320:

BALANCE SHEET							INCOME STATEMENT	
ASSETS		=	LIABILITIES	+	OWNERS' EQUITY	+	REVENUES – EXPENSES	
Allowance for Doubtful Accounts	(980)						Bad Debts Expense	(980)

d. An adjustment is needed to accrue interest on the promissory note ($6,000 × .12 × 45/360 = $\underline{\underline{\$90}}$):

BALANCE SHEET							INCOME STATEMENT	
ASSETS		=	LIABILITIES	+	OWNERS' EQUITY	+	REVENUES – EXPENSES	
Interest Receivable	90						Interest Revenue	90

2. The Current Assets section of Jackson's balance sheet appears as follows:

JACKSON CORP.
PARTIAL BALANCE SHEET
DECEMBER 31, 2004

Current Assets		
Cash and cash equivalents		$ 19,375
Certificate of deposit		10,000
Accounts receivable	$44,000	
Less: Allowance for doubtful accounts	1,320	42,680
Notes receivable		6,000
Interest receivable		165*
Inventory		65,000
Prepaid insurance		4,800
Total current assets		$148,020

*$75 from CD and $90 from promissory note

Chapter Highlights

1. **LO 1** At times, companies invest idle cash in highly liquid financial instruments such as certificates of deposit. They also invest in the debt and equity securities of other companies. Some investments are made without the intention of influencing or controlling the other company. Accountants classify these investments as held-to-maturity securities, trading securities, or available-for-sale securities. Other investments are made to exert significant influence over the policies of the other companies. The equity method is used in these instances. Finally, companies may buy enough of the common stock of another company to control it. This situation normally results in the presentation of consolidated financial statements.
2. **LO 1** Held-to-maturity securities are bonds that are purchased with the intention of holding them until they mature. The cost method results in the recognition of periodic interest income and the recognition of a gain or loss if the securities are sold prior to when they mature.
3. **LO 1** Trading securities are stocks and bonds held for the short term with the intention of profiting from appreciation in their trading price. Interest or dividends are recognized as income. Trading securities are adjusted to their fair value at the end of each period, and any increase or decrease in value is reported on the income statement.
4. **LO 1** Available-for-sale securities are investments that are not classified as either held-to-maturity or trading securities. The accounting and reporting requirements for this category are similar to the rules for trading securities. The primary difference is that unrealized gains and losses from holding available-for-sale securities (changes in fair value from one period to the next) are not recognized on the income statement. Instead, these amounts are reported as a separate component of stockholders' equity.
5. **LO 2** The allowance method of accounting for bad debts matches the cost associated with uncollectible accounts to the revenue of the period in which the sale took place. One of two variations is used to estimate bad debts under the allowance method. Some companies base bad debts on a percentage of net credit sales. Others use an aging schedule as a basis for relating the amount of bad debts to the balance in Accounts Receivable at the end of the period.
6. **LO 3** A promissory note is a written promise to repay a definite sum of money on demand or at a fixed or determinable date in the future. Situations in which a promissory note is used include the purchase of consumer durables, the lending of money to another party, and the replacement of an existing account receivable. Interest earned but not yet collected should be accrued at the end of an accounting period.
7. **LO 4** The interest on certain promissory notes is implicitly included in the agreement instead of stated explicitly as a percentage of the principal amount of the note. Any difference between the cash purchase price of an item or, in the case of a loan, the amount borrowed and the amount to be repaid at maturity is interest. As is the case for interest-bearing notes, any interest earned but not yet collected is recognized as income at the end of an accounting period.
8. **LO 5** Many businesses accept credit cards in lieu of cash. In return for a fee, the credit card company assumes responsibility for collecting the customer charges. A credit card draft or invoice is the basis for recording a credit card sale and an account receivable. When the drafts are presented to the credit card company for payment, the excess of accounts receivable for these sales over the amount of cash received represents the expense associated with accepting credit cards. In some instances, companies do not have to wait to collect from the credit card company but can instead present the drafts for deposit to their bank account.
9. **LO 5** Because a promissory note is negotiable, it can be sold to another party, such as a bank. The sale of a note is called *discounting* and is a way for a company to accelerate the inflow of cash. If the note is sold or discounted with recourse, the company selling it is contingently liable until the maturity date of the loan. A note is used to report this contingency to financial statement readers.
10. **LO 6** Cash equivalents are included with cash on the balance sheet, and therefore changes in them do not appear as significant activities on a statement of cash flows. Purchases and sales of investments do appear in the statement of cash flows. Under the indirect method of preparing the Operating Activities category of the statement of cash flows, increases in accounts and notes receivable are deducted from net income; decreases are added back to net income.

http://porter.swlearning.com

Technology and other resources for your success

If you need additional help, visit the text's Web site. Also, see this text's preface for a description of available technology and other resources. If your instructor is using PERSONAL Trainer in this course, you may complete, on line, the exercises and problems in the text.

Key Terms Quiz

Read each definition below and then write the number of the definition in the blank beside the appropriate term it defines. The quiz solutions appear at the end of the chapter.

_____ **Equity securities**
_____ **Debt securities**
_____ **Held-to-maturity securities**
_____ **Trading securities**
_____ **Available-for-sale securities**
_____ **Subsidiary ledger**
_____ **Control account**
_____ **Direct write-off method**
_____ **Allowance method**
_____ **Aging schedule**
_____ **Promissory note**
_____ **Maker**
_____ **Payee**
_____ **Note receivable**
_____ **Note payable**
_____ **Principal**
_____ **Maturity date**
_____ **Term**
_____ **Maturity value**
_____ **Interest**
_____ **Interest-bearing note**
_____ **Non-interest-bearing note**
_____ **Discounted note**
_____ **Credit card draft**
_____ **Discounting**

1. Securities issued by corporations as a form of ownership in the business.
2. Bonds issued by corporations and governmental bodies as a form of borrowing.
3. Stocks and bonds of other companies bought and held for the purpose of selling them in the near term to generate profits on appreciation in their price.
4. Stocks and bonds that are not classified as either held-to-maturity or trading securities.
5. Investments in bonds of other companies in which the investor has the positive intent and the ability to hold the securities to maturity.
6. A method of estimating bad debts on the basis of either the net credit sales of the period or the amount of accounts receivable at the end of the period.
7. The party that will receive the money from a promissory note at some future date.
8. A written promise to repay a definite sum of money on demand or at a fixed or determinable date in the future.
9. A liability resulting from the signing of a promissory note.
10. A multiple-copy document used by a company that accepts a credit card for a sale.
11. An asset resulting from the acceptance of a promissory note from another company.
12. The process of selling a promissory note.
13. The party that agrees to repay the money for a promissory note at some future date.
14. A promissory note in which the interest rate is explicitly stated.
15. A form used to categorize the various individual accounts receivable according to the length of time each has been outstanding.
16. An alternative name for a non-interest-bearing promissory note.
17. The detail for a number of individual items that collectively make up a single general ledger account.
18. A promissory note in which interest is not explicitly stated but is implicit in the agreement.
19. The recognition of bad debts expense at the point an account is written off as uncollectible.
20. The general ledger account that is supported by a subsidiary ledger.
21. The amount of cash received, or the fair value of the products or services received, by the maker when a promissory note is issued.
22. The date that the promissory note is due.
23. The length of time a note is outstanding; that is, the period of time between the date it is issued and the date it matures.
24. The amount of cash the maker is to pay the payee on the maturity date of the note.
25. The difference between the principal amount of the note and its maturity value.

Answers on p. 295.

Alternate Terms

Allowance for doubtful accounts Allowance for uncollectible accounts

Credit card draft Invoice

Debt securities Bonds

Equity securities Stocks

Net realizable value Net recoverable amount

Non-interest-bearing note Discounted note

Short-term investments Marketable securities

Questions

1. Stanzel Corp. purchased 1,000 shares of IBM common stock. What will determine whether the shares are classified as trading securities or available-for-sale securities?
2. On December 31, Stockton Inc. invests idle cash in two different certificates of deposit. The first is an 8%, 90-day CD, and the second has an interest rate of 9% and matures in 120 days. How is each of these CDs classified on the December 31 balance sheet?
3. What is the primary difference in the accounting requirements for trading securities and those for available-for-sale securities? How is the primary difference justified?
4. Why are changes in the fair value of trading securities reported in the account *Unrealized* Gains/Losses—Trading Securities even though the gains and losses are reported on the income statement?
5. What is the theoretical justification for the allowance method of accounting for bad debts?
6. In estimating bad debts, why is the balance in Allowance for Doubtful Accounts considered when the percentage of accounts receivable approach is used but not when the percentage of net credit sales approach is used?
7. When estimating bad debts on the basis of a percentage of accounts receivable, what is the advantage to using an aging schedule?
8. What is the distinction between an account receivable and a note receivable?
9. How would you evaluate the following statement? "Given the choice, it would always be better to require an interest-bearing note from a customer as opposed to a non-interest-bearing note. This is because interest on a note receivable is a form of revenue and it is only in the case of an interest-bearing note that interest will be earned."
10. Why does the discounting of a note receivable with recourse result in a contingent liability? Should the liability be reported on the balance sheet?

Exercises

Exercise 6-1 ***Certificate of Deposit*** **LO 1**

On May 31, 2004, Elmer Corp. purchased a 120-day, 9% certificate of deposit for $50,000. The CD was redeemed on September 28, 2004. Determine the effect on the accounting equation of:

a. The purchase of the CD.
b. The accrual of interest adjustment for interest earned through June 30, the end of the company's fiscal year.
c. The redemption of the CD.

Assume 360 days in a year.

Exercise 6-2 ***Classification of Cash Equivalents and Investments on a Balance Sheet*** **LO 1**

Classify each of the following items as either a cash equivalent (CE), a short-term investment (STI), or a long-term investment (LTI).

_______ 1. A 120-day certificate of deposit.
_______ 2. Three hundred shares of GM common stock. The company plans on selling the stock in six months.
_______ 3. A six-month U.S. Treasury bill.
_______ 4. A 60-day certificate of deposit.
_______ 5. Ford Motor Co. bonds maturing in 15 years. The company intends to hold the bonds until maturity.
_______ 6. Commercial paper issued by ABC Corp., maturing in four months.
_______ 7. Five hundred shares of Chrysler common stock. The company plans to sell the stock in 60 days to help pay for a note due at that time at the bank.
_______ 8. Two hundred shares of GE preferred stock. The company intends to hold the stock for 10 years and at that point sell it to help finance construction of a new factory.
_______ 9. Ten-year U.S. Treasury bonds. The company plans to sell the bonds on the open market in six months.
_______ 10. A 90-day U.S. Treasury bill.

Exercise 6-3 ***Classification of Investments*** **LO 1**

Red Oak makes the following investments in the stock of other companies during 2004. For each investment, indicate how it would be accounted for and reported on; use the following designations: trading security (T), available-for-sale security (AS), equity investee (E), or a subsidiary included in consolidated statements (S).

________ **1.** 500 shares of ABC common stock to be held for short-term share appreciation

________ **2.** 20,000 shares of the 50,000 shares of Ace common stock to be held for the long term

________ **3.** 100 shares of Creston preferred stock to be held for an indefinite period of time

________ **4.** 80,000 of the 100,000 shares of Orient common stock

________ **5.** 10,000 of the 40,000 shares of Omaha preferred stock to be held for the long term

Exercise 6-4 ***Classification of Investments*** **LO 1**

Fill in the blanks below to indicate whether each of the following investments should be classified as a held-to-maturity security (HM), a trading security (T), or an available-for-sale security (AS):

________ **1.** Shares of IBM stock to be held indefinitely.

________ **2.** GM bonds due in 10 years. The intent is to hold them until they mature.

________ **3.** Shares of Motorola stock. Plans are to hold the stock until the price goes up by 10% and then sell it.

________ **4.** Ford Motor Company bonds due in 15 years. The bonds are part of a portfolio that turns over on the average of every 60 days.

________ **5.** Chrysler bonds due in 10 years. Plans are to hold them indefinitely.

Exercise 6-5 ***Purchase and Sale of Bonds*** **LO 1**

Starship Enterprises enters into the following transactions during 2004 and 2005:

2004

Jan. 1	Purchased $100,000 face value of Northern Lights Inc. bonds at face value. The newly issued bonds have an interest rate of 8% paid semiannually on June 30 and December 31. The bonds mature in five years.
June 30	Received interest on the Northern Lights bonds.
Dec. 31	Received interest on the Northern Lights bonds.

2005

Jan. 1	Sold the Northern Lights Inc. bonds for $102,000.

Assume Starship classifies all bonds as held to maturity.

Required

1. Determine the effect on Starship's accounting equation on each of the preceding dates.
2. Why was Starship able to sell its Northern Lights bonds for $102,000?

Exercise 6-6 ***Investment in Stock*** **LO 1**

On December 1, 2004, Chicago Corp. purchases 1,000 shares of the preferred stock of Denver Corp. for $40 per share. Chicago expects the price of the stock to increase over the next few months and plans to sell it for a profit. On December 20, 2004, Denver declares a dividend of $1 per share to be paid on January 15, 2005. On December 31, 2004, Chicago's accounting year-end, the Denver stock is trading on the market at $42 per share. Chicago sells the stock on February 12, 2005, at a price of $45 per share.

Required

1. Should Chicago classify its investments as held-to-maturity, trading, or available-for-sale securities? Explain your answer.
2. Determine the effects on the accounting equation of Chicago's purchase of the preferred stock on December 1, 2004; the dividend declared on December 20, 2004; the change in market value at December 31, 2004; and the sale on February 12, 2005.
3. In what category of the balance sheet should Chicago classify its investment on its December 31, 2004, balance sheet?

Exercise 6-7 *Investment in Stock* LO 1

On August 15, 2004, Cubs Corp. purchases 5,000 shares of common stock in Sox Inc. at a market price of $15 per share. In addition, Cubs pays brokerage fees of $1,000. Cubs plans to hold the stock indefinitely rather than as a part of its active trading portfolio. The market value of the stock is $13 per share on December 31, 2004, the end of Cubs' accounting year. On July 8, 2005, Cubs sells the Sox stock for $10 per share.

Required

1. Should Cubs classify its investment as held-to-maturity, trading, or available-for-sale securities? Explain your answer.
2. Determine the effects on the accounting equation of Cubs' purchase of the common stock on August 15, 2004; the change in market value at December 31, 2004; and the sale on July 8, 2005.
3. In what category of the balance sheet should Cubs classify its investment on its December 31, 2004, balance sheet?

Exercise 6-8 *Comparison of the Direct Write-Off and Allowance Methods of Accounting for Bad Debts* LO 2

DECISION MAKING

In its first year of business, Rideaway Bikes has net income of $145,000, exclusive of any adjustment for bad debt expense. The president of the company has asked you to calculate net income under each of two alternatives of accounting for bad debts: the direct write-off method and the allowance method. The president would like to use the method that will result in the higher net income. So far, no adjustments have been made to write off uncollectible accounts or to estimate bad debts. The relevant data are as follows:

Write-offs of uncollectible accounts during the year	$ 10,500
Net credit sales	$650,000
Estimated percentage of net credit sales that will be uncollectible	2%

Required

Compute net income under each of the two alternatives. Does Rideaway have a choice as to which method to use? Should it base its choice on which method will result in the higher net income? (Ignore income taxes.)

Exercise 6-9 *Allowance Method of Accounting for Bad Debts—Comparison of the Two Approaches* LO 2

Kandel Company had the following data available for 2004 (before making any adjustments):

Accounts receivable, 12/31/04	$320,100
Allowance for doubtful accounts	2,600
Net credit sales, 2004	834,000

Required

Determine the effect on the accounting equation of the adjustment to recognize bad debts under the following assumptions: (a) bad debts expense is expected to be 2% of net credit sales for the year and (b) Kandel expects it will not be able to collect 6% of the balance in accounts receivable at year-end.

Exercise 6-10 *Accounts Receivable Turnover for General Mills* LO 2

http://www.generalmills.com

The 2002 annual report of General Mills (the makers of Cheerios® and Wheaties®) reported the following amounts (in millions of dollars).

Net Sales, for the year ended May 26, 2002	$7,949
Receivables, less allowance for doubtful accounts of $21, May 26, 2002	1,010
Receivables, less allowance for doubtful accounts of $6, May 27, 2001	664

Required

1. Compute General Mills' accounts receivable turnover ratio for 2002. (Assume that all sales are on credit.)
2. What is the average collection period, in days, for an account receivable? Explain your answer.
3. Give some examples of the types of customers you would expect General Mills to have. Do you think the average collection period for sales to these customers is reasonable? What other information do you need to fully answer this question?

Exercise 6-11 ***Interest-Bearing Notes Receivable*** **LO 3**

On September 1, 2004, Dougherty Corp. accepted a six-month, 7%, $45,000 interest-bearing note from the Rozelle Company in payment of an accounts receivable. Dougherty's year-end is December 31. Rozelle paid the note and interest on the due date.

Required

1. Who is the maker and who is the payee of the note?
2. What is the maturity date of the note?
3. Determine the effect on Dougherty's accounting equation of:
   a. The acceptance of the note.
   b. The accrual of interest earned through December 31, 2004, the end of the company's year.
   c. Receipt of payment of the note and interest.

Exercise 6-12 ***Non-Interest-Bearing Note*** **LO 4**

On May 1, Radtke's Music Mart sold an electronic keyboard to Mary Reynolds. Reynolds made a $300 down payment and signed a 10-month note for $1,625. The normal selling price of the keyboard is $1,800 in cash. Radtke's fiscal year ends December 31. Reynolds paid Radtke in full on the maturity date.

Required

1. How much total interest did Radtke receive on this note?
2. Determine the effect on Radtke's accounting equation on May 1, December 31, and the maturity date.
3. What is the effective interest rate on the note?

Exercise 6-13 ***Credit Card Sales*** **LO 5**

Darlene's Diner accepts American Express credit cards from its customers. Darlene's is closed on Sundays and on that day records the weekly sales and remits the credit card drafts to American Express. For the week ending on Sunday, June 12, cash sales totaled $2,430, and credit card sales amounted to $3,500. On June 15, Darlene's received $3,360 from American Express as payment for the credit card drafts. For the transactions of June 12 and June 15, determine the effect on the accounting equation. As a percentage, what collection fee is American Express charging Darlene?

Exercise 6-14 ***Impact of Transactions Involving Receivables on Statement of Cash Flows*** **LO 6**

From the following list, identify whether the change in the account balance during the year would be added to or deducted from net income when the indirect method is used to determine cash flows from operating activities.

_______ Increase in accounts receivable
_______ Decrease in accounts receivable
_______ Increase in notes receivable
_______ Decrease in notes receivable

Exercise 6-15 ***Cash Collections—Direct Method*** **LO 6**

Emily Enterprises' comparative balance sheets included accounts receivable of $224,600 at December 31, 2003, and $205,700 at December 31, 2004. Sales reported on Emily's 2004 income statement amounted to $2,250,000. What is the amount of cash collections that Emily will report in the Operating Activities category of its 2004 statement of cash flows assuming that the direct method is used?

Multi-Concept Exercise

Exercise 6-16 ***Impact of Transactions Involving Cash, Securities, and Receivables on Statement of Cash Flows*** **LO 1, 2, 3, 6**

From the following list, identify each item as operating (O), investing (I), financing (F), or not separately reported on the statement of cash flows (N). Assume that the indirect method is used to determine the cash flows from operating activities.

(continued)

_______ Purchase of cash equivalents
_______ Redemption of cash equivalents
_______ Purchase of available-for-sale securities
_______ Sale of available-for-sale securities
_______ Write-off of customer account (under the allowance method)

Problems

Problem 6-1 *Investments in Bonds and Stock* LO 1

Swartz Inc. enters into the following transactions during 2004:

July 1	Paid $10,000 to acquire on the open market $10,000 face value of Gallatin bonds. The bonds have a stated annual interest rate of 6% with interest paid semiannually on June 30 and December 31. The bonds mature in $5^1/_2$ years.
Oct. 23	Purchased 600 shares of Eagle Rock common stock at $20 per share.
Nov. 21	Purchased 200 shares of Montana preferred stock at $30 per share.
Dec. 10	Received dividends of $1.50 per share on the Eagle Rock stock and $2.00 per share on the Montana stock.
Dec. 28	Sold 400 shares of Eagle Rock common stock at $25 per share.
Dec. 31	Received interest from the Gallatin bonds.
Dec. 31	Noted market price of $29 per share for the Eagle Rock stock and $26 per share for the Montana stock.

Required

1. Determine the effect on Swartz's accounting equation of each of the preceding transactions. Swartz classifies the bonds as held-to-maturity securities and all stock investments as trading securities.
2. Prepare a partial balance sheet as of December 31, 2004, to indicate the proper presentation of the investments.
3. Indicate the items, and the amount of each, that will appear on the 2004 income statement relative to the investments.

Problem 6-2 *Investments in Stock* LO 1

Atlas Superstores occasionally finds itself with excess cash to invest and consequently entered into the following transactions during 2004:

Jan. 15	Purchased 200 shares of Sears common stock at $50 per share, plus $500 in commissions.
May 23	Received dividends of $2 per share on the Sears stock.
June 1	Purchased 100 shares of Ford Motor Co. stock at $74 per share, plus $300 in commissions.
Oct. 20	Sold all the Sears stock at $42 per share, less commissions of $400.
Dec. 15	Received notification from Ford Motor Co. that a $1.50 per share dividend had been declared. The checks will be mailed to stockholders on January 10, 2005.
Dec. 31	Noted that the Ford Motor Co. stock was quoted on the stock exchange at $85 per share.

Required

1. Determine the effect on Atlas's accounting equation of each of the preceding transactions. Assume that Atlas categorizes all investments as available-for-sale securities.
2. What is the total amount that Atlas should report on its income statement from its investments during 2004?
3. Assume all the same facts except that Atlas categorizes all investments as trading securities. How would your answer to part **2** change? Explain why your answer would change.

Problem 6-3 *Allowance Method for Accounting for Bad Debts* LO 2

At the beginning of 2004, EZ Tech Company's Accounts Receivable balance was $140,000, and the balance in the Allowance for Doubtful Accounts was $2,350. EZ Tech's sales in 2004 were

$1,050,000, 80% of which were on credit. Collections on account during the year were $670,000. The company wrote off $4,000 of uncollectible accounts during the year.

Required

1. Determine the effect on EZ's accounting equation relative to the sale, collections, and write-offs of accounts receivable during 2004.
2. Determine the effect on EZ's accounting equation of the estimate of bad debts assuming (a) bad debt expense is 3% of credit sales and (b) amounts expected to be uncollectible are 6% of the year-end accounts receivable.
3. What is the net realizable value of accounts receivable on December 31, 2004, under each assumption (**a** and **b**) in **2**?
4. What effect does the recognition of bad debt expense have on the net realizable value? What effect does the write-off of accounts have on the net realizable value?

Problem 6-4 *Aging Schedule to Account for Bad Debts* LO 2

SPREADSHEET

Sparkle Jewels distributes fine stones. It sells on credit to retail jewelry stores and extends terms that require the stores to pay in 60 days. For accounts that are not overdue, Sparkle has found that there is a 95% probability of collection. For accounts up to one month past due, the likelihood of collection decreases to 80%. If accounts are between one and two months past due, the probability of collection is 60%, and if an account is more than two months past due, Sparkle Jewels estimates that there is only a 40% chance of collecting the receivable.

On December 31, 2004, the balance in Allowance for Doubtful Accounts is $12,300. The amounts of gross receivables, by age, on this date are as follows:

Category	Amount
Current	$200,000
Past due:	
Less than one month	45,000
One to two months	25,000
More than two months	10,000

Required

1. Prepare a schedule to estimate the amount of uncollectible accounts at December 31, 2004.
2. On the basis of the schedule in Part 1, determine the effect on the accounting equation of the estimate of bad debts at December 31, 2004.
3. Show how accounts receivable would be presented on the December 31, 2004, balance sheet.

Problem 6-5 *Accounts Receivable Turnover for Whirlpool and Maytag* LO 2

The following information was summarized from the 2002 annual report of Whirlpool Corporation: http://www.whirlpool.com

	(in millions)
Trade receivables, less allowances (2002: $94; 2001: $93)	
December 31, 2002	$ 1,781
December 31, 2001	1,515
Net sales for the year ended December 31:	
2002	11,016
2001	10,343

The following information was summarized from the 2002 annual report of Maytag Corporation: http://www.maytag.com

	(in thousands)
Accounts receivable, less allowance for doubtful accounts (2002–$24,451; 2001–$24,121):	
December 31, 2002	$ 586,447
December 31, 2001	618,101
Net sales for the year ended:	
December 31, 2002	4,666,031
December 31, 2001	4,185,051

Required

1. Calculate the accounts receivable turnover ratios for Whirlpool and Maytag for 2002.
2. Calculate the average collection period, in days, for both companies for 2002. Comment on the reasonableness of the collection periods considering the types of companies that you would expect to be customers of Whirlpool and Maytag.
3. Which company appears to be performing better? What other information should you consider to determine how these companies are performing in this regard?

Problem 6-6 ***Non-Interest-Bearing Note Receivable*** **LO 4**

Northern Nursery sells a large stock of trees and shrubs to a landscaping business on May 31, 2004. The landscaper makes a down payment of $5,000 and signs a promissory note agreeing to pay $20,000 on August 29, 2004, the end of its busy season. The cash selling price of the nursery stock on May 31 was $24,000.

Required

1. For the transactions on each of the following dates, determine the effect on the accounting equation:
   a. May 31, 2004, to record the receipt of the down payment and the promissory note
   b. June 30, 2004, the end of Northern's fiscal year
   c. August 29, 2004, to record collection of the note
2. Compute the effective rate of interest earned by Northern on the note. Explain your answer.

Problem 6-7 ***Credit Card Sales*** **LO 5**

Gas stations sometimes sell gasoline at a lower price to customers who pay cash than to customers who use a charge card. A local gas station owner pays 2% of the sales price to the credit card company when customers pay with a credit card. He pays $0.75 per gallon of gasoline and must earn at least $0.25 per gallon of gross margin to stay competitive.

Required

1. Determine the price the owner must charge credit card customers to maintain his gross margin.
2. How much discount could the owner offer to cash customers and still maintain the same gross margin?

Problem 6-8 ***Effects of Changes in Receivable Balances on Statement of Cash Flows*** **LO 6**

Stegner Inc. reported net income of $130,000 for the year ended December 31, 2004. The following items were included on Stegner's balance sheets at December 31, 2004 and 2003:

	12/31/04	12/31/03
Cash	$105,000	$110,000
Accounts receivable	223,000	83,000
Notes receivable	95,000	100,000

Stegner uses the indirect method to prepare its statement of cash flows. Stegner does not have any other current assets or current liabilities and did not enter into any investing or financing activities during 2004.

Required

1. Prepare Stegner's 2004 statement of cash flows.
2. Draft a brief memo to the owner to explain why cash decreased during a profitable year.

Multi-Concept Problem

Problem 6-9 ***Accounts and Notes Receivable*** **LO 2, 3**

Linus Corp. sold merchandise for $5,000 to C. Brown on May 15, 2004, with payment due in thirty days. Subsequent to this, Brown experienced cash flow problems and was unable to pay its debt. On August 10, 2004, Linus stopped trying to collect the outstanding receivable from Brown and wrote the account off as uncollectible. On December 1, 2004, Brown sent Linus a check for $1,000 and offered to sign a two-month, 9%, $4,000 promissory note to satisfy the remaining obligation. Brown paid the entire amount due Linus, with interest, on January 31, 2005. Linus ends its accounting year on December 31 each year, and uses the allowance method to account for bad debts.

Required

1. For each of the transactions during the period from May 15, 2004, to January 31, 2005, determine the effect on Linus's accounting equation.
2. Why would Brown bother to send Linus a check for $1,000 on December 1 and agree to sign a note for the balance, given that such a long period of time had passed since the original purchase?

Alternate Problems

Problem 6-1A ***Investments in Bonds and Stock*** **LO 1**

Vermont Corp. enters into the following transactions during 2004:

July 1	Paid $10,000 to acquire on the open market $10,000 face value of Maine bonds. The bonds have a stated annual interest rate of 8% with interest paid semiannually on June 30 and December 31. The remaining life of the bonds on the date of purchase is $3^1/_2$ years.
Oct. 23	Purchased 1,000 shares of Virginia common stock at $15 per share.
Nov. 21	Purchased 600 shares of Carolina preferred stock at $8 per share.
Dec. 10	Received dividends of $.50 per share on the Virginia stock and $1.00 per share on the Carolina stock.
Dec. 28	Sold 700 shares of Virginia common stock at $19 per share.
Dec. 31	Received interest from the Maine bonds.
Dec. 31	The Virginia Stock and the Carolina stock have market prices of $20 per share and $11 per share, respectively.

Required

1. Determine the effect on Vermont's accounting equation of each of the preceding transactions. Vermont classifies the bonds as held-to-maturity securities and all stock investments as trading securities.
2. Prepare a partial balance sheet as of December 31, 2004, to indicate the proper presentation of the investments.
3. Indicate the items, and the amount of each, that will appear on the 2004 income statement relative to the investments.

Problem 6-2A ***Investments in Stock*** **LO 1**

Trendy Supercenter occasionally finds itself with excess cash to invest and consequently entered into the following transactions during 2004:

Jan. 15	Purchased 100 shares of IBM common stock at $130 per share, plus $250 in commissions.
May 23	Received dividends of $1 per share on the IBM stock.
June 1	Purchased 200 shares of General Motors stock at $60 per share, plus $300 in commissions.
Oct. 20	Sold all of the IBM stock at $140 per share, less commissions of $400.
Dec. 15	Received notification from General Motors that a $0.75 per share dividend had been declared. The checks will be mailed to stockholders on January 10, 2005.
Dec. 31	Noted that the General Motors stock was quoted on the stock exchange at $45 per share.

Required

1. Determine the effect on Trendy's accounting equation of each of the preceding transactions. Assume that Trendy categorizes all investments as available-for-sale securities.
2. What is the total amount of income that Trendy should recognize from its investments during 2004?

(continued)

3. Assume all of the same facts except that Trendy categorizes all investments as trading securities. How would your answer to part 2 change? Explain why your answer would change.

Problem 6-3A *Allowance Method for Accounting for Bad Debts* LO 2

At the beginning of 2004, Miyazaki Company's Accounts Receivable balance was $105,000 and the balance in the Allowance for Doubtful Accounts was $1,950. Miyazaki's sales in 2004 were $787,500, 80% of which were on credit. Collections on account during the year were $502,500. The company wrote off $3,000 of uncollectible accounts during the year.

Required

1. Determine the effect on Miyazaki's accounting equation of the sales, collections, and write-offs of accounts receivable during 2004.
2. Determine the effect on Miyazaki's accounting equation of the estimate of bad debts, assuming (a) bad debt expense is 3% of credit sales or (b) amounts expected to be uncollectible are 6% of the year-end accounts receivable.
3. What is the net realizable value of accounts receivable on December 31, 2004, under each assumption (**a** and **b**) in **2**?
4. What effect does the recognition of bad debt expense have on the net realizable value? What effect does the write-off of accounts have on the net realizable value?

Problem 6-4A *Aging Schedule to Account for Bad Debts* LO 2

SPREADSHEET

Rough Stuff is a distributor of large rocks. It sells on credit to commercial landscaping companies and extends terms which require customers to pay in 60 days. For accounts that are not overdue, Rough has found that there is a 90% probability of collection. For accounts up to one month past due, the likelihood of collection decreases to 75%. If accounts are between one and two months past due, the probability of collection is 65%, and if an account is more than two months past due, Rough estimates that there is only a 25% chance of collecting the receivable.

On December 31, 2004, the credit balance in Allowance for Doubtful Accounts is $34,590. The amounts of gross receivables, by age, on this date are as follows:

Category	Amount
Current	$135,000
Past due:	
Less than one month	60,300
One to two months	35,000
More than two months	45,000

Required

1. Prepare a schedule to estimate the amount of uncollectible accounts at December 31, 2004.
2. Rough knows that $40,000 of the $45,000 amount that is more than two months overdue is due from one customer that is in severe financial trouble. It is rumored that the customer will be filing for bankruptcy in the near future. As controller for Rough Stuff, how would you handle this situation?
3. Show how accounts receivable would be presented on the December 31, 2004, balance sheet.

Problem 6-5A *Accounts Receivable Turnover for Boise Cascade and Georgia-Pacific Corporation* LO 2

http://www.boisecascade.com

The following information was summarized from the 2002 annual report of Boise Cascade Corporation and Subsidiaries (receivables are net of allowances):

	(in thousands)
Receivables, December 31:	
2002	$ 423,976
2001	424,722
Sales for the year ended December 31:	
2002	7,412,329
2001	7,422,175

http://www.gp.com

The following information was summarized from the 2002 annual report of Georgia-Pacific Corporation (receivables are net of allowances):

	(in millions)
Receivables:	
December 28, 2002	$ 1,777
December 29, 2001	2,352
Net sales for the year ended:	
December 28, 2002	23,271
December 29, 2001	25,016

Required

1. Calculate the accounts receivable turnover ratios for Boise Cascade and Georgia-Pacific for 2002.
2. Calculate the average collection period, in days, for both companies for 2002. Comment on the reasonableness of the collection periods considering the types of companies that you would expect to be customers of Boise Cascade and Georgia-Pacific.
3. Which company appears to be performing better? What other information should you consider to determine how these companies are performing in this regard?

Problem 6-6A *Non-Interest-Bearing Note Receivable* LO 4

Midwest Poultry sells a large stock of birds to a processor on May 31, 2004. The processor makes a $12,000 down payment and signs a $36,900 promissory note agreeing to pay the remainder on August 29, 2004, the end of its busy season. The cash selling price of the birds on May 31 was $48,000.

1. Determine the effect on Midwest's accounting equation on August 29, 2004, of recording collection of the note. Midwest's accounting year ends on September 30.
2. Compute the effective rate of interest earned by Midwest on the note. Explain your answer.

Problem 6-7A *Credit Card Sales* LO 5

A local fast-food store is considering the use of major credit cards in its outlets. Current annual sales are $800,000 per outlet. The company can purchase the equipment needed to handle credit cards and have an additional phone line installed in each outlet for approximately $800 per outlet. The equipment will be an expense in the year it is installed. The employee training time is minimal. The credit card company will charge a fee equal to 1.5% of sales for the use of credit cards. The company is unable to determine by how much, if any, sales will increase and whether cash customers will use a credit card rather than cash. No other fast-food stores in the local area accept credit cards for sales payment.

Required

1. Assuming only 5% of existing cash customers will use a credit card, what increase in sales is necessary to pay for the credit card equipment in the first year?
2. What other factors might the company consider in addition to an increase in sales dollars?

Problem 6-8A *Effects of Changes in Receivable Balances on Statement of Cash Flows* LO 6

St. Charles Antique Market reported a net loss of $6,000 for the year ended December 31, 2004. The following items were included on St. Charles Antique Market's balance sheets at December 31, 2004 and 2003:

	12/31/04	12/31/03
Cash	$ 36,300	$ 3,100
Accounts receivable	79,000	126,000
Notes receivable	112,600	104,800

St. Charles Antique Market uses the indirect method to prepare its statement of cash flows. St. Charles Antique Market does not have any other current assets or current liabilities and did not enter into any investing or financing activities during 2004.

Required

1. Prepare St. Charles Antique Market's 2004 statement of cash flows.
2. Draft a brief memo to the owner to explain why cash increased during such an unprofitable year.

Alternate Multi-Concept Problem

Problem 6-9A ***Accounts and Notes Receivable*** **LO 2, 3**

Tweedy Inc. sold merchandise for $6,000 to P.D. Cat on July 31, 2004, with payment due in thirty days. Subsequent to this, Cat experienced cash flow problems and was unable to pay its debt. On December 24, 2004, Tweedy stopped trying to collect the outstanding receivable from Cat and wrote the account off as uncollectible. On January 15, 2005, Cat sent Tweedy a check for $1,500 and offered to sign a two-month, 8%, $4,500 promissory note to satisfy the remaining obligation. Cat paid the entire amount on the note due Tweedy, with interest, on March 15, 2005. Tweedy ends its accounting year on December 31 each year.

Required

1. For each of the transactions during the period from July 31, 2004, to March 15, 2005, determine the effect on Tweedy's accounting equation.
2. Why would Cat bother to send Tweedy a check for $1,500 on January 15 and agree to sign a note for the balance, given that such a long period of time had passed since the original purchase?

Decision Cases

Reading and Interpreting Financial Statements

Decision Case 6-1 ***Reading and Interpreting Winnebago Industries' Financial Statements*** **LO 2**

Refer to the financial statements for 2002 included in Winnebago Industries' annual report. Answer each of the following questions by reference to the account titled "Receivables" rather than the one titled "Dealer Financing Receivables."

Required

1. What is the balance in the Allowance for Doubtful Accounts at the end of each of the two years presented? What is the net realizable value at the end of each year?
2. Calculate the ratio of the Allowance for Doubtful Accounts to Gross Accounts Receivable at the end of each of the two years.
3. Why do you think the balance in the Allowance for Doubtful Accounts was decreased at the end of 2002? Does this mean that the company expects a lesser percentage of bad debts?

http://www.winnebagoind.com
http://www.monacocoach.com

Decision Case 6-2 ***Comparing Two Companies in the Same Industry: Winnebago Industries and Monaco Coach Corporation*** **LO 2**

Refer to the financial statement information of Winnebago Industries and Monaco Coach Corporation in Appendices A and B at the end of the text. Answer the questions below with reference to the account titled "Receivables" for Winnebago Industries and the account titled "Trade Receivables" of Monaco Coach.

1. What is the balance of the Allowance for Doubtful Accounts at the end of each of the two years presented for Monaco Coach? What is the net realizable value at the end of each year?
2. Calculate the ratio of the Allowance for Doubtful Accounts to Gross Receivable at the end of each of the two years for Monaco Coach. How do these ratios compare to those for Winnebago Industries? What does the comparison tell you about the receivables of the two companies? (Refer to your answers to requirement **2** in Case 6-1 for the Winnebago Industries information.)
3. Monaco Coach had an increase in Trade Receivables from 2001 to 2002. What are logical explanations for this increase?
4. Calculate the receivables turnover for Winnebago Industries and Monaco Coach for the year 2002? Compare the two companies on the basis of this ratio.

http://www.pepsico.com

Decision Case 6-3 ***Reading PepsiCo's Statement of Cash Flows*** **LO 1, 6**

The following items appeared in the Investing Activities section of PepsiCo's 2002 statement of cash flows (all amounts are in millions of dollars):

	2002	2001	2000
Short-term investments, by original maturity			
More than three months–purchases	(62)	(2,537)	(4,950)
More than three months–maturities	833	2,078	4,585

Required:

1. What amount did PepsiCo spend in 2002 to purchase short-term investments? How does this amount compare to the amounts spent in the two prior years?
2. What amount did PepsiCo receive from investments that matured in 2002? How does this amount compare to the amounts spent in the two prior years?
3. The amounts from PepsiCo's statement of cash flows indicate that both purchases and maturities of its short-term investments were much less significant in 2002 than in prior years. What are some possible explanations for this?

Making Financial Decisions

Decision Case 6-4 *Liquidity* LO 1, 2

R Montague and J Capulet both distribute films to movie theaters. The following are the current assets for each at the end of the year (all amounts are in millions of dollars):

DECISION MAKING

	R Montague	J Capulet
Cash	$10	$ 5
Six-month certificates of deposit	9	0
Short-term investments in stock	0	6
Accounts receivable	15	23
Allowance for doubtful accounts	(1)	(1)
Total current assets	$33	$33

Required

As a loan officer for the First National Bank of Verona Heights, assume that both companies have come to you asking for a $10 million, six-month loan. If you could lend money to only one of the two, which one would it be? Justify your answer by writing a brief memo to the president of the bank.

Decision Case 6-5 *Notes Receivable* LO 3, 4

DECISION MAKING

Warren Land Development is considering two offers for a lot. Builder A has offered to pay $12,000 down and sign a 10%, $80,000 promissory note, with interest and principal due in one year. Builder B would make a down payment of $20,000 and sign a non-interest-bearing, one-year note for $80,000. The president believes that the deal with Builder A is better because it involves interest and the loan to Builder B does not. The vice president of marketing thinks the offer from Builder B is better because it involves more money "up front." The sales manager is indifferent, reasoning that both builders would eventually pay $100,000 in total and that because the lot was recently appraised at $75,000, both would be paying more than fair market value.

Required

1. Regardless of which offer it accepts, how much revenue should Warren recognize from the sale of the lot? Explain your answer.
2. Which offer do you think Warren should accept? Or is the sales manager correct that it doesn't matter which one is accepted? Explain your answer.

Accounting and Ethics: What Would You Do?

Decision Case 6-6 *Fair Market Values for Investments* LO 1

ETHICS

Kennedy Corp. operates a chain of discount stores. The company regularly holds stock of various companies in a trading securities portfolio. One of these investments is 10,000 shares of Clean Air Inc. stock purchased for $100 per share during December 2004.

Clean Air manufactures highly specialized equipment used to test automobile emissions. Unfortunately, the market price of Clean Air's stock dropped during December 2004 and closed the year trading at $75 per share. Kennedy expects the Clean Air stock to experience a turn around, however, as states pass legislation to require an emissions test on all automobiles.

As controller for Kennedy, you have followed the fortunes of Clean Air with particular interest. You and the company's treasurer are both concerned by the negative impact that a write-down of the stock to fair value would have on Kennedy's earnings for 2004. You have calculated net income for 2004 to be $400,000, exclusive of the recognition of any loss on the stock.

The treasurer comes to you on January 31, 2005, with the following idea:

> Since you haven't closed the books yet for 2004, and we haven't yet released the 2004 financials, let's think carefully about how Clean Air should be classified. I realize that we normally treat these types of investments as trading securities, but if we categorize the Clean Air stock on the balance sheet as available-for-sale rather than a trading security, we won't need to report the adjustment to fair value on the income statement. I don't see anything wrong with this since we would still report the stock at its fair value on the balance sheet.

Required

1. Compute Kennedy's net income for 2004, under two different assumptions: (a) the stock is classified as a trading security and (b) the stock is classified as an available-for-sale security.
2. Which classification do you believe is appropriate, according to accounting standards? Explain your answer.
3. Would you have any ethical concerns in following the treasurer's advice? Explain your answer. If the investment is listed as available-for-sale, does the information faithfully represent what it claims to represent? Who benefits and who is harmed by the decision to reclassify? Explain your answer.

Decision Case 6-7 *Notes Receivable* LO 4

ETHICS

Patterson Company is a large diversified business with a unit that sells commercial real estate. As a company, Patterson has been profitable in recent years with the exception of the real estate business, where economic conditions have resulted in weak sales. The vice president of the real estate division is aware of the poor performance of his group and needs to find ways to "show a profit."

During the current year the division is successful in selling a 100-acre tract of land for a new shopping center. The original cost of the property to Patterson was $4 million. The buyer has agreed to sign a $10 million note with payments of $2 million due at the end of each of the next five years. The property was appraised late last year at a market value of $7.5 million. The vice president has come to you, the controller, and asked that you record a sale for $10 million with a corresponding increase in Notes Receivable for $10 million.

Required

1. Does the suggestion by the vice president as to how to record the sale violate any accounting principle? If so, explain the principle it violates.
2. What would you do? Write a brief memo to the vice president explaining the proper accounting for the sale.

THOMSON ONE Business School Edition Case

Case 6-8 *Using THOMSON ONE for PepsiCo*

http://www.pepsico.com

In the chapter we saw the critical role that receivables and investments play in the success of a company. The ability to manage and control these liquid assets should translate to success in the market for a company's stock in the form of appreciation in its stock price and, if the company chooses, in the form of dividends to the stockholders. We can use THOMSON ONE to obtain information about PepsiCo's performance as measured in its financial statements and in its stock price.

Begin by entering the company's ticker symbol, PEP, and then selecting "GO." On the opening screen you will see background information about the company, key financial ratios, and some recent data concerning stock price. To research the company's stock price further, click on the "Prices" tab. At the top of the Price Chart, click on the "Interactive Chart." To obtain a 1-year chart, go to "Time Frame," click on the down arrow, and select "1 year." Then click on "Draw," and a 1-year chart should appear.

We can also find PepsiCo's most recent financial statements. Near the top of the screen, click on "Financials" and select "Financial Statements." Refer to the comparative statements of earnings, statements of cash flows, and balance sheets.

Based on your use of THOMSON ONE, answer the following questions:

1. What is the dollar amount of short-term investments for the most recent year? What reasons does PepsiCo give for the change in short-term investments in the most recent year?
2. What is the dollar amount of accounts and notes receivable for the most recent year available? Did the amount change significantly from the prior year?
3. What is the accounts and notes receivable turnover ratio for the most recent year? How does this ratio compare with the same one for 2002?
4. What have been PepsiCo's high and low stock prices for the most recent year?
5. How does the company's stock performance compare to the other line on the stock price chart for the S&P 500?

Solutions to Key Terms Quiz

1	Equity securities (p. 253)	11	Note receivable (p. 270)
2	Debt securities (p. 253)	9	Note payable (p. 270)
5	Held-to-maturity securities (p. 256)	21	Principal (p. 271)
3	Trading securities (p. 256)	22	Maturity date (p. 271)
4	Available-for-sale securities (p. 256)	23	Term (p. 271)
17	Subsidiary ledger (p. 264)	24	Maturity value (p. 271)
20	Control account (p. 264)	25	Interest (p. 271)
19	Direct write-off method (p. 265)	14	Interest-bearing note (p. 271)
6	Allowance method (p. 265)	18	Non-interest-bearing note (p. 271)
15	Aging schedule (p. 268)	16	Discounted note (p. 272)
8	Promissory note (p. 270)	10	Credit card draft (p. 273)
13	Maker (p. 270)	12	Discounting (p. 275)
7	Payee (p. 270)		

Chapter 7

Inventories and Cost of Goods Sold

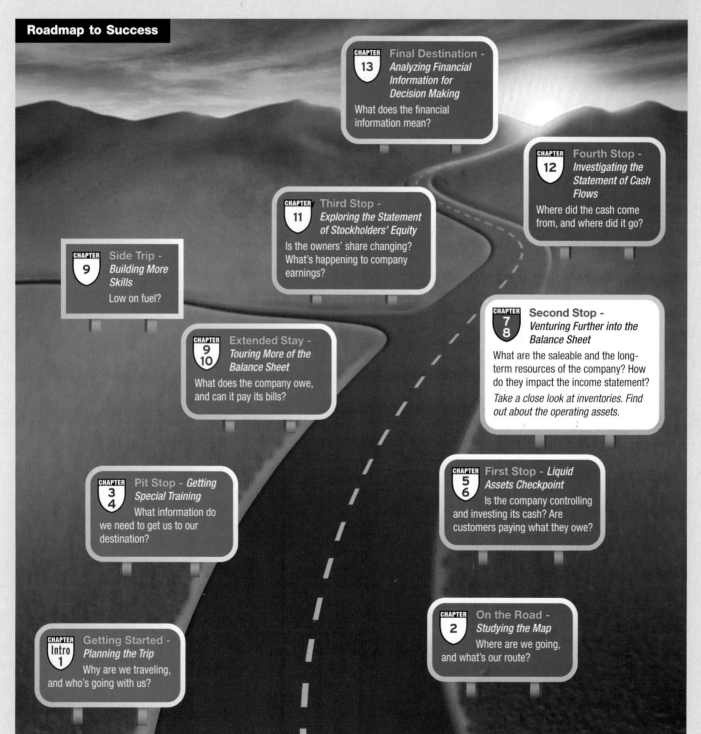

Roadmap to Success

CHAPTER Intro 1 — Getting Started - *Planning the Trip*
Why are we traveling, and who's going with us?

CHAPTER 2 — On the Road - *Studying the Map*
Where are we going, and what's our route?

CHAPTER 3 4 — Pit Stop - *Getting Special Training*
What information do we need to get us to our destination?

CHAPTER 5 6 — First Stop - *Liquid Assets Checkpoint*
Is the company controlling and investing its cash? Are customers paying what they owe?

CHAPTER 7 8 — **Second Stop -** ***Venturing Further into the Balance Sheet***
What are the saleable and the long-term resources of the company? How do they impact the income statement?
Take a close look at inventories. Find out about the operating assets.

CHAPTER 9 10 — Extended Stay - *Touring More of the Balance Sheet*
What does the company owe, and can it pay its bills?

CHAPTER 9 — Side Trip - *Building More Skills*
Low on fuel?

CHAPTER 11 — Third Stop - *Exploring the Statement of Stockholders' Equity*
Is the owners' share changing? What's happening to company earnings?

CHAPTER 12 — Fourth Stop - *Investigating the Statement of Cash Flows*
Where did the cash come from, and where did it go?

CHAPTER 13 — Final Destination - *Analyzing Financial Information for Decision Making*
What does the financial information mean?

Focus on Financial Results

For the last few years the consumer electronics industry has sustained tremendous growth in a fiercely competitive environment. Circuit City remains a top retailer in the U.S. market. High-quality customer service and state-of-the-art merchandise have rewarded Circuit City with sales that reached approximately $10 billion in each of the last three years.

Sales volume is important for any merchandiser but so is managing *inventory* effectively. Inventory is a major issue for Circuit City as it continues to grow; you can see from the accompanying partial balance sheets that merchandise is the largest company asset, representing over one-third of total assets at the end of the 2003 fiscal year.

Both the amount of inventory on hand at year end and the ratio of inventory to total assets increased in 2003. Maintaining large stocks of inventory is costly for any business, and the more a retailer can minimize the amounts it has tied up in merchandise and still meet customer demand, the better off it will be. A combination of efforts to continue to grow sales and to control inventory costs will be two of the most critical factors in the future success of this leading consumer products merchandiser.

Circuit City's 2003 Annual Report

CONSOLIDATED BALANCE SHEETS

(Amounts in thousands except share data)	At February 28 2003	2002
ASSETS		
CURRENT ASSETS:		
Cash and cash equivalents [NOTE 2]	$ 884,670	$1,248,246
Accounts receivable, net of allowance for doubtful accounts of $1,075 and $660	215,125	158,817
Retained interests in securitized receivables [NOTE 6]	560,214	394,456
Merchandise inventory [NOTE 2]	1,409,736	1,234,243
Prepaid expenses and other current assets [NOTE 16]	33,165	39,246
Assets of discontinued operations [NOTE 3]	—	577,703
TOTAL CURRENT ASSETS	3,102,910	3,652,711
Property and equipment, net [NOTES 8 AND 9]	649,593	732,802
Deferred income taxes [NOTES 2 AND 11]	22,362	2,647
Other assets [NOTE 16]	24,252	11,354
Assets of discontinued operations [NOTE 3]	—	142,519
TOTAL ASSETS	$3,799,117	$4,542,033

CONSOLIDATED STATEMENTS OF EARNINGS

(Amounts in thousands except per share data)	Years Ended February 28 2003	%	2002	%	2001	%
NET SALES AND OPERATING REVENUES	$9,953,530	100.0	$9,518,231	100.0	$10,329,982	100.0
Cost of sales, buying and warehousing	7,603,205	76.4	7,180,259	75.4	7,836,093	75.8
Appliance exit costs [NOTE 10]	—	—	10,000	0.1	28,326	0.3
GROSS PROFIT	2,350,325	23.6	2,327,972	24.5	2,465,563	23.9
Finance income [NOTE 4]	62,416	0.7	106,230	1.1	76,800	0.7
Selling, general and administrative expenses [NOTE 2]	2,344,608	23.6	2,226,882	23.4	2,347,545	22.7
Appliance exit costs [NOTE 10]	—	—	—	—	1,670	—
Interest expense [NOTE 9]	1,093	—	881	—	7,273	0.1
Earnings from continuing operations before income taxes	67,040	0.7	206,439	2.2	185,875	1.8
Provision for income taxes [NOTE 11]	25,475	0.3	78,446	0.8	70,637	0.7
NET EARNINGS FROM CONTINUING OPERATIONS	41,565	0.4	127,993	1.4	115,238	1.1
NET EARNINGS FROM DISCONTINUED OPERATIONS [NOTE 3]	64,519	0.7	90,802	0.9	45,564	0.4
NET EARNINGS	$ 106,084	1.1	$ 218,795	2.3	$ 160,802	1.5

You're in the Driver's Seat

http://www.circuitcity.com

Also critical to the success of Circuit City is its management of "inventory turns"—the number of times it turns over its merchandise each year. What will lower or higher inventory turns say about the company's effectiveness in choosing, pricing, and promoting its products? While studying this chapter, consider these questions and select the annual report items you need to estimate Circuit City's inventory turns each year.

LEARNING OBJECTIVES

After studying this chapter, you should be able to:

LO 1 Identify the forms of inventory held by different types of businesses and the types of costs incurred. (p. 299)

LO 2 Demonstrate an understanding of how wholesalers and retailers account for sales of merchandise. (p. 301)

LO 3 Explain the differences between periodic and perpetual inventory systems. (p. 304)

LO 4 Demonstrate an understanding of how wholesalers and retailers account for cost of goods sold. (p. 306)

LO 5 Explain the relationship between the valuation of inventory and the measurement of income. (p. 310)

LO 6 Apply the inventory costing methods of specific identification, weighted average, FIFO, and LIFO using a periodic system. (p. 311)

LO 7 Analyze the effects of the different costing methods on inventory, net income, income taxes, and cash flow. (p. 315)

LO 8 Analyze the effects of an inventory error on various financial statement items. (p. 320)

LO 9 Apply the lower-of-cost-or-market rule to the valuation of inventory. (p. 323)

LO 10 Explain why and how the cost of inventory is estimated in certain situations. (p. 325)

LO 11 Analyze the management of inventory turnover. (p. 328)

LO 12 Explain the effects that inventory transactions have on the statement of cash flows. (p. 329)

LO 13 Apply the inventory costing methods using a perpetual system (Appendix). (p. 336)

WHAT EXTERNAL DECISION MAKERS WANT TO KNOW ABOUT INVENTORY

DECISION MAKING

For a company that sells a product, its inventory is the reason it exists. Without a sufficient supply on hand to meet customer demands, sales will be lost. At the same time, excess inventory on hand can be costly to a company and result in the potential for obsolete or spoiled products that can't be sold. The ability to sell or "turn over" its inventory on a regular basis is a concern to not only management of a company but also to its external stakeholders. Both stockholders and creditors need some assurance that the company is effectively and efficiently managing this important asset. In addition, external decision makers are interested in the relationship between a company's sales and the cost of those sales. Any excess of sales over cost of sales must be sufficient to not only cover other costs of doing business but also provide a profit to investors.

To be successful, decision makers must:

▸ *ASK ESSENTIAL QUESTIONS*

- Will the company be able to sell its inventory on a timely basis?
- Is the inventory adding value to the company?

▸ *FIND BASIC INFORMATION*

The balance sheet and the income statement, along with the supporting notes, provide the information decision makers need about a company's inventory. Specifically, this information tells

- what the nature of the company's inventory is,
- how much has been invested in inventory, and
- how the cost of inventory is being matched with revenues.

▸ *UNDERSTAND ACCOUNTING PRINCIPLES*

To understand the basic information that is found, decision makers must understand the underlying accounting principles (GAAP) that have been applied to create the reported information. For inventory, these principles determine:

- the cost of the inventory
- the methods used to match the cost of the inventory with revenue
- whether the inventory should be written down to reflect a loss in value

▸ *INTERPRET ANALYTICAL INFORMATION*

Decision makers can calculate a company's gross profit ratio to see how well it is performing compared to its competitors and as measured against prior periods. Any significant increases or decreases in this key ratio would interest both stockholders and creditors. Additionally, the inventory turnover ratio provides critical information about how well a company is managing its inventory. For example, a decrease in the inventory turnover ratio, and a corresponding increase in the number of days' sales in inventory, may be a signal to decision makers that a company is experiencing difficulty in selling its products.

THE NATURE OF INVENTORY

LO 1 Identify the forms of inventory held by different types of businesses and the types of costs incurred.

To this point, we have concentrated on the accounting for businesses that sell *services.* Banks, hotels, airlines, health clubs, real estate offices, law firms, and accounting firms are all examples of service companies. In this chapter we turn to accounting by companies that sell products, or what accountants call *inventory.* Companies that sell inventory can be broadly categorized into two types. Retailers and wholesalers purchase inventory in finished form and hold it for resale. For example, as a retailer Circuit City buys its various electronic products directly from wholesalers and then offers them for sale to consumers. This is in contrast to manufacturers, who transform raw materials into a finished product prior to sale. A good example of a manufacturing company is Winnebago Industries. It buys all of the various materials that are needed to build an RV, such as steel, glass, and tires, and then sells the finished product to its distributors, who sell the RVs to consumers.

Whether a company is a wholesaler, retailer, or manufacturer, its inventory is an asset that is held for *resale* in the normal course of business. The distinction between inventory and an operating asset is the *intent* of the owner. For example, some of the computers that Circuit City owns are operating assets because they are used in various activities of the business such as the payroll and accounting functions. Many more of the computers Circuit City owns are inventory, however, because the company intends to sell them. This chapter is concerned with the proper valuation of inventory and the related effect on cost of goods sold.

It is important to distinguish between the *types* of inventory costs incurred and the *form* the inventory takes. Wholesalers and retailers incur a single type of cost, the *purchase price,* of the inventory they sell. On the balance sheet they use a single account for inventory, titled **Merchandise Inventory.** Wholesalers and retailers buy merchandise in finished form and offer it for resale without transforming the product in any way. Because they do not use factory buildings, assembly lines, or production equipment, merchandise companies have a relatively small dollar amount in operating assets and a large amount in inventory. For example, on its balance sheet, Circuit City reported inventory of approximately $1.4 billion and total assets of $3.8 billion. It is not unusual for inventories to account for half of the total assets of a merchandise company.

Merchandise inventory The account wholesalers and retailers use to report inventory held for resale.

The cost of inventory to a *merchandiser* is limited to the product's purchase price, which may include other costs we will mention soon. Conversely, three distinct *types* of costs are incurred by a *manufacturer:* direct materials, direct labor, and manufacturing

Raw materials The inventory of a manufacturer before the addition of any direct labor or manufacturing overhead.

overhead. Direct materials, also called **raw materials,** are the ingredients used in making a product. The costs of direct materials used in manufacturing an automobile include the costs of steel, glass, and rubber. Direct labor consists of the amounts paid to workers to manufacture the product. The $20 per hour paid to an assembly line worker is a primary ingredient in the cost to manufacture the automobile. Manufacturing overhead includes all other costs that are related to the manufacturing process but cannot be directly matched to specific units of output. Depreciation of a factory building and the salary of a supervisor are two examples of overhead costs. Accountants have developed various techniques to assign, or allocate, these manufacturing overhead costs to specific products.

In addition to the three types of costs incurred in a production process, the inventory of a manufacturer takes three distinct *forms.* The three forms or stages in the development of inventory are raw materials, work in process, and finished goods. Direct materials or raw materials enter a production process in which they are transformed into a finished product by the addition of direct labor and manufacturing overhead. At any point in time, including the end of an accounting period, some of the materials have entered the process and some labor costs have been incurred but the product is not finished. The cost of unfinished products is appropriately called **work in process** or *work in progress.* Inventory that has completed the production process and is available for sale is called **finished goods.** Finished goods are the equivalent of merchandise inventory for a retailer or wholesaler in that both represent the inventory of goods held for sale. Many manufacturers disclose the dollar amounts of each of the three forms of inventory in their annual report. For example, Nike disclosed in its 2002 annual report the following amounts, stated in millions of dollars:

Work in process The cost of unfinished products in a manufacturing company.

Finished goods A manufacturer's inventory that is complete and ready for sale.

http://www.nike.com

	MILLIONS
Inventories:	
Finished goods	$1,348.2
Work in progress	13.0
Raw materials	12.6
	$1,373.8

Exhibit 7-1 summarizes the relationships between the types of costs incurred and the forms of inventory for different types of businesses.

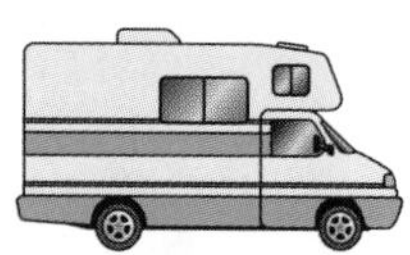

From Concept to Practice 7.1

Reading Winnebago Industries' Notes

Note 3 in Winnebago Industries' 2002 annual report includes information about the composition of its inventory. How does Winnebago Industries categorize these elements of its inventory? What percentage of its total inventory at the end of 2002 is made up of finished goods?

Exhibit 7-1

Relationships between Types of Businesses and Inventory Costs

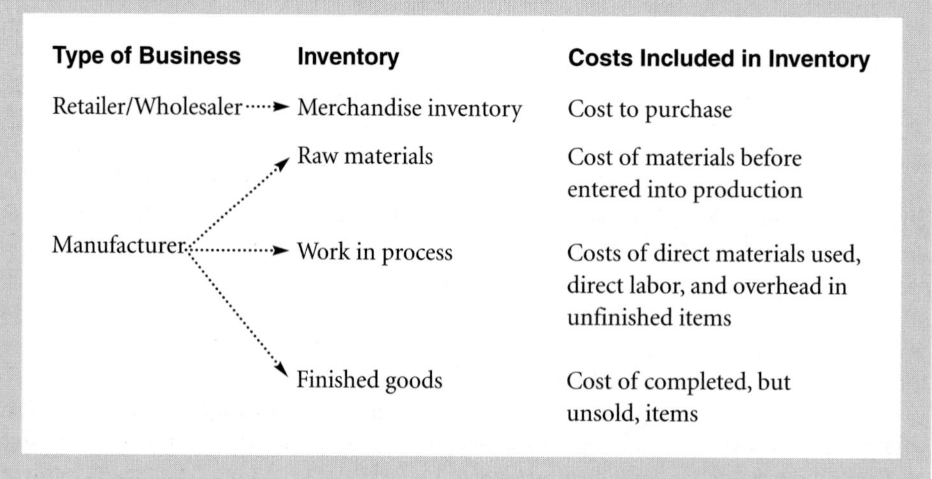

Type of Business	Inventory	Costs Included in Inventory
Retailer/Wholesaler →	Merchandise inventory	Cost to purchase
	Raw materials	Cost of materials before entered into production
Manufacturer →	Work in process	Costs of direct materials used, direct labor, and overhead in unfinished items
	Finished goods	Cost of completed, but unsold, items

THE INCOME STATEMENT FOR A MERCHANDISER

INTERNAL DECISION

Because of the additional complexities involved in valuing the inventory of a manufacturer, we will concentrate in this chapter on the valuation of *merchandise inventory.* (Accounting for the three different forms of inventory for a manufacturer is more complex and is covered in a follow-up course to this one.) A *condensed* multiple-step income statement for Daisy's Flower Depot is presented in Exhibit 7-2. First note the period covered by the statement: for the year ended December 31, 2004. Daisy's ends its fiscal year on December 31; however, many merchandisers end their *fiscal year* on a date other than December 31. Retailers often choose a date toward the end of January because the busy holiday shopping season is over and time can be devoted to closing the records and preparing financial statements. For example, Gap Inc. ends its fiscal year on the Saturday closest to January 31, and Circuit City closes its books on the last day of February each year.

http://www.gap.com
http://www.circuitcity.com

Exhibit 7-2

Condensed Income Statement for a Merchandiser

DAISY'S FLOWER DEPOT
INCOME STATEMENT
FOR THE YEAR ENDED DECEMBER 31, 2004

Net sales	$100,000
Cost of goods sold	60,000
Gross margin	$ 40,000
Selling and administrative expenses	29,300
Net income before tax	$ 10,700
Income tax expense	4,280
Net income	$ 6,420

We will concentrate on the first two items on Daisy's statement: net sales and cost of goods sold. The major difference between this income statement and that for a service company is the inclusion of cost of goods sold. Because a service company does not sell a product, it does not report cost of goods sold. On the income statement of a merchandising company, cost of goods sold is deducted from net sales to arrive at gross margin or gross profit.

Gross margin as a percentage of net sales is a common analytical tool for merchandise companies. Analysts compare the gross margin percentages for various periods or for several companies and express concern if a company's gross margin is dropping. Every industry in the retail sector tracks its average gross margin ratio, and its average sales per square foot of retail space. Analysts can use these facts to see how one company is performing in comparison with others in the same industry.

NET SALES OF MERCHANDISE

LO 2 Demonstrate an understanding of how wholesalers and retailers account for sales of merchandise.

The first section of Daisy's income statement is presented in Exhibit 7-3. Two deductions —for sales returns and allowances and sales discounts—are made from sales revenue to arrive at **net sales.** Sales revenue, or simply sales, is a *representation of the inflow of assets,* either cash or accounts receivable, from the sale of merchandise during the period.

Net sales Sales revenue less sales returns and allowances and sales discounts.

Sales Returns and Allowances

The cornerstone of marketing is to satisfy the customer. Most companies have standard policies that allow the customer to *return* merchandise within a stipulated period of time. Nordstrom, the Seattle-based retailer, has a very liberal policy regarding returns.

http://www.nordstrom.com

Exhibit 7-3

Net Sales Section of the Income Statement

DAISY'S FLOWER DEPOT PARTIAL INCOME STATEMENT FOR THE YEAR ENDED DECEMBER 31, 2004		
Sales revenue	$103,500	
Less: Sales returns and allowances	2,000	
Sales discounts	1,500	
Net sales		$100,000

That policy has, in large measure, fueled its growth. A company's policy might be that a customer who is not completely satisfied can return the merchandise anytime within 30 days of purchase for a full refund. Alternatively, the customer may be given an *allowance* for spoiled or damaged merchandise—that is, the customer keeps the merchandise but receives a credit for a certain amount in the account balance. Typically, a single account, **Sales Returns and Allowances,** is used to account both for returns and for allowances. If the customer has already paid for the merchandise, either a cash refund is given or the credit amount is applied to future purchases.

Sales Returns and Allowances Contra-revenue account used to record both refunds to customers and reductions of their accounts.

Credit Terms and Sales Discounts

Most companies have a standard credit policy. Special notation is normally used to indicate a particular firm's policy for granting credit. For example, credit terms of *n/30* mean that the *net* amount of the selling price, that is, the amount determined after deducting any returns or allowances, is due within 30 days of the date of the invoice. *Net, 10 EOM* means that the net amount is due anytime within 10 days after the end of the month in which the sale took place.

Study Tip

Recall Accumulated Depreciation, a contra account introduced in Chapter 4. It reduces a long-term asset. In other cases, such as this one involving sales, a contra account reduces an income statement account.

Another common element of the credit terms offered to customers is sales discounts, a reduction from the selling price given for early payment. For example, assume that Daisy's offers a customer credit terms of *1/10, n/30.* This means that the customer may deduct 1% from the selling price if the bill is paid within 10 days of the date of the invoice. Normally the discount period begins with the day *after* the invoice date. If the customer does not pay within the first 10 days, the full invoice amount is due within 30 days. Finally, note that the use of *n* for *net* in this notation is really a misnomer. Although the amount due is net of any returns and allowances, it is the *gross* amount that is due within 30 days. That is, no discount is given if the customer does not pay early.

How valuable to the customer is a 1% discount for payment within the first 10 days? Assume that a $1,000 sale is made. If the customer pays at the end of 10 days, the cash paid will be $990, rather than $1,000, a net savings of $10. The customer has saved $10 by paying 20 days earlier than required by the 30-day term. If we assume 360 days in a year, there are 360/20 or 18 periods of 20 days each in a year. Thus, a savings of $10 for 20 days is equivalent to a savings of $10 times 18, or $180 for the year. An annual return of $180/$990, or 18.2%, would be difficult to match with any other type of investment. In fact, a customer might want to consider borrowing the money to pay off the account early.

Sales Discounts Contra-revenue account used to record discounts given customers for early payment of their accounts.

The **Sales Discounts** account is a *contra-revenue* account and thus reduces sales as shown on the income statement in Exhibit 7-3.

THE COST OF GOODS SOLD

The cost of goods sold section of the income statement for Daisy's is shown in Exhibit 7-4. We will soon turn to each line item in this section. First let us take a look at the basic model for cost of goods sold.

DAISY'S FLOWER DEPOT PARTIAL INCOME STATEMENT FOR THE YEAR ENDED DECEMBER 31, 2004			
Cost of goods sold:			
Inventory, January 1, 2004		$15,000	
Purchases	$65,000		
Less: Purchase returns and allowances	1,800		
Purchase discounts	3,700		
Net purchases	$59,500		
Add: Transportation-in	3,500		
Cost of goods purchased		63,000	
Cost of goods available for sale		$78,000	
Less: Inventory, December 31, 2004		18,000	
Cost of goods sold			$60,000

Exhibit 7-4

Cost of Goods Sold Section of the Income Statement

The Cost of Goods Sold Model

The recognition of cost of goods sold as an expense is an excellent example of the *matching principle.* Sales revenue represents the *inflow* of assets, in the form of cash and accounts receivable, from the sale of products during the period. Likewise, cost of goods sold represents the *outflow* of an asset, inventory, from the sale of those same products. The company needs to match the revenue of the period with one of the most important costs necessary to generate the revenue, the *cost* of the merchandise sold.

It may be helpful in understanding cost of goods sold to realize what it is *not. Cost of goods sold is not necessarily equal to the cost of purchases of merchandise during the period.* Except in the case of a new business, a merchandiser starts the year with a certain stock of inventory on hand, called *beginning inventory.* For Daisy's, beginning inventory is the dollar cost of merchandise on hand on January 1, 2004. During the year, Daisy's purchases merchandise. When the cost of goods purchased is added to beginning inventory, the result is **cost of goods available for sale.** Just as the merchandiser starts the period with an inventory of merchandise on hand, a certain amount of *ending inventory* is usually on hand at the end of the year. For Daisy's, this is its inventory on December 31, 2004.

Cost of goods available for sale Beginning inventory plus cost of goods purchased.

As shown in Exhibit 7-5, think of cost of goods available for sale as a "pool" of costs to be distributed between what we sold and what we did not sell. If we subtract from

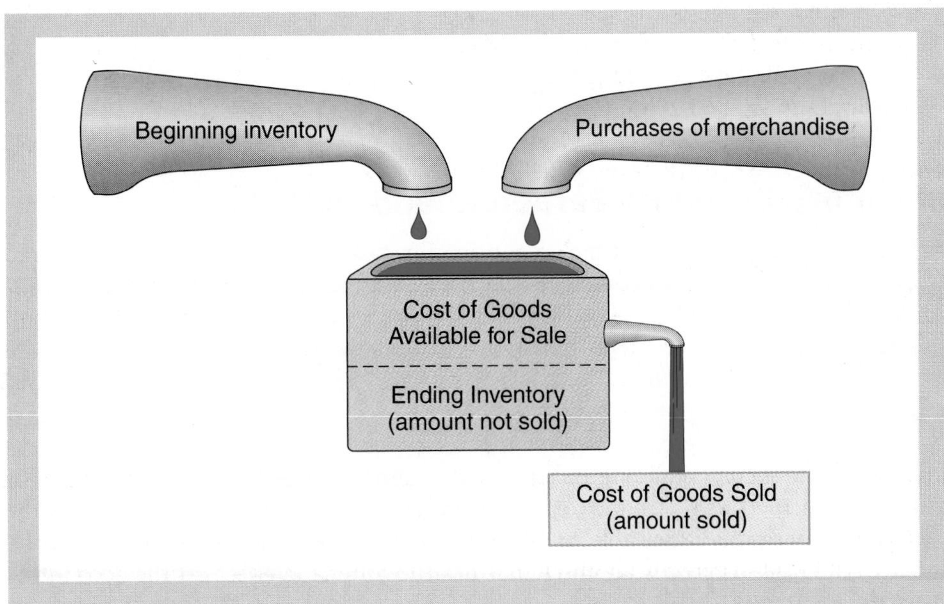

Exhibit 7-5

The Cost of Goods Sold Model

Cost of goods sold Cost of goods available for sale minus ending inventory.

the pool the cost of what we did *not* sell, the *ending inventory,* we will have the amount we *did* sell, the **cost of goods sold.** Cost of goods sold is simply the difference between the cost of goods available for sale and the ending inventory:

Beginning inventory	What is on hand to start the period
+ Purchases	What was acquired for resale during the period
= Cost of goods available for sale	The "pool" of costs to be distributed
− Ending inventory	What was not sold during the period and therefore is on hand to start the next period
= Cost of goods sold	What was sold during the period

The cost of goods sold model for a merchandiser is illustrated in Exhibit 7-6. The amounts used for the illustration are taken from the cost of goods sold section of Daisy's income statement as shown in Exhibit 7-4. Notice that ending inventory exceeds beginning inventory by $3,000. That means that the cost of goods purchased exceeds cost of goods sold by that same amount. Indeed, a key point for stockholders, bankers, and other users is whether inventory is building up, that is, whether a company is not selling as much inventory during the period as it is buying. A buildup may indicate that the company's products are becoming less desirable or that prices are becoming uncompetitive.

Exhibit 7-6 The Cost of Goods Sold Model: Example for a Merchandiser

Description	Item	Amount
Merchandise on hand to start the period	Beginning inventory	$15,000
Acquisitions of merchandise during the period	+ Cost of goods purchased	63,000
The pool of merchandise available for sale during the period	= Cost of goods available for sale	$78,000
Merchandise on hand at end of period	− Ending inventory	(18,000)
The expense recognized on the income statement	= Cost of goods sold	$60,000

A $3,000 excess of ending inventory over beginning inventory means the company bought $3,000 more than it sold ($63,000 bought versus $60,000 sold).

Inventory Systems: Perpetual and Periodic

LO 3 Explain the differences between periodic and perpetual inventory systems.

Perpetual system System in which the Inventory account is increased at the time of each purchase and decreased at the time of each sale.

Periodic system System in which the Inventory account is updated only at the end of the period.

Before we look more closely at the accounting for cost of goods sold, it is necessary to understand the difference between the periodic and the perpetual inventory systems. All businesses use one of these two distinct approaches to account for inventory. With the **perpetual system,** the Inventory account is updated *perpetually,* or after each sale or purchase of merchandise. Conversely, with the **periodic system,** the Inventory account is updated only at the end of the *period.*

In a perpetual system, every time goods are purchased, the Inventory account is increased, with a corresponding increase in Accounts Payable for a credit purchase or a decrease in the Cash account for a cash purchase. In addition to recognizing the increases in Accounts Receivable or Cash and in Sales Revenue when goods are sold, the accountant also records an entry that has the following effect on the accounting equation:

BALANCE SHEET					INCOME STATEMENT
ASSETS	=	LIABILITIES	+	OWNERS' EQUITY	+ REVENUES − EXPENSES
Inventory (xxx)					Cost of Goods Sold (xxx)

Thus, at any point during the period, the inventory account is up to date. It has been increased for the cost of purchases during the period and reduced for the cost of the sales.

Why don't all companies use the procedure we just described, the perpetual system? Depending on the volume of inventory transactions, that is, purchases and sales of merchandise, a perpetual system can be extremely costly to maintain. Historically, businesses that have a relatively small volume of sales at a high unit price have used perpetual systems. For example, dealers in automobiles, furniture, appliances, and jewelry normally use a perpetual system. Each purchase of a unit of merchandise, such as an automobile, can be easily identified and an increase recorded in the Inventory account. When the auto is sold, the dealer can easily determine the cost of the particular car sold by looking at a perpetual inventory record.

Can you imagine, however, a similar system for a supermarket or a hardware store? Consider a checkout stand in a grocery store. Through the use of a cash register tape, the sales revenue for that particular stand is recorded at the end of the day. Because of the tremendous volume of sales of various items of inventory, from cans of vegetables to boxes of soap, it may not be feasible to record the cost of goods sold every time a sale takes place. This illustrates a key point in financial information: the cost of the information should never exceed its benefit. If a store manager had to stop and update the records each time a can of **Campbell's** soup was sold, the retailer's business would obviously be disrupted.

To a certain extent, the ability of mass merchandisers to maintain perpetual inventory records has improved with the advent of point-of-sale terminals. When a cashier runs a can of corn over the sensing glass at the checkout stand and the bar code is read, the company's computer receives a message that a can of corn has been sold. In some companies, however, updating the inventory record is in units only and is used as a means to determine when a product needs to be reordered. The company still relies on a periodic system to maintain the *dollar* amount of inventory. In the remainder of this chapter, we limit our discussion to the periodic system. We discuss the perpetual system in more detail in the appendix to this chapter.

Accounting for Your Decisions

You Are the Entrepreneur

A year ago, you and your brother launched a running shoe company in your garage. You buy shoes from four of the major manufacturers and sell them over the phone. Your accountant suggests that you use a perpetual inventory system. Should you?

ANS: The periodic inventory system has the following advantages: The Inventory account is updated only once per year, not after every purchase; the inventory is physically counted on the last day of each period to determine ending inventory; and its cost is low. By operating out of your garage, you are focusing on keeping administrative costs down. A perpetual inventory system would be more costly and would not provide enough extra benefits at low volume. Your decision may change as your business grows, particularly if you began taking orders over the Internet.

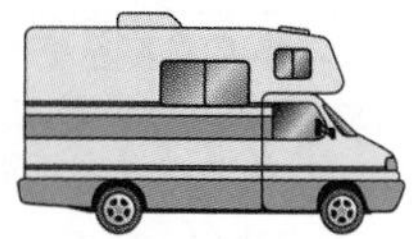

From Concept to Practice 7.2

Understanding Winnebago Industries' Inventory System

Given the nature of its products, would you expect that Winnebago Industries *uses a perpetual or a periodic inventory system? Explain your answer.*

Beginning and Ending Inventories in a Periodic System

In a periodic system, the Inventory account is *not* updated each time a sale or purchase is made. Throughout the year, the Inventory account contains the amount of merchandise on hand at the beginning of the year. The account is adjusted only at the end of the year. A company using the periodic system must physically *count* the units of inventory on hand at the end of the period. The number of units of each product is then multiplied by the cost per unit, to determine the dollar amount of ending inventory. Refer to Exhibit 7-4 for Daisy's Flower Depot. The procedure just described was used to determine its ending inventory of $18,000. Because one period's ending inventory is the next period's beginning inventory, the beginning inventory of $15,000 was based on the count at the end of the prior year.

In summary, the ending inventory in a periodic system is determined by counting the merchandise, not by looking at the Inventory account at the end of the period. The periodic system results in a trade-off. Use of the periodic system reduces record keeping but at the expense of a certain degree of control. Losses of merchandise due to theft, breakage, spoilage, or other reasons may go undetected in a periodic system because management may assume that all merchandise not on hand at the end of the year was sold. In a retail store, some of the merchandise may have been shoplifted rather than sold. In contrast, with a perpetual inventory system, a count of inventory at the end of the period serves as a *control device.* For example, if the Inventory account shows a balance of $45,000 at the end of the year but only $42,000 of merchandise is counted, management is able to investigate the discrepancy. No such control feature exists in a periodic system.

In addition to the loss of control, the use of a periodic system presents a dilemma when a company wants to prepare *interim* financial statements. Because most companies that use a periodic system find it cost-prohibitive to count the entire inventory more than once a year, they use estimation techniques to determine inventory for monthly or quarterly statements. These techniques are discussed later in this chapter.

The Cost of Goods Purchased

LO 4 Demonstrate an understanding of how wholesalers and retailers account for cost of goods sold.

Transportation-in Adjunct account used to record freight costs paid by the buyer.

The cost of goods purchased section of Daisy's income statement is shown in Exhibit 7-7. The company purchased $65,000 of merchandise during the period. Two amounts are deducted from purchases to arrive at net purchases: purchase returns and allowances of $1,800 and purchase discounts of $3,700. The cost of $3,500 incurred by Daisy's to ship the goods to its place of business is called **transportation-in** and is added to net purchases of $59,500 to arrive at the cost of goods purchased of $63,000. Another name for transportation-in is *freight-in.*

Exhibit 7-7
Cost of Goods Purchased

DAISY'S FLOWER DEPOT
PARTIAL INCOME STATEMENT
FOR THE YEAR ENDED DECEMBER 31, 2004

Purchases	$65,000	
Less: Purchase returns and allowances	1,800	
Purchase discounts	3,700	
Net purchases	$59,500	
Add: Transportation-in	3,500	
Cost of goods purchased		$63,000

Purchases Assume that Daisy's buys merchandise on account from one of its wholesalers at a cost of $4,000. **Purchases** is the temporary account used in a periodic inventory system to record acquisitions of merchandise. The effect of this transaction is to increase liabilities and increase cost of goods sold, which is an expense:

Purchases Account used in a periodic inventory system to record acquisitions of merchandise.

BALANCE SHEET								INCOME STATEMENT		
ASSETS	=	LIABILITIES		+	OWNERS' EQUITY		+	REVENUES − EXPENSES	
		Accounts Payable	4,000					Purchases	(4,000)

It is important to understand that Purchases is not an asset account. It is included in the income statement as an integral part of the calculation of cost of goods sold and is therefore shown as a reduction of owners' equity in the accounting equation.

Purchase Returns and Allowances We discussed returns and allowances earlier in the chapter from the seller's point of view. From the standpoint of the buyer, purchase returns and allowances are reductions in the cost to purchase merchandise. Rather than record these reductions directly in the Purchases account, the accountant uses a separate account. The account, **Purchase Returns and Allowances,** is a *contra account* to Purchases. The use of a contra account allows management to monitor the amount of returns and allowances. For example, a large number of returns during the period relative to the amount purchased may signal that the purchasing department is not buying from reputable sources.

Purchase Returns and Allowances Contra-purchases account used in a periodic inventory system when a refund is received from a supplier or a reduction given in the balance owed to a supplier.

Suppose that Daisy's returns $850 of merchandise to a wholesaler for credit on its account. The return decreases both liabilities and purchases. Note that because a return reduces purchases, it actually *increases* net income:

BALANCE SHEET								INCOME STATEMENT		
ASSETS	=	LIABILITIES		+	OWNERS' EQUITY		+	REVENUES − EXPENSES	
		Accounts Payable	(850)					Purchases Returns and Allowances	850

The effect of an allowance for merchandise retained rather than returned is the same as that for a return.

Purchase Discounts Discounts were discussed earlier in the chapter, from the seller's viewpoint. Merchandising companies often purchase inventory on terms that allow for a cash discount for early payment, such as 2/10, net 30. To the buyer, a cash discount is called a *purchase discount* and results in a reduction of the cost to purchase merchandise.

Accounting for Your Decisions

You Are the President

You are the president of a mail-order computer business. Your company buys computers and related parts directly from manufacturers and sells them to consumers via direct mail. Recently, you have noticed an increase in the amount of purchase returns and allowances relative to the amount of purchases. What are some possible explanations for this increase?

ANS: Any number of explanations are possible. It is possible that the products are being damaged while in transit. Or it may be that the company has changed suppliers and the merchandise is not of the quality expected. Or the employees are becoming more demanding in what they accept than they used to be.

For example, assume a purchase of merchandise for $500, with credit terms of 1/10, net 30. The effect of the purchase is:

BALANCE SHEET						INCOME STATEMENT	
ASSETS	=	LIABILITIES		+	OWNERS' EQUITY	+ REVENUES – EXPENSES	
		Accounts Payable	500			Purchases	(500)

Any discount taken by a customer is recorded in the Purchase Discounts account and deducted from purchases on the income statement. Assuming that the customer pays on time, the effect of the collection of the open account is as follows:

BALANCE SHEET							INCOME STATEMENT	
ASSETS		=	LIABILITIES		+	OWNERS' EQUITY	+ REVENUES – EXPENSES	
Cash	(495)		Accounts Payable	(500)			Purchase Discounts	5

Purchase Discounts Contra-purchases account used to record reductions in purchase price for early payment to a supplier.

The **Purchase Discounts** account is contra to the Purchases account and thus increases net income, as shown in the accounting equation above. Also note in Exhibit 7-7 that purchase discounts are deducted from purchases on the income statement. Finally, note that the effect on the income statement is the same as illustrated earlier for a purchase return: because purchases are reduced, net income is increased.

Shipping Terms and Transportation Costs The *cost principle* governs the recording of all assets. All costs necessary to prepare an asset for its intended use should be included in its cost. The cost of an item to a merchandising company is not necessarily limited to its invoice price. For example, any sales tax paid should be included in computing total cost. Any transportation costs incurred by the buyer should likewise be included in the cost of the merchandise.

FOB destination point Terms that require the seller to pay for the cost of shipping the merchandise to the buyer.

FOB shipping point Terms that require the buyer to pay for the shipping costs.

The buyer does not always pay to ship the merchandise. This depends on the terms of shipment. Goods are normally shipped either **FOB destination point** or **FOB shipping point;** *FOB* stands for *free on board.* When merchandise is shipped FOB destination point, it is the responsibility of the seller to deliver the products to the buyer. Thus, the seller either delivers the product to the customer or pays a trucking firm, railroad, or other carrier to transport it. Alternatively, the agreement between the buyer and the seller may provide for the goods to be shipped FOB shipping point. In this case, the merchandise is the responsibility of the buyer as soon as it leaves the seller's premises. When the terms of shipment are FOB shipping point, the buyer incurs transportation costs.

Refer to Exhibit 7-7. Transportation-in represents the freight costs Daisy's paid for in-bound merchandise. These costs are added to net purchases, as shown in the exhibit, and increase the cost of goods purchased. Assume that on delivery of a shipment of goods, Daisy's pays an invoice for $300 from the Rocky Mountain Railroad. The terms of shipment are FOB shipping point. The effect on the accounting equation is as follows:

BALANCE SHEET						INCOME STATEMENT	
ASSETS		=	LIABILITIES	+	OWNERS' EQUITY	+ REVENUES – EXPENSES	
Cash	(300)					Transportation-in	(300)

The Transportation-In account is an *adjunct* account because it is *added* to the net purchases of the period. The total of net purchases and transportation-in is called the *cost of goods purchased.* In summary, cost of goods purchased consists of the following:

Purchases
Less: Purchase returns and allowances
    Purchase discounts
Equals: Net purchases
Add: Transportation-in
Equals: Cost of goods purchased

How should the *seller* account for the freight costs it pays when the goods are shipped FOB destination point? This cost, sometimes called *transportation-out,* is not an addition to the cost of purchases of the seller but is instead one of the costs necessary to *sell* the merchandise. Transportation-out is classified as a *selling expense* on the income statement.

Shipping Terms and Transfer of Title to Inventory Terms of shipment take on additional significance at the end of an accounting period. It is essential that a company establish a proper cutoff at year-end. For example, what if Daisy's purchases merchandise that is in transit at the end of the year? To whom does the inventory belong, Daisy's or the seller? The answer depends on the terms of shipment. If goods are shipped FOB destination point, they remain the legal property of the seller until they reach their destination. Alternatively, legal title to goods shipped FOB shipping point passes to the buyer as soon as the seller turns the goods over to the carrier.

The example in Exhibit 7-8 is intended to summarize our discussion about shipping terms and ownership of merchandise. The example involves a shipment of merchandise in transit at the end of the year. Horton, the seller of the goods, pays the transportation charges only if the terms are FOB destination point. Horton records a sale for goods in transit at year-end, however, only if the terms of shipment are FOB shipping point. If Horton does not record a sale, because the goods are shipped FOB destination point, the inventory appears on its December 31 balance sheet. Daisy's, the buyer, pays freight costs only if the goods are shipped FOB shipping point. Only in this situation does Daisy's record a purchase of the merchandise and include it as an asset on its December 31 balance sheet.

Exhibit 7-8

Shipping Terms and Transfer of Title to Inventory

FACTS **On December 28, 2004, Horton Wholesale ships merchandise to Daisy's Flower Depot. The trucking company delivers the merchandise to Daisy's on January 2, 2005. Daisy's fiscal year-end is December 31.**

		If Merchandise Is Shipped FOB	
COMPANY		DESTINATION POINT	SHIPPING POINT
Horton (seller)	Pay freight costs?	Yes	No
	Record sale in 2004?	No	Yes
	Include inventory on balance sheet at December 31, 2004?	Yes	No
Daisy's (buyer)	Pay freight costs?	No	Yes
	Record purchase in 2004?	No	Yes
	Include inventory on balance sheet at December 31, 2004?	No	Yes

Two-Minute Review

On April 13, 2001, Bitterroot Distributing sells merchandise to Darby Corp. for $1,000 with credit terms of 2/10, net 30. On April 19, Darby returns $150 of defective merchandise and receives a credit on account from Bitterroot. On April 23, Darby pays the amount due.

(continued)

1. *Determine the effects on Bitterroot's accounting equation from April 13 through April 23. Assume Bitterroot uses a periodic inventory system.*
2. *Determine the effects on Darby's accounting equation from April 13 through April 23. Assume Darby uses a periodic inventory system.*

Answers on page 332.

INVENTORY VALUATION AND THE MEASUREMENT OF INCOME

LO 5 Explain the relationship between the valuation of inventory and the measurement of income.

One of the most fundamental concepts in accounting is the relationship between *asset valuation* and the *measurement of income*. Recall a point made in Chapter 4: assets are unexpired costs, and expenses are expired costs. Thus, the value assigned to an asset on the balance sheet determines the amount eventually recognized as an expense on the income statement. For example, the amount recorded as the cost of an item of plant and equipment will dictate the amount of depreciation expense recognized on the income statement over the life of the asset. Similarly, the amount recorded as the cost of inventory determines the amount recognized as cost of goods sold on the income statement when the asset is sold. An error in assigning the proper amount to inventory on the balance sheet will affect the amount recognized as cost of goods sold on the income statement. The relationship between inventory as an asset and cost of goods sold can be understood by recalling the cost of goods sold section of the income statement. Assume the following example:

© KIM STEELE/GETTY IMAGES/PHOTODISC

The inventory of a manufacturer consists of raw material, work in process, and finished goods. The electronic device being built here is part of a firm's work in process inventory. The direct materials probably consist of such items as the individual control knobs purchased from another manufacturer. When the manufacturing process is complete, the inventory of finished goods is ready for sale.

Beginning inventory	$ 500
Add: Purchases	1,200
Cost of goods available for sale	$1,700
Less: Ending inventory	(600)
Cost of goods sold	$1,100

The amount assigned to ending inventory is deducted from cost of goods available for sale to determine cost of goods sold. If the ending inventory amount is incorrect, cost of goods sold will be wrong, and thus the net income of the period will be in error as well. (We will look at inventory errors later in the chapter.)

Inventory Costs: What Should Be Included?

All assets, including inventory, are recorded initially at cost. Cost is defined as "the price paid or consideration given to acquire an asset. As applied to inventories, cost means in principle the sum of the applicable expenditures and charges directly or indirectly incurred in bringing an article to its existing condition and location."[1]

Note the reference to the existing *condition* and *location*. This means that certain costs may also be included in the "price paid." Here are examples:

- As we saw earlier in the chapter, any freight costs incurred by the buyer in shipping inventory to its place of business should be included in the cost of the inventory.
- The cost of insurance taken out during the time that inventory is in transit should be added to the cost of the inventory.
- The cost of storing inventory before the time it is ready to be sold should be included in cost.
- Various types of taxes paid, such as excise and sales taxes, are other examples of costs necessary to put the inventory into a position to be able to sell it.

[1] *Accounting Research Bulletin No. 43*, "Inventory Pricing" (New York: American Institute of Certified Public Accountants, June 1953), Ch. 4, statement 3.

It is often very difficult, however, to allocate many of these incidental costs among the various items of inventory purchased. For example, consider a $500 freight bill that a supermarket paid on a merchandise shipment that includes 100 different items of inventory. To address the practical difficulty in assigning this type of cost to the different products, many companies have a policy by which transportation costs are charged to expense of the period if they are immaterial in amount. Thus, shipments of merchandise are simply recorded at the net invoice price, that is, after taking any cash discounts for early payment. It is a practical solution to a difficult allocation problem. Once again, the company must apply the cost/benefit test to accounting information.

INTERNAL DECISION

INVENTORY COSTING METHODS WITH A PERIODIC SYSTEM

LO 6 Apply the inventory costing methods of specific identification, weighted average, FIFO, and LIFO using a periodic system.

To this point, we have assumed that the cost to purchase an item of inventory is constant. For most merchandisers, however, the unit cost of inventory changes frequently. Consider a simple example. Everett Company purchases merchandise twice during the first year of business. The dates, the number of units purchased, and the costs are as follows:

February 4	200 units purchased at $1.00 per unit	= $200
October 13	200 units purchased at $1.50 per unit	= $300

Everett sells 200 units during the first year. Individual sales of the units take place relatively evenly throughout the year. The question is: *which* 200 units did the company sell, the $1.00 units or the $1.50 units or some combination of each? Recall the earlier discussion of the relationship between asset valuation and income measurement. The question is important because the answer determines not only the value assigned to the 200 units of ending inventory *but also* the amount allocated to cost of goods sold for the 200 units sold.

One possible method of assigning amounts to ending inventory and cost of goods sold is to *specifically identify* which 200 units were sold and which 200 units are on hand. This method is feasible for a few types of businesses in which units can be identified by serial numbers, but it is totally impractical in most situations. As an alternative to specific identification, we could make an *assumption* as to which units were sold and which are on hand. Three different answers are possible:

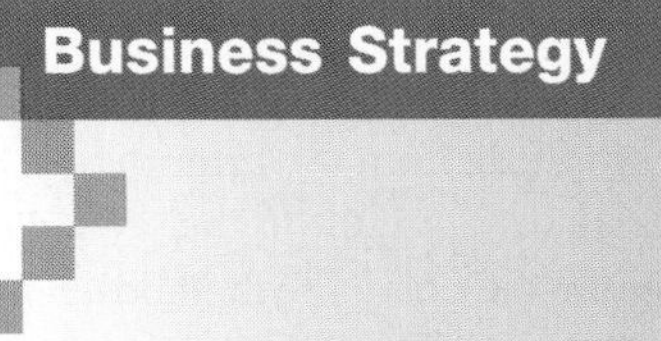

http://www.circuitcity.com

Capitalizing on the Digital Age

New technology is the lifeblood of all consumer electronics retailers in the new millennium, and Circuit City is no exception. The company fully realizes that it must be on the leading edge in offering the latest innovations to its customers if it is to sustain the growth that has made it successful in this highly competitive environment.

At the heart of the new technology is the revolution that has been taking place in digital products. These products generated significant sales increases for Circuit City in a variety of product lines, including big-screen televisions, imaging products, satellite systems, and wireless phones. The company is especially encouraged by the potential for sustained growth in the sales of big-screen TVs, given that their volume and profits are among the highest in the company's line. Circuit City points to the projections of an industry group that anticipates a growth rate in sales in double-digits in calendar 2002 for big-screen televisions. Certainly a key to the company's success in the next few years will be its ability to take advantage of the move to digital technology and to offer its customers products that will satisfy their appetite for the latest electronic gadgetry. ■

Source: Circuit City 2002 Annual Report.

1. 200 units sold at $1.00 each = $200 cost of goods sold
and 200 units on hand at $1.50 each = $300 ending inventory
or

2. 200 units sold at $1.50 each = $300 cost of goods sold
and 200 units on hand at $1.00 each = $200 ending inventory
or

3. 200 units sold at $1.25 each = $250 cost of goods sold
and 200 units on hand at $1.25 each = $250 ending inventory

The third alternative assumes an *average cost* for the 200 units on hand and the 200 units sold. The average cost is the cost of the two purchases of $200 and $300, or $500, divided by the 400 units available to sell, or $1.25 per unit.

If we are concerned with the actual *physical flow* of the units of inventory, all of the three methods illustrated may be incorrect. The only approach that will yield a "correct" answer in terms of the actual flow of *units* of inventory is the specific identification method. In the absence of a specific identification approach, it is impossible to say which particular units were *actually* sold. In fact, there may have been sales from each of the two purchases, that is, some of the $1.00 units may have been sold and some of the $1.50 units may have been sold. To solve the problem of assigning costs to identical units, accountants have developed inventory costing assumptions or methods. Each of these methods makes a specific *assumption* about the *flow of costs* rather than the physical flow of units. The only approach that uses the actual flow of the units in assigning costs is the specific identification method.

To take a closer look at specific identification as well as three alternative approaches to valuing inventory, we will use the following example:

	UNITS	UNIT COST	TOTAL COST
Beginning inventory			
January 1	500	$10	$ 5,000*
Purchases			
January 20	300	11	$ 3,300
April 8	400	12	4,800
September 5	200	13	2,600
December 12	100	14	1,400
Total purchases	1,000 units		$12,100
Available for sale	1,500 units		$17,100
Units sold	900 units		?
Units in ending inventory	600 units		?

*Beginning inventory of $5,000 is carried over as the ending inventory from the prior period. It is highly unlikely that each of the four methods we will illustrate would result in the same dollar amount of inventory at any point in time. It is helpful when first learning the methods, however, to assume the same amount of beginning inventory.

The question marks indicate the dilemma. What portion of the cost of goods available for sale of $17,100 should be assigned to the 900 units sold? What portion should be assigned to the 600 units remaining in ending inventory? The purpose of an inventory costing method is to provide a reasonable answer to these two questions.

Specific Identification Method

Specific identification method An inventory costing method that relies on matching unit costs with the actual units sold.

It is not always necessary to make an assumption about the flow of costs. In certain situations, it may be possible to specifically identify which units are sold and which units are on hand. A serial number on an automobile allows a dealer to identify a car on hand and thus its unit cost. An appliance dealer with 15 refrigerators on hand at the end of the year can identify the unit cost of each by matching a tag number with the purchase records. To illustrate the use of the **specific identification method** for our example, assume that the merchandiser is able to identify the specific units in the inventory at the end of the year and their costs as follows:

Units on Hand

DATE PURCHASED	UNITS	COST	TOTAL COST
January 20	100	$11	$1,100
April 8	300	12	3,600
September 5	200	13	2,600
Ending inventory	600		$7,300

One of two techniques can be used to find cost of goods sold. We can deduct ending inventory from the cost of goods available for sale:

Cost of goods available for sale	$17,100
Less: Ending inventory	7,300
Equals: Cost of goods sold	$ 9,800

Or we can calculate cost of goods sold independently by matching the units sold with their respective unit costs. By eliminating the units in ending inventory from the original acquisition schedule, the units sold and their costs are as follows:

Units Sold

DATE PURCHASED	UNITS	COST	TOTAL COST
Beginning Inventory	500	$10	$5,000
January 20	200	11	2,200
April 8	100	12	1,200
December 12	100	14	1,400
Cost of goods sold	900		$9,800

The practical difficulty in keeping track of individual items of inventory sold is not the only problem with the use of this method. The method also allows management to *manipulate income.* For example, assume that a company is not having a particularly good year. Management may be tempted to do whatever it can to boost net income. One way it can do this is by *selectively selling units with the lowest-possible unit cost.* By doing so, the company can keep cost of goods sold down and net income up. Because of the potential for manipulation with the specific identification method, coupled with the practical difficulty of applying it in most situations, it is not widely used.

Weighted Average Cost Method

The **weighted average cost method** is a relatively easy approach to costing inventory. It assigns the same unit cost to all units available for sale during the period. The weighted average cost is calculated as follows for our example:

Weighted average cost method An inventory costing method that assigns the same unit cost to all units available for sale during the period.

$$\frac{\textbf{Cost of Goods Available for Sale}}{\textbf{Units Available for Sale}} = \textbf{Weighted Average Cost}$$

$$\frac{\$17{,}100}{1{,}500} = \$11.40$$

Ending inventory is found by multiplying the weighted average unit cost by the number of units on hand:

Weighted Average Cost	×	**Number of Units in Ending Inventory**	=	**Ending Inventory**
$11.40	×	600	=	$6,840

Cost of goods sold can be calculated in one of two ways:

Cost of goods available for sale	$17,100
Less: Ending inventory	6,840
Equals: Cost of goods sold	$10,260

or

Weighted Average Cost	×	Number of Units Sold	=	Cost of Goods Sold
$11.40	×	900	=	$10,260

Note that the computation of the weighted average cost is based on the cost of *all* units available for sale during the period, not just the beginning inventory or purchases. Also note that the method is called the *weighted* average cost method. As the name indicates, each of the individual unit costs is multiplied by the number of units acquired at each price. The simple arithmetic average of the unit costs for the beginning inventory and the four purchases is ($10 + $11 + $12 + $13 + $14)/5 = $12. The weighted average cost is slightly less than $12 ($11.40), however, because more units were acquired at the lower prices than at the higher prices.

First-In, First-Out Method (FIFO)

FIFO method An inventory costing method that assigns the most recent costs to ending inventory.

The **FIFO method** assumes that the first units in, or purchased, are the first units out, or sold. The first units sold during the period are assumed to come from the beginning inventory. After the beginning inventory is sold, the next units sold are assumed to come from the first purchase during the period and so forth. Thus, ending inventory consists of the most recent purchases of the period. In many businesses, this cost-flow assumption is a fairly accurate reflection of the *physical* flow of products. For example, to maintain a fresh stock of products, the physical flow in a grocery store is first-in, first-out.

To calculate *ending inventory,* we start with the *most recent* inventory acquired and work *backward:*

Units on Hand

DATE PURCHASED	UNITS	COST	TOTAL COST
December 12	100	$14	$1,400
September 5	200	13	2,600
April 8	300	12	3,600
Ending inventory	600		$7,600

Cost of goods sold can then be found:

Cost of goods available for sale	$17,100
Less: Ending inventory	7,600
Equals: Cost of goods sold	$ 9,500

Or, because the FIFO method assumes that the first units in are the first ones sold, cost of goods sold can be calculated by starting with the *beginning inventory* and working *forward:*

Units Sold

DATE PURCHASED	UNITS	COST	TOTAL COST
Beginning Inventory	500	$10	$5,000
January 20	300	11	3,300
April 8	100	12	1,200
Units sold	900	Cost of goods sold	$9,500

Last-In, First-Out Method (LIFO)

LIFO method An inventory method that assigns the most recent costs to cost of goods sold.

The **LIFO method** assumes that the last units in, or purchased, are the first units out, or sold. The first units sold during the period are assumed to come from the latest purchase made during the period and so forth. Can you think of any businesses where the *physical* flow of products is last-in, first-out? Although this situation is not nearly so common as a first-in, first-out physical flow, a stockpiling operation, such as in a rock quarry, operates on this basis.

Accounting for Your Decisions

You Are the Controller

Your company, Princeton Systems, is a manufacturer of components for personal computers. The company uses the FIFO method to account for its inventory. The CEO, a stickler for accuracy, asks you why you can't identify each unit of inventory and place a cost on it, instead of making an assumption that the first unit of inventory is the first sold when that is not necessarily the case.

ANS: The CEO is suggesting the specific identification method, which works best when there are fewer pieces of unique inventory, not thousands of units of identical pieces. Because the company makes thousands of identical components each year, it would be impractical to assign specific costs to each unit of inventory. The FIFO method, on the other hand, assumes that the first units in are the first units sold, an appropriate assumption under these circumstances.

Study Tip

There may be cases, such as this illustration of LIFO, in which it is easier to determine ending inventory and then deduct it from cost of goods available for sale to find cost of goods sold. This approach is easier in this example because there are fewer layers in ending inventory than in cost of goods sold. In other cases, it may be quicker to determine cost of goods sold first and then plug in ending inventory.

To calculate *ending inventory* using LIFO, we start with the *beginning inventory* and work *forward:*

Units on Hand

DATE PURCHASED	UNITS	COST	TOTAL COST
Beginning inventory	500	$10	$5,000
January 20	100	11	1,100
Ending inventory	600		$6,100

Cost of goods sold can then be found:

Cost of goods available for sale	$17,100
Less: Ending inventory	6,100
Equals: Cost of goods sold	$11,000

Or, because the LIFO method assumes that the last units in are the first ones sold, *cost of goods sold* can be calculated by starting with the *most recent* inventory acquired and working *backward:*

Units Sold

DATE PURCHASED	UNITS	COST	TOTAL COST
December 12	100	$14	$ 1,400
September 5	200	13	2,600
April 8	400	12	4,800
January 20	200	11	2,200
Units sold	900	Cost of goods sold	$11,000

SELECTING AN INVENTORY COSTING METHOD

LO 7 Analyze the effects of the different costing methods on inventory, net income, income taxes, and cash flow.

INTERNAL DECISION

The mechanics of each of the inventory costing methods are straightforward. But how does a company decide on the best method to use to value its inventory? According to the accounting profession, *the primary determinant in selecting an inventory costing method should be the ability of the method to accurately reflect the net income of the period.* But how and why does a particular costing method accurately reflect the net income of the period? Because there is no easy answer to this question, a number of arguments have been raised by accountants to justify the use of one method over the others. We turn now to some of these arguments.

Costing Methods and Cash Flow

Comparative income statements for our example are presented in Exhibit 7-9. Note that with the use of the weighted average method, net income is between the amounts for FIFO and LIFO. Because the weighted average method normally yields results between the other two methods, we concentrate on the two extremes, LIFO and FIFO. The major advantage of using the weighted average method is its simplicity.

Exhibit 7-9

Income Statements for the Inventory Costing Methods

	WEIGHTED AVERAGE	FIFO	LIFO
Sales revenue—$20 each	$18,000	$18,000	$18,000
Beginning inventory	$ 5,000	$ 5,000	$ 5,000
Purchases	12,100	12,100	12,100
Cost of goods available for sale	$17,100	$17,100	$17,100
Ending inventory	**6,840**	**7,600**	**6,100**
Cost of goods sold	**$10,260**	**$ 9,500**	**$11,000**
Gross margin	**$ 7,740**	**$ 8,500**	**$ 7,000**
Operating expenses	2,000	2,000	2,000
Net income before tax	**$ 5,740**	**$ 6,500**	**$ 5,000**
Income tax expense (40%)	**2,296**	**2,600**	**2,000**
Net income	**$ 3,444**	**$ 3,900**	**$ 3,000**

NOTE: Figures that differ among the three methods are in bold.

The original data for our example involved a situation in which prices were *rising* throughout the period: beginning inventory cost $10 per unit, and the last purchase during the year was at $14. With LIFO, the most recent costs are assigned to cost of goods sold; with FIFO, the older costs are assigned to expense. Thus, in a period of rising prices, the assignment of the *higher* prices to cost of goods sold under LIFO results in a *lower gross margin* under LIFO than under FIFO ($7,000 for LIFO and $8,500 for FIFO). Because operating expenses are not affected by the choice of inventory method, the lower gross margin under LIFO results in lower income before tax, which in turn leads to lower taxes. If we assume a 40% tax rate, income tax expense under LIFO is only $2,000, compared with $2,600 under FIFO, a savings of $600 in taxes. Another way to look at the taxes saved by using LIFO is to focus on the difference in the expense under each method:

	LIFO cost of goods sold	$11,000
−	FIFO cost of goods sold	9,500
	Additional expense from use of LIFO	$ 1,500
×	Tax rate	0.40
	Tax savings from the use of LIFO	$ 600

Study Tip

During a period of falling prices, all of the effects shown here would be just the opposite. For example, cost of goods sold would be lower under LIFO than under FIFO.

To summarize, *during a period of rising prices,* the two methods result in the following:

ITEM	LIFO	RELATIVE TO	FIFO
Cost of goods sold	Higher		Lower
Gross margin	Lower		Higher
Income before taxes	Lower		Higher
Taxes	Lower		Higher

In conclusion, lower taxes with the use of LIFO result in cash savings.

The tax savings available from the use of LIFO during a period of rising prices are largely responsible for its popularity. Keep in mind, however, that the cash saved from a lower tax bill with LIFO is only a temporary savings, or what is normally called a *tax deferral.* At some point in the life of the business, the inventory that is carried at the older, lower-priced amounts will be sold. This will result in a tax bill higher than that under FIFO. Yet even a tax deferral is beneficial; given the opportunity, it is better to pay less tax today and more in the future because today's tax savings can be invested.

Two-Minute Review

1. *Which of the inventory methods will result in the least amount of income before taxes, assuming a period of rising prices?*
2. *What is the easiest way to calculate the tax savings from using one method versus another?*

Answers on page 333.

LIFO Liquidation

Recall the assumption made about which costs remain in inventory when LIFO is used. The costs of the oldest units remain in inventory, and if prices are rising, the costs of these units will be lower than the costs of more recent purchases. Now assume that the company *sells more units than it buys during the period.* When a company using LIFO experiences a liquidation, some of the units assumed to be sold will come from the older layers, with a relatively low unit cost. This situation, called a **LIFO liquidation,** presents a dilemma for the company.

LIFO liquidation The result of selling more units than are purchased during the period, which can have negative tax consequences if a company is using LIFO.

A partial or complete liquidation of the older, lower-priced units will result in a low cost of goods sold figure and a correspondingly high gross margin for the period. In turn, the company faces a large tax bill because of the relatively high gross margin. In fact, a liquidation causes the tax advantages of using LIFO to reverse on the company, which is faced with paying off some of the taxes that were deferred in earlier periods. Should a company facing this situation buy inventory at the end of the year to avoid the consequences of a liquidation? This is a difficult question to answer and depends on many factors, including the company's cash position. At the least, the accountant must be aware of the potential for a large tax bill if a liquidation occurs.

Of course, a LIFO liquidation also benefits—and may even distort—reported earnings if the liquidation is large enough. For this reason and the tax problem, many companies are reluctant to liquidate their LIFO inventory. The problem often festers, and companies find themselves with inventory costed at decade-old price levels.

The LIFO Conformity Rule

Would it be possible for a company to have the best of both worlds? That is, could it use FIFO to report its income to stockholders, thus maximizing the amount of net income reported to this group, and use LIFO to report to the IRS, minimizing its taxable income and the amount paid to the government? Unfortunately, the IRS says that if a company chooses LIFO for reporting cost of goods sold on its tax return, then it must also use LIFO on its books, that is, in preparing its income statement. This is called the **LIFO conformity rule.** Note that the rule applies only to the use of LIFO on the tax return. A company is free to use different methods in preparing its tax return and its income statement as long as the method used for the tax return is *not* LIFO.

LIFO conformity rule The IRS requirement that if LIFO is used on the tax return, it must also be used in reporting income to stockholders.

The LIFO Reserve: Estimating LIFO's Effect on Income and on Taxes Paid for Winnebago Industries

If a company decides to use LIFO, an investor can still determine how much more income the company would have reported had it used FIFO. In addition, he or she can approximate the tax savings or the additional taxes to the company from the use of LIFO. Consider Note 3 from the 2002 annual report for Winnebago Industries:

http://www.winnebagoind.com

Note 3: Inventories

Inventories consist of the following: (dollars in thousands)	AUGUST 31, 2002	AUGUST 25, 2001
Finished goods	$ 48,037	$ 36,930
Work-in-process	26,995	21,725
Raw materials	62,194	44,232
	$137,226	$102,887
LIFO reserve	(23,572)	(23,072)
	$113,654	$ 79,815

The above value of inventories, before reduction for the LIFO reserve, approximates replacement cost at the respective dates.

The following steps explain the logic for using the information in the inventory note to estimate LIFO's effect on income and on taxes:

LIFO reserve The excess of the value of a company's inventory stated at FIFO over the value stated at LIFO.

1. The excess of the value of a company's inventory stated at FIFO over the value stated at LIFO is called the **LIFO reserve.** The *cumulative* excess of the value of Winnebago Industries' inventory on a FIFO basis over the value on a LIFO basis is $23,572,000 at the end of 2002.
2. Because Winnebago Industries reports inventory at a lower value on its balance sheet using LIFO, it will report a higher cost of goods sold amount on the income statement. Thus, the LIFO reserve not only represents the excess of the inventory balance on a FIFO basis over that on a LIFO basis but also *represents the cumulative amount by which cost of goods sold on a LIFO basis exceeds cost of goods sold on a FIFO basis.*
3. The increase in Winnebago Industries' LIFO reserve in 2002 was $500,000 ($23,572,000 − $23,072,000). This means that the increase in cost of goods sold for 2002 from using LIFO instead of FIFO was also this amount. Thus, income before tax for 2002 was $500,000 lower because the company used LIFO.
4. If we assume a corporate tax rate of 35%, the tax savings from using LIFO amounted to $500,000 × 0.35, or $175,000.

Costing Methods and Inventory Profits

FIFO, LIFO, and weighted average are all cost-based methods to value inventory. They vary in terms of which costs are assigned to inventory and which to cost of goods sold, but all three assign *historical costs* to inventory. In our previous example, the unit cost for inventory purchases gradually increased during the year from $10 for the beginning inventory to a high of $14 on the date of the last purchase.

Replacement cost The current cost of a unit of inventory.

An alternative to assigning any of the historical costs incurred during the year to ending inventory and cost of goods sold would be to use **replacement cost** to value each of these. Assume that the cost to replace a unit of inventory at the end of the year is $15. Use of a replacement cost system results in the following:

Ending inventory	=	600 units	×	$15 per unit	=	$ 9,000
Cost of goods sold	=	900 units	×	$15 per unit	=	$13,500

Inventory profit The portion of the gross profit that results from holding inventory during a period of rising prices.

A replacement cost approach is not acceptable under the profession's current standards, but many believe that it provides more relevant information to users. Inventory must be replaced if a company is to remain in business. Many accountants argue that the use of historical cost in valuing inventory leads to what is called **inventory profit,** particularly if FIFO is used in a period of rising prices. For example, cost of goods sold in our illustration was only $9,500 on a FIFO basis, compared with $13,500 if the replacement cost of $15 per unit is used. The $4,000 difference between the two cost of goods sold figures is a profit from holding the inventory during a period of rising prices and is called *inventory profit.* To look at this another way, assume that the units are sold for $20 each. The following analysis reconciles the difference between gross margin on a FIFO basis and on a replacement cost basis:

Sales revenue—900 units × $20 =		$18,000
Cost of goods sold—FIFO basis		9,500
Gross margin—FIFO basis		$ 8,500
Cost of goods sold—replacement cost basis	$13,500	
Cost of goods sold—FIFO basis	9,500	
Profit from holding inventory during a period of inflation		4,000
Gross margin on a replacement cost basis		$ 4,500

Those who argue in favor of a replacement cost approach would report only $4,500 of gross margin. They believe that the additional $4,000 of profit reported on a FIFO basis is simply due to holding the inventory during a period of rising prices. According to this viewpoint, if the 900 units sold during the period are to be replaced, a necessity if the company is to continue operating, the use of replacement cost in calculating cost of goods sold results in a better measure of gross margin than if it is calculated using FIFO.

Given that our current standards require the use of historical costs rather than replacement costs, does any one of the costing methods result in a better approximation of replacement cost of goods sold than the others? Because LIFO assigns the cost of the most recent purchases to cost of goods sold, it most nearly approximates the results with a replacement cost system. The other side of the argument, however, is that whereas LIFO results in the best approximation of *replacement cost of goods sold* on the *income statement*, FIFO most nearly approximates replacement cost of the *inventory* on the *balance sheet*. A comparison of the amounts from our example verifies this:

	ENDING INVENTORY	COST OF GOODS SOLD
Weighted average	$6,840	$10,260
FIFO	7,600	9,500
LIFO	6,100	11,000
Replacement cost	9,000	13,500

Accounting for Your Decisions

You Are a Student

The owner/manager of a dairy farm knows that you are an accounting student and has asked your advice about which inventory method to use to measure the cost of both the inventory and the cost of goods sold. Since the inventory of milk and milk byproducts spoils easily, does he have to use the FIFO inventory valuation method? Why or why not?

ANS: No, he does not have to use the FIFO method, just because his products are subject to spoilage. There is a difference between the actual physical flow of the product and the cost flow of that product. From a practical perspective, he would want to sell the milk and milk byproducts on a FIFO basis to minimize spoilage. However, he can keep track of the cost flows for inventory valuation and cost of goods sold purposes using the LIFO method or weighted average cost method.

Changing Inventory Methods

INTERNAL DECISION

The purpose of each of the inventory costing methods is to *match costs with revenues.* If a company believes that a different method will result in a better matching than that being provided by the method currently being used, it should change methods. A company must be able to justify a change in methods, however. Taking advantage of the tax breaks offered by LIFO is *not* a valid justification for a change in methods.

http://www.goodyear.com

It is very important for a company to *disclose* any change in accounting principle, including a change in the method of costing inventory. For example, some companies use the matching principle to justify a change from LIFO to FIFO, as illustrated by this excerpt from **Goodyear Tire & Rubber Company's** 2000 annual report:

> During the fourth quarter of 2000, the Company changed its method of inventory costing from last-in first-out (LIFO) to first-in first-out (FIFO) for domestic inventories. Prior periods have been restated to reflect this change. The method was changed in part to achieve a better matching of revenues and expenses. The change increased net income in 2000 by $44.4 million ($.28 per basic and diluted share), and increased retained earnings for years prior to 1998 by $218.2 million.

Inventory Valuation in Other Countries

The acceptable methods of valuing inventory differ considerably around the world. Although FIFO is the most popular method in the United States, LIFO continues to be widely used, as is the average cost method. Many countries prohibit the use of LIFO for either tax or financial reporting purposes. Countries in which LIFO is either prohibited or rarely used include the United Kingdom, Canada, New Zealand, Sweden, Denmark, and Brazil. On the other hand, Germany, France, Australia, and Japan allow LIFO for inventory valuation of foreign investments but not for domestic reports.

In Chapter 1 we mentioned the attempts by the International Accounting Standards Board (IASB) to develop worldwide accounting standards. This group favors the use of either FIFO or weighted average when specific identification is not feasible. The IASB recognizes LIFO as an acceptable alternative if a company discloses the lower of the net realizable value of its inventory and cost as determined by either FIFO, weighted average, or current cost.

Inventory Errors

LO 8 Analyze the effects of an inventory error on various financial statement items.

Earlier in the chapter we considered the inherent tie between the valuation of assets, such as inventory, and the measurement of income, such as cost of goods sold. The importance of inventory valuation to the measurement of income can be illustrated by considering inventory errors. Many different types of inventory errors exist. Some errors are mathematical; for example, a bookkeeper may incorrectly add a column total. Other errors relate specifically to the physical count of inventory at year-end. For example, the count might inadvertently omit one section of a warehouse. Other errors arise from cutoff problems at year-end.

For example, assume that merchandise in transit at the end of the year is shipped FOB (free on board) shipping point. Under these shipment terms, the inventory belongs to the buyer at the time it is shipped. Because the shipment has not arrived at the end of the year, however, it cannot be included in the physical count. Unless some type of control is in place, the amount in transit may be erroneously omitted from the valuation of inventory at year-end.

To demonstrate the effect of an inventory error on the income statement, consider the following example. Through a scheduling error, two different inventory teams were assigned to count the inventory in the same warehouse on December 31, 2004. The correct amount of ending inventory is $250,000, but because two different teams counted the same inventory in one warehouse, the amount recorded is $300,000. The effect of this error on net income is analyzed in the left half of Exhibit 7-10.

The *overstatement* of *ending inventory* in 2004 leads to an *understatement* of the 2004 cost of goods sold *expense.* Because cost of goods sold is understated, *gross margin* for the year is *overstated.* Operating expenses are unaffected by an inventory error. Thus, *net income* is *overstated* by the same amount of overstatement of gross margin.[2]

[2]An overstatement of gross margin also results in an overstatement of income tax expense. Thus, because tax expense is overstated, the overstatement of net income is not so large as the overstatement of gross margin. For now we will ignore the effect of taxes, however.

Exhibit 7-10 Effects of Inventory Error on the Income Statement

	2004			2005		
	REPORTED	CORRECTED	EFFECT OF ERROR	REPORTED	CORRECTED	EFFECT OF ERROR
Sales	$1,000*	$1,000		$1,500	$1,500	
Cost of goods sold:						
Beginning inventory	$ 200	$ 200		**$ 300**	**$ 250**	$50 OS
Add: Purchases	700	700		1,100	1,100	
Cost of goods available for sale	$ 900	$ 900		**$1,400**	**$1,350**	50 OS
Less: Ending inventory	**300**	**250**	$50 OS†	350	350	
Cost of goods sold	**$ 600**	**$ 650**	50 US‡	**$1,050**	**$1,000**	50 OS
Gross margin	**$ 400**	**$ 350**	50 OS	**$ 450**	**$ 500**	50 US
Operating expenses	100	100		120	120	
Net income	**$ 300**	**$ 250**	50 OS	**$ 330**	**$ 380**	50 US

NOTE: Figures that differ as a result of the error are in bold.
*All amounts are in thousands of dollars.

†OS = Overstatement
‡US = Understatement

The most important conclusion from the exhibit is that an overstatement of ending inventory leads to a corresponding overstatement of net income.

Unfortunately, the effect of a misstatement of the year-end inventory is not limited to the net income for that year. As indicated in the right-hand portion of Exhibit 7-10, the error also affects the income statement for the following year. This happens simply because *the ending inventory of one period is the beginning inventory of the following period.* The *overstatement* of the 2005 *beginning inventory* leads to an *overstatement* of *cost of goods available for sale.* Because cost of goods available for sale is overstated, *cost of goods sold* is also *overstated.* The *overstatement* of cost of goods sold *expense* results in an *understatement* of *gross margin* and thus an *understatement* of *net income.*

Exhibit 7-10 illustrates the nature of a *counterbalancing error.* The effect of the overstatement of net income in the first year, 2004, is offset or counterbalanced by the understatement of net income by the same dollar amount in the following year. If the net incomes of two successive years are misstated in the opposite direction by the same amount, what is the effect on retained earnings? Assume that retained earnings at the beginning of 2004 is correctly stated at $300,000. The counterbalancing nature of the error is seen by analyzing retained earnings. For 2004 the analysis would indicate the following (OS = overstated and US = understated):

	2004 REPORTED	2004 CORRECTED	EFFECT OF ERROR
Beginning retained earnings	$300,000	$300,000	Correct
Add: Net income	300,000	250,000	$50,000 OS
Ending retained earnings	$600,000	$550,000	$50,000 OS

An analysis for 2005 would show the following:

	2005 REPORTED	2005 CORRECTED	EFFECT OF ERROR
Beginning retained earnings	$600,000	$550,000	$50,000 OS
Add: Net income	330,000	380,000	$50,000 US
Ending retained earnings	$930,000	$930,000	Correct

Thus, even though retained earnings is overstated at the end of the first year, it is correctly stated at the end of the second year. This is the nature of a counterbalancing error.

The effect of the error on the balance sheet is shown in Exhibit 7-11. The only accounts affected by the error are Inventory and Retained Earnings. The overstatement

Exhibit 7-11

Effects of Inventory Error on the Balance Sheet

	2004		2005	
	REPORTED	CORRECTED	REPORTED	CORRECTED
Inventory	**$ 300***	**$ 250**	$ 350	$ 350
All other assets	1,700	1,700	2,080	2,080
Total assets	**$2,000**	**$1,950**	$2,430	$2,430
Total liabilities	$ 400	$ 400	$ 500	$ 500
Capital stock	1,000	1,000	1,000	1,000
Retained earnings	**600**	**550**	930	930
Total liabilities and stockholders' equity	**$2,000**	**$1,950**	$2,430	$2,430

NOTE: Figures that differ as a result of the error are in bold.
*All amounts are in thousands of dollars.

of the 2004 ending inventory results in an overstatement of total assets at the end of the first year. Similarly, as our earlier analysis indicates, the overstatement of 2004 net income leads to an overstatement of retained earnings by the same amount. Because the error is counterbalancing, the 2005 year-end balance sheet is correct; that is, ending inventory is not affected by the error, and thus the amount for total assets at the end of 2005 is also correct. The effect of the error on retained earnings is limited to the first year because of the counterbalancing nature of the error.

The effects of inventory errors on various financial statement items are summarized in Exhibit 7-12. Our analysis focused on the effects of an overstatement of inventory. The effects of an understatement are just the opposite and are summarized in the bottom portion of the exhibit.

Not all errors are counterbalancing. For example, if a section of a warehouse *continues* to be omitted from the physical count every year, both the beginning and the ending inventory will be incorrect each year and the error will not counterbalance.

Part of the auditor's job is to perform the necessary tests to obtain reasonable assurance that inventory has not been overstated or understated. If there is an error and inventory is wrong, however, the balance sheet and the income statement will both be distorted. For example, if ending inventory is overstated, inflating total assets, then cost

Exhibit 7-12

Summary of the Effects of Inventory Errors

	Effect of Overstatement of Ending Inventory on	
	CURRENT YEAR	FOLLOWING YEAR
Cost of goods sold	Understated	Overstated
Gross margin	Overstated	Understated
Net income	Overstated	Understated
Retained earnings, end of year	Overstated	Correctly stated
Total assets, end of year	Overstated	Correctly stated

	Effect of Understatement of Ending Inventory on	
	CURRENT YEAR	FOLLOWING YEAR
Cost of goods sold	Overstated	Understated
Gross margin	Understated	Overstated
Net income	Understated	Overstated
Retained earnings, end of year	Understated	Correctly stated
Total assets, end of year	Understated	Correctly stated

Study Tip

Note the logic behind the notion that an overstatement of ending inventory leads to overstatements of both total assets and retained earnings at the end of the year. This is logical because a balance sheet must balance; that is, the left side must equal the right side. If the left side (inventory) is overstated, then the right side (retained earnings) will also be overstated.

of goods sold will be understated, boosting profits. Thus, such an error overstates the financial health of the organization in two ways. A lender or an investor must make a decision based on the current year's statement and cannot wait until the next accounting cycle, when this error is reversed. This is one reason that investors and creditors insist on audited financial statements.

Two-Minute Review

Skipper Corp. omits one section of its warehouse in the year-end inventory count.

1. *Will the omission understate or overstate cost of goods sold on the income statement in the year the error is made?*
2. *Will the omission understate or overstate retained earnings on the balance sheet at the end of the year the error is made?*
3. *Will the omission affect retained earnings on the balance sheet at the end of the following year after the error is made? Explain your answer.*

Answers on page 333.

VALUING INVENTORY AT LOWER OF COST OR MARKET

LO 9 Apply the lower-of-cost-or-market rule to the valuation of inventory.

One of the components sold by an electronics firm has become economically obsolete. A particular style of suit sold by a retailer is outdated and can no longer be sold at regular price. In each of these instances, it is likely that the retailer will have to sell the merchandise for less than the normal selling price. In these situations, a departure from the cost basis of accounting may be necessary because the *market value* of the inventory may be less than its *cost* to the company. The departure is called the **lower-of-cost-or-market (LCM) rule.**

Lower-of-cost-or-market (LCM) rule A conservative inventory valuation approach that is an attempt to anticipate declines in the value of inventory before its actual sale.

At the end of each accounting period, the original cost, as determined using one of the costing methods such as FIFO, is compared with the market price of the inventory. If market is less than cost, the inventory is written down to the lower amount.

For example, if cost is $100,000 and market value is $85,000, the accountant makes an adjustment, which has the following effect:

BALANCE SHEET							INCOME STATEMENT	
ASSETS		=	LIABILITIES	+	OWNERS' EQUITY	+	REVENUES − EXPENSES	
Inventory	(15,000)						Loss on Decline in Value of Inventory	(15,000)

Note that the adjustment reduces both assets, in the form of inventory, and net income. The reduction in net income is the result of reporting the Loss on Decline in Value of Inventory on the income statement as an item of Other Expense.

Why Replacement Cost Is Used as a Measure of Market

A better name for the lower-of-cost-or-market rule would be the lower-of-cost-or-replacement-cost rule because accountants define *market* as *replacement cost.*[3] To

[3]Technically, the use of replacement cost as a measure of market value is subject to two constraints. First, market cannot be more than the net realizable value of the inventory. Second, inventory should not be recorded at less than net realizable value less a normal profit margin. The rationale for these two constraints is covered in intermediate accounting texts. For our purposes, we assume that replacement cost falls between the two constraints.

understand why replacement cost is used as a basis to compare with original cost, consider the following example. A clothier pays $150 for a man's double-breasted suit and normally sells it for $200. Thus, the normal markup on selling price is $50/$200, or 25%, as indicated in the column Before Price Change in Exhibit 7-13. Now assume that double-breasted suits fall out of favor with the fashion world. The retailer checks with the distributor and finds that because of the style change, the cost to the retailer to replace a double-breasted suit is now only $120. The retailer realizes that if double-breasted suits are to be sold at all, they will have to be offered at a reduced price. The selling price is dropped from $200 to $160. If the retailer now buys a suit for $120 and sells it for $160, the gross margin will be $40 and the gross margin percentage will be maintained at 25%, as indicated in the right-hand column of Exhibit 7-13.

Exhibit 7-13
Gross Margin Percentage before and after Price Change

	BEFORE PRICE CHANGE	AFTER PRICE CHANGE
Selling price	$200	$160
Cost	150	120
Gross margin	$ 50	$ 40
Gross margin percentage	25%	25%

To compare the results with and without the use of the LCM rule, assume that the facts are the same as before and that the retailer has 10 double-breasted suits in inventory on December 31, 2004. In addition, assume that all 10 suits are sold at a clearance sale in January 2005 at the reduced price of $160 each. If the lower-of-cost-or-market rule is not used, the results for the two years will be as follows:

LCM RULE NOT USED	2004	2005	TOTAL
Sales revenue ($160 per unit)	$ 0	$1,600	$1,600
Cost of goods sold			
(original cost of $150 per unit)	0	(1,500)	(1,500)
Gross margin	$ 0	$ 100	$ 100

If the LCM rule is not applied, the gross margin is distorted. Instead of the normal 25%, a gross margin percentage of $100/$1,600, or 6.25%, is reported in 2005 when the 10 suits are sold. If the LCM rule is applied, however, the results for the two years are as follows:

LCM RULE USED	2004	2005	TOTAL
Sales revenue ($160 per unit)	$ 0	$1,600	$1,600
Cost of goods sold			
(replacement cost of $120 per unit)	0	(1,200)	(1,200)
Loss on decline in value of inventory: 10 units × ($150 − $120)	(300)	0	(300)
Gross margin	$(300)	$ 400	$ 100

The use of the LCM rule serves two important functions: (1) to report the loss in value of the inventory, $30 per suit or $300 in total, in the year the loss occurs and (2) to report in the year the suits are actually sold the normal gross margin of $400/$1,600, or 25%, which is not affected by a change in the selling price.

Conservatism Is the Basis for the Lower-of-Cost-or-Market Rule

The departure from the cost basis is normally justified on the basis of *conservatism.* According to the accounting profession, conservatism is "a prudent reaction to uncertainties to try to insure that uncertainties and risks inherent in business situations are adequately considered."[4] In our example, the future selling price of a suit is uncertain because of the style changes. The use of the LCM rule serves two purposes. First, the inventory of suits is written down from $150 to $120 each. Second, the decline in value of the inventory is recognized at the time it is first observed rather than waiting until the suits are sold. An investor in a company with deteriorating inventory has good reason to be alarmed. Merchandisers who do not make the proper adjustments to their product lines go out of business as they compete with the lower prices of warehouse clubs and the lower overhead of e-business and home shopping networks.

You should realize that the write-down of the suits violates the historical cost principle, which says that assets should be carried on the balance sheet at their original cost. But the LCM rule is considered a valid exception to the principle because it is a prudent reaction to the uncertainty involved and, thus, an application of conservatism in accounting.

From Concept to Practice 7.3

Reading Circuit City's Notes

A note to Circuit City's financial statements states "Inventory is comprised of finished goods held for sale and is stated at the lower of cost or market." Why do you think the application of the lower-of-cost-or-market rule would be important to a business like Circuit City?

Application of the LCM Rule

We have yet to consider how the LCM rule is applied to the entire inventory of a company. Three different interpretations of the rule are possible:

1. The lower of total cost or total market value for the entire inventory could be reported.
2. The lower of cost or market value for each individual product or item could be reported.
3. The lower of cost or market value for groups of items could be reported. A company is free to choose any one of these approaches in applying the lower-of-cost-or-market rule. Three different answers are possible, depending on the approach selected.

The item-by-item (No. 2 above) approach is the most popular of the three approaches, for two reasons. First, it produces the most conservative result. The reason is that with either a group-by-group or a total approach, increases in the values of some items of inventory will offset declines in the values of other items. The item-by-item approach, however, ignores increases in value and recognizes all declines in value. Second, the item-by-item approach is the method required for tax purposes, although unlike LIFO, it is not required for book purposes merely because it is used for tax computations.

Consistency is important in deciding which of these approaches to use in applying the LCM rule. As is the case with the selection of one of the inventory costing methods discussed earlier in the chapter, the approach chosen to apply the rule should be used consistently from one period to the next.

METHODS FOR ESTIMATING INVENTORY VALUE

LO 10 Explain why and how the cost of inventory is estimated in certain situations.

Situations arise in which it may not be practicable or even possible to measure inventory at cost. At times it may be necessary to *estimate* the amount of inventory. Two similar methods are used for very different purposes to estimate the amount of inventory. They are the gross profit method and the retail inventory method.

[4]*Statement of Financial Accounting Concepts No. 2,* "Qualitative Characteristics of Accounting Information" (Stamford, Conn.: Financial Accounting Standards Board, May 1980), par. 95.

Which Way to Go? Cost or Lower Market?

It's October, and the accountants at Taz Industries are beginning to prepare the annual financial statements for the fiscal year that ended September 30. One of the staff members, Hudson Clark, is responsible for determining the inventory valuation. Since Taz is a manufacturing company, its inventory includes raw materials, work in process, and finished goods. The inventory costing method used at Taz is LIFO.

In the current economic downturn, the depressed economy has greatly reduced the company's current replacement cost for its ending inventory. While he understands that inventory should be valued at the lower of cost or market, Hudson is quite concerned about writing down ending inventory because that will reduce the income reported to creditors and investors. It also will mean total assets will be much lower in value on the September 30 balance sheet.

In a recent discussion with his manager, Hudson stressed the need to report the inventory at cost. After all, he reasoned, the leading economists are saying that the recovery is beginning. Already, by late October, the company is seeing a slight rise in the cost of raw materials. Certainly, by the end of the new fiscal year, the market will have recovered. Reducing the inventory to the lower market value will make the analysis of the current year's financial information appear significantly worse off than prior years. Yet, once the economy recovers, the numbers will return to "normal." Wouldn't it be best to leave the inventory at cost?

Is Hudson correct in his reasoning? Should Taz Industries report its September 30 inventory at cost or at the lower market value? Explain your reasoning.

Gross Profit Method

A company that uses a periodic inventory system may experience a problem if inventory is stolen or destroyed by fire, flooding, or some other type of damage. Without a perpetual inventory record, what is the cost of the inventory stolen or destroyed? The **gross profit method** is a useful technique to estimate the cost of inventory lost in these situations. The method relies *entirely* on the ability to reliably estimate the *ratio of gross profit to sales.*[5]

Exhibit 7-14 illustrates how the normal income statement model that we use to find cost of goods sold can be rearranged to estimate inventory. The model on the left shows the components of cost of goods sold as they appear on the income statement. Assuming a periodic system, the inventory on hand at the end of the period is counted and is subtracted from cost of goods available for sale to determine cost of goods sold. The model is rearranged on the right as a basis for estimating inventory under the gross profit method. The only difference in the two models is in the reversal of the last two components: ending inventory and cost of goods sold. Rather than attempting to estimate *ending* inventory, we are trying to estimate the amount of inventory that should be on hand at a specific date, such as the date of a fire or flood. The estimate of cost of goods sold is found by estimating gross profit and deducting this estimate from sales revenue.

To understand this method, assume that on March 12, 2004, a portion of Hardluck Company's inventory is destroyed in a fire. The company determines, by a physical count, that the cost of the merchandise not destroyed is $200. Hardluck needs to estimate the cost of the inventory lost for purposes of insurance reimbursement. If the insurance company pays Hardluck an amount equivalent to the cost of the inventory destroyed, no loss will be recognized. If the cost of the inventory destroyed exceeds the amount reimbursed by the insurance company, a loss will be recorded for the excess amount.

Gross profit method A technique used to establish an estimate of the cost of inventory stolen, destroyed, or otherwise damaged or of the amount of inventory on hand at an interim date.

Assume that the insurance company agrees to pay Hardluck $250 as full settlement for the inventory lost in the fire. From its records, Hardluck is able to determine the following amounts for the period from January 1 to the date of the fire, March 12:

Net sales from January 1 to March 12	$6,000
Beginning inventory—January 1	1,200
Purchases from January 1 to March 12	3,500

Exhibit 7-14
The Gross Profit Method for Estimating Inventory

INCOME STATEMENT MODEL	GROSS PROFIT METHOD MODEL
Beginning Inventory	Beginning Inventory
+ Purchases	+ Purchases
= Cost of Goods Available for Sale	= Cost of Goods Available for Sale
− Ending Inventory (per count)	− Estimated Cost of Goods Sold
= Cost of Goods Sold	= Estimated Inventory

[5]The terms *gross profit* and *gross margin* are synonymous in this context. Although we have used *gross margin* in referring to the excess of sales over cost of goods sold, the method is typically called the *gross profit method.*

Assume that based on recent years' experience, Hardluck estimates its gross profit ratio as 30% of net sales. The steps it will take to estimate the lost inventory follow:

1. Determine gross profit:

Net Sales	×	**Gross Profit Ratio**	=	**Gross Profit**
\$6,000	×	30%	=	\$1,800

2. Determine cost of goods sold:

Net Sales	−	**Gross Profit**	=	**Cost of Goods Sold**
\$6,000	−	\$1,800	=	\$4,200

3. Determine cost of goods available for sale at time of fire:

Beginning Inventory	+	**Purchases**	=	**Cost of Goods Available for Sale**
\$1,200	+	\$3,500	=	\$4,700

4. Determine inventory at time of the fire:

Cost of Goods Available for Sale	−	**Cost of Goods Sold**	=	**Inventory**
\$4,700	−	\$4,200	=	\$500

5. Determine amount of inventory destroyed:

Inventory at Time of Fire	−	**Inventory Not Destroyed**	=	**Inventory Destroyed**
\$500	−	\$200	=	\$300

Hardluck would make an adjustment to recognize a loss for the excess of the cost of the lost inventory over the amount of reimbursement from the insurance company. The effect of the adjustment is as follows:

BALANCE SHEET							INCOME STATEMENT	
ASSETS		=	LIABILITIES	+	OWNERS' EQUITY	+	REVENUES − EXPENSES	
Cash	250						Loss on Insurance Settlement	(50)
Inventory	(300)							

Another situation in which the gross profit method is used is for *interim financial statements.* Most companies prepare financial statements at least once every three months. In fact, the Securities and Exchange Commission requires a quarterly report from corporations whose stock is publicly traded. Companies using the periodic inventory system, however, find it cost-prohibitive to count the inventory every three months. The gross profit method is used to estimate the cost of the inventory at these interim dates. A company is allowed to use the method only in interim reports. Inventory reported in the annual report must be based on actual, not estimated, cost.

http://www.sec.gov

Retail Inventory Method

The counting of inventory in most retail businesses is an enormous undertaking. Imagine the time involved to count all of the various items stocked in a hardware store. Because of the time and cost involved in counting inventory, most retail businesses take a physical inventory only once a year. The **retail inventory method** is used to estimate inventory for interim statements, typically prepared monthly.

Retail inventory method A technique used by retailers to convert the retail value of inventory to a cost basis.

The retail inventory method has another important use. Consider the year-end inventory count in a large supermarket. One employee counts the number of tubes of toothpaste on the shelf and relays the relevant information either to another employee or to a tape-recording device: "16 tubes of 8-ounce ABC brand toothpaste at \$1.69." The key is that the price recorded is the *selling price* or *retail price* of the product, not its cost. It is much quicker to count the inventory at retail than it would be to trace the cost of each item to purchase invoices. The retail method can then be used to convert the inventory from retail to cost. The methodology used with the retail inventory method, whether for interim statements or at year-end, is similar to the approach used with the gross profit method and is covered in detail in intermediate accounting textbooks.

ANALYZING THE MANAGEMENT OF INVENTORY TURNOVER

LO 11 Analyze the management of inventory turnover.

Managers must strike a balance between maintaining enough inventory to meet customers' needs and incurring the high cost of carrying inventory. The cost of storage and the lost income from the money tied up to own inventory make it very expensive to keep on hand. Investors are also concerned with a company's inventory management. They pay particular attention to a company's **inventory turnover ratio:**

Inventory turnover ratio A measure of the number of times inventory is sold during a period.

$$\textbf{Inventory Turnover Ratio} = \frac{\textbf{Cost of Goods Sold}}{\textbf{Average Inventory}}$$

http://www.circuitcity.com

Refer to Circuit City's financial statements as displayed in the chapter opener. From the information presented, we can compute the company's inventory turnover ratio for fiscal year 2003 (amounts are in thousands of dollars):

$$\text{Inventory Turnover Ratio} = \frac{\text{Cost of Goods Sold}}{\text{Average Inventory}} = \frac{\$7{,}603{,}205}{(\underbrace{\$1{,}409{,}736}_{\text{(2/28/03 balance sheet)}} + \underbrace{\$1{,}234{,}243}_{\text{(2/28/02 balance sheet)}})/2}$$

$$= \frac{\$7{,}603{,}205}{\$1{,}321{,}990}$$

$$= 5.8 \text{ times}$$

This ratio tells us that in fiscal year 2003, Circuit City turned over its inventory 5.8 times. An alternative way to look at a company's efficiency in managing inventory is to calculate the number of days, on average, that inventory is on hand before it is sold. This measure is called the **number of days' sales in inventory** and is calculated as follows (we will assume 360 days in a year):

Number of days' sales in inventory A measure of how long it takes to sell inventory.

$$\textbf{Number of Days' Sales in Inventory} = \frac{\textbf{Number of Days in the Period}}{\textbf{Inventory Turnover Ratio}}$$

$$= \frac{360}{5.8}$$

$$= 62 \text{ days}$$

How efficient was Circuit City in managing its inventory if it took an average of 62 days, or about two months, to sell an item of inventory in fiscal year 2003? There are no easy answers to this question, but a starting point would be to compare this statistic with the same measure for prior years. Another basis for evaluation is to compare the measure with that for other companies in the same industry or business, in this case consumer electronics. As you can imagine, inventory turnover varies considerably from one industry to the next because of the differences in products. For example, consider Safeway, a large regional grocery chain. Safeway's average inventory turnover ratio in 2002 was approximately 9.2 times. This means that on average it takes Safeway only about 360/9.2, or 39 days, to sell its inventory. Given the perishable nature of its products, we would expect Safeway to turn over its inventory more rapidly than a consumer electronics company such as Circuit City. Exhibit 7-15 summarizes the differences in inventory turnover between the two companies.

http://www.safeway.com

Interpret: You Decide. Compute Winnebago Industries' inventory turnover ratio for 2002. What is the average length of time it takes to sell its inventory? Does this seem

COMPANY	TYPES OF PRODUCTS SOLD	INVENTORY TURNOVER	NUMBER OF DAYS' SALES IN INVENTORY
Circuit City	Televisions, VCRs, personal computers	5.8 times	62 days
Safeway	Grocery items	9.2 times	39 days

Exhibit 7-15

Inventory Turnover for Different Types of Companies

reasonable for the type of business the company is in? Is inventory adding value to the company? Support your answers with your analysis and explain your reasoning.

HOW INVENTORIES AFFECT THE CASH FLOWS STATEMENT

LO 12 Explain the effects that inventory transactions have on the statement of cash flows.

The effects on the income statement and the statement of cash flows from inventory-related transactions differ significantly. We have focused our attention in this chapter on how the purchase and the sale of inventory are reported on the income statement. We found that the cost of the inventory sold during the period is deducted on the income statement as cost of goods sold.

The appropriate reporting on a statement of cash flows for inventory transactions depends on whether the direct or indirect method is used. If the direct method is used to prepare the Operating Activities category of the statement, the amount of cash paid to suppliers of inventory is shown as a deduction in this section of the statement.

If the more popular indirect method is used, it is necessary to make adjustments to net income for the changes in two accounts: Inventories and Accounts Payable. These adjustments are summarized in Exhibit 7-16. An increase in inventory is deducted because it indicates that the company is building up its stock of inventory and thus expending cash. A decrease in inventory is added to net income. An increase in accounts payable is added because it indicates that during the period, the company has increased the amount it owes suppliers and has therefore conserved its cash. A decrease in accounts payable is deducted because the company actually reduced the amount owed suppliers during the period.

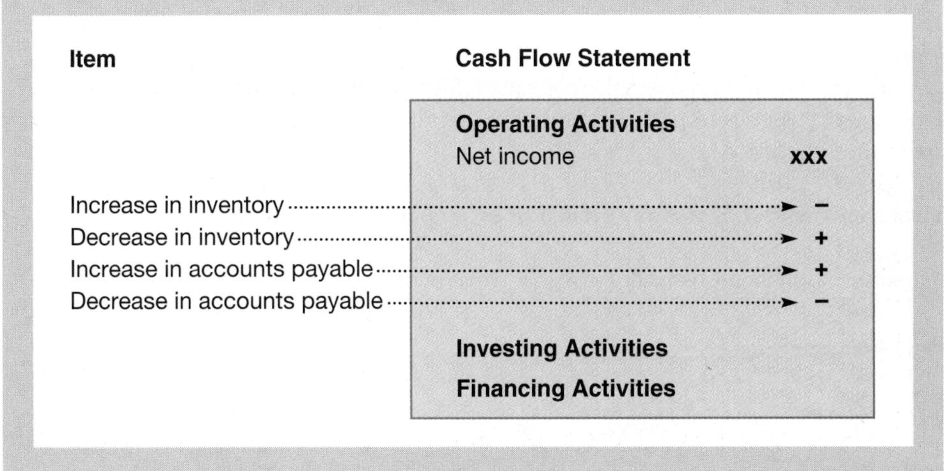

Exhibit 7-16

Inventories and the Statement of Cash Flows

The Operating Activities category of the statement of cash flows for Circuit City is presented in Exhibit 7-17. The increase in inventory is deducted because the increase in this asset uses the company's cash. A decrease in accounts payable also uses Circuit City's cash. Thus, the decrease in this item in 2003 is deducted from net earnings.

Exhibit 7-17 Partial Consolidated Statement of Cash Flows for Circuit City

CONSOLIDATED STATEMENTS OF CASH FLOWS

(Amounts in thousands)	Years Ended February 28 or 29 2003	2002	2001
OPERATING ACTIVITIES:			
Net earnings	**$ 106,084**	$ 218,795	$ 160,802
Adjustments to reconcile net earnings to net cash (used in) provided by operating activities of continuing operations:			
Earnings from discontinued operations [NOTE 3]	**(64,519)**	(90,802)	(45,564)
Depreciation and amortization	**157,469**	134,371	126,297
Amortization of restricted stock awards	**20,828**	15,678	11,365
Loss on dispositions of property and equipment	**15,659**	13,735	4,259
Provision for deferred income taxes	**5,717**	28,004	11,007
Changes in operating assets and liabilities:			
(Increase) decrease in accounts receivable, net	**(56,308)**	46,185	108,630
Increase in retained interests in securitized receivables	**(165,758)**	(148,345)	(95,680)
(Increase) decrease in merchandise inventory	**(175,493)**	176,284	(4,910)
Decrease (increase) in prepaid expenses and other current assets	**6,081**	16,071	(41,964)
(Increase) decrease in other assets	**(12,898)**	(2,359)	588
(Decrease) increase in accounts payable	**(55,818)**	202,289	(59,334)
(Decrease) increase in accrued expenses and other current liabilities and accrued income taxes	**(64,954)**	120,187	(7,680)
Increase (decrease) in accrued straight-line rent and other liabilities	**25,366**	69,606	(17,442)
NET CASH PROVIDED BY OPERATING ACTIVITIES OF CONTINUING OPERATIONS	**(258,544)**	799,699	150,374

Increase here uses cash and thus is deducted.

Decrease here uses cash and thus is deducted.

Ratios for Decision Making

By comparing the gross margin as a percentage of net sales (gross margin percentage) from one year to the next as shown below, positive or negative changes become apparent. When the percentage decreases, it indicates that a greater amount of each net sales dollar is needed to cover the cost of the merchandise sold, which leaves fewer dollars to cover the cost of other operating expenses.

When a company has a high (or an increasing) average sales per square foot of retail space ratio, it indicates more efficient use of the retail space available. A decreasing ratio or a ratio significantly lower than others in the industry indicates inefficient use of the retail space.

Reporting and Analyzing Financial Statement Information Related to a Company's Retail Sales

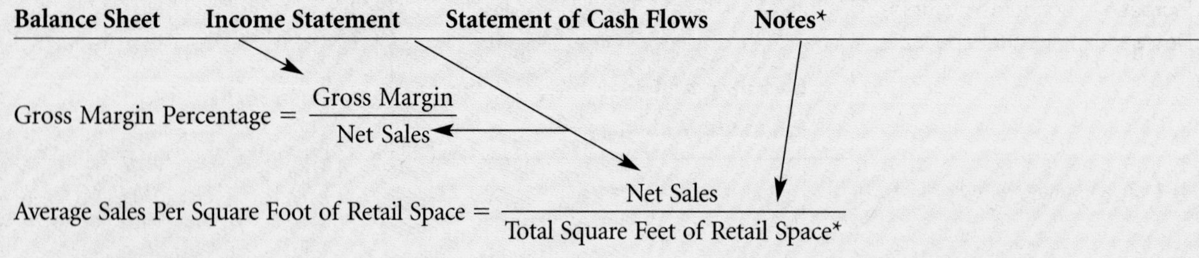

Balance Sheet
Income Statement
Statement of Cash Flows
Notes*
Gross Margin Percentage = Gross Margin / Net Sales
Average Sales Per Square Foot of Retail Space = Net Sales / Total Square Feet of Retail Space*

*This information may be found in the multi-year comparison provided in the annual report. Such comparisons may appear in the Financial Highlights section rather than in the Notes section.

Reporting and analyzing financial statement information related to a company's inventory:
The inventory turnover ratio and the number of days sales in inventory provide a good estimate of how many times throughout the period the inventory was replaced with new goods and how long products remained in inventory before they were sold. A high inventory turnover ratio indicates inventory is coming in and being sold relatively quickly. A lower ratio means inventory is sitting on the shelf or in the warehouse and is not selling very well. A high number of days will result from a low turnover ratio and indicates the business probably does not need to reorder or manufacture much inventory very soon.

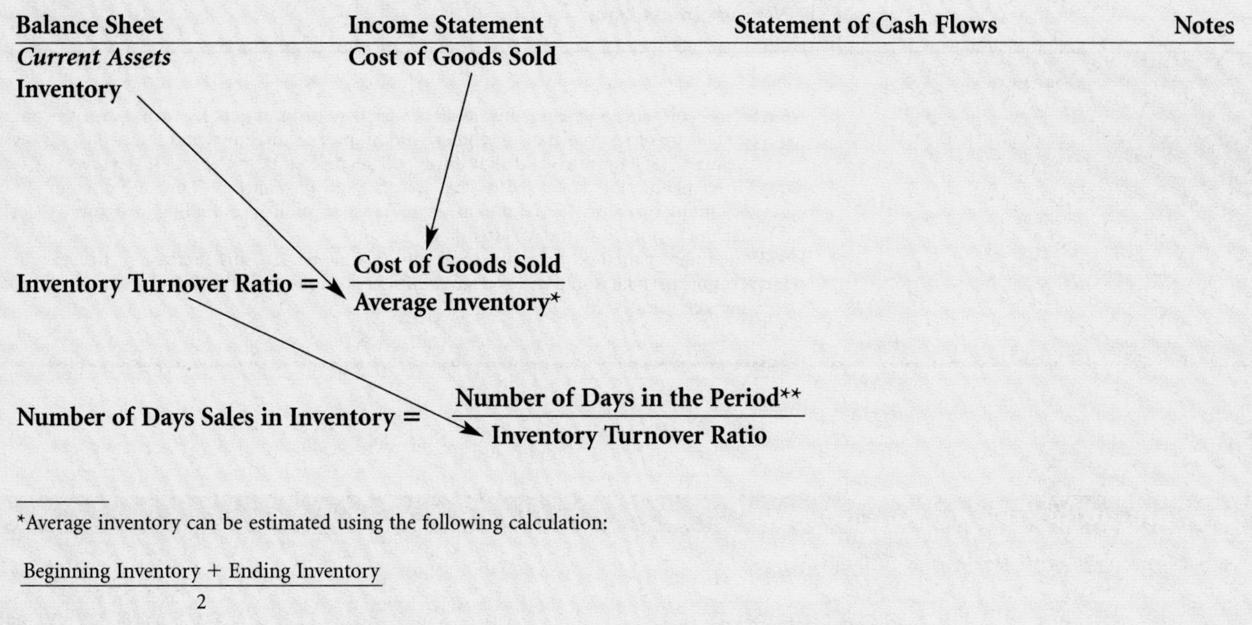

*Average inventory can be estimated using the following calculation:

$$\frac{\text{Beginning Inventory} + \text{Ending Inventory}}{2}$$

**Generally, 360 days is a good estimate unless the period is more or less than one year in length.

Impact on the Financial Reports

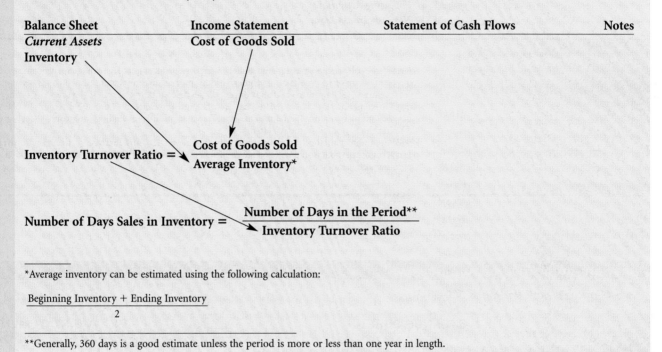

BALANCE SHEET
Current Assets
Inventory[1]
Noncurrent Assets
Current Liabilities
Accounts payable
Noncurrent Liabilities
Stockholders' Equity

INCOME STATEMENT
Revenues
Sales revenue[2]
Expenses
Cost of goods sold[2]
Selling and administrative expenses (including transportation-out expenses)
Income tax expenses
Other
Loss on declines in value of inventory
Loss on insurance settlement

(continued)

STATEMENT OF STOCKHOLDERS' EQUITY	STATEMENT OF CASH FLOWS	NOTES
Contributed Capital *Retained Earnings*	*Operating Activities*[3] Cash received from sales and paid for purchases Cash received for accounts receivable Cash paid for accounts payable *Investing Activities* *Financing Activities* *Noncash Transactions*	The basis (cost or LCM) and the method (FIFO, LIFO, average cost, etc.) used to determine cost are disclosed.

[1]For retailer/wholesaler companies, this would be merchandise inventory; for manufacturing companies, this would be made up of raw materials inventory, work in process inventory, and finished goods inventory.
[2]Sales revenue − (Sales returns and allowances + Sales discounts) = Net sales; Net sales − Cost of goods sold = Gross margin; Purchases − (Purchase returns and allowances + Purchase discounts) = Net purchases; Beginning inventory + Net purchases + Transportation-in − Ending inventory = Cost of goods sold under the periodic inventory system.
[3]Under the indirect method (explained in detail in Chapter 12), any increase or decrease in inventory and in accounts payable would be reflected in this section and would replace the items listed above under "Operating Activities."

Answers to the Two-Minute Reviews

Two-Minute Review on Pages 309–310

BALANCE SHEET							INCOME STATEMENT	
ASSETS		=	LIABILITIES		+	OWNERS' EQUITY	+ REVENUES − EXPENSES	
1. April 13:								
Accounts Receivable	1,000						Sales Revenue	1,000
April 19:								
Accounts Receivable	(150)						Sales Returns and Allowances	(150)
April 23:								
Cash	833						Sales Discounts	(17)
Accounts Receivable	(850)							
2. April 13:			Accounts Payable	1,000			Purchases	(1,000)
April 19:			Accounts Payable	(150)			Purchases Returns and Allowances	150
April 23:							Purchases Returns	
Cash	(833)		Accounts Payable	(850)			Purchases Discounts	17

Answers to the Two-Minute Reviews

Two-Minute Review on Page 317

1. *LIFO*
2. *The easiest approach to calculating the tax savings is to multiply the tax rate times the difference in cost of goods sold between the two methods.*

Two-Minute Review on Page 323

1. *Cost of goods sold will be overstated because the ending inventory is understated.*
2. *Retained earnings at the end of the year in which the error is made will be understated because cost of goods sold is overstated, and thus net income, which goes into retained earnings, is understated.*
3. *Retained earnings at the end of the following year will not be affected because of the counterbalancing nature of this error. Net income in the year of the error is understated, as described above. However, net income of the following year is overstated because cost of goods sold is understated as the result of an understatement of that year's beginning inventory.*

Warmup Exercises

Warmup Exercise 7-1 ***Net Sales*** **LO 2**

Victor Merchandising reported sales revenue, sales returns and allowances, and sales discounts of $57,000, $1500, and $900, respectively, in 2004.

Required

Prepare the net sales section of Victor's 2004 income statement.

Key to the Solution

Refer to Exhibit 7-3.

Warmup Exercise 7-2 ***Cost of Goods Sold*** **LO 4**

The following amounts are taken from Redfield Inc.'s records (all amounts are for 2004):

Inventory, January 1	$14,200
Inventory, December 31	10,300
Purchases	87,500
Purchase Discounts	4,200
Purchase Returns and Allowances	1,800
Transportation-in	4,500

Required

Prepare the cost of goods sold section of Redfield's 2004 income statement.

Key to the Solution

Refer to Exhibit 7-4.

Warmup Exercise 7-3 ***Inventory Valuation*** **LO 6**

Busby Corp. began the year with 75 units of inventory that it paid $2 each to acquire. During the year it purchased an additional 100 units for $3 each. Busby sold 150 units during the year.

Required

1. Compute cost of goods sold and ending inventory assuming Busby uses FIFO.
2. Compute cost of goods sold and ending inventory assuming Busby uses LIFO.

Key to the Solution

Review the mechanics of the methods, beginning on page 314.

Warmup Exercise 7-4 ***Lower of Cost or Market*** **LO 9**

Glendive reports its inventory on a FIFO basis and has inventory with a cost of $78,000 on December 31. The cost to replace the inventory on this date would be only $71,000.

Required

Determine the effect on the accounting equation from any adjustment necessary on December 31.

Key to the Solution

Recall the need to write down inventory when market is less than cost.

Warmup Exercise 7-5 ***Inventory Turnover*** **LO 11**

Sidney began the year with $130,000 in merchandise inventory and ended the year with $190,000. Sales and cost of goods sold for the year were $900,000 and $640,000, respectively.

Required

1. Compute Sidney's inventory turnover ratio.
2. Compute the number of days' sales in inventory.

Key to the Solution

Review how these two statistics are computed on page 328.

Solutions to Warmup Exercises

Warmup Exercise 7-1

VICTOR MERCHANDISING
PARTIAL INCOME STATEMENT
FOR THE YEAR ENDED DECEMBER 31, 2004

Sales revenue	$57,000	
Less: Sales returns and allowances	1,500	
Sales discounts	900	
Net sales		$54,600

Warmup Exercise 7-2

REDFIELD INC.
PARTIAL INCOME STATEMENT
FOR THE YEAR ENDED DECEMBER 31, 2004

Inventory, January 1, 2004		$ 14,200	
Purchases	$87,500		
Less: Purchase returns and allowances	1,800		
Purchase discounts	4,200		
Net purchases	$81,500		
Add: Transportation-in	4,500		
Cost of goods purchased		86,000	
Cost of goods available for sale		$100,200	
Less: Inventory, December 31, 2004		10,300	
Cost of goods sold			$ 89,900

Warmup Exercise 7-3

1. Cost of goods sold: (75 × $2) + (75 × $3) = $375
   Ending inventory: 25 × $3 = $ 75
2. Cost of goods sold: (100 × $3) + (50 × $2) = $400
   Ending inventory: 25 × $2 = $ 50

Warmup Exercise 7-4

BALANCE SHEET							INCOME STATEMENT	
ASSETS		=	LIABILITIES	+	OWNERS' EQUITY	+	REVENUES − EXPENSES	
Inventory	(7,000)						Loss on Decline in Value of Inventory	(7,000)

Warmup Exercise 7-5

1. $$\text{Inventory Turnover Ratio} = \frac{\text{Cost of Goods Sold}}{\text{Average Inventory}}$$
$$= \frac{\$640{,}000}{(\$130{,}000 + \$190{,}000)/2}$$
$$= \frac{\$640{,}000}{\$160{,}000} = 4 \text{ times}$$

2.
$$\frac{\text{Number of Days'}}{\text{Sales in Inventory}} = \frac{\text{Number of Days in the Period}}{\text{Inventory Turnover Ratio}}$$
$$= \frac{360}{4} = 90 \text{ days}$$

Review Problem

Stewart Distributing Company sells a single product for $2 per unit and uses a periodic inventory system. The following data are available for the year:

WebTUTOR™ Advantage

Date	Transaction	Number of Units	Unit Cost	Total
1/1	Beginning inventory	500	$1.00	$500.00
2/5	Purchase	350	1.10	385.00
4/12	Sale	(550)		
7/17	Sale	(200)		
9/23	Purchase	400	1.30	520.00
11/5	Sale	(300)		

Required

1. Compute cost of goods sold, assuming the use of the weighted average costing method.
2. Compute the dollar amount of ending inventory, assuming the FIFO costing method.
3. Compute gross margin, assuming the LIFO costing method.
4. Assume a 40% tax rate. Compute the amount of taxes saved if Stewart uses the LIFO method rather than the FIFO method.

Solution to Review Problem

1. Cost of goods sold, weighted average cost method:

Cost of goods available for sale	
$500 + $385 + $520 =	$1,405
Divided by:	
Units available for sale:	
500 + 350 + 400 =	÷ 1,250 units
Weighted average cost	$1.124 per unit
× Number of units sold:	
550 + 200 + 300 =	× 1,050 units
Cost of goods sold	$1,180.20

2. Ending inventory, FIFO cost method:

Units available for sale		1,250
− Units sold		− 1,050
= Units in ending inventory		200
× Most recent purchase price of		× $ 1.30
= Ending inventory		$ 260

3. Gross margin, LIFO cost method:

Sales revenue: 1,050 units × $2 each		$2,100
Cost of goods sold		
400 units × $1.30 =	$520	
350 units × $1.10 =	385	
300 units × $1.00 =	300	− 1,205
Gross margin		$ 895

4. Taxes saved from using LIFO instead of FIFO:

LIFO Cost of goods sold		$1,205
− FIFO Cost of goods sold:		
Cost of goods available for sale	$1,405	
Ending inventory from part 2	260	
Cost of goods sold		− 1,145
Additional expense from use of LIFO		$ 60
× Tax rate		× 0.40
Tax savings from the use of LIFO		$ 24

Appendix: Accounting Tools: Inventory Costing Methods with the Use of a Perpetual Inventory System

LO 13 Apply the inventory costing methods using a perpetual system.

The illustrations of the inventory costing methods in the chapter assumed the use of a periodic inventory system. In this appendix, we will see how the methods are applied when a company maintains a perpetual inventory system. It is important to understand the difference between inventory *costing systems* and inventory *methods*. The two inventory systems differ in terms of how often the inventory account is updated: periodically or perpetually. However, when a company sells identical units of product and the cost to purchase each unit is subject to change, it also must choose an inventory costing method, such as FIFO, LIFO, or weighted average.

Earlier in the chapter, we illustrated the various costing methods with a periodic system. We now use the same data to illustrate how the methods differ when a perpetual system is used. Keep in mind that if a company uses specific identification, the results will be the same regardless of whether it uses the periodic or the perpetual system. To compare the periodic and perpetual systems for the other methods, we must add one important piece of information: the date of each of the sales. The original data as well as number of units sold on the various dates are summarized below:

DATE	PURCHASES	SALES	BALANCE
Beginning inventory			500 units @ $10
January 20	300 units @ $11		800 units
February 18		450 units	350 units
April 8	400 units @ $12		750 units
June 19		300 units	450 units
September 5	200 units @ $13		650 units
October 20		150 units	500 units
December 12	100 units @ $14		600 units

FIFO COSTING WITH A PERPETUAL SYSTEM

Exhibit 7-18 illustrates the FIFO method on a perpetual basis. The basic premise of FIFO applies whether a periodic or a perpetual system is used: the first units purchased are assumed to be the first units sold. With a perpetual system, however, this concept is applied *at the time of each sale.* For example, note in the exhibit which 450 units are assumed to be sold on February 18. The 450 units sold are taken from the beginning inventory of 500 units with a unit cost of $10. Thus, the inventory or balance after this sale as shown in the last three columns is 50 units at $10 and 300 units at $11, for a total of $3,800. The purchase on April 8 of 400 units at $12 is added to the running balance. On a FIFO basis, the sale of 300 units on June 19 comes from the remainder of the beginning inventory of 50 units and another 250 units from the first purchase at $11 on January 20. The balance after this sale is 50 units at $11 and 400 units at $12. You should follow through the last three transactions in the exhibit to make sure that you understand the application of FIFO on a perpetual basis. An important point to note about the ending inventory of $7,600 is that it is the same amount that we calculated for FIFO periodic earlier in the chapter:

FIFO periodic (Exhibit 7-9)	$7,600
FIFO perpetual (Exhibit 7-18)	$7,600

Whether the method is applied each time a sale is made or only at the end of the period, the earliest units in are the first units out, and the two systems will yield the same ending inventory under FIFO.

Exhibit 7-18 Perpetual System: FIFO Cost-Flow Assumption

	Purchases			Sales			Balance		
DATE	UNITS	UNIT COST	TOTAL COST	UNITS	UNIT COST	TOTAL COST	UNITS	UNIT COST	BALANCE
1/1							500	$10	$5,000
1/20	300	$11	$3,300				500	10	
							300	11	8,300
2/18				450	$10	$4,500	50	10	
							300	11	3,800
4/8	400	12	4,800				50	10	
							300	11	
							400	12	8,600
6/19				50	10	500	50	11	
				250	11	2,750	400	12	5,350
9/5	200	13	2,600				50	11	
							400	12	
							200	13	7,950
10/20				50	11	550	300	12	
				100	12	1,200	200	13	6,200
12/12	100	14	1,400				300	12	
							200	13	
							100	14	7,600

LIFO COSTING WITH A PERPETUAL SYSTEM

A LIFO cost flow with the use of a perpetual system is illustrated in Exhibit 7-19. First, note which 450 units are assumed to be sold on February 18. The sale consists of the

Exhibit 7-19 Perpetual System: LIFO Cost-Flow Assumption

	Purchases			Sales			Balance		
DATE	UNITS	UNIT COST	TOTAL COST	UNITS	UNIT COST	TOTAL COST	UNITS	UNIT COST	BALANCE
1/1							500	$10	$5,000
1/20	300	$11	$3,300				500	10	
							300	11	8,300
2/18				300	$11	$3,300			
				150	10	1,500	350	10	3,500
4/8	400	12	4,800				350	10	
							400	12	8,300
6/19				300	12	3,600	350	10	
							100	12	4,700
9/5	200	13	2,600				350	10	
							100	12	
							200	13	7,300
10/20				150	13	1,950	350	10	
							100	12	
							50	13	5,350
12/12	100	14	1,400				350	10	
							100	12	
							50	13	
							100	14	6,750

most recent units acquired, 300 units at $11, and then 150 units from the beginning inventory at $10. Thus, the balance after this sale is simply the remaining 350 units from the beginning inventory priced at $10. The purchase on April 8 results in a balance of 350 units at $10 and 400 units at $12.

Note what happens with LIFO when it is applied on a perpetual basis. In essence, a gap is created. Units acquired at the earliest price of $10 and units acquired at the most recent price of $12 are on hand, but none of those at the middle price of $11 remain. This situation arises because LIFO is applied every time a sale is made rather than only at the end of the year. Because of this difference, the amount of ending inventory differs, depending on which system is used:

LIFO periodic (Exhibit 7-9)	$6,100
LIFO perpetual (Exhibit 7-19)	$6,750

MOVING AVERAGE WITH A PERPETUAL SYSTEM

Moving average The name given to an average cost method when it is used with a perpetual inventory system.

When a weighted average cost assumption is applied with a perpetual system, it is sometimes called a **moving average.** As indicated in Exhibit 7-20, each time a purchase is made, a new weighted average cost must be computed, thus the name *moving average.* For example, the goods available for sale after the January 20 purchase consist of 500 units at $10 and 300 units at $11, which results in an average cost of $10.38. This is the unit cost applied to the 450 units sold on February 18. The 400 units purchased on April 8 require the computation of a new unit cost, as indicated in the second footnote to the exhibit. As you might have suspected, the ending inventory with an average cost flow differs, depending on whether a periodic or a perpetual system is used:

Weighted average periodic (Exhibit 7-9)	$6,840
Moving average perpetual (Exhibit 7-20)	$7,290

Exhibit 7-20 Perpetual System: Moving Average Cost-Flow Assumption

	Purchases			Sales			Balance		
DATE	UNITS	UNIT COST	TOTAL COST	UNITS	UNIT COST	TOTAL COST	UNITS	UNIT COST	BALANCE
1/1							500	$10.00	$5,000
1/20	300	$11	$3,300				800	10.38*	8,304
2/18				450	$10.38	$4,671	350	10.38	3,633
4/8	400	12	4,800				750	11.24†	8,430
6/19				300	11.24	3,372	450	11.24	5,058
9/5	200	13	2,600				650	11.78‡	7,657
10/20				150	11.78	1,767	500	11.78	5,890
12/12	100	14	1,400				600	12.15§	7,290

The moving average prices per unit are calculated as follows:
*($5,000 + $3,300) / 800 units = $10.38 (rounded to nearest cent)
†($3,633 + $4,800) / 750 units = $11.24
‡($5,058 + $2,600) / 650 units = $11.78
§($5,890 + $1,400) / 600 units = $12.15

Chapter Highlights

1. **LO 1** A manufacturer's inventory consists of raw materials, work in process, and finished goods. The inventory of a retailer or wholesaler is in a single form called *merchandise inventory.*
2. **LO 2** Merchandise is inventory purchased in finished form and held for resale. Both wholesalers and retailers sell merchandise. Sales revenue is a representation of the inflow of assets from the sale of merchandise during the period. Two deductions are made from sales revenue on the income statement. Sales returns and allowances and sales discounts are both subtracted from sales revenue to arrive at net sales.
3. **LO 3** A perpetual inventory system requires the updating of the Inventory account at the time of each purchase and each sale of merchandise. With the periodic system, the Inventory account is updated only at the end of the year. Separate accounts are used during the period to record purchases, purchase returns and allowances, purchase discounts, and transportation-in. The periodic system relies on a count of the inventory on the last day of the period to determine ending inventory.
4. **LO 4** Cost of goods sold is recognized as an expense under the matching principle. It represents the cost associated with the merchandise sold during the period and is matched with the revenue of the period.
5. **LO 4** The purchases of the period are reduced by purchase returns and allowances and by purchase discounts. Any freight costs paid to acquire the merchandise, called *transportation-in,* are added. The result, cost of goods purchased, is added to the beginning inventory to determine cost of goods available for sale. Cost of goods sold is found by deducting ending inventory from cost of goods available for sale.
6. **LO 4** *FOB destination point* means that the seller is responsible for the cost of delivering the merchandise to the buyer. Title to the goods does not transfer to the buyer until the buyer receives the merchandise from the carrier. *FOB shipping point* means that the buyer pays shipping costs. Title to the goods transfers to the buyer as soon as the seller turns them over to the carrier.
7. **LO 5** The amount of cost of goods sold reported on the income statement is inherently tied to the value assigned to ending inventory on the balance sheet. All costs necessary to put inventory into a condition and location for sale should be included in its cost. Freight costs, storage costs, excise and sales taxes, and insurance during the time the merchandise is in transit are all candidates for inclusion in the cost of the asset. As a practical matter, however, some of these costs are very difficult to allocate to individual products and are therefore accounted for as expenses of the period.
8. **LO 6** The purchase of identical units of a product at varying prices necessitates the use of a costing method to assign a dollar amount to ending inventory and cost of goods sold. As alternatives to the use of a specific identification method, which is impractical in many instances as well as subject to manipulation, accountants have devised cost-flow assumptions.
9. **LO 6** The weighted average method assigns the same average unit cost to all units available for sale during the period. It is widely used because of its simplicity.
10. **LO 6** The FIFO method assigns the most recent costs to ending inventory. The older costs are assigned to cost of goods sold. A first-in, first-out approach does tend to parallel the physical flow of products in many businesses, although the actual flow is not our primary concern in choosing a costing method.
11. **LO 6** LIFO assigns the most recent costs to cost of goods sold, and the older costs remain in inventory. In a period of rising prices, this method results in a relatively higher amount assigned to cost of goods sold and, thus, a lower amount of reported net income. Lower net income results in a lower

amount of taxes due, and the tax advantages have resulted in the widespread use of the LIFO method.

A company that chooses to take advantage of the tax break from using LIFO on its tax return must also use the method in preparing the income statement. A concern with the use of LIFO is the possibility of a liquidation. If more units are sold than are bought in any one period, some of the units sold will come from the older, lower-priced units, resulting in a low cost of goods sold and a high gross margin. The high gross margin will necessitate a larger tax amount due.

12. **LO 7** Many accountants favor LIFO because it results in the nearest approximation to the current cost of goods sold. On the other hand, under LIFO, the inventory amount on the balance sheet is, in many cases, very outdated. FIFO gives a much closer approximation to current cost on the balance sheet. It leads, however, to what accountants describe as inventory profit: the portion of the gross margin that is due simply to holding the inventory during an inflationary period.

13. **LO 8** Errors in valuing inventory affect cost of goods sold and thus affect the amount of income reported for the period. An understatement of ending inventory will result in an understatement of net income; an overstatement of ending inventory will result in an overstatement of net income.

14. **LO 9** As used in the lower-of-cost-or-market rule, *market* means *replacement cost.* The purpose of valuing inventory at original cost or replacement cost, whichever is lower, is to anticipate declines in the selling price of goods subject to obsolescence, spoilage, and other types of loss. By being conservative and reducing the carrying value of the inventory at the end of the year, a company is more likely to report its normal gross margin when the units are sold at a reduced price in the next period. The rule can be applied to each item, to a group of items, or to the entire inventory.

15. **LO 10** The gross profit method is used to estimate the cost of inventory lost by theft, fire, flooding, and other types of damage. The method is also useful to estimate the amount of inventory on hand for interim reports, such as quarterly financial statements. It relies on a trustworthy estimate of the gross profit ratio.

16. **LO 10** Retailers use the retail inventory method to estimate the cost of inventory for interim financial statements and to convert the year-end inventory, per a physical count, from retail to cost.

17. **LO 11** Different measures are available to analyze how well a company is managing its inventory levels. The inventory turnover ratio indicates how many times during a period a company sells or turns over its inventory, and the number of days' sales in inventory indicates how long it takes, on average, to sell inventory.

18. **LO 12** The payment of cash to suppliers of inventory represents a cash outflow from operating activities on the statement of cash flows. If a company uses the indirect method, however, adjustments are made to net income for the increase or decrease in the Inventory and Accounts Payable accounts.

19. **LO 13** Ending inventory costed at FIFO will be the same whether the periodic system or the perpetual system is used. This is not the case when the LIFO method is used: the results under the periodic and the perpetual systems differ. Likewise, ending inventory differs in the periodic system and the perpetual system when a weighted average approach is applied. The average method with a perpetual system is really a moving average approach. (Appendix)

http://

Technology and other resources for your success

http://porter.swlearning.com

If you need additional help, visit the text's Web site. Also, see this text's preface for a description of available technology and other resources. If your instructor is using PERSONAL Trainer in this course, you may complete, on line, the exercises and problems in the text.

Key Terms Quiz

Because of the large number of terms introduced in this chapter, there are two key terms quizzes. Read each definition below and then write the number of the definition in the blank beside the appropriate term it defines. The quiz solutions appear at the end of the chapter.

Quiz 1: Merchandise Accounting

_____	Net sales	_____	Transportation-in
_____	Sales Returns and Allowances	_____	Purchases
_____	Sales Discounts	_____	Purchase Returns and Allowances
_____	Cost of goods available for sale	_____	Purchase Discounts
_____	Cost of goods sold	_____	FOB destination point
_____	Perpetual system	_____	FOB shipping point
_____	Periodic system		

1. The contra-revenue account used to record both refunds to customers and reductions of their accounts.
2. The adjunct account used to record freight costs paid by the buyer.
3. The system in which the Inventory account is increased at the time of each purchase of merchandise and decreased at the time of each sale.
4. The contra-purchases account used in a periodic inventory system when a refund is received from a supplier or a reduction given in the balance owed to the supplier.
5. The contra-revenue account used to record discounts given customers for early payment of their accounts.
6. Terms that require the seller to pay for the cost of shipping the merchandise to the buyer.
7. Terms that require the buyer to pay the shipping costs.
8. The system in which the Inventory account is updated only at the end of the period.
9. Beginning inventory plus cost of goods purchased.
10. The contra-purchases account used to record reductions in purchase price for early payment to the supplier.
11. The account used in a periodic inventory system to record acquisitions of merchandise.
12. Sales revenue less sales returns and allowances and sales discounts.
13. Cost of goods available for sale minus ending inventory.

Quiz 2: Inventory Valuation

_____ Merchandise Inventory
_____ Raw materials
_____ Work in process
_____ Finished goods
_____ Specific identification method
_____ Weighted average cost method
_____ FIFO method
_____ LIFO method
_____ LIFO liquidation
_____ LIFO conformity rule
_____ LIFO reserve
_____ Inventory profit
_____ Replacement cost
_____ Lower-of-cost-or-market (LCM) rule
_____ Gross profit method
_____ Retail inventory method
_____ Inventory turnover ratio
_____ Number of days' sales in inventory
_____ Moving average (Appendix)

1. The name given to an average cost method when it is used with a perpetual inventory system.
2. The cost of unfinished products in a manufacturing company.
3. An inventory costing method that assigns the same unit cost to all units available for sale during the period.
4. The account that wholesalers and retailers use to report inventory held for sale.
5. A conservative inventory valuation approach that is an attempt to anticipate declines in the value of inventory before its actual sale.
6. An inventory costing method that assigns the most recent costs to ending inventory.
7. The inventory of a manufacturer before the addition of any direct labor or manufacturing overhead.
8. The current cost of a unit of inventory.
9. An inventory costing method that assigns the most recent costs to cost of goods sold.
10. A measure of how long it takes to sell inventory.
11. A technique used to establish an estimate of the cost of inventory stolen, destroyed, or otherwise damaged or of the amount of inventory on hand at an interim date.
12. A manufacturer's inventory that is complete and ready for sale.
13. A technique used by retailers to convert the retail value of inventory to a cost basis.
14. The IRS requirement that if LIFO is used on the tax return, it must also be used in reporting income to stockholders.
15. An inventory costing method that relies on matching unit costs with the actual units sold.
16. The portion of the gross profit that results from holding inventory during a period of rising prices.
17. The result of selling more units than are purchased during the period, which can have negative tax consequences if a company is using LIFO.
18. The excess of the value of a company's inventory stated at FIFO over the value stated at LIFO.
19. A measure of the number of times inventory is sold during a period.

Answers on p. 365.

Alternate Terms

Gross margin Gross profit

Interim statements Quarterly or monthly statements

Market (value for inventory) Replacement cost

Merchandiser Wholesaler, retailer

Raw materials Direct materials

Retail price Selling price

Sales revenue Sales

Transportation-in Freight-in

Work in process Work in progress

Questions

1. What are three distinct types of costs that manufacturers incur? Describe each of them.
2. When a company gives a cash refund on returned merchandise, why doesn't it just reduce Sales Revenue instead of using a contra-revenue account?
3. What do credit terms of *3/20, n/60* mean? How valuable to the customer is the discount offered in these terms?
4. What is the difference between a periodic inventory system and a perpetual inventory system?
5. How have point-of-sale terminals improved the ability of mass merchandisers to use a perpetual inventory system?
6. In a periodic inventory system, what kind of account is Purchases? Is it an asset or an expense or neither?
7. Why are shipping terms, such as FOB shipping point or FOB destination point, important in deciding ownership of inventory at the end of the year?
8. How and why are transportation-in and transportation-out recorded differently?
9. What is the relationship between the valuation of inventory as an asset on the balance sheet and the measurement of income?
10. What is the justification for including freight costs incurred in acquiring incoming goods in the cost of the inventory rather than simply treating the cost as an expense of the period? What is the significance of this decision for accounting purposes?
11. What are the inventory characteristics that would allow a company to use the specific identification method? Give at least two examples of inventory for which the method is appropriate.
12. How can the specific identification method allow management to manipulate income?
13. What is the significance of the adjective *weighted* in the weighted average cost method? Use an example to illustrate your answer.
14. Which inventory method, FIFO or LIFO, more nearly approximates the physical flow of products in most businesses? Explain your answer.
15. York Inc. manufactures notebook computers and has experienced noticeable declines in the purchase price of many of the components it uses, including computer chips. Which inventory costing method should York use if it wants to maximize net income? Explain your answer.
16. Which inventory costing method should a company use if it wants to minimize taxes? Does your response depend on whether prices are rising or falling? Explain your answers.
17. The president of Ace Retail is commenting on the company's new controller: "The woman is brilliant! She has shown us how we can maximize our income and at the same time minimize the amount of taxes we have to pay the government. Because the cost to purchase our inventory constantly goes up, we will use FIFO to calculate cost of goods sold on the income statement to minimize the amount charged to cost of goods sold and thus maximize net income. For tax purposes, however, we will use LIFO because this will minimize taxable income and thus minimize the amount we have to pay in taxes." Should the president be enthralled with the new controller? Explain your answer.
18. What does the term *LIFO liquidation* mean? How can it lead to poor buying habits?
19. Historical-based costing methods are sometimes criticized for leading to inventory profits. In a period of rising prices, which inventory costing method will lead to the most "inventory profit"? Explain your answer.
20. Is it acceptable for a company to disclose, in its annual report, that it is switching from some other inventory costing method to LIFO *to save on taxes?*
21. Delevan Corp. uses a periodic inventory system and is counting its year-end inventory. Due to a lack of communication, two different teams count the same section of the warehouse. What effect will this error have on net income?
22. What is the rationale for valuing inventory at the lower of cost or market?
23. Why is it likely that the result from applying the lower-of-cost-or-market rule using a total approach, that is, by comparing total cost to total market value, and the result from applying the rule on an item-by-item basis will differ?
24. Patterson's controller makes the following suggestion: "I have a brilliant way to save us money. Because we are already using the gross profit method for our quarterly statements, we start using it to estimate the year-end inventory for the annual report and save the money normally spent to have the inventory counted on December 31." What do you think of his suggestion?
25. Why does a company save time and money by using the retail inventory method at the end of the year?
26. Ralston Corp.'s cost of sales has remained steady over the last two years. During this same time period, however, its inventory has increased considerably. What does this information tell you about the company's inventory turnover? Explain your answer.
27. Why is the weighted average cost method called a *moving* average when a company uses a perpetual inventory system? (Appendix)

Exercises

Exercise 7-1 ***Classification of Inventory Costs*** **LO 1**

Put an X in the appropriate column next to the inventory item to indicate its most likely classification on the books of a company that manufactures furniture and then sells it in retail company stores.

Inventory Item	Classification			
	Raw Material	Work in Process	Finished Goods	Merchandise Inventory
Fabric				
Lumber				
Unvarnished tables				
Chairs on the showroom floor				
Cushions				
Decorative knobs				
Drawers				
Sofa frames				
Chairs in the plant warehouse				
Chairs in the retail storeroom				

Exercise 7-2 *Inventoriable Costs* LO 1

During the first month of operations, ABC Company incurred the following costs in ordering and receiving merchandise for resale. No inventory has been sold.

List price, $100, 200 units purchased
Volume discount, 10% off list price
Paid freight costs, $56
Insurance cost while goods were in transit, $32
Long-distance phone charge to place orders, $4.35
Purchasing department salary, $1,000
Supplies used to label goods at retail price, $9.75
Interest paid to supplier, $46

Required

What amount do you recommend the company record as merchandise inventory on its balance sheet? Explain your answer. For any items not to be included in inventory, indicate their appropriate treatment in the financial statements.

Exercise 7-3 *Perpetual and Periodic Inventory Systems* LO 3

Following is a partial list of account balances for two different merchandising companies. The amounts in the accounts represent the balances at the end of the year *before* any adjustments are made or the banks are closed.

Company A		Company B	
Sales revenue	$50,000	Sales revenue	$85,000
Sales discounts	3,000	Sales discounts	2,000
Merchandise inventory	12,000	Merchandise inventory	9,000
Cost of goods sold	38,000	Purchases	41,000
		Purchase discounts	4,000
		Purchases returns and allowances	1,000

Required

1. Identify which inventory system, perpetual or periodic, each of the two companies uses. Explain how you know which system each uses by looking at the types of accounts on their books.
2. How much inventory does Company A have on hand at the end of the year? What is its cost of goods sold for the year?
3. Explain why you cannot determine Company B's cost of goods sold for the year from the information available.

Exercise 7-4 *Perpetual and Periodic Inventory Systems* LO 3

From the following list, identify whether the merchandisers described would most likely use a perpetual or periodic inventory system.

____________ Appliance store
____________ Car dealership

(continued)

______________ Drugstore
______________ Furniture store
______________ Grocery store
______________ Hardware store
______________ Jewelry store

How might changes in technology affect the ability of merchandisers to use perpetual inventory systems?

Exercise 7-5 ***Missing Amounts in Cost of Goods Sold Model*** **LO 4**

For each of the following independent cases, fill in the missing amounts:

	Case 1	Case 2	Case 3
Beginning inventory	$ (a)	$2,350	$1,890
Purchases (gross)	6,230	5,720	(e)
Purchase returns and allowances	470	800	550
Purchase discounts	200	(c)	310
Transportation-in	150	500	420
Cost of goods available for sale	7,110	(d)	8,790
Ending inventory	(b)	1,750	1,200
Cost of goods sold	5,220	5,570	(f)

Exercise 7-6 ***Purchase Discounts*** **LO 4**

For each of the following transactions of Buckeye Corporation, determine the effect on the accounting equation (all purchases on credit are made with terms of 1/10, net 30, and Buckeye uses the periodic system of inventory):

July 3: Purchased merchandise on credit from Wildcat Corp. for $3,500.

July 6: Purchased merchandise on credit from Cyclone Company for $7,000.

July 12: Paid amount owed to Wildcat Corp.

August 5: Paid amount owed to Cyclone Company.

Exercise 7-7 ***Purchases—Periodic System*** **LO 4**

For each of the following transactions of Wolverine Corporation, determine the effect on the accounting equation. The company uses the periodic system.

March 3: Purchased merchandise from Spartan Corp. for $2,500 with terms of 2/10, net/30. Shipping costs of $250 were paid to Neverlate Transit Company.

March 7: Purchased merchandise from Boilermaker Company for $1,400 with terms of net/30.

March 12: Paid amount owed to Spartan Corp.

March 15: Received a credit of $500 on defective merchandise purchased from Boilermaker Company. The merchandise was kept.

March 18: Purchased merchandise from Gopher Corp. for $1,600 with terms of 2/10, net 30.

March 22: Received a credit of $400 from Gopher Corp. for spoiled merchandise returned to them. This is the amount of credit exclusive of any discount.

April 6: Paid amount owed to Boilermaker Company.

April 18: Paid amount owed to Gopher Corp.

Exercise 7-8 ***Shipping Terms and Transfer of Title*** **LO 4**

On December 23, 2004, Miller Wholesalers ships merchandise to Michael Retailers with terms of FOB destination point. The merchandise arrives at Michael's warehouse on January 3, 2005.

Required

1. Identify who pays to ship the merchandise.
2. Determine whether the inventory should be included as an asset on Michael's December 31, 2004, balance sheet. Should the sale be included on Miller's 2004 income statement?
3. Explain how your answers to part 2 would have been different if the terms of shipment had been FOB shipping point.

Exercise 7-9 *Transfer of Title to Inventory* LO 4

From the following list, identify whether the transactions described should be recorded by Cameron Companies during December 2004 or January 2005.

Purchases of merchandise that are in transit from vendors to Cameron Companies on December 31, 2004:

_______________ Shipped FOB shipping point
_______________ Shipped FOB destination point

Sales of merchandise that are in transit to customers of Cameron Companies on December 31, 2004:

_______________ Shipped FOB shipping point
_______________ Shipped FOB destination point

Exercise 7-10 *Inventory and Income Manipulation* LO 5

ETHICS

The president of SOS Inc. is concerned that the net income at year-end will not reach the expected figure. When the sales manager receives a large order on the last day of the fiscal year, the president tells the accountant to record the sale but to ignore any inventory adjustment because the physical inventory has already been taken. How will this affect the current year's net income? next year's income? What would you do if you were the accountant? Assume that SOS uses a periodic inventory system.

Exercise 7-11 *Inventory Costing Methods* LO 6

VanderMeer Inc. reported the following information for the month of February:

Inventory, February 1	65 units @ $20
Purchases:	
February 7	50 units @ $22
February 18	60 units @ $23
February 27	45 units @ $24

During February, VanderMeer sold 140 units. The company uses a periodic inventory system.

Required

What is the value of ending inventory and cost of goods sold for February under the following assumptions:

1. Of the 140 units sold, 55 cost $20, 35 cost $22, 45 cost $23, and 5 cost $24.
2. FIFO
3. LIFO
4. Weighted average

Exercise 7-12 *Evaluation of Inventory Costing Methods* LO 7

Write the letter of the method that is most applicable to each statement.

a. Specific identification
b. Average cost
c. First-in, first-out (FIFO)
d. Last-in, first-out (LIFO)

_______________ 1. Is the most realistic ending inventory.
_______________ 2. Results in cost of goods sold being closest to current product costs.
_______________ 3. Results in highest income during periods of inflation.
_______________ 4. Results in highest ending inventory during periods of inflation.
_______________ 5. Smooths out costs during periods of inflation.
_______________ 6. Is not practical for most businesses.
_______________ 7. Puts more weight on the cost of the larger number of units purchased.
_______________ 8. Is an assumption that most closely reflects the physical flow of goods for most businesses.

Exercise 7-13 *Inventory Errors* LO 8

For each of the following independent situations, fill in the blanks to indicate the effect of the error on each of the various financial statement items. Indicate an understatement (U), an overstatement (O), or no effect (NE). Assume that each of the companies uses a periodic inventory system.

	Balance Sheet		Income Statement	
Error	**Inventory**	**Retained Earnings**	**Cost of Goods Sold**	**Net Income**
1. Goods in transit at year end are not included in the physical count: they were shipped FOB shipping point.	______	______	______	______
2. One section of a warehouse is counted twice during the year-end count of inventory.	______	______	______	______
3. During the count at year-end, the inventory sheets for one of the stores of a discount retailer are lost.	______	______	______	______

Exercise 7-14 *Transfer of Title to Inventory* LO 8

For each of the following transactions, indicate which company should include the inventory on its December 31, 2004 balance sheet:

1. Michelson Supplies Inc. shipped merchandise to PJ Sales on December 28, 2004, terms FOB destination. The merchandise arrives at PJ's on January 4, 2005.
2. Quarton Inc. shipped merchandise to Filbrandt on December 25, 2004, FOB destination. Filbrandt received the merchandise on December 31, 2004.
3. James Bros. Inc. shipped merchandise to Randall Company on December 27, 2004, FOB shipping point. Randall Company received the merchandise on January 3, 2005.
4. Hinz Company shipped merchandise to Barner Inc. on December 24, 2004, FOB shipping point. The merchandise arrived at Barner's on December 29, 2004.

Exercise 7-15 *Gross Profit Method* LO 10

On February 12, a hurricane destroys the entire inventory of Suncoast Corporation. An estimate of the amount of inventory lost is needed for insurance purposes. The following information is available:

Inventory on January 1	$ 15,400
Net sales from January 1 to February 12	105,300
Purchases from January 1 to February 12	84,230

Suncoast estimates its gross profit ratio as 25% of net sales. The insurance company has agreed to pay Suncoast $10,000 as a settlement for the inventory destroyed.

Required

Determine the effect on the accounting equation of the adjustment to recognize the inventory lost and the insurance reimbursement.

Exercise 7-16 *Inventory Turnover for Sears* LO 11

http://www.sears.com

The following amounts are available from the 2002 annual report of Sears, Roebuck & Co. (all amounts are in millions of dollars):

Cost of sales, buying, and occupancy	$25,646
Merchandise inventories, end of 2002	5,115
Merchandise inventories, end of 2001	4,912

Required

1. Compute Sears' inventory turnover ratio for 2002.
2. What is the average length of time it takes to sell an item of inventory? Explain your answer.
3. Do you think the average length of time it took Sears to sell inventory in 2002 is reasonable? What other information do you need to fully answer this question?

Exercise 7-17 ***Impact of Transactions Involving Inventories on Statement of Cash Flows*** **LO 12**

From the following list, identify whether the change in the account balance during the year would be added to (A) or deducted from (D) net income when the indirect method is used to determine cash flows from operating activities.

_______ Increase in accounts payable
_______ Decrease in accounts payable
_______ Increase in inventories
_______ Decrease in inventories

Exercise 7-18 ***Effects of Transactions Involving Inventories on the Statement of Cash Flows—Direct Method*** **LO 12**

Masthead Company's comparative balance sheets included inventory of $180,400 at December 31, 2003, and $241,200 at December 31, 2004. Masthead's comparative balance sheets also included accounts payable of $85,400 at December 31, 2003, and $78,400 at December 31, 2004. Masthead's accounts payable balances are composed solely of amounts due to suppliers for purchases of inventory on account. Cost of goods sold, as reported by Masthead on its 2004 income statement, amounted to $1,200,000.

Required

What is the amount of cash payments for inventory that Masthead will report in the Operating Activities category of its 2004 statement of cash flows assuming that the direct method is used?

Exercise 7-19 ***Effects of Transactions Involving Inventories on the Statement of Cash Flows—Indirect Method*** **LO 12**

Refer to all of the facts in Exercise 7-18.

Required

Assume instead that Masthead uses the indirect method to prepare its statement of cash flows. Indicate how each item will be reflected as an adjustment to net income in the Operating Activities category of the statement of cash flows.

Multi-Concept Exercises

Exercise 7-20 ***Income Statement for a Merchandiser*** **LO 2, 4**

Fill in the missing amounts in the following income statement for Carpenters Department Store Inc.:

Sales revenue		$125,600	
Less: Sales returns and allowances		(a)	
Net sales			$122,040
Cost of goods sold:			
Beginning inventory		$ 23,400	
Purchases	$ (b)		
Less: Purchase discounts	1,300		
Net purchases	$ (c)		
Add: Transportation-in	6,550		
Cost of goods purchased		81,150	
Cost of goods available for sale		$104,550	
Less: Ending inventory		(e)	
Cost of goods sold			(d)
Gross margin			$ 38,600
Operating expenses			(f)
Income before tax			$ 26,300
Income tax expense			10,300
Net income			$ (g)

Exercise 7-21 ***Partial Income Statement—Periodic System*** **LO 2, 4**

LaPine Company has the following account balances as of December 31, 2004:

(continued)

Purchase returns and allowances	$ 400
Inventory, January 1	4,000
Sales	80,000
Transportation-in	1,000
Sales returns and allowances	500
Purchase discounts	800
Inventory, December 31	3,800
Purchases	30,000
Sales discounts	1,200

Required

Prepare a partial income statement for LaPine Company for 2004 through gross margin. Calculate LaPine's gross margin (gross profit) ratio for 2004.

SPREADSHEET

Exercise 7-22 ***Inventory Costing Methods—Periodic System*** **LO 6, 7**

The following information is available concerning the inventory of Carter Inc.:

	Units	Unit Cost
Beginning inventory	200	$10
Purchases:		
March 5	300	11
June 12	400	12
August 23	250	13
October 2	150	15

During the year, Carter sold 1,000 units. It uses a periodic inventory system.

Required

1. Calculate ending inventory and cost of goods sold for each of the following three methods:
   - **a.** Weighted average
   - **b.** FIFO
   - **c.** LIFO
2. Assume an estimated tax rate of 30%. How much more or less (indicate which) will Carter pay in taxes by using FIFO instead of LIFO? Explain your answer.

Exercise 7-23 ***Lower-of-Cost-or-Market Rule*** **LO 5, 9**

Awards Etc. carries an inventory of trophies and ribbons for local sports teams and school clubs. The cost of trophies has dropped in the past year, which pleases the company except for the fact that it has on hand considerable inventory that was purchased at the higher prices. The president is not pleased with the lower profit margin the company is earning. "The lower profit margin will continue until we sell all of this old inventory," he grumbled to the new staff accountant. "Not really," replied the accountant. "Let's write down the inventory to the replacement cost this year, and then next year our profit margin will be in line with the competition."

Required

Explain why the inventory can be carried at an amount less than its cost. Which accounts will be affected by the write-down? What will be the effect on income in the current year and future years?

Exercise 7-24 ***Inventory Costing Methods—Perpetual System (Appendix)*** **LO 7, 13**

The following information is available concerning Stillwater Inc.:

	Units	Unit Cost
Beginning inventory	200	$10
Purchases:		
March 5	300	11
June 12	400	12
August 23	250	13
October 2	150	15

Stillwater, which uses a perpetual system, sold 1,000 units for $22 each during the year. Sales occurred on the following dates:

	Units
February 12	150
April 30	200
July 7	200
September 6	300
December 3	150

Required

1. Calculate ending inventory and cost of goods sold for each of the following three methods:
   a. Moving average
   b. FIFO
   c. LIFO
2. For each of the three methods, compare the results with those for Carter in Exercise 7-22. Which of the methods gives a different answer depending on whether a company uses a periodic or a perpetual inventory system?
3. Assume the use of the perpetual system and an estimated tax rate of 30%. How much more or less (indicate which) will Stillwater pay in taxes by using LIFO instead of FIFO? Explain your answer.

Problems

Problem 7-1 ***Inventory Costs in Various Businesses*** **LO 1**

Businesses incur various costs in selling goods and services. Each business must decide which costs are expenses of the period and which should be included in the cost of the inventory. Various types of businesses are listed below, along with certain types of costs they incur:

		Accounting Treatment		
Business	**Types of Costs**	**Expense of the Period**	**Inventory Cost**	**Other Treatment**
Retail shoe store	Shoes for sale			
	Shoe boxes			
	Advertising signs			
Grocery store	Canned goods on the shelves			
	Produce			
	Cleaning supplies			
	Cash registers			
Frame shop	Wooden frame supplies			
	Nails			
	Glass			
Walk-in print shop	Paper			
	Copy machines			
	Toner cartridges			
Restaurant	Frozen food			
	China and silverware			
	Prepared food			
	Spices			

Required

Fill in the table to indicate the correct accounting for each of these types of costs by placing an X in the appropriate column. For any costs that receive other treatment, explain what the appropriate treatment is for accounting purposes.

Problem 7-2 ***Calculation of Gross Margin for Wal-Mart and Kmart*** **LO 2**

The following information was summarized from the consolidated statements of income of Wal-Mart Stores Inc. and Subsidiaries for the years ended January 31, 2003, and 2002, and the consolidated statements of operations of Kmart Corporation for the years ended January 29, 2003, and January 30, 2002 (for each company, years are labeled as 2002 and 2001, respectively):

http://www.walmart.com
http://www.kmart.com

(in Millions)	2002 Sales	2002 Cost of Sales*	2001 Sales	2001 Cost of Sales*
Wal-Mart	$244,524	$191,838	$217,799	$171,562
Kmart	30,762	26,258	36,151	29,853

*Described as "cost of sales, buying and occupancy" by Kmart Corporation.

Required

1. Calculate the gross margin (gross profit) ratios for Wal-Mart and Kmart for 2002 and 2001.
2. Which company appears to be performing better? What factors might cause the difference in the gross margin ratios of the two companies? What other information should you consider to determine how these companies are performing in this regard?

Problem 7-3 *Evaluation of Inventory Costing Methods* LO 7

Users of financial statements rely on the information available to them to decide whether to invest in a company or lend it money. As an investor, you are comparing three companies in the same industry. The cost to purchase inventory is rising in the industry. Assume that all expenses incurred by the three companies are the same except for cost of goods sold. The companies use the following methods to value ending inventory:

Company A—weighted average cost
Company B—first-in, first-out (FIFO)
Company C—last-in, first-out (LIFO)

Required

1. Which of the three companies will report the highest net income? Explain your answer.
2. Which of the three companies will pay the least in income taxes? Explain your answer.
3. Which method of inventory costing do you believe is superior to the others in providing information to potential investors? Explain.
4. Explain how your answers to **1, 2,** and **3** would change if the costs to purchase inventory had been falling instead of rising.

Problem 7-4 *Inventory Error* LO 8

The following highly condensed income statements and balance sheets are available for Budget Stores for a two-year period (all amounts are stated in thousands of dollars):

Income Statements	2004	2003
Revenues	$20,000	$15,000
Cost of goods sold	13,000	10,000
Gross profit	$ 7,000	$ 5,000
Operating expenses	3,000	2,000
Net income	$ 4,000	$ 3,000

Balance Sheets	December 31, 2004	December 31, 2003
Cash	$ 1,700	$ 1,500
Inventory	4,200	3,500
Other current assets	2,500	2,000
Long-term assets	15,000	14,000
Total assets	$23,400	$21,000
Liabilities	$ 8,500	$ 7,000
Capital stock	5,000	5,000
Retained earnings	9,900	9,000
Total liabilities and owners' equity	$23,400	$21,000

Before releasing the 2004 annual report, Budget's controller learns that the inventory of one of the stores (amounting to $600,000) was inadvertently omitted from the count on December 31, 2003. The inventory of the store was correctly included in the December 31, 2004, count.

Required

1. Prepare revised income statements and balance sheets for Budget Stores for each of the two years. Ignore the effect of income taxes.
2. If Budget did not prepare revised statements before releasing the 2004 annual report, what would be the amount of overstatement or understatement of net income for the two-year period? What would be the overstatement or understatement of retained earnings at December 31, 2004, if revised statements were not prepared?
3. Given your answers in **2,** does it matter if Budget bothers to restate the financial statements of the two years to rectify the error? Explain your answer.

Problem 7-5 *Gross Profit Method of Estimating Inventory Losses* LO 10

On August 1, an office supply store was destroyed by an explosion in its basement. A small amount of inventory valued at $4,500 was saved. An estimate of the amount of inventory lost is needed for insurance purposes. The following information is available:

Inventory, January 1	$ 3,200
Purchases, January–July	164,000
Sales, January–July	113,500

The normal gross profit ratio is 40%. The insurance company will pay the store $65,000.

Required

1. Using the gross profit method, estimate the amount of inventory lost in the explosion.
2. An adjustment will be made to recognize the inventory loss and the insurance reimbursement. Determine the effect on the accounting equation.

Problem 7-6 *Inventory Turnover for Apple Computer and Dell Computer* LO 11

The following information was summarized from the 2002 annual report of Apple Computer Inc.: http://www.apple.com

	(in millions)
Cost of sales for the year ended:	
September 28, 2002	$4,139
September 29, 2001	4,128
Inventories:	
September 28, 2002	$ 45
September 29, 2001	11
Net sales for the year ended:	
September 28, 2002	5,742
September 29, 2001	5,363

The following information was summarized from the fiscal year 2003 annual report of Dell Computer Corporation: http://www.dell.com

	(in millions)
Cost of sales* for the year ended December 31:	
January 31, 2003	$29,055
February 1, 2002	25,661
Inventories:	
January 31, 2003	306
February 1, 2002	278
Net revenue for the year ended:	
January 31, 2003	35,404
February 1, 2002	31,168

*Described as "cost of revenue" by Dell.

Required

1. Calculate the gross margin (gross profit) ratios for Apple Computer and Dell for each of the two years presented.
2. Calculate the inventory turnover ratios for both companies for the most recent year.
3. Which company appears to be performing better? What other information should you consider to determine how these companies are performing in this regard?

Problem 7-7 ***Effects of Changes in Inventory and Accounts Payable Balances on Statement of Cash Flows*** **LO 12**

Copeland Antiques reported a net loss of $33,200 for the year ended December 31, 2004. The following items were included on Copeland's balance sheets at December 31, 2004 and 2003:

	12/31/04	12/31/03
Cash	$ 65,300	$ 46,100
Trade accounts payable	123,900	93,700
Inventories	192,600	214,800

Copeland uses the indirect method to prepare its statement of cash flows. Copeland does not have any other current assets or current liabilities and did not enter into any investing or financing activities during 2004.

Required

1. Prepare Copeland's 2004 statement of cash flows.
2. Draft a brief memo to the president to explain why cash increased during such an unprofitable year.

Multi-Concept Problems

Problem 7-8 ***Purchases and Sales of Merchandise, Cash Flows*** **LO 2, 3, 4, 12**

Two Wheeler, a bike shop, opened for business on April 1. It uses a periodic inventory system. The following transactions occurred during the first month of business:

April 1: Purchased five units from Duhan Co. for $500 total, with terms 3/10, net 30, FOB destination.

April 10: Paid for the April 1 purchase.

April 15: Sold one unit for $200 cash.

April 18: Purchased 10 units from Clinton Inc. for $900 total, with terms 3/10, net/30, FOB destination.

April 25: Sold three units for $200 each, cash.

April 28: Paid for the April 18 purchase.

Required

1. For each of the preceding transactions of Two Wheeler, determine the effect on the accounting equation.
2. Determine net income for the month of April. Two Wheeler incurred and paid $100 for rent and $50 for miscellaneous expenses during April. Ending inventory is $967 (ignore income taxes).
3. Assuming that the only transactions during April are given (including rent and miscellaneous expenses), compute net cash flow from operating activities.
4. Explain why cash outflow is so much larger than expenses on the income statement.

Problem 7-9 ***Gap Inc.'s Sales, Cost of Goods Sold, and Gross Margin*** **LO 2, 4**

http://www.gap.com

The consolidated balance sheets of Gap Inc. included merchandise inventory in the amount of $2,047,879,000 as of February 1, 2003 (the end of fiscal year 2002) and $1,768,613,000 as of February 2, 2002 (the end of fiscal year 2001). Net sales were $14,454,709,000 and $13,847,873,000 at the end of fiscal years 2002 and 2001, respectively. Cost of goods sold and occupancy expenses were $9,541,558,000 and $9,704,389,000 at the end of fiscal years 2002 and 2001, respectively.

Required

1. Unlike most other merchandisers, Gap Inc. doesn't include accounts receivable on its balance sheet. Why doesn't Gap Inc.'s balance sheet include this account?
2. Determine the effect on the accounting equation for sales during the year ended February 1, 2003.
3. Gap Inc. sets forth net sales but not gross sales on its income statement. What type(s) of deduction(s) would be made from gross sales to arrive at the amount of net sales reported? Why might the company decide not to report the amount(s) of the deduction(s) separately?
4. Reconstruct the cost of goods sold section of Gap Inc.'s 2002 income statement.

5. Calculate the gross margin (gross profit) ratios for Gap Inc. for 2002 and 2001, and comment on the change noted, if any. Is the company's performance improving? What factors might have caused the change in the gross margin ratio?

Problem 7-10 ***Financial Statements*** **LO 2, 4**

A list of accounts for Maple Inc. at 12/31/04 follows:

Accounts Receivable	$ 2,359
Advertising Expense	4,510
Buildings and Equipment, Net	55,550
Capital Stock	50,000
Cash	590
Depreciation Expense	2,300
Dividends	6,000
Income Tax Expense	3,200
Income Tax Payable	3,200
Interest Receivable	100
Inventory:	
January 1, 2004	6,400
December 31, 2004	7,500
Land	20,000
Purchase Discounts	800
Purchases	40,200
Retained Earnings, January 1, 2004	32,550
Salaries Expense	25,600
Salaries Payable	650
Sales	84,364
Sales Returns	780
Transportation-in	375
Utilities Expense	3,600

Required

1. Determine cost of goods sold for 2004.
2. Determine net income for 2004.
3. Prepare a balance sheet dated December 31, 2004.

Problem 7-11 ***Comparison of Inventory Costing Methods—Periodic System*** **LO 5, 6, 7**

Bitten Company's inventory records show 600 units on hand on October 1 with a unit cost of $5 each. The following transactions occurred during the month of October:

Date		Unit Purchases	Unit Sales
October	4		500 @ $10.00
	8	800 @ $5.40	
	9		700 @ $10.00
	18	700 @ $5.76	
	20		800 @ $11.00
	29	800 @ $5.90	

All expenses other than cost of goods sold amount to $3,000 for the month. The company uses an estimated tax rate of 30% to accrue monthly income taxes.

Required

1. Prepare a chart comparing cost of goods sold and ending inventory using the periodic system and the following costing methods:

	Cost of Goods Sold	Ending Inventory	Total
Weighted average			
FIFO			
LIFO			

2. What does the Total column represent?
3. Prepare income statements for each of the three methods.
4. Will the company pay more or less tax if it uses FIFO rather than LIFO? How much more or less?

Problem 7-12 *Comparison of Inventory Costing Methods—Perpetual System (Appendix)* **LO 5, 7, 13**

Repeat Problem 7-11 using the perpetual system.

SPREADSHEET

Problem 7-13 *Inventory Costing Methods—Periodic System* **LO 5, 6, 7**

Oxendine Company's inventory records for the month of November reveal the following:

Inventory, November 1	200 units @ $18.00
November 4, purchase	250 units @ $18.50
November 7, sale	300 units @ $42.00
November 13, purchase	220 units @ $18.90
November 18, purchase	150 units @ $19.00
November 22, sale	380 units @ $42.50
November 24, purchase	200 units @ $19.20
November 28, sale	110 units @ $43.00

Selling and administrative expenses for the month were $10,800. Depreciation expense was $4,000. Oxendine's tax rate is 35%.

Required

1. Calculate the cost of goods sold and ending inventory under each of the following three methods (assume a periodic inventory system): (a) FIFO, (b) LIFO, and (c) weighted average.
2. Calculate the gross margin and net income under each costing assumption.
3. Under which costing method will Oxendine pay the least taxes? Explain your answer.

DECISION MAKING

Problem 7-14 *Inventory Costing Methods—Periodic System* **LO 5, 6, 7**

Following is an inventory acquisition schedule for Weaver Corp. for 2004:

	Units	Unit Cost
Beginning inventory	5,000	$10
Purchases:		
February 4	3,000	9
April 12	4,000	8
September 10	2,000	7
December 5	1,000	6

During the year, Weaver sold 12,500 units at $12 each. All expenses except cost of goods sold and taxes amounted to $20,000. The tax rate is 30%.

Required

1. Compute cost of goods sold and ending inventory under each of the following three methods (assume a periodic inventory system): (a) weighted average, (b) FIFO, and (c) LIFO.
2. Prepare income statements under each of the three methods.
3. Which method do you recommend so that Weaver pays the least amount of taxes during 2004? Explain your answer.
4. Weaver anticipates that unit costs for inventory will increase throughout 2005. Will it be able to switch from the method you recommended it use in 2004 to another method to take advantage for tax purposes of the increase in prices? Explain your answer.

Problem 7-15 *Interpreting Tribune Company's Inventory Accounting Policy* **LO 1, 7**

http://www.tribune.com

The 2002 annual report of Tribune Company and Subsidiaries includes the following in the note that summarizes its accounting policies:

> **Inventories** Inventories are stated at the lower of cost or market. Cost is determined on the last-in, first-out ("LIFO") basis for newsprint and on the first-in, first-out ("FIFO") or average basis for all other inventories.

Required

1. What *types* of inventory cost does Tribune Company carry? What about newspapers? Are newspapers considered inventory?
2. Why would the company choose three different methods to value its inventory?

Problem 7-16 *Interpreting Sears' Inventory Accounting Policy* LO 6, 10

The 2002 annual report of Sears, Roebuck and Co. includes the following information in the note that describes its accounting policies relating to merchandise inventories:

http://www.sears.com

> Approximately 89% of merchandise inventories are valued at the lower of cost or market, with cost determined using the retail inventory method ("RIM") under the last-in, first-out ("LIFO") cost flow assumption. To estimate the effects of inflation on inventories, the Company utilizes internally developed price indices.

Your grandfather knows you are studying accounting and asks you what this information means.

Required

1. Sears uses the LIFO cost flow assumption. Does this mean it sells its newest merchandise first? Explain your answer.
2. Does Sears report merchandise inventories on its balance sheet at their retail value? Explain your answer.

Alternate Problems

Problem 7-1A *Inventory Costs in Various Businesses* LO 1

DECISION MAKING

Sound Traxs Inc. sells and rents videos to retail customers. The accountant is aware that at the end of the year she must account for inventory but is unsure what videos are considered inventory and how to value them. Videos purchased by the company are placed on the shelf for rental. Every three weeks the company performs a detailed analysis of the rental income from each video and decides whether to keep it as a rental or to offer it for sale in the resale section of the store. Resale videos sell for $10 each regardless of the price Sound Traxs paid for the tape.

Required

1. How should Sound Traxs account for each of the two types of tapes—rentals and resales—on its balance sheet?
2. How would you suggest Sound Traxs account for the videos as they are transferred from one department to another?

Problem 7-2A *Calculation of Gross Margins for Sears and J.C. Penney* LO 2

The following information was summarized from the 2002 and 2001 consolidated statements of income of Sears, Roebuck and Co. (for the years ended December 28, 2002, and December 29, 2001), and J.C. Penney Company, Inc. and Subsidiaries (for the years ended January 25, 2003, and January 26, 2002). For each company, years are labeled as 2002 and 2001, respectively.

http://www.sears.com
http://www.jcpenney.com

	2002		2001	
(in Millions)	**Sales***	**Cost of Sales****	**Sales***	**Cost of Sales****
Sears	$35,698	$25,646	$35,755	$26,234
J.C.Penney	32,347	22,573	32,004	22,789

*Described as "merchandise sales and services" by Sears and "retail sales, net" by J.C. Penney.
**Described as "cost of sales, buying and occupancy" by Sears and "cost of goods sold" by J.C. Penney.

Required

1. Calculate the gross margin (gross profit) ratios for Sears and J.C. Penney for 2002 and 2001.
2. Which company appears to be performing better? What factors might cause the difference in the gross margin ratios of the two companies? What other information should you consider to determine how these companies are performing in this regard?

Problem 7-3A *Evaluation of Inventory Costing Methods* LO 7

Three large mass merchandisers use the following methods to value ending inventory:

Company X—weighted average cost
Company Y—first-in, first-out (FIFO)
Company Z—last-in, first-out (LIFO)

(continued)

The cost of inventory has steadily increased over the past 10 years of the product life. Recently, however, prices have started to decline slightly due to foreign competition.

Required

1. Will the effect on net income of the decline in cost of goods sold be the same for all three companies? Explain your answer.
2. Company Z would like to change its inventory costing method from LIFO to FIFO. Write an acceptable note for its annual report to justify the change.

Problem 7-4A *Inventory Error* LO 8

The following condensed income statements and balance sheets are available for Planter Stores for a two-year period (all amounts are stated in thousands of dollars):

Income Statements	2004	2003
Revenues	$35,982	$26,890
Cost of goods sold	12,594	9,912
Gross profit	$23,388	$16,978
Operating expenses	13,488	10,578
Net income	$ 9,900	$ 6,400

Balance Sheets	December 31, 2004	December 31, 2003
Cash	$ 9,400	$ 4,100
Inventory	4,500	5,400
Other current assets	1,600	1,250
Long-term assets, net	24,500	24,600
Total assets	$40,000	$35,350
Current liabilities	$ 9,380	$10,600
Capital stock	18,000	18,000
Retained earnings	12,620	6,750
Total liabilities and owners' equity	$40,000	$35,350

Before releasing the 2004 annual report, Planter's controller learns that the inventory of one of the stores (amounting to $500,000) was counted twice in the December 31, 2003, inventory. The inventory was correctly counted in the December 31, 2004, inventory count.

Required

1. Prepare revised income statements and balance sheets for Planter Stores for each of the two years. Ignore the effect of income taxes.
2. Compute the current ratio at December 31, 2003, before the statements are revised, and then compute the current ratio at the same date after the statements are revised. If Planter applied for a loan in early 2004 and the lender required a current ratio of at least 1-to-1, would the error have affected the loan? Explain your answer.
3. If Planter did not prepare revised statements before releasing the 2004 annual report, what would be the amount of overstatement or understatement of net income for the two-year period? What would be the overstatement or understatement of retained earnings at December 31, 2004, if revised statements were not prepared?
4. Given your answers to **2** and **3**, does it matter if Planter bothers to restate the financial statements of the two years to correct the error? Explain your answer.

Problem 7-5A *Gross Profit Method of Estimating Inventory Losses* LO 10

On July 1, an explosion destroyed a fireworks supply company. A small amount of inventory valued at $4,500 was saved. An estimate of the amount of inventory lost is needed for insurance purposes. The following information is available:

Inventory, January 1	$14,200
Purchases, January–June	77,000
Sales, January–June	93,500

The normal gross profit ratio is 70%. The insurance company will pay the supply company $50,000.

Required

1. Using the gross profit method, estimate the amount of inventory lost in the explosion.
2. An adjustment will be made to recognize the inventory loss and the insurance reimbursement. Determine the effect on the accounting equation.

Problem 7-6A *Inventory Turnover for Wal-Mart and Kmart* LO 11

The following information was summarized from the 2003 annual report of Wal-Mart Stores, Inc.: http://www.walmart.com

	(in millions)
Cost of sales for the year ended January 31:	
2003	$191,838
2002	171,562
Inventories, January 31:	
2003	24,891
2002	22,614

The following information was summarized from the fiscal year 2002 annual report of Kmart Corporation: http://www.kmart.com

	(in millions)
Cost of sales, buying, and occupancy for the year ended:	
January 29, 2003	$26,258
January 30, 2002	29,853
Merchandise inventories:	
January 29, 2003	4,825
January 30, 2002	5,796

Required

1. Calculate the inventory turnover ratios for Wal-Mart for the year ending January 31, 2003, and Kmart for the year ending January 29, 2003.
2. Which company appears to be performing better? What other information should you consider to determine how these companies are performing in this regard?

Problem 7-7A *Effects of Changes in Inventory and Accounts Payable Balances on Statement of Cash Flows* LO 12

Carpetland City reported net income of $78,500 for the year ended December 31, 2004. The following items were included on Carpetland's balance sheet at December 31, 2004 and 2003:

	12/31/04	12/31/03
Cash	$ 14,400	$26,300
Trade accounts payable	23,900	93,700
Inventories	105,500	84,900

Carpetland uses the indirect method to prepare its statement of cash flows. Carpetland does not have any other current assets or current liabilities and did not enter into any investing or financing activities during 2004.

Required

1. Prepare Carpetland's 2004 statement of cash flows.
2. Draft a brief memo to the president to explain why cash decreased during a profitable year.

Alternate Multi-Concept Problems

Problem 7-8A *Purchases and Sales of Merchandise, Cash Flows* LO 2, 3, 4, 12

Chestnut Corp., a ski shop, opened for business on October 1. It uses a periodic inventory system. The following transactions occurred during the first month of business:

October 1: Purchased three units from Elm Inc. for $249 total, terms 2/10, net 30, FOB destination.

October 10: Paid for the October 1 purchase.

(continued)

October 15:	Sold one unit for $200 cash.
October 18:	Purchased 10 units from Wausau Company for $800 total, with terms 2/10, net/30, FOB destination.
October 25:	Sold three units for $200 each, cash.
October 30:	Paid for the October 18 purchase.

Required

1. For each of the preceding transactions of Chestnut, determine the effect on the accounting equation.
2. Determine the number of units on hand on October 31.
3. If Chestnut started the month with $2,000, determine its balance in cash at the end of the month, assuming that these are the only transactions that occurred during October. Why has the cash balance decreased when the company reported net income?

Problem 7-9A *Walgreen's Sales, Cost of Goods Sold, and Gross Margin* LO 2, 4

http://www.walgreens.com

The following information was summarized from the consolidated balance sheets of Walgreen Co. and Subsidiaries as of August 31, 2002, and August 31, 2001, and the consolidated statements of income for the years ended August 31, 2002, and August 31, 2001.

(in millions)	2002	2001
Accounts receivable, net	$ 954.8	$ 798.3
Cost of sales	21,076.1	18,048.9
Inventories	3,645.2	3,482.4
Net sales	28,681.1	24,623.0

Required

1. Determine the effect on the accounting equation related to the collection of accounts receivable and sales during 2002. Assume hypothetically that all of Walgreen's sales are on account.
2. Walgreen Co. sets forth net sales but not gross sales on its income statement. What type(s) of deduction(s) would be made from gross sales to arrive at the amount of net sales reported? Why might the company decide not to report the amount(s) of the deduction(s) separately?
3. Reconstruct the cost of goods sold section of Walgreen's 2002 income statement.
4. Calculate the gross margin (gross profit) ratios for Walgreen Co. for 2002 and 2001 and comment on the change noted, if any. Is the company's performance improving? What factors might have caused the change in the gross margin ratio?

Problem 7-10A *Financial Statements* LO 2, 4

SPREADSHEET

A list of accounts for Lloyd Inc. at December 31, 2004, follows:

Accounts Receivable	$ 56,359
Advertising Expense	12,900
Capital Stock	50,000
Cash	22,340
Dividends	6,000
Income Tax Expense	1,450
Income Tax Payable	1,450
Inventory	
January 1, 2004	6,400
December 31, 2004	5,900
Purchase Discounts	1,237
Purchases	62,845
Retained Earnings, January 1, 2004	28,252
Salaries Payable	650
Sales	112,768
Sales Returns	1,008
Transportation-in	375
Utilities Expense	1,800
Wages and Salaries Expense	23,000
Wages Payable	120

Required

1. Determine cost of goods sold for 2004.
2. Determine net income for 2004.
3. Prepare a balance sheet dated December 31, 2004.

Problem 7-11A ***Comparison of Inventory Costing Methods—Periodic System*** **LO 5, 6, 7**

Stellar Inc.'s inventory records show 300 units on hand on November 1 with a unit cost of $4 each. The following transactions occurred during the month of November:

Date		Unit Purchases	Unit Sales
November	4		200 @ $9.00
	8	500 @ $4.50	
	9		500 @ $9.00
	18	700 @ $4.75	
	20		400 @ $9.50
	29	600 @ $5.00	

All expenses other than cost of goods sold amount to $2,000 for the month. The company uses an estimated tax rate of 25% to accrue monthly income taxes.

Required

1. Prepare a chart comparing cost of goods sold and ending inventory using the periodic system and the following costing methods:

	Cost of Goods Sold	Ending Inventory	Total
Weighted average			
FIFO			
LIFO			

2. What does the Total column represent?
3. Prepare income statements for each of the three methods.
4. Will the company pay more or less tax if it uses FIFO rather than LIFO? How much more or less?

Problem 7-12A ***Comparison of Inventory Costing Methods—Perpetual System*** **LO 5, 7, 13**

Repeat Problem 7-11A, using the perpetual system.

Problem 7-13A ***Inventory Costing Methods—Periodic System*** **LO 5, 6, 7**

SPREADSHEET

Story Company's inventory records for the month of November reveal the following:

Inventory, November 1	300 units @ $27.00
November 4, purchase	375 units @ $26.50
November 7, sale	450 units @ $63.00
November 13, purchase	330 units @ $26.00
November 18, purchase	225 units @ $25.40
November 22, sale	570 units @ $63.75
November 24, purchase	300 units @ $25.00
November 28, sale	165 units @ $64.50

Selling and administrative expenses for the month were $16,200. Depreciation expense was $6,000. Story's tax rate is 35%.

Required

1. Calculate the cost of goods sold and ending inventory under each of the following three methods (assume a periodic inventory system): (a) FIFO, (b) LIFO, and (c) weighted average.
2. Calculate the gross margin and net income under each costing assumption.
3. Under which costing method will Story pay the least taxes? Explain your answer.

DECISION MAKING

Problem 7-14A ***Inventory Costing Methods—Periodic System*** **LO 5, 6, 7**

Following is an inventory acquisition schedule for Fees Corp. for 2004:

	Units	Unit Cost
Beginning inventory	4,000	$20
Purchases:		
February 4	2,000	18
April 12	3,000	16
September 10	1,000	14
December 5	2,500	12

During the year, Fees sold 11,000 units at $30 each. All expenses except cost of goods sold and taxes amounted to $60,000. The tax rate is 30%.

Required

1. Compute cost of goods sold and ending inventory under each of the following three methods (assume a periodic inventory system): (a) weighted average, (b) FIFO, and (c) LIFO.
2. Prepare income statements under each of the three methods.
3. Which method do you recommend so that Fees pays the least amount of taxes during 2004? Explain your answer.
4. Fees anticipates that unit costs for inventory will increase throughout 2005. Will it be able to switch from the method you recommended it use in 2004 to another method to take advantage for tax purposes of the increase in prices? Explain your answer.

Problem 7-15A ***Interpreting the New York Times Company's Financial Statements*** **LO 1, 7**

http://www.nytimes.com

The 2002 annual report of the New York Times Company includes the following note:

> Inventories. Inventories are stated at the lower of cost or current market value. Inventory cost is generally based on the last-in, first-out ("LIFO") method for newsprint and the first-in, first-out ("FIFO") method for other inventories.

Required

1. What *types* of inventory costs does the New York Times Company have? What about newspapers? Aren't these considered inventory?
2. Why did the company choose two different methods to value its inventory?

Problem 7-16A ***Interpreting Home Depot's Financial Statements*** **LO 6, 10**

http://www.homedepot.com

The 2002 annual report for Home Depot includes the following in the note that summarizes its accounting policies:

> Merchandise Inventories. The majority of the company's inventory is stated at the lower of cost (first-in, first-out) or market, as determined by the retail inventory method.

A friend knows that you are studying accounting and asks you what this note means.

Required

1. Home Depot uses the first-in, first-out method. Does this mean that it always sells its oldest merchandise first?
2. Does Home Depot report inventories on its balance sheet at their retail value?

Decision Cases

Reading and Interpreting Financial Statements

Decision Case 7-1 ***Comparing Two Companies in the Same Industry: Winnebago Industries and Monaco Coach Corporation*** **LO 1, 3**

http://www.winnebagoind.com
http://www.monacocoach.com

Refer to the financial information for Winnebago Industries and Monaco Coach Corporation in Appendices A and B at the end of the book and answer the following questions.

Required

1. Are Winnebago Industries and Monaco Coach merchandisers, manufacturers, or service providers?

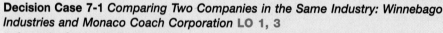

2. What is the dollar amount of inventories that each company reports on its balance sheet at the end of 2002? What percentage of total assets do inventories represent for each company?
3. Refer to note 3 in Winnebago Industries' annual report. What components make up the company's inventory? Which is the largest of these components?
4. Refer to the note in Monaco Coach's annual report titled "Inventories." What components make up the company's inventory? Are you able to determine the dollar amount of each of these components?
5. Given the nature of their businesses, which inventory system, periodic or perpetual, would you expect both Winnebago Industries and Monaco Coach to use? Explain your answer.

Decision Case 7-2 ***Comparing Two Companies in the Same Industry: Winnebago Industries and Monaco Coach Corporation*** **LO 7, 11**

Refer to the financial information for Winnebago Industries and Monaco Coach Corporation reproduced in Appendices A and B at the end of the book.

http://www.winnebagoind.com
http://www.monacocoach.com

Required

1. Compute the inventory turnover ratio for each company for 2002. Which company turned over its inventory more often during the year?
2. Compute the number of days' sales in inventory for each company for 2002. Which company had a fewer number of days' sales in inventory during the year? Is this consistent with your answer in question 1 above? Explain your answer.
3. Locate the note in each company's annual report in which they describe the inventory costing method they use. What inventory method does each company use? Should you be concerned if you are trying to compare Winnebago Industries and Monaco Coach that they do not use the same inventory method? Explain your answer.

Decision Case 7-3 ***Reading and Interpreting Winnebago Industries' Annual Report*** **LO 1, 6**

Refer to Winnebago Industries' financial statements included in its annual report.

http://www.winnebagoind.com

Required

1. Before you look at Winnebago Industries' annual report, what types of inventory accounts do you expect? What types of inventory accounts does Winnebago Industries actually report? (Refer to the note on inventories.)
2. What inventory costing method does Winnebago Industries use? Look in the notes to the financial statements.
3. What portion of total assets is represented by inventory at the end of 2001? at the end of 2002? Do these portions seem reasonable for a company in this business? Explain your answer.
4. Look at the statement of cash flows. Under the operating activities, you will find an adjustment for depreciation, yet there is no mention of depreciation on the income statement. Depreciation on equipment and buildings used in the manufacturing process is included in cost of sales. Make a list of other expenses that you would expect to be included in Winnebago Industries' cost of sales rather than listed separately on the income statement.

Decision Case 7-4 ***Reading Winnebago Industries' Statement of Cash Flows*** **LO 12**

Refer to the statement of cash flows in Winnebago Industries' 2002 annual report and answer the following questions:

http://www.winnebagoind.com

1. Did inventories increase or decrease during 2002? Why was the change in the Inventories account deducted from net income in the Operating Activities category of the statement?
2. Comment on the size of change in inventories over the last three years. Does the level of inventory at the end of 2002 seem appropriate?
3. Did accounts payable and accrued expenses increase or decrease during 2002? Why was the change in the accounts added to net income in the Operating Activities category of the statement?

Decision Case 7-5 ***Reading and Interpreting J.C. Penney's Financial Statements*** **LO 7**

J.C.Penney reports merchandise inventory in the Current Assets section of the balance sheet in its 2002 annual report as follows (amounts in millions of dollars):

http://www.jcpenney.com

(continued)

	2002	2001
Merchandise inventory (net of LIFO reserves of $403 and $377)	$4,945	$4,930

Required

1. What method does J.C.Penney use to report the value of its inventory?
2. What is the amount of the LIFO reserve at the end of each of the two years?
3. Explain the meaning of the increase or decrease in the LIFO reserve during 2002. What does this tell you about inventory costs for the company? Are they rising or falling? Explain your answer.

Decision Case 7-6 *Reading and Interpreting Circuit City's Inventory Note* LO 1, 6, 9

http://www.circuitcity.com

Note 1M in Circuit City's 2002 annual report is titled "Merchandise Inventory" and reads as follows:

> Inventory is comprised of finished goods held for sale and is stated at the lower of cost or market. Cost is determined by the average cost method. The company estimates the realizable value of inventory based on assumptions about forecasted consumer demand, market conditions and obsolescence expectations. If the estimated realizable value is less than cost, the inventory value is reduced to its realizable value. If estimates regarding consumer demand are inaccurate or unexpected technology changes affect demand, the company could be exposed to losses in excess of amounts recorded.

Required

1. What inventory costing method does Circuit City use to value its inventory? Does this method seem appropriate for the type of business that the company operates? Explain your answer.
2. Circuit City states its inventory at the lower of cost or market value. How does the company define "market"? What factors does it take into account in estimating the market value of its inventory?
3. Why do you think the company included the last sentence above which concludes with "the company could be exposed to losses in excess of amounts recorded"?

Making Financial Decisions

DECISION MAKING

Decision Case 7-7 *Gross Margin for a Merchandiser* LO 2, 4

Emblems For You sells specialty sweatshirts. The purchase price is $10 per unit, plus 10% tax and a shipping cost of 50¢ per unit. When the units arrive, they must be labeled, at an additional cost of 75¢ per unit. Emblems purchased, received, and labeled 1,500 units, of which 750 units were sold during the month for $20 each. The controller has prepared the following income statement:

Sales	$15,000
Cost of sales ($11 × 750)	8,250
Gross margin	$ 6,750
Shipping expense	750
Labeling expense	1,125
Net income	$ 4,875

Emblems is aware that a gross margin of 40% is standard for the industry. The marketing manager believes that Emblems should lower the price because the gross margin is higher than the industry average.

Required

1. Calculate Emblems' gross margin ratio.
2. Explain why you believe that Emblems should or should not lower its selling price.

DECISION MAKING

Decision Case 7-8 *Pricing Decision* LO 2, 4

Caroline's Candy Corner sells gourmet chocolates. The company buys chocolates, in bulk, for $5.00 per pound plus 5% sales tax. Credit terms are 2/10, net 25, and the company always pays promptly in order to take advantage of the discount. The chocolates are shipped to Caroline FOB shipping point. Shipping costs are $0.05 per pound. When the chocolates arrive at the shop, Caroline's Candy repackages them into one-pound boxes labeled with the store name. Boxes cost $0.70 each. The company pays its employees an hourly wage of $5.25 plus a commission of $0.10 per pound.

Required

1. What is the cost per one-pound box of chocolates?
2. What price must Caroline's Candy charge in order to have a 40% gross margin?
3. Do you believe this is a sufficient margin for this kind of business? What other costs might the company still incur?

Decision Case 7-9 *Use of a Perpetual Inventory System* LO 3

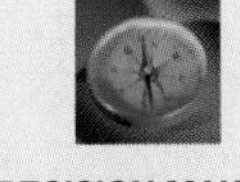
DECISION MAKING

Darrell Keith is starting a new business. He would like to keep a tight control over it. Therefore, he wants to know *exactly* how much gross profit he earns on each unit he sells. Darrell has set up an elaborate numbering system to identify each item as it is purchased and then to match the item with a sales price. Each unit is assigned a number as follows:

0000-000-00-000

a. The first four numbers represent the month and day an item was received.
b. The second set of numbers is the last three numbers of the purchase order that authorized the purchase of the item.
c. The third set of numbers is the two-number department code assigned to different types of products.
d. The last three numbers are a chronological code assigned to units as they are received during a given day.

Required

1. Write a short memo to Darrell explaining the benefits and costs involved in a perpetual inventory system in conjunction with his quest to know exactly how much he will earn on each unit.
2. Comment on Darrell's inventory system, assuming that he is selling (a) automobiles or (b) trees, shrubs, and plants.

Decision Case 7-10 *Inventory Costing Methods* LO 6, 7

DECISION MAKING

You are the controller for Georgetown Company. At the end of its first year of operations, the company is experiencing cash flow problems. The following information has been accumulated during the year:

Purchases	
January	1,000 units @ $8
March	1,200 units @ 8
October	1,500 units @ 9

During the year, Georgetown sold 3,000 units at $15 each. The expected tax rate is 35%. The president doesn't understand how to report inventory in the financial statements because no record of the cost of the units sold was kept as each sale was made.

Required

1. What inventory *system* must Georgetown use?
2. Determine the number of units on hand at the end of the year.
3. Explain cost-flow assumptions to the president and the method you recommend. Prepare income statements to justify your position, comparing your recommended method with at least one other method.

Decision Case 7-11 *Inventory Errors* LO 8

DECISION MAKING

You are the controller of a rapidly growing mass merchandiser. The company uses a periodic inventory system. As the company has grown and accounting systems have developed, errors have occurred in both the physical count of inventory and the valuation of inventory on the balance sheet. You have been able to identify the following errors as of December 2004:

- In 2002 one section of the warehouse was counted twice. The error resulted in inventory overstated on December 31, 2002, by approximately $45,600.
- In 2003 the replacement cost of some inventory was less than the FIFO value used on the balance sheet. The inventory would have been $6,000 less on the balance sheet dated December 31, 2003.

(continued)

- In 2004 the company used the gross profit method to estimate inventory for its quarterly financial statements. At the end of the second quarter, the controller made a math error and understated the inventory by $20,000 on the quarterly report. The error was not discovered until the end of the year.

Required

What, if anything, should you do to correct each of these errors? Explain your answers.

Accounting and Ethics: What Would You Do?

ETHICS

Decision Case 7-12 *Sales Returns and Allowances* LO 2

You are the controller for a large chain of discount merchandise stores. You receive a memorandum from the sales manager for the midwestern region. He raises an issue regarding the proper treatment of sales returns. The manager urges you to discontinue the "silly practice" of recording Sales Returns and Allowances each time a customer returns a product. In the manager's mind, this is a waste of time and unduly complicates the financial statements. The manager recommends, "Things could be kept a lot simpler by just reducing Sales Revenue when a product is returned."

Required

1. What do you think the sales manager's *motivation* might be for writing you the memo? Is it that he believes the present practice is a waste of time and unduly complicates the financial statements?
2. Do you agree with the sales manager's recommendation? Explain why you agree or disagree.
3. Write a brief memo to the sales manager outlining your position on this matter.

ETHICS

Decision Case 7-13 *Selection of an Inventory Method* LO 7

As controller of a widely held public company, you are concerned with making the best decisions for the stockholders. At the end of its first year of operations, you are faced with the choice of method to value inventory. Specific identification is out of the question because the company sells a large quantity of diversified products. You are trying to decide between FIFO and LIFO. Inventory costs have increased 33% over the year. The chief executive officer has instructed you to do whatever it takes in all areas to report the highest income possible.

Required

1. Which method will satisfy the CEO?
2. Which method do you believe is in the best interest of the stockholders? Explain your answer.
3. Write a brief memo to the CEO to convince him that reporting the highest income is not always the best approach for the shareholders.

ETHICS

Decision Case 7-14 *Write-Down of Obsolete Inventory* LO 9

As a newly hired staff accountant, you are assigned the responsibility of physically counting inventory at the end of the year. The inventory count proceeds in a timely fashion. The inventory is outdated, however. You suggest that the inventory could not be sold for the cost at which it is carried and that the inventory should be written down to a much lower level. The controller replies that experience has taught her how the market changes and she knows that the units in the warehouse will be more marketable again. The company plans to keep the goods until they are back in style.

Required

1. What effect will writing off the inventory have on the current year's income?
2. What effect does not writing off the inventory have on the year-end balance sheet?
3. What factors should you consider in deciding whether to persist in your argument that the inventory should be written down?
4. If you fail to write down the inventory, do outside readers of the statements have reliable information? Explain your answer.

THOMSON ONE Business School Edition Case

Case 7-15 *Using THOMSON ONE for Circuit City*

In the chapter we saw how inventory and the efficient management of it play a critical role in the success of a company. The ability to manage and control inventory should translate to success in the market for a company's stock in the form of appreciation in its stock price and, if the company chooses, in the form of dividends to the stockholders. We can use THOMSON ONE to obtain information about both Circuit City's performance as measured in its financial statements and in its stock price.

http://www.circuitcity.com

Begin by entering the company's ticker symbol, CC, and then selecting "GO." On the opening screen you will see background information about the company, key financial ratios, and some recent data concerning stock price. To research the company's stock price further, click on the "Prices" tab. At the top of the Price Chart, click on the "Interactive Chart." To obtain a 1-year chart, go to "Time Frame," click on the down arrow, and select "1 year." Then click on "Draw," and a 1-year chart should appear.

We can also find Circuit City's most recent financial statements. Near the top of the screen, click on "Financials" and select "Financial Statements." Refer to the comparative statements of earnings, statements of cash flows, and balance sheets.

Based on your use of THOMSON ONE, answer the following questions:

1. What is the inventory amount shown for the most recent year? By what amount did inventory increase or decrease from the prior year?
2. What is Circuit City's gross margin ratio for the most recent year available? How does this compare with the company's ratio for the 2003 fiscal year?
3. What is the inventory turnover for Circuit City for the most recent year? How does this ratio compare with that reported in Exhibit 7-15 for the 2003 fiscal year?
4. What have been Circuit City's high and low stock prices for the most recent year?
5. How does the company's stock performance compare to the other line on the stock price chart for the S&P 500?

Solutions to Key Terms Quiz

Quiz 1: Merchandise Accounting

12	Net sales (p. 301)	2	Transportation-in (p. 306)
1	Sales Returns and Allowances (p. 302)	11	Purchases (p. 307)
5	Sales Discounts (p. 302)	4	Purchase Returns and Allowances (p. 307)
9	Cost of goods available for sale (p. 303)	10	Purchase Discounts (p. 308)
13	Cost of goods sold (p. 304)	6	FOB destination point (p. 308)
3	Perpetual system (p. 304)	7	FOB shipping point (p. 308)
8	Periodic system (p. 304)		

Quiz 2: Inventory Valuation

4	Merchandise Inventory (p. 299)	8	Replacement cost (p. 318)
7	Raw materials (p. 300)	16	Inventory profit (p. 318)
2	Work in process (p. 300)	5	Lower-of-cost-or-market (LCM) rule (p. 323)
12	Finished goods (p. 300)	11	Gross profit method (p. 326)
15	Specific identification method (p. 312)	13	Retail inventory method (p. 327)
3	Weighted average cost method (p. 313)	19	Inventory turnover ratio (p. 328)
6	FIFO method (p. 314)	10	Number of days' sales in inventory (p. 328)
9	LIFO method (p. 314)	1	Moving average (Appendix) (p. 338)
17	LIFO liquidation (p. 317)		
14	LIFO conformity rule (p. 317)		
18	LIFO reserve (p. 318)		

Chapter 8

Operating Assets: Property, Plant, and Equipment, Natural Resources, and Intangibles

Roadmap to Success

CHAPTER Intro 1 — Getting Started - *Planning the Trip*
Why are we traveling, and who's going with us?

CHAPTER 2 — On the Road - *Studying the Map*
Where are we going, and what's our route?

CHAPTER 3 4 — Pit Stop - *Getting Special Training*
What information do we need to get us to our destination?

CHAPTER 5 6 — First Stop - *Liquid Assets Checkpoint*
Is the company controlling and investing its cash? Are customers paying what they owe?

CHAPTER 7 8 — Second Stop - *Venturing Further into the Balance Sheet*
What are the saleable and the long-term resources of the company? How do they impact the income statement?
Take a close look at inventories. Find out about the operating assets.

CHAPTER 9 — Side Trip - *Building More Skills*
Low on fuel?

CHAPTER 9 10 — Extended Stay - *Touring More of the Balance Sheet*
What does the company owe, and can it pay its bills?

CHAPTER 11 — Third Stop - *Exploring the Statement of Stockholders' Equity*
Is the owners' share changing? What's happening to company earnings?

CHAPTER 12 — Fourth Stop - *Investigating the Statement of Cash Flows*
Where did the cash come from, and where did it go?

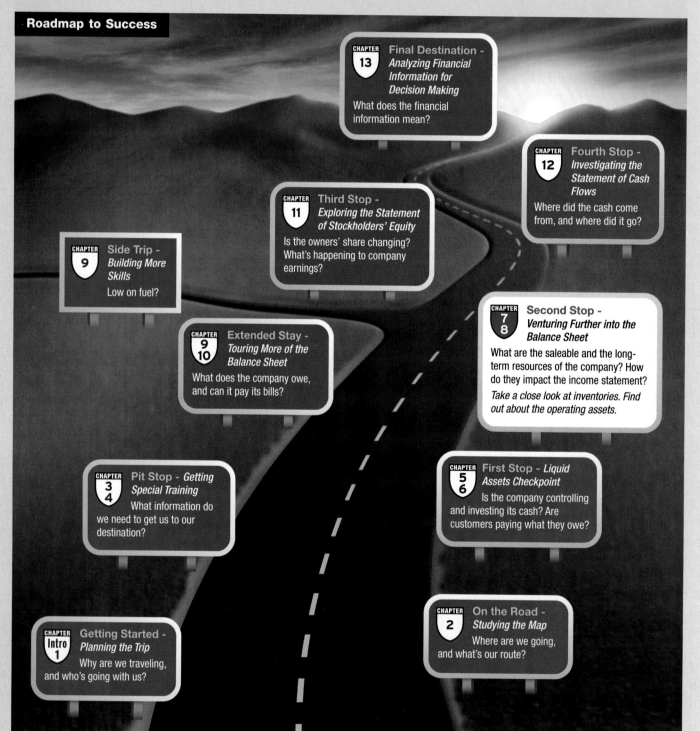

CHAPTER 13 — Final Destination - *Analyzing Financial Information for Decision Making*
What does the financial information mean?

Focus on Financial Results

The Walt Disney Company is a diversified worldwide entertainment company with operations around the world. The company is well known for its Disney Resorts in Florida and California and its Disney Cruise Line. In fact, the Disney trade name and company logo are among the most recognizable in the world. This allows the company to license the name Walt Disney, as well as its characters and visual and literary properties, to various manufacturers, retailers, show promoters, and publishers worldwide. Walt Disney also sells a host of games and toys through the Disney Stores. In addition, the Walt Disney Company is also a television, cable, and satellite broadcasting company. It owns and operates the ABC television network, ESPN, and recently acquired the Fox Family Worldwide network. It also produces and acquires live-action and animated motion pictures for distribution to the theater and home video markets.

The company believes that the diversity of its product offerings and their appeal to a wide audience will lead to a profitable future in the long run. However, the economic slowdown of 2001 was difficult for the company. Attendance at Disney theme parks declined and advertising revenue also dipped. Revenue began to rebound somewhat in 2002 and 2003 but the company's stock price was slow to respond. Throughout the turbulent times, the company has maintained its focus on a growth strategy and a dominant market position.

For sustainable growth, the company will use its tangible assets of *property, plant, and equipment* to increase profitability. But *intangible assets*, like the company's brand name, logo, trademark, film copyrights, and licenses are probably its most important assets. The importance of intangible assets cannot be overstated for a media company, or for many other companies where technology plays an important role.

Investors must be able to read Walt Disney's financial statements and understand how their assests influence the value of the company. Those investor decisions have a major impact on the company's stock price. Hopefully, the stock price accurately reflects the value of the company's assets and the company's ability to use those assets wisely. But it is always difficult to gauge the value of intangible assets and to know how long those assets will last. Accountants have had to consider carefully the proper accounting for all long-lived assets, but especially how to account for intangible assets in a company such as Walt Disney Company.

Walt Disney's 2002 Annual Report

Walt Disney and Co.
Consolidated Balance Sheets
(In millions)

SEPTEMBER 30,	2002	2001
ASSETS		
Current Assets		
Cash and cash equivalents	$ 1,239	$ 618
Receivables	4,049	3,343
Inventories	697	671
Television costs	661	769
Deferred income taxes	624	622
Other assets	579	582
Total current assets	7,849	6,605
Film and television costs	5,959	5,641
Investments	1,810	2,112
Parks, resorts and other property, at cost		
Attractions, buildings and equipment	18,917	18,846
Accumulated depreciation	(8,133)	(7,662)
	10,784	11,184
Projects in progress	1,148	911
Land	848	811
	12,780	12,906
Intangible assets, net	2,776	2,736
Goodwill	17,083	12,106
Other assets	1,788	1,704
Total assets	$50,045	$43,810

http://disney.go.com

You're in the Driver's Seat

If you were a Walt Disney manager, how would you establish the value of intangibles on the balance sheet? How would you determine the life of such assets? How would you evaluate whether the merged company has effectively utilized the intangibles? As you study this chapter, compare the ways organizations report tangible and intangible assets on the balance sheet.

LEARNING OBJECTIVES

After studying this chapter, you should be able to:

LO 1 Understand balance sheet disclosures for operating assets. (p. 369)

LO 2 Determine the acquisition cost of an operating asset. (p. 369)

LO 3 Explain how to calculate the acquisition cost of assets purchased for a lump sum. (p. 370)

LO 4 Describe the impact of capitalizing interest as part of the acquisition cost of an asset. (p. 371)

LO 5 Compare depreciation methods and understand the factors affecting the choice of method. (p. 372)

LO 6 Understand the impact of a change in the estimate of the asset life or residual value. (p. 377)

LO 7 Determine which expenditures should be capitalized as asset costs and which should be treated as expenses. (p. 378)

LO 8 Analyze the effect of the disposal of an asset at a gain or loss. (p. 379)

LO 9 Understand the balance sheet presentation of intangible assets. (p. 383)

LO 10 Describe the proper amortization of intangible assets. (p. 386)

LO 11 Explain the impact that long-term assets have on the statement of cash flows. (p. 388)

LO 12 Understand how investors can analyze a company's operating asets. (p. 390)

WHAT EXTERNAL DECISION MAKERS WANT TO KNOW ABOUT OPERATING ASSETS

DECISION MAKING

External decision makers are very interested in how the company's management has invested its resources to promote long-term stability and growth. Investors seek companies that will not only provide a steady return on investment but also have the potential to increase that return. Creditors want reassurance that the company is stable and that the operating assets provide a secure basis as security (collateral) for loans. All external decision makers want to know how well the company is managing its operating assets, how soon will they be replaced, and if there is any key intangible asset that is nearing the end of its legal life.

To be successful, decision makers must:

▶ *ASK ESSENTIAL QUESTIONS*

- Is the company investing in its future?
- Are the operating assets adding value to the company?

▶ *FIND BASIC INFORMATION*

The balance sheet, the income statement, and the statement of cash flows, along with the supporting notes, are the key sources of information about a company's long-term resources. This information tells:

- what resources have been invested in operating assets,
- whether the investments are recent,
- how much has been invested,
- what liabilities, if any, have been incurred to obtain the operating assets, and
- how the cost of the assets is being matched with revenues

▶ *UNDERSTAND ACCOUNTING PRINCIPLES*

To understand the basic information that is found, decision makers must understand the underlying accounting principles (GAAP) that have been applied to create the reported information. For operating assets, these principles determine:

- the asset cost, and
- the methods used to match asset cost to revenue.

▶ *INTERPRET ANALYTICAL INFORMATION*

Decision makers can calculate the estimated average life and the estimated average age of a company's investment in the long-term assets. These provide insight into how much longer these investments are likely to be useful and how soon the company may need to use resources to replace them. It helps external decision makers determine if the company is investing in its future growth. In addition, the asset turnover ratio provides an estimate of how many sales dollars are generated from the investment in total assets. This analysis can help determine if the operating assets are adding value to the company.

OPERATING ASSETS: PROPERTY, PLANT, AND EQUIPMENT

Balance Sheet Presentation

LO 1 Understand balance sheet disclosures for operating assets.

Operating assets constitute the major productive assets of many companies. Current assets are important to a company's short-term liquidity; operating assets are absolutely essential to its long-term future. These assets must be used to produce the goods or services the company sells to customers. The dollar amount invested in operating assets may be very large, as is the case with most manufacturing companies. On the other hand, operating assets on the balance sheet may be insignificant to a company's value, as is the case with a computer software firm or many of the so-called Internet firms. Users of financial statements must assess the operating assets to make important decisions. For example, lenders are interested in the value of the operating assets as collateral when making lending decisions. Investors must evaluate whether the operating assets indicate long-term potential and can provide a return to the stockholders.

The terms used to describe the operating assets and the balance sheet presentation of those assets vary somewhat by company. Some firms refer to this category of assets as *fixed* or *plant assets.* Other firms prefer to present operating assets in two categories: *tangible assets* and *intangible assets.* The balance sheet of Johnson Controls, Inc., uses another way to classify operating assets. The company presents one line item for *property, plant, and equipment* and presents the details in the notes. Because the term *other assets* can encompass a variety of items, we will use the more descriptive term *intangible assets* for the second category. We begin by examining the accounting issues concerned with the first category: property, plant, and equipment.

http://www.johnsoncontrols.com

The September 30, 2002, notes of Johnson Controls, Inc., present property, plant, and equipment shown at the top of the following page (in millions). Note that the acquisition costs of the buildings and improvements, machinery and equipment, construction in progress, and land are stated and the amount of accumulated depreciation is deducted to determine the net amount. The accumulated depreciation is related to the first three assets, since land is not a depreciable item.

Acquisition of Property, Plant, and Equipment

LO 2 Determine the acquisition cost of an operating asset.

Assets classified as property, plant, and equipment are initially recorded at acquisition cost (also referred to as *historical cost*). As indicated in Johnson Control's notes, these assets are normally presented on the balance sheet at original acquisition cost minus accumulated depreciation. It is important, however, to define the term *acquisition cost* (also known as *original cost*) in a more exact manner. What items should be included as part of the original acquisition? **Acquisition cost** should include all of the costs that

Acquisition cost The amount that includes all of the cost normally necessary to acquire an asset and prepare it for its intended use.

Property, Plant, and Equipment

	September 30, 2002 (in millions)
Buildings and improvements	$ 1,349.2
Machinery and equipment	3,508.2
Construction in progress	267.9
	$ 5,125.3
Land	231.3
	$ 5,356.6
Less accumulated depreciation	(2,911.1)
Property, plant, and equipment (net)	$ 2,445.5

are normal and necessary to acquire the asset and prepare it for its intended use. Items included in acquisition cost would generally include the following:

Purchase price

Taxes paid at time of purchase (for example, sales tax)

Transportation charges

Installation costs

INTERNAL DECISION

An accountant must exercise careful judgment to determine which costs are "normal" and "necessary" and should be included in the calculation of the acquisition cost of operating assets. Acquisition cost should not include expenditures unrelated to the acquisition (for example, repair costs if an asset is damaged during installation) or costs incurred after the asset was installed and use had begun.

Accounting for Your Decisions

You Are an Attorney

You are a newly licensed attorney who just opened a legal firm. As part of your office operations, you have purchased some slightly used computers. Should the cost of repairing the computers be considered as part of the acquistion cost?

ANS: If you were aware that the computers needed to be repaired when purchased, the repair costs are part of the cost of acquisition. If the computers were damaged after they were purchased, the costs should be treated as an expense on the income statement.

LO 3 Explain how to calculate the acquisition cost of assets purchased for a lump sum.

Group Purchase Quite often a firm purchases several assets as a group and pays a lump-sum amount. This is most common when a company purchases land and a building situated on it and pays a lump-sum amount for both. It is important to measure separately the acquisition cost of the land and of the building. Land is not a depreciable asset, but the amount allocated to the building is subject to depreciation. In cases such as this, the purchase price should be allocated between land and building on the basis of the proportion of the *fair market values* of each.

For example, assume that on January 1, Payton Company purchased a building and the land that it is situated on for $100,000. The accountant was able to establish that the fair market values of the two assets on January 1 were as follows:

Land	$ 30,000
Building	90,000
Total	$120,000

On the basis of the estimated market values, the purchase price should be allocated as follows:

To land	$100,000 × $30,000/$120,000 = $25,000
To building	$100,000 × $90,000/$120,000 = $75,000

BALANCE SHEET							INCOME STATEMENT
ASSETS		=	LIABILITIES	+	OWNERS' EQUITY	+	REVENUES − EXPENSES
Land	25,000						
Building	75,000						
Cash	(100,000)						

Market value is best established by an independent appraisal of the property. If such appraisal is not possible, the accountant must rely on the market value of other similar assets, on the value of the assets in tax records, or on other available evidence.

These efforts to allocate dollars between land and buildings will permit the appropriate allocation for depreciation. But **when an investor or lender views the balance sheet,** he or she is often more interested in the current market value. The best things that can be said about historical cost are that it is a verifiable number and that it is conservative. But it is still up to the lender or the investor to determine the appropriate value for these assets.

LO 4 Describe the impact of capitalizing interest as part of the acquisition cost of an asset.

Capitalization of Interest We have seen that acquisition cost may include several items. But should the acquisition cost of an asset include the interest cost necessary to finance the asset? That is, should interest be treated as an asset, or should it be treated as an expense of the period?

Generally, the interest on borrowed money should be treated as an expense of the period. If a company buys an asset and borrows money to finance the purchase, the interest on the borrowed money is not considered part of the asset's cost. Financial statements generally treat investing and financing as separate decisions. Purchase of an asset, an investing activity, is treated as a business decision that is separate from the decision concerning the financing of the asset. Therefore, interest is treated as a period cost and should appear on the income statement as interest expense in the period incurred.

There is one exception to this general guideline, however. If a company constructs an asset over a period of time and borrows money to finance the construction, the amount of interest incurred during the construction period is not treated as interest expense. Instead, the interest must be included as part of the acquisition cost of the asset. This is referred to as **capitalization of interest**. The amount of interest that is capitalized (treated as an asset) is based on the *average accumulated expenditures.* The logic of using the average accumulated expenditures is that this number represents an average amount of money tied up in the project over a year. If it takes $400,000 to construct a building, the interest should not be figured on the full $400,000 because there were times during the year when less than the full amount was being used.

Capitalization of interest Interest on constructed assets is added to the asset account.

When it costs $400,000 to build an asset and the amount of interest to be capitalized is $10,000, the acquisition cost of the asset is $410,000. The asset should appear on the balance sheet at that amount. Depreciation of the asset should be based on $410,000, less any residual value.

Study Tip

Land improvements represent a depreciable asset with a limited life. Land itself is not depreciable.

Land Improvements It is important to distinguish between land and other costs associated with it. The acquisition cost of land should be kept in a separate account because land has an unlimited life and is not subject to depreciation. Other costs associated with land should be recorded in an account such as Land Improvements. For example, the costs of paving a parking lot or landscaping costs are properly treated as **land improvements,** which have a limited life. Therefore, the acquisition costs of land improvements should be depreciated over their useful lives.

Land improvements Costs that are related to land but that have a limited life.

LO 5 Compare depreciation methods and understand the factors affecting the choice of method.

Challenges to Internal Decision Makers: Use, Depreciation, and Disposal of Property, Plant, and Equipment

INTERNAL DECISION

All property, plant, and equipment, except land, have a limited life and decline in usefulness over time. The accrual accounting process requires a proper *matching* of expenses and revenue to accurately measure income. Therefore, the accountant must estimate the decline in usefulness of operating assets and allocate the acquisition cost in a manner consistent with the decline in usefulness. This allocation is the process generally referred to as **depreciation.**

Depreciation The allocation of the original cost of an asset to the periods benefited by its use.

Unfortunately, proper matching for operating assets is not easy because of the many factors involved. An asset's decline in usefulness is related to *physical deterioration* factors such as wear and tear. In some cases, the physical deterioration results from heavy use of the asset in the production process, but it may also result from the passage of time or exposure to the elements.

The decline in an asset's usefulness is also related to *obsolescence* factors. Some operating assets, such as computers, decline in usefulness simply because they have been surpassed by a newer model or newer technology. Finally, the decline in an asset's usefulness is related to a company's *repair and maintenance* policy. A company with an aggressive and extensive repair and maintenance program will not experience a decline in usefulness of operating assets as rapidly as one without such a policy.

Because the decline in an asset's usefulness is related to a variety of factors, several depreciation methods have been developed. In theory, a company should use a depreciation method that allocates the original cost of the asset to the periods benefited and that allows the company to accurately match the expense to the revenue generated by the asset. We will present three methods of depreciation: *straight line, units of production,* and *double declining balance.*

From Concept to Practice 8.1

Reading the Balance Sheets of Winnebago Industries and Monaco Coach

What amount did Winnebago Industries *and* Monaco Coach *report as depreciation in fiscal year 2002? Where is this information disclosed? What depreciation method(s) did each company use?*

INTERNAL DECISION

All depreciation methods are based on the asset's original acquisition cost. In addition, all methods require an estimate of two additional factors: the asset's *life* and its *residual value.* The residual value (also referred to as *salvage value*) should represent the amount that could be obtained from selling or disposing of the asset at the end of its useful life. Often, this may be a small amount or even zero.

Straight-line method A method by which the same dollar amount of depreciation is recorded in each year of asset use.

Straight-Line Method The **straight-line method** of depreciation allocates the cost of the asset evenly over time. This method calculates the annual depreciation as follows:

Depreciation = (Acquisition Cost − Residual Value)/Life

For example, assume that on January 1, 2004, Kemp Company purchased a machine for $20,000. The company estimated that the machine's life would be five years and its residual value at the end of 2008 would be $2,000. The annual depreciation should be calculated as follows:

Depreciation = (Acquisition Cost − Residual Value)/Life

Depreciation = ($20,000 − $2,000)/5

= $3,600

Book value The original cost of an asset minus the amount of accumulated depreciation.

An asset's **book value** is defined as its acquisition cost minus its total amount of accumulated depreciation. Thus, the book value of the machine in this example is $16,400 at the end of 2004:

Book Value = Acquisition Cost − Accumulated Depreciation

Book Value = \$20,000 − \$3,600

= \$16,400

The book value at the end of 2005 is \$12,800:

Book Value = Acquisition Cost − Accumulated Depreciation

Book Value = \$20,000 − (2 × \$3,600)

= \$12,800

The most attractive features of the straight-line method are its ease and its simplicity. It is the most popular method for presenting depreciation in the annual report to stockholders.

Units-of-Production Method In some cases, the decline in an asset's usefulness is directly related to wear and tear as a result of the number of units it produces. In those cases, depreciation should be calculated by the **units-of-production method.** With this method, the asset's life is expressed in terms of the number of units that the asset can produce. The depreciation *per unit* can be calculated as follows:

Units-of-production method Depreciation is determined as a function of the number of units the asset produces.

Depreciation per Unit = (Acquisition Cost − Residual Value)/ Total Number of Units in Asset's Life

The annual depreciation for a given year can be calculated based on the number of units produced during that year, as follows:

Annual Depreciation = Depreciation per Unit × Units Produced in Current Year

For example, assume that Kemp Company in the previous example wanted to use the units-of-production method for 2004. Also assume that Kemp has been able to estimate that the total number of units that will be produced during the asset's five-year life is 18,000. During 2004 Kemp produced 4,000 units. The depreciation per unit for Kemp's machine can be calculated as follows:

Depreciation per Unit = (Acquisition Cost − Residual Value)/Life in Units

Depreciation per Unit = (\$20,000 − \$2,000)/18,000

= \$1 per Unit

The amount of depreciation that should be recorded as an expense for 2004 is \$4,000:

Annual Depreciation = Depreciation per Unit × Units Produced in 2004

Annual Depreciation = \$1 per Unit × 4,000 Units

= \$4,000

Depreciation will be recorded until the asset produces 18,000 units. The machine cannot be depreciated below its residual value of \$2,000.

The units-of-production method is most appropriate when the accountant is able to estimate the total number of units that will be produced over the asset's life. For example, if a factory machine is used to produce a particular item, the life of the asset may be expressed in terms of the number of units produced. Further, the units produced must be related to particular time periods so that depreciation expense can be matched accurately with the related revenue.

Accelerated Depreciation Methods In some cases, more cost should be allocated to the early years of an asset's use and less to the later years. For those assets, an accelerated method of depreciation is appropriate. The term **accelerated depreciation** refers to several depreciation methods by which a higher amount of depreciation is recorded in the early years than in later ones.

Accelerated depreciation A higher amount of depreciation is recorded in the early years and a lower amount in the later years.

One form of accelerated depreciation is the **double-declining-balance method.** Under this method, depreciation is calculated at double the straight-line rate but on a

Double-declining-balance method Depreciation is recorded at twice the straight-line rate, but the balance is reduced each period.

declining amount. The first step is to calculate the straight-line rate as a percentage. The straight-line rate for the Kemp asset with a five-year life is

100%/5 Years = 20%

Study Tip

Residual value is deducted for all depreciation methods except for the double-declining-balance method.

The second step is to double the straight-line rate:

$$2 \times 20\% = 40\%$$

This rate will be applied in all years to the asset's book value at the beginning of each year. As depreciation is recorded, the book value declines. Thus, a constant rate is applied to a declining amount. This constant rate is applied to the full cost or initial book value, not to cost minus residual value as in the other methods. However, the machine cannot be depreciated below its residual value.

The amount of depreciation for 2004 would be calculated as follows:

Depreciation = Beginning Book Value × Rate

Depreciation = $20,000 × 40%

= $8,000

The amount of depreciation for 2005 would be calculated as follows:

Depreciation = Beginning Book Value × Rate

Depreciation = ($20,000 − $8,000) × 40%

= $4,800

The complete depreciation schedule for Kemp Company for all five years of the machine's life would be as follows:

YEAR	RATE	BOOK VALUE AT BEGINNING OF YEAR	DEPRECIATION	BOOK VALUE AT END OF YEAR
2004	40%	$20,000	$ 8,000	$12,000
2005	40	12,000	4,800	7,200
2006	40	7,200	2,880	4,320
2007	40	4,320	1,728	2,592
2008	40	2,592	592	2,000
Total			$18,000	

In the Kemp Company example, the depreciation for 2008 cannot be calculated as $2,592 × 40% because this would result in an accumulated depreciation amount of more than $18,000. The total amount of depreciation recorded in Years 1 through 4 is $17,408. The accountant should record only $592 depreciation ($18,000 − $17,408) in 2008 so that the remaining value of the machine is $2,000 at the end of 2008.

The double-declining-balance method of depreciation results in an accelerated depreciation pattern. It is most appropriate for assets subject to a rapid decline in usefulness as a result of technical or obsolescence factors. Double-declining-balance depreciation is not widely used for financial statement purposes but may be appropriate for certain assets. As discussed earlier, most companies use straight-line depreciation for financial statement purposes because it generally produces the highest net income, especially in growing companies that have a stable or expanding base of assets.

Comparison of Depreciation Methods In this section, you have learned about several methods of depreciating operating assets. Exhibit 8-1 presents a comparison of the depreciation and book values of the Kemp Company asset for 2004–2008 using the straight-line and double-declining-balance methods (we have excluded the units-of-production method). Note that both methods result in a depreciation total of $18,000 over the five-year time period. The amount of depreciation per year depends, however, on the method of depreciation chosen.

YEAR	Straight-Line DEPRECIATION	Straight-Line BOOK VALUE	Double-Declining-Balance DEPRECIATION	Double-Declining-Balance BOOK VALUE
2004	$ 3,600	$16,400	$ 8,000	$12,000
2005	3,600	12,800	4,800	7,200
2006	3,600	9,200	2,880	4,320
2007	3,600	5,600	1,728	2,592
2008	3,600	2,000	592	2,000
Totals	$18,000		$18,000	

Exhibit 8-1

Comparison of Depreciation and Book Values of Straight-Line and Double-Declining-Balance Methods

Nonaccountants often misunderstand the accountant's concept of depreciation. Accountants do not consider depreciation to be a process of *valuing* the asset. That is, depreciation does not describe the increase or decrease in the market value of the asset. **Accountants consider depreciation to be a process of *cost allocation*.** The purpose is to allocate the original acquisition cost to the periods benefited by the asset. The depreciation method chosen should be based on the decline in the asset's usefulness. A company can choose a different depreciation method for each individual fixed asset or for each class or category of fixed assets.

The choice of depreciation method can have a significant impact on the bottom line. If two companies are essentially identical in every other respect, a different depreciation method for fixed assets can make one company look more profitable than another. Or a company that uses accelerated depreciation for one year can find that its otherwise declining earnings are no longer declining if it switches to straight-line depreciation. Investors should pay some attention to depreciation methods when comparing companies. **Statement users must be aware of the different depreciation methods** to understand the calculation of income and to compare companies that may not use the same methods.

Some investors ignore depreciation altogether when evaluating a company, not because they do not know that assets depreciate but **because they want to focus on cash flow instead of earnings.** Depreciation is a "noncash" charge that reduces net income.

INTERNAL DECISION

Depreciation and Income Taxes Financial accounting involves the presentation of financial statements to external users of accounting information, users such as investors and creditors. When depreciating an asset for financial accounting purposes, the accountant should choose a depreciation method that is consistent with the asset's decline in usefulness and that properly allocates its cost to the periods that benefit from its use.

Depreciation is also deducted for income tax purposes. Sometimes depreciation is referred to as a *tax shield* because it reduces (as do other expenses) the amount of income tax that would otherwise have to be paid. When depreciating an asset for tax purposes, a company should generally choose a depreciation method that reduces the present value of its tax burden to the lowest-possible amount over the life of the asset. Normally, this is best accomplished with an accelerated depreciation method, which allows a company to save more income tax in the early years of the asset. This happens because the higher depreciation charges reduce taxable income more than the straight-line method does. The method allowed for tax purposes is referred to as MACRS, which stands for Modified Accelerated Cost Recovery System. As a form of accelerated depreciation, it results in a larger amount of depreciation in the early years of asset life and a smaller amount in later years.

INTERNAL DECISION

Key Decision: Choice of Depreciation Method As we have stated, in theory a company should choose the depreciation method that best allocates the original cost of the asset to the periods benefited by the use of the asset. Theory aside, it is important to examine the other factors that affect a company's decision in choosing a depreciation method or methods. Exhibit 8-2 presents the factors that affect this decision and the likely choice that arises from each factor. Usually, the factors that are the most important are whether depreciation is calculated for presentation on the financial statements to stockholders or is calculated for income tax purposes.

Exhibit 8-2

Management's Choice of Depreciation Method

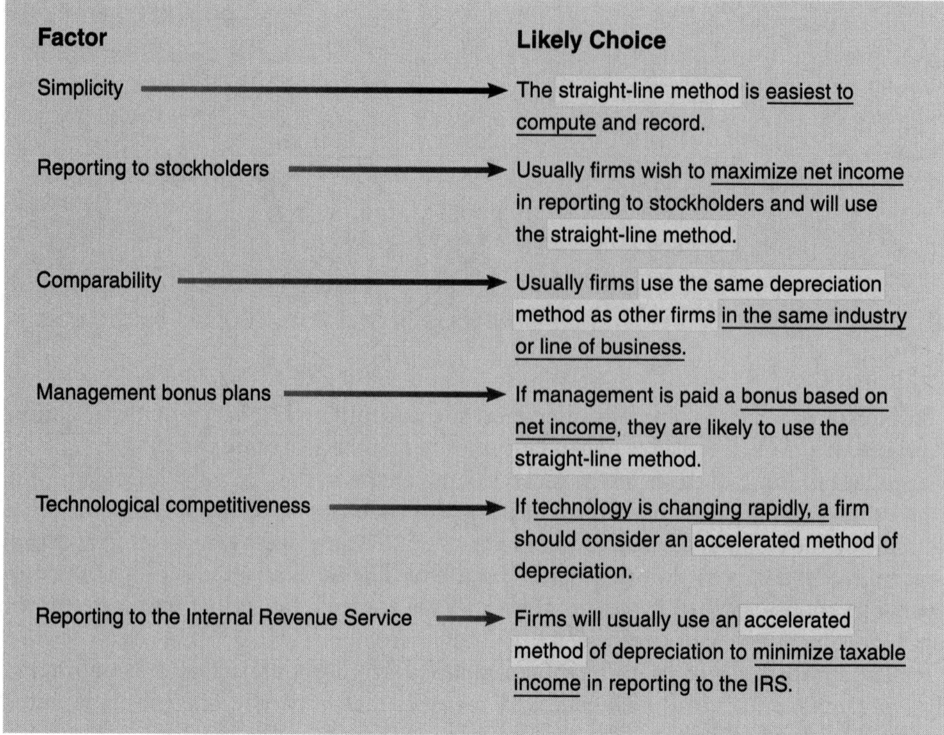

Factor
Likely Choice
Simplicity
The straight-line method is easiest to compute and record.
Reporting to stockholders
Usually firms wish to maximize net income in reporting to stockholders and will use the straight-line method.
Comparability
Usually firms use the same depreciation method as other firms in the same industry or line of business.
Management bonus plans
If management is paid a bonus based on net income, they are likely to use the straight-line method.
Technological competitiveness
If technology is changing rapidly, a firm should consider an accelerated method of depreciation.
Reporting to the Internal Revenue Service
Firms will usually use an accelerated method of depreciation to minimize taxable income in reporting to the IRS.

When depreciation is calculated for financial statement purposes, a company generally wants to present the most favorable impression (the highest income) possible. Therefore, most companies choose the straight-line method of depreciation. In fact, more than 90 percent of large companies use the straight-line method for financial statement purposes.

If the objective of the company's management is to minimize its income tax liability, then the company will generally not choose the straight-line method for tax purposes. As discussed in the preceding section, accelerated depreciation allows the company to save more on income taxes because depreciation is a tax shield.

Therefore, it is not unusual for a company to use *two* depreciation methods for the same asset, one for financial reporting purposes and another for tax purposes. This may seem somewhat confusing, but it is the direct result of the differing goals of financial and tax accounting. See Chapter 10 for more about this issue.

Accounting for Your Decisions

You Are the Sole Owner

Your accountant has presented you with three sets of financial statements—each with a different depreciation method—and asks you which depreciation method you prefer. You answer that other than for tax purposes, you don't really care. Should you?

ANS: For tax purposes you would prefer to use the accelerated depreciation method, which minimizes your net income so that you can pay the minimum allowable taxes. For financial statement purposes you may use a different method. As a sole owner, you may believe that the depreciation method chosen does not matter because you are more concerned with the cash flow of the firm and depreciation is a noncash item. However, the depreciation method is important if you are going to show your statements to external parties—for example, if you must present your statements to a banker in order to get a loan.

Two-Minute Review

1. *What items should be included when calculating the acquisition cost of an asset?*
2. *Which will be higher in the early years of an asset's life—straight-line depreciation or accelerated depreciation? Which will be higher in the later years? Which will be higher in total over the entire life of the asset?*

Answers on page 394.

Key Decision: Change in Depreciation Estimate An asset's acquisition cost is known at the time it is purchased, but its life and its residual value must be estimated. These estimates are then used as the basis for depreciating it. Occasionally, an estimate of the asset's life or residual value must be altered after the depreciation process has begun. This is an example of an accounting change that is referred to as a **change in estimate.**

LO 6 Understand the impact of a change in the estimate of the asset life or residual value.

INTERNAL DECISION

Change in estimate A change in the life of the asset or in its residual value.

Assume the same facts as in the Kemp Company example. The company purchased a machine on January 1, 2004, for $20,000. Kemp estimated that the machine's life would be five years and its residual value at the end of five years would be $2,000. Assume that Kemp has depreciated the machine using the straight-line method for two years. At the beginning of 2006, Kemp believes that the total machine life will be seven years, or another five years beyond the two years the machine has been used. Thus, depreciation must be adjusted to reflect the new estimate of the asset's life.

A change in estimate should be recorded *prospectively,* meaning that the depreciation recorded in prior years is not corrected or restated. Instead, the new estimate should affect the current year and future years. Kemp Company should depreciate the remaining depreciable amount during 2006 through 2010. The amount to be depreciated over that time period should be calculated as follows:

Acquisition Cost, January 1, 2004	$20,000
Less: Accumulated Depreciation	
(2 years at $3,600 per year)	7,200
Book Value, January 1, 2006	$12,800
Less: Residual Value	2,000
Remaining Depreciable Amount	$10,800

The remaining depreciable amount should be recorded as depreciation over the remaining life of the machine. In the Kemp Company case, the depreciation amount for 2006 and the following four years would be $2,160:

Depreciation = Remaining Depreciable Amount/Remaining Life

Depreciation = $10,800/5 Years

= $2,160

If the change in estimate is a material amount, the company should disclose in the notes to the 2006 financial statements that depreciation has changed as a result of a change in estimate. The company's auditors have to be very careful that management's decision to change its estimate of the depreciable life of the asset is not simply an attempt to manipulate earnings. Particularly in capital-intensive manufacturing concerns, lengthening the useful life of equipment can have a material impact on earnings.

A change in estimate of an asset's residual value is treated in a manner similar to a change in an asset's life. There should be no attempt to correct or restate the income statements of past periods that were based on the original estimate. Instead, the accountant should use the new estimate of residual value to calculate depreciation for the current and future years.

A change in estimate is not treated the same way as a *change in principle.* If a company changes its *method* of depreciation, for example, from accelerated depreciation to the straight-line method, this constitutes a change in accounting principle and must be disclosed separately on the income statement.

LO 7 Determine which expenditures should be capitalized as asset costs and which should be treated as expenses.

Capital expenditure A cost that improves the asset and is added to the asset account.

Revenue expenditure A cost that keeps an asset in its normal operating condition and is treated as an expense.

INTERNAL DECISION

Key Decision: Capital versus Revenue Expenditures Accountants must often decide whether certain expenditures related to operating assets should be treated as an addition to the cost of the asset or as an expense. One of the most common examples involving this decision concerns repairs to an asset. Should the repairs constitute capital expenditures or revenue expenditures? A **capital expenditure** is a cost that is added to the acquisition cost of the asset. A **revenue expenditure** is not treated as part of the cost of the asset but as an expense on the income statement. Thus, the company must decide whether to treat an item as an asset (balance sheet) and depreciate its cost over its life or to treat it as an expense (income statement) of a single period.

The distinction between capital and revenue expenditures is a matter of judgment. Generally, the guideline that should be followed is that if an expenditure increases the life of the asset or its productivity, it should be treated as a capital expenditure and added to the asset account. If an expenditure simply maintains an asset in its normal operating condition, however, it should be treated as an expense. The *materiality* of the expenditure must also be considered. Most companies establish a policy of treating an expenditure smaller than a specified amount as a revenue expenditure (an expense on the income statement).

It is very important that a company not improperly capitalize a material expenditure that should have been written off right away. The capitalization policies of companies are closely watched by Wall Street analysts who try to assess the value of these companies. When a company is capitalizing rather than expensing certain items to artificially boost earnings, that revelation can be very damaging to the stock price.

Expenditures related to operating assets may be classified in several categories. For each type of expenditure, its treatment as capital or revenue should be as follows:

CATEGORY	EXAMPLE	ASSET OR EXPENSE
Normal maintenance	Repainting	Expense
Minor repair	Replace spark plugs	Expense
Major repair	Replace a vehicle's engine	Asset, if life or productivity is enhanced
Addition	Add a wing to a building	Asset

An item treated as a capital expenditure affects the amount of depreciation that should be recorded over the asset's remaining life. We return to the Kemp Company example to illustrate. Assume again that Kemp purchased a machine on January 1, 2004, for \$20,000. Kemp estimated that its residual value at the end of five years would be \$2,000 and has depreciated the machine using the straight-line method for 2004 and 2005. At the beginning of 2006, Kemp made a \$3,000 overhaul to the machine, extending its life by three years. Because the expenditure qualifies as a capital expenditure, the cost of overhauling the machine should be added to the asset account.

BALANCE SHEET							INCOME STATEMENT
ASSETS		=	LIABILITIES	+	OWNERS' EQUITY	+	REVENUES − EXPENSES
Machine	3,000						
Cash	(3,000)						

For the years 2004 and 2005, Kemp recorded depreciation of \$3,600 per year:

$$\text{Depreciation} = (\text{Acquisition Cost} - \text{Residual Value})/\text{Life}$$

$$\text{Depreciation} = (\$20{,}000 - \$2{,}000)/5$$

$$= \$3{,}600$$

Beginning in 2006, Kemp should record depreciation of \$2,300 per year, computed as follows:

Original Cost, January 1, 2004	\$20,000
Less: Accumulated Depreciation (2 years × \$3,600)	7,200
Book Value, January 1, 2006	\$12,800
Plus: Major Overhaul	3,000
Less: Residual Value	(2,000)
Remaining Depreciable Amount	\$13,800

Depreciation = Remaining Depreciable Amount/Remaining Life

Depreciation per year = \$13,800/6 Years

= \$2,300

Accounting for Your Decisions

You Are the Owner

You are a realtor whose business car has just had its transmission rebuilt for \$400. Would you classify this "repair" as a capital expenditure or a revenue expenditure? Why is it important to properly classify the \$400?

ANS: If the business car's life is not extended, then the repair should be treated as a revenue expenditure, in which the cost is expensed on the income statement. It is important to properly classify capital and revenue expenditures because capitalizing rather than expensing costs can artificially boost earnings. The opposite effect would occur if costs are expensed and not capitalized.

Environmental Aspects of Operating Assets

As the number of the government's environmental regulations has increased, businesses have been required to expend more money complying with them. A common example involves costs to comply with federal requirements to clean up contaminated soil surrounding plant facilities. In some cases, the costs are very large and may exceed the value of the property. Should such costs be considered an expense and recorded entirely in one accounting period, or should they be treated as a capital expenditure and added to the cost of the asset? If there is a legal obligation to clean up the property or to restore the property to its original condition, companies are required to record the cost of asset retirement obligations as part of the cost of the asset. For example, if a company owns a factory and has made a binding promise to restore the property that is used by the factory to its original condition, then the costs of restoring the property must be added to the asset account. Of course, it is sometimes difficult to determine whether a legal obligation exists. It is important, however, for companies at least to conduct a thorough investigation to determine the potential environmental considerations that may affect the value of operating assets and to ponder carefully the accounting implications of new environmental regulations.

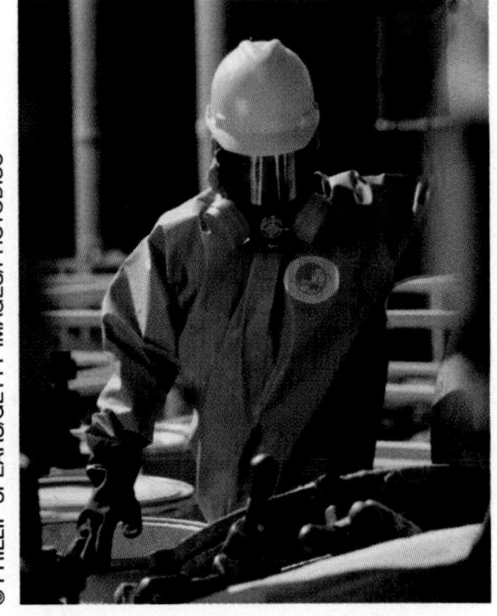

Should the costs of cleaning up a contaminated factory be considered an expense of one period or a capital expenditure added to the cost of the plant asset? To make the best decision, management should gather all the facts about the extent of the cleanup and its environmental impact.

Disposal of Property, Plant, and Equipment

LO 8 Analyze the effect of the disposal of an asset at a gain or loss.

An asset may be disposed of in any of several different ways. One common method is to sell the asset for cash. Sale of an asset involves two important considerations. First, depreciation must be recorded up to the date of sale. If the sale does not occur at the fiscal year-end, usually December 31, depreciation must be recorded for a partial period from the beginning of the year to the date of sale. Second, the company selling the asset must calculate and record the gain or loss on its sale.

Refer again to the Kemp Company example. Assume that Kemp purchased a machine on January 1, 2004, for $20,000, estimating its life to be five years and the residual value to be $2,000. Kemp used the straight-line method of depreciation. Assume that Kemp sold the machine on July 1, 2006, for $12,400. Depreciation for the six-month time period from January 1 to July 1, 2006, is $1,800 ($3,600 per year × 1/2 year = $1,800).

As of July 1, the balance of the Acumulated Depreciation—Machine account is $9,000, which reflects depreciation for the $2^1/_2$ years from the date of purchase to the date of sale. When an asset is sold, all accounts related to it must be removed.

BALANCE SHEET				INCOME STATEMENT	
ASSETS		= LIABILITIES	+ OWNERS' EQUITY	+ REVENUES − EXPENSES	
Accumulated Depreciation	9,000			Gain on Sale of Asset	1,400
Cash	12,400				
Machine	(20,000)				

In the preceding transaction, the Machine account is reduced to eliminate the account, and the Accumulated Depreciation—Machine account is reduced to eliminate it. The **Gain on Sale of Asset** account indicates the amount by which the sale price of the machine *exceeds* the book value. Thus, the gain can be calculated as follows:

Gain on sale of asset The excess of the selling price over the asset's book value.

Asset cost	$20,000
Less: Accumulated depreciation	9,000
Book value	$11,000
Sale price	12,400
Gain on sale of asset	$ 1,400

The account Gain on Sale of Asset is an income statement account and should appear in the Other Income/Expense category of the statement. The Gain on Sale of Asset account is not treated as revenue because it does not constitute the company's ongoing or central activity. Instead, it appears as income but in a separate category to denote its incidental nature.

The calculation of a loss on the sale of an asset is similar to that of a gain. Assume in the above example that Kemp had sold the machine on July 1, 2006, for $10,000 cash. As in the previous example, depreciation must be recorded to the date of sale, July 1.

BALANCE SHEET				INCOME STATEMENT	
ASSETS		= LIABILITIES	+ OWNERS' EQUITY	+ REVENUES − EXPENSES	
Accumulated Depreciation	9,000			Loss on Sale of Asset	(1,000)
Cash	10,000				
Machine	(20,000)				

Loss on sale of asset The amount by which selling price is less than book value.

The **Loss on Sale of Asset** account indicates the amount by which the asset's sales price *is less than* its book value. Thus, the loss could be calculated as follows:

Asset cost	$20,000
Less: Accumulated depreciation	9,000
Book value	$11,000
Sale price	10,000
Loss on sale of asset	$ 1,000

The Loss on Sale of Asset account is an income statement account and should appear in the Other Income/Expense category of the income statement.

OPERATING ASSETS: NATURAL RESOURCES

Balance Sheet Presentation

Natural resources Assets that are consumed during their use.

Important operating assets for some companies consists of **natural resources** such as coalfields, oil wells, other mineral deposits, and timberlands. Natural resources share one characteristic: the resource is consumed as it is used. For example, the coal a utility company uses to make electricity is consumed in the process. Most natural resources cannot be replenished in the foreseeable future. Coal and oil, for example, can be replenished only by nature over millions of years. Timberlands may be replenished in a shorter time period, but even trees must grow for many years to be usable for lumber.

Natural resources should be carried in the Property, Plant, and Equipment category of the balance sheet as an operating asset. Like other assets in the category, natural resources should initially be recorded at *acquisition cost.* Acquisition cost should include the cost of acquiring the natural resource and the costs necessary to prepare the asset for use. The preparation costs for natural resources may often be very large; for example, a utility may spend large sums to remove layers of dirt before the coal can be mined. These preparation costs should be added to the cost of the asset.

The acquisition cost of natural resources is important information to investors. Even more important, however, is the *value* of the natural resources, which is often very hard to determine. For example, the value of an oil well depends on the amount of oil that can be produced but also depends on the price that the oil can be sold for in the oil market, and that often fluctuates a great deal. Investors in companies that have natural resources need to be aware of all of the factors that affect the value of those assets.

Depletion of Natural Resources

When a natural resource is used or consumed, it should be treated as an expense. The process of recording the expense is similar to the depreciation or amortization process but is usually referred to as *depletion.* The amount of depletion expense each period should reflect the portion of the natural resource that was used up during the current year. It is often difficult to determine the total amount of the resource that can be produced. For example, how could a company determine the amount of coal in a coalfield? Usually, a company would have to rely on engineering and geological studies to determine the total amount of coal. The company's accountants need to work with these experts to develop accurate estimates. The amount of depletion can then be based on the portion of the total that was produced during the current period.

INTERNAL DECISION

Assume, for example, that Local Coal Company purchased a coalfield on January 1, 2004, for $1 million. The company employed a team of engineering experts who estimated the total coal in the field to be 200,000 tons and who determined that the field's residual value after removal of the coal would be zero. Local Coal should calculate the depletion per ton as follows:

Depletion per Ton = (Acquisition Cost − Residual Value)/
Total Number of Tons in Asset's Life

= ($1,000,000 − 0)/200,000 tons

= $5 per ton

Depletion expense for each year should be calculated as follows:

Depletion Expense = Depletion per Ton × Tons Mined during Year

Assume that Local Coal Company mined 10,000 tons of coal during 2004. The depletion expense for 2004 for Local Coal follows:

$5 × 10,000 tons = $50,000

Local Coal should record the depletion in an Accumulated Depletion—Coalfield account, which would appear as a contra-asset on the balance sheet.

Rather than using an accumulated depletion account, some companies may decrease (credit) the asset account directly.

There is an interesting parallel between depletion of natural resources and depreciation of plant and equipment. That is, depletion is very similar to depreciation using the units-of-production method. Both require an estimate of the useful life of the asset in terms of the total amount that can be produced (for units-of-production method) or consumed (for depletion) over the asset's life.

http://www.boisecascade.com

Natural resources may be important assets for some companies. For example, Exhibit 8-3 highlights the asset portion of the 2002 balance sheet and the accompanying note of Boise Cascade Corporation. Boise Cascade had timber and timberlands, net of depletion, of $328,720,000 as of December 31, 2002. The note indicates that the company records the cost of timber harvested on the basis of annual amount of timber cut in relation to the total amount of recoverable timber.

Exhibit 8-3 Boise Cascade Corporation and Subsidiaries 2002 Assets Section and Natural Resources Note

	December 31	
Property and equipment (in thousands):	2002	2001
Land and land improvements	$ 70,731	$ 68,482
Buildings and improvements	709,127	675,905
Machinery and equipment	4,678,112	4,606,102
	$5,457,970	$5,350,489
Accumulated depreciation	(2,915,940)	(2,742,650)
	$2,542,030	$2,607,839
Timber, timberlands, and timber deposits	328,720	322,132
	$2,870,750	$2,929,971

Cost of company timber harvested and amortization of logging roads are determined on the basis of the annual amount of timber cut in relation to the total amount of recoverable timber. Timber and timberlands are stated at cost, less the accumulated cost of timber previously harvested.

OPERATING ASSETS: INTANGIBLE ASSETS

Intangible assets Assets with no physical properties.

Intangible assets are long-term assets with no physical properties. Because one cannot see or touch most intangible assets, it is easy to overlook their importance. Intangibles are recorded as assets, however, because they provide future economic benefits to the company. In fact, an intangible asset may be the most important asset a company owns or controls. For example, a pharmaceutical company may own some property, plant, and equipment, but its most important asset may be its patent for a particular drug or process. Likewise, the company that publishes this textbook may consider the copyrights to textbooks to be among its most important revenue-producing assets.

Investors and creditors want to know how the intangible assets will contribute to the future profit of the company. When reading a balance sheet they need to be especially careful in evaluating intangible assets for two reasons. First, the balance sheet includes only the intangibles that meet the accounting definition of an asset. Patents, copyrights, and brand names are included because they are owned by the company and will produce a future benefit that can be measured and identified. But there are other *hidden assets* that are not on the balance sheet. A company's employees, its management team, its location, or the intellectual capital of its scientists may well provide future benefits and value. However, they are not recorded on the balance sheet because they do not meet the accountant's definition of assets. Investors need to be aware of these hidden assets to know the true value of the company.

From Concept to Practice 8.2

Determining Walt Disney's Intangible Assets

Which items on Walt Disney's balance sheet should be considered intangible assets? Intangible assets constitute what portion of total assets on Disney's balance sheet of September 30, 2002?

Second, investors need to be aware that the balance sheet reveals only the *cost* of the intangible assets. It does not reveal what the assets are really worth. For example, the logo and trademark that Walt Disney Company owns for its characters, such as Donald Duck, or its television networks, such as ESPN, are some of its most valuable assets. Yet, they are recorded on the balance sheet at a fraction of their true value.

Balance Sheet Presentation

LO 9 Understand the balance sheet presentation of intangible assets.

Intangible assets are long-term assets and should be shown separately from property, plant, and equipment. Exhibit 8-4 contains a list of the most common intangible assets. Some companies develop a separate category, Intangible Assets, for the various types of intangibles. For example, Exhibit 8-5 presents the Assets section and the accompanying note of the 2002 balance sheet of Nike, Inc. Nike presents only one line for intangible assets, but the note indicates that intangibles consist primarily of goodwill (see below), which is amortized on a straight-line basis. The presentation of intangible assets varies widely, however.

http://nike.com

Exhibit 8-4

Most Common Intangible Assets

INTANGIBLE ASSET	DESCRIPTION
Patent	Right to use, manufacture, or sell a product; granted by the U.S. Patent Office. Patents have a legal life of 20 years.
Copyright	Right to reproduce or sell a published work. Copyrights are granted for 50 years plus the life of the creator.
Trademark	A symbol or name that allows a product or service to be identified; provides legal protection for 20 years plus an indefinite number of renewal periods.
Goodwill	The excess of the purchase price to acquire a business over the value of the individual net assets acquired.

Exhibit 8-6, on page 385, presents the Assets section and the accompanying note of the 2002 balance sheet of Alberto-Culver Company. Alberto-Culver presents the intangible assets of goodwill and trade names immediately after the Property, Plant, and Equipment category. Both accounts are presented net of the accumulated amortization. The note indicates that amortization was computed on the straight-line basis.

http://www.alberto-culver.com

The nature of many intangibles is fairly evident, but goodwill is not so easily understood. **Goodwill** represents the amount of the purchase price paid in excess of the market value of the individual net assets when a business is purchased. Goodwill is recorded only when a business is purchased. It is not recorded when a company engages in activities that do not involve the purchase of another business entity. For example, customer loyalty or a good management team may represent "goodwill," but neither meets the accountants' criteria to be recorded as an asset on a firm's financial statements.

Goodwill The excess of the purchase price to acquire a business over the value of the individual net assets acquired.

International accounting standards allow firms *either* to present goodwill separately as an asset or to deduct it from stockholders' equity at the time of purchase. The result is that the presentation of goodwill on the financial statements of non-U.S. companies can look much different from that for U.S. companies. Similarly, some investors in U.S. companies believe that goodwill is not an asset because it is difficult to determine the

Exhibit 8-5 The Nike, Inc., Consolidated Assets Section and Intangibles Note

Consolidated Balance Sheets

	May 31	
	2002	2001
Assets (in millions)		
Current Assets:		
Cash and equivalents	$ 575.5	$ 304.0
Accounts receivable, less allowance for doubtful accounts of $77.4 and $72.1	1,807.1	1,621.4
Inventories (Note 2)	1,373.8	1,424.1
Deferred income taxes (Notes 1 and 6)	140.8	113.3
Prepaid expenses and other current assets (Note 1)	260.5	162.5
Total current assets	4,157.7	3,625.3
Property, plant and equipment, net (Note 3)	1,614.5	1,618.8
Identifiable intangible assets and goodwill, net (Note 1)*	437.8	397.3
Deferred income taxes and other assets (Notes 1 and 6)	233.0	178.2
Total assets	$6,443.0	$5,819.6

Identifiable intangible assets and goodwill:

At May 31, 2002 and 2001, the Company had patents, trademarks and other identifiable intangible assets recorded at a cost of $264.2 million and $218.6 million, respectively. The Company's excess of purchase cost over the fair value of net assets of businesses acquired (goodwill) was $333.6 million and $322.5 million at May 31, 2002 and 2001, respectively.

Identifiable intangible assets and goodwill are being amortized over their estimated useful lives on a straight-line basis over five to forty years. Accumulated amortization was $160.0 million and $143.8 million at May 31, 2002 and 2001, respectively. Amortization expense, which is included in other income/expense, was $15.7 million, $15.6 million and $18.5 million for the years ended May 31, 2002, 2001, and 2000, respectively.

*Note that the company recorded amortization of goodwill for 2002 and 2001. Beginning in July 2002, amortization of goodwill is no longer allowed under GAAP.

factors that caused this asset. They prefer to focus their attention on a company's tangible assets. These investors simply reduce the amount shown on the balance sheet by the amount of goodwill, deducting it from total assets and reducing stockholders' equity by the same amount.

Acquisition Cost of Intangible Assets

As was the case with property, plant, and equipment, the acquisition cost of an intangible asset includes all of the costs to acquire the asset and prepare it for its intended use. This should include all necessary costs such as legal costs incurred at the time of acquisition. Acquisition cost also should include those costs that are incurred after acquisition and that are necessary to the existence of the asset. For example, if a firm must pay legal fees to protect a patent from infringement, the costs should be considered part of the acquisition cost and should be included in the patent account.

Research and development costs Costs incurred in the discovery of new knowledge.

You should also be aware of one item that is similar to intangible assets but is *not* on the balance sheet. **Research and development costs** are expenditures incurred in the discovery of new knowledge and the translation of research into a design or plan for a new product or service or in a significant improvement to an existing product or service. Firms that engage in research and development do so because they believe such activities provide future benefit to the company. In fact, many firms have become leaders in an industry by engaging in research and development and the discovery of new products or technology. It is often very difficult, however, to identify the amount of

Exhibit 8-6 Alberto-Culver Company and Subsidiaries 2002 Consolidated Assets Section and Intangibles Note

CONSOLIDATED BALANCE SHEETS

Alberto-Culver Company and Subsidiaries

(In thousands, except share data)	September 30,	
Assets	2002	2001
Current assets:		
Cash and equivalents	**$ 217,485**	$ 201,970
Short-term investments	**—**	869
Receivables, less allowance for doubtful accounts of $17,550 in 2002 and $11,387 in 2001 (Note 3)	**209,010**	169,657
Inventories:		
Raw materials	**39,932**	41,521
Work-in-process	**5,545**	4,782
Finished goods	**476,731**	432,008
Total inventories	**522,208**	478,311
Other current assets	**35,514**	26,142
Total current assets	**984,217**	876,949
Property, plant, and equipment:		
Land	**12,981**	13,593
Buildings and leasehold improvements	**166,700**	151,306
Machinery and equipment	**339,338**	306,958
Total property, plant, and equipment	**519,019**	471,857
Accumulated depreciation	**271,169**	236,035
Property, plant, and equipment, net	**247,850**	235,822
Goodwill, net	**343,431**	264,339
Trade names, net	**79,681**	79,532
Other assets	**74,312**	59,859
	$1,729,491	$1,516,501

Prior to October 1, 2001, the cost of goodwill and trade names was amortized on a straight-line basis over periods ranging from ten to forty years. As required, the company implemented the Financial Accounting Standards Board's (FASB) Statement of Financial Accounting Standards (SFAS) No. 142, Goodwill and Other Intangible Assets, for previously acquired intangibles and discontinued the amortization of goodwill effective October 1, 2001. In accordance with SFAS No. 142, the company determined that its trade names have indefinite lives and, therefore, ceased amortization of trade names effective October 1, 2001.

future benefits of research and development and to associate those benefits with specific time periods. Because of the difficulty in predicting future benefits, the FASB has ruled that firms are not allowed to treat research and development costs as assets; all such expenditures must be treated as expenses in the period incurred. Many firms, especially high-technology ones, argue that this accounting rule results in seriously understated balance sheets. In their view, an important "asset" is not portrayed on their balance sheet. They also argue that they are at a competitive disadvantage when compared with foreign companies that are allowed to treat at least a portion of research and development as an asset. Users of financial statements somehow need to be aware of those "hidden assets" when analyzing the balance sheets of companies that must expense research and development costs.

It is important to distinguish between patent costs and research and development costs. Patent costs include legal and filing fees necessary to acquire a patent. Such costs are capitalized as an intangible asset, Patent. However, the Patent account should not include the costs of research and development of a new product. Those costs are not capitalized but are treated as an expense, Research and Development.

Business Strategy

Valuing Intangible Assets

Two of the most important, and most profitable, divisions of Walt Disney Company are the Media Networks Division that produces television programming and the Studio Entertainment Division that produces movies for the theater and cable television markets. While these divisions are important sources of revenue and profitability, it is very difficult for investors to determine the value of their assets. Walt Disney Company has copyrights and licenses for nearly all of its television programming and films. It has become unclear, however, whether those copyright protections will prevent people from copying films and television programs.

Recording companies won important legal protection against Napster to prevent the copying and exchanging of music files over the Internet. Now the legal battles have shifted to films and television programs. Copying and sharing programming is at the heart of what many consumer electronics and PC manufacturers want to pursue. Companies such as Sony, Hewlett-Packard, and Microsoft want to sell products that would allow consumers to record a show from a TV to a computer hard drive, and then watch it later on any TV or computer screen in the home. Companies such as Walt Disney believe that they have the right to protect their assets. "Disney has no asset more valuable than the film *The Lion King*," says Preston Haddon, a Disney executive vice president. "We have presented, and would like to present again, *The Lion King* free over the air on Sunday night on ABC's *Wonderful World of Disney*. But if doing so means that perfect digital copies will be posted to file-sharing sites on the Internet, then we would have to seriously reconsider."

How should assets such as television programs and films be valued, and how will the legal questions surrounding such assets affect the value? ■

Source: Recording Restricted by Arik Hesseldahl, February 10, 2003, Forbes.com.

LO 10 Describe the proper amortization of intangible assets.

Amortization of Intangibles

There has been considerable discussion over the past few years about whether intangible assets should be amortized and, if so, over what period of time. The term *amortization* is very similar to depreciation of property, plant, and equipment. Amortization involves allocating the acquistion cost of an intangible asset to the periods benefited by the use of the asset. If an intangible asset is amortized, most companies use the straight-line method of amortization, and we will use that method for illustration purposes. Occasionally, however, you may see instances of an accelerated form of amortization if the decline in usefulness of the intangible asset does not occur evenly over time.

If an intangible asset has a finite life, amortization must be recognized. A finite life exists when an intangible asset is legally valid only for a certain length of time. For example, a patent is granted for a time period of 20 years and gives the patent holder the legal right to exclusive use of the patented design or invention. A copyright is likewise granted for a specified legal life. A finite life also exists when there is no legal life but the management of the company knows for certain that they will only be able to use the intangible asset for a specified period of time. For example, a company may have purchased the right to use a list of names and addresses of customers for a two-year time period. In that case, the intangible asset can only be used for two years and has a finite life.

When an intangible asset with a finite life is amortized, the time period over which amortization should be recorded must be considered carefully. The general guideline that should be followed is that *amortization should be recorded over the legal life or the useful life, whichever is shorter.* For example, patents may have a legal life of 20 years, but many are not useful for that long because new products and technology make the patent obsolete. The patent should be amortized over the number of years in which the firm receives benefits, which may be a period shorter than the legal life.

Assume that ML Company developed a patent for a new product on January 1, 2004. The costs involved with patent approval were $10,000, and the company wants to record amortization on the straight-line basis over a five-year life with no residual value. The effect on the accounting equation of the amortization is as follows:

BALANCE SHEET					INCOME STATEMENT	
ASSETS		= LIABILITIES	+ OWNERS' EQUITY	+	REVENUES – EXPENSES	
Accumulated Amortization	(2,000)				Patent Expense	(2,000)

Rather than use an accumulated amortization account, some companies decrease the intangible asset account directly. The asset should be reported on the balance sheet at acquisition cost ($10,000) less accumulated amortization ($2,000), or $8,000, as of December 31, 2004.

While intangibles such as patents and copyrights have a finite life, many others do not. *If an intangible asset has an indefinite life, amortization should not be recognized.* For example, a television or radio station may have paid to acquire a broadcast license. A broadcast license is usually for a certain time period but can be renewed at the end of that time period. In that case, the life of the asset is indefinite, and amortization of the intangible asset representing the broadcast rights should not be recognized. A second example would be a trademark. For many companies, such as Coca-Cola or Walt Disney, a trademark is a very valuable asset that provides name recognition and enhances sales. But a trademark is not subject to a legal life, and the life may be quite indefinite. The value of some trademarks may continue for a long time. Because the life of an intangible asset represented by trademarks is indefinite, amortization should not be recorded.

Goodwill is an important intangible asset on the balance sheet of many companies. Until 2001, accounting rules had required companies to record amortization of goodwill over a time period not to exceed 40 years. However, in 2001, the FASB ruled that goodwill should be treated as an intangible asset with an *indefinite* life and companies should no longer record amortization expense related to goodwill. Companies have generally favored the new accounting stance. Hopefully, it will allow companies to more accurately inform statement users of their true value.

While companies should not record amortization of intangible assets with an indefinite life, they are required each year to determine whether the asset has been *impaired.* A discussion of asset impairment is beyond the scope of this text, but generally, it means a loss should be recorded when the value of the asset has declined. For example, some trademarks, such as Xerox and Polaroid, that were quite powerful in the past have declined in value over time. By recognizing an impairment of the asset, the loss is recorded in the time period that the value declines rather than when the asset is sold. It requires a great deal of judgment to determine when intangible assets have been impaired because the true value of an intangible asset is often difficult to determine. A rather drastic example of impairment occurs when a company realizes that an intangible asset has become completely worthless and should be written off.

Assume in the ML example that ML learns on January 1, 2005, when accumulated amortization is $2,000 (or the book value of the patent is $8,000), that a competing company has developed a new product that renders ML's patent worthless. ML has a loss of $8,000, which is the book value of the patent at the time it is deemed to be worthless. The effect on the accounting equation of the patent write-off is as follows:

BALANCE SHEET					INCOME STATEMENT	
ASSETS		= LIABILITIES	+ OWNERS' EQUITY	+	REVENUES – EXPENSES	
Accumulated Amortization	2,000				Loss on Patent	(8,000)
Patent	(10,000)					

Two-Minute Review

1. *What are some examples of intangible assets?*
2. *Over what time period should intangibles with a finite life be amortized? What method is generally used?*

Answers on page 394.

Ethics in Accounting

AOL Time Warner

In the late 1990s, America Online, Inc. negotiated a highly publicized merger with Time Warner, Inc.—at a $156.4 billion price tag. Shortly after the merger (which became effective in January 2001), the Securities and Exchange Commission investigators accused AOL of overstating advertising revenues during the merger period. In addition, AOL had significant problems with declining advertising revenue, very little growth in subscriber sales, and criminal and civil investigations into its accounting practices.

In January 2002, AOL Time Warner made history when it wrote off (expensed) $54.2 billion of the value of goodwill from the acquisition of Time Warner. It was an indication that the goodwill asset recorded at the time of the merger did not have nearly the value that was anticipated when it was recorded.

The two major sources of income for America Online, Inc., prior to the merger were advertising revenue and subscriber sales. In what way could overstating revenues affect the merger arrangement between the two companies? Since the goodwill write-off occurred one year after the merger, what does that tell you about the $156.4 billion price? Were stockholders harmed? Is the write-down of goodwill an ethical issue for business executives? Why or why not?

Source: Jonathan Weil, "AOL could soon need to take another gargantuan write-off," *The Wall Street Journal*, August 23, 2002.

Additional note: In September 2003, the company's board of directors announced that it was changing the company name to Time Warner, Inc.

HOW LONG-TERM ASSETS AFFECT THE STATEMENT OF CASH FLOWS

CASH FLOW

LO 11 Explain the impact that long-term assets have on the statement of cash flows.

The balance sheet tells investors about the cost of the operating assets that the company has at the balance sheet date. The income statement tells investors how much depreciation was recorded on those assets. But, often investors need to know the amount of *cash* that was spent on operating assets or the amount of *cash* that was generated by the sale of operating assets. To determine the amount of cash involved, investors must refer to the statement of cash flows. This is especially important for operating assets because the amount spent to acquire assets is usually the largest expenditure for most companies. Investors need to know whether a company is buying enough assets to ensure that the company can continue to operate profitably in the future. The acquisition, depreciation, and sale of operating assets all have an impact on the statement of cash flows. Exhibit 8-7 illustrates the items discussed in this chapter and their effect on the statement of cash flows.

The acquisition of a long-term asset is an investing activity and should be reflected in the Investing Activities category of the statement of cash flows. The acquisition should appear as a deduction or negative item in that section because it requires the use of cash to purchase the asset. This applies whether the long-term asset is property, plant, and equipment or an intangible asset.

The depreciation or amortization of a long-term asset is not a cash item. It was referred to earlier as a noncash charge to earnings. Nevertheless, it must be presented

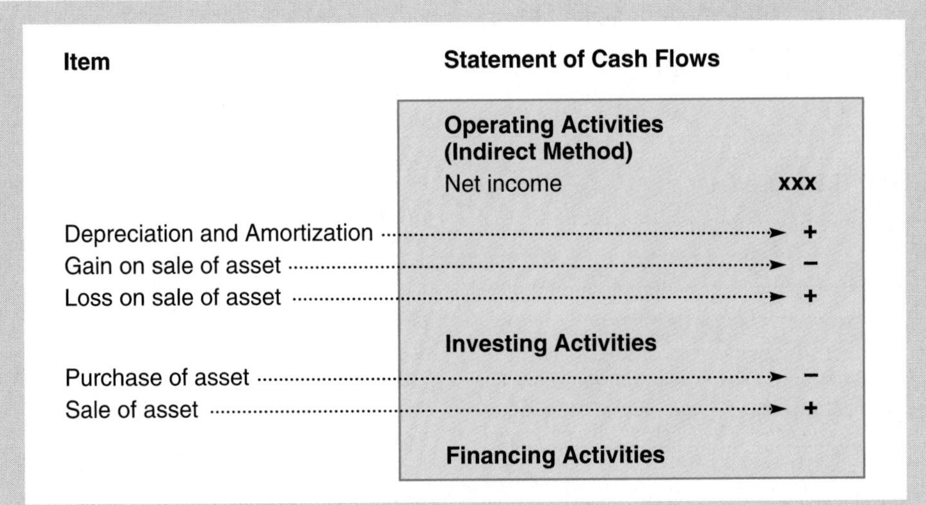

Exhibit 8-7

Long-Term Assets and the Statement of Cash Flows

on the statement of cash flows (if the indirect method is used for the statement). The reason is that it was deducted from earnings in calculating the net income figure. Therefore, it must be eliminated or "added back" if the net income amount is used to indicate the amount of cash generated from operations. Thus, depreciation and amortization should be presented in the Operating Activities category of the statement of cash flows as an addition to net income.

The sale or disposition of long-term assets is an investing activity. When an asset is sold, the amount of cash received should be reflected as an addition or plus amount in the Investing Activities category of the statement of cash flows. If the asset was sold at a gain or loss, however, one additional aspect should be reflected. Because the gain or loss was reflected on the income statement, it should be eliminated from the net income amount presented in the Operating Activities category (if the indirect method is used). A sale of an asset is not an activity related to normal, ongoing operations, and all amounts involved with the sale should be removed from the Operating Activities category. Exhibit 8-8 indicates the Operating and Investing categories of the 2002 statement of cash flows of Walt Disney. The company had a net income during 2002; that income of $1,236 million, is the first line of the Operations category of the cash flow statement. Walt Disney's performance is an excellent example of the difference between the net income on the income statement and actual cash flow. Note that the company had a positive cash flow from operations of $2,286 million. One of the major factors in this positive cash flow was that depreciation and amortization do not involve cash, so $1,021 million was added back to the net income amount in the Operating Activities category. However, the Investing Activities section of the statement of cash flows indicates that the company used a considerable amount of cash ($1,086 million) to invest in its parks and properties. The company spent even more ($2,845 million) for a major acquisition that occurred during the year. After considering all of the items in the Investing Activities category, the company used cash in the amount of $3,176 million. Thus, in spite

Which Way To Go?

R&D Expense or Long-Term Asset? *For the past six months, Taz Industries has been struggling with a problem in its production line. The number of units produced each day has been steadily dropping. The company believes worn-out equipment is partly the cause. Three months ago, the plant manager put an engineer and the senior machinist to work, full time, to solve the problem. They created a new electronic tool that, when used in the assembly process, significantly improves production. It is expected that this tool will be useful for at least the next five years.*

The total cost of the salaries for the engineer and machinist for three months, plus the cost of materials used in the development process, is $35,000. This includes the cost of time and materials for creating early models that did not solve the problem.

Even though the company plans to use the new tool only for internal production and has no intention of selling it, management believes obtaining a patent is a good idea. The various fees involved in obtaining the patent are expected to total $10,000.

How should the company record the costs? Why should they be recorded in this manner?

Exhibit 8-8 Walt Disney Partial Consolidated Statement of Cash Flows

Year Ended September 30,	2002	2001	2000
NET INCOME (LOSS)	$ 1,236	$ (158)	$ 920
OPERATING ITEMS NOT REQUIRING CASH			
Depreciation	1,021	987	962
Amortization of intangible assets	21	767	1,233
Gain on sale of businesses	(34)	(22)	(489)
Equity in the income of investees	(225)	(300)	(208)
Restructuring and impairment charges	—	1,247	92
Minority interests	101	104	107
Cumulative effect of accounting changes	—	278	—
Film and television costs	(97)	(13)	(210)
Other	364	402	164
CHANGES IN WORKING CAPITAL	(101)	(244)	1,184
Cash provided by operations	2,286	3,048	3,755
INVESTING ACTIVITIES			
Investments in parks, resorts and other property	(1,086)	(1,795)	(2,013)
Acquisitions (net of cash acquired)	(2,845)	(480)	(34)
Dispositions	200	137	913
Proceeds from sale of investments	601	235	207
Purchases of investments	(9)	(88)	(82)
Investments in Euro Disney	—	—	(91)
Other	(37)	(24)	9
Cash used by investing activities	(3,176)	(2,015)	(1,091)

of the positive cash amount generated by operations, the company had considerable needs for cash, as indicated in the Investing Activities section, and used more cash than it generated.

For Winnebago Industries the asset turnover is calculated as follows:

Asset Total Assets = (Beginning of year Assets + End of year Assets)/2
= ($342,033,000 + $337,077,000)/2
= $339,055,000

Asset Turnover = Net Sales/Average Total Assets
= $828,269,000/$339,055,000
= 2.44

This indicates that for each dollar of assets that Winnebago Industries has, it is capable of producing $2.44 of sales (Winnebago Industries refers to sales as net revenues). The company must constantly monitor this ratio to ensure that its assets are being used efficiently.

ANALYZING LONG-TERM ASSETS FOR AVERAGE LIFE AND ASSET TURNOVER

ANALYSIS

Because long-term assets constitute the major productive assets of most companies, it is important to analyze the age and composition of these assets. We will analyze the assets of Winnebago Industries in the following section. Analysis of the age of the assets can be accomplished fairly easily for those companies that use the straight-line method of depreciation. A rough measure of the *average life* of the assets can be calculated as follows:

Average Life = Property, Plant, and Equipment/Depreciation Expense

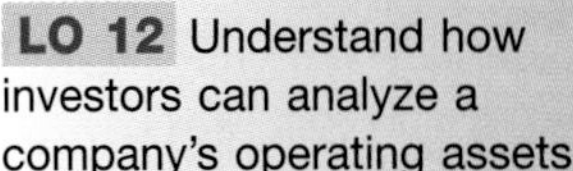

LO 12 Understand how investors can analyze a company's operating assets.

The *average age* of the assets can be calculated as follows:

Average Age = Accumulated Depreciation/Depreciation Expense

On August 25, 2002, Winnebago Industries had property and equipment of $141,310,000 and accumulated depreciation of $92,383,000. A careful reading of the annual report also indicates depreciation expense of $7,879,000 for the year ended August 25, 2002. Therefore, the average life of Winnebago Industries' assets is calculated as follows:

Average Life = Property, Plant, and Equipment/Depreciation Expense

Average Life = $141,310,000/$7,879,000

= 17.94 years

This is a rough estimate because it assumes that the company has purchased assets fairly evenly over time. Because it is an average, it indicates that some assets have a life longer than 17.94 years and others shorter lives.[1]

The average age of Winnebago Industries' assets is calculated as follows:

Average Age = Accumulated Depreciation/Depreciation Expense

Average Age = $92,383,000/$7,879,000

= 11.7 years

This indicates that Winnebago Industries' assets are, on average, aging, and the company may need to invest fairly heavily in new assets in the future.

The asset category of the balance sheet is also important in analyzing the company's *profitability.* The asset turnover ratio is a measure of the productivity of the assets and is measured as follows:

Asset Turnover = Net Sales/Average Total Assets

This ratio is a measure of how many dollars of assets are necessary for every dollar of sales. If a company is using its assets efficiently, each dollar of assets will create a high amount of sales. Technically, the ratio is based on average *total assets,* but long-term assets often constitute the largest portion of a company's total assets.

Interpret: You Decide. Take a close look at the Walt Disney Company's operating assets in the balance sheet at the beginning of the chapter. Additional information from the 2002 annual report is provided in Exhibit 8-9. Analyze the information using what you have learned in this chapter. Calculate the average life, average age, and asset turnover for Disney. Do you think the company is investing in its future? Are the operating assets adding value to the company? Support your responses with your analysis and explain your reasoning.

Accounting for Your Decisions

You Are the Student Intern

Your colleagues at the investment house where you are doing a summer internship insist that the intangible assets on the Nike and Alberto-Culver balance sheets are worthless and should be removed before any analysis can be completed on the two companies. Would you agree or disagree with their position?

ANS: Intangible assets are not worthless. Just because an asset is "intangible" and difficult to quantify doesn't mean it should be removed. Intangible assets such as goodwill and trademarks are frequently listed on balance sheets. They represent assets from an accounting viewpoint and may indeed be some of the most important assets of the company. The patents and trademarks of Nike and Alberto-Culver are assets because they will provide future benefits in the form of sales of products.

[1]The amount of $7,879,000 used to calculate the age of assets is not technically correct because it includes both depreciation and amortization. Winnebago Industries does not disclose the amount of depreciation by itself. Because the amount of intangible assets is fairly small, we have used the combined amount for our calculations.

Exhibit 8-9 **Walt Disney Company Operating Assets—Additional Information**

Income statement information:

Year Ended September 30,	**2002**	2001	2000
Revenues	$25,329	$25,172	$25,325

Information from the notes to the financial statements:

Significant Accounting Policies

Parks, Resorts and Other Property

Parks, resorts and other property are carried at cost. Depreciation is computed on the straight-line method based upon estimated useful lives as follows:

Attractions	25–40 years
Buildings and improvements	40 years
Leasehold improvements	Life of lease
Land improvements	25 years
Equipment	2–10 years
Furniture and fixtures	2–10 years

Intangible Assets

Amortizable intangible assets are amortized on a straight-line basis based upon estimated useful lives as follows:

Intellectual property and copyrights	10–31 years
Stadium facility leases	33 years
Other	4–50 years

Significant Acquisitions and Dispositions

On October 24, 2001, the Company acquired Fox Family Worldwide, Inc. (FFW) for $5.2 billion, funded with $2.9 billion of new long-term borrowings plus the assumption of $2.3 billion of FFW long-term debt. Among the businesses acquired were the Fox Family Channel, which has been renamed ABC Family Channel, a programming service that currently reaches approximately 85 million cable and satellite television subscribers throughout the U.S.; a 76% interest in Fox Kids Europe, which reaches more than 31 million subscribers across Europe; Fox Kids channels in Latin America, and the Saban library and entertainment production businesses.

Our motivation for the acquisition was to acquire a fully integrated cable channel as well as a significant international cable presence and therefore increase shareholder value. We believe that we can reach this objective through the use of new strategies that include cross promotion with our other television properties, repurposing a portion of the programming of the ABC Television Network, utilizing programming from the Disney and ABC libraries, developing original programming and by reducing operating costs.

Source: Walt Disney Company's 2002 Annual Report.

Ratios for Decision Making

Long-term assets are used to produce the products and services that allow a company to operate profitably. Therefore, it is important for investors and creditors to analyze whether the long-term assets are sufficient to support the company's activities. Investors and creditors should analyze the average life of the assets, the average age of the assets, and the asset turnover. The asset turnover is a measure of how many dollars of assets are necessary to generate a dollar of sales. The following ratios can be used to calculate the life, age, and turnover of the long-term assets (assuming the company is using the straight-line method of depreciation):

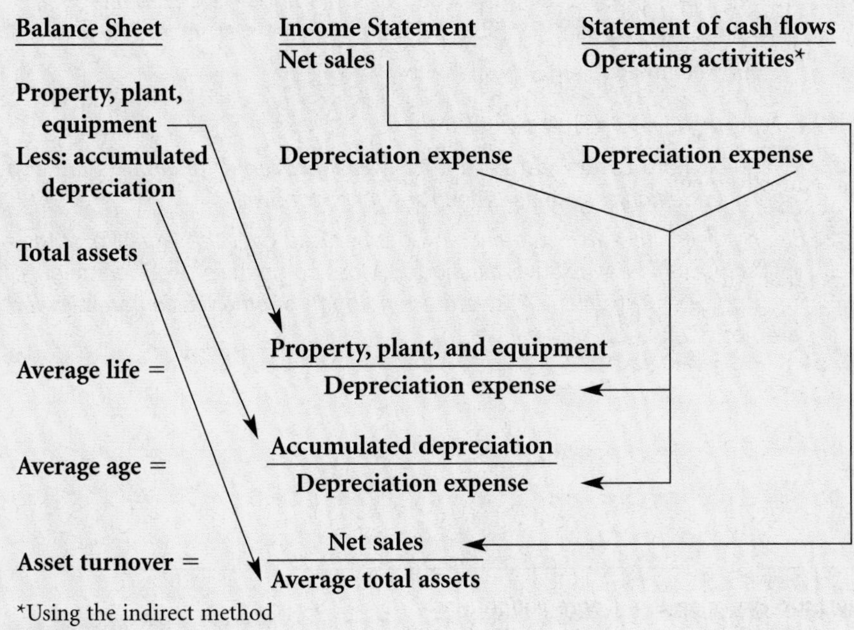

*Using the indirect method

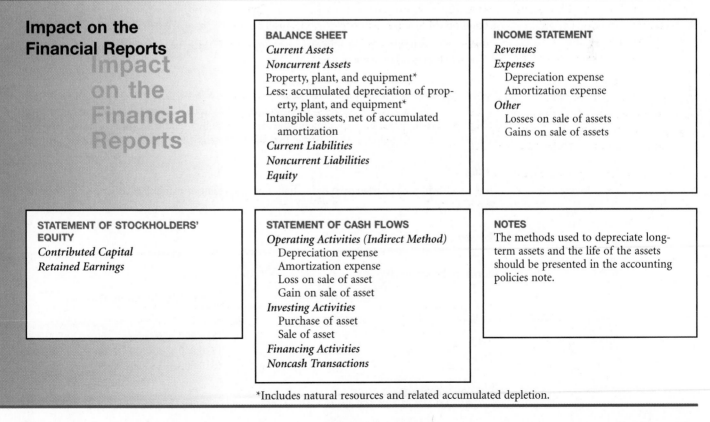

Impact on the Financial Reports

BALANCE SHEET
Current Assets
Noncurrent Assets
Property, plant, and equipment*
Less: accumulated depreciation of property, plant, and equipment*
Intangible assets, net of accumulated amortization
Current Liabilities
Noncurrent Liabilities
Equity

INCOME STATEMENT
Revenues
Expenses
Depreciation expense
Amortization expense
Other
Losses on sale of assets
Gains on sale of assets

STATEMENT OF STOCKHOLDERS' EQUITY
Contributed Capital
Retained Earnings

STATEMENT OF CASH FLOWS
Operating Activities (Indirect Method)
Depreciation expense
Amortization expense
Loss on sale of asset
Gain on sale of asset
Investing Activities
Purchase of asset
Sale of asset
Financing Activities
Noncash Transactions

NOTES
The methods used to depreciate long-term assets and the life of the assets should be presented in the accounting policies note.

*Includes natural resources and related accumulated depletion.

Answers to the Two-Minute Reviews

Two-Minute Review on Page 377

1. *The general rule for calculating the acquisition cost of an asset is to include all of the costs that were necessary to acquire the asset and prepare it for use. Normally, that would include the purchase price but would also include costs such as freight costs, taxes, and installation costs if they were necessary to prepare the asset for use.*
2. *Accelerated depreciation will be higher in the early years of the asset, and straight-line will be higher in the later years. Over the life of the asset, the total amount of depreciation will be the same under all of the methods, assuming that the same amount of salvage value is estimated for each of the methods.*

Two-Minute Review on Page 388

1. *Intangibles are assets that have no physical properties. Examples are copyrights, trademarks, patents, franchises, and goodwill.*
2. *Intangibles with a finite life should be amortized over the legal life of the asset or the useful life, whichever is shorter. Most companies use the straight-line method of amortization. Accelerated methods of amortization are allowed but are not often used.*

Warmup Exercises

Warmup Exercise 8-1 ***Depreciation Methods*** **LO 5**

Assume that a company purchases a depreciable asset on January 1 for $10,000. The asset has a four-year life and will have zero residual value at the end of the fourth year.

Required

Calculate depreciation expense for each of the four years using the straight-line method and the double-declining-balance method.

Warmup Exercise 8-2 ***Depreciation and Cash Flow*** **LO 5**

Use the information from Exercise 8-1. Assume that the double-declining-balance method will be used for tax purposes and the straight-line method will be used for the financial statement to be given to the stockholders. Also assume that the tax rate is 40%.

Required

How much will the tax savings be in the first year as a result of using the accelerated method of depreciation?

Solutions to Warmup Exercises

Warmup Exercise 8-1

	Straight Line	Double Declining Balance	
Year 1	$2,500*	$10,000 × .50** =	$5,000
2	2,500	($10,000 − $5,000) × .50 =	2,500
3	2,500	($10,000 − $7,500) × .50 =	1,250
4	2,500	($10,000 − $8,750) × .50 =	625

**$10,000/4 years*

***Straight-line rate as a percentage is 1 year/4 year, or 25%. Double the rate is 25% × 2, or 50%.*

Warmup Exercise 8-2

The tax savings is equal to the difference in depreciation between the two methods times the tax rate. Therefore, the tax savings is ($5,000 − $2,500) × .40 = $1,000.

Review Problem

WebTUTOR™ Advantage

The accountant for Becker Company wants to develop a balance sheet as of December 31, 2004. A review of the asset records has revealed the following information:

a. Asset A was purchased on July 1, 2002, for $40,000 and has been depreciated on the straight-line basis using an estimated life of six years and a residual value of $4,000.

b. Asset B was purchased on January 1, 2003, for $66,000. The straight-line method has been used for depreciation purposes. Originally, the estimated life of the asset was projected to be six years with a residual value of $6,000; however, at the beginning of 2004, the accountant learned that the remaining life of the asset was only three years with a residual value of $2,000.

c. Asset C was purchased on January 1, 2003, for $50,000. The double-declining-balance method has been used for depreciation purposes, with a four-year life and a residual value estimate of $5,000.

Required

1. Assume that these assets represent pieces of equipment. Calculate the acquisition cost, accumulated depreciation, and book value of each asset as of December 31, 2004.
2. How would the assets appear on the balance sheet on December 31, 2004?
3. Assume that Becker Company sold Asset B on January 2, 2005, for $25,000. Calculate the amount of the resulting gain or loss, and determine the effect on the accounting equation of the sale. Where would the gain or loss appear on the income statement?

Solution to Review Problem

1.

Asset A

2002	Depreciation	($40,000 − $4,000)/6 × 1/2 Year	=	$ 3,000
2003		($40,000 − $4,000)/6	=	6,000
2004		($40,000 − $4,000)/6	=	6,000
Accumulated Depreciation				$15,000

Asset B

2003	Depreciation	($66,000 − $6,000)/6	=	$10,000
2004		($66,000 − $10,000 − $2,000)/3	=	18,000
Accumulated Depreciation				$28,000

Note the impact of the change in estimate on 2004 depreciation.

Asset C

2003	Depreciation	$50,000 × 25% × 2	=	$25,000
2004		($50,000 − $25,000) × (25% × 2)	=	12,500
Accumulated Depreciation				$37,500

BECKER COMPANY
SUMMARY OF ASSET COST AND ACCUMULATED DEPRECIATION
DECEMBER 31, 2004

Asset	Acquisition Cost	Accumulated Depreciation	Book Value
A	$ 40,000	$15,000	$25,000
B	66,000	28,000	38,000
C	50,000	37,500	12,500
Totals	$156,000	$80,500	$75,500

2. The assets would appear in the Property, Plant, and Equipment category of the balance sheet as follows:

Equipment	$156,000	
Less: Accumulated depreciation	80,500	
Equipment (net)		$75,500

3.

Asset B book value	$ 38,000
Selling price	25,000
Loss on sale of asset	$ 13,000

BALANCE SHEET							INCOME STATEMENT
ASSETS		=	LIABILITIES	+	OWNERS' EQUITY	+	REVENUES – EXPENSES
Cash	25,000						Loss on Sale of Asset (13,000)
Asset B	(66,000)						
Accumulated Depreciation	28,000						

The Loss on Sale of Asset account should appear in the Other Income/Other Expense category of the income statement. It is similar to an expense but is not the company's major activity.

Chapter Highlights

1. **LO 1** Operating assets are normally presented on the balance sheet in one category for property, plant, and equipment and a second category for intangibles.
2. **LO 1** Operating assets should be presented at original acquisition cost less accumulated depreciation or amortization.
3. **LO 2** Acquisition cost should include all costs necessary to acquire the asset and prepare it for its intended use.
4. **LO 3** When assets are purchased for a lump sum, acquisition cost should be determined as the proportion of the market values of the assets purchased.
5. **LO 4** Interest on assets constructed over time should be capitalized. The amount of interest capitalized should be the average accumulated expenditures times an interest rate.
6. **LO 5** Several depreciation methods are available to describe the decline in usefulness of operating assets. The straight-line method is the most commonly used and assigns the same amount of depreciation to each time period over the asset's life.
7. **LO 5** Accelerated depreciation allocates a greater expense to the earlier years of an asset's life and less to later years. The double-declining-balance method is one form of accelerated depreciation.
8. **LO 6** Depreciation is based on an estimate of the life of the asset and the residual value. When it is necessary to change the estimate, the amount of depreciation expense is adjusted for the current year and future years. Past depreciation amounts are not restated.
9. **LO 7** Capital expenditures are costs that increase an asset's life or its productivity. Capital expenditures should be added to the cost of the asset. Revenue expenditures should be treated as an expense in the period in which they are incurred because they benefit only the current period.
10. **LO 8** The gain or loss on the disposal of an asset is the difference between the asset's book value and its selling price.
11. **LO 9** Intangible assets should be presented on the balance sheet at acquisition cost less accumulated amortization, if any. Acquisition cost should include all costs necessary to acquire the asset.
12. **LO 10** Research and development costs are not treated as an intangible asset. Instead, they are treated as an expense in the year they are incurred.
13. **LO 10** Intangibles with a finite life should be amortized over the shorter of their legal or useful life
14. **LO 11** The acquisition of long-term assets should be reflected in the Investing Activities category of the statement of cash flows.
15. **LO 12** Investors can analyze the age and composition of the operating assets by calculating the average life of the assets and the average age of the assets. The profitability of the assets can be evaluated by calculating the asset turnover ratio, a measure of how effective the assets are in creating sales for the company.

http://

Technology and other resources for your success

http://porter.swlearning.com

If you need additional help, visit the text's Web site. Also, see this text's preface for a description of available technology and other resources. If your instructor is using PERSONAL *Trainer* in this course, you may complete, on line, the exercises and problems in the text.

Key Terms Quiz

Read each definition below and then write the number of the definition in the blank beside the appropriate term it defines. The quiz solutions appear at the end of the chapter.

_____	Acquisition cost	_____	Change in estimate
_____	Capitalization of interest	_____	Capital expenditure
_____	Land improvements	_____	Revenue expenditure
_____	Depreciation	_____	Gain on sale of asset
_____	Straight-line method	_____	Loss on sale of asset
_____	Book value	_____	Natural resources
_____	Units-of-production method	_____	Intangible assets
_____	Accelerated depreciation	_____	Goodwill
_____	Double-declining-balance method	_____	Research and development costs

1. The amount that includes all of the costs normally necessary to acquire an asset and prepare it for its intended use.
2. Additions made to a piece of property such as paving or landscaping a parking lot. The costs are treated separately from land for purposes of recording depreciation.
3. A method by which the same dollar amount of depreciation is recorded in each year of asset use.
4. A method by which depreciation is determined as a function of the number of units the asset produces.
5. The process of treating the cost of interest on constructed assets as a part of the asset cost rather than as an expense.
6. A change in the life of an asset or in its expected residual value.
7. The allocation of the original acquisition cost of an asset to the periods benefited by its use.
8. A cost that improves an operating asset and is added to the asset account.
9. The original acquisition cost of an asset minus the amount of accumulated depreciation.
10. A cost that keeps an operating asset in its normal operating condition and is treated as an expense of the period.
11. An account whose amount indicates that the selling price received on an asset's disposal exceeds its book value.
12. An account whose amount indicates that the book value of an asset exceeds the selling price received on its disposal.
13. A term that refers to several methods by which a higher amount of depreciation is recorded in the early years of an asset's life and a lower amount is recorded in the later years.
14. Long-term assets that have no physical properties; for example, patents, copyrights, and goodwill.
15. A method by which depreciation is recorded at twice the straight-line rate but the depreciable balance is reduced in each period.
16. The amount indicating that the purchase price of a business exceeded the total fair market value of the individual net assets at the time the business was acquired.
17. Expenditures incurred in the discovery of new knowledge and the translation of research into a design or plan for a new product.
18. Assets that are consumed during their use; for example, coal or oil.

Answers on p. 411.

Alternate Terms

Accumulated depreciation Allowance for depreciation

Acquisition cost Historical cost

Capitalize Treat as asset

Construction in progress Construction in process

Goodwill Purchase price in excess of the market value of assets

Hidden assets Unrecorded or off–balance-sheet assets

Property, Plant, and Equipment Fixed assets

Prospective Current and future years

Residual value Salvage value

Revenue expenditure An expense of the period

Questions

1. What are several examples of operating assets? Why are operating assets essential to a company's long-term future?
2. What is the meaning of the term acquisition cost of operating assets? Give some examples of costs that should be included in the acquisition cost.
3. When assets are purchased as a group, how should the acquisition cost of the individual assets be determined?
4. Why is it important to account separately for the cost of land and building, even when the two assets are purchased together?

5. Under what circumstances should interest be capitalized as part of the cost of an asset?
6. What factors may contribute to the decline in usefulness of operating assets? Should the choice of depreciation method be related to these factors? Must a company choose just one method of depreciation for all assets?
7. Why do you think that most companies use the straight-line method of depreciation?
8. How should the residual value of an operating asset be treated when using the straight-line method? How should it be treated when using the double-declining-balance method?
9. Why do many companies use one method to calculate depreciation for the income statement developed for stockholders and another method for income tax purposes?
10. What should a company do if it finds that the original estimate of the life of an asset or the residual value of the asset must be changed?
11. What are the meanings of the terms capital expenditures and revenue expenditures? What determines whether an item is a capital or revenue expenditure?
12. How is the gain or loss on the sale of an operating asset calculated? Where would the Gain on Sale of Asset account appear on the financial statements?
13. What are several examples of items that constitute intangible assets? In what category of the balance sheet should intangible assets appear?
14. What is the meaning of the term goodwill? Give an example of a transaction that would result in the recording of goodwill on the balance sheet.
15. Do you agree with the FASB's ruling that all research and development costs should be treated as an expense on the income statement? Why or why not?
16. Do you agree with some accountants who argue that intangible assets have an indefinite life and therefore should not be subject to amortization?
17. When an intangible asset is amortized, should the asset's amortization occur over its legal life or over its useful life? Give an example in which the legal life exceeds the useful life.
18. Suppose that an intangible asset is being amortized over a 10-year time period but a competitor has just introduced a new product that will have a serious negative impact on the asset's value. Should the company continue to amortize the intangible asset over the 10-year life?

Exercises

Exercise 8-1 *Acquisition Cost* LO 2

Ruby Company purchased a piece of equipment with a list price of $60,000 on January 1, 2004. The following amounts were related to the equipment purchase:

- Terms of the purchase were 2/10, net 30. Ruby paid for the purchase on January 8.
- Freight costs of $1,000 were incurred.
- A state agency required that a pollution-control device be installed on the equipment at a cost of $2,500.
- During installation, the equipment was damaged and repair costs of $4,000 were incurred.
- Architect's fees of $6,000 were paid to redesign the work space to accommodate the new equipment.
- Ruby purchased liability insurance to cover possible damage to the asset. The three-year policy cost $8,000.
- Ruby financed the purchase with a bank loan. Interest of $3,000 was paid on the loan during 2004.

Required

Determine the acquisition cost of the equipment.

Exercise 8-2 *Lump-Sum Purchase* LO 3

To add to his growing chain of grocery stores, on January 1, 2004, Danny Marks bought a grocery store of a small competitor for $520,000. An appraiser, hired to assess the value of the assets acquired, determined that the land had a market value of $200,000, the building a market value of $150,000, and the equipment a market value of $250,000.

Required

1. What is the acquisition cost of each asset?
2. Danny plans to depreciate the operating assets on a straight-line basis for 20 years. Determine the amount of depreciation expense for 2004 on these newly acquired assets.
3. How would the assets appear on the balance sheet as of December 31, 2004?

Exercise 8-3 *Straight-Line and Units-of-Production Methods* LO 5

DECISION MAKING

Assume that Sample Company purchased factory equipment on January 1, 2004, for $60,000. The equipment has an estimated life of five years and an estimated residual value of $6,000. Sample's accountant is considering whether to use the straight-line or the units-of-production method to depreciate the asset. Because the company is beginning a new production process, the equipment will be used to produce 10,000 units in 2004, but production subsequent to 2004 will increase by 10,000 units each year.

Required

Calculate the depreciation expense, the accumulated depreciation, and the book value of the equipment under both methods for each of the five years of the asset's life. Do you think that the units-of-production method yields reasonable results in this situation?

Exercise 8-4 *Accelerated Depreciation* LO 5

DECISION MAKING

Koffman's Warehouse purchased a forklift on January 1, 2004, for $6,000. It is expected to last for five years and have a residual value of $600. Koffman's uses the double-declining-balance method for depreciation.

Required

1. Calculate the depreciation expense, the accumulated depreciation, and the book value for each year of the forklift's life.
2. Determine the effect on the accounting equation of the depreciation expense for 2004.
3. Refer to Exhibit 8-2. What factors may have influenced Koffman to use the double-declining-balance method?

Exercise 8-5 *Change in Estimate* LO 6

Assume that Bloomer Company purchased a new machine on January 1, 2004, for $80,000. The machine has an estimated useful life of nine years and a residual value of $8,000. Bloomer has chosen to use the straight-line method of depreciation. On January 1, 2006, Bloomer discovered that the machine would not be useful beyond December 31, 2009, and estimated its value at that time to be $2,000.

Required

1. Calculate the depreciation expense, the accumulated depreciation, and the book value of the asset for each year, 2004 to 2009.
2. Was the depreciation recorded in 2004 and 2005 wrong? If so, why was it not corrected?

Exercise 8-6 *Asset Disposal* LO 8

Assume that Gonzalez Company purchased an asset on January 1, 2002, for $60,000. The asset had an estimated life of six years and an estimated residual value of $6,000. The company used the straight-line method to depreciate the asset. On July 1, 2004, the asset was sold for $40,000 cash.

Required

1. Determine the amount of depreciation for 2004. Also determine the effect on the accounting equation of the sale of the asset.
2. How should the gain or loss on the sale of the asset be presented on the income statement?

Exercise 8-7 *Asset Disposal* LO 8

Refer to Exercise 8-6. Assume that Gonzalez Company sold the asset on July 1, 2004, and received $15,000 cash and a note for an additional $15,000.

Required

1. Determine the amount of depreciation for 2004. Also determine the effect on the accounting equation of the sale of the asset.
2. How should the gain or loss on the sale of the asset be presented on the income statement?

Exercise 8-8 *Amortization of Intangibles* LO 10

For each of the following intangible assets, indicate the amount of amortization expense that should be recorded for the year 2004 and the amount of accumulated amortization on the balance sheet as of December 31, 2004.

	Trademark	Patent	Copyright
Cost	$40,000	$50,000	$80,000
Date of purchase	1/1/97	1/1/99	1/1/02
Useful life	indefinite	10 yrs.	20 yrs.
Legal life	undefined	20 yrs.	50 yrs.
Method	SL*	SL	SL

Represents the straight-line method.

Exercise 8-9 *Impact of Transactions Involving Operating Assets on Statement of Cash Flows* LO 11

From the following list, identify each item as operating (O), investing (I), financing (F), or not separately reported on the statement of cash flows (N).

_______ Purchase of land
_______ Proceeds from sale of land
_______ Gain on sale of land
_______ Purchase of equipment
_______ Depreciation expense
_______ Proceeds from sale of equipment
_______ Loss on sale of equipment

Exercise 8-10 *Impact of Transactions Involving Intangible Assets on Statement of Cash Flows* LO 11

From the following list, identify each item as operating (O), investing (I), financing (F), or not separately reported on the statement of cash flows (N).

_______ Cost incurred to acquire copyright
_______ Proceeds from sale of patent
_______ Gain on sale of patent
_______ Research and development costs
_______ Amortization of patent

Multi-Concept Exercises

Exercise 8-11 *Capital versus Revenue Expenditures* LO 1, 7

On January 1, 2002, Jose Company purchased a building for $200,000 and a delivery truck for $20,000. The following expenditures have been incurred during 2004, related to the building and the truck:

- The building was painted at a cost of $5,000.
- To prevent leaking, new windows were installed in the building at a cost of $10,000.
- To allow an improved flow of production, a new conveyor system was installed at a cost of $40,000.
- The delivery truck was repainted with a new company logo at a cost of $1,000.
- To allow better handling of large loads, a hydraulic lift system was installed on the truck at a cost of $5,000.
- The truck's engine was overhauled at a cost of $4,000.

Required

1. Determine which of these costs should be capitalized. Also determine the effect on the accounting equation of the capitalized costs. Assume that all costs were incurred on January 1, 2004.
2. Determine the amount of depreciation for the year 2004. The company uses the straight-line method and depreciates the building over 25 years and the truck over 6 years. Assume zero residual value for all assets.
3. How would the assets appear on the balance sheet of December 31, 2004?

Exercise 8-12 ***Capitalization of Interest and Depreciation*** **LO 4, 5**

During 2004, Mercator Company borrowed $80,000 from a local bank and, in addition, used $120,000 of cash to construct a new corporate office building. Based on average accumulated expenditures, the amount of interest capitalized during 2004 was $8,000. Construction was completed and the building was occupied on January 1, 2005.

Required

1. Determine the acquisition cost of the new building.
2. The building has an estimated useful life of 20 years and a $5,000 salvage value. Assuming that Mercator uses the straight-line basis to depreciate its operating assets, determine the amount of depreciation expense for 2004 and 2005.

Exercise 8-13 ***Research and Development and Patents*** **LO 9, 10**

Erin Company incurred the following costs during 2004.

a. Research and development costs of $20,000 were incurred. The research was conducted to discover a new product to sell to customers in future years. A product was successfully developed, and a patent for the new product was granted during 2004. Erin is unsure of the period benefited by the research but believes the product will result in increased sales over the next five years.
b. Legal costs and application fees of $10,000 for the patent were incurred on January 1, 2004. The patent was granted for a life of 20 years.
c. A patent infringement suit was successfully defended at a cost of $8,000. Assume that all costs were incurred on January 1, 2005.

Required

Determine how the costs in parts **a** and **b** should be presented on Erin's financial statements as of December 31, 2004. Also determine the amount of amortization of intangible assets that Erin should record in 2004 and 2005.

Problems

Problem 8-1 ***Lump-Sum Purchase of Assets and Subsequent Events*** **LO 3**

DECISION MAKING

Carter Development Company purchased, for cash, a large tract of land that was immediately platted and deeded into smaller sections:

Section 1, retail development with highway frontage
Section 2, multifamily apartment development
Section 3, single-family homes in the largest section

Based on recent sales of similar property, the fair market values of the three sections are as follows:

Section 1, $630,000
Section 2, $378,000
Section 3, $252,000

Required

1. What value is assigned to each section of land if the tract was purchased for (a) $1,260,000, (b) $1,560,000, or (c) $1,000,000?
2. How does the purchase of the land affect the balance sheet?
3. Why would Carter be concerned with the value assigned to each section? Would Carter be more concerned with the values assigned if instead of purchasing three sections of land, it purchased land with buildings? Why or why not?

Problem 8-2 ***Depreciation as a Tax Shield*** **LO 5**

The term *tax shield* refers to the amount of income tax saved by deducting depreciation for income tax purposes. Assume that Supreme Company is considering the purchase of an asset as of January 1, 2004. The cost of the asset with a five-year life and zero residual value is $100,000. The company will use the straight-line method of depreciation.

Supreme's income for tax purposes before recording depreciation on the asset will be $50,000 per year for the next five years. The corporation is currently in the 35% tax bracket.

Required

Calculate the amount of income tax that Supreme must pay each year if the asset is not purchased. Calculate the amount of income tax that Supreme must pay each year if the asset is purchased. What is the amount of the depreciation tax shield?

Problem 8-3 ***Book versus Tax Depreciation*** **LO 5**

Griffith Delivery Service purchased a delivery truck for $33,600. The truck has an estimated useful life of six years and no salvage value. For the purposes of preparing financial statements, Griffith is planning to use straight-line depreciation. For tax purposes, Griffith follows MACRS. Depreciation expense using MACRS is $6,720 in Year 1, $10,750 in Year 2, $6,450 in Year 3, $3,870 in each of Years 4 and 5, and $1,940 in Year 6.

Required

1. What is the difference between straight-line and MACRS depreciation expense for each of the six years?
2. Griffith's president has asked why you have used one method for the books and another for calculating taxes. "Can you do this? Is it legal? Don't we take the same total depreciation either way?" he asked. Write a brief memo answering his questions and explaining the benefits of using two methods for depreciation.

Problem 8-4 ***Depreciation and Cash Flow*** **LO 11**

O'hare Company's only asset as of January 1, 2004, was a limousine. During 2004, only three transactions occurred:

Provided services of $100,000 on account.

Collected all accounts receivable.

Depreciation on the limousine was $15,000.

Required

1. Develop an income statement for O'hare for 2004.
2. Determine the amount of the net cash inflow for O'hare for 2004.
3. Explain in one or more sentences why the amount of the net income on O'hare's income statement does not equal the amount of the net cash inflow.
4. If O'hare developed a cash flow statement for 2004 using the indirect method, what amount would appear in the category titled Cash Flow from Operating Activities?

Problem 8-5 ***Reconstruct Net Book Values Using Statement of Cash Flows*** **LO 11**

Centralia Stores Inc. had property, plant, and equipment, net of accumulated depreciation of $4,459,000; and intangible assets, net of accumulated amortization, of $673,000 at December 31, 2004. The company's 2004 statement of cash flows, prepared using the indirect method, included the following items.

The Cash Flows from Operating Activities section included three additions to net income: (1) depreciation expense in the amount of $672,000, (2) amortization expense in the amount of $33,000, and (3) the loss on the sale of equipment in the amount of $35,000. The Cash Flows from Operating Activities section also included a subtraction from net income for the gain on the sale of a copyright of $55,000. The Cash Flows from Investing Activities section included outflows for the purchase of a building in the amount of $292,000 and $15,000 for the payment of legal fees to protect a patent from infringement. The Cash Flows from Investing Activities section also included inflows from the sale of equipment in the amount of $315,000 and the sale of a copyright in the amount of $75,000.

Required

1. Determine the book values of the assets that were sold during 2004.
2. Reconstruct the amount of property, plant, and equipment, net of accumulated depreciation, that was reported on the company's balance sheet at December 31, 2003.
3. Reconstruct the amount of intangibles, net of accumulated amortization, that was reported on the company's balance sheet at December 31, 2003.

SPREADSHEET

Problem 8-6 ***Balance Sheet and Note Disclosures for Delta Air Lines*** **LO 12**

The December 31, 2002, balance sheet of Delta Air Lines Inc. revealed the following information in the property and equipment category (in millions):

	2002	2001
Flight equipment	$20,295	$19,427
Less: Accumulated depreciation	(6,109)	5,730
	$14,186	$13,697
Ground property and equipment	$ 4,270	$ 4,412
Less: Accumulated depreciation	(2,206)	2,355
	$ 2,064	$ 2,057

http://www.deltaairlines.com

The notes that accompany the financial statements revealed the following:

Depreciation and Amortization—We record our property and equipment at cost and depreciate or amortize these assets on a straight-line basis to residual values over its estimated life. Flight equipment is depreciated on a straight-line basis over its estimated service lives, which range from 15 years to 25 years.

Required

1. Assume that Delta Air Lines did not dispose of any flight equipment during the fiscal year 2002. Calculate the amount of depreciation expense for the year.
2. What was the average life of the flight equipment as of 2002?
3. What was the average age of the flight equipment as of 2002?

Multi-Concept Problems

Problem 8-7 *Cost of Assets, Subsequent Book Values, and Balance Sheet Presentation* LO 1, 3, 5, 7, 8

The following events took place at Pete's Painting Company during 2004:

a. On January 1, Pete bought a used truck for $14,000. He added a tool chest and side racks for ladders for $4,800. The truck is expected to last four years and then be sold for $800. Pete uses straight-line depreciation.

b. On January 1, he purchased several items at an auction for $2,400. These items had fair market values as follows:

10 cases of paint trays and roller covers	$ 200
Storage cabinets	600
Ladders & scaffolding	2,400

Pete will use all the paint trays and roller covers this year. The storage cabinets are expected to last nine years, and the ladders and scaffolding for four years.

c. On February 1, Pete paid the city $1,500 for a three-year license to operate the business.

d. On September 1, Pete sold an old truck for $4,800. The truck had cost $12,000 when it was purchased on September 1, 1999. It had been expected to last eight years and have a salvage value of $800.

Required

1. For each situation, explain the value assigned to the asset when it is purchased (or for part **d,** the book value when sold).
2. Determine the amount of depreciation or other expense to be recorded for each asset for 2004.
3. How would these assets appear on the balance sheet as of December 31, 2004?

Problem 8-8 *Cost of Assets and the Effect on Depreciation* LO 2, 5

Early in its first year of business, Toner Company, a fitness and training center, purchased new workout equipment. The acquisition included the following costs:

Purchase price	$150,000
Tax	15,000
Transportation	4,000
Setup*	25,000
Painting*	3,000

**The equipment was adjusted to Toner's specific needs and painted to match the other equipment in the gym.*

The bookkeeper recorded an asset, Equipment, $165,000 (purchase price and tax). The remaining costs were expensed for the year. Toner used straight-line depreciation. The equipment was expected to last 10 years with zero salvage value.

Required

1. How much depreciation did Toner report on its income statement related to this equipment in Year 1? What do you believe is the correct amount of depreciation to report in Year 1 related to this equipment?
2. Income is $100,000, before costs related to the equipment are reported. How much income will Toner report in Year 1? What amount of income should it report? You may ignore income tax.
3. Using the equipment as an example, explain the difference between a cost and an expense.

Problem 8-9 *Capital Expenditures, Depreciation, and Disposal* LO 5, 7, 8

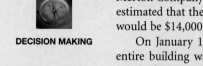

DECISION MAKING

Merton Company purchased an office building at a cost of $364,000 on January 1, 2003. Merton estimated that the building's life would be 25 years and the residual value at the end of 25 years would be $14,000.

On January 1, 2004, the company made several expenditures related to the building. The entire building was painted and floors were refinished at a cost of $21,000. A federal agency required Merton to install additional pollution-control devices in the building at a cost of $42,000. With the new devices, Merton believed it was possible to extend the life of the building by an additional six years.

In 2005 Merton altered its corporate strategy dramatically. The company sold the factory building on April 1, 2005, for $392,000 in cash and relocated all operations in another state.

Required

1. Determine the amount of depreciation that should be reflected on the income statement for 2003 and 2004.
2. Explain why the cost of the pollution-control equipment was not expensed in 2004. What conditions would have allowed Merton to expense the equipment? If Merton has a choice, would it prefer to expense or capitalize the equipment?
3. What amount of gain or loss did Merton record when it sold the building? What amount of gain or loss would have been reported if the pollution-control equipment had been expensed in 2004?

Problem 8-10 *Amortization of Intangible, Revision of Rate* LO 6, 10

During 1999, Reynosa Inc.'s R&D department developed a new manufacturing process. R&D costs were $85,000. The process was patented on October 1, 1999. Legal costs to acquire the patent were $11,900. Reynosa decided to expense the patent over a 20-year time period. Reynosa's fiscal year ends on September 30.

On October 1, 2004, Reynosa's competition announced that it had obtained a patent on a new process that would make Reynosa's patent completely worthless.

Required

1. How should Reynosa record the $85,000 and $11,900 costs?
2. How much amortization expense should Reynosa report in each year through the year ended September 30, 2004?
3. What amount of loss should Reynosa report in the year ended September 30, 2005?

Problem 8-11 *Purchase and Disposal of Operating Asset and Effects on Statement of Cash Flows* LO 8, 11

On January 1, 2004, Castlewood Company purchased some machinery for its production line for $104,000. Using an estimated useful life of eight years and a residual value of $8,000, the annual straight-line depreciation of the machinery was calculated to be $12,000. Castlewood used the machinery during 2004 and 2005 but then decided to automate its production process. On December 31, 2005, Castlewood sold the machinery at a loss of $5,000 and purchased new, fully automated machinery for $205,000.

Required

1. How would the transactions described above be presented on Castlewood's statements of cash flows for the years ended December 31, 2004 and 2005?

2. Why would Castlewood sell at a loss machinery that had a remaining useful life of six years and purchase new machinery with a cost almost twice that of the old?

Problem 8-12 ***Amortization of Intangibles and Effects on Statement of Cash Flows*** **LO 9, 10, 11**

Tableleaf Inc. purchased a patent a number of years ago. The patent is being amortized on a straight-line basis over its estimated useful life. The company's comparative balance sheets as of December 31, 2004 and 2003, included the following line item:

	12/31/04	12/31/03
Patent, less accumulated amortization of $119,000 (2004) and $102,000 (2003)	$170,000	$187,000

Required

1. How much amortization expense was recorded during 2004?
2. What was the patent's acquisition cost? When was it acquired? What is its estimated useful life? How was the acquisition of the patent reported on that year's statement of cash flows?
3. Assume that Tableleaf uses the indirect method to prepare its statement of cash flows. How is the amortization of the patent reported annually on the statement of cash flows?
4. How would the sale of the patent on January 1, 2005, for $200,000 be reported on the 2005 statement of cash flows?

Alternate Problems

Problem 8-1A ***Lump-Sum Purchase of Assets and Subsequent Events*** **LO 3**

Dixon Manufacturing purchased, for cash, three large pieces of equipment. Based on recent sales of similar equipment, the fair market values are as follows:

Piece 1	$200,000
Piece 2	$200,000
Piece 3	$440,000

Required

1. What value is assigned to each piece of equipment if the equipment was purchased for (a) $960,000, (b) $680,000, or (c) $800,000?
2. How does the purchase of the equipment affect total assets?

Problem 8-2A ***Depreciation as a Tax Shield*** **LO 5**

DECISION MAKING

The term *tax shield* refers to the amount of income tax saved by deducting depreciation for income tax purposes. Assume that Rummy Company is considering the purchase of an asset as of January 1, 2004. The cost of the asset with a five-year life and zero residual value is $60,000. The company will use the double-declining-balance method of depreciation.

Rummy's income for tax purposes before recording depreciation on the asset will be $62,000 per year for the next five years. The corporation is currently in the 30% tax bracket.

Required

Calculate the amount of income tax that Rummy must pay each year if the asset is not purchased and then the amount of income tax that Rummy must pay each year if the asset is purchased. What is the amount of tax shield over the life of the asset? What is the amount of tax shield for Rummy if it uses the straight-line method over the life of the asset? Why would Rummy choose to use the accelerated method?

Problem 8-3A ***Book versus Tax Depreciation*** **LO 5**

Payton Delivery Service purchased a delivery truck for $28,200. The truck will have a useful life of six years and zero salvage value. For the purposes of preparing financial statements, Payton is planning to use straight-line depreciation. For tax purposes, Payton follows MACRS. Depreciation expense using MACRS is $5,650 in Year 1, $9,025 in Year 2, $5,400 in Year 3, $3,250 in each of Years 4 and 5, and $1,625 in Year 6.

Required

1. What would be the difference between straight-line and MACRS depreciation expense for each of the six years?
2. Payton's president has asked why you have used one method for the books and another for calculating taxes. "Can you do this? Is it legal? Don't we take the same total depreciation either way?" he asked. Write a brief memo answering his questions and explaining the benefits of using two methods for depreciation.

Problem 8-4A ***Amortization and Cash Flow*** **LO 11**

Book Company's only asset as of January 1, 2004, was a copyright. During 2004, only three transactions occurred:

Royalties earned from copyright use, $500,000 in cash

Cash paid for advertising and salaries, $62,500

Depreciation, $50,000

Required

1. What amount of income will Book report in 2004?
2. What is the amount of cash on hand at December 31, 2004?
3. Explain how the cash balance increased from zero at the beginning of the year to its end-of-year balance. Why does the increase in cash not equal the income?

Problem 8-5A ***Reconstruct Net Book Values Using Statement of Cash Flows*** **LO 11**

E-Gen Enterprises Inc. had property, plant, and equipment, net of accumulated depreciation, of $1,555,000; and intangible assets, net of accumulated amortization, of $34,000 at December 31, 2004. The company's 2004 statement of cash flows, prepared using the indirect method, included the following items.

The Cash Flows from Operating Activities section included three additions to net income: (1) depreciation expense in the amount of $205,000, (2) amortization expense in the amount of $3,000, and (3) the loss on the sale of land in the amount of $17,000. The Cash Flows from Operating Activities section also included a subtraction from net income for the gain on the sale of a trademark of $7,000. The Cash Flows from Investing Activities section included outflows for the purchase of equipment in the amount of $277,000 and $6,000 for the payment of legal fees to protect a copyright from infringement. The Cash Flows from Investing Activities section also included inflows from the sale of land in the amount of $187,000 and the sale of a trademark in the amount of $121,000.

Required

1. Determine the book values of the assets that were sold during 2004.
2. Reconstruct the amount of property, plant, and equipment, net of accumulated depreciation, that was reported on the company's balance sheet at December 31, 2003.
3. Reconstruct the amount of intangibles, net of accumulated amortization, that was reported on the company's balance sheet at December 31, 2003.

Problem 8-6A ***Disclosures of Operating Assets*** **LO 12**

SPREADSHEET

The notes to the December 31, 2004, financial statements of TBW included the following disclosures for the Property, Plant, and Equipment account:

Property, Plant, and Equipment (in millions)	2004	2003
Land and Buildings	$ 963	$ 962
Cable Television Equipment	1,035	941
Furniture, Fixtures, and other Equipment	1,400	1,337
	$3,398	$3,240
Less: Accumulated Depreciation	(1,407)	(1,151)
Total	$1,991	$2,089

Required

Assume that TBW disposed of Property, Plant, and Equipment during 2004 with accumulated depreciation of $600 million.

1. Based on the note disclosures, what was the amount of depreciation expense for fiscal year 2004 for Property, Plant, and Equipment?
2. What was the average life of the assets in the Property, Plant, and Equipment category?
3. What was the average age of the assets in the Property, Plant, and Equipment category?

Alternate Multi-Concept Problems

Problem 8-7A *Cost of Assets, Subsequent Book Values, and Balance Sheet Presentation* LO 1, 5, 8, 9, 10

The following events took place at Tasty-Toppins Inc., a pizza shop that specializes in home delivery, during 2004:

a January 1, purchased a truck for $16,000 and added a cab and oven at a cost of $10,900. The truck is expected to last five years and be sold for $300 at the end of that time. The company uses straight-line depreciation for its trucks.

b. January 1, purchased equipment for $2,700 from a competitor who was retiring. The equipment is expected to last three years with zero salvage value. The company uses the double-declining-balance method to depreciate its equipment.

c. April 1, sold a truck for $1,500. The truck had been purchased for $8,000 exactly five years earlier, had an expected salvage value of $1,000, and was depreciated over an eight-year life using the straight-line method.

d. July 1, purchased a $14,000 patent for a unique baking process to produce a new product. The patent is valid for 15 more years; however, the company expects to produce and market the product for only four years. The patent's value at the end of the four years will be zero.

Required

For each situation, explain the amount of depreciation or amortization recorded for each asset in the current year and the book value of each asset at the end of the year. For part **c,** indicate the accumulated depreciation and book value at the time of sale.

Problem 8-8A *Cost of Assets and the Effect on Depreciation* LO 2, 5

Early in its first year of business, Key Inc., a locksmith and security consultant, purchased new equipment. The acquisition included the following costs:

Purchase price	$168,000
Tax	16,500
Transportation	4,400
Setup*	1,100
Operating Cost for First Year	26,400

**The equipment was adjusted to Key's specific needs.*

The bookkeeper recorded the asset, Equipment, at $216,400. Key used straight-line depreciation. The equipment was expected to last 10 years with zero residual value.

Required

1. Was $216,400 the proper amount to record for the acquisition cost? If not, explain how each expenditure should be recorded.
2. How much depreciation did Key report on its income statement related to this equipment in Year 1? How much should have been reported?
3. If Key's income before the costs associated with the equipment is $55,000, what amount of income did Key report? What amount should it have reported? You may ignore income tax.
4. Explain how Key should determine the amount to capitalize when recording an asset. What is the effect on the income statement and balance sheet of Key's error?

Problem 8-9A *Capital Expenditures, Depreciation, and Disposal* LO 7, 8

DECISION MAKING

Wagner Company purchased a retail shopping center at a cost of $612,000 on January 1, 2003. Wagner estimated that the life of the building would be 25 years and the residual value at the end of 25 years would be $12,000.

On January 1, 2004, the company made several expenditures related to the building. The entire building was painted and floors were refinished at a cost of $115,200. A local zoning agency required Wagner to install additional fire-protection equipment, including sprinklers

(continued)

and built-in alarms, at a cost of $87,600. With the new protection, Wagner believed it was possible to increase the residual value of the building to $30,000.

In 2005 Wagner altered its corporate strategy dramatically. The company sold the retail shopping center on January 1, 2005, for $360,000 of cash.

Required

1. Determine the amount of depreciation that should be reflected on the income statement for 2003 and 2004.
2. Explain why the cost of the fire-protection equipment was not expensed in 2004. What conditions would have allowed Wagner to expense it? If Wagner has a choice, would it prefer to expense or capitalize the improvement?
3. What amount of gain or loss did Wagner record when it sold the building? What amount of gain or loss would have been reported if the fire-protection equipment had been expensed in 2004?

Problem 8-10A *Amortization of Intangible, Revision of Rate* LO 6, 10

During 1999, Maciel Inc.'s R&D department developed a new manufacturing process. R&D costs were $350,000. The process was patented on October 1, 1999. Legal costs to acquire the patent were $23,800. Maciel decided to expense the patent over a 20-year time period using the straight-line method. Maciel's fiscal year ends on September 30.

On October 1, 2004, Maciel's competition announced that it had obtained a patent on a new process that would make Maciel's patent completely worthless.

Required

1. How should Maciel record the $350,000 and $23,800 costs?
2. How much amortization expense should Maciel report in each year through the year ended September 30, 2004?
3. What amount of loss should Maciel report in the year ended September 30, 2005?

Problem 8-11A *Purchase and Disposal of Operating Asset and Effects on Statement of Cash Flows* LO 8, 11

On January 1, 2004, Mansfield Inc. purchased a medium-sized delivery truck for $45,000. Using an estimated useful life of five years and a residual value of $5,000, the annual straight-line depreciation of the trucks was calculated to be $8,000. Mansfield used the truck during 2004 and 2005 but then decided to purchase a much larger delivery truck. On December 31, 2005, Mansfield sold the delivery truck at a loss of $12,000 and purchased a new, larger delivery truck for $80,000.

Required

1. How would the transactions described above be presented on Mansfield's statements of cash flows for the years ended December 31, 2004 and 2005?
2. Why would Mansfield sell a truck that had a remaining useful life of three years at a loss and purchase a new truck with a cost almost twice that of the old?

Problem 8-12A *Amortization of Intangibles and Effects on Statement of Cash Flows* LO 9, 10, 11

Quickster Inc. acquired a patent a number of years ago. The patent is being amortized on a straight-line basis over its estimated useful life. The company's comparative balance sheets as of December 31, 2004 and 2003, included the following line item:

	12/31/04	12/31/03
Patent, less accumulated amortization of $1,661,000 (2004) and $1,510,000 (2003)	$1,357,000	$1,508,000

Required

1. How much amortization expense was recorded during 2004?
2. What was the patent's acquisition cost? When was it acquired? What is its estimated useful life? How was the acquisition of the patent reported on that year's statement of cash flows?
3. Assume that Quickster uses the indirect method to prepare its statement of cash flows. How is the amortization of the patent reported annually on the statement of cash flows?
4. How would the sale of the patent on January 1, 2005, for $1,700,000 be reported on the 2005 statement of cash flows?

Decision Cases

Reading and Interpreting Financial Statements

Decision Case 8-1 ***Winnebago Industries*** **LO 1, 9**

Refer to the financial statements and notes included in the 2002 annual report of Winnebago Industries.

http://www.winnebagoind.com

Required

1. What items does Winnebago Industries list in the Property and Equipment category?
2. What method is used to depreciate the operating assets?
3. What is the estimated useful life of the operating assets?
4. What are the accumulated depreciation and book values of property and equipment for the most recent fiscal year?
5. Were any assets purchased or sold during the most recent fiscal year?

Decision Case 8-2 ***Winnebago Industries' Statement of Cash Flows*** **LO 11**

Refer to the statement of cash flows in Winnebago Industries' 2002 annual report and answer the following questions:

1. What amount of cash was used to purchase property and equipment during 2002?
2. Did Winnebago Industries sell any property and equipment during 2002?
3. What amount was reported for depreciation and amortization during 2002? Does the fact that depreciation and amortization are listed in the Cash Flow from Operating Activities section mean that Winnebago Industries created cash by reporting depreciation?

http://www.winnebagoind.com

Decision Case 8-3 ***Comparing Two Companies in the Same Industry: Winnebago Industries and Monaco Coach Corporation*** **LO 1, 9**

The 2002 annual report of Monaco Coach Corporation, one of Winnebago Industries' competitors in the recreational vehicle industry, is provided in Appendix B at the end of the text. Refer to that annual report and the 2002 annual report of Winnebago Industries, in Appendix A at the end of the text, for any information you might need.

http://www.winnebagoind.com
http://www.monacocoach.com

Required

1. Compare the list of property, plant, and equipment represented in the Monaco Coach note to the list on the Winnebago Industries' balance sheet. How are these lists similar? Note the differences between these lists and provide a logical reason for the differences.
2. What method is used by each company to depreciate the assets? Why do you think each company has chosen the method it uses?
3. What are the accumulated depreciation and book values of the property and equipment for each company? What does this information tell you about these competitors?
4. What is the estimated life of the Monaco Coach assets? How does this compare to the estimated life of the Winnebago Industries assets?
5. Refer to the Investing Activities portion of the cash flow statements of the two companies. Were any assets purchased or sold by either company during the year? This section of the statements does not tell if there was a gain or loss on the sale of long-term assets. Where would you find that information?
6. Do you think these two companies are investing in their future? Are their operating assets adding value to the company? Explain your answers.

Making Financial Decisions

Decision Case 8-4 ***Comparing Companies*** **LO 1, 5**

Assume that you are a financial analyst attempting to compare the financial results of two companies. The 2004 income statement of Straight Company is as follows:

Sales	$720,000
Cost of goods sold	360,000
Gross profit	$360,000

(continued)

Administrative costs	$ 96,000	
Depreciation expense	120,000	216,000
Income before tax		$144,000
Tax expense (40%)		57,600
Net income		$ 86,400

Straight Company depreciates all operating assets using the straight-line method for tax purposes and for the annual report provided to stockholders. All operating assets were purchased on the same date, and all assets had an estimated life of five years when purchased and zero salvage value. Straight Company's balance sheet reveals that on December 31, 2004, the balance of the Accumulated Depreciation account was $240,000.

You want to compare the annual report of Straight Company to that of Accelerated Company. Both companies are in the same industry, and both have exactly the same assets, sales, and expenses except that Accelerated uses the double-declining-balance method for depreciation for income tax purposes and for the annual report provided to stockholders.

Required

Develop Accelerated Company's 2004 income statement. As a financial analyst interested in investing in one of the companies, do you find Straight or Accelerated more attractive? Because depreciation is a "noncash" expense, should you be indifferent between the two companies? Explain your answer.

Decision Case 8-5 ***Depreciation Alternatives*** **LO 5**

DECISION MAKING

Medsupply Inc. produces supplies used in hospitals and nursing homes. Its sales, production, and costs to produce are expected to remain constant over the next five years. The corporate income tax rate is expected to increase over the next three years. The current rate, 15%, is expected to increase to 20% next year and then to 25% and continue at that rate indefinitely.

Medsupply is considering the purchase of new equipment that is expected to last for five years and to cost $150,000 with zero salvage value. As the controller, you are aware that the company can use one method of depreciation for accounting purposes and another method for tax purposes. You are trying to decide between the straight-line and the double-declining-balance methods.

Required

Recommend which method to use for accounting purposes and which to use for tax purposes. Be able to justify your answer on both a numerical and a theoretical basis. How does a noncash adjustment to income, such as depreciation, affect cash flow?

Accounting and Ethics: What Would You Do?

Decision Case 8-6 ***Valuing Assets*** **LO 3**

ETHICS

Denver Company recently hired Terry Davis as an accountant. He was given responsibility for all accounting functions related to fixed asset accounting. Tammy Sharp, Terry's boss, asked him to review all transactions involving the current year's acquisition of fixed assets and to take necessary action to ensure that acquired assets were recorded at proper values. Terry is satisfied that all transactions are proper except for an April 15 purchase of an office building and the land on which it is situated. The purchase price of the acquisition was $200,000. Denver Company has not separately reported the land and building, however.

Terry hired an appraiser to determine the market values of the land and the building. The appraiser reported that his best estimates of the values were $150,000 for the building and $70,000 for the land. When Terry proposed that these values be used to determine the acquisition cost of the assets, Tammy disagreed. She told Terry to request another appraisal of the property and asked him to stress to the appraiser that the land component of the acquisition could not be depreciated for tax purposes. The second appraiser estimated that the values were $180,000 for the building and $40,000 for the land. Terry and Tammy agreed that the second appraisal should be used to determine the acquisition cost of the assets.

Required

Did Terry and Tammy act ethically in this situation? Explain your answer.

Decision Case 8-7 ***Depreciation Estimates*** **LO 5**

ETHICS

Langsom's Mfg. is planning for a new project. Usually Langsom's depreciates long-term equipment for 10 years. The equipment for this project is specialized and will have no further use at the end of the project in three years. The manager of the project wants to depreciate the equipment over the usual 10 years and plans on writing off the remaining book value at the end of Year 3 as a loss. You believe that the equipment should be depreciated over the three-year life.

Required

According to generally accepted accounting principles, should the equipment be depreciated for 3 or 10 years? Is there an ethical dilemma in this decision? If so, what is it? If not, why not? If the manager uses 3 years, does this choice provide useful information to readers of the financial statements? What would your answer be if 10 years is used?

THOMSON ONE Business School Edition Case

Case 8-8 ***Using THOMSON ONE for Walt Disney Company***

Use THOMSON ONE to obtain current information about the financial position and stock price of Walt Disney.

Begin by entering the company's ticker symbol, DIS, and then selecting "GO." On the opening screen you will see background information about the company, key financial ratios, and some recent data concerning stock price. To research their stock price further, you click the Prices tab. At the top of the Price Chart, click on the "Interactive Chart." To obtain a 1-year chart, go to "Time Frame," click on the down arrow, and select 1 year. Then click on "Draw," and a 1-year chart should appear.

http://disney.go.com

You can also find Walt Disney's recent financial statements. Near the top of the screen, click on "Financials" and select "Financial Statements." Refer to the stockholders equity portion of the company's balance sheet.

Based on your use of THOMSON ONE, answer the following questions:

1. Has the amount of intangible assets increased or decreased since the 2002 annual report? Which intangible assets have changed the most?
2. What is the current market price of the stock? How has the stock price responded since the relatively low stock prices of mid-2002?
3. What are the most important new television programs introduced by Walt Disney Company? What are the most important new movies developed by Walt Disney Company?

Solutions to Key Terms Quiz

1	Acquisition cost (p. 369)	6	Change in estimate (p. 377)
5	Capitalization of interest (p. 371)	8	Capital expenditure (p. 378)
2	Land improvements (p. 371)	10	Revenue expenditure (p. 378)
7	Depreciation (p. 372)	11	Gain on Sale of Asset (p. 380)
3	Straight-line method (p. 372)	12	Loss on Sale of Asset (p. 380)
9	Book value (p. 372)	18	Natural resources (p. 381)
4	Units-of-production method (p. 373)	14	Intangible assets (p. 382)
13	Accelerated depreciation (p. 373)	16	Goodwill (p. 383)
15	Double-declining-balance method (p. 373)	17	Research and development costs (p. 384)

Part II

Integrative Problem

SPREADSHEET

Correct an income statement and statement of cash flows and assess the impact of a change in inventory method; compute the effect of a bad-debt recognition.

The following income statement, statement of cash flows, and additional information are available for PEK Company:

PEK COMPANY
INCOME STATEMENT
FOR THE YEAR ENDED DECEMBER 31, 2004

Sales revenue		$1,250,000
Cost of goods sold		636,500
Gross profit		$ 613,500
Depreciation on plant equipment	$58,400	
Depreciation on buildings	12,000	
Interest expense	33,800	
Other expenses	83,800	188,000
Income before taxes		$ 425,500
Income tax expense (30% rate)		127,650
Net income		$ 297,850

PEK COMPANY
STATEMENT OF CASH FLOWS
FOR THE YEAR ENDED DECEMBER 31, 2004

Cash flows from operating activities:	
Net income	$297,850
Adjustments to reconcile net income to net cash provided by operating activities (includes depreciation expense)	83,200
Net cash provided by operating activities	$381,050
Cash flows from financing activities:	
Dividends	(35,000)
Net increase in cash	$346,050

Additional information:

a. Beginning inventory and purchases for the one product the company sells are as follows:

	Units	Unit Cost
Beginning inventory	50,000	$2.00
Purchases:		
February 5	25,000	2.10
March 10	30,000	2.20
April 15	40,000	2.50
June 16	75,000	3.00
September 5	60,000	3.10
October 3	40,000	3.25

b. During the year, the company sold 250,000 units at $5 each.

c. PEK uses the periodic FIFO method to value its inventory and the straight-line method to depreciate all of its long-term assets.

d. During the year-end audit, it was discovered that a January 3, 2004, transaction for the lump-sum purchase of a mixing machine and a boiler was not recorded. The fair market values of the mixing machine and the boiler were $200,000 and $100,000, respectively. Each asset has an estimated useful life of 10 years with no residual value expected. The purchase of the assets was financed by issuing a $270,000 five-year promissory note directly to the seller. Interest of 8% is paid annually on December 31.

Required

1. Prepare a revised income statement and a revised statement of cash flows to take into account the omission of the entry to record the purchase of the two assets. (Hint: You will need to take into account any change in income taxes as a result of changes in any income statement items. Assume that income taxes are paid on December 31 of each year.)
2. Assume the same facts as above, except that the company is considering the use of an accelerated method rather than the straight-line method for the assets purchased on January 3, 2004. All other assets would continue to be depreciated on a straight-line basis. Prepare a revised income statement and a revised statement of cash flows, assuming the company decides to use the accelerated method for these two assets rather than the straight-line method resulting in depreciation of $49,091 for 2004.

Treat the answers in requirements **3** and **4** as independent of the other parts.

3. Assume PEK decides to use the LIFO method rather than the FIFO method to value its inventory and recognize cost of goods sold for 2004. Compute the effect (amount of increase or decrease) this would have on cost of goods sold, income tax expense, and net income.
4. Assume PEK failed to record an estimate of bad debts for 2004 (bad debt expense is normally included in "other expenses"). Before any adjustment, the balance in Allowance for Doubtful Accounts is $8,200. The credit manager estimates that 3% of the $800,000 of sales on account will prove to be uncollectible. Based on this information, compute the effect (amount of increase or decrease) of recognition of the bad-debt estimate on other expenses, income tax expense, and net income.

Part III

Accounting for Liabilities and Owners' Equity

A Word to Students about Part III

By now it's clear that this book is organized along the lines of a balance sheet. That is, Part II covered assets; Part III will cover liabilities and owner's equity. As we'll see, taking on liabilities to pay for assets is one way to provide financing for the future of the company; the other alternative is to issue stock.

Also, the chapters in Part III continue to discuss how the related transactions affect the statement of cash flows, which is key to understanding how companies' statements—and their activities—are interrelated.

Chapter 9

Current Liabilities, Contingencies, and the Time Value of Money

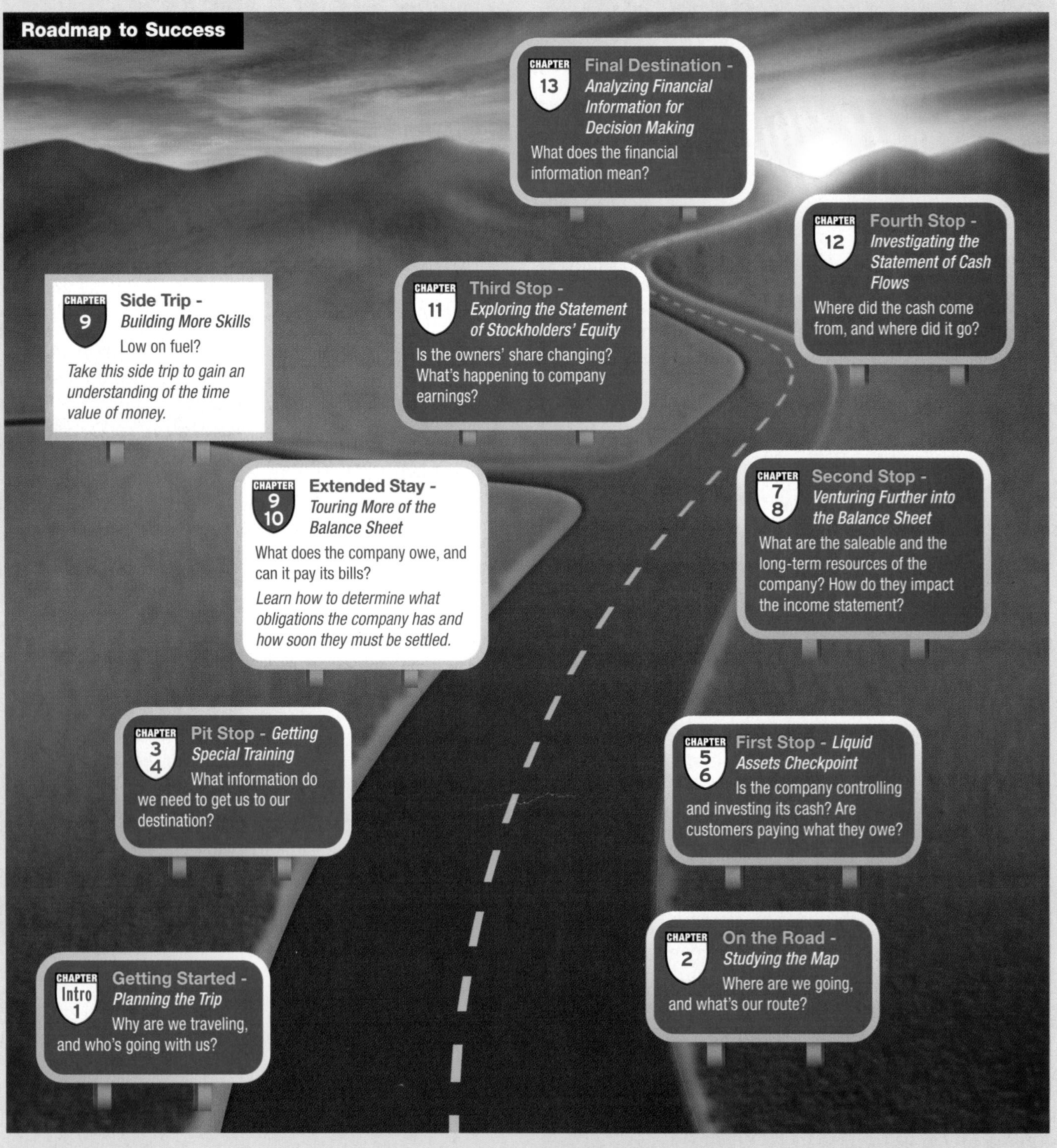

Roadmap to Success

CHAPTER 13 **Final Destination -** *Analyzing Financial Information for Decision Making*
What does the financial information mean?

CHAPTER 12 **Fourth Stop -** *Investigating the Statement of Cash Flows*
Where did the cash come from, and where did it go?

CHAPTER 9 **Side Trip -** *Building More Skills*
Low on fuel?
Take this side trip to gain an understanding of the time value of money.

CHAPTER 11 **Third Stop -** *Exploring the Statement of Stockholders' Equity*
Is the owners' share changing? What's happening to company earnings?

CHAPTER 9 10 **Extended Stay -** *Touring More of the Balance Sheet*
What does the company owe, and can it pay its bills?
Learn how to determine what obligations the company has and how soon they must be settled.

CHAPTER 7 8 **Second Stop -** *Venturing Further into the Balance Sheet*
What are the saleable and the long-term resources of the company? How do they impact the income statement?

CHAPTER 3 4 **Pit Stop -** *Getting Special Training*
What information do we need to get us to our destination?

CHAPTER 5 6 **First Stop -** *Liquid Assets Checkpoint*
Is the company controlling and investing its cash? Are customers paying what they owe?

CHAPTER 2 **On the Road -** *Studying the Map*
Where are we going, and what's our route?

CHAPTER Intro 1 **Getting Started -** *Planning the Trip*
Why are we traveling, and who's going with us?

Focus on Financial Results

J. C. Penney has stated that its objective is "to provide our target customers with timely and competitive selections of fashionable, quality merchandise with unquestionable day-in, day-out value."[1] J. C. Penney wants to be the customer's first choice for the products and services they offer. In 2002, the 100-year-old firm was in the No. 5 spot among U.S. retailers.

Through its 1,100 stores located in the 50 U.S. states, Puerto Rico, and Mexico, its well-known catalog, and a Web site, the familiar retailer offers family apparel, jewelry, shoes, accessories, and home furnishings that bear national, as well as exclusive and private, brand names.

Yet, Penney's retail business did not perform well recently and the company admits that its performance was disappointing and that conditions have been "exceptionally challenging."[2] Improving profitability has become a key goal for the firm in future years. Allen Questrom, Penney's CEO, may well continue the short- and long-term strategies that have been in place for several years. These strategies focus on overhauling the department store merchandising process, simplifying pricing, closing underperforming stores, lowering operating costs, and becoming a major e-commerce retailer.

The first two of these objectives have implications for inventory. During 2001 and 2002, the company worked on reacting more quickly to fast- and slow-selling items to reduce inventory, hoping to take fewer markdowns and yield more profit. Suppliers became an integral part of inventory management during the year.

Managing inventory well also means managing *accounts payable,* one of J. C. Penney's *current liabilities.* That, in turn, means having enough current assets on hand to pay current liabilities, such as suppliers' bills, on time. So Penney's realizes that its profitability goals are directly linked to the effective management of inventory and the related current liabilities.

J. C. Penney's 2002 Annual Report

Consolidated Balance Sheets

J. C. Penney Company, Inc. and Subsidiaries

($ in millions, except per share data)	January 25 2003	January 26 2002
Current assets		
Cash and short-term investments	$ 2,474	$ 2,840
Receivables (net of bad debt reserves of $14 and $27)	705	698
Merchandise inventory (net of LIFO reserves of $403 and $377)	4,945	4,930
Prepaid expenses	229	209
Total current assets	8,353	8,677
Property and equipment		
Land and buildings	2,940	2,987
Furniture and fixtures	3,946	4,105
Leasehold improvements	1,268	1,225
Accumulated depreciation	(3,253)	(3,328)
Property and equipment, net	4,901	4,989
Goodwill	2,304	2,321
Intangible assets (net of accumulated amortization of $322 and $304)	494	527
Other assets	1,815	1,534
Total assets	**$17,867**	**$18,048**
Liabilities and stockholders' equity		
Current liabilities		
Accounts payable and accrued expenses	$ 3,791	$ 3,465
Short-term debt	13	15
Current maturities of long-term debt	275	920
Deferred taxes	80	99
Total current liabilities	4,159	4,499
Long-term debt	4,940	5,179
Deferred taxes	1,391	1,231
Other liabilities	1,007	1,010
Total liabilities	11,497	11,919
Stockholders' equity		
Preferred stock, no par value and stated value of $600 per share; authorized, 25 million shares; issued and outstanding, 0.6 million and 0.6 million shares Series B ESOP convertible preferred	333	363
Common stock, par value $0.50 per share; authorized, 1,250 million shares; issued and outstanding 269 million and 264 million shares	3,423	3,330
Reinvested earnings	2,817	2,573
Accumulated other comprehensive (loss)	(203)	(137)
Total stockholders' equity	6,370	6,129
Total liabilities and stockholders' equity	$17,867	$18,048

The accompanying notes are an integral part of these Consolidated Financial Statements.

[1] J. C. Penney's Annual Report, 2001, p. 1.
[2] Ibid., p. 1.

You're in the Driver's Seat

http://www.jcpenney.com

If you were a bank loan officer looking for information about J. C. Penney Company, Inc.'s credit rating, what information would you want about current liabilities? While you study this chapter, consider which accounts on Penney's balance sheet are current liabilities and how they might influence its financial position.

LEARNING OBJECTIVES

After studying this chapter, you should be able to:

LO 1 Identify the components of the current liability category of the balance sheet. (p. 419)

LO 2 Examine how accruals affect the current liability category. (p. 424)

LO 3 Demonstrate an understanding of how changes in current liabilities affect the statement of cash flows. (p. 425)

LO 4 Determine when contingent liabilities should be presented on the balance sheet or disclosed in notes and how to calculate their amounts. (p. 426)

LO 5 Explain the difference between simple and compound interest. (p. 434)

LO 6 Calculate amounts using the future value and present value concepts. (p. 434)

LO 7 Apply the compound interest concepts to some common accounting situations. (p. 442)

LO 8 Demonstrate an understanding of the deductions and expenses for payroll accounting (Appendix A). (p. 454)

LO 9 Determine when compensated absences must be accrued as a liability (Appendix A). (p. 457)

WHAT EXTERNAL DECISION MAKERS WANT TO KNOW ABOUT CURRENT LIABILITIES

DECISION MAKING

The current liability classification is important because it indicates how many liabilities will come due within a short time after the balance sheet date. Investors are interested in companies that will be able to pay their liabilities when they are due. In the same manner, creditors will only lend money to companies if they are assured that the companies can pay the interest and principal when it is due. Companies that do not have sufficient resources to pay their current liabilities are often said to have a *liquidity problem.* This chapter also covers contingent liabilities. External decision makers want to know about the company's contingent liabilities because they are usually a large dollar amount that will come due in a future time. Investors are not eager to buy stock in a company that has contingent liabilities on the balance sheet or in the notes that accompany the financial statements.

To be successful, decision makers must:

▸ *ASK ESSENTIAL QUESTIONS*

- Will there be cash available to pay current debts when the payments are due?
- What contingent liabilities exist and how likely are they to negatively impact the company?

▸ *FIND BASIC INFORMATION*

The balance sheet, along with the supporting notes, is the key source of information about a company's current liabilities. This information tells:

- the amount of the current liabilities,
- when the liabilities may come due,
- what contingent liabilities exist, and
- whether a company has sufficient assets to pay their current and contingent liabilities.

▶ UNDERSTAND ACCOUNTING PRINCIPLES

To understand the basic information that is found, decision makers must understand the underlying accounting principles (GAAP) that have been applied to create the reported information. These principles determine:

- when a liability is considered to be current, and
- what contingent liabilities must be disclosed and which ones must be recorded.

▶ INTERPRET ANALYTICAL INFORMATION

Decision makers can assess the liquidity of the company in at least three ways. The amount of working capital indicates in dollar amount whether current assets exceed current liabilities. The current ratio indicates the ratio of current assets to current liabilities. The quick ratio measures the ratio of assets that can be converted into cash very quickly to current liabilities. The analysis should also include a careful reading of the notes to the statements to learn more information about recorded liabilities and to determine whether unrecorded liabilities, such as contingencies, exist

CURRENT LIABILITIES

LO 1 Identify the components of the current liability category of the balance sheet.

A classified balance sheet presents financial statement items by category in order to provide more information to financial statement users. The balance sheet generally presents two categories of liabilities, current and long-term.

Current liabilities finance the working capital of the company. At any given time during the year, current liabilities may fluctuate substantially. It is important that the company generates sufficient cash flow to retire these debts as they come due. As long as the company's ratio of current assets to current liabilities stays fairly constant from quarter to quarter or year to year, financial statement users are not going to be too concerned.

http://www.mcdonalds.com

The current liability portion of the 2002 balance sheet of McDonald's Corporation is highlighted in Exhibit 9-1. Some companies list the accounts in the current liability category in the order of payment due date. That is, the account that requires payment first is listed first, the account requiring payment next is listed second, and so forth. This allows users of the statement to assess the cash flow implications of each account. McDonald's uses a different approach and lists Notes Payable as the first account.

Current liability Accounts that will be satisfied within one year or the current operating cycle.

Current liabilities were first introduced to you in Chapter 2 of this text. In general, a **current liability** is an obligation that will be satisfied within one year. Although current liabilities are not due immediately, they are still recorded at face value; that is, the time until payment is not taken into account. If it were, current liabilities would be recorded at a slight discount to reflect interest that would be earned between now and the due date. The face value amount is generally used for all current liabilities because the time period involved is short enough that it is not necessary to record or calculate an interest factor. In addition, when interest rates are low, one need not worry about the interest that could be earned in this short period of time. In Chapter 10 we will find that many long-term liabilities must be stated at their present value on the balance sheet.

From Concept to Practice 9.1

Reading J. C. Penney's Balance Sheet

Refer to J. C. Penney's January 25, 2003 balance sheet in the chapter opener. What accounts are listed as current liabilities? How much did Accounts Payable and Accrued Expenses change from 2002 to 2003?

Exhibit 9-1 McDonald's Corporation 2002 Consolidated Balance Sheet

Consolidated Balance Sheet

IN MILLIONS, EXCEPT PER SHARE DATA	December 31, **2002**	2001
Assets		
Current assets		
Cash and equivalents	$ 330.4	$ 418.1
Accounts and notes receivable	855.3	881.9
Inventories, at cost, not in excess of market	111.7	105.5
Prepaid expenses and other current assets	418.0	413.8
Total current assets	1,715.4	1,819.3
Other assets		
Investments in and advances to affiliates	1,037.7	990.2
Goodwill, net	1,559.8	1,320.4
Miscellaneous	1,074.2	1,115.1
Total other assets	3,671.7	3,425.7
Property and equipment		
Property and equipment, at cost	26,218.6	24,106.0
Accumulated depreciation and amortization	(7,635.2)	(6,816.5)
Net property and equipment	18,583.4	17,289.5
Total assets	$23,970.5	$22,534.5
Liabilities and shareholders' equity		
Current liabilities		
Notes payable	$ 0.3	$ 184.9
Accounts payable	635.8	689.5
Income taxes	16.3	20.4
Other taxes	191.8	180.4
Accrued interest	199.4	170.6
Accrued restructuring and restaurant closing costs	328.5	144.2
Accrued payroll and other liabilities	774.7	680.7
Current maturities of long-term debt	275.5	177.6
Total current liabilities	2,422.3	2,248.3
Long-term debt	9,703.6	8,555.5
Other long-term liabilities and minority interests	560.0	629.3
Deferred income taxes	1,003.7	1,112.2
Common equity put options and forward contracts		
Shareholders' equity		
Preferred stock, no par value; authorized-165.0 million shares; issued-none		500.8
Common stock, $.01 par value; authorized-3.5 billion shares; issued-1,660.6 million shares	16.6	16.6
Additional paid-in capital	1,747.3	1,591.2
Unearned ESOP compensation	(98.4)	(106.7)
Retained earnings	19,204.4	18,608.3
Accumulated other comprehensive income (loss)	(1,601.3)	(1,708.8)
Common stock in treasury, at cost; 392.4 and 379.9 million shares	(8,987.7)	(8,912.2)
Total shareholders' equity	10,280.9	9,488.4
Total liabilities and shareholders' equity	$23,970.5	$22,534.5

Highlighted items will require payments within one year.

See notes to consolidated financial statements.

A handy ratio to help creditors or potential creditors determine a company's liquidity is the current ratio. A current ratio of current assets to current liabilities of 2:1 is usually a very comfortable margin. If the firm has a large amount of inventory, it is sometimes useful to exclude inventory (prepayments are also excluded) when computing the ratio. That provides the "quick" ratio. Usually, one would want a quick ratio of at least 1.5:1 to feel secure that the company could pay its bills on time. Of course, the guidelines given for the current ratio, 2:1, and the quick ratio, 1.5:1, are only rules of thumb. The actual current and quick ratios of companies vary widely and depend on the company, the management policies, and the type of industry. Exhibit 9-2 presents the current and quick ratios for the companies that are used as examples in this chapter. The ratios do vary from company to company, yet all are solid companies without liquidity problems.

Exhibit 9-2

Current and Quick Ratios of Selected Companies for 2002

COMPANY	INDUSTRY	CURRENT RATIO	QUICK RATIO
Georgia-Pacific	building products/lumber	1.16	0.64
J. C. Penney	retailing	2.00	0.76
Johnson Controls	auto	1.03	0.82
McDonald's	fast food	0.71	0.49
Pfizer	drug	1.34	1.09

Accounting for current liabilities is an area in which U.S. accounting standards are very similar to those of most other countries. Nearly all countries encourage firms to provide a breakdown of liabilities into current and long-term in order to allow users to evaluate liquidity.

Interpret: You Decide. Take a close look at the current liabilities of J. C. Penney's indicated in the balance sheet of the chapter opener for this chapter. Analyze the liquidity of the company in three ways. First, calculate the amount of working capital for the current year and the previous year. Second, calculate current ratio for the current year and previous year. Finally, calculate the quick ratio of the company for the current year and the previous year. What do each of these measures tell you about the ability of the company to pay its current liabilities when they come due?

Ethics in Accounting

Rent-Way

http://www.rentway.com

Rent-Way, the nation's second-largest company of rent-to-own stores, was started in 1981. In 1993, it began selling its stock on the stock exchange. In 2001, when the company was operating more than 1,000 stores, it was determined that company expenses had been improperly understated by an estimated $25 to $35 million. Two months later, the company raised its estimate of the understatement to $55 to $65 million, and six months after that the estimate of understatement was more than doubled to about $127 million over a two-year period. During that time, the company's new chief financial officer, William McDonnell, discovered that several weeks before each year-end, the company stopped recording accounts payable to reduce its reported expenses.

What is the company doing that is an ethical concern? Why is this an issue? Why would understating expenses also affect current liabilities? What responsibility does management have to design, detect, or prevent errors in the financial statements?

Source: Queena Sook Kim, "Rent-Way details improper bookkeeping," *The Wall Street Journal*, June 8, 2001.

Accounts Payable

Accounts payable Amounts owed for inventory, goods, or services acquired in the normal course of business.

Accounts payable represent amounts owed for the purchase of inventory, goods, or services acquired in the normal course of business. Often, Accounts Payable is the first account listed in the current liability category because it requires the payment of cash before other current liabilities. **McDonald's** is different from most other companies because it lists Notes Payable before Accounts Payable.

Normally, a firm has an established relationship with several suppliers, and formal contractual arrangements with those suppliers are unnecessary. Accounts payable usually do not require the payment of interest, but terms may be given to encourage early payment. For example, terms may be stated as 2/10, n30, which means that a 2% discount is available if payment occurs within the first 10 days and that if payment is not made within 10 days, the full amount must be paid within 30 days.

INTERNAL DECISION

Timely payment of accounts payable is an important aspect of the management of cash flow. Generally, it is to the company's benefit to take advantage of discounts when they are available. After all, if your supplier is going to give you a 2% discount for paying on Day 10 instead of Day 30, that means you are earning 2% on your money over 20/360 of a year. If you took the 2% discount throughout the year, you would be getting a 36% annual return on your money, since there are 18 periods of 20 days each in a year. It is essential, therefore, that the accounts payable system be established in a manner that alerts management to take advantage of offered discounts.

Notes Payable

The first current liability on McDonald's 2002 balance sheet is notes payable of $0.3 million. How is a note payable different from an account payable? The most important difference is that an account payable is not a formal contractual arrangement, whereas a **note payable** is represented by a formal agreement or note signed by the parties to the transaction. Notes payable may arise from dealing with a supplier or from acquiring a cash loan from a bank or creditor. Those notes that are expected to be paid within one year of the balance sheet date should be classified as current liabilities.

Notes payable Amounts owed that are represented by a formal contract.

The accounting for notes payable depends on whether the interest is paid on the note's due date or is deducted before the borrower receives the loan proceeds. With the first type of note, the terms stipulate that the borrower receives a short-term loan and agrees to repay the principal and interest at the note's due date. For example, assume that Lamanski Company receives a one-year loan from First National Bank on January 1. The face amount of the note of $1,000 must be repaid on December 31 along with interest at the rate of 12%. The effect of the loan on the financial statements as of January 1 is as follows:

BALANCE SHEET								INCOME STATEMENT	
ASSETS		=	LIABILITIES		+	OWNERS' EQUITY	+	REVENUES − EXPENSES	
Cash	1,000		Notes Payable	1,000					

When the loan is repaid on December 31, Lamanski must pay $1,120 ($1,000 of principal and $120 of interest) and must eliminate the Notes Payable account. The effect of the repayment is as follows:

BALANCE SHEET								INCOME STATEMENT	
ASSETS		=	LIABILITIES		+	OWNERS' EQUITY	+	REVENUES − EXPENSES	
Cash	(1,120)		Notes Payable	(1,000)				Interest Expense	(120)

Banks also use another form of note, one in which the interest is deducted in advance. Suppose that on January 1, 2004, First National Bank granted to Lamanski a $1,000 loan, due on December 31, 2004, but deducted the interest in advance and gave Lamanski the remaining amount of $880 ($1,000 face amount of the note less interest of $120). This is sometimes referred to as *discounting a note* because a Discount on Notes Payable account is established on January 1. The effect is as follows:

BALANCE SHEET							INCOME STATEMENT
ASSETS		=	LIABILITIES		+	OWNERS' EQUITY	+ REVENUES – EXPENSES
Cash	880		Notes Payable	1,000			
			Discount on Notes Payable	(120)			

The **Discount on Notes Payable** account should be treated as a reduction of Notes Payable. If a balance sheet was developed immediately after the January 1 loan, the note would appear in the current liability category as follows:

Discount on notes payable A contra liability that represents interest deducted from a loan in advance.

Notes Payable	$1,000
Less: Discount on Notes Payable	120
Net Liability	$ 880

Study Tip

Discount on Notes Payable is a contra-liability account

The original balance in the Discount on Notes Payable account represents interest that must be transferred to interest expense over the life of the note. Before Lamanski presents its year-end financial statements, it must make an adjustment to transfer the discount to interest expense. The effect of the adjustment on December 31 is as follows:

BALANCE SHEET						INCOME STATEMENT	
ASSETS	=	LIABILITIES		+	OWNERS' EQUITY	+ REVENUES – EXPENSES	
		Discount on Notes Payable	120			Interest Expense	(120)

Thus, the balance of the Discount on Notes Payable account is zero, and $120 has been transferred to interest expense. When the note is repaid on December 31, 2004, Lamanski must repay the full amount of the note.

It is important to compare the two types of notes payable. In the previous two examples, the stated interest rate on each note was 12%. The dollar amount of interest incurred in each case was $120. However, the interest *rate* on a discounted note, the second example, is always higher than it appears. Lamanski received the use of only $880, yet it was required to repay $1,000. Therefore, the interest rate incurred on the note was actually $120/$880, or approximately 13.6%.

Current Maturities of Long-Term Debt

Another account that appears in the current liability category of McDonald's balance sheet is **Current Maturities of Long-Term Debt.** On other companies' balance sheets, this item may appear as Long-Term Debt, Current Portion. This account should appear when a firm has a liability and must make periodic payments. For example, assume that on January 1, 2004, your firm obtained a $10,000 loan from the bank. The terms of the loan require you to make payments in the amount of $1,000 per year for 10 years, payable each January 1, beginning January 1, 2005.

Current maturities of long-term debt The portion of a long-term liability that will be paid within one year.

The December 31, 2004, balance sheet should indicate that the liability for the note payable is classified into two portions: a $1,000 current liability that must be repaid within one year and a $9,000 long-term liability. On January 1, 2005, the company must pay $1,000, and the entry should eliminate the current liability of $1,000.

On December 31, 2005, the company should again record the current portion of the liability. Therefore, the 2005 year-end balance sheet should indicate that the liability is classified into two portions: a $1,000 current liability and an $8,000 long-term liability. The process should be repeated each year until the bank loan has been fully paid. When an investor or creditor reads a balance sheet, he or she wants to distinguish between debt that is long-term and debt that is short-term. Therefore, it is important to segregate that portion of the debt that becomes due within one year.

The balance sheet account labeled Current Maturities of Long-Term Debt should include only the amount of principal to be paid. The amount of interest that has been incurred but is unpaid should be listed separately in an account such as Interest Payable.

Taxes Payable

LO 2 Examine how accruals affect the current liability category.

Corporations pay a variety of taxes, including federal and state income taxes, property taxes, and other taxes. Usually, the largest dollar amount is incurred for state and federal income taxes. Taxes are an expense of the business and should be accrued in the same manner as any other business expense. A company that ends its accounting year on December 31 is not required to calculate the amount of tax owed to the government until the following March 15 or April 15, depending on the type of business. Therefore, year-end financial statements should reflect the amount of taxes incurred as an expense on the income statement and the amount of taxes that will be paid on March 15 or April 15 as a current liability on the balance sheet.

The calculation of the amount of tax a business owes is very complex. For now, the important point is that taxes are an expense when incurred (not when they are paid) and must be recorded as a liability as incurred.

Some analysts prefer to measure a company's profits before it pays taxes for several reasons. For one thing, tax rates change from year to year. A small change in the tax rate may drastically change a firm's profitability. Also, investors should realize that taxes occur in every year but that tax changes are not a recurring element of a business. Additionally, taxes are somewhat beyond the control of a company's management. For these reasons, it is important to consider a firm's operations *before* taxes to better evaluate management's ability to control operations.

Other Accrued Liabilities

McDonald's 2002 balance sheet listed an amount of $774.7 million as current liability under the category of Accrued Payroll and Other Liabilities. What items might be included in this category?

Accrued liability A liability that has been incurred but not yet paid.

In previous chapters, especially Chapter 4, we covered many examples of accrued liabilities. **Accrued liabilities** include any amount that has been incurred due to the passage of time but has not been paid as of the balance sheet date. A common example is salary or wages payable. Suppose that your firm has a payroll of $1,000 per day, Monday through Friday, and that employees are paid at the close of work each Friday. Also suppose that December 31 is the end of your accounting year and falls on a Tuesday. Your firm should reflect the $2,000 of salary incurred, but unpaid, as an expense on the income statement and as a current liability on the balance sheet at the year end. The amount of the salary payable would be classified as a current liability and could appear in a category such as Other Accrued Liabilities.

Interest is another item that often must be accrued at year-end. Assume that you received a one-year loan of $10,000 on December 1. The loan carries an interest rate of

12%. The income statement developed for the year ending December 31 should reflect one month's interest ($100) as expense even though it may not actually be due. The interest has been incurred and is therefore an expense. The balance sheet should reflect $100 as interest payable. An Interest Payable account representing one month's interest ($100) should be classified as a current liability, assuming that it is to be paid within one year of the December 31 date.

From Concept to Practice 9.2

Reading the Winnebago Industries and Monaco Coach Balance Sheets and Notes

What accounts are listed as Accrued Expenses on Winnebago Industries' balance sheet? In the notes to its financial statements, Monaco Coach provides details supporting the Accrued Expenses line on the balance sheet. What accounts are listed in its Note 5? Why do you think these items are not included in the Accounts Payable account?

Accounting for Your Decisions

You Are a Student

What types of current liabilities could you, as a student, have? What makes them liabilities? What makes them current?

ANS: Your current liabilities might include the current payments due from (1) student loans, (2) car loans, (3) loans from family members, (4) rent or mortgage payments, (5) credit card charges, (6) cafeteria charges, and similar charges. These items are current liabilities because they are obligations that will be satisfied within a year.

Reading the Statement of Cash Flows for Changes in Current Liabilities

It is important to understand the impact that current liabilities have on a company's cash flows. Exhibit 9-3 illustrates the placement of current liabilities on the statement

CASH FLOW

Exhibit 9-3

Current Liabilities on the Statement of Cash Flows

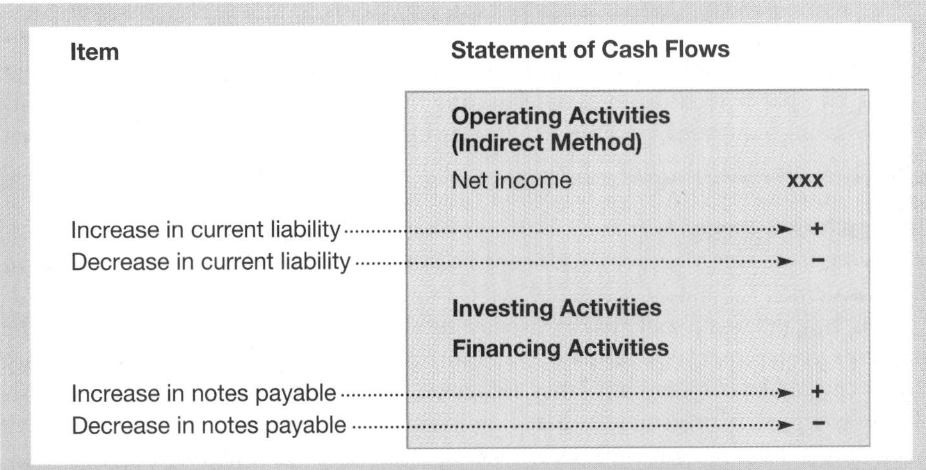

LO 3 Demonstrate an understanding of how changes in current liabilities affect the statement of cash flows.

Which Way to Go?

Is It Really a Current Liability? *Taz Industries has signed a contract with Wile E. Industrial Builders. It will take Wile E. two years to build a new manufacturing plant behind the existing one. Under the agreement, Wile E. will bill Taz for part of the agreed upon price each time one-fourth of the project has been completed. Taz, therefore, will make four equal payments to Wile E., with the last one being made when the building is completed.*

On June 30, 2003, Taz's fiscal year-end, Wile E. began the building process. By the end of July, the accountants at Taz were about to release the year-end balance sheet information. In anticipation of the building being 50% complete before June 30, 2004, and the need to make two payments to Wile E. during the year, the accountants classified half of the contract price as a current liability.

Have the accountants correctly reported the obligation? Why or why not? Would your answer change if, on July 25, 2003, the accountants learned that Wile E. had run into a problem with the building process and there probably would be a six to nine-month delay in construction so the second payment would not be due before January 1, 2005? Why or why not?

of cash flows (using the indirect method) and their effect. Most current liabilities are directly related to a firm's ongoing operations. Therefore, the change in the balance of each current liability account should be reflected in the Operating Activities category of the statement of cash flows. A decrease in a current liability account indicates that cash has been used to pay the liability and should appear as a deduction on the cash flow statement. An increase in a current liability account indicates a recognized expense that has not yet been paid. Look for it as an increase in the Operating Activities category of the cash flow statement.

The cash flow statement of McDonald's Corporation is presented in Exhibit 9-4. Note that one of the items in the 2002 Operating Activities category is listed as Taxes and Other Accrued Liabilities of $448.0 million. This means that the balance of those current liabilities increased by $448.0 million, resulting in an increase of cash.

Almost all current liabilities appear in the Operating Activities category of the statement of cash flows, but there are exceptions. If a current liability is not directly related to operating activities, it should not appear in that category. For example, McDonald's uses some notes payable as a means of financing, distinct from operating activities. Therefore, note borrowings and repayments are reflected in the Financing Activities rather than the Operating Activities category (see Exhibit 9-4).

Two-Minute Review

1. *What is the definition of current liabilities? Give some examples of items that are typically in the current liability category.*
2. *How is the current ratio calculated? What is it intended to measure?*
3. *In which category of the cash flow statement do most current liability items appear?*

Answers on page 445.

CONTINGENT LIABILITIES

LO 4 Determine when contingent liabilities should be presented on the balance sheet or disclosed in notes and how to calculate their amounts.

Contingent liability An existing condition for which the outcome is not known but depends on some future event.

We have seen that accountants must exercise a great deal of expertise and judgment in deciding what to record and in determining the amount to record. This is certainly true regarding contingent liabilities. A **contingent liability** is an obligation that involves an existing condition for which the outcome is not known with certainty and depends on some event that will occur in the future. The actual amount of the liability must be estimated because we cannot clearly predict the future. The important accounting issues are whether contingent liabilities should be recorded and, if so, in what amounts.

This is a judgment call that is usually resolved through discussions among the company's management and its outside auditors. Management usually would rather not disclose contingent liabilities until they come due. The reason is that investors' and creditors' judgment of management is based on the company's earnings, and the recording of a contingent liability must be accompanied by a charge to (reduction in) earnings. Auditors, on the other hand, want management to disclose as much as possible because

Exhibit 9-4 McDonald's Corporation 2002 Consolidated Statement of Cash Flows

Consolidated Statement of Cash Flows

IN MILLIONS Years ended December 31,	**2002**	2001	2000
Operating activities			
Net income	$ 893.5	$1,636.6	$1,977.3
Adjustments to reconcile to cash provided by operations			
Cumulative effect of accounting change	98.6		
Depreciation and amortization	1,050.8	1,086.3	1,010.7
Deferred income taxes	(44.6)	(87.6)	60.5
Changes in working capital items			
Accounts receivable	1.6	(104.7)	(67.2)
Inventories, prepaid expenses and other current assets	(38.1)	(62.9)	(29.6)
Accounts payable	(11.2)	10.2	89.7
Taxes and other accrued liabilities	448.0	270.4	(45.8)
Other (including noncash portion of significant items)	491.5	(60.0)	(244.1)
Cash provided by operations	2,890.1	2,688.3	2,751.5
Investing activities			
Property and equipment expenditures	(2,003.8)	(1,906.2)	(1,945.1)
Purchases of restaurant businesses	(548.4)	(331.6)	(425.5)
Sales of restaurant businesses and property	369.5	375.9	302.8
Other	(283.9)	(206.3)	(144.8)
Cash used for investing activities	(2,466.6)	(2,068.2)	(2,212.6)
Financing activities			
Net short-term borrowings (repayments)	(606.8)	(248.0)	59.1
Long-term financing issuances	1,502.6	1,694.7	2,381.3
Long-term financing repayments	(750.3)	(919.4)	(761.9)
Treasury stock purchases	(670.2)	(1,068.1)	(2,023.4)
Common stock dividends	(297.4)	(287.7)	(280.7)
Other	310.9	204.8	88.9
Cash used for financing activities	(511.2)	(623.7)	(536.7)
Cash and equivalents increase (decrease)	(87.7)	(3.6)	2.2
Cash and equivalents at beginning of year	418.1	421.7	419.5
Cash and equivalents at end of year	$ 330.4	$ 418.1	421.7
Supplemental cash flow disclosures			
Interest paid	$ 359.7	$ 446.9	$ 469.7
Income taxes paid	572.2	773.8	854.2

Note the impact of changes in current liabilities on cash flow

See notes to consolidated financial statements.

the auditors are essentially representing the interests of investors and creditors, who want to have as much information as possible.

Study Tip

Contingent liabilities are recorded only if they are probable and if the amount can be reasonably estimated.

Contingent Liabilities That Are Recorded

A contingent liability should be accrued and presented on the balance sheet if it is probable and if the amount can be reasonably estimated. But when is an event *probable*, and what does *reasonably estimated* mean? The terms must be defined based on the facts of each situation. A financial statement user would want the company to err on the side of full disclosure. On the other hand, the company should not be required to disclose every remote possibility.

A common contingent liability that must be presented as a liability by firms involves product warranties or guarantees. Many firms sell products for which they provide the

Business Strategy

http://www.jcpenney.com

http://www.gap.com

Effectively Expanding into Different Market Segments

Few department stores today focus on a narrow band of customers. Most savvy retailers realize the value of appealing to as many different market segments as possible while still establishing a distinctive identity for the store, to set it apart from its competitors.

J. C. Penney uses a wide array of private and national clothing brands to attract customers from many different demographic groups. National brands like Dockers®, Vanity Fair®, Jockey®, Haggar®, Adidas®, Crazy Horse®, and Joneswear® are all featured in Penney's stores. Private (store) brands such as Arizona Jeans®, Worthington®, Stafford®, and St. John's Bay® have proved successful enough to earn their own store-within-a-store departments, which J. C. Penney plans to expand. Despite this differentiation by brand, accounting information for all brands is added together for financial reporting purposes.

Gap, Inc., on the other hand, sells only its own brand of clothes and accessories in its stores. When the company decided in 1994 to develop a new brand of trendy, budget-priced clothing, it spun off a whole new line of stores to showcase the clothing, and Old Navy® was born. This strategy had already allowed Gap to open the Banana Republic chain of slightly upscale clothing stores and contributed to Old Navy's initial success. Gap has faltered badly in recent years, and many investors are now questioning whether Gap adopted the right strategy. With so many competitors selling the kind of snappy casual clothes that Gap and its Banana Republic and Old Navy offshoots were famous for, the retailer has decided it is time for a new approach. The trendier offerings seem to have turned off mainstream shoppers, store sales have declined, and profits have fallen dramatically. In addition, the past several quarters of fashion misfires have been hard lessons for the company, but Gap appears to have become more disciplined in ways that will carry it through a few more quarters of disappointing sales. "Into the late '90s, Gap didn't have much use for operational controls. But now that product is falling off, they do," says Kindra Devaney, an analyst with Fulcrum Global Partners. Investors hope the company can rekindle some of the old magic and return to profitability. ■

Sources: *Business Week* online, December 17, 2001, by Amy Tsao and J. C. Penney's 2000 Annual Report.

customer a warranty against defects that may develop in the products. If a product becomes defective within the warranty period, the selling firm ensures that it will repair or replace the item. This is an example of a contingent liability because the expense of fixing a product depends on some of the products becoming defective—an uncertain, although likely, event.

Estimated liability A contingent liability that is accrued and reflected on the balance sheet.

At the end of each period, the selling firm must estimate how many of the products sold in the current year will become defective in the future and the cost of repair or replacement. This type of contingent liability is often referred to as an **estimated liability** to emphasize that the costs are not known at year-end and must be estimated.

As an example, assume that Quickkey Computer sells a computer product for $5,000. When the customer buys the product, Quickkey provides a one-year warranty in case it must be repaired. Assume that in 2004 Quickkey sold 100 computers for a total sales revenue of $500,000. At the end of 2004, Quickkey must record an estimate of the warranty costs that will occur on 2004 sales. Using an analysis of past warranty records, Quickkey estimates that repairs will average 2% of total sales. The 2004 balance sheet should indicate a liability of $10,000 in the account Estimated Liability for Warranty. This liability is classified as a current liability because Quickkey provides a one-year warranty. Quickkey's income statement should reflect a warranty expense of $10,000 to accrue the estimated amount of expense incurred.

The amount of warranty costs that a company presents as an expense is of interest to investors and potential creditors. If the expense as a percentage of sales begins to rise, one might conclude that the product is becoming less reliable.

Warranties are an excellent example of the matching principle. In our Quickkey example, the warranty costs related to 2004 sales were estimated and recorded in 2004. This was done to match the 2004 sales with the expenses related to those sales. If actual repairs of the computers occurred in 2005, they do not result in an expense. The repair costs incurred in 2005 should be treated as a reduction in the liability that had previously been estimated.

Because items such as warranties involve estimation, you may wonder what happens if the amount estimated is not accurate. The company must analyze past warranty records carefully and incorporate any changes in customer buying habits, usage, technological changes, and other changes. Still, even with careful analysis, the actual amount of the expense is not likely to equal the estimated amount. Generally, firms do not change the amount of the expense recorded in past periods for such differences. They may adjust the amount recorded in future periods, however.

Warranties provide an example of a contingent liability that must be estimated and recorded. Another example is premium or coupon offers that accompany many products. Cereal boxes are an everyday example of premium offers. The boxes often allow customers to purchase a toy or game at a reduced price if the purchase is accompanied by cereal box tops or proof of purchase. The offer given to cereal customers represents a contingent liability. At the end of each year, the cereal company must estimate the number of premium offers that will be redeemed and the cost involved and must report a contingent liability for that amount.

Legal claims that have been filed against a firm are also examples of contingent liabilities. In today's business environment, lawsuits and legal claims are a fact of life. They represent a contingent liability because an event has occurred but the outcome of that event, the resolution of the lawsuit, is not known. The defendant in the lawsuit must make a judgment about the outcome of the lawsuit in order to decide whether the item should be recorded on the balance sheet or should be disclosed in the notes. If an unfavorable outcome to the legal claim is deemed to be probable, then an amount should be recorded as a contingent liability on the balance sheet. Exhibit 9-5 provides portions of a note disclosure that accompanied the 2002 financial statements of Georgia-Pacific

Product warranties represent a contingent liability that must be presented on the balance sheet. This is because some amount of warranty work is probable and can be estimated. As the level of warranty expense rises, often so does investors' skepticism toward these retailers.

http://www.gp.com

Exhibit 9-5

Note Disclosure for Contingent Liability from Georgia-Pacific's 2002 Financial Statements

Note 15

The Corporation is involved in environmental remediation activities at approximately 172 sites, both owned by the Corporation and owned by others, where it has been notified that it is or may be a potentially responsible party (PRP) under the United States Comprehensive Environmental Response, Compensation and Liability Act (CERCLA) or similar state superfund laws.

The Corporation has established reserves for environmental remediation costs for these sites that it believes are probable and reasonably able to be estimated. To the extent that the Corporation is aware of unasserted claims, considers them probable, and can estimate their potential costs, the Corporation includes appropriate amounts in the reserves. Based on analyses of currently available information and previous experience with respect to the cleanup of hazardous substances, the Corporation believes it is reasonably possible that costs associated with these sites may exceed current reserves by amounts that may prove insignificant or that could range, in the aggregate, up to approximately $127 million.

Corporation. The note concerned litigation over environmental damage that is alleged to have occurred as a result of the company's activities. Environmental remediation claims are very common for companies in many industries. In this case, Georgia-Pacific believed that an unfavorable outcome had become probable and, as a result, recorded a contingent liability of $127 million as an estimate of the amount that will be owed at the eventual outcome of this claim.

INTERNAL DECISION

As you might imagine, firms are not usually eager to record contingent lawsuits as liabilities because the amount of loss is often difficult to estimate. Also, some may view the accountant's decision as an admission of guilt if a lawsuit is recorded as a liability before the courts have finalized a decision. Accountants must often consult with lawyers or other legal experts to determine the probability of the loss of a lawsuit. In cases involving contingencies, it is especially important that the accountant make an independent judgment based on the facts and not be swayed by the desires of other parties.

Contingent Liabilities That Are Disclosed

Any contingent liability that both is probable and can be reasonably estimated must be reported as a liability. We now must consider contingent liabilities that do not meet the probable criterion or cannot be reasonably estimated. In either case, a contingent liability must be disclosed in the financial statement notes but not reported on the balance sheet if the contingent liability is at least reasonably possible.

Although information in the notes to the financial statements contains very important data on which investors base decisions, some accountants believe that note disclosure does not have the same impact as does recording a contingent liability on the balance sheet. For one thing, note disclosure does not affect the important financial ratios that investors use to make decisions.

In the previous section, we presented a legal claim involving Georgia-Pacific as an example of a contingent liability that was probable and therefore was recorded on the balance sheet as a liability. Most lawsuits, however, are not recorded as liabilities either because the risk of loss is not considered probable or because the amount of the loss cannot be reasonably estimated. If a company does not record a lawsuit as a liability, it must still consider whether the lawsuit should be disclosed in the notes to the financial statements. If the risk of loss is at least *reasonably possible,* then the company should provide note disclosure. This is the course of action taken for most contingent liabilities involving lawsuits.

http://www.pfizer.com

Exhibit 9-6 contains excerpts from the notes to the 2002 financial statements of Pfizer, a large drug and pharmaceutical company. The first portion of Exhibit 9-6 indicates that Pfizer is subject to a variety of lawsuits and legal actions, which arise from patent, product liability, environmental, tax claims, and other matters. The second portion of the exhibit concerns some of the most common types of lawsuits in our economy—claims concerning asbestos. Note that in this case Pfizer acquired another company with products containing asbestos, and as a result, several hundred lawsuits are now being filed against Pfizer alleging injury as far back as the 1960s.

You should note that the excerpts in Exhibit 9-6 are examples of contingent liabilities that have been disclosed in the notes to the financial statements *but have not been recorded as liabilities on the balance sheet.* **Readers of the financial statements, and analysts,** must carefully read the notes to determine the impact of such contingent liabilities.

The amount and the timing of the cash outlays associated with contingent liabilities are especially difficult to determine. Lawsuits, for example, may extend several years into the future, and the dollar amount of possible loss may be subject to great uncertainty.

Contingent Liabilities versus Contingent Assets

Contingent liabilities that are probable and can be reasonably estimated must be presented on the balance sheet before the outcome of the future events is known. This

Exhibit 9-6 Note Disclosure for Contingencies from Pfizer's 2002 Annual Report

The following are selected excerpts from Note 20 (Legal Proceedings and Contingencies):

We and certain of our subsidiaries are involved in various patent, product liability, consumer, commercial, environmental, and tax litigations and claims; government investigations; and other legal proceedings that arise from time to time in the ordinary course of our business. We do not believe any of them will have a material adverse effect on our financial position. Litigation is inherently unpredictable, and excessive verdicts do occur. Although we believe we have valid defenses in these matters, we could in the future incur judgments or enter into settlements of claims that could have a material adverse effect on our results of operations in any particular period.

.
.
.
.
.

Asbestos

In the 1960s, Pfizer acquired two businesses, the Gibsonburg Lime Products Company and Quigley Company, Inc., that sold, among other things, products containing small amounts of asbestos. The sale of these products was discontinued in the early 1970s. Gibsonburg Lime was operated as an unincorporated division of Pfizer, whereas Quigley has been and continues to be a separately incorporated subsidiary of Pfizer. As of December 31, 2002, approximately 128,000 claims naming Pfizer and/or Quigley and numerous other defendants were pending in various federal and state courts seeking damages for alleged asbestos exposure. The majority of these claims involve alleged activities of Quigley, for which any liability is solely the responsibility of Quigley. While Quigley continues to have insurance covering asbestos claims, that insurance is limited and going forward contains substantial self-insurance aspects. Quigley has conducted no active trade or business since 1992. Its sole activity is management of its asbestos-related claims.

.
.
.
.
.

Based upon available data and our experience in handling asbestos claims, we believe that a substantial portion of the plaintiffs alleging injury from Pfizer, Quigley and American Optical products do not have any impairing medical condition. For those claimants who do, we believe we have meritorious defenses.

accounting rule applies only to contingent losses or liabilities. It does not apply to contingencies by which the firm may gain. Generally, contingent gains or **contingent assets** are not reported until the gain actually occurs. That is, contingent liabilities may be accrued, but contingent assets are not accrued. Exhibit 9-7 contains a portion of the notes from the 2002 financial statements of **Johnson Controls, Inc.**, a large company that is a supplier to the auto makers. Like many other companies,

Contingent assets An existing condition for which the outcome is not known but by which the company stands to gain.

http://www.johnsoncontrols.com

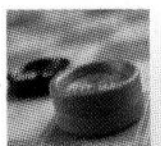

Accounting for Your Decisions

You Are the CEO

You run a high-technology company that grows fast some quarters and disappoints investors in other quarters. As a result, your company's stock price fluctuates widely, and you have attracted the unwanted attention of a law firm that filed a lawsuit on behalf of disgruntled shareholders. How do you reflect this lawsuit on your financial statements?

ANS: Your legal counsel should be consulted to determine whether the plaintiff's case has merit. If a loss is probable and the amount can be estimated, the lawsuit should be recorded as a liability. Unfortunately, lawsuits have become very common for many companies. In some cases, the lawsuits are totally without merit and are frivolous. If your attorneys agree that this case will not result in a loss, then no disclosure would be required.

Exhibit 9-7

Note Disclosure for Contingent Asset (Proceeds from Insurance) from Johnson Controls' 2002 Financial Statements

NOTE

14 Contingencies

The Company is involved in a number of proceedings relating to environmental matters. At September 30, 2002, the Company had an accrued liability of approximately $32 million relating to environmental matters compared with $28 million one year ago. The Company's environmental liabilities do not take into consideration any possible recoveries of future insurance proceeds. Because of the uncertainties associated with environmental remediation activities, the Company's future expenses to remediate the currently identified sites could be considerably higher than the accrued liability. Although it is difficult to estimate the liability of the Company related to these environmental matters, the Company believes that these matters will not have a materially adverse effect upon its capital expenditures, earnings or competitive position.

Additionally, the Company is involved in a number of product liability and various other suits incident to the operation of its businesses. Insurance coverages are maintained and estimated costs are recorded for claims and suits of this nature. It is management's opinion that none of these will have a materially adverse effect on the Company's financial position, results of operations or cash flows.

Johnson Controls has had to accrue rather large amounts for environmental remediation costs. The note indicates that Johnson Controls believes that its insurance policies should cover part of the costs. This is an example of a contingent asset because the company may receive some amounts at a future time. The financial statements reveal that Johnson Controls has recorded liabilities related to the remediation costs but has not recorded any of the potential recoveries from insurance even though it appears quite likely that some amount will be received. This may seem inconsistent—it is. Remember, however, that accounting is a discipline based on a conservative set of principles. It is prudent and conservative to delay the recording of a gain until an asset is actually received but to record contingent liabilities in advance.

Of course, even though the contingent assets are not reported, the information may still be important to investors. Wall Street analysts make their living trying to place a value on contingent assets that they believe will result in future benefits. By buying stock of a company that has unrecorded assets, or advising their clients to do so, investment analysts hope to make money when those assets become a reality.

Two-Minute Review

1. *Under what circumstances should contingent liabilities be reported in the financial statements?*
2. *Under what circumstances should contingent liabilities be disclosed in the notes and not recorded in the financial statements?*
3. *Are contingent assets treated the same as contingent liabilities?*

Answers on page 445.

TIME VALUE OF MONEY CONCEPTS

In this section we will study the impact that interest has on decision making because of the time value of money. The **time value of money** concept means that people prefer a payment at the present time rather than in the future because of the interest factor. If an amount is received at the present time, it can be invested, and the resulting accumulation will be larger than if the same amount is received in the future. Thus, there is a *time value* to cash receipts and payments. This time value concept is important to every student for two reasons: it affects your personal financial decisions, and it affects accounting valuation decisions.

Time value of money An immediate amount should be preferred over an amount in the future.

Exhibit 9-8 indicates some of the personal and accounting decisions affected by the time value of money concept. In your personal life, you make decisions based on the time value of money concept nearly every day. When you invest money, you are interested in how much will be accumulated, and you must determine the *future value* based on the amount of interest that will be compounded. When you borrow money, you must determine the amount of the payments on the loan. You may not always realize it, but the amount of the loan payment is based on the *present value* of the loan, another time value of money concept.

Exhibit 9-8

Importance of the Time Value of Money

DECISION MAKING

Personal Financial Decision	Action
■ How much money will accumulate if you invest in a CD or money market account? →	Calculate the future value based on compound interest.
■ If you take out an auto loan, what will be the monthly loan payments? →	Calculate the payments based on the present value of the loan.
■ If you invest in the bond market, what should you pay for a bond? →	Calculate the present value of the bond based on compound interest.
■ If you win the lottery, should you take an immediate payment or payment over time? →	Calculate the present value of the alternatives based on compound interest.

Valuation Decisions on the Financial Statements	Valuation
■ Long-term assets →	Historical cost, but not higher than present value of the cash flows
■ Notes receivable →	Present value of the cash flows
■ Loan payments →	Based on the present value of the loan
■ Bond issue price →	Present value of the cash flows
■ Leases →	Present value of the cash flows

Time value of money is also important because of its implications for accounting valuations. We will discover in Chapter 10 that the issue price of a bond is based on the present value of the cash flows that the bond will produce. The valuation of the bond and the recording of the bond on the balance sheet are based on this concept. Further, the amount that is considered interest expense on the financial statements is also based on time value of money concepts. The bottom portion of Exhibit 9-8 indicates that the valuations of many other accounts, including Notes Receivable and Leases, are based on compound interest calculations.

The time value of money concept is used in virtually every advanced business course. Investment courses, marketing courses, and many other business courses will use the time value of money concept. *In fact, it is probably the most important decision-making tool to master in preparation for the business world.* This section of the text begins with an explanation of how simple interest and compound interest differ and then proceeds to the concepts of present values and future values.

Simple Interest

LO 5 Explain the difference between simple and compound interest.

Simple interest Interest is calculated on the principal amount only.

Simple interest is interest earned on the principal amount. If the amount of principal is unchanged from year to year, the interest per year will remain the same. Interest can be calculated by the following formula:

$$I = P \times R \times T$$

where

I = Dollar amount of interest per year

P = Principal

R = Interest rate as a percentage

T = Time in years

For example, assume that our firm has signed a two-year note payable for $3,000. Interest and principal are to be paid at the due date with simple interest at the rate of 10% per year. The amount of interest on the note would be $600, calculated as $3,000 × 0.10 × 2. We would be required to pay $3,600 on the due date: $3,000 principal and $600 interest.

Compound Interest

Compound interest Interest calculated on the principal plus previous amounts of interest.

Compound interest means that interest is calculated on the principal plus previous amounts of accumulated interest. Thus, interest is compounded, or we can say that there is interest on interest. For example, assume a $3,000 note payable for which interest and principal are due in two years with interest compounded annually at 10% per year. Interest would be calculated as follows:

YEAR	PRINCIPAL AMOUNT AT BEGINNING OF YEAR	INTEREST AT 10%	ACCUMULATED AT YEAR-END
1	$3,000	$300	$3,300
2	3,300	330	3,630

We would be required to pay $3,630 at the end of two years, $3,000 principal and $630 interest. A comparison of the note payable with 10% simple interest in the first example with the note payable with 10% compound interest in the second example clearly indicates that the amount accumulated with compound interest is always a higher amount because of the interest-on-interest feature.

Interest Compounding

LO 6 Calculate amounts using the future value and present value concepts.

For most accounting problems, we will assume that compound interest is compounded annually. In actual business practice, compounding usually occurs over much shorter intervals. This can be confusing because the interest rate is often stated as an annual rate even though it is compounded over a shorter period. If compounding is not done annually, you must adjust the interest rate by dividing the annual rate by the number of compounding periods per year.

For example, assume that the note payable from the previous example carried a 10% interest rate compounded semiannually for two years. The 10% annual rate should be converted to 5% per period for four semiannual periods. The amount of interest would be compounded, as in the previous example, but for four periods instead of two. The compounding process is as follows:

PERIOD	PRINCIPAL AMOUNT AT BEGINNING OF YEAR	INTEREST AT 5% PER PERIOD	ACCUMULATED AT END OF PERIOD
1	$3,000	$150	$3,150
2	3,150	158	3,308
3	3,308	165	3,473
4	3,473	174	3,647

The example illustrates that compounding more frequently results in a larger amount accumulated. In fact, many banks and financial institutions now compound interest on savings accounts on a daily basis.

Accounting for Your Decisions

You Invest Some Unexpected Cash

You want to invest some extra money you received from a long-lost uncle. You have narrowed your options down to two: (1) invest in a bond that offers 10% interest compounded semiannually, or (2) invest in a certificate of deposit that offers 10% interest compounded quarterly. Both options cover a one-year time period. Using the time value of money concepts you have learned in this accounting course, would you choose Option 1 or 2? Why?

ANS: You should choose Option 2, offering the same interest rate as the first option but compounding on a quarterly basis instead of a semiannual basis. More frequent compounding results in more interest, thus making Option 2's quarterly compounding more appealing than Option 1's semiannual compounding.

In the remainder of this section, we will assume that compound interest is applicable. Four compound interest calculations must be understood:

1. Future value of a single amount
2. Present value of a single amount
3. Future value of an annuity
4. Present value of an annuity

Future Value of a Single Amount

We are often interested in the amount of interest plus principal that will be accumulated at a future time. This is called a *future amount* or *future value.* The future amount is always larger than the principal amount (payment) because of the interest that accumulates. The formula to calculate the **future value of a single amount** is as follows:

Future value of a single amount Amount accumulated at a future time from a single payment or investment.

$$FV = p(1 + i)^n,$$

where

FV = Future value to be calculated

p = Present value or principal amount

i = Interest rate

n = Number of periods of compounding

Example 1: Your three-year-old son, Robert, just inherited $50,000 in cash and securities from his grandfather. If the funds were left in the bank and in the stock market and received an annual return of 10%, how much would be there in 15 years when Robert starts college?

Assume you won the lottery and this check is yours. Which payment option would you take—a lump sum or an amount every year for 10 years? Only by understanding time value of money concepts could you make an intelligent choice.

Solution:

$$\begin{aligned} FV &= \$50{,}000(1 + 0.10)^{15} \\ &= \$50{,}000(4.177) \\ &= \$208{,}850 \end{aligned}$$

In some cases, we will use time diagrams to illustrate the relationships. A time diagram to illustrate a future value would be of the following form:

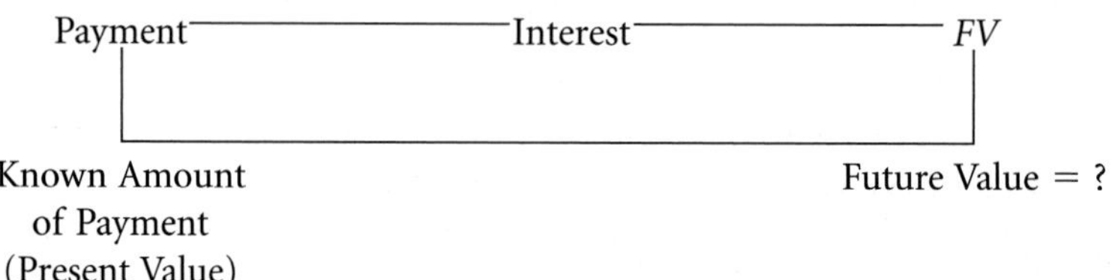

Example 2: Consider a $2,000 note payable that carries interest at the rate of 10% compounded annually. The note is due in two years, and the principal and interest must be paid at that time. The amount that must be paid in two years is the future value. The future value can be calculated in the manner we have used in the previous examples:

YEAR	PRINCIPAL AMOUNT AT BEGINNING OF YEAR	INTEREST AT 10%	ACCUMULATED AT YEAR-END
1	$2,000	$200	$2,200
2	2,200	220	2,420

The future value can also be calculated by using the following formula:

$$\begin{aligned} FV &= \$2{,}000(1 + 0.10)^{2} \\ &= \$2{,}000(1.21) \\ &= \$2{,}420 \end{aligned}$$

Rather than using a formula, there are other methods to calculate future value. Tables can be constructed to assist in the calculations. Table 9-1 on page 450 indicates the future value of $1 at various interest rates and for various time periods. To find the future value of a two-year note at 10% compounded annually, you read across the line for two periods and down the 10% column and see an interest rate factor of 1.210. Because the table has been constructed for future values of $1, we would determine the future value of $2,000 as follows:

$$FV = \$2{,}000 \times 1.210$$
$$= \$2{,}420$$

Many financial calculators are also available to perform future value calculations. We will illustrate the calculations with a widely used calculator, Texas Instrument's Advanced Business Analyst® (BA II). All financial calculators perform the calculations in the same manner, but you should be aware that the methods to enter the data, the keystrokes, might vary somewhat from one calculator to another.[3]

To calculate the future value in our example, you should perform the following steps:

ENTER	DISPLAY
2 N	N = 2
10 I/Y	I/Y = 10
0 PMT	PMT= 0
2000 PV	PV = 2,000
CPT FV	FV = 2,420

A third method used to perform the calculations is to use the built-in functions of a computerized spreadsheet. In Appendix B, we will illustrate how to use a common spreadsheet, Microsoft® Excel, to perform the same calculations. *Note that the numbers produced by each method may differ by a few dollars because of rounding differences. You should ignore those small differences and concentrate on the methods used to perform the interest rate calculations.*

We mentioned that compounding does not always occur annually. How does this affect the calculation of future value amounts?

Example 3: Suppose we want to find the future value of a $2,000 note payable due in two years. The note payable requires interest to be compounded quarterly at the rate of 12% per year. To calculate the future value, we must adjust the interest rate to a quarterly basis by dividing the 12% rate by the number of compounding periods per year, which in the case of quarterly compounding is four:

$$12\%/4 \text{ quarters} = 3\% \text{ per Quarter}$$

Also, the number of compounding periods is eight—four per year times two years.

The future value of the note can be found in two ways. First, we can insert the proper values into the future value formula:

$$FV = \$2{,}000(1 + 0.03)^8$$
$$= \$2{,}000(1.267)$$
$$= \$2{,}534$$

We can arrive at the same future value amount with the use of Table 9-1. Refer to the interest factor in the table indicated for 8 periods and 3%. The future value would be calculated as follows:

[3]Some preliminary steps are necessary before using the calculator for the calculations we will illustrate. First, we will assume that your calculator is set to accommodate annual payments, rather than monthly payments. See your calculator instruction manual to set it to annual payments if necessary. Second, when we calculate the present value or future value of an annuity of payments, we will assume that the payments constitute an ordinary annuity, also called an annuity in arrears. That is, we will assume the payments occur at the end of each period. Your calculator should be set to end-of-period payments. Again, refer to your instruction manual to make sure it is set correctly.

$$FV = \$2{,}000(\text{interest factor})$$
$$= \$2{,}000(1.267)$$
$$= \$2{,}534$$

The steps using the calculator are as follows:

ENTER	DISPLAY
8 N	N = 8
3 I/Y	I/Y = 3
0 PMT	PMT= 0
2000 PV	PV = 2,000
CPT FV	FV = 2,534

Present Value of a Single Amount

Present value of a single amount Amount at a present time that is equivalent to a payment or investment at a future time.

In many situations, we do not want to calculate how much will be accumulated at a future time. Rather, we want to determine the present amount that is equivalent to an amount at a future time. This is the present value concept. The **present value of a single amount** represents the value today of a single amount to be received or paid at a future time. This can be portrayed in a time diagram as follows:

PV ——— Discount ——— Payment

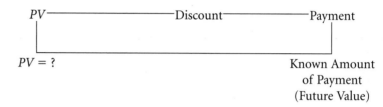

PV = ?   Known Amount of Payment (Future Value)

The time diagram portrays discount, rather than interest, because we often speak of "discounting" the future payment back to the present time.

Example 4: Suppose you know that you will receive \$2,000 in two years. You also know that if you had the money now, it could be invested at 10% compounded annually. What is the present value of the \$2,000? Another way to ask the same question is, What amount must be invested today at 10% compounded annually in order to have \$2,000 accumulated in two years?

The formula used to calculate present value is as follows:

$$PV = \text{Future value} \times (1 + i)^{-n}$$

where

PV = Present value amount in dollars

Future value = Amount to be received in the future

i = Interest rate or discount rate

n = Number of periods

We can use the present value formula to solve for the present value of the \$2,000 note as follows:

$$PV = \$2{,}000 \times (1 + 0.10)^{-2}$$
$$= \$2{,}000 \times (0.826)$$
$$= \$1{,}652$$

Study Tip

When interest rates *increase*, present values *decrease*. This is called an *inverse relationship*.

Example 5: A recent magazine article projects that it will cost \$120,000 to attend a four-year college 10 years from now. If that is true, how much money would you have to put into an account today to fund that education, assuming a 5% rate of return?

$$PV = \$120{,}000(1 + 0.05)^{-10}$$
$$= \$12{,}000(0.614)$$
$$= \$73{,}680$$

Tables have also been developed to determine the present value of $1 at various interest rates and number of periods. Table 9-2 on page 451 presents the present value or discount factors for an amount of $1 to be received at a future time. To use the table for our two-year note example, you must read across the line for two periods and down the 10% column to the discount factor of 0.826. The present value of $2,000 would be calculated as follows:

$$PV = \$2{,}000(\text{discount factor})$$
$$= \$2{,}000(0.826)$$
$$= \$1{,}652$$

The steps using the calculator are as follows:

ENTER	DISPLAY
2 N	N = 2
10 I/Y	I/Y = 10
0 PMT	PMT= 0
2000 FV	FV = 2,000
CPT PV	PV = 1,653

Two other points are important. First, the example illustrates that the present value amount is always less than the future payment. This happens because of the discount factor. In other words, if we had a smaller amount at the present (the present value), we could invest it and earn interest that would accumulate to an amount equal to the larger amount (the future payment). Second, study of the present value and future value formulas indicates that each is the reciprocal of the other. When we want to calculate a present value amount, we normally use Table 9-2 and multiply a discount factor times the payment. However, we could also use Table 9-1 and divide by the interest factor. Thus, the present value of the $2,000 to be received in the future could also be calculated as follows:

$$PV = \$2{,}000/1.210$$
$$= \$1{,}652$$

Future Value of an Annuity

The present value and future value amounts are useful when a single amount is involved. Many accounting situations involve an annuity, however. **Annuity** means a series of payments of equal amounts. We will now consider the calculation of the future value when a series of payments is involved.

Annuity A series of payments of equal amounts.

Example 6: Suppose that you are to receive $3,000 per year at the end of each of the next four years. Also assume that each payment could be invested at an interest rate of 10% compounded annually. How much would be accumulated in principal and interest by the end of the fourth year? This is an example of an annuity of payments of equal amounts. A time diagram would portray the payments as follows:

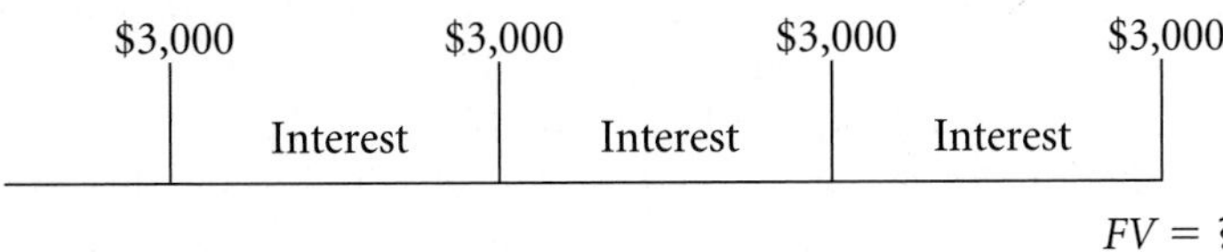

Because we are interested in calculating the future value, we could use the future value of $1 concept and calculate the future value of each $3,000 payment using Table 9-1 as follows:

$3,000 × 1.331 Interest for 3 Periods	$ 3,993
3,000 × 1.210 Interest for 2 Periods	3,630
3,000 × 1.100 Interest for 1 Period	3,300
3,000 × 1.000 Interest for 0 Periods	3,000
Total Future Value	$13,923

It should be noted that four payments would be received but that only three of them would draw interest because the payments are received at the end of each period.

Future value of an annuity Amount accumulated in the future when a series of payments is invested and accrues interest.

Fortunately, there is an easier method to calculate the **future value of an annuity.** Table 9-3 on page 452 has been constructed to indicate the future value of a series of payments of $1 per period at various interest rates and number of periods. The table can be used for the previous example by reading across the four-period line and down the 10% column to a table factor of 4.641. The future value of an annuity of $3,000 per year can be calculated as follows:

$$\begin{aligned} FV &= \$3{,}000(\text{table factor}) \\ &= \$3{,}000(4.641) \\ &= \$13{,}923 \end{aligned}$$

The steps using the calculator are as follows:

ENTER	DISPLAY
4 N	N = 4
10 I/Y	I/Y = 10
3000 PMT	PMT= 3,000
0 PV	PV = 0
CPT FV	FV = 13,923

Example 7: Your cousin just had a baby girl two weeks ago and is already thinking about sending her to college. When the girl is 15, how much money would be in her college account if your cousin deposits $2,000 into it on each of her 15 birthdays? The interest rate is 10%.

$$\begin{aligned} FV &= \$2{,}000(\text{table factor}) \\ &= \$2{,}000(31.772) \\ &= \$63{,}544 \end{aligned}$$

The steps using the calculator are as follows:

ENTER	DISPLAY
15 N	N = 15
10 I/Y	I/Y = 10
2000 PMT	PMT= 2,000
0 PV	PV = 0
CPT FV	FV = 63,545

When compounding occurs more frequently than annually, adjustments must be made to the interest rate and number of periods, adjustments similar to those discussed previously for single amounts.

Example 8: How would the future value be calculated if the previous example was modified so that we deposited $1,000 semiannually and the interest rate was 10% compounded semiannually (or 5% per period) for 15 years? Table 9-3 could be used by reading across the line for 30 periods and down the column for 5% to obtain a table factor of 66.439. The future value would be calculated as follows:

$$\begin{aligned} FV &= \$1{,}000(\text{table factor}) \\ &= \$1{,}000(66.439) \\ &= \$66{,}439 \end{aligned}$$

The steps using the calculator are as follows:

ENTER	DISPLAY
30 N	N = 30
5 I/Y	I/Y = 5
1000 PMT	PMT= 1,000
0 PV	PV = 0
CPT FV	FV = 66,439

Comparing the two examples illustrates once again that more frequent compounding results in larger accumulated amounts.

Present Value of an Annuity

Many accounting applications of the time value of money concept concern situations for which we want to know the present value of a series of payments that will occur in the future. This involves calculating the present value of an annuity. An annuity is a series of payments of equal amounts.

Example 9: Suppose that you will receive an annuity of $4,000 per year for four years, with the first received one year from today. The amounts received can be invested at a rate of 10% compounded annually. What amount would you need at the present time to have an amount equivalent to the series of payments and interest in the future? To answer this question, you must calculate the **present value of an annuity.** A time diagram of the series of payments would appear as follows:

Present value of an annuity The amount at a present time that is equivalent to a series of payments and interest in the future.

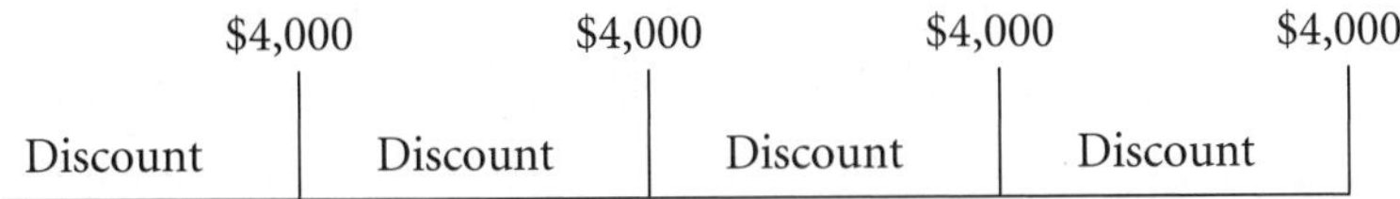

PV = ?

Because you are interested in calculating the present value, you could refer to the present value of $1 concept and discount each of the $4,000 payments individually using table factors from Table 9-2 as follows:

$4,000 × 0.683 Factor for Four Periods	$ 2,732
4,000 × 0.751 Factor for Three Periods	3,004
4,000 × 0.826 Factor for Two Periods	3,304
4,000 × 0.909 Factor for One Period	3,636
Total Present Value	$12,676

For a problem of any size, it is very cumbersome to calculate the present value of each payment individually. Therefore, tables have been constructed to ease the computational burden. Table 9-4 on page 453 provides table factors to calculate the present value of an annuity of $1 per year at various interest rates and number of periods. The previous example can be solved by reading across the four-year line and down the 10% column to obtain a table factor of 3.170. The present value would then be calculated as follows:

$$\begin{aligned} PV &= \$4{,}000(\text{table factor}) \\ &= \$4{,}000(3.170) \\ &= \$12{,}680 \end{aligned}$$

You should note that there is a $4 difference in the present value calculated by the first and second methods. This difference is caused by a small amount of rounding in the table factors that were used.

The steps using the calculator are as follows:

ENTER	DISPLAY
4 N	N = 4
10 I/Y	I/Y = 10
4000 PMT	PMT= 4,000
0 FV	FV = 0
CPT PV	PV = 12,680

Example 10: You just won the lottery. You can take your $1 million in a lump sum today, or you can receive $100,000 per year over the next 12 years. Assuming a 5% interest rate, which would you prefer, ignoring tax considerations?

Solution:

$$\begin{aligned} PV &= \$100{,}000(\text{table factor}) \\ &= \$100{,}000(8.863) \\ &= \$886{,}300 \end{aligned}$$

The steps using the calculator are as follows:

ENTER	DISPLAY
12 N	N = 12
5 I/Y	I/Y = 5
100,000 PMT	PMT= 100,000
0 FV	FV = 0
CPT PV	PV = 886,325

Because the present value of the payments over 12 years is less than the $1 million immediate payment, you should prefer the immediate payment.

Solving for Unknowns

LO 7 Apply the compound interest concepts to some common accounting situations.

In some cases, the present value or future value amounts will be known but the interest rate or the number of payments must be calculated. The formulas that have been presented thus far can be used for such calculations, but you must be careful to analyze each problem to be sure that you have chosen the correct relationship. We will use two examples to illustrate the power of the time value of money concepts.

Assume that you have just purchased a new automobile for $14,420 and must decide how to pay for it. Your local bank has graciously granted you a five-year loan. Because you are a good credit risk, the bank will allow you to make annual payments on the loan at the end of each year. The amount of the loan payments, which include principal and interest, is $4,000 per year. You are concerned that your total payments will be $20,000 ($4,000 per year for five years) and want to calculate the interest rate that is being charged on the loan.

Because the market or present value of the car, as well as the loan, is $14,420, a time diagram of our example would appear as follows:

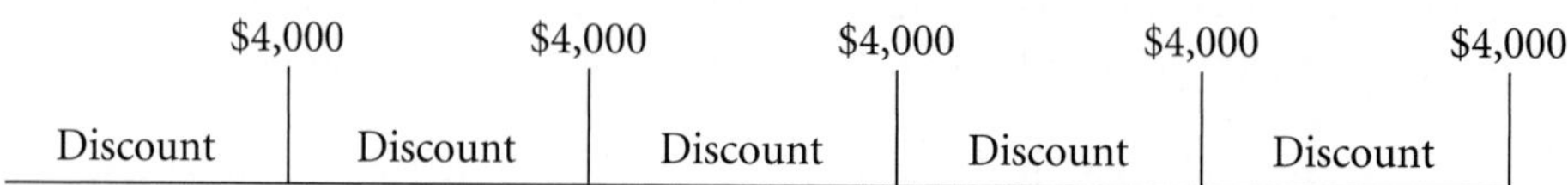

$PV = 14{,}420$

The interest rate that we must solve for represents the discount rate that was applied to the $4,000 payments to result in a present value of $14,420. Therefore, the applicable formula is the following:

$$PV = \$4{,}000(\text{table factor})$$

In this case, PV is known, so the formula can be rearranged as follows:

$$\begin{aligned} \text{Table factor} &= PV/\$4{,}000 \\ &= \$14{,}420/\$4{,}000 \\ &= 3.605 \end{aligned}$$

The value of 3.605 represents a table factor in Table 9-4. We must read across the five-year line until we find a table factor of 3.605. In this case, that table factor is found in the 12% column. Therefore, the rate of interest being paid on the auto loan is 12%.

The steps using the calculator are as follows:

ENTER	DISPLAY
5 N	N = 5
14420 PV	PV = 14,420
4000 PMT +/−	PMT= −4,000
0 FV	FV = 0
CPT I/Y	I/Y = 11.99

[*Note:* On many calculators, including Texas Instrument's BA II, the payment amount (PMT) must be entered as a negative value in order to calculate I/Y.]

The second example involves solving for the number of interest periods. Assume that you want to accumulate $12,000 as a down payment on a home. You believe that you can save $1,000 per semiannual period, and your bank will pay interest of 8% per year, or 4% per semiannual period. How long will it take you to accumulate the desired amount?

The accumulated amount of $12,000 represents the future value of an annuity of $1,000 per semiannual period. Therefore, we can use the interest factors of Table 9-3 to assist in the solution. The applicable formula in this case is the following:

$$FV = \$1{,}000(\text{table factor})$$

The future value is known to be $12,000, and we must solve for the interest factor or table factor. Therefore, we can rearrange the formula as follows:

$$\begin{aligned} \text{Table factor} &= FV/\$1{,}000 \\ &= \$12{,}000/\$1{,}000 \\ &= 12.00 \end{aligned}$$

Using Table 9-3, we must scan down the 4% column until we find a table value that is near 12.00. The closest table value we find is 12.006. That table value corresponds to 10 periods. Therefore, if we deposit $1,000 per semiannual period and invest the money at 4% per semiannual period, it will take 10 semiannual periods (five years) to accumulate $12,000.

The steps using the calculator are as follows:

ENTER	DISPLAY
4 I/Y	I/Y = 4
1000 PMT +/−	PMT= −1,000
12,000 FV	FV = 12,000
CPT N	N = 10

[*Note:* On many calculators, including Texas Instrument's BA II, the payment amount (PMT) must be entered as a negative value in order to calculate N.]

Ratios for Decision Making

Checking the working capital information on the balance sheet to make sure there are enough current assets to cover the current liabilities is a simple way to get an idea about a company's liquidity. Then, calculating the current ratio provides decision makers with information about how adequate that coverage is. The quick ratio is a more conservative measure because inventory generally is not as quick to convert to cash as other current assets. The quick ratio also does not include prepaid items, short-term investments, or other items that can not be converted to cash quickly. Thus, the quick ratio will be lower than the current ratio for any company that has inventory. The higher the working capital, the current ratio, and the quick ratio, the better the company's position to meet its current obligations as shown as follows.

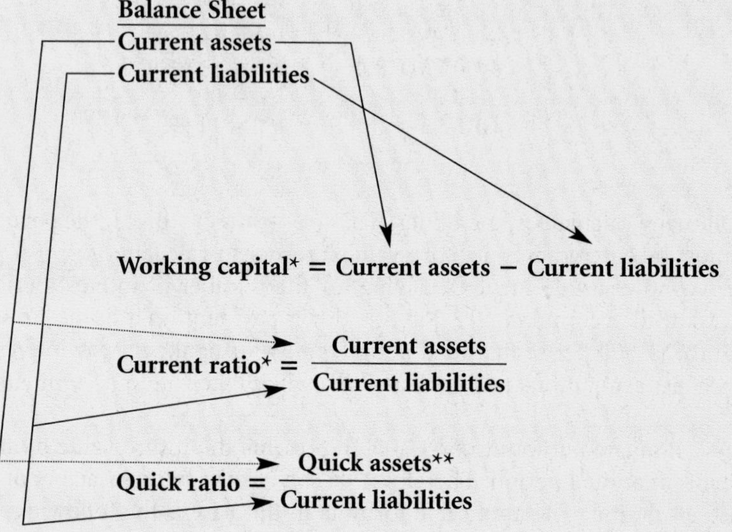

Balance Sheet
Current assets
Current liabilities
Working capital* = Current assets − Current liabilities
Current ratio* = Current assets / Current liabilities
Quick ratio = Quick assets** / Current liabilities

*From Chapter 2
**Current assets − Inventory − Prepaids

Impact on the Financial Reports

Impact on the Financial Reports

BALANCE SHEET
Cash
Current Assets
Noncurrent Assets
Current Liabilities
Notes payable
Discount on notes payable
Interest payable
Tax payable
Estimated warranty liability
Current portion of long-term liability
Noncurrent Liabilities
Stockholders' Equity

INCOME STATEMENT
Revenues
Expenses
Warranty expense
Other
Interest expense
Tax expense

STATEMENT OF STOCKHOLDERS' EQUITY
Contributed Capital
Retained Earnings

STATEMENT OF CASH FLOWS
Operating Activities
Increase in current liabilities
Decrease in current liabilities
Investing Activities
Financing Activities
Cash from short-term borrowings
Cash repayments of short-term borrowings
Noncash Transactions

NOTES
Disclosures of contingent liabilities*

*These are contingent liabilities that cannot be reasonably estimated or are not probable.

Answers to the Two-Minute Reviews

Two-Minute Review on Page 426

1. *Current liabilities are defined as items that will be paid within one year of the balance sheet date. Examples of current liabilities include accounts payable, notes payable if due within one year, taxes payable, and other accrued liabilities. Also, if a portion of a long-term debt will be paid within one year, that portion should be reported as a current liability.*
2. *The current ratio is calculated as total current assets divided by total current liabilities. It is a measure of the liquidity of the company, or the ability of the company to pay its short-term obligations.*
3. *Most current liabilities are reported in the operating activities category of the cash flow statement. You should note that it is the change in the balance of the current liability that is reported.*

Two-Minute Review on Page 432

1. *Contingent liabilities should be reported in the financial statements if they are* probable *and the amount of the liability can be* reasonably estimated.
2. *Contingent liabilities should be disclosed in the notes if they are* reasonably possible.
3. *Contingent assets are generally not recorded until the amount is received. They are not treated in the same manner as contingent liabilities. This indicates the conservative nature of accounting.*

Warmup Exercises

Warmup Exercise 9-1 ***Current Ratio and Quick Ratio*** **LO 1**

A company has the following current assets: Cash, $10,000; Accounts Receivable, $70,000; and Inventory, $20,000. The company also has current liabilities of $40,000. Calculate the company's current ratio and quick ratio.

Warmup Exercise 9-2 ***Current Liabilities on the Statement of Cash Flows*** **LO 3**

A company has the following current liabilities at the beginning of the period: Accounts Payable, $30,000; Taxes Payable $10,000. At the end of the period the balances of the account are as follows: Accounts Payable, $20,000; Taxes Payable, $15,000. What amounts will appear in the statement of cash flows, and in what category of the statement will they appear?

Warmup Exercise 9-3 ***Future Value and Present Value*** **LO 6**

A. You invest $1,000 at the beginning of the year. How much will be accumulated in five years if you earn 10% interest compounded annually?

B. You invest $1,000 *per year* at the end of each year for five years. How much will be accumulated in five years if you earn 10% interest compounded annually?

C. You will receive $1,000 in five years. What is the present value of that amount if you can earn 10% interest compounded annually?

D. You will receive $1,000 *per year* at the end of each year for five years. What is the present value of that amount if you can earn 10% interest compounded annually?

Solutions to Warmup Exercises

Warmup Exercise 9-1

Current Ratio: Current Assets/Current Liabilities

Cash ($10,000) + Accounts Receivable ($70,000) + Inventory ($20,000) = $100,000

$100,000/$40,000 = 2.5 Current Ratio

Quick Ratio: Quick Assets/Current Liabilities

Cash ($10,000) + Accounts Receivable ($70,000) = $80,000

$80,000/$40,000 = 2.0 Quick Ratio

Warmup Exercise 9-2

The amounts appearing in the statement of cash flows should be in the Operating Activities category of the statement. The amounts shown should be the *changes* in the balances of the accounts.

Accounts Payable decreased by $10,000 and should appear as a decrease in the statement of cash flows.

Taxes Payable increased by $5,000 and should appear as an increase in the statement of cash flows.

Warmup Exercise 9-3

A. $FV = \$1,000(\text{table factor})$ using Table 9-1
$= \$1,000(1.611)$ where $i = 10\%$, $n = 5$
$= \$1,611$

A.

ENTER	DISPLAY
5 N	N = 5
10 I/Y	I/Y = 10
0 PMT	PMT= 0
1000 PV	PV = 1,000
CPT FV	FV = 1,611

B. $FV = \$1,000(\text{table factor})$ using Table 9-3
$= \$1,000(6.105)$ where $i = 10\%$, $n = 5$
$= \$6,105$

B.

ENTER	DISPLAY
5 N	N = 5
10 I/Y	I/Y = 10
1000 PMT	PMT= 1,000
0 PV	PV = 0
CPT FV	FV = 6,105

C. $PV = \$1{,}000(\text{table factor})$ using Table 9-2
$= \$1{,}000(0.621)$ where $i = 10\%$, $n = 5$
$= \$621$

C.

ENTER	DISPLAY
5 N	N = 5
10 I/Y	I/Y = 10
0 PMT	PMT= 0
1000 FV	FV = 1,000
CPT PV	PV = 621

D. $PV = \$1{,}000(\text{table factor})$ using Table 9-4
$= \$1{,}000(3.791)$ where $i = 10\%$, $n = 5$
$= \$3{,}791$

D.

ENTER	DISPLAY
5 N	N = 5
10 I/Y	I/Y = 10
1000 PMT	PMT= 1,000
0 FV	FV = 0
CPT PV	PV = 3,791

Review Problem

WebTUTOR™ Advantage

Part A

The accountant for Lunn Express wants to develop a balance sheet as of December 31, 2004. The following items pertain to the liability category and must be considered in order to determine the items that should be reported in the Current Liabilities section of the balance sheet. You may assume that Lunn began business on January 1, 2004, and therefore the beginning balance of all accounts was zero.

a. During 2004 Lunn purchased $100,000 of inventory on account from suppliers. By year-end, $40,000 of the balance has been eliminated as a result of payments. All items were purchased on terms of 2/10, n/30. Lunn uses the gross method of recording payables.

b. On April 1, 2004, Lunn borrowed $10,000 on a one-year note payable from Philips Bank. Terms of the loan indicate that Lunn must repay the principal and 12% interest at the due date of the note.

c. On October 1, 2004, Lunn also borrowed $8,000 from Dove Bank on a one-year note payable. Dove Bank deducted 10% interest in advance and gave to Lunn the net amount. At the due date, Lunn must repay the principal of $8,000.

d. On January 1, 2004, Lunn borrowed $20,000 from Owens Bank by signing a 10-year note payable. Terms of the note indicate that Lunn must make annual payments of principal each January 1 beginning in 2005 and also must pay interest each January 1 in the amount of 8% of the outstanding balance of the loan.

e. The accountant for Lunn has completed an income statement for 2004 that indicates that income before taxes was $10,000. Lunn must pay tax at the rate of 40% and must remit the tax to the U.S. Treasury by April 15, 2005.

f. As of December 31, 2004, Lunn owes to employees salaries of $3,000 for work performed in 2004. The employees will be paid on the first payday of 2005.

g. During 2004 two lawsuits were filed against Lunn. In the first lawsuit, a customer sued for damages because of an injury that occurred on Lunn's premises. Lunn's legal counsel advised that it is probable that the lawsuit will be settled in 2005 at an amount of $7,000. The second lawsuit involves a patent infringement suit of $14,000 filed against Lunn by a competitor. The legal counsel has advised that there is some possibility that Lunn may be at fault but that a loss does not appear probable at this time.

Part B

a. What amount will be accumulated by January 1, 2008, if $5,000 is invested on January 1, 2004, at 10% interest compounded semiannually?

b. Assume that we are to receive $5,000 on January 1, 2008. What amount at January 1, 2004, is equivalent to the $5,000 that is to be received in 2008? Assume that interest is compounded annually at 10%.

c. What amount will be accumulated by January 1, 2008, if $5,000 is invested each semiannual period for eight periods beginning with June 30, 2004, and ending December 31, 2007? Interest will accumulate at 10% compounded semiannually.

d. Assume that we are to receive $5,000 each semiannual period for eight periods beginning on June 30, 2004. What amount at January 1, 2004, is equivalent to the future series of payments? Assume that interest will accrue at 10% compounded semiannually.

e. Assume that a new bank has begun a promotional campaign to attract savings accounts. The bank advertisement indicates that customers who invest $1,000 will double their money in 10 years. Assuming annual compounding of interest, what rate of interest is the bank offering?

Required

1. Consider all items in part **A.** Develop the Current Liabilities section of Lunn's balance sheet at December 31, 2004. To make investment decisions about this company, what additional data would you need? You do not need to consider the notes that accompany the balance sheet.
2. Answer the five questions in part **B.**

Solution to Part A

The accountant's decisions for items **a** through **g** of part **A** should be as follows:

a. The balance of the Accounts Payable account should be $60,000. The payables should be reported at the gross amount, and discounts would not be reported until the time of payment.

b. The note payable to Philips Bank of $10,000 should be included as a current liability. Also, interest payable of $900 ($10,000 × 12% × 9/12) should be considered a current liability.

c. The note payable to Dove Bank should be considered a current liability and listed at $8,000 minus the contra account Discount on Note Payable of $600 ($8,000 × 10% × 9/12 remaining).

d. The debt to Owens Bank should be split between current liability and long-term liability with the current portion shown as $2,000. Also, interest payable of $1,600 ($20,000 × 8% × 1 year) should be considered a current liability.

e. Income taxes payable of $4,000 ($10,000 × 40%) is a current liability.

f. Salaries payable of $3,000 represent a current liability.

g. The lawsuit involving the customer must be reported as a current liability of $7,000 because the possibility of loss is probable. The second lawsuit should not be reported but should be disclosed as a note to the balance sheet.

LUNN EXPRESS
PARTIAL BALANCE SHEET
AS OF DECEMBER 31, 2004

Current Liabilities		
Accounts payable		$60,000
Interest payable ($900 + $1,600)		2,500
Salaries payable		3,000
Taxes payable		4,000
Note payable to Philips Bank		10,000
Note payable to Dove Bank	$8,000	
Less: Discount on note payable	(600)	7,400
Current maturity of long-term debt		2,000
Contingent liability for pending lawsuit		7,000
Total Current Liabilities		$95,900

Other data necessary to make an investment decision might include current assets, total assets, and current liabilities as of December 31, 2003 and 2004. If current assets are significantly larger than current liabilities, you can be comfortable that the company is capable of paying its short-term debt. The dollar amount of current assets and liabilities must be evaluated with regard to the size of the company. The larger the company, the less significant $95,900 in current liabilities would be. Knowing last year's current liabilities would give you an idea about the trend in current liabilities. If they are rising, you would want to know why.

Solution to Part B

a. $FV = \$5{,}000(\text{table factor})$ using Table 9-1
$= \$5{,}000(1.477)$ where $i = 5\%$, $n = 8$
$= \$7{,}385$

a.

ENTER	DISPLAY
8 N	N = 8
5 I/Y	I/Y = 5
0 PMT	PMT= 0
5000 PV	PV = 5,000
CPT FV	FV = 7,387

b. $PV = \$5{,}000(\text{table factor})$ using Table 9-2
$= \$5{,}000(0.683)$ where $i = 10\%$, $n = 4$
$= \$3{,}415$

b.

ENTER	DISPLAY
4 N	N = 4
10 I/Y	I/Y = 10
0 PMT	PMT= 0
5000 FV	FV = 5,000
CPT PV	PV = 3,415

c. FV annuity $= \$5{,}000(\text{table factor})$ using Table 9-3
$= \$5{,}000(9.549)$ where $i = 5\%$, $n = 8$
$= \$47{,}745$

c.

ENTER	DISPLAY
8 N	N = 8
5 I/Y	I/Y = 5
5000 PMT	PMT= 5,000
0 PV	PV = 0
CPT FV	FV = 47,746

d. PV annuity $= \$5{,}000(\text{table factor})$ using Table 9-4
$= \$5{,}000(6.463)$ where $i = 5\%$, $n = 8$
$= \$32{,}315$

d.

ENTER	DISPLAY
8 N	N = 8
5 I/Y	I/Y = 5
5000 PMT	PMT= 5,000
0 FV	FV = 0
CPT PV	PV = 32,316

e. $FV = \$1{,}000(\text{table factor})$ using Table 9-1

Because the future value is known to be $2,000, the formula can be written as

$\$2{,}000 = \$1{,}000(\text{table factor})$

and rearranged as

$\text{Table factor} = \$2{,}000/\$1{,}000 = 2.0.$

In Table 9-1, the table factor of 2.0 and 10 years corresponds with an interest rate of between 7% and 8%.

(*Note:* In this case, the present value must be entered as a negative amount.)

e.

ENTER	DISPLAY
10 N	N = 10
0 PMT	PMT= 0
1000 PV +/−	PV = −1,000
2000 FV	FV = 2,000
CPT I/Y	I/Y = 7.177

TABLE 9-1 Future Value of $1

(N) PERIODS	Rate of Interest in % 1	2	3	4	5	6	7	8	9	10	11	12	15
1	1.010	1.020	1.030	1.040	1.050	1.060	1.070	1.080	1.090	1.100	1.110	1.120	1.150
2	1.020	1.040	1.061	1.082	1.103	1.124	1.145	1.166	1.188	1.210	1.232	1.254	1.323
3	1.030	1.061	1.093	1.125	1.158	1.191	1.225	1.260	1.295	1.331	1.368	1.405	1.521
4	1.041	1.082	1.126	1.170	1.216	1.262	1.311	1.360	1.412	1.464	1.518	1.574	1.749
5	1.051	1.104	1,159	1.217	1.276	1.338	1.403	1.469	1.539	1.611	1.685	1.762	2.011
6	1.062	1.126	1.194	1.265	1.340	1.419	1.501	1.587	1.677	1.772	1.870	1.974	2.313
7	1.072	1.149	1.230	1.316	1.407	1.504	1.606	1.714	1.828	1.949	2.076	2.211	2.660
8	1.083	1.172	1.267	1.369	1.477	1.594	1.718	1.851	1.993	2.144	2.305	2.476	3.059
9	1.094	1.195	1.305	1.423	1.551	1.689	1.838	1.999	2.172	2.358	2.558	2.773	3.518
10	1.105	1.219	1.344	1.480	1.629	1.791	1.967	2.159	2.367	2.594	2.839	3.106	4.046
11	1.116	1.243	1.384	1.539	1.710	1.898	2.105	2.332	2.580	2.853	3.152	3.479	4.652
12	1.127	1.268	1.426	1.601	1.796	2.012	2.252	2.518	2.813	3.138	3.498	3.896	5.350
13	1.138	1.294	1.469	1.665	1.886	2.133	2.410	2.720	3.066	3.452	3.883	4.363	6.153
14	1.149	1.319	1.513	1.732	1.980	2.261	2.579	2.937	3.342	3.797	4.310	4.887	7.076
15	1.161	1.346	1.558	1.801	2.079	2.397	2.759	3.172	3.642	4.177	4.785	5.474	8.137
16	1.173	1.373	1.605	1.873	2.183	2.540	2.952	3.426	3.970	4.595	5.311	6.130	9.358
17	1.184	1.400	1.653	1.948	2.292	2.693	3.159	3.700	4.328	5.054	5.895	6.866	10.761
18	1.196	1.428	1.702	2.026	2.407	2.854	3.380	3.996	4.717	5.560	6.544	7.690	12.375
19	1.208	1.457	1.754	2.107	2.527	3.026	3.617	4.316	5.142	6.116	7.263	8.613	14.232
20	1.220	1.486	1.806	2.191	2.653	3.207	3.870	4.661	5.604	6.727	8.062	9.646	16.367
21	1.232	1.516	1.860	2.279	2.786	3.400	4.141	5.034	6.109	7.400	8.949	10.804	18.822
22	1.245	1.546	1.916	2.370	2.925	3.604	4.430	5.437	6.659	8.140	9.934	12.100	21.645
23	1.257	1.577	1.974	2.465	3.072	3.820	4.741	5.871	7.258	8.954	11.026	13.552	24.891
24	1.270	1.608	2.033	2.563	3.225	4.049	5.072	6.341	7.911	9.850	12.239	15.179	28.625
25	1.282	1.641	2.094	2.666	3.386	4.292	5.427	6.848	8.623	10.835	13.585	17.000	32.919
26	1.295	1.673	2.157	2.772	3.556	4.549	5.807	7.396	9.399	11.918	15.080	19.040	37.857
27	1.308	1.707	2.221	2.883	3.733	4.822	6.214	7.988	10.245	13.110	16.739	21.325	43.535
28	1.321	1.741	2.288	2.999	3.920	5.112	6.649	8.627	11.167	14.421	18.580	23.884	50.066
29	1.335	1.776	2.357	3.119	4.116	5.418	7.114	9.317	12.172	15.863	20.624	26.750	57.575
30	1.348	1.811	2.427	3.243	4.322	5.743	7.612	10.063	13.268	17.449	22.892	29.960	66.212

TABLE 9-2 Present Value of $1

(N) PERIODS	Rate of Interest in % 1	2	3	4	5	6	7	8	9	10	11	12	15
1	0.990	0.980	0.971	0.962	0.952	0.943	0.935	0.926	0.917	0.909	0.901	0.893	0.870
2	0.980	0.961	0.943	0.925	0.907	0.890	0.873	0.857	0.842	0.826	0.812	0.797	0.756
3	0.971	0.942	0.915	0.889	0.864	0.840	0.816	0.794	0.772	0.751	0.731	0.712	0.658
4	0.961	0.924	0.888	0.855	0.823	0.792	0.763	0.735	0.708	0.683	0.659	0.636	0.572
5	0.951	0.906	0.863	0.822	0.784	0.747	0.713	0.681	0.650	0.621	0.593	0.567	0.497
6	0.942	0.888	0.837	0.790	0.746	0.705	0.666	0.630	0.596	0.564	0.535	0.507	0.432
7	0.933	0.871	0.813	0.760	0.711	0.665	0.623	0.583	0.547	0.513	0.482	0.452	0.376
8	0.923	0.853	0.789	0.731	0.677	0.627	0.582	0.540	0.502	0.467	0.434	0.404	0.327
9	0.914	0.837	0.766	0.703	0.645	0.592	0.544	0.500	0.460	0.424	0.391	0.361	0.284
10	0.905	0.820	0.744	0.676	0.614	0.558	0.508	0.463	0.422	0.386	0.352	0.322	0.247
11	0.896	0.804	0.722	0.650	0.585	0.527	0.475	0.429	0.388	0.350	0.317	0.287	0.215
12	0.887	0.788	0.701	0.625	0.557	0.497	0.444	0.397	0.356	0.319	0.286	0.257	0.187
13	0.879	0.773	0.681	0.601	0.530	0.469	0.415	0.368	0.326	0.290	0.258	0.229	0.163
14	0.870	0.758	0.661	0.577	0.505	0.442	0.388	0.340	0.299	0.263	0.232	0.205	0.141
15	0.861	0.743	0.642	0.555	0.481	0.417	0.362	0.315	0.275	0.239	0.209	0.183	0.123
16	0.853	0.728	0.623	0.534	0.458	0.394	0.339	0.292	0.252	0.218	0.188	0.163	0.107
17	0.844	0.714	0.605	0.513	0.436	0.371	0.317	0.270	0.231	0.198	0.170	0.146	0.093
18	0.836	0.700	0.587	0.494	0.416	0.350	0.296	0.250	0.212	0.180	0.153	0.130	0.081
19	0.828	0.686	0.570	0.475	0.396	0.331	0.277	0.232	0.194	0.164	0.138	0.116	0.070
20	0.820	0.673	0.554	0.456	0.377	0.312	0.258	0.215	0.178	0.149	0.124	0.104	0.061
21	0.811	0.660	0.538	0.439	0.359	0.294	0.242	0.199	0.164	0.135	0.112	0.093	0.053
22	0.803	0.647	0.522	0.422	0.342	0.278	0.226	0.184	0.150	0.123	0.101	0.083	0.046
23	0.795	0.634	0.507	0.406	0.326	0.262	0.211	0.170	0.138	0.112	0.091	0.074	0.040
24	0.788	0.622	0.492	0.390	0.310	0.247	0.197	0.158	0.126	0.102	0.082	0.066	0.035
25	0.780	0.610	0.478	0.375	0.295	0.233	0.184	0.146	0.116	0.092	0.074	0.059	0.030
26	0.772	0.598	0.464	0.361	0.281	0.220	0.172	0.135	0.106	0.084	0.066	0.053	0.026
27	0.764	0.586	0.450	0.347	0.268	0.207	0.161	0.125	0.098	0.076	0.060	0.047	0.023
28	0.757	0.574	0.437	0.333	0.255	0.196	0.150	0.116	0.090	0.069	0.054	0.042	0.020
29	0.749	0.563	0.424	0.321	0.243	0.185	0.141	0.107	0.082	0.063	0.048	0.037	0.017
30	0.742	0.552	0.412	0.308	0.231	0.174	0.131	0.099	0.075	0.057	0.044	0.033	0.015

TABLE 9-3 Future Value of Annuity of $1

(N) PERIODS	Rate of Interest in % 1	2	3	4	5	6	7	8	9	10	11	12	15
1	1.000	1.000	1.000	1.000	1.000	1.000	1.000	1.000	1.000	1.000	1.000	1.000	1.000
2	2.010	2.020	2.030	2.040	2.050	2.060	2.070	2.080	2.090	2.100	2.110	2.120	2.150
3	3.030	3.060	3.091	3.122	3.153	3.184	3.215	3.246	3.278	3.310	3.342	3.374	3.473
4	4.060	4.122	4.184	4.246	4.310	4.375	4.440	4.506	4.573	4.641	4.710	4.779	4.993
5	5.101	5.204	5.309	5.416	5.526	5.637	5.751	5.867	5.985	6.105	6.228	6.353	6.742
6	6.152	6.308	6.468	6.633	6.802	6.975	7.153	7.336	7.523	7.716	7.913	8.115	8.754
7	7.214	7.434	7.662	7.898	8.142	8.394	8.654	8.923	9.200	9.487	9.783	10.089	11.067
8	8.286	8.583	8.892	9.214	9.549	9.897	10.260	10.637	11.028	11.436	11.859	12.300	13.727
9	9.369	9.755	10.159	10.583	11.027	11.491	11.978	12.488	13.021	13.579	14.164	14.776	16.786
10	10.462	10.950	11.464	12.006	12.578	13.181	13.816	14.487	15.193	15.937	16.722	17.549	20.304
11	11.567	12.169	12.808	13.486	14.207	14.972	15.784	16.645	17.560	18.531	19.561	20.655	24.349
12	12.683	13.412	14.192	15.026	15.917	16.870	17.888	18.977	20.141	21.384	22.713	24.133	29.002
13	13.809	14.680	15.618	16.627	17.713	18.882	20.141	21.495	22.953	24.523	26.212	28.029	34.352
14	14.947	15.974	17.086	18.292	19.599	21.015	22.550	24.215	26.019	27.975	30.095	32.393	40.505
15	16.097	17.293	18.599	20.024	21.579	23.276	25.129	27.152	29.361	31.772	34.405	37.280	47.580
16	17.258	18.639	20.157	21.825	23.657	25.673	27.888	30.324	33.003	35.950	39.190	42.753	55.717
17	18.430	20.012	21.762	23.698	25.840	28.213	30.840	33.750	36.974	40.545	44.501	48.884	65.075
18	19.615	21.412	23.414	25.645	28.132	30.906	33.999	37.450	41.301	45.599	50.396	55.750	75.836
19	20.811	22.841	25.117	27.671	30.539	33.760	37.379	41.446	46.018	51.159	56.939	63.440	88.212
20	22.019	24.297	26.870	29.778	33.066	36.786	40.995	45.762	51.160	57.275	64.203	72.052	102.444
21	23.239	25.783	28.676	31.969	35.719	39.993	44.865	50.423	56.765	64.002	72.265	81.699	118.810
22	24.472	27.299	30.537	34.248	38.505	43.392	49.006	55.457	62.873	71.403	81.214	92.503	137.632
23	25.716	28.845	32.453	36.618	41.430	46.996	53.436	60.893	69.532	79.543	91.148	104.603	159.276
24	26.973	30.422	34.426	39.083	44.502	50.816	58.177	66.765	76.790	88.497	102.174	118.155	184.168
25	28.243	32.030	36.459	41.646	47.727	54.865	63.249	73.106	84.701	98.347	114.413	133.334	212.793
26	29.526	33.671	38.553	44.312	51.113	59.156	68.676	79.954	93.324	109.182	127.999	150.334	245.712
27	30.821	35.344	40.710	47.084	54.669	63.706	74.484	87.351	102.723	121.100	143.079	169.374	283.569
28	32.129	37.051	42.931	49.968	58.403	68.528	80.698	95.339	112.968	134.210	159.817	190.699	327.104
29	33.450	38.792	45.219	52.966	62.323	73.640	87.347	103.966	124.135	148.631	178.397	214.583	377.170
30	34.785	40.568	47.575	56.085	66.439	79.058	94.461	113.283	136.308	164.494	199.021	241.333	434.745

TABLE 9-4 Present Value of Annuity of $1

(N) PERIODS	Rate of Interest in % 1	2	3	4	5	6	7	8	9	10	11	12	15
1	0.990	0.980	0.971	0.962	0.952	0.943	0.935	0.926	0.917	0.909	0.901	0.893	0.870
2	1.970	1.942	1.913	1.886	1.859	1.833	1.808	1.783	1.759	1.736	1.713	1.690	1.626
3	2.941	2.884	2.829	2.775	2.723	2.673	2.624	2.577	2.531	2.487	2.444	2.402	2.283
4	3.902	3.808	3.717	3.630	3.546	3.465	3.387	3.312	3.240	3.170	3.102	3.037	2.855
5	4.853	4.713	4.580	4.452	4.329	4.212	4.100	3.993	3.890	3.791	3.696	3.605	3.352
6	5.795	5.601	5.417	5.242	5.076	4.917	4.767	4.623	4.486	4.355	4.231	4.111	3.784
7	6.728	6.472	6.230	6.002	5.786	5.582	5.389	5.206	5.033	4.868	4.712	4.564	4.160
8	7.652	7.325	7.020	6.733	6.463	6.210	5.971	5.747	5.535	5.335	5.146	4.968	4.487
9	8.566	8.162	7.786	7.435	7.108	6.802	6.515	6.247	5.995	5.759	5.537	5.328	4.772
10	9.471	8.983	8.530	8.111	7.722	7.360	7.024	6.710	6.418	6.145	5.889	5.650	5.019
11	10.368	9.787	9.253	8.760	8.306	7.887	7.499	7.139	6.805	6.495	6.207	5.938	5.234
12	11.255	10.575	9.954	9.385	8.863	8.384	7.943	7.536	7.161	6.814	6.492	6.194	5.421
13	12.134	11.348	10.635	9.986	9.394	8.853	8.358	7.904	7.487	7.103	6.750	6.424	5.583
14	13.004	12.106	11.296	10.563	9.899	9.295	8.745	8.244	7.786	7.367	6.982	6.628	5.724
15	13.865	12.849	11.938	11.118	10.380	9.712	9.108	8.559	8.061	7.606	7.191	6.811	5.847
16	14.718	13.578	12.561	11.652	10.838	10.106	9.447	8.851	8.313	7.824	7.379	6.974	5.954
17	15.562	14.292	13.166	12.166	11.274	10.477	9.763	9.122	8.544	8.022	7.549	7.120	6.047
18	16.398	14.992	13.754	12.659	11.690	10.828	10.059	9.372	8.756	8.201	7.702	7.250	6.128
19	17.226	15.678	14.324	13.134	12.085	11.158	10.336	9.604	8.950	8.365	7.839	7.366	6.198
20	18.046	16.351	14.877	13.590	12.462	11.470	10.594	9.818	9.129	8.514	7.963	7.469	6.259
21	18.857	17.011	15.415	14.029	12.821	11.764	10.836	10.017	9.292	8.649	8.075	7.562	6.312
22	19.660	17.658	15.937	14.451	13.163	12.042	11.061	10.201	9.442	8.772	8.176	7.645	6.359
23	20.456	18.292	16.444	14.857	13.489	12.303	11.272	10.371	9.580	8.883	8.266	7.718	6.399
24	21.243	18.914	16.936	15.247	13.799	12.550	11.469	10.529	9.707	8.985	8.348	7.784	6.434
25	22.023	19.523	17.413	15.622	14.094	12.783	11.654	10.675	9.823	9.077	8.422	7.843	6.464
26	22.795	20.121	17.877	15.983	14.375	13.003	11.826	10.810	9.929	9.161	8.488	7.896	6.491
27	23.560	20.707	18.327	16.330	14.643	13.211	11.987	10.935	10.027	9.237	8.548	7.943	6.514
28	24.316	21.281	18.764	16.663	14.898	13.406	12.137	11.051	10.116	9.307	8.602	7.984	6.534
29	25.066	21.844	19.188	16.984	15.141	13.591	12.278	11.158	10.198	9.370	8.650	8.022	6.551
30	25.808	22.396	19.600	17.292	15.372	13.765	12.409	11.258	10.274	9.427	8.694	8.055	6.566

Appendix A: Accounting Tools: Payroll Accounting

LO 8 Demonstrate an understanding of the deductions and expenses for payroll accounting.

Salaries payable was one of the current liabilities discussed in Chapter 2. At the end of each accounting period, the accountant must accrue salaries that have been earned by the employees but have not yet been paid. To this point, we have not considered the accounting that must be done for payroll deductions and other payroll expenses.

Payroll deductions and expenses occur not only at year-end but every time, throughout the year, that employees are paid. The amount of cash paid for salaries and wages is the largest cash outflow for many firms. It is imperative that sufficient cash be available not only to meet the weekly or monthly payroll but also to remit the payroll taxes to the appropriate government agencies when required. The purpose of this appendix is to introduce the calculations and the accounting entries that are necessary when payroll is recorded.

The issue of payroll expenses is of great concern to businesses, particularly small entrepreneurial ones. One of the large issues facing companies is how to meet the increasing cost of hiring people. Salary is just one component. How are they going to pay salaries plus benefits such as health insurance, life insurance, disability, unemployment benefits, workers' compensation, and so on? More and more companies are trying to keep their payrolls as small as possible in order to avoid these costs. Unfortunately, this has been a contributing factor in the trends of using more part-time employees and of outsourcing some business functions. Outsourcing, or hiring independent contractors, allows the company to reduce salary expense and the expenses related to fringe benefits. However, it does not necessarily improve the company's profitability. The expenses that are increased as a result of hiring outside contractors must also be considered. A manager must carefully consider all of the costs that are affected before deciding whether to hire more employees or go with an independent contractor.

CALCULATION OF GROSS WAGES

Gross wages The amount of wages before deductions.

We will cover the payroll process by indicating the basic steps that must be performed. The first step is to calculate the **gross wages** of all employees. The gross wage represents the wage amount before deductions. Companies often have two general classes of employees, hourly and salaried. The gross wage of each hourly employee is calculated by multiplying the number of hours worked times his or her hourly wage rate. Salaried employees are not paid on a per-hour basis but at a flat rate per week, month, or year. For both hourly and salaried employees, the payroll accountant must also consider any overtime, bonus, or other salary supplement that may affect gross wages.

CALCULATION OF NET PAY

Net pay The amount of wages after deductions.

The second step in the payroll process is to calculate the deductions from each employee's paycheck to determine **net pay.** Deductions from the employees' checks represent a current liability to the employer because the employer must remit the amounts at a future time to the proper agencies or government offices, for example to the U.S. Treasury Service. The deductions that are made depend on the type of company and the employee. The most important deductions are indicated in the following sections.

Income Tax

The employer must withhold federal income tax from most employees' paychecks. The amount withheld depends on the employee's earnings and the number of *exemptions* claimed by that employee. An exemption reflects the number of dependents a taxpayer can claim. The more exemptions, the lower is the withholding amount required by the government. Tables are available from the Internal Revenue Service to calculate the proper amount that should be withheld. This amount must be remitted to the U.S. Treasury Service periodically; the frequency depends on the company's size and its payroll. Income tax withheld represents a liability to the employer and is normally classified as a current liability.

Many states also have an income tax, and the employer must often withhold additional amounts for the state tax.

FICA—Employees' Share

FICA stands for Federal Insurance Contributions Act; it is commonly called the *social security tax*. The FICA tax is assessed on both the employee and the employer. The employees' portion must be withheld from paychecks at the applicable rate. Currently, the tax is assessed at the rate of 7.65% on the first $84,900 paid to the employee each year. Other rates and special rules apply to certain types of workers and to self-employed individuals. The amounts withheld from the employees' checks must be remitted to the federal government periodically.

FICA taxes withheld from employees' checks represent a liability to the employer until remitted. It is important to remember that the employees' portion of the FICA tax does not represent an expense to the employer.

Voluntary Deductions

If you have ever received a paycheck, you are probably aware that a variety of items was deducted from the amount you earned. Many of these are voluntary deductions chosen by the employee. They may include health insurance, pension or retirement contributions, savings plans, contributions to charities, union dues, and others. Each of these items is deducted from the employees' paychecks, is held by the employer, and is remitted at a future time. Therefore, each represents a current liability to the employer until remitted.

EMPLOYER PAYROLL TAXES

The payroll items discussed thus far do not represent expenses to the employer because they are assessed on the employees and deducted from their paychecks. However, there are taxes that the employer must pay. The two most important are FICA and unemployment taxes.

FICA—Employer's Share

The FICA tax is assessed on both the employee and the employer. The employee amount is withheld from the employees' paychecks and represents a liability but is not an expense to the employer. Normally, an equal amount is assessed on the employer. Therefore, the employer must pay an additional 7.65% of employee wages to the federal government. The employer's portion represents an expense to the employer and should be reflected in a Payroll Tax Expense account or similar type of account. This portion is a liability to the employer until it is remitted.

Unemployment Tax

Most employers must also pay unemployment taxes. The state and federal governments jointly sponsor a program to collect unemployment tax from employers and to pay workers who lose their jobs. The maximum rate of unemployment taxes is 6.2%, of which 5.4% is the state portion and 0.8% the federal, on an employee's first $7,000 of wages earned each year. The rate is adjusted according to a company's employment history, however. If a company has been fairly stable and few of its employees have filed for unemployment benefits, the rate is adjusted downward.

Unemployment taxes are levied against the employer, not the employee. Therefore, the tax represents an expense to the employer and should be reflected in a Payroll Tax Expense account or similar type of account. The tax also represents a liability to the employer until it is remitted.

AN EXAMPLE

Assume that Kori Company has calculated the gross wages of all employees for the month of July to be $100,000. Also assume that the following amounts have been withheld from the employees' paychecks:

Income Tax	$20,000
FICA	7,650
United Way Contributions	5,000
Union Dues	3,000

In addition, assume that Kori's unemployment tax rate is 6% (for the state and federal portions), that no employees have reached the $7,000 limit, and that Kori's portion of FICA matches the employees' share. The transactions to record payroll, to pay the employees, and to record the employer's payroll expenses have the following effects on the accounting equation.

BALANCE SHEET						INCOME STATEMENT	
ASSETS		= LIABILITIES		+ OWNERS' EQUITY		+ REVENUES – EXPENSES	
		Salary Payable	64,350			Salary Expense	(100,000)
		Income Tax Payable	20,000				
		FICA Payable	7,650				
		United Way Payable	5,000				
		Union Dues Payable	3,000				

BALANCE SHEET						INCOME STATEMENT	
ASSETS		= LIABILITIES		+ OWNERS' EQUITY		+ REVENUES – EXPENSES	
Cash	(64,350)	Salary Payable	(64,350)				

BALANCE SHEET						INCOME STATEMENT	
ASSETS		= LIABILITIES		+ OWNERS' EQUITY		+ REVENUES – EXPENSES	
		FICA Payable	7,650			Payroll Tax Expense	(13,650)
		Unemployment Tax Payable	6,000				

Periodically, Kori must remit amounts to the appropriate government body or agency. The accounting entry to record remittance, assuming remittance at the end of July, is as follows:

BALANCE SHEET					INCOME STATEMENT
ASSETS	=	LIABILITIES		+ OWNERS' EQUITY	+ REVENUES − EXPENSES
Cash	(49,300)	Income Tax Payable	(20,000)		
		FICA Payable	(15,300)		
		United Way Payable	(5,000)		
		Union Dues Payable	(3,000)		
		Unemployment Tax Payable	(6,000)		

COMPENSATED ABSENCES

LO 9 Determine when compensated absences must be accrued as a liability.

Most employers allow employees to accumulate a certain number of sick days and to take a certain number of paid vacation days each year. This causes an accounting question when recording payroll amounts. When should the sick days and vacation days be treated as an expense—in the period they are earned or in the period they are taken by the employee?

Compensated absences Employee absences for which the employee will be paid.

The FASB has coined the term **compensated absences.** These are absences from employment, such as vacation, illness, and holidays, for which it is expected that employees will be paid. The FASB has ruled that an expense should be accrued if certain conditions are met: the services have been rendered, the rights (days) accumulate, and payment is probable and can be reasonably estimated. The result of the FASB ruling is that most employers are required to record a liability and expense for vacation days when earned but sick days are not recorded until employees are actually absent.

Compensated absences is another example of the matching principle at work, and so it is consistent with good accounting theory. Unfortunately, it has also resulted in some complex calculations and additional work for payroll accountants. Part of the complexity is due to unresolved legal issues about compensated absences.

U.S. accounting standards on this issue are much more detailed and extensive than the standards of many foreign countries. As a result, U.S. companies may believe that they are subject to higher record-keeping costs than their foreign competitors.

Appendix B: Accounting Tools: Using Excel for Problems Involving Interest Calculations

The purpose of Appendix B is to illustrate how the functions built in to the Excel spreadsheet can be used to calculate future value and present value amounts. We will illustrate the use of Excel with the same examples that are used in the body of Chapter 9.

To view the Excel functions, you should click on the PASTE function of the Excel toolbar (the paste function is on the top of the Excel toolbar and is noted by the symbol *fx*) and then choose the FINANCIAL option. Several different calculations are available. We will illustrate two of them: FV and PV.

Example 1: Your three-year-old son, Robert, just inherited $50,000 in cash and securities from his grandfather. If the funds were left in the bank and in the stock market and received an annual return of 10%, how much would be there in 15 years when Robert starts college?

Solution: In Excel, you should use the FV function and enter the values as follows:

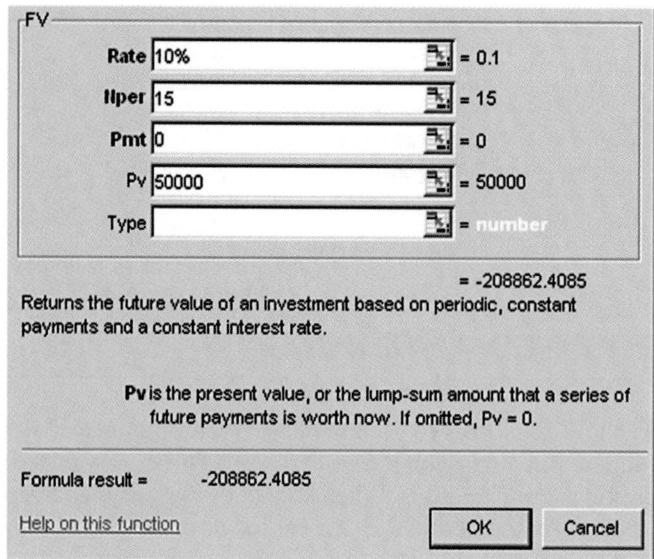

Note that the future value of $208,862 (you may ignore the negative sign in this case) is slightly different than that given in the body of the text because of rounding when using the table factors.

Example 2: Consider a $2,000 note payable that carries interest at the rate of 10% compounded annually. The note is due in two years, and the principal and interest must be paid at that time. What amount must be paid in two years?

Solution: In Excel, you should use the FV function and enter the values as follows:

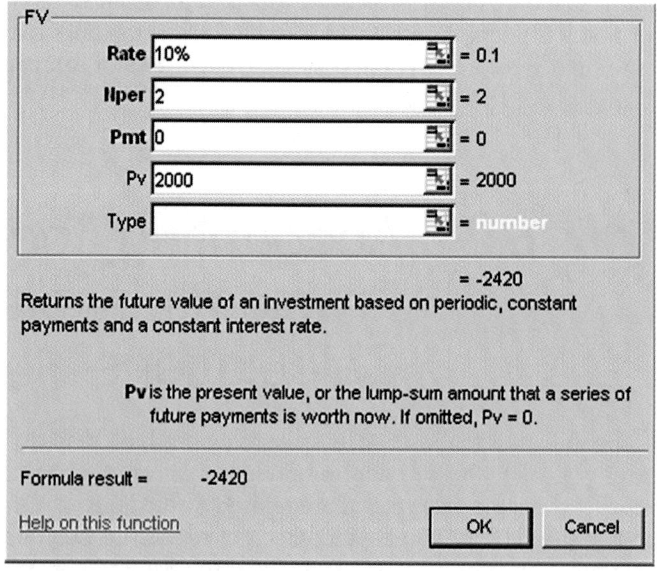

The future value is $2,420.

Example 3: Suppose we want to find the future value of a $2,000 note payable due in two years. The note payable requires interest to be compounded quarterly at the rate of 12% per year. What future amount must be paid in two years?

Solution: In Excel, you should use the FV function and enter the values as follows:

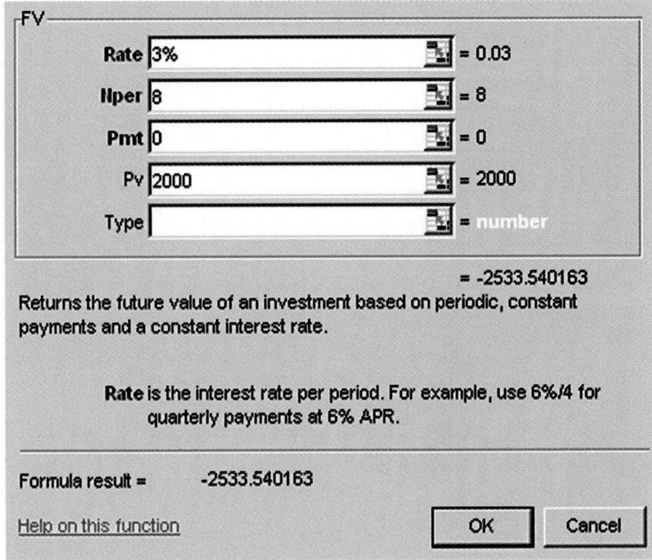

The future value is $2,534 (rounded to the nearest dollar).

Example 4: Suppose you know that you will receive $2,000 in two years. You also know that if you had the money now, it could be invested at 10% compounded annually. What is the present value of the $2,000?

Solution: Since this problem requires the calculation of a present value, the PV function of Excel should be chosen and used as follows:

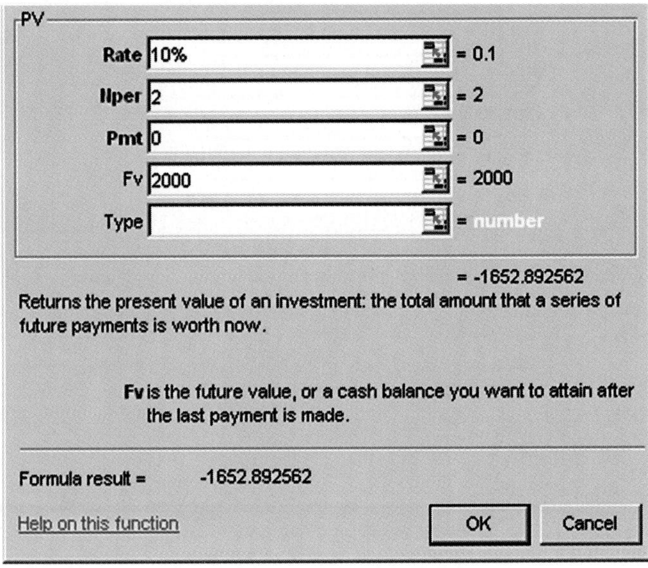

The present value is $1,653 (rounded to the nearest dollar).

Example 5: A recent magazine article projects that it will cost $120,000 to attend a four-year college 10 years from now. If that is true, how much money would you have to put into an account today to fund that education, assuming a 5% rate of return?

Solution: The PV function of Excel should again be used as follows:

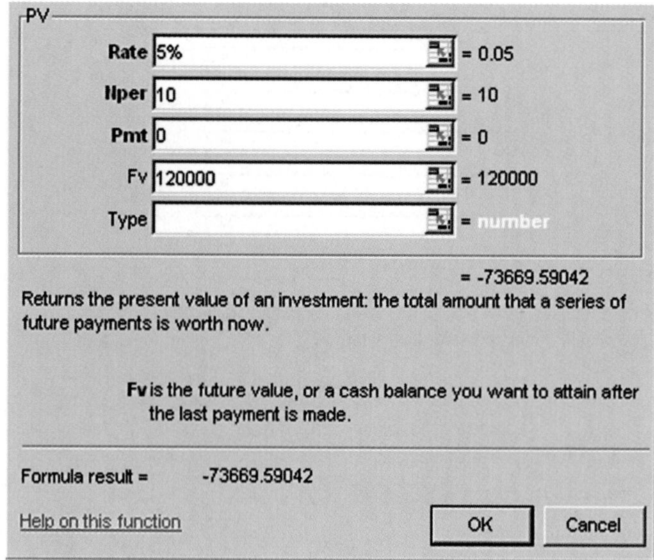

The present value calculated ($73,670—rounded to the nearest dollar) differs slightly from that derived when using the table factors because of rounding in the tables.

Example 6: Suppose that you are to receive $3,000 per year at the end of each of the next four years. Also assume that each payment could be invested at an interest rate of 10% compounded annually. How much would be accumulated in principal and interest by the end of the fourth year?

Solution: This problem involves the calculation of the future value of an annuity, and you should use the FV function of Excel as follows:

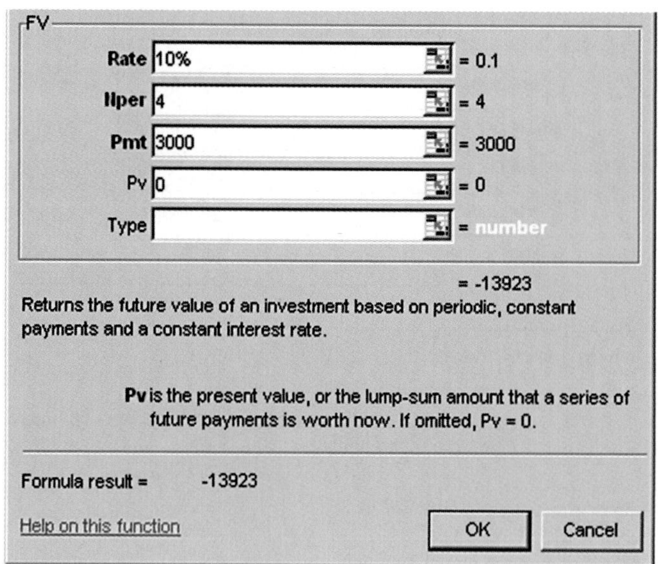

The future value of the series of payments is $13,923. Note that the payments are simply entered as the Pmt variable in the spreadsheet.

Example 7: Your cousin just had a baby girl two weeks ago and is already thinking about sending her to college. When the girl is 15, how much money would be in her college account if your cousin deposits $2,000 into it on each of her 15 birthdays? The interest rate is 10%.

Solution: You should again use the Excel FV function as follows:

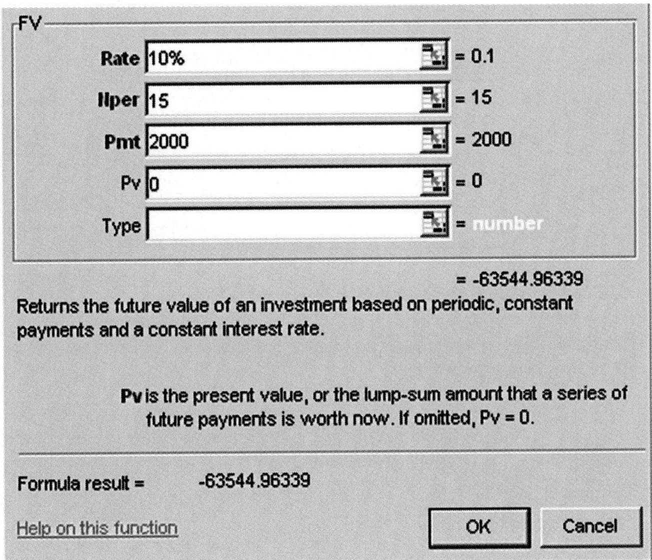

The future value amount is $63,545 (rounded to the nearest dollar).

Example 8: How would the future value be calculated if the previous example was modified so that we deposited $1,000 semiannually and the interest rate was 10% compounded semiannually (or 5% per period) for 15 years?

Solution: Because the compounding is semiannually, you should use the FV function of Excel as follows:

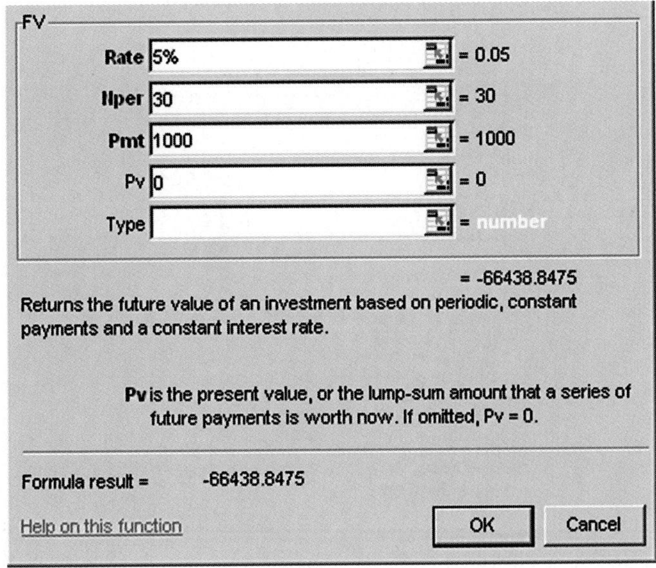

The future value is $66,439 (rounded to the nearest dollar).

Example 9: Suppose that you will receive an annuity of $4,000 per year for four years, with the first received one year from today. The amounts received can be invested at a rate of 10% compounded annually. What amount would you need at the present time to have an amount equivalent to the series of payments and interest in the future?

Solution: This problem involves the calculation of the present value of an annuity, and you should use the PV function of Excel as follows:

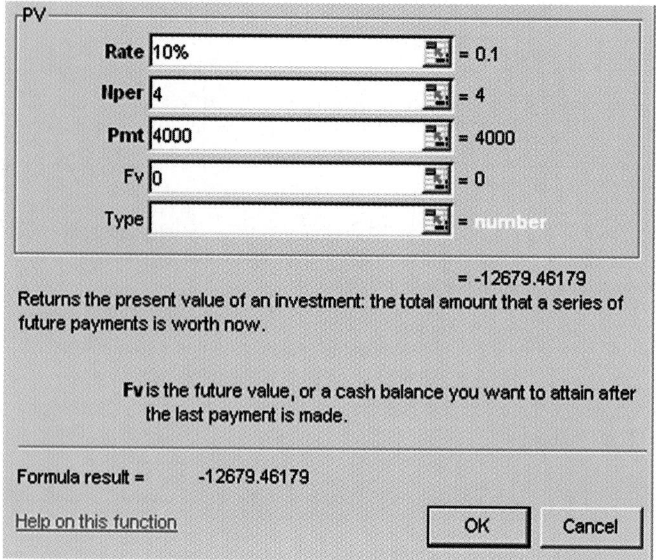

The present value of $12,679 (rounded to the nearest dollar) differs slightly from that derived when using the tables because of rounding in the table factors.

Example 10: You just won the lottery. You can take your $1 million in a lump sum today, or you can receive $100,000 per year over the next 12 years. Assuming a 5% interest rate, which would you prefer, ignoring tax considerations?

Solution: You should use the PV function of Excel as follows:

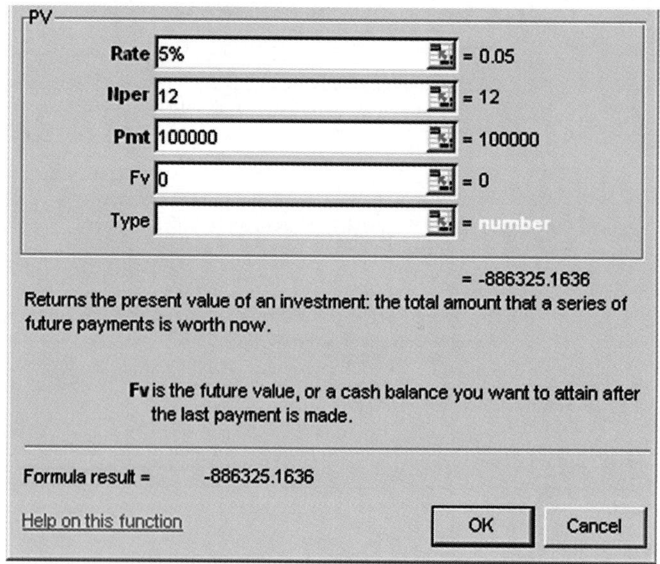

Because the present value of the payments over 12 years is $886,325 (rounded to the nearest dollar) and is less than the $1 million that can be received immediately, you should choose the immediate payment.

Chapter Highlights

1. **LO 1** Balance sheets generally have two categories of liability: current liabilities and long-term liabilities. Current liabilities are obligations that will be satisfied within one year or within the next operating cycle.
2. **LO 2** Accruals are expenses that have been incurred, but not paid, by the balance sheet date. They increase current liabilities and should be valued at the face amount or the amount necessary to settle the obligation. They are not reported at the present value because of the short time span until payment.
3. **LO 2** Accounts payable represent amounts owed for the purchase of inventory, goods, or services. Accounts payable usually do not require the payment of interest, but a discount may be available to encourage prompt payment.
4. **LO 2** The accounting for notes payable depends on the terms of the note. Some notes payable require the payment of interest at the due date. If so, accounting entries must be made to accrue interest expense to the proper periods. Interest is an expense when incurred, not when paid. Alternatively, the terms of the note may require interest to be deducted in advance. The interest deducted should initially be recorded in a Discount on Notes Payable account and transferred to Interest Expense over the life of the note.
5. **LO 2** Accrued liabilities include any amount that is owed but not actually due as of the balance sheet date. These liabilities may be grouped together in an account such as Other Accrued Liabilities.
6. **LO 3** The changes in current liabilities affect the statement of cash flows and, for most items, are reflected in the Operating Activities category. Decreases in current liabilities indicate a reduction of cash; increases in current liabilities indicate an increase in cash.
7. **LO 4** Contingent liabilities involve an existing condition whose outcome depends on some future event. If a contingent liability is probable and the amount of loss can be reasonably estimated, it should be reported on the balance sheet. If a contingent liability is reasonably possible, it must be disclosed but not reported.
8. **LO 5** Simple interest is interest earned on the principal amount. It is often calculated by the well-known formula of principal times rate times time. Compound interest is calculated on the principal plus previous amounts of interest accumulated.
9. **LO 6** The future value of a single amount represents the amount of interest plus principal that will be accumulated at a future time. The future value of a single amount can be calculated by formula or by the use of Table 9-1.
10. **LO 6** The present value of a single amount represents the amount at a present time that is equivalent to an amount at a future time. The present value of a single amount can be calculated by formula or by the use of Table 9-2.
11. **LO 6** An annuity is a series of payments of equal amount. The future value of an annuity represents the amount that will be accumulated in principal and interest if a series of payments is invested for a specified time and for a specified rate. The future value of an annuity can be calculated by formula or by the use of Table 9-3.
12. **LO 6** The present value of an annuity represents the amount at a present time that is equivalent to a series of payments in the future that will occur for a specified time and at a specified interest or discount rate. The present value of an annuity can be calculated by formula or by the use of Table 9-4.
13. **LO 7** The compound interest concepts are also useful when solving for unknowns such as the number of interest periods or the interest rate on a series of payments using compound interest techniques.
14. **LO 8** There are two types of payroll deductions and expenses. Deductions from the employee's check are made to determine net pay and represent a current liability to the employer. Employer's payroll taxes are also assessed directly on the employer and represent an expense. (Appendix A)
15. **LO 9** Compensated absences such as sick pay and vacation pay are expenses and must be accrued by the employer if certain conditions are met. (Appendix A)

http://porter.swlearning.com

Technology and other resources for your success

If you need additional help, visit the text's Web site. Also, see this text's preface for a description of available technology and other resources. If your instructor is using PERSONAL *Trainer* in this course, you may complete, on line, the exercises and problems in the text.

Key Terms Quiz

Read each definition below, and then write the number of the definition in the blank beside the appropriate term it defines. The quiz solutions appear at the end of the chapter.

_____ Current liability
_____ Accounts payable
_____ Notes payable
_____ Discount on Notes Payable
_____ Current Maturities of Long-Term Debt
_____ Accrued liability
_____ Contingent liability
_____ Estimated liability
_____ Contingent asset
_____ Time value of money
_____ Simple interest
_____ Compound interest
_____ Future value of a single amount
_____ Present value of a single amount
_____ Annuity
_____ Future value of an annuity
_____ Present value of an annuity
_____ Gross wages (Appendix A)
_____ Net pay (Appendix A)
_____ Compensated absences (Appendix A)

1. Accounts that will be satisfied within one year or the next operating cycle.
2. The amount needed at the present time to be equivalent to a series of payments and interest in the future.
3. Amounts owed for the purchase of inventory, goods, or services acquired in the normal course of business.
4. A contra-liability account that represents interest deducted from a loan or note in advance.
5. A series of payments of equal amount.
6. The portion of a long-term liability that will be paid within one year of the balance sheet date.
7. A liability that has been incurred but has not been paid as of the balance sheet date.
8. Amounts owed that are represented by a formal contractual agreement. These amounts usually require the payment of interest.
9. A liability that involves an existing condition for which the outcome is not known with certainty and depends on some future event.
10. Interest that is earned or paid on the principal amount only.
11. A contingent liability that is accrued and is reflected on the balance sheet. Common examples are warranties, guarantees, and premium offers.
12. An amount that involves an existing condition dependent on some future event by which the company stands to gain. These amounts are not normally reported.
13. Interest calculated on the principal plus previous amounts of interest accumulated.
14. The concept that indicates that people should prefer to receive an immediate amount at the present time over an equal amount in the future.
15. The amount that will be accumulated in the future when one amount is invested at the present time and accrues interest until the future time.
16. The amount that will be accumulated in the future when a series of payments is invested and accrues interest until the future time.
17. The present amount that is equivalent to an amount at a future time.
18. The amount of an employee's wages before deductions.
19. Employment absences, such as sick days and vacation days, for which it is expected that employees will be paid.
20. The amount of an employee's paycheck after deductions.

Answers on p. 483.

Alternate Terms

Accrued Interest Interest payable

Compensated Absences Accrued vacation or sick pay

Compound Interest Interest on interest

Contingent Asset Contingent gain

Contingent Liability Contingent loss

Current Liability Short-term liability

Current Maturities of Long-Term Debt Long-term debt, current portion

Discounting a Note Interest in advance

FICA Social Security

Future Value of an Annuity Amount of an annuity

Gross Wages Gross pay

Income Tax Liability Income tax payable

Warranties Guarantees

Questions

1. What is the definition of *current liabilities?* Why is it important to distinguish between current and long-term liabilities?
2. Most firms attempt to pay their accounts payable within the discount period to take advantage of the discount. Why is that normally a sound financial move?
3. Assume that your local bank gives you a $1,000 loan at 10% per year but deducts the interest in advance. Is 10% the "real" rate of interest that you will pay? How could the true interest rate be calculated?
4. Is the account Discount on Notes Payable an income statement or balance sheet account? Does it have a debit or credit balance?
5. A firm's year ends on December 31. Its tax is computed and submitted to the U.S. Treasury on March 15 of the following year. When should the taxes be reported as a liability?
6. What is a contingent liability? Why are contingent liabilities accounted for differently than contingent assets?
7. Many firms believe that it is very difficult to estimate the amount of a possible future contingency. Should a contingent liability be reported even if the dollar amount of the loss is not known? Should it be disclosed in the notes to financial statements?
8. Assume that a lawsuit has been filed against your firm. Your legal counsel has assured you that the likelihood of loss is not probable. How should the lawsuit be disclosed on the financial statements?
9. What is the difference between simple interest and compound interest? Would the amount of interest be higher or lower if the interest is simple rather than compound?
10. What is the effect if interest is compounded quarterly versus annually?
11. What is the meaning of the terms *present value* and *future value?* How can you determine whether to calculate the present value of an amount versus the future value?
12. What is the meaning of the word *annuity?* Could the present value of an annuity be calculated as a series of single amounts? If so, how?
13. Assume that you know the total dollar amount of a loan and the amount of the monthly payments on the loan. How could you determine the interest rate as a percentage of the loan?
14. The present value and future value concepts are applied to measure the amount of several accounts commonly encountered in accounting. What are some accounts that are valued in this manner?
15. Your employer withholds federal income tax from your paycheck and remits it to the U.S. Treasury. How is the federal tax treated on the employer's financial statements? (Appendix A)
16. Unemployment tax is a tax on the employer rather than on the employee. How should unemployment taxes be treated on the employer's financial statements? (Appendix A)
17. What is the meaning of the term *compensated absences?* Give some examples. (Appendix A)
18. Do you agree or disagree with the following statement: "Vacation pay should be reported as an expense when the employee takes the vacation"? (Appendix A)

Exercises

Exercise 9-1 ***Current Liabilities*** **LO 1**

The items listed below are accounts on Smith's balance sheet of December 31, 2004.

Taxes Payable
Accounts Receivable
Notes Payable, 9%, due in 90 days
Investment in Bonds
Capital Stock
Accounts Payable
Estimated Warranty Payable in 2005
Retained Earnings
Trademark
Mortgage Payable ($10,000 due every year until 2021)

Required

Identify which of the above accounts should be classified as a current liability on Smith's balance sheet. For each item that is not a current liability, indicate the category of the balance sheet in which it would be classified.

Exercise 9-2 ***Current Liabilities*** **LO 1**

The following items all represent liabilities on a firm's balance sheet.

a. An amount of money owed to a supplier based on the terms 2/20, net 40, for which *no* note was executed
b. An amount of money owed to a creditor on a note due April 30, 2005
c. An amount of money owed to a creditor on a note due August 15, 2006

(continued)

d. An amount of money owed to employees for work performed during the last week in December

e. An amount of money owed to a bank for the use of borrowed funds due on March 1, 2005

f. An amount of money owed to a creditor as an annual installment payment on a 10-year note

g. An amount of money owed to the federal government, based on the company's annual income

Required

1. For each lettered item, state whether it should be classified as a current liability on the December 31, 2004, balance sheet. Assume that the operating cycle is shorter than one year. If the item should not be classified as a current liability, indicate where on the balance sheet it should be presented.
2. For each item identified as a current liability in part **1**, state the account title that is normally used to report the item on the balance sheet.
3. Why would an investor or creditor be interested in whether an item is a current or a long-term liability?

Exercise 9-3 *Current Liabilities Section* LO 1

Jackie Company had the following accounts and balances on December 31, 2004:

Income Taxes Payable	$61,250
Allowance for Doubtful Accounts	17,800
Accounts Payable	24,400
Interest Receivable	5,000
Unearned Revenue	4,320
Wages Payable	6,000
Notes Payable, 10%, due June 2, 2005	1,000
Accounts Receivable	67,500
Discount on Notes Payable	150
Current Maturities of Long-Term Debt	6,900
Interest Payable	3,010

Required

Prepare the Current Liabilities section of Jackie Company's balance sheet as of December 31, 2004.

Exercise 9-4 *Transaction Analysis* LO 2

Polly's Cards & Gifts Shop had the following transactions during the year:

a. Polly's purchased inventory on account from a supplier for $8,000. Assume that Polly's uses a periodic inventory system.

b. On May 1, land was purchased for $44,500. A 20% down payment was made, and an 18-month, 8% note was signed for the remainder.

c. Polly's returned $450 worth of inventory purchased in item **a,** which was found broken when the inventory was received.

d. Polly's paid the balance due on the purchase of inventory.

e. On June 1, Polly signed a one-year, $15,000 note to 1st State Bank and received $13,800.

f. Polly's sold 200 gift certificates for $25 each for cash. Sales of gift certificates are recorded as a liability. At year-end, 35% of the gift certificates had been redeemed.

g. Sales for the year were $120,000, of which 90% were for cash. State sales tax of 6% applied to all sales and must be remitted to the state by January 31.

Required

1. Determine the effect on the accounting equation of items **a** through **g.**
2. Assume that Polly's accounting year ends on December 31. Prepare any necessary adjusting journal entries.
3. What is the total of the current liabilities at the end of the year?

Exercise 9-5 *Current Liabilities and Ratios* LO 2

Listed below are several accounts that appeared on Kruse's 2004 balance sheet.

Accounts Payable	$ 55,000
Marketable Securities	40,000
Accounts Receivable	180,000
Notes Payable, 12%, due in 60 days	20,000
Capital Stock	1,150,000
Salaries Payable	10,000
Cash	15,000
Equipment	950,000
Taxes Payable	15,000
Retained Earnings	250,000
Inventory	85,000
Allowance for Doubtful Accounts	20,000
Land	600,000

Required

1. Prepare the Current Liabilities section of Kruse's 2004 balance sheet.
2. Compute Kruse's working capital.
3. Compute Kruse's current ratio. What does this ratio indicate about Kruse's condition?

Exercise 9-6 *Discounts* LO 2

Each of the following situations involves the use of discounts.

1. How much discount may Seals Inc. take in each of the following transactions? What was the annualized interest rate?
   - **a.** Seals purchases inventory costing $450, 2/10, n/40.
   - **b.** Seals purchases new office furniture costing $1,500, terms 1/10, n/30.
2. Calculate the discount rate Croft Co. received in each of these transactions.
   - **a.** Croft purchased office supplies costing $200 and paid within the discount period with a check for $196.
   - **b.** Croft purchased merchandise for $2,800. It paid within the discount period with a check for $2,674.

Exercise 9-7 *Notes Payable and Interest* LO 2

On July 1, 2004, Jo's Flower Shop borrowed $25,000 from the bank. Jo signed a 10-month, 8% promissory note for the entire amount. Jo's uses a calendar year-end.

Required

1. Determine the effect on the accounting equation when the note was issued on July 1.
2. What adjustments would be required at year end? Determine the effect on the accounting equation.
3. Determine the effect of the May 1 payment of principal and interest.

Exercise 9-8 *Non-Interest-Bearing Notes Payable* LO 2

On October 1, 2004, Ratkowski Inc. borrowed $18,000 from 2nd National Bank by issuing a 12-month note. The bank discounted the note at 9%.

Required

1. Determine the effect on the accounting equation of the issuance of the note.
2. What is the effect of the accrual of interest on December 31?
3. Determine the effect of the payment of the note on October 1, 2005.
4. What effective rate of interest did Ratkowski pay?

Exercise 9-9 *Impact of Transactions Involving Current Liabilities on Statement of Cash Flows* LO 3

From the following list, identify whether the change in the account balance during the year would be reported as an operating (O), investing (I), or financing (F) activity, or not separately reported on the statement of cash flows (N). Assume that the indirect method is used to determine the cash flows from operating activities.

(continued)

_______ Accounts payable
_______ Current maturities of long-term debt
_______ Notes payable
_______ Other accrued liabilities
_______ Salaries and wages payable
_______ Taxes payable

Exercise 9-10 ***Impact of Transactions Involving Contingent Liabilities on Statement of Cash Flows*** **LO 3**

From the following list, identify whether the change in the account balance during the year would be reported as an operating (O), investing (I), or financing (F) activity, or not separately reported on the statement of cash flows (N). Assume that the indirect method is used to determine the cash flows from operating activities.

_______ Estimated liability for warranties
_______ Estimated liability for product premiums
_______ Estimated liability for probable loss relating to litigation

Exercise 9-11 ***Impact of Transactions Involving Payroll Liabilities on Statement of Cash Flows (Appendix A)*** **LO 3**

From the following list, identify whether the change in the account balance during the year would be reported as an operating (O), investing (I), or financing (F) activity, or not separately reported on the statement of cash flows (N). Assume that the indirect method is used to determine the cash flows from operating activities.

_______ Accrued vacation days (compensated absences)
_______ Health insurance premiums payable
_______ FICA payable
_______ Union dues payable
_______ Salary payable
_______ Unemployment taxes payable

Exercise 9-12 ***Warranties*** **LO 4**

Clean Corporation manufactures and sells dishwashers. Clean provides all customers with a two-year warranty guaranteeing to repair, free of charge, any defects reported during this time period. During the year, it sold 100,000 dishwashers, for $325 each. Analysis of past warranty records indicates that 12% of all sales will be returned for repair within the warranty period. Clean expects to incur expenditures of $14 to repair each dishwasher. The account Estimated Liability for Warranties had a balance of $120,000 on January 1. Clean incurred $150,000 in actual expenditures during the year.

Required

Determine the effect on the accounting equation of the events related to the warranty transactions during the year. Determine the adjusted ending balance in the Estimated Liability for Warranties account.

Exercise 9-13 ***Simple Versus Compound Interest*** **LO 5**

Part 1. For each of the following notes, calculate the simple interest due at the end of the term.

Note	Face Value (Principal)	Rate	Term
1	$20,000	4%	6 years
2	20,000	6%	4 years
3	20,000	8%	3 years

Part 2. Now assume that the interest on the notes is compounded annually. Calculate the amount of interest due at the end of the term for each note.

Part 3. Now assume that the interest on the notes is compounded semiannually. Calculate the amount of interest due at the end of the term for each note.

What conclusion can you draw from a comparison of your results in parts **1, 2,** and **3?**

Exercise 9-14 ***Present Value, Future Value*** **LO 6**

Brian Inc. estimates it will need $150,000 in 10 years to expand its manufacturing facilities. A bank has agreed to pay Brian 5% interest, compounded annually, if the company deposits the entire amount now needed to accumulate $150,000 in 10 years. How much money does Brian need to deposit now?

Exercise 9-15 ***Effect of Compounding Period*** **LO 6**

Kern Company deposited $1,000 in the bank on January 1, 2004, earning 8% interest. Kern Company withdraws the deposit plus accumulated interest on January 1, 2006. Compute the amount of money Kern withdraws from the bank, assuming that interest is compounded (a) annually, (b) semiannually, and (c) quarterly.

Exercise 9-16 ***Present Value, Future Value*** **LO 6**

The following situations involve time value of money calculations.

1. A deposit of $7,000 is made on January 1, 2004. The deposit will earn interest at a rate of 8%. How much will be accumulated on January 1, 2009, assuming that interest is compounded (a) annually, (b) semiannually, and (c) quarterly?
2. A deposit is made on January 1, 2004, to earn interest at an annual rate of 8%. The deposit will accumulate to $15,000 by January 1, 2009. How much money was originally deposited, assuming that interest is compounded (a) annually, (b) semiannually, and (c) quarterly?

Exercise 9-17 ***Present Value, Future Value*** **LO 6**

The following are situations requiring the application of the time value of money.

1. On January 1, 2004, $16,000 is deposited. Assuming an 8% interest rate, calculate the amount accumulated on January 1, 2009, if interest is compounded (a) annually, (b) semiannually, and (c) quarterly.
2. Assume that a deposit made on January 1, 2004, earns 8% interest. The deposit plus interest accumulated to $20,000 on January 1, 2009. How much was invested on January 1, 2004, if interest was compounded (a) annually, (b) semiannually, and (c) quarterly?

Exercise 9-18 ***Annuity*** **LO 7**

Steve Jones has decided to start saving for his son's college education by depositing $2,000 at the end of every year for 15 years. A bank has agreed to pay interest at the rate of 4% compounded annually. How much will Steve have in the bank immediately after his 15th deposit?

Exercise 9-19 ***Calculation of Years*** **LO 7**

Kelly Seaver has decided to start saving for her daughter's college education. She wants to accumulate $41,000. The bank will pay interest at the rate of 4% compounded annually. If Kelly plans to make payments of $1,600 at the end of each year, how long will it take her to accumulate $41,000?

Exercise 9-20 ***Value of Payments*** **LO 7**

DECISION MAKING

On graduation from college, Susana Lopez signed an agreement to buy a used car. Her annual payments, due at the end of each year for two years, are $1,480. The car dealer used a 12% rate compounded annually to determine the amount of the payments.

Required

1. What should Susana consider the value of the car to be?
2. If she had wanted to make quarterly payments, what would her payments have been, based on the value of the car as determined in part **1**? How much less interest would she have had to pay if she had been making quarterly payments instead of annual payments? What do you think would have happened to the amount of the payment and the interest if she had asked for monthly payments?

Exercise 9-21 ***Payroll Transactions (Appendix A)*** **LO 8**

During the month of January, VanderSalm Company's employees earned $385,000. The following rates apply to VanderSalm's gross payroll:

Federal Income Tax Rate	28%
State Income Tax Rate	5%
FICA Tax Rate	7.65%
Federal Unemployment Tax Rate	0.8%
State Unemployment Tax Rate	5.4%

In addition, employee deductions were $7,000 for health insurance and $980 for union dues.

Required

1. Calculate the withholdings and net pay for wages for the company. Also determine the effect on the accounting equation of the payroll. You may assume that FICA tax applies to all employees.
2. Calculate the employer's portion of payroll taxes for January. Determine the effect on the accounting equation of accruing the employer's portion of the taxes.
3. If the company paid fringe benefits, such as employees' health insurance coverage, how would these contributions affect the payroll entries?

Exercise 9-22 ***Payroll, Employer's Portion (Appendix A)*** **LO 8**

Tasty Bakery Shop has six employees on its payroll. Payroll records include the following information on employee earnings for each employee:

Name	Earnings from 1/1 to 6/30/2004	Earnings for 3rd Quarter, 2004
Dell	$ 23,490	$11,710
Fin	4,240	2,660
Hook	34,100	15,660
Patty	63,300	26,200
Tuss	30,050	19,350
Woo	6,300	3,900
Totals	$161,480	$79,480

FICA taxes are levied at 7.65% on the first $84,900 of each employee's current year's earnings. The unemployment tax rates are 0.8% for federal and 5.4% for state unemployment. Assume that unemployment taxes are levied on the first $7,000 of each employee's current year's earnings.

Required

1. Calculate the employer's portion of payroll taxes incurred by Tasty Bakery for each employee for the third quarter of 2004. Round your answers to the nearest dollar.
2. Determine the effect on the accounting equation of the employer's portion of payroll taxes.

Exercise 9-23 ***Compensated Absences (Appendix A)*** **LO 9**

Wonder Inc. has a monthly payroll of $72,000 for its 24 employees. In addition to their salary, employees earn one day of vacation and one sick day for each month that they work. There are 20 workdays in a month.

Required

1. Determine the effect on the accounting equation if any, of recording (a) vacation benefits and (b) sick days.
2. From the owner's perspective, should the company offer the employees vacation and sick pay that accumulates year to year?

Multi-Concept Exercises

DECISION MAKING

Exercise 9-24 ***Compare Alternatives*** **LO 6, 7**

Jane Bauer has won the lottery and has four options for receiving her winnings:

1. Receive $100,000 at the beginning of the current year
2. Receive $108,000 at the end of the year
3. Receive $20,000 at the end of each year for 8 years
4. Receive $10,000 at the end of each year for 30 years

Jane can invest her winnings at an interest rate of 8% compounded annually at a major bank. Which of the payment options should Jane choose?

Exercise 9-25 ***Two Situations*** **LO 6, 7**

The following situations involve the application of the time value of money concepts.

1. Sampson Company just purchased a piece of equipment with a value of $53,300. Sampson financed this purchase with a loan from the bank and must make annual loan payments of $13,000 at the end of each year for the next five years. Interest is compounded annually on the loan. What is the interest rate on the bank loan?
2. Simon Company needs to accumulate $200,000 to repay bonds due in six years. Simon estimates it can save $13,300 at the end of each semiannual period at a local bank offering an annual interest rate of 8% compounded semiannually. Will Simon have enough money saved at the end of six years to repay the bonds?

Problems

Problem 9-1 *Notes and Interest* LO 2

Glencoe Inc. operates with a June 30 year-end. During 2004, the following transactions occurred:

a. January 1: Signed a one-year, 10% loan for $25,000. Interest and principal are to be paid at maturity.
b. January 10: Signed a line of credit with the Little Local Bank to establish a $400,000 line of credit. Interest of 9% will be charged on all borrowed funds.
c. February 1: Issued a $20,000 non-interest-bearing, six-month note to pay for a new machine. Interest on the note, at 12%, was deducted in advance.
d. March 1: Borrowed $150,000 on the line of credit.
e. June 1: Repaid $100,000 on the line of credit, plus accrued interest.
f. June 30: Made all necessary adjusting entries.
g. August 1: Repaid the non-interest-bearing note.
h. September 1: Borrowed $200,000 on the line of credit.
i. November 1: Issued a three-month, 8%, $12,000 note in payment of an overdue open account.
j. December 31: Repaid the one-year loan (from item **a**) plus accrued interest.

Required

1. Determine the effect on the accounting equation of items **a** through **j**.
2. As of December 31, which notes are outstanding, and how much interest is due on each?

Problem 9-2 *Effects of Sara Lee's Current Liabilities on Its Statement of Cash Flows* LO 3

http://www.saralee.com

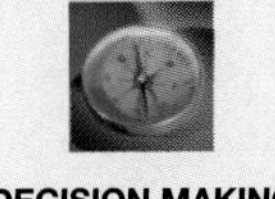

DECISION MAKING

The following items are classified as current liabilities on Sara Lee Corporation's consolidated balance sheet at June 29, 2002 and June 30, 2001 (in millions):

	2002	2001
Notes payable	$ 468	$ 101
Accounts payable	1,321	1,505
Accrued liabilities:		
Payroll and employee benefits	1,147	812
Advertising and promotions	469	343
Taxes other than payroll and income	102	84
Income taxes	122	423
Other	1,113	1,210
Current maturities of long-term debt	721	480

Required

1. Sara Lee uses the indirect method to prepare its statement of cash flows. Prepare the Operating Activities section of the cash flow statement, which indicates how each item will be reflected as an adjustment to net income. If you did not include any of the items set forth above, explain why not.
2. How would you decide whether Sara Lee has the ability to pay these liabilities as they become due?

Problem 9-3 ***Effects of Tommy Hilfiger's Changes in Current Assets and Liabilities on Statement of Cash Flows*** **LO 3**

http://www.tommy.com

SPREADSHEET

The following items are included in the Current Assets and Current Liabilities categories on the consolidated balance sheet of Tommy Hilfiger Corporation at March 31, 2002 and 2001 (in thousands):

	2002	2001
Accounts payable	$ 28,950	$ 38,628
Accounts receivable	224,395	237,414
Accrued expenses and other liabilities	210,270	171,640
Short-term borrowings	62,749	–0–
Inventories	184,972	205,446
Other current assets	97,274	90,353

Required

1. Tommy Hilfiger uses the indirect method to prepare its statement of cash flows. Prepare the Operating Activities section of the cash flow statement, which indicates how each item will be reflected as an adjustment to net income.
2. If you did not include any of the items set forth above in your answer to part **1**, explain how these items would be reported on the statement of cash flows.

Problem 9-4 ***Warranties*** **LO 4**

DECISION MAKING

Clearview Company manufactures and sells high-quality television sets. The most popular line sells for $1,000 each and is accompanied by a three-year warranty to repair, free of charge, any defective unit. Average costs to repair each defective unit will be $90 for replacement parts and $60 for labor. Clearview estimates that warranty costs of $12,600 will be incurred during 2004. The company actually sold 600 television sets and incurred replacement part costs of $3,600 and labor costs of $5,400 during the year. The adjusted 2004 ending balance in the Estimated Liability for Warranties account is $10,200.

Required

1. How many defective units from this year's sales does Clearview Company estimate will be returned for repair?
2. What percentage of sales does Clearview Company estimate will be returned for repair?
3. What steps should Clearview take if actual warranty costs incurred during 2005 are significantly higher than the estimated liability recorded at the end of 2004?

Problem 9-5 ***Warranties*** **LO 4**

Bombeck Company sells a product for $1,500. When the customer buys it, Bombeck provides a one-year warranty. Bombeck sold 120 products during 2004. Based on analysis of past warranty records, Bombeck estimates that repairs will average 3% of total sales.

Required

1. Determine the effect on the accounting equation of the estimated liability.
2. Assume that products under warranty must be repaired during 2004 using repair parts from inventory costing $4,950. Prepare the journal entry to record the repair of products.

Problem 9-6 ***Comparison of Simple and Compound Interest*** **LO 5**

On June 30, 2004, Rolf Inc. borrowed $25,000 from its bank, signing a 8%, two-year note.

Required

1. Assuming that the bank charges simple interest on the note, prepare the journal entry Rolf will record on each of the following dates:

   December 31, 2004
   December 31, 2005
   June 30, 2006

2. Assume instead that the bank charges 8% on the note, which is compounded semiannually. Prepare the necessary journal entries on the dates in part **1**.
3. How much additional interest expense will Rolf have in part **2** over part **1**?

Problem 9-7 *Investment with Varying Interest Rate* LO 6

Shari Thompson invested $1,000 in a financial institution on January 1, 2004. She leaves her investment in the institution until December 31, 2008. How much money does Shari accumulate if she earned interest, compounded annually, at the following rates?

2004	4%
2005	5
2006	6
2007	7
2008	8

Problem 9-8 *Comparison of Alternatives* LO 6

DECISION MAKING

On January 1, 2004, Chen Yu's Office Supply Store plans to remodel the store and install new display cases. Chen has the following options of payment. Chen's interest rate is 8%.

a. Pay $180,000 on January 1, 2004.

b. Pay $196,200 on January 1, 2005.

c. Pay $220,500 on January 1, 2006.

d. Make four annual payments of $55,000 beginning on December 31, 2004.

Required

Which option should he choose? (*Hint:* Calculate the present value of each option as of January 1, 2004.)

Problem 9-9 *Payroll Transactions (Appendix A)* LO 8

Vivian Company has calculated the gross wages of all employees for the month of August to be $210,000. The following amounts have been withheld from the employees' paychecks:

Income Tax	$42,500
FICA	16,000
Heart Fund Contributions	5,800
Union Dues	3,150

Vivian's unemployment tax rate is 6%, and its portion of FICA matches the employees' share.

Required

1. Determine the effect on the accounting equation of accruing the amount payable to employees.
2. Determine the effect on the accounting equation when the employees are paid.
3. Determine the effect on the accounting equation of recording the employer's payroll costs.
4. Determine the effect on the accounting equation when the withholdings were remitted.

Problem 9-10 *Compensated Absences (Appendix A)* LO 9

Hetzel Inc. pays its employees every Friday. For every four weeks that employees work, they earn one vacation day. For every six weeks that they work without calling in sick, they earn one sick day. If employees quit or retire, they can receive a lump-sum payment for their unused vacation days and unused sick days.

Required

Write a short memo to the bookkeeper to explain how and when he should report vacation and sick days. Explain how the matching principle applies and why you believe that the timing you recommend is appropriate.

Multi-Concept Problems

Problem 9-11 *Interest in Advance versus Interest Paid When Loan Is Due* LO 2, 5

On July 1, 2004, Leach Company needs exactly $103,200 in cash to pay an existing obligation. Leach has decided to borrow from State Bank, which charges 14% interest on loans. The loan will be due in one year. Leach is unsure, however, whether to ask the bank for (a) an interest-bearing loan with interest and principal payable at the end of the year or (b) a loan due in one year but with interest deducted in advance.

Required

1. What will be the face value of the note assuming that
   a. interest is paid when the loan is due?
   b. interest is deducted in advance?
2. Calculate the effective interest rate on the note assuming that
   a. interest is paid when the loan is due.
   b. interest is deducted in advance.
3. Assume that Leach negotiates and signs the one-year note with the bank on July 1, 2004. Also assume that Leach's accounting year ends December 31. Determine the effect on the accounting equation of the issuance of the note and the interest on the note, assuming that
   a. interest is paid when the loan is due.
   b. interest is deducted in advance.
4. Prepare the appropriate balance sheet presentation for July 1, 2004, immediately after the note has been issued, assuming that
   a. interest is paid when the loan is due.
   b. interest is deducted in advance.

Problem 9-12 *Contingent Liabilities* LO 1, 4

Listed below are several items for which the outcome of events is unknown at year-end.

a. A company offers a two-year warranty on sales of new computers. It believes that 4% of the computers will require repairs.
b. The company is involved in a trademark infringement suit. The company's legal experts believe an award of $500,000 in the company's favor will be made.
c. A company is involved in an environmental clean-up lawsuit. The company's legal counsel believes it is possible the outcome will be unfavorable but has not been able to estimate the costs of the possible loss.
d. A soap manufacturer has included a coupon offer in the Sunday newspaper supplements. The manufacturer estimates that 25% of the 50-cent coupons will be redeemed.
e. A company has been sued by the federal government for price fixing. The company's legal counsel believes there will be an unfavorable verdict and has made an estimate of the probable loss.

Required

1. Identify which of the items **a** through **e** should be recorded at year-end.
2. Identify which of the items **a** through **e** should not be recorded but should be disclosed in the year-end financial statements.

Problem 9-13 *Time Value of Money Concepts* LO 6, 7

The following situations involve the application of the time value of money concept.

1. Janelle Carter deposited $9,750 in the bank on January 1, 1987, at an interest rate of 11% compounded annually. How much has accumulated in the account by January 1, 2004?
2. Mike Smith deposited $21,600 in the bank on January 1, 1994. On January 2, 2004, this deposit has accumulated to $42,487. Interest is compounded annually on the account. What is the rate of interest that Mike earned on the deposit?
3. Lee Spony made a deposit in the bank on January 1, 1997. The bank pays interest at the rate of 8% compounded annually. On January 1, 2004, the deposit has accumulated to $15,000. How much money did Lee originally deposit on January 1, 1997?
4. Nancy Holmes deposited $5,800 in the bank on January 1 a few years ago. The bank pays an interest rate of 10% compounded annually, and the deposit is now worth $15,026. How many years has the deposit been invested?

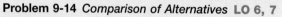

DECISION MAKING

Problem 9-14 *Comparison of Alternatives* LO 6, 7

Brian Imhoff's grandparents want to give him some money when he graduates from high school. They have offered Brian three choices:

a. Receive $15,000 immediately. Assume that interest is compounded annually.

b. Receive $2,250 at the end of each six months for four years. The first check will be received in six months.

c. Receive $4,350 at the end of each year for four years. Assume interest is compounded annually.

Required

Brian wants to have money for a new car when he graduates from college in four years. Assuming an interest rate of 8%, what option should he choose to have the most money in four years?

Alternate Problems

Problem 9-1A *Notes and Interest* LO 2

McLaughlin Inc. operates with a June 30 year-end. During 2004, the following transactions occurred:

a. January 1: Signed a one-year, 10% loan for $35,000. Interest and principal are to be paid at maturity.

b. January 10: Signed a line of credit with the Little Local Bank to establish a $560,000 line of credit. Interest of 9% will be charged on all borrowed funds.

c. February 1: Issued a $28,000 non-interest-bearing, six-month note to pay for a new machine. Interest on the note, at 12%, was deducted in advance.

d. March 1: Borrowed $210,000 on the line of credit.

e. June 1: Repaid $140,000 on the line of credit, plus accrued interest.

f. June 30: Made all necessary adjusting entries.

g. August 1: Repaid the non-interest-bearing note.

h. September 1: Borrowed $280,000 on the line of credit.

i. November 1: Issued a three-month, 8%, $16,800 note in payment of an overdue open account.

j. December 31: Repaid the one-year loan (from item **a**) plus accrued interest.

Required

1. Determine the effect on the accounting equation of items **a** through **g**.
2. As of December 31, which notes are outstanding, and how much interest is due on each?

Problem 9-2A *Effects of Boeing's Current Liabilities on Its Statement of Cash Flows* LO 3

The following items are classified as current liabilities on **Boeing Company's** consolidated statements of financial condition (or balance sheet) at December 31 (in millions):

http://www.boeing.com

DECISION MAKING

	2002	2001
Accounts payable and other liabilities	$13,739	$14,237
Advances in excess of related costs	3,123	4,021
Income taxes payable	1,134	909
Short-term debt and current portion of long-term debt	1,814	1,399

Required

1. Boeing uses the indirect method to prepare its statement of cash flows. Prepare the Operating Activities section of the cash flow statement, which indicates how each item will be reflected as an adjustment to net income. If you did not include any of the items set forth above, explain why not.
2. How would you decide whether Boeing has the ability to pay these liabilities as they become due?

Problem 9-3A *Effects of Nike's Changes in Current Assets and Liabilities on Its Statement of Cash Flows* LO 3

http://www.nike.com

SPREADSHEET

The following items are included in the Current Assets and Current Liabilities categories on the consolidated balance sheet of Nike Inc. at May 31, 2002 and 2001 (in millions):

	2002	2001
Accounts payable	$ 504.4	$ 432.0
Accounts receivable	1,807.1	1,621.4
Accrued liabilities	768.3	472.1
Current portion of long-term debt	55.3	5.4
Income taxes payable	83.0	21.9
Inventories	1,373.8	1,424.1
Notes payable	425.2	855.3
Prepaid expenses	260.5	162.5
Deferred income tax	140.8	113.3

Required

1. Nike uses the indirect method to prepare its statement of cash flows. Prepare the Operating Activities section of the cash flow statement, which indicates how each item will be reflected as an adjustment to net income.
2. If you did not include any of the items set forth above in your answer to part **1,** explain how these items would be reported on the statement of cash flows.

Problem 9-4A *Warranties* LO 4

Sound Company manufactures and sells high-quality stereo sets. The most popular line sells for $2,000 each and is accompanied by a three-year warranty to repair, free of charge, any defective unit. Average costs to repair each defective unit will be $180 for replacement parts and $120 for labor. Sound estimates that warranty costs of $25,200 will be incurred during 2004. The company actually sold 600 sets and incurred replacement part costs of $7,200 and labor costs of $10,800 during the year. The adjusted 2004 ending balance in the Estimated Liability for Warranties account is $20,400.

Required

1. How many defective units from this year's sales does Sound Company estimate will be returned for repair?
2. What percent of sales does Sound Company estimate will be returned for repair?

Problem 9-5A *Warranties* LO 4

Beck Company sells a product for $3,200. When the customer buys it, Beck provides a one-year warranty. Beck sold 120 products during 2004. Based on analysis of past warranty records, Beck estimates that repairs will average 4% of total sales.

Required

1. Determine the effect on the accounting equation of the estimated liability.
2. Assume that during 2004, products under warranty must be repaired using repair parts from inventory costing $10,200. Determine the effect on the accounting equation of the repair of products.
3. Assume that the balance of the Estimated Liabilities for Warranties account as of the beginning of 2004 was $1,100. Calculate the balance of the account as of the end of 2004.

Problem 9-6A *Comparison of Simple and Compound Interest* LO 5

On June 30, 2004, Rolloff Inc. borrowed $25,000 from its bank, signing a 6% note. Principal and interest are due at the end of two years.

Required

1. Assuming that the note earns simple interest for the bank, calculate the amount of interest accrued on each of the following dates:

    December 31, 2004
    December 31, 2005
    June 30, 2006

2. Assume instead that the note earns 6% for the bank but is compounded semiannually. Calculate the amount of interest accrued on the same dates as in part **1**.
3. How much additional interest expense will Rolloff have to pay with semiannual interest?

Problem 9-7A ***Investment with Varying Interest Rate*** **LO 6**

Trena Thompson invested $2,000 in a financial institution on January 1, 2004. She leaves her investment in the institution until December 31, 2008. How much money did Trena accumulate if she earned interest, compounded annually, at the following rates?

2004	4%
2005	5
2006	6
2007	7
2008	8

Problem 9-8A ***Comparison of Alternatives*** **LO 6**

On January 1, 2004, Li Ping's Office Supply Store plans to remodel the store and install new display cases. Li Ping has the following options of payment. Li's interest rate is 8%.

DECISION MAKING

a. Pay $270,000 on January 1, 2004.
b. Pay $294,300 on January 1, 2005.
c. Pay $334,750 on January 1, 2006.
d. Make four annual payments of $82,500 beginning on December 31, 2004.

Required

Which option should Li choose? (*Hint:* Calculate the present value of each option as of January 1, 2004.)

Problem 9-9A ***Payroll Transactions (Appendix A)*** **LO 8**

Calvin Company has calculated the gross wages of all employees for the month of August to be $336,000. The following amounts have been withheld from the employees' paychecks:

Income Tax	$68,000
FICA	25,600
Heart Fund Contributions	9,280
Union Dues	5,040

Calvin's unemployment tax rate is 6%, and its portion of FICA matches the employees' share.

Required

1. Determine the effect on the accounting equation of accruing the amount payable to employees.
2. Determine the effect on the accounting equation when the employees are paid.
3. Determine the effect on the accounting equation of recording the employer's payroll costs.
4. Determine the effect on the accounting equation when the withholdings were remitted.

Problem 9-10A ***Compensated Absences (Appendix A)*** **LO 9**

Assume that you are the accountant for a large company with several divisions. The manager of Division B has contacted you with a concern. During 2004, several employees retired from Division B. The company's policy is that employees can be paid for days of sick leave accrued at the time they retire. Payment occurs in the year following retirement. The manager has been told by corporate headquarters that she cannot replace the employees in 2005 because the payment of the accrued sick pay will be deducted from Division B's budget in that year.

DECISION MAKING

Required

In a memo to the manager of Division B, explain the proper accounting for accrued sick pay. Do you think that the policies of corporate headquarters should be revised?

Alternate Multi-Concept Problems

Problem 9-11A ***Interest in Advance versus Interest Paid When Loan Is Due*** **LO 2, 5**

On July 1, 2004, Moton Company needs exactly $206,400 in cash to pay an existing obligation. Moton has decided to borrow from State Bank, which charges 14% interest on loans. The loan will be due in one year. Moton is unsure, however, whether to ask the bank for (a) an interest-bearing loan with interest and principal payable at the end of the year or (b) a non-interest-bearing loan due in one year but with interest deducted in advance.

Required

1. What will be the face value of the note, assuming that
   a. interest is paid when the loan is due?
   b. interest is deducted in advance?
2. Calculate the effective interest rate on the note, assuming that
   a. interest is paid when the loan is due.
   b. interest is deducted in advance.
3. Assume that Moton negotiates and signs the one-year note with the bank on July 1, 2004. Also assume that Moton's accounting year ends December 31. Determine the effect on the accounting equation of the issuance of the note and the interest on it, assuming that
   a. interest is paid when the loan is due.
   b. interest is deducted in advance.
4. Prepare the appropriate balance sheet presentation for July 1, 2004, immediately after the note has been issued, assuming that
   a. interest is paid when the loan is due.
   b. interest is deducted in advance.

Problem 9-12A *Contingent Liabilities* LO 1, 4

Listed below are several events for which the outcome is unknown at year-end.

a. A company has been sued by the federal government for price fixing. The company's legal counsel believes there will be an unfavorable verdict and has made an estimate of the probable loss.

b. A company is involved in an environmental clean-up lawsuit. The company's legal counsel believes it is possible the outcome will be unfavorable but has not been able to estimate the costs of the possible loss.

c. The company is involved in a trademark infringement suit. The company's legal experts believe an award of $750,000 in the company's favor will be made.

d. A company offers a three-year warranty on sales of new computers. It believes that 6% of the computers will require repairs.

e. A snack food manufacturer has included a coupon offer in the Sunday newspaper supplements. The manufacturer estimates that 30% of the 40-cent coupons will be redeemed.

Required

1. Identify which of the items **a** through **e** should be recorded at year-end.
2. Identify which of the items **a** through **e** should not be recorded but should be disclosed on the year-end financial statements.

Problem 9-13A *Time Value of Money Concepts* LO 6, 7

The following situations involve the application of the time value of money concept.

1. Jan Cain deposited $19,500 in the bank on January 1, 1987, at an interest rate of 11% compounded annually. How much has been accumulated in the account by January 1, 2004?
2. Mark Schultz deposited $43,200 in the bank on January 1, 1994. On January 2, 2004, this deposit has accumulated to $84,974. Interest is compounded annually on the account. What is the rate of interest that Mark earned on the deposit?
3. Les Hinckle made a deposit in the bank on January 1, 1997. The bank pays interest at the rate of 8% compounded annually. On January 1, 2004, the deposit has accumulated to $30,000. How much money did Les originally deposit on January 1, 1997?
4. Val Hooper deposited $11,600 in the bank on January 1 a few years ago. The bank pays an interest rate of 10% compounded annually, and the deposit is now worth $30,052. For how many years has the deposit been invested?

Problem 9-14A *Comparison of Alternatives* **LO 6, 7**

DECISION MAKING

Darlene Page's grandparents want to give her some money when she graduates from high school. They have offered Darlene three choices.

a. Receive $16,000 immediately. Assume that interest is compounded annually.

b. Receive $2,400 at the end of each six months for four years. The first check will be received in six months.

c. Receive $4,640 at the end of each year for four years. Assume interest is compounded annually.

Required

Darlene wants to have money for a new car when she graduates from college in four years. Assuming an interest rate of 8%, what option should she choose to have the most money in four years?

Decision Cases

Reading and Interpreting Financial Statements

Decision Case 9-1 *Winnebago Industries' Current Liability* **LO 1, 2**

http://www.winnebagoind.com

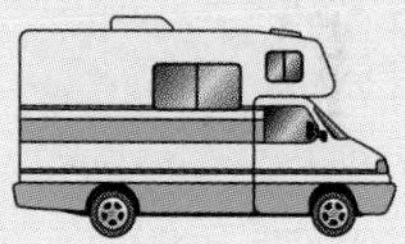

Refer to **Winnebago Industries'** 2002 annual report. Using the company balance sheet and accompanying notes, write a response to the following questions:

Required

1. Determine the company's current ratio for fiscal years 2002 and 2001. What do the ratios indicate about the liquidity of the company?
2. Explain why accrued compensation and product warranties are considered current liabilities on the company's balance sheet.
3. Refer to the company's notes. Does the company have any contingent liabilities for lawsuits or litigation? If so, how were these contingent liabilities treated on the financial statements?

Decision Case 9-2 *Winnebago Industries' Statement of Cash Flows* **LO 3**

http://www.winnebagoind.com

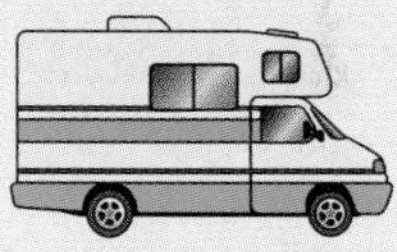

Refer to **Winnebago Industries'** statement of cash flows in its 2002 annual report to answer the following questions:

Required

1. The net cash provided by operating activities was less than the amount of net income in fiscal year 2002. What were the primary reasons?
2. In fiscal year 2002, receivables and inventories appear as negative amounts while accounts payable appears as a positive amount on the statement of cash flows. Explain whether these accounts actually increased or decreased. What do the changes in these accounts indicate about the company's liquidity and its future performance?

Decision Case 9-3 *Comparing Two Companies in the Same Industry: Winnebago Industries and Monaco Coach Corporation* **LO 3**

http://www.winnebagoind.com
http://www.monacocoach.com

Refer to the 2002 statements of cash flows of **Monaco Coach Corporation** and of **Winnebago Industries** in Appendices A and B at the end of the text. (*Note:* Monaco Coach presents the most recent statement in the right-hand column.)

Required

1. Monaco Coach's net cash provided by operating activities decreased significantly in fiscal year 2002. What were the primary reasons for the decrease?
2. Compare the operating activities category of each company's cash flow statement. What company was able to generate more cash from its operating activities? What appears to be the top three reasons for the difference?
3. For each company, look at the following line items listed in the operating section of its 2002 cash flow statement:
   - Monaco Coach: trade receivables, inventories, and accounts payable

(continued)

- Winnebago Industries: receivables and other assets, inventories, and accounts payable and accrued expenses.

Did cash flow increase or decrease for each of these line items? What do the changes in these accounts indicate about each company's liquidity and its future performance?

4. Reach each company's disclosure about warranty claims in its Note 1 to the 2002 financial statements. How are these disclosures similar? How are they different? What information is most helpful for evaluating the company's risk?

Decision Case 9-4 *R J Reynolds' Contingent Liability* LO 3, 4

The following is an excerpt from the 2002 financial disclosures of R J Reynolds regarding a contingency:

> Legal Proceedings
> Various legal actions, proceedings and claims, including legal actions claiming that lung cancer and other diseases, as well as addiction, have resulted from the use of, or exposure to, RJR s operating subsidiaries products, are pending or may be instituted against RJR or its affiliates, including RJR Tobacco, or indemnitees. In July 2000, a jury in the Florida state court case Engle v. R.J. Reynolds Tobacco Co. rendered a verdict in favor of the Florida class of plaintiffs of approximately $145 billion, with approximately $36.3 billion being assigned to RJR Tobacco. RJR Tobacco and other defendants have appealed this verdict. RJR Tobacco believes it has numerous bases for a successful appeal, although it cannot predict the outcome of the appellate process. Even though RJR s management continues to conclude that the loss of any particular smoking and health tobacco litigation claim against RJR Tobacco or its affiliates, when viewed on an individual basis, is not probable, the possibility of material losses related to tobacco litigation is more than remote. However, RJR s management is unable to predict the outcome of such litigation or to reasonably estimate the amount or range of any possible loss. Moreover, notwithstanding the quality of defenses available to it and its affiliates in tobacco-related litigation matters, it is possible that RJR's results of operations, cash flows or financial condition could be materially adversely affected by the ultimate outcome of certain pending or future litigation matters.

Required:

1. Is disclosure of the contingency all that is required of R J Reynolds, or should an amount be recorded on the balance sheet as a liability?
2. If an amount would be recorded, how would it affect the income statement?
3. What steps could be taken to "reasonably estimate" the amount of the loss in a situation such as that facing this company?

Decision Case 9-5 *Ford Motor Company's Contingent Liability* LO 4

http://www.ford.com

The following is an excerpt from Ford Motor Company's notes that accompanied its financial statements for the year ended December 31, 2000.

> In the United States, the recall of certain Firestone tires, most of which were installed as original equipment on Ford Explorers, has led to a significant number of personal injury and class action lawsuits against Ford and Firestone. Plaintiffs in the personal injury cases typically allege that their injuries were caused by defects in the tire that caused it to lose its tread and/or by defects in the Explorer that caused the vehicle to roll over. For those cases involving Explorer rollovers in which damages have been specified, the damages specified by the plaintiffs, including both actual and punitive damages, aggregated approximately $590 million. However, in most of the actions described above, no dollar amount of damages is specified or the specific amount referred to is only the jurisdictional minimum. It has been our experience that in cases that allege a specific amount of damages in excess of the jurisdictional minimum, such amounts, on average, bear little relation to the actual amounts of damages, if any, paid by Ford in resolving such cases.

Required

1. Based on this excerpt, how should Ford's contingencies be treated on its financial statements for the year ended December 31, 2000?
2. Find more recent financial statements of Ford Motor Company. At what point did the company record amounts related to the Firestone tire legal issues?

Making Financial Decisions

Decision Case 9-6 *Current Ratio Loan Provision* LO 1, 2

DECISION MAKING

Assume that you are the controller of a small, growing sporting goods company. The prospects for your firm in the future are quite good, but like most other firms, it has been experiencing some cash flow difficulties because all available funds have been used to purchase inventory and finance start-up costs associated with a new business. At the beginning of the current year, your local bank advanced a loan to your company. Included in the loan is the following provision:

> The company is obligated to pay interest payments each month for the next five years. Principal is due and must be paid at the end of Year 5. The company is further obligated to maintain a current assets to current liabilities ratio of 2 to 1 as indicated on quarterly statements to be submitted to the bank. If the company fails to meet any loan provisions, all amounts of interest and principal are due immediately upon notification by the bank.

You, as controller, have just gathered the following information as of the end of the first month of the current quarter:

Current liabilities:	
Accounts payable	$400,000
Taxes payable	100,000
Accrued expenses	50,000
Total current liabilities	$550,000

You are concerned about the loan provision that requires a 2:1 ratio of current assets to current liabilities.

Required

1. Indicate what actions could be taken during the next two months to meet the loan provision. Which of the available actions should be recommended?
2. What is the meaning of the term *window-dressing* financial statements? What are the long-run implications of actions taken to window-dress financial statements?

Decision Case 9-7 *Alternative Payment Options* LO 7

DECISION MAKING

Kathy Clark owns a small company that makes ice machines for restaurants and food-service facilities. Kathy knows a lot about producing ice machines but is less familiar with the best terms to extend to her customers. One customer is opening a new business and has asked Kathy to consider any of the following options to pay for his new $20,000 ice machine.

a. Term 1: 10% down, the remainder paid at the end of the year plus 8% simple interest.

b. Term 2: 10% down, the remainder paid at the end of the year plus 8% interest, compounded quarterly.

c. Term 3: $0 down, but $21,600 due at the end of the year.

Required

Make a recommendation to Kathy. She believes that 8% is a fair return on her money at this time. Should she accept option **a, b,** or **c,** or take the $20,000 cash at the time of the sale? Justify your recommendation with calculations. What factors, other than the actual amount of cash received from the sale, should be considered?

Accounting and Ethics: What Would You Do?

Decision Case 9-8 *Warranty Cost Estimate* LO 4

ETHICS

John Walton is an accountant for ABC Auto Dealers, a large auto dealership in a metropolitan area. ABC sells both new and used cars. New cars are sold with a five-year warranty, the cost of which is carried by the manufacturer. For several years, however, ABC has offered a two-year warranty on used cars. The cost of the warranty is an expense to ABC, and John has been asked by his boss, Mr. Sawyer, to review warranty costs and recommend the amount to accrue on the year-end financial statements.

For the past several years, ABC has recorded as warranty expense 5% of used car sales. John has analyzed past repair records and found that repairs, although fluctuating somewhat from year to year, have averaged near the 5% level. John is convinced, however, that 5% is inadequate for the coming year. He bases his judgment on industry reports of increased repair costs and on the fact that several cars that were recently sold on warranty have experienced very high repair costs. John believes that the current-year repair accrual will be at least 10%. He discussed the higher expense amount with Mr. Sawyer, who is the controller of ABC.

Mr. Sawyer was not happy with John's decision concerning warranty expense. He reminded John of the need to control expenses during the recent sales downturn. He also reminded John that ABC is seeking a large loan from the bank and that the bank loan officers may not be happy with recent operating results, especially if ABC begins to accrue larger amounts for future estimated amounts such as warranties. Finally, Mr. Sawyer reminded John that most of the employees of ABC, including Mr. Sawyer, were members of the company's profit-sharing plan and would not be happy with the reduced share of profits. Mr. Sawyer thanked John for his judgment concerning warranty cost but told him that the accrual for the current year would remain at 5%.

John left the meeting with Mr. Sawyer somewhat frustrated. He was convinced that his judgment concerning the warranty costs was correct. He knew that the owner of ABC would be visiting the office next week and wondered whether he should discuss the matter with him personally at that time. John also had met one of the loan officers from the bank several times and considered calling her to discuss his concern about the warranty expense amount on the year-end statements.

Required

Discuss the courses of action available to John. What should John do concerning his judgment of warranty costs? Which alternative would readers of the financial statements prefer? Explain why. If the company decides to record warranty expense at 5% rather than 10%, does this choice provide information that is free from bias to readers of the financial statements?

Decision Case 9-9 *Retainer Fees as Sales* LO 4

ETHICS

Bunch o' Balloons markets balloon arrangements to companies who want to thank clients and employees. Bunch o' Balloons has a unique style that has put it in high demand. Consequently, Bunch o' Balloons has asked clients to establish an account. Clients are asked to pay a retainer fee equal to about three months of client purchases. The fee will be used to cover the cost of arrangements delivered and will be reevaluated at the end of each month. At the end of the current month Bunch o' Balloons has $43,900 of retainer fees in its possession. The controller is eager to show this amount as sales because "it represents certain sales for the company."

Required

Do you agree with the controller? When should the sales be reported? Why would the controller be eager to report the cash receipts as sales?

THOMSON ONE Business School Edition Case

Case 9-10 *Using THOMSON ONE for J. C. Penney*

http://www.jcpenney.com

J. C. Penney hopes a network of retail stores, augmented by catalog sales and a burgeoning e-commerce business, will help the company meet its strategic growth goals and respond to intense competition from other retailers. In recent years, J. C. Penney has established the company as a family of businesses—department stores and catalog, Eckerd drugstores, direct marketing, and international operations. Their mission is to change business processes so as to contain expenses, increase revenue and, especially, raise net income.

Use THOMSON ONE to obtain current information about the company's liquidity and other financial information. Begin by entering the company's ticker symbol, JCP, and then selecting "GO." On the opening screen you will see background information about the company, key financial ratios, and some recent data concerning stock price. We can also find the company's recent financial statements. Near the top of the screen, click on "Financials" and select "Financial Statements." Refer to the current asset and current liabilities portions of the company's balance sheet.

Based on your use of THOMSON ONE, answer the following questions.

1. Determine the total current assets and total liabilities for J. C. Penney. How do these compare with the amounts of the previous year?
2. Calculate J. C. Penney's current ratio based on the latest information available.

3. If you were a supplier of merchandise to J. C. Penney, how might its current ratio affect your willingness to extend credit to the company?
4. What major changes in J. C. Penney's operations have been implemented in the latest year available? What do you see as the effect, if any, on the financial statements and notes?

Solutions to Key Terms Quiz

1 Current liability (p. 419)
3 Accounts payable (p. 422)
8 Notes payable (p. 422)
4 Discount on Notes Payable (p. 423)
6 Current Maturities of Long-Term Debt (p. 423)
7 Accrued liability (p. 424)
9 Contingent liability (p. 426)
11 Estimated liability (p. 428)
12 Contingent asset (p. 431)
14 Time value of money (p. 433)
10 Simple interest (p. 434)
13 Compound interest (p. 434)
15 Future value of a single amount (p. 435)
17 Present value of a single amount (p. 438)
5 Annuity (p. 439)
16 Future value of an annuity (p. 440)
2 Present value of an annuity (p. 441)
18 Gross wages (p. 454)
20 Net pay (p. 454)
19 Compensated absences (p. 457)

Chapter 10

Long-Term Liabilities

© TERRI MILLER/E-VISUAL COMMUNICATIONS, INC.

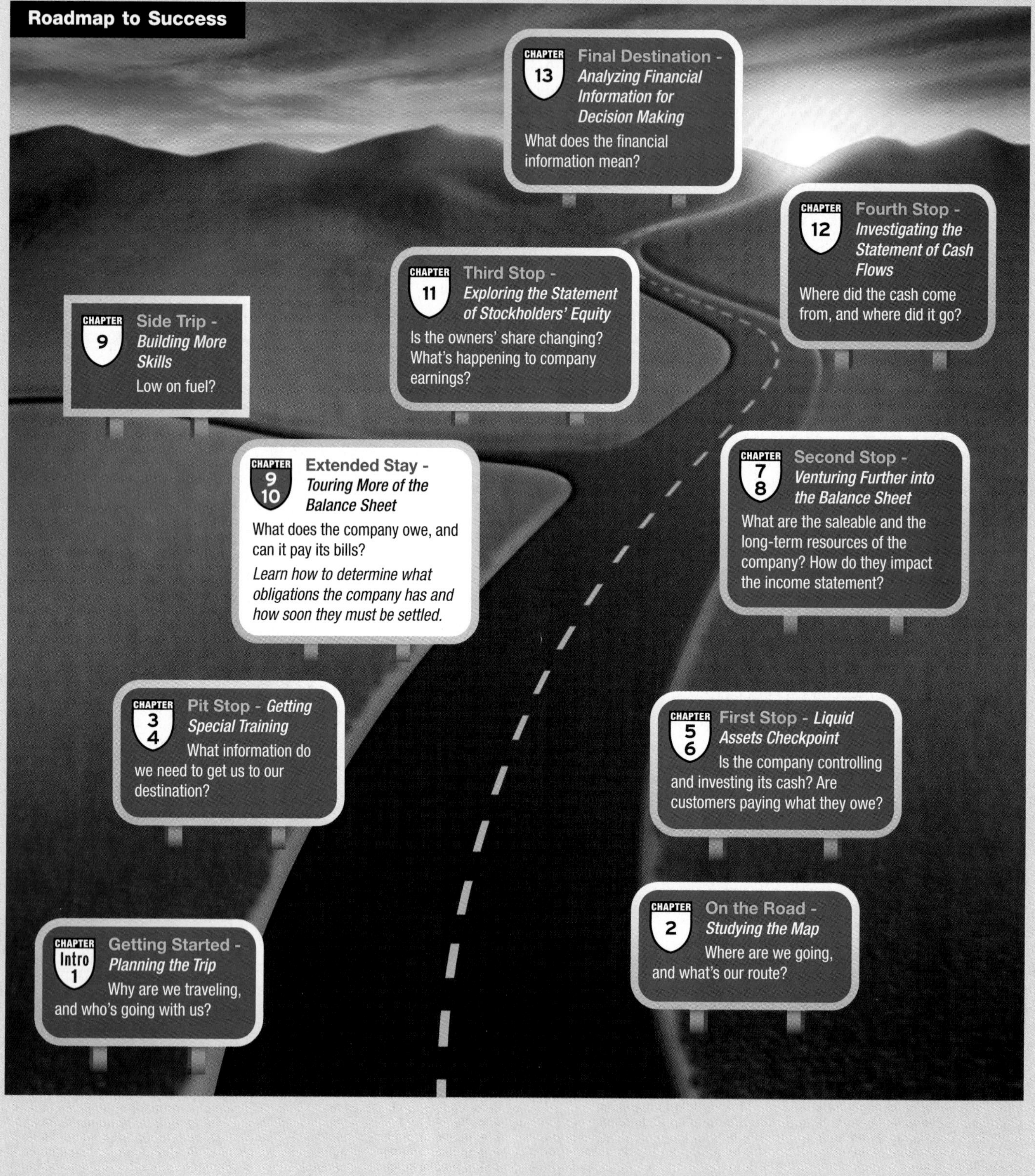

Roadmap to Success

CHAPTER Intro 1 — **Getting Started** - *Planning the Trip*
Why are we traveling, and who's going with us?

CHAPTER 2 — **On the Road** - *Studying the Map*
Where are we going, and what's our route?

CHAPTER 3 4 — **Pit Stop** - *Getting Special Training*
What information do we need to get us to our destination?

CHAPTER 5 6 — **First Stop** - *Liquid Assets Checkpoint*
Is the company controlling and investing its cash? Are customers paying what they owe?

CHAPTER 9 10 — **Extended Stay** - *Touring More of the Balance Sheet*
What does the company owe, and can it pay its bills?
Learn how to determine what obligations the company has and how soon they must be settled.

CHAPTER 7 8 — **Second Stop** - *Venturing Further into the Balance Sheet*
What are the saleable and the long-term resources of the company? How do they impact the income statement?

CHAPTER 9 — **Side Trip** - *Building More Skills*
Low on fuel?

CHAPTER 11 — **Third Stop** - *Exploring the Statement of Stockholders' Equity*
Is the owners' share changing? What's happening to company earnings?

CHAPTER 12 — **Fourth Stop** - *Investigating the Statement of Cash Flows*
Where did the cash come from, and where did it go?

CHAPTER 13 — **Final Destination** - *Analyzing Financial Information for Decision Making*
What does the financial information mean?

Focus on Financial Results

Coca-Cola® is one of the world's foremost brands with worldwide sales of nearly $20 billion in 2002. The company is truly a global corporation with nearly 300 brands in almost 200 countries. While it began many years ago in the United States, now more than 70% of Coca-Cola Company's income comes from business outside the United States. Recently, the growth in company sales has slowed to 3% or less per year, and the company has faced new challenges in the beverage industry. Despite continued turbulence in worldwide markets and challenges from competitors, the firm maintains its focus on growth.

To meet long-term growth objectives, Coca-Cola must make significant investments to support its products. The process also involves investment to develop new global brands and to acquire local or global brands, when appropriate. In addition, the company makes significant marketing investments to encourage consumer loyalty. Coca-Cola has developed relationships with many sports organizations, including the NBA and NASCAR, to enhance consumer awareness and promote sales of its products. Outside the United States, there is a strong push to sell in many other markets, including those in India and Brazil.

To expand profitably, Coca-Cola requires more money than it generates in profits. Therefore, it uses a common financing tool: *long-term debt.* In fact, the balance sheet of December 31, 2002, indicates the company has over $2.7 billion of long-term debt and other liabilities. The 2001 annual report states, "We use debt financing to lower our overall cost of capital, which increases our return on share-owners equity."[1] The company monitors interest rates conditions carefully and in 2002 retired nearly $2.4 billion in debt and replaced it with other debt to take advantage of falling interest rates. Because it is a global company, Coca-Cola has access to key financial markets around the world, which allows it to borrow at the lowest possible rates. While most of its loans are in U.S. dollars, management continually adjusts the composition of the debt to accommodate shifting interest rates and currency exchange rates to minimize the overall cost.

http://www.cocacola.com

Coca-Cola 2002 Annual Report

The Coca-Cola Company and Subsidiaries

December 31, *(In millions except share data)*	**2002**	2001
LIABILITIES AND SHARE-OWNERS' EQUITY		
CURRENT		
Accounts payable and accrued expenses	**$ 3,692**	$ 3,679
Loans and notes payable	**2,475**	3,743
Current maturities of long-term debt	**180**	156
Accrued income taxes	**994**	851
TOTAL CURRENT LIABILITIES	**7,341**	8,429
LONG-TERM DEBT	**2,701**	1,219
OTHER LIABILITIES	**2,260**	961
DEFERRED INCOME TAXES	**399**	442
SHARE-OWNERS' EQUITY		
Common stock, $.25 par value		
Authorized: 5,600,000,000 shares;		
issued: 3,490,818,627 shares in 2002 and 3,491,465,016 shares in 2001	**873**	873
Capital surplus	**3,857**	3,520
Reinvested earnings	**24,506**	23,443
Accumulated other comprehensive income (loss) and unearned compensation on restricted stock	**(3,047)**	(2,788)
	26,189	25,048
Less treasury stock, at cost (1,019,839,490 shares in 2002; 1,005,237,693 shares in 2001)	**14,389**	13,682
	11,800	11,366
TOTAL LIABILITIES AND SHARE-OWNERS' EQUITY	**$ 24,501**	$ 22,417

Coca-Cola's long-term debt.

See Notes to Consolidated Financial Statements.

NET OPERATING REVENUES BY OPERATING SEGMENT*

The Coca-Cola Company and Subsidiaries

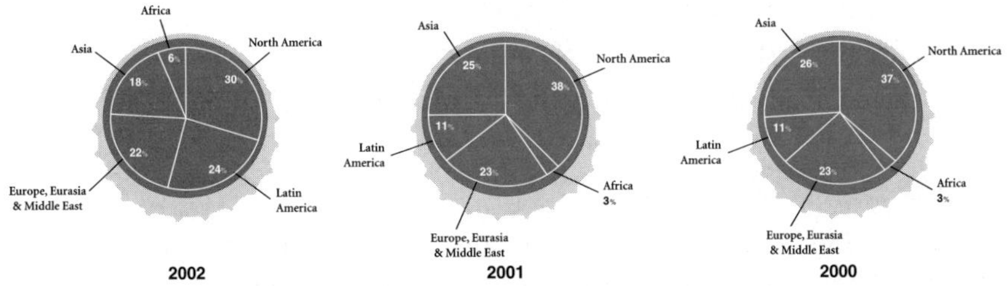

*Charts and percentages are calculated excluding Corporate.

You're in the Driver's Seat

What interest rates does Coca-Cola Company have to pay on long-term debt? How do accountants record the transactions related to long-term debt? Look for the answers as you study this chapter. Check Coca-Cola's most recent annual report to identify any changes in its long-term liabilities.

[1]Coca-Cola's 2001 annual report, p. 44.

LEARNING OBJECTIVES

After studying this chapter, you should be able to:

LO 1 Identify the components of the long-term liability category of the balance sheet. (p. 487)

LO 2 Define the important characteristics of bonds payable. (p. 489)

LO 3 Determine the issue price of a bond using compound interest techniques. (p. 490)

LO 4 Demonstrate an understanding of the effect on the balance sheet of issuance of bonds. (p. 493)

LO 5 Find the amortization of premium or discount using effective interest amortization. (p. 494)

LO 6 Find the gain or loss on retirement of bonds. (p. 498)

LO 7 Determine whether a lease agreement must be reported as a liability on the balance sheet. (p. 500)

LO 8 Explain the effects that transactions involving long-term liabilities have on the statement of cash flows. (p. 505)

LO 9 Explain deferred taxes and calculate the deferred tax liability. (Appendix) (p. 513)

LO 10 Demonstrate an understanding of the meaning of a pension obligation and the effect of pensions on the long-term liability category of the balance sheet. (Appendix) (p. 515)

WHAT EXTERNAL DECISION MAKERS WANT TO KNOW ABOUT LONG-TERM LIABILITIES

DECISION MAKING

External decision makers want to know how a company obtained its funds to finance the business. Companies can finance the business by borrowing (debt) or by issuing stock (equity). Most well-managed companies use a combination of debt and equity. Borrowing money is usually wise but only up to a certain point. Creditors want to lend to companies that will make a profit and be able to pay the interest and principal on the loans. They also want to know whether there is sufficient collateral for the loans. Stockholders want to invest in companies that have financed the company wisely and can generate a steady return to the stockholders.

▶ *ASK ESSENTIAL QUESTIONS*

- What is the return to the bondholders?
- What are the company's lease obligations?
- Will the company be able to pay the interest and principal on its debt?

▶ *FIND BASIC INFORMATION*

The balance sheet, the income statement, and the statement of cash flows, along with the supporting notes, are the key sources of information about a company's long-term resources. This information tells:

- the dollar amount of long-term liabilities,
- the interest rates and due dates of the liabilities,
- the impact of liabilities on the income of the company, and
- how much cash has been generated as a result of the long-term liabilities.

▶ *UNDERSTAND ACCOUNTING PRINCIPLES*

To understand the basic information that is found, decision makers must understand the underlying accounting principles (GAAP) that have been applied to create the reported information. For long-term liabilities, these principles determine:

- how bond and lease information is reported, and
- the classification and accounting treatment of a lease.

▶ INTERPRET ANALYTICAL INFORMATION

The manner in which a company has financed its operations can be measured by the debt-to-equity ratio. A high debt-to-equity ratio indicates the company has used a large amount of debt. Lenders want to know whether borrowers can pay the interest and principal on the debt. This can be determined by examining the times interest earned ratio, a measure of whether sufficient income has been generated to meet interest payments. Decision makers can also calculate the debt service coverage ratio to determine whether sufficient cash has been generated to meet obligations. Of course, external decision makers must also read the notes carefully to determine the interest rates and terms of the liabilities.

BALANCE SHEET PRESENTATION

LO 1 Identify the components of the long-term liability category of the balance sheet.

Long-term liability An obligation that will not be satisfied within one year or the current operating cycle.

In general, **long-term liabilities** are obligations that will not be satisfied within one year. Essentially, all liabilities that are not classified as current liabilities are classified as long-term. We will concentrate on the long-term liabilities of bonds or notes, leases, deferred taxes, and pension obligations. On the balance sheet, the items are listed after current liabilities. For example, the Noncurrent Liabilities section of **PepsiCo, Inc.'s** balance sheet is highlighted in Exhibit 10-1. PepsiCo has acquired financing through a combination of long-term debt, stock issuance, and internal growth or retained earnings. Exhibit 10-1 indicates that long-term debt is one portion of the long-term liability category of the balance sheet. But the balance sheet also reveals two other items that must be considered part of the long-term liability category: deferred income taxes and other liabilities. We begin by looking at a particular type of long-term debt, bonds payable.

Ethics in Accounting

Enron Corporation

In late 2001, Enron, the nation's largest marketer of electricity and natural gas, reported massive losses and reductions in shareholder equity. At that time, the company issued a major restatement of their previously issued financial statements that covered a four-year period and then filed for bankruptcy.

Enron management, working closely with its chief consultant and auditor, Arthur Andersen, had set up several partnerships. These were owned by the Enron Corporation. Then, Enron accountants recorded a significant amount of Enron's long-term debt on the books of the partnerships rather than on the corporation's books. By doing this, Enron avoided reporting billions of dollars of debt on its own balance sheets.

During the period of these transactions, Enron executives were paid large bonuses that were based on Enron's earnings performance and increases in its stock price.

What did the company do that was of ethical concern? Why should Enron have disclosed the debt on its balance sheet instead of on that of the partnerships? How did not having the debt on Enron's books affect the company's earnings and its executives' bonuses?

Sources: Mitchell Pacelle, "Enron report gives details of deals that masked debt," *The Wall Street Journal*, September 23, 2002; "The Fall of Enron," *Business News Online*, December 17, 2001.

Exhibit 10-1 PepsiCo Balance Sheet

Consolidated Balance Sheet

December 28, 2002 and December 29, 2001

PepsiCo, Inc. and Subsidiaries

(In millions except per share amounts)	2002	2001
ASSETS		
Current Assets		
Cash and cash equivalents	$ 1,638	$ 683
Short-term investments, at cost	207	966
	1,845	1,649
Accounts and notes receivable, net	2,531	2,142
Inventories	1,342	1,310
Prepaid expenses and other current assets	695	752
Total Current Assets	6,413	5,853
Property, Plant and Equipment, net	7,390	6,876
Amortizable Intangible Assets, net	801	875
Nonamortizable Intangible Assets	4,418	3,966
Investments in Noncontrolled Affiliates	2,611	2,871
Other Assets	1,841	1,254
Total Assets	$23,474	$21,695
LIABILITIES AND SHAREHOLDERS' EQUITY		
Current Liabilities		
Short-term obligations	$ 562	$ 354
Accounts payable and other current liabilities	4,998	4,461
Income taxes payable	492	183
Total Current Liabilities	6,052	4,998
Long-Term Debt Obligations	2,187	2,651
Other Liabilities	4,226	3,876
Deferred Income Taxes	1,718	1,496
Preferred Stock, no par value	41	41
Repurchased Preferred Stock	(48)	(15)
Common Shareholders' Equity		
Common stock, par value 1⅔¢ per share (issued 1,782 shares)	30	30
Capital in excess of par value		13
Retained earnings	13,464	11,519
Accumulated other comprehensive loss	(1,672)	(1,646)
Less: repurchased common stock, at cost (60 and 26 shares, respectively)	11,822	9,916
Total Common Shareholders' Equity	(2,524)	(1,268)
Total Liabilities and Shareholders' Equity	9,298	8,648
	$23,474	$21,695

PepsiCo's long-term debt

See accompanying notes to consolidated financial statements.

From Concept to Practice 10.1

Reading Coca-Cola's Balance Sheet

Coca-Cola lists three items as long-term liabilities on its 2002 balance sheet. What are those items? Did they increase or decrease?

BONDS PAYABLE

Characteristics of Bonds

LO 2 Define the important characteristics of bonds payable.

A bond is a security or financial instrument that allows firms to borrow money and repay the loan over a long period of time. The bonds are sold, or *issued,* to investors who have amounts to invest and want a return on their investment. The *borrower* (issuing firm) promises to pay interest on specified dates, usually annually or semiannually. The borrower also promises to repay the principal on a specified date, the *due date* or maturity date.

A bond certificate, illustrated in Exhibit 10-2, is issued at the time of purchase and indicates the *terms* of the bond. Generally, bonds are issued in denominations of $1,000. The denomination of the bond is usually referred to as the **face value** or par value. This is the amount that the firm must pay at the maturity date of the bond.

Face value The principal amount of the bond as stated on the bond certificate.

Firms issue bonds in very large amounts, often in millions in a single issue. After bonds are issued, they may be traded on a bond exchange in the same way that stocks are sold on the stock exchanges. Therefore, bonds are not always held until maturity by the initial investor but may change hands several times before their eventual due date. Because bond maturities are as long as 30 years, the "secondary" market in bonds—the market for bonds already issued—is a critical factor in a company's ability to raise money. Investors in bonds may want to sell them if interest rates paid by competing investments become more attractive or if the issuer becomes less creditworthy. Buyers of these bonds may be betting that interest rates will reverse course or

Exhibit 10-2 Bond Certificate

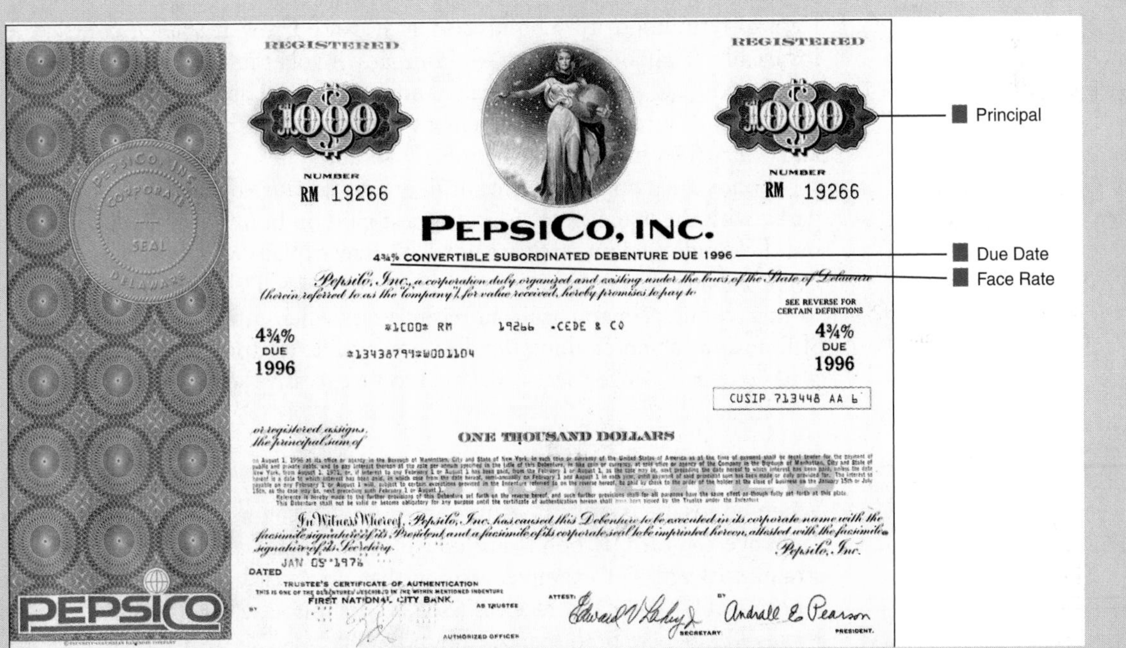

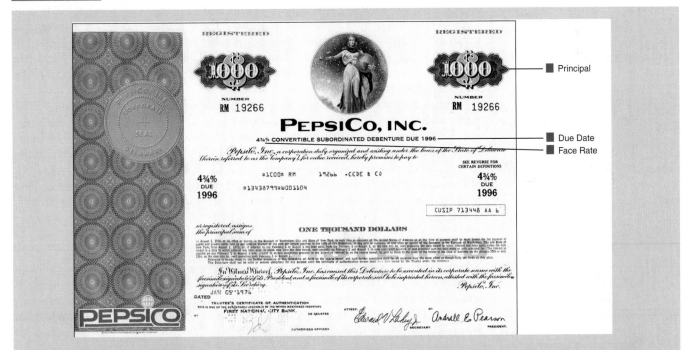

Debenture bonds, like this one from PepsiCo, Inc., are backed by the general creditworthiness of the issuing company, not by the assets as collateral. Buyers of such bonds should check the issuer's credit rating, should know how to read the firm's financial statements, and should learn as much as possible about its operations.

that the company will get back on its feet. Trading in the secondary market does not affect the financial statements of the issuing company.

We have described the general nature of bonds, but it should not be assumed that all bonds have the same terms and features. Following are some important features that often appear in the bond certificate.

Debenture bonds Bonds that are not backed by specific collateral.

Collateral The bond certificate should indicate the *collateral* of the loan. Collateral represents the assets that back the bonds in case the issuer cannot make the interest and principal payments and must default on the loan. **Debenture bonds** are not backed by specific collateral of the issuing company. Rather, the investor must examine the general creditworthiness of the issuer. If a bond is a *secured bond,* the certificate indicates specific assets that serve as collateral in case of default.

Serial bonds Bonds that do not all have the same due date; a portion of the bonds comes due each time period.

Due Date The bond certificate specifies the date that the bond principal must be repaid. Normally, bonds are *term bonds,* meaning that the entire principal amount is due on a single date. Alternatively, bonds may be issued as **serial bonds,** meaning that not all of the principal is due on the same date. For example, a firm may issue serial bonds that have a portion of the principal due each year for the next 10 years. Issuing firms may prefer serial bonds because a firm does not need to accumulate the entire amount for principal repayment at one time.

Other Features Some bonds are issued as convertible or callable bonds. *Convertible bonds* can be converted into common stock at a future time. This feature allows the investor to buy a security that pays a fixed interest rate but that can be converted at a future date into an equity security (stock) if the issuing firm is growing and profitable. The conversion feature is also advantageous to the issuing firm because convertible bonds normally carry a lower rate of interest.

Callable bonds Bonds that may be redeemed or retired before their specified due date.

Callable bonds may be retired before their specified due date. *Callable* generally refers to the issuer's right to retire the bonds. If the buyer or investor has the right to retire the bonds, they are referred to as *redeemable bonds.* Usually, callable bonds stipulate the price to be paid at redemption; this price is referred to as the *redemption price* or the *reacquisition price.* The callable feature is like an insurance policy for the company. Say a bond pays 10%, but interest rates plummet to 6%. Rather than continuing to pay 10%, the company is willing to offer a slight premium over face value for the right to retire those 10% bonds so that it can borrow at 6%. Of course, the investor is invariably disappointed when the company invokes its call privilege.

INTERNAL DECISION

As you can see, various terms and features are associated with bonds. Each firm seeks to structure the bond agreement in the manner that best meets its financial needs and will attract investors at the most favorable rates.

Bonds are a popular source of financing because of the tax advantages when compared with the issuance of stock. Interest paid on bonds is deductible for tax purposes, but dividends paid on stock are not. This may explain why the amount of debt on many firms' balance sheets has increased in recent years. Debt became popular in the 1980s to finance mergers and again in recent years when interest rates reached 20-year lows. Still, investors and creditors tend to downgrade a company when the amount of debt it has on the balance sheet is deemed to be excessive.

Issuance of Bonds

When bonds are issued, the issuing firm must recognize the incurrence of a liability in exchange for cash. If bonds are issued at their face amount, the accounting entry is straightforward. For example, assume that on April 1 a firm issues bonds with a face amount of $10,000 and receives $10,000. In this case, the asset Cash and the liability Bonds Payable are both increased by $10,000.

LO 3 Determine the issue price of a bond using compound interest techniques.

Factors Affecting Bond Price

Face rate of interest The rate of interest on the bond certificate.

With bonds payable, two interest rates are always involved. The **face rate of interest** (also called the *stated rate, nominal rate, contract rate, or coupon rate*) is the rate specified on the bond certificate. It is the amount of interest that will be paid each interest period. For example, if $10,000 worth of bonds is issued with an 8% annual face rate of interest, then interest of $800 ($10,000 × 8% × 1 year) would be paid at the end of each annual period. Alternatively, bonds often require the payment of interest semiannually. If the bonds in our example required the 8% annual face rate to be paid semiannually (at 4%), then interest of $400 ($10,000 × 8% × $^1/_2$ year) would be paid each semiannual period.

The second important interest rate is the **market rate of interest** (also called the *effective rate* or *bond yield*). The market rate of interest is the rate that bondholders could obtain by investing in other bonds that are similar to the issuing firm's bonds. The issuing firm does not set the market rate of interest. That rate is determined by the bond market on the basis of many transactions for similar bonds. The market rate incorporates all of the "market's" knowledge about economic conditions and all its expectations about future conditions. Normally, issuing firms try to set a face rate that is equal to the market rate. However, because the market rate changes daily, there are almost always small differences between the face rate and the market rate at the time bonds are issued.

Market rate of interest The rate that investors could obtain by investing in other bonds that are similar to the issuing firm's bonds.

Study Tip

Calculating the issue price of a bond always involves a calculation of the present value of the cash flows.

In addition to the number of interest payments and the maturity length of the bond, the face rate and the market rate of interest must both be known in order to calculate the issue price of a bond. The **bond issue price** equals the *present value* of the cash flows that the bond will produce. Bonds produce two types of cash flows for the investor: interest receipts and repayment of principal (face value). The interest receipts constitute an annuity of payments each interest period over the life of the bonds. The repayment of principal (face value) is a one-time receipt that occurs at the end of the term of the bonds. We must calculate the present value of the interest receipts (using Table 9-4) and the present value of the principal amount (using Table 9-2). The total of the two present-value calculations represents the issue price of the bond.

Bond issue price The present value of the annuity of interest payments plus the present value of the principal.

An Example Suppose that on January 1, 2004, Discount Firm wants to issue bonds with a face value of $10,000. The face or coupon rate of interest has been set at 8%. The bonds will pay interest annually, and the principal amount is due in four years. Also suppose that the market rate of interest for other similar bonds is currently 10%. Because the market rate of interest exceeds the coupon rate, investors will not be willing to pay $10,000 but something less. We want to calculate the amount that will be obtained from the issuance of Discount Firm's bonds.

Discount's bond will produce two sets of cash flows for the investor: an annual interest payment of $800 ($10,000 × 8%) per year for four years and repayment of the principal of $10,000 at the end of the fourth year. To calculate the issue price, we must calculate the present value of the two sets of cash flows. A time diagram portrays the cash flows as follows:

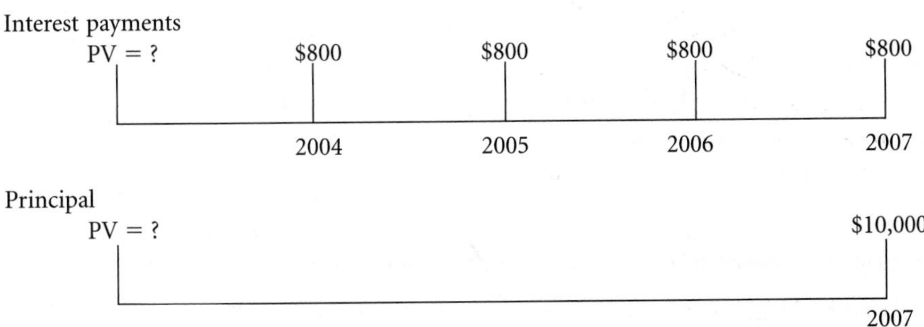

We can calculate the issue price by using the compound-interest tables found in Chapter 9, as follows:

$800 × 3.170 (factor from Table 9-4 for 4 periods, 10%)	$2,536
$10,000 × 0.683 (factor from Table 9-2 for 4 periods, 10%)	6,830
Issue price	$9,366

You should perform the following steps when using a calculator to determine the present value in our example:

ENTER	DISPLAY
4 N	N = 4
10 I/Y	I/Y = 10
800 PMT	PMT = 800
10000 FV	FV = 10,000
CPT PV	PV = 9,366

The factors used to calculate the present value represent four periods and 10% interest. This is a key point. The issue price of a bond is always calculated using the market rate of interest. The face rate of interest determines the amount of the interest payments, but the market rate determines the present value of the payments and the present value of the principal (and therefore the issue price).

Our example of Discount Firm reveals that the bonds with a $10,000 face value amount would be issued for $9,366. The bond markets and the financial press often state the issue price as a percentage of the face amount. The percentage for Discount's bonds can be calculated as ($9,366/$10,000) × 100, or 93.66%.

http://www.ibm.com

Exhibit 10-3 illustrates how bonds are actually listed in the reporting of the bond markets. The exhibit lists two types of **IBM** bonds that were traded on a particular day. The portion immediately after the company name, for example "6⅜ 06," indicates that the face rate of interest is 6⅜% and the due date of the bonds is the year 2006. The next column, for example "6.5," indicates that the bond investor who purchased the bonds on that day will receive a yield of 6.5%. The column labeled "vol" indicates the number of bonds, in thousands, that were bought and sold during the day. The column labeled "close" indicates the market price of the bonds at the end of the day. For example, the first issue of IBM bonds closed at 98¾, which means that the price was 98¾% of the face value of the bonds, or $987.50 per bond. These bonds are trading at a discount because the face rate (6⅜%) is less than the market rate of 6.5%. The bonds in the second issue—"7¼ 08"—have a face rate of 7¼%, will become due in the year 2008, and closed at 101½, or at a premium. The net change column indicates the change in the bond price that occurred for the day's trading.

Exhibit 10-3

Listing of Bonds on the Bond Market

BONDS	CUR YLD	VOL	CLOSE	NET CHG
IBM 6⅜06	6.5	280	98¾	−¼
IBM 7¼08	7.1	68	101½	+¼

Accounting for Your Decisions

You Rate the Bonds

One of the factors that determine the rate of interest on a bond is a rating by a rating agency such as Standard & Poor's or Moody's Investor Service. Bonds with a higher rating are considered less risky and can be issued for a lower rate of interest. You have been given an assignment to rate the bonds issued by PepsiCo. What factors would you consider in your rating?

ANS: There are many factors that affect your evaluation of the riskiness of the company's bonds. One factor would be the amount of debt on PepsiCo's books, which can be found by examining the liability section of the balance sheet. It is important to relate the amount of debt to the total equity of the company; this is often done by computing the debt-to-equity ratio. Another important factor is the company's competitive position within its industry. If PepsiCo can operate profitably, it will generate cash that can be used to pay the interest and principal on the bonds.

Premium or Discount on Bonds

LO 4 Demonstrate an understanding of the effect on the balance sheet of issuance of bonds.

Premium or **discount** represents the difference between the face value and the issue price of a bond. We may state the relationship as follows:

Premium = Issue Price – Face Value
Discount = Face Value – Issue Price

In other words, when issue price exceeds face value, the bonds have sold at a premium, and when the face value exceeds the issue price, the bonds have sold at a discount.

We will continue with the Discount Firm example to illustrate the accounting for bonds sold at a discount. Discount Firm's bonds sold at a discount calculated as follows:

Premium The excess of the issue price over the face value of the bonds.

Discount The excess of the face value of bonds over the issue price.

Discount = $10,000 – $9,366
= $634

The effect on Discount Firm's accounting equation as a result of the issuance of the bonds is as follows:

BALANCE SHEET						INCOME STATEMENT
ASSETS		=	LIABILITIES		+ OWNERS' EQUITY	+ REVENUES – EXPENSES
Cash	9,366		Bonds Payable	10,000		
			Discount on Bonds Payable	(634)		

The Discount on Bonds Payable account is shown as a contra liability on the balance sheet in conjunction with the Bonds Payable account and is a deduction from that account. If Discount Firm prepared a balance sheet immediately after the bond issuance, the following would appear in the Long-Term Liabilities category of the balance sheet:

Long-term liabilities:	
Bonds payable	$10,000
Less: Discount on bonds payable	634
	$ 9,366

The Discount Firm example has illustrated a situation in which the market rate of a bond issue is higher than the face rate. Now we will examine the opposite situation, when the face rate exceeds the market rate. Again, we are interested in calculating the issue price of the bonds.

Issuing at a Premium Suppose that on January 1, 2004, Premium Firm wants to issue the same bonds as in the previous example: $10,000 face value bonds, with an 8% face rate of interest and with interest paid annually each year for four years. Assume, however, that the market rate of interest is 6% for similar bonds. The issue price is calculated as the present value of the annuity of interest payments plus the present value of the principal at the market rate of interest. The calculations are as follows:

$800 × 3.465 (factor from Table 9-4 for 4 periods, 6%)	$ 2,772
$10,000 × 0.792 (factor from Table 9-2 for 4 periods, 6%)	7,920
Issue price	$10,692

You should perform the following steps when using a calculator to determine the present value in our example:

ENTER	DISPLAY
4 N	N = 4
6 I/Y	I/Y = 6
800 PMT	PMT = 800
10000 FV	FV = 10,000
CPT PV	PV = 10,693*
*(rounded)	

We have calculated that the bonds would be issued for $10,692. Because the bonds would be issued at an amount that is higher than the face value amount, they would be issued at a premium. The amount of the premium is calculated as follows:

$$\text{Premium} = \$10{,}692 - \$10{,}000$$
$$= \$692$$

The effect on the accounting equation of the isuance of the bonds at a premium is as follows:

BALANCE SHEET							INCOME STATEMENT
ASSETS		=	LIABILITIES		+	OWNERS' EQUITY	+ REVENUES – EXPENSES
Cash	10,692		Bonds Payable	10,000			
			Discount on Bonds Payable	692			

Study Tip

When interest rates increase, present values decrease. This is called an *inverse relationship.*

The account Premium on Bonds Payable is an addition to the Bonds Payable account. If Premium Firm presented a balance sheet immediately after the bond issuance, the Long-Term Liabilities category of the balance sheet would appear as follows:

Long-term liabilities:	
Bonds payable	$10,000
Plus: Premium on bonds payable	692
	$10,692

You should learn two important points from the Discount Firm and Premium Firm examples. First, you should be able to determine whether a bond will sell at a premium or discount by the relationship that exists between the face rate and the market rate of interest. *Premium* and *discount* do not mean "good" and "bad." Premium or discount arises solely because of the difference that exists between the face rate and the market rate of interest for a bond issue. The same relationship always exists, so that the following statements hold true:

If Market Rate = Face Rate, THEN bonds are issued at face value amount.
If Market Rate > Face Rate, THEN bonds are issued at a discount.
If Market Rate < Face Rate, THEN bonds are issued at a premium.

The examples also illustrate a second important point. The relationship between interest rates and bond prices is always inverse. To understand the term *inverse relationship,* refer to the Discount Firm and Premium Firm examples. The bonds of the two firms are identical in all respects except for the market rate of interest. When the market rate was 10%, the bond issue price was $9,366 (the Discount Firm example). When the market rate was 6%, the bond issue price increased to $10,692 (the Premium Firm example). The examples illustrate that as interest rates decrease, prices on the bond markets increase and that as interest rates increase, bond prices decrease.

Many investors in the stock market perceive that they are taking a great deal of risk with their capital. In truth, **bond investors** are taking substantial risks too. The most obvious risk is that the company will fail and not be able to pay its debts. But another risk is that interest rates on comparable investments will rise. Interest rate risk can have a devastating impact on the current market value of bonds. One way to minimize interest rate risk is to hold the bond to maturity, at which point the company must pay the face amount.

LO 5 Find the amortization of premium or discount using effective interest amortization.

Bond Amortization

Purpose of Amortization The amount of interest expense that should be reflected on a firm's income statement for bonds payable is the true, or effective, interest. The effective interest should reflect the face rate of interest as well as interest that results from issuing the bond at a premium or discount. To reflect that interest component, the amount initially recorded in the Premium on Bonds Payable or the Discount on Bonds Payable account must be amortized or spread over the life of the bond.

Amortization refers to the process of transferring an amount from the discount or premium account to interest expense each time period to adjust interest expense. One commonly used method of amortization is the effective interest method. We will illustrate how to amortize a discount amount and then how to amortize a premium amount.

To illustrate amortization of a discount, we need to return to our Discount Firm example introduced earlier. We have seen that the issue price of the bond could be calculated as $9,366, resulting in a contra-liability balance of $634 in the Discount on Bonds Payable account (see the accounting equation on page 493). But what does the initial balance of the Discount account really represent? The discount should be thought of as additional interest that Discount Firm must pay over and above the 8% face rate. Remember that Discount received only $9,366 but must repay the full principal of $10,000 at the bond due date. For that reason, the $634 discount is an additional interest cost that must be reflected as interest expense. It is reflected as interest expense by the process of amortization. In other words, interest expense is made up of two components: cash interest and amortization. We will now consider how to amortize premium or discount.

Effective Interest Method: Impact on Expense The **effective interest method of amortization** amortizes discount or premium in a manner that produces a constant effective interest rate from period to period. The *dollar amount* of interest expense will vary from period to period, but the rate of interest will be constant. This interest rate is referred to as the *effective interest rate* and is equal to the market rate of interest at the time the bonds are issued.

Effective interest method of amortization The process of transferring a portion of the premium or discount to interest expense; this method results in a constant effective interest rate.

To illustrate this point, we introduce two new terms. The **carrying value** of bonds is represented by the following:

Carrying value The face value of a bond plus the amount of unamortized premium or minus the amount of unamortized discount.

Carrying Value = Face Value − Unamortized Discount

For example, the carrying value of the bonds for our Discount Firm example, as of the date of issuance of January 1, 2004, could be calculated as follows:

$10,000 − $634 = $9,366

In those situations in which there is a premium instead of a discount, carrying value is represented by the following:

Carrying Value = Face Value + Unamortized Premium

For example, the carrying value of the bonds for our Premium Firm example, as of the date of issuance of January 1, 2004, could be calculated as follows:

$10,000 + $692 = $10,692

The second term has been suggested earlier. The *effective rate of interest* is represented by the following:

Effective Rate = Annual Interest Expense/Carrying Value

Effective Interest Method: An Example The amortization table in Exhibit 10-4 illustrates effective interest amortization of the bond discount for our Discount Firm example.

As illustrated in Exhibit 10-4, the effective interest method of amortization is based on several important concepts. The relationships can be stated in equation form as follows:

Cash Interest (in Column 1) = Bond Face Value × Face Rate
Interest Expense (in Column 2) = Carrying Value × Effective Rate
Discount Amortized (in Column 3) = Interest Expense − Cash Interest

Exhibit 10-4

Discount Amortization: Effective Interest Method of Amortization

DATE	COLUMN 1 CASH INTEREST	COLUMN 2 INTEREST EXPENSE	COLUMN 3 DISCOUNT AMORTIZED	COLUMN 4 CARRYING VALUE
	8%	**10%**	**Col. 2 − Col. 1**	
1/1/2004	—	—	—	$ 9,366
12/31/2004	$800	$937	$137	9,503
12/31/2005	800	950	150	9,653
12/31/2006	800	965	165	9,818
12/31/2007	800	982	182	10,000

The first column of the exhibit indicates that the cash interest to be paid is $800 ($10,000 × 8%). The second column indicates the annual interest expense at the effective rate of interest (market rate at the time of issuance). This is a constant rate of interest (10% in our example) and is calculated by multiplying the carrying value *as of the beginning of the period* by the market rate of interest. In 2004, the interest expense is $937 ($9,366 × 10%). Note that the amount of interest expense changes each year because the carrying value changes as discount is amortized. The amount of discount amortized each year in Column 3 is the difference between the cash interest in Column 1 and the interest expense in Column 2. Again, note that the amount of discount amortized changes in each of the four years. Finally, the carrying value in Column 4 is the previous year's carrying value plus the discount amortized in Column 3. When bonds are issued at a discount, the carrying value starts at an amount less than face value and increases each period until it reaches the face value amount.

Exhibit 10-4 is the basis for determining the effect of amortization on the firm's financial statements. The effect of the interest payment and the amortization of discount for 2004 (note the December 31, 2004, line of the table) is as follow:

BALANCE SHEET						INCOME STATEMENT	
ASSETS		=	LIABILITIES		+ OWNERS' EQUITY	+ REVENUES − EXPENSES	
Cash	(800)		Discount on Bonds Payable	137		Interest Expense	(937)

The balance of the Discount on Bonds Payable account as of December 31, 2004, would be calculated as follows:

Beginning balance, January 1, 2004	$634
Less: Amount amortized	137
Ending balance, December 31, 2004	$497

The December 31, 2004, balance represents the amount *unamortized*, or the amount that will be amortized in future time periods. On the balance sheet presented as of December 31, 2004, the unamortized portion of the discount appears as the balance of the Discount on Bonds Payable account as follows:

Long-term liabilities	
Bonds payable	$10,000
Less: Discount on bonds payable	497
	$ 9,503

The process of amortization would continue for four years, until the balance of the Discount on Bonds Payable account has been reduced to zero. By the end of 2007, all of the balance of the Discount on Bonds Payable account will have been transferred to the Interest Expense account and represents an increase in interest expense each period.

The amortization of a premium has an impact opposite that of the amortization of a discount. We will use our Premium Firm example to illustrate. Recall that on January

1, 2004, Premium Firm issued $10,000 face value bonds with a face rate of interest of 8%. At the time the bonds were issued, the market rate was 6%, resulting in an issue price of $10,692 and a credit balance in the Premium on Bonds Payable account of $692.

The amortization table in Exhibit 10-5 illustrates effective interest amortization of the bond premium for Premium Firm. As the exhibit illustrates, effective interest amortization of a premium is based on the same concepts as amortization of a discount. The following relationships still hold true:

Cash Interest (in Column 1) = Bond Face Value × Face Rate
Interest Expense (in Column 2) = Carrying Value × Effective Rate

The first column of the exhibit indicates that the cash interest to be paid is $800 ($10,000 × 8%). The second column indicates the annual interest expense at the effective rate. In 2004 the interest expense is $642 ($10,692 × 6%). Note, however, two differences between Exhibit 10-4 and Exhibit 10-5. In the amortization of a premium, the cash interest in Column 1 exceeds the interest expense in Column 2. Therefore, the premium amortized is defined as follows:

Study Tip

Amortization of a discount increases interest expense. Amortization of a premium reduces interest expense.

Premium Amortized (in Column 3) = Cash Interest − Interest Expense

Also note that the carrying value in Column 4 starts at an amount higher than the face value of $10,000 ($10,692) and is amortized downward until it reaches face value. Therefore, the carrying value at the end of each year is the carrying value at the beginning of the period minus the premium amortized for that year. For example, the carrying value in Exhibit 10-5 at the end of 2004 ($10,534) was calculated by subtracting the premium amortized for 2004 ($158 in Column 3) from the carrying value at the beginning of 2004 ($10,692).

Exhibit 10-5 is the basis for determining the effect of amortization of a premium on the firm's financial statements. The effect of the interest payment and the amortization of premium for 2004 (note the December 31, 2004, line of the table) is as follows:

BALANCE SHEET						INCOME STATEMENT	
ASSETS		= LIABILITIES		+ OWNERS' EQUITY		+ REVENUES − EXPENSES	
Cash	(800)	Premium on Bonds Payable	(158)			Interest Expense	(642)

The balance of the Premium on Bonds payable account as of December 31, 2004, would be calculated as follows:

Beginning balance, January 1, 2004	$692
Less: Amount amortized	158
Ending balance, December 31, 2004	$534

The December 31, 2004, balance represents the amount *unamortized*, or the amount that will be amortized in future time periods. On the balance sheet presented as of

Exhibit 10-5

Premium Amortization: Effective Interest Method of Amortization

DATE	COLUMN 1 CASH INTEREST	COLUMN 2 INTEREST EXPENSE	COLUMN 3 PREMIUM AMORTIZED	COLUMN 4 CARRYING VALUE
	8%	6%	Col. 1 − Col. 2	
1/1/2004	—	—	—	$10,692
12/31/2004	$800	$642	$158	10,534
12/31/2005	800	632	168	10,366
12/31/2006	800	622	178	10,188
12/31/2007	800	612	188	10,000

December 31, 2004, the unamortized portion of the premium appears as the balance of the Premium on Bonds payable account as follows:

Long-term liabilities:	
Bonds payable	$10,000
Plus: Premium on bonds payable	534
	$10,534

The process of amortization would continue for four years, until the balance of the Premium on Bonds Payable account has been reduced to zero. By the end of 2007, all of the balance of the Premium on Bonds Payable account will have been transferred to the Interest Expense account and represents a reduction of interest expense each period.

Two-Minute Review

1. *How do you calculate the issue price of a bond?*
2. *What effect does amortizing a premium have on the amount of interest expense for the bond? What effect does amortizing a discount have?*

Answers on p. 508.

INTERNAL DECISION

Redemption of Bonds

Redemption at Maturity The term *redemption* refers to retirement of bonds by repayment of the principal. If bonds are retired on their due date, the accounting entry is not difficult. Refer again to the Discount Firm example. If Discount Firm retires its bonds on the due date of December 31, 2007, it must repay the principal of $10,000, and Cash is reduced by $10,000. No gain or loss is incurred because the carrying value of the bond at that point is $10,000.

LO 6 Find the gain or loss on retirement of bonds.

Retired Early at a Gain A firm may want to retire bonds before their due date for several reasons. A firm may simply have excess cash and may determine that the best use of those funds is to repay outstanding bond obligations. Bonds may also be retired early because of changing interest rate conditions. If interest rates in the economy decline, firms may find it advantageous to retire bonds that have been issued at higher rates. Of course, what is advantageous to the issuer is not necessarily so for the investor. Early retirement of callable bonds is always a possibility that must be anticipated. Large institutional investors expect such a development and merely reinvest the money elsewhere. Many individual investors are more seriously inconvenienced when a bond issue is called.

Bond terms generally specify that if bonds are retired before their due date, they are not retired at the face value amount but at a call price or redemption price indicated on the bond certificate. Also, the amount of unamortized premium or discount on the bonds must be considered when bonds are retired early. The retirement results in a **gain or loss on redemption** that must be calculated as follows:

Gain or loss on redemption The difference between the carrying value and the redemption price at the time bonds are redeemed.

Gain = Carrying Value − Redemption Price
Loss = Redemption Price − Carrying Value

In other words, the issuing firm must calculate the carrying value of the bonds at the time of redemption and compare it with the total redemption price. If the carrying value is higher than the redemption price, the issuing firm must record a gain. If the carrying value is lower than the redemption price, the issuing firm must record a loss.

We will use the Premium Firm example to illustrate the calculation of gain or loss. Assume that on December 31, 2004, Premium Firm wants to retire its bonds due in 2007. Assume, as in the previous section, that the bonds were issued at a premium of $692 at the beginning of 2004. Premium Firm has used the effective interest method of amortization and has recorded the interest and amortization entries for the year (see page 497). This has resulted in a balance of \$534 in the Premium on Bonds Payable account as of December 31, 2004. Assume also that Premium Firm's bond certificates indicate that the bonds may be retired early at a call price of 102 (meaning 102% of face value). Thus, the redemption price is 102% of \$10,000, or \$10,200.

Premium Firm's retirement of bonds would result in a gain. The gain can be calculated using two steps. First, we must calculate the carrying value of the bonds as of the date they are retired. The carrying value of Premium Firm's bonds at that date is calculated as follows:

$$\begin{aligned}\textbf{Carrying Value} &= \textbf{Face Value} + \textbf{Unamortized Premium}\\ &= \$10{,}000 + \$534\\ &= \$10{,}534\end{aligned}$$

Note that the carrying value we have calculated is the same amount indicated for December 31, 2004, in Column 4 of the effective interest amortization table of Exhibit 10-5.

The second step is to calculate the gain:

$$\begin{aligned}\textbf{Gain} &= \textbf{Carrying Value} - \textbf{Redemption Price}\\ &= \$10{,}534 - (\$10{,}000 \times 1.02)\\ &= \$10{,}534 - \$10{,}200\\ &= \$334\end{aligned}$$

It is important to remember that when bonds are retired, the balance of the Bonds Payable account and the remaining balance of the Premium on Bonds Payable account must be eliminated from the balance sheet.

Retired Early at a Loss To illustrate retirement of bonds at a loss, assume that Premium Firm retires bonds at December 31, 2004, as in the previous section. However, assume that the call price for the bonds is 107 (or 107% of face value).

We can again perform the calculations in two steps. The first step is to calculate the carrying value:

$$\begin{aligned}\text{Carrying Value} &= \text{Face Value} + \text{Unamortized Premium}\\ &= \$10{,}000 + \$534\\ &= \$10{,}534\end{aligned}$$

The second step is to compare the carrying value with the redemption price to calculate the amount of the loss:

$$\begin{aligned}\text{Loss} &= \text{Redemption Price} - \text{Carrying Value}\\ &= (\$10{,}000 \times 1.07) - \$10{,}534\\ &= \$10{,}700 - \$10{,}534\\ &= \$166\end{aligned}$$

In this case, a loss of \$166 has resulted from the retirement of Premium Firm bonds. A loss means that the company paid more to retire the bonds than the amount at which the bonds were recorded on the balance sheet.

Financial Statement Presentation of Gain or Loss The accounts Gain on Bond Redemption and Loss on Bond Redemption are income statement accounts. A gain on bond redemption increases Premium Firm's income; a loss decreases its income. In most cases, a gain or loss should not be considered "unusual" or "infrequent" and therefore should not be placed in the section of the income statement where extraordinary items are presented. While gains and losses should be treated as part of the company's operating income, some statement users may consider them

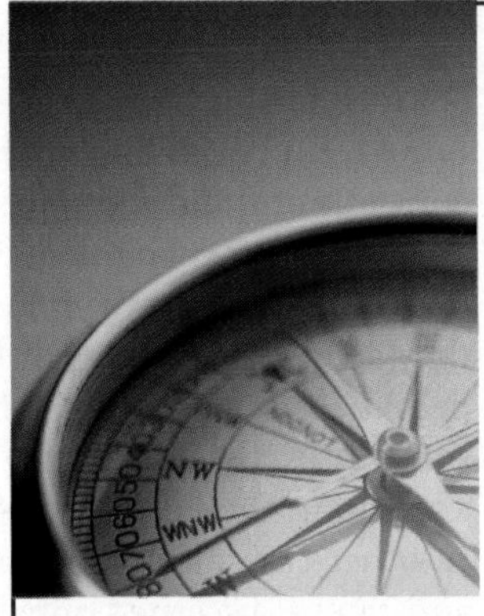

Which Way to Go?

Does the Debt Really Have to Be Reported on the Balance Sheet?

The fiscal year-end for Taz Industries is June 30. To improve the price of the company's common stock in the market, management has been working hard to pay off the company's long-term debt. On July 15 of the current year, a large payment was made to buy back from the market 25% of the outstanding Taz Industry bonds, which were immediately retired.

Generally, it takes six weeks after the fiscal year-end for Taz Industries' annual report information to be prepared, submitted to the SEC, and posted on the company's Web site. Because the significant debt retirement occurred so soon after June 30, the president of Taz wants the June 30 balance sheet to show the lower debt amount. Certainly, there will be disclosure of the transaction in the notes, but why not show the company's balance sheet in the best position possible? After all, people will be reading the annual report information after July 15. Wouldn't it be more accurate to show the debt on the balance sheet at its more current, lower amount?

What debt amount should be shown on the June 30 balance sheet and why?

Business Strategy

http://www.cocacola.com
http://www.pepsico.com

Product Strategy to Meet Competition

Competition in the beverage industry is fierce, and Coca-Cola must constantly adjust its strategy to match its competitors. Coca-Cola continues to be the world's No. 1 soft drink company, but it has lost some momentum in competition with PepsiCo and other companies. In fact, PepsiCo's Gatorade sports drink has been outselling Coca-Cola's Powerade drink. Other companies have begun to make inroads into the market with noncarbonated drinks and even drinking water, such as Evian's.

Coca-Cola's first strategic priority is to increase sales of its carbonated drink brands including Coca-Cola, Cherry Coke, and Diet Coke with lemon. It also unveiled a new vanilla-flavored version of its flagship Coke brand. "It has a broad range of appeal all the way from teens to young adults and adults," said Chris Lowe, Coca-Cola's senior vice president for worldwide brands and advertising. "Vanilla seems to cross the generational gap the same way that Coca-Cola does." But Coca-Cola's second priority is to broaden its brands to include noncarbonated drinks such as Minute Maid fruit drinks and Dasani water. Analysts have said the product launches highlight the intense see-saw battle for soft drink supremacy in the U.S. market. Although both companies have scored successes, Coca-Cola believes its management and marketing strategies will allow it to continue to be in the No. 1 spot around the world. ■

Source: Elizabeth S. Armbuster, "Stocks on the Move: Pepsi Bumps Coke off United Planes," March 25, 2002, Morningstar.com and 2002 Annual Report.

as "one-time" events and wish to exclude them when predicting a company's future income. For that reason, it would be very helpful if companies would present their gains and losses separately on the income statement so that readers could determine whether such amounts will affect future periods.

LIABILITY FOR LEASES

Long-term bonds and notes payable are important sources of financing for many large corporations and are quite prominent in the long-term liability category of the balance sheet for many firms. But other important elements of that category of the balance sheet also represent long-term obligations. We will introduce you to leases because they are a major source of financing for many companies. We will introduce two other liabilities, deferred taxes and pensions, in the appendix at the end of this chapter. In some cases, these liabilities are required to be reported on the financial statements and are important components of the Long-Term Liabilities section of the balance sheet. In other cases, the items are not required to be presented in the financial statements and can be discerned only by a careful reading of the notes to the financial statements.

Leases

LO 7 Determine whether a lease agreement must be reported as a liability on the balance sheet.

INTERNAL DECISION

A *lease,* a contractual arrangement between two parties, allows one party, the *lessee,* the right to use an asset in exchange for making payments to its owner, the *lessor.* A common example of a lease arrangement is the rental of an apartment. The tenant is the lessee and the landlord is the lessor.

Lease agreements are a form of financing. In some cases, it is more advantageous to lease an asset than to borrow money to purchase it. The lessee can conserve cash because a lease does not require a large initial cash outlay. A wide variety of lease arrangements exists, ranging from simple agreements to complex ones that span a long time period. Lease arrangements are popular because of their flexibility. The terms of a lease can be structured in many ways to meet the needs of the lessee and lessor. This results in difficult accounting questions:

1. Should the right to use property be reported as an asset by the lessee?
2. Should the obligation to make payments be reported as a liability by the lessee?
3. Should all leases be accounted for in the same manner regardless of the terms of the lease agreement?

The answers are that some leases should be reported as an asset and a liability by the lessee and some should not. The accountant must examine the terms of the lease agreement and compare those terms with an established set of criteria.

Accounting for Your Decisions

Should You Lease or Buy?

You want to acquire a new car and are considering leasing instead of buying. What factors should you consider to determine whether leasing is the better alternative?

ANS: To make this decision, answer the following questions: Do you have the cash to buy the car? If not, what is the cost of borrowing? How long will the car be used? Will another car be needed in the near future? What is the purpose of the car? How will the lease payments compare with the purchase payments? Will you own the car at the end of the lease?

Lease Criteria From the viewpoint of the lessee, there are two types of lease agreements: operating and capital leases. In an **operating lease,** the lessee acquires the right to use an asset for a limited period of time. The lessee is *not* required to record the right to use the property as an asset or to record the obligation for payments as a liability. Therefore, the lessee is able to attain a form of *off–balance-sheet financing.* That is, the lessee has attained the right to use property but has not recorded that right, or the accompanying obligation, on the balance sheet. By escaping the balance sheet, the lease does not add to debt or impair the debt-to-equity ratio that investors usually calculate. Management has a responsibility to make sure that such off–balance-sheet financing is not in fact a long-term obligation. The company's auditors are supposed to analyze the terms of the lease carefully to make sure that management has exercised its responsibility.

Operating lease A lease that does not meet any of the four criteria and is not recorded as an asset by the lessee.

The second type of lease agreement is a **capital lease.** In this type of lease, the lessee has acquired sufficient rights of ownership and control of the property to be considered its owner. The lease is called a *capital lease* because it is capitalized (recorded) on the balance sheet by the lessee.

Capital lease A lease that is recorded as an asset by the lessee.

A lease should be considered a capital lease by the lessee if one or more of the following criteria are met:[2]

1. The lease transfers ownership of the property to the lessee at the end of the lease term.
2. The lease contains a bargain-purchase option to purchase the asset at an amount lower than its fair market value.
3. The lease term is 75% or more of the property's economic life.
4. The present value of the minimum lease payments is 90% or more of the fair market value of the property at the inception of the lease.

INTERNAL DECISION

If none of the criteria are met, the lease agreement is accounted for as an operating lease. This is an area in which it is important for the accountant to exercise professional judgment. In some cases, firms may take elaborate measures to evade or manipulate the criteria that would require lease capitalization. The accountant should

[2] *Statement of Financial Accounting Standards No. 13,* "Accounting for Leases" (Stamford, Conn.: FASB, 1976).

determine what is full and fair disclosure based on an unbiased evaluation of the substance of the transaction.

Operating Leases You have already accounted for operating leases in previous chapters when recording rent expense and prepaid rent. A rental agreement for a limited time period is also a lease agreement.

Suppose, for example, that Lessee Firm wants to lease a car for a new salesperson. A lease agreement is signed with Lessor Dealer on January 1, 2004, to lease a car for the year for $4,000, payable on December 31, 2004. Typically, a car lease does not transfer title at the end of the term, does not include a bargain-purchase price, and does not last for more than 75% of the car's life. In addition, the present value of the lease payments is not 90% of the car's value. Because the lease does not meet any of the specified criteria, it should be presented as an operating lease. Lessee Firm would simply record lease expense, or rent expense, of $4,000 for the year.

http://www.fasb.org

http://www.tommy.com

Although operating leases are not recorded on the balance sheet by the lessee, they are mentioned in financial statement notes. The FASB requires note disclosure of the amount of future lease obligations for leases that are considered operating leases. Exhibit 10-6 provides a portion of the note from Tommy Hilfiger Corporation's 2002 annual report. The note reveals that Tommy Hilfiger has used operating leases as an important source of financing and has significant off–balance-sheet commitments in future periods as a result. An investor might want to add this off–balance-sheet item to the debt on the balance sheet to get a conservative view of the company's obligations.

Exhibit 10-6

Tommy Hilfiger Corporation 2002 Note Disclosure of Leases

Operating leases can be used as an important source of financing.

Note 8–Commitments and Contingencies

Leases (in millions)

The Company leases office, warehouse and showroom space, retail stores and office equipment under operating leases, which expire not later than 2022. The Company normalizes fixed escalations in rental expense under its operating leases. Minimum annual rentals under non-cancelable operating leases, excluding operating cost escalations and contingent rental amounts based upon retail sales, are payable as follows:

Fiscal Year Ending March 31,	
2003	$ 43,396
2004	41,933
2005	35,683
2006	29,151
2007	25,771
Thereafter	123,213

Rent expense, including operating cost escalations and contingent rental amounts based upon retail sales, was $34,781, $22,561 and $20,092 for the years ended March 31, 2002, 2001, and 2000, respectively.

Capital Leases Capital leases are presented as assets and liabilities by the lessee because they meet one or more of the lease criteria. Suppose that Lessee Firm in the previous example wanted to lease a car for a longer period of time. Assume that on January 1, 2004, Lessee signs a lease agreement with Lessor Dealer to lease a car. The terms of the agreement specify that Lessee will make annual lease payments of $4,000 per year for five years, payable each December 31. Assume also that the lease specifies that at the end of the lease agreement, the title to the car is transferred to Lessee Firm. Lessee must decide how to account for the lease agreement.

Study Tip

It is called a *capital lease* because the lease is capitalized, or put on the books of the lessee as an asset.

The contractual arrangement between Lessee Firm and Lessor Dealer is called a lease agreement, but clearly the agreement is much different from a year-to-year lease arrangement. Essentially, Lessee Firm has acquired the right to use the asset for its entire life and does not need to return it to Lessor Dealer. You may call this agreement a lease, but it actually represents a purchase of the asset by Lessee with payments made over time.

The lease should be treated as a capital lease by Lessee because it meets at least one of the four criteria (it meets the first criteria concerning transfer of title). A capital lease must be recorded at its present value by Lessee as an asset and as an obligation. As of January 1, 2004, we must calculate the present value of the annual payments. If we assume an interest rate of 8%, the present value of the payments is $15,972 ($4,000 × an annuity factor of 3.993 from Table 9-4).

You should perform the following steps when using a calculator to determine the present value in our example:

ENTER	DISPLAY
5 N	N = 5
8 I/Y	I/Y = 8
4000 PMT	PMT = 4,000
0 FV	FV = 0
CPT PV	PV = 15,971*
*(rounded)	

The effect on Lessee Firm's accounting equation of treating the lease as a capital lease is as follows:

BALANCE SHEET					INCOME STATEMENT
ASSETS	=	LIABILITIES	+	OWNERS' EQUITY	+ REVENUES − EXPENSES
Leased Asset 15,972		Lease Obligation 15,972			

The Leased Asset account is a long-term asset similar to plant and equipment and represents the fact that Lessee has acquired the right to use and retain the asset. Because the leased asset represents depreciable property, depreciation must be reported for each of the five years of asset use. On December 31, 2004, Lessee records depreciation of $3,194 ($15,972/5 years), assuming that the straight-line method is adopted. The effect of the depreciation is as follows:

BALANCE SHEET					INCOME STATEMENT
ASSETS	=	LIABILITIES	+	OWNERS' EQUITY	+ REVENUES − EXPENSES
Accumulated Depreciation—Leased Asset (3,194)					Depreciation Expense (3,194)

Depreciation of leased assets is referred to as *amortization* by some firms.

On December 31, Lessee Firm also must make a payment of $4,000 to Lessor Dealer. A portion of each payment represents interest on the obligation (loan), and the remainder represents a reduction of the principal amount. Each payment must be separated into its principal and interest components. Generally, the effective interest method is used for that purpose. An effective interest table can be established using the same concepts as were used to amortize a premium or discount on bonds payable.

Exhibit 10-7 illustrates the effective interest method applied to the Lessee Firm example. Note that the table begins with an obligation amount equal to the present value of the payments of $15,972. Each payment is separated into principal and interest amounts so that the amount of the loan obligation at the end of the lease agreement equals zero. The amortization table is the basis for the amounts that are reflected on the financial statement. Exhibit 10-7 indicates that the $4,000 payment in 2004

Exhibit 10-7

Lease Amortization: Effective Interest Method of Amortization

DATE	COLUMN 1 LEASE PAYMENT	COLUMN 2 INTEREST EXPENSE	COLUMN 3 REDUCTION OF OBLIGATION	COLUMN 4 LEASE OBLIGATION
		8%	**Col. 1 − Col. 2**	
1/1/2004	—	—	—	$15,972
12/31/2004	$4,000	$1,278	$2,722	13,250
12/31/2005	4,000	1,060	2,940	10,310
12/31/2006	4,000	825	3,175	7,135
12/31/2007	4,000	571	3,429	3,706
12/31/2008	4,000	294	3,706	–0–

should be considered as interest of $1,278 (8% of $15,972) and reduction of principal of $2,722. The effect on the accounting equation of the December 31, 2004, payment is as follows:

BALANCE SHEET					INCOME STATEMENT	
ASSETS		= LIABILITIES		+ OWNERS' EQUITY	+ REVENUES − EXPENSES	
Cash	(4,000)	Lease Obligation	(2,722)		Interest Expense	(1,278)

Therefore, for a capital lease, Lessee Firm must record both an asset and a liability. The asset is reduced by the process of depreciation. The liability is reduced by reductions of principal using the effective interest method. According to Exhibit 10-7, the total lease obligation as of December 31, 2004, is $13,250. This amount must be separated into current and long-term categories. The portion of the liability that will be paid within one year of the balance sheet should be considered a current liability. Reference to Exhibit 10-7 indicates that the liability will be reduced by $2,940 in 2005, and that amount should be considered a current liability. The remaining amount of the liability, $10,310 ($13,250 − $2,940), should be considered long-term. On the balance sheet as of December 31, 2004, Lessee Firm reports the following balances related to the lease obligation:

Assets:		
Leased assets	$15,972	
Less: Accumulated depreciation	3,194	
		$12,778
Current liabilities:		
Lease obligation		$ 2,940
Long-term liabilities:		
Lease obligation		$10,310

Notice that the depreciated asset does not equal the present value of the lease obligation. This is not unusual. For example, an automobile often may be completely depreciated but still have payments due on it.

The criteria used to determine whether a lease is an operating or a capital lease have provided a standard accounting treatment for all leases. The accounting for leases in foreign countries generally follows guidelines similar to those used in the United States. The criteria used in foreign countries to determine whether a lease is a capital lease are usually less detailed and less specific, however. As a result, capitalization of leases occurs less frequently in foreign countries than in the United States because of the increased use of judgment necessary in applying the accounting rules.

Two-Minute Review

1. *When a lease is considered a capital lease to the lessee, what entry is made to initially record the lease agreement?*
2. *When the lessee makes a lease payment on a capital lease, how is the payment recorded?*

Answers on p. 508.

HOW LONG-TERM LIABILITIES AFFECT THE STATEMENT OF CASH FLOWS

CASH FLOW

LO 8 Explain the effects that transactions involving long-term liabilities have on the statement of cash flows.

Exhibit 10-8 indicates the impact that long-term liabilities have on a company's cash flow and their placement on the statement of cash flows.

Most long-term liabilities are related to a firm's financing activities. Therefore, the change in the balance of each long-term liability account should be reflected in the Financing Activities category of the statement of cash flows. The decrease in a long-term liability account indicates that cash has been used to pay the liability. Therefore, in the statement of cash flows, a decrease in a long-term liability account should appear as a subtraction or reduction. The increase in a long-term liability account indicates that the firm has obtained additional cash via a long-term obligation. Therefore, an increase in a long-term liability account should appear in the statement of cash flows as an addition.

The statement of cash flows of Coca-Cola Company is presented in Exhibit 10-9. Note that the Financing Activities category contains two items related to long-term liabilities. In 2002, long-term debt was issued for $1,622 million and is an addition to cash. This indicates that Coca-Cola increased its cash position by borrowings. Second, the payment of debt is listed as a deduction of $2,378 million. This indicates that Coca-Cola paid long-term liabilities resulting in a reduction of cash.

Although most long-term liabilities are reflected in the Financing Activities category of the statement of cash flows, there are exceptions. The most notable exception involves the Deferred Tax account (discussed in the appendix at the end of this chapter). The change in this account is reflected in the Operating Activities category of the statement of cash flows. This presentation is necessary because the Deferred Tax account is related to an operating item, income tax expense. For example, in Exhibit 10-9, Coca-Cola listed $40 million in the Operating Activities category of the 2002 statement of cash flows. This indicates that $40 million more was recorded as expense than was paid out in cash. Therefore, the amount is a positive amount in, or an addition to, the Operating Activities category.

Exhibit 10-8

Long-Term Liabilities on the Statement of Cash Flows

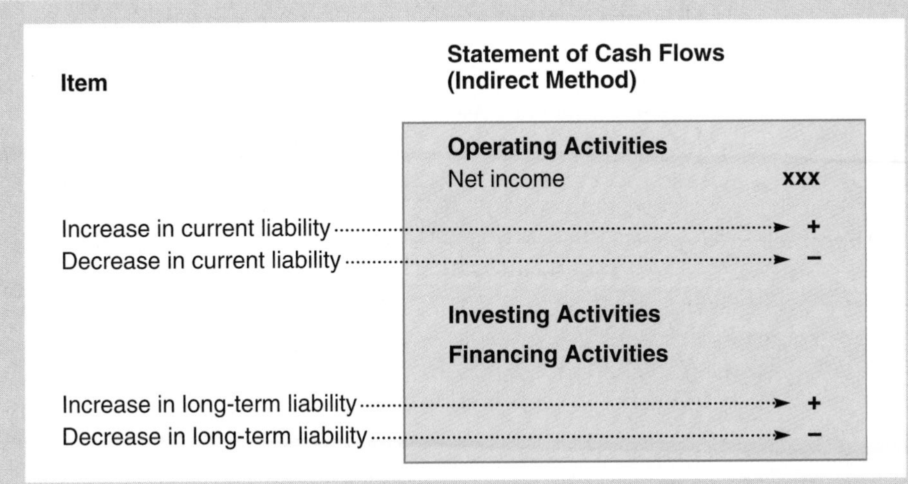

Exhibit 10-9 Coca-Cola Company and Subsidiaries 2002 Consolidated Statements of Cash Flows

CONSOLIDATED STATEMENTS OF CASH FLOWS

The Coca-Cola Company and Subsidiaries

Year Ended December 31, (In millions)	2002	2001	2000
OPERATING ACTIVITIES			
Net income	$ 3,050	$ 3,969	$ 2,177
Depreciation and amortization	806	803	773
Stock-based compensation expense	365	41	43
Deferred income taxes	40	56	3
Equity income or loss, net of dividends	(256)	(54)	380
Foreign currency adjustments	(76)	(60)	196
Gain on issuances of stock by equity investee	—	(91)	—
(Gains) losses on sales of assets, including bottling interests	3	(85)	(127)
Cumulative effect of accounting changes	926	10	—
Other operating charges	—	—	916
Other items	291	(17)	76
Net change in operating assets and liabilities	(407)	(462)	(852)
Net cash provided by operating activities	4,742	4,110	3,585
INVESTING ACTIVITIES			
Acquisitions and investments, principally trademarks and bottling companies	(544)	(651)	(397)
Purchases of investments and other assets	(156)	(456)	(508)
Proceeds from disposals of investments and other assets	243	455	290
Purchases of property, plant and equipment	(851)	(769)	(733)
Proceeds from disposals of property, plant and equipment	69	91	45
Other investing activities	52	142	138
Net cash used in investing activities	(1,187)	(1,188)	(1,165)
FINANCING ACTIVITIES			
Issuances of debt	1,622	3,011	3,671
Payments of debt	(2,378)	(3,937)	(4,256)
Issuances of stock	107	164	331
Purchases of stock for treasury	(691)	(277)	(133)
Dividends	(1,987)	(1,791)	(1,685)
Net cash used in financing activities	(3,327)	(2,830)	(2,072)
EFFECT OF EXCHANGE RATE CHANGES ON CASH AND CASH EQUIVALENTS	32	(45)	(140)
CASH AND CASH EQUIVALENTS			
Net increase during the year	260	47	208
Balance at beginning of year	1,866	1,819	1,611
Balance at end of year	$ 2,126	$ 1,866	$ 1,819

Changes in long-term debt generally affect the financing activities category.

See Notes to Consolidated Financial Statements.

ANALYZING DEBT TO ASSESS A FIRM'S ABILITY TO PAY ITS LIABILITIES

ANALYSIS

Long-term liabilities are a component of the "capital structure" of the company and are included in the calculation of the debt-to-equity ratio:

$$\textbf{Debt-to-Equity Ratio} = \frac{\textbf{Total Liabilities}}{\textbf{Total Stockholders' Equity}}$$

For example, refer to the liability category of PepsiCo's balance sheet given in Exhibit 10-1. PepsiCo's total liabilities are $14,183 million (current liabilities of $6,052, long-term obligations of $2,187, other liabilities of $4,226, and deferred income taxes of $1,718). Its total shareholders' equity is $9,298 million (including the preferred stock). (See Chapter 11 for more discussion of preferred stock.) Therefore, the debt-to-equity ratio is $14,183/$9,298, or 1.53, which means that PepsiCo has 1.53 times as much debt as equity, a situation that is not uncommon for companies in the beverage industry.

Most investors would prefer to see equity rather than debt on the balance sheet. Debt, and its interest charges, make up a fixed obligation that must be repaid in a finite period of time. In contrast, equity never has to be repaid, and the dividends that are declared on it are optional. Stock investors view debt as a claim against the company that must be satisfied before they get a return on their money.

Other ratios used to measure the degree of debt obligation include the times interest earned ratio and the debt service coverage ratio:

$$\textbf{Times Interest Earned Ratio} = \frac{\textbf{Income before Interest and Tax}}{\textbf{Interest Expense}}$$

$$\textbf{Debt Service Coverage Ratio} = \frac{\textbf{Cash Flow from Operations before Interest and Tax}}{\textbf{Interest and Principal Payments}}$$

Lenders want to be sure that borrowers can pay the interest and repay the principal on a loan. Both of the preceding ratios, which will be explored in more detail in Chapter 13, reflect the degree to which a company can make its debt payments out of current cash flow.

From Concept to Practice 10.2

Reading the Winnebago Industries and Monaco Coach Corporation Balance Sheets

Calculate the 2001 and 2002 debt-to-equity ratios for Winnebago Industries and Monaco Coach Corporation. Did the 2002 ratio go up or down from the previous year?

Interpret: You Decide. Take a close look at the liabilities section of the balance sheet for Coca-Cola provided in the chapter opener for this chapter. Calculate the debt-to-equity ratio for the company for 2002. What does it indicate about the capital structure of the company? Calculate the times interest earned ratio and the debt service coverage ratios. What do these ratios indicate about the ablity of the company to pay the interest and principal payments on its debt?

Ratios for Decision Making

Reporting and analyzing financial statement information related to a company's long-term debt:
The impact of debt in investment and credit decisions can be significant. Because the company must meet its debt obligations in order to remain in business, investors and creditors carefully review its financial information. The following ratios are key to determining whether the company is likely to have resources to pay its liabilities: (a) the proportion of current earnings, before interest and tax expenses, to the current interest expense and (b) the amount of net cash, before interest and taxes have been paid, currently created by company operations when compared to the amount of interest and principal payments that have been paid in the current period. In addition, the ratio of total debt to total equity indicates how heavily the company is burdened by its liabilities.

In this chapter, you learned about three new ratios used for decision making. These ratios and the sources of the information needed for the analysis are presented below:

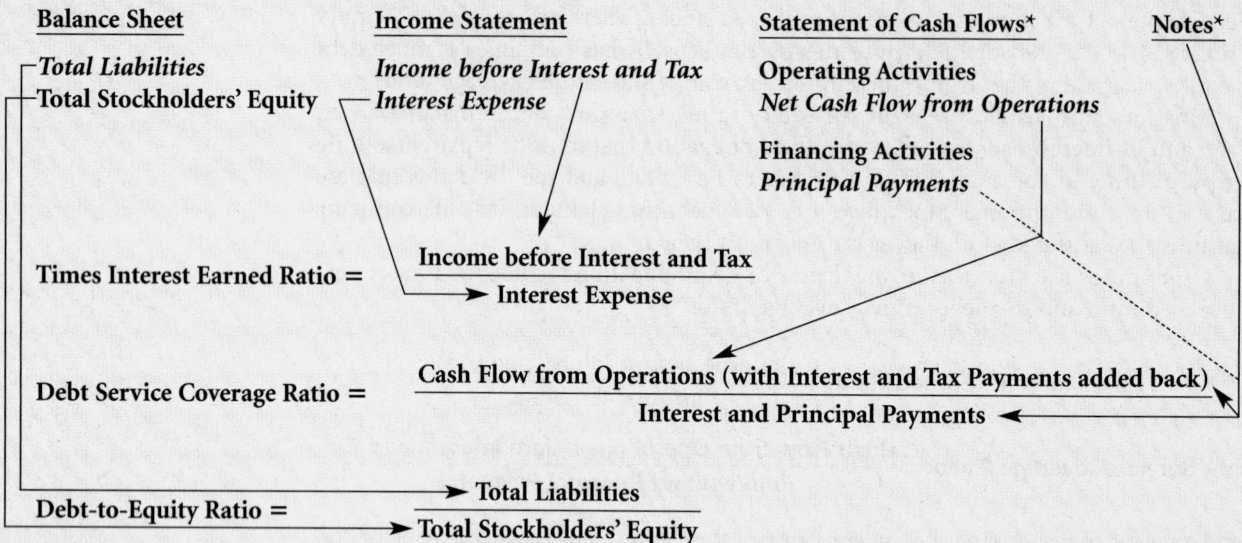

*When the statement of cash flows is prepared under the indirect method, the interest payment amount is disclosed in the notes to the financial statements. Under the direct method, explained in detail in Chapter 12, the interest amount appears on the statement of cah flows in the operating activities section.

Answers to the Two-Minute Reviews

Two-Minute Review on Page 498

1. *To calculate the issue price of a bond, you must calculate the present value of the annuity of interest payments and add to it the present value of the principal to be repaid, using the market rate of interest as the rate in the calculations.*
2. *When a premium is amortized, it decreases the amount of interest on the bond, and when a discount is amortized, it increases the amount of interest expense on the bond.*

Two-Minute Review on Page 505

1. *A capital lease is recorded as an asset, in an account such as Leased Asset, and as a liability, in an account such as Lease Obligation. The lease is recorded at the amount of the present value of the lease payments.*
2. *When a lease payment is made, the portion of the payment that is interest would be recorded to the Interest Expense account, and the portion of the payment that is principal is considered a reduction in the Lease Obligation account.*

Impact on the Financial Reports

Impact on the Financial Reports

BALANCE SHEET

Current Assets

Noncurrent Assets

Leased Assets, net of accumulated depreciation, obtained under capital lease agreements

Current Liabilities

Current liabilities, such as Accounts Payable and Wages Payable, that will require payment within the next fiscal year

Current portion of long-term debt, both interest and principal, that will require payment within the next fiscal year

Noncurrent Liabilities

Obligations, such as Bonds Payable and Lease Obligations, that will not require asset resources within the next fiscal year

Equity

INCOME STATEMENT

Revenues

Expenses

Rent expense under operating lease agreements

Current-period depreciation expense on assets under capital lease agreements

Other

Current-period interest expense on current and long-term obligations

Gain or loss on early retirement of debt

STATEMENT OF STOCKHOLDERS' EQUITY

Contributed Capital

Retained Earnings

STATEMENT OF CASH FLOWS (INDIRECT METHOD)

*Operating Activities**

Depreciation expense for a leased asset is added back, which increases the cash amount from operating activities

Investing Activities

Financing Activities

Decrease due to principal payments on capital leases

Increase/decrease due to borrowing/paying off long-term debt (notes, bonds)

Noncash Transactions

NOTES

Disclosure includes basic information about lease obligations and bonds, such as the scheduled repayments of the debt.

*When the direct method, explained in Chapter 12, is used to prepare the statement of cash flows, the operating section would show a decrease due to payments for operating leases and would not show any depreciation amount since depreciation expense does not use cash.

Warmup Exercises

Warmup Exercise 10-1 ***Bond Payable*** **LO 3, 5**

A bond due in 10 years, with face value of $1,000 and face rate of interest of 8%, is issued when the market rate of interest is 6%.

Required

1. What is the issue price of the bond?
2. What is the amount of premium or discount on the bond at the time of issuance?
3. What amount of interest expense will be shown on the income statement for the first year of the bond?
4. What amount of the premium or discount will be amortized during the first year of the bond?

Warmup Exercise 10-2 ***Lease*** **LO 7**

You have signed an agreement to lease a car for four years and will make annual payments of $4,000 at the end of each year. (Assume that the lease meets the criteria for a capital lease.)

Required

1. Calculate the present value of the lease payments, assuming an 8% interest rate.
2. What is the effect on the accounting equation of the signing of the lease?
3. When the first lease payment is made, what portion of the payment will be considered interest?

Solutions to Warmup Exercises

Warmup Exercise 10-1

1. The issue price of the bond would be calculated at the present value:

$80 (7.360) =	$ 588.80	using Table 9-4, where i = 6% and n = 10
$1,000 (0.558) =	558.00	using Table 9-2, where i = 6% and n = 10
Issue price	$1,146.80	

You should perform the following steps when using a calculator to determine the present value:

ENTER	DISPLAY
10 N	N = 10
6 I/Y	I/Y = 8
80 PMT	PMT = 80
1000 FV	FV = 1000
CPT PV	PV = 1,147*
*(rounded)	

2. The amount of the premium is the difference between the issue price and the face value:

$$\text{Premium} = \$1{,}146.80 - \$1{,}000 = \$146.80$$

3. The amount of interest expense can be calculated as follows:

$$\text{Interest Expense} = \$1{,}146.80 \times 0.06 = \$68.81$$

4. The amount that will be amortized can be calculated as follows:

$$\begin{aligned}\text{Amortized} &= \text{Cash Interest} - \text{Interest Expense}\\ &= (\$1{,}000 \times 0.08) - (\$1{,}146.80 \times 0.06)\\ &= \$80.00 - \$68.81\\ &= \$11.19\end{aligned}$$

Warmup Exercise 10-2

1. The present value of the lease payments can be calculated as follows:

$$\begin{aligned}\text{Present Value} &= \$4{,}000\ (3.312) \text{ using Table 9-4, where i} = 8\%, \text{n} = 4\\ &= \$13{,}248\end{aligned}$$

You should perform the following steps when using a calculator to determine the present value:

ENTER	DISPLAY
4 N	N = 4
8 I/Y	I/Y = 8
4000 PMT	PMT = 4,000
0 FV	FV = 0
CPT PV	PV = 13,248*
*(rounded)	

2.

BALANCE SHEET						INCOME STATEMENT
ASSETS	=	LIABILITIES		+	OWNERS' EQUITY	+ REVENUES – EXPENSES
Leased Asset 13,248		Lease Obligation 13,248				

3. The amount of interest can be calculated as follows:

Interest = $13,248 × 0.08
= $1,059.84

Review Problem

WebTUTOR™ Advantage

The following items pertain to the liabilities of Brent Foods. You may assume that Brent Foods began business on January 1, 2004, and therefore the beginning balance of all accounts was zero.

a. On January 1, 2004, Brent Foods issued bonds with a face value of $50,000. The bonds are due in five years and have a face interest rate of 10%. The market rate on January 1 for similar bonds was 12%. The bonds pay interest annually each December 31. Brent has chosen to use the effective interest method of amortization for any premium or discount on the bonds.

b. On December 31, Brent Foods signed a lease agreement with Cordova Leasing. The agreement requires Brent to make annual lease payments of $3,000 per year for four years, with the first payment due on December 31, 2005. The agreement stipulates that ownership of the property is transferred to Brent at the end of the four-year lease. Assume that an 8% interest rate is used for the leasing transaction.

c. On January 1, 2005, Brent redeems its bonds payable at the specified redemption price of 101. Because this item occurs in 2005, it does not affect the balance sheet prepared for year-end 2004.

Required

1. Determine the effect on the accounting equation of the December 31, 2004 interest adjustment in item **a** and the signing of the lease in item **b.**
2. Develop the Long-Term Liabilities section of Brent Foods' balance sheet as of December 31, 2004, based on items **a** and **b.** You do not need to consider the notes that accompany the balance sheet.
3. Would the company prefer to treat the lease in item **b** as an operating lease? Why or why not?
4. Calculate the gain or loss on the bond redemption for item **c.**

Solution to Review Problem

1. **a.** The issue price of the bonds on January 1 must be calculated at the present value of the interest payments and the present value of the principal, as follows:

$5,000 × 3.605	$18,025
$50,000 × 0.567	28,350
Issue price	$46,375

You should perform the following steps when using a calculator to determine the present value:

ENTER	DISPLAY
5 N	N = 5
12 I/Y	I/Y = 12
5000 PMT	PMT = 5,000
50000 FV	FV = 50,000
CPT PV	PV = 46,395

Note: The difference is caused by rounding that occurs when using the factors from Tables 9-2 and 9-4.

The amount of the discount is calculated as follows:

$50,000 – $46,375 = $3,625

The effect of the interest and amortization as of December 31, 2004, is as follows:

BALANCE SHEET						INCOME STATEMENT	
ASSETS		= LIABILITIES		+ OWNERS' EQUITY	+	REVENUES − EXPENSES	
Cash	(5,000)	Discount on Bonds Payable	565			Interest Expense	(5,565)

The interest expense is calculated using the effective interest method by multiplying the carrying value of the bonds times the market rate of interest ($46,375 × 12%).

Brent must show two accounts in the Long-Term Liabilities section of the balance sheet: Bonds Payable of $50,000 and Discount on Bonds Payable of $3,060 ($3,625 less $565 amortized).

b. The lease meets the criteria to be a capital lease. Brent must report the lease as an asset and report the obligation for lease payments as a liability. The transaction should be reported at the present value of the lease payments, $9,936 (computed by multiplying $3,000 by the annuity factor of 3.312). The effect of treating the lease as a caital lease is as follows:

BALANCE SHEET						INCOME STATEMENT	
ASSETS		= LIABILITIES		+ OWNERS' EQUITY	+	REVENUES − EXPENSES	
Leased Asset	9,936	Lease Obligation	9,936				

Because the lease agreement was signed on December 31, 2004, it is not necessary to amortize the Lease Obligation account in 2004. The account should be stated in the Long-Term Liabilities section of Brent's balance sheet at $9,936.

2. The Long-Term Liabilities section of Brent's balance sheet for December 31, 2004, on the basis of items **a** and **b** is as follows:

BRENT FOODS
PARTIAL BALANCE SHEET
AS OF DECEMBER 31, 2004

Long-term liabilities:		
Bonds payable	$50,000	
Less: Unamortized discount on bonds payable	3,060	$46,940
Lease obligation		9,936
Total long-term liabilities		$56,876

3. The company would prefer that the lease be an operating lease because it would not have to report the asset or liability on the balance sheet. This off–balance-sheet financing may give a more favorable impression of the company.

4. Brent must calculate the loss on the bond redemption as the difference between the carrying value of the bonds ($46,940) and the redemption price ($50,000 × 1.01). The amount of the loss is calculated as follows:

$50,500 − $46,940 = $3,560 loss on redemption

Appendix: Accounting Tools: Other Liabilities

In this appendix we will discuss two additional items that are found in the long-term liabilities category of many companies: deferred taxes and pensions. Both items are complex financial arrangements, and our primary purpose is to make you aware of their existence when reading financial statements.

Deferred Tax

LO 9 Explain deferred taxes and calculate the deferred tax liability.

http://www.pepsico.com
http://www.cocacola.com

http://www.tribune.com

The financial statements of most major firms include an item titled Deferred Income Taxes or Deferred Tax (see PepsiCo's deferred taxes in Exhibit 10-1 and Coca-Cola's in the chapter opening). In most cases, the account appears in the Long-Term Liabilities section of the balance sheet, and the dollar amount may be large enough to catch the user's attention. For another example, Exhibit 10-10 illustrates the presentation of deferred tax in the liability portion of 2002 comparative balance sheets of Tribune Company and Subsidiaries. The Deferred Income Taxes account is listed immediately after Long-Term Debt and for Tribune Company should be considered a long-term liability. At the end of 2002, the firm had more than $2,081 million of deferred tax. The size of that account relative to the other liabilities should raise questions concerning its exact meaning. In fact, deferred income taxes represent one of the most misunderstood aspects of financial statements. In this section, we will attempt to address some of the questions concerning deferred taxes.

Deferred tax The account used to reconcile the difference between the amount recorded as income tax expense and the amount that is payable as income tax.

Deferred tax is an amount that reconciles the differences between the accounting done for purposes of financial reporting to stockholders ("book" purposes) and the accounting done for tax purposes. It may surprise you that U.S. firms are allowed to use accounting methods for financial reporting that differ from those used for tax calculations. The reason is that the Internal Revenue Service defines income and expense differently than does the Financial Accounting Standards Board. As a result, companies tend to use accounting methods that minimize income for tax purposes but maximize income in the annual report to stockholders. This is not true in some foreign countries where financial accounting and tax accounting are more closely aligned. Firms in those countries do not report deferred tax, because the difference between methods is not significant.

http://www.irs.gov
http://www.fasb.org

When differences between financial and tax reporting do occur, we can classify them into two types: permanent and temporary. **Permanent differences** occur when an item is included in the tax calculation and is never included for book purposes—or vice versa, when an item is included for book purposes but not for tax purposes.

Permanent difference A difference that affects the tax records but not the accounting records, or vice versa.

For example, the tax laws allow taxpayers to exclude interest on certain investments, usually state and municipal bonds, from their income. These are generally called *tax-exempt bonds.* If a corporation buys tax-exempt bonds, it does not have to declare the interest as income for tax purposes. When the corporation develops its income statement for stockholders (book purposes), however, the interest is included and appears in the Interest Income account. Therefore, tax-exempt interest represents a permanent difference between tax and book calculations.

Temporary differences occur when an item affects both the book and the tax calculations but not in the same time period. A difference caused by depreciation methods is the most common type of temporary difference. In previous chapters you have learned that depreciation may be calculated using a straight-line method or an accelerated method such as the double-declining-balance method. Most firms do not use the same depreciation method for book and tax purposes, however. Generally, straight-line depreciation is used for book purposes and an accelerated method is used for tax purposes because accelerated depreciation lowers taxable income—at least in early years—and therefore reduces the tax due. The IRS refers to this accelerated method as the *Modified Accelerated Cost Recovery System (MACRS).* It is similar to other accelerated depreciation methods in that it allows the firm to take larger depreciation deductions for tax purposes in the early years of the asset and smaller deductions in the later years. Over the life of the depreciable asset, the total depreciation using straight-line is equal to that using MACRS. Therefore, this difference is an example of a temporary difference between book and tax reporting.

Temporary difference A difference that affects both book and tax records but not in the same time period.

The Deferred Tax account is used to reconcile the differences between the accounting for book purposes and for tax purposes. It is important to distinguish between permanent and temporary differences because the FASB has ruled that not all differences should affect the Deferred Tax account. The Deferred Tax account should reflect temporary differences but not items that are permanent differences between book accounting and tax reporting.[3]

[3]*Statement of Financial Accounting Standards No. 109,* "Accounting for Income Taxes" (Stamford, Conn.: FASB, 1992).

Exhibit 10-10 Tribune Company and Subsidiaries 2002 Liabilities and Shareholders' Equity

TRIBUNE COMPANY AND SUBSIDIARIES
CONSOLIDATED BALANCE SHEETS

(In thousands of dollars)

	Dec. 29, 2002	Dec. 30, 2001
Current Liabilities		
Long-term debt due within one year	$ 46,368	$ 410,890
Accounts payable	192,098	223,563
Employee compensation and benefits	208,551	159,979
Contracts payable for broadcast rights	334,545	298,165
Deferred income	87,962	84,167
Other	284,452	339,791
Total current liabilities	1,153,976	1,516,555
Long-Term Debt		
PHONES debt related to AOL Time Warner stock	523,440	684,000
Other long-term debt (less portions due within one year)	2,703,262	3,000,692
Other Non-Current Liabilities		
Deferred income taxes	2,081,092	2,143,205
Contracts payable for broadcast rights	578,034	522,854
Deferred compensation and benefits	385,181	372,204
Other obligations	13,243	594,189
Total other non-current liabilities	3,557,550	3,632,452

Deferred tax is a liability for Tribune Company and Subsidiaries

See Notes to Consolidated Financial Statements.

Example of Deferred Tax Assume that Startup Firm begins business on January 1, 2004. During 2004 the firm has sales of $6,000 and has no expenses other than depreciation and income tax at the rate of 40%. Startup has depreciation on only one asset. That asset was purchased on January 1, 2004, for $10,000 and has a four-year life. Startup has decided to use the straight-line depreciation method for financial reporting purposes. Startup's accountants have chosen to use MACRS for tax purposes, however, resulting in $4,000 depreciation in 2004 and a decline of $1,000 per year thereafter.

The depreciation amounts for each of the four years for Startup's asset are as follows:

Year	Tax Depreciation	Book Depreciation	Difference
2004	$ 4,000	$ 2,500	$1,500
2005	3,000	2,500	500
2006	2,000	2,500	(500)
2007	1,000	2,500	(1,500)
Totals	$10,000	$10,000	$ 0

Startup's tax calculation for 2004 is based on the accelerated depreciation of $4,000, as follows:

Sales	$6,000
Depreciation Expense	4,000
Taxable Income	$2,000
× Tax Rate	40%
Tax Payable to IRS	$ 800

For the year 2004, Startup owes $800 of tax to the Internal Revenue Service. This amount is ordinarily recorded as tax payable until the time it is remitted.

Startup wants also to develop an income statement to send to the stockholders. What amount should be shown as tax expense on the income statement? You may guess that the Tax Expense account on the income statement should reflect $800 because that is the amount to be paid to the IRS. That is not true in this case, however. Remember that the tax payable amount was calculated using the depreciation method that Startup chose for tax purposes. The income statement must be calculated using the straight-line method, which Startup uses for book purposes. Therefore, Startup's income statement for 2004 appears as follows:

Sales	$6,000
Depreciation Expense	2,500
Income before Tax	$3,500
Tax Expense (40%)	1,400
Net Income	$2,100

The effect on Startup's financial statements is as follows:

BALANCE SHEET					INCOME STATEMENT	
ASSETS	= LIABILITIES		+	OWNERS' EQUITY	+ REVENUES – EXPENSES	
	Tax Payable	800			Tax Expense	(1,400)
	Deferred Tax	600				

The Deferred Tax account is a balance sheet account. A balance in it reflects the fact that Startup has received a tax benefit by recording accelerated depreciation, in effect delaying the ultimate obligation to the IRS. To be sure, the amount of deferred tax still represents a liability of Startup. The Deferred Tax account balance of $600 represents the amount of the 2004 temporary difference of $1,500 times the tax rate of 40% ($1,500 × 40% = $600).

What can we learn from the Startup example? First, when you see a firm's income statement, the amount listed as tax expense does not represent the amount of cash paid to the government for taxes. Accrual accounting procedures require that the tax expense amount be calculated using the accounting methods chosen for book purposes.

Second, when you see a firm's balance sheet, the amount in the Deferred Tax account reflects all of the temporary differences between the accounting methods chosen for tax and book purposes. The accounting and financial communities are severely divided on whether the Deferred Tax account represents a "true" liability. For one thing, many investment analysts do not view it as a real liability because they have noticed that it continues to grow year after year. Others look at it as a bookkeeping item that is simply there to balance the books. The FASB has taken the stance that deferred tax is an amount that results in a future obligation and meets the definition of a liability. The controversy concerning deferred taxes is likely to continue for many years.

Pensions

LO 10 Demonstrate an understanding of the meaning of a pension obligation and the effect of pensions on the long-term liability category of the balance sheet.

Many large firms establish pension plans to provide income to employees after their retirement. These pension plans often cover a large number of employees and involve millions of dollars. The large amounts in pension funds have become a major force in our economy, representing billions of dollars in stocks and bonds. In fact, pension funds are among the major "institutional investors" that have an enormous economic impact on our stock and bond exchanges.

Pensions are complex financial arrangements that involve difficult estimates and projections developed by specialists and actuaries. Pension plans also involve very difficult accounting issues requiring a wide range of estimates and assumptions about future cash flows.

Pension An obligation to pay employees for service rendered while employed.

We will concern ourselves with two accounting questions related to pensions. First, the employer must report the cost of the pension plan as an expense over some time period. How should that expense be reported? Second, the employer's financial statements should reflect a measure of the liability associated with a pension plan. What is the liability for future pension amounts, and how should it be recorded or disclosed? Our discussion will begin with the recording of pension expense.

Pensions on the Income Statement Most pension plans are of the following form:

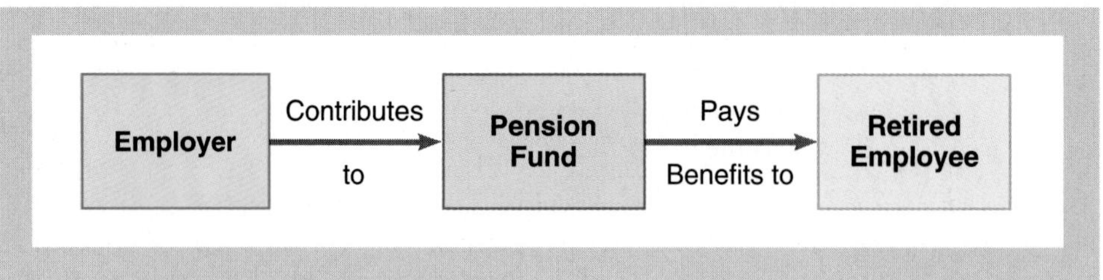

Funding payment A payment made by the employer to the pension fund or its trustee.

Normally, the employer must make payments to the pension fund at least annually, perhaps more frequently. This is often referred to as *funding the pension* or as the **funding payment.** *Funding* simply means that the employer has contributed cash to the pension fund. The pension fund is usually administered by a trustee, often a bank or other financial institution. The trustee must invest the employer's funds so that they earn interest and dividends sufficient to pay the amounts owed to retired employees.

Our first accounting question concerns the amount that should be shown by the employer as pension expense. This is another example of the difference between cash-basis accounting and accrual accounting. The cash paid as the funding payment is not the same as the expense. When using the accrual basis of accounting, we must consider the amount of pension cost incurred, not the amount paid. Pension expense should be accrued in the period that the employee earns the benefits, regardless of the amount paid to the pension trustee. The amount expensed and the amount paid involve two separate decisions.

The FASB has specified the methods that should be used to calculate the amount of annual pension expense to record on the employer's income statement.[4] The accountant must determine the costs of the separate components of the pension and total them to arrive at the amount of pension expense. The components include the employee's service during the current year, the interest cost, the earnings on pension investments, and other factors. The details of those calculations are beyond our discussion.

To illustrate, suppose that Employer Firm has calculated its annual pension expense to be $80,000 for 2004. Also suppose that Employer has determined that it will make a funding payment of $60,000 to the pension fund. The effect of those decisions on Employer's financial statements is as follows:

BALANCE SHEET						INCOME STATEMENT	
ASSETS		= LIABILITIES		+ OWNERS' EQUITY		+ REVENUES − EXPENSES	
Cash	(60,000)	Accrued Pension Cost	20,000			Pension Expense	(80,000)

The Pension Expense account is an income statement account and is reflected on Employer's 2004 income statement.

Accrued pension cost The difference between the amount of pension recorded as an expense and the amount of the funding payment.

Pensions on the Balance Sheet The **Accrued Pension Cost** account in the preceding example is a balance sheet account. The account could represent an asset or

[4] *Statement of Financial Accounting Standards No. 87,* "Employers' Accounting for Pension Plans" (Stamford, Conn.: FASB, 1985).

a liability, depending on whether the amount expensed is more or less than the amount of the funding payment. If the amount expensed is less than the amount paid, it is reported by Employer Firm as an asset and labeled as Prepaid Pension Cost. Normally, the amount expensed is greater than the amount paid, as in the example here. In that case, the Accrued Pension Cost is reported by Employer Firm as a long-term liability.

But what is the meaning of the Accrued Pension Cost account? Is it really a liability? It certainly is not a measure of the amount that is owed to employees at the time of retirement. In fact, the only true meaning that can be given to the account is to say that it is the difference between the amount expensed and the amount funded.[5] In that regard, the Accrued Pension Cost account is inadequate in determining a firm's liability to its employees for future retirement benefits. The FASB requires a great deal of note information for pension plans. This note section can be used to develop a clearer picture of the status of a firm's pension obligation.

Pension Note Information Readers of financial statements are often interested in the *funding status* of pension plans. This indicates whether sufficient assets are available in the pension fund to cover the amounts to be paid to employees as retirement benefits. We will use the note disclosures of an actual firm to illustrate the use of pension information.

Exhibit 10-11 presents portions of the 2002 pension note for PepsiCo Company. PepsiCo is a large company with thousands of employees who are covered by the company's pension plans. Analysts who follow the industry must assess whether PepsiCo's pension is adequate for its employees. The amounts on the balance sheet give some indication about the status of the plan, but a more complete picture is provided in the company's notes. Fortunately, the notes can assist us as we determine whether the pension plans could be considered underfunded. Several items in the note need to be defined. First, PepsiCo has disclosed the amount of *plan assets* at fair value. This is a measure of the total dollar amount of assets that has been accumulated in the pension fund. The footnote indicates that as of year-end 2002, PepsiCo had assets of $3,537 million. Second, PepsiCo disclosed a $4,324 million obligation to retirees at the end of 2002. When the obligation is larger than the amount of assets available in the pension fund, the fund is referred to as *underfunded.* At December 28, 2002, PepsiCo's pension funds were underfunded, but the difference between assets and obligation was small enough that it should not be cause for concern.

http://www.pepsico.com

PepsiCo's pension plans may be underfunded, but overall their pension plans certainly appear to be quite healthy. Not all firms are as fortunate. There have been many press reports of firms whose pension plans are seriously underfunded and for which it is quite questionable whether sufficient assets are available to pay impending retirement benefits. Such underfunded plans must be considered an off–balance-sheet liability by investors or creditors in assessing the company's health.

Users of the financial statements of U.S. firms are somewhat fortunate because the disclosure of pensions on the balance sheet and in the notes is quite extensive. The accounting

Exhibit 10-11

PepsiCo Company's Pension Note for 2002

	Pension (in millions)	
	2002	2001
Fair value of plan assets	$3,537	$3,129
Obligation at end of year	4,324	3,556
Selected information for plans with accumulated benefit obligation in excess of plan assets:		

[5]Some pension plans that are underfunded may be required to report an additional amount as a liability. This is referred to as the *minimum liability provision.*

for pensions by firms outside the United States varies considerably. Many countries do not require firms to accrue pension costs, and the expense is reported only when paid to retirees. Furthermore, within the statements and notes, there is much less disclosure, making an assessment of the funding status of pensions much more difficult.

Postretirement Benefits

Pensions represent a benefit paid to employees after their retirement. In addition to pensions, other benefits may be paid to employees after their retirement. For example, many firms promise to pay a portion of retirees' health care costs. The accounting question is whether postretirement benefits should be considered an expense when paid or during the period that the employee worked for the firm.

A few years ago, most firms treated postretirement benefits as an expense when they were paid to the retiree. It was widely believed that costs such as those for health care after retirement were too uncertain to be accrued as an expense and that such costs did not meet the definition of a liability and thus did not merit recording. The result of this expense-as-you-pay accounting was that firms had an obligation that was not recorded as a liability. As health care costs began to escalate, this unrecorded—and often undisclosed—cost became a concern for many firms as well as for stockholders, analysts, and employees.

The FASB has modified the accounting for other postemployment benefits to be consistent with pension costs. Under the matching principle, postretirement costs must now be accrued as an expense during the period that the employee helps the firm generate revenues and thus *earns* the benefits. The accountant must determine the costs of the separate components of postretirement benefits and total them to calculate the amount of the expense. The amount of the expense is reflected on the income statement in the Postretirement Expense account. The balance sheet should normally reflect the Accrued Postretirement Cost account. That account should be classified as a liability in the long-term liability category; it indicates the employer's obligation to present and future retirees.

The dollar amount of the liability represented by postretirement obligations is very large for many companies. For example, in 2002 PepsiCo's notes to the financial statement reveal the obligation to its employees for these retirement costs was $1,120 million (in addition to its pension plan amounts, disclosed in Exhibit 10-11).

There is still much controversy concerning the accounting for postretirement costs. Many firms object to the accounting requirements because of the uncertainty involved in measuring an obligation that extends far into the future. They also object because the requirements result in reduced profits on the income statement and huge liabilities on the balance sheet. Interestingly, this accounting rule had little impact on the stock market because the investment community already knew the magnitude of the postretirement obligations.

Chapter Highlights

1. **LO 1** Balance sheets generally have two categories of liabilities: current liabilities and long-term liabilities. Long-term liabilities are obligations that will not be satisfied within one year.
2. **LO 2** The terms of a bond payable are given in the bond certificate. The denomination of a bond is its face value. The interest rate stated in the bond certificate is referred to as the *face rate* or *stated rate of interest.* Term bonds all have the same due date. Serial bonds are not all due on the same date. Convertible bonds can be converted into common stock by the bondholders. Callable bonds may be redeemed or retired before their due date.
3. **LO 3** The issue price of a bond is the present value of the cash flows that the bond will provide to the investor. To determine the price, you must calculate the present values of the annuity of interest payments and of the principal amount. The present values must be calculated at the market rate of interest.
4. **LO 4** A bond sells at a discount or premium, depending on the relationship of the face rate to the market rate of interest. If the face rate exceeds the market rate, a bond is issued at a premium. If the face rate is less than the market rate, it will be issued at a discount.

5. **LO 5** Premiums or discounts must be amortized by transferring a portion of the premium or the discount each period to interest expense. The effective interest method of amortization reduces the balance of the premium or discount such that the effective interest rate on the bond is constant over its life.

6. **LO 5** The carrying value of the bond equals the face value plus unamortized premium or minus unamortized discount.

7. **LO 6** When bonds are redeemed before their due date, a gain or loss on redemption results. The gain or loss is the difference between the bond carrying value at the date of redemption and the redemption price.

8. **LO 7** A lease, a contractual arrangement between two parties, allows the lessee the right to use property in exchange for making payments to the lessor.

9. **LO 7** There are two major categories of lease agreements: operating and capital. The lessee does not report an operating lease as an asset and does not present the obligation to make payments as a liability. Capital leases are reported as assets and liabilities by the lessee. Leases are reported as capital leases if they meet one or more of four criteria.

10. **LO 7** Capital lease assets must be depreciated by the lessee over the life of the lease agreement. Capital lease payments must be separated into interest expense and reduction of principal using the effective interest method.

11. **LO 8** Long-term liabilities represent methods of financing. Therefore, changes in the balances of long-term liability accounts should be reflected in the Financing Activities category of the statement of cash flows.

12. **LO 9** There are many differences between the accounting for tax purposes and the accounting for financial reporting purposes. Permanent differences occur when an item affects one calculation but never affects the other. Temporary differences affect both book and tax calculations but not in the same time period. (Appendix)

13. **LO 9** The amount of tax payable is calculated using the accounting method chosen for tax purposes. The amount of tax expense is calculated using the accounting method chosen for financial reporting purposes. The Deferred Tax account reconciles the differences between tax expense and tax payable. It reflects all of the temporary differences times the tax rate. Deferred taxes is a controversial item on the balance sheet, raising questions as to whether it is a true liability. (Appendix)

14. **LO 10** Pensions represent an obligation to compensate retired employees for service performed while employed. (Appendix)

15. **LO 10** Pension expense is represented on the income statement and is calculated on the basis of several complex components that have been specified by the FASB. (Appendix)

16. **LO 10** Pension expense does not represent the amount of cash paid by the employer to the pension fund. The cash payment is referred to as the *funding payment.* The Accrued Pension account is recorded as the difference between the amount of pension expense and the amount of the funding. (Appendix)

17. **LO 10** The required note information on pensions can be used to evaluate the funding status of a firm's pension plan. If the amount of assets in the pension fund exceeds the pension obligation, the fund is considered to be overfunded, generally indicating that it is healthy and well managed. An overfunded plan is an example of an "off–balance-sheet" asset that an investor can count toward the value of the company's stock. (Appendix)

http://

http://porter.swlearning.com

Technology and other resources for your success

If you need additional help, visit the text's Web site. Also, see this text's preface for a description of available technology and other resources. If your instructor is using PERSONAL Trainer in this course, you may complete, on line, the exercises and problems in the text.

Key Terms Quiz

Read each definition below and then write the number of that definition in the blank beside the appropriate term it defines. The quiz solutions appear at the end of the chapter.

_____ Long-term liability
_____ Face value
_____ Debenture bonds
_____ Serial bonds
_____ Callable bonds
_____ Face rate of interest
_____ Market rate of interest
_____ Bond issue price
_____ Premium
_____ Discount
_____ Effective interest method of amortization
_____ Carrying value
_____ Gain or loss on redemption
_____ Operating lease
_____ Capital lease
_____ Deferred tax (Appendix)
_____ Permanent difference (Appendix)
_____ Temporary difference (Appendix)
_____ Pension (Appendix)
_____ Funding payment (Appendix)
_____ Accrued pension cost (Appendix)

1. The principal amount of the bond as stated on the bond certificate.
2. Bonds that do not all have the same due date. A portion of the bonds comes due each time period.
3. The interest rate stated on the bond certificate. It is also called the *nominal or coupon rate.*
4. The total of the present value of the cash flows produced by a bond. It is calculated as the present value of the annuity of interest payments plus the present value of the principal.
5. An obligation that will not be satisfied within one year.
6. The excess of the issue price over the face value of bonds. It occurs when the face rate on the bonds exceeds the market rate.
7. Bonds that are backed by the general creditworthiness of the issuer and are not backed by specific collateral.
8. The excess of the face value of bonds over the issue price. It occurs when the market rate on the bonds exceeds the face rate.
9. Bonds that may be redeemed or retired before their specified due date.
10. The process of transferring a portion of premium or discount to interest expense. This method transfers an amount resulting in a constant effective interest rate.
11. The face value of a bond plus the amount of unamortized premium or minus the amount of unamortized discount.
12. The interest rate that bondholders could obtain by investing in other bonds that are similar to the issuing firm's bonds.
13. The difference between the carrying value and the redemption price at the time bonds are redeemed. This amount is presented as an income statement account.
14. A lease that does not meet any of four criteria and is not recorded by the lessee.
15. A payment made by the employer to the pension fund or its trustee.
16. A lease that meets one or more of four criteria and is recorded as an asset by the lessee.
17. A difference between the accounting for tax purposes and the accounting for financial reporting purposes. This type of difference affects both book and tax calculations but not in the same time period.
18. The account used to reconcile the difference between the amount recorded as income tax expense and the amount that is payable as income tax.
19. A difference between the accounting for tax purposes and the accounting for financial reporting purposes. This type of difference occurs when an item affects one set of calculations but never affects the other set.
20. An obligation to pay retired employees as compensation for service performed while employed.
21. An account that represents the difference between the amount of pension recorded as an expense and the amount of the funding payment made to the pension fund.

Answers on p. 534.

Alternate Terms

Accumulated Benefit Obligation ABO

Bond Face Value Bond par value

Bonds Payable Notes payable

Bond Retirement Extinguishment of bonds

Carrying Value of Bond Book value of bond

Effective Interest Amortization Interest method of amortization

Face Rate of Interest Stated rate or nominal rate or coupon rate of interest

Long-Term Liabilities Noncurrent liabilities

Market Rate of Interest Yield or effective rate of interest

Postretirement Costs Other postemployment benefits

Projected Benefit Obligation PBO

Redemption Price Reacquisition price

Temporary Difference Timing difference

Questions

1. Which interest rate, the face rate or the market rate, should be used when calculating the issue price of a bond? Why?
2. What is the tax advantage that companies experience when bonds are issued instead of stock?
3. Does the issuance of bonds at a premium indicate that the face rate is higher or lower than the market rate of interest?
4. How does the effective interest method of amortization result in a constant rate of interest?
5. What is the meaning of the following sentence: "Amortization affects the amount of interest expense"? How does amortization of premium affect the amount of interest expense? How does amortization of discount affect the amount of interest expense?
6. Does amortization of a premium increase or decrease the bond carrying value? Does amortization of a discount increase or decrease the bond carrying value?
7. Is there always a gain or loss when bonds are redeemed? How is the gain or loss calculated?
8. What are the reasons that not all leases are accounted for in the same manner? Do you think it would be possible to develop a new accounting rule that would treat all leases in the same manner?

9. What is the meaning of the term *off–balance-sheet financing?* Why do some firms want to engage in off–balance-sheet transactions?

10. What are the effects on the financial statements if a lease is considered an operating rather than a capital lease?

11. Should depreciation be reported on leased assets? If so, over what period of time should depreciation occur?

12. Why do firms have a Deferred Tax account? Where should that account be shown on the financial statements? (Appendix)

13. How can you determine whether an item should reflect a permanent or a temporary difference when calculating the deferred tax amount? (Appendix)

14. Does the amount of income tax expense presented on the income statement represent the amount of tax actually paid? Why or why not? (Appendix)

15. When an employer has a pension plan for employees, what information is shown on the financial statements concerning the pension plan? (Appendix)

16. How can you determine whether a pension plan is overfunded or underfunded? (Appendix)

17. Do you agree with this statement: "All liabilities could be legally enforced in a court of law"? (Appendix)

Exercises

Exercise 10-1 *Relationships* LO 2

The following components are computed annually when a bond is issued for other than its face value:

- Cash interest payment
- Interest expense
- Amortization of discount/premium
- Carrying value of bond

Required

State whether each component will increase (I), decrease (D), or remain constant (C) as the bond approaches maturity, given the following situations:

1. Issued at a discount.
2. Issued at a premium.

Exercise 10-2 *Issue Price* LO 3

Youngblood Inc. plans to issue $500,000 face value bonds with a stated interest rate of 8%. They will mature in 10 years. Interest will be paid semiannually. At the date of issuance, assume the market rate is (a) 8%, (b) 6%, and (c) 10%.

Required

For each market interest rate, answer the following questions:

1. What is the amount due at maturity?
2. How much cash interest will be paid every six months?
3. At what price will the bond be issued?

Exercise 10-3 *Issue Price* LO 3

The following terms relate to independent bond issues:

a. 500 bonds; $1,000 face value; 8% stated rate; 5 years; annual interest payments

b. 500 bonds; $1,000 face value; 8% stated rate; 5 years; semiannual interest payments

c. 800 bonds; $1,000 face value; 8% stated rate; 10 years; semiannual interest payments

d. 2,000 bonds; $500 face value; 12% stated rate; 15 years; semiannual interest payments

Required

Assuming the market rate of interest is 10%, calculate the selling price for each bond issue.

Exercise 10-4 *Impact of Two Bond Alternatives* LO 4

Yung Chong Company wants to issue 100 bonds, $1,000 face value, in January. The bonds will have a 10-year life and pay interest annually. The market rate of interest on January 1 will be 9%. Yung Chong is considering two alternative bond issues: (a) bonds with a face rate of 8% and (b) bonds with a face rate of 10%.

DECISION MAKING

Required

1. Could the company save money by issuing bonds with an 8% face rate? If it chooses alternative (a), what would be the interest cost as a percentage?
2. Could the company benefit by issuing bonds with a 10% face rate? If it chooses alternative (b), what would be the interest cost as a percentage?

Exercise 10-5 ***Redemption of Bonds*** **LO 6**

Reynolds Corporation issued $75,000 face value bonds at a discount of $2,500. The bonds contain a call price of 103. Reynolds decides to redeem the bonds early when the unamortized discount is $1,750.

Required

1. Calculate Reynolds Corporation's gain or loss on the early redemption of the bonds.
2. Describe how the gain or loss would be reported on the income statement and in the notes to the financial statements.

Exercise 10-6 ***Redemption of a Bond at Maturity*** **LO 6**

On March 31, 2004, Sammonds Inc. issued $250,000 face value bonds at a discount of $7,000. The bonds were retired at their maturity date, March 31, 2014.

Required

Assuming the last interest payment and the amortization of discount have already been recorded, calculate the gain or loss on the redemption of the bonds on March 31, 2014. Indicate the effect on the accounting equation of the redemption of the bonds.

Exercise 10-7 ***Leased Asset*** **LO 7**

Hopper Corporation signed a 10-year capital lease on January 1, 2004. The lease requires annual payments of $8,000 every December 31.

Required

1. Assuming an interest rate of 9%, calculate the present value of the minimum lease payments.
2. Explain why the value of the leased asset and the accompanying lease obligation are not initially reported on the balance sheet at $80,000.

Exercise 10-8 ***Financial Statement Impact of a Lease*** **LO 7**

Benjamin's Warehouse signed a six-year capital lease on January 1, 2004, with payments due every December 31. Interest is calculated annually at 10%, and the present value of the minimum lease payments is $13,065.

Required

1. Calculate the amount of the annual payment that Benjamin's must make every December 31.
2. Calculate the amount of the lease obligation that would be presented on the December 31, 2005, balance sheet (after two lease payments have been made).

Exercise 10-9 ***Leased Assets*** **LO 7**

Koffman and Sons signed a four-year lease for a forklift on January 1, 2004. Annual lease payments of $1,510, based on an interest rate of 8%, are to be made every December 31, beginning with December 31, 2004.

Required

1. Assume the lease is treated as an operating lease.
   a. Will the value of the forklift appear on Koffman's balance sheet?
   b. What account will indicate lease payments have been made?
2. Assume the lease is treated as a capital lease.
   a. Indicate the effect on the accounting equation when the lease is signed. Explain why the value of the leased asset is not recorded at $6,040 ($1,510 × 4).
   b. Indicate the effect on the accounting equation of the first lease payment on December 31, 2004.
   c. Calculate the amount of depreciation expense on December 31, 2004.

d. At what amount would the lease obligation be presented on the balance sheet as of December 31, 2004?

Exercise 10-10 *Impact of Transactions Involving Bonds on Statement of Cash Flows* LO 8

From the following list, identify each item as operating (O), investing (I), financing (F), or not separately reported on the statement of cash flows (N).

_______ Proceeds from issuance of bonds payable
_______ Interest expense
_______ Redemption of bonds payable at maturity

Exercise 10-11 *Impact of Transactions Involving Capital Leases on Statement of Cash Flows* LO 8

Assume that Garnett Corporation signs a lease agreement with Duncan Company to lease a piece of equipment and determines that the lease should be treated as a capital lease. Garnett records a leased asset in the amount of $53,400 and a lease obligation in the same amount on its balance sheet.

Required

1. Indicate how this transaction would be reported on Garnett's statement of cash flows.
2. From the following list of transactions relating to this lease, identify each item as operating (O), investing (I), financing (F), or not separately reported on the statement of cash flows (N).

   _______ Reduction of lease obligation (principal portion of lease payment)
   _______ Interest expense
   _______ Depreciation expense—leased assets

Exercise 10-12 *Impact of Transactions Involving Tax Liabilities on Statement of Cash Flows* LO 8

From the following list, identify each item as operating (O), investing (I), financing (F), or not separately reported on the statement of cash flows (N). For items identified as operating, indicate whether the related amount would be added to or deducted from net income in determining the cash flows from operating activities.

_______ Decrease in taxes payable
_______ Increase in deferred taxes

Exercise 10-13 *Temporary and Permanent Differences (Appendix)* LO 9

Madden Corporation wants to determine the amount of deferred tax that should be reported on its 2004 financial statements. It has compiled a list of differences between the accounting conducted for tax purposes and the accounting used for financial reporting (book) purposes.

Required

For each of the following items, indicate whether the difference should be classified as a permanent or a temporary difference.

1. During 2004, Madden received interest on state bonds purchased as an investment. The interest can be treated as tax-exempt interest for tax purposes.
2. During 2004, Madden paid for a life insurance premium on two key executives. Madden's accountant has indicated that the amount of the premium cannot be deducted for income tax purposes.
3. During December 2004, Madden received money for renting a building to a tenant. Madden must report the rent as income on its 2004 tax form. For book purposes, however, the rent will be considered income on the 2005 income statement.
4. Madden owns several pieces of equipment that it depreciates using the straight-line method for book purposes. An accelerated method of depreciation is used for tax purposes, however.
5. Madden offers a warranty on the product it sells. The corporation records the expense of the warranty repair costs in the year the product is sold (the accrual method) for book purposes.

(continued)

For tax purposes, however, Madden is not allowed to deduct the expense until the period when the product is repaired.

6. During 2004, Madden was assessed a large fine by the federal government for polluting the environment. Madden's accountant has indicated that the fine cannot be deducted as an expense for income tax purposes.

Exercise 10-14 ***Deferred Tax (Appendix)*** **LO 9**

On January 1, 2004, Kunkel Corporation purchased an asset for $32,000. Assume this is the only asset owned by the corporation. Kunkel has decided to use the straight-line method to depreciate it. For tax purposes, it will be depreciated over three years. It will be depreciated over five years, however, for the financial statements provided to stockholders. Assume that Kunkel Corporation is subject to a 40% tax rate.

Required

Calculate the balance that should be reflected in the Deferred Tax account for Kunkel Corporation for each year 2004 through 2008.

Multi-Concept Exercises

Exercise 10-15 ***Issuance of a Bond at Face Value*** **LO 4, 5**

On January 1, 2004, Whitefeather Industries issued 300, $1,000 face value bonds. The bonds have a five-year life and pay interest at the rate of 10%. Interest is paid semiannually on July 1 and January 1. The market rate of interest on January 1 was 10%.

Required

1. Calculate the issue price of the bonds and record the issuance of the bonds on January 1, 2004.
2. Explain how the issue price would have been affected if the market rate of interest had been higher than 10%.
3. Determine the effect on the accounting equation of the payment of interest on July 1, 2004.
4. Calculate the amount of interest accrued on December 31, 2004.

Exercise 10-16 ***Impact of a Discount*** **LO 4, 5**

Berol Corporation sold 20-year bonds on January 1, 2004. The face value of the bonds was $100,000, and they carry a 9% stated rate of interest, which is paid on December 31 of every year. Berol received $91,526 in return for the issuance of the bonds when the market rate was 10%. Any premium or discount is amortized using the effective interest method.

Required

1. Determine the effect on the accounting equation of the sale of the bonds on January 1, 2004, and the proper balance sheet presentation on this date.
2. Determine the effect on the accounting equation of the payment of interest on December 31, 2004, and the proper balance sheet presentation on this date.
3. Explain why it was necessary for Berol to issue the bonds for only $91,526 rather than $100,000.

Exercise 10-17 ***Impact of a Premium*** **LO 4, 5**

Assume the same set of facts for Berol Corporation as in Exercise 10-16 except that it received $109,862 in return for the issuance of the bonds when the market rate was 8%.

Required

1. Determine the effect on the accounting equation of the sale of the bonds on January 1, 2004, and the proper balance sheet presentation on this date.
2. Determine the effect on the accounting equation of the payment of interest on December 31, 2004, and the proper balance sheet presentation on this date.
3. Explain why the company was able to issue the bonds for $109,862 rather than for the face amount.

Problems

Problem 10-1 *Factors That Affect the Bond Issue Price* LO 3

Becca Company is considering the issue of $100,000 face value, 10-year term bonds. The bonds will pay 6% interest each December 31. The current market rate is 6%; therefore, the bonds will be issued at face value.

Required

1. For each of the following independent situations, indicate whether you believe that the company will receive a premium on the bonds or will issue them at a discount or at face value. Without using numbers, explain your position.
   - **a.** Interest is paid semiannually instead of annually.
   - **b.** Assume instead that the market rate of interest is 7%; the nominal rate is still 6%.
2. For each situation in part **1**, prove your statement by determining the issue price of the bonds given the changes in parts **a** and **b.**

Problem 10-2 *Amortization of Discount* LO 5

Stacy Company issued five-year, 10% bonds with face value of $10,000 on January 1, 2004. Interest is paid annually on December 31. The market rate of interest on this date is 12%, and Stacy Company receives proceeds of $9,275 on the bond issuance.

Required

1. Prepare a five-year table (similar to Exhibit 10-4) to amortize the discount using the effective interest method.
2. What is the total interest expense over the life of the bonds? cash interest payment? discount amortization?
3. Determine the effect on the accounting equation of the payment of interest and the amortization of discount on December 31, 2006 (the third year), and determine the balance sheet presentation of the bonds on that date.

Problem 10-3 *Amortization of Premium* LO 5

Assume the same set of facts for Stacy Company as in Problem 10-2 except that the market rate of interest of January 1, 2004, is 8% and the proceeds from the bond issuance equal $10,803.

Required

1. Prepare a five-year table (similar to Exhibit 10-5) to amortize the premium using the effective interest method.
2. What is the total interest expense over the life of the bonds? cash interest payment? premium amortization?
3. Determine the effect on the accounting equation of the payment of interest and the amortization of premium on December 31, 2006 (the third year), and determine the balance sheet presentation of the bonds on that date.

Problem 10-4 *Redemption of Bonds* LO 6

McGee Company issued $200,000 face value bonds at a premium of $4,500. The bonds contain a call provision of 101. McGee decides to redeem the bonds, due to a significant decline in interest rates. On that date, McGee had amortized only $1,000 of the premium.

SPREADSHEET

Required

1. Calculate the gain or loss on the early redemption of the bonds.
2. Calculate the gain or loss on the redemption, assuming that the call provision is 103 instead of 101.
3. Indicate where the gain or loss should be presented on the financial statements.
4. Why do you suppose the call price is normally higher than 100?

Problem 10-5 *Financial Statement Impact of a Lease* LO 7

On January 1, 2004, Muske Trucking Company leased a semitractor and trailer for five years. Annual payments of $28,300 are to be made every December 31, beginning December 31, 2004. Interest expense is based on a rate of 8%. The present value of the minimum lease payments is $113,000 and has been determined to be greater than 90% of the fair market value of the asset on January 1, 2004. Muske uses straight-line depreciation on all assets.

Required

1. Prepare a table similar to Exhibit 10-7 to show the five-year amortization of the lease obligation.
2. Determine the effect on the accounting equation of the lease transaction on January 1, 2004.
3. Determine the effect on the accounting equation of the annual payment, interest expense, and depreciation on December 31, 2005 (the second year of the lease).
4. Prepare the balance sheet presentation as of December 31, 2005, for the leased asset and the lease obligation.

Problem 10-6 *Deferred Tax (Appendix)* LO 9

Erinn Corporation has compiled its 2004 financial statements. Included in the Long-Term Liabilities category of the balance sheet are the following amounts:

	2004	2003
Deferred tax	$180	$100

Included in the income statement are the following amounts related to income taxes:

	2004	2003
Income before tax	$500	$400
Tax expense	200	160
Net income	$300	$240

In the notes that accompany the 2004 statement are the following amounts:

	2004
Current provision for tax	$120
Deferred portion	80

Required

1. Determine the effect on the accounting equation in 2004 for income tax expense, deferred tax, and income tax payable.
2. Assume that a stockholder has inquired about the meaning of the numbers recorded and disclosed about deferred tax. Explain why the Deferred Tax liability account exists. Also, what do the terms *current provision* and *deferred portion* mean? Why is the deferred amount in the note $80 when the deferred amount on the 2004 balance sheet is $180?

Problem 10-7 *Deferred Tax Calculations (Appendix)* LO 9

Wyhowski Inc. reported income from operations, before taxes, for 2002–2004 as follows:

2002	$210,000
2003	240,000
2004	280,000

When calculating income, Wyhowski deducted depreciation on plant equipment. The equipment was purchased January 1, 2002, at a cost of $88,000. The equipment is expected to last three years and have $8,000 salvage value. Wyhowski uses straight-line depreciation for book purposes. For tax purposes, depreciation on the equipment is $50,000 in 2002, $20,000 in 2003, and $10,000 in 2004. Wyhowski's tax rate is 35%.

Required

1. How much did Wyhowski pay in income tax each year?
2. How much income tax expense did Wyhowski record each year?
3. What is the balance in the Deferred Income Tax account at the end of 2002, 2003, and 2004?

Problem 10-8 ***Financial Statement Impact of a Pension (Appendix)*** **LO 10**

Smith Financial Corporation prepared the following schedule relating to its pension expense and pension-funding payment for the years 2002 through 2004.

Year	Expense	Payment
2002	$100,000	$ 90,000
2003	85,000	105,000
2004	112,000	100,000

At the beginning of 2002, the Prepaid/Accrued Pension Cost account was reported on the balance sheet as an asset with a balance of $4,000.

Required

1. Determine the effect on the accounting equation of Smith Financial Corporation's pension expense for 2002, 2003, and 2004.
2. Calculate the balance in the Prepaid/Accrued Pension Cost account at the end of 2004. Does this represent an asset or a liability?
3. Explain the effects that pension expense, the funding payment, and the balance in the Prepaid/Accrued Pension Cost account have on the 2004 income statement and balance sheet.

Multi-Concept Problems

Problem 10-9 ***Bond Transactions*** **LO 4, 5**

Brand Company issued $1,000,000 face value, eight-year, 12% bonds on April 1, 2004, when the market rate of interest was 12%. Interest payments are due every October 1 and April 1. Brand uses a calendar year-end.

Required

1. Determine the effect on the accounting equation of the issuance of the bonds on April 1, 2004.
2. Determine the effect on the accounting equation of the interest payment on October 1, 2004.
3. Explain why additional interest must be recorded on December 31, 2004. What impact does this have on the amounts paid on April 1, 2005?
4. Determine the total cash inflows and outflows that occurred on the bonds over the eight-year life.

Problem 10-10 ***Partial Classified Balance Sheet for Walgreens*** **LO 1, 9, 10**

The following items, listed alphabetically, appear on Walgreens' consolidated balance sheet at August 31, 2002 (in millions).

http://www.walgreens.com

Accrued expenses and other liabilities	$ 1,017.9
Deferred income tax (long-term)	176.5
Income taxes payable	100.9
Other noncurrent liabilities	516.9
Trade accounts payable	1,836.4

Required

1. Prepare the Current Liabilities and Long-Term Liabilities sections of Walgreens' classified balance sheet at August 31, 2002.
2. Walgreens' had total liabilities of $3,626.6 million and total shareholders' equity of $5,207.2 at August 31, 2001. Total shareholders' equity at August 31, 2002, amounted to $6,230.2. Compute the company's debt-to-equity ratio at August 31, 2002 and 2001, respectively. As an investor, how would you react to the changes in this ratio?
3. What other related ratios would the company's lenders use to assess the company? What do these ratios measure?

Alternate Problems

Problem 10-1A *Factors that Affect the Bond Issue Price* **LO 3**

Rivera Inc. is considering the issuance of $500,000 face value, 10-year term bonds. The bonds will pay 5% interest each December 31. The current market rate is 5%; therefore, the bonds will be issued at face value.

Required

1. For each of the following independent situations, indicate whether you believe that the company will receive a premium on the bonds or will issue them at a discount or at face value. Without using numbers, explain your position.
   a. Interest is paid semiannually instead of annually.
   b. Assume instead that the market rate of interest is 4%; the nominal rate is still 5%.
2. For each situation in part **1**, prove your statement by determining the issue price of the bonds given the changes in parts **a** and **b**.

Problem 10-2A *Amortization of Discount* **LO 5**

SPREADSHEET

Ortega Company issued five-year, 5% bonds with face value of $50,000 on January 1, 2004. Interest is paid annually on December 31. The market rate of interest on this date is 8%, and Ortega Company receives proceeds of $44,011 on the bond issuance.

Required

1. Prepare a five-year table (similar to Exhibit 10-4) to amortize the discount using the effective interest method.
2. What is the total interest expense over the life of the bonds? cash interest payment? discount amortization?
3. Determine the effect on the accounting equation of the payment of interest on December 31, 2006 (the third year), and the balance sheet presentation of the bonds on that date.

Problem 10-3A *Amortization of Premium* **LO 5**

Assume the same set of facts for Ortega Company as in Problem 10-2A except that the market rate of interest of January 1, 2004, is 4% and the proceeds from the bond issuance equal $52,230.

Required

1. Prepare a five-year table (similar to Exhibit 10-5) to amortize the premium using the effective interest method.
2. What is the total interest expense over the life of the bonds? cash interest payment? premium amortization?
3. Determine the effect on the accounting equation of the payment of interest on December 31, 2006 (the third year), and the balance sheet presentation of the bonds on that date.

Problem 10-4A *Redemption of Bonds* **LO 6**

Elliot Company issued $100,000 face value bonds at a premium of $5,500. The bonds contain a call provision of 101. Elliot decides to redeem the bonds, due to a significant decline in interest rates. On that date, Elliot has amortized only $2,000 of the premium.

Required

1. Calculate the gain or loss on the early redemption of the bonds.
2. Calculate the gain or loss on the redemption, assuming that the call provision is 104 instead of 101.
3. Indicate how the gain or loss would be reported on the income statement and in the notes to the financial statements.
4. Why do you suppose that the call price of the bonds is normally an amount higher than 100?

Problem 10-5A *Financial Statement Impact of a Lease* **LO 7**

On January 1, 2004, Kiger Manufacturing Company leased a factory machine for six years. Annual payments of $21,980 are to be made every December 31, beginning December 31, 2004. Interest expense is based on a rate of 9%. The present value of the minimum lease payments is $98,600 and has been determined to be greater than 90% of the fair market value of the machine on January 1, 2004. Kiger uses straight-line depreciation on all assets.

Required

1. Prepare a table similar to Exhibit 10-7 to show the six-year amortization of the lease obligation.
2. Determine the effect on the accounting equation of of the lease on January 1, 2004.
3. Determine the effect on the accounting equation of the annual payment, interest expense, and depreciation on December 31, 2005 (the second year of the lease).
4. Prepare the balance sheet presentation as of December 31, 2005, for the leased asset and the lease obligation.

Problem 10-6A *Deferred Tax (Appendix)* LO 9

Thad Corporation has compiled its 2004 financial statements. Included in the Long-Term Liabilities category of the balance sheet are the following amounts:

	2004	2003
Deferred tax	$180	$200

Included in the income statement are the following amounts related to income taxes:

	2004	2003
Income before tax	$500	$400
Tax expense	100	150
Net income	$400	$250

Required

1. Determine the effect on the accounting equation in 2004 for income tax expense, deferred tax, and income tax payable.
2. Assume that a stockholder has inquired about the meaning of the numbers recorded. Explain why the Deferred Tax liability account exists.

Problem 10-7A *Deferred Tax Calculations (Appendix)* LO 9

Clemente Inc. has reported income for book purposes as follows for the past three years:

(in Thousands)	Year 1	Year 2	Year 3
Income before taxes	$120	$120	$120

Clemente has identified two items that are treated differently in the financial records and in the tax records. The first one is interest income on municipal bonds, which is recognized on the financial reports to the extent of $5,000 each year but does not show up as a revenue item on the company's tax return. The other item is equipment that is depreciated using the straight-line method, at the rate of $20,000 each year, for financial accounting but is depreciated for tax purposes at the rate of $30,000 in Year 1, $20,000 in Year 2, and $10,000 in Year 3.

Required

1. Determine the amount of cash paid for income taxes each year by Clemente. Assume that a 40% tax rate applies to all three years.
2. Calculate the balance in the Deferred Tax account at the end of Years 1, 2, and 3. How does this account appear on the balance sheet?

Problem 10-8A *Financial Statement Impact of a Pension (Appendix)* LO 10

Premier Consulting Corporation prepared the following schedule relating to its pension expense and pension-funding payment for the years 2002 through 2004:

Year	Expense	Payment
2002	$100,000	$110,000
2003	85,000	80,000
2004	112,000	100,000

(continued)

At the beginning of 2002, the Prepaid/Accrued Pension Cost account was reported on the balance sheet as an asset with a balance of $5,000.

Required

1. Determine the effect on the accounting equation of Premier Consulting Corporation's pension expense for 2002, 2003, and 2004.
2. Calculate the balance in the Prepaid/Accrued Pension Cost account at the end of 2004.
3. Explain the effects that pension expense, the funding payment, and the balance in the Prepaid/Accrued Pension Cost account have on the 2004 income statement and balance sheet.

Alternate Multi-Concept Problems

Problem 10-9A ***Financial Statement Impact of a Bond*** **LO 4, 6**

Worthington Company issued $1,000,000 face value, six-year, 10% bonds on July 1, 2004, when the market rate of interest was 12%. Interest payments are due every July 1 and January 1. Worthington uses a calendar year-end.

Required

1. Determine the effect on the accounting equation of the issuance of the bonds on July 1, 2004.
2. Determine the effect on the accounting equation of accrual of interest on December 31, 2004.
3. Determine the effect on the accounting equation of the interest payment on January 1, 2005.
4. Calculate the amount of cash that will be paid for the retirement of the bonds on the maturity date.

Problem 10-10A ***Partial Classified Balance Sheet for Boeing*** **LO 1, 9, 10**

http://www.boeing.com

The following items appear on the consolidated balance sheet of Boeing Inc. at December 31, 2002 (in millions). The information in parentheses was added to aid in your understanding.

Accounts payable and other liabilities	$13,739
Accrued retiree healthcare	5,434
Advances in excess of related costs	3,123
Short-term debt and current portion of long-term debt	1,814
Income tax payable	1,134
Long-term debt	12,589
Deferred lease income (long-term)	542
Accrued pension plan liability (long-term)	6,271

Required

1. Prepare the Current Liabilities and Long-Term Liabilities sections of Boeing's classified balance sheet at December 31, 2002.
2. Boeing had total liabilities of $38,153 and total shareholders' equity of $10,825 at December 31, 2002. Total stockholders' equity amounted to $7,696 at December 31, 2002. (All amounts are in millions.) Compute Boeing's debt-to-equity ratio at December 31, 2002 and 2001. As an investor, how would you react to the change in this ratio?
3. What other related ratios would the company's lenders use to assess the company? What do these ratios measure?

Decision Cases

Reading and Interpreting Financial Statements

Decision Case 10-1 ***Comparing Two Companies in the Same Industry: Winnebago Industries and Monaco Coach Corporation*** **LO 1, 7**

http://www.winnebagoind.com
http://www.monacocoach.com

The Current Liabilities and Long-Term Liabilities sections of Monaco Coach Corporation's balance sheet as of December 28, 2002 and December 29, 2001, are as follows (in thousands):

	December 28, 2001	December 29, 2002
LIABILITIES		
Current liabilities:		
Book overdraft	$ 5,889	$ 3,518
Line of credit	26,004	51,413
Current portion of long-term note payable	10,000	21,667
Accounts payable	66,859	78,055
Product liability reserve	19,856	21,322
Product warranty reserve	27,799	31,745
Income taxes payable	0	4,536
Accrued expenses and other liabilities	19,249	29,633
Total current liabilities	175,656	241,889
Long-term note payable	30,000	30,333
Deferred income taxes	8,312	14,568
Total liabilities	213,968	286,790

Refer to the annual reports in Appendices A and B at the end of the text for any additional information you might need about Monaco Coach Corporation or Winnebago Industries.

Required

1. Calculate the debt-to-equity ratio on December 28, 2002 for Monaco Coach and on August 31, 2002 for Winnebago Industries. How do the two ratios compare? What does that tell you about the two companies?
2. Comment on the reasons for the change in Monaco Coach's total liabilities from December 29, 2001, to December 28, 2002. What are the most important changes? What impact do these changes have on the company's cash flow?
3. A note to Monaco Coach's 2002 financial statements indicates:

   The Company s line of credit facility consists of a revolving line of credit of up to $70.0 million (the Revolving Loan). At the election of the Company, the Revolving Loan bears interest at variable rates based on the Prime Rate or LIBOR. At December 28, 2002, the interest rate was 4.3%. The Revolving Loan is due and payable in full on September 30, 2004, and requires monthly interest payments. The balance outstanding under the Revolving Loan at December 28, 2002, was $51.4 million. The Revolving Loan is collateralized by all of the assets of the Company, and include various restrictions and financial covenants.

   What does the term "collateralized by all of the assets" mean? If you were a lender to the company, what factors should you have considered before lending money to the company?
4. Look at Note 4 to Winnebago Industries' 2002 financial statements. How does the disclosed information in that note compare with Monaco Coach's disclosure above?

Decision Case 10-2 *Evaluating Winnebago Industries' Competitor* LO 1

The Current Liabilities and Long-Term Liabilities sections of Coachmen Industries' balance sheet as of December 31, 2002, are as follows (in thousands):

http://www.coachmen.com

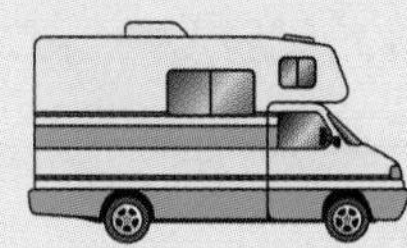

	2002	2001
CURRENT LIABILITIES		
Accounts payable, trade	$ 18,801	$ 18,944
Accrued income taxes	1,222	494
Accrued expenses and other liabilities	39,856	38,846
Current maturities of long-term debt	902	917
Total current liabilities	60,781	59,201
Long-term debt	10,097	11,001
Deferred income taxes	4,123	1,257
Other	8,768	8,461
Total liabilities	83,769	79,920

Required

1. Explain why current maturities of long-term debt is shown as a current liability for the company.
2. The notes to the balance sheet provide the following information:

   The Company maintains an Amended and Restated Revolving Credit Facility that provides a secured line of credit aggregating $30 million through June 30, 2003. This agreement was amended on November 5, 2001, to modify available borrowings to $30 million from $50 million, to provide certain collateral to the bank, and to modify certain financial covenants to reflect current business conditions.

   What is meant by a "line of credit?" Explain what is meant by "financial covenants." Why would a lender specify financial covenants when extending a loan?
3. If you were a lender, what measures or ratios would you calculate to determine whether a loan should be extended to the company?

Decision Case 10-3 ***Reading PepsiCo's Statement of Cash Flows (Appendix)*** **LO 8, 9**

http://www.pepsico.com

A portion of the financing activities section of PepsiCo's statement of cash flows for the year ended December 28, 2002, follows (in millions):

Financing Activities:	
Proceeds from the issuance of long-term debt	$ 11
Payment of long-term debt	(353)
Short-term borrowings by original maturity:	
More than three months—proceeds	707
More than three months—payments	(809)
Three months or less, net	(40)

Required

1. Explain why proceeds from debt is shown as a positive amount and payment of debt is shown as a negative amount.
2. During 2002, interest rates had declined to low levels. Explain why the company paid off debt during such conditions.
3. PepsiCo has a Deferred Income Tax account listed in the asset category of its balance sheet. Would an increase in that account result in an addition or a subtraction on the statement of cash flows? In which category?

Making Financial Decisions

Decision Case 10-4 ***Making a Loan Decision*** **LO 1**

DECISION MAKING

Assume that you are a loan officer in charge of reviewing loan applications from potential new clients at a major bank. You are considering an application from Molitor Corporation, which is a fairly new company with a limited credit history. It has provided a balance sheet for its most recent fiscal year as follows:

MOLITOR CORPORATION
BALANCE SHEET
DECEMBER 31, 2004

Assets		Liabilities	
Cash	$ 10,000	Accounts payable	$100,000
Receivables	50,000	Notes payable	200,000
Inventory	100,000		
Equipment	500,000	**Stockholders' Equity**	
		Common stock	80,000
		Retained earnings	280,000
Total assets	$660,000	Total liabilities and stockholders' equity	$660,000

Your bank has established certain guidelines that must be met before making a favorable loan recommendation. These include minimum levels for several financial ratios. You are particularly concerned about the bank's policy that loan applicants must have a total-assets-to-debt ratio of at least 2-to-1 to be acceptable. Your initial analysis of Molitor's balance sheet has indicated that the firm has met the minimum total-assets-to-debt ratio requirement. On reading the notes that accompany the financial statements, however, you discover the following statement:

Molitor has engaged in a variety of innovative financial techniques resulting in the acquisition of $200,000 of assets at very favorable rates. The company is obligated to make a series of payments over the next five years to fulfill its commitments in conjunction with these financial instruments. Current generally accepted accounting principles do not require the assets acquired or the related obligations to be reflected on the financial statements.

Required

1. How should this note affect your evaluation of Molitor's loan application? Calculate a revised total-assets-to-debt ratio for Molitor.
2. Do you believe that the bank's policy concerning a minimum total-assets-to-debt ratio can be modified to consider financing techniques that are not reflected on the financial statements? Write a statement that expresses your position on this issue.

Decision Case 10-5 *Bond Redemption Decision* LO 6

DECISION MAKING

Armstrong Areo Ace, a flight training school, issued $100,000 of 20-year bonds at face value when the market rate was 10%. The bonds have been outstanding for 10 years. The company pays annual interest on January 1. The current rate for similar bonds is 4%. On January 1, the controller would like to purchase the bonds on the open market, retire the bonds, then issue $100,000 of 10-year bonds to pay 4% annual interest.

Required

Draft a memo to the controller advising him to retire the outstanding bonds and issue new debt. Ignore taxes. (*Hint:* Find the selling price of bonds that pay 10% when the market rate is 4%.)

Accounting and Ethics: What Would You Do?

Decision Case 10-6 *Determination of Asset Life* LO 7

ETHICS

Jen Latke is an accountant for Hale's Manufacturing Company. Hale's has entered into an agreement to lease a piece of equipment from EZ Leasing. Jen must decide how to report the lease agreement on Hale's financial statements.

Jen has reviewed the lease contract carefully. She has also reviewed the four lease criteria specified in the accounting rules. She has been able to determine that the lease does not meet three of the criteria. However, she is concerned about the criterion that indicates that if the term of the lease is 75% or more of the life of the property, the lease should be classified as a capital lease. Jen is fully aware that Hale's does not want to record the lease agreement as a capital lease but prefers to show it as a type of off–balance-sheet financing.

Jen's reading of the lease contract indicates that the asset has been leased for seven years. She is unsure of the life of such assets, however, and has consulted two sources to determine it. One of them states that equipment similar to that owned by Hale's is depreciated over nine years. The other, a trade publication of the equipment industry, indicates that equipment of this type will usually last for 12 years.

Required

1. How should Jen report the lease agreement in the financial statements?
2. If Jen decides to present the lease as an off–balance-sheet arrangement, has she acted ethically? Is she following generally accepted accounting principles? Does the information disclosed to outsiders communicate the economic reality of the transaction?

Decision Case 10-7 *Overfunded Pension Plan (Appendix)* LO 10

ETHICS

Witty Company has sponsored a pension plan for employees for several years. Each year Witty has paid cash to the pension fund, and the pension trustee has used that cash to invest in stocks and bonds. Because the trustee has invested wisely, the amount of the pension assets exceeds the accumulated benefit obligation as of December 31, 2004.

The president of Witty Company wants to pay a dividend to the stockholders at the end of 2004. The president believes that it is important to maintain a stable dividend pattern. Unfortunately, the company, though profitable, does not have enough cash on hand to pay a dividend and must find a way to raise the necessary cash if the dividend is declared. Several executives of the company have recommended that assets be withdrawn from the pension fund. They have pointed out that the fund is currently "overfunded." Further, they have stated that a withdrawal of assets will not have an impact on the financial statements because the overfunding is an "off–balance-sheet item."

Required

Comment on the proposal to withdraw assets from the pension fund to pay a dividend to stockholders. Do you believe it is unethical?

THOMSON ONE Business School Edition Case

Case 10-8 ***Using THOMSON ONE for Coca-Cola***

http://www.cocacola.com

The chapter opener discussed the beverage in general and focused on the long-term liabilities of Coca-Cola. Sold in over 200 countries, Coca-Cola is the most recognized brand name in the world. Sales of Classic Coke, Diet Coke, Sprite, and other new products continue to provide the company with the cash necessary to pay off its debts as they come due. Use THOMSON ONE to obtain current information about the company's debt and its new products.

Begin by entering the company's ticker symbol, KO, and then selecting "GO." On the opening screen you will see background information about the company, key financial ratios, and some recent data concerning stock price. We can also find the company's recent financial statements. Near the top of the screen, click on "Financials" and select "Financial Statements." Refer to the long-term liabilities portion of the company's balance sheet. Also refer to the company's most recent income statement.

Based on your use of THOMSON ONE, answer the following questions:

1. Based on the most recent information, what is the amount of Coca-Cola's long-term debt? How does it compare to the amount of debt in the financial statements of the chapter opener?
2. By what percentage have the sales of Coca-Cola products increased from the previous year?
3. What amount of interest expense is reflected on the most recent income statement? Has interest expense increased or decreased from the previous year?
4. Click on the "News" tab near the top of the screen. Has the company introduced any new beverage products recently?

Solutions to Key Terms Quiz

5	Long-term liability (p. 487)	11	Carrying value (p. 495)
1	Face value (p. 489)	13	Gain or loss on redemption (p. 498)
7	Debenture bonds (p. 490)	14	Operating lease (p. 501)
2	Serial bonds (p. 490)	16	Capital lease (p. 501)
9	Callable bonds (p. 490)	18	Deferred tax (p. 513)
3	Face rate of interest (p. 490)	19	Permanent difference (p. 513)
12	Market rate of interest (p. 491)	17	Temporary difference (p. 513)
4	Bond issue price (p. 491)	20	Pension (p. 515)
6	Premium (p. 493)	15	Funding payment (p. 516)
8	Discount (p. 493)	21	Accrued pension cost (p. 516)
10	Effective interest method of amortization (p. 495)		

Chapter 11

Stockholders' Equity

AP/WIDE WORLD PHTOS

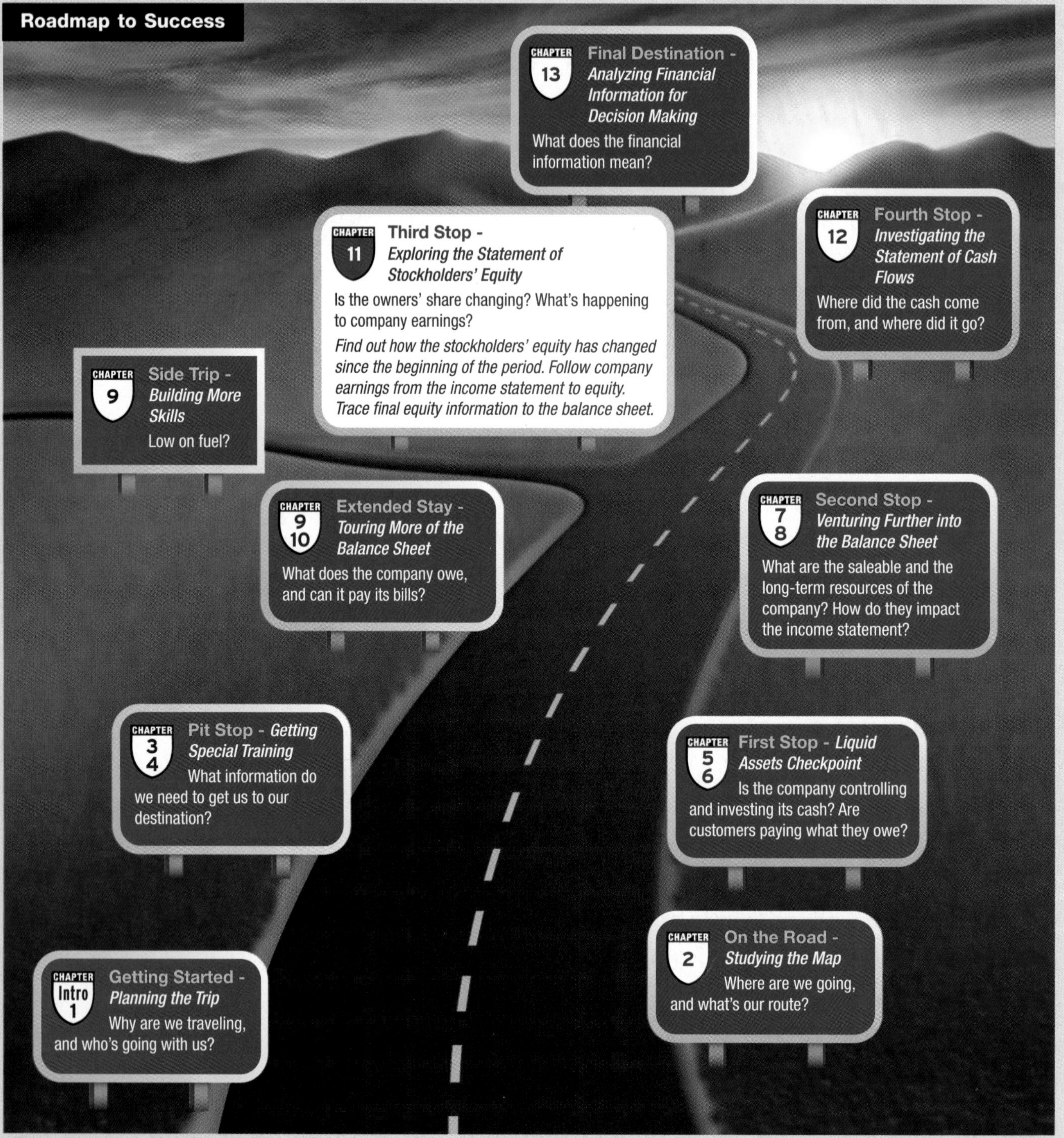

Roadmap to Success

CHAPTER 13 **Final Destination -** *Analyzing Financial Information for Decision Making*
What does the financial information mean?

CHAPTER 11 **Third Stop -** *Exploring the Statement of Stockholders' Equity*
Is the owners' share changing? What's happening to company earnings?
Find out how the stockholders' equity has changed since the beginning of the period. Follow company earnings from the income statement to equity. Trace final equity information to the balance sheet.

CHAPTER 12 **Fourth Stop -** *Investigating the Statement of Cash Flows*
Where did the cash come from, and where did it go?

CHAPTER 9 **Side Trip -** *Building More Skills*
Low on fuel?

CHAPTER 9 10 **Extended Stay -** *Touring More of the Balance Sheet*
What does the company owe, and can it pay its bills?

CHAPTER 7 8 **Second Stop -** *Venturing Further into the Balance Sheet*
What are the saleable and the long-term resources of the company? How do they impact the income statement?

CHAPTER 3 4 **Pit Stop -** *Getting Special Training*
What information do we need to get us to our destination?

CHAPTER 5 6 **First Stop -** *Liquid Assets Checkpoint*
Is the company controlling and investing its cash? Are customers paying what they owe?

CHAPTER 2 **On the Road -** *Studying the Map*
Where are we going, and what's our route?

CHAPTER Intro 1 **Getting Started -** *Planning the Trip*
Why are we traveling, and who's going with us?

Focus on Financial Results

The airline industry is very volatile and has certainly experienced difficulties since the September 11, 2001, tragedy. With reduced revenues, weak demand, high fixed costs, high fuel costs, and increasing expenses for security and insurance, the results for many of the airline companies have been grim. United Airlines declared bankruptcy in order to restructure and several other airlines were also near bankruptcy. But throughout all the bad times, Southwest Airlines has performed fairly well and has become the model for the future of the industry. The other airlines know they must cut costs and become more efficient in order to compete with Southwest.

How does Southwest do it? Southwest Airlines Company provides short-haul, high-frequency, point-to-point, low-fare air transportation services. Southwest's 375 aircraft provide service between 58 cities in 30 states throughout the U.S. In addition, Southwest serves many conveniently located satellite or downtown airports, such as Dallas Love Field, Houston Hobby, and Chicago Midway. The company's operating strategy also permits Southwest to achieve high-asset utilization. Aircraft are scheduled to minimize the amount of time they are at the gate, pegged at approximately 25 minutes, consequently reducing the number of aircraft and gate facilities that would otherwise be required.

Southwest Airlines has consistently been an innovator in the industry. In January 1995, Southwest introduced a ticketless travel option, eliminating the need to print and then process a paper ticket. The company provides air travel at a low cost while being firmly committed to customer service. Southwest employees are trained to be friendly and efficient and are rewarded for their efforts.

All of the company's efforts are consistent with its financial strategy to build shareholder value, which contributes to the stockholders' equity portion of the balance sheet shown here. Since the company has been consistently profitable for many years, the stockholders have benefited and shareholder value will likely continue to grow in the future.

Southwest Airlines 2002 Annual Report

Southwest Airlines Partial Balance Sheet

(In thousands, except per share amounts)

	December 31, 2002	2001
Stockholders' equity:		
Common stock, $1.00 par value: 2,000,000 shares authorized; 776,663 and 766,774 shares issued in 2002 and 2001 respectively	**776,663**	766,774
Capital in excess of par value	**135,848**	50,409
Retained earnings	**3,455,448**	3,228,408
Accumulated other comprehensive income (loss)	**53,658**	(31,538)
Total stockholder's equity	**4,421,617**	4,014,053
	$8,953,750	$8,997,141

You're in the Driver's Seat

http://www.southwest.com

If you were a Southwest Airlines stockholder, what information about the stock would you want to learn from Southwest's balance sheet? What additional information would you want about the company's plans? Use this chapter to develop your answers, and look at Southwest's most recent annual report to see whether the stock has responded to the company's attempts to build shareholder value.

LEARNING OBJECTIVES

After studying this chapter, you should be able to:

LO 1 Identify the components of the Stockholders' Equity category of the balance sheet and the accounts found in each component. (p. 542)

LO 2 Demonstrate an understanding of the characteristics of common and preferred stock and the differences between the classes of stock. (p. 545)

LO 3 Determine the financial statement impact when stock is issued for cash or for other consideration. (p. 546)

LO 4 Describe the financial statement impact of stock treated as treasury stock. (p. 547)

LO 5 Compute the amount of cash dividends when a firm has issued both preferred and common stock. (p. 550)

LO 6 Demonstrate an understanding of the difference between cash and stock dividends and the effect of stock dividends. (p. 551)

LO 7 Determine the difference between stock dividends and stock splits. (p. 553)

LO 8 Demonstrate an understanding of the statement of stockholders' equity and comprehensive income. (p. 554)

LO 9 Understand how investors use ratios to evaluate owners' equity. (p. 557)

LO 10 Explain the effects that transactions involving stockholders' equity have on the statement of cash flows. (p. 559)

LO 11 Describe the important differences between the sole proprietorship and partnership forms of organization versus the corporate form (Appendix). (p. 566)

WHAT EXTERNAL DECISION MAKERS WANT TO KNOW ABOUT STOCKHOLDERS' EQUITY

DECISION MAKING

External decision makers want to know whether or not to buy stock in a company. They want to know what classes of stock the company currently has. They also want to know whether the company will issue dividends to the stockholders and whether the stock price will increase after the stock is purchased. Most importantly, they want to know whether the company will be profitable and how the company will use that profit. When profits are retained in the business, investors want to know how it will be used.

▶ *ASK ESSENTIAL QUESTIONS*

- Should potential investors buy stock in the company?
- Should existing stockholders continue or should they sell their stock?
- Can stockholders expect to receive a dividend from the company?
- Will the company need to issue more stock to finance its operations?

▶ *FIND BASIC INFORMATION*

The balance sheet and the statement of cash flows, along with the supporting notes, are the key sources of information about a company's stock and stockholders' equity. This information tells:

- the dollar amount of stock that has been issued,
- the different types or classes of stock,

- the amount of the profits that has been retained in the company,
- whether dividends have been declared by the company, and
- how much cash has been generated as a result of the stock

▶ *UNDERSTAND ACCOUNTING PRINCIPLES*

To understand the basic information that is found, decision makers must understand the underlying accounting principles (GAAP) that have been applied to create the reported information. For stockholders' equity, these principles determine:

- the amount of equity contributed to stockholders
- the equity earned by the company and retained within the company

▶ *INTERPRET ANALYTICAL INFORMATION*

The most important measure of the stock is the market value of the stock on the stock market or stock exchange. The amount of the dividends can be measured by computing the dividend payout ratio that indicates what portion of the company's profit has been paid out to stockholders. Another measure of the company's stock is the book value per share that indicates the rights of the stockholders if the company were liquidated.

AN OVERVIEW OF STOCKHOLDERS' EQUITY

Equity as a Source of Financing

INTERNAL DECISION

Whenever a company needs to raise money, it must choose from the alternative financing sources that are available. Financing can be divided into two general categories: debt (borrowing from banks or other creditors) and equity (issuing stock). The company's management must consider the advantages and disadvantages of each alternative. Exhibit 11-1 indicates a few of the factors that must be considered.

Issuing stock is a very popular method of financing because of its flexibility. It provides advantages for the issuing company and the investors (stockholders). Investors are primarily concerned with the return on their investment. With stock, the return may be in the form of dividends paid to the investors but may also be the price appreciation of the stock. Stock is popular because it generally provides a higher rate of return (but also a higher degree of risk) than can be obtained by creditors

Accounting for Your Decisions

You Are the Investor

You have the opportunity to buy a company's bonds that pay 8% interest or the same company's stock. The stock has paid a dividend at an 8% rate for the last few years. The company is a large, reputable firm and has been profitable during recent times. Should you be indifferent between the two alternatives?

ANS: Interest on bonds is a fixed obligation. Unless the company goes out of business, you can count on receiving the 8% interest if you invest in the bonds. Dividends on stock are not fixed. There is no guarantee that the company will continue to pay 8% as the dividend on your investment. If the company is not profitable, it may decrease the size of the dividend. On the other hand, if the company becomes more profitable, it may pay a larger dividend.

Exhibit 11-1

Advantages and Disadvantages of Stock versus Debt Financing

DECISION MAKING

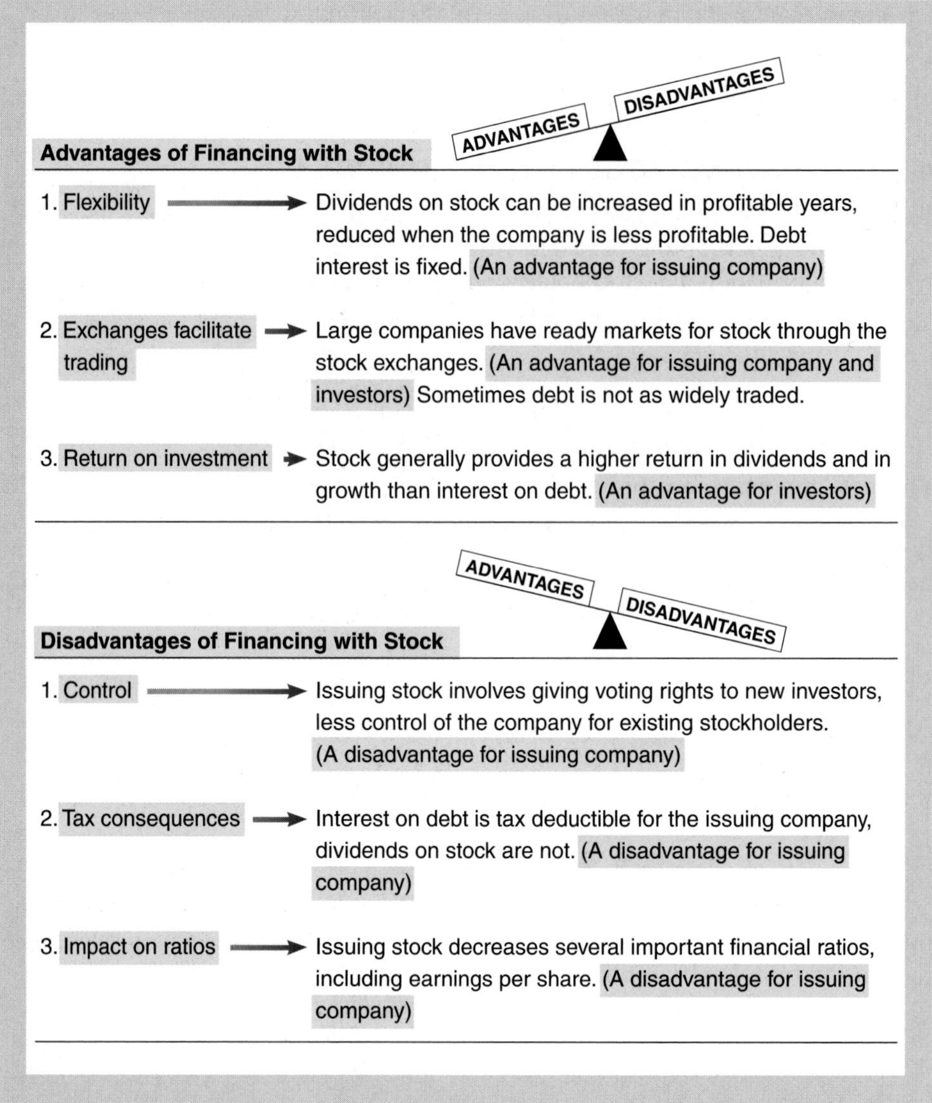

who receive interest from lending money. Stock is popular with issuing companies because dividends on stock can be adjusted according to the company's profitability; higher dividends can be paid when the firm is profitable and lower dividends when it is not. Interest on debt financing, on the other hand, is generally fixed and is a legal liability that cannot be adjusted when a company experiences lower profitability.

ADVANTAGES
DISADVANTAGES
Advantages of Financing with Stock
1. Flexibility → Dividends on stock can be increased in profitable years, reduced when the company is less profitable. Debt interest is fixed. (An advantage for issuing company)
2. Exchanges facilitate trading → Large companies have ready markets for stock through the stock exchanges. (An advantage for issuing company and investors) Sometimes debt is not as widely traded.
3. Return on investment → Stock generally provides a higher return in dividends and in growth than interest on debt. (An advantage for investors)
ADVANTAGES
DISADVANTAGES
Disadvantages of Financing with Stock
1. Control → Issuing stock involves giving voting rights to new investors, less control of the company for existing stockholders. (A disadvantage for issuing company)
2. Tax consequences → Interest on debt is tax deductible for the issuing company, dividends on stock are not. (A disadvantage for issuing company)
3. Impact on ratios → Issuing stock decreases several important financial ratios, including earnings per share. (A disadvantage for issuing company)

There are several disadvantages in issuing stock. Stock usually has voting rights, and issuing stock allows new investors to vote. Existing investors may not want to share the control of the company with new stockholders. From the issuing company's viewpoint, there is also a serious tax disadvantage to stock versus debt. As indicated in Chapter 10, interest on debt is tax deductible and results in lower taxes. Dividends on stock, on the other hand, are not tax deductible and do not result in tax savings to the issuing company. Finally, the following sections of this chapter indicate the impact that issuing stock has on the company's financial statements. Issuing stock decreases several important financial ratios, such as earnings per share. Issuing debt does not have a similar effect on the earnings per share ratio.

Management should consider many other factors in deciding between debt and equity financing. The company's goal should be financing the company in a manner that results in the lowest overall cost of capital to the firm. Usually, companies attain that goal by having a reasonable balance of both debt and equity financing.

Stockholders' Equity on the Balance Sheet

The basic accounting equation is often stated as follows:

Assets = Liabilities + Owners' Equity

Owners' equity is viewed as a residual amount. That is, the owners of a corporation have a claim to all assets after the claims represented by liabilities to creditors have been satisfied.

In this chapter, we concentrate on the corporate form of organization and refer to the owners' equity as *stockholders' equity*. Therefore, the basic accounting equation for a corporation can be restated as follows:

Assets = Liabilities + Stockholders' Equity

The stockholders are the owners of a corporation. They have a residual interest in its assets after the claims of all creditors have been satisfied.

The stockholders' equity category of all corporations has two major components or subcategories:

Total Stockholders' Equity = Contributed Capital
+
Retained Earnings

Contributed capital represents the amount the corporation has received from the sale of stock to stockholders. Retained earnings is the amount of net income that the corporation has earned but not paid as dividends. Instead, the corporation retains and reinvests the income.

Although all corporations maintain the two primary categories of contributed capital and retained earnings, within these categories they use a variety of accounts that have several alternative titles. The next section examines two important items: income and dividends, and their impact on the Retained Earnings account.

From Concept to Practice 11.1

Reading Winnebago Industries' Annual Report

Winnebago Industries' retained earnings is titled Reinvested Earnings. What was the balance of the reinvested earnings at the end of 2002? Did the balance increase from the end of 2001?

How Income and Dividends Affect Retained Earnings

The Retained Earnings account plays an important role because it serves as a link between the income statement and the balance sheet. The term *articulated statements* refers to the fact that the information on the income statement is related to the information on the balance sheet. The bridge (or link) between the two statements is the Retained Earnings account. Exhibit 11-2 presents this relationship graphically. As the exhibit indicates, the income statement is used to calculate a company's net income for a given period of time. The amount of the net income is transferred to the statement of retained earnings and is added to the beginning balance of retained earnings (with dividends deducted) to calculate the ending balance of retained earnings. The ending balance of retained earnings is the amount that is portrayed on the balance sheet in the stockholders' equity category. That is why you must always prepare the income statement before you prepare the balance sheet, as you have discovered when developing financial statements in previous chapters of the text.

Exhibit 11-2

Retained Earnings Connects the Income Statement and the Balance Sheet

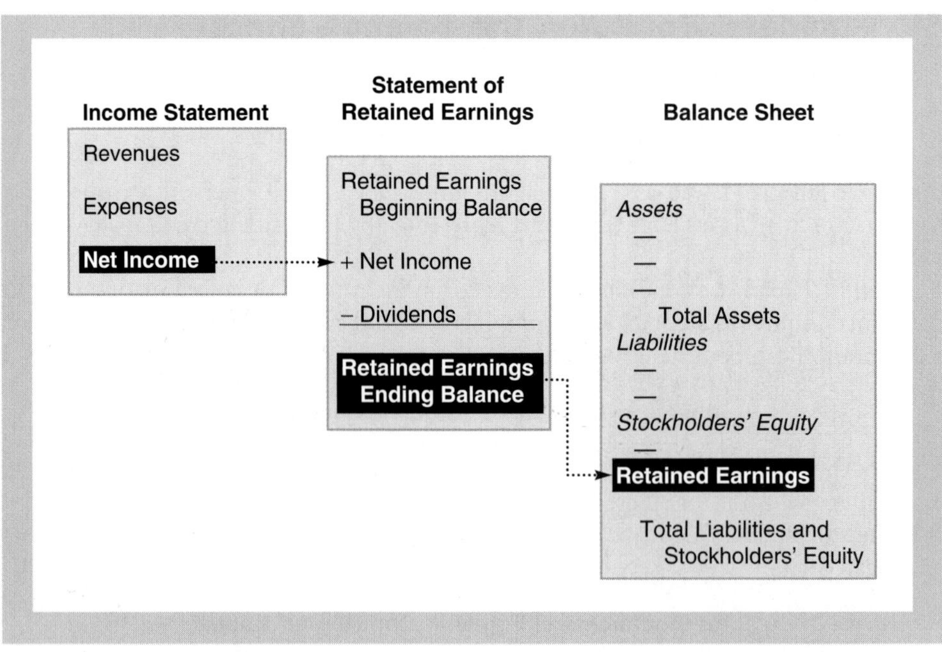

Identifying the Components of the Stockholders' Equity Section of the Balance Sheet

LO 1 Identify the components of the Stockholders' Equity category of the balance sheet and the accounts found in each component.

http://www.delta.com

http://www.continental.com

The stockholders' equity portion of the balance sheet of **Delta Air Lines** is provided in Exhibit 11-3. We will focus on the Stockholders' (Shareholders') Equity category of the balance sheet. All corporations, including Delta Air Lines, begin the Stockholders' Equity category with a list of the firm's contributed capital. In some cases, there are two categories of stock: common stock and preferred stock (the latter is discussed later in this chapter). Common stock normally carries voting rights. The common stockholders elect the officers of the corporation and establish its bylaws and governing rules. It is not unusual for corporations to have more than one type of common stock, each with different rights or terms. For example, **Continental Airlines, Inc.**, one of Delta's competitors, has two classes of common stock listed on its 2002 balance sheet.

Authorized shares The maximum number of shares a corporation may issue as indicated in the corporate charter.

Issued shares The number of shares sold or distributed to stockholders.

Outstanding shares The number of shares issued less the number of shares held as treasury stock.

Number of Shares It is important to determine the number of shares of stock for each stock account. Corporate balance sheets report the number of shares in three categories: **authorized, issued,** and **outstanding shares.**

To become incorporated, a business must develop articles of incorporation and apply to the proper state authorities for a corporate charter. The corporation must specify the maximum number of shares that it will be allowed to issue. This maximum number of shares is called the *authorized stock.* A corporation applies for authorization to issue many more shares than it will issue immediately, to allow for future growth and other events that may occur over its long life. For example, Delta Air Lines indicates that it has 450,000,000 shares of common stock authorized but that only 180,903,373 shares had been issued as of December 31, 2002.

The number of shares *issued* indicates the number of shares that have been sold or transferred to stockholders. The number of shares issued does not necessarily mean, however, that those shares are currently outstanding. The term *outstanding* indicates shares actually in the hands of the stockholders. Shares that have been issued by the corporation and then repurchased are counted as shares issued but not as shares outstanding. Quite often corporations repurchase their own stock as treasury stock (explained in more detail later in this chapter). Treasury stock reduces the number of shares outstanding. The number of Delta Air Lines' shares of common stock outstanding at December 31, 2002, could be calculated as follows:

Exhibit 11-3 Delta Air Lines' Partial Balance Sheet

Delta Air Lines Inc.

Partial balance sheet *(in millions)*	December 31, 2002	2001
Employee Stock Ownership Plan Preferred Stock:		
Series B ESOP Convertible Preferred Stock, $1.00 par value, $72.00 stated and liquidation value; 6,065,489 shares issued and outstanding at December 31, 2002, and 6,278,210 shares issued and outstanding at December 31, 2001	**437**	452
Unearned compensation under Employee Stock Ownership Plan	**(173)**	(197)
Total Employee Stock Ownership Plan Preferred Stock	**264**	255
Shareowners' Equity:		
Common stock, $1.50 par value; 450,000,000 shares authorized; 180,903,373 shares issued at December 31, 2002, and 180,890,356 shares issued at December 31, 2001	**271**	271
Additional paid-in capital	**3,263**	3,267
Retained earnings	**1,639**	2,930
Accumulated other comprehensive income (loss)	**(1,562)**	25
Treasury stock at cost, 57,544,168 shares at December 31, 2002, and 57,644,690 shares at December 31, 2001	**(2,718)**	(2,724)
Total shareowners' equity	**893**	3,769
Total liabilities and shareowners' equity	**$24,720**	$23,605

Delta's contributed capital (common stock and additional paid-in capital)

Number of shares issued	180,903,373
Less: Treasury stock	57,544,168
Number of shares outstanding	123,359,205

Study Tip

Treasury stock is included in the number of shares issued. It is not part of the number of shares outstanding.

Par Value: The Firm's "Legal Capital" The Stockholders' Equity category of many balance sheets refers to an amount as the *par value* of the stock. For example, Delta's common stock has a par value of $1.50 per share. **Par value** is an arbitrary amount stated on the face of the stock certificate and represents the legal capital of the corporation. Most corporations set the par value of the stock at very low amounts because there are legal difficulties if stock is sold at less than par. Therefore, par value does not indicate the stock's value or the amount that is obtained when it is sold on the stock exchange; it is simply an arbitrary amount that exists to fulfill legal requirements. A company's legal requirement depends on its state of incorporation. Some states do not require corporations to indicate a par value; others require them to designate the *stated value* of the stock. A stated value is accounted for in the same manner as a par value and appears in the Stockholders' Equity category in the same manner as a par value.

Par value An arbitrary amount that represents the legal capital of the firm.

The amount of the par value is the amount that is presented in the stock account. That is, the dollar amount in a firm's stock account can be calculated as its par value per share times number of shares issued. For Delta, the dollar amount appearing in the common stock account can be calculated as follows:

$1.50 Par Value per Share × 180,903,373 Shares Issued =
$271 million (rounded to millions) Balance in the Common Stock Account

Additional Paid-in Capital The dollar amounts of the stock accounts in the Stockholders' Equity category do not indicate the amount that was received when the stock was sold to stockholders. The Common Stock and Preferred Stock accounts

Additional paid-in capital The amount received for the issuance of stock in excess of the par value of the stock.

indicate only the par value of the stock. When stock is issued for an amount higher than the par value, the excess is reported as **additional paid-in capital.** Several alternative titles are used for this account, including Paid-in Capital in Excess of Par, Capital Surplus (an old term that should no longer be used), and Premium on Stock. Regardless of the title, the account represents the amount received in excess of par when stock was issued.

Delta's balance sheet indicates additional paid-in capital of $3,263 million at December 31, 2002. Delta, as well as many other corporations, presents only one amount for additional paid-in capital for all stock transactions. Therefore, we are unable to determine whether the amount resulted from the issuance of common stock or other stock transactions. As a result, it is often impossible to determine the issue price of each category of stock even with a careful analysis of the balance sheet and the accompanying notes.

Retained earnings Net income that has been made by the corporation but not paid out as dividends.

Retained Earnings: The Amount *Not* Paid as Dividends **Retained earnings** represents net income that the firm has earned but has *not* paid as dividends. Remember that retained earnings is an amount that is accumulated over the entire life of the corporation and does not represent the income or dividends for a specific year. For example, the balance of the Retained Earnings account on Delta's balance sheet at December 31, 2002, is $1,639 million. That does not mean that Delta had a net income of this amount in 2002; it simply means that over the life of the corporation, Delta has retained $1,639 million more net income than it paid out as dividends to stockholders.

It is also important to remember that the balance of the Retained Earnings account does not mean that liquid assets of that amount are available to the stockholders. Corporations decide to retain income because they have needs other than paying dividends to stockholders. The needs may include the purchase of assets, the retirement of debt, or other financial needs. Money spent for those needs usually benefits the stockholders in the long run, but liquid assets equal to the balance of the Retained Earnings account are not necessarily available to stockholders. In theory, income should be retained whenever the company can reinvest the money and get a better return within the business than the shareholders can get on their own. In summary, retained earnings is a stockholders' equity account. Although the company's assets have increased, retained earnings does not represent a pool of liquid assets.

A prospective stockholder may purchase shares and receive certificates, like this one, either directly from the company or through a stockbroker. Usually, a broker purchases shares in its own name for the investor's account—and the investor never sees a certificate.

COURTESY OF SOUTH-WESTERN PUBLISHING

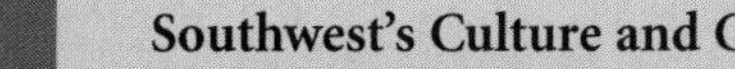

Business Strategy

Southwest's Culture and Compensation

Southwest Airlines has always sought to create a positive corporate culture that would enhance employee performance and shareholder value. The culture was a reflection of one of its founders, Herbert D. Kelleher, who loved to joke with employees and dole out hugs and kisses as greetings. Fun and humor were essential, he preached. Employees wanted to please and emulate him. Workers routinely went above and beyond the call of duty to help the airline thrive. Such efforts have helped Southwest post 30 consecutive years of profits and turn it into the fourth-biggest airline in terms of U.S. domestic service. Many carriers, new and old, are trying to emulate Southwest's low-cost, no-frills formula.

The employees were not just motivated by company loyalty. In the mid-1970s, Southwest became the first airline to start a profit-sharing plan and added a stock-purchase plan in 1984. In 1991, it started a stock-option plan that now includes many employees. The stock has produced millionaires throughout company ranks, down to mechanics and flight attendants. Even with the stock declines, a $10,000 investment in early July of 1984 would be worth just over $200,000 today.

Yet that formula is under mounting pressure. Many employees of the airline have complained that they have worked increasingly hard to boost productivity and profits, but without matching pay raises. Southwest, which led the industry in on-time performance for most of the 1990s, slipped to second in 1999 and has bounced in and out of the lead ever since. Southwest executives say recent complaints from employees don't necessarily indicate waning loyalty. An overwhelming number of employees remain devoted to the company's success and are proud of their high productivity, executives say.

CEO Jim Parker says the airline's work ethic remains critical to its success. "Our cost advantage is not based on low wages," he says. "We pay very competitive wages. It is based on our employees' hard work." ■

Source: Melanie Trottman, "Inside Southwest Airlines, Storied Culture Feels Strains," *Wall Street Journal*, July 11, 2003.

WHAT IS PREFERRED STOCK?

LO 2 Demonstrate an understanding of the characteristics of common and preferred stock and the differences between the classes of stock.

Many companies have a class of stock called *preferred stock*. One of the advantages of preferred stock is the flexibility it provides because its terms and provisions can be tailored to meet the firm's needs. These terms and provisions are detailed in the stock certificate. Generally, preferred stock offers holders a preference to dividends declared by the corporation. That is, if dividends are declared, the preferred stockholders must receive dividends first, before the holders of common stock.

The dividend rate on preferred stock may be stated in two ways. First, it may be stated as a percentage of the stock's par value. For example, if a stock is presented on the balance sheet as $100 par, 7% preferred stock, its dividend rate is $7 per share ($100 times 7%). Second, the dividend may be stated as a per-share amount. For example, a stock may appear on the balance sheet as $100 par, $7 preferred stock, meaning that the dividend rate is $7 per share. Investors in common stock should note the dividend requirements of the preferred shareholder. The greater the obligation to the preferred shareholder, the less desirable the common stock becomes.

Cumulative feature The right to dividends in arrears before the current-year dividend is distributed.

Several important provisions of preferred stock relate to the payment of dividends. Some preferred stock issues have a **cumulative feature,** which means that if a dividend is not declared to the preferred stockholders in one year, dividends are considered to be *in arrears*. Before a dividend can be declared to common stockholders in a subsequent period, the preferred stockholders must be paid all dividends in arrears as well as the current year's dividend. The cumulative feature ensures that the preferred stockholders will receive a dividend before one is paid to common stockholders. It does not guarantee a dividend to preferred stockholders, however. There is no legal requirement mandating that a corporation declare a dividend, and preferred stockholders have a legal right to receive a dividend only when it has been declared.

Participating feature Allows preferred stockholders to share on a percentage basis in the distribution of an abnormally large dividend.

Some preferred stocks have a **participating feature.** Its purpose is to allow the preferred stockholders to receive a dividend in excess of the regular rate when a firm has been particularly profitable and declares an abnormally large dividend. When the participating feature is present and a firm declares a dividend, the preferred stockholders first have a right to the current year's dividend, and then the common stockholders must receive an equal portion (usually based on the par or stated value of the stocks) of the dividend. The participating feature then applies to any dividend declared in excess of the amounts in the first two steps. The preferred stockholders are allowed to share in the excess, normally on the basis of the total par value of the preferred and common stock.

Convertible feature Allows preferred stock to be exchanged for common stock.

Callable feature Allows the firm to eliminate a class of stock by paying the stockholders a specified amount.

Preferred stock may also be convertible or callable. The **convertible feature** allows the preferred stockholders to convert their stockholdings to common stock. Convertible preferred stock offers stockholders the advantages of the low risk generally associated with preferred stock and the possibility of the higher return that is associated with common stock. The **callable feature** allows the issuing firm to retire the stock after it has been issued. Normally, the call price is specified as a fixed dollar amount. Firms may exercise the call option to eliminate a certain class of preferred stock so that control of the corporation is maintained in the hands of fewer stockholders. The call option also may be exercised when the dividend rate on the preferred stock is too high and other, more cost-effective financing alternatives are available.

Preferred stock is attractive to many investors because it offers a return in the form of a dividend at a level of risk that is lower than that of most common stocks. Usually, the dividend available on preferred stock is more stable from year to year, and as a result, the market price of the stock is also more stable. In fact, if preferred stock carries certain provisions, the stock is very similar to bonds or notes payable. Management must evaluate whether such securities really represent debt and should be presented in the liability category of the balance sheet or whether they represent equity and should be presented in the equity category. Such a decision involves the concept of *substance over form.* That is, a company must look not only at the legal form but also at the economic substance of the security to decide whether it is debt or equity.

ISSUANCE OF STOCK

Stock Issued for Cash

LO 3 Determine the financial statement impact when stock is issued for cash or for other consideration.

Stock may be issued in several different ways. It may be issued for cash or for noncash assets. When stock is issued for cash, the amount of its par value should be reported in the stock account and the amount in excess of par should be reported in an additional paid-in capital account. For example, assume that on July 1 a firm issued 1,000 shares of $10 par common stock for $15 per share. The effect on the balance sheet is as follows:

BALANCE SHEET							INCOME STATEMENT
ASSETS		=	LIABILITIES	+	OWNERS' EQUITY		+ REVENUES − EXPENSES
Cash	15,000				Common Stock	10,000	
					Additional Paid-in Capital—Common	5,000	

As noted earlier, the Common Stock account and the Additional Paid-in Capital account are both presented in the Stockholders' Equity category of the balance sheet and represent the contributed capital component of the corporation.

If no-par stock is issued, the corporation does not distinguish between common stock and additional paid-in capital. If the firm in the previous example had issued no-par stock on July 1 for $15 per share, the entire amount of $15,000 would be presented in the Common Stock account.

Stock Issued for Noncash Consideration

Occasionally, stock is issued in return for something other than cash. For example, a corporation may issue stock to obtain land or buildings. When such a transaction occurs, the company faces the difficult task of deciding what value to place on the transaction. This is especially difficult when the market values of the elements of the transaction are not known with complete certainty. According to the general guideline, the transaction should be reported at fair market value. Market value may be indicated by the value of the consideration given (stock) or the value of the consideration received (property), whichever can be most readily determined.

Assume that on July 1 a firm issued 500 shares of $10 par preferred stock to acquire a building. The stock is not widely traded, and the current market value of the stock is not evident. The building has recently been appraised by an independent firm as having a market value of $12,000. In this case, the issuance of the stock affects the balance sheet as follows:

BALANCE SHEET								INCOME STATEMENT
ASSETS		=	LIABILITIES	+	OWNERS' EQUITY		+	REVENUES − EXPENSES
Building	12,000				Preferred Stock	5,000		
					Additional Paid-in Capital—Preferred	7,000		

In other situations, the market value of the stock may be more readily determined and should be used as the best measure of the value of the transaction. Market value may be represented by the current stock market quotation or by a recent cash sale of the stock. The company should attempt to develop the best estimate of the market value of the noncash transaction and should neither intentionally overstate nor intentionally understate the assets received by the issuance of stock.

WHAT IS TREASURY STOCK?

LO 4 Describe the financial statement impact of stock treated as treasury stock.

Treasury stock Stock issued by the firm and then repurchased but not retired.

The Stockholders' Equity category of Delta Air Lines' balance sheet in Exhibit 11-3 includes **treasury stock** in the amount of $2,718 million. The Treasury Stock account is created when a corporation buys its own stock sometime after issuing it. For an amount to be treated as treasury stock, (1) it must be the corporation's own stock, (2) it must have been issued to the stockholders at some point, (3) it must have been repurchased from the stockholders, and (4) it must not be retired but must be held for some purpose. Treasury stock is not considered outstanding stock and does not have voting rights.

A corporation may repurchase stock as treasury stock for several reasons. The most common is to have stock available to distribute to employees for bonuses or as part of an employee-benefit plan. Firms also may buy treasury stock to maintain a favorable market price for the stock or to improve the appearance of the firm's financial ratios. More recently, firms have purchased their stock to maintain control of the ownership and to prevent unwanted takeover or buyout attempts. Of course, the lower the stock price, the more likely a company is to buy back its own stock and wait for the shares to rise in value before reissuing them.

The two methods to account for treasury stock transactions are the cost method and the par value method. We will present the more commonly used cost method.

Assume that the Stockholders' Equity section of Rezin Company's balance sheet on December 31, 2003, appears as follows:

Common stock, $10 par value,	
1,000 shares issued and outstanding	$10,000
Additional paid-in capital—Common	12,000
Retained earnings	15,000
Total stockholders' equity	$37,000

Assume that on February 1, 2004, Rezin buys 100 of its shares as treasury stock at $25 per share. The effect on Rezin's balance sheet is as follows:

BALANCE SHEET								INCOME STATEMENT
ASSETS		=	LIABILITIES	+	OWNERS' EQUITY		+	REVENUES – EXPENSES
Cash	(2,500)				Treasury Stock	(2,500)		

The purchase of treasury stock does not directly affect the Common Stock account itself. The Treasury Stock account is considered to be a contra account and is subtracted from the total of contributed capital and retained earnings in the Stockholders' Equity section. Treasury Stock is *not* an asset account. When a company buys its own stock, it is contracting its size and reducing the equity of stockholders. Therefore, Treasury Stock is a contra-equity account, not an asset.

The Stockholders' Equity section of Rezin's balance sheet on February 1, 2004, after the purchase of the treasury stock, appears as follows:

Common stock, $10 par value,	
1,000 shares issued, 900 outstanding	$10,000
Additional paid-in capital—Common	12,000
Retained earnings	15,000
Total contributed capital and retained earnings	$37,000
Less: Treasury stock, 100 shares at cost	2,500
Total stockholders' equity	$34,500

Corporations may choose to reissue stock to investors after it has been held as treasury stock. When treasury stock is resold for more than it cost, the difference between the sales price and the cost appears in the Additional Paid-in Capital—Treasury Stock account. For example, if Rezin resold 100 shares of treasury stock on May 1, 2004, for $30 per share, the Treasury Stock account would be reduced by $2,500 (100 shares times $25 per share), and the Additional Paid-in Capital—Treasury Stock account would be increased by $500 (100 shares times the difference between the purchase price of $25 and the reissue price of $30).

When treasury stock is resold for an amount less than its cost, the difference between the sales price and the cost is deducted from the Additional Paid-in Capital—Treasury Stock account. If that account does not exist, the difference should be deducted from the Retained Earnings account. For example, assume that Rezin Company had resold 100 shares of treasury stock on May 1, 2004, for $20 per share, instead of $30 in the previous example. In this example, Rezin has had no other treasury stock transactions, and therefore, no balance existed in the Additional Paid-in Capital—Treasury Stock account. Rezin would then reduce the Treasury Stock account by $2,500 (100 shares times $25 per share) and would reduce Retained Earnings by $500 (100 shares times the difference between the purchase price of $25 and the reissue price of $20 per share). Thus, the Additional Paid-in Capital—Treasury Stock account may have a positive balance, but entries that result in a negative balance in the account should not be made.

Note that *income statement accounts are never involved* in treasury stock transactions. Regardless of whether treasury stock is reissued for more or less than its cost, the effect is reflected in the stockholders' equity accounts. It is simply not possible for a firm to engage in transactions involving its own stock and have the result affect the performance of the firm as reflected on the income statement.

Two-Minute Review

1. *Where does the Treasury Stock account appear on the balance sheet?*
2. *What is the effect on stockholders' equity when stock is purchased as treasury stock?*
3. *How does treasury stock affect the number of shares issued and outstanding?*

Answers on page 562.

RETIREMENT OF STOCK

Retirement of stock occurs when a corporation buys back stock after it has been issued to investors and does not intend to reissue the stock. Retirement often occurs because the corporation wants to eliminate a particular class of stock or a particular group of stockholders. When stock is repurchased and retired, the balances of the stock account and the paid-in capital account that were created when the stock was issued must be eliminated. When the original issue price is higher than the repurchase price of the stock, the difference is reflected in the Paid-in Capital from Stock Retirement account. When the repurchase price of the stock is more than the original issue price, the difference reduces the Retained Earnings account. The general principle for retirement of stock is the same as for treasury stock transactions. No income statement accounts are affected by the retirement. The effect is reflected in the Cash account and the stockholders' equity accounts.

Retirement of stock When the stock is repurchased with no intention to reissue at a later date.

DIVIDENDS: DISTRIBUTION OF INCOME TO SHAREHOLDERS

Cash Dividends

INTERNAL DECISION

Corporations may declare and issue several different types of dividends, the most common of which is a cash dividend to stockholders. Cash dividends may be declared quarterly, annually, or at other intervals. Normally, cash dividends are declared on one date, referred to as the *date of declaration,* and are paid out on a later date, referred to as the *payment date.* The dividend is paid to the stockholders that own the stock as of a particular date, the *date of record.*

Generally, two requirements must be met before the board of directors can declare a cash dividend. First, sufficient cash must be available by the payment date to pay to the stockholders. Second, the Retained Earnings account must have a sufficient positive balance. Dividends reduce the balance of the account, and therefore Retained Earnings must have a balance before the dividend declaration. Most firms have an established policy concerning the portion of income that will be declared as dividends. The **dividend payout ratio** is calculated as the annual dividend amount divided by the annual net income. The dividend payout ratios of three members of the retail industry are given in Exhibit 11-4. The dividend payout ratio for many firms is 50% or 60% and seldom

Dividend payout ratio The annual dividend amount divided by the annual net income.

Exhibit 11-4

2002 Dividend Payout Ratios to Common Stockholders in the Retail Industry

http://www.jcpenney.com
http://www.walmart.com
http://www.dillards.com

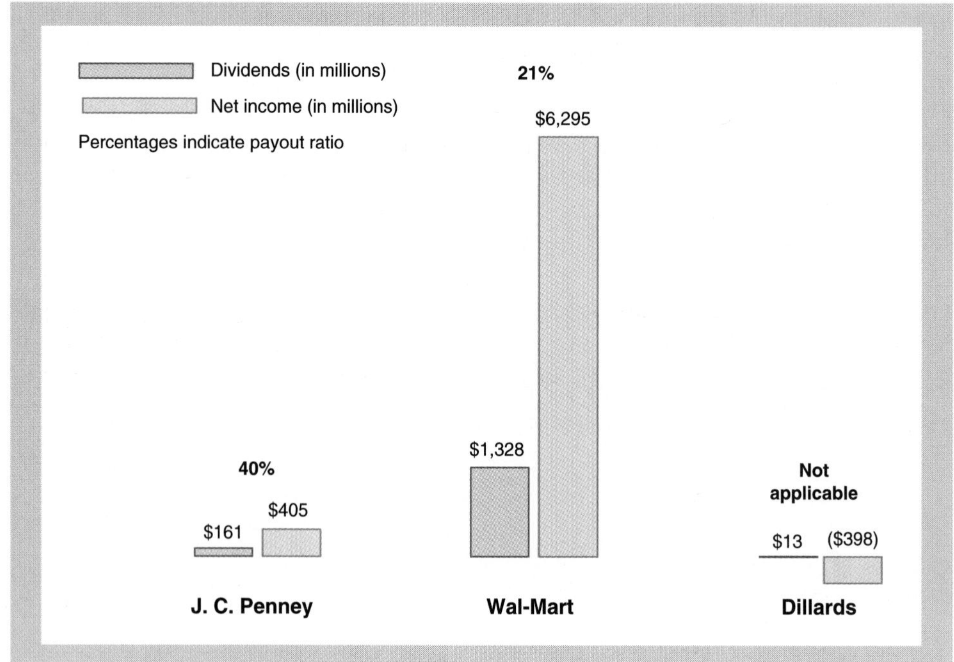

Study Tip A dividend is not an expense on the income statement. It is a reduction of retained earnings and appears on the retained earnings statement. If it is a cash dividend, it also reduces the cash balance when paid.

exceeds 70%. Typically, utilities pay a high proportion of their earnings. In contrast, fast-growing companies in technology often pay nothing to shareholders. Some investors want and need the current income of a high-dividend payout, but others would rather not receive dividend income and prefer to gamble that the stock price will appreciate.

Cash dividends become a liability on the date they are declared. An accounting transaction should be recorded on that date to acknowledge the liability and reduce the balance of the Retained Earnings account. For example, assume that on July 1 the board of directors of Grant Company declared a cash dividend of $7,000 to be paid on September 1. Grant reflects the declaration as a reduction of Retained Earnings and an increase in Cash Dividend Payable.

The Cash Dividend Payable account is a liability and is normally shown in the Current Liabilities section of the balance sheet.

The important point to remember is that dividends reduce the amount of retained earnings *when declared.* When dividends are paid, the company reduces the liability to stockholders reflected in the Cash Dividend Payable account.

Cash Dividends for Preferred and Common Stock

LO 5 Compute the amount of cash dividends when a firm has issued both preferred and common stock.

When cash dividends involving more than one class of stock are declared, the corporation must determine the proper amount to allocate to each class of stock. As indicated earlier, the amount of dividends that preferred stockholders have rights to depends on the terms and provisions of the preferred stock. We will illustrate the proper allocation of cash dividends with an example of a firm that has two classes of stock, preferred and common.

Assume that on December 31, 2004, Stricker Company has outstanding 10,000 shares of $10 par, 8% preferred stock and 40,000 shares of $5 par common stock. Stricker was unable to declare a dividend in 2002 or 2003 but wants to declare a $70,000 dividend for 2004. The dividend is to be allocated to preferred and common stockholders in accordance with the terms of the stock agreements.

Noncumulative Preferred Stock If the terms of the stock agreement indicate that the preferred stock is not cumulative, the preferred stockholders do not have a right to dividends in arrears. The dividends that were not declared in 2002 and 2003 are simply lost and do not affect the distribution of the dividend in 2004. Therefore, the cash dividend declared in 2004 is allocated between preferred and common stockholders as follows:

	TO PREFERRED	TO COMMON
Step 1: Distribute current year dividend to preferred (10,000 shares × $10 par × 8% × 1 year)	$8,000	
Step 2: Distribute remaining dividend to common ($70,000 − $8,000)		$62,000
Total allocated	$8,000	$62,000
Dividend per share		
Preferred: $8,000/10,000 shares	$0.80	
Common: $62,000/40,000 shares		$1.55

Cumulative Preferred Stock If the terms of the stock agreement indicate that the preferred stock is cumulative, the preferred stockholders have a right to dividends in arrears before the current year's dividend is distributed. Therefore, Stricker performs the following steps:

	TO PREFERRED	TO COMMON
Step 1: Distribute dividends in arrears to preferred (10,000 shares × $10 par × 8% × 2 years)	$16,000	
Step 2: Distribute current-year dividend to preferred (10,000 shares × $10 par × 8% × 1 year)	8,000	
Step 3: Distribute remainder to common ($70,000 − $24,000)		$46,000
Total allocated	$24,000	$46,000
Dividend per share		
Preferred: $24,000/10,000 shares	$2.40	
Common: $46,000/40,000 shares		$1.15

The Stricker Company example illustrates the flexibility available with preferred stock. The provisions and terms of the preferred stock can be established to make the stock attractive to investors and to provide an effective form of financing for the corporation. The cumulative and participating features make the preferred stock more attractive. However, these features may make the *common stock* less attractive because more dividends for the preferred stockholders may mean less dividends for the common stockholders.

Stock Dividends

LO 6 Demonstrate an understanding of the difference between cash and stock dividends and the effect of stock dividends.

Stock dividend The issuance of additional shares of stock to existing stockholders.

Cash dividends are the most popular and widely used form of dividend, but corporations may at times use stock dividends instead of, or in addition to, cash dividends. A **stock dividend** occurs when a corporation declares and issues additional shares of its own stock to its existing stockholders. Firms use stock dividends for several reasons. First, a corporation may simply not have sufficient cash available to declare a cash dividend. Stock dividends do not require the use of the corporation's resources and allow cash to be retained for other purposes. Second, stock dividends result in additional shares of stock outstanding and may decrease the market price per share of stock if the dividend is large (small stock dividends tend to have little effect on market price). The lower price may make the stock more attractive to a wider range of investors and allow enhanced financing opportunities. Finally, stock dividends normally do not represent taxable income to the recipients and may be attractive to some wealthy stockholders.

Similar to cash dividends, stock dividends are normally declared by the board of directors on a specific date, and the stock is distributed to the stockholders at a later date. The corporation recognizes the stock dividend on the date of declaration. Assume that Shah Company's Stockholders' Equity category of the balance sheet appears as follows as of January 1, 2004:

Common stock, $10 par, 5,000 shares issued and outstanding	$ 50,000
Additional paid-in capital—Common	30,000
Retained earnings	70,000
Total stockholders' equity	$150,000

Assume that on January 2, 2004, Shah declares a 10% stock dividend to common stockholders to be distributed on April 1, 2004. Small stock dividends (usually those of 20 to 25% or less) normally are recorded at the *market value* of the stock as of the date of declaration. Assume that Shah's common stock is selling at $40 per share on that date. Therefore, the total market value of the stock dividend is $20,000 (10% of 5,000 shares outstanding, or 500 shares, times $40 per share). The effect of the stock dividend on January 2, the date of declaration, is as follows:

BALANCE SHEET							INCOME STATEMENT
ASSETS	=	LIABILITIES	+	OWNERS' EQUITY		+	REVENUES – EXPENSES
				Retained Earnings	(20,000)		
				Common Stock Dividend Distributable	5,000		
				Additional Paid-in Capital—Common	15,000		

The Common Stock Dividend Distributable account represents shares of stock to be issued; it is not a liability account because no cash or assets are to be distributed to the stockholders. Thus, it should be treated as an account in the Stockholders' Equity section of the balance sheet and is a part of the contributed capital component of equity.

Note that the declaration of a stock dividend does not affect the total stockholders' equity of the corporation, although the retained earnings are reduced. That is, the Stockholders' Equity section of Shah's balance sheet on January 2, 2004, is as follows after the declaration of the dividend:

Common stock, $10 par, 5,000 shares issued and outstanding	$ 50,000
Common stock dividend distributable, 500 shares	5,000
Additional paid-in capital—Common	45,000
Retained earnings	50,000
Total stockholders' equity	$150,000

The account balances are different, but total stockholders' equity is $150,000 both before and after the declaration of the stock dividend. In effect, retained earnings has been capitalized (transferred permanently to the contributed capital accounts). When a corporation actually issues a stock dividend, it is necessary to transfer an amount from the Stock Dividend Distributable account to the appropriate stock account.

Our stock dividend example has illustrated the general rule that stock dividends should be reported at fair market value. That is, in the transaction to reflect the stock dividend, retained earnings is decreased in the amount of the fair market value per share of the stock times the number of shares to be distributed. When a large stock dividend is declared, however, accountants do not follow the general rule we have illustrated. A large stock dividend is a stock dividend of more than 20% to 25% of the number of shares of stock outstanding. In that case, the stock dividend is reported at *par value* rather than at fair market value. That is, Retained Earnings is decreased in the amount of the par value per share times the number of shares to be distributed.

Refer again to the Shah Company example. Assume that instead of a 10% dividend, on January 2, 2004, Shah

Which Way to Go?

Is It Better to Issue Stocks or Bonds?

Taz Industries' president has asked Fleming LaRue, the controller, and Clarissa Ping, the treasurer, to determine the best way for the company to raise cash to pay for expanding operations. Fleming feels strongly that it is in the best interest of the company to issue bonds. Clarissa does not agree and wants the company to issue more shares of common stock. They have decided to compromise and recommend issuing cumulative, convertible preferred stock. Currently, Taz has only common stock outstanding.

The president is very concerned about how the board of directors and the current stockholders will react to the recommendation. Should she be concerned? Why might the board and stockholders be unhappy with issuing the new stock? What can the president say to convince them that this would be a good solution?

declares and distributes a 100% stock dividend to be distributed on April 1, 2004. The stock dividend results in 5,000 additional shares being issued and certainly meets the definition of a large stock dividend. The effect on the accounting equation on the declaration date is:

BALANCE SHEET						INCOME STATEMENT
ASSETS	=	LIABILITIES	+	OWNERS' EQUITY	+	REVENUES – EXPENSES
				Retained Earnings (50,000)		
				Common Stock Dividend Distributable 50,000		

When the stock is actually distributed, the amount of $50,000 is transferred from the Common Stock Dividend Distributable account to the Common Stock account. The Stockholders' Equity category of Shah's balance sheet as of April 1 after the stock dividend is as follows:

Common stock, $10 par, 10,000 shares issued and outstanding	$100,000
Additional paid-in capital—Common	30,000
Retained earnings	20,000
Total stockholders' equity	$150,000

Again, you should note that the stock dividend has not affected total stockholders' equity. Shah has $150,000 of stockholders' equity both before and after the stock dividend. The difference between large and small stock dividends is the amount transferred from retained earnings to the contributed capital portion of equity.

Stock Splits

LO 7 Determine the difference between stock dividends and stock splits.

Stock split The creation of additional shares of stock with a reduction of the par value of the stock.

A **stock split** is similar to a stock dividend in that it results in additional shares of stock outstanding and is nontaxable. In fact, firms may use a stock split for nearly the same reasons as a stock dividend: to increase the number of shares, reduce the market price per share, and make the stock more accessible to a wider range of investors. There is an important legal difference, however. Stock dividends do not affect the par value per share of the stock, whereas stock splits reduce the par value per share. There also is an important accounting difference. An accounting transaction is *not recorded* when a corporation declares and executes a stock split. None of the stockholders' equity accounts are affected by the split. Rather, the note information accompanying the balance sheet must disclose the additional shares and the reduction of the par value per share.

Return to the Shah Company example. Assume that on January 2, 2004, Shah issued a 2-for-1 stock split instead of a stock dividend. The split results in an additional 5,000 shares of stock outstanding but should not be recorded in a formal accounting transaction. Therefore, the Stockholders' Equity section of Shah Company immediately after the stock split on January 2, 2004, is as follows:

Common stock, $5 par, 10,000 shares issued and outstanding	$ 50,000
Additional paid-in capital—Common	30,000
Retained earnings	70,000
Total stockholders' equity	$150,000

You should note that the par value per share has been reduced from $10 to $5 per share of stock as a result of the split. Like a stock dividend, the split does not affect total stockholders' equity because no assets have been transferred. Therefore, the split simply results in more shares of stock with claims to the same net assets of the firm.

http://www.microsoft.com

For example, on January 16, 2003, **Microsoft Corporation** (ticker symbol MSFT) announced a two-for-one stock split on its common stock. As a result of the stock split, shareholders were to receive one additional common share for every share held on the record date of January 27, 2003. Because Microsoft stock is very widely held and there are many individual stockholders, Microsoft wanted to effectively communicate to its stockholders what the effect of the stock split would be. Exhibit 11-5 is an excerpt of the answers to frequently asked questions that the company provided on its Web site. After a stock split, each stockholder still has the same *proportional* ownership of the company. When a company has a stock split, it restates the number of shares for all previous years also. Although a stock split does not increase the wealth of the shareholder, it is usually a good sign. Companies with rising stock prices declare a stock split to make the stock more marketable to the small investor, who would be more likely to buy a stock at $50 per share than at $100.

Exhibit 11-5 Microsoft's Answers to Stockholders Regarding Stock Splits

How does a 2-for-1 stock split actually work?
A 2-for-1 split means the investor will have twice as many shares as he had before, at half the market price. Here's an example: As of the record date (January 27, 2003) if an investor owns 100 shares of MSFT and the market price is $50.00/share, that investor's total value is $5,000.00. After the split, the investor will have 200 shares of stock, but the market price will be approximately $25.00/share. The investor's total investment value in MSFT remains the same at $5,000.00 until the stock price moves up or down.

Why did you split the stock now?
The decision to split the stock was made by Microsoft's Board of Directors, based on a desire to make our stock more accessible to a broader range of investors.

STATEMENT OF STOCKHOLDERS' EQUITY

LO 8 Demonstrate an understanding of the statement of stockholders' equity and comprehensive income.

Statement of stockholders' equity Reflects the differences between beginning and ending balances for all accounts in the Stockholders' Equity category of the balance sheet.

http://www.walgreens.com

In addition to a balance sheet, an income statement, and a cash flow statement, many annual reports contain a **statement of stockholders' equity.** The purpose of this statement is to explain all the reasons for the difference between the beginning and the ending balance of each of the accounts in the Stockholders' Equity category of the balance sheet. Of course, if the only changes are the result of income and dividends, a statement of retained earnings is sufficient. When other changes have occurred in stockholders' equity accounts, this more complete statement is necessary.

The statement of stockholders' equity of **Walgreens** is presented in Exhibit 11-6 for the year 2002. The statement starts with the beginning balances of each of the accounts as of August 31, 2001. Walgreens stockholders' equity is presented in four categories (the columns on the statement) as of August 31, 2001, as follows (in millions):

Number of shares	1,019,425,052
Common stock	$79.6
Paid-in capital	$596.7
Retained earnings	$4,530.9

The statement of stockholders' equity indicates the items or events that affected stockholders' equity during the year. The items or events were as follows:

Exhibit 11-6 Walgreens' Statement of Stockholders' Equity, 2001

Walgreens Co. and Subsidiaries
For the Year Ended August 31, 2002
(Dollars in millions, except per share data)

	Shareholders' Equity	Common Stock Shares	Common Stock Amount	Paid-In Capital*	Retained Earnings
	Balance, August 31, 2001	1,019,425,052	79.6	596.7	4,530.9
1	Net earnings	—	—	—	1,019.2
2	Cash dividends declared ($0.145 per share)	—	—	—	(148.4)
3	Employee stock purchase and option plans	5,483,224	0.5	151.7	—
	Balance, August 31, 2002	1,024,908,276	$80.1	$748.4	$5,401.7

*This represents additional paid-in capital and is a good example of how terminology varies from company to company.

ITEM OR EVENT	EFFECT ON STOCKHOLDERS' EQUITY
Net earnings →	Increased retained earnings by $1,019.2 million
Dividends →	Decreased retained earnings by $148.4 million
Shares issued →	Increased common stock by $0.5 million and Increased paid-in capital by $151.7 million

The last line of the statement of stockholders' equity indicates the ending balances of the stockholders' equity accounts as of the balance sheet date, August 31, 2002. You should note that each of the stockholders' equity accounts increased during 2002. The statement of stockholders' equity is useful in explaining the reasons for the changes that occurred.

WHAT IS COMPREHENSIVE INCOME?

There has always been some question about which items or transactions should be shown on the income statement and should be included in the calculation of net income. Generally, the accounting rule-making bodies have held that the income statement should reflect an *all-inclusive* approach. That is, all events and transactions that affect income should be shown on the income statement. This approach prevents the manipulation of the income figure by those who would like to show "good news" on the income statement and "bad news" directly on the retained earnings statement or the statement of stockholders' equity. The result of the all-inclusive approach is that the income statement includes items that are not necessarily under management's control, such as losses from natural disasters, and thus the income statement may not be a true reflection of a company's future potential.

The FASB has accepted certain exceptions to the all-inclusive approach and has allowed items to be recorded directly to the stockholders' equity category. This text has discussed one such item: unrealized gains and losses on investment securities. Exhibit 11-7 presents several additional items that are beyond the scope of this text. Items such as these have been excluded from the income statement for various reasons. Quite often, the justification is a concern for the volatility of the net income number. The items we have cited are often large dollar amounts; if included in the income statement, they would cause income to fluctuate widely from period to period. Therefore, the income statement is deemed to be more useful if the items are excluded.

Ethics in Accounting

BOSTON CHICKEN

In 1995, Arthur Andersen advised its client Boston Chicken not to include the operating results of its franchises, even though the company had loaned the franchisees as much as 80% of their capital. The franchisees paid license and royalty fees to Boston Chicken, and that was included as income. However, Boston Chicken did not include the sales and expenses (operating results) of the franchises. For many of the franchises, the sales were less than expenses, resulting in a loss.

In 1996, the SEC required Boston Chicken to report the total losses of the franchisees and to include the results on its books. When Boston Chicken complied, franchisees' losses exceeded the parent company's net income, and Boston Chicken filed for bankruptcy in 1998.

What is the company doing that is an ethical concern? Why is this important, and to whom?

Source: Bill Richards and Scott Thurm, "Boston Chicken cases mirrors Enron failure," *The Wall Street Journal*, March 13, 2002.

Comprehensive income The total change in net assets from all sources except investments by or distributions to the owners.

A new term has been coined to incorporate the "income-type" items that escape the income statement. **Comprehensive income** is the net assets increase resulting from all transactions during a time period (except for investments by owners and distributions to owners). Exhibit 11-7 presents the statement of comprehensive income and its relationship to the traditional income statement. It illustrates that comprehensive income encompasses all the revenues and expenses that are presented on the income statement to calculate net income and also includes items that are not presented on the income statement but affect total stockholders' equity.[1] The compre-

Exhibit 11-7 The Relationship of the Income Statement and Statement of Comprehensive Income

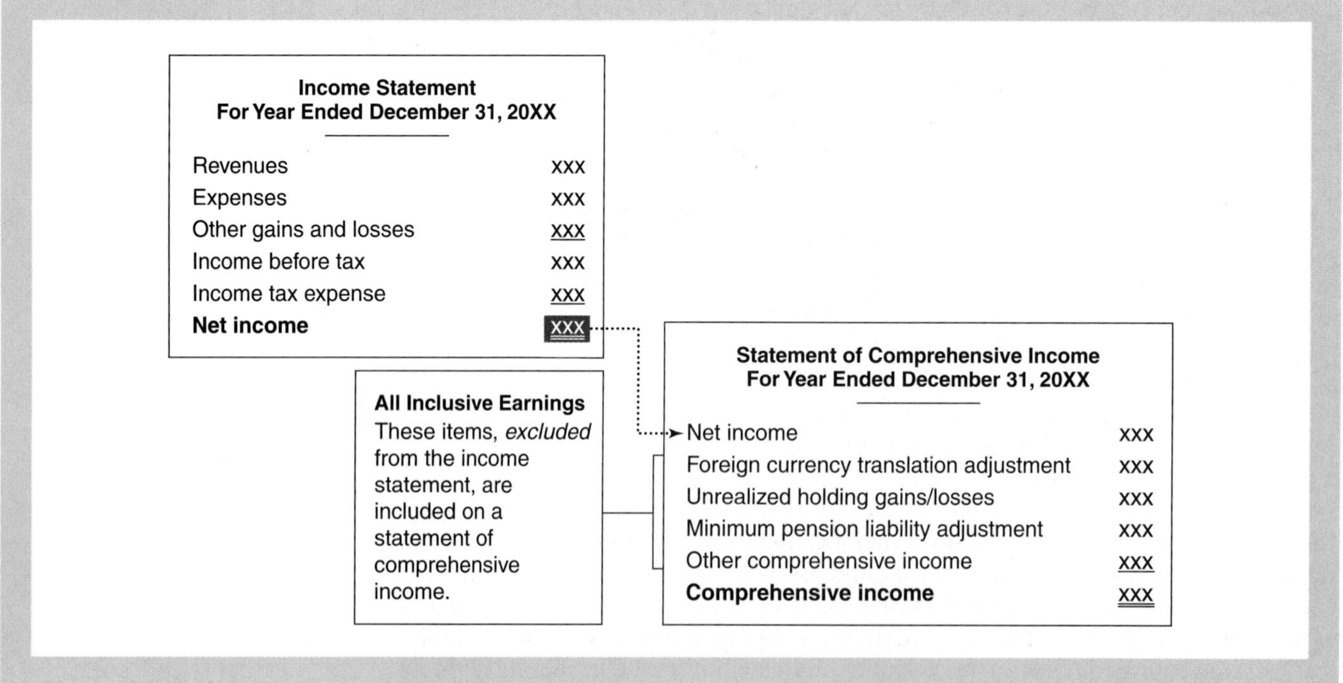

[1]The format of Exhibit 11-7 is suggested by the FASB. The FASB also allows other possible formats of the statement of comprehensive income.

hensive income measure is truly all-inclusive because it includes such transactions as unrealized gains and prior period adjustments that affect stockholders' equity. Firms are required to disclose comprehensive income because it provides a more complete measure of performance.

WHAT ANALYZING OWNERS' EQUITY REVEALS ABOUT A FIRM'S VALUE

ANALYSIS

Book Value per Share

LO 9 Understand how investors use ratios to evaluate owners' equity.

Book value per share Total stockholders' equity divided by the number of shares of common stock outstanding.

Users of financial statements are often interested in computing the value of a corporation's stock. This is a difficult task because *value* is not a well-defined term and means different things to different users. One measure of value is the book value of the stock. **Book value per share** of common stock represents the rights that each share of common stock has to the net assets of the corporation. The term *net assets* refers to the total assets of the firm minus total liabilities. In other words, net assets equal the total stockholders' equity of the corporation. Therefore, when only common stock is present, book value per share is measured as follows:

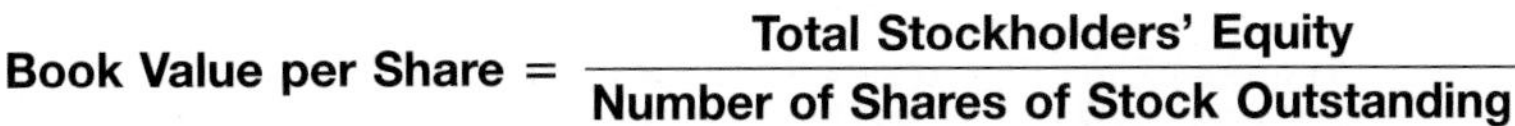

$$\text{Book Value per Share} = \frac{\text{Total Stockholders' Equity}}{\text{Number of Shares of Stock Outstanding}}$$

Refer again to the statement of stockholders' equity of Walgreens that appears in Exhibit 11-6. As of August 31, 2002, the total stockholders' equity is \$6,230.2 million (\$80.1 + \$748.4 + \$5,401.7), and the number of outstanding shares of common stock is 1,024.9 million. Therefore, the book value per share for Walgreens is \$6.08, calculated as follows:

$$\$6{,}230.2/1{,}024.9 = \$6.08$$

This means that the company's common stockholders have the right to \$6.08 per share of net assets in the corporation.

The book value per share indicates the recorded minimum value per share of the stock. In a sense, it indicates the rights of the common stockholders in the event that the company is liquidated. It does not indicate the market value of the common stock. That is, book value per share does not indicate the price that should be paid by those who want to buy or sell the stock on the stock exchange. Book value is also an incomplete measure of value because the corporation's net assets are normally measured on the balance sheet at the original historical cost, not at the current value of the assets. Thus, book value per share does not provide a very accurate measure of the price that a stockholder would be willing to pay for a share of stock. The book value of a stock is often thought to be the "floor" of a stock price. An investor's decision to pay less than book value for a share of stock suggests that he or she thinks that the company is going to continue to lose money, thus shrinking book value.

Calculating Book Value When Preferred Stock Is Present

The focus of the computation of book value per share is always on the value per share of the *common* stock. Therefore, the computation must be adjusted for corporations that have both preferred and common stock. The numerator of the fraction, total stockholders' equity, should be reduced by the rights that preferred stockholders have to the corporation's net assets. Normally, this can be accomplished by deducting the redemption value or liquidation value of the preferred stock along with any dividends in arrears on cumulative preferred stock. The denominator should not include the number of shares of preferred stock.

To illustrate the computation of book value per share when both common and preferred stock are present, we will refer to the stockholders' equity category of **Delta Air Lines,** presented again in Exhibit 11-8. When calculating book value per share, we want to consider only the *common* stockholders' equity. Exhibit 11-8 indicates **1** that Delta's total stockholders' equity in 2002 was $893 million but also **2** that preferred stockholders had a right to $437 million in the event of liquidation. Therefore, $437 million must be deducted to calculate the rights of the common stockholders:

$893 − $437 = $455 million common stockholders' equity

The number of shares of common stock *outstanding* can be calculated from Exhibit 11-8 as follows:

180,903,373	shares issued
− 57,544,168	treasury shares
123,359,205	shares outstanding

Therefore, the computation of book value per share is as follows:

$455,000,000/123,359,205 = $3.69 Book Value per Share

This indicates that if the company was liquidated and the assets sold at their recorded values, the common stockholders would receive $3.69 per share. Of course, if the company went bankrupt and had to liquidate assets at distressed values, stockholders would receive something less than book value.

Two-Minute Review

1. *What effect does a stock dividend have on a firm's stockholders' equity?*
2. *What effect does a stock split have on a firm's stockholders' equity?*
3. *How is book value per share calculated?*

Answers on page 562.

Exhibit 11-8 Delta Air Lines Stockholders' Equity Section

	SHAREOWNERS' EQUITY	2002	2001
	(In Millions, Except Share Data)		
	Employee Stock Ownership Plan Preferred Stock:		
2	Series B ESOP Convertible Preferred Stock, $1.00 par value, $72.00 stated and liquidation value; 6,065,489 shares issued and outstanding at December 31, 2002, and 6,278,210 shares issued and outstanding at December 31, 2001	437	452
	Unearned compensation under Employee Stock Ownership Plan	(173)	(197)
	Total Employee Stock Ownership Plan Preferred Stock	264	255
	Shareowners' Equity:		
	Common stock, $1.50 par value; 450,000,000 shares authorized; 180,903,373 shares issued at December 31, 2002, and 180,890,356 shares issued at December 31, 2001	271	271
	Additional paid-in capital	3,263	3,267
	Retained earnings	1,639	2,930
	Accumulated other comprehensive income (loss)	(1,562)	25
	Treasury stock at cost, 57,544,168 shares at December 31, 2002, and 57,644,690 shares at December 31, 2001	(2,718)	(2,724)
1	Total shareowners' equity	893	3,769
	Total liabilities and shareowners' equity	$24,720	$23,605

Deduct preferred stock before calculating book value per share.

Market Value per Share

The market value of the stock is a more meaningful measure of the value of the stock to those financial statement users interested in buying or selling shares of stock. The **market value per share** is the price at which stock is currently selling. When stock is sold on a stock exchange, the price can be determined by its most recent selling price. For example, the listing for General Motors stock on the Internet may indicate the following[2]:

52-Week			Daily			
HIGH	LOW	SYM	HIGH	LOW	LAST	CHANGE
68.17	39.17	GM	43.3	42.01	42.93	+0.48 (1.13%)

The two left-hand columns indicate the stock price for the last 52-week period. General Motors sold as high as $68.17 and as low as $39.17 during that time period. The right-hand portion indicates the high and low for the previous day's trading and the closing price. General Motors sold as high as $43.30 per share and as low as $42.01 per share and closed at $42.93. For the day, the stock increased by 1.13% or $0.48 per share.

The market value of the stock depends on many factors. Stockholders must evaluate a corporation's earnings and liquidity as indicated in the financial statements. They must also consider a variety of economic factors and project all of the factors into the future to determine the proper market value per share of the stock. Many investors use sophisticated investment techniques, including large databases, to identify factors that affect a company's stock price.

Interpret: You Decide. Take a close look at the stockholders' equity section of the balance sheet of Southwest Airlines provided in the chapter opener for this chapter. What is the number of shares authorized and number of shares issued at the balance sheet date? What does this indicate about the company's use of treasury stock? Also, use the Internet or *The Wall Street Journal* to find the company's stock price. What have been the high and low prices over the last year? What does this indicate about the company's stock as a potential investment?

HOW CHANGES IN STOCKHOLDERS' EQUITY AFFECT THE STATEMENT OF CASH FLOWS

CASH FLOW

LO 10 Explain the effects that transactions involving stockholders' equity have on the statement of cash flows.

It is important to determine the effect that the issuance of stock, the repurchase of stock, and the payment of dividends have on the statement of cash flows. Each of these business activities' impact on cash must be reflected on the statement. Exhibit 11-9 indicates how these stockholders' equity transactions affect cash flow and where the items should be placed on the statement of cash flows.

The issuance of stock is a method to finance business. Therefore, the cash *inflow* from the sale of stock to stockholders should be reflected as an inflow in the Financing Activities section of the statement of cash flows. Generally, companies do not disclose separately the amount received for the par value of the stock and the amount received in excess of par. Rather, one amount is listed to indicate the total inflow of cash.

The repurchase or retirement of stock also represents a financing activity. Therefore, the cash *outflow* should be reflected as a reduction of cash in the Financing Activities section of the statement of cash flows. Again, companies do not distinguish between the amount paid for the par of the stock and the amount paid in excess of par. One amount is generally listed to indicate the total cash outflow to retire stock.

[2]On-line at http://www.gm.com, Investor Relations—Stock Performance, September 20, 2002.

Exhibit 11-9

The Effect of Stockholders' Equity Items on the Statement of Cash Flows

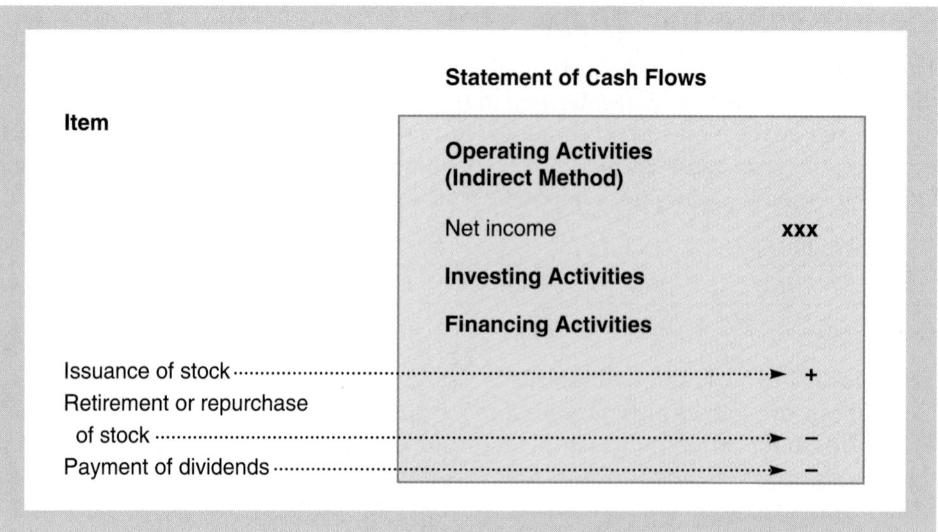

Study Tip

Transactions affecting the Stockholders' Equity category of the balance sheet will appear in the Financing Activities category of the cash flow statement. Dividends are included in the cash flow statement when actually paid rather than when they are declared.

Dividends paid to stockholders represent a cost of financing the business with stock. Therefore, dividends paid should be reflected as a cash *outflow* in the Financing Activities section of the statement of cash flows. It is important to distinguish between the declaration of dividends and the payment of dividends. The cash outflow occurs at the time the dividend is paid and should be reflected on the statement of cash flows in that period.

A partial 2002 statement of cash flows for Southwest Airlines is given in Exhibit 11-10. Note in particular two lines in the Financing Activities category of the cash flow statement. First, the cash dividends line indicates cash payments of $13,872,000 for the payment of dividends. Also, Southwest did not repurchase stock during the year, but that line indicates that cash payments of $108,674,000 were made to repurchase the stock during 2000.

Exhibit 11-10 Southwest Airlines 2002 Financing Activities Section of the Statement of Cash Flows

(In thousands)	Years Ended December 31, 2002	2001	2000
Cash Flows from Financing Activities:			
Issuance of long-term debt	385,000	$614,250	—
Proceeds from revolving credit facility	—	475,000	—
Proceeds from trust arrangement	119,142	266,053	—
Proceeds from Employee stock plans	56,757	43,541	70,424
Payments of long-term debt and capital lease obligations	(64,568)	(110,600)	(10,238)
Payments of trust arrangement	(385,195)	—	—
Payment of revolving credit facility	(475,000)	—	—
Payments of cash dividends	(13,872)	(13,440)	(10,978)
Repurchases of common stock	—	—	(108,674)
Other, net	(3,922)	(4,703)	—
Net cash provided by (used in) financing activities	(381,658)	1,270,101	(59,466)

Ratios for Decision Making

Reporting and analyzing financial statement information related to a company's stockholders' equity:

The book value per share represents the *right* each share of common stock has to the net assets of the company. This is an estimate since, should the company be sold, the amount received by shareholders for each share of stock owned may be more or less than the book value per share.

Balance Sheet	Income Statement	Statement of Cash Flows	Notes
Preferred Stock**			
Common Stock (number of shares authorized, issued, and outstanding)*			
Total Stockholders' Equity			

$$\textbf{Book Value per Share} = \frac{\textbf{Total Stockholders' Equity**}}{\textbf{Number of Shares of Stock Outstanding*}}$$

*If the number of shares of common stock outstanding is not stated on the common stock line, it can be determined by subtracting the total number of treasury stock shares from the total number of common stock shares issued.

**When there is preferred stock outstanding, the redemption value or liquidation value (disclosed on the preferred stock line or in the notes) of the preferred stock must be subtracted from total stockholders' equity.

Impact on the Financial Reports

Impact on the Financial Reports

BALANCE SHEET	INCOME STATEMENT
Current Assets	*Revenues*
Cash	*Expenses*
Noncurrent Assets	*Other*
Current Liabilities	
Cash dividend payable	
Noncurrent Liabilities	
Stockholders' Equity	
Contributed Capital[1]	
Preferred stock[2]	
Additional paid-in capital—preferred	
Common stock	
Additional paid-in capital—common (or Paid-in capital in excess of par)	
Paid-in capital from stock retirement	
Common stock dividend distributable	
Total Contributed Capital	
Retained earnings	
Treasury stock[3]	
Total Stockholders' Equity	

[1]The number of shares in each of the following categories is disclosed for each class of stock: (a) authorized, (b) issued, and (c) outstanding.

[2]The most common features for preferred stock are (a) cumulative, (b) participating, (c) convertible, and (d) callable.

[3]This reduces stockholders' equity.

STATEMENT OF STOCKHOLDERS' EQUITY	STATEMENT OF CASH FLOWS	NOTES
Contributed Capital Number of shares issued Number of shares repurchased Paid-in capital (par and excess) from shares issued Amount paid for repurchase of stock (for treasury or retirement) *Retained Earnings* Current period net income (net loss) Cash dividends declared	*Operating Activities* *Investing Activities* *Financing Activities* Cash received from issuance of stock Cash paid for treasury shares Cash received from sale of treasury shares Cash paid to retire stock Cash paid for dividends *Noncash Transactions*	

Answers to the Two-Minute Reviews

Two-Minute Review on Page 549

1. *Treasury Stock is a contra-equity account, and the balance should appear as a reduction in the Stockholders' Equity category of the balance sheet.*
2. *When treasury stock is purchased, it reduces total stockholders' equity.*
3. *Treasury stock is still stock that has been issued and so does not affect the number of shares issued. But it is stock that is held by the company, rather than the stockholders, and the purchase of treasury stock reduces the number of shares of stock outstanding.*

Two-Minute Review on Page 558

1. *A stock dividend does not change a firm's total stockholders' equity but does affect the balances of accounts within that category of the balance sheet. Generally, a stock dividend will reduce the retained earnings account and will increase the capital stock account.*
2. *A stock split does not affect total stockholders' equity or the accounts within stockholders' equity. No accounting entry is made for a stock split.*
3. *Book value per share is determined by dividing total stockholders' equity (less an amount representing the rights of preferred shareholders) by the number of shares of common stock outstanding.*

Warmup Exercises

Warmup Exercise 11-1 ***Retained Earnings*** **LO 1**

A company has a retained earnings account with a January 1 balance of $500,000. The accountant has reviewed the following information for the current year:

Increase in cash balance	$50,000
Net income	80,000
Dividends declared	30,000
Dividends paid	20,000
Decrease in accounts receivable balance	10,000

Required

Calculate the ending balance of the Retained Earnings account.

Key to the Solution

Cash and accounts receivable do not affect retained earnings. Also note that dividends are deducted from retained earnings at the time they are declared rather than when they are paid.

Warmup Exercise 11-2 ***Stock Issued and Outstanding*** **LO 2**

A company begins business on January 1 and issues 100,000 shares of common stock. On July 1, the company declares and issues a 2-for-1 stock split. On October 15, the company purchases 20,000 shares of stock as treasury stock and reissues 5,000 shares by the end of the month.

Required

Calculate the number of shares issued and the number of shares outstanding as of the end of the first year of operations.

Warmup Exercise 11-3 ***Analysis of Stockholders' Equity*** **LO 9**

A. Company A has total stockholders' equity at year-end of $500,000 and has 10,000 shares of stock.

B. Company B has total stockholders' equity at year-end of $500,000 and has 10,000 shares of stock. The company also has 50,000 shares of preferred stock, which has a $1 par value and a liquidation value of $3 per share.

Required

Calculate the book value per share for Company A and Company B.

Key to the Solution

Book value per share is calculated for the common stockholder. If preferred stock is present, an amount must be deducted that represents the amount the preferred stockholder would receive at liquidation.

Solution to Warmup Exercises

Warmup Exercise 11-1

The ending balance of the Retained Earnings account should be calculated as follows:

Beginning balance	$500,000
Plus: Net income	80,000
Less: Dividends declared	(30,000)
Ending balance	$550,000

Warmup Exercise 11-2

The number of shares of stock issued is 200,000, or 100,000 times 2 because of the stock split. The number of shares outstanding is 185,000, calculated as follows:

Number of shares after split	100,000 × 2 =	200,000
Less purchase of treasury stock		(20,000)
Plus stock reissued		5,000
Total outstanding		185,000 shares

Warmup Exercise 11-3

A. Book value per share is $50, or $500,000/10,000.

B. Book value per share is $35, or ($500,000 − $150,000)/10,000.

Review Problem

Andrew Company was incorporated on January 1, 2004, under a corporate charter that authorized the issuance of 50,000 shares of $5 par common stock and 20,000 shares of $100 par, 8% preferred stock. The following events occurred during 2004. Andrew wants to record the events and develop financial statements on December 31, 2004.

WebTUTOR™ Advantage

a. Issued for cash 10,000 shares of common stock at $25 per share and 1,000 shares of preferred stock at $110 per share on January 15, 2004.

b. Acquired a patent on April 1 in exchange for 2,000 shares of common stock. At the time of the exchange, the common stock was selling on the local stock exchange for $30 per share.

c. Repurchased 500 shares of common stock on May 1 at $20 per share. The corporation is holding the stock to be used for an employee bonus plan.

d. Declared a cash dividend of $1 per share to common stockholders and an 8% dividend to preferred stockholders on July 1. The preferred stock is noncumulative, nonparticipating. The dividend will be distributed on August 1.

e. Distributed the cash dividend on August 1.

f. Declared and distributed to preferred stockholders a 10% stock dividend on September 1. At the time of the dividend declaration, preferred stock was valued at $130 per share.

g. On December 31, calculated the annual net income for the year to be $200,000.

Required

1. Indicate the effect on the accounting equation for items **a** through **f.**
2. Develop the Stockholders' Equity section of Andrew Company's balance sheet at December 31, 2004. You do not need to consider the notes that accompany the balance sheet.
3. Determine the book value per share of the common stock. Assume that the preferred stock can be redeemed at par.

Solution to Review Problem

1. The effects of items **a** through **f** on the accounting equation are as follows:

a.

BALANCE SHEET							INCOME STATEMENT
ASSETS		=	LIABILITIES	+	OWNERS' EQUITY		+ REVENUES – EXPENSES
Cash	360,000				Common Stock	50,000	
					Additional Paid-in Capital—Common	200,000	
					Preferred Stock	100,000	
					Additional Paid-in Capital—Preferred	10,000	

b. The patent received for stock should be recorded at the value of the stock:

BALANCE SHEET							INCOME STATEMENT
ASSETS		=	LIABILITIES	+	OWNERS' EQUITY		+ REVENUES – EXPENSES
Patent	60,000				Common Stock	10,000	
					Additional Paid-in Capital—Common	50,000	

c. Stock reacquired constitutes treasury stock and should be recorded as follows:

BALANCE SHEET							INCOME STATEMENT
ASSETS		=	LIABILITIES	+	OWNERS' EQUITY		+ REVENUES – EXPENSES
Cash	(10,000)				Treasury Stock	(10,000)	

d. A cash dividend should be declared on the number of shares of stock outstanding as of July 1. The effect is as follows:

BALANCE SHEET							INCOME STATEMENT
ASSETS	=	LIABILITIES		+	OWNERS' EQUITY		+ REVENUES − EXPENSES
		Dividends Payable—Common	11,500		Retained Earnings	(19,500)	
		Dividends Payable—Preferred	8,000				

The number of common shares outstanding should be calculated as the number of shares issued (12,000) less the number of shares of treasury stock (500). The preferred stock dividend should be calculated as 1,000 shares times $100 par times 8%.

e.

BALANCE SHEET							INCOME STATEMENT
ASSETS		= LIABILITIES		+	OWNERS' EQUITY		+ REVENUES − EXPENSES
Cash	(19,500)	Dividends Payable—Common	(11,500)				
		Dividends Payable—Preferred	(8,000)				

f. A stock dividend should be based on the number of shares of stock outstanding and should be declared and recorded at the market value of the stock. The impact is as follows:

BALANCE SHEET					INCOME STATEMENT
ASSETS	= LIABILITIES	+	OWNERS' EQUITY		+ REVENUES − EXPENSES
			Retained Earnings	(13,000)	
			Preferred Stock	10,000	
			Additional Paid-in Capital—Preferred	3,000	

The amount of the reduction of retained earnings should be calculated as the number of shares outstanding (1,000) times 10% times $130 per share.

2. The Stockholders' Equity for Andrew Company after completing these transactions appears as follows:

Preferred stock, $100 par, 8%, 20,000 shares authorized, 1,100 issued	$110,000
Common stock, $5 par, 50,000 shares authorized, 12,000 issued	60,000
Additional paid-in capital—Preferred	13,000
Additional paid-in capital—Common	250,000
Retained earnings	167,500*
Total contributed capital and retained earnings	$600,500
Less: Treasury stock, 500 shares, common	(10,000)
Total stockholders' equity	$590,500

*$200,000 − $19,500 − $13,000 = $167,500

3. The book value per share of the common stock is calculated as follows:

($590,500 − $110,000)/11,500 shares = $41.78

Appendix: Accounting Tools: Unincorporated Businesses

LO 11 Describe the important differences between the sole proprietorship and partnership forms of organization versus the corporate form.

The focus of Chapter 11 has been on the corporate form of organization. Most of the large, influential companies in the United States are organized as corporations. They have a legal and economic existence that is separate from that of the owners of the business, the stockholders. Yet many other companies in the economy are organized as sole proprietorships or partnerships. The purpose of this appendix is to show briefly how the characteristics of such organizations affect the accounting, particularly the accounting for the Owners' Equity category of the balance sheet.

Sole Proprietorships

Sole proprietorship A business with a single owner.

A **sole proprietorship** is a business owned by one person. Most sole proprietorships are small in size, with the owner serving as the operator or manager of the company. The primary advantage of the sole proprietorship form of organization is its simplicity. The Owner's Equity category of the balance sheet consists of one account, the owner's capital account. The owner answers to no one but himself or herself. A disadvantage of the sole proprietorship is that all the responsibility for the success or failure of the venture attaches to the owner, who often has limited resources.

There are three important points to remember about this form of organization. First, a sole proprietorship is not a separate entity for legal purposes. This means that the law does not distinguish between the assets of the business and those of its owner. If an owner loses a lawsuit, for example, the law does not limit an owner's liability to the amount of assets of the business but extends liability to the owner's personal assets. Thus, the owner is said to have *unlimited liability.*

Second, accountants adhere to the *entity principle* and maintain a distinction between the owner's personal assets and the assets of the sole proprietorship. The balance sheet of a sole proprietorship should reflect only the "business" assets and liabilities, with the difference reflected as owner's capital.

Third, a sole proprietorship is not treated as a separate entity for federal income tax purposes. That is, the sole proprietorship does not pay tax on its income. Rather, the business income must be declared as income on the owner's personal tax return, and income tax is assessed at the personal tax rate rather than the rate that applies to companies organized as corporations. This may or may not be advantageous, depending on the amount of income involved and the owner's tax situation.

Typical Transactions When the owners of a corporation, the stockholders, invest in the corporation, they normally do so by purchasing stock. When investing in a sole proprietorship, the owner simply contributes cash, or other assets, into the business. For example, assume that on January 1, 2004, Peter Tom began a new business by investing $10,000 cash. The effect on the accounting equation of Peter Tom Company is as follows:

BALANCE SHEET							INCOME STATEMENT
ASSETS		=	LIABILITIES	+	OWNERS' EQUITY		+ REVENUES − EXPENSES
Cash	10,000				Peter Tom, Capital	10,000	

The Peter Tom, Capital account is an owner's equity account and reflects the rights of the owner to the business assets.

An owner's withdrawal of assets from the business is recorded as a reduction of owner's equity. Assume that on July 1, 2004, Peter Tom took an auto valued at $6,000 from the business to use as his personal auto. The effect on the accounting equation is as follows:

BALANCE SHEET						INCOME STATEMENT
ASSETS	=	LIABILITIES	+	OWNERS' EQUITY	+	REVENUES – EXPENSES
Equipment (6,000)				Peter Tom, Drawing (6,000)		

The Peter Tom, Drawing account is a contra-equity account. Sometimes a drawing account is referred to as a *withdrawals account,* as in Peter Tom, Withdrawals. An increase in the account reduces the owner's equity. At the end of the fiscal year, the drawing account should be closed to the capital account and the effect is as follows:

BALANCE SHEET						INCOME STATEMENT
ASSETS	=	LIABILITIES	+	OWNERS' EQUITY	+	REVENUES – EXPENSES
				Peter Tom, Capital (6,000)		
				Peter Tom, Drawing 6,000		

The amount of the net income of the business should also be reflected in the capital account. Assume that all revenue and expense accounts of Peter Tom Company have been closed to the Income Summary account, resulting in a credit balance of $4,000, the net income for the year. The Income Summary account is then closed to capital and the capital account is increased.

The Owner's Equity section of the balance sheet for Peter Tom Company consists of one account, the capital account, calculated as follows:

Beginning balance, Jan. 1, 2004	$ 0
Plus: Investments	10,000
Net income	4,000
Less: Withdrawals	(6,000)
Ending balance, Dec. 31, 2004	$ 8,000

Partnerships

A **partnership** is a company owned by two or more persons. Like sole proprietorships, most partnerships are fairly small businesses formed when individuals combine their capital and managerial talents for a common business purpose. Other partnerships are large, national organizations. For example, the major public accounting firms are very large, national companies but are organized in most states as partnerships.

Partnership A business owned by two or more individuals and with the characteristic of unlimited liability.

Partnerships have characteristics similar to those of sole proprietorships. The following are the most important characteristics of partnerships:

1. *Unlimited liability.* Legally, the assets of the business are not separate from the partners' personal assets. Each partner is personally liable for the debts of the partnership. Creditors have a legal claim first to the assets of the partnership and then to the assets of the individual partners.
2. *Limited life.* Corporations have a separate legal existence and an unlimited life; partnerships do not. The life of a partnership is limited; it exists as long as the contract between the partners is valid. The partnership ends when a partner withdraws or a new partner is added. A new partnership must be created for the business to continue.
3. *Not taxed as a separate entity.* Partnerships are subject to the same tax features as sole proprietorships. The partnership itself does not pay federal income tax. Rather, the income of the partnership is treated as personal income on each of the partners' individual tax returns and is taxed as personal income. All partnership income is subject to federal income tax on the individual partners' returns even if it is not distributed to the partners. A variety of other factors affects the tax consequences of partnerships versus the corporate form of organization. These aspects are quite complex and beyond the scope of this text.

Partnership agreement Specifies how much the owners will invest, their salaries, and how profits will be shared.

A partnership is based on a **partnership agreement.** It is very important that the partners agree, in writing, about all aspects of the partnership. The agreement should detail items such as how much capital each partner is to invest, the time each is expected to devote to the business, the salary of each, and how income of the partnership is to be divided. If a partnership agreement is not present, the courts may be forced to settle disputes among partners. Therefore, the partners should develop a partnership agreement when the firm is first established and should review the agreement periodically to determine whether changes are necessary.

Investments and Withdrawals In a partnership, it is important to account separately for the capital of each of the partners. A capital account should be established in the Owners' Equity section of the balance sheet for each partner of the company. Investments into the company should be credited to the partner making the investment. For example, assume that on January 1, 2004, Page Thoms and Amy Rebec begin a partnership named AP Company. Page contributes $10,000 cash, and Amy contributes equipment valued at $5,000. The effect on the accounting equation is as follows:

BALANCE SHEET									INCOME STATEMENT
ASSETS		=	LIABILITIES	+	OWNERS' EQUITY			+	REVENUES – EXPENSES
Cash	10,000				Page Thoms, Capital	10,000			
Equipment	5,000				Amy Rebec, Capital	5,000			

A drawing account also should be established for each owner of the company to account for withdrawals of assets. Assume that on April 1, 2004, each owner withdraws $2,000 of cash from AP Company. The effect is as follows:

BALANCE SHEET									INCOME STATEMENT
ASSETS		=	LIABILITIES	+	OWNERS' EQUITY			+	REVENUES – EXPENSES
Cash	(4,000)				Page Thoms, Drawing	(2,000)			
					Amy Rebec, Drawing	(2,000)			

Distribution of Income The partnership agreement governs the manner in which income should be allocated to partners. The distribution may recognize the partners' relative investment in the business, their time and effort, their expertise and talents, or other factors. We will illustrate three methods of income allocation, but you should be aware that partnerships use many other allocation methods. Although these allocation methods are straightforward, partnerships dissolve often because one or more of the partners believes that the allocation is unfair. It is very difficult to devise a method that will make all partners happy.

One way to allocate income is to divide it evenly between or among the partners. In fact, when a partnership agreement is not present, the courts specify that an equal allocation must be applied, regardless of the relative contributions or efforts of the partners. For example, assume that AP Company has $30,000 of net income for the period and has established an agreement that income should be allocated evenly between the two partners, Page and Amy. Each capital account would be increased by $15,000. An equal distribution of income to all partners is easy to apply but is not fair to those partners who have contributed more in money or time to the partnership.

Another way to allocate income is to specify in the partnership agreement that income be allocated according to a *stated ratio.* For example, Page and Amy may specify that all income of AP Company should be allocated on a 2-to-1 ratio, with Page receiving the larger portion. If that allocation method is applied to the preceding example, Page Thoms, Capital would be increased by $20,000 and Amy Rebec, Capital would be increased by $10,000:

Finally, we illustrate an allocation method that more accurately reflects the partners' input. It is based on salaries, interest on invested capital, and a stated ratio. Assume that the partnership agreement of AP Company specifies that Page and Amy be allowed a salary of $6,000 and $4,000 respectively, that each partner receive 10% on her capital balance, and that any remaining income be allocated equally. Assume that AP Company has been in operation for several years and the capital balances of the owners at the end of 2004, before the income distribution, are as follows:

Page Thoms, Capital	$40,000
Amy Rebec, Capital	50,000

If AP Company calculated that its 2004 net income (before partner salaries) was $30,000, income would be allocated between the partners as follows:

	PAGE	AMY
Distributed for salaries:	$ 6,000	$ 4,000
Distributed for interest:		
Page: ($40,000 × 10%)	4,000	
Amy: ($50,000 × 10%)		5,000
Remainder = $30,000 − $10,000 − $9,000 = $11,000		
Remainder distributed equally:		
Page: ($11,000/2)	5,500	
Amy: ($11,000/2)		5,500
Total distributed	$15,500	$14,500

Page Thoms, Capital would be increased by $15,500 and Amy Rebec, Capital by $14,500.

This does not indicate the amount actually paid to (or withdrawn by) the partners. However, for tax purposes, the income of the partnership is treated as personal income on the partners' individual tax returns regardless of whether the income is actually paid in cash to the partners. This aspect often encourages partners to withdraw income from the business and makes it difficult to retain sufficient capital for the business to operate profitably.

Chapter Highlights

1. **LO 1** The Stockholders' Equity category is composed of two parts. Contributed capital is the amount derived from stockholders and other external parties. Retained earnings is the amount of net income not paid as dividends.
2. **LO 1** The Stockholders' Equity category reveals the number of shares authorized, issued, and outstanding. Treasury stock is stock that the firm has issued and repurchased but not retired.
3. **LO 2** *Preferred stock* refers to a stock that has preference to dividends declared. If a dividend is declared, the preferred stockholders must receive a dividend before the common stockholders.
4. **LO 3** When stock is issued for cash, the par value of the stock should be reported in the stock account and the amount in excess of par should be reported in an additional paid-in capital account.
5. **LO 3** When stock is issued for a noncash asset, the transaction should reflect the value of the stock given or the value of the property received, whichever is more evident.
6. **LO 4** Treasury stock is accounted for as a reduction of stockholders' equity. When treasury stock is reissued and the cost is less than reissue price, the difference is added to additional paid-in capital. When cost exceeds reissue price, additional paid-in capital or retained earnings is reduced for the difference.
7. **LO 5** The amount of cash dividends to be paid to common and preferred stockholders depends on the terms of the preferred stock. If the stock is cumulative, preferred stockholders have the right to dividends in arrears before current-year dividends are paid. Participating preferred stock indicates that preferred stockholders can share in the dividend amount that exceeds a specified amount.
8. **LO 6** Stock dividends involve the issuance of additional shares of stock. The dividend should normally reflect the fair market value of the additional shares.
9. **LO 7** Stock splits are similar to stock dividends except that splits reduce the par value per share of the stock. No accounting transaction is necessary for splits.
10. **LO 8** The statement of stockholders' equity reflects the changes in the balances of all stockholder equity accounts.
11. **LO 9** Book value per share is calculated as net assets divided by the number of shares of common stock outstanding. It indicates the rights that stockholders have, based on recorded values, to the net assets in the event of liquidation and is therefore not a measure of the market value of the stock.
12. **LO 9** When a corporation has both common and preferred stock, the net assets attributed to the rights of the preferred stockholders must be deducted from the amount of net assets to determine the book value per share of the common stock.

13. **LO 10** Transactions involving stockholders' equity accounts should be reflected in the Financing Activities category of the statement of cash flows.

14. **LO 11** A sole proprietorship is a business owned by one person. It is not a separate entity for legal purposes and does not pay taxes on its income. However, a balance sheet should present the assets and liabilities of the business separate from those of the owner. (Appendix)

15. **LO 11** A partnership is a company owned by two or more persons. Like sole proprietorships, partnerships are not a separate legal or tax entity. The balance sheet of the partnership should present the assets and liabilities of the business separate from those of the owners. (Appendix)

http://

Technology and other resources for your success

http://porter.swlearning.com

If you need additional help, visit the text's Web site. Also, see this text's preface for a description of available technology and other resources. If your instructor is using PERSONAL*Trainer* in this course, you may complete, on line, the exercises and problems in the text.

Key Terms Quiz

Read each definition below and then write the number of the definition in the blank beside the appropriate term it defines. The quiz solutions appear at the end of the chapter.

_____ Authorized shares
_____ Issued shares
_____ Outstanding shares
_____ Par value
_____ Additional paid-in capital
_____ Retained earnings
_____ Cumulative feature
_____ Participating feature
_____ Convertible feature
_____ Callable feature
_____ Treasury stock
_____ Retirement of stock
_____ Dividend payout ratio
_____ Stock dividend
_____ Stock split
_____ Statement of stockholders' equity
_____ Comprehensive income
_____ Book value per share
_____ Market value per share
_____ Sole proprietorship (Appendix)
_____ Partnership (Appendix)
_____ Partnership agreement (Appendix)

1. The number of shares sold or distributed to stockholders.
2. An arbitrary amount that is stated on the face of the stock certificate and that represents the legal capital of the firm.
3. Net income that has been made by the corporation but not paid out as dividends.
4. The right to dividends in arrears before the current-year dividend is distributed.
5. Allows preferred stock to be returned to the corporation in exchange for common stock.
6. Stock issued by the firm and then repurchased but not retired.
7. The annual dividend amount divided by the annual net income.
8. A statement that reflects the differences between beginning and ending balances for all accounts in the Stockholders' Equity category.
9. Creation of additional shares of stock and reduction of the par value of the stock.
10. Total stockholders' equity divided by the number of shares of common stock outstanding.
11. The total change in net assets from all sources except investments by or distributions to the owners.
12. The selling price of the stock as indicated by the most recent stock transactions on, for example, the stock exchange.
13. The maximum number of shares a corporation may issue as indicated in the corporate charter.
14. The number of shares issued less the number of shares held as treasury stock.
15. The amount received for the issuance of stock in excess of the par value of the stock.
16. A provision allowing the preferred stockholders to share, on a percentage basis, in the distribution of an abnormally large dividend.
17. Allows the issuing firm to eliminate a class of stock by paying the stockholders a fixed amount.
18. When the stock of a corporation is repurchased with no intention to reissue at a later date.
19. A corporation's declaration and issuance of additional shares of its own stock to existing stockholders.

20. A business owned by two or more individuals and with the characteristic of unlimited liability.
21. A document that specifies how much each owner should invest, the salary of each owner, and how profits are to be shared.
22. A business with a single owner.

Answers on p. 588.

Alternate Terms

Additional paid-in capital Paid-in capital in excess of par value

Additional paid-in capital—treasury stock Paid-in capital from treasury stock transactions

Callable Redeemable

Capital account Owners' equity account

Contributed capital Paid-in capital

Retained earnings Retained income

Small stock dividend Stock dividend less than 20%

Stockholders' equity Owners' equity

Questions

1. What are the two major components of stockholders' equity? Which accounts generally appear in each component?
2. Corporations disclose the number of shares authorized, issued, and outstanding. What is the meaning of these terms? What causes a difference between the number of shares issued and the number outstanding?
3. Why do firms designate an amount as the par value of stock? Does par value indicate the selling price or market value of the stock?
4. If a firm has a net income for the year, will the balance in the Retained Earnings account equal the net income? What is the meaning of the balance of the account?
5. What is the meaning of the statement that preferred stock has a preference to dividends declared by the corporation? Do preferred stockholders have the right to dividends in arrears on preferred stock?
6. Why might some stockholders be inclined to buy preferred stock rather than common stock? What are the advantages of investing in preferred stock?
7. Why are common shareholders sometimes called *residual owners* when a company has both common and preferred stock outstanding?
8. When stock is issued in exchange for an asset, at what amount should the asset be reported? How could the fair market value be determined?
9. What is treasury stock? Why do firms use it? Where does it appear on a corporation's financial statements?
10. When treasury stock is bought and sold, the transactions do not result in gains or losses reported on the income statement. What account or accounts are used instead? Why are no income statement amounts recorded?
11. Many firms operate at a dividend payout ratio of less than 50%. Why do firms not pay a larger percentage of income as dividends?
12. What is a *stock dividend?* How should it be recorded?
13. Would you rather receive a cash dividend or a stock dividend from a company? Explain.
14. What is the difference between stock dividends and stock splits? How should stock splits be recorded?
15. How is the book value per share calculated? Does the amount calculated as book value per share mean that stockholders will receive a dividend equal to the book value?
16. Can the market value per share of stock be determined by the information on the income statement?
17. What is the difference between a statement of stockholders' equity and a retained earnings statement?
18. What is an advantage of organizing a company as a corporation rather than a partnership? Why don't all companies incorporate? (Appendix)
19. What are some ways that partnerships could share income among the partners? (Appendix)

Exercises

Exercise 11-1 *Stockholders' Equity Accounts* LO 1

MJ Company has identified the following items. Indicate whether each item is included in an account in the Stockholders' Equity category of the balance sheet and identify the account title. Also indicate whether the item would increase or decrease stockholders' equity.

1. Preferred stock issued by MJ
2. Amount received by MJ in excess of par value when preferred stock was issued
3. Dividends in arrears on MJ preferred stock

(continued)

4. Cash dividend declared but unpaid on MJ stock
5. Stock dividend declared but unissued by MJ
6. Treasury stock
7. Amount received in excess of cost when treasury stock is reissued by MJ
8. Retained earnings

Exercise 11-2 ***Solve for Unknowns*** **LO 1**

The Stockholders' Equity category of Zache Company's balance sheet appears below.

Common stock, $10 par, 10,000 shares issued, 9,200 outstanding	$??
Additional paid-in capital	??
Total contributed capital	$350,000
Retained earnings	100,000
Treasury stock, ?? shares at cost	10,000
Total stockholders' equity	$??

Required

1. Determine the missing values that are indicated by question marks.
2. What was the cost per share of the treasury stock?

Exercise 11-3 ***Stock Issuance*** **LO 3**

Horace Company had the following transactions during 2004, its first year of business.

a. Issued 5,000 shares of $5 par common stock for cash at $15 per share.
b. Issued 7,000 shares of common stock on May 1 to acquire a factory building from Barkley Company. Barkley had acquired the building in 2000 at a price of $150,000. Horace estimated that the building was worth $175,000 on May 1, 2004.
c. Issued 2,000 shares of stock on June 1 to acquire a patent. The accountant has been unable to estimate the value of the patent but has determined that Horace's common stock was selling at $25 per share on June 1.

Required

1. Determine the effect on the accounting equation of the events.
2. Determine the balance sheet amounts for common stock and additional paid-in capital.

Exercise 11-4 ***Stock Issuances*** **LO 3**

The following transactions are for Weber Corporation in 2004:

a. On March 1, the corporation was organized and received authorization to issue 5,000 shares of 8%, $100 par value preferred stock and 2,000,000 shares of $10 par value common stock.
b. On March 10, Weber issued 5,000 shares of common stock at $35 per share.
c. On March 18, Weber issued 100 shares of preferred stock at $120 per share.
d. On April 12, Weber issued another 10,000 shares of common stock at $45 per share.

Required

1. Determine the effect on the accounting equation of each of the events.
2. Prepare the Stockholders' Equity section of the balance sheet as of December 31, 2004.
3. Does the balance sheet indicate the market value of the stock at year-end? Explain.

Exercise 11-5 ***Treasury Stock*** **LO 4**

The Stockholders' Equity category of Bradford Company's balance sheet on January 1, 2004, appeared as follows:

Common stock, $10 par, 10,000 shares issued and outstanding	$100,000
Additional paid-in capital	50,000
Retained earnings	80,000
Total stockholders' equity	$230,000

The following transactions occurred during 2004:

a. Reacquired 2,000 shares of common stock at $20 per share on July 1.

b. Reacquired 400 shares of common stock at $18 per share on August 1.

Required

1. Determine the effect on the accounting equation of the events.
2. Assume the company resold the shares of treasury stock at $28 per share on October 1. Did the company benefit from the treasury stock transaction? If so, where is the "gain" presented on the balance sheet?

Exercise 11-6 ***Treasury Stock Transactions*** **LO 4**

The stockholders' equity category of Little Joe's balance sheet on January 1, 2004, appeared as follows:

Common stock, $5 par, 40,000 shares issued and outstanding	$200,000
Additional paid-in capital	90,000
Retained earnings	100,000
Total stockholders' equity	$390,000

The following transactions occurred during 2004:

a. Reacquired 5,000 shares of common stock at $20 per share on February 1.

b. Reacquired 1,200 shares of common stock at $13 per share on March 1.

Required

1. Determine each event's impact on the accounting equation.
2. Assume that the treasury stock was reissued on October 1 at $12 per share. Did the company benefit from the treasury stock reissuance? Where is the "gain" or "loss" presented on the financial statements?
3. What effect did the two transactions to purchase treasury stock and the later reissuance of that stock have on the Stockholders' Equity section of the balance sheet?

Exercise 11-7 ***Cash Dividends*** **LO 5**

Kerry Company has 1,000 shares of $100 par value, 9% preferred stock and 10,000 shares of $10 par value common stock outstanding. The preferred stock is cumulative and nonparticipating. Dividends were paid in 2000. Since 2000, Kerry has declared and paid dividends as follows:

2001	$ 0
2002	10,000
2003	20,000
2004	25,000

Required

1. Determine the amount of the dividends to be allocated to preferred and common stockholders for each year, 2002 to 2004.
2. If the preferred stock had been noncumulative, how much would have been allocated to the preferred and common stockholders each year?

Exercise 11-8 ***Cash Dividends*** **LO 5**

The Stockholders' Equity category of Jackson Company's balance sheet as of January 1, 2004, appeared as follows:

Preferred stock, $100 par, 8%, 2,000 shares issued and outstanding	$200,000
Common stock, $10 par, 5,000 shares issued and outstanding	50,000
Additional paid-in capital	300,000
Total contributed capital	$550,000
Retained earnings	400,000
Total stockholders' equity	$950,000

The notes that accompany the financial statements indicate that Jackson has not paid dividends for the two years prior to 2004. On July 1, 2004, Jackson declares a dividend of $100,000 to be paid to preferred and common stockholders on August 1.

Required

1. Determine the amounts of the dividend to be allocated to preferred and common stockholders, assuming that the preferred stock is noncumulative, nonparticipating stock.
2. Determine the effect on the accounting equation of the July 1 and August 1, 2004, events.
3. Determine the amounts of the dividend to be allocated to preferred and common stockholders, assuming instead that the preferred stock is cumulative, nonparticipating stock.

Exercise 11-9 ***Stock Dividends*** **LO 6**

The Stockholders' Equity category of Worthy Company's balance sheet as of January 1, 2004, appeared as follows:

Common stock, $10 par,	
40,000 shares issued and outstanding	$400,000
Additional paid-in capital	100,000
Retained earnings	400,000
Total stockholders' equity	$900,000

The following transactions occurred during 2004:

a. Declared a 10% stock dividend to common stockholders on January 15. At the time of the dividend, the common stock was selling for $30 per share. The stock dividend was to be issued to stockholders on January 30, 2004.

b. Distributed the stock dividend to the stockholders on January 30, 2004.

Required

1. Determine the effect on the accounting equation of the 2004 events.
2. Develop the Stockholders' Equity category of Worthy Company's balance sheet as of January 31, 2004, after the stock dividend was issued. What effect did these transactions have on total stockholders' equity?

Exercise 11-10 ***Stock Dividends versus Stock Splits*** **LO 7**

Campbell Company wants to increase the number of shares of its common stock outstanding and is considering a stock dividend versus a stock split. The Stockholders' Equity of the firm on its most recent balance sheet appeared as follows:

Common stock, $10 par,	
50,000 shares issued and outstanding	$ 500,000
Additional paid-in capital	750,000
Retained earnings	880,000
Total stockholders' equity	$2,130,000

If a stock dividend is chosen, the firm wants to declare a 100% stock dividend. Because the stock dividend qualifies as a "large stock dividend," it must be recorded at par value. If a stock split is chosen, Campbell will declare a 2-for-1 split.

Required

1. Compare the effects of the stock dividends and stock splits on the accounting equation.
2. Develop the Stockholders' Equity category of Campbell's balance sheet (a) after the stock dividend and (b) after the stock split.

Exercise 11-11 ***Stock Dividends and Stock Splits*** **LO 7**

Whitacre Company's Stockholders' Equity section of the balance sheet on December 31, 2003, was as follows:

Common stock, $10 par value,	
60,000 shares issued and outstanding	$ 600,000
Additional paid-in capital	480,000
Retained earnings	1,240,000
Total stockholders' equity	$2,320,000

nonparticipating preferred stock and 10,000 shares of $5 par common stock. On January 10, Peeler issued for cash 500 shares of preferred stock at $120 per share and 4,000 shares of common at $80 per share. On January 20, it issued 1,000 shares of common stock to acquire a building site, at a time when the stock was selling for $70 per share.

During 2004, Peeler established an employee benefit plan and acquired 500 shares of common stock at $60 per share as treasury stock for that purpose. Later in 2004, it resold 100 shares of the stock at $65 per share.

On December 31, 2004, Peeler determined its net income for the year to be $40,000. The firm declared the annual cash dividend to preferred stockholders and a cash dividend of $5 per share to the common stockholders. The dividends will be paid in 2005.

Required

Develop the Stockholders' Equity category of Peeler's balance sheet as of December 31, 2004. Indicate on the statement the number of shares authorized, issued, and outstanding for both preferred and common stock.

Problem 11-2 *Evaluating Alternative Investments* LO 2

DECISION MAKING

Ellen Hays received a windfall from one of her investments. She would like to invest $100,000 of the money in Linwood Inc., which is offering common stock, preferred stock, and bonds on the open market. The common stock has paid $8 per share in dividends for the past three years and the company expects to be able to perform as well in the current year. The current market price of the common stock is $100 per share. The preferred stock has an 8% dividend rate, cumulative and nonparticipating. The bonds are selling at par with an 8% stated rate.

1. What are the advantages and disadvantages of each type of investment?
2. Recommend one type of investment over the others to Ellen, and justify your reason.

Problem 11-3 *Dividends for Preferred and Common Stock* LO 5

The Stockholders' Equity category of Greenbaum Company's balance sheet as of December 31, 2004, appeared as follows:

Preferred stock, $100 par, 8%,	
1,000 shares issued and outstanding	$ 100,000
Common stock, $10 par,	
20,000 shares issued and outstanding	200,000
Additional paid-in capital	250,000
Total contributed capital	$ 550,000
Retained earnings	450,000
Total stockholders' equity	$1,000,000

The notes to the financial statements indicate that dividends were not declared or paid for 2002 or 2003. Greenbaum wants to declare a dividend of $59,000 for 2004.

Required

Determine the total and the per-share amounts that should be declared to the preferred and common stockholders under the following assumptions:

1. The preferred stock is noncumulative, nonparticipating.
2. The preferred stock is cumulative, nonparticipating.

Problem 11-4 *Effect of Stock Dividend* LO 6

Favre Company has a history of paying cash dividends on its common stock. The firm did not have a particularly profitable year, however, in 2004. At the end of the year, Favre found itself without the necessary cash for a dividend and therefore declared a stock dividend to its common stockholders. A 50% stock dividend was declared to stockholders on December 31, 2004. The board of directors is unclear about a stock dividend's effect on Favre's balance sheet and has requested your assistance.

Required

1. Write a statement to indicate the effect that the stock dividend has on the financial statements of Favre Company.
2. A group of common stockholders has contacted the firm to express its concern about the effect of the stock dividend and to question the effect the stock dividend may have on the market price of the stock. Write a statement to address the stockholders' concerns.

Problem 11-5 ***Dividends and Stock Splits*** **LO 7**

On January 1, 2004, Frederiksen's Inc.'s Stockholders' Equity category appeared as follows:

Preferred stock, $80 par value, 7%, 3,000 shares issued and outstanding	$ 240,000
Common stock, $10 par value, 15,000 shares issued and outstanding	150,000
Additional paid-in capital—Preferred	60,000
Additional paid-in capital—Common	225,000
Total contributed capital	$ 675,000
Retained earnings	2,100,000
Total stockholders' equity	$2,775,000

The preferred stock is noncumulative and nonparticipating. During 2004, the following transactions occurred:

a. On March 1, declared a cash dividend of $16,800 on preferred stock. Paid the dividend on April 1.

b. On June 1, declared a 5% stock dividend on common stock. The current market price of the common stock was $18. The stock was issued on July 1.

c. On September 1, declared a cash dividend of $0.50 per share on the common stock; paid the dividend on October 1.

d. On December 1, issued a 2-for-1 stock split of common stock, when the stock was selling for $50 per share.

Required

1. Explain each transaction's effect on the stockholders' equity accounts and the total stockholders' equity.
2. Develop the Stockholders' Equity category of the December 31, 2004, balance sheet. Assume the net income for the year was $650,000.
3. Write a paragraph that explains the difference between a stock dividend and a stock split.

Problem 11-6 ***Statement of Stockholders' Equity*** **LO 8**

Refer to all the facts in Problem 11-1.

Required

Develop a statement of stockholders' equity for Peeler Company for 2004. The statement should start with the beginning balance of each stockholders' equity account and explain the changes that occurred in each account to arrive at the 2004 ending balances.

Problem 11-7 ***Wal-Mart's Comprehensive Income*** **LO 8**

http://www.walmart.com

The consolidated statement of shareholders' equity of Wal-Mart Stores, Inc. for the year ended January 31, 2003, appears below:

Consolidated Statement of Shareholders' Equity
(Amounts in millions)

	Number of Shares	Common Stock	Capital in Excess of Par Value	Retained Earnings	Other Accumulated Comprehensive Income	Total
Balance, January 31, 2002	4,453	$445	$1,484	$34,441	$(1,268)	$35,102
Comprehensive Income						
Net income				8,039		8,039
Other accumulated comprehensive income						
Foreign currency translation adjustment					1,113	1,113
Hedge accounting adjustment					(148)	(148)
Minimum pension liability adjustment					(206)	(206)
Total Comprehensive Income						8,798
Cash dividends ($0.30 per share)				(1,328)		(1,328)
Purchase of Company stock	(63)	(5)	(150)	(3,228)		(3,383)
Stock options exercised and other	5		148			148
Balance, January 31, 2003	4,395	$440	$1,482	$37,924	$ (509)	$39,337

Required

1. Which items were included in comprehensive income? If these items had been included on the income statement as part of net income, what would have been the effect?
2. Do you think that the concept of comprehensive income would be useful to explain the impact of all the events that took place during 2002 to the stockholders of Wal-Mart?

Problem 11-8 *Effects of Stockholders' Equity Transactions on Statement of Cash Flows* LO 10

Refer to all the facts in Problem 11-1.

Required

Indicate how each of the transactions affects the cash flows of Peeler Company, by preparing the Financing Activities section of the 2004 statement of cash flows. Provide an explanation for the exclusion of any of these transactions from the Financing Activities section of the statement.

Problem 11-9 *Income Distribution of a Partnership (Appendix)* LO 11

Louise Abbott and Buddie Costello are partners in a comedy club business. The partnership agreement specifies the manner in which income of the business is to be distributed. Louise is to receive a salary of $20,000 for managing the club, and Buddie is to receive interest at the rate of 10% on her capital balance of $300,000. Remaining income is to be distributed on a 2-to-1 ratio.

Required

Determine the amount that should be distributed to each partner, assuming the following business net incomes:

1. $50,000
2. $80,000
3. $100,000

Problem 11-10 *Sole Proprietorships (Appendix)* LO 11

On May 1, Chong Yu deposited $120,000 of his own savings in a separate bank account to start a printing business. He purchased copy machines for $42,000. Expenses for the year, including depreciation on the copy machines, were $84,000. Sales for the year, all in cash, were $108,000. Chong withdrew $12,000 during the year.

Required

1. What is the balance in Chong's capital account at the end of the year?
2. Explain why the balance in Chong's capital account is different from the amount of cash on hand.

Problem 11-11 *Partnerships (Appendix)* LO 11

Kirin Nerise and Milt O'Brien agreed to form a partnership to operate a sandwich shop. Kirin contributed $25,000 cash and will manage the store. Milt contributed computer equipment worth $8,000 and $92,000 cash. Milt will keep the financial records. During the year, sales were $90,000 and expenses (including a salary to Kirin) were $76,000. Kirin withdrew $500 per month. Milt withdrew $4,000 (total). Their partnership agreement specified that Kirin would receive a salary of $7,200 for the year. Milt would receive 6% interest on his initial capital investment. All remaining income or loss would be equally divided.

Required

Calculate the ending balance in the equity account of each of the partners.

Multi-Concept Problems

Problem 11-12 *Analysis of Stockholders' Equity* LO 1, 4

The Stockholders' Equity section of the December 31, 2004, balance sheet of Eldon Company appeared as follows:

Preferred stock, $30 par value, 5,000 shares authorized, ? shares issued	$120,000
Common stock, ? par, 10,000 shares authorized, 7,000 shares issued	70,000
Additional paid-in capital—Preferred	6,000

(continued)

Additional paid-in capital—Common	560,000
Additional paid-in capital—Treasury stock	1,000
Total contributed capital	$757,000
Retained earnings	40,000
Less: Treasury stock, preferred, 100 shares	(3,200)
Total stockholders' equity	$??

Required

Determine the following items, based on Eldon's balance sheet:

1. The number of shares of preferred stock issued
2. The number of shares of preferred stock outstanding
3. The average per-share sales price of the preferred stock when issued
4. The par value of the common stock
5. The average per-share sales price of the common stock when issued
6. The cost of the treasury stock per share
7. The total stockholders' equity
8. The per-share book value of the common stock, assuming that there are no dividends in arrears and that the preferred stock can be redeemed at its par value

Problem 11-13 ***Effects of Stockholders' Equity Transactions on the Balance Sheet*** **LO 3, 4, 7**

The following transactions occurred at Horton Inc. during its first year of operation:

a. Issued 100,000 shares of common stock at $5 each; 1,000,000 shares are authorized at $1 par value.
b. Issued 10,000 shares of common stock for a building and land. The building was appraised for $20,000, but the value of the land is undeterminable. The stock is selling for $10 on the open market.
c. Purchased 1,000 shares of its own common stock on the open market for $16 per share.
d. Declared a dividend of $0.10 per share on outstanding common stock. The dividend is to be paid after the end of the first year of operations. Market value of the stock is $26.
e. Declared a 2-for-1 stock split. The market value of the stock was $37 before the stock split.
f. Reported $180,000 of income for the year.

Required

1. Indicate each transaction's effect on the assets, liabilities, and owners' equity of Horton Inc.
2. Prepare the Stockholders' Equity section of the balance sheet.
3. Write a paragraph that explains the number of shares of stock issued and outstanding at the end of the year.

Problem 11-14 ***Stockholders' Equity Section of the Balance Sheet*** **LO 1, 4**

The newly hired accountant at Ives Inc. prepared the following balance sheet:

Assets	
Cash	$ 3,500
Accounts receivable	5,000
Treasury stock	500
Plant, property, and equipment	108,000
Retained earnings	1,000
Total assets	$118,000
Liabilities	
Accounts payable	$ 5,500
Dividends payable	1,500
Owners' Equity	
Common stock, $1 par, 100,000 shares issued	100,000
Additional paid-in capital	11,000
Total liabilities and owners' equity	$118,000

Required

1. Prepare a corrected balance sheet. Write a short explanation for each correction.
2. Why does the Retained Earnings account have a negative balance?

Alternate Problems

Problem 11-1A ***Stockholders' Equity Category*** **LO 1**

Kebler Company was incorporated as a new business on January 1, 2004. The corporate charter approved on that date authorized the issuance of 2,000 shares of $100 par 7% cumulative, nonparticipating preferred stock and 20,000 shares of $5 par common stock. On January 10, Kebler issued for cash 1,000 shares of preferred stock at $120 per share and 8,000 shares of common at $80 per share. On January 20, it issued 2,000 shares of common stock to acquire a building site, at a time when the stock was selling for $70 per share.

During 2004 Kebler established an employee benefit plan and acquired 1,000 shares of common stock at $60 per share as treasury stock for that purpose. Later in 2004, it resold 100 shares of the stock at $65 per share.

On December 31, 2004, Kebler determined its net income for the year to be $80,000. The firm declared the annual cash dividend to preferred stockholders and a cash dividend of $5 per share to the common stockholders. The dividend will be paid in 2005.

Required

Develop the Stockholders' Equity category of Kebler's balance sheet as of December 31, 2004. Indicate on the statement the number of shares authorized, issued, and outstanding for both preferred and common stock.

Problem 11-2A ***Evaluating Alternative Investments*** **LO 2**

DECISION MAKING

Rob Lowe would like to invest $100,000 in Franklin Inc., which is offering common stock, preferred stock, and bonds on the open market. The common stock has paid $1 per share in dividends for the past three years, and the company expects to be able to double the dividend in the current year. The current market price of the common stock is $10 per share. The preferred stock has an 8% dividend rate. The bonds are selling at par with a 5% stated rate.

Required

1. Explain Franklin's obligation to pay dividends or interest on each instrument.
2. Recommend one type of investment over the others to Rob, and justify your reason.

Problem 11-3A ***Dividends for Preferred and Common Stock*** **LO 5**

The Stockholders' Equity category of Rausch Company's balance sheet as of December 31, 2004, appeared as follows:

Preferred stock, $100 par, 8%, 2,000 shares issued and outstanding	$ 200,000
Common stock, $10 par, 40,000 shares issued and outstanding	400,000
Additional paid-in capital	500,000
Total contributed capital	$1,100,000
Retained earnings	900,000
Total stockholders' equity	$2,000,000

The notes to the financial statements indicate that dividends were not declared or paid for 2002 or 2003. Rausch wants to declare a dividend of $118,000 for 2004.

Required

Determine the total and the per-share amounts that should be declared to the preferred and common stockholders under the following assumptions:

1. The preferred stock is noncumulative, nonparticipating.
2. The preferred stock is cumulative, nonparticipating.

Problem 11-4A ***Effect of Stock Dividend*** **LO 6**

Travanti Company has a history of paying cash dividends on its common stock. Although the firm has been profitable this year, the board of directors has been planning construction of a second manufacturing plant. To reduce the amount that they must borrow to finance the expansion, the directors are contemplating replacing their usual cash dividend with a 40% stock dividend. The board is unsure what the effect of a stock dividend will be on the company's balance sheet and has requested your assistance.

Required

1. Write a statement to indicate the effect that the stock dividend has on the financial statements of Travanti Company.
2. A group of common stockholders has contacted the firm to express its concern about the effect of the stock dividend and to question the effect that the stock dividend may have on the market price of the stock. Write a statement to address the stockholders' concerns.

Problem 11-5A *Dividends and Stock Splits* LO 7

On January 1, 2004, Svenberg Inc.'s Stockholders' Equity category appeared as follows:

Preferred stock, $80 par value, 8%, 1,000 shares issued and outstanding	$ 80,000
Common stock, $10 par value, 10,000 shares issued and outstanding	100,000
Additional paid-in capital—Preferred	60,000
Additional paid-in capital—Common	225,000
Total contributed capital	$ 465,000
Retained earnings	1,980,000
Total stockholders' equity	$2,445,000

The preferred stock is noncumulative and nonparticipating. During 2004, the following transactions occurred:

a. On March 1, declared a cash dividend of $6,400 on preferred stock. Paid the dividend on April 1.

b. On June 1, declared an 8% stock dividend on common stock. The current market price of the common stock was $26. The stock was issued on July 1.

c. On September 1, declared a cash dividend of $0.70 per share on the common stock; paid the dividend on October 1.

d. On December 1, issued a 3-for-1 stock split of common stock, when the stock was selling for $30 per share.

Required

1. Explain each transaction's effect on the stockholders' equity accounts and the total stockholders' equity.
2. Develop the Stockholders' Equity category of the balance sheet. Assume the net income for the year was $720,000.
3. Write a paragraph that explains the difference between a stock dividend and a stock split.

Problem 11-6A *Statement of Stockholders' Equity* LO 8

Refer to all the facts in Problem 11-1A.

Required

Develop a statement of stockholders' equity for Kebler Company for 2004. The statement should start with the beginning balance of each stockholders' equity account and explain the changes that occurred in each account to arrive at the 2004 ending balances.

Problem 11-7A *Southwest Airlines Comprehensive Income* LO 8

http://www.southwest.com

The consolidated statement of stockholders' equity of Southwest Airlines, Co. for the year ended December 31, 2002, appears on the following page.

Consolidated Statement of Stockholders' Equity

SOUTHWEST AIRLINES CO.
CONSOLIDATED STATEMENT OF STOCKHOLDERS' EQUITY

(In thousands, except per share amounts)	Common Stock	Capital in Excess of Par Value	Retained Earnings	Accumulated Other Comprehensive Income (Loss)	Treasury Stock	Total
Balance at December 31, 2001	$766,774	$ 50,409	$3,228,408	$(31,538)	—	$4,014,053
Issuance of common stock pursuant to Employee stock plans	9,889	46,868	—	—	—	56,757
Tax benefit of options exercised	—	38,571	—	—	—	38,571
Cash dividends, $.018 per share	—	—	(13,929)	—	—	(13,929)
Comprehensive income (loss)	—	—	—	—	—	
Net income	—	—	240,969	—	—	240,969
Unrealized gain on derivative instruments	—	—	—	87,213	—	87,213
Other	—	—	—	(2,017)	—	(2,017)
Total comprehensive income				326,165		
Balance at December 31, 2002	$776,663	$135,848	$3,455,448	$53,658	$—	$4,421,617

Required

1. Was Southwest's net income higher or lower than its comprehensive income? Explain the items that caused Southwest's net income to be different from its comprehensive income. What does the term *unrealized gain* mean?
2. Do you think that Southwest's stockholders would find the concept of comprehensive income useful to evaluate the performance of the company?

Problem 11-8A *Effects of Stockholders' Equity Transactions on the Statement of Cash Flows* LO 10

Refer to all the facts in Problem 11-1A.

Required

Indicate how each of the transactions affects the cash flows of Kebler Company, by preparing the Financing Activities section of the 2004 statement of cash flows. Provide an explanation for the exclusion of any of these transactions from the Financing Activities section of the statement.

Problem 11-9A *Income Distribution of a Partnership (Appendix)* LO 11

Kay Katz and Doris Kan are partners in a dry-cleaning business. The partnership agreement specifies the manner in which income of the business is to be distributed. Kay is to receive a salary of $40,000 for managing the business. Doris is to receive interest at the rate of 10% on her capital balance of $600,000. Remaining income is to be distributed on a 2-to-1 ratio.

Required

Determine the amount that should be distributed to each partner, assuming the following business net incomes:

1. $100,000
2. $160,000
3. $200,000

Problem 11-10A *Sole Proprietorships (Appendix)* LO 11

On May 1, Chen Chien Lao deposited $150,000 of her own savings in a separate bank account to start a printing business. She purchased copy machines for $52,500. Expenses for the year, including depreciation on the copy machines, were $105,000. Sales for the year, all in cash, were $135,000. Chen withdrew $15,000 during the year.

Required

1. What is the balance in Chen's capital account at the end of the year?
2. Explain why the balance in Chen's capital account is different from the amount of cash on hand.

Problem 11-11A ***Partnerships (Appendix)*** **LO 11**

Karen Locke and Gina Keyes agreed to form a partnership to operate a sandwich shop. Karen contributed $35,000 cash and will manage the store. Gina contributed computer equipment worth $11,200 and $128,800 cash. Gina will keep the financial records. During the year, sales were $126,000 and expenses (including a salary to Karen) were $106,400. Karen withdrew $700 per month. Gina withdrew $5,600 (total). Their partnership agreement specified that Karen would receive a salary of $10,800 for the year. Gina would receive 6% interest on her initial capital investment. All remaining income or loss would be equally divided.

Required

Calculate the ending balance in the equity account of each of the partners.

Alternate Multi-Concept Problems

Problem 11-12A ***Analysis of Stockholders' Equity*** **LO 1, 4**

The Stockholders' Equity section of the December 31, 2004, balance sheet of Carter Company appeared as follows:

Preferred stock, $50 par value,	
10,000 shares authorized, ? shares issued	$ 400,000
Common stock, ? par value,	
20,000 shares authorized, 14,000 shares issued	280,000
Additional paid-in capital—Preferred	12,000
Additional paid-in capital—Common	980,000
Additional paid-in capital—Treasury stock	2,000
Total contributed capital	$1,674,000
Retained earnings	80,000
Less: Treasury stock, preferred, 200 shares	(12,800)
Total stockholders' equity	$??

Determine the following items, based on Carter's balance sheet.

1. The number of shares of preferred stock issued
2. The number of shares of preferred stock outstanding
3. The average per-share sales price of the preferred stock when issued
4. The par value of the common stock
5. The average per-share sales price of the common stock when issued
6. The cost of the treasury stock per share
7. The total stockholders' equity
8. The per-share book value of the common stock, assuming that there are no dividends in arrears and that the preferred stock can be redeemed at its par value

Problem 11-13A ***Effects of Stockholders' Equity Transactions on Balance Sheet*** **LO 3, 4, 7**

The following transactions occurred at Hilton Inc. during its first year of operation:

a. Issued 10,000 shares of common stock at $10 each; 100,000 shares are authorized at $1 par value.

b. Issued 10,000 shares of common stock for a patent, which is expected to be effective for the next 15 years. The value of the patent is undeterminable. The stock is selling for $10 on the open market.

c. Purchased 1,000 shares of its own common stock on the open market for $10 per share.

d. Declared a dividend of $0.50 per share of outstanding common stock. The dividend is to be paid after the end of the first year of operations. Market value of the stock is $10.

e. Income for the year is reported as $340,000.

Required

1. Indicate each transaction's effect on the assets, liabilities, and owners' equity of Hilton Inc.
2. Hilton's president has asked you to explain the difference between contributed capital and retained earnings. Discuss these terms as they relate to Hilton.
3. Determine the book value per share of the stock at the end of the year.

Problem 11-14A ***Stockholders' Equity Section of the Balance Sheet*** **LO 1, 4**

The newly hired accountant at Grainfield Inc. is considering the following list of accounts as he prepares the balance sheet. All of the accounts have positive balances. The company is authorized to issue 1,000,000 shares of common stock and 10,000 shares of preferred stock. The treasury stock was purchased at $5 per share.

Treasury stock (common)	$ 15,000
Retained earnings	54,900
Dividends payable	1,500
Common stock, $1 par	100,000
Additional paid-in capital	68,400
Preferred stock, $10 par, 5%	50,000

Required

1. Prepare the Stockholders' Equity section of the balance sheet for Grainfield.
2. Explain why some of the listed accounts are not shown in the Stockholders' Equity section.

Decision Cases

Reading and Interpreting Financial Statements

Decision Case 11-1 ***Winnebago Industries' Stockholders' Equity Category*** **LO 1, 2**

Refer to Winnebago Industries' 2002 annual report.

http://www.winnebagoind.com

Required

1. What are the numbers of shares of common stock authorized, issued, and outstanding as of the balance sheet date?
2. Calculate the book value per share of the common stock.
3. The balance of the Reinvested Earnings account increased during the year. What are the possible factors that affect its balance?
4. The total stockholders' equity as of August 31, 2002, is $179,815,000. Does that mean that stockholders will receive that amount if the company is liquidated?

Decision Case 11-2 ***Comparing Two Companies in the Same Industry: Winnebago Industries and Monaco Coach Corporation*** **LO 1, 8**

Refer to the stockholders' equity section of the balance sheets of Monaco Coach Corporation as of December 28, 2002, and of Winnebago Industries as of August 31, 2002, that are provided in Appendices A and B at the end of the text.

http://www.winnebagoind.com
http://www.monacocoach.com

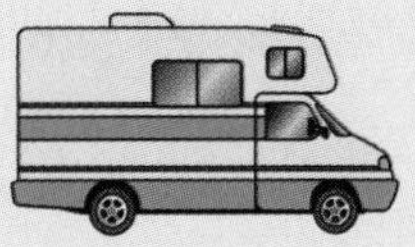

Required

1. For each company, what are the numbers of shares of common stock authorized, issued, and outstanding as of the balance sheet date?
2. Calculate the book value per share for each company on its balance sheet date. What does this information tell you?
3. Did the balance of the Retained Earnings account of each company increase or decrease during the year? What are the possible factors that affect the Retained Earnings balance?
4. How does the total stockholders' equity of each company compare to the other company? Does the difference mean that one company's stock is more valuable than the others? Explain your answer.

Decision Case 11-3 ***Reading Winnebago Industries' Statement of Cash Flows*** **LO 10**

A portion of the cash flow statement of Winnebago Industries for the year ended August 25, 2002, is as follows:

(In thousands)	Year Ended August 31, 2002	August 25, 2001	August 26, 2000
Cash flows from financing activities and capital transactions:			
Payments for purchase of common stock	(86,072)	(10,686)	(19,726)
Payments of cash dividends	(3,954)	(4,121)	(4,324)
Proceeds from issuance of common and treasury stock	4,357	3,449	1,176
Net cash used by financing activities and capital transactions	(85,669)	(11,358)	(22,874)

http://www.winnebagoind.com

Required

1. Explain how each of the items in the Financing Activities category affected the amount of the company's cash.
2. Winnebago Industries generated cash by selling treasury stock during the year. What are possible reasons for buying stock as treasury stock? Why would a company resell treasury stock after it has been purchased?
3. The cash flow statement indicates a use of cash for dividends paid. How do dividends affect the Stockholders' Equity category of the balance sheet?

Making Financial Decisions

DECISION MAKING

Decision Case 11-4 *Debt versus Preferred Stock* LO 1, 2

Assume that you are an analyst attempting to compare the financial structures of two companies. In particular, you must analyze the debt and equity categories of the two firms and calculate a debt-to-equity ratio for each firm. The liability and equity categories of First Company at year-end appeared as follows:

Liabilities	
Accounts payable	$ 500,000
Loan payable	800,000
Stockholders' Equity	
Common stock	300,000
Retained earnings	600,000
Total liabilities and equity	$2,200,000

First Company's loan payable bears interest at 8%, which is paid annually. The principal is due in five years.

The liability and equity categories of Second Company at year-end appeared as follows:

Liabilities	
Accounts payable	$ 500,000
Stockholders' Equity	
Common stock	300,000
Preferred stock	800,000
Retained earnings	600,000
Total liabilities and equity	$2,200,000

Second Company's preferred stock is 8%, cumulative stock. A provision of the stock agreement specifies that the stock must be redeemed at face value in five years.

Required

1. It appears that the loan payable of First Company and the preferred stock of Second Company are very similar. What are the differences between the two securities?
2. When calculating the debt-to-equity ratio, do you believe that the Second Company preferred stock should be treated as debt or as stockholders' equity? Write a statement expressing your position on this issue.

Decision Case 11-5 *Preferred versus Common Stock* **LO 2**

DECISION MAKING

Rohnan Inc. needs to raise $500,000. It is considering two options:

a. Issue preferred stock, $100 par, 8%, cumulative, nonparticipating, callable at $110. The stock could be issued at par.

b. Issue common stock, $1 par, market $10. Currently, the company has 400,000 shares outstanding equally in the hands of five owners. The company has never paid a dividend.

Required

Rohnan has asked you to consider both options and make a recommendation. It is equally concerned with cash flow and company control. Write your recommendations.

Accounting and Ethics: What Would You Do?

Decision Case 11-6 *Inside Information* **LO 9**

ETHICS

Jim Brock was an accountant with Hubbard Inc., a large corporation with stock that was publicly traded on the New York Stock Exchange. One of Jim's duties was to manage the corporate reporting department, which was responsible for developing and issuing Hubbard's annual report. At the end of 2004, Hubbard closed its accounting records, and initial calculations indicated a very profitable year. In fact, the net income exceeded the amount that had been projected during the year by the financial analysts who followed Hubbard's stock.

Jim was very pleased with the company's financial performance. In January 2005, he suggested that his father buy Hubbard's stock because he was sure the stock price would increase when the company announced its 2004 results. Jim's father followed the advice and bought a block of stock at $25 per share.

On February 15, 2005, Hubbard announced its 2004 results and issued the annual report. The company received favorable press coverage about its performance, and the stock price on the stock exchange increased to $32 per share.

Required

What was Jim's professional responsibility to Hubbard Inc. concerning the issuance of the 2004 annual report? Did Jim act ethically in this situation?

Decision Case 11-7 *Dividend Policy* **LO 5**

ETHICS

Hancock Inc. is owned by nearly 100 shareholders. Judith Stitch owns 48% of the stock. She needs cash to fulfill her commitment to donate the funds to construct a new art gallery. Some of her friends have agreed to vote for Hancock to pay a larger-than-normal dividend to shareholders. Judith has asked you to vote for the large dividend because she knows that you also support the arts. When informed that the dividend may create a working capital hardship on Hancock, Judith responded: "There is plenty of money in Retained Earnings. The dividend will not affect the cash of the company."

1. Is Judith correct in stating that the dividend payment will not affect the cash of the company because there is money in Retained Earnings?
2. Is there an ethical conflict between Judith's personal interest to support the arts and the company's interest? Does she have the right to persuade other stockholders to support her cause?
3. Is this a significant enough issue to influence your vote? Explain your reasoning. How might you react if you were a large creditor?

THOMSON ONE Business School Edition Case

Case 11-8 *Using THOMSON ONE for Southwest Airlines*

http://www.southwest.com

The chapter opener discussed the airline industry in general and Southwest Airlines' place in the industry. For several years, Southwest Airlines has been a leader in the industry with superior performance and profitability. That performance has been reflected in its stock price. We can use THOMSON ONE to obtain information about its financial position and its stock price.

Begin by entering the company's ticker symbol, LUV, and then selecting "GO." On the opening screen you will see background information about the company, key financial ratios, and some recent data concerning stock price. To research its stock price further, click the Prices tab. At the top of the Price Chart, click on the "Interactive Chart." To obtain a 1-year chart, go to

"Time Frame," click on the down arrow, and select 1 year. Then, click on "Draw," and a 1-year chart should appear.

We can also find Southwest Airlines' recent financial statements. Near the top of the screen, click on "Financials" and select "Financial Statements." Refer to the stockholders' equity portion of the company's balance sheet.

Based on your use of THOMSON ONE, answer the following questions.

1. What have been the high and low stock prices for the company over the past year?
2. How does the company's stock performance compare to the other line on the stock price chart for the S&P 500?
3. What was the amount of retained earnings for the most recent balance sheet?
4. By what percentage has the company's total stockholders' equity increased from the year prior to the most recent year?

Solutions to Key Terms Quiz

13	Authorized shares (p. 542)
1	Issued shares (p. 542)
14	Outstanding shares (p. 542)
2	Par value (p. 543)
15	Additional paid-in capital (p. 544)
3	Retained earnings (p. 544)
4	Cumulative feature (p. 545)
16	Participating feature (p. 546)
5	Convertible feature (p. 546)
17	Callable feature (p. 546)
6	Treasury stock (p. 547)
18	Retirement of stock (p. 549)
7	Dividend payout ratio (p. 549)
19	Stock dividend (p. 551)
9	Stock split (p. 553)
8	Statement of stockholders' equity (p. 554)
11	Comprehensive income (p. 556)
10	Book value per share (p. 557)
12	Market value per share (p. 559)
22	Sole proprietorship (p. 566)
20	Partnership (p. 567)
21	Partnership agreement (p. 567)

Part III

Integrative Problem

Evaluating financing options for asset acquisition and their impact on financial statements

Following are the financial statements for Griffin Inc. for the year 2004.

GRIFFIN INC.
BALANCE SHEET
DECEMBER 31, 2004
(IN MILLIONS)

Assets		**Liabilities**	
Cash	$ 1.6	Current portion of lease obligation	$ 1.0
Other current assets	6.4	Other current liabilities	3.0
Leased assets (net of accumulated depreciation)	7.0	Lease obligation—Long-term	6.0
Other long-term assets	45.0	Other long-term liabilities	6.0
		Total liabilities	$16.0
		Stockholders' Equity	
		Preferred stock	$ 1.0
		Additional paid-in capital on preferred stock	2.0
		Common stock	4.0
		Additional paid-in capital on common stock	16.0
		Retained earnings	21.0
		Total stockholders' equity	$44.0
Total assets	$60.0	Total liabilities and stockholders' equity	$60.0

GRIFFIN INC.
INCOME STATEMENT
FOR THE YEAR ENDED DECEMBER 31, 2004
(IN MILLIONS)

Revenues		$50.0
Expenses:		
Depreciation of leased asset	$ 1.0	
Depreciation—Other assets	3.2	
Interest on leased asset	0.5	
Other expenses	27.4	
Income tax (30% rate)	5.4	
Total expenses		(37.5)
Income before extraordinary loss		$12.5
Extraordinary loss (net of $0.9 taxes)		(2.1)
Net income		$10.4
EPS before extraordinary loss		$3.10
EPS extraordinary loss		(0.53)
EPS—Net income		$2.57

Additional Information:

Griffin Inc. has authorized 500,000 shares of 10%, $10 par value cumulative preferred stock. There were 100,000 shares issued and outstanding at all times during 2004. The firm has also authorized 5 million shares of $1 par common stock, with 4 million shares issued and outstanding.

On January 1, 2004, Griffin Inc. acquired an asset, a piece of specialized heavy equipment, for $8 million with a capital lease. The lease contract indicates that the term of the lease is eight years. Payments of $1.5 million are to be made each December 31. The first lease payment was made December 31, 2004 and consisted of $1 million principal and $0.5 million of interest expense. The capital lease is depreciated using the straight-line method over eight years with zero salvage value.

Required

1. Assuming the equipment was acquired using a capital lease, indicate the effect on the accounting equation of the acquisition, depreciation, and lease payments.
2. The management of Griffin Inc. is considering the financial statement impact of methods of financing, other than the capital lease, that could have been used to acquire the equipment. For each alternative **a**, **b**, and **c**, indicate the effect on the accounting equation and prepare revised 2004 financial statements and calculate, as revised, the following amounts or ratios:

    Current ratio
    Debt-to-equity ratio
    Net income
    EPS—Net income

Assume that the following alternative actions would have taken place on January 1, 2004.

a. Instead of acquiring the equipment with a capital lease, the company negotiated an operating lease to use the asset. The lease requires annual year-end payments of $1.5 million and results in "off-balance sheet" financing. (*Hint:* The $1.5 million should be treated as rental expense.)

b. Instead of acquiring the equipment with a capital lease, Griffin Inc. issued bonds for $8 million and purchased the equipment with the proceeds of the bond issue. Assume the bond interest of $0.5 million was accrued and paid on December 31, 2004. A portion of the principal also is paid each year for eight years. On December 31, 2004, the company paid $1 million of principal and anticipated another $1 million of principal to be paid in 2005. Assume the equipment would have an eight-year life and would be depreciated on a straight-line basis with zero salvage value.

c. Instead of acquiring the equipment with a capital lease, Griffin Inc. issued 200,000 additional shares of 10% preferred stock to raise $8 million and purchased the equipment for $8 million with the proceeds from the stock issue. Dividends on the stock are declared and paid annually. Assume that a dividend payment was made on December 31, 2004. Assume the equipment would have an eight-year life and would be depreciated on a straight-line basis with zero salvage value.

Part IV

Additional Topics in Financial Reporting

A Word to Students about Part IV

Part IV will be fascinating and even fun—as long as you *keep practicing the concepts and reading the links from chapter to chapter.* **How does the corporation report cash flows?** See Chapter 12 to learn how to evaluate a company based on its cash flows. **Can you find the trends in a company's performance?** Use any set of financial statements you can find to practice the analysis concepts and skills presented in Chapter 13.

Chapter 12

The Statement of Cash Flows

Appendix

Accounting Tools: A Work-Sheet Approach to the Statement of Cash Flows

Chapter 13

Financial Statement Analysis

Appendix

Accounting Tools: Reporting and Analyzing Other Income Statement Items

Chapter 12

The Statement of Cash Flows

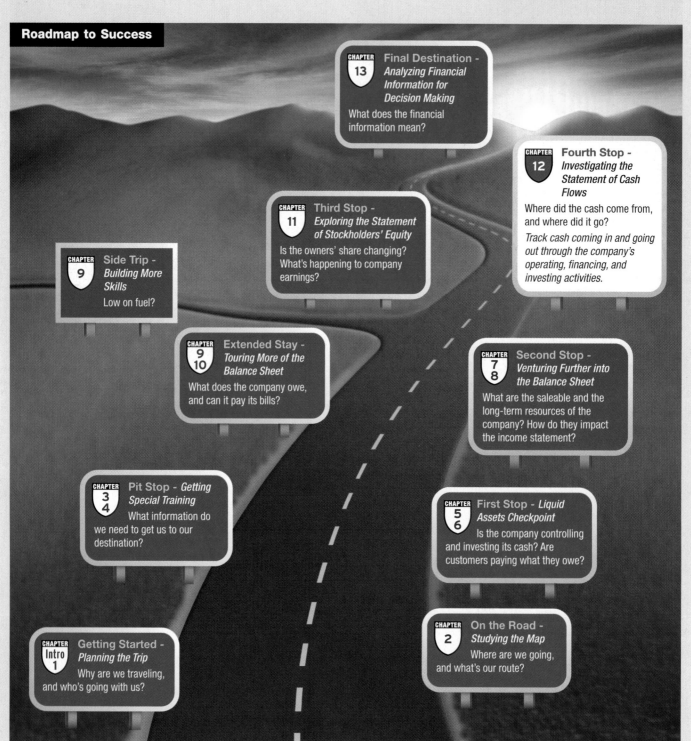

Roadmap to Success

CHAPTER 13 **Final Destination -** *Analyzing Financial Information for Decision Making*
What does the financial information mean?

CHAPTER 12 **Fourth Stop -** *Investigating the Statement of Cash Flows*
Where did the cash come from, and where did it go?
Track cash coming in and going out through the company's operating, financing, and investing activities.

CHAPTER 11 **Third Stop -** *Exploring the Statement of Stockholders' Equity*
Is the owners' share changing? What's happening to company earnings?

CHAPTER 9 **Side Trip -** *Building More Skills*
Low on fuel?

CHAPTER 9 10 **Extended Stay -** *Touring More of the Balance Sheet*
What does the company owe, and can it pay its bills?

CHAPTER 7 8 **Second Stop -** *Venturing Further into the Balance Sheet*
What are the saleable and the long-term resources of the company? How do they impact the income statement?

CHAPTER 3 4 **Pit Stop -** *Getting Special Training*
What information do we need to get us to our destination?

CHAPTER 5 6 **First Stop -** *Liquid Assets Checkpoint*
Is the company controlling and investing its cash? Are customers paying what they owe?

CHAPTER Intro 1 **Getting Started -** *Planning the Trip*
Why are we traveling, and who's going with us?

CHAPTER 2 **On the Road -** *Studying the Map*
Where are we going, and what's our route?

Focus on Financial Results

Cash, and the steady flow of it, is the lifeblood of any business, and IBM is no exception. As shown on the accompanying consolidated statement of cash flows, IBM ended 2002 with over $5.3 billion in cash and cash equivalents, an amount that was down about $1 billion from a year earlier. Cash flow from operating activities in 2002 of $13.788 billion was only slightly less than that generated in 2001.

What a company does with the cash it generates from its operations is crucial to its future success. For example, how much of this cash does it use to invest in new plant and equipment? As seen in the investing activities section of its statement of cash flows, IBM spent approximately $5 billion in each of the last three years for "purchases of plant, rental machines and other property." Another important use of cash for many businesses, including IBM, is to acquire other companies. As explained in the notes to its statements, the company's most significant acquisition in 2002 was the purchase of PricewaterhouseCoopers Consulting for $3.474 billion.

How much cash generated from buying and selling products and services remains after investing in new plant and equipment and other businesses? For IBM in 2002, this was about $7 billion, an amount that in turn was used for a variety of financing activities, including the repayment of various forms of debt, the repurchase of its own stock on the market, and the payment of dividends to stockholders.

In the highly competitive technology industry, the management of cash is critical to the long-term success of companies such as IBM. Not only will the computer giant need to continue to generate significant amounts from its operations, it will need to strive to find the best uses for the cash it raises.

Source: IBM 2002 Annual Report

IBM's 2002 Annual Report

Consolidated Statement of Cash Flows

(dollars in millions)

FOR THE YEAR ENDED DECEMBER 31:	2002	2001*	2000*
CASH FLOW FROM OPERATING ACTIVITIES FROM CONTINUING OPERATIONS:			
Income from continuing operations	$ 5,334	$ 8,146	$ 7,874
Adjustments to reconcile net income from continuing operations to cash provided by operating activities:			
Depreciation	3,691	3,881	4,224
Amortization of software	688	625	482
Deferred income taxes	(67)	664	44
Net gain on asset sales and other	(343)	(340)	(751)
Other than temporary declines in securities and other investments	58	405	—
Noncash portion of special actions	1,350	—	—
Change in operating assets and liabilities, net of acquisitions/divestitures:			
Receivables	4,125	2,837	(4,692)
Inventories	793	287	(22)
Pension assets	(4,227)	(1,758)	(1,333)
Other assets	70	1,244	673
Accounts payable	(55)	(918)	2,134
Pension liabilities	83	(69)	(237)
Other liabilities	2,288	(1,038)	441
NET CASH PROVIDED BY OPERATING ACTIVITIES FROM CONTINUING OPERATIONS	13,788	13,966	8,837
CASH FLOW FROM INVESTING ACTIVITIES FROM CONTINUING OPERATIONS:			
Payments for plant, rental machines and other property	(4,753)	(5,400)	(5,319)
Proceeds from disposition of plant, rental machines and other property	775	1,149	1,569
Investment in software	(597)	(655)	(565)
Purchases of marketable securities and other investments	(1,582)	(778)	(750)
Proceeds from disposition of marketable securities and other investments	1,185	738	1,393
Divestiture of businesses	1,233	—	—
Acquisition of businesses	(3,158)	(916)	(329)
NET CASH USED IN INVESTING ACTIVITIES FROM CONTINUING OPERATIONS	(6,897)	(5,862)	(4,001)
CASH FLOW FROM FINANCING ACTIVITIES FROM CONTINUING OPERATIONS:			
Proceeds from new debt	6,726	4,535	9,604
Short-term (repayments)/borrowings less than 90 days - net	(4,087)	2,926	(1,400)
Payments to settle debt	(5,812)	(7,898)	(7,561)
Preferred stock transactions - net	—	(254)	—
Common stock transactions - net	(3,087)	(3,652)	(6,073)
Cash dividends paid	(1,005)	(966)	(929)
NET CASH USED IN FINANCING ACTIVITIES FROM CONTINUING OPERATIONS	(7,265)	(5,309)	(6,359)
Effect of exchange rate changes on cash and cash equivalents	148	(83)	(147)
Net cash (used in)/provided by discontinued operations	(722)	55	190
Net change in cash and cash equivalents	(948)	2,767	(1,480)
Cash and cash equivalents at January 1	6,330	3,563	5,043
CASH AND CASH EQUIVALENTS AT DECEMBER 31	$ 5,382	$ 6,330	$ 3,563
SUPPLEMENTAL DATA:			
Cash paid during the year for the total company:			
Income taxes	$ 1,841	$ 2,279	$ 2,697
Interest	$ 831	$ 1,247	$ 1,447

NONCASH INVESTING AND FINANCING ACTIVITIES:

The noncash portion of the purchase price paid for PwCC is a *significant noncash investing activity*.

*Reclassified to conform with 2002 presentation.

The accompanying *notes* in the 2002 IBM Annual Report are an integral part of the financial statements.

You're in the Driver's Seat

IBM's 2002 statement of cash flows portrays a company ready to take advantage of its strong cash position and use this strength to create new opportunities in the highly competitive and constantly changing technology industry. Look up IBM's most recent annual report. Has the company continued to generate healthy profits and at the same time maintained a strong cash position? If you owned shares of IBM stock, would you be satisfied with the amount of dividends it is currently paying? Has the amount of dividends paid gone up, gone down, or remained relatively steady since 2002?

http://www.ibm.com

LEARNING OBJECTIVES

After studying this chapter, you should be able to:

LO 1 Explain the purpose of a statement of cash flows. (p. 596)

LO 2 Explain what cash equivalents are and how they are treated on the statement of cash flows. (p. 598)

LO 3 Describe operating, investing, and financing activities, and give examples of each. (p. 599)

LO 4 Describe the difference between the direct and the indirect methods of computing cash flow from operating activities. (p. 603)

LO 5 Prepare a statement of cash flows, using the direct method to determine cash flow from operating activities. (p. 608)

LO 6 Prepare a statement of cash flows, using the indirect method to determine cash flow from operating activities. (p. 617)

LO 7 Use a work sheet to prepare a statement of cash flows, using the indirect method to determine cash flow from operating activities (Appendix). (p. 626)

WHAT EXTERNAL DECISION MAKERS WANT TO KNOW ABOUT THE STATEMENT OF CASH FLOWS

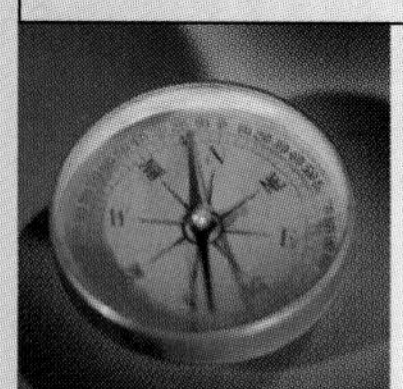

DECISION MAKING

Throughout earlier chapters in this book, we have considered what decision makers want to know about the various items that appear on a company's financial statements. In this chapter, we look more closely at one of the statements, specifically the statement of cash flows. All external parties have an interest in a company's cash flows. Stockholders need some assurance that enough cash is being generated from operations to pay dividends and invest in the company's future. Creditors want to know whether cash from operations is sufficient to repay their loans along with interest.

To be successful, decision makers must:

▶ *ASK ESSENTIAL QUESTIONS*

- Is the company able to maintain sufficient cash balances to satisfy its current obligations?
- Is the company generating sufficient cash from operations to invest in its future?

▶ *FIND BASIC INFORMATION*

The statement of cash flows, along with supporting notes, provides the information decision makers need to assess how well a company is managing its cash resources.

▶ *UNDERSTAND ACCOUNTING PRINCIPLES*

To understand the basic information that is found on a statement of cash flows and the supporting notes, decision makers must understand the underlying accounting principles (GAAP) that have been applied to create the reported information. These principles determine:

- the categories into which the various activities that affect cash flows are classified
- the acceptable methods a company can use to report cash flow from operations

▶ INTERPRET ANALYTICAL INFORMATION

Comparison of cash flows with those of prior periods as well as with those of competitors can help decision makers assess a company's overall financial performance. In addition, various measures can be employed to better understand how well a company is managing its cash flows. For example, the cash flow adequacy ratio gives an indication of a company's ability to meet its principal and interest obligations on its debt.

CASH FLOWS AND ACCRUAL ACCOUNTING

The *bottom line* is a phrase used in many different ways in today's society. "I wish politicians would cut out all of the rhetoric and get to the bottom line." "The bottom line is that the manager was fired because the team wasn't winning." "Our company's bottom line is twice what it was last year." This last use of the phrase, in reference to a company's net income, is probably the way in which *bottom line* was first used. In recent years, managers, stockholders, creditors, analysts, and other users of financial statements have become more and more wary of focusing on any one number as an indicator of a company's overall performance. Most experts now agree that there has been a tendency to rely far too heavily on net income and its companion, earnings per share, and in many cases to ignore a company's cash flows. As you know by now from your study of accounting, you can't pay bills with net income; you need cash!

To understand the difference between a company's bottom line and its cash flow, consider the case of IBM Corporation in 2002. IBM reported net earnings (income) of $3.579 billion in 2002. However, as shown in the chapter opener, during this same time period its cash actually decreased by $948 million. How is this possible? First, net income is computed on an accrual basis, not a cash basis. Second, the income statement primarily reflects events related to the operating activities of a business, that is, selling products or providing services.

http://www.ibm.com

If you think about it, any one of four combinations is possible. That is, a company's cash position can increase or decrease during a period, and it can report a net profit or a net loss. Exhibit 12-1 illustrates this point by showing the performance of four well-known computer companies, including IBM, during 2002. Dell Computer Corporation is the only one of the four companies that both improved its cash position in 2002 and reported a net profit. IBM reported a net profit but saw its cash decline in 2002. Hewlett-Packard Company reported a net loss in 2002 but improved its cash position. Finally, Gateway, Inc. both experienced a net loss in 2002 and saw its cash decline. To summarize, a company with a profitable year does not necessarily increase its cash position, nor does a company with an unprofitable year always experience a decrease in cash.

http://www.dell.com

http://www.hp.com

http://www.gateway.com

Exhibit 12-1

Cash Flows and Net Income for Four Computer Companies in 2002 (all amounts in millions of dollars)

COMPANY	BEGINNING BALANCE IN CASH	ENDING BALANCE IN CASH	INCREASE (DECREASE) IN CASH	NET INCOME (LOSS)
Dell Computer Corporation (fiscal year ended January 31, 2002)	3,641	4,232	591	2,122
IBM	$5,382	$6,330	(948)	$3,579
Hewlett-Packard Company (fiscal year ended October 31, 2002)	4,197	11,192	6,995	(903)
Gateway, Inc.	731	466	(265)	(298)

PURPOSE OF THE STATEMENT OF CASH FLOWS

LO 1 Explain the purpose of a statement of cash flows.

Statement of cash flows The financial statement that summarizes an entity's cash receipts and cash payments during the period from operating, investing, and financing activities.

The **statement of cash flows** is an important complement to the other major financial statements. It summarizes the operating, investing, and financing activities of a business over a period of time. The balance sheet summarizes the cash on hand and the balances in other assets, liabilities, and owners' equity accounts, providing a snapshot at a specific point in time. The statement of cash flows reports the changes in cash over a period of time and, most important, *explains these changes.*

The income statement summarizes performance on an accrual basis. As you have learned in your study of accrual accounting, income on this basis is considered a better indicator of *future* cash inflows and outflows than is a statement limited to current cash flows. The statement of cash flows complements the accrual-based income statement by allowing users to assess a company's performance on a cash basis. As we will see in the following simple example, however, it also goes beyond presenting data related to operating performance and looks at other activities that affect a company's cash position.

An Example

Consider the following discussion between the owner of Fox River Realty and the company accountant. After a successful first year in business in 2003, in which it earned a profit of $100,000, the owner reviews the income statement for the second year, as presented in Exhibit 12-2.

Exhibit 12-2

Income Statement for Fox River Realty

FOX RIVER REALTY
INCOME STATEMENT
FOR THE YEAR ENDED DECEMBER 31, 2004

Revenues	$400,000
Depreciation expense	$ 50,000
All other expenses	100,000
Total expenses	$150,000
Net income	$250,000

The owner is pleased with the results and asks to see the balance sheet. Comparative balance sheets for the first two years are presented in Exhibit 12-3.

Where Did the Cash Go? At first glance, the owner is surprised to see the significant decline in the Cash account. She immediately presses the accountant for answers. With such a profitable year, where has the cash gone? Specifically, why has cash decreased from $150,000 to $50,000, even though income rose from $100,000 in the first year to $250,000 in the second year?

The accountant begins his explanation to the owner by pointing out that income on a cash basis is even *higher* than the reported $250,000. Because depreciation expense is an expense that does not use cash (cash is used when the plant and equipment are purchased, not when they are depreciated), cash provided from operating activities is calculated as follows:

Net income	$250,000
Add back: Depreciation expense	50,000
Cash provided by operating activities	$300,000

Further, the accountant reminds the owner of the additional $50,000 that she invested in the business during the year. Now the owner is even more bewildered: with cash from operations of $300,000 and her own infusion of $50,000, why did cash *decrease* by $100,000? The accountant refreshes the owner's memory on three major outflows of cash during the year. First, even though the business earned $250,000, she withdrew

Exhibit 12-3

Comparative Balance Sheets for Fox River Realty

FOX RIVER REALTY COMPARATIVE BALANCE SHEETS DECEMBER 31		
	2004	**2003**
Cash	$ 50,000	$150,000
Plant and equipment	600,000	350,000
Accumulated depreciation	(150,000)	(100,000)
Total assets	$500,000	$400,000
Notes payable	$100,000	$150,000
Common stock	250,000	200,000
Retained earnings	150,000	50,000
Total equities	$500,000	$400,000

$150,000 in dividends during the year. Second, the comparative balance sheets indicate that notes payable with the bank were reduced from $150,000 to $100,000, requiring the use of $50,000 in cash. Finally, the comparative balance sheets show an increase in plant and equipment for the year from $350,000 to $600,000—a sizable investment of $250,000 in new long-term assets.

Statement of Cash Flows To summarize what happened to the cash, the accountant prepares a statement of cash flows as shown in Exhibit 12-4. Although the owner is not particularly happy with the decrease in cash for the year, she is at least satisfied with the statement as an explanation of where the cash came from and how it was used. The statement summarizes the important cash activities for the year and fills a void created with the presentation of just an income statement and a balance sheet.

REPORTING REQUIREMENTS FOR A STATEMENT OF CASH FLOWS

Accounting standards specify both the basis for preparing the statement of cash flows and the classification of items on the statement.[1] First, the statement must be prepared on a cash basis. Second, the cash flows must be classified into three categories:

Exhibit 12-4

Statement of Cash Flows for Fox River Realty

FOX RIVER REALTY STATEMENT OF CASH FLOWS FOR THE YEAR ENDED DECEMBER 31, 2004	
Cash provided (used) by operating activities:	
Net income	$ 250,000
Add back: Depreciation expense	50,000
Net cash provided (used) by operating activities	$ 300,000
Cash provided (used) by investing activities:	
Purchase of new plant and equipment	$(250,000)
Cash provided (used) by financing activities:	
Additional investment by owner	$ 50,000
Cash dividends paid to owner	(150,000)
Repayment of notes payable to bank	(50,000)
Net cash provided (used) by financing activities	$(150,000)
Net increase (decrease) in cash	$(100,000)
Cash balance at beginning of year	150,000
Cash balance at end of year	$ 50,000

[1] *Statement of Financial Accounting Standards No. 95*, "Statement of Cash Flows" (Stamford, Conn.: Financial Accounting Standards Board, November 1987).

- Operating activities
- Investing activities
- Financing activities

We now take a closer look at each of these important requirements in preparing a statement of cash flows.

The Definition of Cash: Cash and Cash Equivalents

LO 2 Explain what cash equivalents are and how they are treated on the statement of cash flows.

The purpose of the statement of cash flows is to provide information about a company's cash inflows and outflows. Thus, it is essential to have a clear understanding of what the definition of *cash* includes. According to accounting standards, certain items are recognized as being equivalent to cash and are combined with cash on the balance sheet and the statement of cash flows.

Cash equivalent An item readily convertible to a known amount of cash and with a maturity to the investor of three months or less.

Commercial paper (short-term notes issued by corporations), money market funds, and Treasury bills are examples of cash equivalents. To be classified as a **cash equivalent,** an item must be readily convertible to a known amount of cash and have a maturity *to the investor* of three months or less. For example, a three-year Treasury note purchased two months before its maturity is classified as a cash equivalent. The same note purchased two years before maturity would be classified as an investment instead.

To understand why cash equivalents are combined with cash when preparing a statement of cash flows, assume that a company has a cash balance of $10,000 and no assets that qualify as cash equivalents. Further assume that the $10,000 is used to purchase 90-day Treasury bills. The effect on the accounting equation of the purchase is as follows:

BALANCE SHEET							INCOME STATEMENT
ASSETS		=	LIABILITIES	+	OWNERS' EQUITY	+	REVENUES − EXPENSES
Investment in Treasury Bills	10,000						
Cash	(10,000)						

For record-keeping purposes, it is important to recognize this transaction as a transfer between cash in the bank and an investment in a government security. In the strictest sense, the investment represents an outflow of cash. The purchase of a security with such a short maturity does not, however, involve any significant degree of risk in terms of price changes and thus is not reported on the statement of cash flows as an outflow. Instead, for purposes of classification on the balance sheet and the statement of cash flows, this is merely a transfer *within* the cash and cash equivalents category. The point is that before the purchase of the Treasury bills the company had $10,000 in cash and cash equivalents, and after the purchase it still had $10,000 in cash and cash equivalents. *Because nothing changed, the transaction is not reported on the statement of cash flows.*

Now, assume a different transaction in which a company purchases shares of GM common stock for cash. The effect on the accounting equation of this purchase is as follows:

BALANCE SHEET							INCOME STATEMENT
ASSETS		=	LIABILITIES	+	OWNERS' EQUITY	+	REVENUES − EXPENSES
Investment in GM Common Stock	10,000						
Cash	(10,000)						

This purchase involves a certain amount of risk for the company making the investment. The GM stock is not convertible to a known amount of cash because its market value is subject to change. Thus, for balance sheet purposes, the investment is not considered a cash equivalent and is not therefore combined with cash but is classified as either a trading security or an available-for-sale security, depending on the company's intent in holding the stock (the distinction between these two types was discussed in Chapter 6). In the preparation of a statement of cash flows, the *investment in stock of another company is considered a significant activity and thus is reported on the statement of cash flows.*

Classification of Cash Flows

LO 3 Describe operating, investing, and financing activities, and give examples of each.

For the statement of cash flows, companies are required to classify activities into three categories: operating, investing, or financing. These categories represent the major functions of an entity, and classifying activities in this way allows users to look at important relationships. For example, one important financing activity for many businesses is borrowing money. Grouping the cash inflows from borrowing money during the period with the cash outflows from repayments of loans during the period makes it easier for analysts and other users of the statements to evaluate the company.

Each of the three types of activities can result both in cash inflows and in cash outflows to the company. Thus, the general format for the statement is as shown in Exhibit 12-5. Note the direct tie between the bottom portion of this statement and the balance sheet. The beginning and ending balances in cash and cash equivalents, shown as the last two lines on the statement of cash flows, are taken directly from the comparative balance sheets. Some companies end their statement of cash flows with the figure for the net increase or decrease in cash and cash equivalents and do not report the beginning and ending balances in cash and cash equivalents directly on the statement of cash flows. Instead, the reader must turn to the balance sheet for these amounts. We now take a closer look at the types of activities that appear in each of the three categories on the statement of cash flows.

Operating activities Activities concerned with the acquisition and sale of products and services.

Operating Activities

Operating activities involve acquiring and selling products and services. The specific activities of a business depend on its type. For example, the purchase of raw materials is an important operating activity for a manufacturer. For a retailer, the purchase of inventory from a distributor constitutes an operating activity. For a realty company, the payment of a commission to a salesperson is an operating activity. All three types of businesses sell either products or services, and their sales are important operating activities.

A statement of cash flows reflects the cash effects, either inflows or outflows, associated with each of these activities. For example, the manufacturer's payment for purchases

Exhibit 12-5

Format for the Statement of Cash Flows

THE SMITH CORPORATION STATEMENT OF CASH FLOWS FOR THE YEAR ENDED DECEMBER 31, 2004		
Cash flows from operating activities:		
Inflows	$ xxx	
Outflows	(xxx)	
Net cash provided (used) by operating activities		$xxx
Cash flows from investing activities:		
Inflows	$ xxx	
Outflows	(xxx)	
Net cash provided (used) by investing activities		xxx
Cash flows from financing activities:		
Inflows	$ xxx	
Outflows	(xxx)	
Net cash provided (used) by financing activities		xxx
Net increase (decrease) in cash and cash equivalents		$xxx
Cash and cash equivalents at beginning of year		xxx
Cash and cash equivalents at end of year		$xxx

of raw materials results in a cash outflow. The receipt of cash from collecting an account receivable results in a cash inflow. The income statement reports operating activities on an accrual basis. The statement of cash flows reflects a company's operating activities on a cash basis.

Investing activities Activities concerned with the acquisition and disposal of long-term assets.

Investing Activities **Investing activities** involve acquiring and disposing of long-term assets. Replacing worn-out plant and equipment and expanding the existing base of long-term assets are essential to all businesses. In fact, cash paid for these acquisitions, often called *capital expenditures,* is usually the largest single item in the Investing Activities section of the statement. The following excerpt from IBM's 2002 statement of cash flows (also shown in the chapter opener) indicates that the company spent $4,753 million for 1 plant, rental machines, and other property during 2002 (all amounts are in millions of dollars):

	Cash flow from investing activities from continuing operations:	
1	Payments for plant, rental machines and other property	(4,753)
2	Proceeds from disposition of plant, rental machines and other property	775
	Investment in software	(597)
4	Purchases of marketable securities and other investments	(1,582)
5	Proceeds from disposition of marketable securities and other investments	1,185
6	Divestiture of businesses	1,233
3	Acquisitions of businesses	(3,158)
	Net cash used in investing activities from continuing operations	(6,897)

Sales of long-term assets, such as plant and equipment, are not generally a significant source of cash. These assets are acquired to be used in producing goods and services, or to support this function, rather than to be resold, as is true for inventory. Occasionally, however, plant and equipment may wear out or no longer be needed and are offered for sale. In fact, the excerpt from IBM's report indicates that it generated $775 million of cash in 2002 from 2 disposals of plant, rental machines and other property.

In Chapter 6, we explained why companies sometimes invest in the stocks and bonds of other companies. The classification of these investments on the statement of cash flows depends on the type of investment. The acquisition of one company by another, whether in the form of a merger or a stock acquisition, is an important *investing* activity to bring to the attention of statement readers. IBM spent $3,158 million to 3 acquire other companies during 2002. Note also that in 2002 IBM spent $1,582 million to 4 buy marketable securities and other investments and 5 generated $1,185 million from selling these investments. According to a note to IBM's statements, the company classifies marketable securities as available for sale. Finally, the company 6 generated $1,233 million by selling or divesting of certain businesses during 2002.

Cash flows from purchases, sales, and maturities of held-to-maturity securities (bonds) and available-for-sale securities (stocks and bonds) are classified as *investing* activities. On the other hand, these same types of cash flows for trading securities are classified as *operating* activities. This apparent inconsistency in the accounting rules is based on the idea that trading securities are held for the express purpose of generating short-term profits and thus are operating in nature.

From Concept to Practice 12.1

Reading Winnebago Industries' and Monaco Coach Corporation's Statements of Cash Flows

According to Winnebago Industries' and Monaco Coach Corporation's Investing Activities sections of their statements of cash flows, how much did each company spend in 2002 to acquire property and equipment? What types of expenditures would you expect to find in this category?

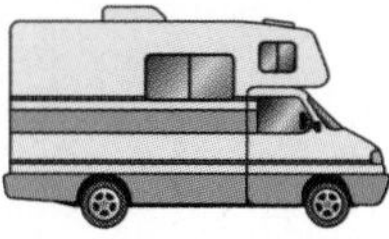

Financing Activities All businesses rely on internal financing, external financing, or a combination of the two in meeting their needs for cash. Initially, a new business must have a certain amount of investment by the owners to begin operations. After this, many companies use notes, bonds, and other forms of debt to provide financing.[2] Issuing stock and various forms of debt results in cash inflows that appear as **financing activities** on the statement of cash flows. On the other side, the repurchase of a company's own stock and the repayment of borrowings are important cash outflows to be reported in the Financing Activities section of the statement. Another important activity listed in the Financing Activities section of the statement is the payment of dividends to stockholders. IBM's 2002 statement of cash flows lists most of the common cash inflows and outflows from financing activities (amounts in millions of dollars):

Financing activities Activities concerned with the raising and repayment of funds in the form of debt and equity.

	Cash flow from financing activities from continuing operations:	
1	Proceeds from new debt	6,726
	Short-term (repayments)/borrowings less than 90 days—net	(4,087)
2	Payments to settle debt	(5,812)
	Common stock transactions—net	(3,087)
	Cash dividends paid	(1,005)
	Net cash used in financing activities from continuing operations	(7,265)

In 2002, IBM 1 received $6,726 million from issuing new debt and 2 paid $5,812 million to retire old debt. In analyzing IBM, you would probably next read the long-term debt note to see whether the company essentially refinanced the old debt with new

Business Strategy

Investing in the Future

As mentioned in the chapter opener, **IBM** completed an important strategic acquisition in 2002 when it bought PwC Consulting. For approximately $3.5 billion, Big Blue acquired the management and consulting services unit of one of the Big Four accounting firms, PricewaterhouseCoopers. For the latter, the sale completed the firm's reorganization plan to divest itself of its consulting unit from regulatory restraints imposed on firms that provide audit services. For IBM, the deal added 30,000 new consulting professionals to a similar number already working for the computer giant.

IBM paid about $2.9 billion of the $3.5 billion price tag for PwC Consulting in cash. Only time will tell whether this heavy investment proves to be wise. However, a glance at IBM's 2002 revenues provides some insight into why the acquisition was made. Of the approximately $81 million of total revenues earned in 2002, nearly 45% of this, or $36 million, came from Global Services. This is the unit of IBM that provides outsourcing, business consulting, and integrated technology services to customers. With the addition of PwC Consulting, IBM doubled the number of professionals working directly with these customers.

In its 2002 annual report, Sam Palmisano, IBM's CEO, talks about "e-business on demand." The concept is that companies can provide products and services to customers "on demand" and in the process convert fixed costs to variable costs and significantly reduce the cost of carrying inventories. IBM hopes to work closely with these customers to implement this concept and views the acquisition of PwC Consulting as a strategic move in this direction. ■

Sources: 2002 IBM Annual Report; "IBM, PricewaterhouseCoopers Complete Sale of PwC Consulting," Press Release, October 2, 2002.

[2]Wm. Wrigley Jr. Company is unusual in this regard in that it relies almost solely on funds generated from stockholders, in the form of common stock, for financing. The company had no short-term notes payable at December 31, 2002, and total long-term liabilities accounted for less than 10% of the total liabilities and stockholders' equity on the balance sheet on that date.

debt at a lower interest rate and, if it did, what the interest saving is, because this will continue to be a benefit for many years.

Summary of the Three Types of Activities To summarize the categorization of the activities of a business as operating, investing, and financing, refer to Exhibit 12-6. The exhibit lists examples of each of the three activities along with the related accounts on the balance sheet and the account classifications on the balance sheet.

Study Tip

Later in the chapter, you will learn a technique to use in preparing the statement of cash flows. Recall the observations made here regarding what types of accounts affect each of the three activities when you get to that section of the chapter.

In the exhibit, operating activities center on the acquisition and sale of products and services and related costs, such as wages and taxes. Two important observations can be made about the cash flow effects from the operating activities of a business. *First, the cash flows from these activities are the cash effects of transactions that enter into the determination of net income.* For example, the sale of a product enters into the calculation of net income. The cash effect of this transaction—that is, the collection of the account receivable—results in a cash inflow from operating activities. *Second, cash flows from operating activities usually relate to an increase or decrease in either a current asset or a current liability.* For example, the payment of taxes to the government results in a decrease in taxes payable, which is a current liability on the balance sheet.

Note that investing activities normally relate to long-term assets on the balance sheet. For example, the purchase of new plant and equipment increases long-term assets, and the sale of these same assets reduces long-term assets on the balance sheet.

Finally, *note that financing activities usually relate to either long-term liabilities or stockholders' equity accounts.* There are exceptions to these observations about the type of balance sheet account involved with each of the three types of activities, but these rules of thumb are useful as we begin to analyze transactions and attempt to determine their classification on the statement of cash flows.

Exhibit 12-6 Classification of Items on the Statement of Cash Flows

ACTIVITY	EXAMPLES	EFFECT ON CASH	RELATED BALANCE SHEET ACCOUNT	CLASSIFICATION ON BALANCE SHEET
Operating	Collection of customer accounts	Inflow	Accounts receivable	Current asset
	Payment to suppliers for inventory	Outflow	Accounts payable	Current liability
			Inventory	Current asset
	Payment of wages	Outflow	Wages payable	Current liability
	Payment of taxes	Outflow	Taxes payable	Current liability
Investing	Capital expenditures	Outflow	Plant and equipment	Long-term asset
	Purchase of another company	Outflow	Long-term investment	Long-term asset
	Sale of plant and equipment	Inflow	Plant and equipment	Long-term asset
	Sale of another company	Inflow	Long-term investment	Long-term asset
Financing	Issuance of capital stock	Inflow	Capital stock	Stockholders' equity
	Issuance of bonds	Inflow	Bonds payable	Long-term liability
	Issuance of bank note	Inflow	Notes payable	Long-term liability
	Repurchase of stock	Outflow	Treasury stock	Stockholders' equity
	Retirement of bonds	Outflow	Bonds payable	Long-term liability
	Repayment of notes	Outflow	Notes payable	Long-term liability
	Payment of dividends	Outflow	Retained earnings	Stockholders' equity

Two Methods of Reporting Cash Flow from Operating Activities

INTERNAL DECISION

Companies use one of two different methods to report the amount of cash flow from operating activities. The first approach, called the **direct method,** involves reporting major classes of gross cash receipts and cash payments. For example, cash collected from customers is reported separately from any interest and dividends received. Each of the major types of cash payments related to the company's operations follows, such as cash paid for inventory, for salaries and wages, for interest, and for taxes. An acceptable alternative to this approach is the **indirect method.** Under the indirect method, net cash flow from operating activities is computed by adjusting net income to remove the effect of all deferrals of past operating cash receipts and payments and all accruals of future operating cash receipts and payments.

LO 4 Describe the difference between the direct and the indirect methods of computing cash flow from operating activities.

Direct method For preparing the Operating Activities section of the statement of cash flows, the approach in which cash receipts and cash payments are reported.

Indirect method For preparing the Operating Activities section of the statement of cash flows, the approach in which net income is reconciled to net cash flow from operations.

Although the direct method is preferred by the Financial Accounting Standards Board, it is used much less frequently than the indirect method in practice. In fact, an annual survey of 600 companies reported that 592 companies used the indirect method and only 8 companies used the direct method.[3]

To compare and contrast the two methods, assume that Boulder Company begins operations as a corporation on January 1, 2004, with the owners' investment of $10,000 in cash. An income statement for 2004 and a balance sheet as of December 31, 2004, are presented in Exhibits 12-7 and 12-8, respectively.

Direct Method To report cash flow from operating activities under the direct method, we look at each of the items on the income statement and determine how much cash each of these activities either generated or used. For example, revenues for the period were $80,000. Since the balance sheet at the end of the period shows a balance in Accounts Receivable of $13,000, however, Boulder collected only $80,000 − $13,000,

Exhibit 12-7

Boulder Company Income Statement

BOULDER COMPANY
INCOME STATEMENT
FOR THE YEAR ENDED DECEMBER 31, 2004

Revenues	$80,000
Operating expenses	(64,000)
Income before tax	$16,000
Income tax expense	(4,000)
Net income	$12,000

Exhibit 12-8

Boulder Company Balance Sheet

BOULDER COMPANY
BALANCE SHEET
AS OF DECEMBER 31, 2004

Assets		Liabilities and Stockholders' Equity	
Cash	$15,000	Accounts payable	$ 6,000
Accounts receivable	13,000	Capital stock	10,000
		Retained earnings	12,000
Total	$28,000	Total	$28,000

or $67,000, from its sales of the period. Thus, the first line on the statement of cash flows in Exhibit 12-9 reports $67,000 in cash collected from customers. Remember that the *net increase* in Accounts Receivable must be deducted from sales to find cash collected. For a new company, this is the same as the ending balance because the company starts the year without a balance in Accounts Receivable.

The same logic can be applied to determine the amount of cash expended for operating purposes. Operating expenses on the income statement are reported at $64,000. According to the balance sheet, however, $6,000 of the expense is unpaid at the end of the period as evidenced by the balance in Accounts Payable. Thus, the amount of cash expended for operating purposes as reported on the statement of cash flows in Exhibit

[3] *Accounting Trends & Techniques*, 56th ed. (New York: American Institute of Certified Public Accountants, 2002).

Exhibit 12-9

Statement of Cash Flows Using the Direct Method

BOULDER COMPANY STATEMENT OF CASH FLOWS FOR THE YEAR ENDED DECEMBER 31, 2004	
Cash flows from operating activities	
Cash collected from customers	$ 67,000
Cash payments for operating purposes	(58,000)
Cash payments for taxes	(4,000)
Net cash inflow from operating activities	$ 5,000
Cash flows from financing activities	
Issuance of capital stock	$ 10,000
Net increase in cash	$ 15,000
Cash balance, beginning of period	–0–
Cash balance, end of period	$ 15,000

12-9 is $64,000 − $6,000, or $58,000. The other cash payment in the Operating Activities section of the statement is $4,000 for income taxes. Because no liability for income taxes is reported on the balance sheet, we know that $4,000 represents both the income tax expense of the period and the amount paid to the government. The only other item on the statement of cash flows in Exhibit 12-9 is the cash inflow from financing activities for the amount of cash invested by the owner in return for capital stock.

Indirect Method When the indirect method is used, the first line in the Operating Activities section of the statement of cash flows as shown in Exhibit 12-10 is the net income of the period. Net income is then *adjusted* to reconcile it to the amount of cash provided by operating activities. As reported on the income statement, this net income figure includes the sales of $80,000 for the period. As we know, however, the amount of cash collected was $13,000 less than this because not all customers paid Boulder the amount due. *The increase in Accounts Receivable for the period is deducted from net income on the statement because the increase indicates that the company sold more during the period than it collected in cash.*

The logic for the addition of the increase in Accounts Payable is similar, although the effect is the opposite. The amount of operating expenses deducted on the income statement was $64,000. We know, however, that the amount of cash paid was $6,000 less than this, as the balance in Accounts Payable indicates. *The increase in Accounts Payable for the period is added back to net income on the statement because the increase indicates that the company paid less during the period than it recognized in expense on the income statement.* One observation can be noted about this example. Because this is the first

Exhibit 12-10

Statement of Cash Flows Using the Indirect Method

BOULDER COMPANY STATEMENT OF CASH FLOWS FOR THE YEAR ENDED DECEMBER 31, 2004	
Cash flows from operating activities	
Net income	$ 12,000
Adjustments to reconcile net income to net cash from operating activities:	
Increase in accounts receivable	(13,000)
Increase in accounts payable	6,000
Net cash inflow from operating activities	$ 5,000
Cash flows from financing activities	
Issuance of capital stock	$ 10,000
Net increase in cash	$ 15,000
Cash balance, beginning of period	–0–
Cash balance, end of period	$ 15,000

year of operations for Boulder, we wouldn't be too concerned that accounts receivable is increasing faster than accounts payable. If this becomes a trend, however, we would try to improve the accounts receivable collections process.

Two important observations should be made in comparing the two methods illustrated in Exhibits 12-9 and 12-10. First, the amount of cash provided by operating activities is the same under the two methods: $5,000; the two methods are simply different computational approaches to arrive at the cash generated from operations. Second, the remainder of the statement of cash flows is the same, regardless of which method is used. The only difference between the two methods is in the Operating Activities section of the statement.

From Concept to Practice 12.2

Reading IBM's Statement of Cash Flows

Does IBM use the direct or the indirect method in the Operating Activities section of its statement of cash flows? How can you tell which it is?

Noncash Investing and Financing Activities

Occasionally, companies engage in important investing and financing activities that do not affect cash. For example, assume that at the end of the year Wolk Corp. issues capital stock to an inventor in return for the exclusive rights to a patent. Although the patent has no ready market value, the stock could have been sold on the open market for $25,000. The effect on the accounting equation of this transaction is as follows:

BALANCE SHEET								INCOME STATEMENT
ASSETS		=	LIABILITIES	+	OWNERS' EQUITY		+	REVENUES – EXPENSES
Patent	25,000				Capital Stock	25,000		

This transaction does not involve cash and is therefore not reported on the statement of cash flows. However, what if we changed the scenario slightly? Assume that Wolk wants the patent but the inventor is not willing to accept stock in return for it. So instead Wolk sells stock on the open market for $25,000 and then pays this amount in cash to the inventor for the rights to the patent. Consider the effects on the accounting equation of these two transactions. First, the sale of stock increases Cash and Owners' Equity:

BALANCE SHEET								INCOME STATEMENT
ASSETS		=	LIABILITIES	+	OWNERS' EQUITY		+	REVENUES – EXPENSES
Cash	25,000				Capital Stock	25,000		

Next, the acquisition of the patent has the following effect:

BALANCE SHEET								INCOME STATEMENT
ASSETS		=	LIABILITIES	+	OWNERS' EQUITY		+	REVENUES – EXPENSES
Patent	25,000							
Cash	(25,000)							

How would each of these two transactions be reported on a statement of cash flows? The first transaction appears as a cash inflow in the Financing Activities section of the statement; the second is reported as a cash outflow in the Investing Activities section. The point is that even though the *form* of this arrangement (with stock sold for cash and then the cash paid to the inventor) differs from the form of the first arrangement (with stock exchanged directly for the patent), the *substance* of the two arrangements is the same. That is, both involve a significant financing activity, the issuance of stock, and an important investing activity, the acquisition of a patent. Because the substance is what matters, accounting standards require that any significant noncash transactions be reported either in a separate schedule or in a note to the financial statements. For our transaction in which stock was issued directly to the inventor, presentation in a schedule is as follows:

Supplemental schedule of noncash investing and financing activities	
Acquisition of patent in exchange for capital stock	$25,000

To this point, we have concentrated on the purpose of a statement of cash flows and the major reporting requirements related to it. We turn our attention next to a methodology to use in actually preparing the statement.

Two-Minute Review

1. *What are cash equivalents, and why are any increases or decreases in them not reported on a statement of cash flows?*
2. *What are the three types of activities reported on a statement of cash flows?*
3. *What are the two methods of reporting cash flow from operating activities, and how do they differ?*

Answers on page 623.

HOW THE STATEMENT OF CASH FLOWS IS PUT TOGETHER

Two interesting observations can be made about the statement of cash flows. First, the "answer" to a statement of cash flows is known before we start to prepare it. That is, the change in cash for the period is known by comparing two successive balance sheets. Thus, it is not the change in cash itself that is emphasized on the statement of cash flows but the *explanations* for the change in cash. That is, each item on a statement of cash flows helps to explain why cash changed by the amount it did during the period. The second important observation about the statement of cash flows relates even more specifically to how we prepare it. Both an income statement and a balance sheet are prepared simply by taking the balances in each of the various accounts in the general ledger and putting them in the right place on the right statement. This is not true for the statement of cash flows, however. Instead, it is necessary to analyze the transactions during the period and attempt to (1) determine which of these affected cash and (2) classify each of the cash effects into one of the three categories.

In the simple examples presented so far in the chapter, we prepared the statement of cash flows without the use of any special tools. In more complex situations, however, some type of methodology is needed. We first will review the basic accounting equation and then illustrate a systematic approach for preparing the statement. The chapter appendix presents a work-sheet approach to the preparation of the statement of cash flows.

The Accounting Equation and the Statement of Cash Flows

The basic accounting equation is as follows:

Assets = Liabilities + Owners' Equity

Next, consider this refinement of the equation:

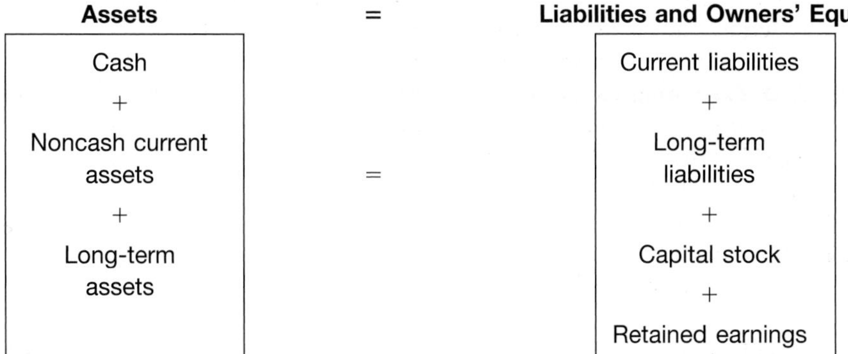

The equation can be rearranged so that only cash is on the left side and all other items are on the right side:

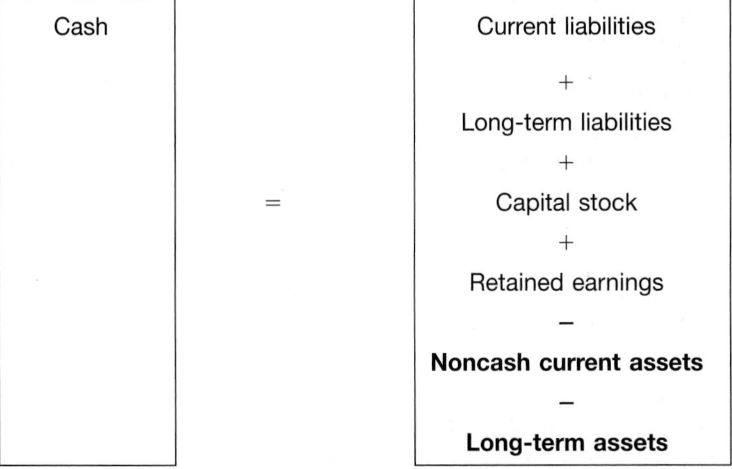

Cash
=
Current liabilities
+
Long-term liabilities
+
Capital stock
+
Retained earnings
−
Noncash current assets
−
Long-term assets

Therefore, any changes in cash must be accompanied by a corresponding change in the right side of the equation. For example, an increase or inflow of cash could result from an *increase* in long-term liabilities in the form of issuing bonds payable, an important financing activity for many companies. Or an increase in cash could come from a *decrease* in long-term assets in the form of a sale of fixed assets. The various possibilities for inflows (+) and outflows (−) of cash can be summarized by activity as follows:

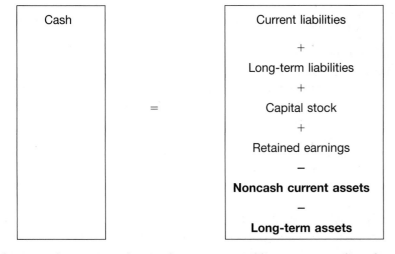

ACTIVITY	LEFT SIDE	RIGHT SIDE	EXAMPLE
Operating			
	+ Cash	− Noncash current assets	Collect accounts receivable
	− Cash	+ Noncash current assets	Prepay insurance
	+ Cash	+ Current liabilities	Collect customer's deposit
	− Cash	− Current liabilities	Pay suppliers
	+ Cash	+ Retained earnings	Make a cash sale
Investing			
	+ Cash	− Long-term assets	Sell equipment
	− Cash	+ Long-term assets	Buy equipment
Financing			
	+ Cash	+ Long-term liabilities	Issue bonds
	− Cash	− Long-term liabilities	Retire bonds
	+ Cash	+ Capital stock	Issue capital stock
	− Cash	− Capital stock	Buy capital stock
	− Cash	− Retained earnings	Pay dividends

By considering these examples we see that inflows and outflows of cash relate to increases and decreases in the various balance sheet accounts. We now turn to analyzing these accounts as a way to assemble a statement of cash flows.

Preparing the Statement of Cash Flows: Direct Method

LO 5 Prepare a statement of cash flows, using the direct method to determine cash flow from operating activities.

The following steps can be used to prepare a statement of cash flows:

1. **Set up three schedules with the following headings:**
   a. Cash Flows from Operating Activities
   b. Cash Flows from Investing Activities
   c. Cash Flows from Financing Activities

   As we analyze the transactions that affect each of the noncash balance sheet accounts, any cash effects are entered on the appropriate master account. When completed, the three schedules contain all of the information needed to prepare a statement of cash flows.
2. **Determine the cash flows from operating activities.** Generally, this requires analyzing each item on the *income statement* and the *current asset* and *current liability* accounts. As cash flows are identified in this analysis, they are entered on the schedule of cash flows from operating activities.
3. **Determine the cash flows from investing activities.** Generally, this requires analyzing the *long-term asset* accounts and any additional information provided. As cash flows are identified in this analysis, they are entered on the schedule of cash flows from investing activities. Any significant noncash activities are entered on a supplemental schedule.
4. **Determine the cash flows from financing activities.** Generally, this requires analyzing the *long-term liability* and *stockholders' equity* accounts and any additional information provided. As cash flows are identified in this analysis, they are entered on the schedule of cash flows from investing activities. Any significant noncash activities are entered on a supplemental schedule.

Remember that these are general rules that the cash effects of changes in current accounts are reported in the operating section, those relating to long-term asset accounts in the investing section, and those relating to long-term liabilities and stockholders' equity in the financing section. The general rules for classification of activities have a few exceptions, but we will not concern ourselves with them.

To illustrate this approach, we will refer to the income statement in Exhibit 12-11 and to the comparative balance sheets and the additional information provided for Julian Corp. in Exhibit 12-12.

Exhibit 12-11
Julian Corp. Income Statement

JULIAN CORP.
INCOME STATEMENT
FOR THE YEAR ENDED DECEMBER 31, 2004

Revenues and gains:		
Sales revenue	$670,000	
Interest revenue	15,000	
Gain on sale of machine	5,000	
Total revenues and gains		$690,000
Expenses and losses:		
Cost of goods sold	$390,000	
Salaries and wages	60,000	
Depreciation	40,000	
Insurance	12,000	
Interest	15,000	
Income taxes	50,000	
Loss on retirement of bonds	3,000	
Total expenses and losses		570,000
Net income		$120,000

Exhibit 12-12

Julian Corp. Comparative Balance Sheets

JULIAN CORP.
COMPARATIVE BALANCE SHEETS

	December 31	
	2004	**2003**
Cash	$ 35,000	$ 46,000
Accounts receivable	63,000	57,000
Inventory	84,000	92,000
Prepaid insurance	12,000	18,000
Total current assets	$194,000	$213,000
Long-term investments	$120,000	$ 90,000
Land	150,000	100,000
Property and equipment	320,000	280,000
Accumulated depreciation	(100,000)	(75,000)
Total long-term assets	$490,000	$395,000
Total assets	$684,000	$608,000
Accounts payable	$ 38,000	$ 31,000
Salaries and wages payable	7,000	9,000
Income taxes payable	8,000	5,000
Total current liabilities	$ 53,000	$ 45,000
Notes payable	$ 85,000	$ 35,000
Bonds payable	200,000	260,000
Total long-term liabilities	$285,000	$295,000
Capital stock	$100,000	$ 75,000
Retained earnings	246,000	193,000
Total stockholders' equity	$346,000	$268,000
Total liabilities and stockholders' equity	$684,000	$608,000

Additional Information

1. Long-term investments were purchased for $30,000. The securities are classified as available for sale.
2. Land was purchased by issuing a $50,000 note payable.
3. Equipment was purchased for $75,000.
4. A machine with an original cost of $35,000 and a book value of $20,000 was sold for $25,000.
5. Bonds with a face value of $60,000 were retired by paying $63,000 in cash.
6. Capital stock was issued in exchange for $25,000 in cash.
7. Dividends of $67,000 were paid.

Determine the Cash Flows from Operating Activities To do this, we need to consider each of the items on the income statement and any related current assets or liabilities from the balance sheet.

Sales Revenue and Accounts Receivable Sales as reported on the income statement in Exhibit 12-11 amounted to $670,000.

Based on the beginning and ending balances in Exhibit 12-12, Accounts Receivable increased during the year by $6,000, from $57,000 to $63,000. *This indicates that Julian had $6,000 more in sales to its customers than it collected in cash from them* (assuming that all sales are on credit). Thus, cash collections must have been $670,000 − $6,000, or $664,000. Another way to look at this is as follows:

Beginning accounts receivable	$ 57,000
+ Sales revenue	670,000
− Cash collections	(*X*)
= Ending accounts receivable	$ 63,000

Solving for X, we can find cash collections:

$$57{,}000 + 670{,}000 - X = 63{,}000$$
$$X = \underline{\underline{664{,}000}}$$

At this point, note the inflow of Cash for $664,000 as shown in the Schedule of Cash Flows from Operating Activities, in Exhibit 12-13.

Exhibit 12-13

Schedule of Cash Flows from Operating Activities

Cash Flows from Operating Activities	
Cash receipts from:	
Sales on account	664,000
Interest	15,000
Cash payments for:	
Inventory purchases	(375,000)
Salaries and wages	(62,000)
Insurance	(6,000)
Interest	(15,000)
Taxes	(47,000)

Interest Revenue Julian reported interest revenue on the income statement of $15,000. Did the company actually receive this amount of cash, or was it merely an accrual of revenue earned but not yet received? The answer can be found by examining the Current Assets section of the balance sheet. *Because there is no Interest Receivable account, the amount of interest earned was the amount of cash received.*

The cash received should be entered in the Schedule of Cash Flows from Operating Activities, as shown in Exhibit 12-13.

Gain on Sale of Machine A gain on the sale of machine of $5,000 is reported as the next line on the income statement. Any cash received from the sale of a long-term asset is reported in the Investing Activities section of the statement of cash flows. Thus, we ignore the gain when reporting cash flows from operating activities under the direct method.

Cost of Goods Sold, Inventory, and Accounts Payable Cost of goods sold, as reported on the income statement, amounts to $390,000. Recall that $390,000 is not the amount of cash expended to pay suppliers of inventory. First, cost of goods sold represents the cost of the inventory sold during the period, not the amount purchased. Thus, we must analyze the Inventory account to determine the purchases of the period. Second, the amount of purchases is not the same as the cash paid to suppliers, because purchases are normally on account. Thus, we must analyze the Accounts Payable account to determine the cash payments.

Based on the beginning and ending balances from Exhibit 12-12, inventory decreased during the year by $8,000 from $92,000 to $84,000. *This means that the cost of inventory sold was $8,000 more than the purchases of the period.* Thus, purchases must have been $390,000 − $8,000, or $382,000. Another way to look at this is as follows:

	Beginning inventory	$ 92,000
+	Purchases	X
−	Cost of goods sold	(390,000)
=	Ending inventory	$ 84,000

Solving for X, we can find purchases:

$$92{,}000 + X - 390{,}000 = 84{,}000$$
$$X = \underline{\underline{382{,}000}}$$

Note from Exhibit 12-12 that Accounts Payable increased during the year by $7,000, from $31,000 to $38,000. *This means that Julian's purchases were $7,000 more during the period than its cash payments.* Also, recall that we determined earlier that purchases were $382,000. Thus, cash payments must have been $382,000 − $7,000, or $375,000. Another way to look at this is as follows:

Beginning accounts payable	$ 31,000
+ Purchases	382,000
− Cash payments	(*X*)
= Ending accounts payable	$ 38,000

Solving for *X*, we can find cash payments:

$$31{,}000 + 382{,}000 - X = 38{,}000$$
$$X = \underline{\underline{375{,}000}}$$

At this point, we indicate in the schedule in Exhibit 12-13 that the cash payments for inventory total $375,000.

Salaries and Wages Expense and Salaries and Wages Payable The second expense listed on the income statement in Exhibit 12-11 is salaries and wages of $60,000. However, did Julian *pay* this amount to employees during the year? The answer can be found by examining the Salaries and Wages Payable account in the balance sheet in Exhibit 12-12. From the balance sheet, we note that the liability account decreased by $2,000, from $9,000 to $7,000. *This means that the amount of cash paid to employees was $2,000 more than the amount of expense accrued.* Another way to look at the cash payments of $60,000 + $2,000, or $62,000, is as follows:

Beginning salaries and wages payable	$ 9,000
+ Salaries and wages expense	60,000
− Cash payments to employees	(*X*)
= Ending salaries and wages payable	$ 7,000

Solving for *X*, we can find cash payments:

$$9{,}000 + 60{,}000 - X = 7{,}000$$
$$X = \underline{\underline{62{,}000}}$$

As you see in Exhibit 12-13, cash paid of $62,000 appears as a cash outflow in the Schedule of Cash Flows from Operating Activities.

Depreciation Expense The next item on the income statement is depreciation of $40,000. Depreciation of tangible long-term assets, amortization of intangible assets, and depletion of natural resources are different from most other expenses in that they have no effect on cash flow. The only related cash flows are from the purchase and the sale of these long-term assets, and these are reported in the Investing Activities section of the statement of cash flows. Thus, depreciation is not reflected on the Schedule of Cash Flows from Operating Activities when the direct method is used as in Exhibit 12-13.

Insurance Expense and Prepaid Insurance According to the income statement in Exhibit 12-11, Julian recorded Insurance Expense of $12,000 during 2004. This amount is not the cash payments for insurance, however, because Julian has a Prepaid Insurance account on the balance sheet. Recall from Chapter 4 that as a company buys insurance, it increases its Prepaid Insurance account. As the insurance expires, this account is reduced and an expense is recognized. Note from the balance sheets in Exhibit 12-12 that the Prepaid Insurance account decreased during the year by $6,000, from $18,000 to $12,000. *This means that the amount of cash paid for insurance was $6,000 less than the amount of expense recognized.* Thus, the cash payments must have been $12,000 − $6,000, or $6,000. Another way to look at the cash payments is as follows:

Accounting for Your Decisions

You Are an Entrepreneur

You operate a coffee cart in the lobby of an office building. You started the business this year by investing $5,000 of your own money to buy the coffee cart. Even though you think the cart will last for five years, a friend who has studied accounting has advised you to recognize the entire cost of the cart as an expense the first year. He reasons that "the first year is very crucial to any business and since depreciation is added back in the Operating Activities section of the statement of cash flows, why not add back the maximum amount so that you will maximize the cash flow from operations?" Is your friend's reasoning sound?

ANS: Your friend is correct in stating that depreciation is added back in the Operating Activities section, assuming use of the indirect method. The only reason that depreciation is added back, however, is because it was deducted as an expense on the income statement but does not use any cash. Depreciation is not a cash flow, and any manipulation of the amount of depreciation expensed in any one year will not affect the amount of cash generated from operations.

Beginning prepaid insurance	$18,000
+ Cash payments for insurance	*X*
− Insurance expense	(12,000)
= Ending prepaid insurance	$12,000

Solving for *X*, we can find the amount of cash paid:

$$18{,}000 + X - 12{,}000 = 12{,}000$$
$$X = \underline{\underline{6{,}000}}$$

Note the cash outflow of $6,000 as entered in Exhibit 12-13 of the Schedule of Cash Flows from Operating Activities.

Interest Expense The amount of interest expense reported on the income statement is $15,000. Because the balance sheet does not report an accrual of interest owed but not yet paid (an Interest Payable account), we know that $15,000 is also the amount of cash paid. The schedule in Exhibit 12-13 reflects the cash outflow of $15,000 for interest. Whether interest paid is properly classified as an operating activity is subject to considerable debate. The Financial Accounting Standards Board decided in favor of classification of *interest* as an *operating* activity because, unlike dividends, it appears on the income statement. This, it was argued, provides a direct link between the statement of cash flows and the income statement. Many argue, however, that it is inconsistent to classify dividends paid as a financing activity but interest paid as an operating activity. After all, both represent returns paid to providers of capital: interest to creditors and dividends to stockholders.

Income Tax Expense and Income Taxes Payable The income statement in Exhibit 12-11 reports income tax expense of $50,000. We know, however, that this is not necessarily the amount paid to the government during the year. In fact, note the increase in the Income Taxes Payable account on the balance sheets in Exhibit 12-12. The liability increased by $3,000, from $5,000 to $8,000. *This means that the amount of cash paid to the government in taxes was $3,000 less than the amount of expense accrued.* Another way to look at the cash payments of $50,000 − $3,000, or $47,000, is as follows:

Beginning income taxes payable	$ 5,000
+ Income tax expense	50,000
− Cash payments for taxes	(*X*)
= Ending income taxes payable	$ 8,000

Solving for X, we can find the amount of cash paid:

$$5{,}000 + 50{,}000 - X = 8{,}000$$
$$X = \underline{\underline{47{,}000}}$$

As you see by examining Exhibit 12-13, the cash payments for taxes is the last item on the Schedule of Cash Flows from Operating Activities.

Loss on Retirement of Bonds A $3,000 loss on the retirement of bonds is reported as the last item under expenses and losses on the income statement in Exhibit 12-11. Any cash paid to retire a long-term liability is reported in the Financing Activities section of the statement of cash flows. Thus, we ignore the loss when reporting cash flows from operating activities under the direct method.

Compare Net Income with Net Cash Flow from Operating Activities

At this point, all of the items on the income statement have been analyzed, as have all of the current asset and current liability accounts. All of the information needed to prepare the Operating Activities section of your statement of cash flows has been gathered.

To summarize, the preparation of the Operating Activities section of the statement of cash flows requires the conversion of each item on the income statement to a cash basis. The current asset and current liability accounts are analyzed to discover the cash effects of each item on the income statement. Exhibit 12-14 summarizes this conversion process.

Note in the exhibit the various adjustments made to put each income statement item on a cash basis. For example, the $6,000 increase in accounts receivable for the period is deducted from sales revenue of $670,000 to arrive at cash collected from customers. Similar adjustments are made to each of the other income statement items with the exception of depreciation, the gain, and the loss. Depreciation is ignored because it does not have an effect on cash flow. The gain relates to the sale of a long-term asset, and any cash effect is reflected in the Investing Activities section of the statement of cash flows. Similarly, the loss resulted from the retirement of bonds, and any cash flow effect is reported in the Financing Activities section. The bottom of the exhibit highlights an important point: Julian reported net income of $120,000 but actually generated $174,000 in cash from operations.

Determine the Cash Flows from Investing Activities At this point, we turn our attention to the long-term asset accounts and any additional information available about these accounts. Julian has three long-term assets on its balance sheet: Long-Term Investments, Land, and Property and Equipment.

Long-Term Investments Item 1 in the additional information in Exhibit 12-12 indicates that Julian purchased $30,000 of investments during the year. The $30,000 net increase in the Long-Term Investments account from $90,000 to $120,000 confirms this (no mention is made of the sale of any investments during 2004). The purchase of investments required the use of $30,000 of cash, as indicated on the Schedule of Cash Flows from Investing Activities in Exhibit 12-15 on page 615.

Land Note from the balance sheets in Exhibit 12-12 the $50,000 net increase in land, from $100,000 to $150,000. Item 2 in the additional information indicates that Julian purchased land by issuing a $50,000 note payable. This transaction obviously does not involve cash. It does have both an important financing element and an investing component, however. The issuance of the note is a financing activity, and the acquisition of land is an investing activity. Because no cash was involved, the transaction is reported in a separate schedule instead of directly on the statement of cash flows:

Supplemental schedule of noncash investing and financing activities	
Acquisition of land in exchange for note payable	$50,000

Property and Equipment Property and equipment increased by $40,000 during 2004. However, Julian both acquired equipment and sold a machine (items 3 and 4 in the additional information). As we discussed earlier in the chapter, acquisitions of new plant and equipment are important investing activities for most businesses. Thus, the

Exhibit 12-14 Conversion of Income Statement Items to Cash Basis

INCOME STATEMENT	AMOUNT	ADJUSTMENTS	CASH FLOWS
Sales revenue	$670,000		$670,000
		+ Decreases in accounts receivable	–0–
		− Increases in accounts receivable	(6,000)
		Cash collected from customers	$664,000
Interest revenue	15,000		$ 15,000
		+ Decreases in interest receivable	–0–
		− Increases in interest receivable	–0–
		Cash collected in interest	$ 15,000
Gain on sale of machine	5,000	*Not an operating activity*	$ –0–
Cost of goods sold	390,000		$390,000
		+ Increases in inventory	–0–
		− Decreases in inventory	(8,000)
		+ Decreases in accounts payable	–0–
		− Increases in accounts payable	(7,000)
		Cash paid to suppliers	$375,000
Salaries and wages	60,000		$ 60,000
		+ Decreases in salaries/wages payable	2,000
		− Increases in salaries/wages payable	–0–
		Cash paid to employees	$ 62,000
Depreciation	40,000	*No cash flow effect*	$ –0–
Insurance	12,000		$ 12,000
		+ Increases in prepaid insurance	–0–
		− Decreases in prepaid insurance	(6,000)
		Cash paid for insurance	$ 6,000
Interest	15,000		$ 15,000
		+ Decreases in interest payable	–0–
		− Increases in interest payable	–0–
		Cash paid for interest	$ 15,000
Income taxes	50,000		$ 50,000
		+ Decreases in income taxes payable	–0–
		− Increases in income taxes payable	(3,000)
		Cash paid for taxes	$ 47,000
Loss on retirement of bonds	3,000	*Not an operating activity*	$ –0–
Net income	$120,000	Net cash flow from operating activities	$174,000

$75,000 expended to acquire new property and equipment appears in the schedule in Exhibit 12-15 as a cash outflow.

As reported in the balance sheets in Exhibit 12-12, the Property and Equipment account increased during the year by only $40,000, from $280,000 to $320,000. Since Julian *added* to this account $75,000, however, we know that it must have *disposed* of some assets as well. In fact, item 4 in the additional information in Exhibit 12-12 reports the sale of a machine with an original cost of $35,000. An analysis of the Property and Equipment account at this point confirms this amount:

	Beginning property and equipment	$280,000
+	Acquisitions	75,000
−	Disposals	(*X*)
=	Ending property and equipment	$320,000

Solving for X, we can find the *cost* of the fixed assets sold during the year:

$$280{,}000 + 75{,}000 - X = 320{,}000$$
$$X = \underline{\underline{\$35{,}000}}$$

The additional information also indicates that the book value of the machine sold was $20,000. This means that if the original cost was $35,000 and the book value was $20,000, the Accumulated Depreciation on the machine sold must have been $35,000 − $20,000, or $15,000. An analysis similar to the one we just looked at for Property and Equipment confirms this amount:

	Beginning accumulated depreciation	$ 75,000
+	Depreciation expense (entry i)	40,000
−	Accumulated depreciation on assets sold	(X)
=	Ending accumulated depreciation	$100,000

Solving for X, we can find the accumulated depreciation on the assets disposed of during the year:

$$75{,}000 + 40{,}000 - X = 100{,}000$$
$$X = \underline{\underline{\$15{,}000}}$$

Finally, we are told in the additional information that the machine was sold for $25,000. *If the selling price was $25,000 and the book value was $20,000, Julian reports a gain on sale of $5,000, an amount that is confirmed on the income statement in Exhibit 12-11.* To summarize, the machine was sold for $25,000, an amount that exceeded its book value of $20,000, thus generating a gain of $5,000. The cash inflow of $25,000 is entered on the Schedule of Cash Flows from Investing Activities in Exhibit 12-15.

Exhibit 12-15

Schedule of Cash Flows from Investing Activities

Cash Flows from Investing Activities	
Cash inflows from:	
Sale of machine	25,000
Cash outflows for:	
Purchase of investments	(30,000)
Purchase of property and equipment	(75,000)

Determine the Cash Flows from Financing Activities These activities generally involve long-term liabilities and stockholders' equity. We first consider Julian's two long-term liabilities, Notes Payable and Bonds Payable, and then the two stockholders' equity accounts: Capital Stock and Retained Earnings.

Notes Payable Recall that item 2 in the additional information reported that Julian purchased land in exchange for a $50,000 note payable. This amount is confirmed on the balance sheets, which show an increase in notes payable of $50,000, from $35,000 to $85,000. In our discussion of investing activities, we already entered this transaction on a supplemental schedule of noncash activities because it was a significant financing activity but did not involve cash.

Bonds Payable The balance sheets in Exhibit 12-12 report a decrease in bonds payable of $60,000, from $260,000 to $200,000. Item 5 in the additional information in Exhibit 12-12 indicates that bonds with a face value of $60,000 were retired by paying $63,000 in cash. The book value of the bonds retired is the same as the face value of $60,000 because there is no unamortized discount or premium on the records. *When a company has to pay more in cash ($63,000) to settle a debt than the book value of the debt*

($60,000), it reports a loss. In this case, the loss is $3,000, as reported on the income statement in Exhibit 12-11. For purposes of preparing a statement of cash flows with the direct method, however, the important amount is the $63,000 in cash paid to retire the bonds. This amount appears as a cash outflow in the Schedule of Cash Flows from Financing Activities in Exhibit 12-16.

Exhibit 12-16

Schedule of Cash Flows from Financing Activities

Cash Flows from Financing Activities	
Cash inflows from:	
Issuance of stock	25,000
Cash outflows for:	
Retirement of bonds	(63,000)
Payment of cash dividends	(67,000)

Capital Stock Exhibit 12-12 indicates an increase in capital stock of $25,000, from $75,000 to $100,000. Julian issued capital stock in exchange for $25,000 in cash, according to item 6 in the additional information in Exhibit 12-12. Some companies issue additional stock after the initial formation of a corporation to raise needed capital. The increase in Cash from this issuance is presented as a cash inflow in the Schedule of Cash Flows from Financing Activities, as shown in Exhibit 12-16.

Retained Earnings This account increased during the year by $53,000, from $193,000 to $246,000. Because we know from Exhibit 12-11 that net income was $120,000, however, the company must have declared some dividends. We can determine the amount of cash dividends for 2004 in the following manner:

Beginning retained earnings	$193,000
+ Net income	120,000
− Cash dividends	(*X*)
= Ending retained earnings	$246,000

Solving for *X*, we can find the amount of cash dividends paid during the year:[4]

$$193{,}000 + 120{,}000 - X = 246{,}000$$

$$X = \underline{\underline{\$67{,}000}}$$

Accounting for Your Decisions

You Decide for Your Investment Club

You are a member of an investment club and have been given the assignment of analyzing the statements of cash flows for the Norfolk Corp. for the last three years. The company has neither issued nor retired any stock during this time period. You notice that the company's cash balance has increased steadily during this period but that a majority of the increase is due to a large net inflow of cash from financing activities in each of the three years. Should you be concerned?

ANS: The net inflow of cash from financing activities indicates that the company is borrowing more than it is repaying. Certainly borrowing can be an attractive means of financing the purchase of new plant and equipment. At some point, however, the debt, along with interest, will need to be repaid. The company must be able to generate sufficient cash from its operations to make these payments.

[4]Any decrease in Retained Earnings represents the dividends *declared* during the period rather than the amount paid. If there had been a Dividends Payable account, we would analyze it to find the amount of dividends paid. The lack of a balance in such an account at either the beginning or the end of the period tells us that Julian paid the same amount of dividends that it declared during the period.

Item 7 in the additional information confirms that this was in fact the amount of dividends paid during the year. The dividends paid appear in the Schedule of Cash Flows from Financing Activities, as presented in Exhibit 12-16.

Using the Three Schedules to Prepare a Statement of Cash Flows

All of the information needed to prepare a statement of cash flows is now available in the three schedules, along with the supplemental schedule prepared earlier. From the information gathered in Exhibits 12-13, 12-15, and 12-16, a completed statement of cash flows appears in Exhibit 12-17.

What does Julian's statement of cash flows tell us? Cash flow from operations totaled $174,000. Cash used to acquire investments and equipment amounted to $80,000, after receiving $25,000 from the sale of a machine. A net amount of $105,000 was used for financing activities. Thus, Julian used more cash than it generated, and that's why the cash balance declined. That's okay for a year or two, but if this continues, the company won't be able to pay its bills.

An Approach to Preparing the Statement of Cash Flows: Indirect Method

LO 6 Prepare a statement of cash flows, using the indirect method to determine cash flow from operating activities.

The purpose of the Operating Activities section of the statement changes when we use the indirect method. Instead of reporting cash receipts and cash payments, *the objective*

Exhibit 12-17

Completed Statement of Cash Flows for Julian Corp.

JULIAN CORP. STATEMENT OF CASH FLOWS FOR THE YEAR ENDED DECEMBER 31, 2004	
Cash flows from operating activities	
Cash receipts from:	
Sales on account	$ 664,000
Interest	15,000
Total cash receipts	$ 679,000
Cash payments for:	
Inventory purchases	$(375,000)
Salaries and wages	(62,000)
Insurance	(6,000)
Interest	(15,000)
Taxes	(47,000)
Total cash payments	$(505,000)
Net cash provided by operating activities	$ 174,000
Cash flows from investing activities	
Purchase of investments	$ (30,000)
Purchase of property and equipment	(75,000)
Sale of machine	25,000
Net cash used by investing activities	$ (80,000)
Cash flows from financing activities	
Retirement of bonds	$ (63,000)
Issuance of stock	25,000
Payment of cash dividends	(67,000)
Net cash used by financing activities	$(105,000)
Net decrease in cash	$ (11,000)
Cash balance, December 31, 2003	46,000
Cash balance, December 31, 2004	$ 35,000
Supplemental schedule of noncash investing and financing activities	
Acquisition of land in exchange for note payable	$ 50,000

is to reconcile net income to net cash flow from operating activities. The other two sections of the completed statement in Exhibit 12-17, the investing and financing sections, are unchanged. The use of the indirect or the direct method for presenting cash flow from operating activities does not affect these two sections.

An approach similar to that used for the direct method can be used to prepare the Operating Activities section of the statement of cash flows under the indirect method.

Net Income Recall that the first line in the Operating Activities section of the statement under the indirect method is net income. That is, we start with the assumptions that all revenues and gains reported on the income statement increase cash flow and that all expenses and losses decrease cash flow. Julian's net income of $120,000, as reported on its income statement in Exhibit 12-11, is reported as the first item in the Operating Activities section of the statement of cash flows as shown in Exhibit 12-18.

Increase in Accounts Receivable Recall from the balance sheets in Exhibit 12-12 the net increase in Accounts Receivable of $6,000. Because net income includes sales, as opposed to cash collections, the $6,000 *net increase* must be *deducted* to adjust net income to cash from operations, as shown in Exhibit 12-18.

From Concept to Practice 12.3

Reading IBM's Statement of Cash Flows

Did IBM's Receivables increase or decrease during 2002? Why is the change in this account added on the statement of cash flows?

Gain on Sale of Machine The gain itself did not generate any cash, but the *sale* of the machine did. And as we found earlier, the cash generated by selling the machine was reported in the Investing Activities section of the statement. The cash proceeds included the gain. Because the gain is included in the net income figure, it must be *deducted* to determine cash from operations. Also note that the gain is included twice in cash inflows if it is not deducted from the net income figure in the Operating Activities section. Note the deduction of $5,000 in Exhibit 12-18.

Decrease in Inventory As the $8,000 net decrease in the Inventory account indicates, Julian liquidated a portion of its stock of inventory during the year. A net decrease in this account indicates that the company sold more products than it purchased during the year. As shown in Exhibit 12-18, the *net decrease* of $8,000 is *added back* to net income.

Exhibit 12-18

Indirect Method for Reporting Cash Flows from Operating Activities

JULIAN CORP.
PARTIAL STATEMENT OF CASH FLOWS
FOR THE YEAR ENDED DECEMBER 31, 2004

Net cash flows from operating activities	
Net income	$120,000
Adjustments to reconcile net income to net cash provided by operating activities:	
Increase in accounts receivable	(6,000)
Gain on sale of machine	(5,000)
Decrease in inventory	8,000
Increase in accounts payable	7,000
Decrease in salaries and wages payable	(2,000)
Depreciation expense	40,000
Decrease in prepaid insurance	6,000
Increase in income taxes payable	3,000
Loss on retirement of bonds	3,000
Net cash provided by operating activities	$174,000

Increase in Accounts Payable According to Exhibit 12-12, Julian owed suppliers $31,000 at the start of the year. By the end of the year, the balance had grown to $38,000. Effectively, the company saved cash by delaying the payment of some of its outstanding accounts payable. The *net increase* of $7,000 in this account is *added back* to net income, as shown in Exhibit 12-18.

Decrease in Salaries and Wages Payable Salaries and Wages Payable decreased during the year by $2,000. The rationale for *deducting* the $2,000 *net decrease* in this liability in Exhibit 12-18 follows from what we just said about an increase in Accounts Payable. The payment to employees of $2,000 more than the amount included in expense on the income statement requires an additional deduction under the indirect method.

Depreciation Expense Depreciation is a noncash expense. Because it was deducted to arrive at net income, we must *add back* $40,000, the amount of depreciation, to find cash from operations. The same holds true for amortization of intangible assets and depletion of natural resources.

Decrease in Prepaid Insurance This account decreased by $6,000, according to Exhibit 12-12. A decrease in this account indicates that Julian deducted more on the income statement for the insurance expense of the period than it paid in cash for new policies. That is, the cash outlay for insurance protection was not as large as the amount of expense reported on the income statement. Thus, the *net decrease* in the account of $6,000 is *added back* to net income in Exhibit 12-18.

Increase in Income Taxes Payable Exhibit 12-12 reports a net increase of $3,000 in Income Taxes Payable. The *net increase* of $3,000 in this liability is *added back* to net income in Exhibit 12-18 because the payments to the government were $3,000 less than the amount included on the income statement.

Loss on Retirement of Bonds The $3,000 loss from retiring bonds was reported on the income statement as a deduction. There are two parts to the explanation for *adding back* the loss to net income to eliminate its effect in the Operating Activities section of the statement. First, any cash outflow from retiring bonds is properly classified as a financing activity, not an operating activity. The entire cash outflow should be reported in one classification rather than being allocated between two classifications. Second, the amount of the cash outflow is $63,000, not $3,000. To summarize, to convert net income to a cash basis, we add the loss back in the Operating Activities section to eliminate its effect. The actual use of cash to retire the bonds is shown in the financing section of the statement.

Summary of Adjustments to Net Income under the Indirect Method

The following is a list of the most common adjustments to net income when the indirect method is used to prepare the Operating Activities section of the statement of cash flows:

ADDITIONS TO NET INCOME	DEDUCTIONS FROM NET INCOME
Decrease in accounts receivable	Increase in accounts receivable
Decrease in inventory	Increase in inventory
Decrease in prepayments	Increase in prepayments
Increase in accounts payable	Decrease in accounts payable
Increase in accrued liabilities	Decrease in accrued liabilities
Losses on sales of long-term assets	Gains on sales of long-term assets
Losses on retirements of bonds	Gains on retirements of bonds
Depreciation, amortization, and depletion	

Study Tip

Note from this list how changes in current assets and current liabilities are treated on the statement. For example, because accounts receivable and accounts payable are on opposite sides of the balance sheet, increases in each of them are handled in opposite ways. But an increase in one and a decrease in the other are treated in the same way.

Comparison of the Indirect and Direct Methods

Earlier in the chapter we pointed out that the amount of cash provided by operating activities is the same under the direct and the indirect methods. The relative merits of the two methods, however, have stirred considerable debate in the accounting profession. The Financial Accounting Standards Board has expressed a strong preference for the direct method but allows companies to use the indirect method.

If a company uses the indirect method, it must separately disclose two important cash payments: income taxes paid and interest paid. Thus, if Julian uses the indirect method, it reports the following either at the bottom of the statement of cash flows or in a note to the financial statements:

Income taxes paid	$47,000
Interest paid	$15,000

Advocates of the direct method believe that the information provided with this approach is valuable in evaluating a company's operating efficiency. **For example, the use of the direct method allows the analyst to follow any trends in cash receipts from customers and compare them with cash payments to suppliers.** The information presented in the Operating Activities section of the statement under the direct method is certainly user-friendly. Someone without a technical background in accounting can easily tell where cash came from and where it went during the period.

Advocates of the indirect method argue two major points. Many companies believe that the use of the direct method reveals too much about their business by telling readers exactly the amount of cash receipts and cash payments from operations. Whether the use of the direct method tells the competition too much about a company is subject to debate. The other argument made for the indirect method is that it focuses attention on the differences between income on an accrual basis and a cash basis. In fact, this reconciliation of net income and cash provided by operating activities is considered to be important enough that *if a company uses the direct method, it must present a separate schedule to reconcile net income to net cash from operating activities.* This schedule, in effect, is the same as the Operating Activities section for the indirect method.

THE USE OF CASH FLOW INFORMATION

The statement of cash flows is a critical disclosure to a company's investors and creditors. Many investors focus on cash flow from operations, rather than net income, as their key statistic. Similarly, many bankers are as concerned with cash flow from operations as they are with net income because they care about a company's ability to pay its bills. There is the concern that accrual accounting can mask cash flow problems. For example, a company with smooth earnings could be building up accounts receivable and inventory. This may not become evident until the company is in deep trouble.

The statement of cash flows provides investors, analysts, bankers, and other users with a valuable starting point as they attempt tò evaluate a company's financial health. From this point, these groups must decide *how* to use the information presented on the statement. They pay particular attention to the *relationships* among various items on the statement, as well as to other financial statement items. In fact, many large banks have their own cash flow models, which typically involve a rearrangement of the items on the statement of cash flows to suit their needs. We now turn our attention to two examples of how various groups use cash flow information.

Creditors and Cash Flow Adequacy

Bankers and other creditors are especially concerned with a company's ability to meet its principal and interest obligations. *Cash flow adequacy* is a measure intended to help in this regard.[5] It gauges the cash available to meet future debt obligations after paying taxes and interest costs and making capital expenditures. Because capital expenditures

[5] An article appearing in the January 10, 1994, edition of *The Wall Street Journal* reported that Fitch Investors Service Inc. has published a rating system to compare the cash flow adequacy of companies that it rates single-A in its credit ratings. The rating system is intended to help corporate bond investors assess the ability of these companies to meet their maturing debt obligations. Lee Berton, "Investors Have a New Tool for Judging Issuers' Health: 'Cash-Flow Adequacy,'" p. C1.

on new plant and equipment are a necessity for most companies, analysts are concerned with the cash available to repay debt *after* the company has replaced and updated its existing base of long-term assets.

Cash flow adequacy can be computed as follows:

$$\text{Cash Flow Adequacy} = \frac{\text{Cash Flow from Operating Activities} - \text{Capital Expenditures}}{\text{Average Amount of Debt Maturing over Next Five Years}}$$

How could you use the information in an annual report to measure a company's cash flow adequacy? First, whether a company uses the direct or indirect method to report cash flow from operating activities, this number represents cash flow *after* paying interest and taxes. The numerator of the ratio is determined by deducting capital expenditures, as they appear in the Investing Activities section of the statement, from cash flow from operating activities. A disclosure required by the Securities and Exchange Commission provides the information needed to calculate the denominator of the ratio. This regulatory body requires companies to report the annual amount of long-term debt maturing over each of the next five years.

IBM's Cash Flow Adequacy As an example of the calculation of this ratio, consider the following amounts from IBM's statement of cash flows for the year ended December 31, 2002 (amounts in millions of dollars):

Net cash provided from operating activities from continuing operations	$13,788
Payments for plant, rental machines and other property	$ 4,753

Note k in IBM's 2002 annual report provides the following information:

> Annual contractual maturities on long-term debt outstanding at December 31, 2002, are as follows: (dollars in millions)
>
> | | |
> |---|---|
> | 2003 | $3,949 |
> | 2004 | 3,613 |
> | 2005 | 1,670 |
> | 2006 | 2,705 |
> | 2007 | 846 |
> | 2008 and beyond | 9,940 |

We can now compute IBM's cash flow adequacy for the year ended December 31, 2002, as follows:

$$\text{Cash Flow Adequacy} = \frac{\$13{,}788 - \$4{,}753}{(\$3{,}949 + \$3{,}613 + \$1{,}670 + \$2{,}705 + \$846)/5}$$

$$= \frac{\$9{,}035}{\$2{,}556.6} = 3.53$$

Would you feel comfortable lending to IBM if you knew that its ratio of cash flow from operations, after making necessary capital expenditures, to average maturities of debt over the next five years was over 3 to 1? Before answering this question, you would want to compare the ratio with the ratios for prior years as well as with the ratio for companies of similar size and in lines of business similar to those of IBM. As a starting point, however, IBM's ratio of 3.53 to 1 indicates that its 2002 cash flow was more than sufficient to repay its average annual debt over the next five years.

Stockholders and Cash Flow per Share

As we will see in Chapter 13, one measure of the relative worth of an investment in a company is the ratio of the stock's market price per share to the company's earnings per share (that is, the price/earnings ratio). But many stockholders and Wall Street analysts are even more interested in the price of the stock in relation to the company's cash flow per share. Cash flow for purposes of this ratio is normally limited to cash flow from operating activities. This ratio has been used by these groups to evaluate

© AP/WIDE WORLD PHOTOS

Managers, investors, and brokers gauge the relative strengths of retailers by observing which stores are the most popular. But they also study the financial statements, particularly the statement of cash flows and its indicators of cash flow adequacy, as the most fundamental way to measure a firm's strength.

http://www.sec.gov
http://www.ibm.com

investments—even though the accounting profession has expressly forbidden the reporting of cash flow per share information in the financial statements. The accounting profession's belief is that this type of information is not an acceptable alternative to earnings per share as an indicator of company performance.

Interpret: You Decide Refer to the chapter opener in which IBM's statement of cash flows is presented. Also, review the company's cash flow adequacy ratio, as determined on page 621. As a creditor of IBM, would you feel confident in the company's ability to repay its debt over the next five years? Explain your reasoning.

Accounting for Your Decisions

You Are the Banker

You and your old college roommate are having an argument. You say that cash flow is all that matters when looking at a company's prospects. Your roommate says that the most important number is earnings per share. Who's right?

ANS: You're both wrong. True, bankers are interested in cash flow to make sure that a company can pay back its loans. But earnings per share is important also because it is less easily manipulated. After all, companies can decide when they want to finance expansion, pay down debt, or invest in new businesses. A company with strong earnings can appear weak from a cash flow perspective if it invests too much in new operating assets or other businesses. On the other hand, a company that wants to appear cash-rich can avoid making all of the investments that it ought to be making. Although companies can manipulate earnings to some extent, the matching principle ensures that revenues and expenses relating to those revenues take place during the same period.

Ratios for Decision Making

Reporting and analyzing financial statement information related to a company's cash flows:
Of critical importance to companies, their creditors, and their investors is the company's ability to pay its debts when required. For long-term debts, the statement of cash flows and the disclosure in the notes of the upcoming maturities of those debts are very helpful to project whether or not the company will be able to meet its obligations in the future. The cash flow adequacy ratio tells how many times the current amount of net cash inflows from operating activities, after deducting capital expenditures, could pay for the upcoming maturities of long-term debts. The higher the number, the better the company's position. The ratio assumes the current net cash inflow from operating activities and the expenditures for capital assets are typical of the company over time.

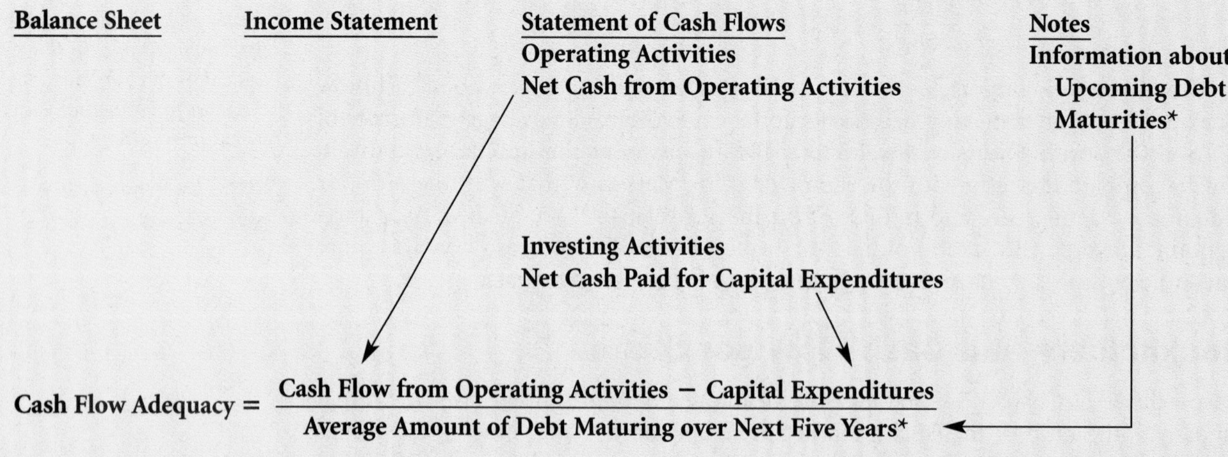

*Total debt that will be paid off over the next five years ÷ 5

Answers to the Two-Minute Review

Two-Minute Review on Page 606

1. *A cash equivalent is an item readily convertible to a known amount of cash and with an original maturity to the investor of three months or less. Because the maturity date of these items, such as a 60-day certificate of deposit, is so near, they are not considered to carry any significant risks in terms of price changes. Thus, any changes in cash equivalents are not reported on the statement of cash flows.*
2. *Operating, investing, and financing activities.*
3. *Direct and indirect methods. The direct method involves reporting major classes of gross cash receipts and cash payments. Under the indirect method, net cash flow from operating activities is computed by adjusting net income to remove the effect of all deferrals of past operating cash receipts and payments and all accruals of future operating cash receipts and payments.*

Warmup Exercises

Warmup Exercise 12-1 ***Purpose of the Statement of Cash Flows*** **LO 1**

Most companies begin the statement of cash flows by indicating the amount of net income and ending it with the beginning and ending cash balances. Why is the statement necessary if net income already appears on the income statement and the cash balances can be found on the balance sheet?

Key to the Solution

Recall the *purpose* of the statement of cash flows as described in the beginning of the chapter.

Warmup Exercise 12-2 ***Classification of Activities*** **LO 3**

For each of the following activities, indicate whether it should appear on the statement of cash flows as an operating (O), investing (I), or financing (F) activity. Assume the company uses the direct method of reporting in the Operating Activities section.

________ **1.** New equipment is acquired for cash.
________ **2.** Thirty-year bonds are issued.
________ **3.** Cash receipts from the cash register are recorded.
________ **4.** The bi-weekly payroll is paid.
________ **5.** Common stock is issued for cash.
________ **6.** Land that was being held for future expansion is sold at book value.

Key to the Solution

Recall the general rules for each of the categories: operating activities involve acquiring and selling products and services; investing activities deal with acquiring and disposing of long-term assets; and financing activities are concerned with the raising and repayment of funds in the form of debt and equity.

Warmup Exercise 12-3 ***Adjustments to Net Income with the Indirect Method*** **LO 6**

Assume that a company uses the indirect method to prepare the Operating Activities section of the statement of cash flows. For each of the following items, indicate whether it would be added to net income (A), deducted from net income (D), or not reported in this section of the statement under the indirect method (NR).

________ **1.** Decrease in accounts payable
________ **2.** Increase in accounts receivable
________ **3.** Decrease in prepaid insurance
________ **4.** Purchase of new factory equipment
________ **5.** Depreciation expense
________ **6.** Gain on retirement of bonds

Key to the Solution

Refer to the summary of adjustments to net income under the indirect method on page 619.

Solutions to Warmup Exercises

Warmup Exercise 12-1

The statement of cash flows is a complement to the other statements in that it summarizes the operating, investing, and financing activities over a period of time. Even though the net income and cash balances are available on other statements, the statement of cash flows explains to the reader *why* net income is different than cash flow from operations and *why* cash changed by the amount it did during the period.

Warmup Exercise 12-2

1. I **2.** F **3.** O **4.** O **5.** F **6.** I

Warmup Exercise 12-3

1. D **2.** D **3.** A **4.** NR **5.** A **6.** D

Review Problem

WebTUTOR™ Advantage

An income statement and comparative balance sheets for Dexter Company are shown below:

DEXTER COMPANY
INCOME STATEMENT
FOR THE YEAR ENDED DECEMBER 31, 2004

Sales revenue	$89,000
Cost of goods sold	57,000
Gross margin	$32,000
Depreciation expense	6,500
Advertising expense	3,200
Salaries expense	12,000
Total operating expenses	$21,700
Operating income	$10,300
Loss on sale of land	2,500
Income before tax	$ 7,800
Income tax expense	2,600
Net income	$ 5,200

DEXTER COMPANY
COMPARATIVE BALANCE SHEETS

	December 31	
	2004	2003
Cash	$ 12,000	$ 9,500
Accounts receivable	22,000	18,400
Inventory	25,400	20,500
Prepaid advertising	10,000	8,600
Total current assets	$ 69,400	$ 57,000
Land	$120,000	$ 80,000
Equipment	190,000	130,000
Accumulated depreciation	(70,000)	(63,500)
Total long-term assets	$240,000	$146,500
Total assets	$309,400	$203,500
Accounts payable	$ 15,300	$ 12,100
Salaries payable	14,000	16,400
Income taxes payable	1,200	700
Total current liabilities	$ 30,500	$ 29,200

Capital stock	$200,000	$100,000
Retained earnings	78,900	74,300
Total stockholders' equity	$278,900	$174,300
Total liabilities and stockholders' equity	$309,400	$203,500

Additional Information

1. Land was acquired during the year for $70,000.
2. An unimproved parcel of land was sold during the year for $27,500. Its original cost to Dexter was $30,000.
3. A specialized piece of equipment was acquired in exchange for capital stock in the company. The value of the capital stock was $60,000.
4. In addition to the capital stock issued in item **3**, stock was sold for $40,000.
5. Dividends of $600 were paid.

Required

Prepare a statement of cash flows for 2004 using the direct method in the Operating Activities section of the statement. Include supplemental schedules to report any noncash investing and financing activities and to reconcile net income to net cash provided by operating activities.

Solution to Review Problem

DEXTER COMPANY
STATEMENT OF CASH FLOWS
FOR THE YEAR ENDED DECEMBER 31, 2004

Cash flows from operating activities	
Cash collections from customers	$ 85,400
Cash payments:	
To suppliers	$(58,700)
For advertising	(4,600)
To employees	(14,400)
For income taxes	(2,100)
Total cash payments	$(79,800)
Net cash provided by operating activities	$ 5,600
Cash flows from investing activities	
Purchase of land	$(70,000)
Sale of land	27,500
Net cash used by investing activities	$(42,500)
Cash flows from financing activities	
Issuance of capital stock	$ 40,000
Payment of cash dividends	(600)
Net cash provided by financing activities	$ 39,400
Net increase in cash	$ 2,500
Cash balance, December 31, 2003	9,500
Cash balance, December 31, 2004	$ 12,000
Supplemental schedule of noncash investing and financing activities	
Acquisition of specialized equipment in exchange for capital stock	$ 60,000
Reconciliation of net income to net cash provided by operating activities	
Net income	$ 5,200
Adjustments to reconcile net income to net cash provided by operating activities:	
Increase in accounts receivable	(3,600)
Increase in inventory	(4,900)
Increase in prepaid advertising	(1,400)
Increase in accounts payable	3,200
Decrease in salaries payable	(2,400)
Increase in income taxes payable	500
Depreciation expense	6,500
Loss on sale of land	2,500
Net cash provided by operating activities	$ 5,600

Appendix: Accounting Tools: A Work-Sheet Approach to the Statement of Cash Flows

LO 7 Use a work sheet to prepare a statement of cash flows, using the indirect method to determine cash flow from operating activities.

In the chapter, we illustrated a systemic approach to aid in the preparation of a statement of cash flows. We now consider the use of a work sheet as an alternative tool to organize the information needed to prepare the statement. We will use the information given in the chapter for Julian Corp. (refer to Exhibits 12-11 and 12-12 for the income statements and comparative balance sheets). Although it is possible to use a work sheet to prepare the statement when the Operating Activities section is prepared under the direct method, we illustrate the use of a work sheet using the more popular *indirect* method.

A work sheet for Julian Corp. is presented in Exhibit 12-19.

Exhibit 12-19 Julian Corp. Statement of Cash Flows Work Sheet

JULIAN CORP.
STATEMENT OF CASH FLOWS WORK SHEET (INDIRECT METHOD)
(ALL AMOUNTS IN THOUSANDS OF DOLLARS)

	Balances			Cash Inflows (Outflows)			
ACCOUNTS	12/31/04	12/31/03	CHANGES	OPERATING	INVESTING	FINANCING	NONCASH ACTIVITIES
Cash	35	46	(11)[16]				
Accounts Receivable	63	57	6[10]	(6)[10]			
Inventory	84	92	(8)[11]	8[11]			
Prepaid Insurance	12	18	(6)[12]	6[12]			
Long-Term Investments	120	90	30[1]		(30)[1]		
Land	150	100	50[2]				(50)[2]
Property and Equipment	320	280	75[3]		(75)[3]		
			(35)[4]		25[4]		
Accumulated Depreciation	(100)	(75)	15[4]				
			(40)[9]	40[9]			
Accounts Payable	(38)	(31)	(7)[13]	7[13]			
Salaries and Wages Payable	(7)	(9)	2[14]	(2)[14]			
Income Taxes Payable	(8)	(5)	(3)[15]	3[15]			
Notes Payable	(85)	(35)	(50)[2]				50[2]
Bonds Payable	(200)	(260)	60[5]			(63)[5]	
Capital Stock	(100)	(75)	(25)[6]			25[6]	
Retained Earnings	(246)	(193)	67[7]	(5)[4]		(67)[7]	
				3[5]			
			(120)[8]	120[8]	—	—	—
Totals	–0–	–0–	–0–	174	(80)	(105)	–0–
Net decrease in cash				(11)[16]			

SOURCE: The authors are grateful to Jeannie Folk for the development of this work sheet.

The following steps were followed in preparing the work sheet:

Step 1: The balances in each account at the end and at the beginning of the period are entered in the first two columns of the work sheet. For Julian, these balances can be found in its comparative balance sheets in Exhibit 12-12. Note that contra assets, liabilities, and owners' equity accounts are bracketed on the work sheet. Because the work sheet lists all balance sheet accounts, the total of the asset balances must equal the total of the liability and owner's equity balances, and thus, the totals at the bottom for these first two columns equal $0.

Step 2: The additional information listed at the bottom of Exhibit 12-12 is used to record the various investing and financing activities on the work sheet (the item numbers discussed below correspond to the superscript numbers on the work sheet in Exhibit 12-19):

1. Long-term investments were purchased for $30,000. Because this transaction required the use of cash, it is entered as a bracketed amount in the Investing column and as an addition to the Long-Term Investments account in the Changes column.
2. Land was acquired by issuing a $50,000 note payable. This transaction is entered on two lines on the work sheet. First, $50,000 is added to the Changes column for Land and as a corresponding deduction in the Noncash column (the last column on the work sheet). Likewise, $50,000 is added for Notes Payable to the Changes column and to the Noncash column.
3. Item 3 in the additional information indicates the acquisition of equipment for $75,000. This amount appears on the work sheet as an addition to Property and Equipment in the Changes column and as a deduction (cash outflow) in the Investing column.
4. A machine with an original cost of $35,000 and a book value of $20,000 was sold for $25,000, resulting in four entries on the work sheet. First, the amount of cash received, $25,000, is entered as an addition in the Investing column on the line for property and equipment. On the same line, the cost of the machine, $35,000, is entered as a deduction in the Changes column. The difference between the cost of the machine, $35,000, and its book value, $20,000, is its accumulated depreciation of $15,000. This amount is shown as a deduction from this account in the Changes column. Because the gain of $5,000 is included in net income, it is deducted in the Operating column (on the Retained Earnings line).
5. Bonds with a face value of $60,000 were retired by paying $63,000 in cash, resulting in the entry of three amounts on the work sheet. The face value of the bonds, $60,000, is entered as a reduction of Bonds Payable in the Changes column. The amount paid to retire the bonds, $63,000, is entered on the same line in the Financing column. The loss of $3,000 is added in the Operating column because it was a deduction to arrive at net income.
6. Capital stock was issued for $25,000. This amount is entered on the Capital Stock line under the Changes column (as an increase in the account) and under the Financing column as an inflow.
7. Dividends of $67,000 were paid. This amount is entered as a reduction in Retained Earnings in the Changes column and as a cash outflow in the Financing Activities column.

Step 3: Because the indirect method is being used, net income of $120,000 for the period is entered as an addition to Retained Earnings in the Operating column of the work sheet (entry 8). The amount is also entered as an increase (bracketed) in the Changes column.

Step 4: Any noncash revenues or expenses are entered on the work sheet on the appropriate lines. For Julian, depreciation expense of $40,000 is added (bracketed) to Accumulated Depreciation in the Changes column and in the Operating column. This entry is identified on the work sheet as entry 9.

Step 5: Each of the changes in the noncash current asset and current liability accounts is entered in the Changes column and in the Operating column. These entries are identified on the work sheet as entries 10 through 15.

Step 6: Totals are determined for the Operating, Investing, and Financing columns and entered at the bottom of the work sheet. The total for the final column, Noncash Activities, of $0, is also entered.

Step 7: The net cash inflow (outflow) for the period is determined by adding the totals of the operating, investing, and financing columns. For Julian, the net cash *outflow* is $11,000, shown as entry 16 at the bottom of the statement. This same amount is then transferred to the line for Cash in the Changes column. Finally, the total of the Changes column at this point should net to $0.

Chapter Highlights

1. **LO 1** The purpose of a statement of cash flows is to summarize the cash flows of an entity during a period of time. The cash inflows and outflows are categorized into three activities: operating, investing, and financing.
2. **LO 2** Cash equivalents are convertible to a known amount of cash and are therefore included with cash on the balance sheet. Because such items as commercial paper, money market funds, and Treasury bills do not involve any significant risk, neither their purchase nor their sale is shown as an investing activity on the statement of cash flows.
3. **LO 3** Operating activities are generally the effects of items that enter into the determination of net income, such as the effects of buying and selling products and services. Other operating activities include payments of compensation to employees, taxes to the government, and interest to creditors. Preparation of the Operating Activities section of the statement of cash flows requires an analysis of the current assets and current liabilities.
4. **LO 3** Investing activities are critical to the success of a business because they involve the replacement of existing productive assets and the addition of new ones. Capital expenditures are normally the single largest cash outflow for most businesses. Occasionally, companies generate cash from the sale of existing plant and equipment. The information needed to prepare the Investing Activities section of the statement of cash flows is found by analyzing the long-term asset accounts.
5. **LO 3** All businesses rely on financing in one form or another. At least initially, all corporations sell stock to raise funds. Many turn to external sources as well, generating cash from the issuance of promissory notes and bonds. The repayment of debt and the reacquisition of capital stock are important uses of cash for some companies. Given the nature of financing activities, long-term liability and stockholders' equity accounts must be examined in preparing this section of the statement of cash flows.
6. **LO 4** Two different methods are acceptable to report cash flow from operating activities. Under the direct method, cash receipts and cash payments related to operations are reported. Under the indirect method, net income is reconciled to net cash flow from operating activities. Regardless of which method is used, the amount of cash generated from operations is the same.
7. **LO 5** Preparation of the Operating Activities section under the direct method requires the conversion of income statement items from an accrual basis to a cash basis. Certain items, such as depreciation, do not have a cash effect and are not included on the statement. Gains and losses typically relate to either investing or financing activities and are not included in the Operating Activities section of the statement. When the direct method is used to present cash flow from operating activities, a separate schedule is required to reconcile net income to net cash flow from operating activities. This schedule is the same as the Operating Activities section under the indirect method.
8. **LO 6** When the indirect method is used, the reconciliation of net income to net cash flow from operating activities appears on the face of the statement. Adjustments are made for the changes in each of the operating-related current asset and current liability accounts, as well as adjustments for noncash items, such as depreciation. The effects of gains and losses on net income must also be removed to convert to a cash basis. If the indirect method is used, a company must separately disclose the amount of cash paid for taxes and for interest.
9. **LO 7** A work sheet is sometimes used in preparing a statement of cash flows. The work sheet acts as a tool to aid in the preparation of the statement. (Appendix)

http://porter.swlearning.com

Technology and other resources for your success

If you need additional help, visit the text's Web site. Also, see this text's preface for a description of available technology and other resources. If your instructor is using PERSONAL Trainer in this course, you may complete, on line, the exercises and problems in the text.

Key Terms Quiz

Read each definition below and then write the number of that definition in the blank beside the appropriate term it defines. The quiz solutions appear at the end of the chapter.

_____ Statement of cash flows
_____ Cash equivalent
_____ Operating activities
_____ Investing activities
_____ Financing activities
_____ Direct method
_____ Indirect method

1. Activities concerned with the acquisition and sale of products and services.
2. For preparing the Operating Activities section of the statement of cash flows, the approach in which net income is reconciled to net cash flow from operations.
3. The financial statement that summarizes an entity's cash receipts and cash payments during the period from operating, investing, and financing activities.
4. An item readily convertible to a known amount of cash and with a maturity to the investor of three months or less.
5. Activities concerned with the acquisition and disposal of long-term assets.
6. For preparing the Operating Activities section of the statement of cash flows, the approach in which cash receipts and cash payments are reported.
7. Activities concerned with the raising and repayment of funds in the form of debt and equity.

Answers on p. 653.

Alternate Terms

Bottom line Net income

Cash flow from operating activities Cash flow from operations

Statement of cash flows Cash flows statement

Questions

1. What is the purpose of the statement of cash flows? As a flows statement, explain how it differs from the income statement.
2. What is a cash equivalent? Why is it included with cash for purposes of preparing a statement of cash flows?
3. Preston Corp. acquires a piece of land by signing a $60,000 promissory note and making a down payment of $20,000. How should this transaction be reported on the statement of cash flows?
4. Hansen Inc. made two purchases during December. One was a $10,000 Treasury bill that matures in 60 days from the date of purchase. The other was a $20,000 investment in Motorola common stock that will be held indefinitely. How should each of these be treated for purposes of preparing a statement of cash flows?
5. Companies are required to classify cash flows as operating, investing, or financing. Which of these three categories do you think will most likely have a net cash *outflow* over a number of years? Explain your answer.
6. A fellow student says to you: "The statement of cash flows is the easiest of the basic financial statements to prepare because you know the answer before you start. You compare the beginning and ending balances in cash on the balance sheet and compute the net inflow or outflow of cash. What could be easier?" Do you agree? Explain your answer.
7. What is your evaluation of the following statement? "Depreciation is responsible for providing some of the highest amounts of cash for capital-intensive businesses. This is obvious by examining the Operating Activities section of the statement of cash flows. Other than the net income of the period, depreciation is often the largest amount reported in this section of the statement."
8. Which method for preparing the Operating Activities section of the statement of cash flows, the direct or the indirect method, do you believe provides more information to users of the statement? Explain your answer.
9. Assume that a company uses the indirect method to prepare the Operating Activities section of the statement of cash flows. Why would a decrease in accounts receivable during the period be added back to net income?
10. Why is it necessary to analyze both inventory and accounts payable in trying to determine cash payments to suppliers when the direct method is used?
11. A company has a very profitable year. What explanations might there be for a decrease in cash?
12. A company reports a net loss for the year. Is it possible that cash could increase during the year? Explain your answer.
13. What effect does a decrease in income taxes payable for the period have on cash generated from operating activities? Does it matter whether the direct or the indirect method is used?
14. Why do accounting standards require a company to separately disclose income taxes paid and interest paid if it uses the indirect method?

15. Is it logical that interest paid is classified as a cash outflow in the *Operating* Activities section of the statement of cash flows but that dividends paid are included in the *Financing* Activities section? Explain your answer.

16. Jackson Company prepays the rent on various office facilities. The beginning balance in Prepaid Rent was $9,600, and the ending balance was $7,300. The income statement reports Rent Expense of $45,900. Under the direct method, what amount would appear for cash paid in rent in the Operating Activities section of the statement of cash flows?

17. Baxter Inc. buys 2,000 shares of its own common stock at $20 per share as treasury stock. How is this transaction reported on the statement of cash flows?

18. Duke Corp. sold a delivery truck for $9,000. Its original cost was $25,000, and the book value at the time of the sale was $11,000. How does the transaction to record the sale appear on a statement of cash flows prepared under the indirect method?

19. Billings Company has a patent on its books with a balance at the beginning of the year of $24,000. The ending balance for the asset was $20,000. The company neither bought nor sold any patents during the year, nor does it use an Accumulated Amortization account. Assuming that the company uses the indirect method in preparing a statement of cash flows, how is the decrease in the Patents account reported on the statement?

20. Ace Inc. declared and distributed a 10% stock dividend during the year. Explain how, if at all, you think this transaction should be reported on a statement of cash flows.

Exercises

Exercise 12-1 ***Cash Equivalents*** **LO 2**

Metropolis Industries invested its excess cash in the following instruments during December 2004:

Certificate of deposit, due January 31, 2005	$ 35,000
Certificate of deposit, due June 30, 2005	95,000
Investment in City of Elgin bonds, due May 1, 2006	15,000
Investment in Quantum Data stock	66,000
Money Market Fund	105,000
90-day Treasury bills	75,000
Treasury note, due December 1, 2005	200,000

Required

Determine the amount of cash equivalents that should be combined with cash on the company's balance sheet at December 31, 2004, and for purposes of preparing a statement of cash flows for the year ended December 31, 2004.

Exercise 12-2 ***Classification of Activities*** **LO 3**

For each of the following transactions reported on a statement of cash flows, fill in the blank to indicate if it would appear in the Operating Activities section (O), in the Investing Activities section (I), or in the Financing Activities section (F). Put an *S* in the blank if the transaction does not affect cash but is reported in a supplemental schedule of noncash activities. Assume the company uses the direct method in the Operating Activities section.

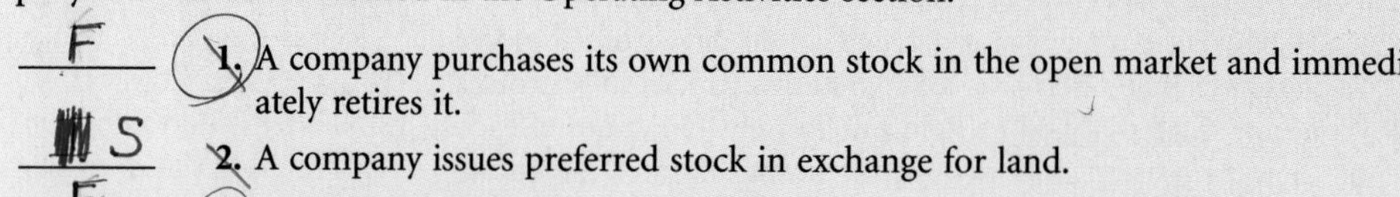

_______ 1. A company purchases its own common stock in the open market and immediately retires it.

_______ 2. A company issues preferred stock in exchange for land.

_______ 3. A six-month bank loan is obtained.

_______ 4. Twenty-year bonds are issued.

_______ 5. A customer's open account is collected.

_______ 6. Income taxes are paid.

_______ 7. Cash sales for the day are recorded.

_______ 8. Cash dividends are declared and paid.

_______ 9. A creditor is given shares of common stock in the company in return for cancellation of a long-term loan.

_______ 10. A new piece of machinery is acquired for cash.

_______ 11. Stock of another company is acquired as an investment.

_______ 12. Interest is paid on a bank loan.

_______ 13. Factory workers are paid.

Exercise 12-3 ***Retirement of Bonds Payable on the Statement of Cash Flows—Indirect Method*** **LO 3**

Redstone Inc. has the following debt outstanding on December 31, 2004:

10% bonds payable, due 12/31/08	$500,000	
Discount on bonds payable	(40,000)	$460,000

On this date, Redstone retired the entire bond issue by paying cash of $510,000.

Required

1. Determine the effect on the accounting equation of the bond retirement.
2. Describe how the bond retirement would be reported on the statement of cash flows, assuming that Redstone uses the indirect method.

Exercise 12-4 ***Cash Collections—Direct Method*** **LO 5**

Stanley Company's comparative balance sheets included accounts receivable of $80,800 at December 31, 2003, and $101,100 at December 31, 2004. Sales reported by Stanley on its 2004 income statement amounted to $1,450,000. What is the amount of cash collections that Stanley will report in the Operating Activities section of its 2004 statement of cash flows assuming that the direct method is used?

Exercise 12-5 ***Cash Payments—Direct Method*** **LO 5**

Lester Enterprises' comparative balance sheets included inventory of $90,200 at December 31, 2003, and $70,600 at December 31, 2004. Lester's comparative balance sheets also included accounts payable of $57,700 at December 31, 2003, and $39,200 at December 31, 2004. Lester's accounts payable balances are composed solely of amounts due to suppliers for purchases of inventory on account. Cost of goods sold, as reported by Lester on its 2004 income statement, amounted to $770,900. What is the amount of cash payments for inventory that Lester will report in the Operating Activities section of its 2004 statement of cash flows assuming that the direct method is used?

Exercise 12-6 ***Operating Activities Section—Direct Method*** **LO 5**

The following account balances for the noncash current assets and current liabilities of Labrador Company are available:

	December 31	
	2004	**2003**
Accounts receivable	$ 4,000	$ 6,000
Inventory	32,000	25,000
Office supplies	7,000	10,000
Accounts payable	7,500	4,500
Salaries and wages payable	1,500	2,500
Interest payable	500	1,000
Income taxes payable	4,500	3,000

In addition, the income statement for 2004 is as follows:

	2004
Sales revenue	$100,000
Cost of goods sold	75,000
Gross profit	$ 25,000
General and administrative expense	$ 8,000
Depreciation expense	3,000
Total operating expenses	$ 11,000
Income before interest and taxes	$ 14,000
Interest expense	3,000
Income before tax	$ 11,000
Income tax expense	5,000
Net income	$ 6,000

Required

1. Prepare the Operating Activities section of the statement of cash flows using the direct method.
2. What does the use of the direct method reveal about a company that the indirect method does not?

Exercise 12-7 *Determination of Missing Amounts—Cash Flow from Operating Activities* LO 5

The computation of cash provided by operating activities requires analysis of the noncash current asset and current liability accounts. Determine the missing amounts for each of the following independent cases:

Case 1	
Accounts receivable, beginning of year	$150,000
Accounts receivable, end of year	100,000
Credit sales for the year	175,000
Cash sales for the year	60,000
Write-offs of uncollectible accounts	35,000
Total cash collections for the year (from cash sales and collections on account)	?
Case 2	
Inventory, beginning of year	$ 80,000
Inventory, end of year	55,000
Accounts payable, beginning of year	25,000
Accounts payable, end of year	15,000
Cost of goods sold	175,000
Cash payments for inventory (assume all purchases of inventory are on account)	?
Case 3	
Prepaid insurance, beginning of year	$ 17,000
Prepaid insurance, end of year	20,000
Insurance expense	15,000
Cash paid for new insurance policies	?
Case 4	
Income taxes payable, beginning of year	$ 95,000
Income taxes payable, end of year	115,000
Income tax expense	300,000
Cash payments for taxes	?

Exercise 12-8 *Dividends on the Statement of Cash Flows* LO 5

The following selected account balances are available from the records of Lewistown Company:

	December 31	
	2004	**2003**
Dividends payable	$ 30,000	$ 20,000
Retained earnings	375,000	250,000

Other information available for 2004 follows:

a. Lewistown reported $285,000 net income for the year.

b. It declared and distributed a stock dividend of $50,000 during the year.

c. It declared cash dividends at the end of each quarter and paid them within the next 30 days of the following quarter.

Required

1. Determine the amount of cash dividends *paid* during the year for presentation in the Financing Activities section of the statement of cash flows.
2. Should the stock dividend described in part **b** appear on a statement of cash flows? Explain your answer.

Exercise 12-9 *Adjustments to Net Income with the Indirect Method* LO 6

Assume that a company uses the indirect method to prepare the Operating Activities section of the statement of cash flows. For each of the following items, fill in the blank to indicate whether it would be added to net income (A), deducted from net income (D), or not reported in this section of the statement under the indirect method (NR).

_______ 1. Depreciation expense
_______ 2. Gain on sale of used delivery truck
_______ 3. Bad debts expense
_______ 4. Increase in accounts payable
_______ 5. Purchase of new delivery truck
_______ 6. Loss on retirement of bonds
_______ 7. Increase in prepaid rent
_______ 8. Decrease in inventory
_______ 9. Increase in short-term investments (classified as available-for-sale securities)
_______ 10. Amortization of patents

Exercise 12-10 ***Operating Activities Section—Indirect Method*** **LO 6**

The following account balances for the noncash current assets and current liabilities of Suffolk Company are available:

	December 31	
	2004	**2003**
Accounts receivable	$43,000	$35,000
Inventory	30,000	40,000
Prepaid rent	17,000	15,000
Totals	$90,000	$90,000
Accounts payable	$26,000	$19,000
Income taxes payable	6,000	10,000
Interest payable	15,000	12,000
Totals	$47,000	$41,000

Net income for 2004 is $40,000. Depreciation expense is $20,000. Assume that all sales and all purchases are on account.

Required

1. Prepare the Operating Activities section of the statement of cash flows using the indirect method.
2. Provide a brief explanation as to why cash flow from operating activities is more or less than the net income of the period.

Multi-Concept Exercises

Exercise 12-11 ***Classification of Activities*** **LO 2, 3**

Use the following legend to indicate how each of the following transactions would be reported on the statement of cash flows (assume that the stocks and bonds of other companies are classified as available-for-sale securities):

II = Inflow from investing activities
OI = Outflow from investing activities
IF = Inflow from financing activities
OF = Outflow from financing activities
CE = Classified as a cash equivalent and included with cash for purposes of preparing the statement of cash flows

_______ 1. Purchased a six-month certificate of deposit.
_______ 2. Purchased a 60-day Treasury bill.
_______ 3. Issued 1,000 shares of common stock.
_______ 4. Purchased 1,000 shares of stock in another company.
_______ 5. Purchased 1,000 shares of its own stock to be held in the treasury.
_______ 6. Invested $1,000 in a money market fund.
_______ 7. Sold 500 shares of stock of another company.
_______ 8. Purchased 20-year bonds of another company.
_______ 9. Issued 30-year bonds.
_______ 10. Repaid a six-month bank loan.

Exercise 12-12 *Classification of Activities* **LO 3, 5**

Use the following legend to indicate how each of the following transactions would be reported on the statement of cash flows (assume that the company uses the direct method in the Operating Activities section):

IO = Inflow from operating activities
OO = Outflow from operating activities
II = Inflow from investing activities
OI = Outflow from investing activities
IF = Inflow from financing activities
OF = Outflow from financing activities
NR = Not reported in the body of the statement of cash flows but included in a supplemental schedule

_______ **1.** Collected $10,000 in cash from customers' open accounts for the period.

_______ **2.** Paid one of the company's inventory suppliers $500 in settlement of an open account.

_______ **3.** Purchased a new copier for $6,000; signed a 90-day note payable.

_______ **4.** Issued bonds at face value of $100,000.

_______ **5.** Made $23,200 in cash sales for the week.

_______ **6.** Purchased an empty lot adjacent to the factory for $50,000. The seller of the land agrees to accept a five-year promissory note as consideration.

_______ **7.** Renewed the property insurance policy for another six months. Cash of $1,000 is paid for the renewal.

_______ **8.** Purchased a machine for $10,000.

_______ **9.** Paid cash dividends of $2,500.

_______ **10.** Reclassified as short-term a long-term note payable of $5,000 that is due within the next year.

_______ **11.** Purchased 500 shares of the company's own stock on the open market for $4,000.

_______ **12.** Sold 500 shares of Nike stock for book value of $10,000 (they had been classified as available-for-sale securities).

Exercise 12-13 *Long-Term Assets on the Statement of Cash Flows—Indirect Method* **LO 3, 6**

The following account balances are taken from the records of Martin Corp. for the past two years:

	December 31	
	2004	**2003**
Plant and equipment	$ 750,000	$ 500,000
Accumulated depreciation	160,000	200,000
Patents	92,000	80,000
Retained earnings	825,000	675,000

Other information available for 2004 follows:

a. Net income for the year was $200,000.

b. Depreciation expense on plant and equipment was $50,000.

c. Plant and equipment with an original cost of $150,000 were sold for $64,000 (you will need to determine the book value of the assets sold).

d. Amortization expense on patents was $8,000.

e. Both new plant and equipment and patents were purchased for cash during the year.

Required

Indicate, with amounts, how all items related to these long-term assets would be reported in the 2004 statement of cash flows, including any adjustments in the Operating Activities section of the statement. Assume that Martin uses the indirect method.

Exercise 12-14 *Income Statement, Statement of Cash Flows (Direct Method), and Balance Sheet* **LO 1, 5**

The following events occurred at Handsome Hounds Grooming Company during its first year of business:

a. To establish the company, the two owners contributed a total of $50,000 in exchange for common stock.

b. Grooming service revenue for the first year amounted to $150,000, of which $40,000 was on account.

c. Customers owe $10,000 at the end of the year from the services provided on account.

d. At the beginning of the year a storage building was rented. The company was required to sign a three-year lease for $12,000 per year and make a $2,000 refundable security deposit. The first year's lease payment and the security deposit were paid at the beginning of the year.

e. At the beginning of the year the company purchased a patent at a cost of $100,000 for a revolutionary system to be used for dog grooming. The patent is expected to be useful for 10 years. The company paid 20% down in cash and signed a four-year note at the bank for the remainder.

f. Operating expenses, including amortization of the patent and rent on the storage building, totaled $80,000 for the first year. No expenses were accrued or unpaid at the end of the year.

g. The company declared and paid a $20,000 cash dividend at the end of the first year.

Required

1. Prepare an income statement for the first year.
2. Prepare a statement of cash flows for the first year, using the direct method in the Operating Activities section.
3. Did the company generate more or less cash flow from operations than it earned in net income? Explain why there is a difference.
4. Prepare a balance sheet as of the end of the first year.

Problems

Problem 12-1 ***Statement of Cash Flows—Indirect Method*** **LO 6**

The following balances are available for Chrisman Company:

	December 31	
	2004	**2003**
Cash	$ 8,000	$ 10,000
Accounts receivable	20,000	15,000
Inventory	15,000	25,000
Prepaid rent	9,000	6,000
Land	75,000	75,000
Plant and equipment	400,000	300,000
Accumulated depreciation	(65,000)	(30,000)
Totals	$462,000	$401,000
Accounts payable	$ 12,000	$ 10,000
Income taxes payable	3,000	5,000
Short-term notes payable	35,000	25,000
Bonds payable	75,000	100,000
Common stock	200,000	150,000
Retained earnings	137,000	111,000
Totals	$462,000	$401,000

Bonds were retired during 2004 at face value, plant and equipment were acquired for cash, and common stock was issued for cash. Depreciation expense for the year was $35,000. Net income was reported at $26,000.

Required

1. Prepare a statement of cash flows for 2004, using the indirect method in the Operating Activities section.
2. Did Chrisman generate sufficient cash from operations to pay for its investing activities? How did it generate cash other than from operations? Explain your answers.

Problem 12-2 ***Statement of Cash Flows Using a Work Sheet—Indirect Method (Appendix)*** **LO 7**

Refer to all of the facts in Problem 12-1.

Required

1. Using the format in the chapter's appendix, prepare a statement of cash flows work sheet.
2. Prepare a statement of cash flows for 2004, using the indirect method in the Operating Activities section.
3. Did Chrisman generate sufficient cash from operations to pay for its investing activities? How did it generate cash other than from operations? Explain your answers.

Problem 12-3 ***Statement of Cash Flows—Direct Method*** **LO 5**

DECISION MAKING

Peoria Corp. has just completed another very successful year, as indicated by the following income statement:

	For the Year Ended December 31, 2004
Sales revenue	$1,250,000
Cost of goods sold	700,000
Gross profit	$ 550,000
Operating expenses	150,000
Income before interest and taxes	$ 400,000
Interest expense	25,000
Income before taxes	$ 375,000
Income tax expense	150,000
Net income	$ 225,000

Presented below are comparative balance sheets:

	December 31	
	2004	**2003**
Cash	$ 52,000	$ 90,000
Accounts receivable	180,000	130,000
Inventory	230,000	200,000
Prepayments	15,000	25,000
Total current assets	$ 477,000	$ 445,000
Land	$ 750,000	$ 600,000
Plant and equipment	700,000	500,000
Accumulated depreciation	(250,000)	(200,000)
Total long-term assets	$1,200,000	$ 900,000
Total assets	$1,677,000	$1,345,000
Accounts payable	$ 130,000	$ 148,000
Other accrued liabilities	68,000	63,000
Income taxes payable	90,000	110,000
Total current liabilities	$ 288,000	$ 321,000
Long-term bank loan payable	$ 350,000	$ 300,000
Common stock	$ 550,000	$ 400,000
Retained earnings	489,000	324,000
Total stockholders' equity	$1,039,000	$ 724,000
Total liabilities and stockholders' equity	$1,677,000	$1,345,000

Other information follows:

a. Dividends of $60,000 were declared and paid during the year.

b. Operating expenses include $50,000 of depreciation.

c. Land and plant and equipment were acquired for cash, and additional stock was issued for cash. Cash was also received from additional bank loans.

The president has asked you some questions about the year's results. She is very impressed with the profit margin of 18% (net income divided by sales revenue). She is bothered, however, by the decline in the cash balance during the year. One of the conditions of the existing bank loan is that the company maintain a minimum cash balance of $50,000.

Required

1. Prepare a statement of cash flows for 2004, using the direct method in the Operating Activities section.
2. On the basis of your statement in requirement 1, draft a brief memo to the president to explain why cash decreased during such a profitable year. Include in your explanation any recommendations for improving the company's cash flow in future years.

Problem 12-4 ***Statement of Cash Flows—Indirect Method*** **LO 6**

Refer to all of the facts in Problem 12-3.

DECISION MAKING

Required

1. Prepare a statement of cash flows for 2004, using the indirect method in the Operating Activities section.
2. On the basis of your statement in requirement 1, draft a brief memo to the president to explain why cash decreased during such a profitable year. Include in your explanation any recommendations for improving the company's cash flow in future years.

Problem 12-5 ***Statement of Cash Flows Using a Work Sheet—Indirect Method (Appendix)*** **LO 7**

Refer to all of the facts in Problem 12-3.

DECISION MAKING

Required

1. Using the format in the chapter's appendix, prepare a statement of cash flows work sheet.
2. Prepare a statement of cash flows for 2004, using the indirect method in the Operating Activities section.
3. On the basis of your statement in requirement 2, draft a brief memo to the president to explain why cash decreased during such a profitable year. Include in your explanation any recommendations for improving the company's cash flow in future years.

Problem 12-6 ***Statement of Cash Flows—Direct Method*** **LO 5**

The income statement for Astro Inc. for 2004 follows:

DECISION MAKING

	For the Year Ended December 31, 2004
Sales revenue	$ 500,000
Cost of goods sold	400,000
Gross profit	$ 100,000
Operating expenses	180,000
Loss before interest and taxes	$ (80,000)
Interest expense	20,000
Net loss	$(100,000)

Presented below are comparative balance sheets:

	December 31	
	2004	2003
Cash	$ 95,000	$ 80,000
Accounts receivable	50,000	75,000
Inventory	100,000	150,000
Prepayments	55,000	45,000
Total current assets	$ 300,000	$ 350,000
Land	$ 475,000	$ 400,000
Plant and equipment	870,000	800,000
Accumulated depreciation	(370,000)	(300,000)
Total long-term assets	$ 975,000	$ 900,000
Total assets	$1,275,000	$1,250,000
Accounts payable	$ 125,000	$ 100,000
Other accrued liabilities	35,000	45,000
Interest payable	15,000	10,000
Total current liabilities	$ 175,000	$ 155,000

(continued)

Long-term bank loan payable	$ 340,000	$ 250,000
Common stock	$ 450,000	$ 400,000
Retained earnings	310,000	445,000
Total stockholders' equity	$ 760,000	$ 845,000
Total liabilities and stockholders' equity	$1,275,000	$1,250,000

Other information follows:

a. Dividends of $35,000 were declared and paid during the year.

b. Operating expenses include $70,000 of depreciation.

c. Land and plant and equipment were acquired for cash, and additional stock was issued for cash. Cash was also received from additional bank loans.

The president has asked you some questions about the year's results. He is disturbed with the $100,000 net loss for the year. He notes, however, that the cash position at the end of the year is improved. He is confused about what appear to be conflicting signals: "How could we have possibly added to our bank accounts during such a terrible year of operations?"

Required

1. Prepare a statement of cash flows for 2004, using the direct method in the Operating Activities section.
2. On the basis of your statement in requirement **1**, draft a brief memo to the president to explain why cash increased during such an unprofitable year. Include in your memo your recommendations for improving the company's bottom line.

Problem 12-7 *Statement of Cash Flows—Indirect Method* LO 6

Refer to all of the facts in Problem 12-6.

DECISION MAKING

Required

1. Prepare a statement of cash flows for 2004, using the indirect method in the Operating Activities section.
2. On the basis of your statement in requirement **1**, draft a brief memo to the president to explain why cash increased during such an unprofitable year. Include in your memo your recommendations for improving the company's bottom line.

Problem 12-8 *Statement of Cash Flows Using a Work Sheet—Indirect Method (Appendix)* LO 7

Refer to all of the facts in Problem 12-6.

DECISION MAKING

Required

1. Using the format in the chapter's appendix, prepare a statement of cash flows work sheet.
2. Prepare a statement of cash flows for 2004, using the indirect method in the Operating Activities section.
3. On the basis of your statement in requirement **2**, draft a brief memo to the president to explain why cash increased during such an unprofitable year. Include in your memo your recommendations for improving the company's bottom line.

Problem 12-9 *Year-End Balance Sheet and Statement of Cash Flows—Indirect Method* LO 6

The balance sheet of Terrier Company at the end of 2003 is presented below, along with certain other information for 2004:

	December 31, 2003
Cash	$ 140,000
Accounts receivable	155,000
Total current assets	$ 295,000
Land	$ 300,000
Plant and equipment	500,000
Accumulated depreciation	(150,000)
Investments	100,000
Total long-term assets	$ 750,000
Total assets	$1,045,000

Current liabilities	$ 205,000
Bonds payable	$ 300,000
Common stock	$ 400,000
Retained earnings	140,000
Total stockholders' equity	$ 540,000
Total liabilities and stockholders' equity	$1,045,000

Other information follows:

a. Net income for 2004 was $70,000.

b. Included in operating expenses was $20,000 in depreciation.

c. Cash dividends of $25,000 were declared and paid.

d. An additional $150,000 of bonds was issued for cash.

e. Common stock of $50,000 was purchased for cash and retired.

f. Cash purchases of plant and equipment during the year were $200,000.

g. An additional $100,000 of bonds was issued in exchange for land.

h. Sales exceeded cash collections on account during the year by $10,000. All sales are on account.

i. The amount of current liabilities remained unchanged during the year.

Required

1. Prepare a statement of cash flows for 2004, using the indirect method in the Operating Activities section. Include a supplemental schedule for noncash activities.
2. Prepare a balance sheet at December 31, 2004.
3. Provide a possible explanation as to why Terrier decided to issue additional bonds for cash during 2004.

Problem 12-10 *Statement of Cash Flows Using a Work Sheet—Indirect Method (Appendix)* LO 7

Refer to all of the facts in Problem 12-9.

Required

1. Prepare a balance sheet at December 31, 2004.
2. Using the format in the chapter's appendix, prepare a statement of cash flows work sheet.
3. Prepare a statement of cash flows for 2004, using the indirect method in the Operating Activities section.
4. Provide a possible explanation as to why Terrier decided to issue additional bonds for cash during 2004.

Multi-Concept Problems

Problem 12-11 *Statement of Cash Flows—Direct Method* LO 4, 5

Glendive Corp. is in the process of preparing its statement of cash flows for the year ended June 30, 2004. An income statement for the year and comparative balance sheets follow:

SPREADSHEET

	For the Year Ended June 30, 2004
Sales revenue	$550,000
Cost of goods sold	350,000
Gross profit	$200,000
General and administrative expenses	$ 55,000
Depreciation expense	75,000
Loss on sale of plant assets	5,000
Total expenses and losses	$135,000
Income before interest and taxes	$ 65,000
Interest expense	15,000
Income before taxes	$ 50,000
Income tax expense	17,000
Net income	$ 33,000

	June 30	
	2004	2003
Cash	$ 31,000	$ 40,000
Accounts receivable	90,000	75,000
Inventory	80,000	95,000
Prepaid rent	12,000	16,000
Total current assets	$213,000	$226,000
Land	$250,000	$170,000
Plant and equipment	750,000	600,000
Accumulated depreciation	(310,000)	(250,000)
Total long-term assets	$690,000	$520,000
Total assets	$903,000	$746,000
Accounts payable	$155,000	$148,000
Other accrued liabilities	32,000	26,000
Income taxes payable	8,000	10,000
Total current liabilities	$195,000	$184,000
Long-term bank loan payable	$100,000	$130,000
Common stock	$350,000	$200,000
Retained earnings	258,000	232,000
Total stockholders' equity	$608,000	$432,000
Total liabilities and stockholders' equity	$903,000	$746,000

Dividends of $7,000 were declared and paid during the year. New plant assets were purchased for $195,000 in cash during the year. Also, land was purchased for cash. Plant assets were sold during 2004 for $25,000 in cash. The original cost of the assets sold was $45,000, and their book value was $30,000. Additional stock was issued for cash, and a portion of the bank loan was repaid.

Required

1. Prepare a statement of cash flows, using the direct method in the Operating Activities section.
2. Evaluate the following statement: "Whether a company uses the direct or the indirect method to report cash flows from operations is irrelevant because the amount of cash flow from operating activities is the same regardless of which method is used."

Problem 12-12 *Statement of Cash Flows—Indirect Method* LO 4, 6

Refer to all of the facts in Problem 12-11.

SPREADSHEET

Required

1. Prepare a statement of cash flows for 2004, using the indirect method in the Operating Activities section.
2. Evaluate the following statement: "Whether a company uses the direct or indirect method to report cash flows from operations is irrelevant because the amount of cash flow from operating activities is the same regardless of which method is used."

Problem 12-13 *Statement of Cash Flows—Direct Method* LO 2, 5

Lang Company has not yet prepared a formal statement of cash flows for 2004. Comparative balance sheets (thousands omitted) as of December 31, 2004 and 2003, and a statement of income and retained earnings for the year ended December 31, 2004, follow:

LANG COMPANY
BALANCE SHEET
DECEMBER 31

Assets	2004	2003
Current assets:		
Cash	$ 60	$ 100
U.S. Treasury bills (six-month)	–0–	50
Accounts receivable	610	500
Inventory	720	600
Total current assets	$1,390	$1,250

Assets	2004	2003
Long-term assets:		
Land	$ 80	$ 70
Buildings and equipment	710	600
Accumulated depreciation	(180)	(120)
Patents (less amortization)	105	130
Total long-term assets	$ 715	$ 680
Total assets	$2,105	$1,930

Liabilities and Owners' Equity	2004	2003
Current liabilities:		
Accounts payable	$ 360	$ 300
Taxes payable	25	20
Notes payable	400	400
Total current liabilities	$ 785	$ 720
Term notes payable—due 2008	200	200
Total liabilities	$ 985	$ 920
Owners' equity:		
Common stock outstanding	$ 830	$ 700
Retained earnings	290	310
Total owners' equity	$1,120	$1,010
Total liabilities and owners' equity	$2,105	$1,930

LANG COMPANY
STATEMENT OF INCOME AND RETAINED EARNINGS
FOR THE YEAR ENDED DECEMBER 31, 2004
(THOUSANDS OMITTED)

Sales		$2,408
Less expenses and interest:		
Cost of goods sold	$1,100	
Salaries and benefits	850	
Heat, light, and power	75	
Depreciation	60	
Property taxes	18	
Patent amortization	25	
Miscellaneous expense	10	
Interest	55	2,193
Net income before income taxes		$ 215
Income taxes		105
Net income		$ 110
Retained earnings—January 1, 2004		310
		$ 420
Stock dividend distributed		130
Retained earnings—December 31, 2004		$ 290

Required

1. For purposes of a statement of cash flows, are the U.S. Treasury bills cash equivalents? If not, how should they be classified? Explain your answers.
2. Prepare a statement of cash flows for 2004, using the direct method in the Operating Activities section.

(CMA adapted)

Alternate Problems

Problem 12-1A ***Statement of Cash Flows—Indirect Method*** **LO 6**

The following balances are available for Madison Company:

	December 31	
	2004	**2003**
Cash	$ 12,000	$ 10,000
Accounts receivable	10,000	12,000
Inventory	8,000	7,000
Prepaid rent	1,200	1,000
Land	75,000	75,000
Plant and equipment	200,000	150,000
Accumulated depreciation	(75,000)	(25,000)
Totals	$231,200	$230,000
Accounts payable	$ 15,000	$ 15,000
Income taxes payable	2,500	2,000
Short-term notes payable	20,000	22,500
Bonds payable	75,000	50,000
Common stock	100,000	100,000
Retained earnings	18,700	40,500
Totals	$231,200	$230,000

Bonds were issued during 2004 at face value, and plant and equipment were acquired for cash. Depreciation expense for the year was $50,000. A net loss of $21,800 was reported.

Required

1. Prepare a statement of cash flows for 2004, using the indirect method in the Operating Activities section.
2. Explain briefly how Madison was able to increase its cash balance during a year in which it incurred a net loss.

Problem 12-2A ***Statement of Cash Flows Using a Work Sheet—Indirect Method (Appendix)*** **LO 7**

Refer to all of the facts in Problem 12-1A.

Required

1. Using the format in the chapter's appendix, prepare a statement of cash flows work sheet.
2. Prepare a statement of cash flows for 2004, using the indirect method in the Operating Activities section.
3. Explain briefly how Madison was able to increase its cash balance during a year in which it incurred a net loss.

Problem 12-3A ***Statement of Cash Flows—Direct Method*** **LO 5**

DECISION MAKING

Wabash Corp. has just completed another very successful year, as indicated by the following income statement:

	For the Year Ended December 31, 2004
Sales revenue	$2,460,000
Cost of goods sold	1,400,000
Gross profit	$1,060,000
Operating expenses	460,000
Income before interest and taxes	$ 600,000
Interest expense	100,000
Income before taxes	$ 500,000
Income tax expense	150,000
Net income	$ 350,000

The following are comparative balance sheets:

	December 31	
	2004	**2003**
Cash	$ 140,000	$ 210,000
Accounts receivable	60,000	145,000
Inventory	200,000	180,000
Prepayments	15,000	25,000
Total current assets	$ 415,000	$ 560,000
Land	$ 600,000	$ 700,000
Plant and equipment	850,000	600,000
Accumulated depreciation	(225,000)	(200,000)
Total long-term assets	$1,225,000	$1,100,000
Total assets	$1,640,000	$1,660,000
Accounts payable	$ 140,000	$ 120,000
Other accrued liabilities	50,000	55,000
Income taxes payable	80,000	115,000
Total current liabilities	$ 270,000	$ 290,000
Long-term bank loan payable	$ 200,000	$ 250,000
Common stock	$ 450,000	$ 400,000
Retained earnings	720,000	720,000
Total stockholders' equity	$1,170,000	$1,120,000
Total liabilities and stockholders' equity	$1,640,000	$1,660,000

Other information follows:

a. Dividends of $350,000 were declared and paid during the year.

b. Operating expenses include $25,000 of depreciation.

c. Land was sold for its book value, and new plant and equipment was acquired for cash.

d. Part of the bank loan was repaid, and additional common stock was issued for cash.

The president has asked you some questions about the year's results. She is very impressed with the profit margin of 14% (net income divided by sales revenue). She is bothered, however, by the decline in the company's cash balance during the year. One of the conditions of the existing bank loan is that the company maintain a minimum cash balance of $100,000.

Required

1. Prepare a statement of cash flows for 2004, using the direct method in the Operating Activities section.
2. On the basis of your statement in requirement **1**, draft a brief memo to the president to explain why cash decreased during such a profitable year. Include in your explanation any recommendations for improving the company's cash flow in future years.

Problem 12-4A *Statement of Cash Flows—Indirect Method* LO 6

Refer to all of the facts in Problem 12-3A.

DECISION MAKING

Required

1. Prepare a statement of cash flows for 2004, using the indirect method in the Operating Activities section.
2. On the basis of your statement in requirement **1**, draft a brief memo to the president to explain why cash decreased during such a profitable year. Include in your explanation any recommendations for improving the company's cash flow in future years.

Problem 12-5A *Statement of Cash Flows Using a Work Sheet—Indirect Method (Appendix)* LO 7

Refer to all of the facts in Problem 12-3A.

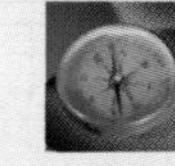

DECISION MAKING

Required

1. Using the format in the chapter's appendix, prepare a statement of cash flows work sheet.
2. Prepare a statement of cash flows for 2004, using the indirect method in the Operating Activities section.

(continued)

3. On the basis of your statement in requirement 2, draft a brief memo to the president to explain why cash decreased during such a profitable year. Include in your explanation any recommendations for improving the company's cash flow in future years.

Problem 12-6A ***Statement of Cash Flows—Direct Method*** **LO 5**

DECISION MAKING

The income statement for Pluto Inc. for 2004 follows:

	For the Year Ended December 31, 2004
Sales revenue	$350,000
Cost of goods sold	150,000
Gross profit	$200,000
Operating expenses	250,000
Loss before interest and taxes	$ (50,000)
Interest expense	10,000
Net loss	$ (60,000)

Presented below are comparative balance sheets:

	December 31	
	2004	2003
Cash	$ 25,000	$ 10,000
Accounts receivable	30,000	80,000
Inventory	100,000	100,000
Prepayments	36,000	35,000
Total current assets	$191,000	$225,000
Land	$300,000	$200,000
Plant and equipment	500,000	250,000
Accumulated depreciation	(90,000)	(50,000)
Total long-term assets	$710,000	$400,000
Total assets	$901,000	$625,000
Accounts payable	$ 50,000	$ 10,000
Other accrued liabilities	40,000	20,000
Interest payable	22,000	12,000
Total current liabilities	$112,000	$ 42,000
Long-term bank loan payable	$450,000	$100,000
Common stock	$300,000	$300,000
Retained earnings	39,000	183,000
Total stockholders' equity	$339,000	$483,000
Total liabilities and stockholders' equity	$901,000	$625,000

Other information follows:

a. Dividends of $84,000 were declared and paid during the year.

b. Operating expenses include $40,000 of depreciation.

c. Land and plant and equipment were acquired for cash. Cash was received from additional bank loans.

The president has asked you some questions about the year's results. He is disturbed with the net loss of $60,000 for the year. He notes, however, that the cash position at the end of the year is improved. He is confused about what appear to be conflicting signals: "How could we have possibly added to our bank accounts during such a terrible year of operations?"

Required

1. Prepare a statement of cash flows for 2004, using the direct method in the Operating Activities section.
2. On the basis of your statement in requirement 1, draft a brief memo to the president to explain why cash increased during such an unprofitable year. Include in your memo your recommendations for improving the company's bottom line.

Problem 12-7A ***Statement of Cash Flows—Indirect Method*** **LO 6**

Refer to all of the facts in Problem 12-6A.

Required

1. Prepare a statement of cash flows for 2004, using the indirect method in the Operating Activities section.
2. On the basis of your statement in requirement **1,** draft a brief memo to the president to explain why cash increased during such an unprofitable year. Include in your memo your recommendations for improving the company's bottom line.

Problem 12-8A ***Statement of Cash Flows Using a Work Sheet—Indirect Method (Appendix)*** **LO 7**

Refer to all of the facts in Problem 12-6A.

Required

1. Using the format in the chapter's appendix, prepare a statement of cash flows work sheet.
2. Prepare a statement of cash flows for 2004, using the indirect method in the Operating Activities section.
3. On the basis of your statement in requirement **2,** draft a brief memo to the president to explain why cash increased during such an unprofitable year. Include in your memo your recommendations for improving the company's bottom line.

Problem 12-9A ***Year-End Balance Sheet and Statement of Cash Flows—Indirect Method*** **LO 6**

The balance sheet of Poodle Company at the end of 2003 is presented below along with certain other information for 2004:

	December 31, 2003
Cash	$ 155,000
Accounts receivable	140,000
Total current assets	$ 295,000
Land	$ 100,000
Plant and equipment	700,000
Accumulated depreciation	(175,000)
Investments	125,000
Total long-term assets	$ 750,000
Total assets	$1,045,000
Current liabilities	$ 325,000
Bonds payable	$ 100,000
Common stock	$ 500,000
Retained earnings	120,000
Total stockholders' equity	$ 620,000
Total liabilities and stockholders' equity	$1,045,000

Other information follows:

a. Net income for 2004 was $50,000.
b. Included in operating expenses was $25,000 in depreciation.
c. Cash dividends of $40,000 were declared and paid.
d. An additional $50,000 of common stock was issued for cash.
e. Bonds payable of $100,000 were purchased for cash and retired at no gain or loss.
f. Cash purchases of plant and equipment during the year were $60,000.
g. An additional $200,000 of land was acquired in exchange for a long-term note payable.
h. Sales exceeded cash collections on account during the year by $15,000. All sales are on account.
i. The amount of current liabilities decreased by $20,000 during the year.

Required

1. Prepare a statement of cash flows for 2004, using the indirect method in the Operating Activities section. Include a supplemental schedule for noncash activities.

(continued)

2. Prepare a balance sheet at December 31, 2004.
3. What primary uses did Poodle make of the cash it generated from operating activities?

Problem 12-10A ***Statement of Cash Flows Using a Work Sheet—Indirect Method (Appendix)*** **LO 7**

Refer to all of the facts in Problem 12-9A.

Required

1. Prepare a balance sheet at December 31, 2004.
2. Using the format in the chapter's appendix, prepare a statement of cash flows work sheet.
3. Prepare a statement of cash flows for 2004, using the indirect method in the Operating Activities section.
4. Provide a possible explanation as to why Poodle decided to purchase and retire bonds during 2004.

Alternate Multi-Concept Problems

Problem 12-11A ***Statement of Cash Flows—Direct Method*** **LO 4, 5**

Bannack Corp. is in the process of preparing its statement of cash flows for the year ended June 30, 2004. An income statement for the year and comparative balance sheets follow:

	For the Year Ended June 30, 2004
Sales revenue	$400,000
Cost of goods sold	240,000
Gross profit	$160,000
General and administrative expenses	$ 40,000
Depreciation expense	80,000
Loss on sale of plant assets	10,000
Total expenses and losses	$130,000
Income before interest and taxes	$ 30,000
Interest expense	15,000
Income before taxes	$ 15,000
Income tax expense	5,000
Net income	$ 10,000

	June 30	
	2004	2003
Cash	$ 25,000	$ 40,000
Accounts receivable	80,000	69,000
Inventory	75,000	50,000
Prepaid rent	2,000	18,000
Total current assets	$ 182,000	$ 177,000
Land	$ 60,000	$ 150,000
Plant and equipment	575,000	500,000
Accumulated depreciation	(310,000)	(250,000)
Total long-term assets	$ 325,000	$ 400,000
Total assets	$ 507,000	$ 577,000
Accounts payable	$ 145,000	$ 140,000
Other accrued liabilities	50,000	45,000
Income taxes payable	5,000	15,000
Total current liabilities	$ 200,000	$ 200,000
Long-term bank loan payable	$ 75,000	$ 150,000
Common stock	$ 100,000	$ 100,000
Retained earnings	132,000	127,000
Total stockholders' equity	$ 232,000	$ 227,000
Total liabilities and stockholders' equity	$ 507,000	$ 577,000

Dividends of $5,000 were declared and paid during the year. New plant assets were purchased for $125,000 in cash during the year. Also, land was sold for cash at its book value. Plant assets were sold during 2004 for $20,000 in cash. The original cost of the assets sold was $50,000, and their book value was $30,000. A portion of the bank loan was repaid.

Required

1. Prepare a statement of cash flows for 2004, using the direct method in the Operating Activities section.
2. Evaluate the following statement: "Whether a company uses the direct or the indirect method to report cash flows from operations is irrelevant because the amount of cash flow from operating activities is the same regardless of which method is used."

Problem 12-12A *Statement of Cash Flows—Indirect Method* LO 4, 6

Refer to all of the facts in Problem 12-11A.

Required

1. Prepare a statement of cash flows for 2004, using the indirect method in the Operating Activities section.
2. Evaluate the following statement: "Whether a company uses the direct or the indirect method to report cash flows from operations is irrelevant because the amount of cash flow from operating activities is the same regardless of which method is used."

Problem 12-13A *Statement of Cash Flows—Direct Method* LO 2, 5

Shepard Company has not yet prepared a formal statement of cash flows for 2004. Comparative balance sheets as of December 31, 2004 and 2003, and a statement of income and retained earnings for the year ended December 31, 2004, follow:

SHEPARD COMPANY
BALANCE SHEET
DECEMBER 31
(THOUSANDS OMITTED)

Assets	**2004**	**2003**
Current assets:		
Cash	$ 50	$ 75
U.S. Treasury bills (six-month)	25	0
Accounts receivable	125	200
Inventory	525	500
Total current assets	$ 725	$ 775
Long-term assets:		
Land	$ 100	$ 80
Buildings and equipment	510	450
Accumulated depreciation	(190)	(150)
Patents (less amortization)	90	110
Total long-term assets	$ 510	$ 490
Total assets	$1,235	$1,265
Liabilities and Owners' Equity		
Current liabilities:		
Accounts payable	$ 370	$ 330
Taxes payable	10	20
Notes payable	300	400
Total current liabilities	$ 680	$ 750
Term notes payable—due 2008	200	200
Total liabilities	$ 880	$ 950
Owners' equity:		
Common stock outstanding	$ 220	$ 200
Retained earnings	135	115
Total owners' equity	$ 355	$ 315
Total liabilities and owners' equity	$1,235	$1,265

SHEPARD COMPANY
STATEMENT OF INCOME AND RETAINED EARNINGS
YEAR ENDED DECEMBER 31, 2004
(THOUSANDS OMITTED)

Sales		$1,416
Less expenses and interest:		
Cost of goods sold	$990	
Salaries and benefits	195	
Heat, light, and power	70	
Depreciation	40	
Property taxes	2	
Patent amortization	20	
Miscellaneous expense	2	
Interest	45	1,364
Net income before income taxes		$ 52
Income taxes		12
Net income		$ 40
Retained earnings—January 1, 2004		115
		$ 155
Stock dividend distributed		20
Retained earnings—December 31, 2004		$ 135

Required

1. For purposes of a statement of cash flows, are the U.S. Treasury bills cash equivalents? If not, how should they be classified? Explain your answers.
2. Prepare a statement of cash flows for 2004, using the direct method in the Operating Activities section. (CMA adapted)

Decision Cases

Reading and Interpreting Financial Statements

Decision Case 12-1 ***Reading and Interpreting Winnebago Industries' Statement of Cash Flows*** **LO 2, 3**

http://www.winnebagoind.com

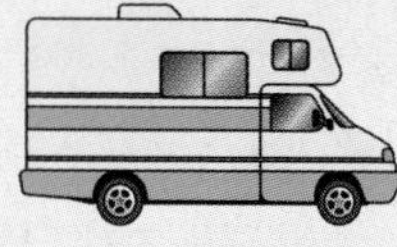

Refer to Winnebago Industries' statement of cash flows for 2002 and any other pertinent information in its annual report.

Required

1. According to a note in the annual report, how does the company define cash equivalents?
2. According to the statement of cash flows, did inventories increase or decrease during the most recent year? Explain your answer.
3. What are the major reasons for the difference between net income and net cash provided by operating activities?
4. Excluding operations, what was Winnebago Industries' largest source of cash during the most recent year? the largest use of cash?
5. In the Financing Activities section of its statement of cash flows, Winnebago Industries reports an amount used for the purchase of common stock. Locate this same amount on the statement of changes in stockholders' equity and explain why it appears on both statements.

Decision Case 12-2 ***Comparing Two Companies in the Same Industry: Winnebago Industries and Monaco Coach Corporation*** **LO 3**

http://www.winnebagoind.com
http://www.monacocoach.com

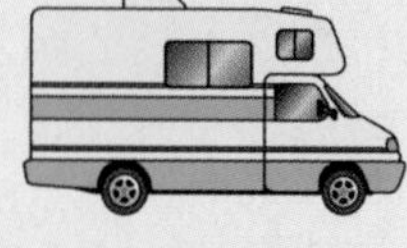

Refer to the financial statement information of Winnebago Industries and Monaco Coach Corporation in Appendices A and B at the end of the text. Use the cash flow statements in the annual reports for 2002 to answer the following questions:

Required

1. Did inventories increase or decrease for Monaco Coach during 2002? How does that compare to the change in inventory levels of Winnebago Industries? What are logical reasons for those changes in inventory levels?

2. The net cash provided by operating activities decreased significantly for both Monaco Coach and Winnebago Industries from 2001 to 2002. What was the most important reason for the decline for each company?
3. What amount did each company spend to purchase property and equipment during 2002? Did each company spend a similar amount, or a significantly different amount, in 2001?
4. What is the primary source of cash for financing activities for each of the two companies? Why do you think the companies did not use stock more extensively in 2002 as a way to acquire cash? Do you think this was a good strategic move? Why or why not?

Decision Case 12-3 *Reading and Interpreting IBM's Statement of Cash Flows and Notes* LO 4

http://www.ibm.com

According to Note C in IBM's 2002 annual report, the company completed 12 acquisitions during the year at a total cost of $3,958 million. The largest of these was the $3,474 million incurred to acquire PricewaterhouseCoopers Consulting (PwCC). However, the total amount of *cash* expended for all acquisitions of other businesses on the 2002 statement of cash flows was only $3,158 million.

Further on in Note C, IBM explains how it paid for the purchase of PwCC:

> The company paid $2,852 million of the purchase price in cash, $294 million primarily in the form of restricted shares of IBM common stock and $328 million in notes convertible into restricted shares of IBM common stock.

Required

1. Explain how it is possible that the total cost incurred to acquire PwCC could be more than the total cash expended to acquire all businesses in 2002.
2. How much cash did IBM pay to acquire PwCC? What other forms of consideration did the company use to buy the other company? Verify for yourself that all of these forms of consideration in total equal $3,474 million.
3. Given that the total cost to acquire PwCC was more than the cash expended, where should the noncash portion of the purchase price be disclosed on the statement of cash flows? Locate where this disclosure appears on IBM's statement of cash flows as displayed in the chapter opener.

Making Financial Decisions

Decision Case 12-4 *Dividend Decision and the Statement of Cash Flows—Direct Method* LO 1, 5

DECISION MAKING

Bailey Corp. just completed the most profitable year in its 25-year history. Reported earnings of $1,020,000 on sales of $8,000,000 resulted in a very healthy profit margin of 12.75%. Each year before releasing the financial statements, the board of directors meets to decide on the amount of dividends to declare for the year. For each of the past nine years, the company has declared a dividend of $1 per share of common stock, which has been paid on January 15 of the following year.

Presented below are the income statement for the year and comparative balance sheets as of the end of the last two years.

	For the Year Ended December 31, 2004
Sales revenue	$8,000,000
Cost of goods sold	4,500,000
Gross profit	$3,500,000
Operating expenses	1,450,000
Income before interest and taxes	$2,050,000
Interest expense	350,000
Income before taxes	$1,700,000
Income tax expense 40%	680,000
Net income	$1,020,000

(continued)

	December 31	
	2004	**2003**
Cash	$ 480,000	$ 450,000
Accounts receivable	250,000	200,000
Inventory	750,000	600,000
Prepayments	60,000	75,000
Total current assets	$1,540,000	$1,325,000
Land	$3,255,000	$2,200,000
Plant and equipment	4,200,000	2,500,000
Accumulated depreciation	(1,250,000)	(1,000,000)
Long-term investments	500,000	900,000
Patents	650,000	750,000
Total long-term assets	$7,355,000	$5,350,000
Total assets	$8,895,000	$6,675,000
Accounts payable	$ 350,000	$ 280,000
Other accrued liabilities	285,000	225,000
Income taxes payable	170,000	100,000
Dividends payable	0	200,000
Notes payable due within next year	200,000	0
Total current liabilities	$1,005,000	$ 805,000
Long-term notes payable	$ 300,000	$ 500,000
Bonds payable	2,200,000	1,500,000
Total long-term liabilities	$2,500,000	$2,000,000
Common stock, $10 par	$2,500,000	$2,000,000
Retained earnings	2,890,000	1,870,000
Total stockholders' equity	$5,390,000	$3,870,000
Total liabilities and stockholders' equity	$8,895,000	$6,675,000

Additional information follows:

a. All sales are on account, as are all purchases.

b. Land was purchased through the issuance of bonds. Additional land (beyond the amount purchased through the issuance of bonds) was purchased for cash.

c. New plant and equipment were acquired during the year for cash. No plant assets were retired during the year. Depreciation expense is included in operating expenses.

d. Long-term investments were sold for cash during the year.

e. No new patents were acquired, and none were disposed of during the year. Amortization expense is included in operating expenses.

f. Notes payable due within next year represents the amount reclassified from long-term to short-term.

g. Fifty thousand shares of common stock were issued during the year at par value.

As Bailey's controller, you have been asked to recommend to the board whether to declare a dividend this year and, if so, whether the precedent of paying a $1 per share dividend can be maintained. The president is eager to keep the dividend at $1 in view of the successful year just completed. He is also concerned, however, about the effect of a dividend on the company's cash position. He is particularly concerned about the large amount of notes payable that comes due next year. He further notes the aggressive growth pattern in recent years, as evidenced this year by large increases in land and plant and equipment.

Required

1. Using the format in Exhibit 12-14, convert the income statement from an accrual basis to a cash basis.
2. Prepare a statement of cash flows, using the direct method in the Operating Activities section.
3. What do you recommend to the board of directors concerning the declaration of a cash dividend? Should the $1 per share dividend be declared? Should a smaller amount be declared? Should no dividend be declared? Support your answer with any necessary computations. Include in your response your concerns, from a cash flow perspective, about the following year.

Decision Case 12-5 ***Equipment Replacement Decision and Cash Flows from Operations*** **LO 1, 6**

DECISION MAKING

Conrad Company has been in operation for four years. The company is pleased with the continued improvement in net income but is concerned about a lack of cash available to replace existing equipment. Land, buildings, and equipment were purchased at the beginning of Year 1. No subsequent fixed asset purchases have been made, but the president believes that equipment will need to be replaced in the near future. The following information is available (all amounts are in millions of dollars):

	Year of Operation			
	Year 1	**Year 2**	**Year 3**	**Year 4**
Net income (loss)	$(10)	$ (2)	$15	$20
Depreciation expense	30	25	15	14
Increase (decrease) in:				
Accounts receivable	32	5	12	20
Inventories	26	8	5	9
Prepayments	0	0	10	5
Accounts payable	15	3	(5)	(4)

Required

1. Compute the cash flow from operations for each of Conrad's first four years of operation.
2. Write a memo to the president explaining why the company is not generating sufficient cash from operations to pay for the replacement of equipment.

Accounting and Ethics: What Would You Do?

Decision Case 12-6 ***Loan Decision and the Statement of Cash Flows—Indirect Method*** **LO 1, 6**

ETHICS

Mega Enterprises is in the process of negotiating an extension of its existing loan agreements with a major bank. The bank is particularly concerned with Mega's ability to generate sufficient cash flow from operating activities to meet the periodic principal and interest payments. In conjunction with the negotiations, the controller prepared the following statement of cash flows to present to the bank:

MEGA ENTERPRISES
STATEMENT OF CASH FLOWS
FOR THE YEAR ENDED DECEMBER 31, 2004
(ALL AMOUNTS IN MILLIONS OF DOLLARS)

Cash flows from operating activities	
Net income	$ 65
Adjustments to reconcile net income to net cash provided by operating activities:	
Depreciation and amortization	56
Increase in accounts receivable	(19)
Decrease in inventory	27
Decrease in accounts payable	(42)
Increase in other accrued liabilities	18
Net cash provided by operating activities	$ 105
Cash flows from investing activities	
Acquisitions of other businesses	$ (234)
Acquisitions of plant and equipment	(125)
Sale of other businesses	300
Net cash used by investing activities	$ (59)
Cash flows from financing activities	
Additional borrowings	$ 150
Repayments of borrowings	(180)
Cash dividends paid	(50)
Net cash used by financing activities	$ (80)
Net decrease in cash	$ (34)
Cash balance, January 1, 2004	42
Cash balance, December 31, 2004	$ 8

During 2004, Mega sold one of its businesses in California. A gain of $150 million was included in 2004 income as the difference between the proceeds from the sale of $450 million and the book value of the business of $300 million. The effect on the accounting equation of the transaction to record the sale is as follows (in millions of dollars):

BALANCE SHEET					INCOME STATEMENT	
ASSETS		= LIABILITIES	+	OWNERS' EQUITY	+ REVENUES – EXPENSES	
Cash	450					
California Properties	(300)				Gain on Sale	150

Required

1. Comment on the presentation of the sale of the California business on the statement of cash flows. Does the way in which the sale was reported violate generally accepted accounting principles? Regardless of whether it violates GAAP, does the way in which the transaction was reported on the statement result in a misstatement of the net decrease in cash for the period? Explain your answers.
2. Prepare a revised statement of cash flows for 2004, with the proper presentation of the sale of the California business.
3. Has the controller acted in an unethical manner in the way the sale was reported on the statement of cash flows? Explain your answer.

Decision Case 12-7 *Cash Equivalents and the Statement of Cash Flows* LO 2, 3

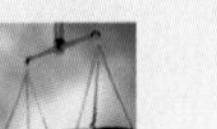

ETHICS

In December 2004, Rangers Inc. invested $100,000 of idle cash in U.S. Treasury notes. The notes mature on October 1, 2005, at which time Rangers expects to redeem them at face value of $100,000. The treasurer believes that the notes should be classified as cash equivalents because of the plans to hold them to maturity and receive face value. He would also like to avoid presentation of the purchase as an investing activity because the company has made sizable capital expenditures during the year. The treasurer realizes that the decision about classification of the Treasury notes rests with you, as controller.

Required

1. According to generally accepted accounting principles, how should the investment in U.S. Treasury notes be classified for purposes of preparing a statement of cash flows for the year ended December 31, 2004? Explain your answer.
2. If the notes are classified as an operating rather than an investing activity, is the information provided to outside readers free from bias? Explain.
3. As controller for Rangers, what would you do in this situation? What would you tell the treasurer?

THOMSON ONE Business School Edition Case

Case 12-8 *Using THOMSON ONE for IBM*

http://www.ibm.com

In the chapter we saw the critical role that cash flow plays in the success of all businesses, and looked specifically at IBM's cash flows. The future of any business is closely tied to its ability to generate cash from its operations and use that money wisely for investing and financing activities. In turn, success as measured in the financial statements should translate to success in the market for that company's stock. We can use THOMSON ONE to obtain information about IBM's cash flows and its stock price.

Begin by entering the company's ticker symbol, IBM, and then selecting "GO." On the opening screen you will see background information about the company, key financial ratios, and some recent data concerning stock price. To research the company's stock price further, you click the Prices tab. At the top of the Price Chart, click on the "Interactive Chart." To obtain a 1-year chart, go to "Time Frame," click on the down arrow, and select 1 year. Then click on "Draw," and a 1-year chart should appear.

We can also find IBM's recent financial statements. Near the top of the screen, click on "Financials" and select "Financial Statements." Refer to the comparative statements of cash flows for IBM.

Based on your use of THOMSON ONE, answer the following questions:

1. What has been the high and low stock price for the company for the most recent year?

2. How does the company's stock performance compare to the other line on the stock price chart for the S&P 500?
3. By what amount did cash and cash equivalents increase or decrease for the most recent year?
4. What was the amount of cash flow that IBM generated from operations in the most recent year? How much more or less is this number than the net income for the same period?

Solutions to Key Terms Quiz

__3__ Statement of cash flows (p. 596)
__4__ Cash equivalent (p. 598)
__1__ Operating activities (p. 599)
__5__ Investing activities (p. 600)
__7__ Financing activities (p. 601)
__6__ Direct method (p. 602)
__2__ Indirect method (p. 603)

Chapter 13

Financial Statement Analysis

WRIGLEY'S SPEARMINT
JUICY FRUIT
DOUBLEMINT

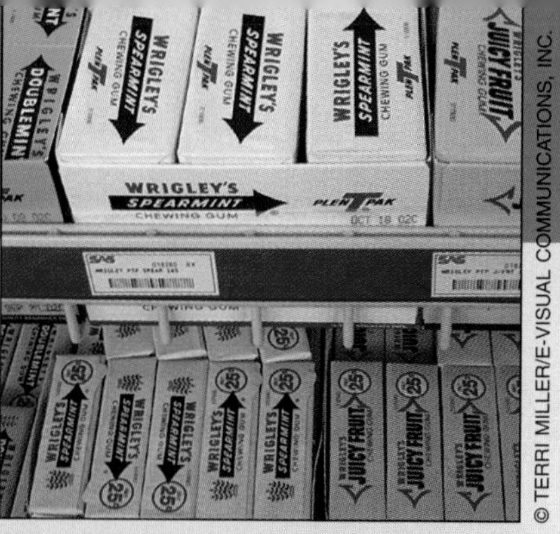

© TERRI MILLER/E-VISUAL COMMUNICATIONS, INC.

Roadmap to Success

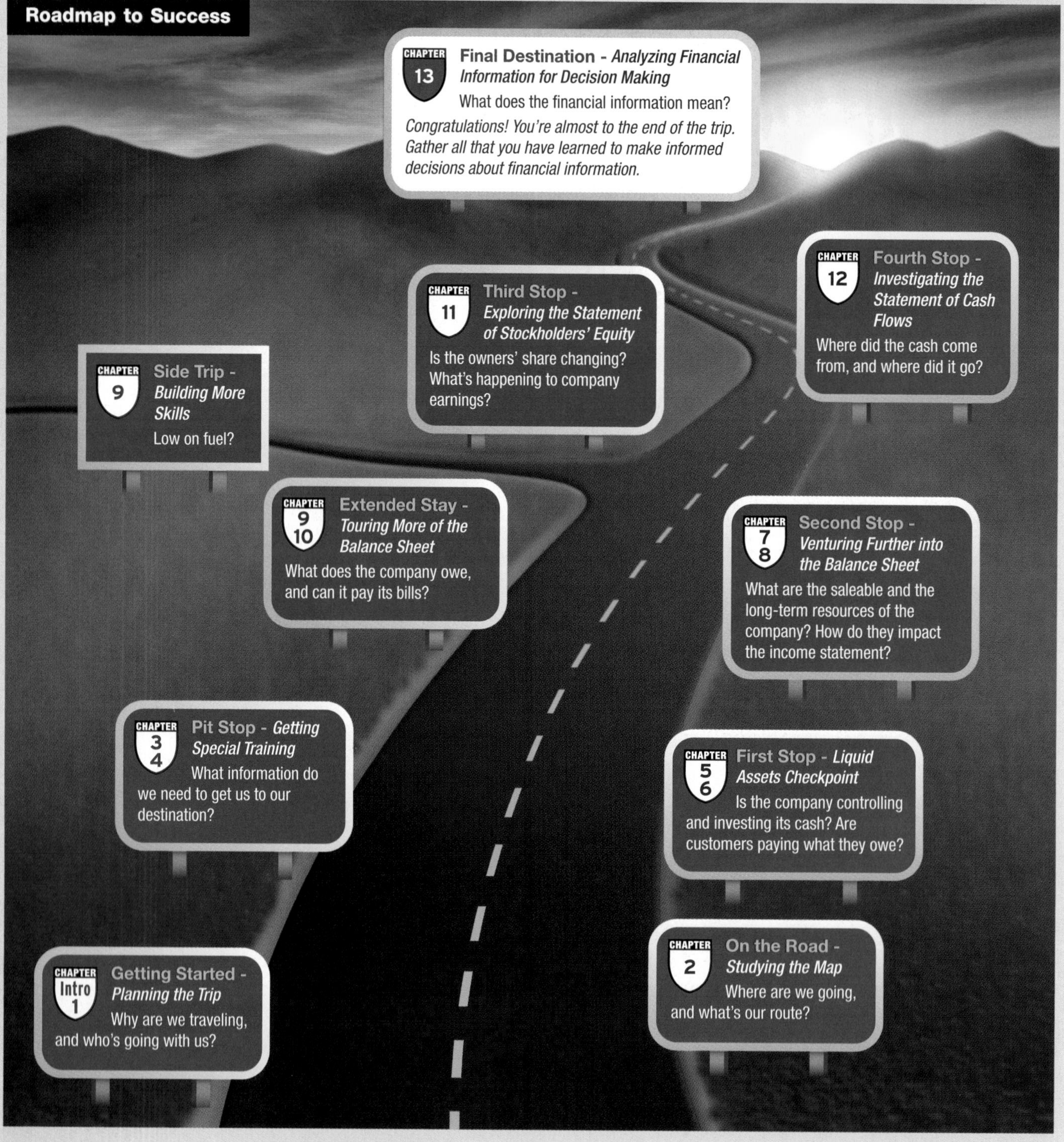

CHAPTER 13 Final Destination - *Analyzing Financial Information for Decision Making*
What does the financial information mean?
Congratulations! You're almost to the end of the trip. Gather all that you have learned to make informed decisions about financial information.
CHAPTER 12 Fourth Stop - *Investigating the Statement of Cash Flows*
Where did the cash come from, and where did it go?
CHAPTER 11 Third Stop - *Exploring the Statement of Stockholders' Equity*
Is the owners' share changing? What's happening to company earnings?
CHAPTER 9 Side Trip - *Building More Skills*
Low on fuel?
CHAPTER 9 10 Extended Stay - *Touring More of the Balance Sheet*
What does the company owe, and can it pay its bills?
CHAPTER 7 8 Second Stop - *Venturing Further into the Balance Sheet*
What are the saleable and the long-term resources of the company? How do they impact the income statement?
CHAPTER 3 4 Pit Stop - *Getting Special Training*
What information do we need to get us to our destination?
CHAPTER 5 6 First Stop - *Liquid Assets Checkpoint*
Is the company controlling and investing its cash? Are customers paying what they owe?
CHAPTER 2 On the Road - *Studying the Map*
Where are we going, and what's our route?
CHAPTER Intro 1 Getting Started - *Planning the Trip*
Why are we traveling, and who's going with us?

Focus on Financial Results

Although its products are variations on a single theme of chewing gum, the 112-year-old Wm. Wrigley Jr. Company has enjoyed a long and highly successful run. Wrigley has customers in more than 150 countries, and it garners about half of all chewing gum profits in Europe alone. The company is the market leader in 18 European markets and has achieved shares of 80% or higher. What accounts for this success?

Basic data for assessing the results of Wrigley's steady investments in marketing and new product innovations appear in the Financial Highlights section of the company's annual report, pictured here. Both net sales and net earnings reached record levels in 2002. Note that nearly half of those earnings ($181 million) were paid out to stockholders in dividends. However, the company has to make some tradeoffs. The more earnings that it pays in dividends, the less it has available to invest in future growth in overseas markets and to acquire new plant and equipment. Regardless, most companies and their stockholders would be envious of the robust return on average equity of nearly 29% that Wrigley achieved in 2002.

Sources: 2002 Wrigley Annual Report and Web site.

Wrigley's 2002 Annual Report

FINANCIAL HIGHLIGHTS

In thousands of dollars except per share amounts

	2002	2001
Net Sales	$2,746,318	$2,401,419
Net Earnings	$ 401,525	$ 362,986
Per Share of Common Stock (basic and diluted)	$ 1.78	$ 1.61
Dividends Paid	$ 181,232	$ 167,922
Per Share of Common Stock	$ .805	$ .745
Additions to Property, Plant and Equipment	$ 216,872	$ 181,760
Stockholders' Equity	$1,522,576	$1,276,197
Return on Average Equity	28.7%	30.1%
Stockholders of Record at Close of Year	40,534	38,701
Average Shares Outstanding (000)	225,145	225,349

About half of the earnings was paid out to owners as dividends.

You're in the Driver's Seat

http://www.wrigley.com

If you were considering buying shares of stock in the Wm. Wrigley Jr. Company, you would want to compare Wrigley with alternative investments and assess its ability to generate income and pay dividends. What measures of financial performance would be most important to you? Find the company's most recent annual report and determine whether those measures have improved since 2002.

LEARNING OBJECTIVES

After studying this chapter, you should be able to:

LO 1 Explain the various limitations and considerations in financial statement analysis. (p. 656)

LO 2 Use comparative financial statements to analyze a company over time (horizontal analysis). (p. 658)

LO 3 Use common-size financial statements to compare various financial statement items (vertical analysis). (p. 661)

LO 4 Compute and use various ratios to assess liquidity. (p. 666)

LO 5 Compute and use various ratios to assess solvency. (p. 671)

LO 6 Compute and use various ratios to assess profitability. (p. 674)

LO 7 Explain how to report on and analyze other income statement items (Appendix). (p. 688)

PRECAUTIONS IN STATEMENT ANALYSIS

Various groups have different purposes for analyzing a company's financial statements. **For example, a banker is primarily interested in the likelihood that a loan will be repaid.** Certain ratios, as we will see, indicate the ability to repay principal and interest. **A stockholder, on the other hand, is concerned with a fair return on the amount invested in the company.** Again, certain ratios are helpful in assessing the return to the stockholder. The managers of a business are also interested in the tools of financial statement analysis because various outside groups judge managers by using certain key ratios. Fortunately, most financial statements provide information about financial performance. Publicly held corporations are required to include in their annual reports a section that reviews the past year, with management's comments on its performance as measured by selected ratios and other forms of analysis.

Before we turn to various techniques commonly used in the financial analysis of a company, it is important to understand some of the limitations and other considerations in statement analysis.

Watch for Alternative Accounting Principles

LO 1 Explain the various limitations and considerations in financial statement analysis.

INTERNAL DECISION

Every set of financial statements is based on various assumptions. For example, a cost-flow method must be assumed in valuing inventory and recognizing cost of goods sold. The accountant chooses FIFO, LIFO, or one of the other acceptable methods. The analyst or other user finds this type of information in the notes to the financial statements. The selection of a particular inventory valuation method has a significant effect on certain key ratios. Recognition of the acceptable alternatives is especially important in comparing two or more companies. *Changes* in accounting methods, such as a change in the depreciation method, also make comparing results for a given company over time more difficult. Again, the reader must turn to the notes for information regarding these changes.

Take Care When Making Comparisons

Users of financial statements often place too much emphasis on summary indicators and key ratios, such as the current ratio and the earnings per share amount. No single ratio is capable of telling the user everything there is to know about a particular company. The calculation of various ratios for a company is only a starting point. One technique we discuss is the comparison of ratios for different periods of time. Has the ratio gone up or down from last year? What is the percentage of increase or decrease in the ratio over the last five years? Recognizing trends in ratios is important in analyzing any company.

The potential investor must also recognize the need to compare one company with others in the same industry. For example, a particular measure of performance may cause an investor to conclude that the company is not operating efficiently. Comparison with an industry standard, however, might indicate that the ratio is normal for companies in that industry. Various organizations publish summaries of selected ratios for a sample of companies in the United States. The ratios are usually organized by industry. Dun & Bradstreet's *Industry Norms and Key Business Ratios,* for example, is an annual review that organizes companies into major industry segments and approximately 800 specific lines of business.

Although industry comparisons are useful, caution is necessary in interpreting the results of such analyses. Few companies in today's economy operate in a single industry. Exceptions exist (Wrigley is almost exclusively in the business of making and selling chewing gum), but most companies cross the boundaries of a single industry. *Conglomerates,* companies operating in more than one industry, present a special challenge to the analyst. Keep in mind also the point made earlier about alternative accounting methods. It is not unusual to find companies in the same industry using different inventory valuation techniques or depreciation methods.

Finally, many corporate income statements contain nonoperating items, such as extraordinary items, cumulative effects from accounting changes, and gains and losses from discontinued operations. When these items exist, the reader must exercise extra caution in making comparisons. To assess the future prospects of a group of companies, you may want to compare income statements *before* taking into account the effects these items have on income.

Understand the Possible Effects of Inflation

Inflation, or an increase in the level of prices, is another important consideration in analyzing financial statements. The statements, to be used by outsiders, are based on historical costs and are not adjusted for the effects of increasing prices. For example, consider the following trend in a company's sales for the past three years:

	2004	2003	2002
Net sales	$121,000	$110,000	$100,000

http://www.wrigley.com
http://www.hersheys.com

Focus on Core Values

How does a company grow its sales and earnings year after year without merging or greatly diversifying its core business of making and selling chewing gum? For Wm. Wrigley Jr. Company, the secret to success is relatively simple: generate a continuous wave of new product activity, while working diligently to improve its stable of time-tested brands.

During 2002, Wrigley took three of the most recognizable brand names in the world—Wrigley's Spearmint, Doublemint, and Juicy Fruit—and improved their formulas, updated the packaging and added new marketing campaigns. But, the 112-year-old Chicago company hasn't achieved its success by resting on its laurels. Another major initiative in 2002 was the rollout of two new products: Eclipse Flash strips and Orbit Drops. The former are breath-freshening dissolvable films and the latter sugar-free lozenges.

Has Wrigley management been content to grow internally and not at least pursue growth by merger, a strategy so popular throughout U.S. business? Although not successful in the end, a recent attempt to diversify externally is evidence that Wrigley is not opposed to this popular strategy. During 2002, the company actively pursued a business combination with another giant in the confectionary business, Hershey Foods. In the annual report, William Wrigley, Jr., CEO of Wrigley, expressed disappointment that the merger did not materialize but reaffirmed the company's interest in pursuing confectionary opportunities globally. In the meantime, stockholders should take comfort in Wrigley's rock-solid financial performance, including an enviable return on average equity that has hovered around 30% over the past decade. ■

Source: 2002 Wrigley Annual Report.

As measured by the actual dollars of sales, sales have increased by 10% each year. Caution is necessary in concluding that the company is better off in each succeeding year because of the increase in sales *dollars*. Assume, for example, that 2002 sales of $100,000 are the result of selling 100,000 units at $1 each. Are 2003 sales of $110,000 the result of selling 110,000 units at $1 each or of selling 100,000 units at $1.10 each? Although on the surface it may seem unimportant which result accounts for the sales increase, the answer can have significant ramifications. If the company found it necessary to increase selling price to $1.10 in the face of increasing *costs,* it may be no better off than it was in 2002 in terms of gross profit. On the other hand, if the company is able to increase sales revenue by 10% primarily based on growth in unit sales, then its performance would be considered stronger than if the increase is merely due to a price increase. The point to be made is one of caution: published financial statements are stated in historical costs and therefore have not been adjusted for the effects of inflation.

Fortunately, inflation has been relatively subdued in the past several years. During the late 1970s, the FASB actually required a separate note in the financial statements to calculate the effects of inflation. The requirement was abandoned in the mid-1980s when inflation had subsided and the profession decided that the cost of providing inflation-adjusted information exceeded the benefits to the users.

ANALYSIS OF COMPARATIVE AND COMMON-SIZE STATEMENTS

Horizontal analysis A comparison of financial statement items over a period of time.

Vertical analysis A comparison of various financial statement items within a single period with the use of common-size statements.

We are now ready to analyze a set of financial statements. We will begin by looking at the comparative statements of a company for a two-year period. The analysis of the statements over a series of years is often called **horizontal analysis.** We will then see how the statements can be recast in what are referred to as *common-size statements.* The analysis of common-size statements is called **vertical analysis.** Finally, we will consider the use of a variety of ratios to analyze a company.

Horizontal Analysis

LO 2 Use comparative financial statements to analyze a company over time (horizontal analysis).

Comparative balance sheets for a hypothetical entity, Henderson Company, are presented in Exhibit 13-1. The increase or decrease in each of the major accounts on the balance sheet is shown in both absolute dollars and as a percentage. The base year for computing the percentage increase or decrease in each account is the first year, 2003, and is normally shown on the right side. By reading across from right to left (thus the term *horizontal analysis*), the analyst can quickly spot any unusual changes in accounts from the previous year. Three accounts stand out: **1** Cash decreased by 76%, **2** Inventory increased by 73%, and **3** Accounts Payable increased by 70%. (These lines are also boldfaced for convenience.) Individually, each of these large changes is a red flag. Taken together, these changes send the financial statement user the warning that the business may be deteriorating. Each of these large changes should be investigated further.

Exhibit 13-2 shows comparative statements of income and retained earnings for Henderson for 2004 and 2003. At first glance, **1** the 20% increase in sales to $24 million appears promising, but management was not able to limit the increase in either **2** cost of goods sold or **3** selling, general, and administrative expense to 20%. The analysis indicates that cost of goods sold increased by 29% and selling, general, and administrative expense increased by 50%. The increases in these two expenses more than offset the increase in sales and resulted in a **4** decrease in operating income of 25%.

Companies that experience sales growth often become lax about controlling expenses. Their managements sometimes forget that it is the bottom line that counts, not the top line. Perhaps the salespeople are given incentives to increase sales without considering the costs of the sales. Maybe management is spending too much on overhead, including its own salaries. The owners of the business will have to address these concerns if they want to get a reasonable return on their investment.

Exhibit 13-1 Comparative Balance Sheets—Horizontal Analysis

Read from earlier year to later year. Usually this is from right to left.

HENDERSON COMPANY
COMPARATIVE BALANCE SHEETS
DECEMBER 31, 2004 AND 2003
(ALL AMOUNTS IN THOUSANDS OF DOLLARS)

The base year is normally on the right.

	December 31		Increase (Decrease)	
	2004	2003	Dollars	Percent
Cash	$ **320**	$ **1,350**	$ **(1,030)** 1	**(76)**%
Accounts receivable	5,500	4,500	1,000	22
Inventory	**4,750**	**2,750**	**2,000** 2	**73**
Prepaid insurance	150	200	(50)	(25)
Total current assets	$10,720	$ 8,800	$ 1,920	22
Land	2,000	2,000	–0–	–0–
Buildings and equipment	6,000	4,500	1,500	33
Accumulated depreciation	(1,850)	(1,500)	(350)	(23)
Total long-term assets	$ 6,150	$ 5,000	$ 1,150	23
Total assets	$16,870	$13,800	$ 3,070	22
Accounts payable	$ **4,250**	$ **2,500**	$ **1,750** 3	**70**
Taxes payable	2,300	2,100	200	10
Notes payable	600	800	(200)	(25)
Current portion of bonds	100	100	–0–	–0–
Total current liabilities	$ 7,250	$ 5,500	$ 1,750	32
Bonds payable	700	800	(100)	(13)
Total liabilities	$ 7,950	$ 6,300	$ 1,650	26
Preferred stock, $5 par	500	500	–0–	–0–
Common stock, $1 par	1,000	1,000	–0–	–0–
Retained earnings	7,420	6,000	1,420	24
Total stockholders' equity	$ 8,920	$ 7,500	$ 1,420	19
Total liabilities and stockholders' equity	$16,870	$13,800	$ 3,070	22

NOTE: Referenced amounts boldfaced for convenience.

Dollar change from year to year.

Percentage change from one year to the next year.

In **horizontal analysis**, read right to left to compare one year's results with the next as a dollar amount of change and as a percentage of change from year to year.

From Concept to Practice 13.1

Reading the Annual Reports of Winnebago Industries and Monaco Coach Corporation

Where do Winnebago Industries' and Monaco Coach Corporation's annual reports provide financial summaries? How many years does each include? In terms of a trend over time, which item on each summary do you think is the most significant?

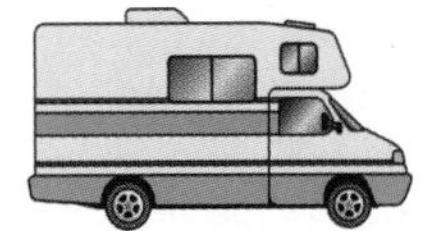

Horizontal analysis can be extended to include more than two years of results. At a minimum, publicly held companies are required to include income statements and statements of cash flows for the three most recent years and balance sheets as of the end of the two most recent years. Many annual reports include, as supplementary information, financial summaries of operations for extended periods of time. As illustrated in Exhibit 13-3 on pages 662–663, for example, Wrigley includes an 11-year summary of selected financial data, such as net sales, dividends paid, return on average equity, and total assets. Note the increase in net sales in every year over the 11-year period. Also note, however, that Wrigley does not include in the summary the gross profit ratio (gross profit divided

Exhibit 13-2 Comparative Statements of Income and Retained Earnings—Horizontal Analysis

HENDERSON COMPANY
COMPARATIVE STATEMENTS OF INCOME AND RETAINED EARNINGS
FOR THE YEARS ENDED DECEMBER 31, 2004 AND 2003
(ALL AMOUNTS IN THOUSANDS OF DOLLARS)

	December 31		Increase (Decrease)	
	2004	2003	Dollars	Percent
Net sales	**$24,000**	**$20,000**	**$ 4,000**	1 **20%**
Cost of goods sold	**18,000**	**14,000**	**4,000**	2 **29**
Gross profit	$ 6,000	$ 6,000	$ -0-	-0-
Selling, general, and administrative expense	**3,000**	**2,000**	**1,000**	3 **50**
Operating income	**$ 3,000**	**$ 4,000**	**$(1,000)**	4 **(25)**
Interest expense	140	160	(20)	(13)
Income before tax	$ 2,860	$ 3,840	$ (980)	(26)
Income tax expense	1,140	1,540	(400)	(26)
Net income	$ 1,720	$ 2,300	$ (580)	(25)
Preferred dividends	50	50		
Income available to common	$ 1,670	$ 2,250		
Common dividends	250	250		
To retained earnings	$ 1,420	$ 2,000		
Retained earnings, 1/1	6,000	4,000		
Retained earnings, 12/31	$ 7,420	$ 6,000		

These three increases in revenue and expenses resulted in an operating income *decrease* of 25%.

NOTE: Referenced amounts boldfaced for convenience.

by net sales). A comparison of the trend in this ratio would help to determine whether the company has effectively controlled the cost to manufacture its products.

Tracking items over a series of years, a practice called *trend analysis,* can be a very powerful tool for the analyst. Advanced statistical techniques are available for analyzing trends in financial data and, most important, for projecting those trends to future periods. Some of the techniques, such as time series analysis, have been used extensively in forecasting sales trends.

From Concept to Practice 13.2

Reading Wrigley's Annual Report

Refer to Wrigley's financial highlights in Exhibit 13-3 on pages 662–663. Compute the company's gross profit ratio for each of the 11 years. Is there a noticeable upward or downward trend in the ratio over this time period?

Historically, attention has focused on the balance sheet and income statement in analyzing a company's position and results of operation. Only recently have analysts and other users begun to appreciate the value in incorporating the statement of cash flows into their analyses.

Comparative statements of cash flows for Henderson appear in Exhibit 13-4. Henderson's financing activities remained constant over the two-year period, as indicated in that section of the statements. Each year the company paid $200,000 on notes, another $100,000 to retire bonds, and $300,000 to stockholders in dividends. Cash outflow from investing activities slowed down somewhat in 2004, with the purchase of $1,500,000 in new buildings, compared with $2,000,000 the year before.

Exhibit 13-4 Comparative Statements of Cash Flow—Horizontal Analysis

HENDERSON COMPANY
COMPARATIVE STATEMENTS OF CASH FLOWS
FOR THE YEARS ENDED DECEMBER 31, 2004 AND 2003
(ALL AMOUNTS IN THOUSANDS OF DOLLARS)

	2004	2003	Increase (Decrease) Dollars	Percent
Net Cash Flows from Operating Activities				
2 Net income	**$1,720**	**$2,300**	**$ (580)**	**(25)%**
Adjustments:				
Depreciation expense	350	300		
Changes in:				
3 Accounts receivable	**(1,000)**	**500**		
4 Inventory	**(2,000)**	**(300)**		
Prepaid insurance	50	50		
Accounts payable	1,750	(200)		
Taxes payable	200	300		
Net cash provided by operating activities 1 Unfavorable	**$1,070**	**$2,950**	**$(1,880)**	**(64)%**
Net Cash Flows from Investing Activities				
Purchase of buildings	**$(1,500)**	**$(2,000)**	**$ (500)**	**(25)%**
Net Cash Flows from Financing Activities				
Repayment of notes	**$ (200)**	**$ (200)**	–0–	–0–
Retirement of bonds	**(100)**	**(100)**	–0–	–0–
Cash dividends—preferred	**(50)**	**(50)**	–0–	–0–
Cash dividends—common	**(250)**	**(250)**	–0–	–0–
Net cash used by financing activities	$ (600)	$ (600)	–0–	–0–
Net increase (decrease) in cash	$(1,030)	$ 350		
Beginning cash balance	1,350	1,000		
Ending cash balance	$ 320	$ 1,350		
Supplemental Information				
Interest paid	$ 140	$ 160		
Income taxes paid	$ 940	$ 1,440		

NOTE: Referenced amounts boldfaced for convenience.

The most noticeable difference between Henderson's statements of cash flows for the two years is in the Operating Activities section. Operations 1 generated almost $2 million less in cash in 2004 than in 2003 ($1.07 million in 2004 versus $2.95 million in 2003). The decrease in net income 2 was partially responsible for this reduction in cash from operations. However, the increases in 3 accounts receivable and 4 inventories in 2004 had a significant impact on the decrease in cash generated from operating activities.

Vertical Analysis

LO 3 Use common-size financial statements to compare various financial statement items (vertical analysis).

Often it is easier to examine comparative financial statements if they have been standardized. *Common-size statements* recast all items on the statement as a percentage of a selected item on the statement. This excludes size as a relevant variable in the analysis. One could use this type of analysis to compare Wal-Mart with the smaller Target or to compare IBM with the much smaller Apple Computer. It is also a convenient way to compare the same company from year to year.

Exhibit 13-3 Wrigley Financial Summary

Selected Financial Data

In thousands of dollars and shares except per share amounts, stockholders of record and employees

Net sales has increased each year in the 11-year period.

	2002	2001	2000	1999
OPERATING DATA				
Net Sales	**$2,746,318**	2,401,419	2,126,114	2,045,227
Cost of Sales	**1,150,215**	997,054	904,266	904,183
Income Taxes	**181,896**	164,380	150,370	136,247
Earnings before cumulative effect of accounting changes in 1992*	**401,525**	362,986	328,942	308,183
Per Share of Common Stock (basic and diluted)	**1.78**	1.61	1.45	1.33
Net Earnings	**401,525**	362,986	328,942	308,183
Per Share of Common Stock (basic and diluted)	**1.78**	1.61	1.45	1.33
Dividends Paid	**181,232**	167,922	159,138	153,812
Per Share of Common Stock	**.805**	.745	.701	.664
As a Percent of Net Earnings	**45%**	46%	48%	50%
Dividends Declared Per Share of Common Stock	**.820**	.760	.701	.740
Average Shares Outstanding	**225,145**	225,349	227,037	231,722
OTHER FINANCIAL DATA				
Net Property, Plant and Equipment	**$ 836,110**	684,379	607,034	559,140
Total Assets	**2,108,296**	1,777,793	1,574,740	1,547,745
Working Capital	**620,205**	581,519	540,505	551,921
Stockholders' Equity	**1,522,576**	1,276,197	1,132,897	1,138,775
Return on Average Equity	**28.7%**	30.1%	29.0%	26.8%
Stockholders of Record at Close of Year	**40,534**	38,701	37,781	38,626
Employees at Close of Year	**11,250**	10,800	9,800	9,300
Market Price of Stock				
High	**58.90**	53.30	48.31	50.31
Low	**44.21**	42.94	29.94	33.25

*(includes amounts related to factory closure—net gain of $6,763 or $.03 per share in 1998, and net costs of $2,145 or $.01 per share and $12,990 or $.06 per share in 1997 and 1996 respectively; and nonrecurring net gain on sale of Singapore property in 1994 of $24,766 or $.11 per share)

Exhibit 13-3 Wrigley Financial Summary (continued)

1998	1997	1996	1995	1994	1993	1992
1,990,286	1,923,963	1,835,987	1,754,931	1,596,551	1,428,504	1,286,921
894,988	892,751	859,414	820,478	737,239	653,687	606,263
136,378	122,614	128,840	126,492	122,746	103,944	83,730
304,501	271,626	230,272	223,739	230,533	174,891	148,573
1.31	1.17	.99	.96	.99	.75	.63
304,501	271,626	230,272	223,739	230,533	174,891	141,295
1.31	1.17	.99	.96	.99	.75	.60
150,835	135,680	118,308	111,401	104,694	87,344	72,511
.650	.585	.510	.480	.450	.375	.310
50%	50%	51%	50%	45%	50%	51%
.655	.595	.510	.495	.470	.375	.315
231,928	231,928	231,966	232,132	232,716	233,022	234,110
520,090	430,474	388,149	347,491	289,420	239,868	222,137
1,520,855	1,343,126	1,233,543	1,099,219	978,834	815,324	711,372
624,546	571,857	511,272	458,683	413,414	343,132	299,149
1,157,032	985,379	897,431	796,852	688,470	575,182	498,935
28.4%	28.9%	27.2%	30.1%	36.5%	32.6%	29.4%
38,052	36,587	34,951	28,959	24,078	18,567	14,546
9,200	8,200	7,800	7,300	7,000	6,700	6,400
52.16	41.03	31.44	27.00	26.94	23.06	19.94
35.47	27.28	24.19	21.44	19.06	14.75	11.06

Vertical analysis involves looking at the relative size and composition of various items on a particular financial statement. Common-size comparative balance sheets for Henderson Company are presented in Exhibit 13-5. Note that all asset accounts are stated as a percentage of total assets. Similarly, all liability and stockholders' equity accounts are stated as a percentage of total liabilities and stockholders' equity. The combination of the comparative balance sheets for the two years and the common-size feature allows the analyst to spot critical changes in the composition of the assets. We noted in Exhibit 13-1 that cash had decreased by 76% over the two years. The decrease of cash from 9.8% of total assets to only 1.9% **1** is highlighted in Exhibit 13-5.

Exhibit 13-5 Common-Size Comparative Balance Sheets—Vertical Analysis

HENDERSON COMPANY
COMMON-SIZE COMPARATIVE BALANCE SHEETS
DECEMBER 31, 2004 AND 2003
(ALL AMOUNTS IN THOUSANDS OF DOLLARS)

	December 31, 2004		December 31, 2003	
	Dollars	Percent	Dollars	Percent
Cash	**$ 320**	**1.9%**	**$ 1,350** [1]	**9.8%**
Accounts receivable	5,500	32.6	4,500	32.6
Inventory	**4,750**	**28.1**	**2,750** [3]	**19.9**
Prepaid insurance	150	0.9	200	1.5
Total current assets	**$10,720**	[2] **63.5%**	**$ 8,800**	**63.8%**
Land	2,000	11.9%	2,000	14.5%
Buildings and equipment, net	4,150	24.6	3,000	21.7
Total long-term assets	$ 6,150	36.5%	$ 5,000	36.2%
Total assets	$16,870	100.0%	$13,800	100.0%
Accounts payable	$ 4,250	25.2%	$ 2,500	18.1%
Taxes payable	2,300	13.6	2,100	15.2
Notes payable	600	3.6	800	5.8
Current portion of bonds	100	0.6	100	0.7
Total current liabilities	**$ 7,250**	[4] **43.0%**	**$ 5,500**	**39.8%**
Bonds payable	700	[5] 4.1	800	5.8
Total liabilities	$ 7,950	47.1%	$ 6,300	45.6%
Preferred stock, $5 par	500	3.0%	500	3.6%
Common stock, $1 par	1,000	5.9	1,000	7.3
Retained earnings	7,420	44.0	6,000	43.5
Total stockholders' equity	**$ 8,920**	[6] **52.9%**	**$ 7,500**	**54.4%**
Total liabilities and stockholders' equity	$16,870	100.0%	$13,800	100.0%

NOTE: Referenced amounts boldfaced for convenience.

Compare percentages across years to spot year-to-year trends.

In **vertical analysis,** compare each line item as a percentage of total (100%) to highlight a company's overall condition.

One can also observe in the exhibit that **2** total current assets have continued to represent just under two-thirds (63.5%) of total assets. If cash has decreased significantly in terms of the percentage of total assets, what accounts have increased to maintain current assets at two-thirds of total assets? We can quickly determine from the data in Exhibit 13-5 that **3** although inventory represented 19.9% of total assets at the end of 2003, the percentage is up to 28.1% at the end of 2004. This change in the relative composition of current assets between cash and inventory may have important implications. The change, for instance, may signal that the company is having trouble selling inventory.

Total current liabilities **4** represent a slightly higher percentage of total liabilities and stockholders' equity at the end of 2004 than at the end of 2003. The increase is balanced by a slight decrease in the relative percentages of 5 long-term debt (the bonds) and of 6 stockholders' equity. We will return later to further analysis of the composition of both the current and the noncurrent accounts.

Common-size comparative income statements for Henderson are presented in Exhibit 13-6. The *base*, or benchmark, on which all other items in the income statement are compared is 1 net sales. Again, observations from the comparative statements alone are further confirmed by examining the common-size statements. Although the **gross profit ratio**—*gross profit as a percentage of net sales*—was 30% in 2003, the same ratio for 2004 is only 25% 2. Recall the earlier observation that although sales increased by 20% from one year to the next, 3 cost of goods sold increased by 29%.

Gross profit ratio Gross profit to net sales.

Exhibit 13-6 Common-Size Comparative Income Statements—Vertical Analysis

HENDERSON COMPANY
COMMON-SIZE COMPARATIVE INCOME STATEMENTS
FOR THE YEARS ENDED DECEMBER 31, 2004 AND 2003
(ALL AMOUNTS IN THOUSANDS OF DOLLARS)

	2004		2003	
	Dollars	Percent	Dollars	Percent
Net sales	**$24,000**	1 **100.0%**	**$20,000**	**100.0%**
Cost of goods sold	3 18,000	75.0	14,000	70.0
Gross profit	**$ 6,000**	2 **25.0%**	**$ 6,000**	**30.0%**
Selling, general, and administrative expense	3,000	12.5	2,000	10.0
Operating income	$ 3,000	12.5%	$ 4,000	20.0%
Interest expense	140	0.6	160	0.8
Income before tax	**$ 2,860**	**11.9%**	**$ 3,840**	**19.2%**
Income tax expense	1,140	4.8	1,540	7.7
Net income	**$ 1,720**	4 **7.1%**	**$ 2,300**	**11.5%**

NOTE: Referenced amounts boldfaced for convenience.

Gross profit as a percentage of sales is the **gross profit ratio.**

The ratio of net income to net sales is the **profit margin ratio.**

In addition to the gross profit ratio, an important relationship from Exhibit 13-6 is the *ratio of net income to net sales*, or **profit margin ratio.** The ratio, an overall indicator of management's ability to control expenses, reflects the amount of income for each dollar of sales. Some analysts prefer to look at income before tax, rather than final net income, because taxes are not typically an expense that can be controlled. Further, if the company does not earn a profit before tax, it will incur no tax expense. Note 4 the decrease in Henderson's profit margin: from 11.5% in 2003 to 7.1% in 2004 (or from 19.2% to 11.9% on a before-tax basis).

Profit margin ratio Net income to net sales.

Two-Minute Review

1. *Explain the basic difference between horizontal and vertical analysis.*
2. *Assume that you are concerned about whether accounts receivable has been increasing over the last few years. Which type of analysis, horizontal or vertical, would you perform to help address your concern?*
3. *Assume that you are concerned about whether selling and administrative expenses were unreasonable this past year given the level of sales. Which type of analysis, horizontal or vertical, would you perform to help address your concern?*

Answers on page 682.

LIQUIDITY ANALYSIS AND THE MANAGEMENT OF WORKING CAPITAL

LO 4 Compute and use various ratios to assess liquidity.

Two ratios were discussed in the last section: the *gross profit ratio* and the *profit margin ratio.* A ratio is simply the relationship, normally stated as a percentage, between two financial statement amounts. In this section, we consider a wide range of ratios used by management, analysts, and others for a variety of purposes. We classify the ratios in three main categories according to their use in performing (1) liquidity analysis, (2) solvency analysis, and (3) profitability analysis.

Liquidity The nearness to cash of the assets and liabilities.

Liquidity is a relative measure of the nearness to cash of the assets and liabilities of a company. Nearness to cash deals with the length of time before cash is realized. Various ratios are used to measure liquidity, and they basically concern the company's ability to pay its debts as they come due. Recall the distinction between the current and long-term classifications on the balance sheet. Current assets are assets that will be either converted into cash or consumed within one year or the operating cycle, if the cycle is longer than one year. The operating cycle for a manufacturing company is the length of time between the purchase of raw materials and the eventual collection of any outstanding account receivable from the sale of the product. Current liabilities are a company's obligations that require the use of current assets or the creation of other current liabilities to satisfy them.

The nearness to cash of the current assets is indicated by their placement on the balance sheet. Current assets are listed on the balance sheet in descending order of their nearness to cash. Liquidity is, of course, a matter of degree, with cash being the most liquid of all assets. With few exceptions, such as prepaid insurance, most current assets are convertible into cash. However, accounts receivable is closer to being converted into cash than is inventory. An account receivable need only be collected to be converted to cash. An item of inventory must first be sold, and then, assuming that sales of inventory are on account, the account must be collected before cash is realized.

Working Capital

Working capital Current assets minus current liabilities.

Working capital is the excess of current assets over current liabilities at a point in time:

Working Capital = Current Assets − Current Liabilities

Reference to Henderson's comparative balance sheets in Exhibit 13-1 indicates the following:

	December 31	
	2004	2003
Current assets	$10,720,000	$8,800,000
Current liabilities	7,250,000	5,500,000
Working capital	$ 3,470,000	$3,300,000

The management of working capital is an extremely important task for any business. A comparison of Henderson's working capital at the end of each of the two years indicates a slight increase in the degree of protection for short-term creditors of the company. Management must always strive for the ideal balance of current assets and current liabilities. The amount of working capital is limited in its informational value, however. For example, it tells us nothing about the composition of the current accounts. Also, the dollar amount of working capital may not be useful for comparison with other companies of different sizes in the same industry. Working capital of $3,470,000 may be adequate for Henderson Company, but it might signal impending bankruptcy for a company much larger than Henderson.

Current Ratio

Current ratio The ratio of current assets to current liabilities.

The **current ratio** is one of the most widely used of all financial statement ratios and is calculated as follows:

$$\text{Current Ratio} = \frac{\text{Current Assets}}{\text{Current Liabilities}}$$

For Henderson Company, the ratio at each year-end is as follows:

December 31	
2004	**2003**
$\frac{\$10,720,000}{\$7,250,000} = 1.48 \text{ to } 1$	$\frac{\$8,800,000}{\$5,500,000} = 1.60 \text{ to } 1$

At the end of 2004, Henderson had $1.48 of current assets for every $1 of current liabilities. Is this current ratio adequate? Or is it a sign of impending financial difficulties? There is no definitive answer to either of these questions. Some analysts use a general rule of thumb of 2:1 for the current ratio as a sign of short-term financial health. The answer depends first on the industry. Companies in certain industries have historically operated with current ratios much less than 2:1.

A second concern in interpreting the current ratio involves the composition of the current assets. Cash is usually the only acceptable means of payment for most liabilities. Therefore, it is important to consider the makeup, or *composition,* of the current assets. Refer to Exhibit 13-5 and Henderson's common-size balance sheets. Not only did the current ratio decline during 2004 but also the proportion of the total current assets made up by inventory increased whereas the proportion made up by accounts receivable remained the same. Recall that accounts receivable is only one step removed from cash, whereas inventory requires both sale and collection of the subsequent account.

Study Tip

Many of the ratios discussed in this chapter, such as the current ratio, were introduced in earlier chapters. Use the information here as a review of those earlier introductions.

Acid-Test Ratio

The **acid-test** or **quick ratio** is a stricter test of a company's ability to pay its current debts as they are due. Specifically, it is intended to deal with the composition problem because it *excludes* inventories and prepaid assets from the numerator of the fraction:

Acid-test or quick ratio A stricter test of liquidity than the current ratio; excludes inventory and prepayments from the numerator.

$$\text{Acid-Test or Quick Ratio} = \frac{\text{Quick Assets}}{\text{Current Liabilities}}$$

where

$$\text{Quick Assets} = \text{Cash} + \text{Marketable Securities} + \text{Current Receivables}$$

Henderson's quick assets consist of only cash and accounts receivable, and its quick ratios are as follows:

December 31	
2004	**2003**
$\frac{\$320,000 + \$5,500,000}{\$7,250,000} = 0.80 \text{ to } 1$	$\frac{\$1,350,000 + \$4,500,000}{\$5,500,000} = 1.06 \text{ to } 1$

Does the quick ratio of less than 1:1 at the end of 2004 mean that Henderson will be unable to pay creditors on time? *For many companies, an acid-test ratio below 1 is not desirable because it may signal the need to liquidate marketable securities to pay bills, regardless of the current trading price of the securities.* Although the quick ratio is a better indication of short-term debt-paying ability than the current ratio, it is still not perfect. For example, we would want to know the normal credit terms that Henderson extends to its customers, as well as the credit terms that the company receives from its suppliers.

Assume that Henderson requires its customers to pay their accounts within 30 days and that the normal credit terms extended by Henderson's suppliers allow payment anytime within 60 days. The relatively longer credit terms extended by Henderson's suppliers give it some cushion in meeting its obligations. The due date of the $2,300,000 in taxes payable could also have a significant effect on the company's ability to remain in business.

Cash Flow from Operations to Current Liabilities

Cash flow from operations to current liabilities ratio A measure of the ability to pay current debts from operating cash flows.

Two limitations exist with either the current ratio or the quick ratio as a measure of liquidity. First, almost all debts require the payment of cash. Thus, a ratio that focuses on cash is more useful. Second, both ratios focus on liquid assets at a *point in time.* Cash flow from operating activities, as reported on the statement of cash flows, can be used to indicate the flow of cash during the year to cover the debts due.[1] The **cash flow from operations to current liabilities ratio** is computed as follows:

$$\frac{\textbf{Cash Flow from Operations}}{\textbf{to Current Liabilities Ratio}} = \frac{\textbf{Net Cash Provided by Operating Activities}}{\textbf{Average Current Liabilities}}$$

Note the use of *average* current liabilities in the denominator. This results in a denominator that is consistent with the numerator, which reports the cash flow over a period of time. Because we need to calculate the *average* current liabilities for both years, it is necessary to add the ending balance sheet for 2002 for use in the analysis. The balance sheet for Henderson on December 31, 2002, is given in Exhibit 13-7. The ratio for Henderson for each year is as follows:

2004	2003
$\frac{\$1{,}070{,}000}{(\$7{,}250{,}000 + \$5{,}500{,}000)/2} = 16.8\%$	$\frac{\$2{,}950{,}000}{(\$5{,}500{,}000 + \$5{,}600{,}000)/2} = 53.2\%$

Two factors are responsible for the large decrease in this ratio from 2003 to 2004. First, cash generated from operations during 2004 was less than half what it was during 2003 (the numerator). Second, average current liabilities were smaller in 2003 than

Exhibit 13-7

Henderson's Balance Sheet, End of 2002

HENDERSON COMPANY BALANCE SHEET DECEMBER 31, 2002 (ALL AMOUNTS IN THOUSANDS OF DOLLARS)	
Cash	$ 1,000
Accounts receivable	5,000
Inventory	2,450
Prepaid insurance	250
Total current assets	$ 8,700
Land	$ 2,000
Buildings and equipment, net	1,300
Total long-term assets	$ 3,300
Total assets	$12,000
Accounts payable	$ 2,700
Taxes payable	1,800
Notes payable	1,000
Current portion of bonds	100
Total current liabilities	$ 5,600
Bonds payable	900
Total liabilities	$ 6,500
Preferred stock, $5 par	$ 500
Common stock, $1 par	1,000
Retained earnings	4,000
Total stockholders' equity	$ 5,500
Total liabilities and stockholders' equity	$12,000

[1]For a detailed discussion on the use of information contained in the statement of cash flows in performing ratio analysis, see Charles A. Carslaw and John R. Mills, "Developing Ratios for Effective Cash Flow Statement Analysis," *Journal of Accountancy* (November 1991), pp. 63–70.

in 2004 (the denominator). In examining the health of the company in terms of its liquidity, an analyst would concentrate on the reason for these decreases.

Accounts Receivable Analysis

The analysis of accounts receivable is an important component in the management of working capital. A company must be willing to extend credit terms that are liberal enough to attract and maintain customers, but at the same time, management must continually monitor the accounts to ensure collection on a timely basis. One measure of the efficiency of the collection process is the **accounts receivable turnover ratio:**

Accounts receivable turnover ratio A measure of the number of times accounts receivable are collected in a period.

$$\text{Accounts Receivable Turnover Ratio} = \frac{\text{Net Credit Sales}}{\text{Average Accounts Receivable}}$$

Note an important distinction between this ratio and either the current or the quick ratio. Although both of those ratios measure liquidity at a point in time and all numbers come from the balance sheet, a turnover ratio is an *activity* ratio and consists of an activity (sales, in this case) divided by a base to which it is naturally related (accounts receivable). Because an activity such as sales is for a period of time (a year, in this case), the base should be stated as an average for that same period of time.

The accounts receivable turnover ratios for both years can now be calculated (we assume that all sales are on account):

2004	2003
$\frac{\$24{,}000{,}000}{(\$5{,}500{,}000 + \$4{,}500{,}000)/2} = 4.8 \text{ times}$	$\frac{\$20{,}000{,}000}{(\$4{,}500{,}000 + \$5{,}000{,}000)/2} = 4.2 \text{ times}$

Accounts turned over, on average, 4.2 times in 2003, compared with 4.8 times in 2004. This means that the average number of times accounts were collected during each year was between four and five times. What does this mean about the average length of time that an account was outstanding? Another way to measure efficiency in the collection process is to calculate the **number of days' sales in receivables:**

Number of days' sales in receivables A measure of the average age of accounts receivable.

$$\text{Number of Days' Sales in Receivables} = \frac{\text{Number of Days in the Period}}{\text{Accounts Receivable Turnover}}$$

For simplicity, we assume 360 days in a year:

2004	2003
$\frac{360 \text{ days}}{4.8 \text{ times}} = 75 \text{ days}$	$\frac{360 \text{ days}}{4.2 \text{ times}} = 86 \text{ days}$

The average number of days an account is outstanding, or the average collection period, is 75 days in 2004, down from 86 days in 2003. Is this acceptable? The answer depends on the company's credit policy. If Henderson's normal credit terms require payment within 60 days, further investigation is needed, even though the number of days outstanding has decreased from the previous year.

Management needs to be concerned with both the collectibility of an account as it ages and the cost of funds tied up in receivables. For example, a $1 million average receivable balance that requires an additional month to collect suggests that the company is forgoing $10,000 in lost profits if we assume that the money could be reinvested in the business to earn 1% per month, or 12% per year.

Inventory Analysis

A similar set of ratios can be calculated to analyze the efficiency in managing inventory. The **inventory turnover ratio** is as follows:

Inventory turnover ratio A measure of the number of times inventory is sold during a period.

$$\text{Inventory Turnover Ratio} = \frac{\text{Cost of Goods Sold}}{\text{Average Inventory}}$$

Accounting for Your Decisions

You Examine Your Business's Trends

You are a small business owner and have noticed that over the past two years, sales have increased but the accounts receivable turnover ratio has decreased. Should you be concerned?

ANS: You should certainly be pleased with an increase in sales, but a decrease in accounts receivable turnover should concern you. A decline in this ratio indicates that the average time to collect an open account is increasing. Regardless of the specific reason for this change (e.g., more liberal credit terms, change in credit-worthiness of customers, lack of follow-up on overdue accounts), the increase in the time to collect may result in cash flow problems for you.

The ratio for each of the two years follows:

2004	2003
$\frac{\$18,000,000}{(\$4,750,000 + \$2,750,000)/2} = 4.8 \text{ times}$	$\frac{\$14,000,000}{(\$2,750,000 + \$2,450,000)/2} = 5.4 \text{ times}$

Henderson was slightly more efficient in 2003 in moving its inventory. The number of "turns" each year varies widely for different industries. For example, a wholesaler of perishable fruits and vegetables may turn over inventory at least 50 times per year. An airplane manufacturer, however, may turn over its inventory once or twice a year. What does the number of turns per year tell us about the average length of time it takes to sell an item of inventory? The **number of days' sales in inventory** is an alternative measure of the company's efficiency in managing inventory. It is the number of days between the date an item of inventory is purchased and the date it is sold:

Number of days' sales in inventory A measure of how long it takes to sell inventory.

$$\textbf{Number of Days' Sales in Inventory} = \frac{\textbf{Number of Days in the Period}}{\textbf{Inventory Turnover}}$$

The number of days' sales in inventory for Henderson is as follows:

2004	2003
$\frac{360 \text{ days}}{4.8 \text{ times}} = 75 \text{ days}$	$\frac{360 \text{ days}}{5.4 \text{ times}} = 67 \text{ days}$

This measure can reveal a great deal about inventory management. For example, an unusually low turnover (and, of course, high number of days in inventory) may sig-

Accounting for Your Decisions

You Are the Analyst

http://www.boeing.com
http://www.safeway.com

You have been presented with two companies—Boeing and Safeway. Boeing, a commercial aircraft company, has a very slow inventory turnover, while Safeway, a grocery chain, has a very fast inventory turnover. Would it be correct to conclude that Safeway is a better investment because its inventory turns over faster?

http://www.albertsons.com

ANS: Not at all. These industries are completely different and not comparable. On the contrary, comparing Safeway's inventory turnover with Albertson's, another grocery chain, might be useful, just as comparing Boeing with Lockheed Martin Marietta might make sense. Ratios can be used when comparing companies in the same industry, but not companies in different industries.

nal a large amount of obsolete inventory or problems in the sales department. Or, it may indicate that the company is pricing its products too high and the market is reacting by reducing demand for the company's products.

Cash Operating Cycle

The **cash to cash operating cycle** is the length of time between the purchase of merchandise for sale, assuming a retailer or wholesaler, and the eventual collection of the cash from the sale. One method to approximate the number of days in a company's operating cycle involves combining two measures:

Cash to cash operating cycle The length of time from the purchase of inventory to the collection of any receivable from the sale.

Cash to Cash Operating Cycle = Number of Days' Sales in Inventory + Number of Days' Sales in Receivables

Henderson's operating cycles for 2004 and 2003 are as follows:

2004	2003
75 days + 75 days = 150 days	67 days + 86 days = 153 days

The average length of time between the purchase of inventory and the collection of cash from sale of the inventory was 150 days in 2004. Note that although the length of the operating cycle did not change significantly from 2003 to 2004, the composition did change: the increase in the average number of days in inventory was offset by the decrease in the average number of days in receivables.

SOLVENCY ANALYSIS

LO 5 Compute and use various ratios to assess solvency.

Solvency refers to a company's ability to remain in business over the long term. It is related to liquidity but differs in time. Although liquidity relates to the firm's ability to pay next year's debts as they come due, solvency concerns the ability of the firm to stay financially healthy over the period of time that existing debt (short- and long-term) will be outstanding.

Solvency The ability of a company to remain in business over the long term.

© TERRI MILLER/E-VISUAL COMMUNICATIONS, INC.

Due to the perishable nature of their products, grocery chains have high inventory turnovers and short cash to cash operating cycles. Firms in other segments have relatively longer cycles.

Debt-to-Equity Ratio

Debt-to-equity ratio The ratio of total liabilities to total stockholders' equity.

Capital structure is the focal point in solvency analysis. This refers to the composition of the right side of the balance sheet and the mix between debt and stockholders' equity. The composition of debt and equity in the capital structure is an important determinant of the cost of capital to a company. We will have more to say later about the effects that the mix of debt and equity has on profitability. For now, consider the **debt-to-equity ratio:**

$$\text{Debt-to-Equity Ratio} = \frac{\text{Total Liabilities}}{\text{Total Stockholders' Equity}}$$

Henderson's debt-to-equity ratio at each year-end is as follows:

December 31	
2004	**2003**
$\frac{\$7{,}950{,}000}{\$8{,}920{,}000} = 0.89$ to 1	$\frac{\$6{,}300{,}000}{\$7{,}500{,}000} = 0.84$ to 1

The 2004 ratio indicates that for every $1 of capital that stockholders provided, creditors provided $0.89. Variations of the debt-to-equity ratio are sometimes used to assess solvency. For example, an analyst might calculate the ratio of total liabilities to the sum of total liabilities and stockholders' equity. This results in a ratio that differs from the debt-to-equity ratio, but the objective of the measure is the same—to determine the degree to which the company relies on outsiders for funds.

Study Tip

The elements in many ratios are intuitive and should not require memorization to remember. For example, it is logical that the debt-to-equity ratio is computed by dividing total liabilities by total stockholders' equity.

What is an *acceptable* ratio of debt to equity? As with all ratios, the answer depends on the company, the industry, and many other factors. You should not assume that a lower debt-to-equity ratio is better. Certainly taking on additional debt is risky. Many companies are able to benefit from borrowing money, however, by putting the cash raised to good uses in their businesses. Later in the chapter we discuss the concept of leverage: using borrowed money to benefit the company and its stockholders.

In the 1980s, investors and creditors tolerated a much higher debt-to-equity ratio than is considered prudent today. The savings and loan crisis in the 1980s prompted the federal government to enact regulations requiring financial institutions to have a lower proportion of debt-to-equity. By the mid-1990s, investors and creditors were demanding that all types of companies display lower debt-to-equity ratios.

Times Interest Earned

Times interest earned ratio An income statement measure of the ability of a company to meet its interest payments.

The debt-to-equity ratio is a measure of the company's overall long-term financial health. Management must also be aware of its ability to meet current interest payments to creditors. The **times interest earned ratio** indicates the company's ability to meet current-year interest payments out of current-year earnings:

$$\text{Times Interest Earned Ratio} = \frac{\text{Net Income + Interest Expense + Income Tax Expense}}{\text{Interest Expense}}$$

Both interest expense and income tax expense are added back to net income in the numerator because interest is a deduction in arriving at the amount of income subject to tax. Stated slightly differently, if a company had just enough income to cover the payment of interest, tax expense would be zero. The greater the interest coverage is, the better, as far as lenders are concerned. Bankers often place more importance on the times interest earned ratio than even on earnings per share. The ratio for Henderson for each of the two years indicates a great deal of protection in this regard:

2004	2003
$\frac{\$1{,}720{,}000 + \$140{,}000 + \$1{,}140{,}000}{\$140{,}000}$	$\frac{\$2{,}300{,}000 + \$160{,}000 + \$1{,}540{,}000}{\$160{,}000}$
= 21.4 to 1	= 25 to 1

Debt Service Coverage

Two problems exist with the times interest earned ratio as a measure of the ability to pay creditors. First, the denominator of the fraction considers only *interest*. Management must also be concerned with the *principal* amount of loans maturing in the next year. The second problem deals with the difference between the cash and the accrual bases of accounting. The numerator of the times interest earned ratio is not a measure of the *cash* available to repay loans. Keep in mind the various noncash adjustments, such as depreciation, that enter into the determination of net income. Also, recall that the denominator of the times interest earned ratio is a measure of interest expense, not interest payments. The **debt service coverage ratio** is a measure of the amount of cash that is generated from operating activities during the year and that is available to repay interest due and any maturing principal amounts (that is, the amount available to "service" the debt):

Debt service coverage ratio A statement of cash flows measure of the ability of a company to meet its interest and principal payments.

$$\textbf{Debt Service Coverage Ratio} = \frac{\textbf{Cash Flow from Operations before Interest and Tax Payments}}{\textbf{Interest and Principal Payments}}$$

Some analysts use an alternative measure in the numerator of this ratio, as well as for other purposes. The alternative is referred to as EBITDA, which stands for earnings before interest, taxes, depreciation, and amortization. Whether EBITDA is a good substitute for cash flow from operations before interest and tax payments depends on whether there were significant changes in current assets and current liabilities during the period. If significant changes in these accounts occurred during the period, cash flow from operations before interest and tax payments is a better measure of a company's ability to cover interest and debt payments.

Cash flow from operations is available on the comparative statement of cash flows in Exhibit 13-4. As was the case with the times interest earned ratio, the net cash provided by operating activities is adjusted to reflect the amount available *before* paying interest and taxes.

Keep in mind that the income statement in Exhibit 13-2 reflects the *expense* for interest and taxes each year. The amounts of interest and taxes *paid* each year are shown as supplemental information at the bottom of the statement of cash flows in Exhibit 13-4 and are relevant in computing the debt service coverage ratio.

We must include any principal payments with interest paid in the denominator of the debt service coverage ratio. According to the Financing Activities section of the statements of cash flows in Exhibit 13-4, Henderson repaid $200,000 each year on the notes payable and $100,000 each year on the bonds. The debt service coverage ratios for the two years are calculated as follows:

2004

$$\frac{\$1{,}070{,}000 + \$140{,}000 + \$940{,}000}{\$140{,}000 + \$200{,}000 + \$100{,}000} = 4.89 \text{ times}$$

2003

$$\frac{\$2{,}950{,}000 + \$160{,}000 + \$1{,}440{,}000}{\$160{,}000 + \$200{,}000 + \$100{,}000} = 9.89 \text{ times}$$

Like Henderson's times interest earned ratio, its debt service coverage ratio decreased during 2004. According to the calculations, however, Henderson still generated almost $5 of cash from operations during 2004 to "cover" every $1 of required interest and principal payments.

Cash Flow from Operations to Capital Expenditures Ratio

One final measure is useful in assessing the solvency of a business. The **cash flow from operations to capital expenditures ratio** measures a company's ability to use operations to finance its acquisitions of productive assets. To the extent that a company is able to

Cash flow from operations to capital expenditures ratio A measure of the ability of a company to finance long-term asset acquisitions with cash from operations.

do this, it should rely less on external financing or additional contributions by the owners to replace and add to the existing capital base. The ratio is computed as follows:

$$\text{Cash Flow from Operations to Capital Expenditures Ratio} = \frac{\text{Cash Flow from Operations} - \text{Total Dividends Paid}}{\text{Cash Paid for Acquisitions}}$$

Note that the numerator of the ratio measures the cash flow *after* meeting all dividend payments.[2] The calculation of the ratios for Henderson follows:

2004	2003
$\frac{\$1,070,000 - \$300,000}{\$1,500,000} = 51.3\%$	$\frac{\$2,950,000 - \$300,000}{\$2,000,000} = 132.5\%$

Although the amount of capital expenditures was less in 2004 than in 2003, the company generated considerably less cash from operations in 2004 to cover these acquisitions. In fact, the ratio of less than 100% in 2004 indicates that Henderson was not able to finance all of its capital expenditures from operations *and* cover its dividend payments.

Two-Minute Review

1. *Explain the difference between liquidity and solvency as it relates to a company's financial position.*
2. *Assume that you are a supplier and are considering whether to sell to a company on account. Which of the two, liquidity or solvency, are you more concerned with?*

Answers on page 682.

PROFITABILITY ANALYSIS

LO 6 Compute and use various ratios to assess profitability.

Profitability How well management is using company resources to earn a return on the funds invested by various groups.

Liquidity analysis and solvency analysis deal with management's ability to repay short- and long-term creditors. Creditors are concerned with a company's profitability because a profitable company is more likely to be able to make principal and interest payments. Of course, stockholders care about a company's profitability because it affects the market price of the stock and the ability of the company to pay dividends. Various measures of **profitability** indicate how well management is using the resources at its disposal to earn a return on the funds invested by various groups. Two frequently used profitability measures, the gross profit ratio and the profit margin ratio, were discussed earlier in the chapter. We now turn to other measures of profitability.

Rate of Return on Assets

Return on assets ratio A measure of a company's success in earning a return for all providers of capital.

Before computing the rate of return, we must answer an important question: *return to whom? Every return ratio is a measure of the relationship between the income earned by the company and the investment made in the company by various groups.* The broadest rate of return ratio is the **return on assets ratio** because it considers the investment made by *all* providers of capital, from short-term creditors to bondholders to stockholders. Therefore, the denominator, or base, for the return on assets ratio is average total liabilities and stockholders' equity—which of course is the same as average total assets.

[2]Dividends paid are reported on the statement of cash flows in the Financing Activities section. The amount *paid* should be used for this calculation rather than the amount declared, which appears on the statement of retained earnings.

The numerator of a return ratio will be some measure of the company's income for the period. The income selected for the numerator must match the investment or base in the denominator. For example, if average total assets is the base in the denominator, it is necessary to use an income number that is applicable to all providers of capital. Therefore, the income number used in the rate of return on assets is income *after* adding back interest expense. This adjustment considers creditors as one of the groups that have provided funds to the company. In other words, we want the amount of income before either creditors or stockholders have been given any distributions (that is, interest to creditors or dividends to stockholders). Interest expense must be added back on a net-of-tax basis. Because net income is on an after-tax basis, for consistency purposes interest must also be placed on a net, or after-tax, basis.

The return on assets ratio is as follows:

$$\textbf{Return on Assets Ratio} = \frac{\textbf{Net Income + Interest Expense, Net of Tax}}{\textbf{Average Total Assets}}$$

If we assume a 40% tax rate (which *is* the actual ratio of income tax expense to income before tax for Henderson), its return on assets ratios are as follows:

		2004		2003
Net income		$ 1,720,000		$ 2,300,000
Add back:				
Interest expense	$140,000		$160,000	
× (1 − tax rate)	× 0.6	84,000	× 0.6	96,000
Numerator		$ 1,804,000		$ 2,396,000
Assets, beginning of year		$13,800,000		$12,000,000
Assets, end of year		16,870,000		13,800,000
Total		$30,670,000		$25,800,000
Denominator:				
Average total assets (total above divided by 2)		$15,335,000		$12,900,000
		$1,804,000 / $15,335,000		$2,396,000 / $12,900,000
Return on assets ratio		= 11.76%		= 18.57%

Components of Return on Assets

What caused Henderson's return on assets to decrease so dramatically from the previous year? The answer can be found by considering the two individual components that make up the return on assets ratio. The first of these components is the **return on sales ratio** and is calculated as follows:

Return on sales ratio A variation of the profit margin ratio; measures earnings before payments to creditors.

$$\textbf{Return on Sales Ratio} = \frac{\textbf{Net Income + Interest Expense, Net of Tax}}{\textbf{Net Sales}}$$

The return on sales ratios for Henderson for the two years follow:

2004	2003
$\frac{\$1,720,000 + \$84,000}{\$24,000,000} = 7.52\%$	$\frac{\$2,300,000 + \$96,000}{\$20,000,000} = 11.98\%$

The ratio for 2004 indicates that for every $1 of sales, the company was able to earn a profit, before the payment of interest, of between 7 and 8 cents, as compared with a return of almost 12 cents on the dollar in 2003.

The other component of the rate of return on assets is the **asset turnover ratio.** The ratio is similar to both the inventory turnover and the accounts receivable turnover

Asset turnover ratio The relationship between net sales and average total assets.

ratios because it is a measure of the relationship between some activity (net sales, in this case) and some investment base (average total assets):

$$\text{Asset Turnover Ratio} = \frac{\text{Net Sales}}{\text{Average Total Assets}}$$

For Henderson, the ratio for each of the two years follows:

2004	2003
$\frac{\$24{,}000{,}000}{\$15{,}335{,}000} = 1.57$ times	$\frac{\$20{,}000{,}000}{\$12{,}900{,}000} = 1.55$ times

It now becomes evident that the explanation for the decrease in Henderson's return on assets lies in the drop in the return on sales, since the asset turnover ratio was almost the same. To summarize, note the relationship among the three ratios:

$$\text{Return on Assets} = \text{Return on Sales} \times \text{Asset Turnover}$$

For 2004, Henderson's return on assets consists of the following:

$$\frac{\$1{,}804{,}000}{\$24{,}000{,}000} \times \frac{\$24{,}000{,}000}{\$15{,}335{,}000} = 7.52\% \times 1.57 = 11.8\%$$

Finally, notice that net sales cancels out of both ratios, leaving the net income adjusted for interest divided by average assets as the return on assets ratio.

Return on Common Stockholders' Equity

Reasoning similar to that used to calculate return on assets can be used to calculate the return on capital provided by the common stockholder. Because we are interested in the return to the common stockholder, our base is no longer average total assets but average common stockholders' equity. Similarly, the appropriate income figure for the numerator is net income less preferred dividends because we are interested in the return to the common stockholder after all claims have been settled. Income taxes and interest expense have already been deducted in arriving at net income, but preferred dividends have not been because dividends are a distribution of profits, not an expense.

Return on common stockholders' equity ratio A measure of a company's success in earning a return for the common stockholders.

The **return on common stockholders' equity ratio** is computed as follows:

$$\text{Return on Common Stockholders' Equity Ratio} = \frac{\text{Net Income} - \text{Preferred Dividends}}{\text{Average Common Stockholders' Equity}}$$

The average common stockholders' equity for Henderson is calculated using information from Exhibits 13-1 and 13-7:

	Account Balances at December 31		
	2004	2003	2002
Common stock, $1 par	$1,000,000	$1,000,000	$1,000,000
Retained earnings	7,420,000	6,000,000	4,000,000
Total common equity	$8,420,000	$7,000,000	$5,000,000

Average common equity:

2003: ($7,000,000 + $5,000,000)/2 = $6,000,000

2004: ($8,420,000 + $7,000,000)/2 = $7,710,000

Net income less preferred dividends—or "income available to common," as it is called—can be found by referring to net income on the income statement and to preferred dividends on the statement of retained earnings. The combined statement of income and retained earnings in Exhibit 13-2 gives the relevant amounts for the numerator. Henderson's return on equity for the two years is as follows:

2004		2003	
$\frac{\$1{,}720{,}000 - \$50{,}000}{\$7{,}710{,}000}$	= 21.66%	$\frac{\$2{,}300{,}000 - \$50{,}000}{\$6{,}000{,}000}$	= 37.50%

Even though Henderson's return on stockholders' equity ratio decreased significantly from one year to the next, most stockholders would be very happy to achieve these returns on their money. Very few investments offer much more than 10% return unless substantial risk is involved.

Return on Assets, Return on Equity, and Leverage

The return on assets for 2004 was 11.8%. But the return to the common stockholders was much higher: 21.7%. How do you explain this phenomenon? Why are the stockholders receiving a higher return on their money than all of the providers of money combined are getting? A partial answer to these questions can be found by reviewing the cost to Henderson of the various sources of capital.

Exhibit 13-1 indicates that notes, bonds, and preferred stock are the primary sources of capital other than common stock (accounts payable and taxes payable are *not* included because they represent interest-free loans to the company from suppliers and the government). These sources and the average amount of each outstanding during 2004 follow:

	Account Balances at December 31		
	2004	2003	AVERAGE
Notes payable	$ 600,000	$ 800,000	$ 700,000
Current portion of bonds	100,000	100,000	100,000
Bonds payable—Long-term	700,000	800,000	750,000
Total liabilities	$1,400,000	$1,700,000	$1,550,000
Preferred stock	$ 500,000	$ 500,000	$ 500,000

What was the cost to Henderson of each of these sources? The cost of the money provided by the preferred stockholders is clearly the amount of dividends of $50,000. The cost as a percentage is $50,000/$500,000, or 10%. The average cost of the borrowed money can be approximated by dividing the 2004 interest expense of $140,000 by the average of the notes payable and bonds payable of $1,550,000. The result is an average cost of these two sources of $140,000/$1,550,000, or approximately 9%.

The concept of **leverage** refers to the practice of using borrowed funds and amounts received from preferred stockholders in an attempt to earn an overall return that is higher than the cost of these funds. Recall the rate of return on assets for 2004: 11.8%. Because this return is on an after-tax basis, it is necessary, for comparative purposes, to convert the average cost of borrowed funds to an after-tax basis. Although we computed an average cost for borrowed money of 9%, the actual cost of the borrowed money is 5.4% [9% × (100% − 40%)] after taxes. Because dividends are *not* tax-deductible, the cost of the money provided by preferred stockholders is 10%, as calculated earlier.

Leverage The use of borrowed funds and amounts contributed by preferred stockholders to earn an overall return higher than the cost of these funds.

Has Henderson successfully employed favorable leverage? That is, has it been able to earn an overall rate of return on assets that is higher than the amounts that it must pay creditors and preferred stockholders? Henderson has been successful in using outside money: neither of the sources must be paid a rate in excess of the 11.8% overall rate on assets used. Also keep in mind that Henderson has been able to borrow some amounts on an interest-free basis. As mentioned earlier, the accounts payable and taxes payable represent interest-free loans from suppliers and the government, although the loans are typically for a short period of time, such as 30 days.

In summary, the excess of the 21.7% return on equity over the 11.8% return on assets indicates that the Henderson management has been successful in employing leverage; that is, there is favorable leverage. Is it possible to be unsuccessful in this pursuit; that is, can there be unfavorable leverage? If the company must pay more for the amounts provided by creditors and preferred stockholders than it can earn overall, as indicated by the return on assets, there will, in fact, be unfavorable leverage. This may occur when interest requirements are high and net income is low. A company would likely have a high debt-to-equity ratio as well when there is unfavorable leverage.

Earnings per Share

Earnings per share A company's bottom line stated on a per-share basis.

Earnings per share is one of the most quoted statistics for publicly traded companies. Stockholders and potential investors want to know what their share of profits is, not just the total dollar amount. Presentation of profits on a per-share basis also allows the stockholder to relate earnings to what he or she paid for a share of stock or to the current trading price of a share of stock.

In simple situations, such as our Henderson Company example, earnings per share (EPS) is calculated as follows:

$$\text{Earnings per Share} = \frac{\text{Net Income} - \text{Preferred Dividends}}{\text{Weighted Average Number of Common Shares Outstanding}}$$

Because Henderson had 1,000,000 shares of common stock outstanding throughout both 2003 and 2004, its EPS for each of the two years is as follows:

2004	2003
$\frac{\$1{,}720{,}000 - \$50{,}000}{1{,}000{,}000 \text{ shares}} = \$1.67 \text{ per share}$	$\frac{\$2{,}300{,}000 - \$50{,}000}{1{,}000{,}000 \text{ shares}} = \$2.25 \text{ per share}$

A number of complications can arise in the computation of EPS, and the calculations can become exceedingly complex for a company with many different types of securities in its capital structure. These complications are beyond the scope of this book and are discussed in more advanced accounting courses.

Price/Earnings Ratio

Earnings per share is an important ratio for an investor because of its relationship to dividends and market price. Stockholders hope to earn a return by receiving periodic dividends or eventually selling the stock for more than they paid for it, or both. Although earnings are related to dividends and market price, the latter two are of primary interest to the stockholder.

Price/earnings (P/E) ratio The relationship between a company's performance according to the income statement and its performance in the stock market.

We mentioned earlier the desire of investors to relate the earnings of the company to the market price of the stock. Now that we have stated Henderson's earnings on a per-share basis, we can calculate the **price/earnings (P/E) ratio.** What market price is relevant? Should we use the market price that the investor paid for a share of stock, or should we use the current market price? Because earnings are based on the most recent evaluation of the company for accounting purposes, it seems logical to use current market price, which is based on the stock market's current assessment of the company. Therefore, the ratio is computed as follows:

$$\text{Price/Earnings Ratio} = \frac{\text{Current Market Price}}{\text{Earnings per Share}}$$

Assume that the current market price for Henderson's common stock is $15 per share at the end of 2004 and $18 per share at the end of 2003. The price/earnings ratio for each of the two years is as follows:

2004	2003
$\frac{\$15 \text{ per share}}{\$1.67 \text{ per share}} = 9 \text{ to } 1$	$\frac{\$18 \text{ per share}}{\$2.25 \text{ per share}} = 8 \text{ to } 1$

What is normal for a P/E ratio? As is the case for all other ratios, it is difficult to generalize as to what is good or bad. The P/E ratio compares the stock market's assessment of a company's performance with its success as reflected on the income statement.

A relatively high P/E ratio may indicate that a stock is overpriced by the market; one that is relatively low could indicate that it is underpriced.

The P/E ratio is often thought to indicate the "quality" of a company's earnings. For example, assume that two companies have identical EPS ratios of $2 per share. Why should investors be willing to pay $20 per share (or 10 times earnings) for the stock of one company but only $14 per share (or 7 times earnings) for the stock of the other company? First, we must realize that many factors in addition to the reported earnings of the company affect market prices. General economic conditions, the outlook for the particular industry, and pending lawsuits are just three examples of the various factors that can affect the trading price of a company's stock. The difference in P/E ratios for the two companies may reflect the market's assessment of the accounting practices of the companies, however. Assume that the company with a market price of $20 per share uses LIFO in valuing inventory and that the company trading at $14 per share uses FIFO. The difference in prices may indicate that investors believe that even though the companies have the same EPS, the LIFO company is "better off" because it will have a lower amount of taxes to pay. (Recall that in a period of inflation, the use of LIFO results in more cost of goods sold, less income, and therefore less income taxes.) Finally, aside from the way investors view the accounting practices of different companies, they also consider the fact that, to a large extent, earnings reflect the use of historical costs, as opposed to fair market values, in assigning values to assets. Investors must consider the extent to which a company's assets are worth more than what was paid for them.

Accounting for Your Decisions

You Are the CEO

You have just been promoted to the chief executive officer position at Orange Computer, a company that has recently fallen on hard times. Sales and earnings have been sluggish. Part of the reason that the prior CEO was dismissed by the board was the lagging stock price. Although the typical computer company stock price is roughly 25 times earnings, Orange Computer is languishing at just 8 times earnings. What can you do to restore the company's stock price?

ANS: The best way to boost your company's stock price is to restore earnings to levels comparable to that of other companies in the industry. If investors see that you are cutting costs, boosting sales, and restoring earnings, they may see a future earnings and dividends stream from Orange Computer that matches other competing investments. Investors' optimism may well translate to an improved stock price.

Dividend Ratios

Two ratios are used to evaluate a company's dividend policies: the **dividend payout ratio** and the **dividend yield ratio.** The dividend payout ratio is the ratio of the common dividends per share to the earnings per share:

Dividend payout ratio The percentage of earnings paid out as dividends.

Dividend yield ratio The relationship between dividends and the market price of a company's stock.

$$\text{Dividend Payout Ratio} = \frac{\text{Common Dividends per Share}}{\text{Earnings per Share}}$$

Exhibit 13-2 indicates that Henderson paid $250,000 in common dividends each year, or with 1 million shares outstanding, $0.25 per share. The two payout ratios are as follows:

2004	2003
$\frac{\$0.25}{\$1.67} = 15.0\%$	$\frac{\$0.25}{\$2.25} = 11.1\%$

Henderson management was faced with an important financial policy decision in 2004. Should the company maintain the same dividend of $0.25 per share, even though EPS dropped significantly? Many companies prefer to maintain a level dividend pattern, hoping that a drop in earnings is only temporary.

From Concept to Practice 13.3

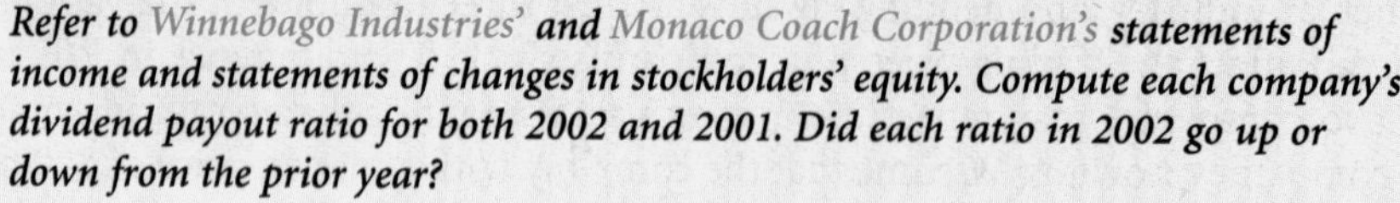

Reading Winnebago Industries' and Monaco Coach Corporation's Annual Reports

Refer to Winnebago Industries' and Monaco Coach Corporation's statements of income and statements of changes in stockholders' equity. Compute each company's dividend payout ratio for both 2002 and 2001. Did each ratio in 2002 go up or down from the prior year?

The second dividend ratio of interest to stockholders is the dividend yield ratio:

$$\text{Dividend Yield Ratio} = \frac{\text{Common Dividends per Share}}{\text{Market Price per Share}}$$

The yield to Henderson's stockholders would be calculated as follows:

2004	2003
$\frac{\$0.25}{\$15} = 1.7\%$	$\frac{\$0.25}{\$18} = 1.4\%$

As we see, Henderson common stock does not provide a high yield to its investors. The relationship between the dividends and the market price indicates that investors buy the stock for reasons other than the periodic dividend return.

The dividend yield is very important to investors who depend on dividend checks to pay their living expenses. Utility stocks are popular among retirees because these shares have dividend yields as high as 5%. That is considered a good investment with relatively low risk and some opportunity for gains in the stock price. On the other hand, investors who want to put money into growing companies are willing to forgo dividends if it means the potential for greater price appreciation.

Summary of Selected Financial Ratios

We have now completed our review of the various ratios used to assess a company's liquidity, solvency, and profitability. For ease of reference, Exhibit 13-8 summarizes the ratios discussed in this chapter. Keep in mind that this list is not all-inclusive and that certain ratios used by analysts and others may be specific to a particular industry or type of business.

Exhibit 13-8 Summary of Selected Financial Ratios

Liquidity Analysis	
Working capital	Current Assets − Current Liabilities
Current ratio	$\frac{\text{Current Assets}}{\text{Current Liabilities}}$
Acid-test ratio (quick ratio)	$\frac{\text{Cash + Marketable Securities + Current Receivables}}{\text{Current Liabilities}}$
Cash flow from operations to current liabilities ratio	$\frac{\text{Net Cash Provided by Operating Activities}}{\text{Average Current Liabilities}}$
Accounts receivable turnover ratio	$\frac{\text{Net Credit Sales}}{\text{Average Accounts Receivable}}$

Exhibit 13-8 Summary of Selected Financial Ratios (*continued*)

Liquidity Analysis (continued)	
Number of days' sales in receivables	$\frac{\text{Number of Days in the Period}}{\text{Accounts Receivable Turnover}}$
Inventory turnover ratio	$\frac{\text{Cost of Goods Sold}}{\text{Average Inventory}}$
Number of days' sales in inventory	$\frac{\text{Number of Days in the Period}}{\text{Inventory Turnover}}$
Cash to cash operating cycle	Number of Days' Sales in Inventory + Number of Days' Sales in Receivables
Solvency Analysis	
Debt-to-equity ratio	$\frac{\text{Total Liabilities}}{\text{Total Stockholders' Equity}}$
Times interest earned ratio	$\frac{\text{Net Income + Interest Expense + Income Tax Expense}}{\text{Interest Expense}}$
Debt service coverage ratio	$\frac{\text{Cash Flow from Operations before Interest and Tax Payments}}{\text{Interest and Principal Payments}}$
Cash flow from operations to capital expenditures ratio	$\frac{\text{Cash Flow from Operations − Total Dividends Paid}}{\text{Cash Paid for Acquisitions}}$
Profitability Analysis	
Gross profit ratio	$\frac{\text{Gross Profit}}{\text{Net Sales}}$
Profit margin ratio	$\frac{\text{Net Income}}{\text{Net Sales}}$
Return on assets ratio	$\frac{\text{Net Income + Interest Expense, Net of Tax}}{\text{Average Total Assets}}$
Return on sales ratio	$\frac{\text{Net Income + Interest Expense, Net of Tax}}{\text{Net Sales}}$
Asset turnover ratio	$\frac{\text{Net Sales}}{\text{Average Total Assets}}$
Return on common stockholders' equity ratio	$\frac{\text{Net Income − Preferred Dividends}}{\text{Average Common Stockholders' Equity}}$
Earnings per share	$\frac{\text{Net Income − Preferred Dividends}}{\text{Weighted Average Number of Common Shares Outstanding}}$
Price/earnings ratio	$\frac{\text{Current Market Price}}{\text{Earnings per Share}}$
Dividend payout ratio	$\frac{\text{Common Dividends per Share}}{\text{Earnings per Share}}$
Dividend yield ratio	$\frac{\text{Common Dividends per Share}}{\text{Market Price per Share}}$

Accounting for Your Decisions

You Decide on a Stock Purchase

You are starting college and your parents have agreed to help pay your tuition. They will put money into a stock fund for four years and allow you to use the dividends from the fund to pay your quarterly tuition. Should you advise your parents to find a stock with a relatively low dividend yield ratio if it has an above-average return on stockholders' equity?

ANS: Regardless of how attractive a company's return on equity ratio might be, you need cash on a regular basis to pay tuition. You should advise your parents to find a stock with a relatively high dividend yield ratio.

Answers to the Two-Minute Reviews

Two-Minute Review on Page 665

1. *Horizontal analysis is used to compare a particular financial statement item over a period of time, whereas vertical analysis allows someone to compare various financial statement items within a single period. With vertical analysis, all of the items are stated as a percentage of a specific item on that statement, such as sales on the income statement or total assets on the balance sheet.*
2. *Horizontal analysis could be used to examine the trend in accounts receivable over recent years.*
3. *Vertical analysis could be used to examine the relationship between selling and administrative expenses and sales. However, you may also want to compare this percentage with the ratio in prior years (thus, you would be performing horizontal analysis as well).*

Two-Minute Review on Page 674

1. Liquidity *is a relative measure of the nearness to cash of the assets and liabilities of a company. Measures of liquidity are intended to determine the company's ability to pay its debts as they come due.* Solvency *refers to a company's ability to remain in business over the long term. Liquidity and solvency are certainly related, but the latter takes a much more long-term view of the financial health of the company.*
2. *Because you need to assess the ability of the company to pay its account on a timely basis, you would be more concerned with the liquidity of the company over the short term.*

Warmup Exercises

Warmup Exercise 13-1 *Types of Ratios* **LO 4, 5, 6**

Fill in the blanks that follow to indicate whether each of the following ratios is concerned with a company's liquidity (L), its solvency (S), or its profitability (P).

______ **1.** Return on assets ratio
______ **2.** Current ratio
______ **3.** Debt-to-equity ratio

_______ 4. Earnings per share

_______ 5. Inventory turnover ratio

_______ 6. Gross profit ratio

Key to the Solution

Review the summary of selected ratios in Exhibit 13-8.

Warmup Exercise 13-2 ***Accounts Receivable Turnover*** **LO 4**

Company A reported sales during the year of $1,000,000. Its average accounts receivable balance during the year was $250,000. Company B reported sales during the same year of $400,000 and had an average accounts receivable balance of $40,000.

Required

1. Compute the accounts receivable turnover for both companies.
2. What is the average length of time each company takes to collect its receivables?

Key to the Solution

Review the summary of selected ratios in Exhibit 13-8.

Warmup Exercise 13-3 ***Earnings Per Share*** **LO 6**

A company reported net income during the year of $90,000 and paid dividends of $15,000 to its common stockholders and $10,000 to its preferred stockholders. During the year, 20,000 shares of common stock were outstanding and 10,000 shares of preferred stock were outstanding.

Required

Compute earnings per share for the year.

Key to the Solution

Recall that earnings per share only has relevance to the common stockholders and therefore it is a measure of the earnings per common share outstanding, after taking into account any claims of preferred stockholders.

Solutions to Warmup Exercises

Warmup Exercise 13-1

1. P **2.** L **3.** S **4.** P **5.** L **6.** P

Warmup Exercise 13-2

1. Company A turns over its accounts receivable, on the average, 4 times during the year ($1,000,000/$250,000) and Company B 10 times during the year ($400,000/$40,000).
2. Assuming 360 days in a year, Company A takes, on the average, 90 days to collect its accounts receivable, and Company B takes, on the average, 36 days.

Warmup Exercise 13-3

Earnings per share: ($90,000 − $10,000)/20,000 shares = $4 per share.

Review Problem

On pages 684–687 are the comparative financial statements for Wm. Wrigley Jr. Company, the chewing gum manufacturer, as shown in its 2002 annual report.

WebTUTOR™ Advantage

Required

1. Compute the following ratios for the two years 2002 and 2001, either for each year or as of the end of each of the years, as appropriate. Beginning balances for 2001 are not available; that is, you do not have a balance sheet as of the end of 2000. Therefore, to be consistent,

(continued)

CONSOLIDATED STATEMENT OF EARNINGS

Wm. Wrigley Jr. Company

In thousands of dollars except per share amounts

	2002	2001	2000
EARNINGS			
Net sales	**$2,746,318**	2,401,419	2,126,114
Cost of sales	**1,150,215**	997,054	904,266
Gross profit	**1,596,103**	1,404,365	1,221,848
Selling, general and adminstrative expense	**1,011,029**	891,009	758,605
Operating income	**585,074**	513,356	463,243
Investment income	**8,918**	18,553	19,185
Other expense	**(10,571)**	(4,543)	(3,116)
Earnings before income taxes	**583,421**	527,366	479,312
Income taxes	**181,896**	164,380	150,370
Net earnings	**401,525**	362,986	328,942
PER SHARE AMOUNTS			
Net earnings per share of common stock (basic and diluted)	**1.78**	1.61	1.45
Dividends paid per share of common stock	**.805**	.745	.701

See accompanying accounting policies and notes.

(continued)

use year-end balances for both years where you would normally use average amounts for the year. To compute the return on assets ratio, you will need to find the tax rate. Use the relationship between income taxes and earnings before taxes to find the rate for each year.

a. Current ratio
b. Quick ratio
c. Cash flow from operations to current liabilities ratio
d. Number of days' sales in receivables
e. Number of days' sales in inventory
f. Debt-to-equity ratio
g. Debt service coverage ratio
h. Cash flow from operations to capital expenditures ratio
i. Return on assets ratio
j. Return on common stockholders' equity ratio

2. Comment on Wrigley's liquidity. Has it improved or declined over the two-year period?
3. Does Wrigley appear to be solvent to you? Does there appear to be anything unusual about its capital structure?
4. Comment on Wrigley's profitability. Would you buy stock in the company?

CONSOLIDATED STATEMENT OF CASH FLOWS

In thousands of dollars

	2002	2001	2000
OPERATING ACTIVITIES			
Net earnings	**$ 401,525**	362,986	328,942
Adjustments to reconcile net earnings to net cash provided by operating activities:			
Depreciation	**85,568**	68,326	57,880
Loss on sales of property, plant and equipment	**1,014**	2,910	778
(Increase) Decrease in:			
Accounts receivable	**(55,288)**	(53,162)	(18,483)
Inventories	**(31,858)**	(29,487)	(2,812)
Other current assets	**1,304**	(8,079)	199
Deferred charges and other assets	**(78,585)**	(15,852)	30,408
Increase (Decrease) in:			
Accounts payable	**756**	20,537	12,988
Accrued expenses	**33,416**	16,360	18,015
Income and other taxes payable	**(3,715)**	9,565	14,670
Deferred income taxes	**19,082**	5,570	2,546
Other noncurrent liabilites	**1,216**	10,817	3,152
Net cash provided by operating activities	**374,435**	390,491	448,283
INVESTING ACTIVITIES			
Additions to property, plant and equipment	**(216,872)**	(181,760)	(125,068)
Proceeds from property retirements	**5,017**	2,376	1,128
Purchases of short-term investments	**(41,177)**	(24,448)	(125,728)
Maturities of short-term investments	**44,858**	26,835	115,007
Net cash used in investing activities	**(208,174)**	(176,997)	(134,661)
FINANCING ACTIVITIES			
Dividends paid	**(181,232)**	(167,922)	(159,138)
Common Stock, purchased, net	**(16,402)**	(34,173)	(131,765)
Net cash used in financing activities	**(197,634)**	(202,095)	(290,903)
Effect of exchange rate changes on cash and cash equivalents	**2,864**	(4,213)	(10,506)
Net increase (decrease) in cash and cash equivalents	**(28,509)**	7,186	12,213
Cash and cash equivalents at beginning of year	**307,785**	300,599	288,386
Cash and cash equivalents at end of year	**279,276**	307,785	300,599
SUPPLEMENTAL CASH FLOW INFORMATION			
Income taxes paid	**173,010**	146,858	136,311
Interest paid	**1,636**	1,101	749
Interest and dividends received	**8,974**	18,570	19,243

See accompanying accounting policies and notes.

(continued)

CONSOLIDATED BALANCE SHEET

In thousands of dollars

	2002	2001
ASSETS		
Curret assets:		
Cash and cash equivalents	**$ 279,276**	307,785
Short-term investments, at amortized cost	**25,621**	25,450
Accounts receivable (less allowance for doubtful accounts: 2002–$5,850; 2001–$7,712)	**312,919**	239,885
Inventories:		
Finished goods	**88,583**	75,693
Raw materials and supplies	**232,613**	203,288
	321,196	278,981
Other current assets	**47,720**	46,896
Deferred income taxes—current	**19,560**	14,846
Total curret assets	**1,006,292**	913,843
Marketable equity securities, at fair value	**19,411**	25,300
Deferred charges and other assets	**213,483**	124,666
Deferred income taxes—noncurrent	**33,000**	29,605
Property, plant and equipment, at cost:		
Land	**48,968**	39,933
Buildings and building equipment	**393,780**	359,109
Machinery and equipment	**1,049,001**	857,054
	1,491,749	1,256,096
Less accumulated depreciation	**655,639**	571,717
Net property, plant and equipment	**836,110**	684,379
TOTAL ASSETS	**$ 2,108,296**	1,777,793

Solution to Review Problem

1. Ratios:
   - **a.** 2002: $1,006,292/$386,087 = 2.61
     2001: $913,843/$332,324 = 2.75
   - **b.** 2002: ($279,276 + $25,621 + $312,919)/$386,087 = 1.60
     2001: ($307,785 + $25,450 + $239,885)/$332,324 = 1.72
   - **c.** 2002: $374,435/$386,087 = .97
     2001: $390,491/$332,324 = 1.18

In thousands of dollars and shares	2002	2001
LIABILITIES AND STOCKHOLDERS' EQUITY		
Curret liabilities:		
Accounts payable	$ 97,705	91,397
Accrued expenses	172,137	128,264
Dividends payable	46,137	42,741
Income and other taxes payable	66,893	68,467
Deferred income taxes—current	3,215	1,455
Total current liabilities	386,087	332,324
Deferred income taxes—noncurrent	70,589	46,430
Other noncurrent liabilities	129,044	122,842
Stockholders' equity:		
Preferred Stock—no par value Authorized: 20,000 shares Issued: None		
Common Stock—no par value		
Common Stock Authorized: 400,000 shares Issued 2002–190,898 shares; 2001–189,800 shares	12,719	12,646
Class B Common Stock—convertible Authorized: 80,000 shares Issued and outstanding: 2002–41,543 shares; 2001–42,641 shares	2,777	2,850
Additional paid-in capital	4,209	1,153
Retained earnings	1,902,990	1,684,337
Common Stock in treasury, at cost (2002–7,385 shares; 2001–7,491 shares)	(297,156)	(289,799)
Accumulated other comprehensive income:		
Foreign currency translation adjustment	(112,303)	(149,310)
Gain (loss) on derivative contracts	(853)	46
Unrealized holding gains on marketable equity securities	10,193	14,274
	(102,963)	(134,990)
Total stockholders' equity	1,522,576	1,276,197
TOTAL LIABILITIES AND STOCKHOLDERS' EQUITY	2,108,296	1,777,793

See accompanying accounting policies and notes.

(continued)

d. 2002: 360 days/[($2,746,318/$312,919)] = 360/8.78 = 41 days

2001: 360 days/[($2,401,419/$239,885)] = 360/10.01 = 36 days

e. 2002: 360 days/[($1,150,215/$321,196)] = 360/3.58 = 101 days

2001: 360 days/[($997,054/$278,981)] = 360/3.57 = 101 days

f. 2002: ($386,087 + $70,589 + $129,044)/$1,522,576 = .38

2001: ($332,324 + $46,430 + $122,842)/$1,276,197 = .39

g. 2002: ($374,435 + $173,010 + $1,636)/$1,636 = 336

2001: ($390,491 + $146,858 + $1,101)/$1,101 = 489

h. 2002: ($374,435 − $181,232)/$216,872 = .89

2001: ($390,491 − $167,922)/$181,760 = 1.22

i. 2002: $401,525 + [$1,636[a](1 − 0.31[b])]/$2,108,296 = 19.1%

2001: $362,986 + [$1,101[a](1 − 0.31[b])]/$1,777,793 = 20.5%

j. 2002: $401,525/$1,522,576[c] = 26.4%

2001: $362,986/$1,276,197[c] = 28.4%

2. Although both the current ratio and the quick ratio declined during 2002, neither was a very significant decrease. Cash flow from operations to current liabilities also declined, but the ratio at the end of 2002 was still nearly 1 to 1. Wrigley appears to be quite liquid and should have no problems meeting its short-term obligations.
3. Wrigley is extremely solvent. Its capital structure reveals that it does not rely in any significant way on long-term debt to finance its business. The amount of noncurrent liabilities is less than 10% of total liabilities and stockholders' equity at the end of each year. In fact, a majority of Wrigley's debt is in the form of interest-free current liabilities. Most revealing is the debt service coverage ratio of 489 times in 2001 and 336 times in 2002. The total interest expense each year is insignificant.
4. The return on assets for 2002 is 19.1%, and the return on common stockholders' equity is 26.4%. Although these return ratios are down slightly from the prior year, they indicate a very profitable company. It should be noted that the company paid nearly half of its 2002 earnings in dividends. Wrigley appears to be a very sound investment, but many other factors, including information on the current market price of the stock, should be considered before making a decision.

---

[a]Wrigley does not separately disclose interest expense on its income statement; the amounts of interest paid that are reported at bottom of statements of cash flows have been used for the calculations.

[b]Tax rate for each of the two years:

2002: $181,896/$583,421 = 0.31

2001: $164,380/$527,366 = 0.31

[c]In addition to its common stock, Wrigley has outstanding Class B common stock. Because this is a second class of stock (similar in many respects to preferred stock), the contributed capital attributable to it should be deducted from total stockholders' equity in the denominator. Similarly, any dividends paid on the Class B common stock should be deducted from net income in the numerator to find the return to the regular common stockholders. We have ignored the difficulties involved in determining these adjustments in our calculations of return on equity.

Appendix: Accounting Tools: Reporting and Analyzing Other Income Statement Items

LO 7 Explain how to report on and analyze other income statement items.

Not all companies have income statements that are as easy to understand and interpret as Wrigley's statement. Some companies report any one or some combination of the following three items on their income statements: discontinued operations, extraordinary items, and cumulative effect of a change in accounting principle. Although the nature of each of these items is very distinct, the three do share some common characteristics. First, they are all reported near the end of the income statement, after income from continuing operations. Second, they are reported separately on the income statement to call the reader's attention to their unique nature and to the fact that any additions to, or deductions from, income that they give rise to may not necessarily reoccur in future periods. Finally, each of these items is shown net of their tax effects. This means that any additional taxes due because of them, or any tax benefits from them, are deducted from the items themselves. Following is a brief description of each item.

Discontinued Operations

When a company decides to either sell or otherwise dispose of one of its operations, it must separately report on that division or segment of the business on its income statement. This includes any gain or loss from the disposal of the business as well as any net income or loss from operating the business until the date of disposal. Because the discontinued segment of the business will not be part of the company's operations in the future, **discontinued operations** are separately disclosed on the income statement. **Analysts and other users would normally only consider income from continuing operations in making their decisions.**

Discontinued operations A line item on the income statement to reflect any gains or losses from the disposal of a segment of the business as well as any net income or loss from operating that segment.

Extraordinary Items

According to accounting standards, certain events that give rise to gains or losses are deemed to be extraordinary and are thus separately disclosed on the income statement. To qualify for extraordinary treatment, the gain or loss must be due to an event that is both unusual in nature and infrequent in occurrence.[3] Under current accounting standards, an **extraordinary item** is relatively rare, such as when a natural catastrophe like a tornado destroys a plant in an area not known for tornadoes. As is the case for discontinued operations, **analysts and others often ignore the amount of such gains and losses in reaching their decisions since they are aware that these items are not likely to reoccur in the future.**

Extraordinary item A line item on the income statement to reflect any gains or losses that arise from an event that is both unusual in nature and infrequent in occurrence.

Cumulative Effect of a Change in Accounting Principle

This line item on the income statement arises when a company makes a change in one of its accounting principles, practices, or methods. For example, when a company changes its depreciation from straight-line to accelerated or its method of valuing inventory from FIFO to average cost, it must report a separate line item on its income statement called **cumulative effect of a change in accounting principle.** The amount of this line item represents the difference in income in all prior years between the old method and the new method.

Cumulative effect of a change in accounting principle A line item on the income statement to reflect the effect on prior years' income from a change in accounting principle.

Sometimes, a change in accounting principle is dictated by a new accounting standard. For example, in response to a pronouncement from the Securities and Exchange Commission, Winnebago Industries changed the timing of when it recognizes revenue. Under the new standard, revenue is reported when the company's products are delivered to dealers, which is when title passes, rather than when the RVs are shipped by Winnebago Industries. The 2001 income statement reflected the cumulative effect from this change in the timing of revenue recognition as follows (all amounts are in thousands of dollars):

http://www.sec.gov
http://www.winnebagoind.com

Income before cumulative effect of change in accounting principle	$43,754
Cumulative effect of change in accounting principle, net of taxes	(1,050)
Net income	$42,704

An analyst trying to predict the future profitability of Winnebago Industries might very well ignore the cumulative effect reported as part of 2001 net income knowing that this item will not likely reoccur in the future.

[3] *APB Opinion No. 30,* "Reporting the Results of Operations," Accounting Principles Board, 1973.

Chapter Highlights

1. **LO 1** Various parties, including management, creditors, stockholders, and others, perform financial statement analysis. Care must be exercised, however, in all types of financial analysis. For example, the existence of alternative accounting principles can make comparing different companies difficult. Published financial statements are not adjusted for the effects of inflation, and thus comparisons over time must be made with caution.
2. **LO 2** Horizontal analysis uses comparative financial statements to examine the increases and decreases in items from one period to the next. The analysis can look at the change in items over an extended period of time. Many companies present a summary of selected financial items for a 5- or 10-year period.
3. **LO 3** Vertical analysis involves stating all items on a particular financial statement as a percentage of one item on the statement. For example, all expenses on a common-size income statement are stated as a percentage of net sales. This technique, along with horizontal analysis, can be useful in spotting problem areas within a company.
4. **LO 4** Ratios can be categorized according to their primary purpose. Liquidity ratios indicate the company's ability to pay its debts as they are due. The focus of liquidity analysis is on a company's current assets and current liabilities.
5. **LO 5** Solvency ratios deal with a company's long-term financial health, that is, its ability to repay long-term creditors. The right side of the balance sheet is informative in this respect because it reports on the various sources of capital to the business.
6. **LO 6** Profitability ratios measure how well management has used the assets at its disposal to earn a return for the various providers of capital. Return on assets indicates the return to all providers; return on common stockholders' equity measures the return to the residual owners of the business. Certain other ratios are used to relate a company's performance according to the financial statements with its performance in the stock market.
7. **LO 7** Certain items must be reported separately at the bottom of the income statement. These include discontinued operations, extraordinary gains and losses, and the cumulative effect of a change in accounting principle. By reporting these items separately, the company allows users of the income statement to determine whether or not to consider them in trying to predict future income.

http://

Technology and other resources for your success

http://porter.swlearning.com

If you need additional help, visit the text's Web site. Also, see this text's preface for a description of available technology and other resources. If your instructor is using *PERSONAL Trainer* in this course, you may complete, on line, the exercises and problems in the text.

Key Terms Quiz

Because of the number of terms introduced in this chapter, there are two key terms quizzes. For each quiz, read each definition below and then write the number of that definition in the blank beside the appropriate term it defines. The quiz solutions appear at the end of the chapter.

Quiz 1:

_____ Horizontal analysis
_____ Vertical analysis
_____ Gross profit ratio
_____ Profit margin ratio
_____ Liquidity
_____ Working capital
_____ Current ratio
_____ Acid-test or quick ratio
_____ Cash flow from operations to current liabilities ratio
_____ Accounts receivable turnover ratio
_____ Number of days' sales in receivables
_____ Inventory turnover ratio
_____ Number of days' sales in inventory
_____ Cash to cash operating cycle

1. A stricter test of liquidity than the current ratio; excludes inventory and prepayments from the numerator.
2. Current assets minus current liabilities.
3. The ratio of current assets to current liabilities.
4. A measure of the average age of accounts receivable.
5. A measure of the ability to pay current debts from operating cash flows.
6. A measure of the number of times accounts receivable are collected in a period.
7. A measure of how long it takes to sell inventory.

8. The length of time from the purchase of inventory to the collection of any receivable from the sale.
9. A measure of the number of times inventory is sold during a period.
10. Gross profit to net sales.
11. A comparison of various financial statement items within a single period with the use of common-size statements.
12. Net income to net sales.
13. The nearness to cash of the assets and liabilities.
14. A comparison of financial statement items over a period of time.

Quiz 2:

_____ Solvency
_____ Debt-to-equity ratio
_____ Times interest earned ratio
_____ Debt service coverage ratio
_____ Cash flow from operations to capital expenditures ratio
_____ Profitability
_____ Return on assets ratio
_____ Return on sales ratio
_____ Asset turnover ratio
_____ Return on common stockholders' equity ratio
_____ Leverage
_____ Earnings per share
_____ Price/earnings (P/E) ratio
_____ Dividend payout ratio
_____ Dividend yield ratio
_____ Discontinued operations (Appendix)
_____ Extraordinary item (Appendix)
_____ Cumulative effect of a change in accounting principle (Appendix)

1. A measure of a company's success in earning a return for the common stockholders.
2. The relationship between a company's performance according to the income statement and its performance in the stock market.
3. The ability of a company to remain in business over the long term.
4. A variation of the profit margin ratio; measures earnings before payments to creditors.
5. A company's bottom line stated on a per-share basis.
6. The percentage of earnings paid out as dividends.
7. The ratio of total liabilities to total stockholders' equity.
8. A measure of the ability of a company to finance long-term asset acquisitions with cash from operations.
9. A measure of a company's success in earning a return for all providers of capital.
10. The relationship between net sales and total assets.
11. The relationship between dividends and the market price of a company's stock.
12. The use of borrowed funds and amounts contributed by preferred stockholders to earn an overall return higher than the cost of these funds.
13. An income statement measure of the ability of a company to meet its interest payments.
14. A statement of cash flows measure of the ability of a company to meet its interest and principal payments.
15. How well management is using company resources to earn a return on the funds invested by various groups.
16. A line item on the income statement to reflect any gains or losses that arise from an event that is both unusual in nature and infrequent in occurrence.
17. A line item on the income statement to reflect the effect on prior years' income from a change in accounting principle.
18. A line item on the income statement to reflect any gains or losses from the disposal of a segment of the business as well as any net income or loss from operating that segment.

Answers on p. 718.

Alternate Terms

Acid-test ratio Quick ratio

Horizontal analysis Trend analysis

Number of days' sales in receivables Average collection period

Price/earnings ratio P/E ratio

Questions

1. Two companies are in the same industry. Company A uses the LIFO method of inventory valuation, and Company B uses FIFO. What difficulties does this present when comparing the two companies?
2. You are told to compare the company's results for the year, as measured by various ratios, with one of the published surveys that arranges information by industry classification. What are some of the difficulties you may encounter when making comparisons using industry standards?

3. What types of problems does inflation cause in analyzing financial statements?
4. Distinguish between horizontal and vertical analysis. Why is the analysis of common-size statements called *vertical* analysis? Why is horizontal analysis sometimes called *trend* analysis?
5. A company experiences a 15% increase in sales over the previous year. However, gross profit actually decreased by 5% from the previous year. What are some of the possible causes for an increase in sales but a decline in gross profit?
6. A company's total current assets have increased by 5% over the prior year. Management is concerned, however, about the composition of the current assets. Why is the composition of current assets important?
7. Ratios were categorized in the chapter according to their use in performing three different types of analysis. What are the three types of ratios?
8. Describe the operating cycle for a manufacturing company. How would the cycle differ for a retailer?
9. What accounts for the order in which current assets are presented on a balance sheet?
10. A company has a current ratio of 1.25 but an acid-test or quick ratio of only 0.65. How can this difference in the two ratios be explained? What are some concerns that you would have about this company?
11. Explain the basic concept underlying all turnover ratios. Why is it advisable in computing a turnover ratio to use an average in the denominator (for example, average inventory)?
12. Sanders Company's accounts receivable turned over nine times during the year. The credit department extends terms of 2/10, net 30. Does the turnover ratio indicate any problems that management should investigate?
13. The turnover of inventory for Ace Company has slowed from 6.0 times per year to 4.5 times. What are some of the possible explanations for this decrease?
14. How does the operating cycle for a manufacturer differ from the operating cycle for a service company, for example, an airline?
15. What is the difference between liquidity analysis and solvency analysis?
16. Why is the debt service coverage ratio a better measure of solvency than the times interest earned ratio?
17. A friend tells you that the best way to assess solvency is by comparing total debt to total assets. Another friend says that solvency is measured by comparing total debt to total stockholders' equity. Which one is right?
18. A company is in the process of negotiating with a bank for an additional loan. Why will the bank be very interested in the company's debt service coverage ratio?
19. What is the rationale for deducting dividends when computing the ratio of cash flow from operations to capital expenditures?
20. The rate of return on assets ratio is computed by dividing net income and interest expense, net of tax, by average total assets. Why is the numerator net income and interest expense, net of tax, rather than just net income?
21. A company has a return on assets of 14% and a return on common stockholders' equity of 11%. The president of the company has asked you to explain the reason for this difference. What causes the difference? How is the concept of financial leverage involved?
22. What is meant by the "quality" of a company's earnings? Explain why the price/earnings ratio for a company may indicate the quality of earnings.
23. Some ratios are more useful for management, whereas others are better suited to the needs of outsiders, such as stockholders and bankers. What is an example of a ratio that is primarily suited to management use? What is one that is more suited to use by outsiders?
24. The needs of service-oriented companies in analyzing financial statements differ from those of product-oriented companies. Why is this true? Give an example of a ratio that is meaningless to a service business.
25. What is the reason for reporting discontinued operations, extraordinary items, and the cumulative effect of a change in accounting principle separately on an income statement? (Appendix)

Exercises

Exercise 13-1 ***Accounts Receivable Analysis*** **LO 4**

The following account balances are taken from the records of the Faraway Travel Agency:

	December 31		
	2004	**2003**	**2002**
Accounts receivable	$150,000	$100,000	$80,000
	2004	**2003**	
Net credit sales	$600,000	$540,000	

Faraway extends credit terms requiring full payment in 60 days, with no discount for early payment.

Required

1. Compute Faraway's accounts receivable turnover ratio for 2004 and 2003.

2. Compute the number of days' sales in receivables for 2004 and 2003. Assume 360 days in a year.
3. Comment on the efficiency of Faraway's collection efforts over the two-year period.

Exercise 13-2 ***Inventory Analysis*** **LO 4**

The following account balances are taken from the records of Lewis Inc., a wholesaler of fresh fruits and vegetables:

	December 31		
	2004	**2003**	**2002**
Merchandise inventory	$ 200,000	$ 150,000	$120,000
	2004	**2003**	
Cost of goods sold	$7,100,000	$8,100,000	

Required

1. Compute Lewis's inventory turnover ratio for 2004 and 2003.
2. Compute the number of days' sales in inventory for 2004 and 2003. Assume 360 days in a year.
3. Comment on your answers in parts **1** and **2** relative to the company's management of inventory over the two years. What problems do you see in its inventory management?

Exercise 13-3 ***Accounts Receivable and Inventory Analyses for Coca-Cola and PepsiCo*** **LO 4**

The following information was obtained from the 2002 and 2001 financial statements of Coca-Cola Company and Subsidiaries and PepsiCo Inc. and Subsidiaries (year ends for PepsiCo are December 28, 2002, and December 29, 2001):

http://www.cocacola.com
http://www.pepsico.com

(in millions)		Coca-Cola	PepsiCo
Accounts and notes receivable, net[a]	12/31/02	$ 2,097	$ 2,531
	12/31/01	1,882	2,142
Inventories	12/31/02	1,294	1,342
	12/31/01	1,055	1,310
Net sales[b]	2002	19,564	25,112
	2001	17,545	23,512
Cost of goods sold[c]	2002	7,105	11,497
	2001	6,044	10,750

[a]Described as "trade accounts receivable" by Coca-Cola.
[b]Described as "net operating revenues" by Coca-Cola.
[c]Described as "cost of sales" by PepsiCo.

Required

1. Using the information provided above, compute the following for each company for 2002:
   a. Accounts receivable turnover ratio
   b. Number of days' sales in receivables
   c. Inventory turnover ratio
   d. Number of days' sales in inventory
   e. Cash to cash operating cycle
2. Comment briefly on the liquidity of each of these two companies.

Exercise 13-4 ***Liquidity Analyses for Coca-Cola and PepsiCo*** **LO 4**

The following information was summarized from the balance sheets of the Coca-Cola Company and Subsidiaries at December 31, 2002, and PepsiCo Inc. and Subsidiaries at December 28, 2002:

(continued)

(in millions)	Coca-Cola	PepsiCo
Cash and cash equivalents	$ 2,126	$1,638
Short-term investments/marketable securities	219	207
Accounts and notes receivables, net	2,097	2,531
Inventories	1,294	1,342
Prepaid expenses and other current assets	1,616	695
Total current assets	$ 7,352	$6,413
Current liabilities	$ 7,341	$6,052
Other liabilities	5,360	8,131
Stockholders' equity	11,800	9,291

Required

1. Using the information provided above, compute the following for each company at the end of 2002:
   a. Current ratio
   b. Quick ratio
2. Comment briefly on the liquidity of each of these two companies. Which appears to be more liquid?
3. What other ratios would help you to more fully assess the liquidity of these companies?

Exercise 13-5 ***Liquidity Analyses for McDonald's and Wendy's*** **LO 4**

http://www.mcdonalds.com
http://www.wendys.com

DECISION MAKING

The following information was summarized from the balance sheets of McDonald's Corporation and Wendy's International Inc. at December 31, 2002, and December 29, 2002, respectively:

	McDonald's (in millions)	Wendy's (in thousands)
Current Assets:		
Cash and cash equivalents	$ 330.4	$ 171,944
Accounts receivable, net*	855.3	86,416
Notes receivable, net	—	11,204
Inventories	111.7	47,433
Other current assets	418.0	13,822
Total current assets	$ 1,715.4	$ 330,819
Current liabilities	$ 2,422.3	$ 360,075
Other liabilities	$11,267.3	$ 858,681
Stockholders' equity	$10,280.9	$1,448,605

*McDonald's combines accounts and notes receivable.

Required

1. Using the information provided above, compute the following for each company at year end:
   a. Working capital
   b. Current ratio
   c. Quick ratio
2. Comment briefly on the liquidity of each of these two companies. Which appears to be more liquid?
3. McDonald's reported cash flows from operations of $2,890.1 million during 2002. Wendy's reported cash flows from operations of $444,256 thousand. Current liabilities reported by McDonald's at December 31, 2001, and Wendy's at December 30, 2001, were $2,248.3 million and $296,687 thousand, respectively. Calculate the cash flow from operations to current liabilities ratio for each company. Does the information provided by this ratio change your opinion as to the relative liquidity of each of these two companies?
4. What steps might be taken by McDonald's to cover its short-term cash requirements?

Exercise 13-6 ***Solvency Analyses for Tommy Hilfiger*** **LO 5**

http://www.tommy.com

The following information was obtained from the comparative financial statements included in Tommy Hilfiger Corporation's 2003 annual report (all amounts are in thousands of dollars):

	March 31, 2003	March 31, 2002
Total liabilities	$ 984,776	$1,096,989
Total shareholders' equity	1,043,375	1,497,462

	For the Fiscal Years Ended March 31	
	2003	2002
Interest and other expense	$ 46,976	$ 41,177
Provision for income taxes	14,144	20,069
Net income (loss)	(513,605)	134,545
Net cash provided by operating activities	230,105	353,100
Total dividends paid	—	—
Cash used to purchase property and equipment	71,903	96,923
Payments on long-term debt	74,234	155,538

Required

1. Using the information provided above, compute the following for 2001 and 2000:
   a. Debt-to-equity ratio (at each year-end)
   b. Times interest earned ratio
   c. Debt service coverage ratio
   d. Cash flow from operations to capital expenditures ratio
2. Comment briefly on the company's solvency.

Exercise 13-7 ***Solvency Analysis*** **LO 5**

The following information is available from the balance sheets at the ends of the two most recent years and the income statement for the most recent year of Impact Company:

	December 31	
	2004	2003
Accounts payable	$ 65,000	$ 50,000
Accrued liabilities	25,000	35,000
Taxes payable	60,000	45,000
Short-term notes payable	0	75,000
Bonds payable due within next year	200,000	200,000
Total current liabilities	$ 350,000	$ 405,000
Bonds payable	$ 600,000	$ 800,000
Common stock, $10 par	$1,000,000	$1,000,000
Retained earnings	650,000	500,000
Total stockholders' equity	$1,650,000	$1,500,000
Total liabilities and stockholders' equity	$2,600,000	$2,705,000

	2004
Sales revenue	$1,600,000
Cost of goods sold	950,000
Gross profit	$ 650,000
Selling and administrative expense	300,000
Operating income	$ 350,000
Interest expense	89,000
Income before tax	$ 261,000
Income tax expense	111,000
Net income	$ 150,000

Other Information

a. Short-term notes payable represents a 12-month loan that matured in November 2004. Interest of 12% was paid at maturity.

b. One million dollars of serial bonds had been issued 10 years earlier. The first series of $200,000 matured at the end of 2004, with interest of 8% payable annually.

c. Cash flow from operations was $185,000 in 2004. The amounts of interest and taxes paid during 2004 were $89,000 and $96,000, respectively.

Required

1. Compute the following for Impact Company:
   a. The debt-to-equity ratio at December 31, 2004, and December 31, 2003
   b. The times interest earned ratio for 2004
   c. The debt service coverage ratio for 2004
2. Comment on Impact's solvency at the end of 2004. Do the times interest earned ratio and the debt service coverage ratio differ in their indication of Impact's ability to pay its debts?

Exercise 13-8 ***Return Ratios and Leverage*** **LO 6**

The following selected data are taken from the financial statements of Evergreen Company:

Sales revenue	$ 650,000
Cost of goods sold	400,000
Gross profit	$ 250,000
Selling and administrative expense	100,000
Operating income	$ 150,000
Interest expense	50,000
Income before tax	$ 100,000
Income tax expense (40%)	40,000
Net income	$ 60,000
Accounts payable	$ 45,000
Accrued liabilities	70,000
Income taxes payable	10,000
Interest payable	25,000
Short-term loans payable	150,000
Total current liabilities	$ 300,000
Long-term bonds payable	$ 500,000
Preferred stock, 10%, $100 par	$ 250,000
Common stock, no par	600,000
Retained earnings	350,000
Total stockholders' equity	$1,200,000
Total liabilities and stockholders' equity	$2,000,000

Required

1. Compute the following ratios for Evergreen Company:
   a. Return on sales
   b. Asset turnover (assume that total assets at the beginning of the year were $1,600,000)
   c. Return on assets
   d. Return on common stockholders' equity (assume that the only changes in stockholders' equity during the year were from the net income for the year and dividends on the preferred stock)
2. Comment on Evergreen's use of leverage. Has it successfully employed leverage? Explain.

Exercise 13-9 ***Relationships among Return on Assets, Return on Sales, and Asset Turnover*** **LO 6**

A company's return on assets is a function of its ability to turn over its investment (asset turnover) and earn a profit on each dollar of sales (return on sales). For each of the *independent* cases below, determine the missing amounts. (*Note:* Assume in each case that the company has no interest expense; that is, net income is used as the definition of income in all calculations.)

Case 1	
Net income	$ 10,000
Net sales	$ 80,000
Average total assets	$ 60,000
Return on assets	?

Case 2	
Net income	$ 25,000
Average total assets	$250,000
Return on sales	2%
Net sales	?

Case 3	
Average total assets	$ 80,000
Asset turnover	1.5 times
Return on sales	6%
Return on assets	?

Case 4	
Return on assets	10%
Net sales	$ 50,000
Asset turnover	1.25 times
Net income	?

Case 5	
Return on assets	15%
Net income	$ 20,000
Return on sales	5%
Average total assets	?

Exercise 13-10 *EPS, P/E Ratio, and Dividend Ratios* LO 6

DECISION MAKING

The stockholders' equity section of the balance sheet for Cooperstown Corp. at the end of 2004 appears as follows:

8%, $100 par, cumulative preferred stock, 200,000 shares authorized, 50,000 shares issued and outstanding	$ 5,000,000
Additional paid-in capital on preferred	2,500,000
Common stock, $5 par, 500,000 shares authorized, 400,000 shares issued and outstanding	2,000,000
Additional paid-in capital on common	18,000,000
Retained earnings	37,500,000
Total stockholders' equity	$65,000,000

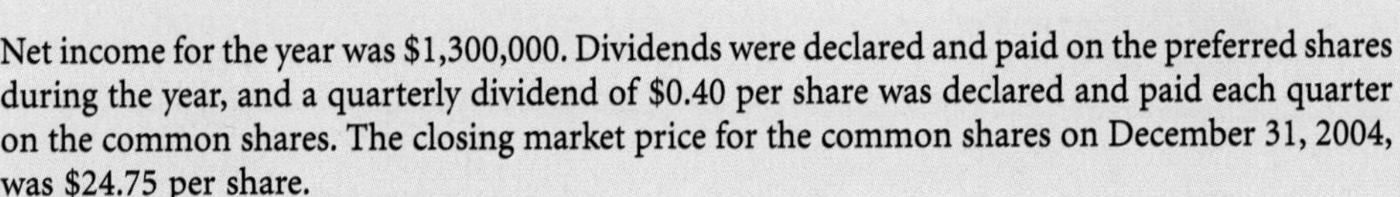

Net income for the year was $1,300,000. Dividends were declared and paid on the preferred shares during the year, and a quarterly dividend of $0.40 per share was declared and paid each quarter on the common shares. The closing market price for the common shares on December 31, 2004, was $24.75 per share.

Required

1. Compute the following ratios for the common stock:
   a. Earnings per share
   b. Price/earnings ratio
   c. Dividend payout ratio
   d. Dividend yield ratio
2. Assume that you are an investment adviser. What other information would you want to have before advising a client regarding the purchase of Cooperstown stock?

Exercise 13-11 *Earnings Per Share and Extraordinary Items* LO 6

The stockholders' equity section of the balance sheet for Lahey Construction Company at the end of 2004 follows:

9%, $10 par, cumulative preferred stock, 500,000 shares authorized, 200,000 shares issued and outstanding	$ 2,000,000
Additional paid-in capital on preferred	7,500,000
Common stock, $1 par, 2,500,000 shares authorized, 1,500,000 shares issued and outstanding	1,500,000
Additional paid-in capital on common	21,000,000
Retained earnings	25,500,000
Total stockholders' equity	$57,500,000

The lower portion of the 2004 income statement indicates the following:

Net income before tax		$ 9,750,000
Income tax expense (40%)		(3,900,000)
Income before extraordinary items		$ 5,850,000
Extraordinary loss from flood	$(6,200,000)	
Less related tax effect (40%)	2,480,000	(3,720,000)
Net income		$ 2,130,000

Assume the number of shares outstanding did not change during the year.

Required

1. Compute earnings per share *before* extraordinary items.
2. Compute earnings per share *after* the extraordinary loss.
3. Which of the two EPS ratios is more useful to management? Explain your answer. Would your answer be different if the ratios were to be used by an outsider, for example, by a potential stockholder? Why?

Multi-Concept Exercises

Exercise 13-12 ***Common-Size Balance Sheets and Horizontal Analysis*** **LO 2, 3**

Comparative balance sheets for Farinet Company for the past two years are as follows:

	December 31	
	2004	**2003**
Cash	$ 16,000	$ 20,000
Accounts receivable	40,000	30,000
Inventory	30,000	50,000
Prepaid rent	18,000	12,000
Total current assets	$104,000	$112,000
Land	$150,000	$150,000
Plant and equipment	800,000	600,000
Accumulated depreciation	(130,000)	(60,000)
Total long-term assets	$820,000	$690,000
Total assets	$924,000	$802,000
Accounts payable	$ 24,000	$ 20,000
Income taxes payable	6,000	10,000
Short-term notes payable	70,000	50,000
Total current liabilities	$100,000	$ 80,000
Bonds payable	$150,000	$200,000
Common stock	$400,000	$300,000
Retained earnings	274,000	222,000
Total stockholders' equity	$674,000	$522,000
Total liabilities and stockholders' equity	$924,000	$802,000

Required

1. Using the format in Exhibit 13-5, prepare common-size comparative balance sheets for the two years for Farinet Company.
2. What observations can you make about the changes in the relative composition of Farinet's accounts from the common-size balance sheets? List at least five observations.
3. Using the format in Exhibit 13-1, prepare comparative balance sheets for Farinet Company, including columns both for the dollars and for the percentage increase or decrease in each item on the statement.
4. Identify the five items on the balance sheet that experienced the largest change from one year to the next. For each of these, explain where you would look to find additional information about the change.

Exercise 13-13 ***Common-Size Income Statements and Horizontal Analysis*** **LO 2, 3**

Income statements for Mariners Corp. for the past two years follow:

	(Amounts in Thousands of Dollars)	
	2004	**2003**
Sales revenue	$60,000	$50,000
Cost of goods sold	42,000	30,000
Gross profit	$18,000	$20,000
Selling and administrative expense	9,000	5,000
Operating income	$ 9,000	$15,000
Interest expense	2,000	2,000
Income before tax	$ 7,000	$13,000
Income tax expense	2,000	4,000
Net income	$ 5,000	$ 9,000

Required

1. Using the format in Exhibit 13-6, prepare common-size comparative income statements for the two years for Mariners Corp.
2. What observations can you make about the common-size statements? List at least four observations.
3. Using the format in Exhibit 13-2, prepare comparative income statements for Mariners Corp., including columns both for the dollars and for the percentage increase or decrease in each item on the statement.
4. Identify the two items on the income statement that experienced the largest change from one year to the next. For each of these, explain where you would look to find additional information about the change.

Problems

Problem 13-1 ***Effect of Transactions on Working Capital, Current Ratio, and Quick Ratio*** **LO 4**

(*Note:* Consider completing Problem 13-2 after this problem to ensure that you obtain a clear understanding of the effect of various transactions on these measures of liquidity.)

The following account balances are taken from the records of Liquiform Inc.:

Cash	$ 70,000
Trading securities (short-term)	60,000
Accounts receivable	80,000
Inventory	100,000
Prepaid insurance	10,000
Accounts payable	75,000
Taxes payable	25,000
Salaries and wages payable	40,000
Short-term loans payable	60,000

Required

1. Use the information provided above to compute the amount of working capital and Liquiform's current and quick ratios (round to three decimal points).
2. Determine the effect that each of the following transactions will have on Liquiform's working capital, current ratio, and quick ratio by recalculating each and then indicating whether the measure is increased, decreased, or not affected by the transaction. (For the ratios, round to three decimal points.) Consider each transaction independently; that is, assume that it is the *only* transaction that takes place.

(continued)

Transaction	Effect of Transaction on Working Capital	Current Ratio	Quick Ratio
a. Purchased inventory on account for $20,000.			
b. Purchased inventory for cash, $15,000.			
c. Paid suppliers on account, $30,000.			
d. Received cash on account, $40,000.			
e. Paid insurance for next year, $20,000.			
f. Made sales on account, $60,000.			
g. Repaid short-term loans at bank, $25,000.			
h. Borrowed $40,000 at bank for 90 days.			
i. Declared and paid $45,000 cash dividend.			
j. Purchased $20,000 of trading securities (classified as current assets).			
k. Paid $30,000 in salaries.			
l. Accrued additional $15,000 in taxes.			

Problem 13-2 *Effect of Transactions on Working Capital, Current Ratio, and Quick Ratio* LO 4

(*Note:* Consider completing this problem after Problem 13-1 to ensure that you obtain a clear understanding of the effect of various transactions on these measures of liquidity.)

The following account balances are taken from the records of Veriform Inc.:

Cash	$ 70,000
Trading securities (short-term)	60,000
Accounts receivable	80,000
Inventory	100,000
Prepaid insurance	10,000
Accounts payable	75,000
Taxes payable	25,000
Salaries and wages payable	40,000
Short-term loans payable	210,000

Required

1. Use the information provided above to compute the amount of working capital and Veriform's current and quick ratios (round to three decimal points).
2. Determine the effect that each of the following transactions will have on Veriform's working capital, current ratio, and quick ratio by recalculating each and then indicating whether the measure is increased, decreased, or not affected by the transaction. (For the ratios, round to three decimal points.) Consider each transaction independently; that is, assume that it is the *only* transaction that takes place.

Transaction	Effect of Transaction on Working Capital	Current Ratio	Quick Ratio
a. Purchased inventory on account for $20,000.			
b. Purchased inventory for cash, $15,000.			
c. Paid suppliers on account, $30,000.			
d. Received cash on account, $40,000.			
e. Paid insurance for next year, $20,000.			
f. Made sales on account, $60,000.			
g. Repaid short-term loans at bank, $25,000.			
h. Borrowed $40,000 at bank for 90 days.			
i. Declared and paid $45,000 cash dividend.			
j. Purchased $20,000 of trading securities (classified as current assets).			
k. Paid $30,000 in salaries.			
l. Accrued additional $15,000 in taxes.			

Problem 13-3 *Goals for Sales and Return on Assets* LO 6

DECISION MAKING

The president of Blue Skies Corp. is reviewing with his vice presidents the operating results of the year just completed. Sales increased by 15% from the previous year to $60,000,000. Average total assets for the year were $40,000,000. Net income, after adding back interest expense, net of tax, was $5,000,000.

The president is happy with the performance over the past year but is never satisfied with the status quo. He has set two specific goals for next year: (1) a 20% growth in sales and (2) a return on assets of 15%.

To achieve the second goal, the president has stated his intention to increase the total asset base by 12.5% over the base for the year just completed.

Required

1. For the year just completed, compute the following ratios:
   a. Return on sales
   b. Asset turnover
   c. Return on assets
2. Compute the necessary asset turnover for next year to achieve the president's goal of a 20% increase in sales.
3. Calculate the income needed next year to achieve the goal of a 15% return on total assets. (*Note:* Assume that *income* is defined as net income plus interest, net of tax.)
4. Based on your answers to parts **2** and **3**, comment on the reasonableness of the president's goals. What must the company focus on to attain these goals?

Problem 13-4 *Goals for Sales and Income Growth* LO 6

DECISION MAKING

SPREADSHEET

Sunrise Corp. is a major regional retailer. The chief executive officer (CEO) is concerned with the slow growth both of sales and of net income and the subsequent effect on the trading price of the common stock. Selected financial data for the past three years follow.

SUNRISE CORP.
(IN MILLIONS)

	2004	2003	2002
1. Sales	$200.0	$192.5	$187.0
2. Net income	6.0	5.8	5.6
3. Dividends declared and paid	2.5	2.5	2.5
December 31 balances:			
4. Owners' equity	70.0	66.5	63.2
5. Debt	30.0	29.8	30.3
Selected year-end financial ratios			
Net income to sales	3.0%	3.0%	3.0%
Asset turnover	2 times	2 times	2 times
6. Return on owners' equity*	8.6%	8.7%	8.9%
7. Debt to total assets	30.0%	30.9%	32.4%

*Based on year-end balances in owners' equity.

The CEO believes that the price of the stock has been adversely affected by the downward trend of the return on equity, the relatively low dividend payout ratio, and the lack of dividend increases. To improve the price of the stock, she wants to improve the return on equity and dividends. She believes that the company should be able to meet these objectives by (1) increasing sales and net income at an annual rate of 10% a year and (2) establishing a new dividend policy that calls for a dividend payout of 50% of earnings or $3,000,000, whichever is larger.

The 10% annual sales increase will be accomplished through a new promotional program. The president believes that the present net income to sales ratio of 3% will be unchanged by the cost of this new program and any interest paid on new debt. She expects that the company can accomplish this sales and income growth while maintaining the current relationship of total assets to sales. Any capital that is needed to maintain this relationship and that is not generated internally would be acquired through long-term debt financing. The CEO hopes that debt would not exceed 35% of total liabilities and owners' equity.

(continued)

Required

1. Using the CEO's program, prepare a schedule that shows the appropriate data for the years 2005, 2006, and 2007 for the items numbered 1 through 7 on the preceding schedule.
2. Can the CEO meet all of her requirements if a 10% per year growth in income and sales is achieved? Explain your answer.
3. What alternative actions should the CEO consider to improve the return on equity and to support increased dividend payments?
4. Explain the reasons that the CEO might have for wanting to limit debt to 35% of total liabilities and owners' equity. (CMA adapted)

Multi-Concept Problems

Problem 13-5 ***Basic Financial Ratios*** **LO 4, 5, 6**

The accounting staff of CCB Enterprises has completed the financial statements for the 2004 calendar year. The statement of income for the current year and the comparative statements of financial position for 2004 and 2003 follow.

CCB ENTERPRISES
STATEMENT OF INCOME
FOR THE YEAR ENDED DECEMBER 31, 2004
(THOUSANDS OMITTED)

Revenue:	
Net sales	$800,000
Other	60,000
Total revenue	$860,000
Expenses:	
Cost of goods sold	$540,000
Research and development	25,000
Selling and administrative	155,000
Interest	20,000
Total expenses	$740,000
Income before income taxes	$120,000
Income taxes	48,000
Net income	$ 72,000

CCB ENTERPRISES
COMPARATIVE STATEMENTS OF FINANCIAL POSITION
DECEMBER 31, 2004 AND 2003
(THOUSANDS OMITTED)

	2004	2003
Assets		
Current assets:		
Cash and short-term investments	$ 26,000	$ 21,000
Receivables, less allowance for doubtful accounts ($1,100 in 2004 and $1,400 in 2003)	48,000	50,000
Inventories, at lower of FIFO cost or market	65,000	62,000
Prepaid items and other current assets	5,000	3,000
Total current assets	$144,000	$136,000
Other assets:		
Investments, at cost	$106,000	$106,000
Deposits	10,000	8,000
Total other assets	$116,000	$114,000
Property, plant, and equipment:		
Land	$ 12,000	$ 12,000
Buildings and equipment, less accumulated depreciation ($126,000 in 2004 and $122,000 in 2003)	268,000	248,000
Total property, plant, and equipment	$280,000	$260,000
Total assets	$540,000	$510,000

Liabilities and Stockholders' Equity		
Current liabilities:		
Short-term loans	$ 22,000	$ 24,000
Accounts payable	72,000	71,000
Salaries, wages, and other	26,000	27,000
Total current liabilities	$120,000	$122,000
Long-term debt	$160,000	$171,000
Total liabilities	$280,000	$293,000
Stockholders' equity:		
Common stock, at par	$ 44,000	$ 42,000
Paid-in capital in excess of par	64,000	61,000
Total paid-in capital	$108,000	$103,000
Retained earnings	152,000	114,000
Total stockholders' equity	$260,000	$217,000
Total liabilities and stockholders' equity	$540,000	$510,000

Required:

1. Calculate the following financial ratios for 2004 for CCB Enterprises:
   a. Times interest earned
   b. Return on total assets
   c. Return on common stockholders' equity
   d. Debt-equity ratio (at December 31, 2004)
   e. Current ratio (at December 31, 2004)
   f. Quick (acid-test) ratio (at December 31, 2004)
   g. Accounts receivable turnover ratio (assume that all sales are on credit)
   h. Number of days' sales in receivables
   i. Inventory turnover ratio (assume that all purchases are on credit)
   j. Number of days' sales in inventory
   k. Number of days in cash operating cycle
2. Prepare a few brief comments on the overall financial health of CCB Enterprises. For each comment, indicate any information that is not provided in the problem and that you would need to fully evaluate the company's financial health. (CMA adapted)

Problem 13-6 ***Projected Results to Meet Corporate Objectives*** **LO 5, 6**

Tablon Inc. is a wholly owned subsidiary of Marbel Co. The philosophy of Marbel's management is to allow the subsidiaries to operate as independent units. Corporate control is exercised through the establishment of minimum objectives for each subsidiary, accompanied by substantial rewards for success and penalties for failure. The time period for performance review is long enough for competent managers to display their abilities.

Each quarter the subsidiary is required to submit financial statements. The statements are accompanied by a letter from the subsidiary president explaining the results to date, a forecast for the remainder of the year, and the actions to be taken to achieve the objectives if the forecast indicates that the objectives will not be met.

Marbel management, in conjunction with Tablon management, had set the objectives listed below for the year ending May 31, 2005. These objectives are similar to those set in previous years.

- Sales growth of 20%
- Return on stockholders' equity of 15%
- A long-term debt-to-equity ratio of not more than 1.0
- Payment of a cash dividend of 50% of net income, with a minimum payment of at least $400,000

Tablon's controller has just completed the financial statements for the six months ended November 30, 2004, and the forecast for the year ending May 31, 2005. The statements are presented on the following page.

After a cursory glance at the financial statements, Tablon's president concluded that not all objectives would be met. At a staff meeting of the Tablon management, the president asked the controller to review the projected results and recommend possible actions that could be taken during the remainder of the year so that Tablon would be more likely to meet the objectives.

TABLON INC.
INCOME STATEMENT
(THOUSANDS OMITTED)

	Year Ended May 31, 2004	Six Months Ended November 30, 2004	Forecast for Year Ending May 31, 2005
Sales	$25,000	$15,000	$30,000
Cost of goods sold	$13,000	$ 8,000	$16,000
Selling expenses	5,000	3,500	7,000
Administrative expenses and interest	4,000	2,500	5,000
Income taxes (40%)	1,200	400	800
Total expenses and taxes	$23,200	$14,400	$28,800
Net income	$ 1,800	$ 600	$ 1,200
Dividends declared and paid	600	0	600
Income retained	$ 1,200	$ 600	$ 600

TABLON INC.
STATEMENT OF FINANCIAL POSITION
(THOUSANDS OMITTED)

	May 31, 2004	November 30, 2004	Forecast for May 31, 2005
Assets			
Cash	$ 400	$ 500	$ 500
Accounts receivable (net)	4,100	6,500	7,100
Inventory	7,000	8,500	8,600
Plant and equipment (net)	6,500	7,000	7,300
Total assets	$18,000	$22,500	$23,500
Liabilities and Equities			
Accounts payable	$ 3,000	$ 4,000	$ 4,000
Accrued taxes	300	200	200
Long-term borrowing	6,000	9,000	10,000
Common stock	5,000	5,000	5,000
Retained earnings	3,700	4,300	4,300
Total liabilities and equities	$18,000	$22,500	$23,500

Required

1. Calculate the projected results for each of the four objectives established for Tablon Inc. State which results will not meet the objectives by year-end.
2. From the data presented, identify the factors that seem to contribute to the failure of Tablon Inc. to meet all of its objectives.
3. Explain the possible actions that the controller could recommend in response to the president's request.

(CMA adapted)

Problem 13-7 *Comparison with Industry Averages* LO 4, 5, 6

Heartland Inc. is a medium-size company that has been in business for 20 years. The industry has become very competitive in the last few years, and Heartland has decided that it must grow if it is going to survive. It has approached the bank for a sizable five-year loan, and the bank has requested its most recent financial statements as part of the loan package.

The industry in which Heartland operates consists of approximately 20 companies relatively equal in size. The trade association to which all of the competitors belong publishes an annual survey of the industry, including industry averages for selected ratios for the competitors. All companies voluntarily submit their statements to the association for this purpose.

Heartland's controller is aware that the bank has access to this survey and is very concerned about how the company fared this past year compared with the rest of the industry. The ratios included in the publication, and the averages for the past year, are as follows:

Ratio	Industry Average
Current ratio	1.23
Acid-test (quick) ratio	0.75
Accounts receivable turnover	33 times
Inventory turnover	29 times
Debt-to-equity ratio	0.53
Times interest earned	8.65 times
Return on sales	6.57%
Asset turnover	1.95 times
Return on assets	12.81%
Return on common stockholders' equity	17.67%

The financial statements to be submitted to the bank in connection with the loan follow:

HEARTLAND INC.
STATEMENT OF INCOME AND RETAINED EARNINGS
FOR THE YEAR ENDED DECEMBER 31, 2004
(THOUSANDS OMITTED)

Sales revenue	$542,750
Cost of goods sold	(435,650)
Gross margin	$107,100
Selling, general, and administrative expenses	$ (65,780)
Loss on sales of securities	(220)
Income before interest and taxes	$ 41,100
Interest expense	(9,275)
Income before taxes	$ 31,825
Income tax expense	(12,730)
Net income	$ 19,095
Retained earnings, January 1, 2004	58,485
	$ 77,580
Dividends paid on common stock	(12,000)
Retained earnings, December 31, 2004	$ 65,580

HEARTLAND INC.
COMPARATIVE STATEMENTS OF FINANCIAL POSITION
(THOUSANDS OMITTED)

	December 31, 2004	December 31, 2003
Assets		
Current assets:		
Cash	$ 1,135	$ 750
Marketable securities	1,250	2,250
Accounts receivable, net of allowances	15,650	12,380
Inventories	12,680	15,870
Prepaid items	385	420
Total current assets	$ 31,100	$ 31,670
Long-term investments	$ 425	$ 425
Property, plant, and equipment:		
Land	$ 32,000	$ 32,000
Buildings and equipment, net of accumulated depreciation	216,000	206,000
Total property, plant, and equipment	$248,000	$238,000
Total assets	$279,525	$270,095

(continued)

	December 31, 2004	December 31, 2003
Liabilities and Stockholders' Equity		
Current liabilities:		
Short-term notes	$ 8,750	$ 12,750
Accounts payable	20,090	14,380
Salaries and wages payable	1,975	2,430
Income taxes payable	3,130	2,050
Total current liabilities	$ 33,945	$ 31,610
Long-term bonds payable	$ 80,000	$ 80,000
Stockholders' equity:		
Common stock, no par	$100,000	$100,000
Retained earnings	65,580	58,485
Total stockholders' equity	$165,580	$158,485
Total liabilities and stockholders' equity	$279,525	$270,095

Required

1. Prepare a columnar report for the controller of Heartland Inc., comparing the industry averages for the ratios published by the trade association with the comparable ratios for Heartland. For Heartland, compute the ratios as of December 31, 2004, or for the year ending December 31, 2004, whichever is appropriate.
2. Briefly evaluate Heartland's ratios relative to the industry averages.
3. Do you think that the bank will approve the loan? Explain your answer.

Alternate Problems

Problem 13-1A ***Effect of Transactions on Debt-to-Equity Ratio*** **LO 5**

(*Note:* Consider completing Problem 13-2A after this problem to ensure that you obtain a clear understanding of the effect of various transactions on this measure of solvency.)

The following account balances are taken from the records of Monet's Garden Inc.:

Current liabilities	$150,000
Long-term liabilities	375,000
Stockholders' equity	400,000

Required

1. Use the information provided above to compute Monet's debt-to-equity ratio (round to three decimal points).
2. Determine the effect that each of the following transactions will have on Monet's debt-to-equity ratio by recalculating the ratio and then indicating whether the ratio is increased, decreased, or not affected by the transaction. (Round to three decimal points.) Consider each transaction independently; that is, assume that it is the *only* transaction that takes place.

Transaction	Effect of Transaction on Debt-to-Equity Ratio
a. Purchased inventory on account for $20,000.	
b. Purchased inventory for cash, $15,000.	
c. Paid suppliers on account, $30,000.	
d. Received cash on account, $40,000.	
e. Paid insurance for next year, $20,000.	
f. Made sales on account, $60,000.	
g. Repaid short-term loans at bank, $25,000.	
h. Borrowed $40,000 at bank for 90 days.	
i. Declared and paid $45,000 cash dividend.	
j. Purchased $20,000 of trading securities (classified as current assets).	
k. Paid $30,000 in salaries.	
l. Accrued additional $15,000 in taxes.	

Problem 13-2A ***Effect of Transactions on Debt-to-Equity Ratio*** **LO 5**

(*Note:* Consider completing this problem after Problem 13-1A to ensure that you obtain a clear understanding of the effect of various transactions on this measure of solvency.)

The following account balances are taken from the records of Degas Inc.:

Current liabilities	$ 25,000
Long-term liabilities	125,000
Stockholders' equity	400,000

Required

1. Use the information provided above to compute Degas' debt-to-equity ratio (round to three decimal points).
2. Determine the effect that each of the following transactions will have on Degas' debt-to-equity ratio by recalculating the ratio and then indicating whether the ratio is increased, decreased, or not affected by the transaction. (Round to three decimal points.) Consider each transaction independently; that is, assume that it is the *only* transaction that takes place.

Transaction	Effect of Transaction on Debt-to-Equity Ratio
a. Purchased inventory on account for $20,000.	
b. Purchased inventory for cash, $15,000.	
c. Paid suppliers on account, $30,000.	
d. Received cash on account, $40,000.	
e. Paid insurance for next year, $20,000.	
f. Made sales on account, $60,000.	
g. Repaid short-term loans at bank, $25,000.	
h. Borrowed $40,000 at bank for 90 days.	
i. Declared and paid $45,000 cash dividend.	
j. Purchased $20,000 of trading securities (classified as current assets).	
k. Paid $30,000 in salaries.	
l. Accrued additional $15,000 in taxes.	

Problem 13-3A ***Goals for Sales and Return on Assets*** LO 6

DECISION MAKING

The president of Blue Moon Corp. is reviewing with her department managers the operating results of the year just completed. Sales increased by 12% from the previous year to $750,000. Average total assets for the year were $400,000. Net income, after adding back interest expense, net of tax, was $60,000.

The president is happy with the performance over the past year but is never satisfied with the status quo. She has set two specific goals for next year: (1) a 15% growth in sales and (2) a return on assets of 20%.

To achieve the second goal, the president has stated her intention to increase the total asset base by 10% over the base for the year just completed.

Required

1. For the year just completed, compute the following ratios:
   a. Return on sales
   b. Asset turnover
   c. Return on assets
2. Compute the necessary asset turnover for next year to achieve the president's goal of a 15% increase in sales.
3. Calculate the income needed next year to achieve the goal of a 20% return on total assets. (*Note:* Assume that *income* is defined as net income plus interest, net of tax.)
4. Based on your answers to parts 2 and 3, comment on the reasonableness of the president's goals. What must the company focus on to attain these goals?

Problem 13-4A ***Goals for Sales and Income Growth*** LO 6

DECISION MAKING

Sunset Corp. is a major regional retailer. The chief executive officer (CEO) is concerned with the slow growth both of sales and of net income and the subsequent effect on the trading price of the common stock. Selected financial data for the past three years follow.

SPREADSHEET

SUNSET CORP.
(IN MILLIONS)

	2004	2003	2002
1. Sales	$100.0	$96.7	$93.3
2. Net income	3.0	2.9	2.8
3. Dividends declared and paid	1.2	1.2	1.2
December 31 balances:			
4. Owners' equity	40.0	38.2	36.5
5. Debt	10.0	10.2	10.2
Selected year-end financial ratios			
Net income to sales	3.0%	3.0%	3.0%
Asset turnover	2 times	2 times	2 times
6. Return on owners' equity*	7.5%	7.6%	7.7%
7. Debt to total assets	20.0%	21.1%	21.8%

*Based on year-end balances in owners' equity.

The CEO believes that the price of the stock has been adversely affected by the downward trend of the return on equity, the relatively low dividend payout ratio, and the lack of dividend increases. To improve the price of the stock, he wants to improve the return on equity and dividends.

He believes that the company should be able to meet these objectives by (1) increasing sales and net income at an annual rate of 10% a year and (2) establishing a new dividend policy that calls for a dividend payout of 60% of earnings or $2,000,000, whichever is larger.

The 10% annual sales increase will be accomplished through a product enhancement program. The president believes that the present net income to sales ratio of 3% will be unchanged by the cost of this new program and any interest paid on new debt. He expects that the company can accomplish this sales and income growth while maintaining the current relationship of total assets to sales. Any capital that is needed to maintain this relationship and that is not generated internally would be acquired through long-term debt financing. The CEO hopes that debt would not exceed 25% of total liabilities and owners' equity.

Required

1. Using the CEO's program, prepare a schedule that shows the appropriate data for the years 2005, 2006, and 2007 for the items numbered 1 through 7 on the preceding schedule.
2. Can the CEO meet all of his requirements if a 10% per-year growth in income and sales is achieved? Explain your answers.
3. What alternative actions should the CEO consider to improve the return on equity and to support increased dividend payments? (CMA adapted)

Alternate Multi-Concept Problems

Problem 13-5A *Basic Financial Ratios* LO 4, 5, 6

The accounting staff of SST Enterprises has completed the financial statements for the 2004 calendar year. The statement of income for the current year and the comparative statements of financial position for 2004 and 2003 follow.

SST ENTERPRISES
STATEMENT OF INCOME
YEAR ENDED DECEMBER 31, 2004
(THOUSANDS OMITTED)

Revenue:	
Net sales	$600,000
Other	45,000
Total revenue	$645,000
Expenses:	
Cost of goods sold	$405,000
Research and development	18,000
Selling and administrative	120,000
Interest	15,000
Total expenses	$558,000
Income before income taxes	$ 87,000
Income taxes	27,000
Net income	$ 60,000

SST ENTERPRISES
COMPARATIVE STATEMENTS OF FINANCIAL POSITION
DECEMBER 31, 2004 AND 2003
(THOUSANDS OMITTED)

	2004	2003
Assets		
Current assets:		
Cash and short-term investments	$ 27,000	$ 20,000
Receivables, less allowance for doubtful accounts ($1,100 in 2004 and $1,400 in 2003)	36,000	37,000
Inventories, at lower of FIFO cost or market	35,000	42,000
Prepaid items and other current assets	2,000	1,000
Total current assets	$100,000	$100,000
Property, plant, and equipment:		
Land	$ 9,000	$ 9,000
Buildings and equipment, less accumulated depreciation ($74,000 in 2004 and $62,000 in 2003)	191,000	186,000
Total property, plant, and equipment	$200,000	$195,000
Total assets	$300,000	$295,000
Liabilities and Stockholders' Equity		
Current liabilities:		
Short-term loans	$ 20,000	$ 15,000
Accounts payable	80,000	68,000
Salaries, wages, and other	5,000	7,000
Total current liabilities	$105,000	$ 90,000
Long-term debt	15,000	40,000
Total liabilities	$120,000	$130,000
Stockholders' equity:		
Common stock, at par	$ 50,000	$ 50,000
Paid-in capital in excess of par	25,000	25,000
Total paid-in capital	$ 75,000	$ 75,000
Retained earnings	105,000	90,000
Total stockholders' equity	$180,000	$165,000
Total liabilities and stockholders' equity	$300,000	$295,000

Required

1. Calculate the following financial ratios for 2004 for SST Enterprises:
   a. Times interest earned
   b. Return on total assets
   c. Return on common stockholders' equity
   d. Debt-equity ratio (at December 31, 2004)
   e. Current ratio (at December 31, 2004)
   f. Quick (acid-test) ratio (at December 31, 2004)
   g. Accounts receivable turnover ratio (assume that all sales are on credit)
   h. Number of days' sales in receivables
   i. Inventory turnover ratio (assume that all purchases are on credit)
   j. Number of days' sales in inventory
   k. Number of days in cash operating cycle
2. Prepare a few brief comments on the overall financial health of SST Enterprises. For each comment, indicate any information that is not provided in the problem and that you would need to fully evaluate the company's financial health.

(CMA adapted)

Problem 13-6A ***Projected Results to Meet Corporate Objectives*** LO 5, 6

Grout Inc. is a wholly owned subsidiary of Slait Co. The philosophy of Slait's management is to allow the subsidiaries to operate as independent units. Corporate control is exercised through the establishment of minimum objectives for each subsidiary, accompanied by substantial rewards for success and penalties for failure. The time period for performance review is long enough for competent managers to display their abilities.

Each quarter the subsidiary is required to submit financial statements. The statements are accompanied by a letter from the subsidiary president explaining the results to date, a forecast for the remainder of the year, and the actions to be taken to achieve the objectives if the forecast indicates that the objectives will not be met.

Slait management, in conjunction with Grout management, had set the objectives listed below for the year ending September 30, 2005. These objectives are similar to those set in previous years.

- Sales growth of 10%
- Return on stockholders' equity of 20%
- A long-term debt-to-equity ratio of not more than 1.0
- Payment of a cash dividend of 50% of net income, with a minimum payment of at least $500,000

Grout's controller has just completed preparing the financial statements for the six months ended March 31, 2005, and the forecast for the year ending September 30, 2005. The statements are presented below.

After a cursory glance at the financial statements, Grout's president concluded that not all objectives would be met. At a staff meeting of the Grout management, the president asked the controller to review the projected results and recommend possible actions that could be taken during the remainder of the year so that Grout would be more likely to meet the objectives.

GROUT INC.
INCOME STATEMENT
(THOUSANDS OMITTED)

	Year Ended September 30, 2004	Six Months Ended March 31, 2005	Forecast for Year Ending September 30, 2005
Sales	$10,000	$6,000	$12,000
Cost of goods sold	$ 6,000	$4,000	$ 8,000
Selling expenses	1,500	900	1,800
Administrative expenses and interest	1,000	600	1,200
Income taxes	500	300	600
Total expenses and taxes	$ 9,000	$5,800	$11,600
Net income	$ 1,000	$ 200	$ 400
Dividends declared and paid	500	0	400
Income retained	$ 500	$ 200	$ 0

GROUT INC.
STATEMENT OF FINANCIAL POSITION
(THOUSANDS OMITTED)

	September 30, 2004	March 31, 2005	Forecast for September 30, 2005
Assets			
Cash	$ 400	$ 500	$ 500
Accounts receivable (net)	2,100	3,400	2,600
Inventory	7,000	8,500	8,400
Plant and equipment (net)	2,800	2,500	3,200
Total assets	$12,300	$14,900	$14,700
Liabilities and Equities			
Accounts payable	$ 3,000	$ 4,000	$ 4,000
Accrued taxes	300	200	200
Long-term borrowing	4,000	5,500	5,500
Common stock	4,000	4,000	4,000
Retained earnings	1,000	1,200	1,000
Total liabilities and equities	$12,300	$14,900	$14,700

Required

1. Calculate the projected results for each of the four objectives established for Grout Inc. State which results will not meet the objectives by year-end.
2. From the data presented, identify the factors that seem to contribute to the failure of Grout Inc. to meet all of its objectives.
3. Explain the possible actions that the controller could recommend in response to the president's request. (CMA adapted)

Problem 13-7A *A Comparison with Industry Averages* LO 4, 5, 6

Midwest Inc. is a medium-size company that has been in business for 20 years. The industry has become very competitive in the last few years, and Midwest has decided that it must grow if it is going to survive. It has approached the bank for a sizable five-year loan, and the bank has requested its most recent financial statements as part of the loan package.

The industry in which Midwest operates consists of approximately 20 companies relatively equal in size. The trade association to which all of the competitors belong publishes an annual survey of the industry, including industry averages for selected ratios for the competitors. All companies voluntarily submit their statements to the association for this purpose.

Midwest's controller is aware that the bank has access to this survey and is very concerned about how the company fared this past year compared with the rest of the industry. The ratios included in the publication, and the averages for the past year, are as follows:

Ratio	Industry Average
Current ratio	1.20
Acid-test (quick) ratio	0.50
Inventory turnover	35 times
Debt-to-equity ratio	0.50
Times interest earned	25 times
Return on sales	3%
Asset turnover	3.5 times
Return on common stockholders' equity	20%

The financial statements to be submitted to the bank in connection with the loan follow:

MIDWEST INC.
STATEMENT OF INCOME AND RETAINED EARNINGS
FOR THE YEAR ENDED DECEMBER 31, 2004
(THOUSANDS OMITTED)

Sales revenue	$420,500
Cost of goods sold	(300,000)
Gross margin	$120,500
Selling, general, and administrative expenses	(85,000)
Income before interest and taxes	$ 35,500
Interest expense	(8,600)
Income before taxes	$ 26,900
Income tax expense	(12,000)
Net income	$ 14,900
Retained earnings, January 1, 2004	12,400
	$ 27,300
Dividends paid on common stock	(11,200)
Retained earnings, December 31, 2004	$ 16,100

(continued)

MIDWEST INC.
COMPARATIVE STATEMENTS OF FINANCIAL POSITION
(THOUSANDS OMITTED)

	December 31, 2004	December 31, 2003
Assets		
Current assets:		
Cash	$ 1,790	$ 2,600
Marketable securities	1,200	1,700
Accounts receivable, net of allowances	400	600
Inventories	8,700	7,400
Prepaid items	350	400
Total current assets	$ 12,440	$ 12,700
Long-term investments	$ 560	$ 400
Property, plant, and equipment:		
Land	$ 12,000	$ 12,000
Buildings and equipment, net of accumulated depreciation	87,000	82,900
Total property, plant, and equipment	$ 99,000	$ 94,900
Total assets	$112,000	$108,000
Liabilities and Stockholders' Equity		
Current liabilities:		
Short-term notes	$ 800	$ 600
Accounts payable	6,040	6,775
Salaries and wages payable	1,500	1,200
Income taxes payable	1,560	1,025
Total current liabilities	$ 9,900	$ 9,600
Long-term bonds payable	$ 36,000	$ 36,000
Stockholders' equity:		
Common stock, no par	$ 50,000	$ 50,000
Retained earnings	16,100	12,400
Total stockholders' equity	$ 66,100	$ 62,400
Total liabilities and stockholders' equity	$112,000	$108,000

Required

1. Prepare a columnar report for the controller of Midwest Inc., comparing the industry averages for the ratios published by the trade association with the comparable ratios for Midwest. For Midwest, compute the ratios as of December 31, 2004, or for the year ending December 31, 2004, whichever is appropriate.
2. Briefly evaluate Midwest's ratios relative to the industry.
3. Do you think that the bank will approve the loan? Explain your answer.

Decision Cases

Reading and Interpreting Financial Statements

Decision Case 13-1 ***Horizontal Analysis for Winnebago Industries*** **LO 2**
Refer to Winnebago Industries' comparative income statements included in its annual report.

Required

1. Prepare a work sheet with the following headings:

	Increase (Decrease) from			
	2001 to 2002		2000 to 2001	
Income Statement Accounts	**Dollars**	**Percent**	**Dollars**	**Percent**

2. Complete the work sheet using each of the account titles on Winnebago Industries' income statement. Round dollar amounts to the nearest one-tenth of $1 million and percentages to the nearest one-tenth of a percent.

3. What observations can you make from this horizontal analysis? What is your overall analysis of operations? Have the company's operations improved over the three-year period?

Decision Case 13-2 *Vertical Analysis for Winnebago Industries* LO 3

Refer to Winnebago Industries' financial statements included in its annual report.

Required

1. Using the format in Exhibit 13-6, prepare common-size comparative income statements for 2002 and 2001. Round dollar amounts to the nearest one-tenth of $1 million and percentages to the nearest one-tenth of a percent.
2. What changes do you detect in the income statement relationships from 2001 to 2002?
3. Using the format in Exhibit 13-5, prepare common-size comparative balance sheets at the end of 2002 and 2001. Round dollar amounts to the nearest one-tenth of $1 million and percentages to the nearest one-tenth of a percent.
4. What observations can you make about the relative composition of Winnebago Industries' assets from the common-size statements? What observations can be made about the changes in the relative composition of liabilities and owners' equity accounts?

Decision Case 13-3 *Comparing Two Companies in the Same Industry: Winnebago Industries and Monaco Coach Corporation* LO 3

http://www.winnebagoind.com
http://www.monacocoach.com

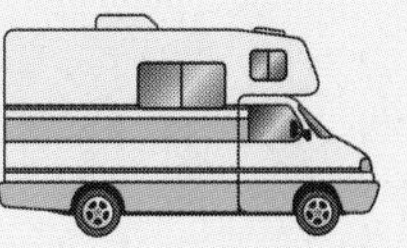

This case should be completed after responding to the requirements in Case 13-2. Refer to the financial statement information of Winnebago Industries and Monaco Coach Corporation in Appendices A and B at the end of the text.

Required:

1. Using the format in Exhibit 13-6, prepare common size comparative income statements for 2002 and 2001 for Monaco Coach. Round dollar amounts to the nearest one-tenth of $1 million and percentages to the nearest one-tenth of a percent.
2. The common size comparative income statements indicates the relative importance of items on the statement. Compare the common size income statements of Monaco Coach and Winnebago Industries. What are the most important differences between the two companies' income statements?
3. Using the format in Exhibit 13-5, prepare common size balance sheets at the end of 2002 and 2001 Monaco Coach. Round the dollar amounts to the nearest one-tenth of $1 million and percentages to the nearest one-tenth of a percent.
4. The common size comparative balance sheets indicates the relative importance of items on the statement. Compare the common size balance sheets of Monaco Coach and Winnebago Industries. What are the most important differences between the two companies' balance sheets?

Decision Case 13-4 *Ratio Analysis for Winnebago Industries* LO 4, 5, 6

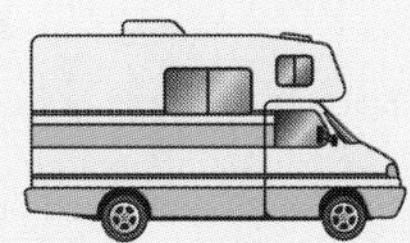

Refer to Winnebago Industries' financial statements included in its annual report.

Required

1. Compute the following ratios and other amounts for each of the two years, 2002 and 2001. Because only two years of data are given on the balance sheets, to be consistent you should use year-end balances for each year in lieu of average balances. Assume a 40% tax rate and 360 days to a year. State any other necessary assumptions in making the calculations. Round all ratios to the nearest one-tenth of a percent.
   a. Working capital
   b. Current ratio
   c. Acid-test ratio
   d. Cash flow from operations to current liabilities
   e. Number of days' sales in receivables
   f. Number of days' sales in inventory
   g. Debt-to-equity ratio
   h. Cash flow from operations to capital expenditures
   i. Asset turnover

(continued)

j. Return on sales

k. Return on assets

l. Return on common stockholders' equity

2. What is your overall analysis of the financial health of Winnebago Industries? What do you believe are the company's strengths and weaknesses?

Making Financial Decisions

DECISION MAKING

Decision Case 13-5 *Acquisition Decision* LO 4, 5, 6

Diversified Industries is a large conglomerate and is continually in the market for new acquisitions. The company has grown rapidly over the last 10 years through buyouts of medium-size companies. Diversified does not limit itself to companies in any one industry but looks for firms with a sound financial base and the ability to stand on their own financially.

The president of Diversified recently told a meeting of the company's officers: "I want to impress two points on all of you. First, we are not in the business of looking for bargains. Diversified has achieved success in the past by acquiring companies with the ability to be a permanent member of the corporate family. We don't want companies that may appear to be a bargain on paper but can't survive in the long run. Second, a new member of our family must be able to come in and make it on its own—the parent is not organized to be a funding agency for struggling subsidiaries."

Ron Dixon is the vice president of acquisitions for Diversified, a position he has held for five years. He is responsible for making recommendations to the board of directors on potential acquisitions. Because you are one of his assistants, he recently brought you a set of financials for a manufacturer, Heavy Duty Tractors. Dixon believes that Heavy Duty is a "can't-miss" opportunity for Diversified and asks you to confirm his hunch by performing basic financial statement analysis on the company. The most recent income statement and comparative balance sheets for the company follow:

HEAVY DUTY TRACTORS INC.
STATEMENT OF INCOME AND RETAINED EARNINGS
FOR THE YEAR ENDED DECEMBER 31, 2004
(THOUSANDS OMITTED)

Sales Revenue	$875,250
Cost of goods sold	542,750
Gross margin	$332,500
Selling, general, and administrative expenses	264,360
Operating income	$ 68,140
Interest expense	45,000
Net income before taxes and extraordinary items	$ 23,140
Income tax expense	9,250
Income before extraordinary items	$ 13,890
Extraordinary gain, less taxes of $6,000	9,000
Net income	$ 22,890
Retained earnings, January 1, 2004	169,820
	$192,710
Dividends paid on common stock	10,000
Retained earnings, December 31, 2004	$182,710

HEAVY DUTY TRACTORS INC.
COMPARATIVE STATEMENTS OF FINANCIAL POSITION
(THOUSANDS OMITTED)

	December 31, 2004	December 31, 2003
Assets		
Current assets:		
Cash	$ 48,500	$ 24,980
Marketable securities	3,750	0
Accounts receivable, net of allowances	128,420	84,120
Inventories	135,850	96,780
Prepaid items	7,600	9,300
Total current assets	$324,120	$215,180
Long-term investments	$ 55,890	$ 55,890

	December 31, 2004	December 31, 2003
Property, plant, and equipment:		
Land	$ 45,000	$ 45,000
Buildings and equipment, less accumulated depreciation of $385,000 in 2004 and $325,000 in 2003	545,000	605,000
Total property, plant, and equipment	$590,000	$650,000
Total assets	$970,010	$921,070
Liabilities and Stockholders' Equity		
Current liabilities:		
Short-term notes	$ 80,000	$ 60,000
Accounts payable	65,350	48,760
Salaries and wages payable	14,360	13,840
Income taxes payable	2,590	3,650
Total current liabilities	$162,300	$126,250
Long-term bonds payable, due 2011	$275,000	$275,000
Stockholders' equity:		
Common stock, no par	$350,000	$350,000
Retained earnings	182,710	169,820
Total stockholders' equity	$532,710	$519,820
Total liabilities and stockholders' equity	$970,010	$921,070

Required

1. How liquid is Heavy Duty Tractors? Support your answer with any ratios that you believe are necessary to justify your conclusion. Also indicate any other information that you would want to have in making a final determination on its liquidity.
2. In light of the president's comments, should you be concerned about the solvency of Heavy Duty Tractors? Support your answer with the necessary ratios. How does the maturity date of the outstanding debt affect your answer?
3. Has Heavy Duty demonstrated the ability to be a profitable member of the Diversified family? Support your answer with the necessary ratios.
4. What will you tell your boss? Should he recommend to the board of directors that Diversified put in a bid for Heavy Duty Tractors?

Decision Case 13-6 *Pricing Decision* LO 3

DECISION MAKING

BPO's management believes that the company has been successful at increasing sales because it has not increased the selling price of the products, even though its competition has increased prices and costs have increased. Price and cost relationships in Year 1 were established because they represented industry averages. The following income statements are available for BPO's first three years of operation:

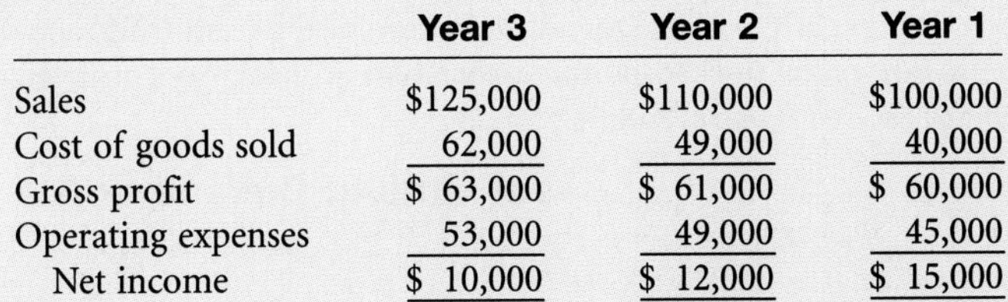

	Year 3	Year 2	Year 1
Sales	$125,000	$110,000	$100,000
Cost of goods sold	62,000	49,000	40,000
Gross profit	$ 63,000	$ 61,000	$ 60,000
Operating expenses	53,000	49,000	45,000
Net income	$ 10,000	$ 12,000	$ 15,000

Required

1. Using the format in Exhibit 13-6, prepare common-size comparative income statements for the three years.
2. Explain why net income has decreased while sales have increased.
3. Prepare an income statement for Year 4. Sales volume in units is expected to increase by 10%, and costs are expected to increase by 8%.
4. Do you think BPO should raise its prices or maintain the same selling prices? Explain your answer.

Accounting and Ethics: What Would You Do?

Decision Case 13-7 *Provisions in a Loan Agreement* LO 4, 5

ETHICS

As controller of Midwest Construction Company, you are reviewing with your assistant, Dave Jackson, the financial statements for the year just ended. During the review, Jackson reminds you of an existing loan agreement with Southern National Bank. Midwest has agreed to the following conditions:

- The current ratio will be maintained at a minimum level of 1.5 to 1.0 at all times.
- The debt-to-equity ratio will not exceed 0.5 to 1.0 at any time.

Jackson has drawn up the following preliminary, condensed balance sheet for the year just ended:

MIDWEST CONSTRUCTION COMPANY
BALANCE SHEET
DECEMBER 31
(IN MILLIONS OF DOLLARS)

Current assets	$16	Current liabilities	$10
Long-term assets	64	Long-term debt	15
		Stockholders' equity	55
Total	$80	Total	$80

Jackson wants to discuss two items with you. First, long-term debt currently includes a $5 million note payable, to Eastern State Bank, that is due in six months. The plan is to go to Eastern before the note is due and ask it to extend the maturity date of the note for five years. Jackson doesn't believe that Midwest needs to include the $5 million in current liabilities because the plan is to roll over the note.

Second, in December of this year, Midwest received a $2 million deposit from the state for a major road project. The contract calls for the work to be performed over the next 18 months. Jackson recorded the $2 million as revenue this year because the contract is with the state; there shouldn't be any question about being able to collect.

Required

1. Based on the balance sheet Jackson prepared, is Midwest in compliance with its loan agreement with Southern? Support your answer with any necessary computations.
2. What would you do with the two items in question? Do you see anything wrong with the way Jackson has handled each of them? Explain your answer.
3. Prepare a revised balance sheet based on your answer to part **2.** Also, compute a revised current ratio and debt-to-equity ratio. Based on the revised ratios, is Midwest in compliance with its loan agreement?

Decision Case 13-8 *Inventory Turnover* LO 4

ETHICS

Garden Fresh Inc. is a wholesaler of fresh fruits and vegetables. Each year it submits a set of financial ratios to a trade association. Even though the association doesn't publish the individual ratios for each company, the president of Garden Fresh thinks it is important for public relations that his company look as good as possible. Due to the nature of the fresh fruits and vegetables business, one of the major ratios tracked by the association is inventory turnover. Garden Fresh's inventory stated at FIFO cost was as follows:

	Year Ending December 31	
	2004	**2003**
Fruits	$10,000	$ 9,000
Vegetables	30,000	33,000
Totals	$40,000	$42,000

Sales revenue for the year ending December 31, 2004, is $3,690,000. The company's gross profit ratio is normally 40%.

Based on these data, the president thinks the company should report an inventory turnover ratio of 90 times per year.

Required

1. Explain, using the necessary calculations, how the president came up with an inventory turnover ratio of 90 times.

2. Do you think the company should report a turnover ratio of 90 times? If not, explain why you disagree and explain, with calculations, what you think the ratio should be.
3. Assume you are the controller for Garden Fresh. What will you tell the president?

THOMSON ONE Business School Edition Case

Case 13-9 ***Using THOMSON ONE for Wrigley***

In the chapter we saw the critical role that financial statements play in the successful analysis of a company's potential for the future. Success as measured in the financial statements should translate to success in the market for a company's stock in the form of appreciation in its stock price and, if the company chooses, in the form of dividends to the stockholders. We can use THOMSON ONE to obtain information about both Wrigley's performance as measured in its financial statements and in its stock price.

http://www.wrigley.com

Begin by entering the company's ticker symbol, WWY, and then selecting "GO." On the opening screen you will see background information about the company, key financial ratios, and some recent data concerning stock price. To research the company's stock price further, you click the "Prices" tab. At the top of the Price Chart, click on the "Interactive Chart." To obtain a 1-year chart, go to "Time Frame," click on the down arrow, and select "1 year." Then click on "Draw," and a 1-year chart should appear.

We can also find Wrigley's most recent financial statements. Near the top of the screen, click on "Financials" and select "Financial Statements." Refer to the comparative statements of earnings, statements of cash flows, and balance sheets.

Based on your use of THOMSON ONE, complete each of the following:

1. Compute the following ratios for the two most recent years available, either for each year or as of the end of each of the years, as appropriate. If beginning balances for the earliest year are not available, use year-end balances for both years where you would normally use average amounts for the year. To compute the return on assets ratio, you will need to find the tax rate. Use the relationship between income taxes and earnings before taxes to find the rate for each year.
   a. Current ratio
   b. Quick ratio
   c. Cash flow from operations to current liabilities ratio
   d. Number of days' sales in receivables
   e. Number of days' sales in inventory
   f. Debt-to-equity ratio
   g. Debt service coverage ratio
   h. Cash flow from operations to capital expenditures ratio
   i. Return on assets ratio
   j. Return on common stockholders' equity ratio
2. Comment on Wrigley's liquidity. Has it improved or declined over the two-year period?
3. Does Wrigley appear to be solvent to you? Does there appear to be anything unusual about its capital structure?
4. Comment on Wrigley's profitability.
5. What have been Wrigley's high and low stock prices for the most recent year?
6. How does the company's stock performance compare to the other line on the stock price chart for the S&P 500?
7. Based on your analysis of Wrigley's financial statements and your review of its stock market performance over the last year, would you buy stock in the company? Explain your reasoning for your answer.

Solutions to Key Terms Quiz

Quiz 1:

14 Horizontal analysis (p. 658)
11 Vertical analysis (p. 658)
10 Gross profit ratio (p. 665)
12 Profit margin ratio (p. 665)
13 Liquidity (p. 666)
2 Working capital (p. 666)
3 Current ratio (p. 666)
1 Acid-test or quick ratio (p. 667)
5 Cash flow from operations to current liabilities ratio (p. 668)
6 Accounts receivable turnover ratio (p. 669)
4 Number of days' sales in receivables (p. 669)
9 Inventory turnover ratio (p. 669)
7 Number of days' sales in inventory (p. 670)
8 Cash to cash operating cycle (p. 671)

Quiz 2:

3 Solvency (p. 671)
7 Debt-to-equity ratio (p. 672)
13 Times interest earned ratio (p. 672)
14 Debt service coverage ratio (p. 673)
8 Cash flow from operations to capital expenditures ratio (p. 673)
15 Profitability (p. 674)
9 Return on assets ratio (p. 674)
4 Return on sales ratio (p. 675)
10 Asset turnover ratio (p. 675)
1 Return on common stockholders' equity ratio (p. 676)
12 Leverage (p. 677)
5 Earnings per share (p. 678)
2 Price/earnings (P/E) ratio (p. 678)
6 Dividend payout ratio (p. 679)
11 Dividend yield ratio (p. 679)
18 Discontinued operations (p. 689)
16 Extraordinary item (p. 689)
17 Cumulative effect of a change in accounting principle (p. 689)

Part IV

Integrative Problem

Presented below are comparative balance sheets and a statement of income and retained earnings for Gallagher, Inc., which operates a national chain of sporting goods stores:

GALLAGHER, INC.
COMPARATIVE BALANCE SHEETS
DECEMBER 31, 2004 AND 2003
(ALL AMOUNTS IN THOUSANDS OF DOLLARS)

	December 31	
	2004	**2003**
Cash	$ 840	$ 2,700
Accounts receivable	12,500	9,000
Inventory	8,000	5,500
Prepaid insurance	100	400
Total current assets	$21,440	$17,600

Land	$ 4,000	$ 4,000
Buildings and equipment	12,000	9,000
Accumulated depreciation	(3,700)	(3,000)
Total long-term assets	$12,300	$10,000
Total assets	$33,740	$27,600
Accounts payable	$ 7,300	$ 5,000
Taxes payable	4,600	4,200
Notes payable	2,400	1,600
Current portion of bonds	200	200
Total current liabilities	$14,500	$11,000
Bonds payable	1,400	1,600
Total liabilities	$15,900	$12,600
Preferred stock, $5 par	$ 1,000	$ 1,000
Common stock, $1 par	2,000	2,000
Retained earnings	14,840	12,000
Total stockholders' equity	$17,840	$15,000
Total liabilities and stockholders' equity	$33,740	$27,600

GALLAGHER, INC.
STATEMENT OF INCOME AND RETAINED EARNINGS
FOR THE YEAR ENDED DECEMBER 31, 2004
(ALL AMOUNTS IN THOUSANDS OF DOLLARS)

Net sales	$48,000
Cost of goods sold	36,000
Gross profit	$12,000
Selling, general and administrative expense	6,000
Operating income	$ 6,000
Interest expense	280
Income before tax	$ 5,720
Income tax expense	2,280
Net income	$ 3,440
Preferred dividends	100
Income available to common	$ 3,340
Common dividends	500
To retained earnings	$ 2,840
Retained earnings, 1/1	12,000
Retained earnings, 12/31	$14,840

Required

1. Prepare a statement of cash flows for Gallagher, Inc. for the year ended December 31, 2004, using the **indirect** method in the Operating Activities section of the statement.
2. Gallagher's management is concerned with both its short-term liquidity and its solvency over the long run. To help it evaluate these, compute the following ratios, rounding all answers to the nearest one-tenth of a percent:
   a. Current ratio
   b. Acid-test ratio
   c. Cash flow from operations to current liabilities ratio
   d. Accounts receivable turnover ratio
   e. Number of days' sales in receivables
   f. Inventory turnover ratio
   g. Number of days' sales in inventory
   h. Debt-to-equity ratio
   i. Debt service coverage ratio
   j. Cash flow from operations to capital expenditures ratio
3. Comment on Gallagher's liquidity and its solvency. What additional information do you need to fully evaluate the company?

2002

WINNEBAGO INDUSTRIES

Annual Report

Table of Contents

Corporate Profile

Winnebago Industries, Inc., headquartered in Forest City, Iowa, is the leading United States (U.S.) manufacturer of motor homes, self-contained recreation vehicles used primarily in leisure travel and outdoor recreation activities. The Company builds quality motor homes with state-of-the-art computer-aided design and manufacturing systems on automotive-styled assembly lines. The Company's products are subjected to what the Company believes is the most rigorous testing in the RV industry. These vehicles are sold through dealers under the Winnebago®, Itasca®, Rialta® and Ultimate® brand names. The Company markets its recreation vehicles on a wholesale basis to a diversified dealer organization located throughout the U.S., and to a limited extent, in Canada. As of August 31, 2002, the motor home dealer organization in the U.S. and Canada included approximately 295 dealer locations. Motor home sales by Winnebago Industries represented at least 89 percent of its revenues in each of the past five fiscal years. In addition, the Company's subsidiary, Winnebago Acceptance Corporation, engages in floor plan financing for a limited number of the Company's dealers. Other products manufactured by the Company consist principally of a variety of component parts for other manufacturers.

Winnebago Industries was incorporated under the laws of the state of Iowa on February 12, 1958, and adopted its present name on February 28, 1961.

Recent Financial Performance

(In thousands, except per share data)

	Fiscal 2002 (53 Weeks)	Fiscal 2001 (52 Weeks)	2002 to 2001 % of Change
Net Revenues	$ 828,403	$ 675,927	22.6%
Gross Profit	$ 119,538	$ 87,366	36.8%
Operating Income	$ 81,197	$ 55,474	46.4%
Net Income	$ 54,671	$ 42,704	28.0%
Diluted Income Per Share	$ 2.68	$ 2.03	32.0%
Diluted Weighted Average Outstanding Shares	20,384	21,040	(3.1%)

Winnebago Industries, Inc.

Mission Statement

Winnebago Industries, Inc. is the leading United States manufacturer of motor homes and related products and services. Our mission is to continually improve our products and services to meet or exceed the expectations of our customers. We emphasize employee teamwork and involvement in identifying and implementing programs to save time and lower production costs while maintaining the highest quality of products. These strategies allow us to prosper as a business with a high degree of integrity and to provide a reasonable return for our shareholders, the ultimate owners of our business.

Values

How we accomplish our mission is as important as the mission itself. Fundamental to the success of the Company are these basic values we describe as the four Ps:

People -- Our employees are the source of our strength. They provide our corporate intelligence and determine our reputation and vitality. Involvement and teamwork are our core corporate values.

Products -- Our products are the end result of our teamwork's combined efforts, and they should be the best in meeting or exceeding our customers' expectations. As our products are viewed, so are we viewed.

Plant -- We believe our facilities to be the most technologically advanced in the RV industry. We continue to review facility improvements that will increase the utilization of our plant capacity and enable us to build the best quality product for the investment.

Profitability -- Profitability is the ultimate measure of how efficiently we provide our customers with the best products for their needs. Profitability is required to survive and grow. As our respect and position within the marketplace grows, so will our profit.

Guiding Principles

Quality comes first -- To achieve customer satisfaction, the quality of our products and services must be our number one priority.

Customers are central to our existence -- Our work must be done with our customers in mind, providing products and services that meet or exceed the expectations of our customers. We must not only satisfy our customers, we must also surprise and delight them.

Continuous improvement is essential to our success -- We must strive for excellence in everything we do: in our products, in their safety and value, as well as in our services, our human relations, our competitiveness and our profitability.

Employee involvement is our way of life -- We are a team. We must treat each other with trust and respect.

Dealers and suppliers are our partners -- The Company must maintain mutually beneficial relationships with dealers, suppliers and our other business associates.

Integrity is never compromised -- The Company must pursue conduct in a manner that is socially responsible and that commands respect for its integrity and for its positive contributions to society.

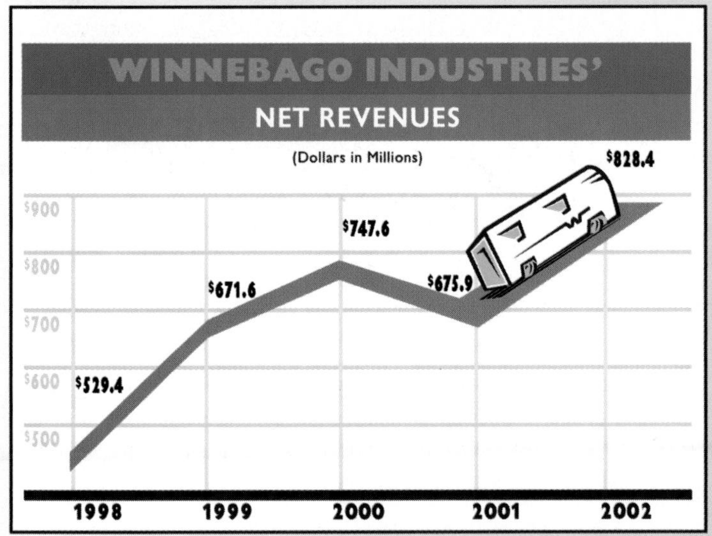

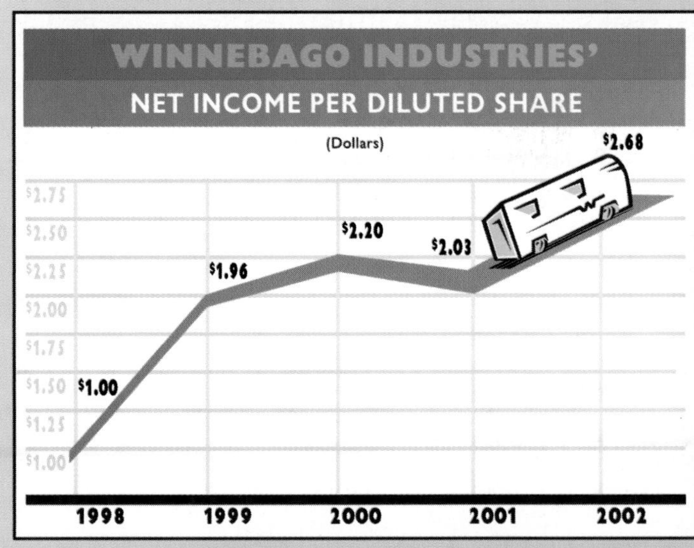

To My Fellow Shareholders:

Leadership is the focus of our 2002 Annual Report. Of course, leadership comes in many forms and we will detail Winnebago Industries' many leadership qualities and their benefit to our shareholders throughout this report.

We were extremely pleased with the record revenues and earnings posted for Winnebago Industries during fiscal 2002.

The Company's revenues for fiscal 2002 (53 weeks) were a record $828.4 million, a 22.6 percent increase compared to revenues of $675.9 million for the previous fiscal year (52 weeks).

Net income and diluted income per share for fiscal 2002 were a record $54.7 million, or $2.68 per share, increases of 28 percent and 32 percent, respectively, compared to net income of $42.7 million and diluted income per share of $2.03 for the previous fiscal year, which includes a $4.5 million one time tax benefit (or 21 cents per diluted share).

Definitely, a lot of hard work by our employees and our dealers proved successful in a less than ideal economic environment.

Starting in 1997, we challenged ourselves to be the most profitable U.S. public company in the recreation vehicle (RV) industry. We measure profitability by using four guidelines: Return on Assets (ROA), Return on Equity (ROE), Operating Income as a percent of revenues and Net Income as a percent of revenues. We have highlighted these statistics in our last two Annual Reports because of their importance as a means to measure ourselves against our competitors. Winnebago Industries and the other public motor home manufacturers used in this analysis account for approximately 75 percent of all U.S.Class A and C motor home sales. The graphs shown demonstrate that we not

Competitive Comparison

(Information obtained from last 12 months public filings)

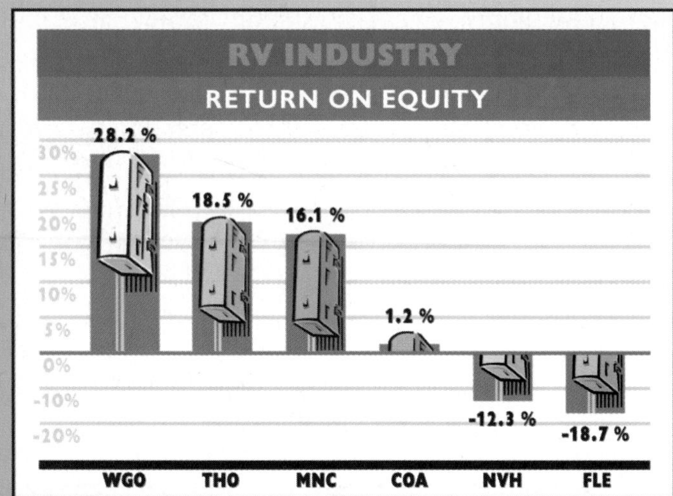

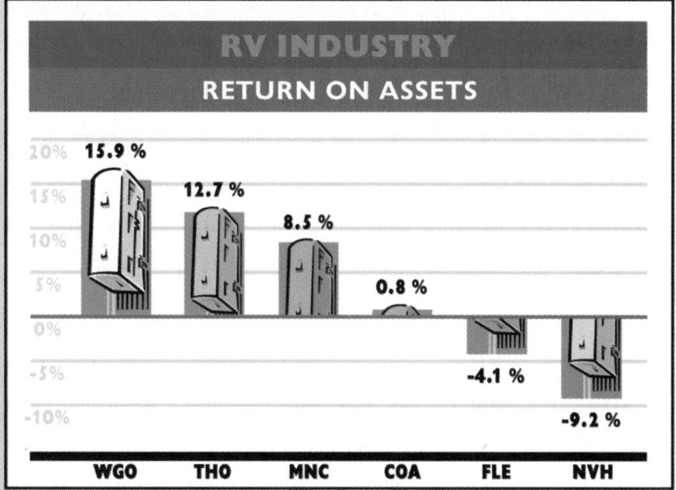

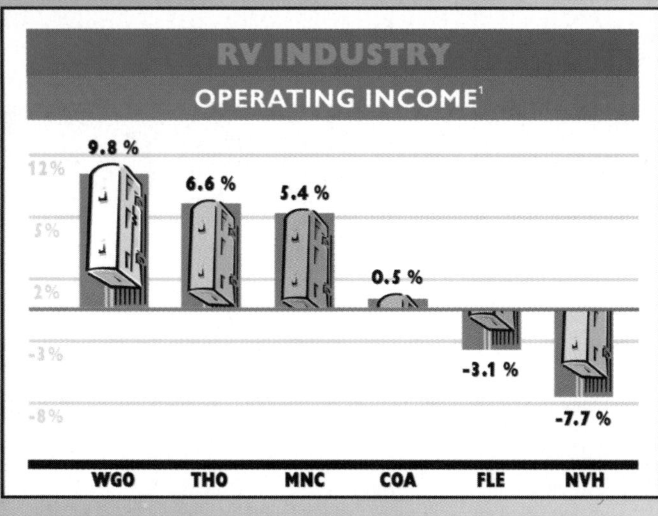

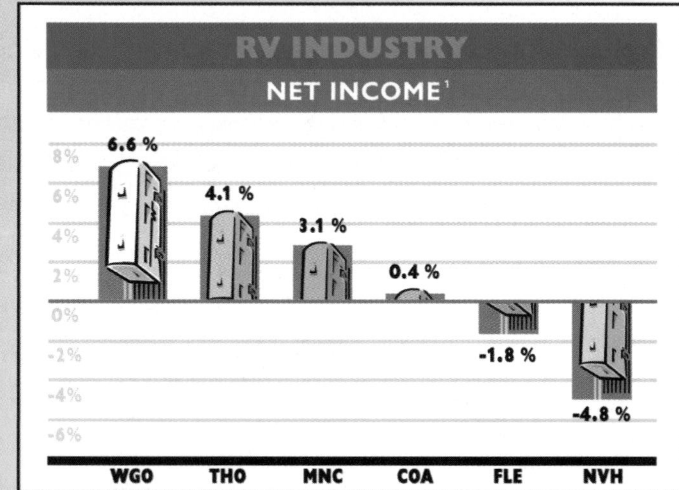

(1) Expressed as a percent of Net Revenues

Winnebago Industries, Inc. | Thor Industries, Inc. | Monaco Coach Corporation

Coachmen Industries, Inc. | Fleetwood Enterprises, Inc. | National RV Holdings, Inc.

only met our goal of being the most profitable public RV company, but that we are leading the RV industry in profitability by substantial margins.

Furthermore, Winnebago Industries has a strong balance sheet, no long-term debt and all recent expansions have been paid for with available cash.

But this financial success was only a portion of Winnebago Industries' achievements during fiscal 2002. We are also the sales leader in the motor home market. According to Statistical Surveys, Inc., an independent retail reporting service, Winnebago Industries' retail market share of the total U.S. Class A and C motor home market leads the industry at 21.0 percent for the calendar year to date through August, compared to 18.8 percent for the same period in calendar 2001. This upward trend began in calendar year 1997 when Winnebago Industries' share of the Class A and C retail market was 15.8 percent as of the end of the year.

Winnebago Industries believes that it also leads the industry in RV manufacturing technology. By utilizing the latest technology for the production of our motor homes we are able to increase quality, while maximizing the productivity of our workforce and facilities.

An annual dealer satisfaction index (DSI) survey by the Recreation Vehicle Dealers Association also shows that Winnebago Industries is viewed by its dealers as the leader in the RV industry. This DSI survey rates manufacturers based on the quality of their sales, product, management and service/warranty/support. Winnebago Industries was the only public RV company to receive the award this year, and has earned this recognition every year since the award's inception in 1996.

The RV market and Winnebago Industries' long-term future look bright. Demographics are in our favor as our target market of consumers age 50 and older is expected to increase for the next 30 years. In addition to growth due to the aging of the baby boom generation, a study conducted by the University of Michigan for the RV industry shows that the age of people interested in purchasing RVs is also expanding to include younger buyers under 35 years of age as well as older buyers over age 75 who are staying healthy and active much later in life. This study also shows an increased interest in owning RVs by a larger percentage of all U.S. households.

In the near term, the current low interest rates are very favorable for continued growth of the RV market. Approximately two-thirds of our customers finance their motor home purchase, due to the tax incentive that allows the deduction of interest on a mortgage loan as many motor

Winnebago Industries' corporate headquarters in Forest City, Iowa.

homes qualify as a second home.

Depressed consumer confidence levels and a weak economy continue to be challenges to the RV industry. In spite of these issues, our market share gains and an overall increase in interest in our motor homes required us to run our factory on overtime from January through September of 2002 to meet demand for the Company's motor homes. In order to continue to grow with the market, we are currently building a state-of-the-art manufacturing facility in Charles City, Iowa, to build Class C motor homes. This will thereby enable us to increase our Class A motor home production in Forest City. Motor home production in the new facility is anticipated to begin by early 2003 with a ramp-up of production throughout the remainder of fiscal 2003. This is the largest expansion to date for Winnebago Industries and will increase our capacity by approximately 30 percent. The additional capacity will help us meet the expected increased demand for our motor homes.

While the RV industry continues to be a very competitive market, Winnebago Industries believes that it has the leadership qualities necessary to continue to grow and enhance our shareholder value well into the future.

Bruce Hertzke

Bruce D. Hertzke
Chairman of the Board,
Chief Executive Officer and President
November 25, 2002

Bruce D. Hertzke

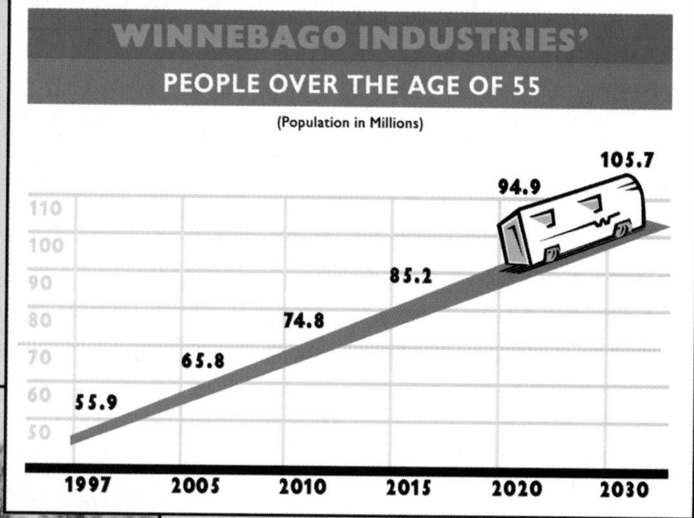

2003 Winnebago Adventurer

Winnebago Industries' 2003 motor home family includes: (left to right) Rialta, Winnebago Minnie, Itasca Suncruiser, and the top of the line Ultimate Freedom.

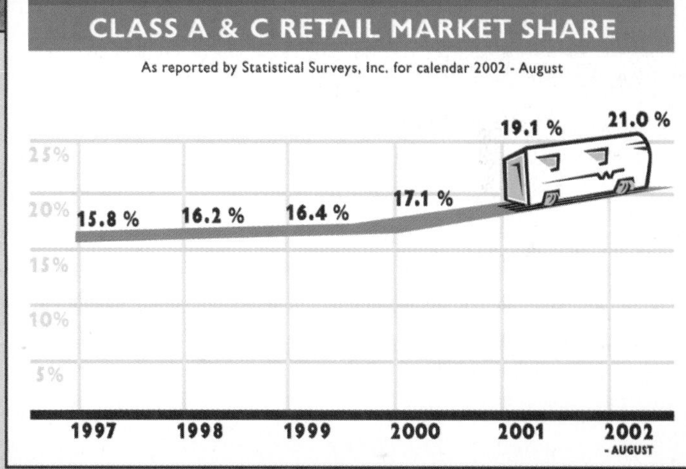

Operations Review

Market Leadership

Winnebago Industries strengthened its market leadership role in fiscal 2002. The Company has a proud history of manufacturing RVs for 44 years. Winnebago Industries now chooses to focus on the motorized portion of the RV market because we believe it to be the most profitable segment of the RV industry.

The Company has grown its retail market share of Class A and C motor homes from 15.8 percent for the 1997 calendar year to 21.0 percent year to date through August 2002. Also, Winnebago Industries grew its market share by 11.4 percent when compared to the same period last year.

This growth in market share has come in large part from the introduction of innovative new products. Winnebago Industries currently manufactures four brands of motor homes: Winnebago, Itasca, Rialta and Ultimate. In total, 65 percent of Winnebago Industries' model lineup was new for 2002, including four brand new product lines: the affordable Class A Winnebago Sightseer™ and Itasca Sunova™ and the fuel-efficient Class C Winnebago Vista® and Itasca Sunstar®. In addition to the four models mentioned above, the 2002 model lineup also included the redesigned Winnebago Chieftain® and Itasca Sunflyer®. These high-line gas motor homes feature luxurious offerings in each of their four floorplans and spaciousness with a dual slideout design.

2003 Winnebago Sightseer

The Company's expanded product offerings created broader exposure for its products at dealerships and the

2003 Itasca Spirit

Company believes this allowed it to reach more customers. These new product lines also created additional opportunities for current owners of Winnebago Industries' products or other brands in the RV industry to trade up or down. Consumers often want the latest and greatest offerings available in the marketplace and we intend to continue to develop new motor home models that will provide them with that opportunity.

The Company introduced its new 2003 motor home lineup to dealers during its annual Dealer Days event in Las Vegas in July. Judging from the order input during and following this event, Winnebago Industries' new motor home lineup was accepted extremely well. Winnebago Industries' motor home sales order backlog at the end of the fourth quarter on August 31, 2002 was 3,248 units, a 103.3 percent increase, compared to 1,598 units on order at the end of the fourth quarter last year.

Winnebago Industries' new lineup includes 76 innovative models for 2003.

Class C Leadership

Winnebago Industries has been the top selling Class C motor home manufacturer since 1998 and continues to expand on its Class C market share lead.

The comprehensive Class C lineup from Winnebago Industries includes the unique, fuel-efficient, Rialta, Vista and Sunstar that are all built on the front-wheel drive Volkswagen® chassis. Winnebago Industries has an exclusive contract with Volkswagen of America to utilize its chassis for the U.S. motor home market.

More traditional-styled Class C products include the Winnebago Minnie® and Minnie Winnie®, as well as the Itasca Spirit® and Sundancer®, which are built on Ford® and/or Chevrolet® chassis.

The Minnie, Minnie Winnie, Spirit and Sundancer models all feature a new advanced radius-style roof design for 2003, which maximizes headroom and provides improved insulation and water runoff.

Class A

Winnebago Industries has experienced solid growth in both the Class A gas and diesel motor home markets, gaining 36.7 percent and 153.7 percent, respectively, since 1997.

Class A gas models include the Winnebago Sightseer, Brave®, Adventurer® and Chieftain, as well as the Itasca Sunova, Sunrise®, Suncruiser® and Sunflyer models, which are built on Ford® and/or Workhorse™ chassis.

New to the market last year, the entry-level Winnebago Sightseer and Itasca Sunova were extremely well received. Winnebago Industries expanded the Sightseer and Sunova lineup with the introduction of a new 33-foot model in each line for 2003.

The best selling Class A motor home line in the industry, the Winnebago Adventurer and Itasca Suncruiser, have new 37-foot models as well as two redesigned models, the most popular floorplan, 35U, and the 38G, for 2003.

Diesel Class A models include the Winnebago Journey® and Journey DL and Itasca Horizon® motor homes that are built on Freightliner® chassis, while the Ultimate Advantage® and Ultimate Freedom® motor homes are built on Spartan® chassis.

The Company introduced new 39-foot models for 2003 in the Winnebago Journey DL and Itasca Horizon line featuring a 330 hp Caterpillar® diesel engine on a 27,910-lb.

2003 Itasca Horizon

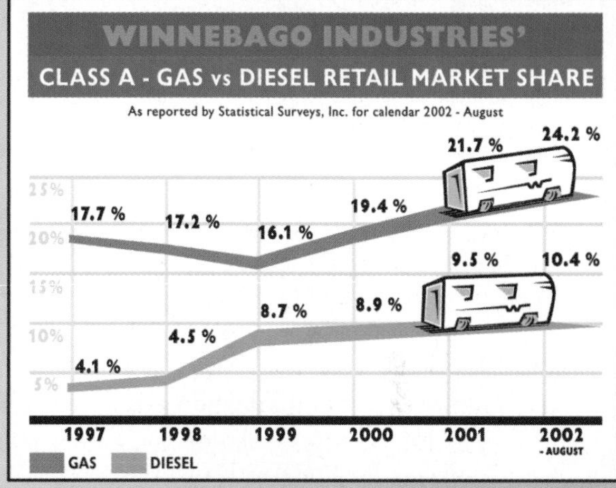

Freightliner chassis with a front galley/sofa slideout and a rear bed slideout. The bedroom also features a convenient second lavatory with dresser.

The Company also introduced its first motor homes with triple slideouts in the Ultimate Advantage and Ultimate Freedom lines for 2003. The Ultimate Advantage 40K and the Ultimate Freedom KD both feature two slideouts in the front portion of the motor home and one in the bedroom, while the Ultimate Freedom ED model features a galley/sofa slideout in the front and two slideouts in the rear bedroom. The bedroom features a bed slideout on the passenger side, as well as a unique lavatory/dresser slideout on the driver's side of the motor home.

Leadership in Feature Innovation

Once again, Winnebago Industries shows its innovation with new motor home features in 2003.

The full comfort BenchMark™ dinette provides abundant storage and easily converts into a comfortable bed. With its sprung seat cushions for added comfort, BenchMark also features attractive fabrics and spacious storage. The seat cushions open fully to reveal maximum access to storage space - perfect for blankets, pillows, games and anything you need to access quickly and easily.

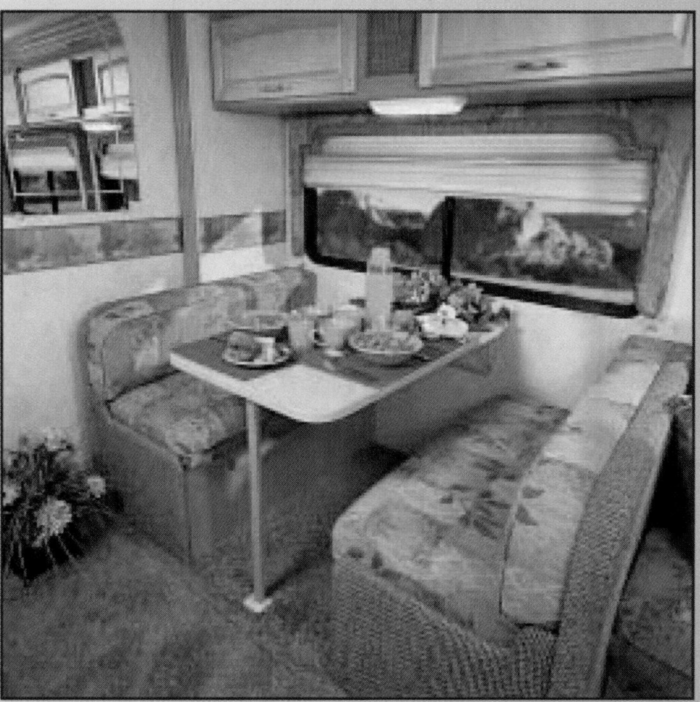

BenchMark full comfort dinette.

Exclusive to Winnebago Industries, the new Sleep Number Bed® by Select Comfort™ is featured on select 2003 motor homes. This queen-size bed features dual hand held remotes so you can quickly and independently adjust the mattress firmness level to your ideal level of comfort and support. The Sleep Number Bed is the "Key to a Perfect

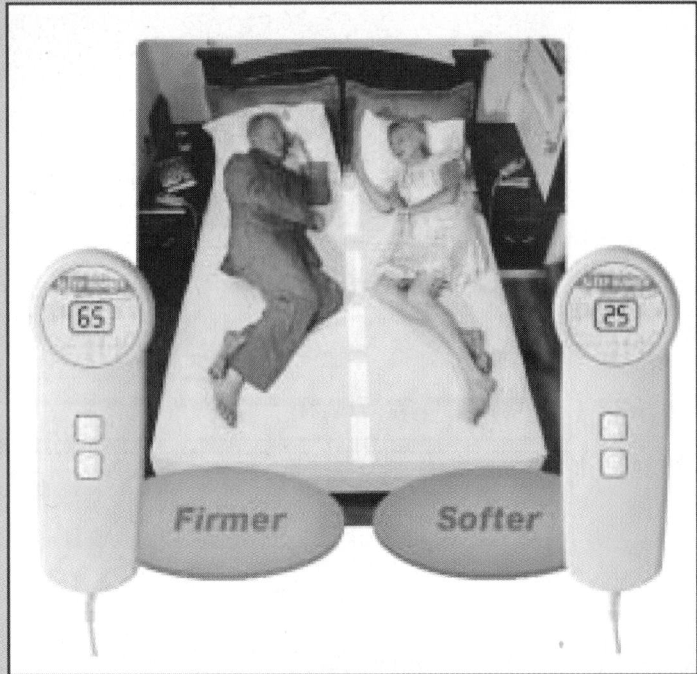

The Sleep Number Bed is exclusive to Winnebago Industries for select motor homes in 2003

Night's Sleep™."

Helping make communication easy, select Winnebago Industries' motor homes feature two-way radios with a docking/charging station.

Unique to the industry, the diesel-powered motor homes from Winnebago Industries feature an improved chassis manifold air supply with a detachable 50-foot hose that provides a ready source of compressed air for pumping up anything from beach toys to tires.

The innovative TripTek™ system, which monitors the engine and provides a predeparture checklist that appears on the rearview monitor system, is also available on select Winnebago Industries' diesel-powered motor homes.

Sturdy powered sunvisors are also featured in 2003. The driver is able to control both front visors, with the passenger also able to control the visor on his or her side. The sunvisors are featured on the Company's higher-line products, such as the Winnebago Chieftain, Itasca Sunflyer and its diesel powered motor homes.

Select Winnebago Industries' motor homes also feature an attractive, new base coat/clear coat full-body paint, providing a low maintenance, high-gloss automotive finish with maximum durability and the highest chip resistance available.

Other unique features to Winnebago Industries' motor homes include the RV Radio™, TrueAir™ Residential Air Conditioning System, StoreMore® Slideout System and the OnePlace™ Systems Center.

The Company is committed to aggressive new product development and has made significant capital expenditures to reach that goal. As an example, by replacing 60 Cad PCs with high-end workstations, adding a laser scanner to the design studio and adding gigabyte Ethernet to the local area network infrastructure within this last fiscal year, the Company increased efficiency in the design process.

Commercial and Specialty Vehicles

Winnebago Industries believes that it leads the RV industry in the construction of commercial and specialty vehicles, manufacturing a broad range of products.

The Commercial Vehicle Division offers several models that can be custom designed for a wide variety of applications including medical, dental, law enforcement and computer training.

The Specialty Vehicle Department is responsible for the

2003 Ultimate Freedom

2003 Rialta

sale of Ability Equipped™ motor homes that are custom-built for individuals with special mobility needs. Ability Equipped motor homes can be outfitted with wider entrance doors, wheelchair lifts, roll-in showers, hand driving controls and other equipment needed to make them wheelchair accessible.

OEM

Winnebago Industries manufactures the majority of the parts used in its motor homes (with the exception of the chassis, engines, auxiliary power units and appliances), allowing the Company to maintain strict quality standards, design parts to unique motor home needs and easily facilitate parts replacement for future needs. Winnebago Industries is able to maximize its production capacity through the sale of original equipment manufacturing (OEM) components, while providing the added benefit of low-cost component parts, contributing to the Company's leadership position in the industry with the highest ROE, ROA, Net Income as a percent of revenues and Operating Income as a percent of revenues in the industry. Winnebago Industries generated revenues of $25 million from the sale of OEM components in fiscal 2002.

Aluminum extrusion parts

The largest portion of OEM revenues were generated by Winnebago Industries' Creative Aluminum Products Company (CAPCO), which produces aluminum extrusion products, primarily for the RV and home building industries.

Marketing Opportunities

Winnebago Industries is able to leverage its strong brand name with excellent marketing opportunities. These opportunities continue to maximize our brand strength while further positioning us as the industry leader.

The Winnebago Adventurer is featured in the upcoming Jack Nicholson film, *About Schmidt*, due to be released nationwide on January 3, 2003. The New Line Cinema film chronicles the life of Warren Schmidt, played by Nicholson, as he attempts to find meaning in his life after his retirement as an insurance actuary and the death of his wife. Warren sets out on a series of exploits in his Adventurer with the ultimate destination to attend the wedding of his daughter,

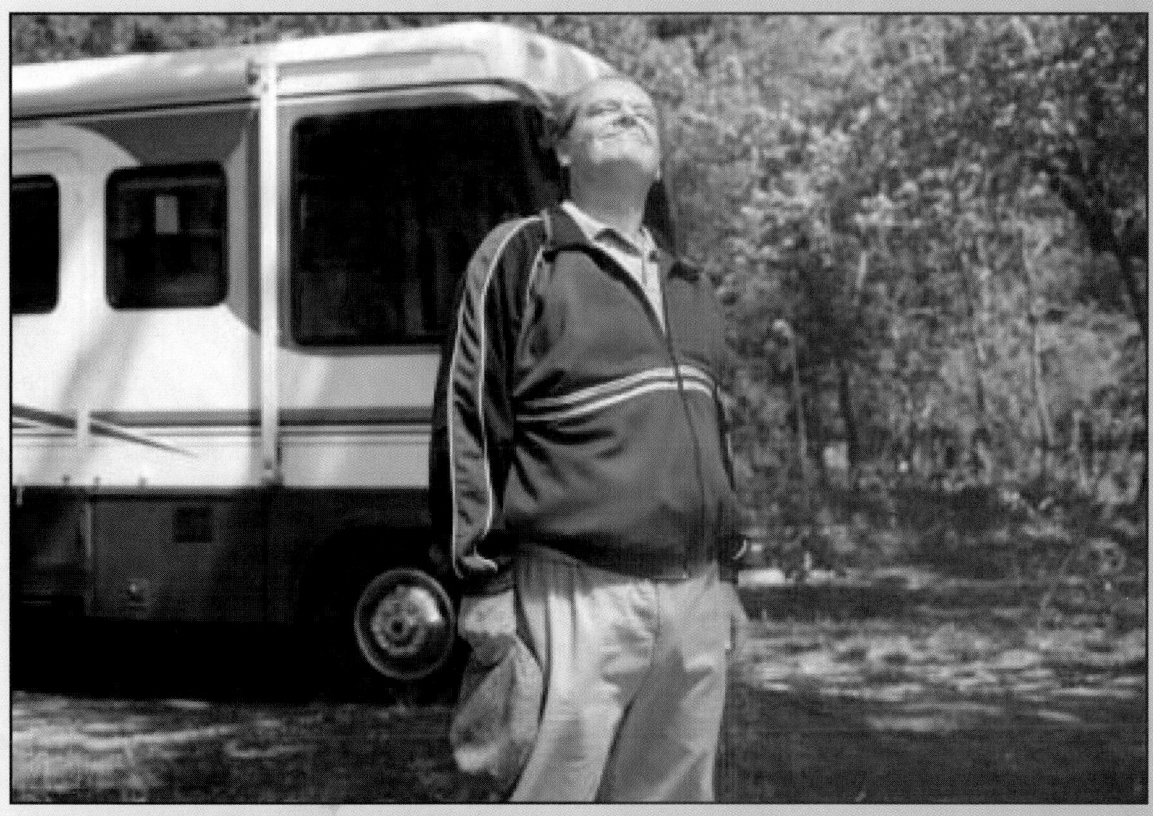

Jack Nicholson and his Winnebago Adventurer in "About Schmidt."

Jeannie, played by Hope Davis, and soon-to-be son-in-law, Randall, an underachieving waterbed salesman played by Dermot Mulroney. The film also stars Kathy Bates and Howard Hesseman as the free-spirited in-laws and is directed by Oscar-nominated director Alexander Payne.

Winnebago Industries participated in a media tour sponsored by the Recreation Vehicle Industry Association (RVIA) during fiscal 2002. During their third season touring as RVIA spokespersons, Brad and Amy Herzog used a 2002 Winnebago Adventurer for their "Baby Makes Three in an RV" tour. Traveling with their young son, Luke, the Herzogs reinforced the ease, cost savings and comfort that RV travel offers for young families.

Winnebago Industries also provided several motor homes during fiscal 2002 for *"Biff Henderson's America"* segments that appeared on the CBS *Late Show with David Letterman* TV show. The Company worked closely with RVIA, CBS and Letterman's staff to support these humorous Charles Kuralt style segments.

Jeopardy and the *Wheel of Fortune* TV shows also utilize Winnebago Braves as their contestant search vehicles. In addition, Winnebago Industries motor homes have been offered as grand prizes for the *Wheel of Fortune* and *The Price Is Right* TV shows.

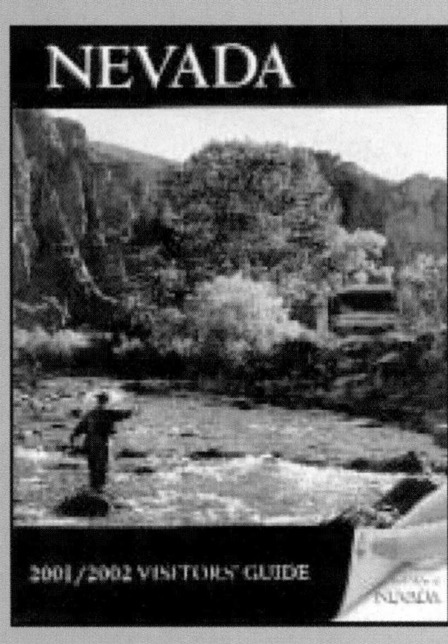

Up to six Winnebago Industries motor homes will be given away in this Nevada Sweepstakes promotion.

The Nevada Commission on Tourism is continuing a three-year campaign that will award up to six Winnebago Industries motor homes as grand prizes throughout the duration of the sweepstakes to the year 2003. The $1 million campaign prominently features a Winnebago Adventurer in the promotional material.

This continued exposure in the media is immeasurable in terms of continued brand recognition.

Sales and Service Support

Winnebago Industries continues to support the most comprehensive sales and service support programs in the RV industry for its dealers and retail customers. The Company believes that providing quality product and service support to our dealers through hands-on training and support materials, such as our on-line WIN NET information system, will ensure that our retail customers are more satisfied; thus, ensuring long-term growth and profitability.

Winnebago Industries also prides itself on providing the highest level of warranty, parts and service programs in the industry and conducts extensive service training for its dealers. In the past few years, Winnebago Industries has implemented industry-leading programs like the 40 percent warranty parts markup program, TripSaver Emergency Warranty Parts Shipments and the enhanced WIN NET on-line data entry system that provides Winnebago Industries' dealers with instant access to service, parts and warranty information.

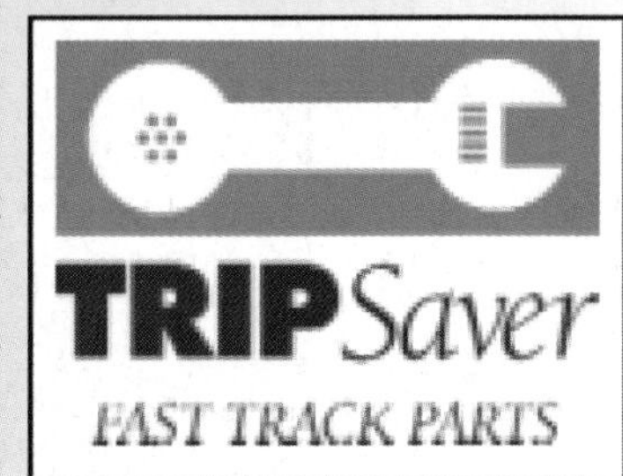

To ensure that our sales and service programs are effective, we continually monitor our customers' satisfaction levels through surveys. From this data, Winnebago Industries has developed a Customer Satisfaction Index (CSI) that is used to shape our sales and service programs and to reward our most effective dealers. In 1986, Winnebago Industries initiated the first dealer recognition program within the RV industry. This "Circle of Excellence Award" recognized 162 dealers with this top honor for the 2002 model year, including six dealers who have achieved this exclusive status each year since the program was initiated 16 years ago, as well as 21 first-time winners.

WIT

The Winnebago-Itasca Travelers (WIT) Club is very important to Winnebago Industries, particularly as club members have proven themselves to be extremely loyal, repeat buyers of the Company's products. The WIT Club enables the Company to stay connected with our Winnebago, Itasca, Rialta and Ultimate motor home owners and provides added benefits to these owners as well. Caravans, rallies and tours held frequently throughout the year provide WIT Club members with a way to use their motor homes, remain active and keep in touch with their club-member friends. Winnebago Industries encourages its dealers to actively participate in local chapters by offering complimentary memberships to new purchasers and to host "Show & Tell" events on the dealership lots. The WIT Club

WIT members in nearly 1,500 Winnebago Industries motor homes participated in the 2002 WIT Grand National Rally for this annual event in Forest City, Iowa

also provides member benefits such as a monthly magazine, professional trip routing, purchasing and service discounts, mail forwarding and various types of insurance.

Technology Leader

Winnebago Industries believes that it is the most technologically advanced RV manufacturer in the industry, and the Company remains on the cutting edge in terms of computerized equipment at all of its facilities. An additional $11 million was spent on capital expenditures in fiscal 2002 to upgrade manufacturing equipment and expand manufacturing capabilities in order to increase productivity and improve the quality of Winnebago Industries' products.

The Company's new motor home manufacturing facility currently under construction will be a state-of-the-art facility that will utilize the latest computer technology, such as computer numerically controlled routers for the manufacture of Winnebago Industries' Class C motor homes.

Computer numerically controlled (CNC) router.

Quality Leadership

Winnebago Industries believes that its high degree of technology, as well as the advanced sales and service programs and aftermarket support we provide our dealers and retail customers, are greatly responsible for our quality leadership within the RV industry.

The Company was pleased to again receive the Quality Circle Award from the Recreation Vehicle Dealers' Association (RVDA). Quality Circle status is the result of outstanding ratings on the RVDA's annual Dealer Satisfaction Index survey. One of 32 companies which qualified for consideration based upon an adequate number of responses, Winnebago Industries was the only public motor home manufacturer to be rated high enough by dealers to receive the Quality Circle Award. Winnebago Industries was also the only public motor home manufacturer to have won this award each year since it was instituted six years ago. The Company is particularly proud of the response to the last question on the survey that names Winnebago Industries with an industry leading figure of

Quality Circle Awards from RVDA

91.7 percent on the topic of "Product Valuable for Dealership's Success."

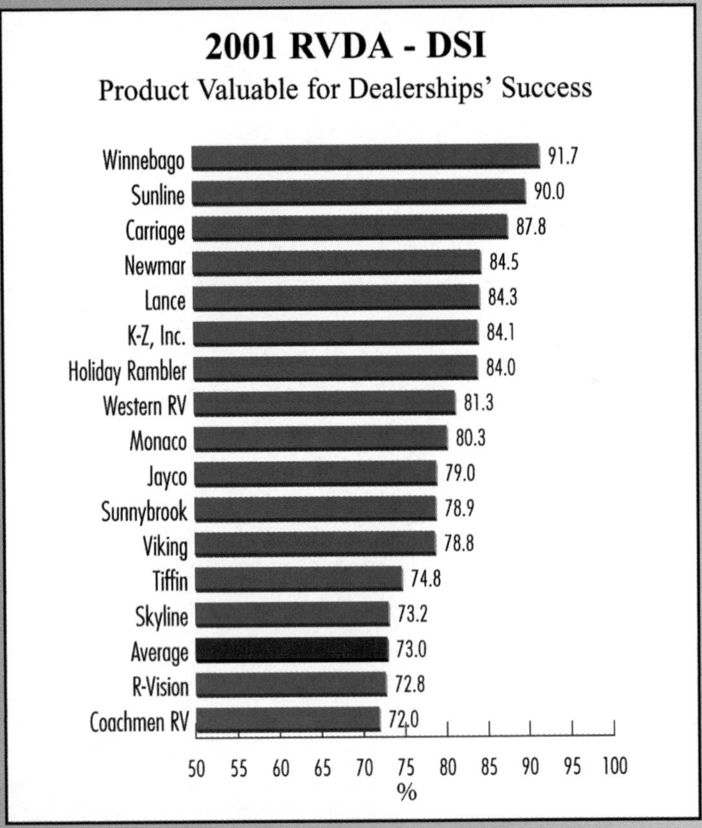

Productivity

Winnebago Industries has committed to Lean Manufacturing philosophies. Lean Manufacturing is a systematic approach of identifying and eliminating waste (non-value-added activities) through continuous organization and processes improvement. There are a series of seven workshops involved in the Lean Manufacturing process. Approximately 1,300 employees have attended the first workshop which involves employees learning the basic fundamentals of Lean Manufacturing. Another 500 employees have attended the second workshop on workplace organization and standardization.

Implementation of Lean Manufacturing in our Lorimor soft goods facility resulted in a 34 percent reduction in the number of machines needed, elimination of 5-10 hours of overtime per employee per week, reduction in work space, waste and inventory, as well as improved material flow.

Leadership Summary

Winnebago Industries is the leading motor home manufacturer in the RV industry. Demographic trends indicate that the RV industry's target market will grow for the next 30 years. Winnebago Industries' brand recognition and recognition as a top quality manufacturer lead us to believe that the Company will continue to be a leader in the industry. Through the development of innovative new products, quality improvement and plant expansion, Winnebago Industries believes it will continue to grow in market share and volume. While it is important to be in the leading position in sales within the industry, it is also the Company's continued goal to remain the most profitable public company in the industry. Winnebago Industries strongly believes it has the leadership position necessary to deliver the best results for its shareholders.

Construction of the new motor home manufacturing facility in Charles City, Iowa is scheduled to be completed in early calendar 2003.

Motor Home Product Classification

Class A Motor Homes

These are conventional motor homes constructed directly on medium-duty truck chassis which include the engine and drivetrain components. The living area and the driver's compartment are designed and produced by the motor home manufacturer. Class A motor homes from Winnebago Industries include: Winnebago Sightseer, Brave, Adventurer, Chieftain, Journey and Journey DL; Itasca Sunova, Sunrise, Suncruiser, Sunflyer and Horizon; and Ultimate Advantage and Ultimate Freedom.

Class B Van Campers

These are panel-type trucks to which sleeping, kitchen, and/or toilet facilities are added. These models also have a top extension to provide more headroom. Winnebago Industries converts the EuroVan Camper, which is distributed by Volkswagen of America and Volkswagen of Canada.

Class C Motor Homes (Mini)

These are mini motor homes built on a van-type chassis onto which motor home manufacturers construct a living area with access to the driver's compartment. Class C motor homes from Winnebago Industries include: Winnebago Vista, Minnie and Minnie Winnie; Itasca Sunstar, Spirit and Sundancer; and Rialta.

Motor Home Family Tree

Winnebago Industries manufactures four brands of Class A and C motor homes. Listed below are the brand names and model designations of the Company's 2003 product line.

- Vista
- Minnie
- Minnie Winnie
- Sightseer
- Brave
- Adventurer
- Chieftain
- Journey/Journey DL

- Sunstar
- Spirit
- Sundancer
- Sunova
- Sunrise
- Suncruiser
- Sunflyer
- Horizon

- Rialta

- Ultimate Advantage
- Ultimate Freedom

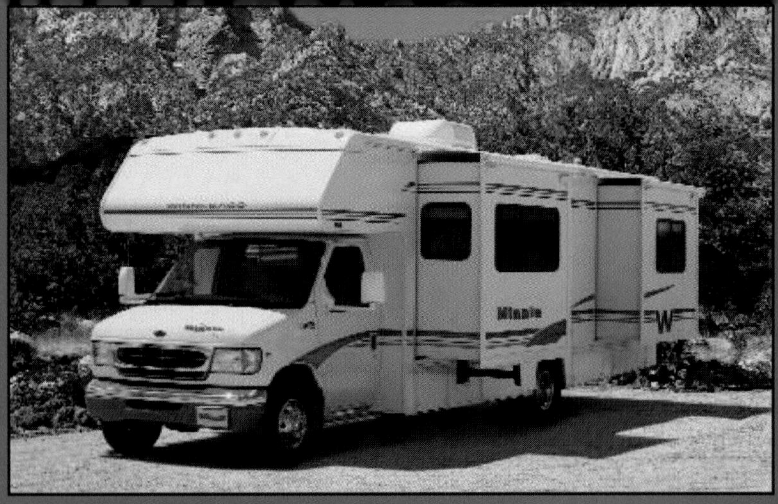

Management's Discussion and Analysis of Financial Condition and Results of Operations

FORWARD LOOKING INFORMATION

Certain of the matters discussed in this Annual Report are "forward looking statements" as defined in the Private Securities Litigation Reform Act of 1995, which involve risks and uncertainties, including, but not limited to, reactions to actual or threatened terrorist attacks, availability and price of fuel, a significant increase in interest rates, a slowdown in the economy, availability of chassis, slower than anticipated sales of new or existing products, new product introductions by competitors, collections of dealer financing receivables and other factors which may be disclosed throughout this Annual Report. Any forecasts and projections in this report are "forward looking statements," and are based on management's current expectations of the Company's near-term results, based on current information available pertaining to the Company, including the aforementioned risk factors; actual results could differ materially. The Company undertakes no obligation to publicly update or revise any forward looking statements whether as a result of new information, future events or otherwise, except as required by law or the rules of the New York Stock Exchange.

CRITICAL ACCOUNTING POLICIES

In preparing the consolidated financial statements, we follow accounting principles generally accepted in the United States of America, which in many cases requires us to make assumptions, estimates and judgments that affect the amounts reported. Many of these policies are straightforward. There are, however, some policies that are critical because they are important in determining the financial condition and results of operations. These policies are described below and involve additional management judgment due to the sensitivity of the methods, assumptions and estimates necessary in determining the related income statement, asset and/or liability amounts.

The Company offers to its customers a variety of warranties on its products ranging from 1 to 10 years in length. Estimated costs related to product warranty are accrued at the time of sale and included in cost of sales. Estimated costs are based upon past warranty claims and unit sales history and adjusted as required to reflect actual costs incurred, as information becomes available.

Beginning in fiscal year 2001, revenue was recorded by the Company upon receipt of products by Winnebago Industries dealers rather than upon shipment as in prior years. This change in accounting principle was made to implement the Securities and Exchange Commission's (SEC) Staff Accounting Bulletin (SAB) No. 101, as amended. SAB No. 101 requires that four basic criteria must be met before revenue can be recognized: (1) persuasive evidence of an arrangement exists; (2) delivery has occurred or services rendered; (3) the fee is fixed and determinable; and (4) collectability is reasonably assured. This change required an adjustment to net income in the Company's first quarter 2001 results, which reflects the cumulative effect on the prior year's results due to the application of SAB No. 101.

The Company has reserves for other loss exposures, such as product liability, litigation and accounts receivable. The Company also has loss exposure on loan guarantees and repurchase agreements (see Note 6 of Condensed Notes to

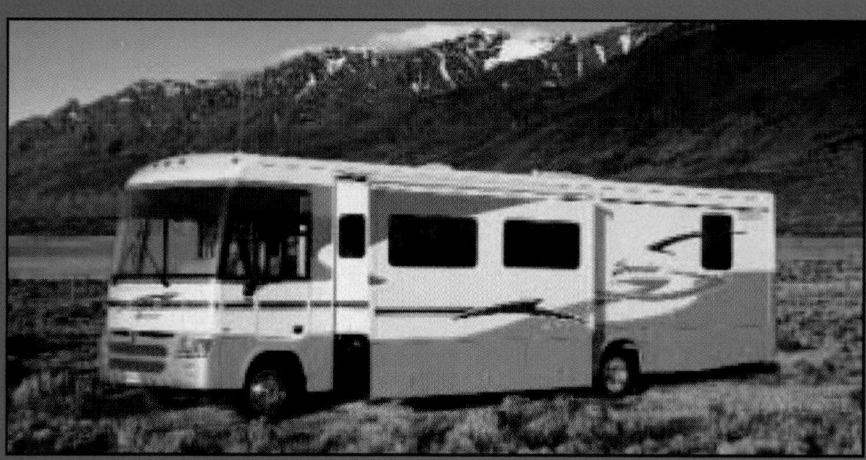

Consolidated Financial Statements). Establishing loss reserves for these matters requires the use of estimates and judgment in regards to risk exposure and ultimate liability. The Company estimates losses under the programs using consistent and appropriate methods; however, changes in assumptions could materially affect the Company's recorded liabilities for loss.

GENERAL

The primary use of recreation vehicles (RVs) for leisure travel and outdoor recreation has historically led to a peak retail selling season concentrated in the spring and summer months. The Company's sales of RVs are generally influenced by this pattern in retail sales, but can also be affected by the level of dealer inventory. The Company's products are generally manufactured against orders from the Company's dealers and from time to time to build inventory to satisfy the peak selling season.

RESULTS OF OPERATIONS

Fiscal 2002 Compared to Fiscal 2001

Net revenues for recreation vehicles and other manufactured products were $825,269,000 for fiscal 2002 (53 weeks), an increase of $153,583,000, or 22.9 percent, from fiscal 2001 (52 weeks). Motor home shipments (Class A and C) during fiscal 2002 were 11,054 units, an increase of 1,978 units, or 21.8 percent, compared to fiscal 2001. The Company's increase in revenues during fiscal 2002 reflects low interest rates, an increase in market share, continued acceptance of the Company's new products, solid performance by the Company's dealers and a high quality reputation of the Company's products.

Net revenues for dealer financing at Winnebago Acceptance Corporation (WAC) were $3,134,000 for fiscal 2002, a decrease of $1,107,000 or 26.1 percent from fiscal 2001. Decreased revenues for dealer financing reflect a significant decrease in interest rates partially offset by higher average outstanding dealer receivable balances when comparing fiscal 2002 to fiscal 2001.

Cost of manufactured products, as a percent of manufactured product revenues, was 85.9 percent for fiscal 2002, compared to 87.6 percent for fiscal 2001. The Company's lower cost of manufacturing during fiscal 2002 can be attributed to increased volume of motor home production and deliveries to dealers.

Selling expenses increased by $1,321,000 to $19,606,000 comparing fiscal 2002 to fiscal 2001 but decreased as a percentage of net revenues to 2.4 percent from 2.7 percent. The increase in dollars can be attributed primarily to increases in advertising expenses and salesperson incentive compensation. The increased sales volume during fiscal 2002 contributed to the decrease in percentage.

General and administrative expenses increased by $5,128,000 to $18,735,000 and to 2.3 percent of net revenues compared to 2.0 percent for fiscal 2001. The increases in dollars and percentage when comparing the two fiscal year-end periods were primarily due to increases in employee incentive programs and to a lesser extent increased legal reserves.

For fiscal 2002, the Company had net financial income of $2,859,000 compared to net financial income of $3,754,000 during fiscal 2001. When comparing the two fiscal years, the average available cash for investing during fiscal 2002 was larger than the average available cash during fiscal 2001. However, the average rate the Company earned on investments was significantly lower than the average rate earned during the fiscal 2001 period.

The effective income tax rate increased from 26.1 percent in fiscal 2001 to 35.0 percent in fiscal 2002. The primary reason for the increase was due to a $4.5 million tax benefit recorded in fiscal 2001 in connection with the expiration of certain tax statutes and a higher provision for state

income taxes in 2002.

For fiscal 2001, the Company adopted Staff Accounting Bulletin (SAB) No. 101 issued by the SEC in December 1999. SAB No. 101 set forth the views of the SEC staff concerning revenue recognition. As a result of SAB No. 101, the Company began recording revenue upon receipt of products by the Company's dealers rather than upon shipment by the Company. Adoption of SAB No. 101 during the 52 weeks ended August 25, 2001 required an adjustment of $1,050,000 to net income, or $.05 per diluted share, in the Company's first quarter 2001 results, which is reflected as a cumulative effect adjustment in the fiscal 2001 statement of income.

For the 53 weeks ended August 31, 2002, the Company had net income of $54,671,000, or $2.68 per diluted share, compared to the 52 weeks ended August 25, 2001 net income of $42,704,000, or $2.03 per diluted share. Net income and diluted income per share for fiscal 2002 increased 43.1 percent and 47.3 percent, respectively, compared to the prior year proforma results of $38.2 million net income and $1.82 per diluted share, which excludes the $4.5 million one time tax benefit. The differences in percentages when comparing net income to net earnings per share were primarily due to a lower number of outstanding shares of the Company's common stock during the 53 weeks ended August 31, 2002 due to the Company's buyback of 2,412,000 shares during fiscal 2002. (See Note 13 to the Company's 2002 Consolidated Financial Statements.)

Fiscal 2001 Compared to Fiscal 2000

Net revenues for recreation vehicles and other manufactured products were $671,686,000 for fiscal 2001, a decrease of $72,043,000, or 9.7 percent, from fiscal 2000. Motor home shipments (Class A and C) during fiscal 2001 were 9,076 units, a decrease of 1,440 units, or 13.7 percent, compared to fiscal 2000. The percentage decrease in net revenues was less than the percentage decrease in motor home unit sales because the Company's fiscal 2001 sales, as a percentage of total unit sales, contained relatively more higher-priced units with slideout features as well as diesel-powered Class A vehicles. The Company's net revenues during fiscal 2001 reflected the decline in consumer confidence levels and a slowdown in the economy. The Company's performance within the RV industry in fiscal 2001 was a result of the excellent acceptance of its new products, solid performance of its dealer partners, brand recognition and strong quality reputation.

Net revenues for dealer financing at WAC were $4,241,000 for fiscal 2001, an increase of $333,000, or 8.5 percent, from fiscal 2000. Increased revenues for dealer financing reflected an increase in dealer receivable balances and, to a lesser extent, an increase in interest rates charged when comparing fiscal 2001 to fiscal 2000.

Cost of manufactured products, as a percent of manufactured product revenues, was 87.6 percent for fiscal 2001 compared to 86.2 percent for fiscal 2000. The Company's higher cost of manufacturing products during 2001 can be attributed to lower volume of production and deliveries to dealers.

Selling expenses decreased by $438,000 to $18,285,000 comparing fiscal 2001 to fiscal 2000 but increased as a percentage of net revenues to 2.7 percent from 2.5 percent. The decrease in dollars can be attributed primarily to reductions in salesperson incentive compensation. Decreased sales volume during fiscal 2001 contributed to the increase in percentage.

General and administrative expenses decreased by $3,515,000 to $13,607,000 and to 2.0 percent of net revenues from 2.3 percent when comparing fiscal 2001 to fiscal 2000. Lower payments for employee incentive programs and reduced product liability costs were primary reasons for the decreases in both dollars and percentages.

For fiscal 2001, the Company had net financial income of $3,754,000 compared to net financial income of $3,338,000 during fiscal 2000. When comparing the two periods, the increase was due primarily to larger cash balances available for investing during fiscal 2001.

The effective income tax rate decreased from 34.6 percent in fiscal 2000 to 26.1 percent in fiscal 2001. The primary reason for the decrease in fiscal 2001 was due to the Company recording a $4.5 million tax benefit in connection with the expiration of certain tax statutes.

For fiscal 2001, the Company had income before cumulative effect of a change in accounting principle (SAB No. 101) of $43,754,000, or $2.08 per diluted share. The comparable results for fiscal 2000 was net income of $48,399,000, or $2.20 per diluted share.

As a result of SAB No. 101, the Company began recording revenue upon the dealers' receipt of products rather than upon shipment by the Company. Adoption of SAB No. 101 during fiscal 2001 required an adjustment of $1,050,000 to net income, or $.05 per diluted share, in the Company's first quarter 2001 results, which is reflected as a cumulative effect adjustment in the fiscal 2001 statement of income.

For fiscal 2001, the Company had net income of $42,704,000, or $2.03 per diluted share compared to fiscal 2000 net income of $48,399,000, or $2.20 per diluted share. Proforma results, excluding the $4.5 million one time tax benefit for fiscal year 2001, were $38.2 million net income and $1.82 per diluted share. Net income and earnings per diluted share for the proforma 2001 results decreased 21.1 percent and 17.3 percent, respectively, compared to fiscal 2000. The differences in percentages when comparing net income to net earnings per share was primarily due to a lower number of outstanding shares of the Company's common stock during the 52 weeks ended August 25, 2001. (See Note 13 to the Company's 2002 Consolidated Financial Statements.)

ANALYSIS OF FINANCIAL CONDITION, LIQUIDITY AND RESOURCES

The Company generally meets its working capital, capital equipment and cash requirements with funds generated from operations.

At August 31, 2002, working capital was $144,995,000, a decrease of $29,253,000 from the amount at August 25, 2001. Cash provided by operations was $36,790,000, $81,912,000 and $51,412,000 during fiscal years ended August 31, 2002, August 25, 2001 and August 26, 2000, respectively. Operating cash flows were provided in fiscal 2002 primarily by income generated from operations. Cash flows used by investing activities were $11,176,000, $19,717,000 and $25,255,000 in fiscal 2002, 2001 and 2000, respectively. Cash flows used by investing activities primarily include investments in capital expenditures. Capital expenditures were $10,997,000 in fiscal 2002, $9,089,000 in fiscal 2001 and $14,548,000 in fiscal 2000. Net cash used by financing activities was $85,669,000 in fiscal 2002, $11,358,000 in fiscal 2001 and $22,874,000 in fiscal 2000. Cash used by financing activities in fiscal 2002, 2001 and 2000 was primarily to repurchase shares of the Company's common stock at a cost of $86,072,000, $10,686,000 and $19,726,000, respectively. (See Consolidated Statements of Cash Flows.)

The Company's sources of liquidity consisted principally of cash and cash equivalents in the amount of $42,225,000 at August 31, 2002 compared to $102,280,000 at August 25, 2001. (See Consolidated Statements of Cash Flows.)

Principal expected demands at August 31, 2002 on the Company's liquid assets for fiscal 2003 include capital expenditures of approximately $23,000,000 and payments of cash dividends, based on the cash dividend described in the following sentence. On October 9, 2002, the Board of Directors declared a cash dividend of $.10 per common

share payable January 6, 2003 to shareholders of record on December 6, 2002. Also, on June 19, 2002, the Board of Directors authorized the repurchase of outstanding shares of the Company's common stock, depending on market conditions, for an aggregate purchase price of up to $15,000,000. As of October 4, 2002, 119,900 shares had been repurchased for an aggregate consideration of approximately $4,294,000 under this authorization.

Management currently expects its cash on hand and funds from operations to be sufficient to cover both short-term and long-term operating requirements.

NEW ACCOUNTING PRONOUNCEMENTS

On August 27, 2000, the Company adopted SEC Staff Accounting Bulletin (SAB) No. 101, Revenue Recognition in Financial Statements, which the SEC staff issued in December 1999. SAB No. 101 sets forth the SEC staff's views concerning revenue recognition. As a result of SAB No. 101, the Company began recording revenue upon receipt of products by Winnebago Industries' dealers rather than upon shipment by the Company. This change required an adjustment to net income in the Company's first quarter 2001 results, which is reflected as a cumulative effect adjustment in the fiscal 2001 statement of income.

In July 2001, the Financial Accounting Standards Board (FASB) issued Statement of Financial Accounting Standards (SFAS) No. 141, Business Combinations. SFAS No. 141 establishes new standards for accounting and reporting requirements for business combinations and requires that the purchase method of accounting be used for all business combinations initiated after June 30, 2001. Use of the pooling-of-interests method will be prohibited. In July 2001, the FASB also issued SFAS No. 142, Goodwill and Other Intangible Assets. SFAS No. 142 establishes new standards for goodwill acquired in a business combination and eliminates amortization of goodwill and instead sets forth methods to periodically evaluate goodwill for impairment. The Company will adopt these statements on September 1, 2002, the beginning of the first quarter of the Company's 2003 fiscal year. Management believes that neither SFAS No. 141 or 142 will affect the Company's consolidated financial statements because it does not have any acquisitions pending, goodwill or other intangible assets.

In August 2001, the FASB issued SFAS No. 143, Accounting for Asset Retirement Obligations. SFAS No. 143 requires entities to record the fair value of a liability for an asset retirement obligation in the period in which it is incurred. Also, in September 2001, the FASB issued SFAS 144, Accounting for the Impairment or Disposal of Long-Lived Assets, which addresses financial accounting and reporting for the impairment or disposal of long-lived assets. While SFAS No. 144 supersedes SFAS No. 121, Accounting for the Impairment of Long-Lived Assets and for Long-Lived Assets to be Disposed Of, it retains many of the fundamental provisions of that statement. The Company is required to adopt SFAS Nos. 143 and 144 in fiscal 2003. The Company is reviewing the impact of SFAS Nos. 143 and 144, and does not believe adoption of either of these new standards will have a material affect on the Company's financial statements.

The Company adopted Emerging Issues Task Force (EITF) Issue No. 01-9, Accounting for Consideration Given by a Vendor to a Customer or a Reseller of the Vendor's Products, at the beginning of the third quarter of fiscal 2002. This guidance was effective for periods beginning after December 15, 2001. EITF No. 01-9 requires that certain payments to customers for cooperative advertising and certain sales incentive offers that were historically classified in selling expense be shown as a reduction in net revenues. The adoption of this new accounting policy had no impact on previously reported operating income, net income, or

earnings per share.

In July 2002, the FASB issued SFAS No. 146, Accounting for Costs Associated with Exit or Disposal Activities. This standard reviews the accounting for certain exit costs and disposal activities currently set forth in EITF Issue No. 94-3, Liability Recognition for Certain Employee Termination Benefits and Other Costs to Exit an Activity (including Certain Costs Incurred in a Restructuring). The principal change of the new statement is that it now requires that a liability for a cost associated with an exit or disposal activity be recognized when the liability is incurred versus the date of commitment to an exit plan. This statement is effective for exit and disposal activities initiated after December 31, 2002. The Company does not believe adoption of this standard will significantly affect the Company's financial condition or operating results.

IMPACT OF INFLATION

Historically, the impact of inflation on the Company's operations has not been significantly detrimental, as the Company has usually been able to adjust its prices to reflect the inflationary impact on the cost of manufacturing its products. The inability of the Company to successfully offset increases in manufacturing costs could have a material adverse effect on the Company's results of operations.

QUANTITATIVE AND QUALITATIVE DISCLOSURES ABOUT MARKET RISK

As of August 31, 2002, the Company had an investment portfolio of fixed income securities, which are classified as cash and cash equivalents of $42,225,000, of which $36,084,000 are fixed income investments that are subject to interest rate risk and a decline in value if market interest rates increase. However, the Company has the ability to hold its fixed income investments until maturity (which approximates 45 days) and, therefore, the Company would not expect to recognize an adverse impact in income or cash flows in such an event.

As of August 31, 2002, the Company had dealer-financing receivables in the amount of $37,880,000. Interest rates charged on these receivables vary based on the prime rate.

COMPANY OUTLOOK

Long-term demographics are favorable to the Company, as the target market of consumers age 50 and older is anticipated to nearly double within the next 30 years. In addition, a 2001 "RV Consumer Demographic Study" conducted by the University of Michigan for the RV industry, found the age of people interested in purchasing recreation vehicles is expanding to include younger buyers as well as older buyers. The study also found an increased interest in owning RVs generally by a larger percentage of all U.S. households. Order backlog for the Company's Class A and Class C motor homes was 3,248 orders at August 31, 2002, 1,598 orders at August 25, 2001 and 1,355 orders at August 26, 2000. The Company includes in its backlog all accepted purchase orders from dealers shippable within the next six months. Orders in backlog can be canceled or postponed at the option of the purchaser at any time without penalty and, therefore, backlog may not necessarily be a measure of future sales.

Consolidated Balance Sheets

(dollars in thousands)	August 31, 2002	August 25, 2001
Assets		
Current assets		
Cash and cash equivalents	$ 42,225	$ 102,280
Receivables, less allowance for doubtful accounts ($120 and $244, respectively)	28,616	21,571
Dealer financing receivables, less allowance for doubtful accounts ($96 and $117, respectively)	37,880	40,263
Inventories	113,654	79,815
Prepaid expenses	4,314	3,604
Deferred income taxes	6,907	6,723
Total current assets	233,596	254,256
Property and equipment, at cost		
Land	972	1,029
Buildings	47,953	45,992
Machinery and equipment	86,744	82,182
Transportation equipment	5,641	5,482
	141,310	134,685
Less accumulated depreciation	92,383	88,149
Total property and equipment, net	48,927	46,536
Investment in life insurance	23,602	22,223
Deferred income taxes	22,438	21,495
Other assets	8,514	7,412
Total assets	$ 337,077	$ 351,922

See notes to consolidated financial statements

(dollars in thousands)	August 31, 2002	August 25, 2001
Liabilities and Stockholders' Equity		
Current liabilities		
Accounts payable, trade	$ 44,230	$ 40,678
Income taxes payable	2,610	4,938
Accrued expenses:		
Accrued compensation	18,673	13,730
Product warranties	8,151	8,072
Insurance	5,967	4,567
Promotional	4,499	3,181
Other	4,471	4,842
Total current liabilities	88,601	80,008
Postretirement health care and deferred compensation benefits	68,661	64,450
Contingent liabilities and commitments		
Stockholders' equity		
Capital stock common, par value $.50; authorized 60,000,000 shares, issued 25,888,000 and 25,886,000 shares, respectively	12,944	12,943
Additional paid-in capital	25,740	22,261
Reinvested earnings	284,856	234,139
	323,540	269,343
Less treasury stock, at cost	143,725	61,879
Total stockholders' equity	179,815	207,464
Total liabilities and stockholders' equity	$ 337,077	$ 351,922

Consolidated Statements of Income

(in thousands, except per share data)	August 31, 2002 (1)	Year Ended August 25, 2001	August 26, 2000
Revenues			
Manufactured products	$ 825,269	$ 671,686	$ 743,729
Dealer financing	3,134	4,241	3,908
Total net revenues	828,403	675,927	747,637
Costs and expenses			
Cost of manufactured products	708,865	588,561	641,138
Selling	19,606	18,285	18,723
General and administrative	18,735	13,607	17,122
Total costs and expenses	747,206	620,453	676,983
Operating income	81,197	55,474	70,654
Financial income	2,859	3,754	3,338
Income before income taxes	84,056	59,228	73,992
Provision for taxes	29,385	15,474	25,593
Income before cumulative effect of change in accounting principle	54,671	43,754	48,399
Cumulative effect of change in accounting principle, net of taxes	- - -	(1,050)	- - -
Net income	$ 54,671	$ 42,704	$ 48,399
Earnings per common share (basic)			
Income before cumulative effect of change in accounting principle	$ 2.74	$ 2.11	$ 2.23
Cumulative effect of change in accounting principle	- - -	(.05)	- - -
Income per share (basic)	$ 2.74	$ 2.06	$ 2.23
Earnings per common share (diluted)			
Income before cumulative effect of change in accounting principle	$ 2.68	$ 2.08	$ 2.20
Cumulative effect of change in accounting principle	- - -	(.05)	- - -
Income per share (diluted)	$ 2.68	$ 2.03	$ 2.20
Weighted average shares of common stock outstanding			
Basic	19,949	20,735	21,680
Diluted	20,384	21,040	22,011

See notes to consolidated financial statements.

(1) Year ended August 31, 2002 contained 53 weeks; all other fiscal years contained 52 weeks.

Consolidated Statements of Cash Flows

(in thousands)	August 31, 2002	Year Ended August 25, 2001	August 26, 2000
Cash flows from operating activities			
Net income	$ 54,671	$ 42,704	$ 48,399
Adjustments to reconcile net income to net cash provided by operating activities			
Depreciation and amortization	7,879	7,380	6,622
(Gain) loss on disposal of property, leases and other assets	(202)	325	350
(Credit) provision for doubtful receivables	(46)	34	203
Tax benefit of stock options	3,349	1,209	- - -
Change in assets and liabilities			
(Increase) decrease in receivables and other assets	(7,766)	10,956	702
(Increase) decrease in inventories	(33,839)	5,892	1,324
Increase in deferred income taxes	(1,127)	(1,499)	(2,674)
Increase (decrease) in accounts payable and accrued expenses	10,921	13,616	(8,306)
(Decrease) increase in income taxes payable	(2,328)	(3,852)	180
Increase in postretirement benefits	5,278	5,147	4,612
Net cash provided by operating activities	36,790	81,912	51,412
Cash flows from investing activities			
Purchases of property and equipment	(10,997)	(9,089)	(14,548)
Proceeds from sale of property and equipment	929	338	531
Investments in dealer receivables	(114,737)	(114,907)	(103,125)
Collections of dealer receivables	117,202	107,261	95,061
Investments in other assets	(3,573)	(3,320)	(3,724)
Proceeds from other assets	- - -	- - -	550
Net cash used in investing activities	(11,176)	(19,717)	(25,255)
Cash flows from financing activities and capital transactions			
Payments for purchase of common stock	(86,072)	(10,686)	(19,726)
Payments of cash dividends	(3,954)	(4,121)	(4,324)
Proceeds from issuance of common and treasury stock	4,357	3,449	1,176
Net cash used in financing activities and capital transactions	(85,669)	(11,358)	(22,874)
Net (decrease) increase in cash and cash equivalents	(60,055)	50,837	3,283
Cash and cash equivalents at beginning of year	102,280	51,443	48,160
Cash and cash equivalents at end of year	$ 42,225	$ 102,280	$ 51,443

See notes to consolidated financial statements.

Consolidated Statements of Changes in Stockholders' Equity

(amounts in thousands except per share data)	Common Shares Number	Common Shares Amount	Additional Paid-In Capital	Reinvested Income	Treasury Stock Number	Treasury Stock Amount
Balance, August 28, 1999	25,874	$12,937	$21,907	$151,482	3,575	$36,942
Proceeds from the sale of common stock to employees	4	2	77	---	---	---
Net cost of treasury stock issued for stock options exercised	---	---	(194)	---	(66)	(729)
Issuance of stock to officers	---	---	204	---	(32)	(359)
Payments for purchase of common stock	---	---	---	---	1,127	19,726
Cash dividends on common stock - $.20 per share	---	---	---	(4,325)	---	---
Net income	---	---	---	48,399	---	---
Balance, August 26, 2000	25,878	12,939	21,994	195,556	4,604	55,580
Proceeds from the sale of common stock to employees	8	4	94	---	---	---
Net cost of treasury stock issued for stock options exercised	---	---	(1,069)	---	(313)	(3,773)
Issuance of stock to officers	---	---	33	---	(51)	(614)
Tax benefit due to sale of common stock to employees	---	---	1,209	---	---	---
Payments for purchase of common stock	---	---	---	---	883	10,686
Cash dividends on common stock - $.20 per share	---	---	---	(4,121)	---	---
Net income	---	---	---	42,704	---	---
Balance, August 25, 2001	25,886	12,943	22,261	234,139	5,123	61,879
Proceeds from the sale of common stock to employees	2	1	49	---	---	---
Net cost of treasury stock issued for stock options exercised	---	---	(453)	---	(280)	(3,650)
Issuance of stock to officers	---	---	534	---	(45)	(576)
Tax benefit due to sale of common stock to employees	---	---	3,349	---	---	---
Payments for purchase of common stock	---	---	---	---	2,412	86,072
Cash dividends on common stock - $.20 per share	---	---	---	(3,954)	---	---
Net income	---	---	---	54,671	---	---
Balance, August 31, 2002	25,888	$12,944	$25,740	$284,856	7,210	$143,725

See notes to consolidated financial statements.

Report of Independent Auditors

To the Board of Directors and Shareholders
Winnebago Industries, Inc.
Forest City, Iowa

We have audited the consolidated balance sheets of Winnebago Industries, Inc. and subsidiaries (the Company) as of August 31, 2002 and August 25, 2001, and the related consolidated statements of income, cash flows, and changes in stockholders' equity for each of the three years in the period ended August 31, 2002. These consolidated financial statements are the responsibility of the Company's management. Our responsibility is to express an opinion on these consolidated financial statements based on our audits.

We conducted our audits in accordance with auditing standards generally accepted in the United States of America. Those standards require that we plan and perform the audit to obtain reasonable assurance about whether the consolidated financial statements are free of material misstatement. An audit includes examining, on a test basis, evidence supporting the amounts and disclosures in the consolidated financial statements. An audit also includes assessing the accounting principles used and significant estimates made by management, as well as evaluating the overall financial statement presentation. We believe that our audits provide a reasonable basis for our opinion.

In our opinion, the consolidated financial statements present fairly, in all material respects, the financial position of the Company as of August 31, 2002 and August 25, 2001; and the results of its operations and its cash flows for each of the three years in the period ended August 31, 2002 in conformity with accounting principles generally accepted in the United States of America.

Deloitte & Touche LLP

Deloitte & Touche LLP
Minneapolis, Minnesota

October 4, 2002

Selected Financial Data

(dollars in thousands, except per share data)	Aug. 31, 2002(2)	Aug. 25, 2001(3)	Aug. 26, 2000	Aug. 28, 1999
For the Year				
Net revenues (4)	$ 828,403	$ 675,927	$ 747,637	$ 671,653
Income before taxes	84,056	59,228	73,992	66,609
Pretax profit % of revenue	10.1%	8.8%	9.9%	9.9%
Provision for income taxes (credits)	$ 29,385	$ 15,474	$ 25,593	$ 22,349
Income tax rate	35.0%	26.1%	34.6%	33.6%
Income from continuing operations	$ 54,671	$ 43,754	$ 48,399	$ 44,260
Gain on sale of Cycle-Sat subsidiary	---	---	---	---
(Loss) income from discontinued operations	---	---	---	---
Cum. effect of change in accounting principle	---	(1,050)	---	---
Net income (loss)	$ 54,671	$ 42,704	$ 48,399	$ 44,260
Income per share				
Continuing operations				
Basic	$ 2.74	$ 2.11	$ 2.23	$ 1.99
Diluted	2.68	2.08	2.20	1.96
Discontinued operations				
Basic	---	---	---	---
Diluted	---	---	---	---
Cum. effect of change in accounting principle				
Basic	---	(.05)	---	---
Diluted	---	(.05)	---	---
Net income per share				
Basic	$ 2.74	$ 2.06	$ 2.23	$ 1.99
Diluted	2.68	2.03	2.20	1.96
Weighted average common shares outstanding (in thousands)				
Basic	19,949	20,735	21,680	22,209
Diluted	20,384	21,040	22,011	22,537
Cash dividends per share	$ .20	$ .20	$ .20	$ .20
Book value	9.63	9.99	8.22	6.69
Return on assets (ROA)	15.9%	12.9%	16.3%	17.1%
Return on equity (ROE)	28.2%	22.3%	29.8%	33.3%
Unit Sales				
Class A	6,725	5,666	6,819	6,054
Class C	4,329	3,410	3,697	4,222
Total Class A & C Motor Homes	11,054	9,076	10,516	10,276
Class B Conversions (EuroVan Campers)	763	703	854	600
At Year End				
Total assets	$ 337,077	$ 351,922	$ 308,686	$ 285,889
Stockholders' equity	179,815	207,464	174,909	149,384
Working capital	144,995	174,248	141,683	123,720
Long-term debt	---	---	---	---
Current ratio	2.6 to 1	3.2 to 1	3.0 to 1	2.5 to 1
Number of employees	3,685	3,325	3,300	3,400

(1) Certain prior periods' information has been reclassified to conform to the current year-end presentation. These reclassifications have no impact on net income as previously reported.

(2) The fiscal years ended August 31, 2002 and August 31, 1996 contained 53 weeks; all other fiscal years contained 52 weeks.

Aug. 29, 1998	Aug. 30, 1997	Aug. 31, 1996(2)	Aug. 26, 1995	Aug. 27, 1994	Aug. 28, 1993
$ 529,363	$ 437,961	$ 487,545	$ 462,760	$ 436,870	$ 368,255
35,927	6,992	21,063	20,006	15,264	11,018
6.8%	1.6%	4.3%	4.3%	3.5%	3.0%
$ 11,543	$ 416	$ 6,639	($7,912)	($1,312)	($1,087)
32.1%	5.9%	31.5%	(39.5%)	(8.6%)	(9.9%)
$ 24,384	$ 6,576	$ 14,424	$ 27,918	$ 16,576	$ 12,105
---	16,472	---	---	---	---
---	---	(2,039)	(162)	869	(2,827)
---	---	---	---	(20,420)	---
$ 24,384	$ 23,048	$ 12,385	$ 27,756	($2,975)	$ 9,278
$ 1.01	$ .26	$ .57	$ 1.11	$ .66	$ .48
1.00	.26	.57	1.10	.65	.48
---	.65	(.08)	(.01)	.03	(.11)
---	.64	(.08)	(.01)	.03	(.11)
---	---	---	---	(.81)	---
---	---	---	---	(.80)	---
$ 1.01	$ .91	$ .49	$ 1.10	$ (.12)	$ .37
1.00	.90	.49	1.09	(.12)	.37
24,106	25,435	25,349	25,286	25,187	25,042
24,314	25,550	25,524	25,462	25,481	25,307
$ .20	$ .20	$ .30	$ .30	$ ---	$ ---
5.11	4.86	4.15	3.96	3.16	3.26
11.0%	10.6%	5.7%	14.1%	(1.8%)	6.3%
20.3%	20.1%	12.0%	30.8%	(3.7%)	12.1%
5,381	4,834	5,893	5,993	6,820	6,095
3,390	2,724	2,857	2,853	1,862	1,998
8,771	7,558	8,750	8,846	8,682	8,093
978	1,205	857	1,014	376	---
$ 230,612	$ 213,475	$ 220,596	$ 211,630	$ 181,748	$ 157,050
116,523	123,882	105,311	100,448	79,710	81,693
92,800	99,935	62,155	69,694	58,523	44,669
---	---	1,692	3,810	2,693	633
2.5 to 1	3.4 to 1	2.0 to 1	2.4 to 1	2.1 to 1	1.9 to 1
3,010	2,830	3,150	3,010	3,150	2,770

(3) Includes a noncash after-tax cumulative effect of change in accounting principle of $1.1 million expense or $.05 per share due to the adoption of SAB No. 101, Revenue Recognition in Financial Statements.
(4) Net revenues for fiscal 2002 required adoption of EITF No. 01-9 Accounting for Consideration Given by a Vendor for a Customer (Including a Reseller of the Vendor's Product) which requires the reduction of net revenues by certain payments to customers for certain sales incentive offers and fiscal 2001 required adoption of EITF 00-10 related to shipping and handling fees and costs.

Notes to Consolidated Financial Statements

Note 1: Nature of Business and Significant Accounting Policies

Winnebago Industries, Inc.'s (the Company) operations are conducted predominantly in two industry segments: the manufacture and sale of recreation vehicles and other manufactured products, and floor plan financing for selected Winnebago, Itasca, Rialta, and Ultimate dealers. The recreation vehicle market is highly competitive, both as to price and quality of the product. The Company believes its principal marketing advantages are its brand name recognition, the quality of its products, its dealer organization, its warranty and service capability and its marketing techniques. The Company also believes that its prices are competitive with the competition's units of comparable size and quality.

Principles of Consolidation. The consolidated financial statements include the parent company and subsidiary companies. All material intercompany balances and transactions with subsidiaries have been eliminated.

Statements of Cash Flows. For purposes of these statements, cash equivalents primarily consisted of commercial paper, tax-exempt money market preferreds, and variable rate auction preferred stock with an original maturity of three months or less. For cash equivalents, the carrying amount is a reasonable estimate of fair value.

Fiscal Period. The Company follows a 52/53-week fiscal year period. The financial statements for fiscal 2002 are based on a 53-week period; the others are on a 52-week basis.

Revenue Recognition. The Company adopted Staff Accounting Bulletin (SAB) No. 101, Revenue Recognition, as of the beginning of fiscal 2001. This accounting principle requires the Company to recognize revenue upon delivery of products to the dealer, which is when title passes, instead of when shipped by the Company. Interest income from dealer floor plan receivables is recorded on the accrual basis in accordance with the terms of the loan agreements.

Shipping Revenues and Expenses. Shipping revenues for products shipped are included within sales, while shipping expenses are included within cost of goods sold, in accordance with Emerging Issues Task Force (EITF) No. 00-10, Accounting for Shipping and Handling Fees and Costs.

Considerations Given by the Company to Its Dealers. Certain payments to customers for cooperative advertising and certain sales incentive offers are shown as a reduction in net revenues, in accordance with EITF No. 01-9, Accounting for Consideration Given by a Vendor to a Customer or a Reseller of the Vendor's Products. Cooperative advertising expense and sales incentives were previously reported as selling expense. Prior period expenses have been reclassified, which had no effect on previously reported net income.

Inventories. Inventories are valued at the lower of cost or market, with cost being determined by using the last-in, first-out (LIFO) method and market defined as net realizable value.

Property and Equipment. Depreciation of property and equipment is computed using the straight-line method on the cost of the assets, less allowance for salvage value where appropriate, at rates based upon their estimated service lives as follows:

Asset Class	Asset Life
Buildings	10-30 yrs.
Machinery and equipment	3-10 yrs.
Transportation equipment	3-6 yrs.

Management periodically reviews the carrying values of long-lived assets for impairment whenever events or changes in circumstances indicate that the carrying value may not be recoverable. In performing the review for recoverability, management estimates the nondiscounted future cash flows expected to result from the use of the asset and its eventual disposition.

Provision for Warranty Claims. Estimated warranty costs are provided at the time of sale of the warranted products. Estimates of future warranty costs are based on prior experience and known current events.

Income Taxes. The Company accounts for income taxes under Statement of Financial Accounting Standards (SFAS) No. 109, Accounting for Income Taxes. This Statement requires recognition of deferred assets and liabilities for the expected future tax consequences of events that have been

included in the financial statements or tax returns. Under this method, deferred tax assets and liabilities are determined based on the differences between the financial statement and tax basis of assets and liabilities using enacted tax rates in effect for the years in which the differences are expected to reverse.

Derivative Instruments and Hedging Activities. All contracts that contain provisions meeting the definition of a derivative also meet the requirements of, and have been designated as, normal purchases or sales. The Company's policy is to not enter into contracts with terms that cannot be designated as normal purchases or sales.

Allowance for Doubtful Accounts. The allowance for doubtful accounts is based on previous loss experience. Additional amounts are provided through charges to income as management believes necessary after evaluation of receivables and current economic conditions. Amounts which are considered to be uncollectible are charged off and recoveries of amounts previously charged off are credited to the allowance upon recovery.

Research and Development. Research and development expenditures are expenses as incurred. Development activities generally relate to creating new products and improving or creating variations of existing products to meet new applications. During fiscal 2002, 2001 and 2000, the Company spent approximately $3,190,000, $3,397,000 and $3,374,000, respectively, on research and development activities.

Income Per Common Share. Basic income per common share is computed by dividing net income by the weighted average common shares outstanding during the period.

Diluted income per common share is computed by dividing net income by the weighted average common shares outstanding plus the incremental shares that would have been outstanding upon the assumed exercise of dilutive stock options (see Note 13).

Fair Value Disclosures of Financial Instruments. All financial instruments are carried at amounts believed to approximate fair value.

Use of Estimates. The preparation of financial statements in conformity with accounting principles generally accepted in the United States of America requires management to make estimates and assumptions that affect the reported amounts of assets and liabilities and disclosure of contingent assets and liabilities at the date of the financial statements and the reported amounts of revenues and expenses during the reporting period. Actual results could differ from those estimates.

Reclassifications. Certain prior year information has been reclassified to conform to the current year presentation. This reclassification had no affect on net income or stockholders' equity as previously reported.

Note 2: Dealer Financing Receivables

Dealer floor plan receivables are collateralized by recreation vehicles and are due upon the dealer's sale of the vehicle, with the entire balance generally due at the end of one year. At August 31, 2002 and August 25, 2001, the Company had a concentration of credit risks whereby $37,388,000 and $39,243,000, respectively, of dealer financing receivables were due from one dealer.

Note 3: Inventories

Inventories consist of the following:

(dollars in thousands)	August 31, 2002	August 25, 2001
Finished goods	$ 48,037	$ 36,930
Work-in-process	26,995	21,725
Raw materials	62,194	44,232
	137,226	102,887
LIFO reserve	(23,572)	(23,072)
	$ 113,654	$ 79,815

The above value of inventories, before reduction for the LIFO reserve, approximates replacement cost at the respective dates.

Note 4: Notes Payable

Short-term lines of credit and related borrowings outstanding at fiscal year-end are as follows:

(dollars in thousands)	August 31, 2002	August 25, 2001
Available credit lines	$ ---	$ 20,000
Outstanding	---	---
Interest rate	---	4.52%

On October 19, 2000, the Company entered into an unsecured credit agreement with Wells Fargo Bank Iowa, National Association. The credit agreement provided the Company with a line of credit of $20,000,000 until January 31, 2002. There were no outstanding borrowings under the credit agreement during fiscal 2002 or 2001. The Company did not renew this agreement when it expired on January 31, 2002.

Note 5: Employee Retirement Plans

The Company has a qualified profit sharing and contributory 401(k) plan for eligible employees. The plan provides for contributions by the Company in such amounts as the Board of Directors may determine. Contributions to the plan in cash for fiscal 2002, 2001 and 2000 were $2,668,000, $2,283,000 and $2,685,000, respectively.

The Company also has a nonqualified deferred compensation program which permits key employees to annually elect (via individual contracts) to defer a portion of their compensation until their retirement. The retirement benefit to be provided is based upon the amount of compensation deferred and the age of the individual at the time of the contracted deferral. An individual generally vests at the later of age 55 and five years of service since the deferral was made. For deferrals prior to December 1992, vesting occurs at the later of age 55 and five years of service from first deferral or 20 years of service. Deferred compensation expense was $1,642,000, $1,659,000 and $1,645,000, in fiscal 2002, 2001 and 2000, respectively. Total deferred compensation liabilities were $24,711,000 and $24,646,000 at August 31, 2002 and August 25, 2001, respectively.

To assist in funding the deferred compensation liability, the Company has invested in corporate-owned life insurance policies. The cash surrender value of these policies (net of borrowings of $14,825,000 and $13,637,000 at August 31, 2002 and August 25, 2001, respectively) are presented as assets of the Company in the accompanying consolidated balance sheets.

The Company provides certain health care and other benefits for retired employees who have fulfilled eligibility requirements at age 55 with 15 years of continuous service. Retirees are required to pay a monthly premium for medical coverage based on years of service at retirement and then current age. The Company's postretirement health care plan currently is not funded. The status of the plan is as follows:

(dollars in thousands)	August 31, 2002	August 25, 2001
Change in benefit obligation		
Accumulated benefit obligation, beginning of year	$ 41,179	$ 36,925
Actuarial loss	6,675	1,225
Interest cost	2,836	2,750
Service cost	2,079	1,955
Net benefits paid	(571)	(587)
Plan amendment	(7,230)	(1,089)
Benefit obligation, end of year	$ 44,968	$ 41,179
Funded status		
Accumulated benefit obligation in excess of plan assets	$ 44,968	$ 41,179
Unrecognized cost		
Net actuarial loss	(9,463)	(2,777)
Prior service cost	8,445	1,402
Accrued benefit cost	$ 43,950	$ 39,804

The discount rate used in determining the accumulated postretirement benefit obligation was 6.75 percent at August 31, 2002 and 7.0 percent at August 25, 2001. The average assumed health care cost trend rate used in measuring the accumulated postretirement benefit obligations as of August 31, 2002 was 9.4 percent, decreasing each successive year until it reaches 5.0 percent in 2023 after which it remains constant.

Net postretirement benefit expense for the fiscal years ended August 31, 2002, August 25, 2001 and August 26, 2000 consisted of the following components:

(dollars in thousands)	Aug. 31, 2002	Aug. 25, 2001	Aug. 26, 2000
Components of net periodic benefit cost			
Interest cost	$ 2,836	$ 2,750	$ 1,953
Service cost	2,079	1,955	1,714
Net amortization and deferral	(193)	(65)	(129)
Net periodic benefit cost	$ 4,722	$ 4,640	$ 3,538

Assumed health care cost trend rates have a significant effect on the amounts reported for the health care plans. A one percentage point change in assumed health care cost trend rates would have the following effects:

(dollars in thousands)	One Percentage Point Increase	One Percentage Point Decrease
Effect on total of service and interest cost components	$ 1,401	$ (1,034)
Effect on postretirement benefit obligation	$ 11,369	$ (8,535)

Summary of postretirement health care and deferred compensation benefits at fiscal year end are as follows:

(dollars in thousands)	August 31, 2002	August 25, 2001
Accrued benefit cost	$ 43,950	$ 39,804
Deferred compensation liability	24,711	24,646
Total postretirement health care and deferred compensation benefits	$ 68,661	$ 64,450

Note 6: Contingent Liabilities and Commitments

It is customary practice for companies in the recreation vehicle industry to enter into repurchase agreements with lending institutions which have provided wholesale floor plan financing to dealers. Most dealers are financed on a "floor plan" basis under which a bank or finance company lends the dealer all, or substantially all, of the purchase price, collateralized by a lien upon, or title to, the merchandise purchased. Upon request of a lending institution financing a dealer's purchases of the Company's products, and after completion of a credit investigation of the dealer involved, the Company will execute a repurchase agreement. These agreements provide that, in the event of default by the dealer on the agreement to pay the lending institution, the Company will repurchase the financed merchandise. The agreements provide that the Company's liability will not exceed 100 percent of the dealer invoice and provide for periodic liability reductions based on the time since the date of the original invoice. The Company's contingent obligations under these repurchase agreements are reduced by the proceeds received upon the sale of any repurchased unit. The Company's contingent liability on all repurchase agreements was approximately $245,828,000 and $216,784,000 at August 31, 2002 and August 25, 2001, respectively. The Company's losses under repurchase agreements were approximately $81,000, $197,000, and $282,000 during fiscal 2002, 2001 and 2000, respectively.

Included in these contingent liabilities are certain dealer receivables subject to full recourse to the Company with Bank of America Specialty Group and Conseco Financing Servicing Group. Contingent liabilities under these recourse agreements were $1,049,000 and $3,276,000 at August 31, 2002 and August 25, 2001, respectively. The Company did not incur any actual losses under these recourse agreements during fiscal 2002, 2001 and 2000.

The Company self-insures for a portion of product liability claims. Self-insurance retention liability varies annually based on market conditions and for the past five fiscal years was at $2,500,000 per occurrence and $6,000,000 in aggregate per policy year. Liabilities in excess of these amounts are the responsibility of the insurer.

The Company and the Winnebago Industries, Inc. Deferred Compensation Plan, Winnebago Industries, Inc. Deferred

Incentive Formula Bonus Plan and Winnebago Industries, Inc. Deferred Compensation Plan and Deferred Bonus Plan Trust are Defendants in a purported class action title Sanft, et al vs. Winnebago Industries, Inc., at al which was filed in the United States District Court, Northern District of Iowa, Central Division, on August 30, 2001 and is currently pending. The Complaint alleges a class consisting of participants in the Winnebago Industries, Inc. Deferred Compensation Plan and the Winnebago Industries, Inc. Deferred Incentive Formula Bonus Plan (the "Plans") and alleges 23 separate causes of action including declaratory and injunctive relief, Federal common law unjust enrichment, breach of fiduciary duty and violation of ERISA vesting provisions and ERISA funding requirements. The suit seeks to negate certain amendments made to the Plans in 1994 which reduced the benefits which some participants would receive under the Plans. This action has not been certified as a class action. The Company believes that the Defendants have meritorious defenses to class certification and as to the Plaintiff's substantive claims. The Company is vigorously defending the lawsuit and will oppose any attempt by the Plaintiffs to have the case certified as a class action. The case is currently set for trial in June 2004. As of August 31, 2002 the Company has accrued estimated legal fees for the defense of the case. However, no other amounts have been accrued for the case because it is not possible at this time to properly assess the risk of an adverse verdict or the magnitude of possible exposure.

The Company is also involved in other various legal proceedings which are ordinary routine litigation incident to its business, many of which are covered in whole or in part by insurance. While it is impossible to estimate with certainty the ultimate legal and financial liability with respect to this litigation, management is of the opinion that while the final resolution of any such litigation may have an impact on the Company's consolidated results for a particular reporting period, the ultimate disposition of such litigation will not have any material adverse effect on the Company's financial position, results of operations or liquidity

Note 7: Income Taxes

The components of the provision for income taxes are as follows:

	Year Ended		
(dollars in thousands)	**Aug. 31, 2002**	**Aug. 25, 2001**	**Aug. 26, 2000**
Current			
Federal	$ 29,666	$ 16,448	$ 27,162
State	846	524	1,105
	30,512	16,972	28,267
Deferred - (principally federal)	(1,127)	(1,498)	(2,674)
Total provision	$ 29,385	$ 15,474	$ 25,593

The following is a reconciliation of the U.S. statutory tax rate to the effective income tax rates (benefit) provided:

	Year Ended		
	August 31, 2002	**August 25, 2001**	**August 26, 2000**
U.S. federal statutory rate	35.0%	35.0%	35.0%
State taxes, net of federal benefit	1.1	0.6	0.8
Life insurance premiums	0.1	0.1	0.1
Previously unrecorded tax benefits	- - -	(7.7)	- - -
Tax credits	(0.1)	(0.5)	(0.3)
Foreign sales corporation commissions	(0.1)	(0.2)	(0.2)
Cash surrender value	(0.5)	(0.7)	(0.6)
Other	(0.5)	(0.5)	(0.2)
Total	35.0%	26.1%	34.6%

The tax effect of significant items comprising the Company's net deferred tax assets are as follows:

(dollars in thousands)	August 31, 2002 Assets	August 31, 2002 Liabilities	August 31, 2002 Total	August 25, 2001 Total
Current				
Warranty reserves	$ 2,847	$ ---	$ 2,847	$ 2,825
Self-insurance reserve	1,544	---	1,544	1,598
Accrued vacation	1,538	---	1,538	1,404
Miscellaneous reserves	1,594	(616)	978	896
Subtotal	7,523	(616)	6,907	6,723
Noncurrent				
Postretirement health care benefits	15,382	---	15,382	13,931
Deferred compensation	10,967	---	10,967	10,788
Property and equipment	---	(3,911)	(3,911)	(3,224)
Subtotal	26,349	(3,911)	22,438	21,495
Total	$ 33,872	$ (4,527)	$ 29,345	$ 28,218

Note 8: Financial Income and Expense

The following is a reconciliation of financial income (expense):

(dollars in thousands)	Year Ended August 31, 2002	August 25, 2001	August 26, 2000
Dividend income	$ 2,726	$ 2,488	$ 2,076
Interest income from investments and receivables	369	1,332	1,478
Gains on foreign currency transactions	62	23	58
Interest expense	(298)	(89)	(274)
	$ 2,859	$ 3,754	$ 3,338

Note 9: Repurchase of Related Party Stock

In April 2002, pursuant to an authorization of the Board of Directors, the Company repurchased 2,100,000 shares of common stock from Hanson Capital Partners, LLC ("HCP"). HCP is a Delaware limited liability company whose members are the Luise V. Hanson Qualified Terminable Interest Property Marital Deduction Trust (the "QTIP Trust"), which has a 34.9 percent membership interest in HCP, and the Luise V. Hanson Revocable Trust, dated September 22, 1984 (the "Revocable Trust"), which has a 65.1 percent membership interest in HCP. John V. Hanson, a director of the Company, Mary Jo Boman, the wife of Gerald E. Boman, a director of the Company, Paul D. Hanson and Bessemer Trust Company, N.A. act as co-trustees under the QTIP trust. Mrs. Luise V. Hanson is trustee of the Revocable Trust. Mrs. Hanson is also a controlling person in the Company. Mrs. Hanson is the mother of John V. Hanson, Mary Jo Boman and Paul D. Hanson and the mother-in-law of Gerald E. Boman. The shares were repurchased for an aggregate purchase price of $77,700,000 ($37 per share), plus interest in the amount of $245,765. On the date of the share repurchase, the high and low prices of the Company's common stock on the New York Stock Exchange were $43.70 and $42.35, respectively. The Company utilized its cash on hand and cash becoming available from maturing fixed income securities to pay the purchase price of the stock in three installments with interest at the rate of four percent per anum on the outstanding balance.

Note 10: Stock Option Plans

The Company's 1987 stock option plan allowed the granting of nonqualified and incentive stock options to key employees at prices not less than 100 percent of fair market value, determined by the mean of the high and low prices, on the date of grant. The plan expired in fiscal 1997; however, exercisable options representing 35,000 shares remain outstanding at August 31, 2002.

The Company's stock option plan for outside directors provided that each director who was not a current or former full-time employee of the Company received an option to purchase 10,000 shares of the Company's common stock at prices equal to 100 percent of the fair market value, determined by the mean of the high and low prices on the date of grant. The Board of Directors has terminated this plan as to future grants. Future grants of options to outside directors are made under the Company's 1997 stock option plan described as follows.

The Company's 1997 stock option plan provides additional incentives to those officers, employees, directors, advisors and consultants of the Company whose substantial contributions are essential to the continued growth and success of the Company's business. A total of 2,000,000 shares of the Company's common stock may be issued or transferred or used as the basis of stock appreciation rights under the 1997 stock option plan. The plan allows the granting of nonqualified and incentive stock options as well as stock appreciation rights. The plan is administered by a committee appointed by the Company's Board of Directors. The option prices for these shares shall not be less than 85 percent of the fair market value of a share at the time of option granting for nonqualified stock options or less than 100 percent for incentive stock options. The term of each option expires and all rights to purchase shares thereunder cease ten years after the date such option is granted or on such date prior thereto as may be fixed by the committee. Options granted under this plan become exercisable six months after the date the option is granted unless otherwise set forth in the agreement. Outstanding options granted to employees generally vest in three equal annual installments provided that all options granted under the 1997 stock option plan shall become vested in full and immediately upon the occurrence of a change in control of the Company.

A summary of stock option activity for fiscal 2002, 2001 and 2000 is as follows:

	2002			2001			2000		
	Shares	Price per Share	Wtd. Avg. Exercise Price/Sh	Shares	Price per Share	Wtd. Avg. Exercise Price/Sh	Shares	Price per Share	Wtd. Avg. Exercise Price/Sh
Outstanding at beginning of year	788,168	$ 7 - $20	$ 12.51	795,514	$ 4 - $20	$ 10.88	680,176	$ 4 - $15	$ 8.56
Options granted	165,950	22 - 39	23.13	312,000	12 - 18	12.83	180,800	19 - 20	18.59
Options exercised	(279,614)	8 - 19	11.44	(312,944)	4 - 19	8.64	(65,462)	6 - 10	8.15
Options canceled	- - -	- - -	- - -	(6,402)	9 - 19	13.84	---	---	---
Outstanding at end of year	674,504	$7 - $39	$15.57	788,168	$7 - $20	$12.51	795,514	$4 - $20	$10.88
Exercisable at end of year	302,271	$7 - $39	$13.89	352,018	$7 - $20	$11.33	469,214	$4 - $20	$8.40

The following table summarizes information about stock options outstanding at August 31, 2002:

Range of Exercise Prices	Number Outstanding at August 31, 2002	Weighted Remaining Years of Contractual Life	Weighted Average Exercise Price	Number Exercisable at August 31, 2002	Weighted Average Exercise Price
$ 7.19 - $ 8.88	64,000	4	$ 8.16	64,000	$ 8.16
10.19 - 15.38	318,359	7	11.94	145,026	11.35
18.00 - 19.72	126,195	7	18.55	76,995	18.58
21.62 - 39.48	165,950	9	23.13	16,250	37.00
	674,504	8	$ 15.57	302,271	$ 13.89

In 1997, the Company adopted SFAS No. 123, Accounting for Stock-Based Compensation. The Company has elected to continue following the accounting guidance of Accounting Principles Board Opinion No. 25, Accounting for Stock Issued to Employees for measurement and recognition of stock-based transactions with employees. No compensation cost has been recognized for options issued under the stock option plans because the exercise price of all options granted was not less than 100 percent of fair market value of the common stock on the date of grant. Had compensation cost for the stock options issued been determined based on the fair value at the grant date, consistent with provisions of SFAS No. 123, the Company's 2002, 2001 and 2000 income and income per share would have been changed to the pro forma amounts indicated as follows:

(dollars in thousands, except per share data)	2002	2001	2000
Net income			
As reported	$ 54,671	$ 42,704	$ 48,399
Pro forma	52,881	41,006	47,143
Income per share (basic)			
As reported	$ 2.74	$ 2.06	$ 2.23
Pro forma	2.65	1.98	2.17
Income per share (diluted)			
As reported	$ 2.68	$ 2.03	$ 2.20
Pro forma	2.59	1.95	2.14

The fair value of each option grant is estimated on the date of grant using the Black-Scholes option-pricing model with the following assumptions:

	2002	2001	2000
Dividend yield	.87%	1.13%	1.21%
Risk-free interest rate	3.22%	4.55%	6.92%
Expected life	5 years	5 years	5 years
Expected volatility	55.82%	49.92%	49.64%
Estimated fair value of options granted per share	$10.08	$5.29	$8.30

Note 11: Supplemental Cash Flow Disclosure

Cash paid during the year for:

(dollars in thousands)	August 31, 2002	Year Ended August 25, 2001	August 26, 2000
Income taxes	$ 29,306	$ 18,205	$ 28,305
Interest	246	3	249

Note 12: Business Segment Information

The Company defines its operations into two business segments: Recreation Vehicles and Other Manufactured Products and Dealer Financing. Recreation Vehicles and Other Manufactured Products includes all data relative to the manufacturing and selling of the Company's Class A, B and C motor home products as well as sales of component products for other manufacturers and recreation vehicle related parts and service revenue. Dealer Financing includes floorplan financing for a limited number of the Company's dealers. Management focuses on operating income as a segment's measure of profit or loss when evaluating a segment's financial performance. Operating income is before interest expense, interest income, and income taxes. A variety of balance sheet ratios are used by management to measure the business. Maximizing the return from each segment's assets excluding cash and cash equivalents is the primary focus. The accounting policies of the segments are the same as those described in the Summary of Significant Accounting Policies (Note 1). Identifiable assets are those assets used in the operations of each industry segment. General Corporate assets consist of cash and cash equivalents, deferred income taxes and other corporate assets not related to the two business segments. General Corporate income and expenses include administrative costs. Intersegment sales and expenses are not significant.

For the years ended August 31, 2002, August 25, 2001 and August 26, 2000, the Company's segment information is as follows:

(dollars in thousands)	Recreation Vehicles & Other Manufactured Products	Dealer Financing	General Corporate	Total
2002 (53 weeks)				
Net revenues	$ 825,269	$ 3,134	$ - - -	$ 828,403
Operating income	79,299	1,224	674	81,197
Identifiable assets	223,792	38,138	75,147	337,077
Depreciation and amortization	7,664	3	212	7,879
Capital expenditures	10,889	20	88	10,997
2001				
Net revenues	$ 671,686	$ 4,241	$ - - -	$ 675,927
Operating income	52,120	1,275	2,079	55,474
Identifiable assets	176,731	40,856	134,335	351,922
Depreciation and amortization	7,158	5	217	7,380
Capital expenditures	8,974	19	96	9,089
2000				
Net revenues	$ 743,729	$ 3,908	$ - - -	$ 747,637
Operating income	67,252	1,152	2,250	70,654
Identifiable assets	191,501	33,508	83,677	308,686
Depreciation and amortization	6,375	4	243	6,622
Capital expenditures	14,412	- - -	136	14,548

Net Revenues By Major Product Class

(dollars in thousands)	August 31, 2002	August 25, 2001	August 26, 2000	August 28, 1999	August 29, 1998
	Fiscal Year Ended (1) (2)				
Motor homes (Class A & C)	$773,125	$624,110	$690,022	$613,813	$470,932
	93.3%	92.4%	92.3%	91.4%	89.0%
Other recreation vehicle revenues (3)	20,486	17,808	18,813	16,620	19,222
	2.5%	2.6%	2.5%	2.5%	3.6%
Other manufactured products revenues (4)	31,658	29,768	34,894	38,225	37,133
	3.8%	4.4%	4.7%	5.7%	7.0%
Total manufactured products revenues	825,269	671,686	743,729	668,658	527,287
	99.6%	99.4%	99.5%	99.6%	99.6%
Finance revenues (5)	3,134	4,241	3,908	2,995	2,076
	.4%	.6%	.5%	.4%	.4%
Total net revenues	$828,403	$675,927	$747,637	$671,653	$529,363
	100.0%	100.0%	100.0%	100.0%	100.0%

(1) Certain prior periods' information has been reclassified to conform to the current year-end presentation. These reclassification's have no impact on net income as previously reported.
(2) The fiscal year ended August 31, 2002 contained 53 weeks; all other fiscal years contained 52 weeks.
(3) Primarily recreation vehicle related parts, EuroVan Campers (Class B motor homes), and recreation vehicle service revenue.
(4) Primarily sales of extruded aluminum, commercial vehicles, and component products for other manufacturers.
(5) WAC revenues from dealer financing.

Note 13: Income Per Share

The following table reflects the calculation of basic and diluted income per share for the past three fiscal years:

(in thousands, except per share data)	August 31, 2002 (1)	August 25, 2001	August 26, 2000
Income per share - basic			
Net income	$ 54,671	$ 42,704	$ 48,399
Weighted average shares outstanding	19,949	20,735	21,680
Net income per share - basic	$ 2.74	$ 2.06	$ 2.23
Income per share - assuming dilution			
Net income	$ 54,671	$ 42,704	$ 48,399
Weighted average shares outstanding	19,949	20,735	21,680
Dilutive impact of options outstanding	435	305	331
Weighted average shares and potential dilutive shares outstanding	20,384	21,040	22,011
Net income per share - assuming dilution	$ 2.68	$ 2.03	$ 2.20

(1) Fiscal year ended August 31, 2002 contained 53 weeks; all other fiscal years contained 52 weeks.

Note 14: Preferred Stock and Shareholders Rights Plan

The Board of Directors may authorize the issuance from time to time of preferred stock in one or more series with such designations, preferences, qualifications, limitations, restrictions, and optional or other special rights as the Board may fix by resolution. In connection with the Rights Plan discussed below, the Board of Directors has reserved, but not issued, 300,000 shares of preferred stock.

In May 2000, the Company adopted a shareholder rights plan providing for a dividend distribution of one preferred share purchase right for each share of common stock outstanding on and after May 26, 2000. The rights can be exercised only if an individual or group acquires or announces a tender offer for 15 percent or more of the Company's common stock. Certain members of the Hanson family (including trusts and estates established by such Hanson family members and the John K. and Luise V. Hanson Foundation) are exempt from the applicability of the Rights Plan as it relates to the acquisition of 15 percent or more of the Company's outstanding common stock. If the rights first become exercisable as a result of an announced tender offer, each right would entitle the holder (other than the individual or group acquiring or announcing a tender offer for 15 percent or more of the Company's common stock) to buy 1/100 of a share of a new series of preferred stock at an exercise price of $67.25. The preferred shares will be entitled to 100 times the per share dividend payable on the Company's common stock and to 100 votes on all matters submitted to a vote of the shareowners. Once an individual or group acquires 15 percent or more of the Company's common stock, each right held by such individual or group becomes void and the remaining rights will then entitle the holder to purchase the number of common shares having a market value of twice the exercise price of the right. In the event the Company is acquired in a merger or 50 percent or more of its consolidated assets or earnings power are sold, each right will then entitle the holder to purchase a number of the acquiring company's common shares having a market value of twice the exercise price of the right. After an individual or group acquires 15 percent of the Company's common stock and before they acquire 50 percent, the Company's Board of Directors may exchange the rights in whole or in part, at an exchange ratio of one share of common stock per right. Before an individual or group acquires 15 percent of the Company's common stock, the rights are redeemable for $.01 per right at the option of the Company's Board of Directors. The Company's Board of Directors is authorized to reduce the 15 percent threshold to no less than 10 percent. Each right will expire on May 3, 2010, unless earlier redeemed by the Company.

Common Stock Data

The Company's common stock is listed on the New York, Chicago and Pacific Stock Exchanges.
Ticker symbol: WGO
Shareholders of record as of November 12, 2002: 4,922.
Below are the New York Stock Exchange high, low and closing prices of Winnebago Industries, Inc. stock for each quarter of fiscal 2002 and fiscal 2001.

Fiscal 2002	High	Low	Close	Fiscal 2001	High	Low	Close
First Quarter	$33.70	$17.30	$33.70	First Quarter	$13.63	$10.75	$11.50
Second Quarter	48.85	32.39	47.45	Second Quarter	19.00	11.56	17.10
Third Quarter	51.43	39.35	44.40	Third Quarter	19.60	15.60	18.77
Fourth Quarter	48.60	31.85	38.19	Fourth Quarter	30.75	18.44	28.02

Cash Dividends Per Share

Fiscal 2002		Fiscal 2001	
Amount	Date Paid	Amount	Date Paid
$ .10	January 7, 2002	$ .10	January 8, 2001
.10	July 8, 2002	.10	July 9, 2001

Interim Financial Information (Unaudited)

(dollars in thousands, except per share data)	Quarter Ended			
Fiscal 2002	December 1, 2001	March 2, 2002	June 1, 2002	August 31, 2002
Net revenues	$177,802	$183,055	$246,636	$220,910
Gross profit	24,232	22,938	37,255	35,113
Operating income	15,311	13,414	27,289	25,183
Net income	10,710	9,448	18,094	16,419
Net income per share (basic)	.52	.46	.93	.88
Net income per share (diluted)	.51	.45	.90	.86

Quarter ended December 1, 2001 contained 14 weeks.

	Quarter Ended			
Fiscal 2001	November 25, 2000	February 24, 2001	May 26, 2001	August 25, 2001
Net revenues	$162,702	$141,308	$195,605	$176,312
Gross profit	20,782	15,779	26,182	24,623
Operating income	13,380	8,550	18,098	15,446
Net income	8,546	6,184	12,444	15,530
Net income per share (basic)	.40	.30	.61	.75
Net income per share (diluted)	.40	.30	.60	.74

Quarter ended November 25, 2000 contains an adjustment of $1,050,000 for the cumulative effect of a change in accounting principle, net of taxes.

During the quarter ended August 25, 2001, the Company recorded a $4.5 million tax benefit in connection with the expiration of certain tax statutes.

Certain prior periods' information has been reclassified to conform to the current year end presentation. This reclassification has no impact on net income as previously reported.

Shareholder Information

Publications
A notice of Annual Meeting of Shareholders and Proxy Statement is furnished to shareholders in advance of the annual meeting.

Copies of the Company's quarterly financial news releases and the annual report on Form 10-K (without exhibits), required to be filed by the Company with the Securities and Exchange Commission, may be obtained without charge from the corporate offices as follows:

Sheila Davis, PR/IR Manager
Winnebago Industries, Inc.
605 W. Crystal Lake Road
P.O. Box 152
Forest City, Iowa 50436-0152
Telephone: (641) 585-3535
Fax: (641) 585-6966
E-Mail: ir@winnebagoind.com

This annual report as well as corporate news releases may also be viewed online in the Investor Relations section of Winnebago Industries website:
http://www.winnebagoind.com

Shareholder Account Assistance
Transfer Agent to contact for address changes, account certificates and stock holdings:

Wells Fargo Bank Minnesota, N.A.
P.O. Box 64854
St. Paul, Minnesota 55164-0854
or
161 North Concord Exchange
South St. Paul, Minnesota 55075-1139
Telephone: (800) 468-9716 or
(651) 450-4064
Inquirees:
www.wellsfargo.com/com/shareowner_services

Annual Meeting
The Annual Meeting of Shareholders is scheduled to be held on Tuesday, January 14, 2003, at 7:30 p.m. (CST) in Friendship Hall, Highway 69 South, Forest City, Iowa.

Auditor
Deloitte & Touche LLP
400 One Financial Plaza
120 South Sixth Street
Minneapolis, Minnesota 55402-1844

Purchase of Common Stock
Winnebago Industries stock may be purchased from Netstock through the Company's website at http://www.winnebagoind.com/investor_relations.htm. Winnebago Industries is not affiliated with Netstock and has no involvement in the relationship between Netstock and any of its customers.

Directors and Officers

Directors

Bruce D. Hertzke (51)
Chairman of the Board,
Chief Executive Officer
and President
Winnebago Industries, Inc.

Gerald E. Boman (67)
Former Senior Vice President
Winnebago Industries, Inc.

Jerry N. Currie (57)
President and Chief Executive Officer
CURRIES Company and GRAHAM
Manufacturing

Joseph W. England (62)
Former Senior Vice President
Deere and Company

John V. Hanson (60)
Former Deputy Chairman of the
Board
Winnebago Industries, Inc.

Gerald C. Kitch (64)
Former Executive Vice President
Pentair, Inc.

Richard C. Scott (68)
Vice President, University
Development
Baylor University

Frederick M. Zimmerman (66)
Professor of Manufacturing Systems
Engineering
The University of St. Thomas

Luise V. Hanson (89)
Director Emeritus

Officers

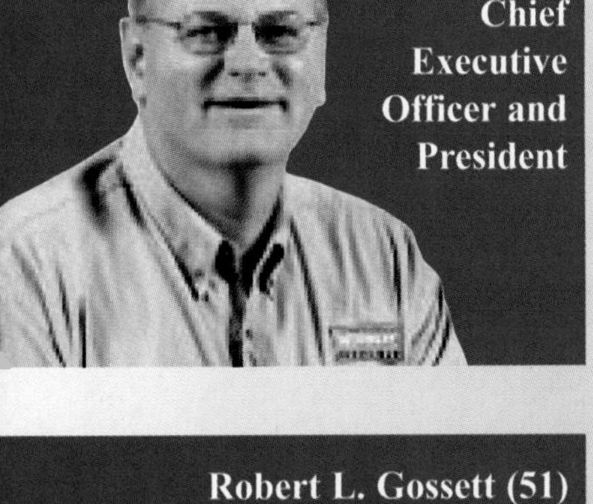

Bruce D. Hertzke (51)
Chairman of the Board, Chief Executive Officer and President

Edwin F. Barker (55)
Vice President, Chief Financial Officer

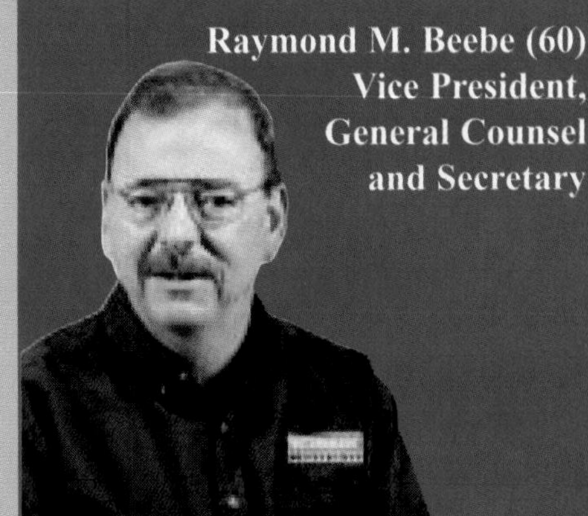

Raymond M. Beebe (60)
Vice President, General Counsel and Secretary

Robert L. Gossett (51)
Vice President, Administration

Brian J. Hrubes (51)
Controller

James P. Jaskoviak (50)
Vice President, Sales and Marketing

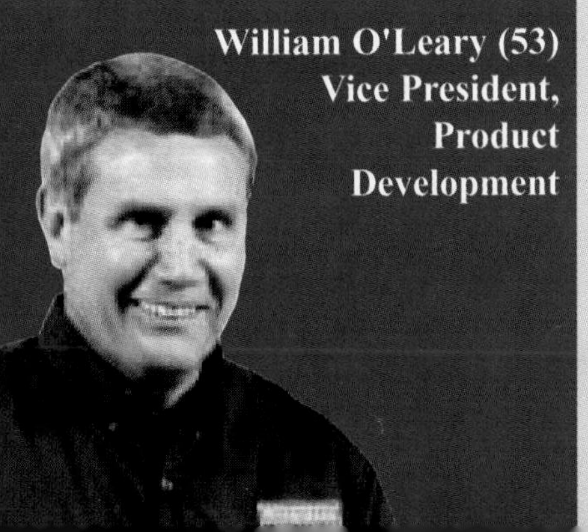

William O'Leary (53)
Vice President, Product Development

Robert J. Olson (51)
Vice President, Manufacturing

Joseph L. Soczek, Jr. (59)
Treasurer

Monaco Coach Corporation
2002 Annual Report
NYSE: MNC
2002

FINANCIAL HIGHLIGHTS

Dollars in thousands, except earnings per share and shares outstanding data.

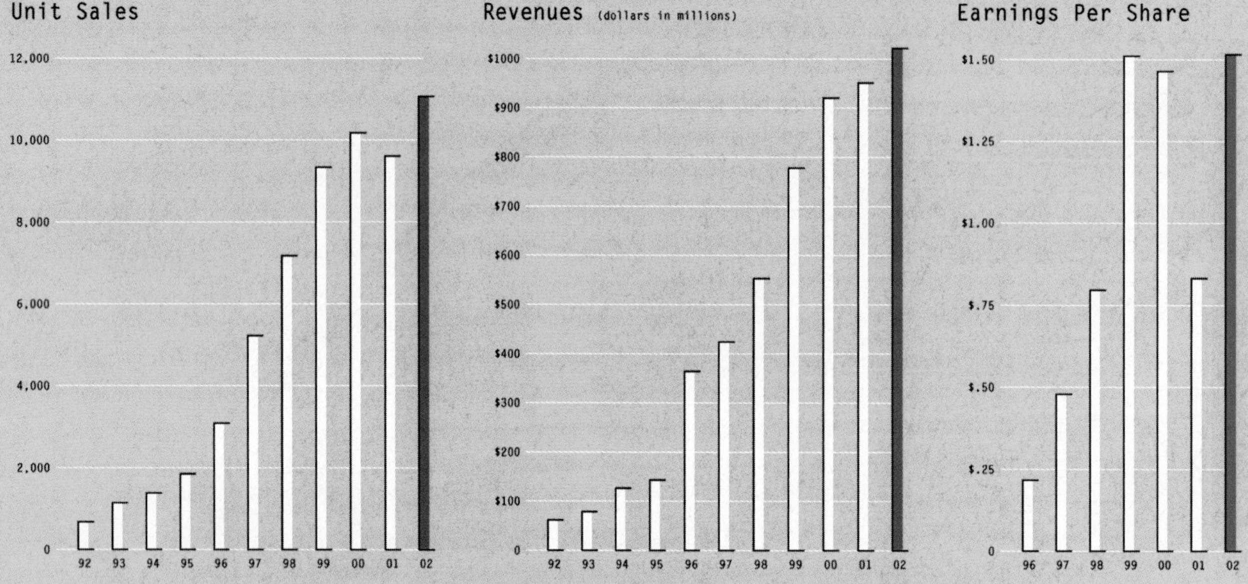

	2000	2001*	2002
Sales	$901,890	$937,073	$1,222,689
Gross Profit	$129,650	$ 113,990	$163,129
Operating Income	$69,830	$42,658	$75,927
Pretax Income	$69,380	$40,635	$73,280
Net Income	$42,521	$24,919	$44,515
Earnings Per Share	$1.47	$0.85	$1.51
Average Common Shares Outstanding	28,978,265	29,288,688	29,573,420

* Includes results from Safari and Beaver divisions acquired on August 6, 2001.

OUR FOUNDATION

As Monaco Coach Corporation continues to broaden its product line, expand its customer base, add more dealerships and attract new stockholders, the Company is committed to maintaining those standards which make the "Monaco Difference" so important to every member of the MNC "family."

To do this, the Company continues to follow our six corporate goals:

To operate the business on the basis of honesty, integrity and superior service.

To produce the highest-quality recreational vehicles at the most competitive prices.

To create and nurture a lifestyle for RV owners that exceeds their dreams.

To offer a working environment in which all employees have the opportunity to realize their personal and professional goals.

To create a bond with our suppliers and retail dealers that ensures our mutual success.

To provide our shareholders with a positive return on their investment.

These are not lofty goals or idealistic statements; rather, they are a continuation of the basic guidelines and principles which have been an integral part of the Company's success.

Maintaining these guidelines and principles throughout the Company's current and future growth will enable MNC to retain the outstanding loyalty of its present customers, employees and dealers, and forge an equally strong link with new customers, employees, dealers and stockholders who are now or soon will be part of the MNC family.

CORPORATE PROFILE

Monaco Coach Corporation is a leading manufacturer of luxury motorcoaches and one of the most prominent companies in the overall recreational vehicle field.

The corporation's broad product line includes diesel and gasoline-powered class A motorhomes, class C mini-motorhomes, travel trailers and fifth wheel towable recreational vehicles. This highly diversified line, ranging in price from $25,000 to more than $1,100,000, is marketed under the Monaco, Holiday Rambler, Beaver, Safari, McKenzie and Royale Coach brand names. Monaco Coach Corporation products are represented by an expanding network of independent retail dealerships.

Headquartered in Coburg, Oregon, with additional facilities in Oregon and Indiana, Monaco Coach Corporation is traded on the NYSE under the symbol MNC. 2002 revenues reached a record $1.22 billion, resulting in earnings of $1.51 per share. Unit sales grew from 550 in 1993 to 11,211 in 2002. The Company's growth rate over that period of time is unmatched by any publicly traded company in the recreational vehicle industry.

Pictured left to right: MNC President John Nepute, CEO Kay Toolson and CFO Marty Daley

TO MY FELLOW SHAREHOLDERS,

On October 25, 2002, Monaco Coach Corporation surpassed one billion dollars in revenue for the year. This milestone marked the first time in our Company's history we have crossed the billion-dollar mark in a given year.

It was a truly happy occasion for all of us, especially those who have been here since the early days. One billion dollars is a far cry from the $17 million we grossed in 1987, my first full year with the Company. We couldn't have realized this accomplishment without employees at every level working together toward the same goals. Through the good times and challenging times, it's been a complete team effort, and everyone at Monaco Coach Corporation deserves to be proud of this special achievement.

When we first heard the news, we were reviewing a letter from an unsatisfied customer. Frankly, we were more concerned about how we were going to make that customer happy than any milestone our Company might have reached that day. As impressive as this accomplishment is, and as proud as we are, we would gladly trade it for 100% customer satisfaction. Unlike realizing a financial goal, our goal to provide an exceptional recreational vehicle experience to every customer has no end. We work hard to achieve it every single day.

2002: A LOOK BACK

Total 2002 industry wholesale unit shipments outpaced 2001 by nearly 20%. Our dealer partners enjoyed increased retail sales despite lingering economic uncertainty. Aided by low interest rates and growing retail demand, dealers allowed inventory to build gradually throughout the year.

Record unit sales of 11,211 allowed Monaco Coach Corporation to

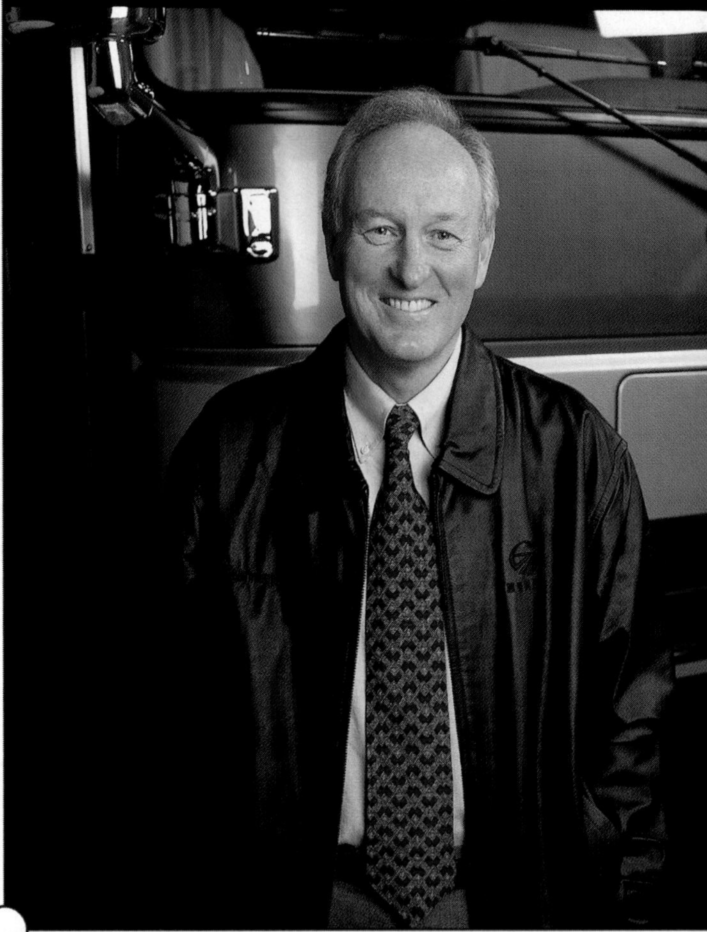

Monaco Coach Corporation Chairman and Chief Executive Officer Kay Toolson

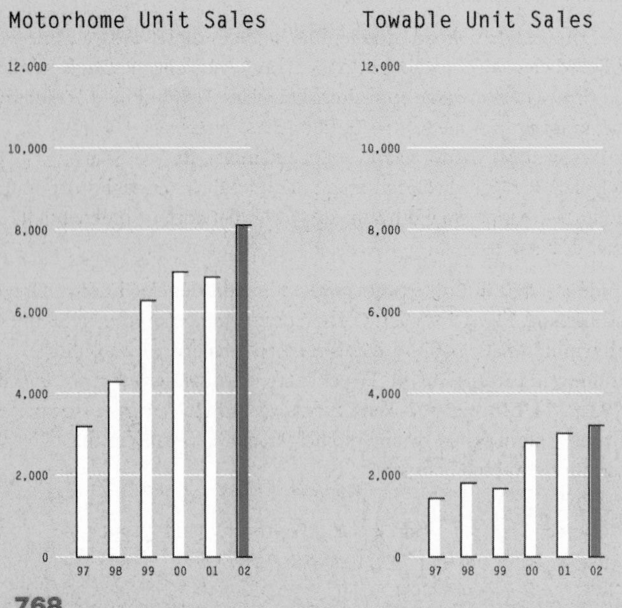

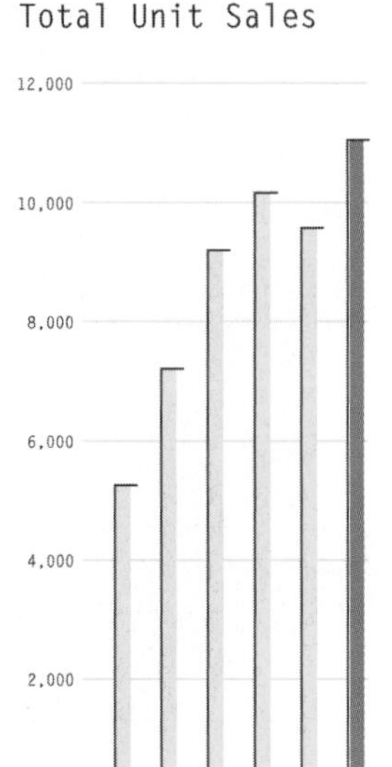

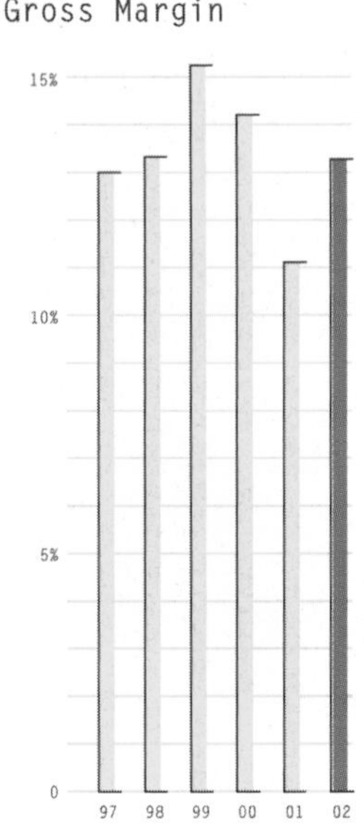

reach $1.22 billion in revenue in 2002. Earnings per share rose to $1.51, up from 85 cents in 2001. Net income reached $44.5 million, up from $25 million a year ago. Gross margin rebounded from 12.2% in 2001 to 13.3% in 2002, and our sales, general and administrative (S, G &A) expenses were reduced from 7.5% in 2001 to 7.1% in 2002. Our motorhome sales grew to a record 8,005 units, and the towable market remained strong in 2002. Although our towable production was capacity constrained in 2002, our travel-trailer and fifth-wheel towable shipments reached 3,206.

Our acquisition of SMC Corporation is more than a year behind us, and we're focused on building value and unique character into the Safari and Beaver product lines. As a result, we've added dealer partners and excited many loyal Safari and Beaver customers. We integrated these SMC models into our operations throughout the year, resulting in production efficiencies and economies of scale that contributed to better gross margins.

We also expanded our customer service capabilities in 2002. Our new 40-bay customer service center in Harrisburg, Oregon, helps our dealer partners meet the service needs of our growing owner family. In addition, we finalized construction of a new, larger regional service center in Wildwood, Florida, which opened in March, 2003. We're working with our dealer partners to provide an exceptional service experience for every customer.

We have known for some time that luxurious RV accommodations are an important part of our customers' lifestyle and critical to the continued growth of our market. That's why two years ago we formed an alliance with Outdoor Resorts of America (ORA), a premier builder of luxury RV resorts. Our original role was that of a lender on three new projects, in Las Vegas, Nevada, in Naples, Florida, and in Indio, California, near Palm Springs.

The downturn in the economy forced a change in our relationship with ORA, and it became necessary for us to acquire the three properties. We have since completed initial development of the Las Vegas and Indio resorts and have decided to sell the undeveloped property in Naples, Florida. We expect to close the sale of that property in mid-2003. ORA continues site management at the Las Vegas and Indio resorts.

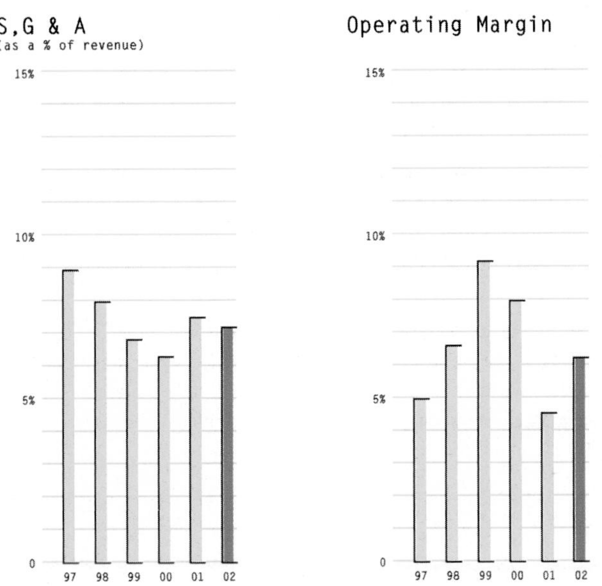

Each ORA resort has a country club atmosphere and a true sense of community for residents and guests. The resorts are subdivided into individual lots, and we realize a return on our investment with each lot sale.

2003: A LOOK AHEAD

Although we remain optimistic, we're mindful of the challenges and uncertainties confronting our market. However, favorable demographic trends, changing attitudes toward leisure travel and innovative products are driving our industry to new heights.

The recreational vehicle industry is very competitive, with new products from many manufacturers offering solid features at aggressive prices. We must continue to pay close attention to our dealer partners and retail customers in order to stay ahead of our competition and attract positive attention to our brands. Product development is a critical element of our strategy for 2003. We'll concentrate on new product innovations, particularly in the competitive gasoline motorhome and entry-level diesel motorhome segments. We're also determined to continue leading the high-end diesel motorhome market, and we see great opportunities in the towable market.

One of our most important assignments as managers is to keep an eye on dealer inventory levels, especially given the recent challenges in the retail market. In early 2003, we launched several retail sales promotions and incentive programs designed to help our dealer partners generate lot traffic, increase sales and turn inventory. These promotions hurt our gross margins and increase our sales expenses, but they also assist in preserving (or in some cases growing) market share in a difficult market. Although we expect our sales expenses to rise, improved manufacturing efficiencies will partially offset gross margin pressure.

We recently announced a towable manufacturing expansion in Elkhart, Indiana. This $5 million investment will double our towable production capacity to approximately 130 units per week. Our towables experienced strong demand in 2002, and the future outlook for this market segment remains favorable. Our plant expansion will be complete mid-year, and we will gradually utilize this additional capacity throughout the second half of 2003.

Cash generated in 2003 will be used to reduce debt and fund capital improvements such as expansion of our towable production facility, our paint facility in Indiana, and our new Florida service facility. One of our goals is to substantially reduce our long-term debt this year.

Thank you for your support. As I've said many times, I feel truly blessed to be a part of this wonderful organization. The success we've enjoyed would not have been possible without the hard work of our dedicated employees, the strength of our supplier relationships, or the thoughtful guidance of our board of directors. We owe an enormous debt of gratitude to our supportive dealer partners and to every happy Monaco Coach Corporation customer on the road today. We also appreciate our past, present and future shareholders. You've supported our growth and your support will allow us to grow for many years to come. On behalf of everyone associated with Monaco Coach Corporation, I thank you.

Sincerely,

Kay L. Toolson

Chairman and Chief Executive Officer

A LOOK BACK

For the RV industry, 2002 was a year of recovery. For Monaco Coach Corporation, 2002 was a banner year.

With total revenues for the year of $1.22 billion, the Company crossed the billion-dollar mark for the first time in its history. It also enjoyed record unit sales of 11,211. Low interest rates and rebounding retail demand spurred a rise in dealer orders, driving revenue growth. At the same time, sales expenses fell and gross margins improved because the Company was operating more efficiently. Earnings nearly doubled in 2002, to $1.51 per share from 85 cents per share in 2001. Net income soared to $44.5 million last year from $25 million the year before.

Near the end of 2001, two events combined to slow the pace of recovery in the RV market. The first, of course, was the terrorist attacks of September 11, 2001. Like merchants in many other segments of the economy, RV dealers feared the worst and adjusted their expectations accordingly. Although retail demand quickly returned, the attacks delayed recovery into the first part of 2002. The second event was Monaco Coach Corporation's acquisition of SMC Corporation in August 2001. The deal made Monaco Coach Corporation an even stronger motorhome manufacturer, specifically in the diesel class A market. But as a result, the Company faced a huge task — consolidating and absorbing manufacturing and service responsibilities of a former rival. Consolidation activities and product redesigns temporarily hurt plant efficiencies and negatively impacted gross margins. Overall retail demand improved in early 2002 and remained relatively healthy throughout the year, although economic anxiety and the prospect of war dampened sales as the year ended.

Earnings rebounded in 2002. Two factors explain the increase. First, low dealer inventories and returning retail demand allowed Monaco Coach Corporation to reduce incentive programs that impacted both sales expenses and gross margins in 2000-2001. Second, the Company continued the process of absorbing SMC throughout 2002. By the end of the year, most of the initial costs incurred through the acquisition were behind the Company. The absorption boosted plant efficiencies and capacity utilization, resulting in gross margin improvement.

Diesel-powered motorhome chassis production is an example of Monaco Coach Corporation's vertically integrated operations. The recent acquisition of SMC Corporation has allowed the company to leverage plant efficiencies to improve gross margins.

PRODUCTION CONSOLIDATION

The absorption of SMC into Monaco Coach Corporation was a complicated process, but one that was well worth the effort.

In 2002, Monaco Coach Corporation finished shifting the manufacturing of the Safari product line into its Coburg, Oregon, factory. The integration allows a greater degree of capacity utilization at the Coburg plant. It makes for more efficient coach production and increased economies of scale. New efficiencies, in turn, enhance margins.

After the purchase, SMC's Beaver and Safari product lines were redesigned. They were also expanded, introducing the brands into new market segments. Safari and Beaver were under-represented in the retail market, and these new products enticed additional dealers to represent the brands. Loyal Beaver and Safari customers finally have new, attractive products to consider. Meanwhile, the brands are penetrating new niches for the first time.

The $1.5 million remodel of the former Safari production facility in Harrisburg, Oregon, as a customer service center was also completed in 2002. With 40 service bays, the new center is much larger than the former customer service facility in Coburg.

Following the SMC acquisition, Safari brand motorhome production was consolidated into Monaco Coach Corporation's Coburg, Oregon, facility. This move allowed the Company to increase capacity utilization and production efficiency.

Motorhome Market

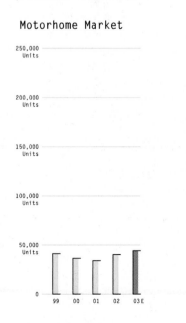

250,000 Units
200,000 Units
150,000 Units
100,000 Units
50,000 Units
0
99 00 01 02 03E

Towable Market

250,000 Units
200,000 Units
150,000 Units
100,000 Units
50,000 Units
0
99 00 01 02 03E

* Courtesy of the Recreational Vehicle Industry Association

Class A Retail Market Share*

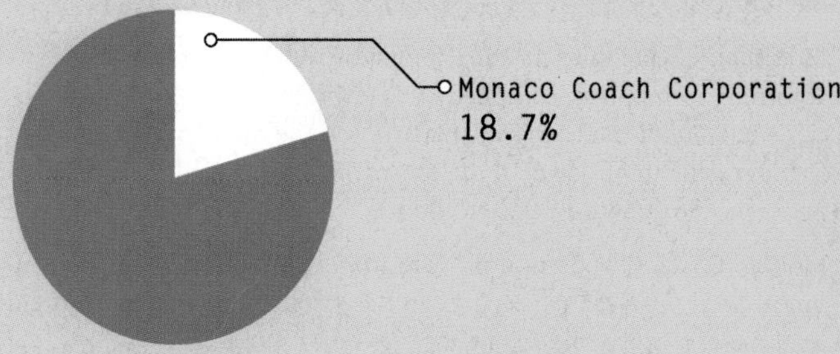

Diesel Retail Market Share*

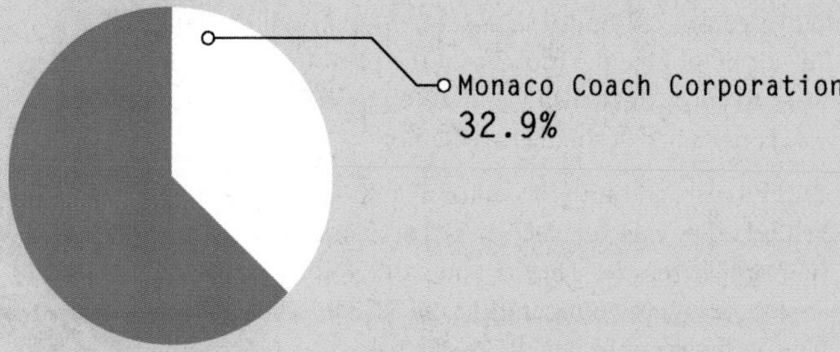

Gas Retail Market Share*

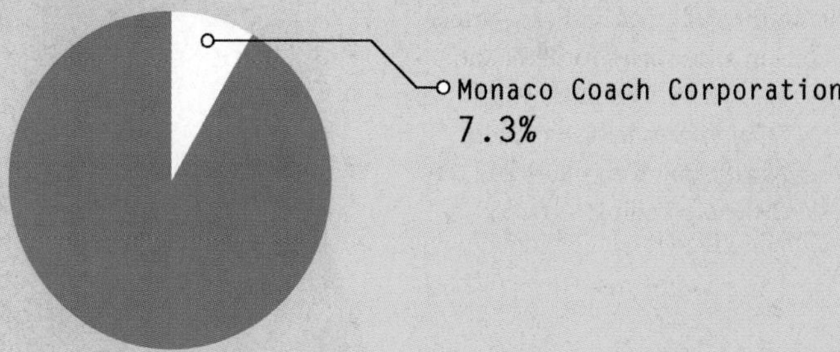

MNC Revenue Breakdown

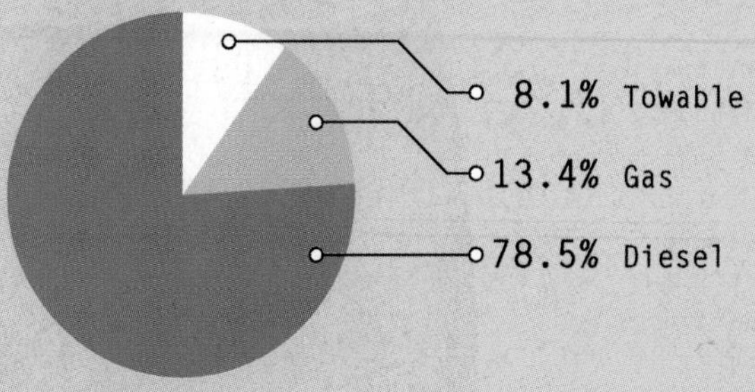

* Courtesy of Statistical Surveys, Inc.

A LOOK AHEAD

While 2002 was a successful year for Monaco Coach Corporation, favorable demographic trends, changing attitudes toward leisure travel and innovative new products provide opportunities for growth well into the future.

Motorhome retail sales in 2002 jumped 9% from the prior year, according to numbers compiled by Statistical Surveys, Inc. This increase came in spite of the economic malaise and the threat of war. Demographic trends favored the RV market in general, as did a growing preference for traveling close to home.

Monaco Coach Corporation plans to introduce a full slate of product innovations this year, particularly in the gasoline motorhome and entry-level diesel motorhome segments.

The steady growth of the market for towables inspired a significant item on the 2003 agenda: a planned expansion of the towable production facility in Elkhart, Indiana.

When completed mid-year, the $5 million addition will effectively double the capacity of the plant from 65 units per week to approximately 130. In 2002, production capacity was constrained at the Elkhart facility.

Travel trailers and fifth wheel towable RVs are towed behind other vehicles, such as pickup trucks or sport utility vehicles. They are often the RVs of choice for a new, younger group of RV buyers (between the age of 35-45) who are starting to enter the market in larger numbers than ever before.

Towables typically cost much less than motorhomes and are perfect add-on accessories for SUVs or pickup trucks. The number of SUVs and personal use pickups on North American roads has skyrocketed, and each owner is a potential towable buyer. Monaco Coach Corporation plans to make use of the expanded capacity in the Elkhart facility at a gradual pace in the second half of 2003. The Company also expects to take advantage of its added flexibility to explore new towable market segments.

Additionally, the Company plans an expansion of its motorhome paint facility in Wakarusa, Indiana. Over the past few years, retail customers have

Customers' preference for more elaborate paint schemes on lower-priced motorhomes has lead to a planned expansion of Monaco Coach Corporation's paint facilities.

demanded increasingly sophisticated paint designs on much lower-priced motorhomes, prompting Monaco Coach Corporation to expand its paint capabilities to meet this market evolution.

A new, larger regional service center in Wildwood, Florida, will also open this year. This state-of-the-art facility consolidates Company-operated service centers in Tampa and Leesburg, Florida.

Last year, the Company initiated enhancements to its quality assurance process that should continue to benefit customers into 2003 and beyond. The "White Glove" inspection process is designed to mimic a retail dealer's delivery activities. Information garnered through these careful inspections is communicated back to the product development, engineering and production teams in order to continually improve overall product quality.

Monaco Coach Corporation also introduced the RV industry's first certified pre-owned program and company-branded extended warranty program in 2002, and these popular programs will continue for 2003. Qualifying pre-owned Monaco Coach Corporation products can be sold by retail dealers as certified after passing a comprehensive inspection. This program, along with Monaco Coach Corporation's branded extended warranty program, provide its retail dealer partners with powerful additional sales tools.

The big question mark heading into 2003 is retail demand. Interest rates remain at low levels, reducing retail dealers' inventory costs. But retail customers' confidence is shaken by the prospect of war on the horizon and an economic forecast which continues to be gloomy in the short term.

At the start of 2003 Monaco Coach Corporation announced incentives to support its dealer partners in this uncertain climate. These incentives are conceptually similar to the Company's successful programs of 2000-2001. The new programs reduce gross margins and increase sales expenses. However, further efficiencies gained in the absorption of SMC will partially offset the incentives' effect on operating margins. Furthermore, the incentives are expected to boost sales until the economy improves and war clouds lift. The Company intends to apply cash generated this year to debt reduction and capital improvements.

When the climate improves, prospects for RV sales are especially bright. Delayed customer purchases create pent-up demand which can drive recovery. Demographic trends show a larger base of potential RV customers than at any other point in history. RV dealers have effectively managed their inventory levels and can respond quickly to growing retail demand. When the political and economic climate becomes sunnier, sales of Monaco Coach Corporation products should blossom.

Monaco Coach Corporation worked quickly to integrate the SMC acquisition into its operations to gain efficiencies and to take advantage of economies of scale. Internalizing production operations improves efficiency as the Company's unit sales increase. Electronic design and assembly and composite materials technology represent areas of vertical production integration that also benefit from increased unit sales.

LUXURY RESORTS ENHANCE THE RV LIFESTYLE

Monaco Coach Corporation has long recognized the need for upscale RV resorts to accommodate luxury motorcoach owners. High-end RV resort lots are becoming a more common accessory for coach owners, who use their spaces as front yard, back yard, porch and patio. They adorn their lots with gardens, outdoor kitchens, entertainment centers, ponds, and even fountains. The resort becomes their neighborhood, a place where they share their lives with fellow RV enthusiasts when they are not on the road.

Because of this trend, Monaco Coach Corporation was interested when Outdoor Resorts of America, the leading developer of RV resorts, asked for help in financing the construction of three new properties, in Las Vegas, Florida and California. Monaco Coach Corporation saw the value in these developments and agreed to act as a lender on the projects.

The Las Vegas resort began marketing developed lots in September 2001, but the economic downturn after the terrorist attacks delayed sales. In order to ensure the viability of the projects, Monaco Coach Corporation agreed to assume ownership of the three locations, a deal that was finalized in November 2002.

The Company is selling the Florida parcel, with the sale expected to be finalized in 2003. Meanwhile, initial development is completed at the Las Vegas and California properties. The Indio, California, resort joined Las Vegas in lot sales in early 2003. ORA contributes development experience and lot sales expertise and manages operations for both resorts.

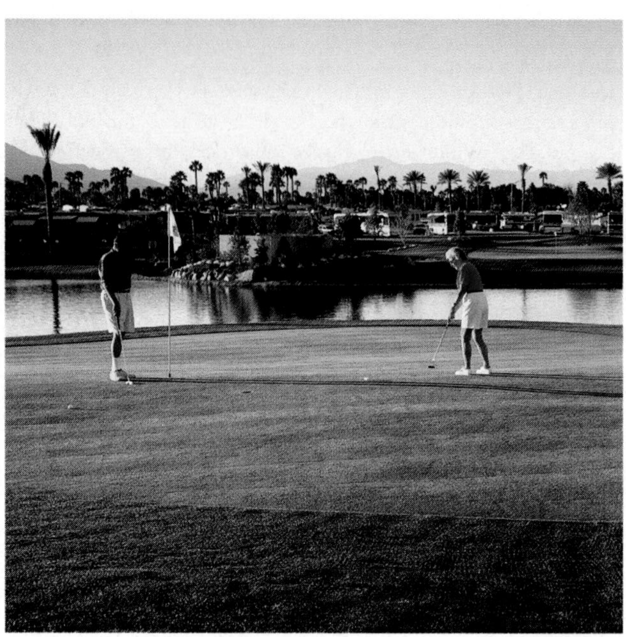

While Monaco Coach Corporation remains focused on its core RV manufacturing business, the Company recognizes the importance of promoting the RV lifestyle. To this end, Monaco Coach Corporation invested capital to facilitate upscale destination development while providing a modest return on its investment.

The resorts offer the amenities and atmosphere of a country club, the social structure and camaraderie of a planned community, and the specialized services of a resort designed for luxury motorcoaches. These resorts bring a whole new dimension of fun and allure to the RV lifestyle.

MONACO COACH CORPORATION ANNOUNCES CHANGES TO ITS BOARD OF DIRECTORS

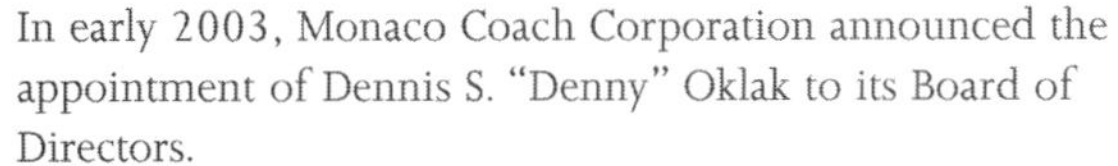

In early 2003, Monaco Coach Corporation announced the appointment of Dennis S. "Denny" Oklak to its Board of Directors.

Mr. Oklak is currently President and Chief Operating Officer of Duke Realty Corporation, one of the largest real estate investment trusts in the United States. From 1986 through January 2003, Mr. Oklak served in various other positions with Duke Realty Corporation, including Co-Chief Operating Officer, Executive Vice President and Chief Administrative Officer and Senior Vice President and Treasurer. Prior to joining Duke Realty Corporation, Mr. Oklak was with Deloitte & Touche, a Big Four public accounting firm. Mr. Oklak has a Bachelor of Science Degree in Accounting from Ball State University and is a Certified Public Accountant.

According to Kay L. Toolson, Monaco Chairman and Chief Executive Officer, "We are pleased to welcome Denny to our Board. His property management and financial expertise are extremely valuable to our Company and strengthen the diverse skills of our Board."

As members of MNC's Board of Directors, Mr. Oklak joins Carl Ring of Liberty Partners (financial services), Roger Vandenberg of Cariad Capital, Inc. (financial services), Richard Rouse (private investor), Robert "Chip" Hanafee (private investor) and L. Ben Lytle, Chairman of Anthem, Inc. (health care). Kay L. Toolson will continue as MNC's Board Chairman.

Country club amenities grace luxury RV resorts. Swimming pools, golf courses, tennis courts and clubhouses offer comfort and atmosphere for residents and guests.Each individual RV lot becomes a personal expression of the resident. Fountains, barbecues, outdoor kitchens and entertainment centers are common lot enhancements.

MARKET FOR THE REGISTRANT'S COMMON STOCK AND RELATED STOCKHOLDER MATTERS The Company's Common Stock is traded on the New York Stock Exchange under the symbol "MNC." The following table sets forth for the periods indicated the high and low closing sale prices for the Common Stock (rounded to the nearest $.01 per share).

2002	High	Low
First Quarter	$29.60	$21.77
Second Quarter	$29.50	$21.30
Third Quarter	$23.00	$15.57
Fourth Quarter	$20.03	$15.00
2001		
First Quarter	$14.49	$10.89
Second Quarter	$22.13	$10.77
Third Quarter	$20.73	$12.10
Fourth Quarter	$22.65	$13.91

As of January 31, 2003, there were approximately 763 holders of record of the Company's Common Stock. The high and low closing sales prices listed above have been adjusted to reflect the stock splits approved by the Board on August 6, 2001, May 19, 1999, November 2, 1998, and March 16, 1998.

The Company has never paid dividends on its Common Stock and currently has no plans to pay dividends on its Common Stock. The Company's existing loan agreements limit the payment of dividends on the Common Stock.

MANAGEMENT'S DISCUSSION AND ANALYSIS OF FINANCIAL CONDITION AND RESULTS OF OPERATIONS

This annual report contains forward-looking statements within the meaning of Section 27A of the Securities Act of 1933, as amended, and Section 21E of the Securities Exchange Act of 1934, as amended. These statements may generally be identified by the words "expect," "anticipate," "believe," "intend," "plan," "will," or similar expressions, and include, but are not necessarily limited to, all of the statements marked below with an asterisk (*). Such forward-looking statements involve known and unknown risks, uncertainties and other factors that may cause actual results, performance or achievements of the Company to differ materially from those expressed or implied by such forward-looking statements, including those set forth below under "Factors That May Affect Future Operating Results" within Management's Discussion and Analysis of Financial Condition and Results of Operations. The Company cautions the reader, however, that these factors may not be exhaustive.

OVERVIEW

The Company has conducted a series of acquisitions during its history, beginning in March 1993 when the Company commenced operations by acquiring substantially all of the assets and liabilities of a predecessor company that had been formed in 1968. In March 1996, the Company acquired from Harley-Davidson certain assets and assumed certain liabilities of its Holiday Rambler Division and acquired certain related dealerships. In August 2001, the Company acquired SMC Corporation, manufacturer of the Beaver and Safari brand motorhomes. In November 2002, the Company acquired from Outdoor Resorts of America ("ORA") three luxury motor coach resort properties being developed by ORA in Las Vegas, Nevada; Indio, California; and Naples, Florida.

Each of these acquisitions was accounted for using the purchase method of accounting, and the acquired operations have in each case been incorporated into the Company's consolidated financial statements. As a result, the consolidated financial statements for fiscal years 2000, 2001, and 2002 contain various acquisition-related expenses including, in 2000 and 2001, amortization of goodwill related to the acquisition of the Company's predecessor and interest expense and amortization of debt issuance costs and goodwill relating to the acquisition of Holiday Rambler. Additionally, the consolidated financial statements for fiscal years 2001 and 2002 contain interest expense and amortization of debt issuance costs related to the acquisition of SMC Corporation and, for fiscal year 2002, interest expense and amortization of debt issuance costs associated with the resort acquisition.

For years prior to 2002, the Company amortized the goodwill resulting from the acquisitions of the predecessor and Holiday Rambler using the straight-line method over a 40-year period. However, in accordance with Statements of Financial Accounting Standards No. 142, "Accounting for Goodwill and Other Intangible Assets" ("SFAS 142"), no goodwill amortization was recorded for the acquisition of SMC Corporation for the fiscal year ended December 29, 2001, and no goodwill amortization was recorded for any of the acquisitions for the fiscal year ended December 28, 2002. Management has completed its annual testing of goodwill during 2002 as required by SFAS 142 and determined that there has been no impairment requiring a write down.

RESULTS OF OPERATIONS
2002 COMPARED WITH 2001

Net sales increased 30.5% from $937.1 million in 2001 to $1.2 billion in 2002. The Company's overall unit sales were up 18.1% from 9,489 in 2001 to 11,211 units in 2002. The Company's units sales were up 28.5% on the motorized side with 16.5% of that increase due to the addition of the Safari and Beaver line of products starting in the second half of 2001. Gross diesel motorized sales revenues were up 30.6%, while gas motorized were up 45.7% and towables were up 8.2%. This reflects a stronger mix of higher priced units in each category in 2002 as the Company's overall average unit selling price increased from $99,900 in 2001 to $110,000 in 2002. The Company's diesel products accounted for 78.5% of total 2002 revenues while gas products were 13.4% and towables were 8.1% of total revenues.

Gross profit increased by $49.1 million from $114.0 million in 2001 to $163.1 million in 2002 and gross margin increased from 12.2% in 2001 to 13.3% in 2002. The increase in gross margin in 2002 was due to lower sales discounts and reductions in material costs as a percentage of sales. Through the first half of 2001, the Company found it necessary to offer above normal discounts to maintain sales to dealers. The discounting returned to normal levels in the second half of 2001 and throughout 2002. Reductions in material costs were attained by leveraging the Company's subassembly fiberglass and cabinet shop operations with higher production levels than in 2001. The Company's overall gross margin may fluctuate in future periods if the mix of products shifts from higher to lower gross margin units or if the Company encounters unexpected manufacturing difficulties or competitive pressures.

Selling, general, and administrative expenses increased by $16.5 million from $70.7 million in 2001 to $87.2 million in 2002 and decreased as a percentage of sales from 7.5% in 2001 to 7.1% in 2002. Increases in spending over the prior year were due to those items that fluctuate with the increase in sales such as sales commissions, product liability expenses, advertising, promotions, general insurance, and printed brochure costs. The reduction as a percentage of sales was mostly due to the large increase in sales compared to overall spending.

Amortization of goodwill declined from $645,000 in 2001 to zero in 2002 due to the application of SFAS 142 discussed above and management's determination that there had been no impairment of goodwill as of December 28, 2002.

Operating income increased $33.3 million from $42.7 million in 2001 to $75.9 million in 2002. The Company's lower level of selling, general, and administrative expense as a percentage of sales combined with the increase in the Company's gross margin, resulted in an increase in operating margin from 4.6% in 2001 to 6.2% in 2002.

Net interest expense increased from $2.4 million in 2001 to $2.8 million in 2002. This increase was related to increased debt levels during 2002 due to higher levels of inventory compared to the prior year, combined with increased capital requirements after the SMC acquisition in August of 2001 and the resort acquisition in November of 2002. No interest was capitalized in 2001 or 2002. The Company's interest expense included $14,000 in 2001 and $314,000 in 2002 related to the amortization of debt issuance costs recorded in conjunction with the Company's credit facilities. The Company also increased its long-term credit facility by $22 million in the fourth quarter of 2002 for the resort acquisition. See "Liquidity and Capital Resources." The Company is expecting increased interest expense for 2003 based on anticipated higher debt levels.

The Company reported a provision for income taxes of $28.8 million, or an effective tax rate of 39.3%, for 2002, compared to $15.7 million, or an effective tax rate of 38.7% for 2001. The change in effective tax rate was due mainly to a decreased benefit in 2002 from foreign sales.

Net income increased by $19.6 million from $24.9 million in 2001 to $44.5 million in 2002, due to the combination of an increase in net sales and an increase in operating margin. The Company does not currently expense stock options granted. However, if option expensing were required, the impact on net income for 2002 for all previously granted options would have been a decrease of $1.3 million. See Note 13 of the Company's consolidated financial statements for information regarding the calculation of the impact of option expense.

2001 COMPARED WITH 2000

Net sales increased 3.9% from $901.9 million in 2000 to $937.1 million in 2001. The Company's overall unit sales were down 5.2% from 10,009 in 2000 to 9,489 units in 2001. The Company's units sales were down 6.1% on the motorized side reflecting lower sales during the first half of 2001 which were nearly offset by increases in the latter part of 2001, mostly from the addition of the Safari and Beaver line of products. Motorized gross sales were up 2.7% reflecting the higher mix of diesel unit sales in 2001. The Company's unit sales of towable products in 2001 were down only 3.4% while gross sales were up 8.2% as sales from the towable operations had a shift in the mix from the prior year of fewer travel trailers and more higher priced fifth wheel units. The Company's overall average unit selling price increased from $91,800 in 2000 to $99,900 in 2001 reflecting the continuing increases in sales of diesel motor coaches.

Gross profit decreased by $15.7 million from $129.7 million in 2000 to $114.0 million in 2001 and gross margin decreased from 14.4% in 2000 to 12.2% in 2001. The decrease in gross margin in 2001 was due to a combination of factors resulting from competitive pressures in the market. Through the first half of 2001, the Company found it necessary to offer above normal discounts to maintain sales to dealers. In addition, throughout 2001, the Company's efforts to match production with the models that were selling well in the market resulted in production inefficiencies caused by shifting volume among production lines and changing the mix of models produced on those lines, as well as integrating the Safari production into the Coburg facility.

Selling, general, and administrative expenses increased by $11.5 million from $59.2 million in 2000 to $70.7 million in 2001 and increased as a percentage of sales from 6.6% in 2000 to 7.5% in 2001. Approximately 42% of the increase was due to retail sales and dealer promotions, as well as show and rally expenses. The remainder of the increase was from administrative and sales wages and commissions, mostly due to the combining of SMC operations which have historically run higher selling, general, and administrative costs as a percentage of sales than the Company.

Operating income decreased $27.1 million from $69.8 million in 2000 to $42.7 million in 2001. The Company's higher level of selling, general, and administrative expense as a percentage of sales combined with the reduction in the Company's gross margin, resulted in a decrease in operating margin from 7.7% in 2000 to 4.6% in 2001.

Net interest expense increased $1.7 million from $632,000 in 2000 to $2.4 million in 2001. This increase was related to increased debt due to higher levels of inventory during the first half of 2001, combined with cash requirements to complete the SMC Acquisition in the third quarter of 2001. The Company capitalized $192,000 of interest expense in 2000 relating to the construction in Indiana and Florida, and no interest was capitalized in 2001. The Company's interest expense included $61,300 in 2000 and $14,000 in 2001 related to the amortization of debt issuance costs recorded in conjunction with the Company's credit facilities. Additionally, interest expense in 2000 included $52,700, from accelerated amortization of debt issuance costs related to the credit facilities. The Company also paid off its revolving credit facility in the third quarter of 2001 and obtained financing from a consortium of lenders.

The Company reported a provision for income taxes of $15.7 million, or an effective tax rate of 38.7%, for 2001, compared to $26.9 million, or an effective tax rate of 38.7% for 2000.

Net income decreased by $17.6 million from $42.5 million in 2000 to $24.9 million in 2001, due to the increase in net sales being more than offset by a lower operating margin.

LIQUIDITY AND CAPITAL RESOURCES

The Company's primary sources of liquidity are internally generated cash from operations and available borrowings under its credit facilities. During 2002, the Company generated cash of $1.3 million from operating activities. The Company generated $53.1 million from net income and non-cash expenses such as depreciation and amortization. This amount was mostly offset by net changes in working capital accounts. Sources of cash included an increase in trade payables of $10.3 million, an increase in accrued liabilities and reserves of $14.0 million and an increase in income taxes payable of $9.6 million. The uses of cash included an increase of $33.9 million in trade receivables and an increase of $48.5 million in inventories. The increase in trade receivables reflects increased shipments near the end of the fourth quarter compared to the prior year end of 2001. Increased inventory levels reflect an increase in raw materials due to higher production run rates and an increase in work in process as the Company implemented a new quality improvement process that added an additional stage to the final completion of the product. The finished goods component of inventory increased by $14 million over the prior year. Increased payables and liabilities are reflective of increased purchases for higher production run rates over the prior year, model change, accruals for current income taxes payable, and various other accrued liabilities.

The Company has credit facilities consisting of a revolving line of credit of up to $70.0 million of which $51.4 million was outstanding at December 28, 2002 (the "Revolving Loan") and term loans with balances of $52.0 million at December 28, 2002 (the "Term Loans"). At the election of the Company, the Revolving Loan and Term Loans bear interest at varying rates that fluctuate based on the Prime rate or LIBOR, and are determined based on the Company's leverage ratio. The Company also pays interest monthly on the unused available portion of the Revolving Loan at varying rates, determined by the Company's leverage ratio. The Revolving loan is due and payable in full on September 30, 2004, and requires monthly interest payments. Additional prepayments for portions of the term notes are required in the event the Company sells substantially all of any motor coach resort location. The Term Loans require monthly interest payments and quarterly principal payments that total $4.3 million. The Revolving Loan and Term Loans are collateralized by all the assets of the Company and include various restrictions and financial covenants. The Company utilizes "zero balance" bank disbursement accounts in which an advance on the line of credit is automatically made for checks clearing each day. Since the balance of the disbursement account at the bank returns to zero at the end of each day, the outstanding checks of the Company are reflected as a liability. The outstanding check liability is combined with the Company's positive cash balance accounts to reflect a net book overdraft or a net cash balance for financial reporting.

The Company's principal working capital requirements are for purchases of inventory and financing of trade receivables. Many of the Company's dealers finance product purchases under wholesale floor plan arrangements with third parties as described below. At December 28, 2002, the Company had working capital of approximately $114.2 million, an increase of $50.5 million from working capital of $63.7 million at December 29, 2001. The Company has been using short-term credit facilities and cash flow to finance its capital expenditures.

The Company believes that cash flow from operations and funds available under its anticipated credit facilities will be sufficient to meet the Company's liquidity requirements for the next 12 months.* The Company's capital expenditures were $18.7 million in 2002, which included costs for routine capital expenditures, completing renovations in the Oregon service center and Indiana cabinet shop, as well as incurring costs for a paint facility addition in Indiana. The Company also incurred a significant portion of the costs required to build a new Florida service center, which will replace it's two existing service facilities in Florida. The Company anticipates that capital expenditures for all of 2003 will be approximately $21 to $22 million, which includes expenditures to complete the Florida service center and Indiana towable plant expansion, an expansion of the Oregon chassis plant, and routine capital expenditures for computer system upgrades and additions, smaller scale plant remodeling projects, and normal replacement of outdated or worn-out equipment.* The Company may require additional equity or debt financing to address working capital and facilities expansion needs, particularly if the Company significantly increases the level of working capital assets such as inventory and accounts receivable. The Company may also from time to time seek to acquire businesses that would complement the Company's current business, and any such acquisition could require additional financing. There can be no assurance that additional financing will be available if required or on terms deemed favorable by the Company.

As is typical in the recreational vehicle industry, many of the Company's retail dealers utilize wholesale floor plan financing arrangements with third party lending institutions to finance their purchases of the Company's products. Under the terms of these floor plan arrangements, institutional lenders customarily require the recreational vehicle manufacturer to agree to repurchase any unsold units if the dealer fails to meet its commitments to the lender, subject to certain conditions. The Company has agreements with several institutional lenders under which the Company currently has repurchase obligations. The Company's contingent obligations under these repurchase agreements are reduced by the proceeds received upon the sale of any repurchased units. The Company's obligations under these repurchase agreements vary from period to period. At December 28, 2002, approximately $490.2 million of products sold by the Company to independent dealers were subject to potential repurchase under existing floor plan financing agreements with approximately 8.4% concentrated with one dealer. Historically, the Company has been successful in mitigating losses associated with repurchase obligations. During 2002, the losses associated with the exercise of repurchase agreements were $300,000. If the Company were obligated to repurchase a significant number of units under any repurchase agreement, its business, operating results and financial condition could be adversely affected.

As part of the normal course of business, the Company incurs certain contractual obligations and commitments which will require future cash payments. The following tables summarize the significant obligations and commitments.

PAYMENTS DUE BY PERIOD

Contractual Obligations (in thousands)	1 year or less	1 to 3 years	4 to 5 years	Thereafter	Total
Long-term debt (1)	$21,667	$30,333	$0	$0	$52,000
Operating Leases (2)	2,598	2,216	2,003	4,477	11,294
Total Contractual Cash Obligations	**$24,265**	**$32,549**	**$2,003**	**$4,477**	**$63,294**

AMOUNT OF COMMITMENT EXPIRATION BY PERIOD

Other Commitments (in thousands)	1 year or less	1 to 3 years	4 to 5 years	Thereafter	Total
Lines of Credit (3)	$0	$51,413	0	0	$51,413
Guarantees	0	16,000(2)	0	0	16,000
Repurchase Obligations (4)	0	490,200	0	0	490,200
Total Commitments	**$0**	**$557,613**	**0**	**0**	**$557,613**

(1) See Note 7 to the financials.
(2) See Note 11 to the financials.
(3) See Note 6 to the financials. The amount listed represents available borrowings on the line of credit at December 28, 2002.
(4) Reflects obligations under manufacturer repurchase commitments. See Note 16 to the financials.

INFLATION

The Company does not believe that inflation has had a material impact on its results of operations for the periods presented.

CRITICAL ACCOUNTING POLICIES

The discussion and analysis of our financial condition and results of operations are based upon our consolidated financial statements, which have been prepared in accordance with accounting principles generally accepted in the United States of America. The preparation of these financial statements requires us to make estimates and judgments that affect the reported amounts of assets, liabilities, revenues and expenses, and related disclosure of contingent assets and liabilities. On an on-going basis, we evaluate our estimates, including those related to warranty costs, product liability, and impairment of goodwill. We base our estimates on historical experience and on various other assumptions that are believed to be reasonable under the circumstances. Actual results may differ from these estimates under different assumptions or conditions. We believe the following critical accounting policies and related judgments and estimates affect the preparation of our consolidated financial statements.

WARRANTY COSTS The Company provides an estimate for accrued warranty costs at the time a product is sold. This estimate is based on historical average repair costs, as well as other reasonable assumptions as have been deemed appropriate by management.

PRODUCT LIABILITY The Company provides an estimate for accrued product liability based on current pending cases, as well as for those cases which are incurred but not reported. This estimate is developed by legal counsel based on professional judgment, as well as historical experience.

IMPAIRMENT OF GOODWILL The Company assesses the potential impairment of goodwill in accordance with Financial Accounting Standards Board (FASB) Statement No. 142. This analysis involves management comparing the market capitalization of the Company, to the carrying amount, including goodwill, of the net book value of the Company, to determine if goodwill has been impaired.

INVENTORY RESERVES The Company writes down its inventory for obsolescence, and the difference between the cost of inventory and its estimated market value. These write-downs are based on assumptions about future sales demand and market conditions. If actual sales demand or market conditions change from those projected by management, additional inventory write-downs may be required.

INCOME TAXES In conjunction with preparing its consolidated financial statements, the Company must estimate its income taxes in each of the jurisdictions in which it operates. This process involves estimating actual current tax expense together with assessing temporary differences resulting from differing treatment of items for tax and accounting purposes. These differences result in deferred tax assets and liabilities, which are included in the consolidated balance sheets. The Company must then assess the likelihood that the deferred tax assets will be recovered from future taxable income, and to the extent management believes that recovery is not likely, a valuation allowance must be established. Significant management judgment is required in determining the Company's provision for income taxes, deferred tax assets and liabilities, and any valuation allowance recorded against net deferred tax assets. A discussion of the income tax provision and the components of the deferred tax assets and liabilities can be found in Note 9 to the Company's consolidated financial statements.

FACTORS THAT MAY AFFECT FUTURE OPERATING RESULTS

WE MAY EXPERIENCE UNANTICIPATED FLUCTUATIONS IN OUR OPERATING RESULTS FOR A VARIETY OF REASONS Our net sales, gross margin, and operating results may fluctuate significantly from period to period due to a number of factors, many of which are not readily predictable. These factors include the following:

- The margins associated with the mix of products we sell in any particular period.
- Our ability to utilize and expand our manufacturing resources efficiently.
- Shortages of materials used in our products.
- A determination by us that goodwill or other intangible assets are impaired and have to be written down to their fair values, resulting in a charge to our results of operations.
- Our ability to introduce new models that achieve consumer acceptance.
- The introduction, marketing and sale of competing products by others, including significant discounting offered by our competitors.
- The addition or loss of our dealers.
- The timing of trade shows and rallies, which we use to market and sell our products.
- Factors affecting the recreational vehicle industry as a whole, including economic and seasonal factors.

Our overall gross margin may decline in future periods to the extent that we increase the percentage of sales of lower gross margin towable products or if the mix of motor coaches we sell shifts to lower gross margin units. In addition, a relatively small variation in the number of recreational vehicles we sell in any quarter can have a significant impact on total sales and operating results for that quarter.

Demand in the recreational vehicle industry generally declines during the winter months, while sales are generally higher during the spring and summer months. With the broader range of products we now offer, seasonal factors could have a significant impact on our operating results in the future. Additionally, unusually severe weather conditions in certain markets could delay the timing of shipments from one quarter to another.

We attempt to forecast orders for our products accurately and commence purchasing and manufacturing prior to receipt of such orders. However, it is highly unlikely that we will consistently accurately forecast the timing, rate, and mix of orders. This aspect of our business makes our planning inexact and, in turn, affects our shipments, costs, inventories, operating results, and cash flow for any given quarter.

THE RECREATIONAL VEHICLE INDUSTRY IS CYCLICAL AND SUSCEPTIBLE TO SLOWDOWNS IN THE GENERAL ECONOMY The recreational vehicle industry has been characterized by cycles of growth and contraction in consumer demand, reflecting prevailing economic, demographic and political conditions that affect disposable income for leisure-time activities. For example, unit sales of recreational vehicles (excluding conversion vehicles) peaked at approximately 259,000 units in 1994 and declined to approximately 247,000 units in 1996. The industry peaked again in 1999 at approximately 321,000 units and declined in 2001 to 257,000 units. In 2002, the industry rebounded up to approximately 307,000 units. Our business is subject to the cyclical nature of this industry. Some of the factors that contribute to this cyclicality include fuel availability and costs, interest rate levels, the level of discretionary spending, and availability of credit and overall consumer confidence. The recent decline in consumer confidence and slowing of the overall economy has adversely affected the recreational vehicle market. An extended continuation of these conditions would materially affect our business, results of operations and financial condition.

OUR RECENT GROWTH HAS PUT PRESSURE ON THE CAPABILITIES OF OUR OPERATING, FINANCIAL, AND MANAGEMENT INFORMATION SYSTEMS In the past few years, we have significantly expanded the size and scope of our business, which has required us to hire additional employees. Some of these new employees include new management personnel. In addition, our current management personnel have assumed additional responsibilities. The increase in our size over a relatively short period of time has put pressure on our operating, financial, and management information systems. If we continue to expand, such growth would put additional pressure on these systems and may cause such systems to malfunction or to experience significant delays.

WE MAY EXPERIENCE UNEXPECTED PROBLEMS AND EXPENSES ASSOCIATED WITH THE EXPANSION OF OUR MANUFACTURING CAPACITY In the past few years, we have significantly increased our manufacturing capacity. In connection with this expansion, we have also integrated some of our manufacturing facilities. We may experience unexpected building and production problems associated with this expansion. In the past, we have had difficulties with the manufacturing of new models and increasing the rates of production of our plants. Our expenses have increased as a result of the expansion and we will be materially and adversely affected if the expansion does not result in an increase in revenue from new or additional products.

This expansion involves risks, including the following:

- We must rely on timely performance by contractors, subcontractors, and government agencies, whose performance we may be unable to control.
- The development of new products involves costs associated with new machinery, training of employees, and compliance with environmental, health, and other government regulations.
- The newly developed products may not be successful in the marketplace.
- We may be unable to complete a planned expansion in a timely manner, which could result in lower production levels and an inability to satisfy customer demand for our products.

WE RELY ON A RELATIVELY SMALL NUMBER OF DEALERS FOR A SIGNIFICANT PERCENTAGE OF OUR SALES Although our products were offered by 420 dealerships located primarily in the United States and Canada as of December 28, 2002, a significant percentage of our sales are concentrated among a relatively small number of independent dealers. For the year ended December 28, 2002, sales to one dealer, Lazy Days RV Center, accounted for 12.3% of total sales compared to 11.7% of sales in the same period ended last year. For fiscal years 2001 and 2002, sales to our 10 largest dealers, including Lazy Days RV Center, accounted for a total of 39.0%. The loss of a significant dealer or a substantial decrease in sales by any of these dealers could have a material impact on our business, results of operations and financial condition.

WE MAY HAVE TO REPURCHASE A DEALER'S INVENTORY OF OUR PRODUCTS IN THE EVENT THAT THE DEALER DOES NOT REPAY ITS LENDER As is common in the recreational vehicle industry, we enter into repurchase agreements with the financing institutions used by our dealers to finance their purchases of our products. These agreements require us to repurchase the dealer's inventory in the event that the dealer does not repay its lender. Obligations under these agreements vary from period to period, but totaled approximately $490.2 million as of December 28, 2002, with approximately 8.4% concentrated with one dealer. If we were obligated to repurchase a significant number of units under any repurchase agreement, our business, operating results, and financial condition could be adversely affected.

OUR ACCOUNTS RECEIVABLE BALANCE IS SUBJECT TO CONCENTRATION RISK We sell our product to dealers who are predominantly located in the United States and Canada. The terms and conditions of payment are a combination of open trade receivables, and commitments from dealer floor plan lending institutions. As of December 28, 2002, total trade receivables were $116.6 million, with approximately $83.6 million, or 71.7% of the outstanding accounts receivable balance concentrated among floor plan lenders. The remaining $33.0 million of trade receivables were concentrated substantially all with one dealer.

WE MAY EXPERIENCE A DECREASE IN SALES OF OUR PRODUCTS DUE TO AN INCREASE IN THE PRICE OR A DECREASE IN THE SUPPLY OF FUEL An interruption in the supply, or a significant increase in the price or tax on the sale, of diesel fuel or gasoline on a regional or national basis could significantly affect our business. Diesel fuel and gasoline have, at various times in the past, been either expensive or difficult to obtain.

WE DEPEND ON SINGLE OR LIMITED SOURCES TO PROVIDE US WITH CERTAIN IMPORTANT COMPONENTS THAT WE USE IN THE PRODUCTION OF OUR PRODUCTS A number of important components for certain of our products are purchased from single or a limited number of sources. These include turbo diesel engines (Cummins and Caterpillar), substantially all of our transmissions (Allison), axles (Dana and Meritor) for all diesel motor coaches and chassis (Workhorse and Ford) for gas motor coaches. We have no long-term supply contracts with these suppliers or their distributors, and we cannot be certain that these suppliers will be able to meet our future requirements. For example, in 1997, Allison placed all chassis manufacturers on allocation with respect to one of the transmissions that we use, and again in 1999 Ford placed one of its gasoline powered chassis on allocation. An extended delay or interruption in the supply of any components that we obtain from a single supplier or from a limited number of suppliers could adversely affect our business, results of operations and financial condition.

OUR INDUSTRY IS VERY COMPETITIVE. WE MUST CONTINUE TO INTRODUCE NEW MODELS AND NEW FEATURES TO REMAIN COMPETITIVE The market for our products is very competitive. We currently compete with a number of manufacturers of motor coaches, fifth wheel trailers, and travel trailers. Some of these companies have greater financial resources than we have and extensive distribution networks. These companies, or new competitors in the industry, may develop products that customers in the industry prefer over our products.

We believe that the introduction of new products and new features is critical to our success. Delays in the introduction of new models or product features, quality problems associated with these introductions, or a lack of market acceptance of new models or features could affect us adversely. For example, unexpected costs associated with model changes have affected our gross margin in the past. Further, new product introductions can divert revenues from existing models and result in fewer sales of existing products.

OUR PRODUCTS COULD FAIL TO PERFORM ACCORDING TO SPECIFICATIONS OR PROVE TO BE UNRELIABLE, CAUSING DAMAGE TO OUR CUSTOMER RELATIONSHIPS AND OUR REPUTATION AND RESULTING IN LOSS OF SALES Our customers require demanding specifications for product performance and reliability. Because our products are complex and often use advanced components, processes and techniques, undetected errors and design flaws may occur. Product defects result in higher product service and warranty and replacement costs and may cause serious damage to our customer relationships and industry reputation, all of which will negatively affect our sales and business.

OUR BUSINESS IS SUBJECT TO VARIOUS TYPES OF LITIGATION, INCLUDING PRODUCT LIABILITY AND WARRANTY CLAIMS We are subject to litigation arising in the ordinary course of our business, typically for product liability and warranty claims that are common in the recreational vehicle industry. While we do not believe that the outcome of any pending litigation, net of insurance coverage, will materially adversely affect our business, results of operations, or financial condition, we cannot provide assurances in this regard because litigation is an inherently uncertain process.*

To date, we have been successful in obtaining product liability insurance on terms that we consider acceptable. The terms of the policy contain a self-insured retention amount of $500,000 per occurrence, with a maximum annual aggregate self-insured retention of $3.0 million. Overall product liability insurance, including umbrella coverage, is available to a maximum amount of $100.0 million for each occurrence, as well as in the aggregate. We cannot be certain we will be able to obtain insurance coverage in the future at acceptable levels or that the costs of such insurance will be reasonable. Further, successful assertion against us of one or a series of large uninsured claims, or of a series of claims exceeding our insurance coverage, could have a material adverse effect on our business, results of operations, and financial condition.

WE MAY BE UNABLE TO ATTRACT AND RETAIN KEY EMPLOYEES, DELAYING PRODUCT DEVELOPMENT AND MANUFACTURING Our success depends in part upon attracting and retaining highly skilled professionals. A number of our employees are highly skilled engineers and other technical professionals, and our failure to continue to attract and retain such individuals could adversely affect our ability to compete in the industry.

NEWLY ISSUED FINANCIAL REPORTING PRONOUNCEMENTS

See "New Accounting Pronouncements" in Note 1 of Notes to the Company's Consolidated Financial Statements.

AUDIT COMMITTEE APPROVAL OF NON-AUDIT SERVICES

In accordance with Section 10A(i)(2) of the Securities Exchange Act of 1934, as added by Section 202 of the Sarbanes-Oxley Act of 2002, we are responsible for listing the non-audit services approved in the three months ended December 28, 2002 by our Audit Committee to be performed by our external auditor. Non-audit services are defined in the law as services other than those provided in connection with an audit or a review of our financial statements. The non-audit services approved by the Audit Committee in the three months ended December 28, 2002 are each considered by the Company to be audit-related services, which are closely related to the financial audit process. During the three months ended December 28, 2002, the Audit Committee approved the engagement of PricewaterhouseCoopers LLP, our external auditor, for the following non-audit services: (1) tax review and consulting services during the three months ended December 28, 2002 not to exceed $10,000; and (2) tax review and consulting services during fiscal year 2003 not to exceed $35,000.

QUANTITATIVE AND QUALITATIVE DISCLOSURES ABOUT MARKET RISK

We are exposed to market risks related to fluctuations in interest rates on our borrowings. We do not currently use rate swaps, futures contracts or options on futures, or other types of derivative financial instruments. Our line of credit and term debt permit a combination of fixed and variable interest rate options which allows us to minimize the effect of rising interest rates by locking in fixed rates for periods of up to 6 months. We believe these features of our credit facilities help us reduce the risk associated with interest rate fluctuations.

CONSOLIDATED BALANCE SHEETS

(in thousands of dollars, except share and per share data)

	December 29, 2001	December 28, 2002
ASSETS		
Current assets:		
Trade receivables, net of $541 and $799, respectively	$82,885	$116,647
Inventories	127,075	175,609
Resort lot inventory	0	26,883
Prepaid expenses	2,063	3,612
Deferred income taxes	27,327	33,379
Total current assets	**239,350**	**356,130**
Notes receivable	8,157	0
Property, plant, and equipment, net	122,795	135,350
Debt issuance costs, net of accumulated amortization of $75 and $389, respectively	940	683
Goodwill, net of accumulated amortization of $5,320 and $5,320, respectively	55,856	55,254
Total assets	**$427,098**	**$547,417**
LIABILITIES		
Current liabilities:		
Book overdraft	$5,889	$3,518
Line of credit	26,004	51,413
Current portion of long-term note payable	10,000	21,667
Accounts payable	66,859	78,055
Product liability reserve	19,856	21,322
Product warranty reserve	27,799	31,745
Income taxes payable	0	4,536
Accrued expenses and other liabilities	19,249	29,633
Total current liabilities	**175,656**	**241,889**
Long-term note payable	30,000	30,333
Deferred income taxes	8,312	14,568
	213,968	**286,790**
Commitments and contingencies (Note 16)		
STOCKHOLDERS' EQUITY		
Common stock, $.01 par value; 50,000,000 shares authorized 28,632,774 and 28,871,144 issued and outstanding, respectively	286	289
Additional paid-in capital	48,522	51,501
Retained earnings	164,322	208,837
Total stockholders' equity	**213,130**	**260,627**
Total liabilities and stockholders' equity	**$427,098**	**$547,417**

The accompanying notes are an integral part of these consolidated financial statements.

CONSOLIDATED STATEMENTS OF INCOME

for the years ended December 30, 2000, December 29, 2001, and December 28, 2002
(in thousands of dollars, except share and per share data)

	2000	2001	2002
Net sales	$901,890	$937,073	$1,222,689
Cost of sales	772,240	823,083	1,059,560
Gross profit	**129,650**	**113,990**	**163,129**
Selling, general and administrative expenses	59,175	70,687	87,202
Amortization of goodwill	645	645	0
Operating income	**69,830**	**42,658**	**75,927**
Other income, net	182	334	105
Interest expense	(632)	(2,357)	(2,752)
Income before income taxes	**69,380**	**40,635**	**73,280**
Provision for income taxes	26,859	15,716	28,765
Net income	**$42,521**	**$24,919**	**$44,515**
Earnings per common share:			
Basic	$ 1.50	$ .87	$ 1.55
Diluted	$ 1.47	$ .85	$ 1.51
Weighted average common shares outstanding:			
Basic	28,377,123	28,531,593	28,812,473
Diluted	28,978,265	29,288,688	29,573,420

The accompanying notes are an integral part of these consolidated financial statements.

CONSOLIDATED STATEMENTS OF STOCKHOLDERS' EQUITY

for the years ended December 30, 2000, December 29, 2001, and December 28, 2002
(in thousands of dollars, except share data)

	Common Stock		Additional Paid-in	Retained	
	Shares	Amount	Capital	Earnings	Total
Balances, January 1, 2000	**18,871,084**	**$189**	**$46,268**	**$96,882**	**$143,339**
Issuance of common stock	81,023	1	727		728
Tax benefit of stock options exercised			37		37
Net income				42,521	42,521
Balances, December 30, 2000	**18,952,107**	**190**	**47,032**	**139,403**	**186,625**
Issuance of common stock	161,848	1	1,115		1,116
Tax benefit of stock options exercised			470		470
Stock splits	9,518,819	95	(95)		0
Net income				24,919	24,919
Balances, December 29, 2001	**28,632,774**	**286**	**48,522**	**164,322**	**213,130**
Issuance of common stock	238,370	3	1,654		1,657
Tax benefit of stock options exercised			1,325		1,325
Net income				44,515	44,515
Balances, December 28, 2002	**28,871,144**	**$289**	**$51,501**	**$208,837**	**$260,627**

The accompanying notes are an integral part of these consolidated financial statements.

CONSOLIDATED STATEMENTS OF CASH FLOWS

for the years ended December 30, 2000, December 29, 2001, and December 28, 2002

(in thousands of dollars)

	2000	2001	2002
Increase (Decrease) in Cash:			
Cash flows from operating activities:			
Net income	$42,521	$24,919	$44,515
Adjustments to reconcile net income to net cash provided by operating activities:			
Depreciation and amortization	6,359	7,543	8,585
Gain on disposal of equipment		(74)	178
Deferred income taxes	3,609	6,005	(1,574)
Change in assets and liabilities:			
Trade receivables, net	(31,460)	(13,154)	(33,932)
Inventories	(26,801)	12,682	(48,534)
Resort lot inventory			(98)
Prepaid expenses	(724)	(903)	(1,650)
Accounts payable	16,186	(10,318)	10,301
Product liability reserve	(1,288)	(1,639)	1,237
Product warranty reserve	314	(1,958)	3,835
Income taxes payable	(1,406)	0	9,597
Accrued expenses and other liabilities	(957)	(2,123)	8,888
Net cash provided by operating activities	**6,353**	**20,980**	**1,348**
Cash flows from investing activities:			
Additions to property, plant and equipment	(19,750)	(10,210)	(18,735)
Proceeds from sale of assets		106	387
Collections on notes receivable			500
Payment for business acquisition, net of cash acquired		(24,320)	(21,085)
Issuance of notes receivable	(2,800)	(5,357)	(385)
Net cash used in investing activities	**(22,550)**	**(39,781)**	**(39,318)**
Cash flows from financing activities:			
Book overdraft	2,700	(10,840)	(2,371)
Borrowings (payments) on line of credit, net	12,732	(10,930)	25,414
Borrowings on long-term notes payable		40,000	22,000
Payments on long-term notes payable			(10,000)
Issuance of common stock	765	1,586	2,982
Debt issuance costs		(1,015)	(55)
Net cash provided by financing activities	**16,197**	**18,801**	**37,970**
Net change in cash	0	0	0
Cash at beginning of period	0	0	0
Cash at end of period	**$0**	**$0**	**$0**

The accompanying notes are an integral part of these consolidated financial statements.

NOTES TO CONSOLIDATED FINANCIAL STATEMENTS

1. BUSINESS AND SIGNIFICANT ACCOUNTING POLICIES:

Business

Monaco Coach Corporation and its subsidiaries (the "Company") manufacture premium motor coaches, bus conversions, and towable recreational vehicles at manufacturing facilities in Oregon and Indiana. These products are sold to independent dealers primarily throughout the United States and Canada. In addition, the Company also owns three motor coach resort properties, the developed lots of which, are sold to retail customers.

Pursuant to Statement of Financial Accounting Standards (SFAS) No. 131, "Disclosures about Segments of an Enterprise and Related Information," the Company has determined that it's core business activities are comprised of two distinct operations. The first is the design, manufacture, and sale of recreational vehicles. The second is the development and sale of motor coach recreation resort lots. While the nature of the Company's business is segregated into two distinct operations, the Company has elected to report its operations as a single entity, based on the relative immateriality of the motor coach resort operations when compared to the Company's operations in its entirety.

Consolidation Policy

The accompanying consolidated financial statements include the accounts of the Company and its wholly-owned subsidiaries. All material intercompany transactions and balances have been eliminated.

Fiscal Period

The Company follows a 52/53 week fiscal year period ending on the Saturday closest to December 31. Interim periods also end on the Saturday closest to the calendar quarter end. For 2000, 2001, and 2002, all fiscal periods were 52 weeks long. All references to years in the consolidated financial statements relate to fiscal years rather than calendar years.

Stock Splits

On August 6, 2001, the Board of Directors declared a three-for-two stock split in the form of a 50% stock dividend on the Company's Common stock. Accordingly, all historical weighted average share and per share amounts have been restated to reflect the stock split. Share amounts presented in the Consolidated Statement of Stockholders' Equity reflect the actual share amounts outstanding for each period presented.

Estimates and Industry Factors

Estimates - The preparation of financial statements in conformity with accounting principles generally accepted in the United States of America, requires management to make estimates and assumptions that affect the reported amounts of assets and liabilities and disclosure of contingent assets and liabilities at the date of the financial statements and the reported amounts of revenues and expenses during the reporting period. The Company bases estimates on various assumptions that are believed to be reasonable under the circumstances. Management is continually evaluating and updating these estimates, and it is possible that these estimates will change in the near future.

Concentration of Credit Risk - The Company distributes its products through an independent dealer network for recreational vehicles. Sales to one customer were approximately 12% of net revenues for fiscal years 2000, 2001, and 2002. No other individual dealers represented over 10% of net revenues in 2000, 2001, or 2002. The loss of a significant dealer or a substantial decrease in sales by such a dealer could have a material adverse effect on the Company's business, results of operations and financial condition. The terms and conditions of payment are a combination of open trade receivables, and commitments from dealer floor plan lending institutions. As of December 28, 2002, total trade receivables were $116.6 million, with approximately $83.6 million, or 71.7% of the outstanding accounts receivable balance, concentrated among floor plan lenders. The remaining open $33.0 million of trade receivables, were concentrated substantially all with one dealer.

Concentrations of credit risk exist for accounts receivable and repurchase agreements (see Note 16), primarily for the Company's largest dealers. As of December 28, 2002, the Company had one dealer that comprised 28.1% of the outstanding trade receivables. The Company generally sells to dealers throughout the United States and there is no geographic concentration of credit risk.

Reliance on Key Suppliers - The Company's production strategy relies on certain key suppliers' ability to deliver subassemblies and component parts in time to meet manufacturing schedules. The Company has a variety of key suppliers, including Allison, Workhorse, Cummins, Caterpillar, Dana, Meritor and Ford. The Company does not have any long-term contracts with these suppliers or their distributors. In 1997, Allison put all chassis manufacturers on allocation with respect to one of the transmissions the Company uses, and in 1999 Ford put one of its gasoline powered chassis on allocation. In light of these dependencies, it is possible that failure of Allison, Ford or any of the other suppliers to meet the Company's future requirements for transmissions, chassis or other key components could have a material near-term impact on the Company's business, results of operations, and financial condition.

Product Warranty Reserve - Estimated warranty costs are provided for at the time of sale of products with warranties covering the products for up to one year from the date of retail sale (five years for the front and sidewall frame structure, and three years on the Roadmaster chassis). These estimates are based on historical average repair costs, as well as other reasonable assumptions as have been deemed appropriate by management. The following table discloses significant changes in the product warranty reserve:

	2000	2001	2002
		(in thousands)	
Beginning balance	$13,436	$13,750	$27,799
Expense	17,474	21,800	34,237
Payments/adjustments	17,160	21,788	30,402
Adjustment for SMC Acquisition	—	14,037	111
Ending balance	**$13,750**	**$27,799**	**$31,745**

Product Liability Reserve - Estimated litigation costs are provided for at the time of sale of products, or at the time a determination is made that an estimable loss has occurred. These estimates are developed by legal counsel based on professional judgment, as well as historical experience. The following table discloses significant changes in the product liability reserve:

	2000	2001	2002
		(in thousands)	
Beginning balance	$9,407	$8,120	$19,856
Expense	5,489	6,108	8,020
Payments/adjustments	6,776	4,246	6,783
Adjustment for SMC Acquisition	—	-9,874	229
Ending balance	**$8,120**	**$19,856**	**$21,322**

Inventories

Inventories consist of raw materials, work-in-process, and finished recreational vehicles and are stated at the lower of cost (first-in, first-out) or market. Cost of work-in-process and finished recreational vehicles includes material, labor, and manufacturing overhead costs.

Resort Lot Inventory

Resort lot inventories consist of construction-in-progress on motor coach properties, as well as fully developed motor coach properties. These properties are stated at the lower of cost (specific identification) or market. Cost of construction in progress, as well as fully developed motor coach properties include costs associated with land, construction, and interest capitalization.

Property, Plant, and Equipment

Property, plant, and equipment, including significant improvements thereto, are stated at cost less accumulated depreciation and amortization. Cost includes expenditures for major improvements, replacements and renewals and the net amount of interest cost associated with significant capital additions during periods of construction. Capitalized interest was $192,000 in 2000, and zero in 2001 and 2002. Maintenance and repairs are charged to expense as incurred. Replacements and renewals are capitalized. When assets are sold, retired or otherwise disposed of, the cost and accumulated depreciation are removed from the accounts and any resulting gain or loss is reflected in income.

The cost of plant and equipment is depreciated using the straight-line method over the estimated useful lives of the related assets. Buildings are generally depreciated over 39 years and equipment is depreciated over 3 to 10 years. Leasehold improvements are amortized under the straight-line method based on the shorter of the lease periods or the estimated useful lives.

At each balance sheet date, management assesses whether there has been permanent impairment in the value of property, plant, and equipment assets. The amount of any such impairment is determined by comparing anticipated undiscounted future cash flows from operating activities with the associated carrying value. The factors considered by management in performing this assessment include current operating results, trends and prospects, as well as the effects of obsolescence, demand, competition, and other economic factors.

Goodwill

Goodwill represents the excess of the cost of acquisition over the fair value of net assets acquired. The Company is the successor to a company formed in

1968 (the "Predecessor") and commenced operations on March 5, 1993 by acquiring substantially all of the assets and liabilities of the Predecessor. As of December 28, 2002, the goodwill arising from the acquisition of the assets and operations of the Company's Predecessor in March 1993 was $16.1 million. In March 1996, the Company acquired the Holiday Rambler Division of Harley-Davidson, Inc. ("Holiday Rambler"). As of December 28, 2002, the goodwill arising from the acquisition of Holiday Rambler was $1.8 million. The Company also recorded $37.3 million of goodwill associated with the August 2, 2001 acquisition of SMC Corporation (SMC). For years ending December 29, 2001 and prior, the Company amortized goodwill using the straight-line method over a 40 year period for the acquisition of the Company's Predecessor, as well as for the Holiday Rambler acquisition. In accordance with Statements of Financial Accounting Standards No. 142 (SFAS 142) "Accounting for Goodwill and Other Intangible Assets," no amortization was recorded for the SMC acquisition for 2001, and no amortization was recorded for any of the acquisitions for fiscal year 2002.

SFAS 142 requires that management assesses annually whether there has been permanent impairment in the value of goodwill. The test for any such impairment is determined by comparing the fair value of the Company's reporting entity with its carrying value, including goodwill. The factors considered by management in performing this assessment can include current operating results, trends and prospects, as well as the effects of obsolescence, demand, competition, and other economic factors. As required by SFAS 142, management has completed its annual testing during 2002 and determined that there has been no impairment of goodwill requiring a write down.

Debt Issuance Costs

Unamortized debt issuance costs of $940,000, and $683,000 (at December 29, 2001 and December 28, 2002, respectively), are being amortized over the terms of the related loans.

Stock-Based Employee Compensation Plans

At December 28, 2002, the Company has three stock-based employee compensation plans (see Note 13). The Company accounts for those plans under the recognition and measurement principles of APB Opinion No. 25, Accounting for Stock Issued to Employees, and related Interpretations. No stock-based employee compensation cost is reflected in net income, as all options granted under those plans had an exercise price equal to the market value of the underlying common stock on the date of grant.

Income Taxes

Deferred taxes are recognized based on the difference between the financial statement and tax basis of assets and liabilities at enacted tax rates in effect in the years in which the differences are expected to reverse. Deferred tax expense or benefit represents the change in deferred tax asset/liability balances. A valuation allowance is established for deferred tax assets when it is more likely than not that the deferred tax asset will not be realized.

Revenue Recognition

The Company recognizes revenue from the sale of recreational vehicles upon shipment and recognizes revenue from resort lot sales upon closing.

In December 1999, the Securities and Exchange Commission issued Staff Accounting Bulletin (SAB) No. 101, Revenue Recognition in Financial Statements. SAB No. 101 provides guidance for revenue recognition under certain circumstances. The Company has complied with the guidance provided by SAB No. 101 for the fiscal years 2000, 2001, and 2002.

Advertising and Promotion Costs

The Company expenses advertising costs as incurred, except for prepaid show costs which are expensed when the event takes place. During 2002, approximately $14.6 million ($7.8 million in 2000 and $10.1 million in 2001) of advertising costs were expensed.

Research and Development Costs

Research and development costs are charged to expense as incurred and were $1.2 million in 2002 ($783,000 in 2000 and $975,000 in 2001).

New Accounting Pronouncements

SFAS 148

In December 2002, the Board issued SFAS 148, Accounting for Stock-Based Compensation - Transition and Disclosure - an amendment of SFAS 123. This statement provides transition guidance for entities that elect to voluntarily adopt the accounting provisions of SFAS 123. The statement does not change the provisions of SFAS 123 that permit entities to continue to apply the intrinsic value method of APB 25, Accounting for Stock Issued to Employees. The statement also requires certain new disclosures that are incremental to those required by SFAS 123. The transition and disclosure provisions are effective for fiscal years ending after December 15, 2002. The Company applies the intrinsic value method of APB 25 in accordance with SFAS 123 and has elected the disclosure provisions of the fair value method of SFAS 123. Therefore, the transitional rules for adopting SFAS 123 do not apply, however, the Company has included the new disclosure requirements of SFAS 148 in its financial statements.

FIN 45

In November 2002, the Board issued FASB Interpretation No. 45 (FIN 45), Guarantor's Accounting and Disclosure Requirements for Guarantees, Including Indirect Guarantees of Indebtedness of Others, and Interpretation of SFAS 5, 57, and 107 and Rescission of FIN 34. The Interpretation requires certain disclosures to be made by a guarantor about its obligations under certain guarantees that it has issued. It also clarifies that a guarantor is required to recognize, at the inception of a guarantee, a liability for the fair value of the obligation undertaken in issuing the guarantee.

The initial recognition and measurement provisions are applicable on a prospective basis to guarantees issued or modified after December 31, 2002. The disclosure requirements are effective for financial statements of interim or annual periods ending after December 15, 2002. The Company has included the disclosure requirements in its financial statements and has determined that the recognition provisions of FIN 45 apply to certain guarantees routinely made by the Company including repurchase obligations to third party lenders for inventory financing of dealer inventories. The Company anticipates recording a liability of approximately $500,000 for potential losses resulting from guarantees on products shipped to dealers starting in 2003. This estimated liability, which will be recorded primarily in the first half of 2003, is based on the Company's experience of losses associated with the repurchase and resale of units in prior years.

FIN 46

In January 2003, the Board issued FASB Interpretation No. 46 (FIN 46), Consolidation of Variable Interest Entities - an Interpretation of ARB No. 51, Consolidated Financial Statements. The Interpretation addresses how variable interest entities are to be identified and how an enterprise assesses its interests in a variable interest entity to decide whether to consolidate that entity. The Interpretation also requires existing unconsolidated variable interest entities to be consolidated by their primary beneficiaries if the entities do not effectively disperse risks among the parties involved.

FIN 46 is effective in the first fiscal year or interim period beginning after June 15, 2003, to variable interest entities in which a company holds a variable interest that is acquired before February 1, 2003.

The provisions of FIN 46 may apply to certain operating leases of the Company that have residual value guarantees.

Supplemental Cash Flow Disclosures:

	2000	2001	2002
		(in thousands)	
Cash paid during the period for:			
Interest, net of amount capitalized of $192 in 2000, $0 in 2001, and $0 in 2002	$632	$2,206	$2,464
Income taxes	28,226	16,231	18,753

2. ACQUISITIONS:

SMC Corporation

The Company announced on June 25, 2001 that it had reached an agreement with Oregon based motor home manufacturer SMC Corporation ("SMC") to acquire all of the outstanding shares of SMC pursuant to a cash tender offer at a price of $3.70 per share. On August 6, 2001, the Company completed the back-end merger, and owned 100% of the shares.

The cash paid for SMC, including transaction costs of $3,062,000, totaled $24,320,000. The total assets acquired and liabilities assumed of SMC, based on estimated fair values at August 6, 2001, is as follows:

	(in thousands)
Receivables	$6,678
Inventories	25,360
Deferred tax asset	17,418
Property and equipment	14,776
Prepaids and other assets	21
Goodwill	37,317
Total assets acquired	**101,570**
Book overdraft	(1,551)
Notes payable	(16,345)
Accounts payable	(23,824)
Accrued liabilities	(35,530)
Total liabilities assumed	**(77,250)**
Total assets acquired and liabilities assumed	**$24,320**

The allocation of the purchase price and the related goodwill has been adjusted for resolution of pre-acquisition contingencies of $602,000. The effects of resolution of pre-acquisition contingencies occurring: (i) within one year of the acquisition date were reflected as an adjustment of the allocation of the purchase price and goodwill, and (ii) after one year were recognized in the determination of net income.

The following unaudited pro forma information presents the consolidated results as if the acquisition had occurred at the beginning of the period and giving effect to the adjustments for the related interest on financing the purchase price, goodwill, and depreciation. The pro forma information does not necessarily reflect results that would have occurred or is it necessarily indicative of future operating results.

	(in thousands, except per share data)	
	2000	2001
Net sales	$1,093,000	$1,015,000
Net income	36,000	14,000
Diluted earnings per common share	$1.25	$0.48

Outdoor Resorts

During the quarter ended September 28, 2002, the Company reached an agreement in principle with Outdoor Resorts of America (ORA) to acquire all of the outstanding stock of Outdoor Resorts of Las Vegas, Inc. (ORLV), Outdoor Resorts of Naples, Inc. (ORN), and Outdoor Resorts Motorcoach Country Club, Inc. (ORMCC), ("the Projects"). The Projects consist of developed and undeveloped luxury motor coach resorts.

On November 27, 2002, the Company completed the acquisition of all of the outstanding stock of ORLV, ORN, and ORMCC. Previous to the acquisition, the Company had provided ORA with loans in the amount of $8.0 million, as well as co-guaranteeing $10 million in bank debt secured by ORA.

As consideration for the acquisition, Monaco assumed the current debt and liabilities of the projects of approximately $30.8 million, including the $8.0 million note payable to the Company, and the $10 million co-guaranteed debt. This acquisition relieves ORA of certain debt pressures associated with resort construction, and will allow ORA to continue to focus on development and lot sales, as well as providing management services for the Company on the Projects.

The cash paid for the Projects, including transaction costs of $522,000 totaled $21,113,000. The total assets acquired and liabilities assumed of the Projects, based on estimated fair values at November 27, 2002, is as follows:

	(in thousands)
Cash	$28
Resort lot inventory	26,784
Deferred tax asset	272
Property and equipment	3,670
Total assets acquired	**30,754**
Notes payable	(8,027)
Accounts payable	(1,165)
Accrued liabilities	(449)
Total liabilities assumed	**(9,641)**
Total assets acquired and liabilities assumed	**$21,113**

The allocation of the purchase price will be subject to adjustment upon resolution of pre-ORA Acquisition contingencies. The effects of resolution of pre-ORA Acquisition contingencies occurring: (i) within one year of the acquisition date will be reflected as an adjustment of the allocation of the purchase price and of goodwill, and (ii) after one year will be recognized in the determination of net income.

The following unaudited pro forma information presents the consolidated results as if the acquisition had occurred at the beginning of the period and giving effect to the adjustments for the related interest on financing the purchase price and depreciation. The pro forma information does not necessarily reflect results that would have occurred or is it necessarily indicative of future operating results.

	(in thousands, except per share data)	
	2001	2002
Net sales	$939,195	$1,223,776
Net income	24,478	44,127
Diluted earnings per common share	$0.84	$1.49

3. INVENTORIES:

Inventories consist of the following:

	December 29, 2001	December 28, 2002
	(in thousands)	
Raw materials	$53,160	$70,021
Work-in-process	44,436	62,022
Finished units	29,479	43,566
	$127,075	**$175,609**

4. PROPERTY, PLANT, AND EQUIPMENT:

Property, plant, and equipment consist of the following:

	December 29, 2001	December 28,2002
	(in thousands)	
Land	$11,999	$15,638
Buildings	99,333	104,043
Equipment	22,838	26,503
Furniture and fixtures	9,479	11,436
Vehicles	1,571	1,763
Leasehold improvements	1,472	2,152
Construction in progress	2,376	7,236
	149,068	**168,771**
Less accumulated depreciation and amortization	26,273	33,421
	$122,795	**$135,350**

5. ACCRUED EXPENSES AND OTHER LIABILITIES:

	December 29, 2001	December 28, 2002
	(in thousands)	
Payroll, vacation, and related accruals	$12,580	$17,317
Payroll and property taxes	1,172	1,517
Promotional and advertising	1,345	3,473
Other	4,152	7,326
	$19,249	**$29,633**

6. LINE OF CREDIT:

The Company's line of credit facility consists of a revolving line of credit of up to $70.0 million (the "Revolving Loan"). At the election of the Company, the Revolving Loan bears interest at variable rates based on the Prime Rate or LIBOR. At December 28, 2002, the interest rate was 4.3%. The Revolving Loan is due and payable in full on September 30, 2004, and requires monthly interest payments. The balance outstanding under the Revolving Loan at December 28, 2002 was $51.4 million. The Revolving Loan is collateralized by all of the assets of the Company, and include various restrictions and financial covenants.

The weighted average interest rate on the outstanding borrowings under the revolving line of credit was 5.8% and 4.3% for 2001 and 2002, respectively. Interest expense on the unused available portion of the line was $85,000 or 0.2% and $141,000 or 0.7% of weighted average outstanding borrowings for 2001 and 2002, respectively. The revolving line of credit is collateralized by all the assets of the Company. The agreement contains restrictive covenants as to the Company's leverage ratio, current ratio, fixed charge coverage ratio, and tangible net worth. As of December 28, 2002, the Company was in compliance with these covenants.

7. LONG-TERM NOTE PAYABLE:

In November 2002, the Company obtained an amendment to the long-term note payable for an additional borrowing of $22 million in association with the purchase of Outdoor Resorts (see Note 2). The Company has long-term notes payable of $52 million outstanding at December 28, 2002. The term notes bear interest at varying rates that fluctuate based on the Prime rate or LIBOR, and are determined based on the Company's leverage ratio. The term notes require monthly interest payments and quarterly principal payments. Additional prepayments for portions of the term notes are required in the event the Company sells substantially all of any motor coach resort location. The term notes are collateralized by all the assets of the Company. The term notes are due and payable in full on September 28, 2005. As of December 28, 2002, the interest rate on the term debt was 3.55%.

The following table displays the scheduled principal payments by year that will be due on the term loan.

Year	Amount of payment due
2003	$21,667
2004	$17,333
2005	$13,000
	$52,000

8. PREFERRED STOCK:

The Company has authorized "blank check" preferred stock (1,934,783 shares authorized, $.01 par value) ("Preferred Stock"), which may be issued from time to time in one or more series upon authorization by the Company's Board of Directors. The Board of Directors, without further approval of the stockholders, is authorized to fix the dividend rights and terms, conversion rights, voting rights, redemption rights and terms, liquidation preferences, and any other rights, preferences, privileges and restrictions applicable to each series of the Preferred Stock. There were no shares of Preferred Stock outstanding as of December 29, 2001 or December 28, 2002.

9. INCOME TAXES:

The provision for income taxes is as follows:

	2000	2001	2002
		(in thousands)	
Current:			
Federal	$19,120	$8,262	$25,303
State	4,130	1,606	5,278
	23,250	**9,868**	**30,581**
Deferred:			
Federal	2,945	4,880	(1,556)
State	664	968	(260)
Provision for income taxes	**$26,859**	**$15,716**	**$28,765**

The reconciliation of the provision for income taxes at the U.S. federal statutory rate to the Company's effective income tax rate is as follows:

	2000	2001	2002
		(in thousands)	
Expected U.S. federal income taxes at statutory rates	$24,283	$14,222	$25,648
State and local income taxes, net of federal benefit	3,116	1,673	3,262
Other	(540)	(179)	(145)
	$26,859	**$15,716**	**$28,765**

The components of the current net deferred tax asset and long-term net deferred tax liability are:

	December 29, 2001	December 28, 2002
Current deferred income tax assets:		
Warranty liability	$11,909	$13,768
Product liability	6,376	7,211
Inventory reserves	3,144	3,922
Payroll and related accruals	1,911	2,057
Insurance reserves	467	1,318
Resort lot inventory	0	921
Other accruals	3,520	4,182
	$27,327	**$33,379**
Long-term deferred income tax liabilities:		
Depreciation	$8,741	$11,509
Amortization	2,846	3,530
Net operating loss (NOL) carryforward	(6,070)	(1,272)
Valuation allowance on NOL carryforward	2,795	801
	$8,312	**$14,568**

Management believes that the temporary differences which gave rise to the deferred income tax assets will be realized in the foreseeable future, except for benefits arising from the NOL carryforward associated with the SMC Acquisition. Accordingly, management has provided a valuation allowance for the portion of the NOL carryforward that may not be fully recognized. During 2002, certain tax law changes were enacted which resulted in the Company's immediate recognition of certain operating losses relating to prior year results of operations. As a result, management has properly reflected a reduction in the valuation allowance. At December 28, 2002, the valuation allowance relates to the deferred tax asset for the state income tax benefit of the net operating loss carryforward.

10. EARNINGS PER SHARE:

Basic earnings per common share is based on the weighted average number of shares outstanding during the period using net income attributable to common stock as the numerator. Diluted earnings per common share is based on the weighted average number of shares outstanding during the period, after consideration of the dilutive effect of stock options and convertible preferred stock, using net income as the numerator. The weighted average number of common shares used in the computation of earnings per common share for the years ended December 30, 2000, December 29, 2001, and December 28, 2002 are as follows:

	2000	2001	2002
Basic			
Issued and outstanding shares (weighted average)	28,377,123	28,531,593	28,812,473
Effect of Dilutive Securities			
Stock options	601,142	757,095	760,947
Diluted	**28,978,265**	**29,288,688**	**29,573,420**

11. LEASES:

The Company has commitments under certain noncancelable operating leases. Total rental expense for the fiscal years ended December 30, 2000, December 29, 2001, and December 28, 2002 related to operating leases amounted to approximately $2.4 million, $2.8 million, and $3.8 million, respectively. The Company's most significant lease is a two-year operating lease for an aircraft with annual renewals for up to three additional years. The future minimum rental commitments under the initial term of this lease is $1.4 million in 2003. In addition, if the Company chooses the return option at the end of the initial lease term in February of 2004, the Company has guaranteed up to $16 million of any deficiency in the event that the Lessor's net sales proceeds of the aircraft are less than $18.5 million.

Approximate future minimum rental commitments under these leases at December 28, 2002 are summarized as follows:

Fiscal Year	(in thousands)
2003	2,598
2004	1,117
2005	1,099
2006	1,023
2007	980
2008 and thereafter	4,477

12. BONUS PLAN:

The Company has a discretionary bonus plan for certain key employees. Bonus expense included in selling, general, and administrative expenses for the years ended December 30, 2000, December 29, 2001, and December 28, 2002 was $9.0 million, $6.1 million, and $11.5 million, respectively.

13. STOCK OPTION PLANS:

The Company has an Employee Stock Purchase Plan (the "Purchase Plan") - 1993, a Non-employee Director Stock Option Plan (the "Director Plan") - 1993, and an Incentive Stock Option Plan (the "Option Plan") - 1993:

Stock Purchase Plan

The Company's Purchase Plan qualifies under Section 423 of the Internal Revenue Code. The Company has reserved 683,438 shares of Common Stock for issuance under the Purchase Plan. During the years ended December 29, 2001, and December 28, 2002, 64,643 shares and 45,875 shares, respectively, were purchased under the Purchase Plan. The weighted-average fair value of purchase rights granted in 2001 and 2002 was $8.74 and $17.88, respectively. Under the Purchase Plan, an eligible employee may purchase shares of common stock from the Company through payroll deductions of up to 10% of base compensation, at a price per share equal to 85% of the lesser of the fair market value of the Company's Common Stock as of the first day (grant date) or the last day (purchase date) of each six-month offering period under the Purchase Plan.

The Purchase Plan is administered by a committee appointed by the Board. Any employee who is customarily employed for at least 20 hours per week and more than five months in a calendar year by the Company, or by any majority-owned subsidiary designated from time to time by the Board, and who does not own 5% or more of the total combined voting power or value of all classes of the Company's outstanding capital stock, is eligible to participate in the Purchase Plan.

Directors' Option Plan

Each non-employee director of the Company is entitled to participate in the Company's "Director Plan." The Board of Directors and the stockholders have authorized a total of 352,500 shares of Common Stock for issuance pursuant to the Director Plan. Under the terms of the Director Plan, each eligible non-employee director is automatically granted an option to purchase 8,000 shares of Common Stock (the "Initial Option") on the later of the effective date of the Company's initial public offering or the date on which the optionee first becomes a director of the Company. Thereafter, each optionee is automatically granted an additional option to purchase 3,500 shares of Common Stock (a "Subsequent Option") on September 30 of each year if, on such date, the optionee has served as a director of the Company for at least six months. Each Initial Option vests over five years at the rate of 20% of the shares subject to the Initial Option at the end of each anniversary following the date of grant. Each Subsequent Option vests in full on the fifth anniversary of its date of grant. The exercise price of each option is the fair market value of the Common Stock as determined by the closing price reported by the New York Stock Exchange on the date of grant. As of December 28, 2002, 89,100 options had been exercised, and options to purchase 79,700 shares of common stock were outstanding.

Option Plan

The Option Plan provides for the grant to employees of incentive stock options within the meaning of Section 422 of the Internal Revenue Code of 1986, as amended (the "Code"), and for the grant to employees and consultants of the Company of nonstatutory stock options. A total of 3,257,813 shares of Common Stock have been reserved for issuance under the Option Plan. As of December 28, 2002, 975,230 options had been excercised, and options to purchase 1,261,823 shares of Common Stock were outstanding. These options vest ratably over five years commencing with the date of grant.

The exercise price of all incentive stock options granted under the Option Plan must be at least equal to the fair market value of a share of the Company's Common Stock on the date of grant. With respect to any participant possessing more than 10% of the voting power of the Company's outstanding capital stock, the exercise price of any option granted must equal at least 110% of the fair market value on the grant date, and the maximum term of the option must not exceed five years. The terms of all other options granted under the Option Plan may not exceed ten years.

Transactions involving the Director Plan and the Option Plan are summarized with corresponding weighted-average exercise prices as follows:

	Shares	Price
Outstanding at January 1, 2000	1,214,188	$ 5.99
Granted	206,851	12.43
Exercised	(68,810)	3.25
Forfeited	(14,661)	7.93
Outstanding at December 30, 2000	**1,337,568**	**6.48**
Granted	218,401	12.42
Exercised	(140,163)	3.95
Forfeited	(45,033)	8.21
Outstanding at December 29, 2001	**1,370,773**	**7.62**
Granted	178,650	23.88
Exercised	(192,495)	4.62
Forfeited	(15,405)	13.77
Outstanding at December 28, 2002	**$1,341,523**	**$10.15**

For various price ranges, weighted average characteristics of all outstanding stock options at December 28, 2002 were as follows:

	Options Outstanding			Options Exercisable	
Range of Exercise Prices	Shares	Remaining Life (years)	Weighted-Average Price	Shares	Weighted-Average Price
$0 - 2.43	75,700	.2	$0.65	75,700	$0.65
$2.44 - 4.86	306,753	3.3	$3.18	306,753	$3.18
$7.29 - 9.72	205,356	5.3	$7.73	148,034	$7.74
$9.73 - 12.15	386,138	7.3	$11.10	135,307	$10.68
$12.16 - 14.58	171,226	7.3	$12.76	58,621	$12.66
$14.59 - 17.01	19,750	8.4	$16.19	3,200	$16.18
$19.44 - 21.87	17,500	9.8	$20.03	-------	------
$21.88 - 24.30	159,100	9.3	$24.30	-------	------
	1,341,523			**727,615**	

At December 28, 2002, the Company has three stock-based employee compensation plans. The Company accounts for those plans under the recognition and measurement principles of APB Opinion No. 25, Accounting for Stock Issued to Employees, and related Interpretations. No stock-based employee compensation cost is reflected in net income, as all options granted under those plans had an exercise price equal to the market value of the underlying common stock on the date of grant. The following table illustrates the effect on net income and earnings per share if the Company had applied the fair value recognition provisions of SFAS 123, Accounting for Stock-based Compensation, to stock-based employee compensation.

	2000	2001	2002
	(In thousands, except per share data)		
Net income - as reported	$42,521	$24,919	$44,515
Deduct: Total stock-based employee compensation expense			
Determined under fair value based method for all awards,			
net of related tax effects	(778)	(1,039)	(1,328)
Net income - pro forma	**$41,743**	**$23,880**	**$43,187**
Earnings per share:			
Basic - as reported	$1.50	$0.87	$1.55
Basic - pro forma	1.47	0.84	1.50
Diluted - as reported	$1.47	$0.85	$1.51
Diluted - pro forma	1.44	0.82	1.46

For purposes of the above pro forma information, the fair value of each option grant was estimated at the date of grant using the Black-Scholes option pricing model with the following weighted average assumptions:

	2000	2001	2002
Risk-free interest rate	6.27%	4.42%	4.22%
Expected life (in years)	5.68	6.23	5.97
Expected volatility	54.63%	55.02%	56.92%
Expected dividend yield	0.00%	0.00%	0.00%

14. FAIR VALUE OF FINANCIAL INSTRUMENTS:

The fair value of the Company's financial instruments are presented below. The estimates require subjective judgments and are approximate. Changes in methodologies and assumptions could significantly affect estimates.

Line of Credit - The carrying amount outstanding on the revolving line of credit is $26.0 million and $51.4 million at December 29, 2001 and December 28, 2002, respectively, which approximates the estimated fair value as this instrument requires interest payments at a market rate of interest plus a margin.

Long-term Note Payable - The carrying amount outstanding on the long-term note payable is $52 million (including $21.7 million of current payable) at December 28, 2002, which approximates the estimated fair value as this instrument requires interest payments at a market rate of interest plus a margin.

15. 401(K) DEFINED CONTRIBUTION PLAN:

The Company sponsors a 401(k) defined contribution plan covering substantially all full-time employees. Company contributions to the plan totaled $593,000 in 2000, $629,000 in 2001, and $748,000 in 2002.

16. COMMITMENTS AND CONTINGENCIES:

Repurchase Agreements

Many of the Company's sales to independent dealers are made on a "floor plan" basis by a bank or finance company which lends the dealer all or substantially all of the wholesale purchase price and retains a security interest in the vehicles. Upon request of a lending institution financing a dealer's purchases of the Company's product, the Company will execute a repurchase agreement. These agreements provide that, for up to 18 months after a unit is shipped, the Company will repurchase a dealer's inventory in the event of a default by a dealer to its lender.

The Company's liability under repurchase agreements is limited to the unpaid balance owed to the lending institution by reason of its extending credit to the dealer to purchase its vehicles, reduced by the resale value of vehicles which may be repurchased. The risk of loss is spread over numerous dealers and financial institutions.

No significant net losses were incurred during the years ended December 30, 2000, December 29, 2001, or December 28, 2002. The approximate amount subject to contingent repurchase obligations arising from these agreements at December 28, 2002 is $490.2 million, with approximately 8.4% concentrated with one dealer. If the Company were obligated to repurchase a significant number of units under any repurchase agreement, its business, operating results, and financial condition could be adversely affected.

Product Liability

The Company is subject to regulations which may require the Company to recall products with design or safety defects, and such recall could have a material adverse effect on the Company's business, results of operations, and financial condition.

The Company has from time to time been subject to product liability claims. To date, the Company has been successful in obtaining product liability insurance on terms the Company considers acceptable. The terms of the policy contain a self-insured retention amount of $500,000 per occurrence, with a maximum annual aggregate self-insured retention of $3.0 million. Overall product liability insurance, including umbrella coverage, is available to a maximum amount of $100.0 million for each occurrence, as well as in the aggregate. There can be no assurance that the Company will be able to obtain insurance coverage in the future at acceptable levels or that the cost of insurance will be reasonable. Furthermore, successful assertion against the Company of one or a series of large uninsured claims, or of one or a series of claims exceeding any insurance coverage, could have a material adverse effect on the Company's business, results of operations, and financial condition.

Litigation

The Company is involved in various legal proceedings which are incidental to the industry and for which certain matters are covered in whole or in part by insurance or, otherwise, the Company has recorded accruals for estimated settlements. Management believes that any liability which may result from these proceedings will not have a material adverse effect on the Company's consolidated financial statements.

17. QUARTERLY RESULTS (UNAUDITED):

Year ended December 30, 2000	1st Quarter	2nd Quarter	3rd Quarter	4th Quarter
(In thousands, except per share data)				
Net sales	$237,983	$226,091	$226,393	$211,423
Gross profit	37,314	32,117	30,908	29,311
Operating income	21,375	18,217	16,143	14,095
Net income	12,918	11,148	9,807	8,648
Earnings per common share:				
Basic	$0.46	$0.39	$0.35	$0.30
Diluted	$0.44	$0.39	$0.34	$0.30

Year ended December 29, 2001	1st Quarter	2nd Quarter	3rd Quarter	4th Quarter
(In thousands, except per share data)				
Net sales	$211,228	$223,424	$240,831	$261,590
Gross profit	25,488	25,804	30,548	32,150
Operating income	9,088	9,153	11,438	12,979
Net income	5,197	5,480	6,623	7,619
Earnings per common share:				
Basic	$0.18	$0.19	$0.23	$0.27
Diluted	$0.18	$0.19	$0.23	$0.26

Year ended December 28, 2002	1st Quarter	2nd Quarter	3rd Quarter	4th Quarter
(In thousands, except per share data)				
Net sales	$293,600	$313,742	$314,680	$300,667
Gross profit	37,745	41,229	42,817	41,338
Operating income	16,579	18,724	20,034	20,590
Net income	9,673	10,970	11,788	12,084
Earnings per common share:				
Basic	$0.34	$0.38	$0.41	$0.42
Diluted	$0.33	$0.37	$0.40	$0.41

Report of Independent Accountants

To the Stockholders and Board of Directors of Monaco Coach Corporation

In our opinion, the accompanying consolidated balance sheets and the related consolidated statements of income, of stockholders' equity, and of cash flows present fairly, in all material respects, the financial position of Monaco Coach Corporation and its Subsidiaries (the Company) at December 29, 2001 and December 28, 2002, and the results of their operations and their cash flows for each of the three years in the period ended December 28, 2002 in conformity with accounting principles generally accepted in the United States of America. These financial statements are the responsibility of the Company's management; our responsibility is to express an opinion on these financial statements based on our audits. We conducted our audits of these statements in accordance with auditing standards generally accepted in the United States of America, which require that we plan and perform the audit to obtain reasonable assurance about whether the financial statements are free of material misstatement. An audit includes examining, on a test basis, evidence supporting the amounts and disclosures in the financial statements, assessing the accounting principles used and significant estimates made by management, and evaluating the overall financial statement presentation. We believe that our audits provide a reasonable basis for our opinion.

As discussed in Note 1 to the consolidated financial statements, the Company adopted the provisions of Statement of Financial Accounting Standards No. 142, Goodwill and Other Intangible Assets.

PricewaterhouseCoopers LLP

PricewaterhouseCoopers LLP
Portland, Oregon
January 28, 2003

Five-Year Selected Financial Data

The following table sets forth financial data of Monaco Coach Corporation for the years indicated (in thousands of dollars, except share and per share data and consolidated operating data).

	Fiscal Year				
	1998	1999	2000	2001	2002
Consolidated Statements of Income Data:					
Net sales	$594,802	$780,815	$901,890	$937,073	$1,222,689
Cost of sales	512,570	658,536	772,240	823,083	1,059,560
Gross profit	**82,232**	**122,279**	**129,650**	**113,990**	**163,129**
Selling, general, and administrative expenses	41,571	48,791	59,175	70,687	87,202
Amortization of goodwill	645	645	645	645	0
Operating income	**40,016**	**72,843**	**69,830**	**42,658**	**75,927**
Other income, net	(607)	(142)	(182)	(334)	(105)
Interest expense	1,861	1,143	632	2,357	2,752
Income before provision for income taxes	**38,762**	**71,842**	**69,380**	**40,635**	**73,280**
Provision for income taxes	16,093	28,081	26,859	15,716	28,765
Net income	**$ 22,669**	**$43,761**	**$42,521**	**$24,919**	**$44,515**
Earnings per common share:					
Basic	$0.81	$1.55	$1.50	$0.87	$1.55
Diluted	$0.79	$1.51	$1.47	$0.85	$1.51
Weighted average shares outstanding:					
Basic	27,987,004	28,213,444	28,377,123	28,531,593	28,812,473
Diluted	28,622,976	29,050,453	28,978,264	29,288,688	29,573,420
Consolidated Operating Data:					
Units sold:					
Motor coaches	4,768	6,233	6,632	6,228	8,005
Towables	2,217	3,269	3,377	3,261	3,206
Dealerships at end of period	263	294	338	385	420
Consolidated Balance Sheet Data:					
Working capital	$23,676	$38,888	$69,299	$63,694	$114,241
Total assets	190,127	246,727	321,610	427,098	547,417
Long-term borrowings, less current portion	5,400	---	---	30,000	30,333
Total stockholders' equity	98,193	143,339	186,625	213,130	260,627

MONACO COACH CORPORATION
BOARD OF DIRECTORS

Kay L. Toolson
Chairman and Chief Executive Officer, Monaco Coach Corporation

Robert P. Hanafee, Jr.
Private Investor

L. Ben Lytle
Chairman, Anthem, Inc. (Healthcare Services)

Dennis D. Oklak
President, Duke Realty (Real Estate Services)

Carl E. Ring, Jr.
Partner, Liberty Partners (Financial Services)

Richard A. Rouse
Private Investor

Roger A. Vandenberg
President, Cariad Capital (Financial Services)

EXECUTIVE OFFICERS

Kay L. Toolson
Chairman and Chief Executive Officer

John W. Nepute
President

Marty Daley
Vice President and Chief Financial Officer

Richard E. Bond
Senior Vice President, Chief Administrative Officer and Secretary

Irv Yoder
Vice President and Director of Indiana Manufacturing

Marty Garriott
Vice President and Director of Oregon Manufacturing

Mike Snell
Vice President of Sales

Patrick Carroll
Vice President of Product Development

John Healey
Vice President of Purchasing

OTHER OFFICERS AND KEY MANAGEMENT PERSONNEL

Kurt W. Anderson, Terri Archambault, Chris A. Ballinger, Joni S. Beachy, Michael R. Becker, Steve Bettis, Mikeal D. Blomme, Marvin P. Burns, Jeffrey P. Butler, Jan Cleveland, Russell Cobb, Dan Cornagey, Lee G. Covey, Arthur N. Deeds, Michael Duncan, Darryl F. Emery, Ron L. Ericson, Jenny Evans, Gordon C. Foster, James A. Fox, Paul E. Freet, Dennis E. Girod, Peter J. Hanes, Garth R. Herring, Scott Hicks, Dale D. Hoogenboom, Brett Howard, Chris G. Hundt, Enoch R. Hutchcraft, Sandra J. Kadash, Mark P. Kealoha, Paul Kellerman, Charles J. Kimball, Edgar F. Kinney, April A. Klein, Aaron Lafleur, Donald J. Lance, Scott A. Lilly, Philip R. Lord, Jim Mac, Richard K. Mackin, Melanie Hoover Marsh, Jack R. Mason, Daryl L. Maurer, John Mayger, Brad McKinney, B. Ray Mehaffey, Gary W. Mehaffey, Ty Meier, Arnold P. Morosky, Wes Murphy, Deanna R. Ota, T. Michael Pangburn, Yvonne Reed, Pat Robbins, D. Page Robertson, T. Alan L. Schmucker, Rick A. Schraw, Defoe A. Shook, Jr., Michael A. Spencer, Lyle D. Stutzman, Charles Tillery, Don Turner, Mike Warren, Dale D. Weins, Terry L. Welles, Scott E. Zimmer, Tom Zoll, Joe Zurbuch

CORPORATE INFORMATION

Corporate Headquarters/Oregon Manufacturing Facilities
91320 Industrial Way, Coburg, OR 97408, Telephone (541) 686-8011

Indiana Facilities
606 Nelson's Parkway, Wakarusa, IN 46573, Telephone (574) 862-7211

On The World Wide Web
www.monaco-online.com

STOCK TRANSFER AGENT
Wells Fargo Bank Minnesota, N.A.
St. Paul, MN

COMMON STOCK
The company's common stock is listed on the New York Stock Exchange. Its trading symbol is MNC.

EMPLOYEES
5,933 total employees.

SERVICE AND WARRANTY CENTERS
30725 Diamond Hill Road, Harrisburg, OR 97446, Telephone (800) 283-0869
1809 West Hively Avenue, Elkhart, IN 46517, Telephone (574) 295-8060
4505 Monaco Way, Wildwood, FL 34785, Telephone (866) 888-8941

INDEPENDENT AUDITORS
PricewaterhouseCoopers LLP, Portland, Oregon

ANNUAL MEETING
The 2003 annual meeting will be held on May 13, 2003 at 1:00 p.m. in Wakarusa, Indiana.

FORM 10-K AND INVESTOR INFORMATION
Copies of the Annual Report on Form 10-K filed with the Securities and Exchange Commission and other investor information may be obtained without charge from the Company upon written request to its Coburg, Oregon office, attention Investor Relations.

CORPORATE COUNSEL
Wilson, Sonsini, Goodrich and Rosati, Professional Corporation, Palo Alto, California

INVESTOR RELATIONS INQUIRIES SHOULD BE DIRECTED TO:
Monaco Coach Corporation
91320 Industrial Way, Coburg, OR 97408
Attention: Investor Relations
Telephone (800) 634-0855 or on the World Wide Web at www.monaco-online.com

Design by Kaufman/Kane, Mark Comstock; Photography by Mark Clifford; Contributing Writer John Strieder

Printed in USA.

MONACO COACH CORPORATION

91320 Industrial Way, Coburg, OR 97408
www.monaco-online.com
Telephone (541) 686-8011
NYSE: MNC

MONACO COACH CORPORATION PRODUCT LINE

DEALER PROFILE

Successful RV manufacturers understand the importance of good relationships with both retail dealers and customers.

For Monaco Coach Corporation, managing a profitable company depends on its healthy relationships with recreational vehicle (RV) dealers.

It's easy to make the mistake of assuming RV dealerships are set up just like automobile dealerships. They aren't. Most dealers don't carry all of Monaco Coach Corporation's brands or models. The typical dealer has developed expertise and a reputation in a particular product segment, such as motorhomes or towable recreational vehicles. As a result, Monaco Coach Corporation products often share dealer space with similar models from competitors. Retail customers seek dealers who can meet their needs and carry a variety of products, and manufacturers want to align themselves with these strong dealers.

Despite its advantages, this system can create challenges for an RV manufacturer. When a competing coach-maker offers a rebate or another financial incentive, Monaco Coach Corporation may choose to respond. Financing throws another wrinkle into the mix. Inventory finance costs are the largest business expense for retail dealers. Fluctuations in interest rates, along with overall dealer inventory and retail demand levels, affect how much new product dealers can afford to (or are willing to) bring into their dealerships.

CREATING DEALER ENTHUSIASM

So Monaco Coach Corporation is competing for floor space, not only with competitors, but with the dealer's temptation to leave a spot on a sales floor empty in tough economic times. But when the going gets tough, Monaco Coach Corporation gets creative.

The most effective and important way to overcome dealer resistance is through product innovation. Customers' confidence and enthusiasm are the two biggest components driving RV sales today. The same axiom holds true for RV dealers. When uncertain times pressure confidence, enthusiasm for new products can overcome a dealer's reluctance. Monaco Coach Corporation continues to launch new and re-designed products that offer unique and innovative features to excite dealers.

Aggressive product development is the most important tactic Monaco Coach Corporation uses to stimulate orders. However, at the start of 2003, the Company introduced retail and wholesale incentives similar to the Company's successful programs of 2000-2001. The incentives are designed to encourage "turns" — replacing retail-sold coaches on dealer lots with new orders filled from the manufacturer. To stimulate sales, the Company may also offer sales incentives through dealers to consumers. Typically, this offer is coupled with a discount given to dealers who replace a retail-sold coach with a factory order. This allows the Company to maintain its presence on sales floors during lean times.

The Company-Dealer relationship has other important aspects. For example, when dealers reduce inventory, the Company may either adjust production, increase incentives, or both. That is why Monaco Coach Corporation works closely with its dealers. If inventories are too high, dealers may order less. If inventories are too low, dealers don't have anything to sell.

EXPANDED DISTRIBUTION

Historically, Monaco Coach Corporation has expanded its dealer representation as it has expanded its product line. For example, the Company introduced Class C "mini-motorhomes" two years ago to allow dealers interested in that market segment to carry one of the Company's products. This way, Monaco Coach Corporation can challenge competitors on many fronts.

The lower the product price, the greater the number of dealers Monaco Coach Corporation needs in its family. Conversely, more expensive coaches require less dealer representation. As Monaco Coach Corporation has expanded into lower-priced product lines, its number of dealers has grown accordingly. Today, the Company has approximately 425 dealer locations throughout the United States and Canada. The Company also employs a "multi-brand" strategy to align itself with more than one strong dealer in a given coverage area.

Monaco Coach Corporation's success is closely tied to the success of its retail dealer partners, so a close manufacturer-dealer relationship is essential. As in any relationship, this bond is strengthened with attentiveness, thoughtfulness and good communication. With careful navigation, more motorcoaches can travel a smooth, easy route from the factory to the dealer to the highways of North America.

CUSTOMER PROFILE

The nature of the typical consumer may be the most misunderstood aspect of the RV industry. Thousands of happy travelers roaming the highways of North America view their RV as much more than a weekend toy. To these loyal RV enthusiasts, the choice to spend leisure time in their RVs is an important lifestyle decision.

This high customer commitment level is a key ingredient in the RV industry's recipe for success. For the RV enthusiast, the coach plays a far greater role in leisure planning than many other luxury purchases, and many RV owners live in their coach on a full-time or part-time basis. Consider, for a moment, the level of commitment these enthusiasts have to the RV lifestyle. RV buyers do their homework before choosing a vehicle. In fact, many buyers will shop for their RV up to 36 months before they decide to buy. It is often said that RV buyers may delay their decisions to purchase, but rarely abandon the idea altogether. This high customer commitment level adds stability to the RV market.

Average enthusiasts purchase three to five RVs during their buying lifetime. Typically, they trade up into new products every three to five years. Why is this important? The frequency with which RV owners trade stresses the importance of aggressive, innovative product development and brand positioning. If a couple with a three-year-old RV visits a retail dealer's sales lot, they want to see a product that is considerably different – and better – than the vehicle they already have. If Monaco Coach Corporation continues to offer new products that are unique and attractive, the Company can entice these buyers to purchase again and again.

Best of all, the target market of potential RV customers is growing by leaps and bounds. Monaco Coach Corporation customers range across all ages but the majority are between the ages of 55-70 years young. This market is projected to grow by over 65% between now and 2010! Not to mention the younger families who are entering the RV market in greater numbers than ever before.

Although the RV industry's potential customer base is growing at an astonishing rate, the industry must still convince this group that the RV lifestyle is for them. Toward that end, the Recreational Vehicle Industry Association is continuing the popular "Go RVing – Life's a Trip" marketing campaign. This national advertising effort has introduced millions of families to the advantages of RV travel and has reaped high rewards for the RV industry. Attitudes toward leisure travel are changing, and more customers are discovering that an RV is the safest, most flexible means of family travel.

continued on back page

RV enthusiasts love the outdoors. These energetic travelers demand the world-class accommodations provided by luxury RV resorts.

SIGNATURE SERIES
$470,000-$520,000

EXECUTIVE
$370,000-$420,000

DYNASTY
$295,000-$330,000

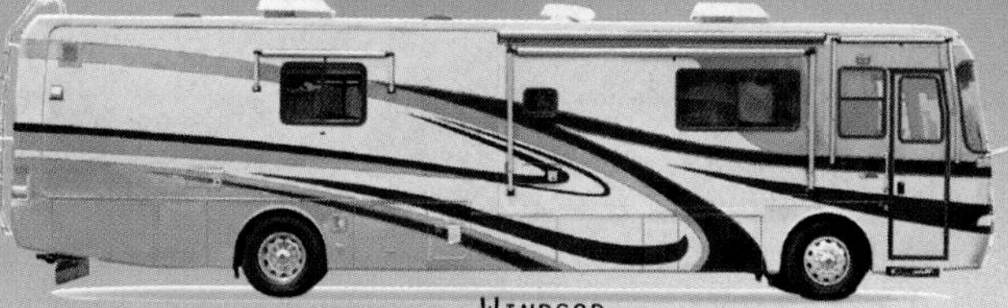

WINDSOR
$225,000-$270,000

Diesel Products

CAMELOT
$220,000-$240,000

LA PALMA
$95,000-$120,000

Class C

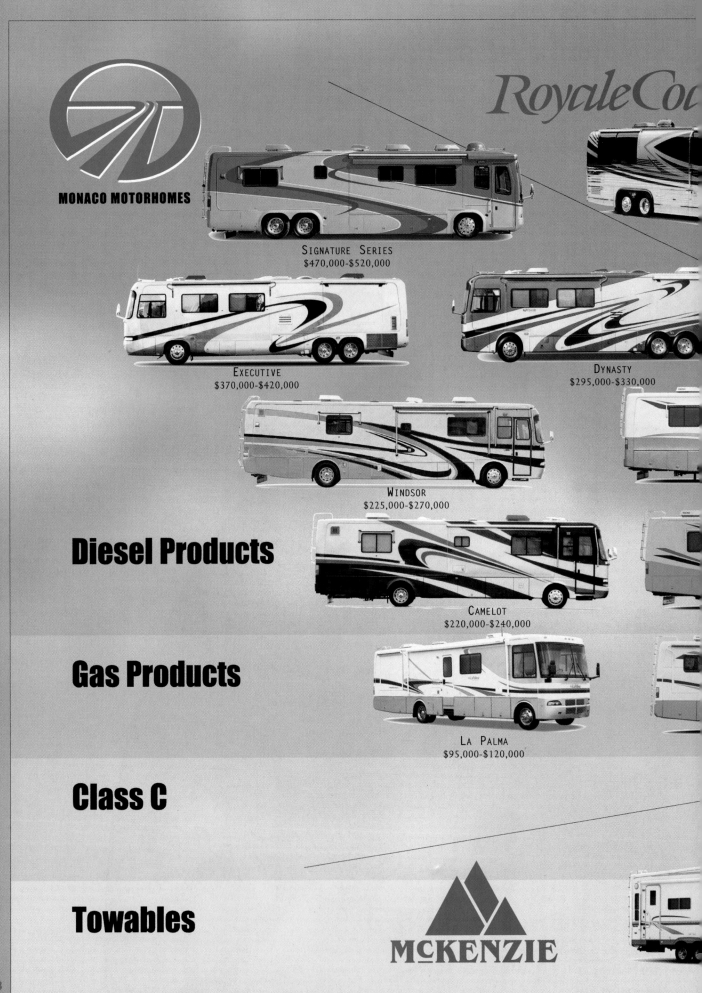

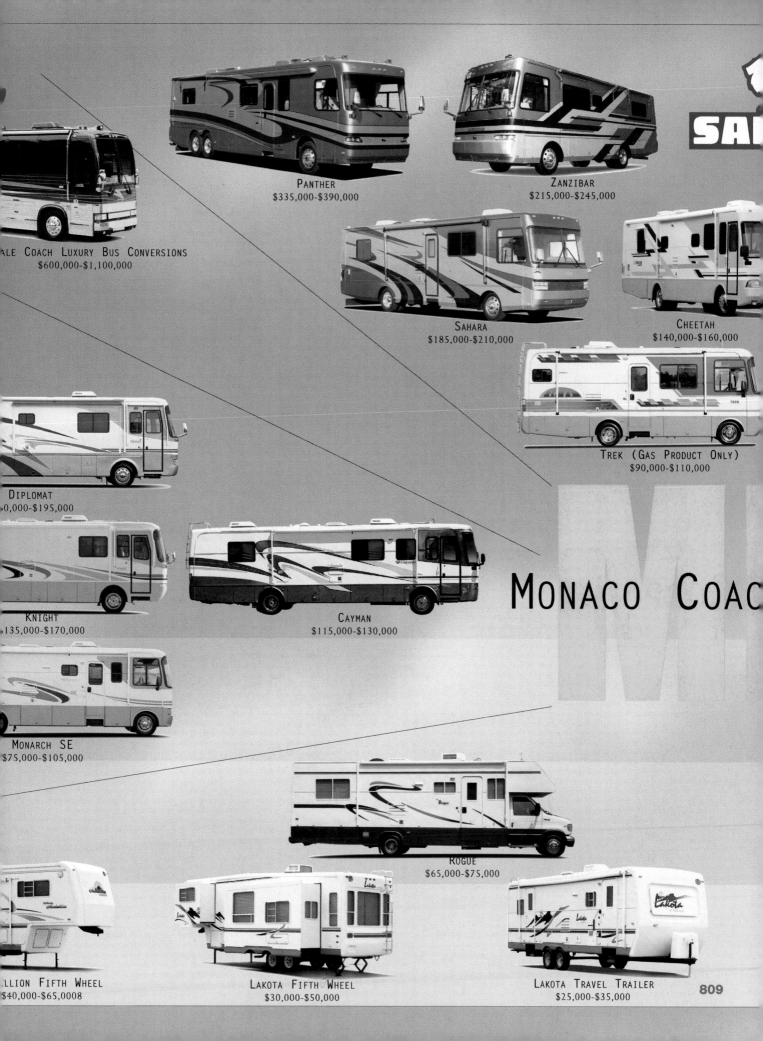

ALE COACH LUXURY BUS CONVERSIONS
$600,000-$1,100,000

PANTHER
$335,000-$390,000

ZANZIBAR
$215,000-$245,000

SA

SAHARA
$185,000-$210,000

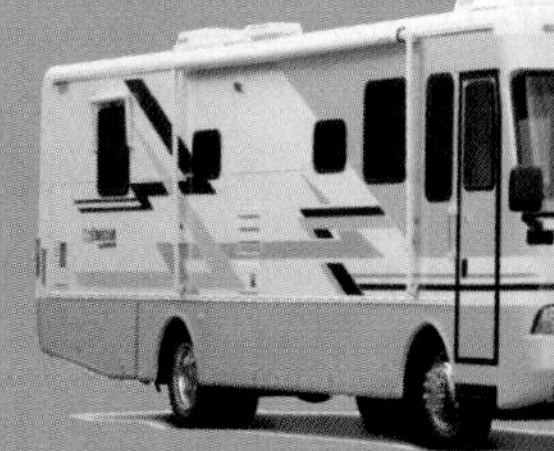

CHEETAH
$140,000-$160,000

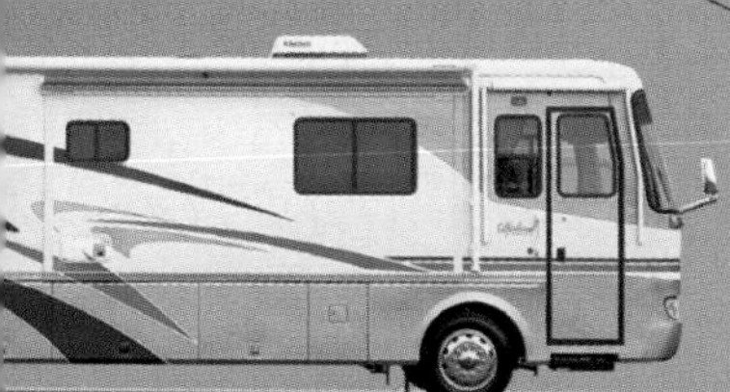

DIPLOMAT
0,000-$195,000

TREK (GAS PRODUCT ONLY)
$90,000-$110,000

KNIGHT
135,000-$170,000

CAYMAN
$115,000-$130,000

MONACO COAC

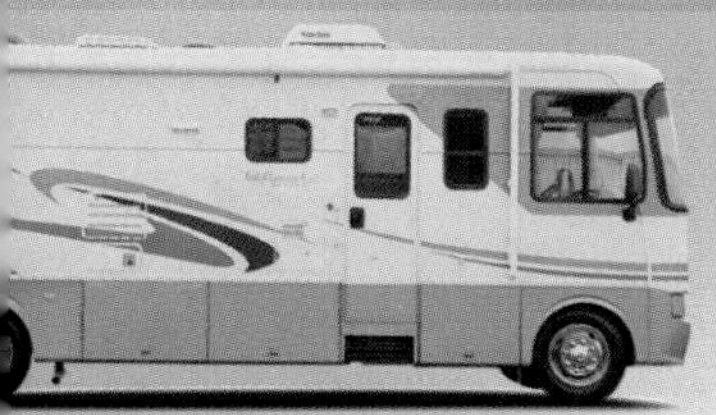

MONARCH SE
$75,000-$105,000

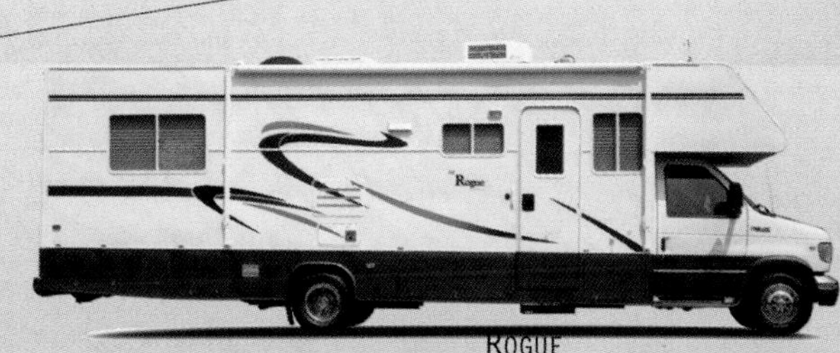

ROGUE
$65,000-$75,000

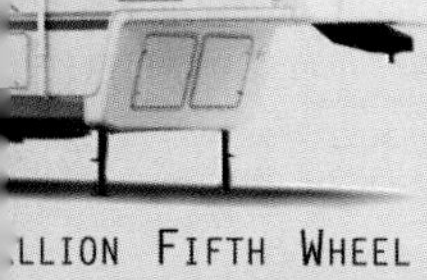

LLION FIFTH WHEEL
$40,000-$65,0008

LAKOTA FIFTH WHEEL
$30,000-$50,000

LAKOTA TRAVEL TRAILER
$25,000-$35,000

MARQUIS
$445,000-$535,000

PATRIOT
$310,000-$360,00

MONTEREY
$210,000-$230,000

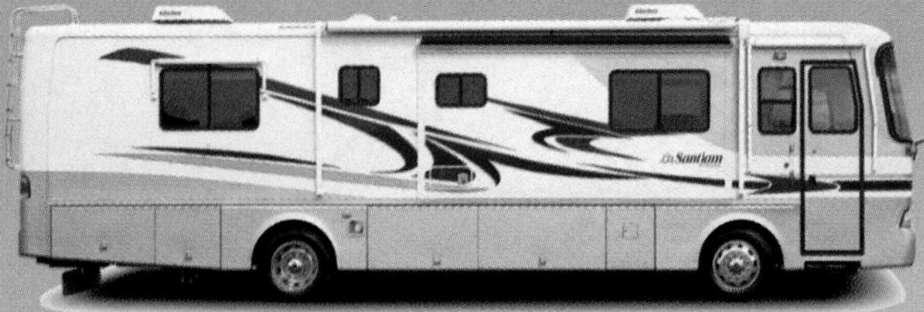
SANTIAM
$155,000-$180,000

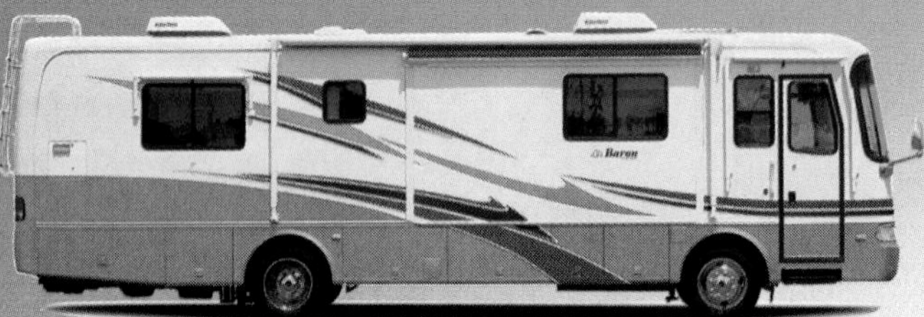
BARON
$135,000-$160,000

CORPORATION

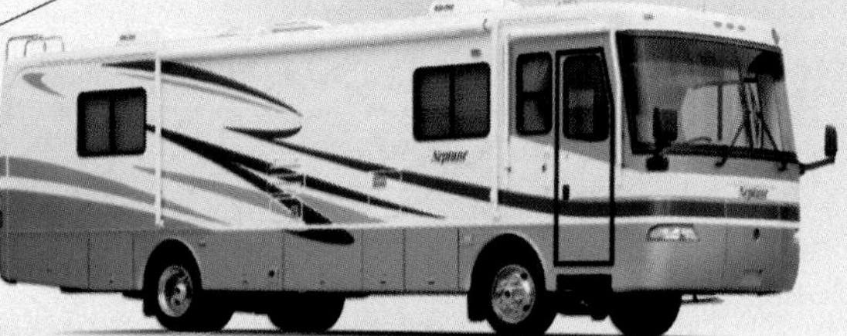
NEPTUNE
$115,000-$135,000

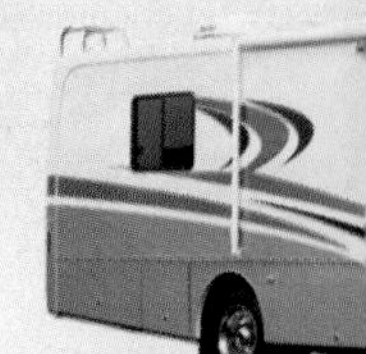
AMBASSA
$135,000-$1

ADMIRAL
$75,000-$105,000

TRAVEL
$85,000-$1

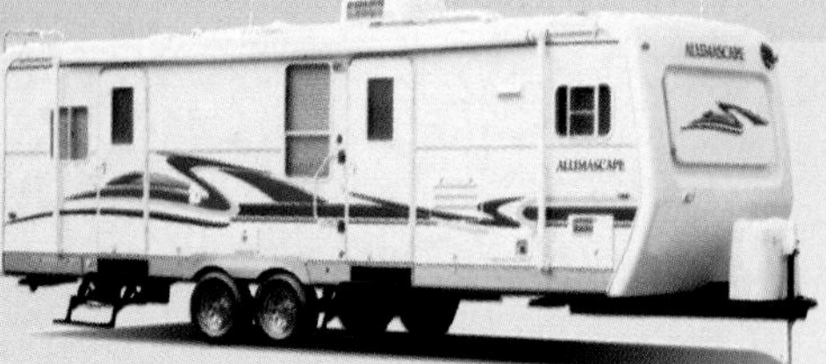
ALUMASCAPE TRAVEL TRAILER
$25,000-$35,000

ALUMASCAPE FIFTH WHEEL
$30,000-$40,000

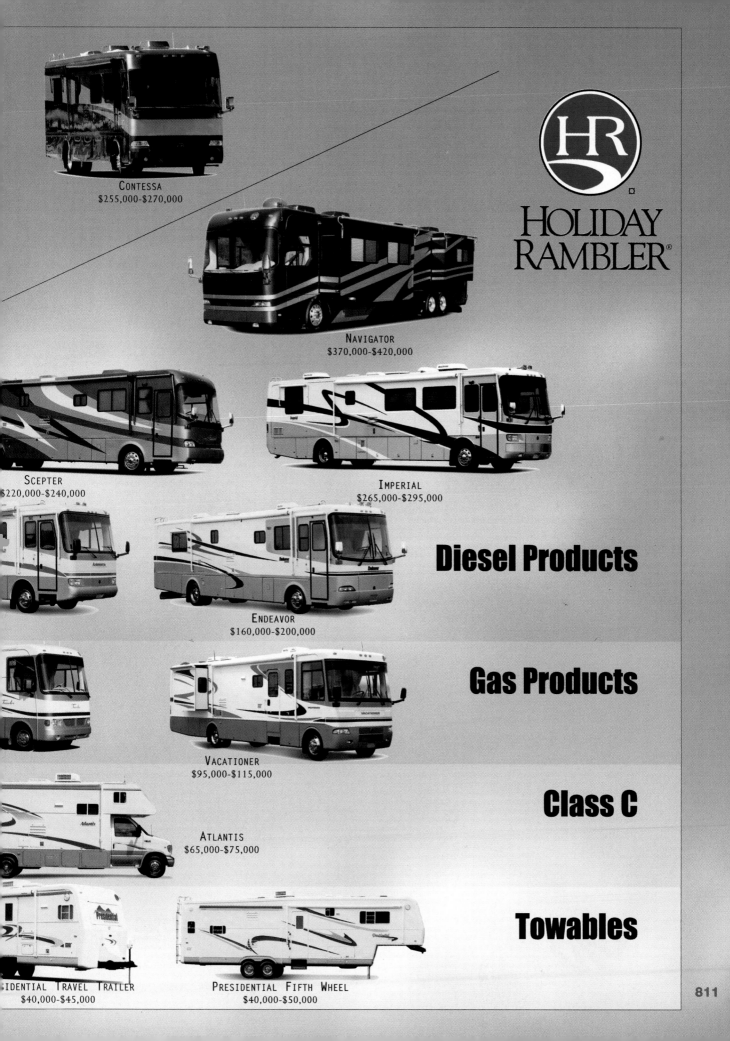

CONTESSA
$255,000-$270,000

NAVIGATOR
$370,000-$420,000

SCEPTER
$220,000-$240,000

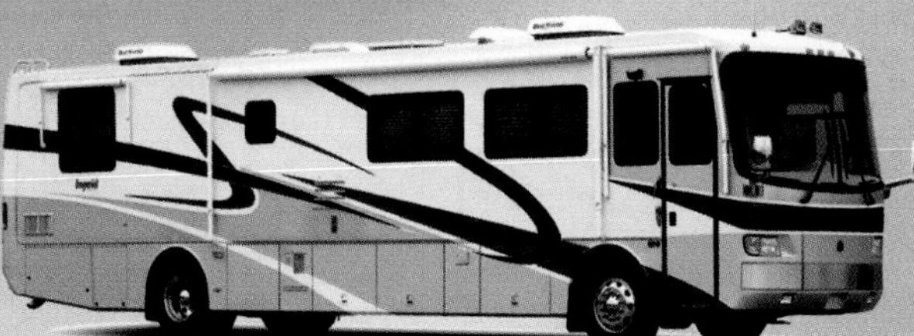

IMPERIAL
$265,000-$295,000

Diesel Products

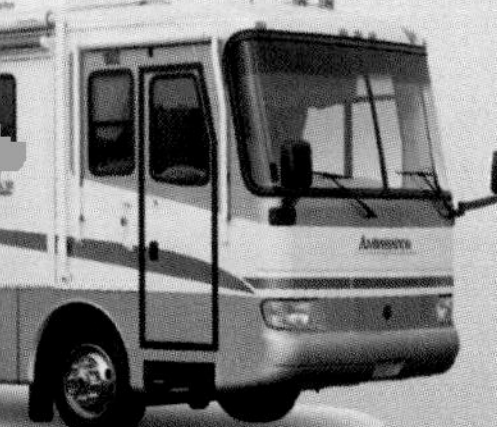

ENDEAVOR
$160,000-$200,000

Gas Products

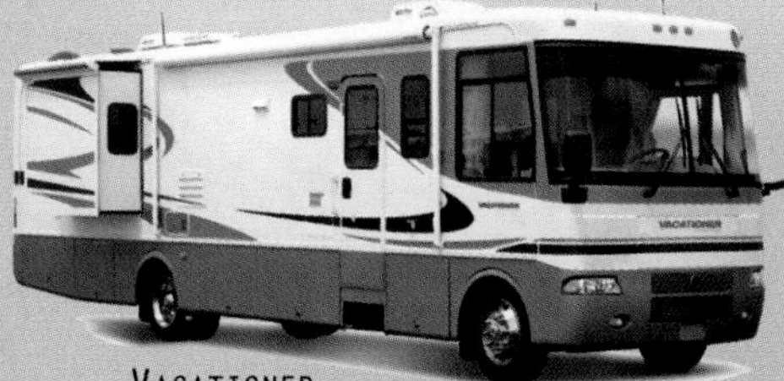

VACATIONER
$95,000-$115,000

Class C

ATLANTIS
$65,000-$75,000

Towables

SIDENTIAL TRAVEL TRAILER
$40,000-$45,000

PRESIDENTIAL FIFTH WHEEL
$40,000-$50,000

When the time comes to decide on the ideal RV for their needs, customers have a greater number of attractive choices than they ever imagined. Enticing features such as slide-out rooms dramatically increase interior living space. Better-performing gasoline and diesel-powered motorhomes are supported by sophisticated service networks, providing owners with comfort, luxury and all-important peace of mind.

Fuel prices and interest rates are often misunderstood as they relate to the RV industry. The average RV owner travels approximately 5,000 miles per year. If a typical RV delivers ten miles per gallon and fuel prices rise 50 cents per gallon, the RV enthusiast will experience an annual operating increase of a mere $250. Compared to airline travel and hotel expenses, RV travel represents a bargain.

Since the majority of RV buyers purchase their new coaches with a combination of earned money and trade-in equity, consumer credit and interest rates have a lower impact than might be expected on their decisions to buy. Furthermore, those buyers who do require financing tend to borrow far less than the purchase price of the vehicle, and they generally make up the difference with a combination of cash and trade. Not to mention that the interest is usually tax deductible, as RVs qualify as a second (or primary) home. Historically, consumer credit has not been a limiting factor for RV industry growth.

Approximately 60% of RV enthusiasts begin their adventures with pre-owned products. This creates a robust pre-owned RV market that provides an important revenue stream for retail dealers. Additionally, healthy pre-owned RV demand helps keep resale values high, further enticing current RV owners to trade their coaches for new models. Owners of pre-owned RVs who enjoy the lifestyle become excellent new-coach customers, further stressing the long-term positive impact of a healthy pre-owned market.

In short, RV consumers are highly committed to their lifestyle, and this commitment is demonstrated through their repeat purchases. Highly committed customers, relatively unfazed by fuel prices and less reliant on interest rates, result in a stable RV market. For Monaco Coach Corporation, innovative products, exceptional customer service, attractive demographic trends and changing attitudes toward leisure travel represent a potential sales bonanza for the next decade and beyond.

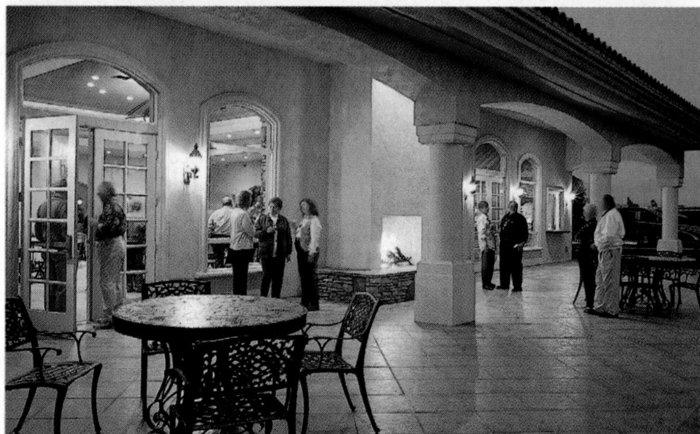

As RVs have become more sophisticated, so have RV resorts. These luxurious resorts defy the common image of a campground. Handsomely appointed RV lots, country club amenities and beautiful clubhouses are common resort features. Day trips, evening events and entertainment create a community with a true neighborhood feel.

MONACO COACH CORPORATION
91320 Industrial Way, Coburg, OR 97408
www.monaco-online.com
Telephone (541) 686-8011
NYSE: MNC

Glossary

Accelerated depreciation A higher amount of depreciation is recorded in the early years and a lower amount in the later years. (p. 373)

Account Record used to accumulate amounts for each individual asset, liability, revenue, expense, and component of owners' equity. (p. 117)

Accounting The process of identifying, measuring, and communicating economic information to various users. (p. 14)

Accounting controls Procedures concerned with safeguarding the assets or the reliability of the financial statements. (p. 228)

Accounting cycle A series of steps performed each period and culminating with the preparation of a set of financial statements. (p. 182)

Accounting system Methods and records used to accurately report an entity's transactions and to maintain accountability for its assets and liabilities. (p. 228)

Accounts payable Amounts owed for inventory, goods, or services acquired in the normal course of business. (p. 422)

Accounts receivable turnover ratio A measure of the number of times accounts receivable are collected in a period. (p. 669)

Accrual Cash has not yet been paid or received, but expense has been incurred or revenue earned. (p. 177)

Accrual basis A system of accounting in which revenues are recognized when earned and expenses when incurred. (p. 161)

Accrued asset An asset resulting from the recognition of a revenue before the receipt of cash. (p. 177)

Accrued liability A liability resulting from the recognition of an expense before the payment of cash. (pp. 177, 424)

Accrued pension cost The difference between the amount of pension recorded as an expense and the amount of the funding payment. (p. 516)

Acid-test or quick ratio A stricter test of liquidity than the current ratio; excludes inventory and prepayments from the numerator. (p. 667)

Acquisition cost The amount that includes all of the cost normally necessary to acquire an asset and prepare it for its intended use. (p. 369)

Additional paid-in capital The amount received for the issuance of stock in excess of the par value of the stock. (p. 544)

Adjusting entries Journal entries made at the end of a period by a company using the accrual basis of accounting. (p. 170)

Administrative controls Procedures concerned with efficient operation of the business and adherence to managerial policies. (p. 228)

Aging schedule A form used to categorize the various individual accounts receivable according to the length of time each has been outstanding. (p. 268)

Allowance method A method of estimating bad debts on the basis of either the net credit sales of the period or the accounts receivable at the end of the period. (p. 265)

American Accounting Association The professional organization for accounting educators. (p. 28)

American Institute of Certified Public Accountants (AICPA) The professional organization for certified public accountants. (p. 24)

Annuity A series of payments of equal amounts. (p. 439)

Asset A future economic benefit. (p. 8)

Asset turnover ratio The relationship between net sales and average total assets. (p. 675)

Audit committee Board of directors subset that acts as a direct contact between stockholders and the independent accounting firm. (p. 226)

Auditing The process of examining the financial statements and the underlying records of a company in order to render an opinion as to whether the statements are fairly represented. (p. 26)

Auditors' report The opinion rendered by a public accounting firm concerning the fairness of the presentation of the financial statements. (p. 26)

Authorized shares The maximum number of shares a corporation may issue as indicated in the corporate charter. (p. 542)

Available-for-sale securities Stocks and bonds that are not classified as either held-to-maturity or trading securities. (p. 256)

Balance sheet The financial statement that summarizes the assets, liabilities, and owners' equity at a specific point in time. (p. 17)

Bank reconciliation A form used by the accountant to reconcile the balance shown on the bank statement for a particular account with the balance shown in the accounting records. (p. 223)

Bank statement A detailed list, provided by the bank, of all the activity for a particular account during the month. (p. 221)

Blind receiving report Form used by the receiving department to account for the quantity and condition of merchandise received from a supplier. (p. 235)

Board of directors Group composed of key officers of a corporation and outside members responsible for general oversight of the affairs of the entity. (p. 226)

Bond A certificate that represents a corporation's promise to repay a certain amount of money and interest in the future. (p. 6)

Bond issue price The present value of the annuity of interest payments plus the present value of the principal. (p. 491)

Book value The original cost of an asset minus the amount of accumulated depreciation. (p. 372)

Book value per share Total stockholders' equity divided by the number of shares of common stock outstanding. (p. 557)

Business All the activities necessary to provide the members of an economic system with goods and services. (p. 4)

Business entity An organization operated to earn a profit. (p. 6)

Callable bonds Bonds that may be redeemed or retired before their specified due date. (p. 490)

Callable feature Allows the firm to eliminate a class of stock by paying the stockholders a specified amount. (p. 546)

Capital expenditure A cost that improves the asset and is added to the asset account. (p. 378)

Capital lease A lease that is recorded as an asset by the lessee. (p. 501)

Capital stock Indicates the owners' contributions to a corporation. (p. 8)

Capitalization of interest Interest on constructed assets is added to the asset account. (p. 371)

Carrying value The face value of a bond plus the amount of unamortized premium or minus the amount of unamortized discount. (p. 495)

Cash basis A system of accounting in which revenues are recognized when cash is received and expenses when cash is paid. (p. 161)

Cash equivalent An investment that is readily convertible to a known amount of cash and a maturity to the investor of three months or less. (pp. 219, 598)

Cash flow from operations to capital expenditures ratio A measure of the ability of a company to finance long-term asset acquisitions with cash from operations. (p. 673)

Cash flow from operations to current liabilities ratio A measure of the ability to pay current debts from operating cash flows. (p. 668)

Cash to cash operating cycle The length of time from the purchase of inventory to the collection of any receivable from the sale. (p. 671)

Certified Public Accountant (CPA) The designation for an individual who has passed a uniform exam administered by the AICPA and met other requirements as determined by individual states. (p. 24)

Change in estimate A change in the life of the asset or in its residual value. (p. 377)

Chart of accounts A numerical list of all the accounts used by a company. (p. 117)

Closing entries Journal entries made at the end of the period to return the balance in all nominal accounts to zero and transfer the net income or loss and the dividends to Retained Earnings. (p. 182)

Comparability For accounting information, the quality that allows a user to analyze two or more companies and look for similarities and differences. (p. 62)

Compensated absences Employee absences for which the employee will be paid. (p. 457)

Compound interest Interest calculated on the principal plus previous amounts of interest. (p. 434)

Comprehensive income The total change in net assets from all sources except investments by or distributions to the owners. (p. 556)

Conservatism The practice of using the least optimistic estimate when two estimates of amounts are about equally likely. (p. 64)

Consistency For accounting information, the quality that allows a user to compare two or more accounting periods for a single company. (p. 63)

Contingent assets An existing condition for which the outcome is not known but by which the company stands to gain. (pp. 431, 447)

Contingent liability An existing condition for which the outcome is not known but depends on some future event. (p. 426)

Contra account An account with a balance that is opposite that of a related account. (p. 171)

Control account The general ledger account that is supported by a subsidiary ledger. (p. 264)

Controller The chief accounting officer for a company. (p. 24)

Convertible feature Allows preferred stock to be exchanged for common stock. (p. 546)

Corporation A form of entity organized under the laws of a particular state; ownership evidenced by shares of stock. (p. 6)

Cost of goods available for sale Beginning inventory plus cost of goods purchased. (p. 303)

Cost of goods sold Cost of goods available for sale minus ending inventory. (p. 304)

Cost principle Assets recorded at the cost to acquire them. (p. 22)

Credit An entry on the right side of an account. (p. 123)

Credit card draft A multiple-copy document used by a company that accepts a credit card for a sale. (p. 273)

Credit memoranda Additions on a bank statement for such items as interest paid on the account and notes collected by the bank for the customer. (p. 223)

Creditor Someone to whom a company or person has a debt. (p. 8)

Cumulative effect of a change in accounting principle A line item on the income statement to reflect the effect on prior years' income from a change in accounting principle. (p. 689)

Cumulative feature The right to dividends in arrears before the current-year dividend is distributed. (p. 545)

Current asset An asset that is expected to be realized in cash or sold or consumed during the operating cycle or within one year if the cycle is shorter than one year. (p. 67)

Current liability An obligation that will be satisfied within the next operating cycle or within one year if the cycle is shorter than one year. (pp. 69, 419)

Current maturities of long-term debt The portion of a long-term liability that will be paid within one year. (p. 423)

Current ratio Current assets divided by current liabilities. (pp. 71, 666)

Current value The amount of cash, or its equivalent, that could be received by selling an asset currently. (p. 160)

Debenture bonds Bonds that are not backed by specific collateral. (p. 490)

Debit An entry on the left side of an account. (p. 123)

Debit memoranda Deductions on a bank statement for such items as NSF checks and various service charges. (p. 223)

Debt securities Bonds issued by corporations and governmental bodies as a form of borrowing. (p. 253)

Debt service coverage ratio A statement of cash flow measure of the ability of a company to meet its interest and principal payments. (p. 673)

Debt-to-equity ratio The ratio of total liabilities to total stockholders' equity. (p. 672)

Deferral Cash has either been paid or received, but expense or revenue has not yet been recognized. (p. 176)

Deferred expense An asset resulting from the payment of cash before the incurrence of expense. (p. 176)

Deferred revenue A liability resulting from the receipt of cash before the recognition of revenue. (p. 177)

Deferred tax The account used to reconcile the difference between the amount recorded as income tax expense and the amount that is payable as income tax. (p. 513)

Deposit in transit A deposit recorded on the books but not yet reflected on the bank statement. (p. 222)

Depreciation The process of allocating the cost of a long-term tangible asset over its useful life. (pp. 62, 372)

Direct method For preparing the Operating Activities section of the statement of cash flows, the approach in which cash receipts and cash payments are reported. (p. 602)

Direct write-off method The recognition of bad debts expense at the point an account is written off as uncollectible. (p. 265)

Discontinued operations A line item on the income statement to reflect any gains or losses from the disposal of a segment of the business as well as any net income or loss from operating that segment. (p. 689)

Discount The excess of the face value of bonds over the issue price. (p. 493)

Discount on notes payable A contra liability that represents interest deducted from a loan in advance. (p. 423)

Discounted note An alternative name for a non-interest-bearing promissory note. (p. 272)

Discounting The process of selling a promissory note. (p. 275)

Dividend payout ratio The annual dividend amount divided by the annual net income. (pp. 549, 679)

Dividend yield ratio The relationship between dividends and the market price of a company's stock. (p. 679)

Dividends A distribution of the net income of a business to its owners. (p. 20)

Double declining-balance method Depreciation is recorded at twice the straight-line rate, but the balance is reduced each period. (p. 373)

Double-entry system A system of accounting in which every transaction is recorded with equal debits and credits and the accounting equation is kept in balance. (p. 126)

Earnings per share A company's bottom line stated on a per-share basis. (p. 678)

Economic entity concept The assumption that a single, identifiable unit must be accounted for in all situations. (p. 6)

Effective interest method of amortization The process of transferring a portion of the premium or discount to interest expense; this method results in a constant effective interest rate. (p. 495)

Equity securities Securities issued by corporations as a form of ownership in the business. (p. 253)

Estimated liability A contingent liability that is accrued and reflected on the balance sheet. (p. 428)

Event A happening of consequence to an entity. (p. 109)

Expenses Outflows of assets or incurrences of liabilities resulting from delivering goods, rendering services, or carrying out other activities. (pp. 9, 169)

External event An event involving interaction between an entity and its environment. (p. 109)

Extraordinary item A line item on the income statement to reflect any gains or losses that arise from an event that is both unusual in nature and infrequent in occurrence. (p. 689)

Face rate of interest The rate of interest on the bond certificate. (p. 490)

Face value The principal amount of the bond as stated on the bond certificate. (p. 489)

FIFO method An inventory costing method that assigns the most recent costs to ending inventory. (p. 314)

Financial Accounting Standards Board (FASB) The group in the private sector with authority to set accounting standards. (p. 24)

Financial accounting The branch of accounting concerned with the preparation of financial statements for outsider use. (p. 15)

Financing activities Activities concerned with the raising and repayment of funds in the form of debt and equity. (p. 601)

Finished goods A manufacturer's inventory that is complete and ready for sale. (p. 300)

FOB destination point Terms that require the seller to pay for the cost of shipping the merchandise to the buyer. (p. 308)

FOB shipping point Terms that require the buyer to pay for the shipping costs. (p. 308)

Foreign Corrupt Practices Act Legislation intended to increase the accountability of management for accurate records and reliable financial statements. (p. 226)

Funding payment A payment made by the employer to the pension fund or its trustee. (p. 516)

Future value of a single amount Amount accumulated at a future time from a single payment or investment. (p. 438)

Future value of an annuity Amount accumulated in the future when a series of payments is invested and accrues interest. (p. 440)

Gain on sale of asset The excess of the selling price over the asset's book value. (p. 380)

Gain or loss on redemption The difference between the carrying value and the redemption price at the time bonds are redeemed. (p. 498)

General journal The journal used in place of a specialized journal. (p. 129)

General ledger A book, file, hard drive, or other device containing all the accounts. (p. 117)

Generally accepted accounting principles (GAAP) The various methods, rules, practices, and other procedures that have evolved over time in response to the need to regulate the preparation of financial statements. (p. 23)

Going concern The assumption that an entity is not in the process of liquidation and that it will continue indefinitely. (p. 22)

Goodwill The excess of the purchase price of a business over the total market value of identifiable assets. (p. 383)

Gross profit Sales less cost of goods sold. (p. 73)

Gross profit method A technique used to establish an estimate of the cost of inventory stolen, destroyed, or otherwise damaged or of the amount of inventory on hand at an interim date. (p. 326)

Gross profit ratio Gross profit to net sales. (pp. 74, 665)

Gross wages The amount of wages before deductions. (p. 454)

Held-to-maturity securities Investments in bonds of other companies in which the investor has the positive intent and the ability to hold the securities to maturity. (p. 256)

Historical cost The amount paid for an asset and used as a basis for recognizing it on the balance sheet and carrying it on later balance sheets. (p. 160)

Horizontal analysis A comparison of financial statement items over a period of time. (p. 658)

Income statement A statement that summarizes revenues and expenses. (p. 19)

Indirect method For preparing the Operating Activities section of the statement of cash flows, the approach in which net income is reconciled to net cash flow from operations. (p. 603)

Installment method The method in which revenue is recognized at the time cash is collected. (p. 167)

Intangible assets Assets with no physical properties. (p. 382)

Interest The difference between the principal amount of the note and its maturity value. (p. 271)

Interest-bearing note A promissory note in which the interest rate is explicitly stated. (p. 271)

Interim statements Financial statements prepared monthly, quarterly, or at other intervals less than a year in duration. (p. 183)

Internal audit staff Department responsible for monitoring and evaluating the internal control system. (p. 226)

Internal auditing The department responsible in a company for the review and appraisal of its accounting and administrative controls. (p. 25)

Internal control system Policies and procedures necessary to ensure the safeguarding of an entity's assets, the reliability of its accounting records, and the accomplishment of overall company objectives. (p. 226)

Internal event An event occurring entirely within an entity. (p. 109)

International Accounting Standards Board (IASB) The organization formed to develop worldwide accounting standards. (p. 24)

Inventory profit The portion of the gross profit that results from holding inventory during a period of rising prices. (p. 318)

Inventory turnover ratio A measure of the number of times inventory is sold during a period. (pp. 328, 669)

Investing activities Activities concerned with the acquisition and disposal of long-term assets. (p. 600)

Invoice Form sent by the seller to the buyer as evidence of a sale. (p. 235)

Invoice approval form Form the accounting department uses before making payment to document the accuracy of all the information about a purchase. (p. 236)

Issued shares The number of shares sold or distributed to stockholders. (p. 542)

Journal A chronological record of transactions, also known as the book of original entry. (p. 128)

Journalizing The act of recording journal entries. (p. 128)

Land improvements Costs that are related to land but that have a limited life. (p. 371)

Leverage The use of borrowed funds and amounts contributed by preferred stockholders to earn an overall return higher than the cost of these funds. (p. 677)

Liability An obligation of a business. (p. 8)

LIFO conformity rule The IRS requirement that if LIFO is used on the tax return, it must also be used in reporting income to stockholders. (p. 317)

LIFO liquidation The result of selling more units than are purchased during the period, which can have negative tax consequences if a company is using LIFO. (p. 317)

LIFO method An inventory method that assigns the most recent costs to cost of goods sold. (p. 314)

LIFO reserve The excess of the value of a company's inventory stated at FIFO over the value stated at LIFO. (p. 318)

Liquidity The nearness to cash of the assets and liabilities. (pp. 70, 666)

Long-term liability An obligation that will be settled within one year or the current operating cycle. (p. 487)

Loss on sale of asset The amount by which selling price is less than book value. (p. 380)

Lower-of-cost-or-market (LCM) rule A conservative inventory valuation approach that is an attempt to anticipate declines in the value of inventory before its actual sale. (p. 323)

Maker The party that agrees to repay the money for a promissory note at some future date. (p. 270)

Management accounting The branch of accounting concerned with providing management with information to facilitate planning and control. (p. 14)

Market rate of interest The rate that investors could obtain by investing in other bonds that are similar to the issuing firm's bonds. (p. 491)

Market value per share The selling price of the stock as indicated by the most recent transactions. (p. 559)

Matching principle The association of revenue of a period with all of the costs necessary to generate that revenue. (p. 168)

Materiality The magnitude of an accounting information omission or misstatement that will affect the judgment of someone relying on the information. (p. 64)

Maturity date The date that the promissory note is due. (p. 271)

Maturity value The amount of cash the maker is to pay the payee on the maturity date of the note. (p. 271)

Merchandise inventory The account wholesalers and retailers use to report inventory held for resale. (p. 299)

Monetary unit The yardstick used to measure amounts in financial statements; the dollar in the United States. (p. 23)

Moving average The name given to an average cost method when it is used with a perpetual inventory system. (p. 338)

Multiple-step income statement An income statement that shows classifications of revenues and expenses as well as important subtotals. (p. 73)

Natural resources Assets that are consumed during their use. (p. 381)

Net income The excess of revenues over expenses. (p. 19)

Net pay The amount of wages after deductions. (p. 454)

Net sales Sales revenue less sales returns and allowances and sales discounts. (p. 301)

Nominal accounts The name given to revenue, expense, and dividend accounts because they are temporary and are closed at the end of the period. (p. 182)

Non-interest-bearing note A promissory note in which interest is not explicitly stated but is implicit in the agreement. (p. 271)

Note payable A liability resulting from the signing of a promissory note. (pp. 270, 422)

Note receivable An asset resulting from the acceptance of a promissory note from another company. (p. 270)

Number of days' sales in inventory A measure of how long it takes to sell inventory. (pp. 328, 670)

Number of days' sales in receivables A measure of the average age of accounts receivable. (p. 669)

Operating activities Activities concerned with the acquisition and sale of products and services. (p. 599)

Operating cycle The period of time between the purchase of inventory and the collection of any receivable from the sale of the inventory. (p. 65)

Operating lease A lease that does not meet any of the four criteria and is not recorded as an asset by the lessee. (p. 501)

Outstanding check A check written by a company but not yet presented to the bank for payment. (p. 222)

Outstanding shares The number of shares issued less the number of shares held as treasury stock. (p. 542)

Owners' equity The owners' claim on the assets of an entity. (p. 17)

Par value An arbitrary amount that represents the legal capital of the firm. (p. 543)

Participating feature Allows preferred stockholders to share on a percentage basis in the distribution of an abnormally large dividend. (p. 546)

Partnership A business owned by two or more individuals and with the characteristic of unlimited liability. (pp. 6, 567)

Partnership agreement Specifies how much the owners will invest, their salaries, and how profits will be shared. (p. 567)

Payee The party that will receive the money from a promissory note at some future date. (p. 270)

Pension An obligation to pay employees for service rendered while employed. (p. 515)

Percentage-of-completion method The method used by contractors to recognize revenue before the completion of a long-term contract. (p. 166)

Periodic system System in which the inventory account is updated only at the end of the period. (p. 304)

Permanent difference A difference that affects the tax records but not the accounting records, or vice versa. (p. 513)

Perpetual system System in which the inventory account is increased at the time of each purchase and decreased at the time of each sale. (p. 304)

Petty cash fund Money kept on hand for making minor disbursements in coin and currency rather than by writing checks. (p. 225)

Posting The process of transferring amounts from a journal to the ledger accounts. (p. 128)

Premium The excess of the issue price over the face value of the bonds. (p. 493)

Present value of a single amount Amount at a present time that is equivalent to a payment or investment at a future time. (p. 438)

Present value of an annuity The amount at a present time that is equivalent to a series of payments and interest in the future. (p. 441)

Price/earnings (P/E) ratio The relationship between a company's performance according to the income statement and its performance in the stock market. (p. 678)

Principal The amount of cash received, or the fair value of the products or services received, by the maker when a promissory note is issued. (p. 271)

Production method The method in which revenue is recognized when a commodity is produced rather than when it is sold. (p. 167)

Profit margin Net income divided by sales. (p. 74)

Profit margin ratio Net income to net sales. (p. 665)

Profitability How well management is using company resources to earn a return on the funds invested by various groups. (p. 674)

Promissory note A written promise to repay a definite sum of money on demand or at a fixed or determinable date in the future. (p. 270)

Purchase Discounts Contra-purchases account used to record reductions in purchase price for early payment to a supplier. (p. 308)

Purchase order Form sent by the purchasing department to the supplier. (p. 234)

Purchase requisition form Form a department uses to initiate a request to order merchandise. (p. 232)

Purchase Returns and Allowances Contra-purchases account used in a periodic inventory system when a refund is received from a supplier or a reduction given in the balance owed to a supplier. (p. 307)

Purchases Account used in a periodic inventory system to record acquisitions of merchandise. (p. 307)

Raw materials The inventory of a manufacturer before the addition of any direct labor or manufacturing overhead. (p. 300)

Real accounts The name given to balance sheet accounts because they are permanent and are not closed at the end of the period. (p. 182)

Recognition The process of recording an item in the financial statements as an asset, liability, revenue, expense, or the like. (p. 159)

Relevance The capacity of information to make a difference in a decision. (p. 61)

Reliability The quality that makes accounting information dependable in representing the events that it purports to represent. (p. 62)

Replacement cost The current cost of a unit of inventory. (p. 318)

Report of management Written statement in the annual report indicating the responsibility of management for the financial statements. (p. 226)

Research and development costs Costs incurred in the discovery of new knowledge. (p. 384)

Retail inventory method A technique used by retailers to convert the retail value of inventory to a cost basis. (p. 327)

Retained earnings The part of owners' equity that represents the income earned less dividends paid over the life of an entity. (pp. 17, 544)

Retirement of stock When the stock is repurchased with no intention to reissue at a later date. (p. 549)

Return on assets ratio A measure of a company's success in earning a return for all providers of capital. (p. 674)

Return on common stockholders' equity ratio A measure of a company's success in earning a return for the common stockholders. (p. 676)

Return on sales ratio A variation of the profit margin ratio; measures earnings before payments to creditors. (p. 675)

Revenue Inflow of assets resulting from the sale of goods and services. (p. 9)

Revenue expenditure A cost that keeps an asset in its normal operating condition and is treated as an expense. (p. 378)

Revenue recognition principle Revenues are recognized in the income statement when they are realized, or realizable, and earned. (p. 165)

Revenues Inflows of assets or settlements of liabilities from delivering or producing goods, rendering services, or conducting other activities. (p. 164)

Sales Discounts Contra-revenue account used to record discounts given customers for early payment of their accounts. (p. 302)

Sales Returns and Allowances Contra-revenue account used to record both refunds to customers and reductions of their accounts. (p. 302)

Sarbanes-Oxley Act An act of Congress in 2002 intended to bring reform to corporate accountability and stewardship in the wake of a number of major corporate scandals. (p. 32)

Securities and Exchange Commission (SEC) The federal agency with ultimate authority to determine the rules in preparing statements for companies whose stock is sold to the public. (p. 24)

Serial bonds Bonds that do not all have the same due date; a portion of the bonds comes due each time period. (p. 490)

Share of stock A certificate that acts as ownership in a corporation. (p. 6)

Simple interest Interest is calculated on the principal amount only. (pp. 434, 449)

Single-step income statement An income statement in which all expenses are added together and subtracted from all revenues. (p. 72)

Sole proprietorship A business with a single owner. (pp. 6, 566)

Solvency The ability of a company to remain in business over the long term. (p. 671)

Source document A piece of paper that is used as evidence to record a transaction. (p. 110)

Specific identification method An inventory costing method that relies on matching unit costs with the actual units sold. (p. 312)

Statement of cash flows The financial statement that summarizes an entity's cash receipts and cash payments during the period from operating, investing, and financing activities. (p. 596)

Statement of stockholders' equity Reflects the differences between beginning and ending balances for all accounts in the Stockholders' Equity category of the balance sheet. (p. 554)

Stock dividend The issuance of additional shares of stock to existing stockholders. (p. 551)

Stock split The creation of additional shares of stock with a reduction of the par value of the stock. (p. 553)

Stockholder One of the owners of a corporation. Also called a shareholder. (p. 8)

Stockholders' equity The owners' equity in a corporation. (p. 17)

Straight-line method A method by which the same dollar amount of depreciation is recorded in each year of asset use. (pp. 171, 372)

Subsidiary ledger The detail for a number of individual items that collectively make up a single general ledger account. (p. 264)

Temporary difference A difference that affects both book and tax records but not in the same time period. (p. 513)

Term The length of time a note is outstanding; that is, the period of time between the date it is issued and the date it matures. (p. 271)

Time period Artificial segment on the calendar, used as the basis for preparing financial statements. (p. 23)

Time value of money An immediate amount should be preferred over an amount in the future. (p. 433)

Times interest earned ratio An income statement measure of the ability of a company to meet its interest payments. (p. 672)

Trading securities Stock and bonds of other companies bought and held for the purpose of selling them in the near term to generate profits on appreciation in their price. (p. 256)

Transaction Any event that is recognized in a set of financial statements. (p. 109)

Transportation-in Adjunct account used to record freight costs paid by the buyer. (p. 306)

Treasurer The officer responsible in an organization for the safeguarding and efficient use of a company's liquid assets. (p. 24)

Treasury stock Stock issued by the firm and then repurchased but not retired. (p. 547)

Trial balance A list of each account and its balance; used to prove equality of debits and credits. (p. 130)

Understandability The quality of accounting information that makes it comprehensible to those willing to spend the necessary time. (p. 61)

Units-of-production method Depreciation is determined as a function of the number of units the asset produces. (p. 373)

Vertical analysis A comparison of various financial statement items within a single period with the use of common-size statements. (p. 658)

Weighted average cost method An inventory costing method that assigns the same unit cost to all units available for sale during the period. (p. 313)

Work in process The cost of unfinished products in a manufacturing company. (p. 300)

Work sheet A device used at the end of the period to gather the information needed to prepare financial statements without actually recording and posting adjusting entries. (p. 182)

Working capital Current assets minus current liabilities. (pp. 70, 666)

Company Index

Subject Index